D1075082

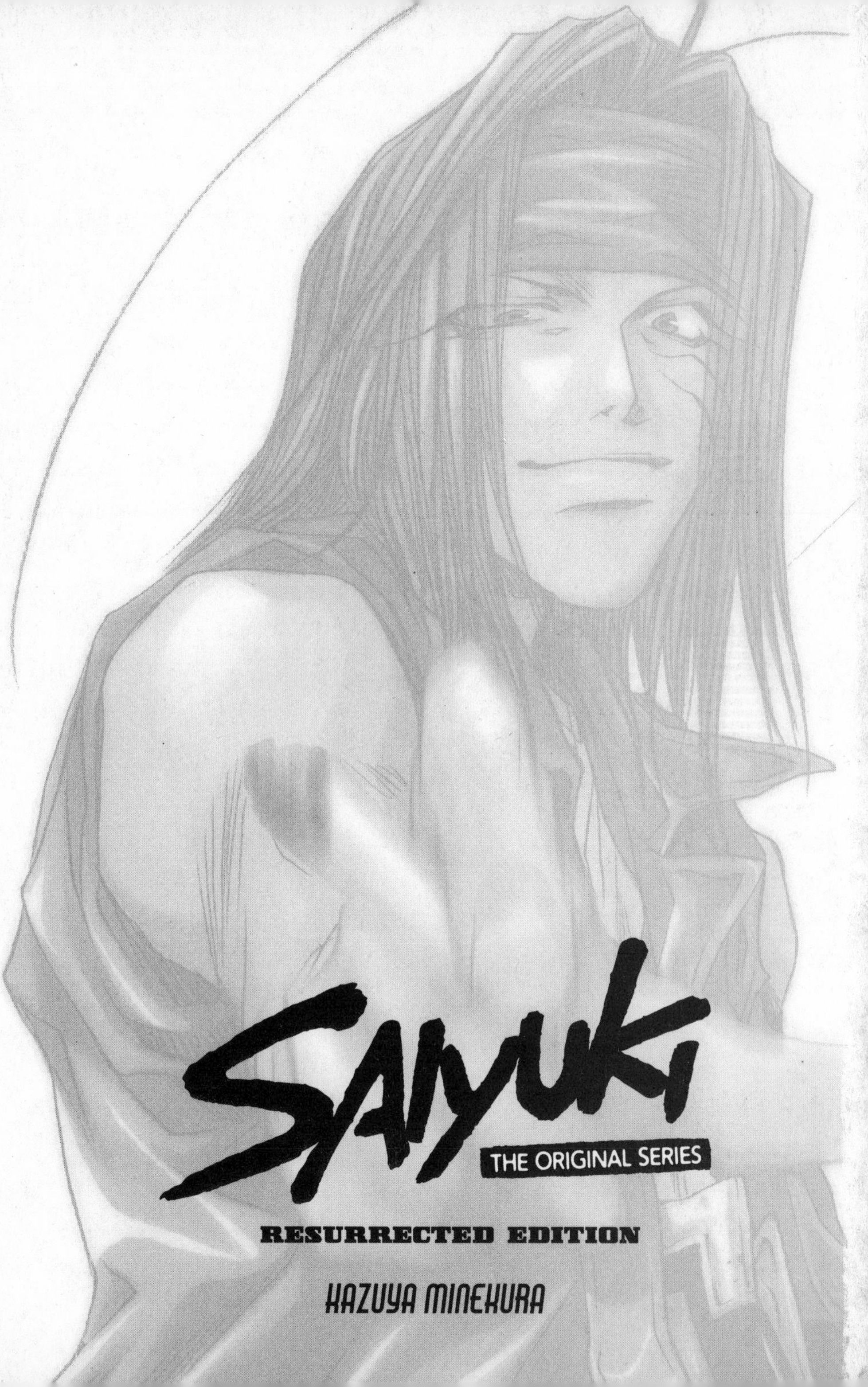

SAIYUKI

THE ORIGINAL SERIES

RESURRECTED EDITION

KAZUYA MINEKURA

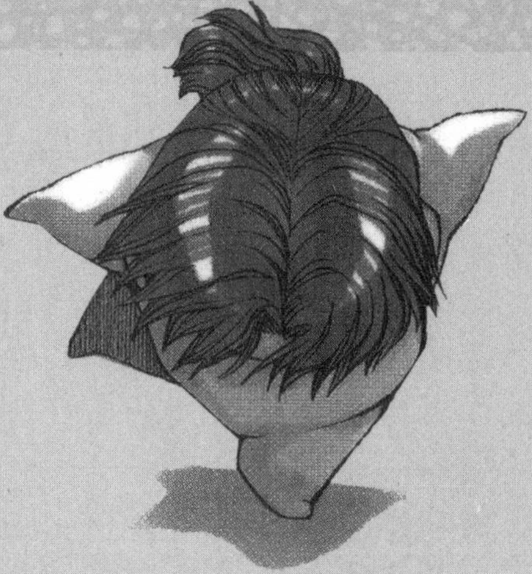

A note from the author

KAZUYA MINEKURA

Looking at him now, Kami-sama looks like a whole other person in this volume…ʖ

VOLUME 4 CONTENTS

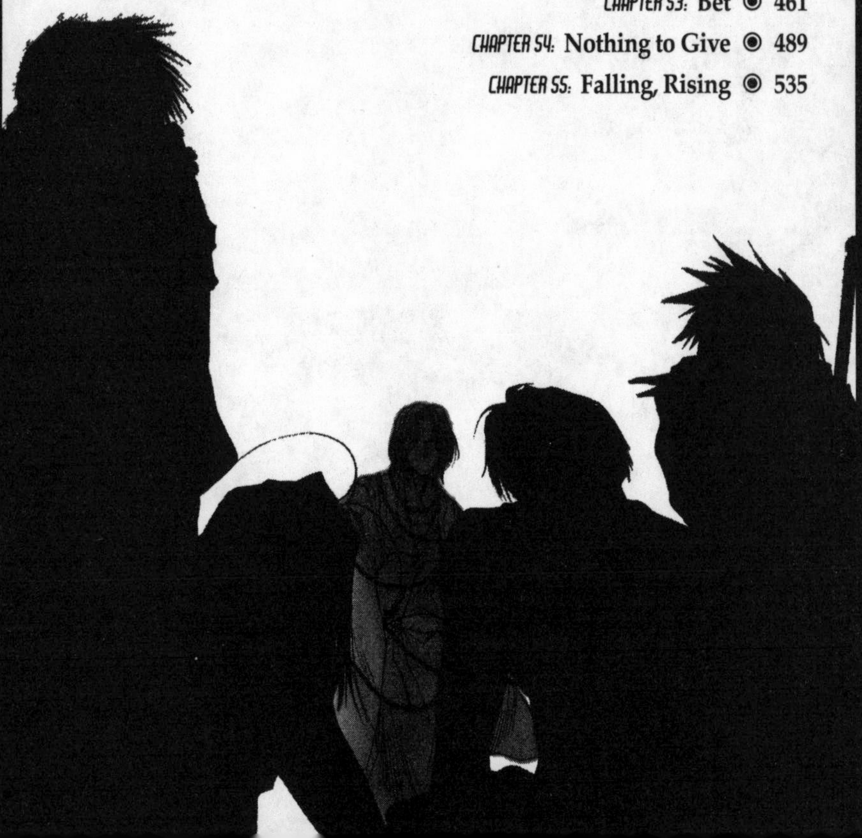

SAIYUKI

7

KAZUYA MINEKURA

— VOLUME VI SYNOPSIS —

A Negative Wave has spread across the fount of culture and faith, Togenkyo. Four lawless desperados set out on a journey to the West to stop the experiments to revive the great yokai Gyumaoh—experiments believed to be the cause of this calamity.

Sanzo is felled by a fatal dose of poison, and the castle of sand begins to crumble around them, until Kougaiji saves our heroes just in the nick of time.

Kougaiji challenges Goku to a duel over the sutra. Goku hesitates, but the thought of losing someone he cares about strengthens his resolve —and he removes his power inhibitor.

Goku's rampage does not stop with Kougaiji's defeat, and Gojyo and Hakkai struggle to restrain him until a single shot rings out...

The Gang stops in a town to rest and recuperate. Gojyo goes out to do the shopping, and he comes across a strange boy. Little does he know that this was the beginning of a whole new adventure.

CHAPTER 37
Out of Gear

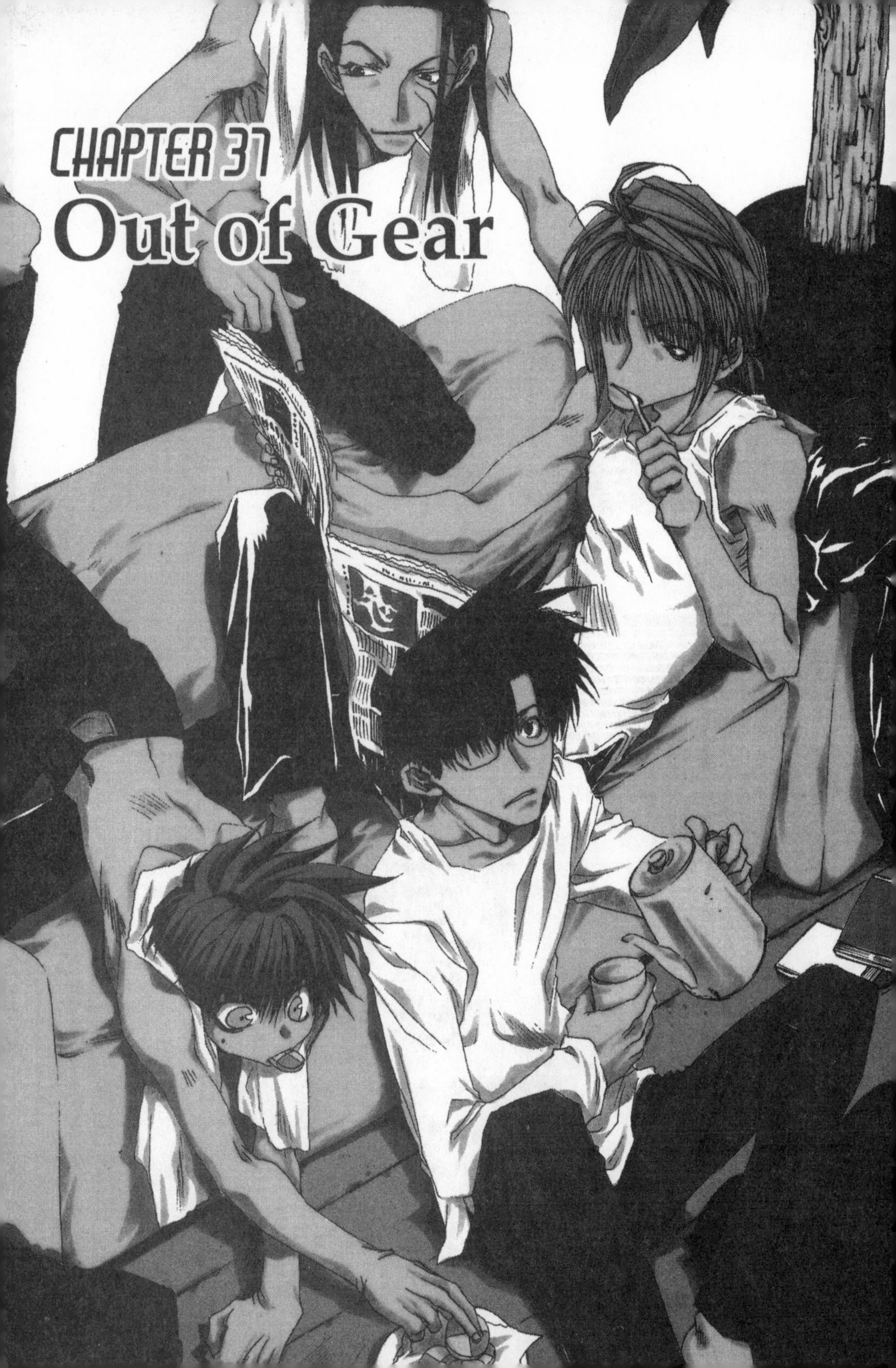

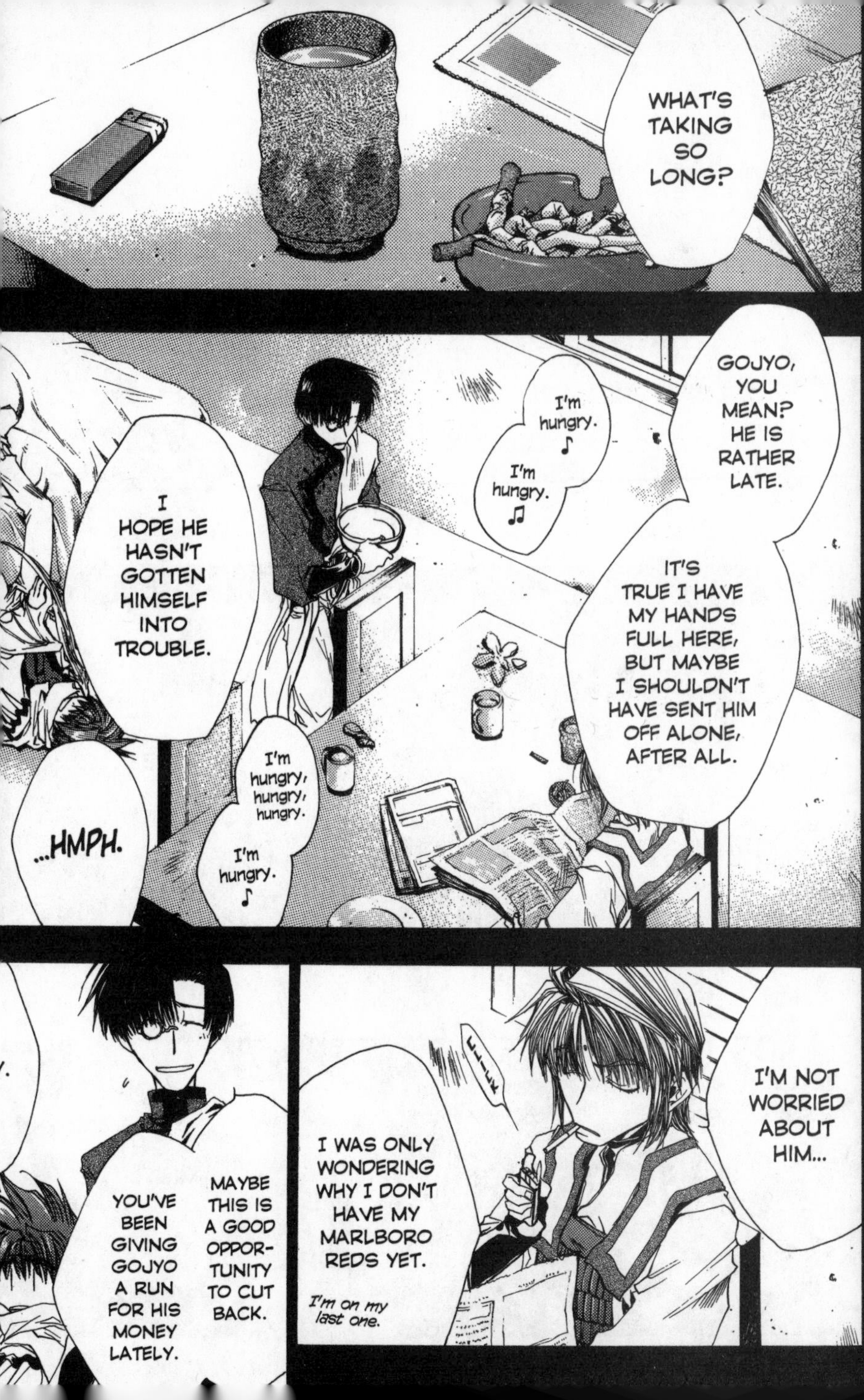
WHAT'S TAKING SO LONG?
GOJYO, YOU MEAN? HE IS RATHER LATE.
I'm hungry. ♪
I'm hungry. ♫
IT'S TRUE I HAVE MY HANDS FULL HERE, BUT MAYBE I SHOULDN'T HAVE SENT HIM OFF ALONE, AFTER ALL.
I HOPE HE HASN'T GOTTEN HIMSELF INTO TROUBLE.
I'm hungry, hungry, hungry.
I'm hungry. ♪
...HMPH.
I'M NOT WORRIED ABOUT HIM...
I WAS ONLY WONDERING WHY I DON'T HAVE MY MARLBORO REDS YET.
I'm on my last one.
MAYBE THIS IS A GOOD OPPORTUNITY TO CUT BACK.
YOU'VE BEEN GIVING GOJYO A RUN FOR HIS MONEY LATELY.

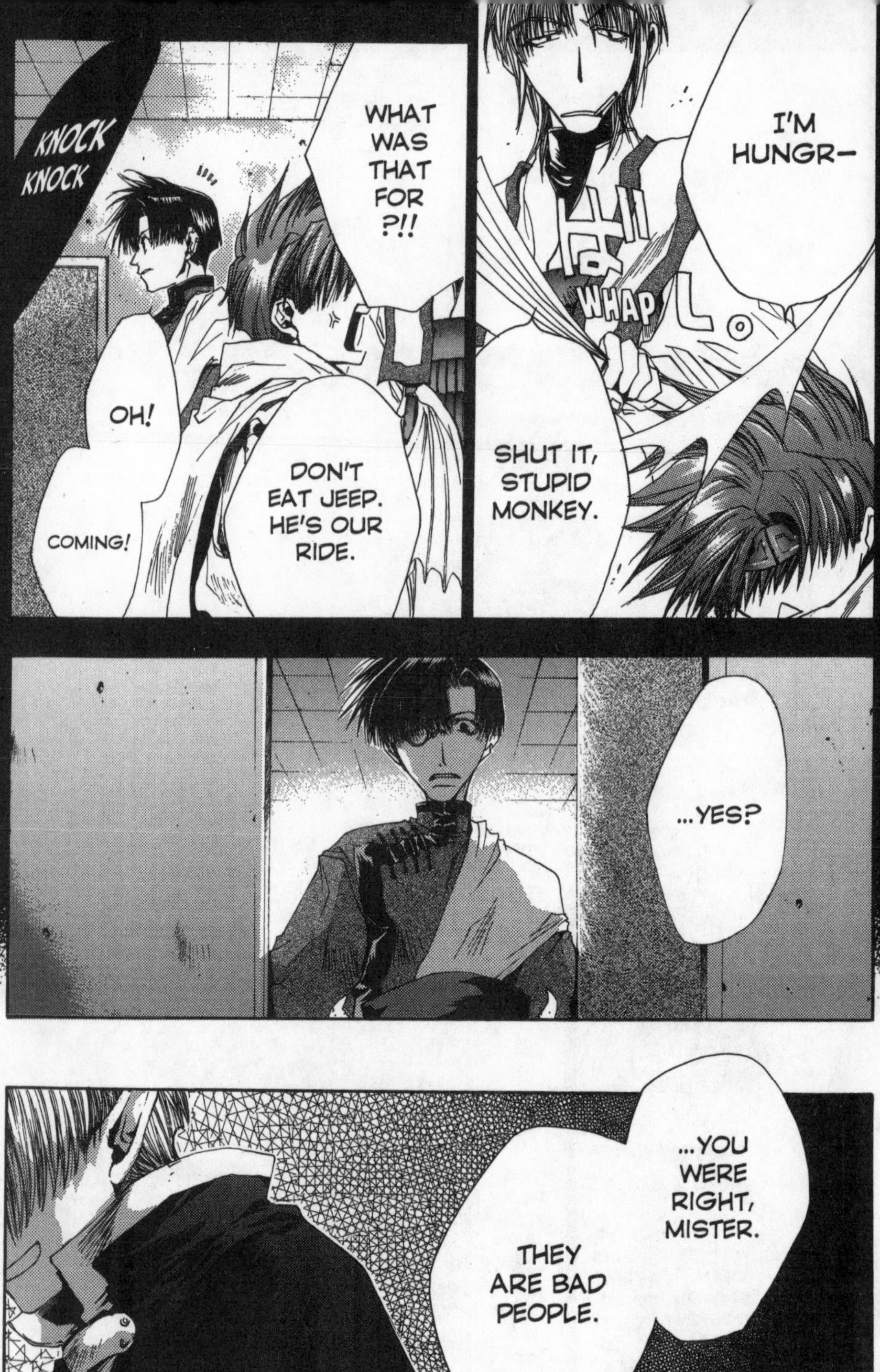
I'M HUNGR—
WHAP
SHUT IT, STUPID MONKEY.
WHAT WAS THAT FOR ?!!
KNOCK KNOCK
DON'T EAT JEEP. HE'S OUR RIDE.
OH!
COMING!
...YES?
...YOU WERE RIGHT, MISTER.
THEY ARE BAD PEOPLE.

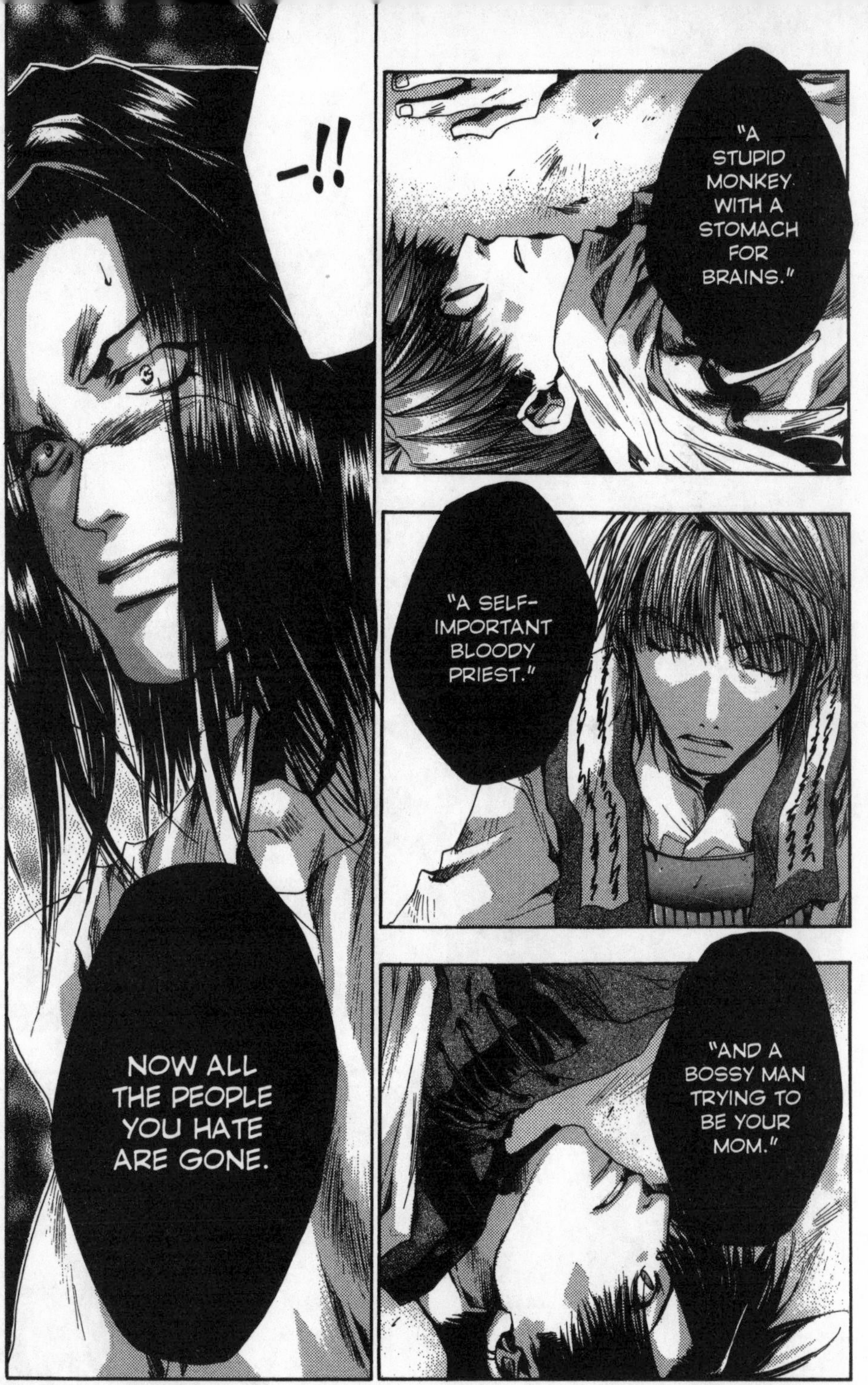
"A STUPID MONKEY WITH A STOMACH FOR BRAINS."
"A SELF-IMPORTANT BLOODY PRIEST."
"AND A BOSSY MAN TRYING TO BE YOUR MOM."
—!!
NOW ALL THE PEOPLE YOU HATE ARE GONE.

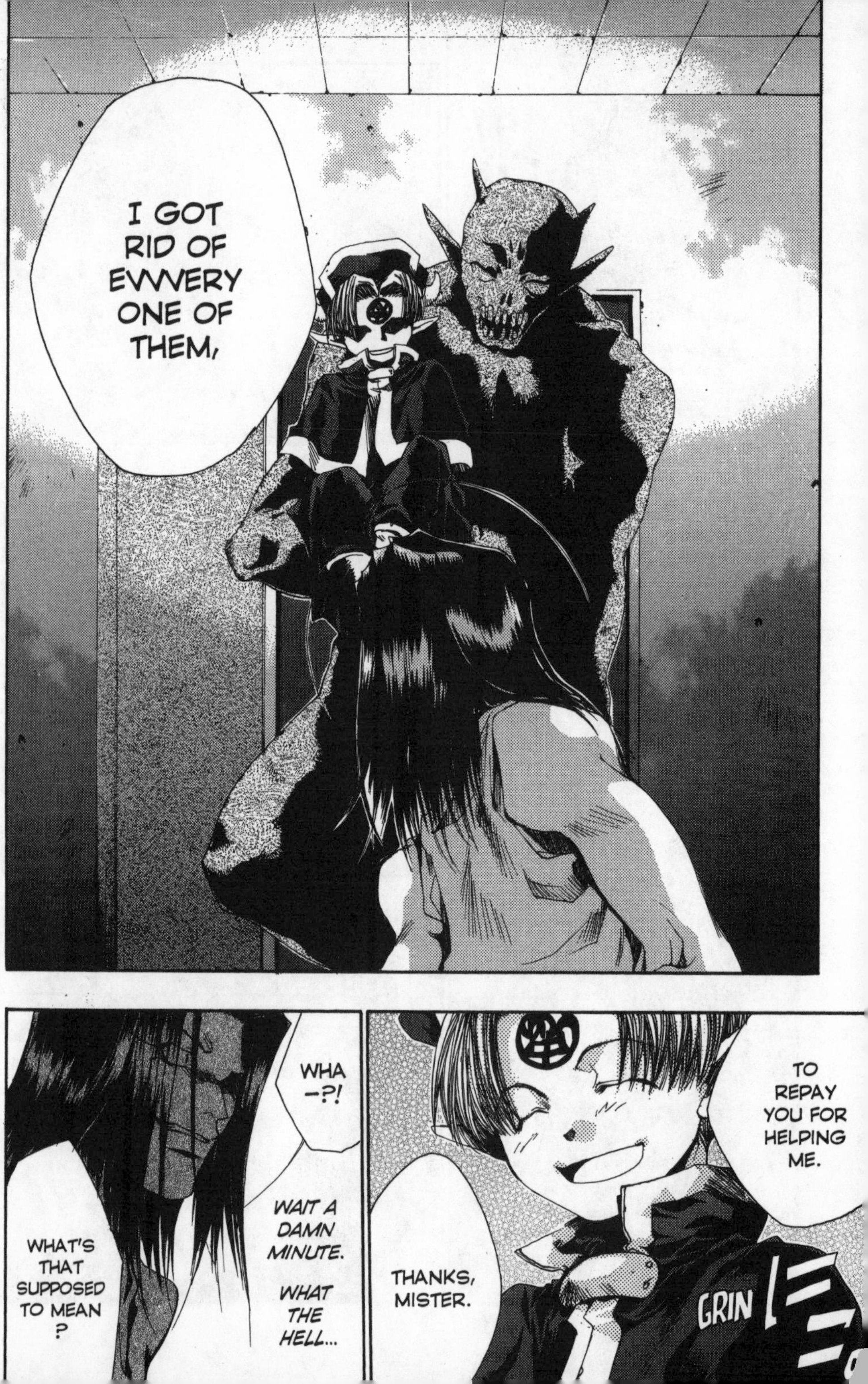
I GOT RID OF EVVVERY ONE OF THEM,
TO REPAY YOU FOR HELPING ME.
THANKS, MISTER.
GRIN
WHA-?!
WAIT A DAMN MINUTE.
WHAT THE HELL...
WHAT'S THAT SUPPOSED TO MEAN?

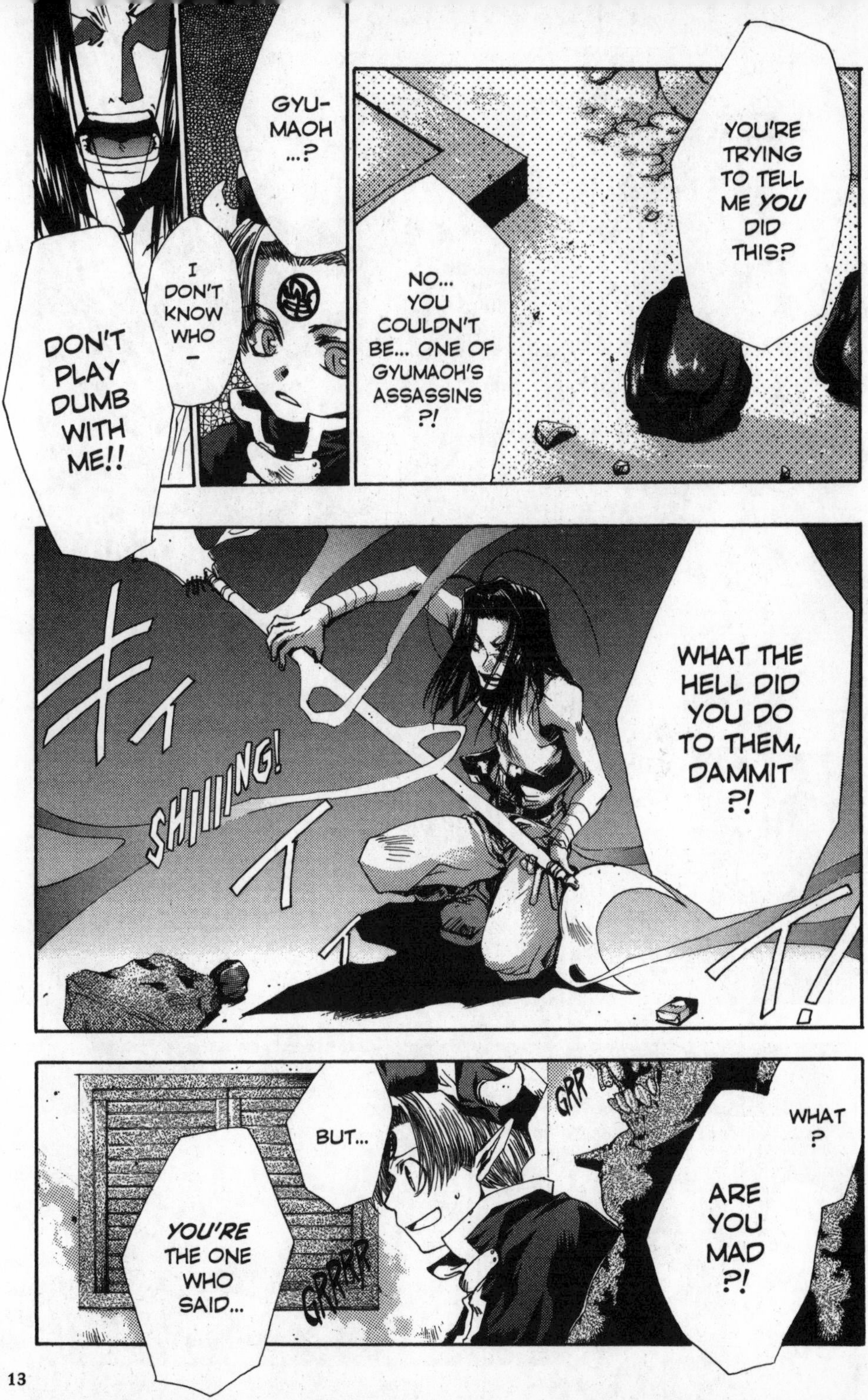
YOU'RE TRYING TO TELL ME YOU DID THIS?
NO... YOU COULDN'T BE... ONE OF GYUMAOH'S ASSASSINS ?!
GYU-MAOH ...?
I DON'T KNOW WHO –
DON'T PLAY DUMB WITH ME!!
WHAT THE HELL DID YOU DO TO THEM, DAMMIT ?!
SHIIIING!
WHAT ?
ARE YOU MAD ?!
GRR
BUT...
YOU'RE THE ONE WHO SAID...
GRRRR

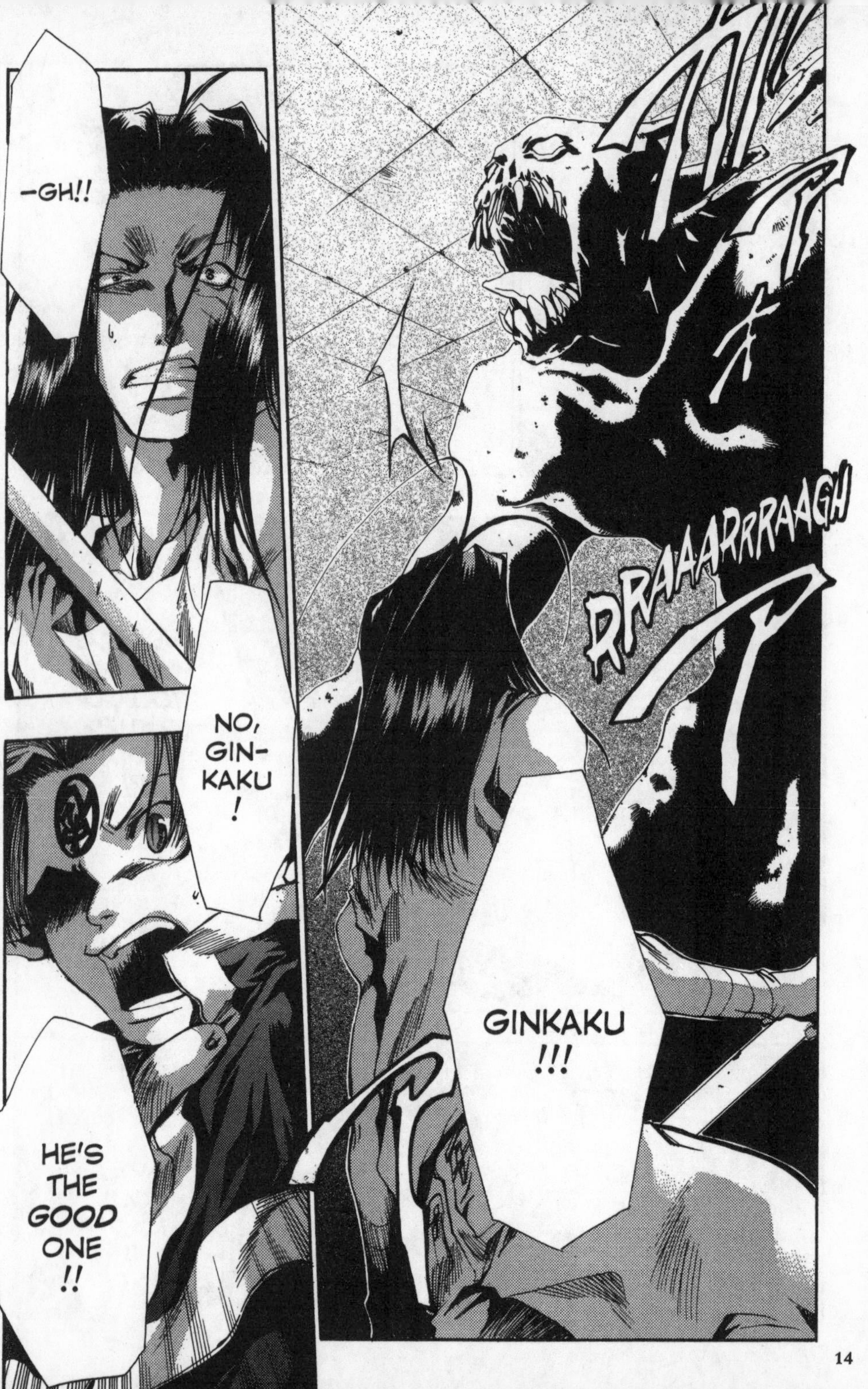
DRAAARRRAAGH
GINKAKU!!!
-GH!!
NO, GINKAKU!
HE'S THE GOOD ONE!!

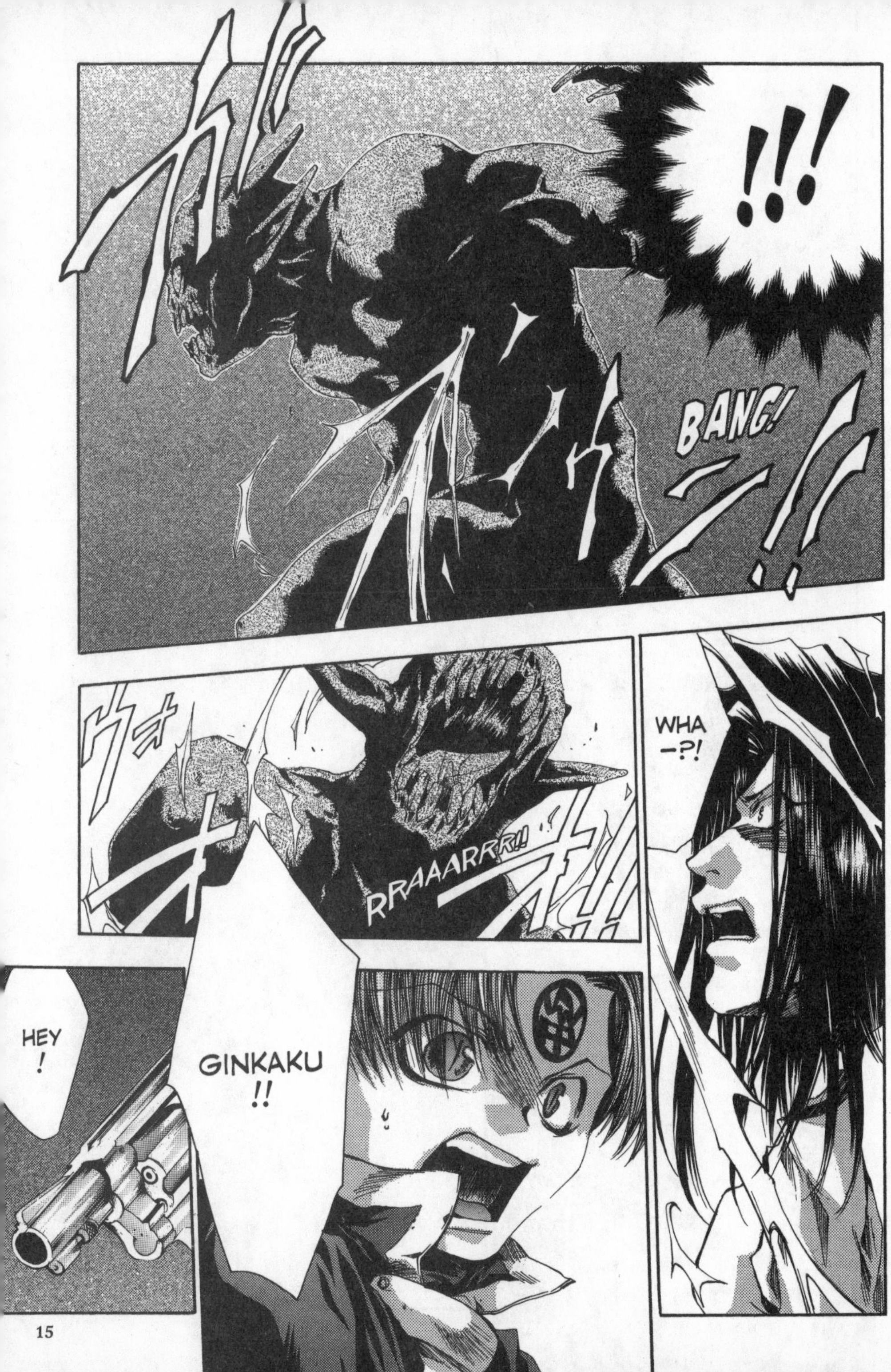
!!!
BANG!
WHA —?!
RRAAARRR!!
GINKAKU !!
HEY !

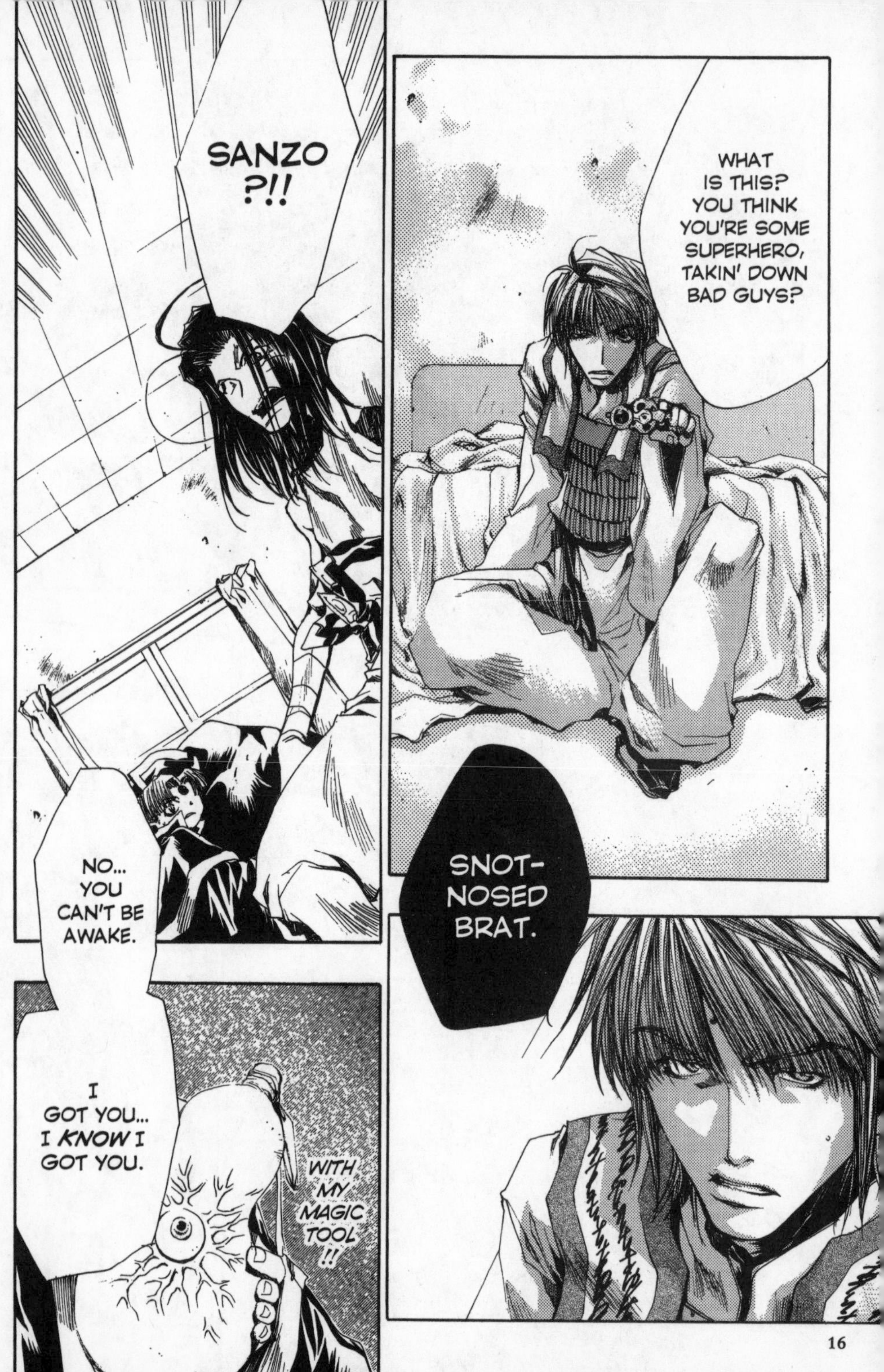
WHAT IS THIS? YOU THINK YOU'RE SOME SUPERHERO, TAKIN' DOWN BAD GUYS?
SANZO ?!!
NO... YOU CAN'T BE AWAKE.
SNOT-NOSED BRAT.
I GOT YOU... I *KNOW* I GOT YOU.
WITH MY MAGIC TOOL !!

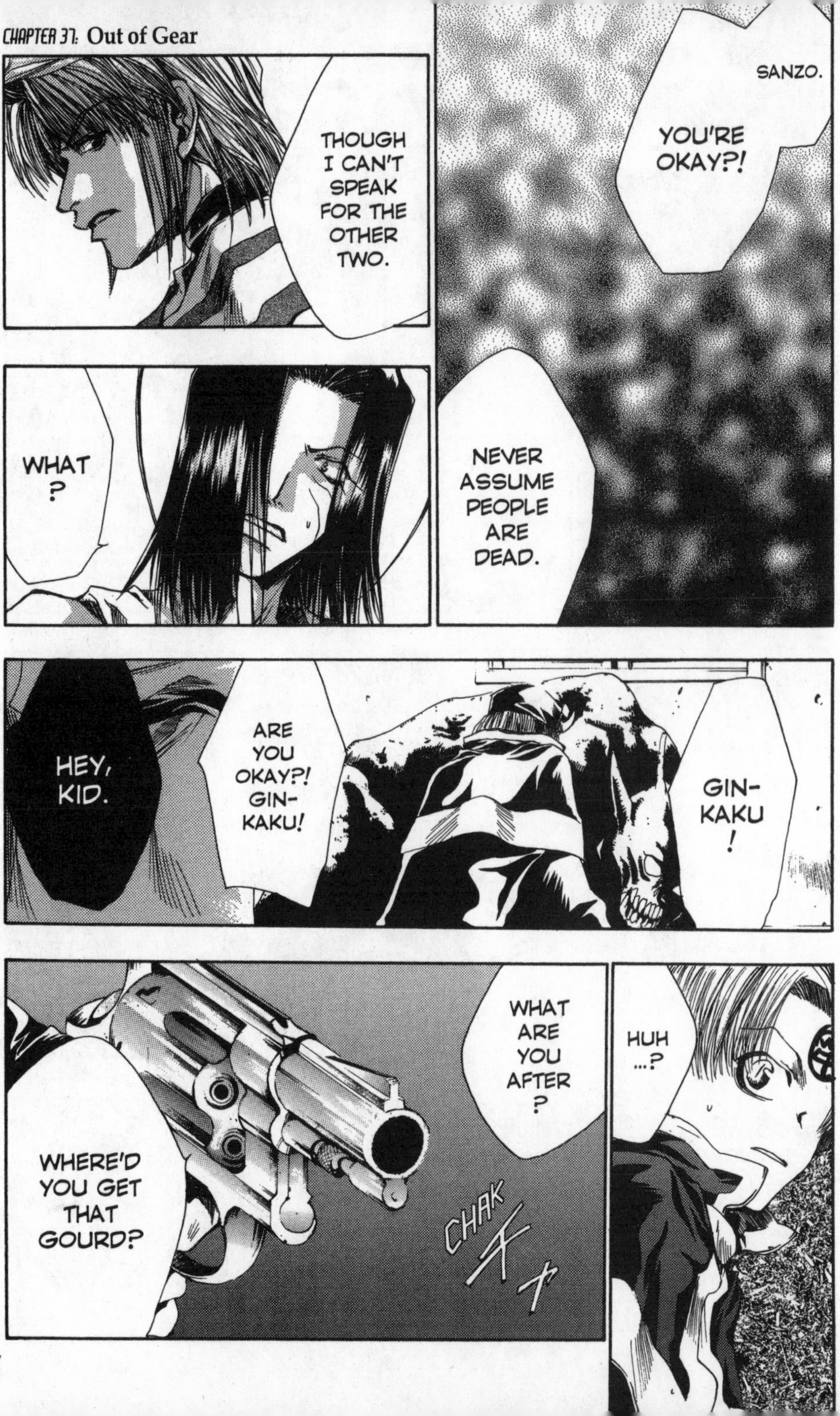
SANZO.
YOU'RE OKAY?!
NEVER ASSUME PEOPLE ARE DEAD.
THOUGH I CAN'T SPEAK FOR THE OTHER TWO.
WHAT?
GIN-KAKU!
ARE YOU OKAY?! GIN-KAKU!
HEY, KID.
HUH...?
WHAT ARE YOU AFTER?
CHAK
WHERE'D YOU GET THAT GOURD?

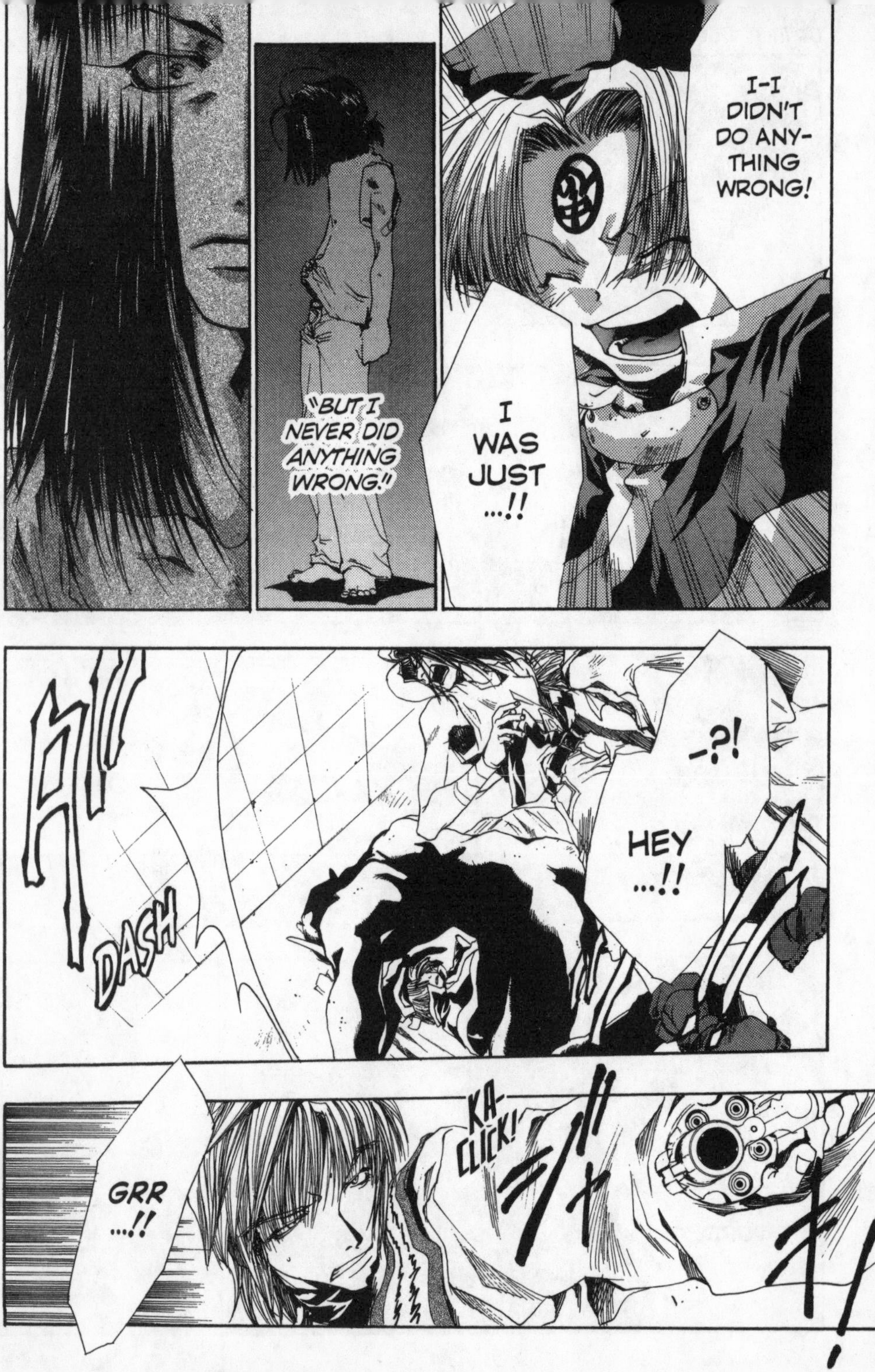
I-I DIDN'T DO ANY-THING WRONG!
I WAS JUST ...!!
"BUT I NEVER DID ANYTHING WRONG."
-?!
HEY ...!!
DASH
KA-CLICK!
ジャキ!
GRR ...!!

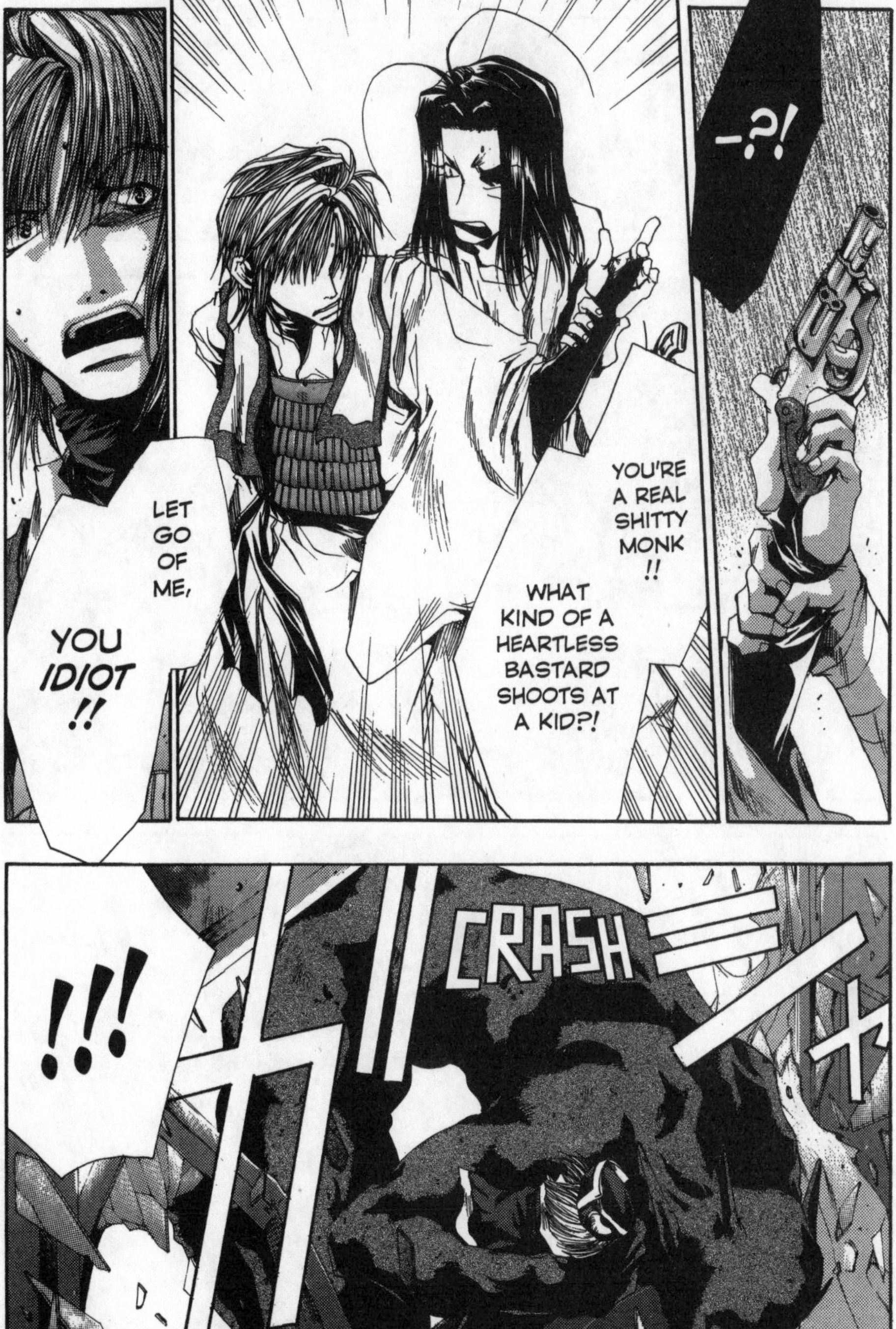
-?!
YOU'RE A REAL SHITTY MONK!!
WHAT KIND OF A HEARTLESS BASTARD SHOOTS AT A KID?!
LET GO OF ME,
YOU IDIOT!!
CRASH
!!!

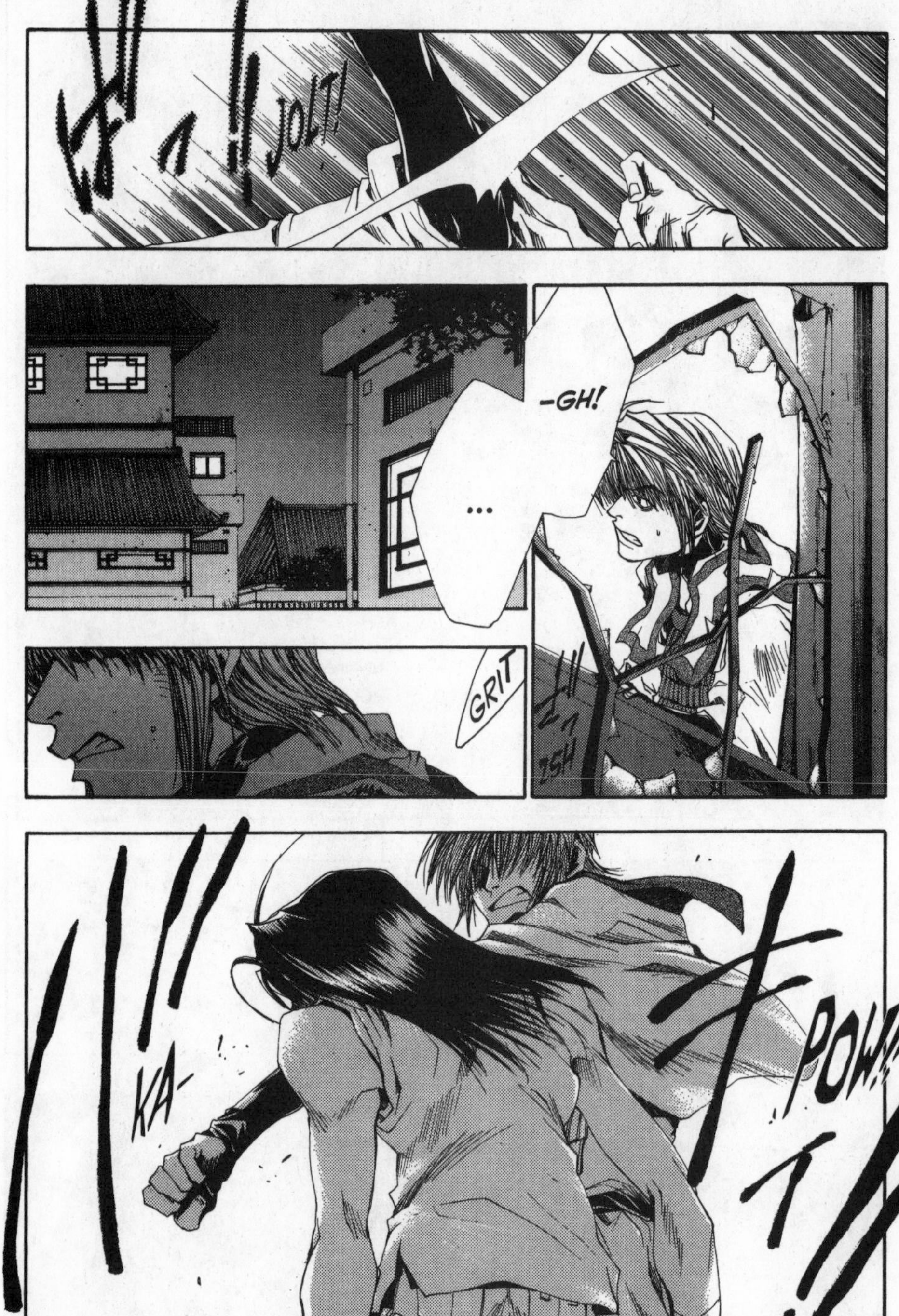
JOLT!
-GH!
...
ZSH
GRIT
POW!!!
KA-

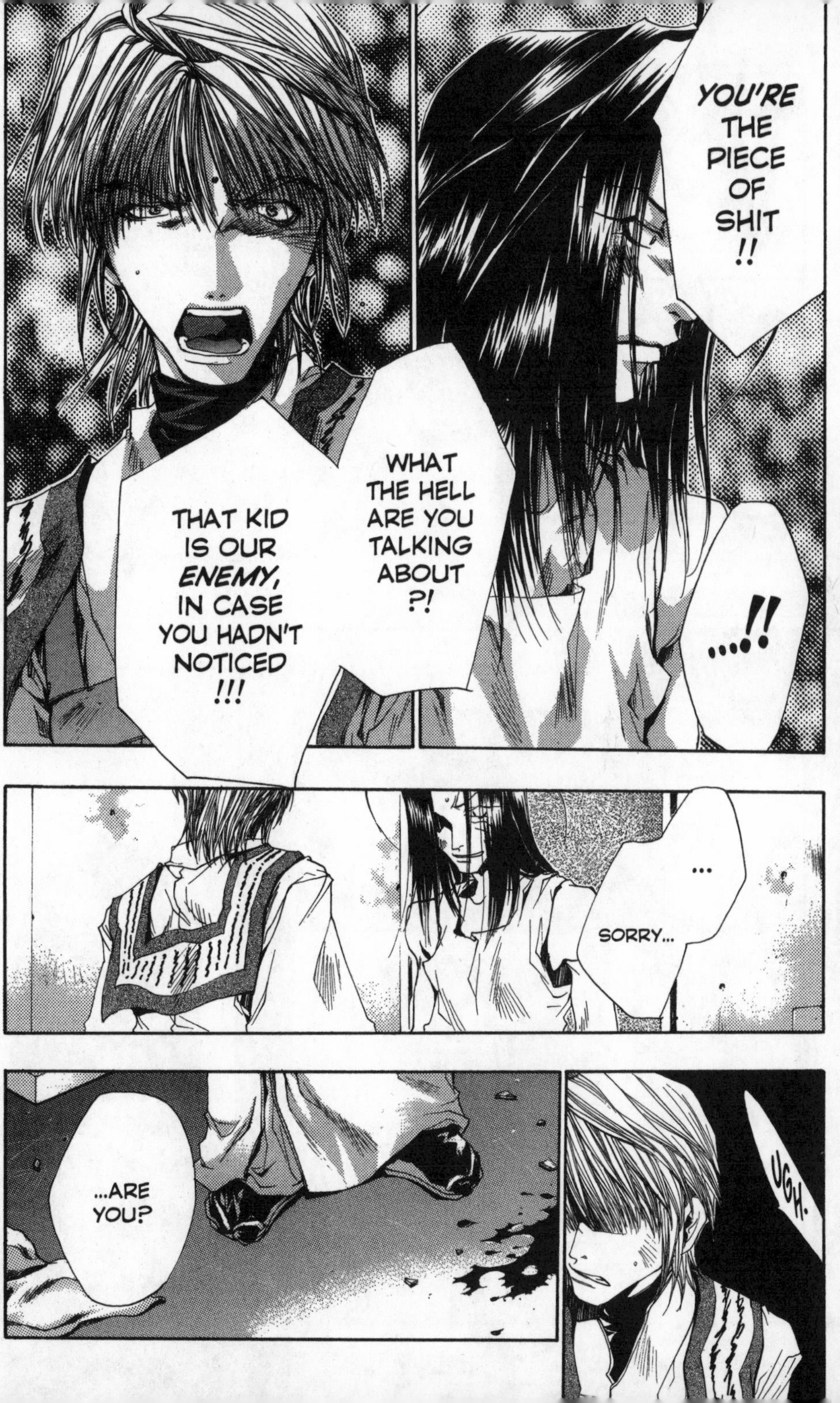
YOU'RE THE PIECE OF SHIT !!
...!!
WHAT THE HELL ARE YOU TALKING ABOUT ?!
THAT KID IS OUR *ENEMY*, IN CASE YOU HADN'T NOTICED !!!
...
SORRY...
UGH.
...ARE YOU?

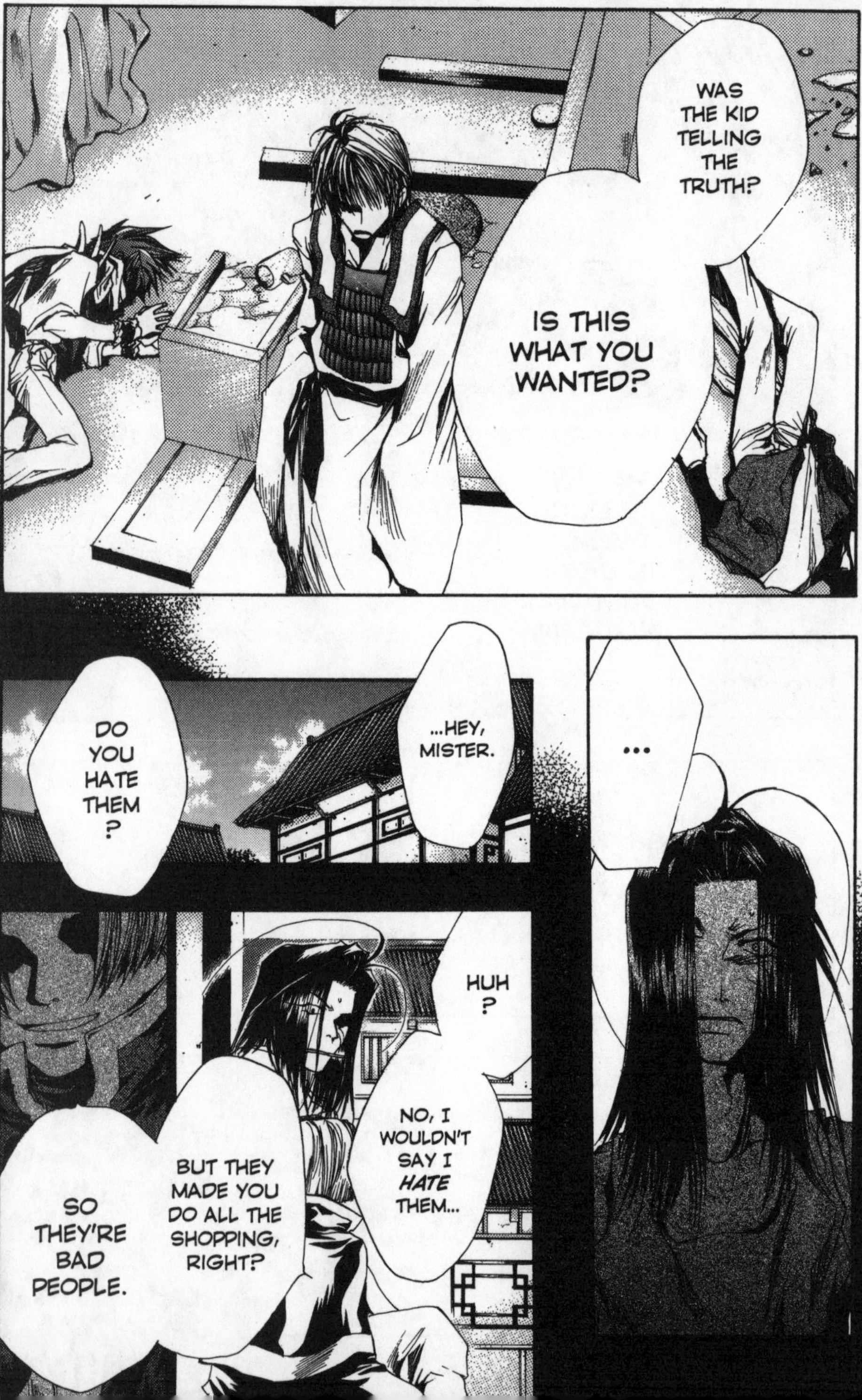
WAS THE KID TELLING THE TRUTH?
IS THIS WHAT YOU WANTED?
...
...HEY, MISTER.
DO YOU HATE THEM ?
HUH ?
NO, I WOULDN'T SAY I *HATE* THEM...
BUT THEY MADE YOU DO ALL THE SHOPPING, RIGHT?
SO THEY'RE BAD PEOPLE.

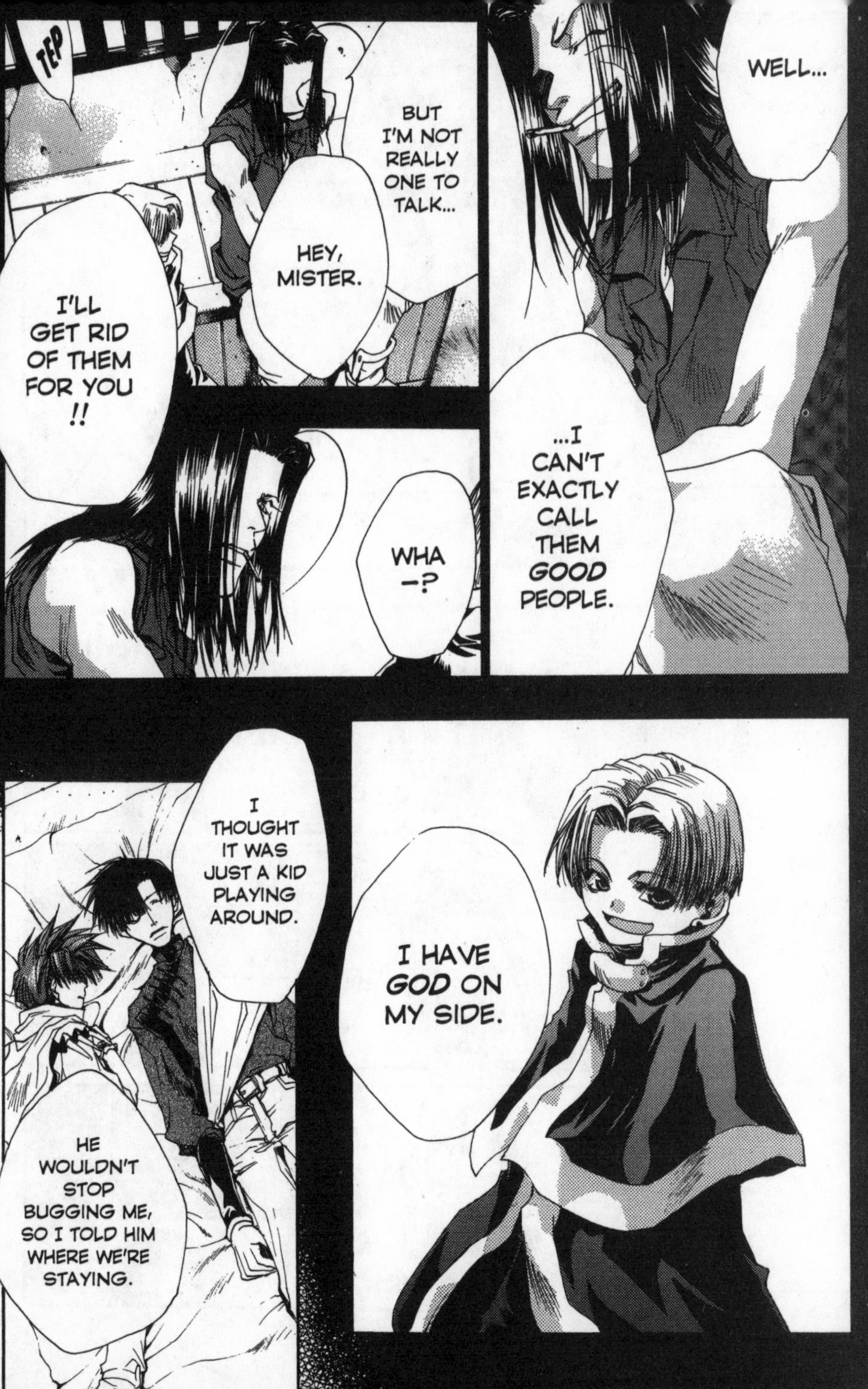
WELL...
...I CAN'T EXACTLY CALL THEM *GOOD* PEOPLE.
TEP
BUT I'M NOT REALLY ONE TO TALK...
HEY, MISTER.
I'LL GET RID OF THEM FOR YOU!!
WHA–?
I HAVE *GOD* ON MY SIDE.
I THOUGHT IT WAS JUST A KID PLAYING AROUND.
HE WOULDN'T STOP BUGGING ME, SO I TOLD HIM WHERE WE'RE STAYING.

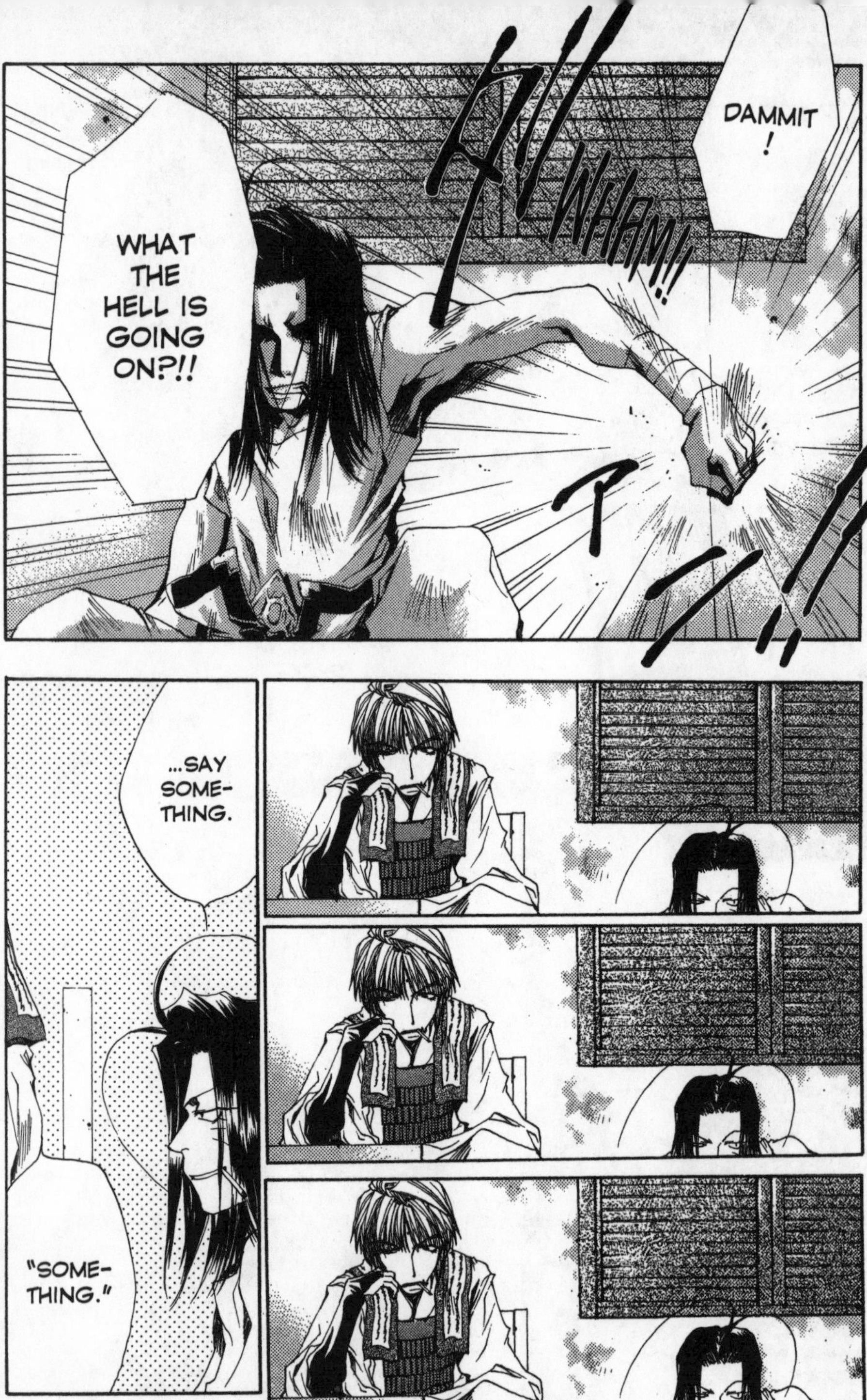
DAMMIT!
WHAM!!
WHAT THE HELL IS GOING ON?!!
...SAY SOME-THING.
"SOME-THING."

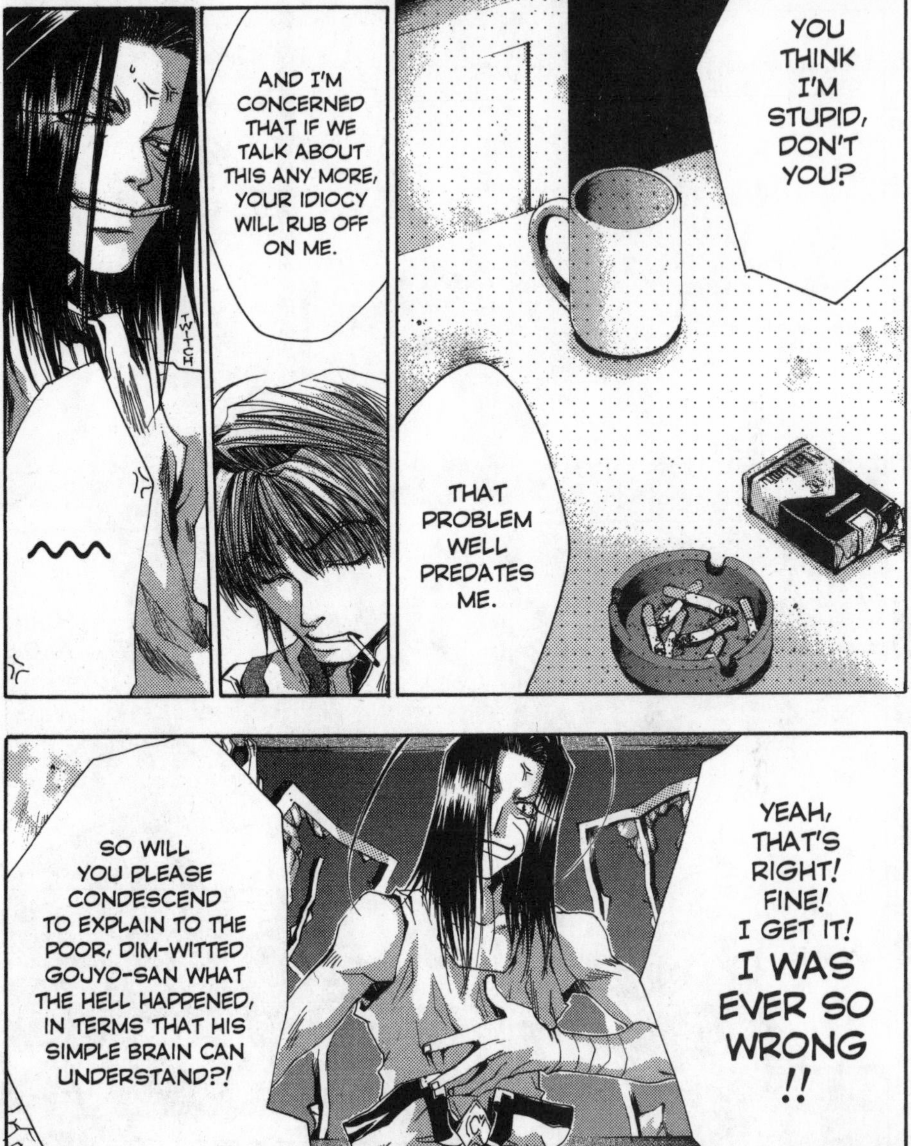
YOU THINK I'M STUPID, DON'T YOU?
THAT PROBLEM WELL PREDATES ME.
AND I'M CONCERNED THAT IF WE TALK ABOUT THIS ANY MORE, YOUR IDIOCY WILL RUB OFF ON ME.
TWITCH
YEAH, THAT'S RIGHT! FINE! I GET IT! I WAS EVER SO WRONG!!
SO WILL YOU PLEASE CONDESCEND TO EXPLAIN TO THE POOR, DIM-WITTED GOJYO-SAN WHAT THE HELL HAPPENED, IN TERMS THAT HIS SIMPLE BRAIN CAN UNDERSTAND?!
IS THAT TOO MUCH TO ASK, O GREAT SANZO-SAMA!!
...

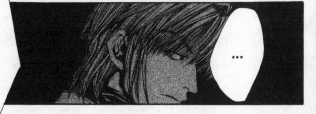

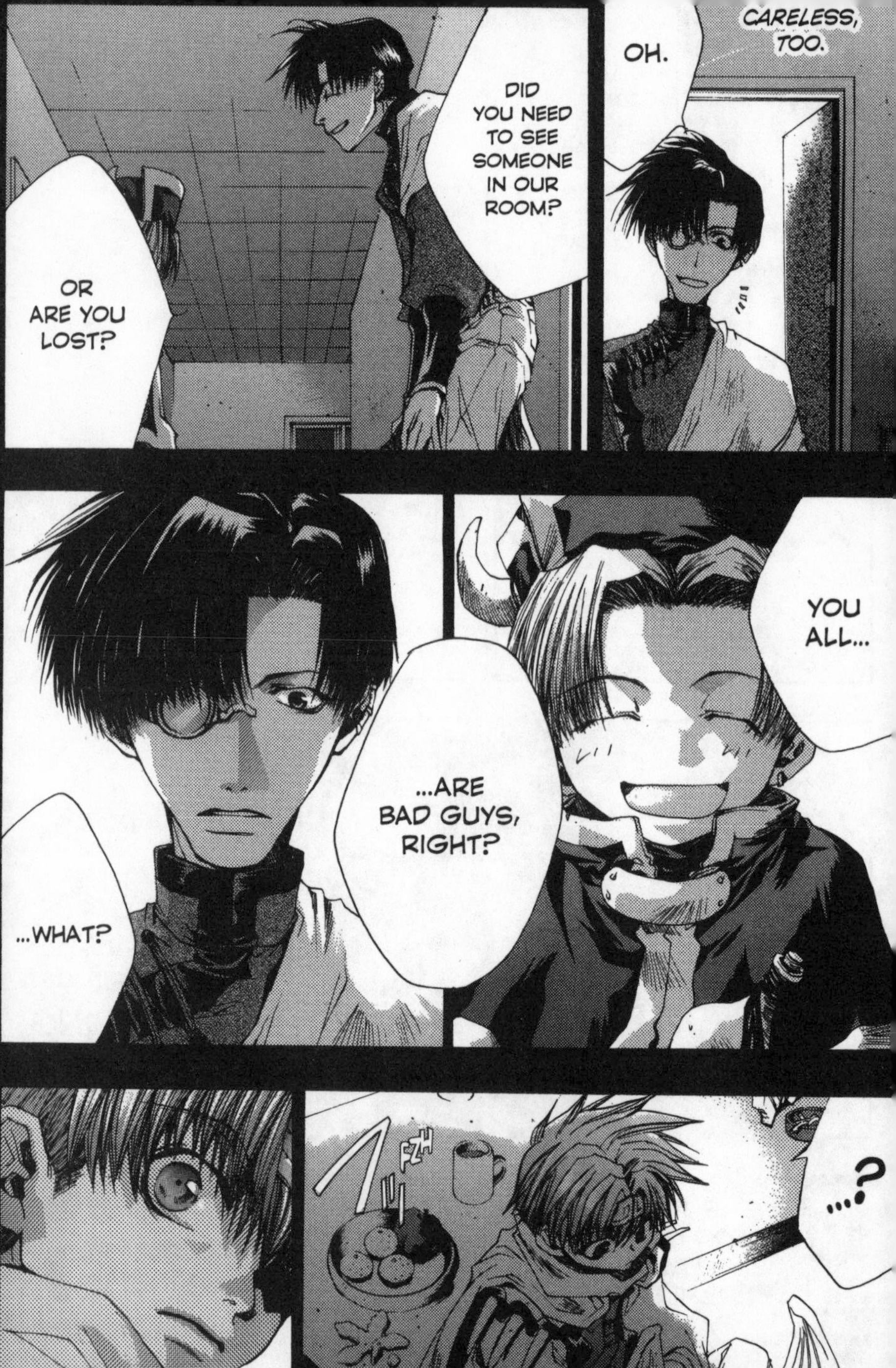
CARELESS, TOO.
OH.
DID YOU NEED TO SEE SOMEONE IN OUR ROOM?
OR ARE YOU LOST?
YOU ALL...
...ARE BAD GUYS, RIGHT?
...WHAT?
...?
FZH

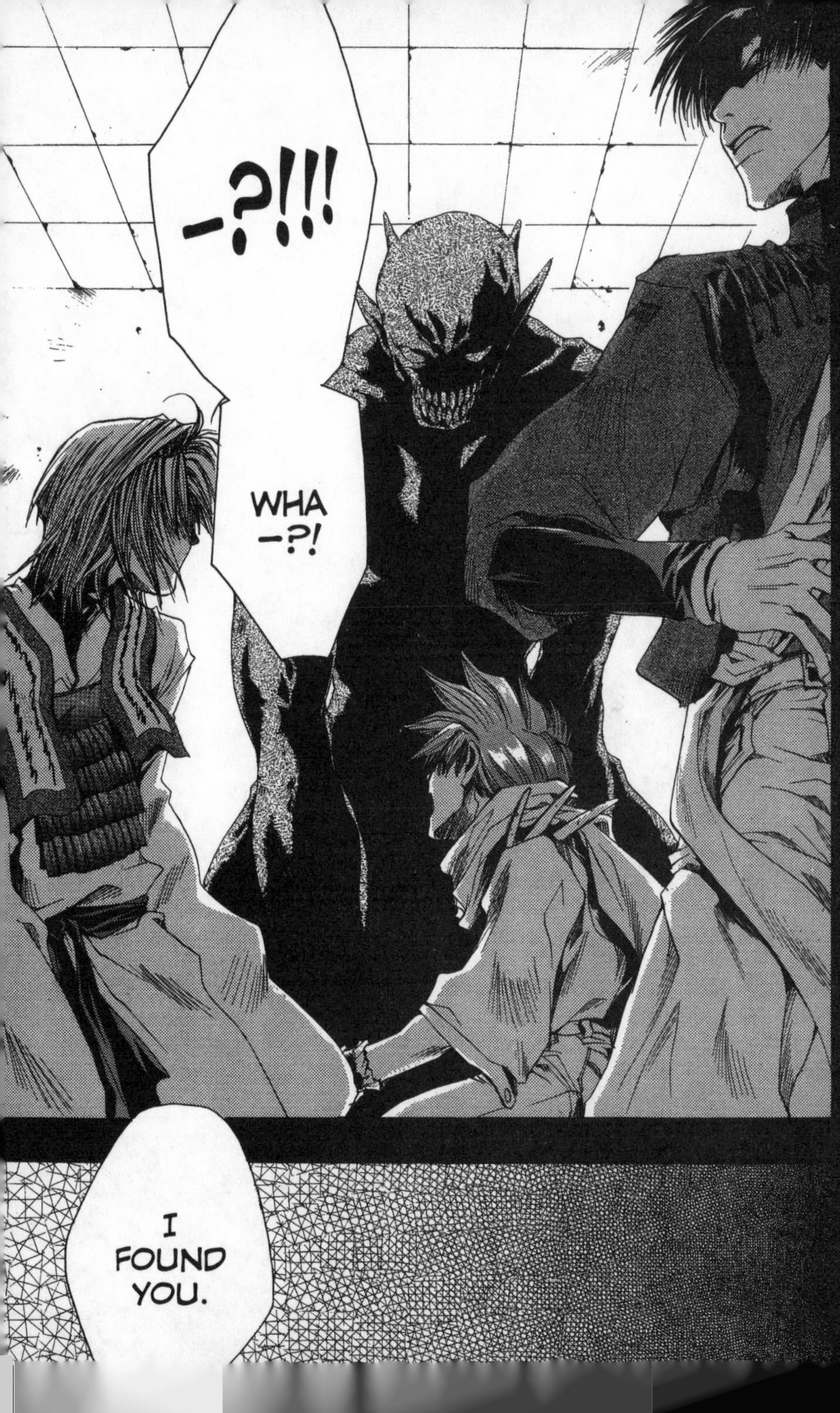
–?!!!
WHA –?!
I FOUND YOU.

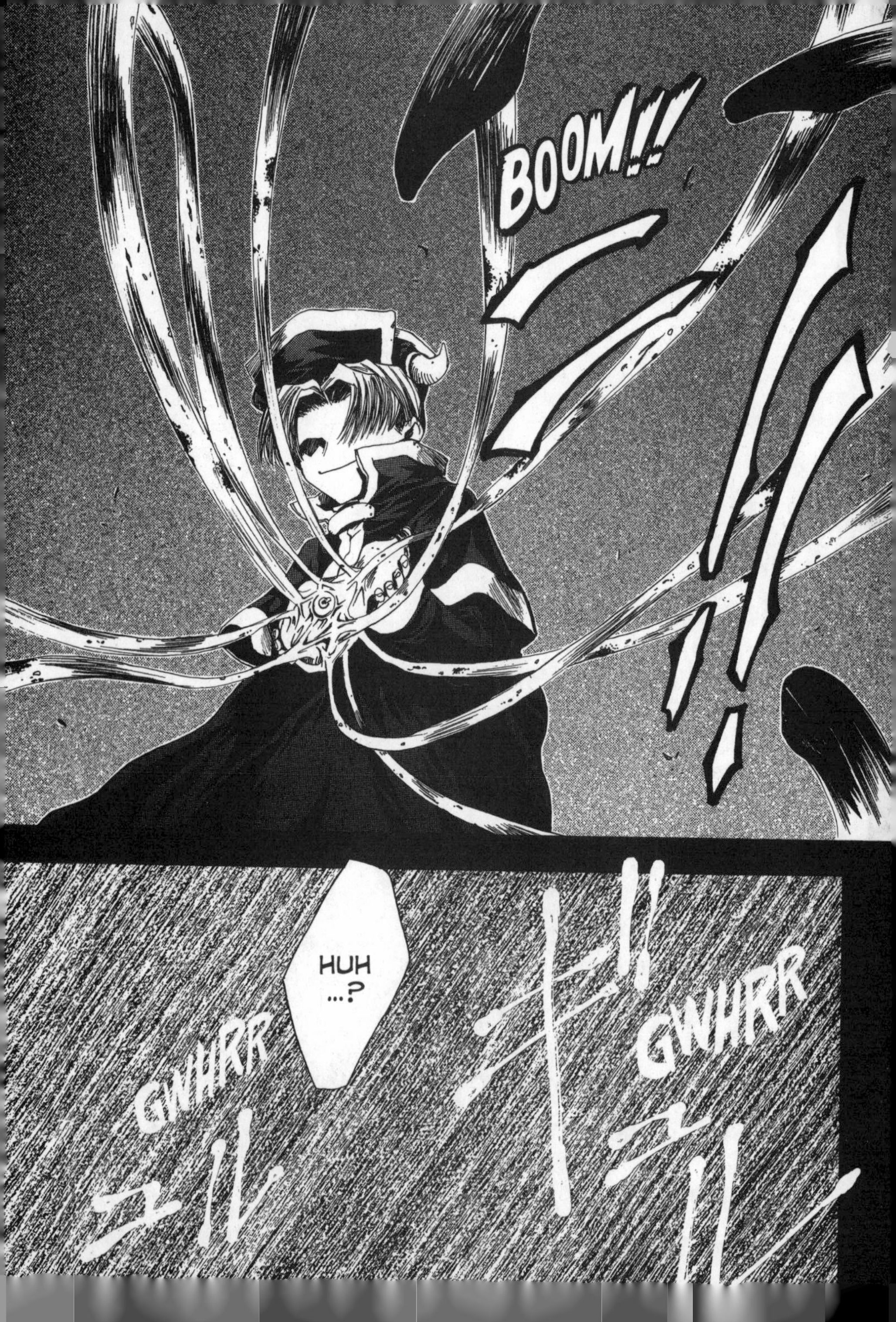
BOOM!!
GWHRR
HUH ...?
GWHRR

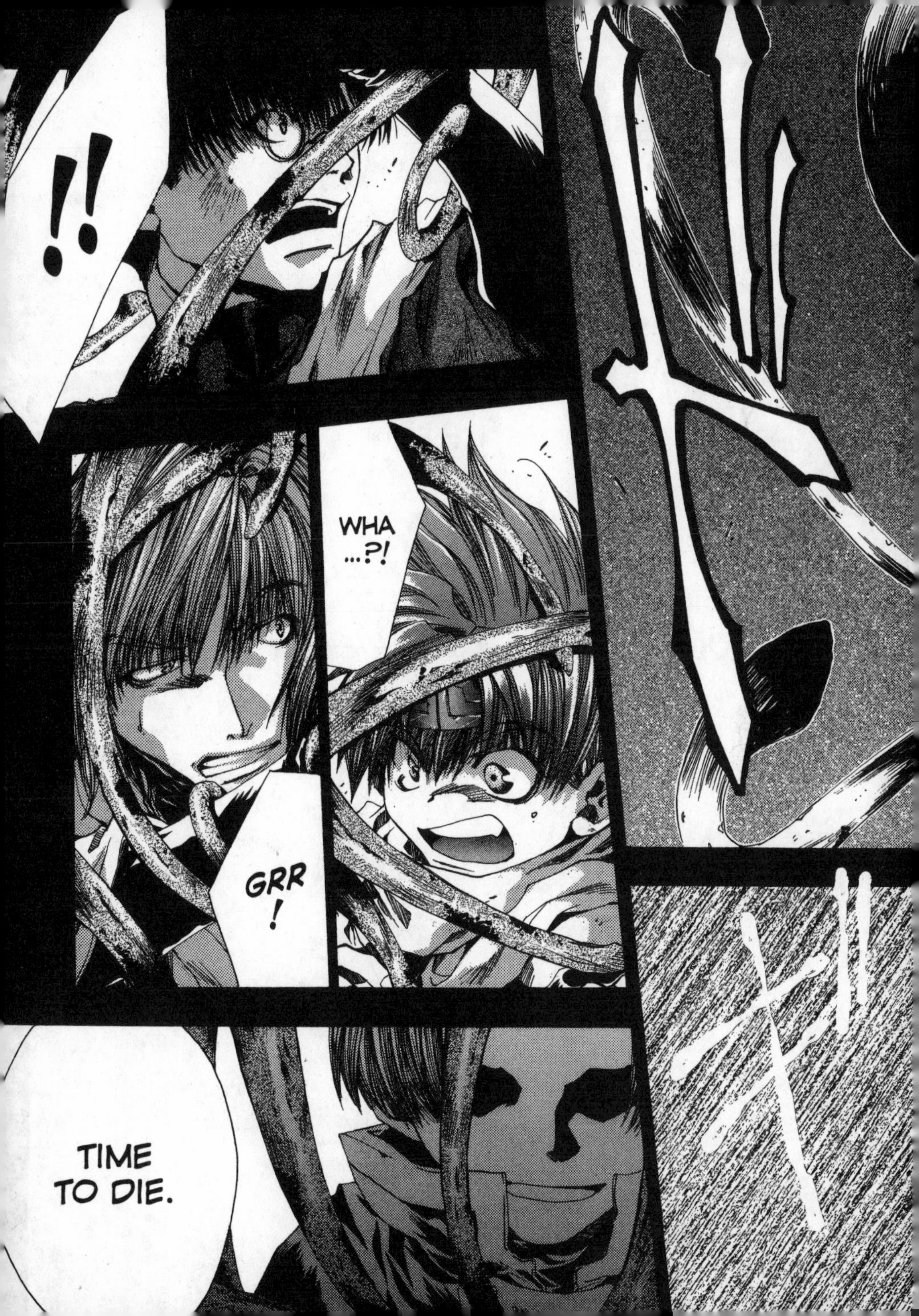
!!
WHA ...?!
GRR !
TIME TO DIE.

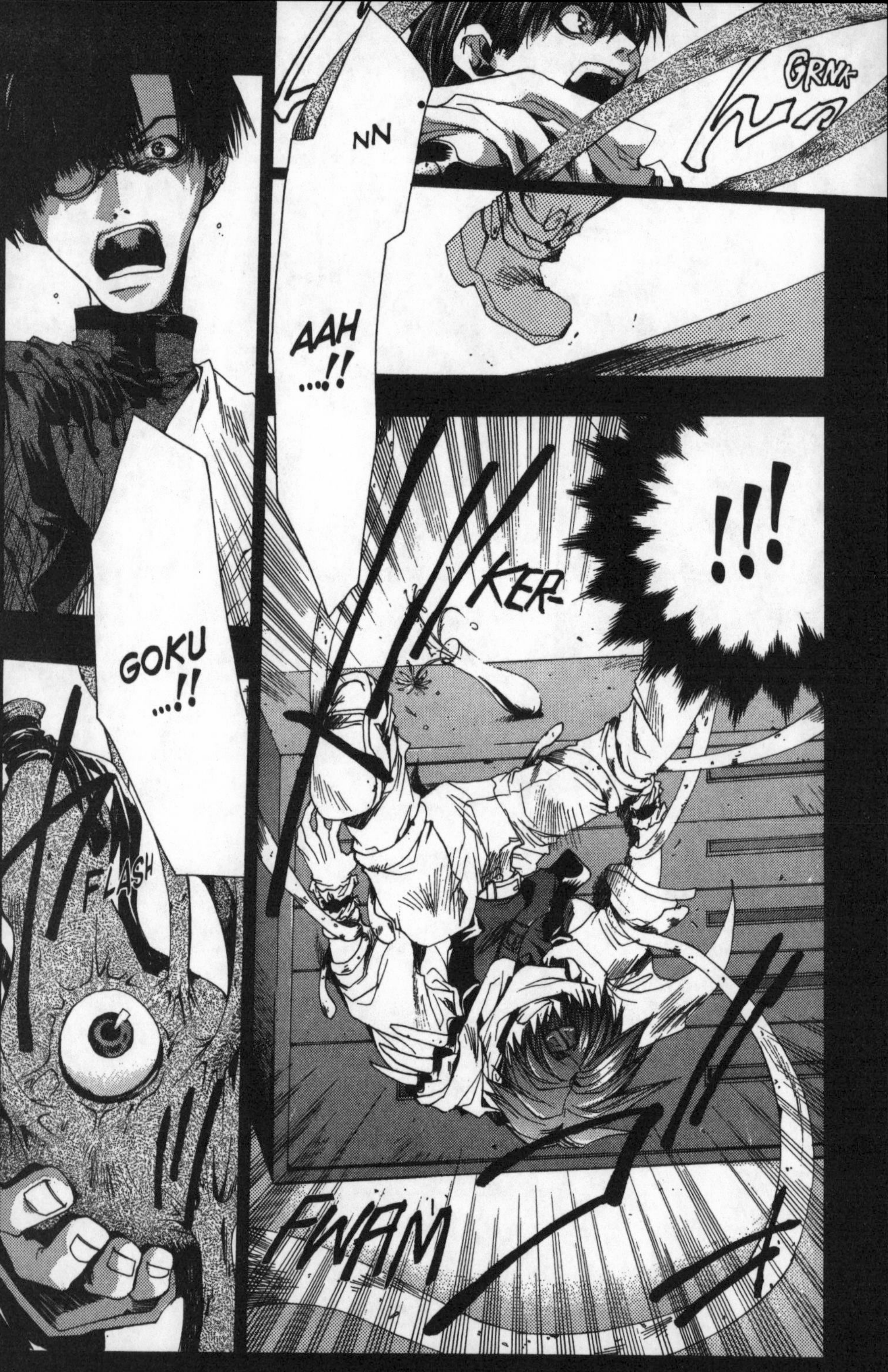
GRNK
NN
AAH ...!!
!!!
KER-
FWAM
GOKU ...!!
FLASH

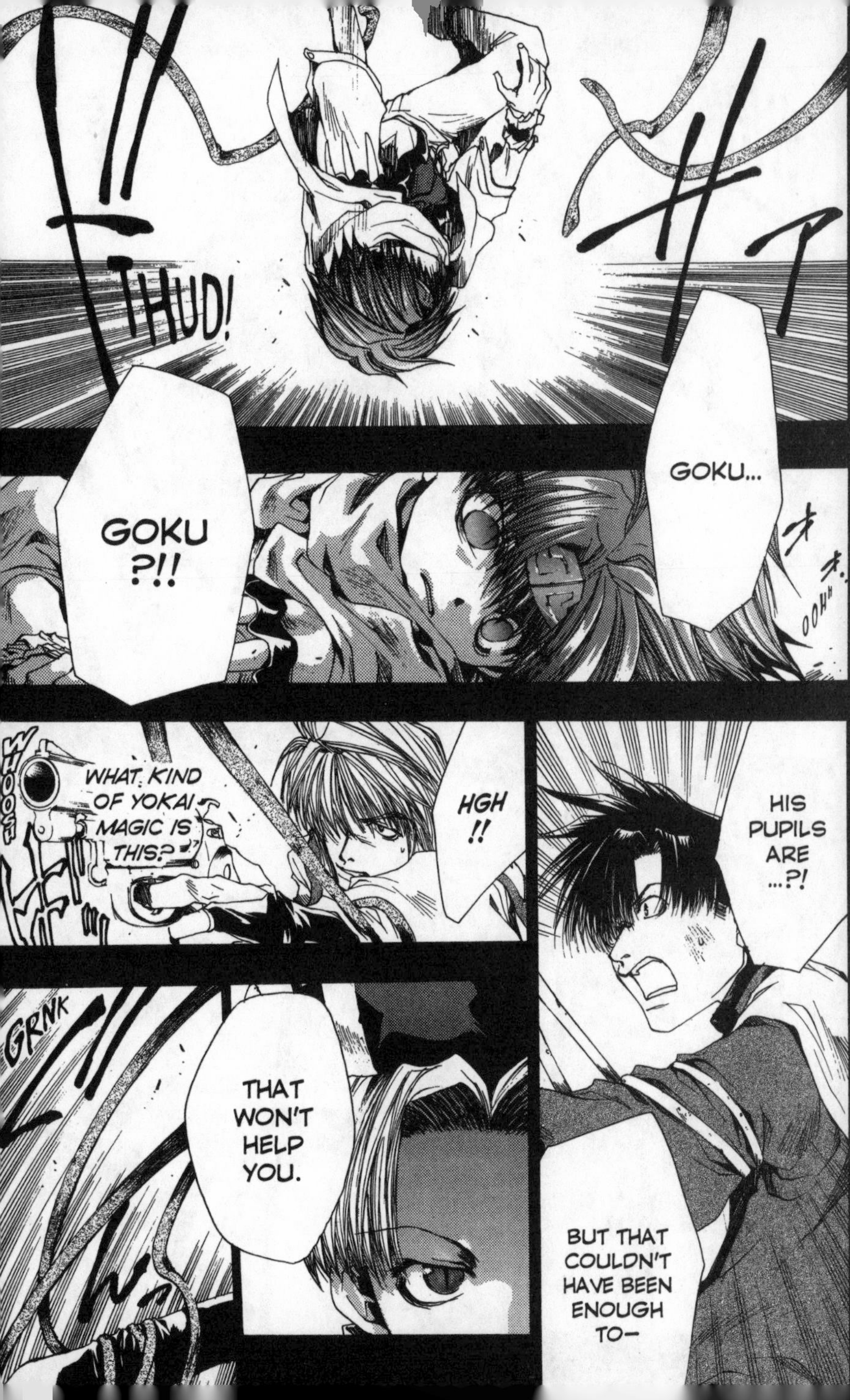
THUD!
GOKU...
OOH
GOKU ?!!
HIS PUPILS ARE ...?!
BUT THAT COULDN'T HAVE BEEN ENOUGH TO—
HGH !!
WHAT KIND OF YOKAI MAGIC IS THIS?
WHOOF
THAT WON'T HELP YOU.
GRNK

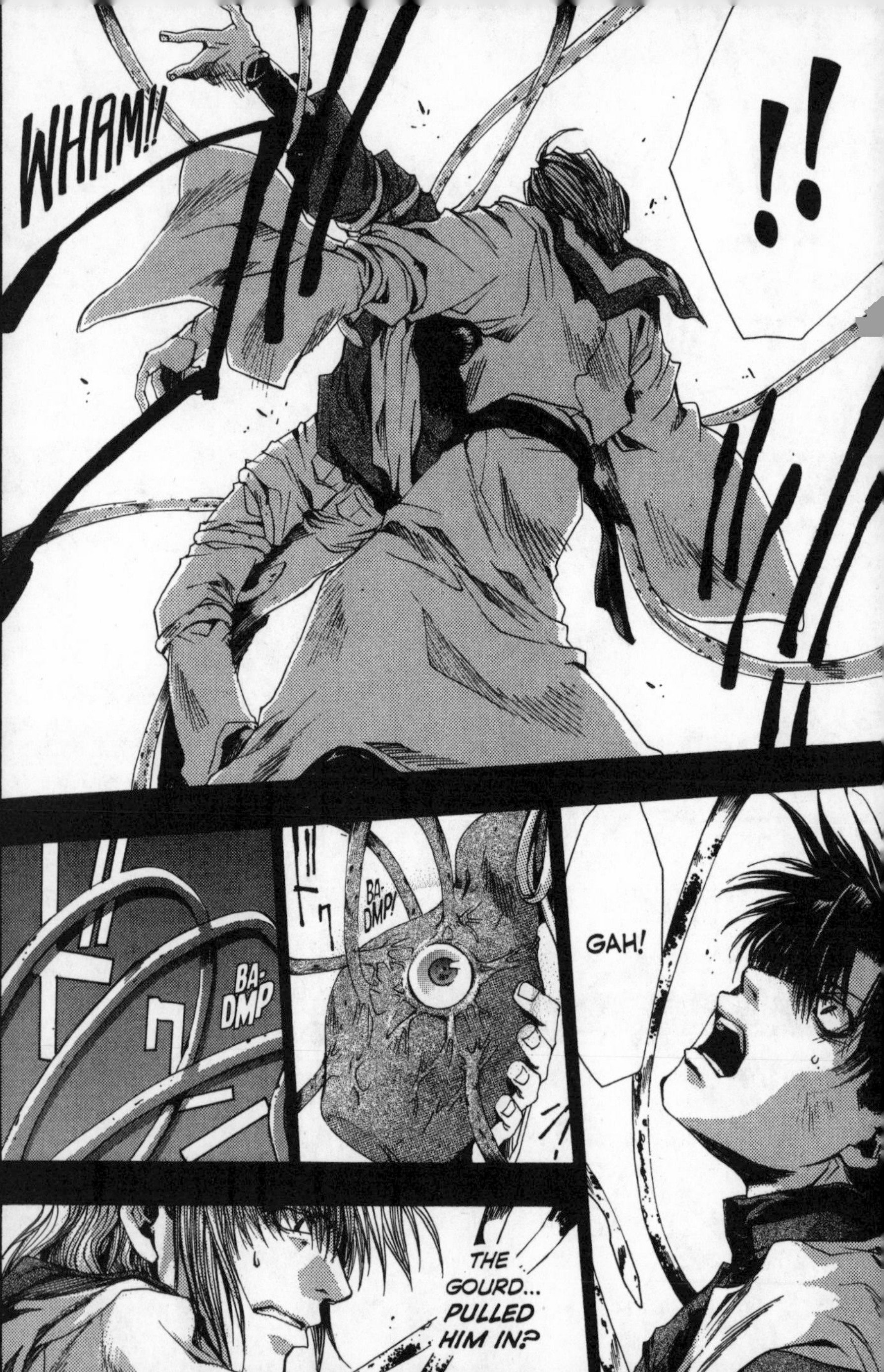
!!
WHAM!!
GAH!
BA-DMP!
BA-DMP
THE GOURD... PULLED HIM IN?

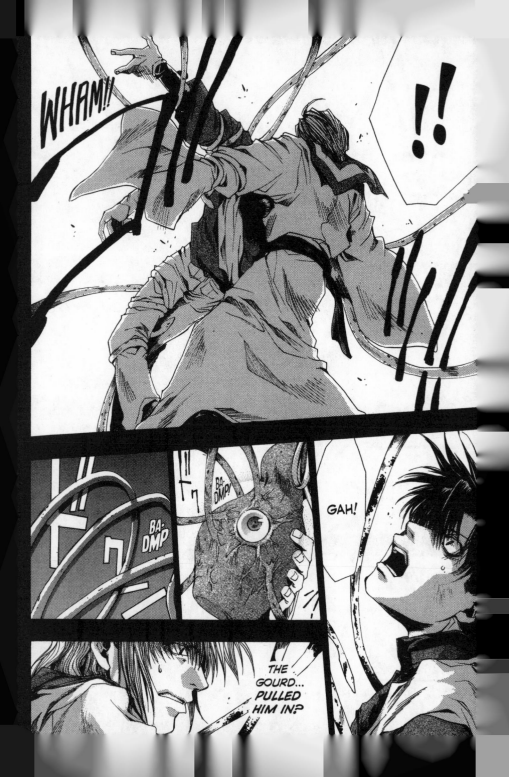

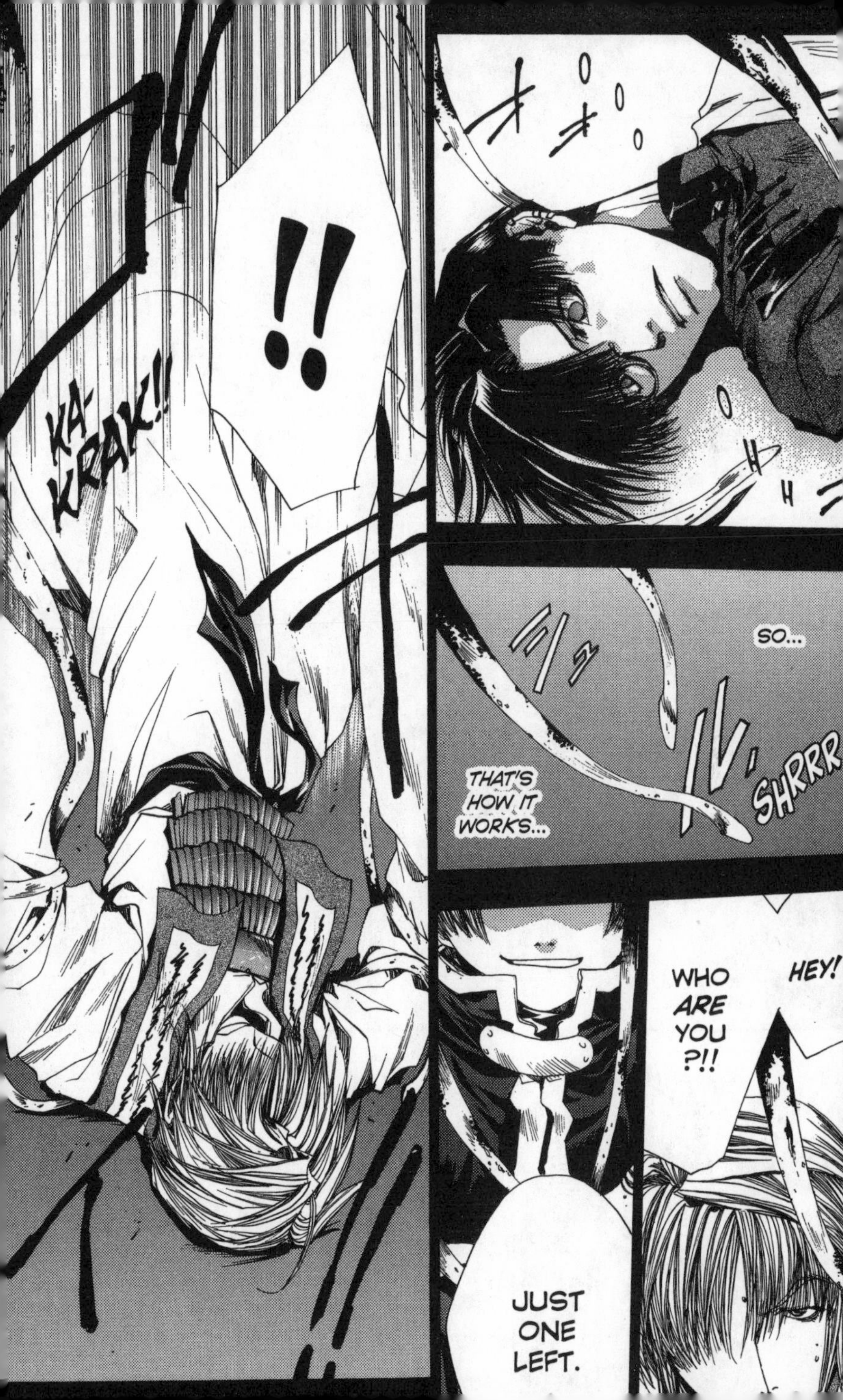
SO...
THAT'S HOW IT WORKS...
SHRRR
HEY!
WHO ARE YOU ?!!
JUST ONE LEFT.
!!
KA-KRAK!!

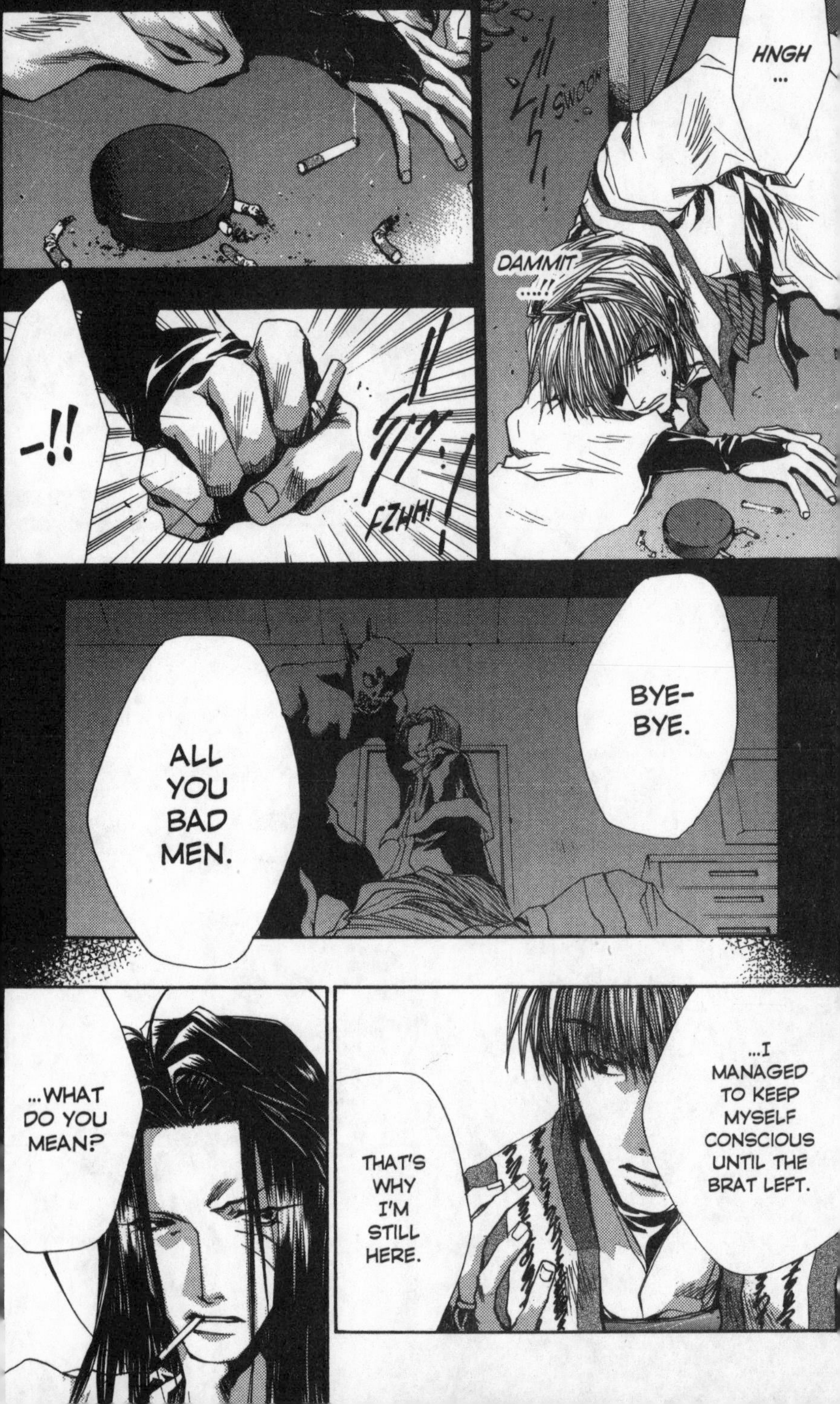
HNGH ...
SWOON
DAMMIT ...!!
FZHH!
–!!
BYE-BYE.
ALL YOU BAD MEN.
...I MANAGED TO KEEP MYSELF CONSCIOUS UNTIL THE BRAT LEFT.
THAT'S WHY I'M STILL HERE.
...WHAT DO YOU MEAN?

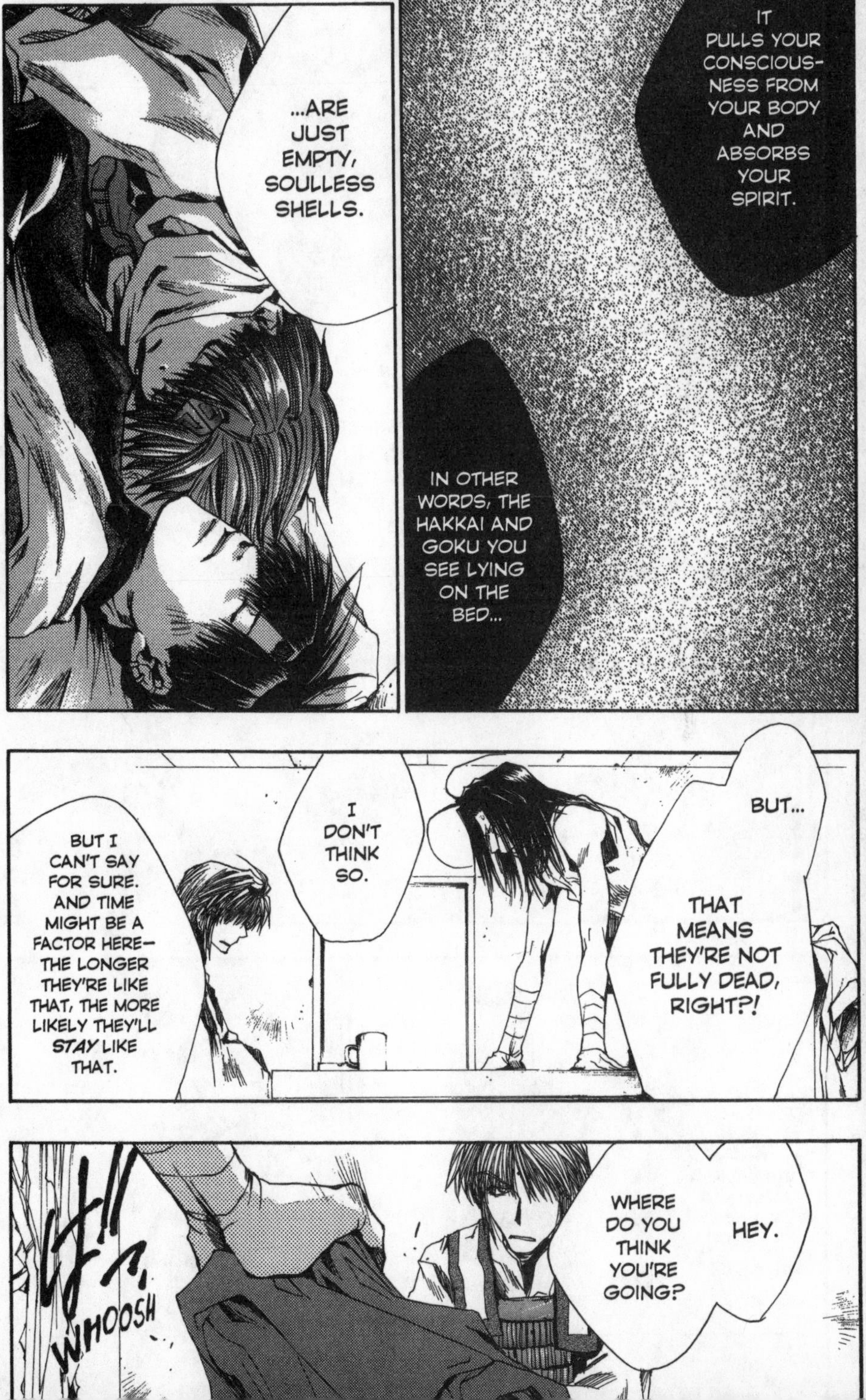
IT PULLS YOUR CONSCIOUSNESS FROM YOUR BODY AND ABSORBS YOUR SPIRIT.
IN OTHER WORDS, THE HAKKAI AND GOKU YOU SEE LYING ON THE BED...
...ARE JUST EMPTY, SOULLESS SHELLS.
BUT...
THAT MEANS THEY'RE NOT FULLY DEAD, RIGHT?!
I DON'T THINK SO.
BUT I CAN'T SAY FOR SURE. AND TIME MIGHT BE A FACTOR HERE—THE LONGER THEY'RE LIKE THAT, THE MORE LIKELY THEY'LL STAY LIKE THAT.
HEY.
WHERE DO YOU THINK YOU'RE GOING?
!
WHOOSH

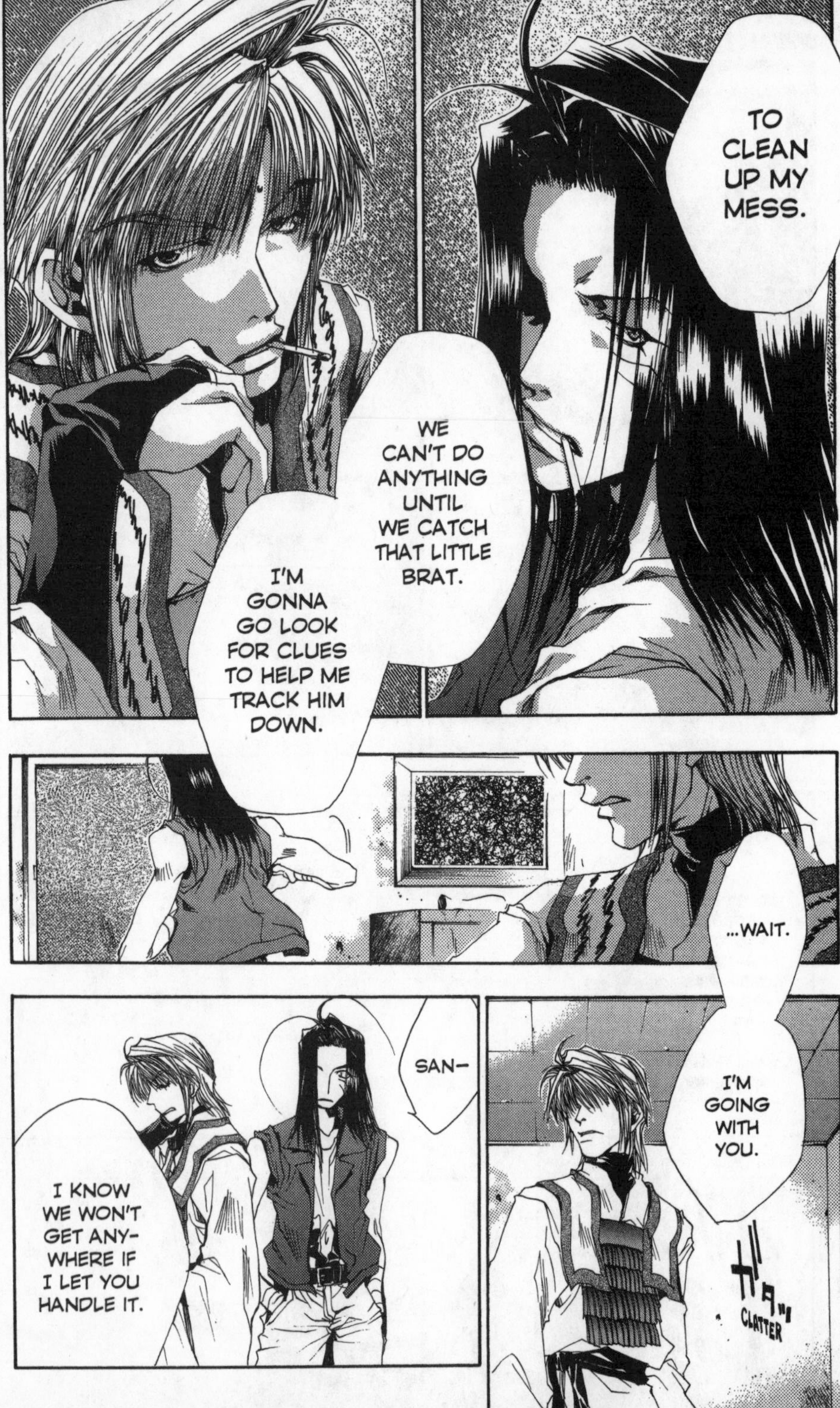
TO CLEAN UP MY MESS.
WE CAN'T DO ANYTHING UNTIL WE CATCH THAT LITTLE BRAT.
I'M GONNA GO LOOK FOR CLUES TO HELP ME TRACK HIM DOWN.
...WAIT.
I'M GOING WITH YOU.
CLATTER
SAN-
I KNOW WE WON'T GET ANY-WHERE IF I LET YOU HANDLE IT.

CHAPTER 37: Out of Gear

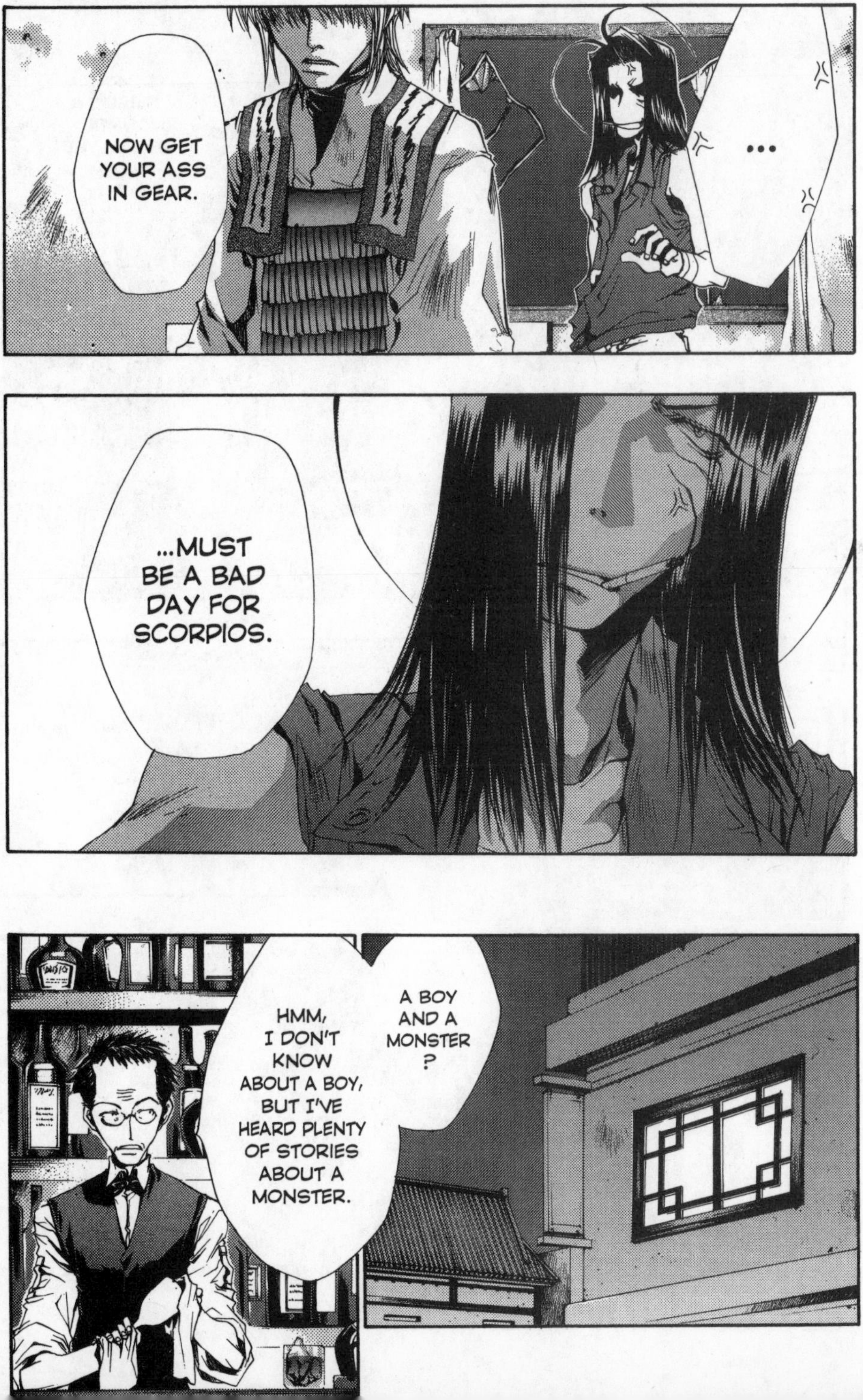
...
NOW GET YOUR ASS IN GEAR.
...MUST BE A BAD DAY FOR SCORPIOS.
A BOY AND A MONSTER ?
HMM, I DON'T KNOW ABOUT A BOY, BUT I'VE HEARD PLENTY OF STORIES ABOUT A MONSTER.

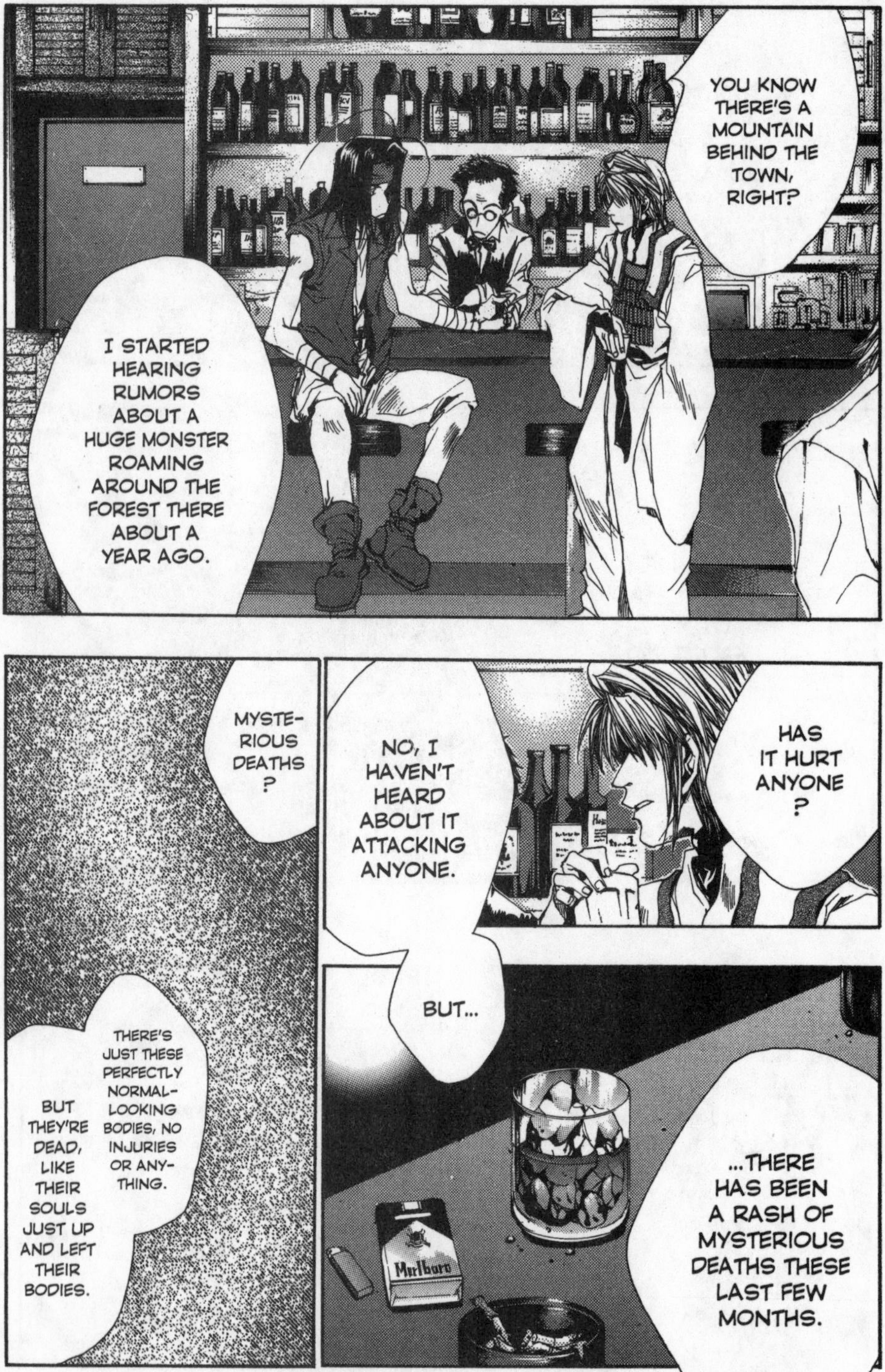
YOU KNOW THERE'S A MOUNTAIN BEHIND THE TOWN, RIGHT?
I STARTED HEARING RUMORS ABOUT A HUGE MONSTER ROAMING AROUND THE FOREST THERE ABOUT A YEAR AGO.
HAS IT HURT ANYONE?
NO, I HAVEN'T HEARD ABOUT IT ATTACKING ANYONE.
BUT...
...THERE HAS BEEN A RASH OF MYSTERIOUS DEATHS THESE LAST FEW MONTHS.
MYSTE-RIOUS DEATHS?
THERE'S JUST THESE PERFECTLY NORMAL-LOOKING BODIES, NO INJURIES OR ANY-THING.
BUT THEY'RE DEAD, LIKE THEIR SOULS JUST UP AND LEFT THEIR BODIES.

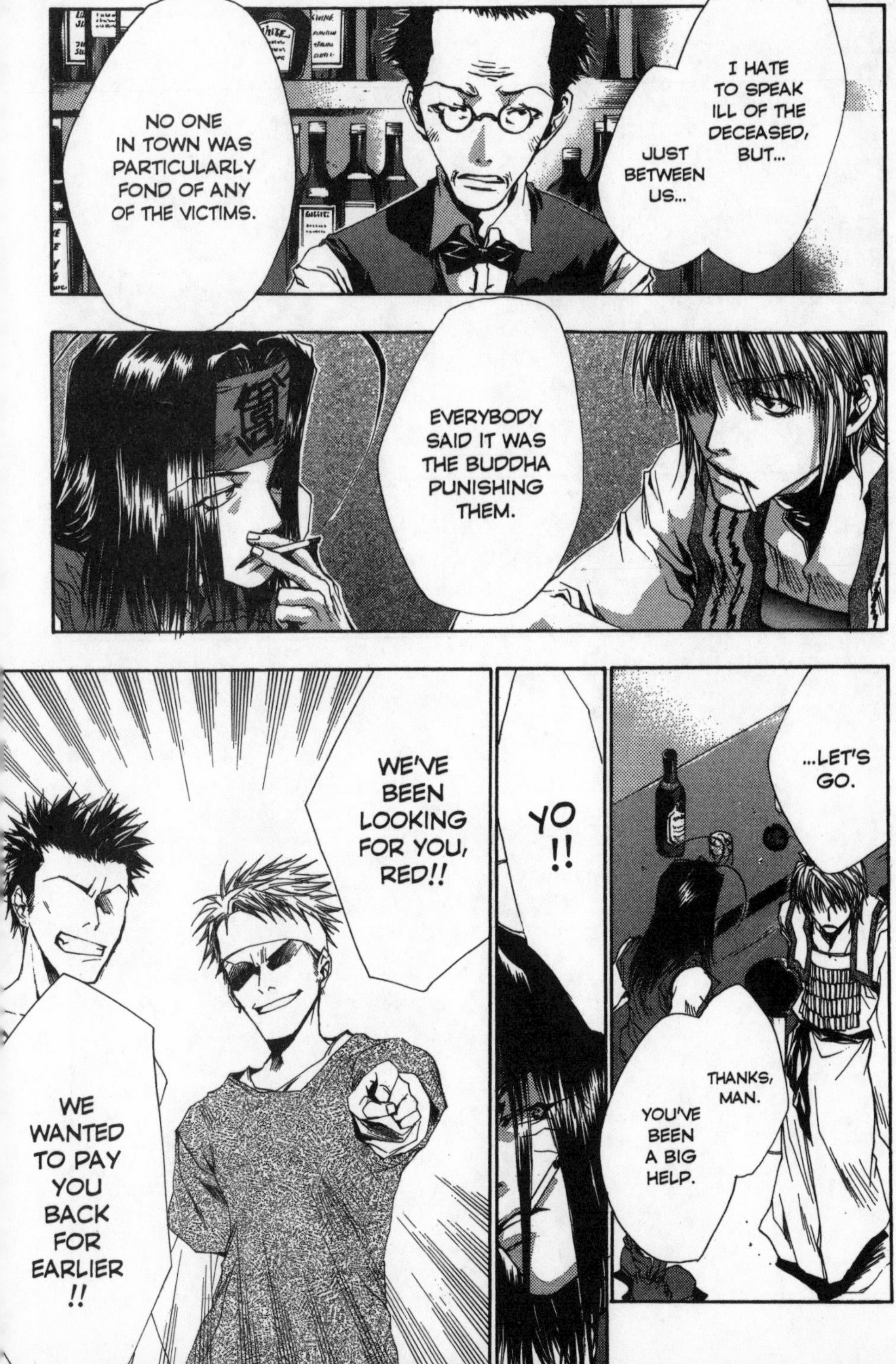
I HATE TO SPEAK ILL OF THE DECEASED, BUT...
JUST BETWEEN US...
NO ONE IN TOWN WAS PARTICULARLY FOND OF ANY OF THE VICTIMS.
EVERYBODY SAID IT WAS THE BUDDHA PUNISHING THEM.
...LET'S GO.
THANKS, MAN.
YOU'VE BEEN A BIG HELP.
YO !!
WE'VE BEEN LOOKING FOR YOU, RED!!
WE WANTED TO PAY YOU BACK FOR EARLIER !!

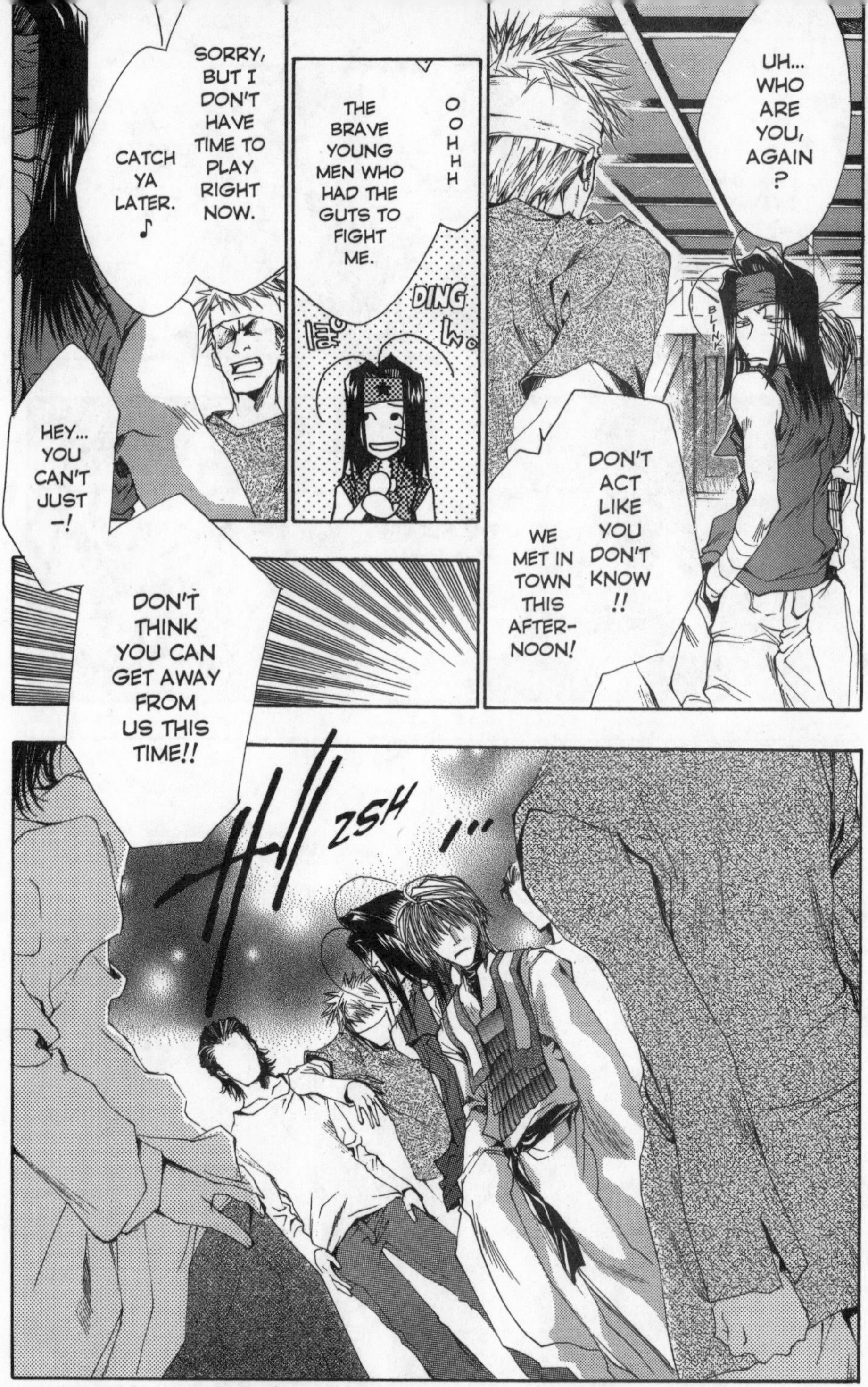
UH... WHO ARE YOU, AGAIN?
BLINK
DON'T ACT LIKE YOU DON'T KNOW!!
WE MET IN TOWN THIS AFTERNOON!
OOHHH
THE BRAVE YOUNG MEN WHO HAD THE GUTS TO FIGHT ME.
DING
SORRY, BUT I DON'T HAVE TIME TO PLAY RIGHT NOW.
CATCH YA LATER. ♪
HEY... YOU CAN'T JUST -!
DON'T THINK YOU CAN GET AWAY FROM US THIS TIME!!
ZSH

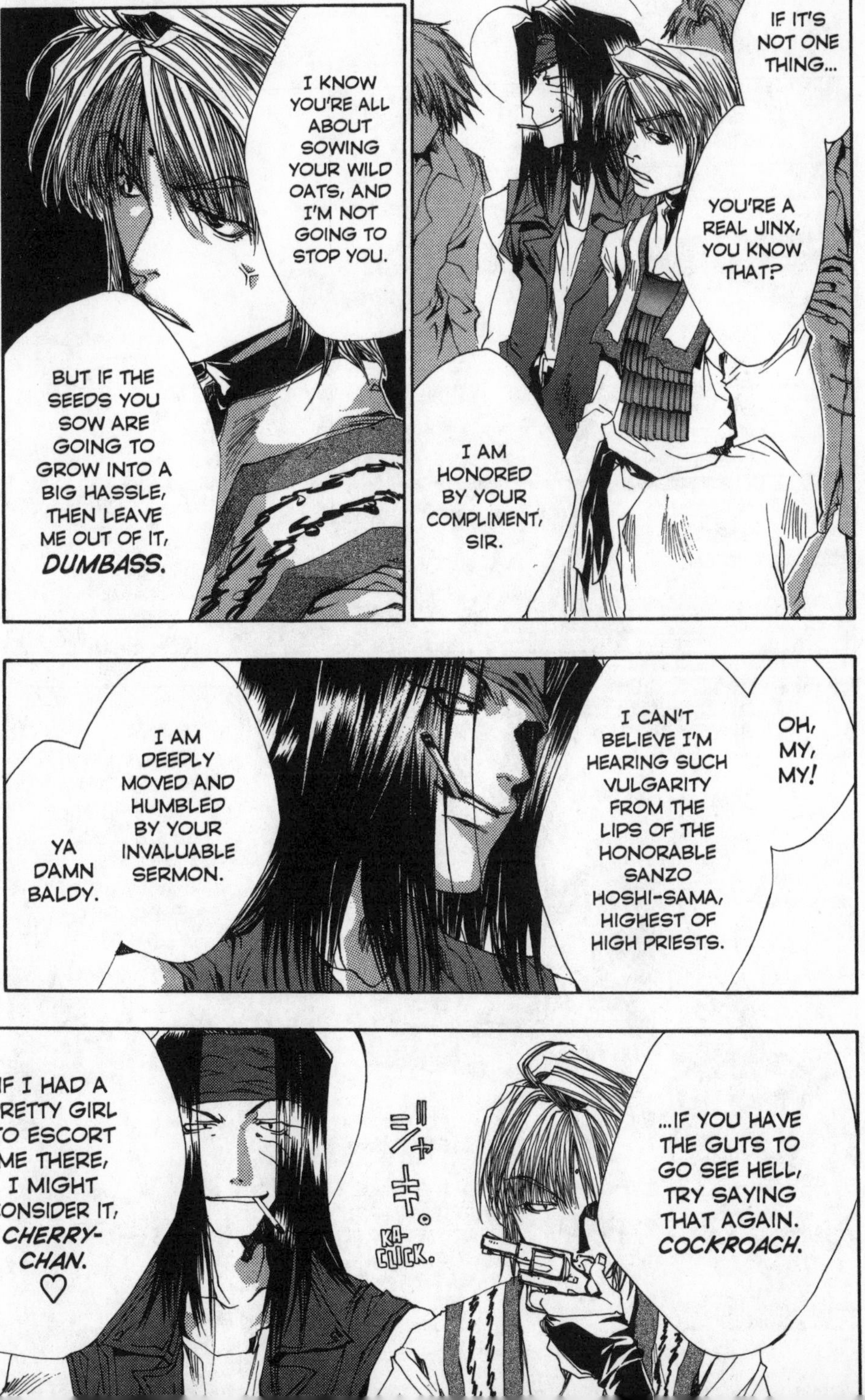
IF IT'S NOT ONE THING...
YOU'RE A REAL JINX, YOU KNOW THAT?
I AM HONORED BY YOUR COMPLIMENT, SIR.
I KNOW YOU'RE ALL ABOUT SOWING YOUR WILD OATS, AND I'M NOT GOING TO STOP YOU.
BUT IF THE SEEDS YOU SOW ARE GOING TO GROW INTO A BIG HASSLE, THEN LEAVE ME OUT OF IT, DUMBASS.
OH, MY, MY!
I CAN'T BELIEVE I'M HEARING SUCH VULGARITY FROM THE LIPS OF THE HONORABLE SANZO HOSHI-SAMA, HIGHEST OF HIGH PRIESTS.
I AM DEEPLY MOVED AND HUMBLED BY YOUR INVALUABLE SERMON.
YA DAMN BALDY.
...IF YOU HAVE THE GUTS TO GO SEE HELL, TRY SAYING THAT AGAIN. COCKROACH.
KA-CLICK.
IF I HAD A PRETTY GIRL TO ESCORT ME THERE, I MIGHT CONSIDER IT, CHERRY-CHAN. ♡

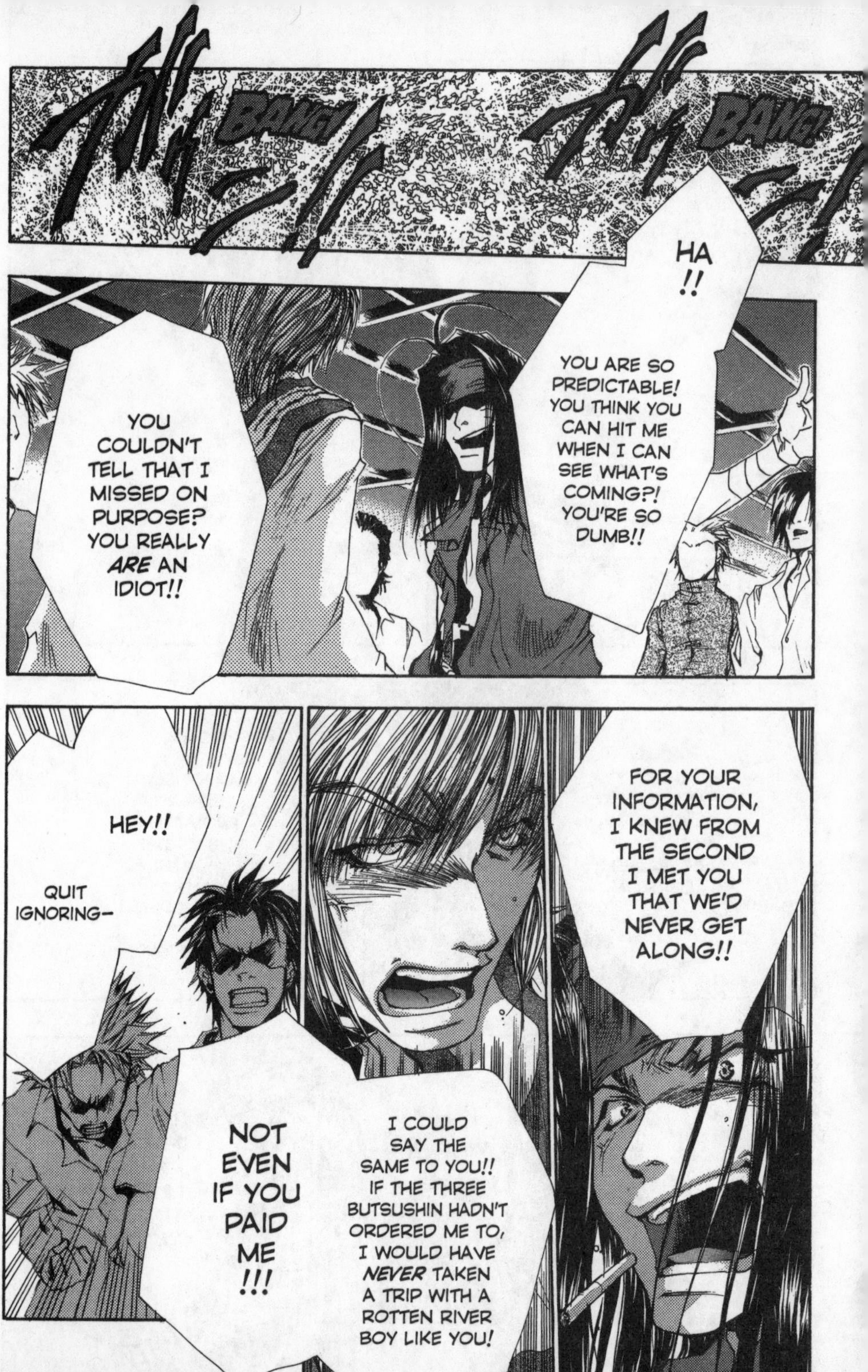
BANG!
BANG!
HA!!
YOU ARE SO PREDICTABLE! YOU THINK YOU CAN HIT ME WHEN I CAN SEE WHAT'S COMING?! YOU'RE SO DUMB!!
YOU COULDN'T TELL THAT I MISSED ON PURPOSE? YOU REALLY *ARE* AN IDIOT!!
FOR YOUR INFORMATION, I KNEW FROM THE SECOND I MET YOU THAT WE'D NEVER GET ALONG!!
I COULD SAY THE SAME TO YOU!! IF THE THREE BUTSUSHIN HADN'T ORDERED ME TO, I WOULD HAVE *NEVER* TAKEN A TRIP WITH A ROTTEN RIVER BOY LIKE YOU!
NOT EVEN IF YOU PAID ME!!!
HEY!!
QUIT IGNORING-

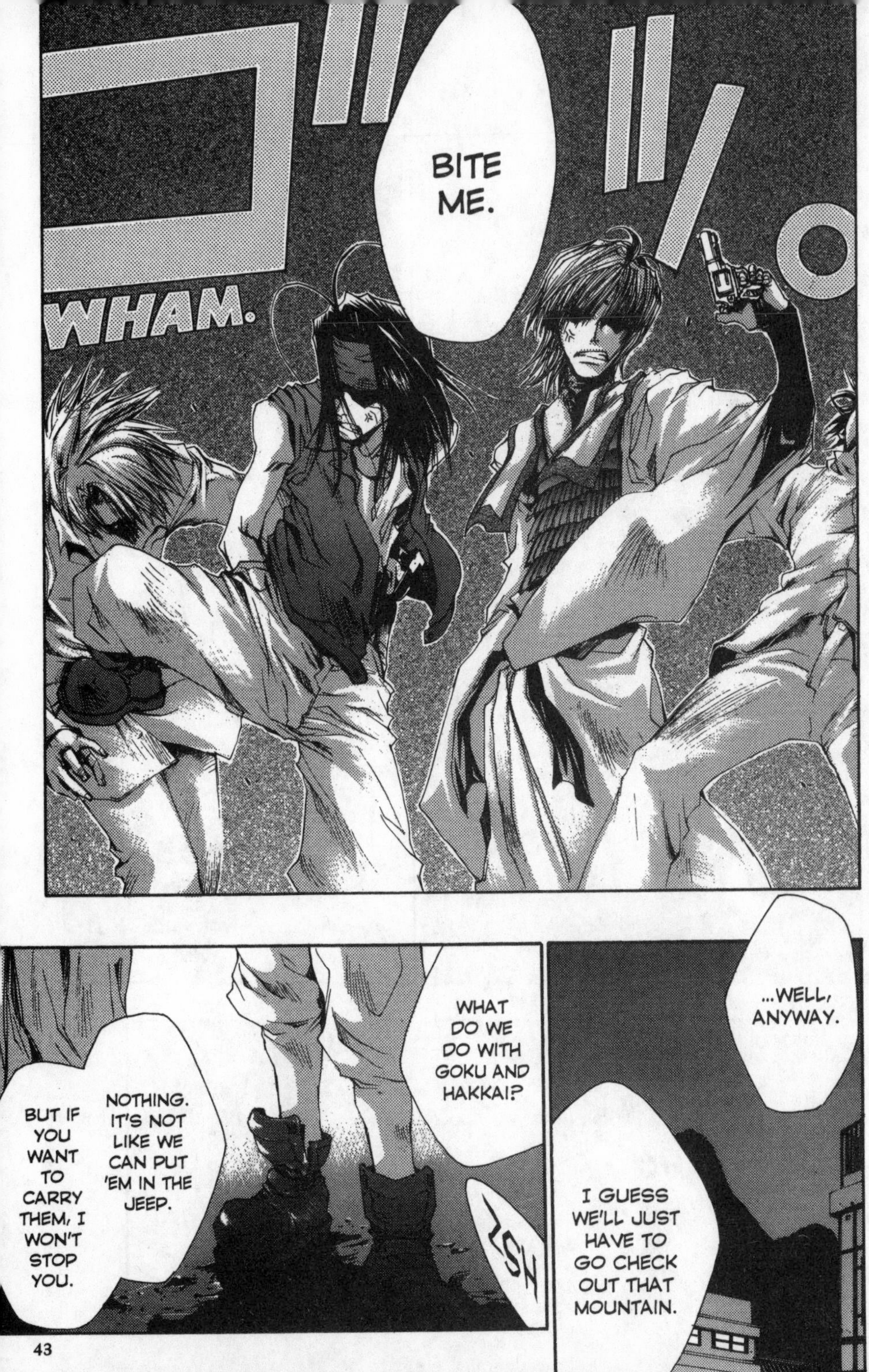
BITE ME.
WHAM.
...WELL, ANYWAY.
I GUESS WE'LL JUST HAVE TO GO CHECK OUT THAT MOUNTAIN.
WHAT DO WE DO WITH GOKU AND HAKKAI?
ZSH
NOTHING. IT'S NOT LIKE WE CAN PUT 'EM IN THE JEEP.
BUT IF YOU WANT TO CARRY THEM, I WON'T STOP YOU.

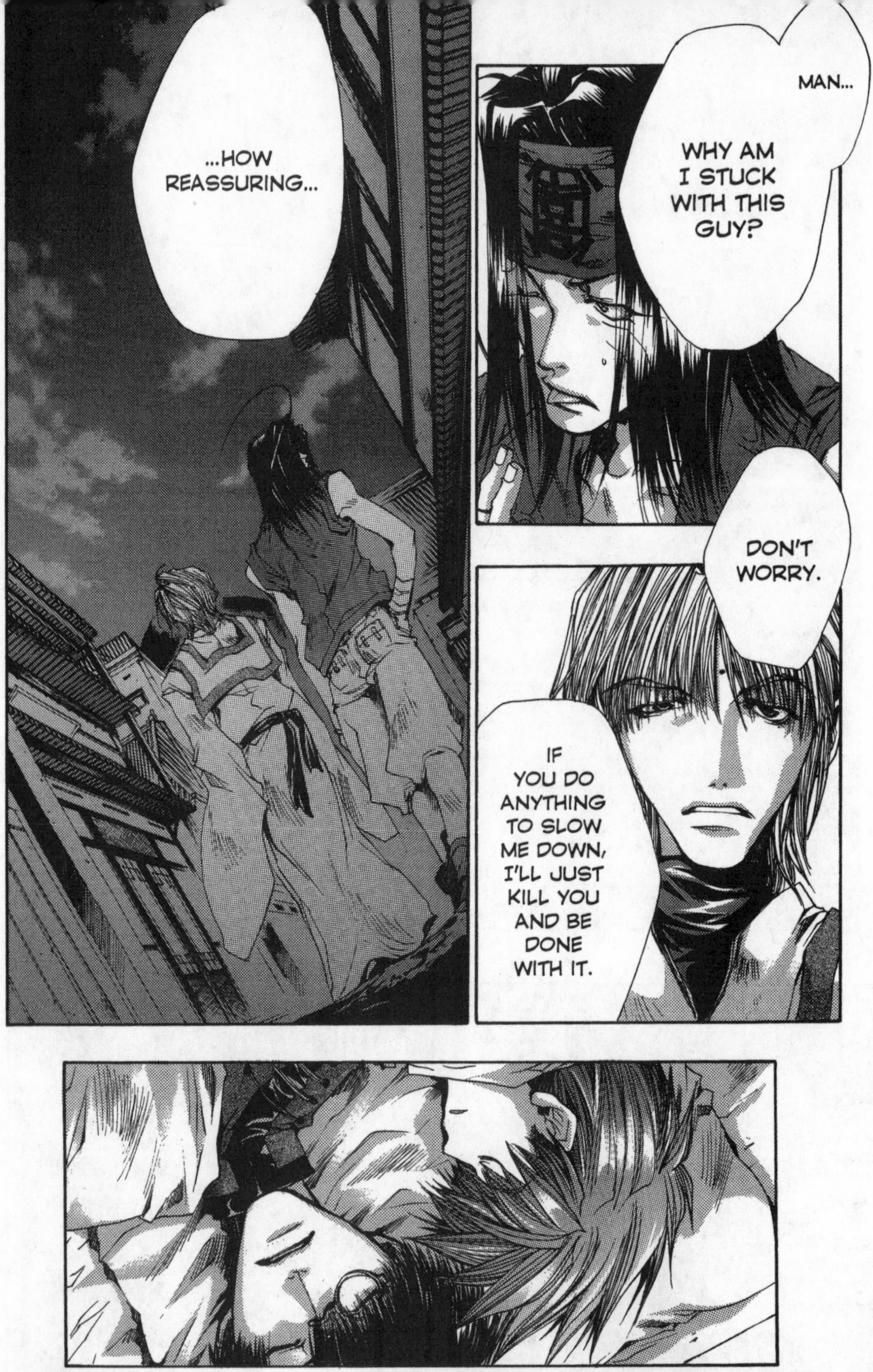
MAN...
WHY AM I STUCK WITH THIS GUY?
DON'T WORRY.
IF YOU DO ANYTHING TO SLOW ME DOWN, I'LL JUST KILL YOU AND BE DONE WITH IT.
...HOW REASSURING...

CHAPTER 38: Branches

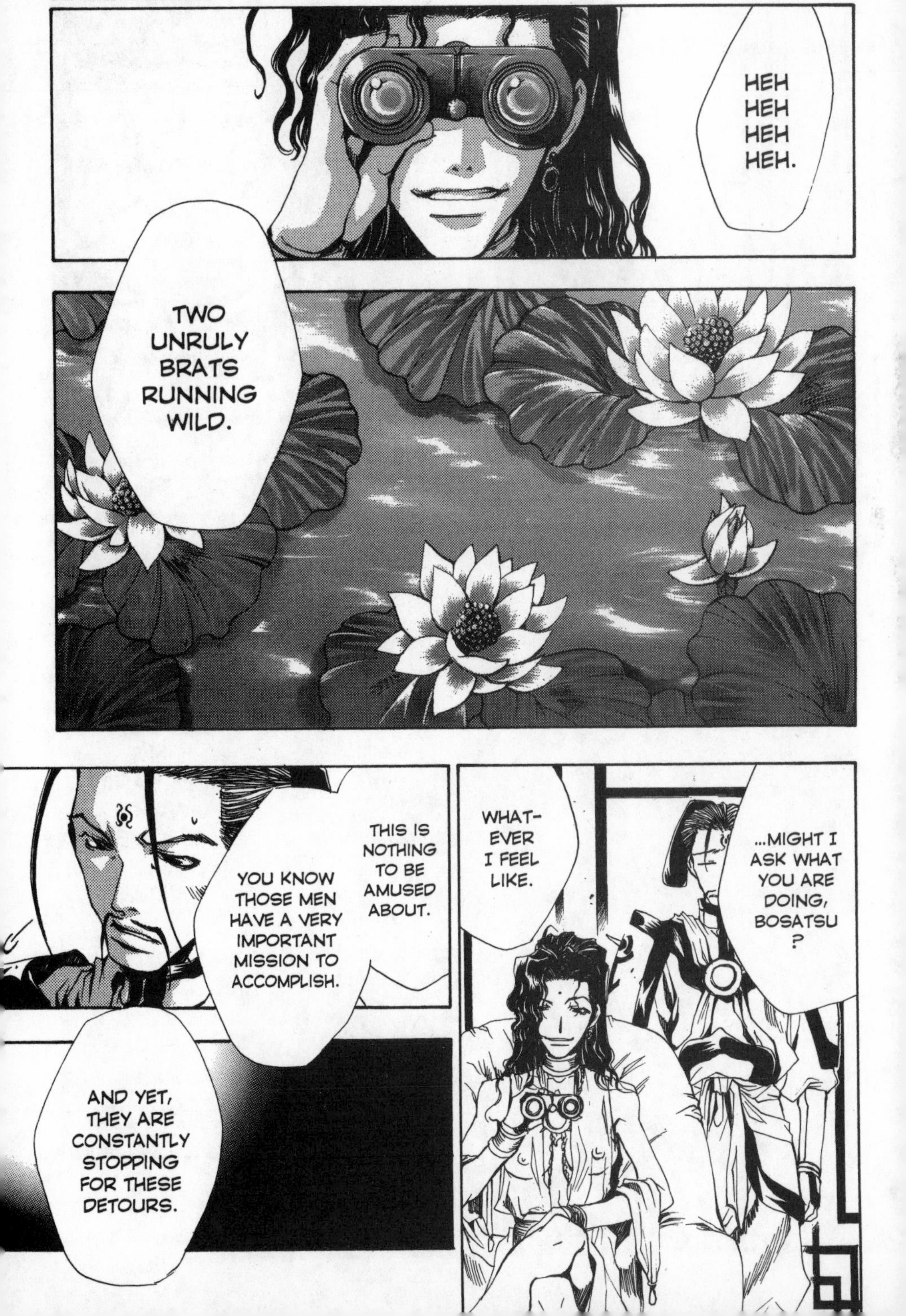
HEH HEH HEH HEH.
TWO UNRULY BRATS RUNNING WILD.
...MIGHT I ASK WHAT YOU ARE DOING, BOSATSU?
WHAT-EVER I FEEL LIKE.
THIS IS NOTHING TO BE AMUSED ABOUT.
YOU KNOW THOSE MEN HAVE A VERY IMPORTANT MISSION TO ACCOMPLISH.
AND YET, THEY ARE CONSTANTLY STOPPING FOR THESE DETOURS.

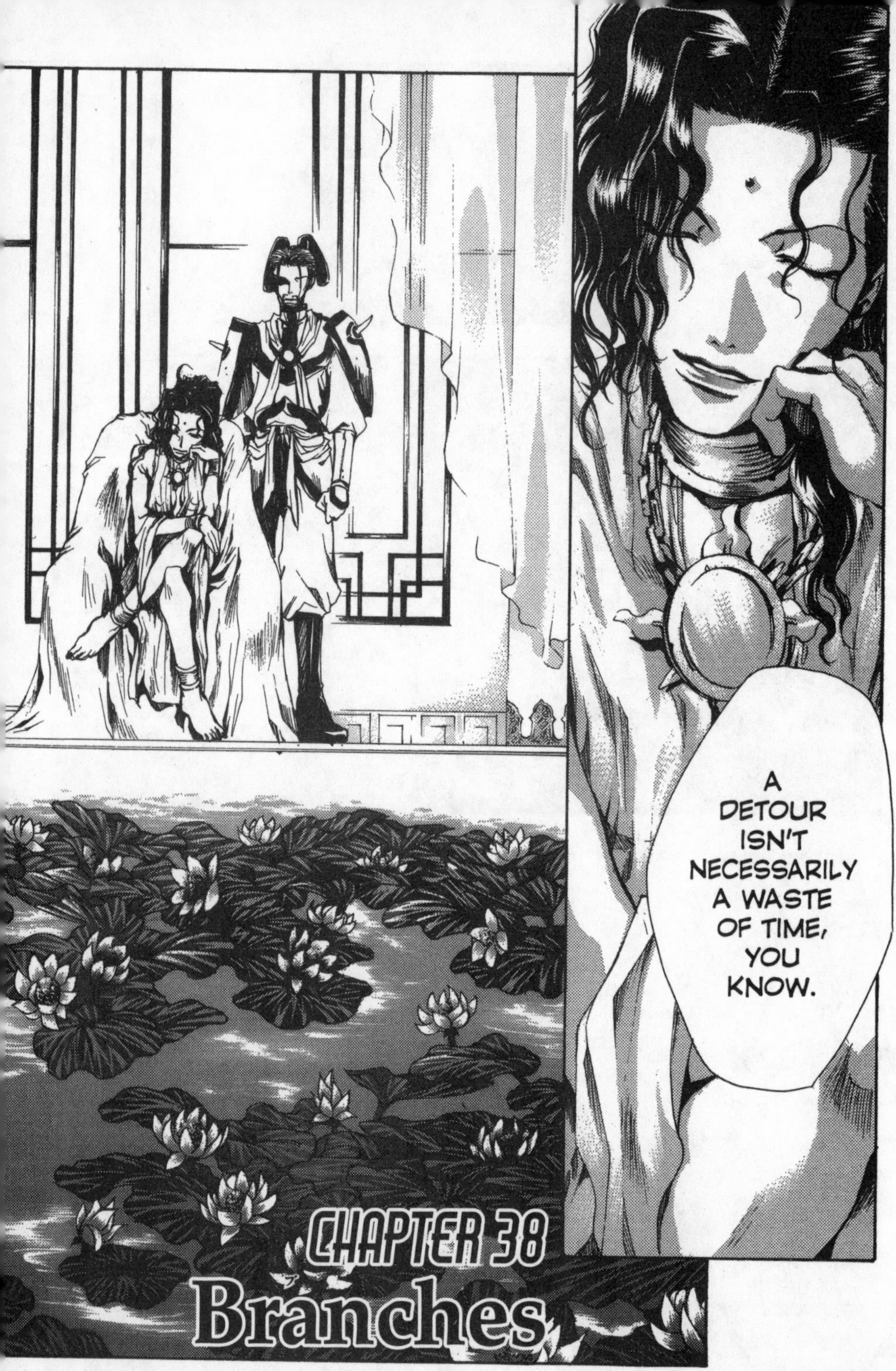
A DETOUR ISN'T NECESSARILY A WASTE OF TIME, YOU KNOW.
CHAPTER 38
Branches

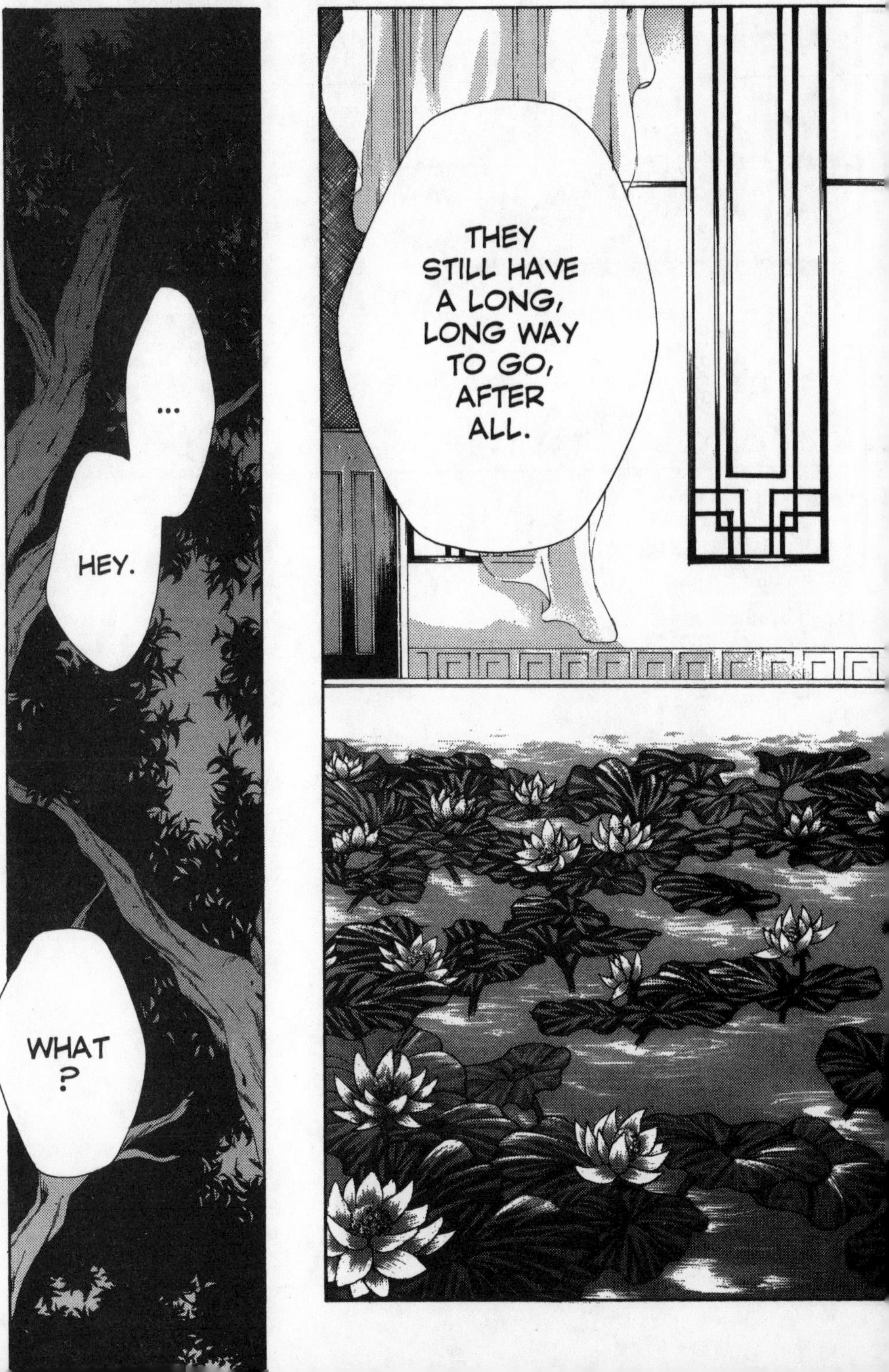
THEY STILL HAVE A LONG, LONG WAY TO GO, AFTER ALL.
...
HEY.
WHAT?

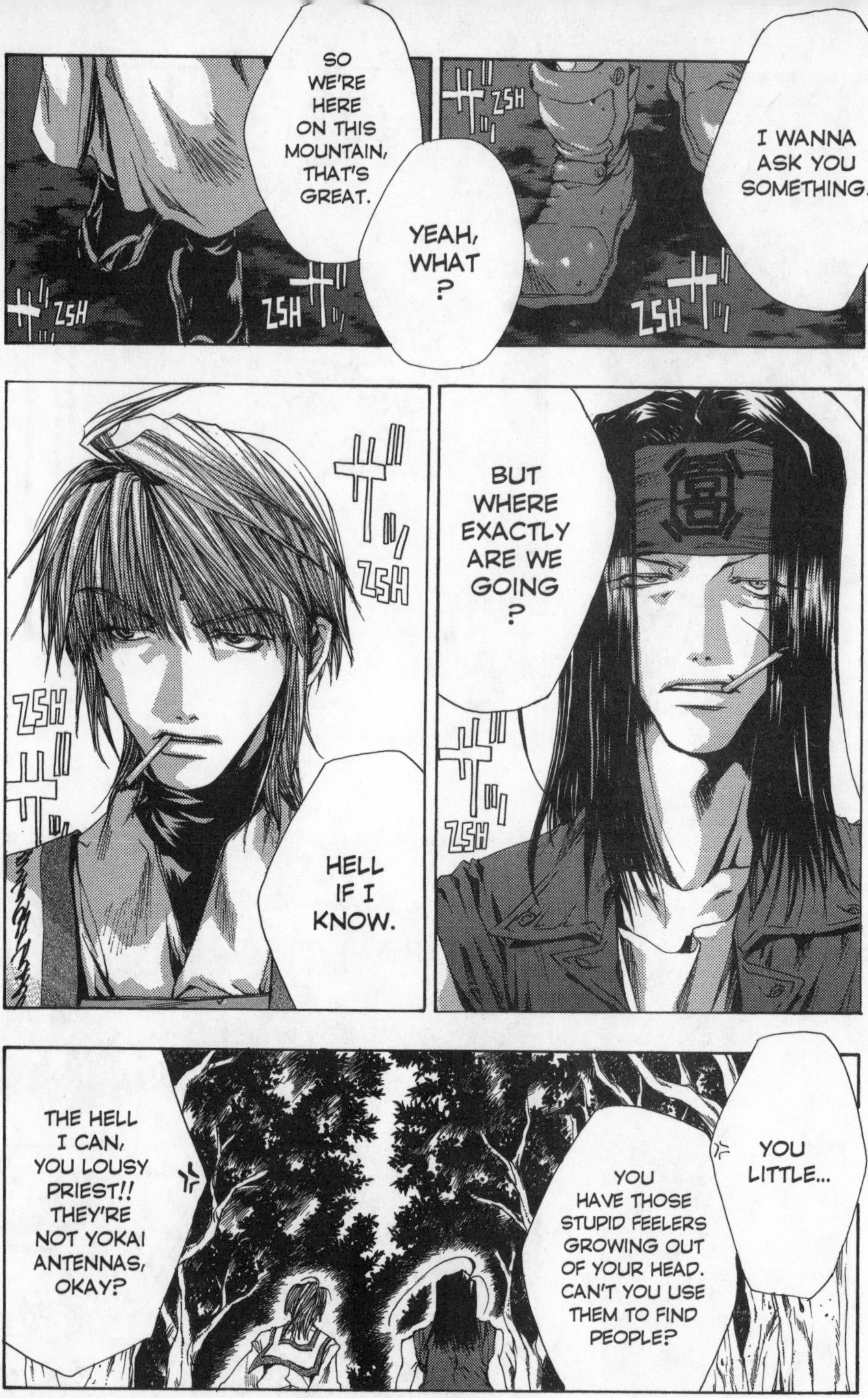
I WANNA ASK YOU SOMETHING.
ZSH
YEAH, WHAT?
SO WE'RE HERE ON THIS MOUNTAIN, THAT'S GREAT.
ZSH
ZSH
ZSH
BUT WHERE EXACTLY ARE WE GOING?
ZSH
ZSH
HELL IF I KNOW.
ZSH
YOU LITTLE...
YOU HAVE THOSE STUPID FEELERS GROWING OUT OF YOUR HEAD. CAN'T YOU USE THEM TO FIND PEOPLE?
THE HELL I CAN, YOU LOUSY PRIEST!! THEY'RE NOT YOKAI ANTENNAS, OKAY?

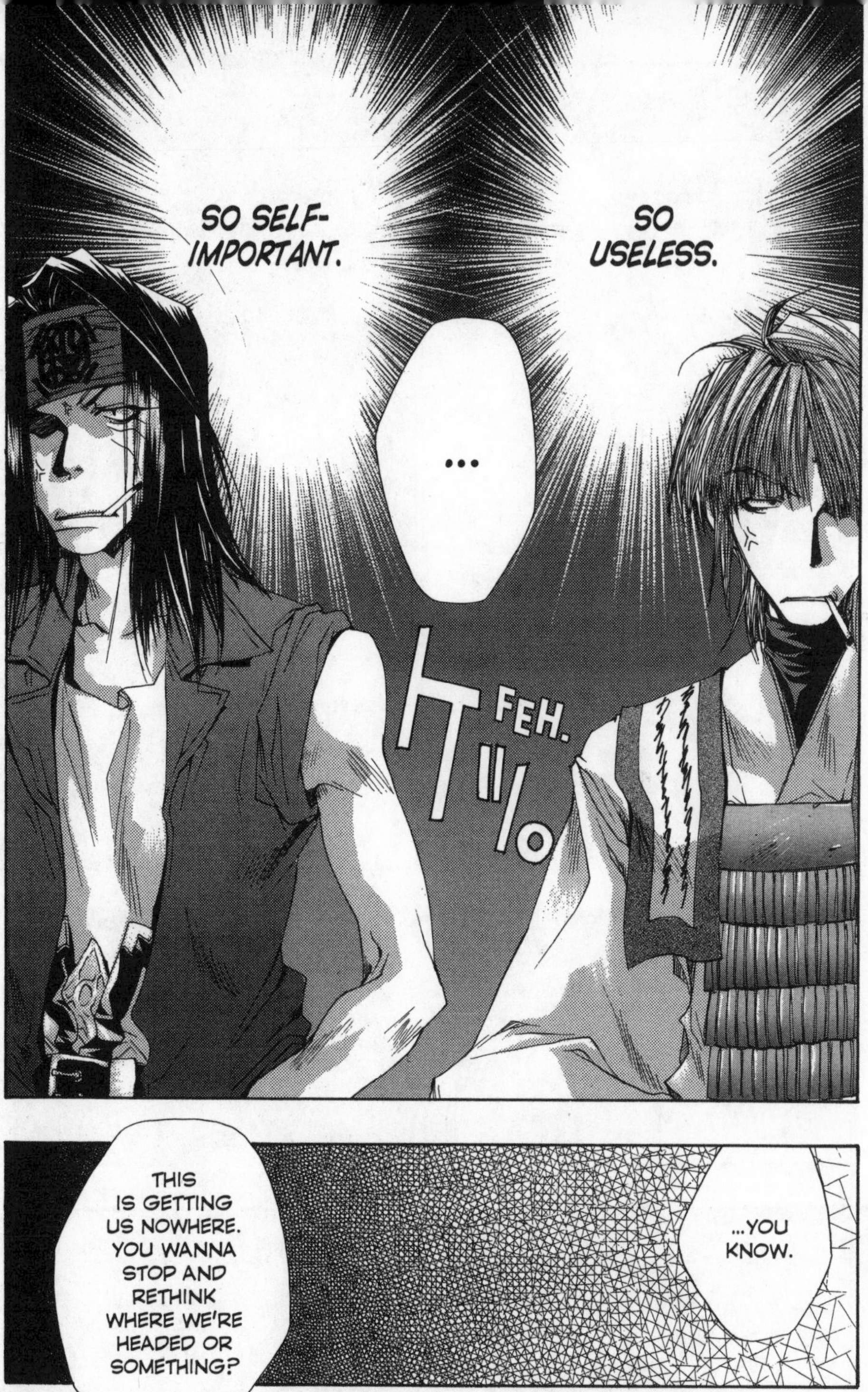
SO USELESS.
SO SELF-IMPORTANT.
...
FEH.
...YOU KNOW.
THIS IS GETTING US NOWHERE. YOU WANNA STOP AND RETHINK WHERE WE'RE HEADED OR SOMETHING?

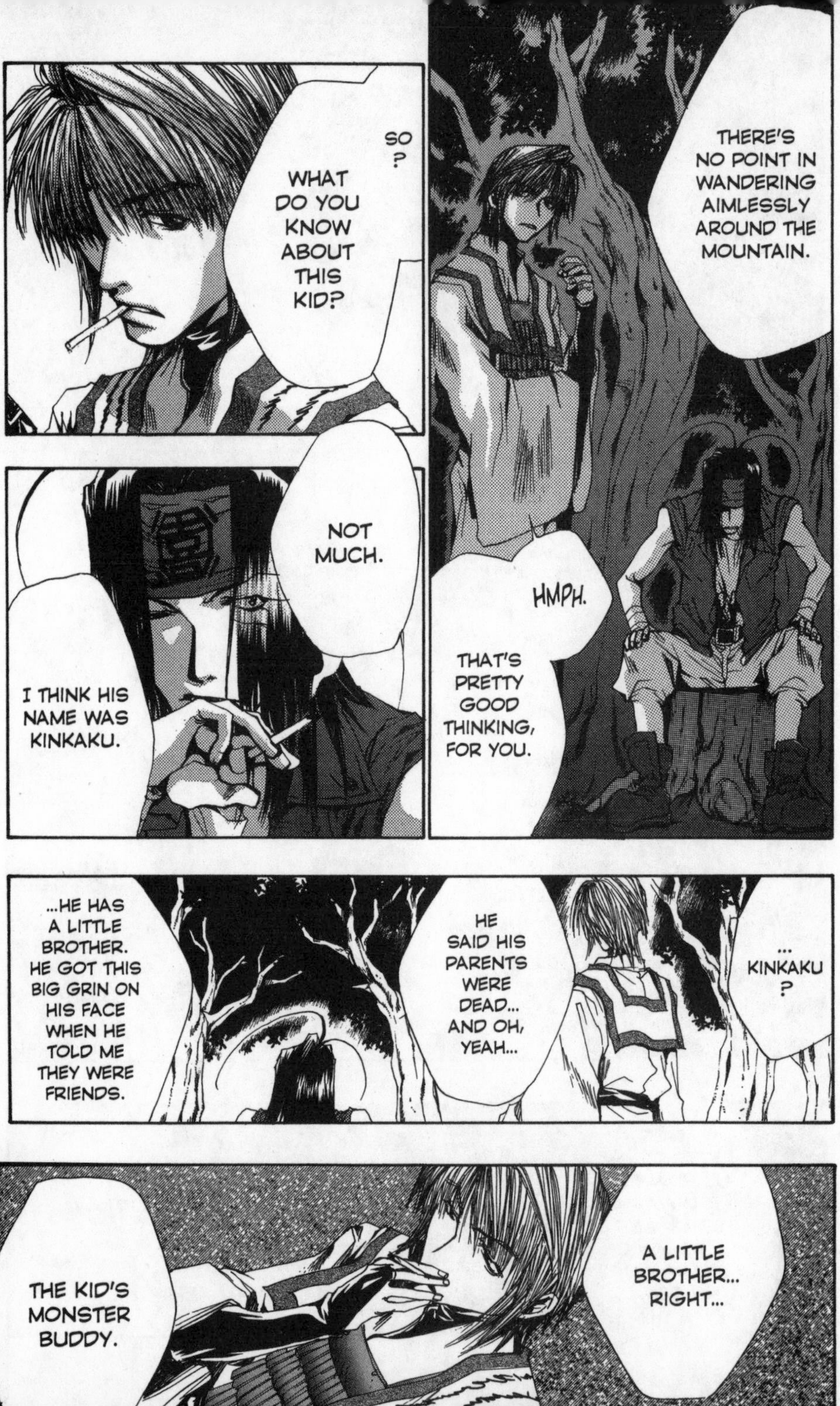
THERE'S NO POINT IN WANDERING AIMLESSLY AROUND THE MOUNTAIN.
HMPH.
THAT'S PRETTY GOOD THINKING, FOR YOU.
SO ?
WHAT DO YOU KNOW ABOUT THIS KID?
NOT MUCH.
I THINK HIS NAME WAS KINKAKU.
... KINKAKU ?
HE SAID HIS PARENTS WERE DEAD... AND OH, YEAH...
...HE HAS A LITTLE BROTHER. HE GOT THIS BIG GRIN ON HIS FACE WHEN HE TOLD ME THEY WERE FRIENDS.
A LITTLE BROTHER... RIGHT...
THE KID'S MONSTER BUDDY.

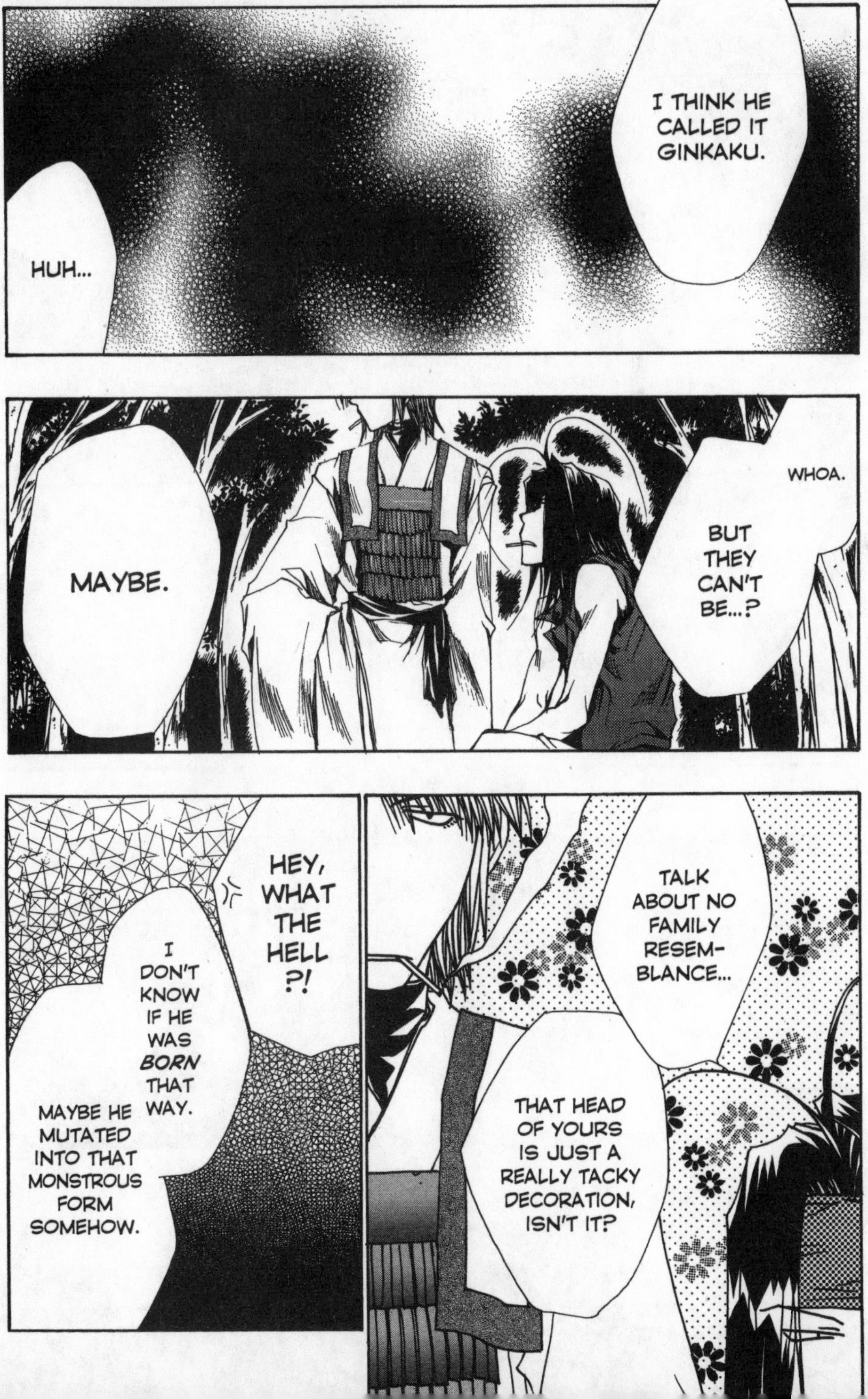
I THINK HE CALLED IT GINKAKU.
HUH...
WHOA.
BUT THEY CAN'T BE...?
MAYBE.
TALK ABOUT NO FAMILY RESEM-BLANCE...
THAT HEAD OF YOURS IS JUST A REALLY TACKY DECORATION, ISN'T IT?
HEY, WHAT THE HELL ?!
I DON'T KNOW IF HE WAS *BORN* THAT WAY.
MAYBE HE MUTATED INTO THAT MONSTROUS FORM SOMEHOW.

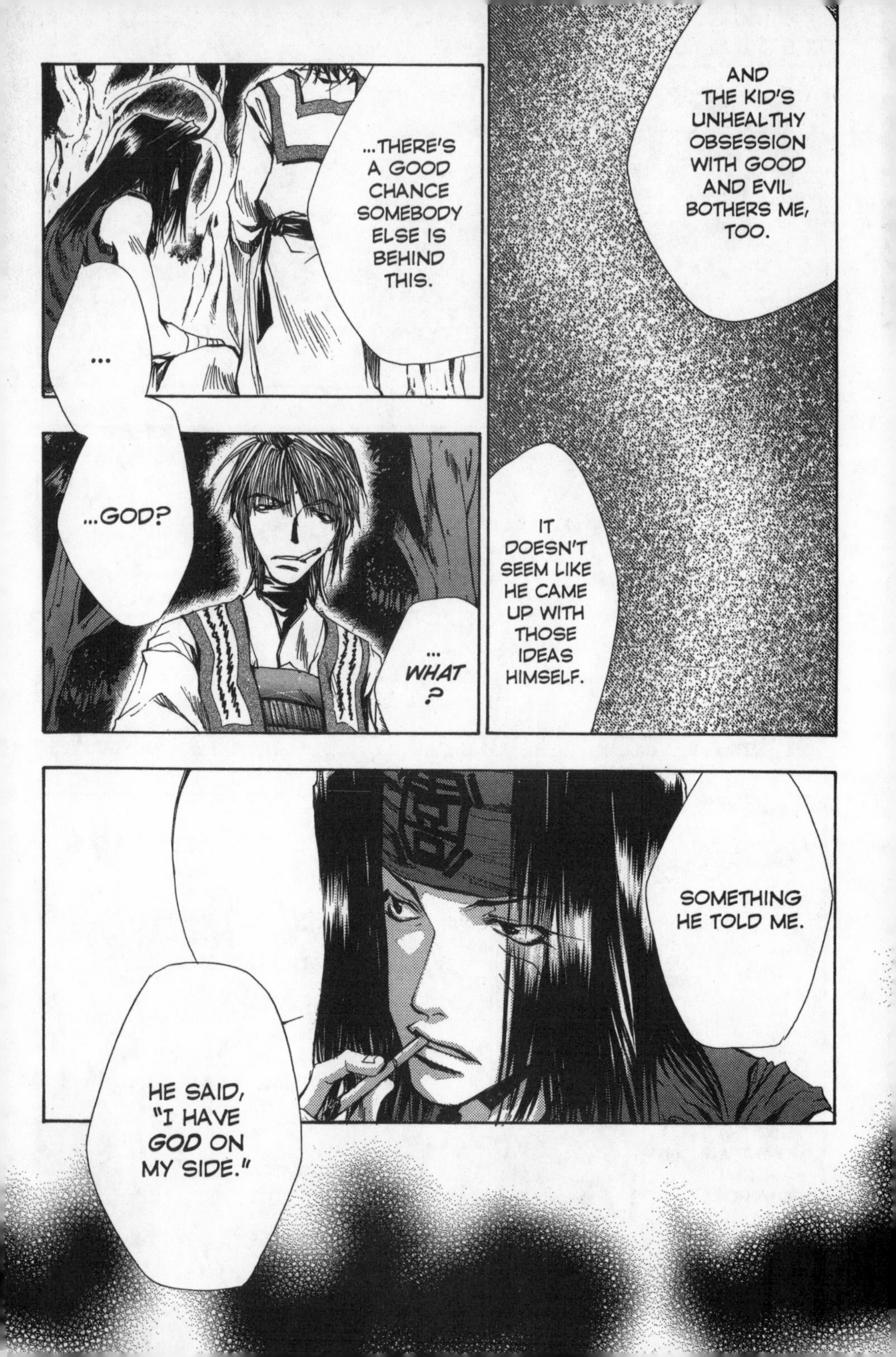
AND THE KID'S UNHEALTHY OBSESSION WITH GOOD AND EVIL BOTHERS ME, TOO.
IT DOESN'T SEEM LIKE HE CAME UP WITH THOSE IDEAS HIMSELF.
...THERE'S A GOOD CHANCE SOMEBODY ELSE IS BEHIND THIS.
...
... *WHAT*?
...GOD?
SOMETHING HE TOLD ME.
HE SAID, "I HAVE *GOD* ON MY SIDE."

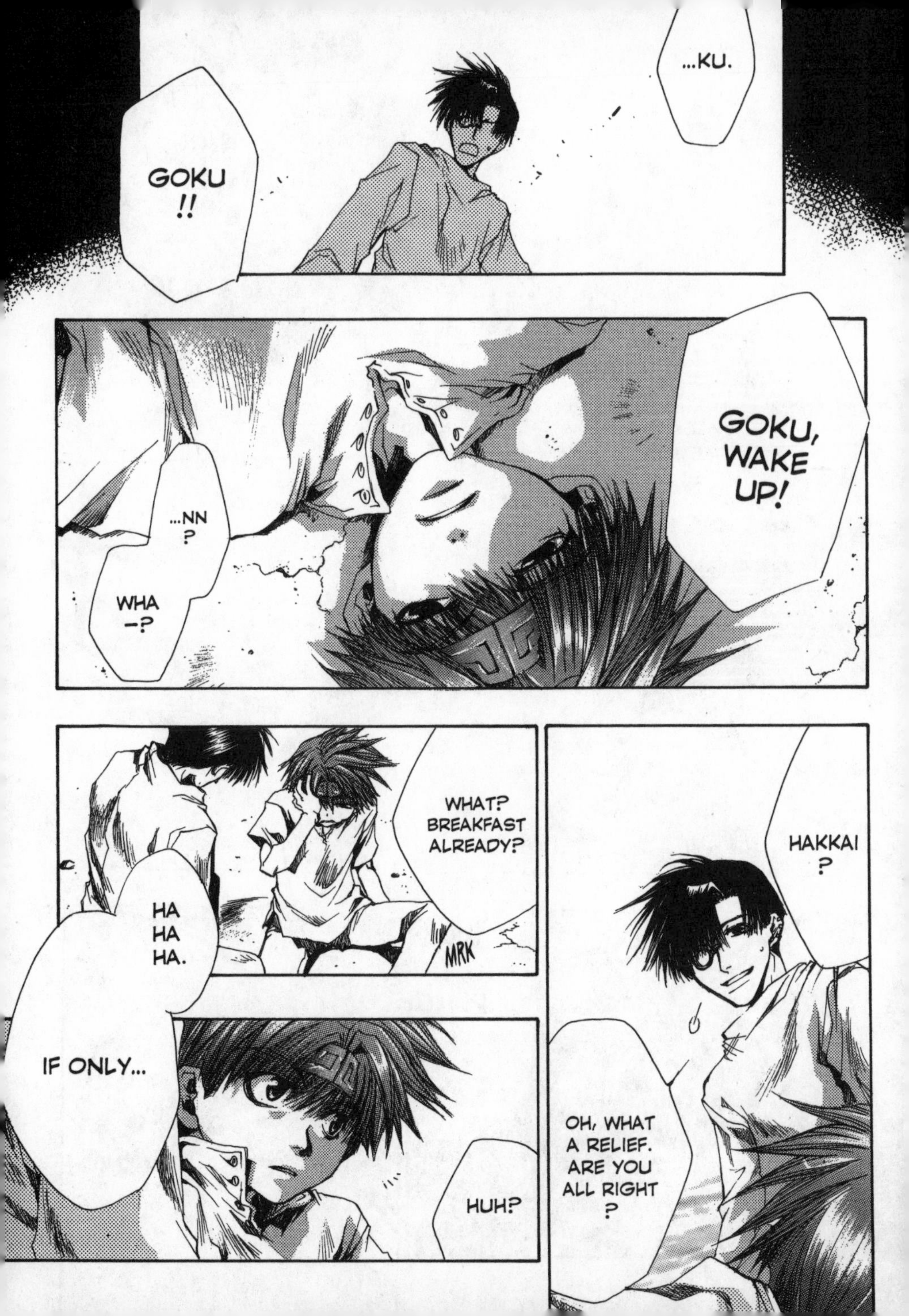
...KU.
GOKU !!
GOKU, WAKE UP!
...NN ?
WHA -?
HAKKAI ?
OH, WHAT A RELIEF. ARE YOU ALL RIGHT ?
WHAT? BREAKFAST ALREADY?
MRK
HA HA HA.
IF ONLY...
HUH?

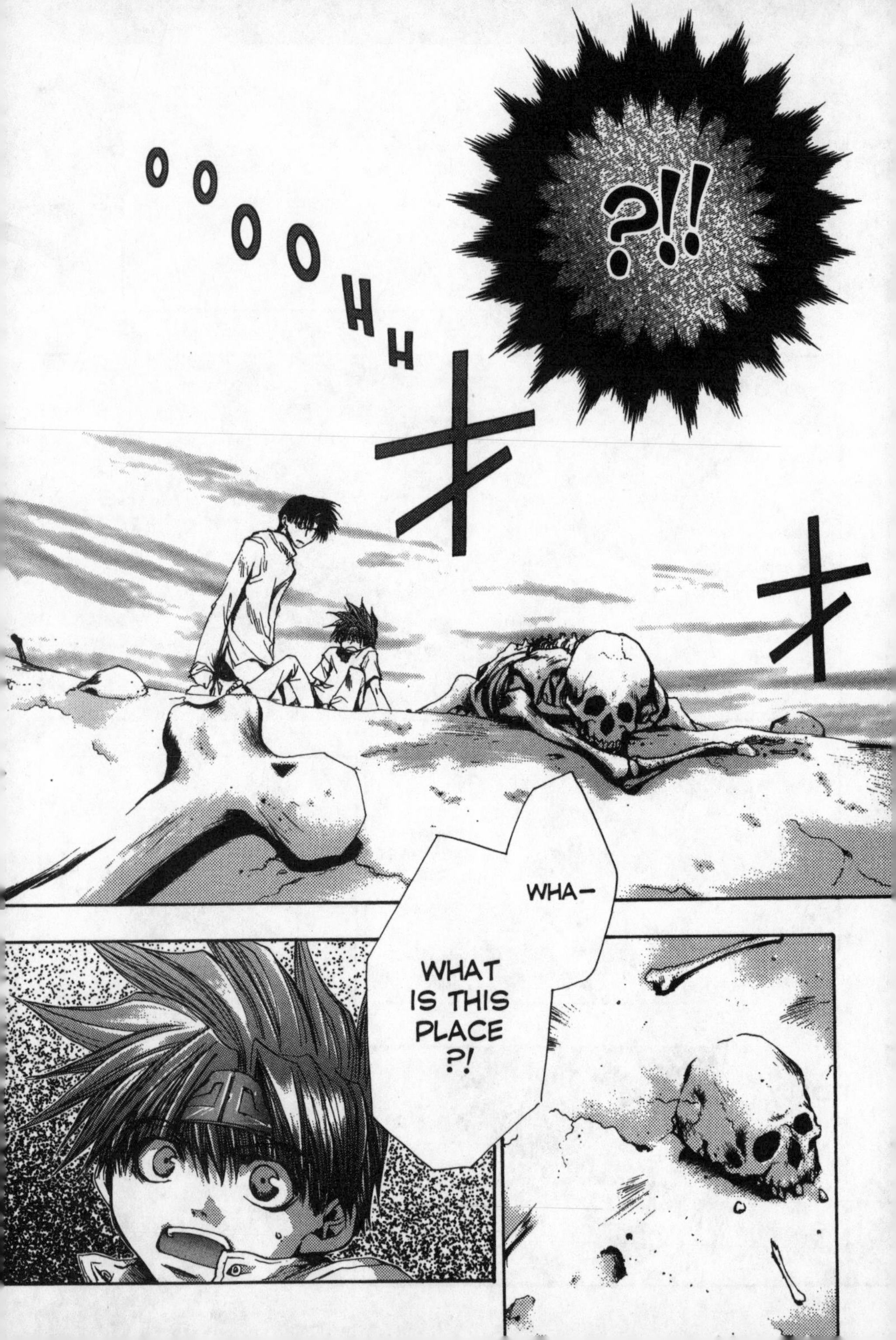
?!!
OOOOHH
WHA-
WHAT IS THIS PLACE ?!

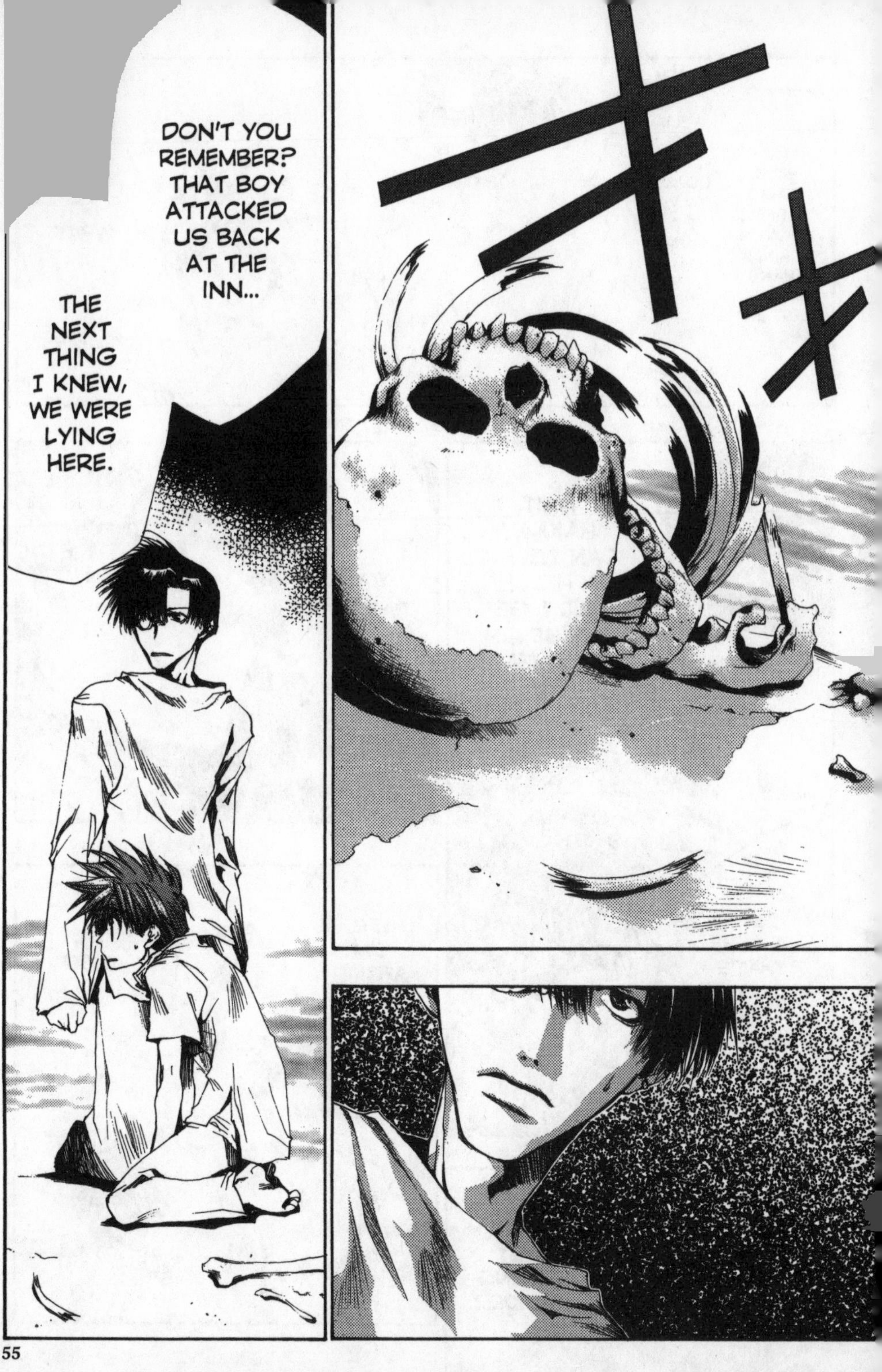
DON'T YOU REMEMBER? THAT BOY ATTACKED US BACK AT THE INN...
THE NEXT THING I KNEW, WE WERE LYING HERE.

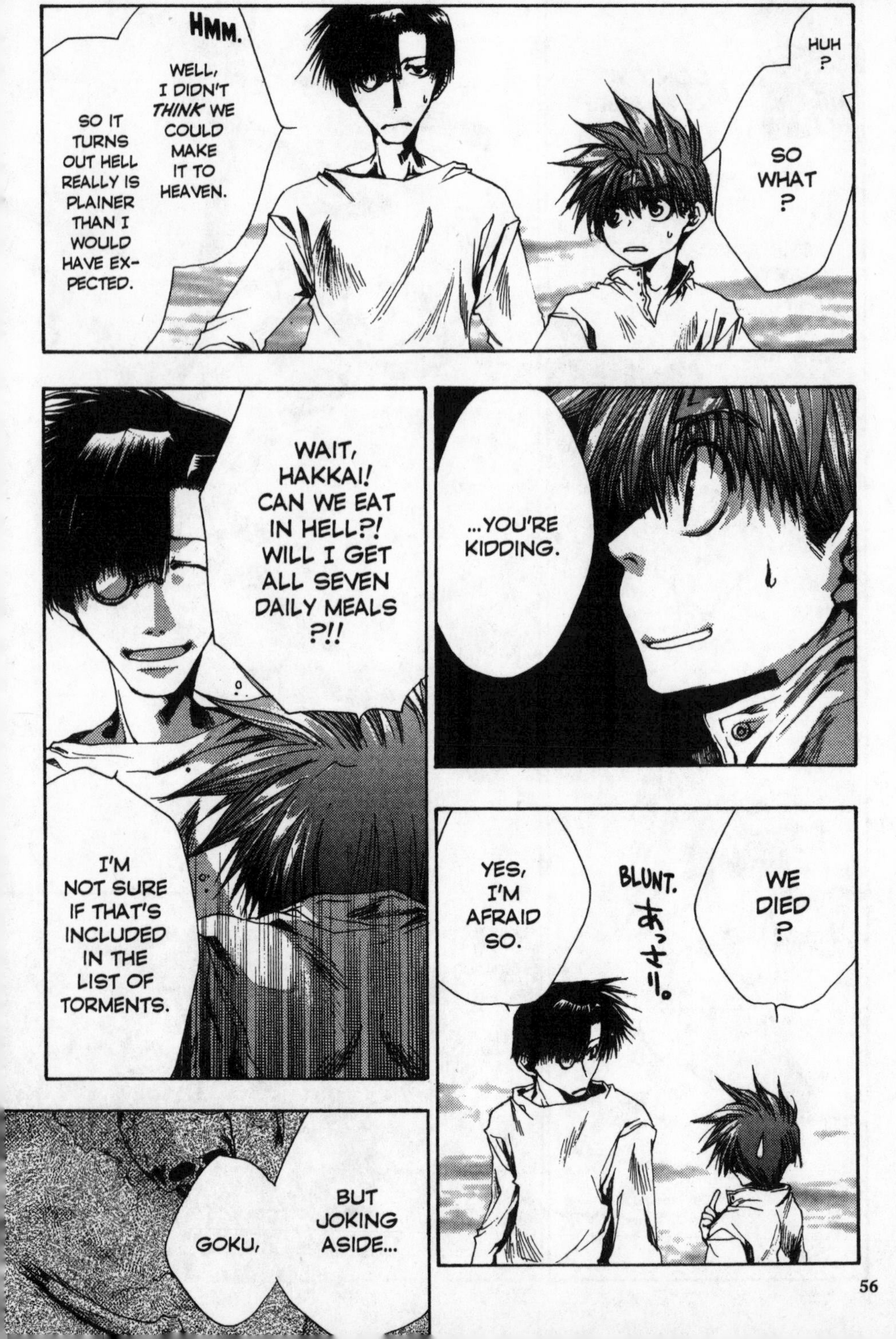
HUH?
SO WHAT?
HMM.
WELL, I DIDN'T *THINK* WE COULD MAKE IT TO HEAVEN.
SO IT TURNS OUT HELL REALLY IS PLAINER THAN I WOULD HAVE EX-PECTED.
...YOU'RE KIDDING.
WAIT, HAKKAI! CAN WE EAT IN HELL?! WILL I GET ALL SEVEN DAILY MEALS?!!
I'M NOT SURE IF THAT'S INCLUDED IN THE LIST OF TORMENTS.
WE DIED?
BLUNT.
あっさり。
YES, I'M AFRAID SO.
BUT JOKING ASIDE...
GOKU,

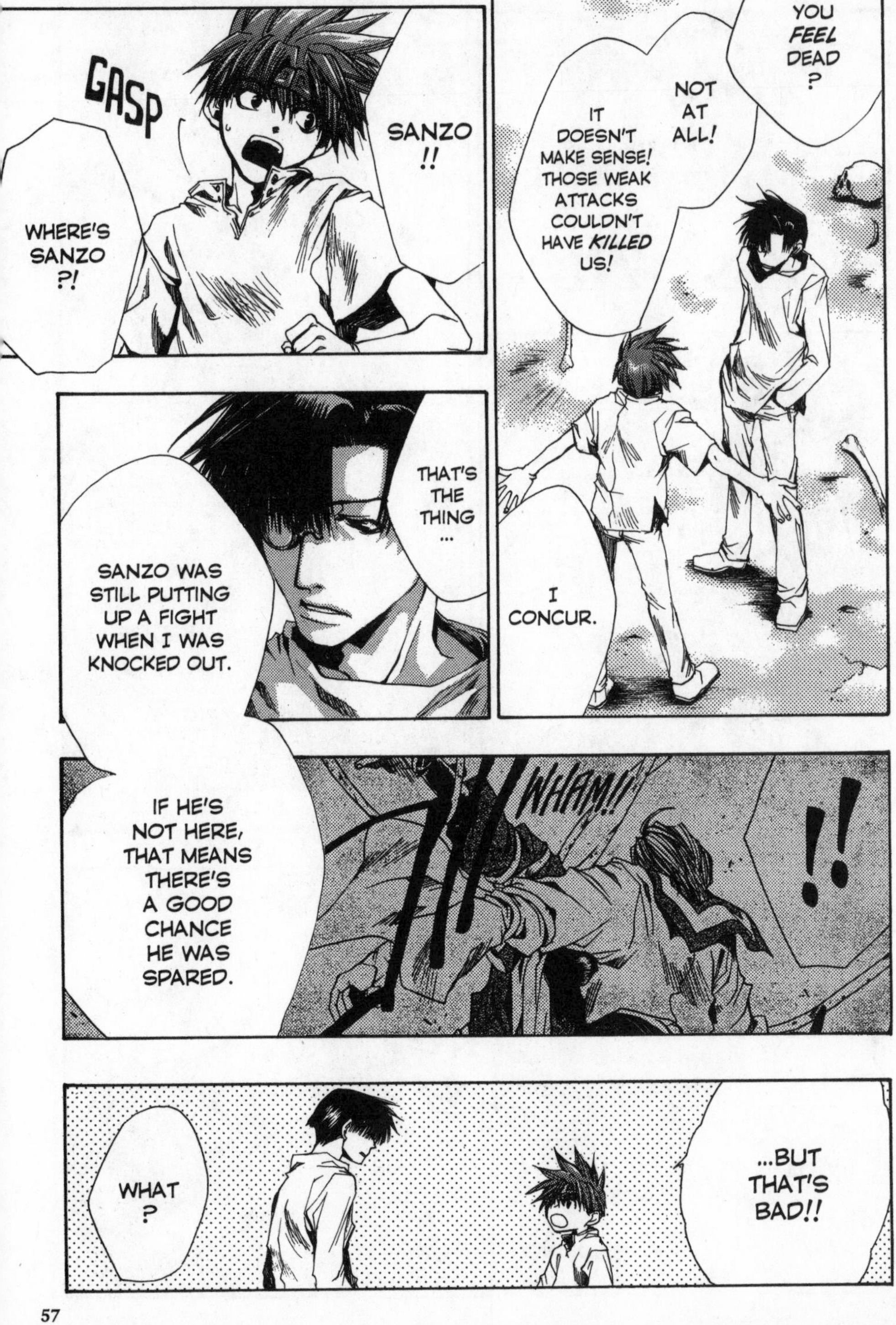
DO YOU FEEL DEAD?
NOT AT ALL!
IT DOESN'T MAKE SENSE! THOSE WEAK ATTACKS COULDN'T HAVE KILLED US!
I CONCUR.
GASP
SANZO!!
WHERE'S SANZO?!
THAT'S THE THING...
SANZO WAS STILL PUTTING UP A FIGHT WHEN I WAS KNOCKED OUT.
!!
WHAM!!
IF HE'S NOT HERE, THAT MEANS THERE'S A GOOD CHANCE HE WAS SPARED.
...BUT THAT'S BAD!!
WHAT?

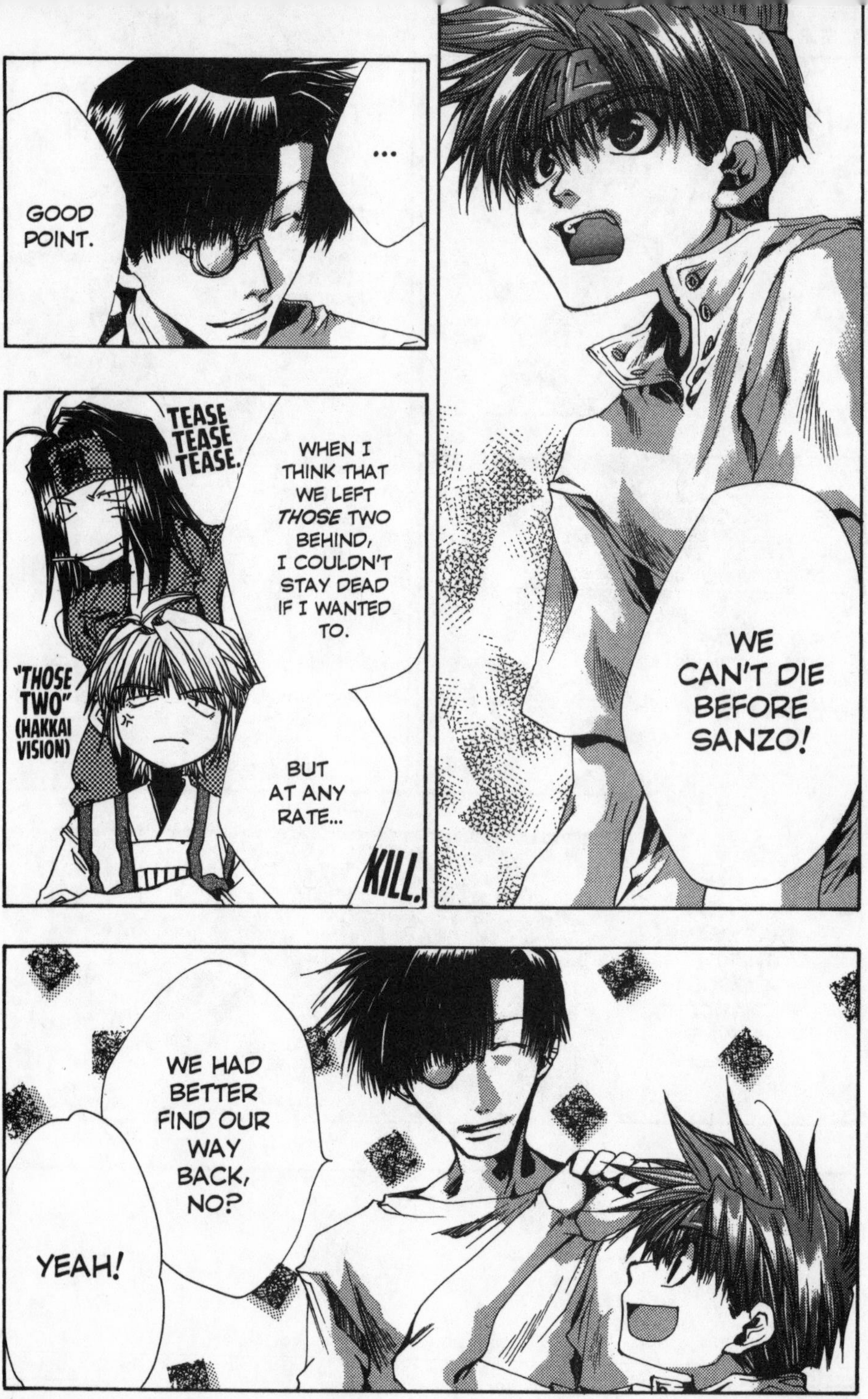
WE CAN'T DIE BEFORE SANZO!
...
GOOD POINT.
WHEN I THINK THAT WE LEFT *THOSE* TWO BEHIND, I COULDN'T STAY DEAD IF I WANTED TO.
TEASE TEASE TEASE.
BUT AT ANY RATE...
KILL.
"THOSE TWO" (HAKKAI VISION)
WE HAD BETTER FIND OUR WAY BACK, NO?
YEAH!

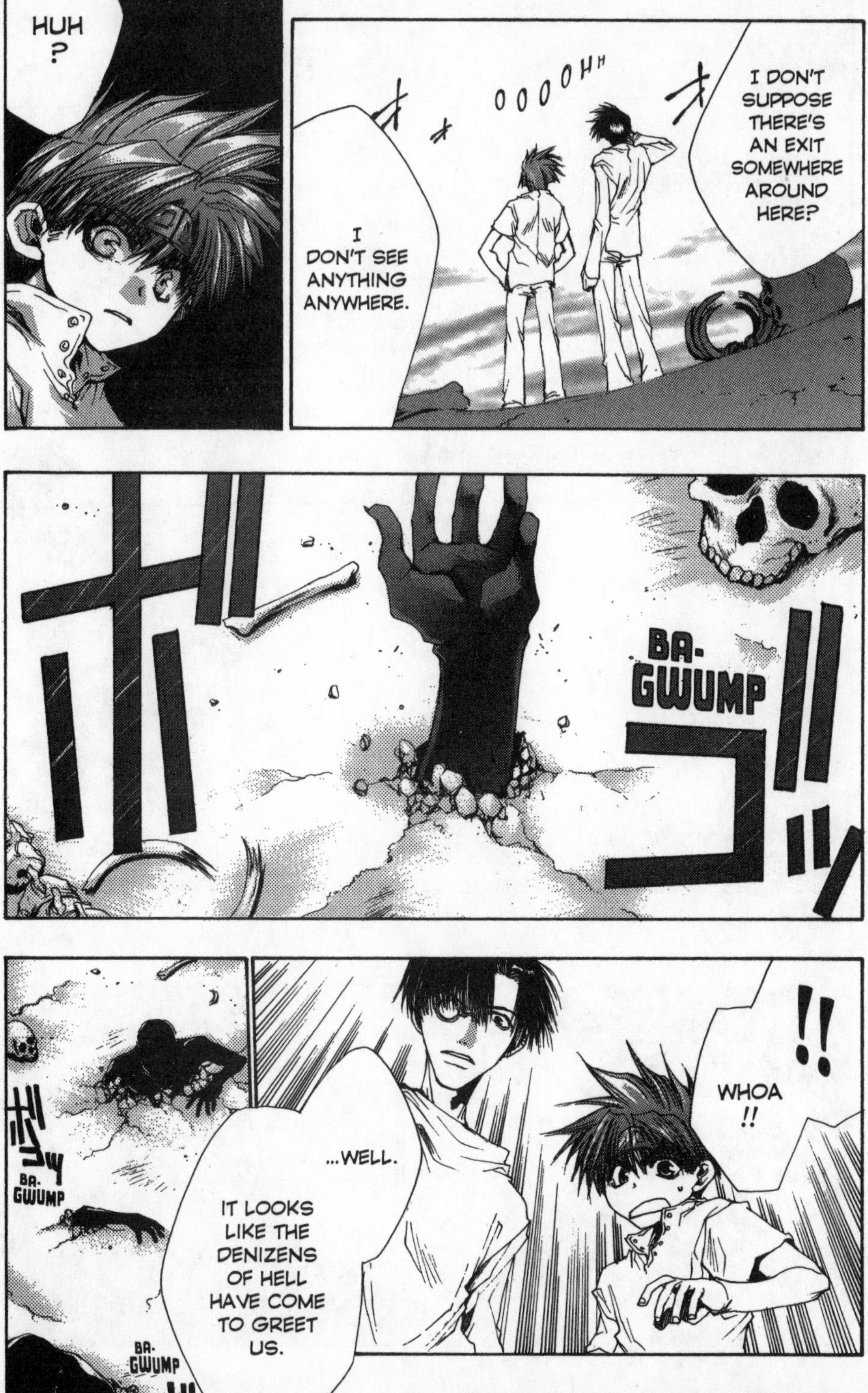
I DON'T SUPPOSE THERE'S AN EXIT SOMEWHERE AROUND HERE?
OOOOHH
I DON'T SEE ANYTHING ANYWHERE.
HUH ?
BA-GWUMP
!!
WHOA !!
...WELL.
IT LOOKS LIKE THE DENIZENS OF HELL HAVE COME TO GREET US.
BA-GWUMP
BA-GWUMP

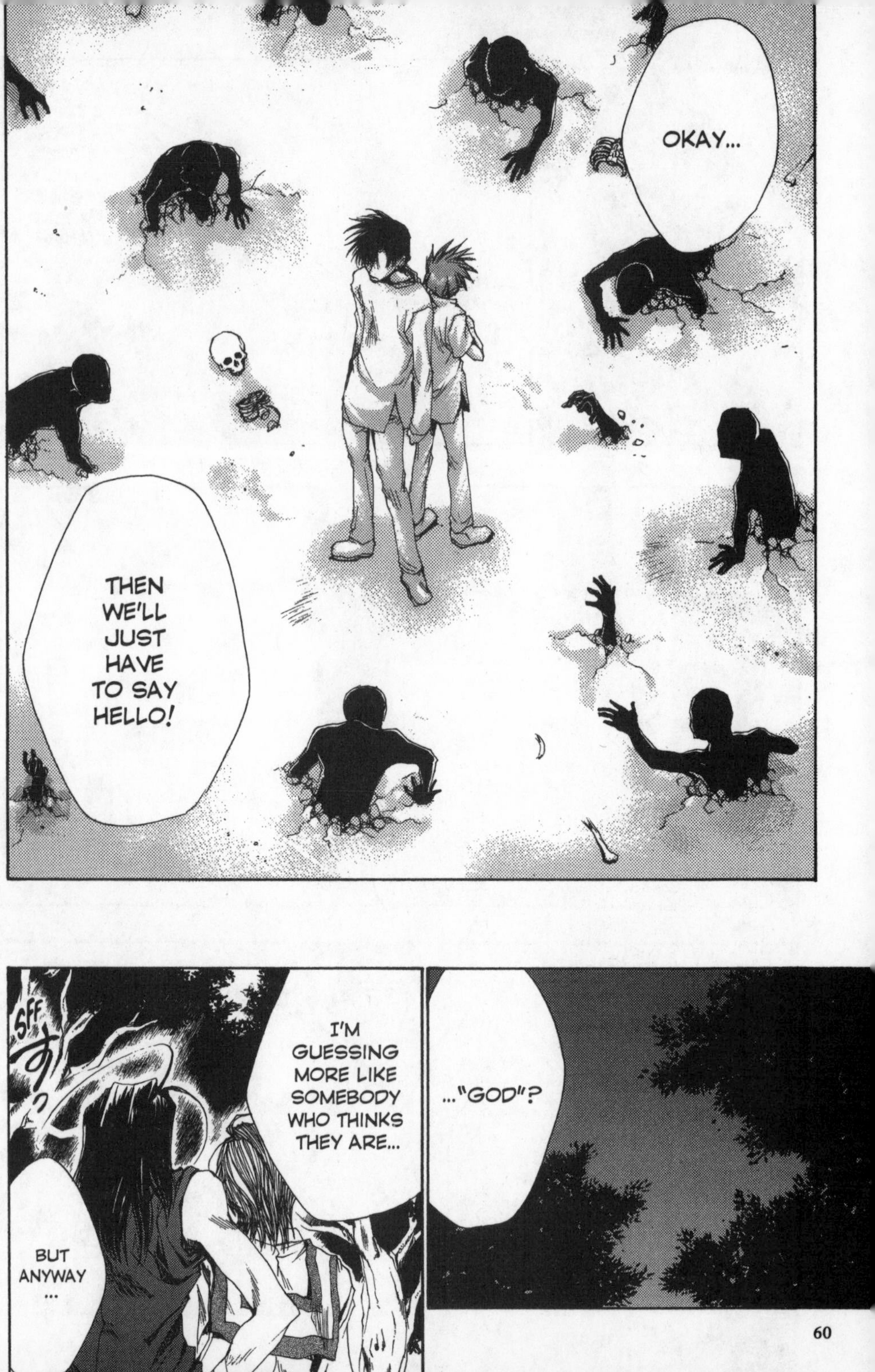
OKAY...
THEN WE'LL JUST HAVE TO SAY HELLO!
..."GOD"?
I'M GUESSING MORE LIKE SOMEBODY WHO THINKS THEY ARE...
SFF
BUT ANYWAY ...

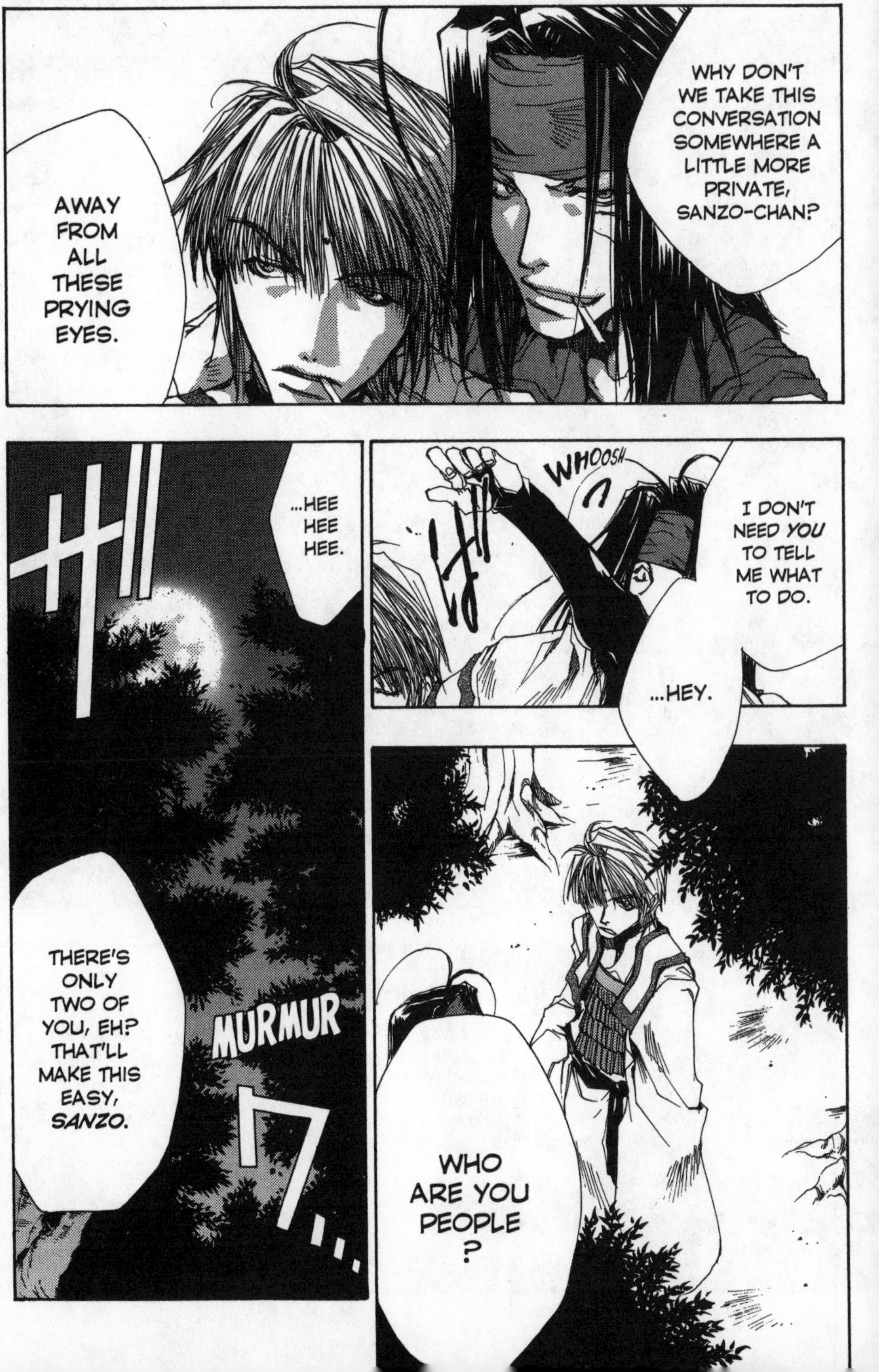
WHY DON'T WE TAKE THIS CONVERSATION SOMEWHERE A LITTLE MORE PRIVATE, SANZO-CHAN?
AWAY FROM ALL THESE PRYING EYES.
WHOOSH
I DON'T NEED *YOU* TO TELL ME WHAT TO DO.
...HEY.
WHO ARE YOU PEOPLE ?
...HEE HEE HEE.
MURMUR
THERE'S ONLY TWO OF YOU, EH? THAT'LL MAKE THIS EASY, *SANZO*.

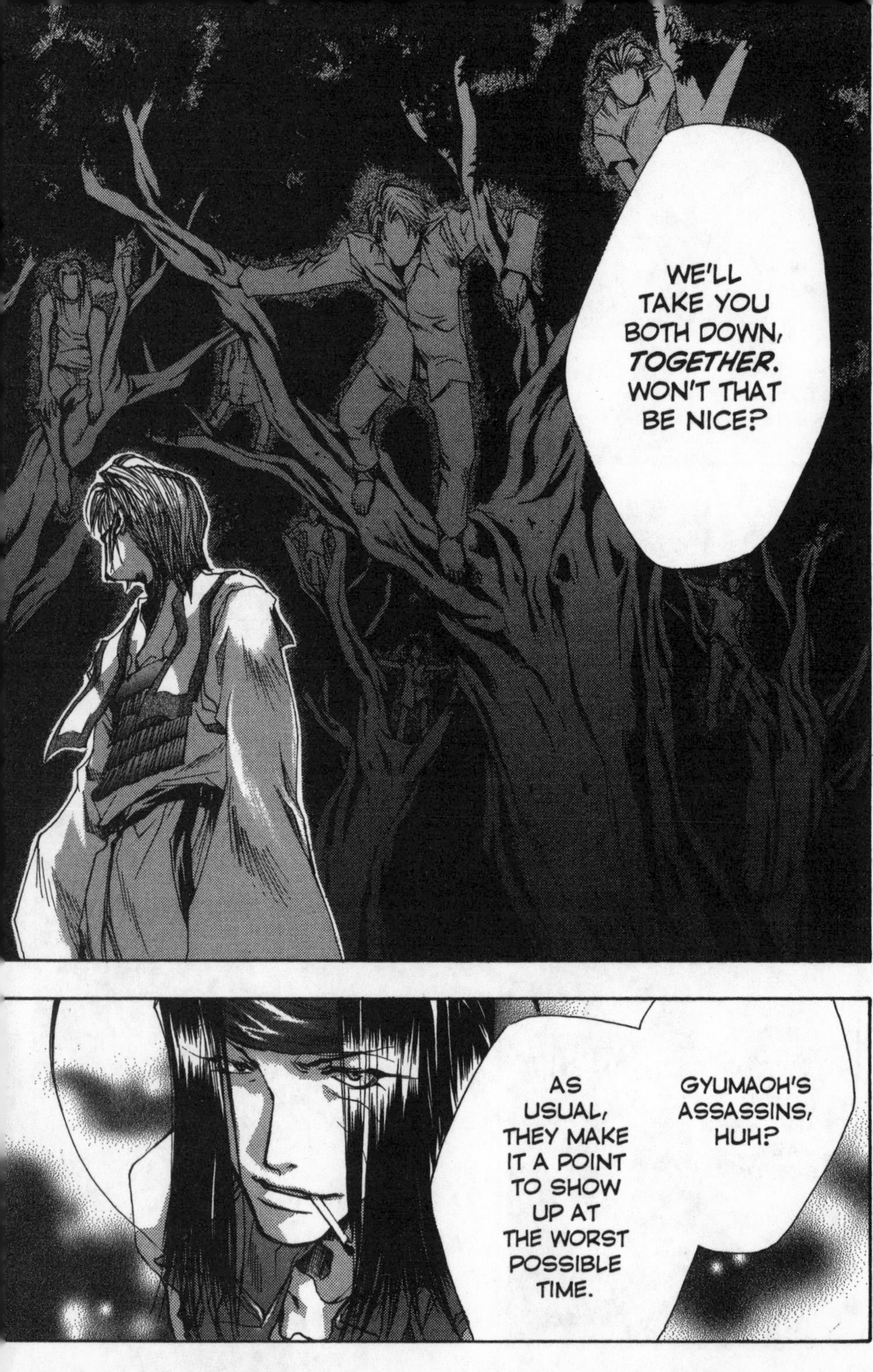
WE'LL TAKE YOU BOTH DOWN, *TOGETHER*. WON'T THAT BE NICE?
GYUMAOH'S ASSASSINS, HUH?
AS USUAL, THEY MAKE IT A POINT TO SHOW UP AT THE WORST POSSIBLE TIME.

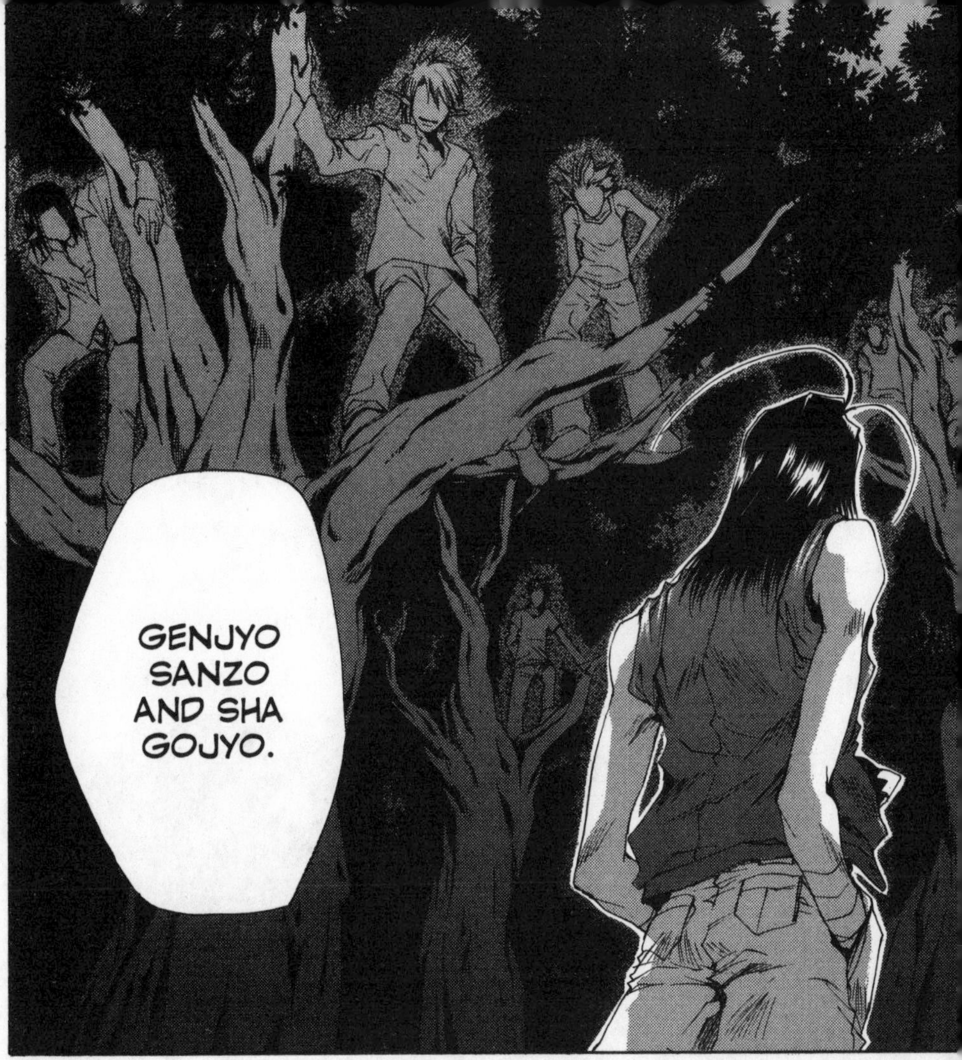
GENJYO SANZO AND SHA GOJYO.
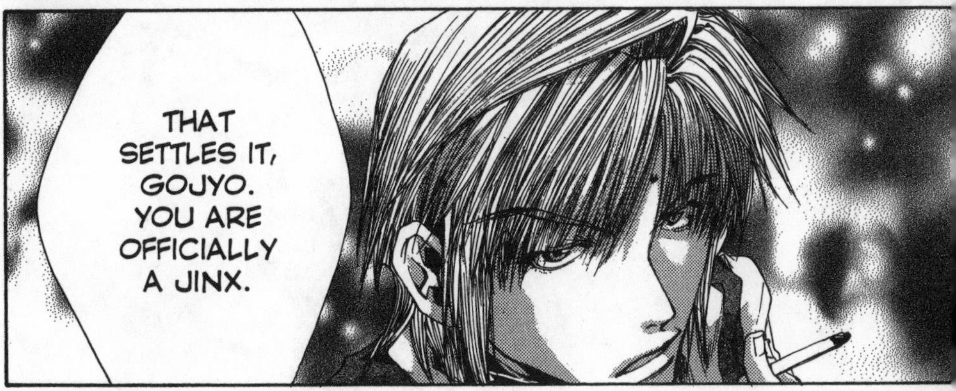
THAT SETTLES IT, GOJYO. YOU ARE OFFICIALLY A JINX.

CHAPTER 39 Critical Day

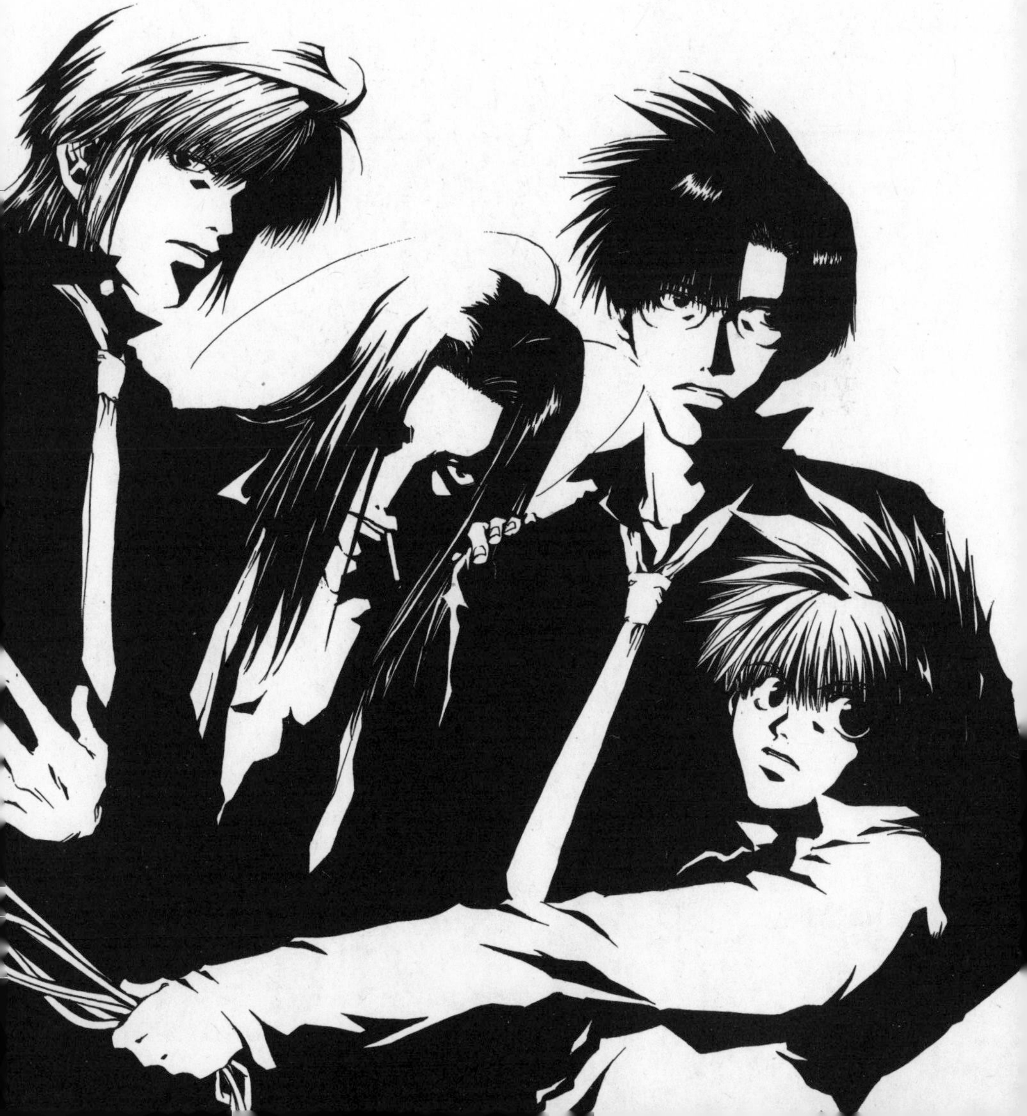

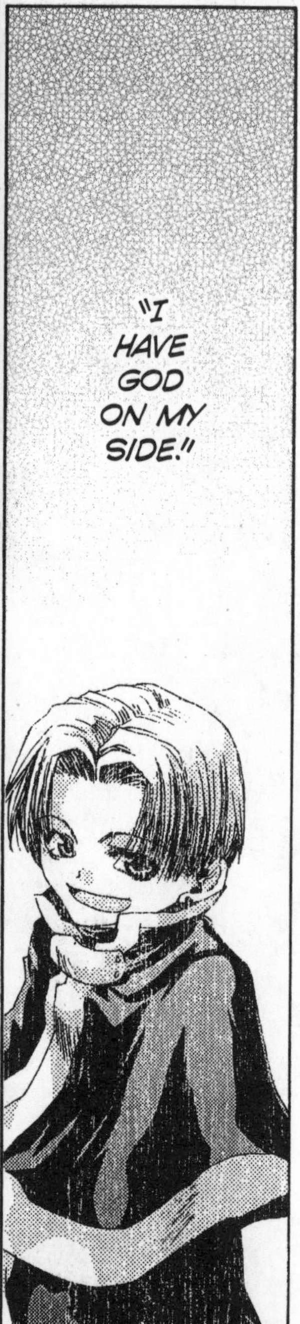
"I HAVE GOD ON MY SIDE."

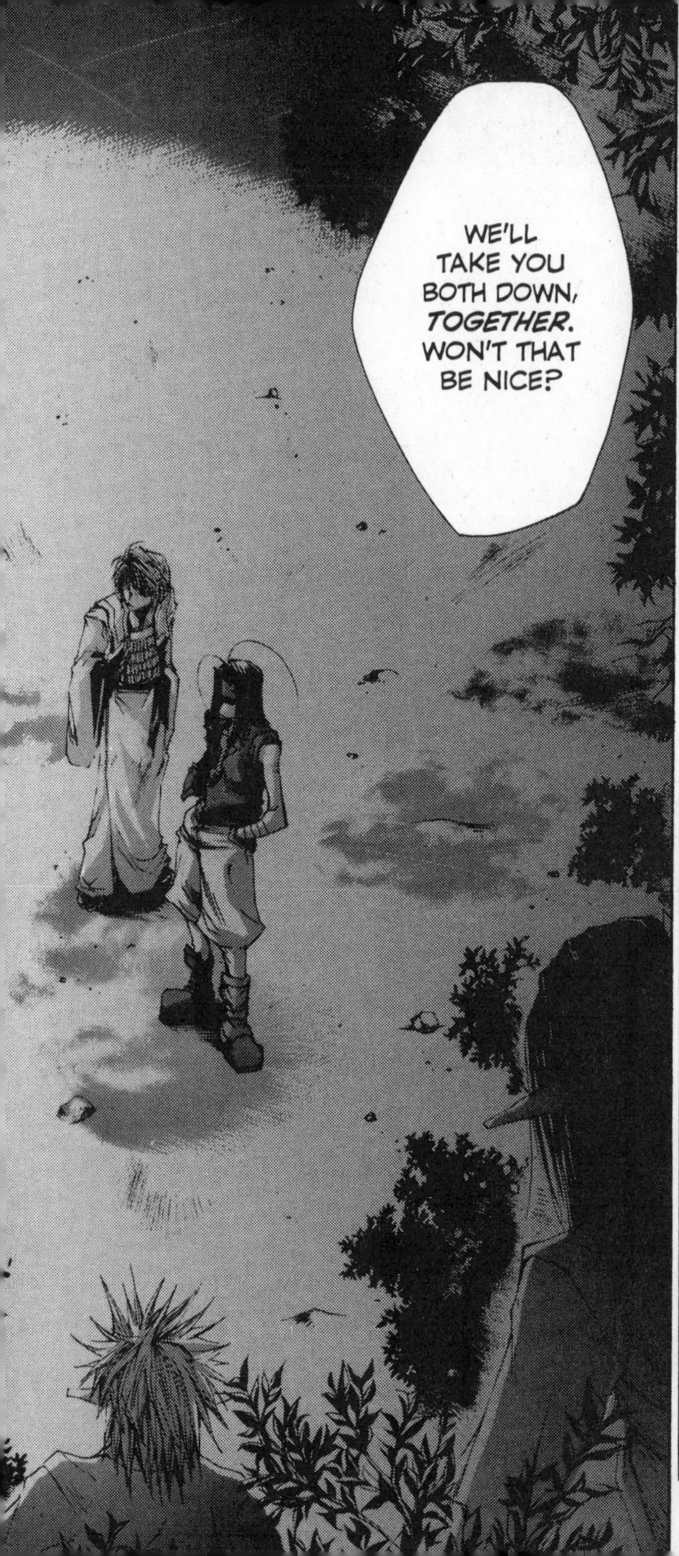
WE'LL TAKE YOU BOTH DOWN, *TOGETHER*. WON'T THAT BE NICE?

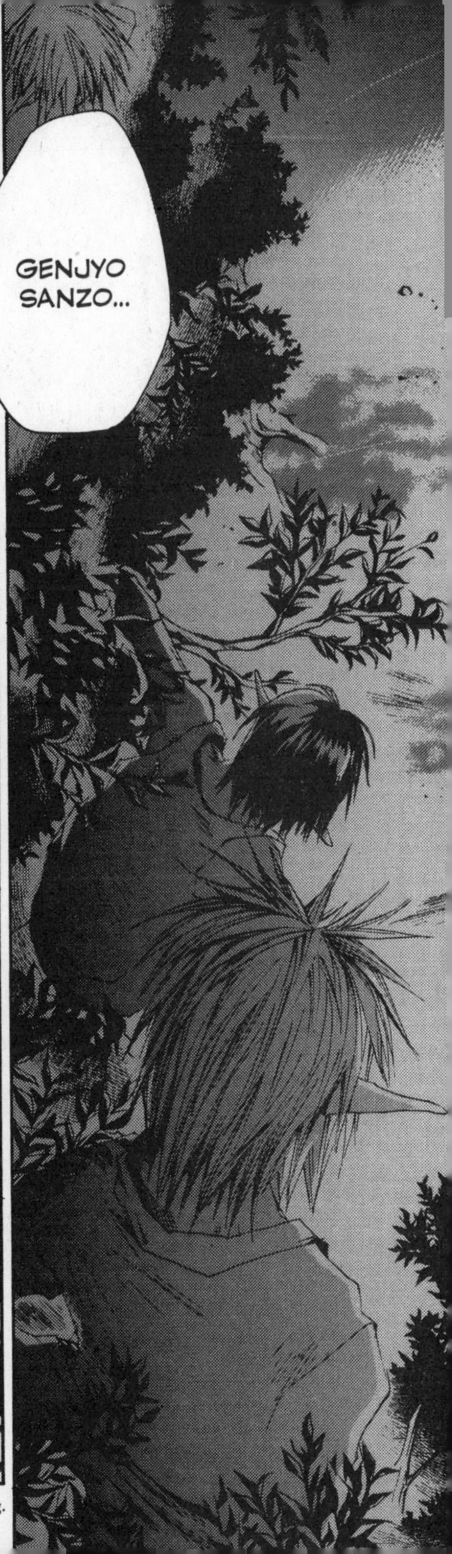
GENJYO SANZO...

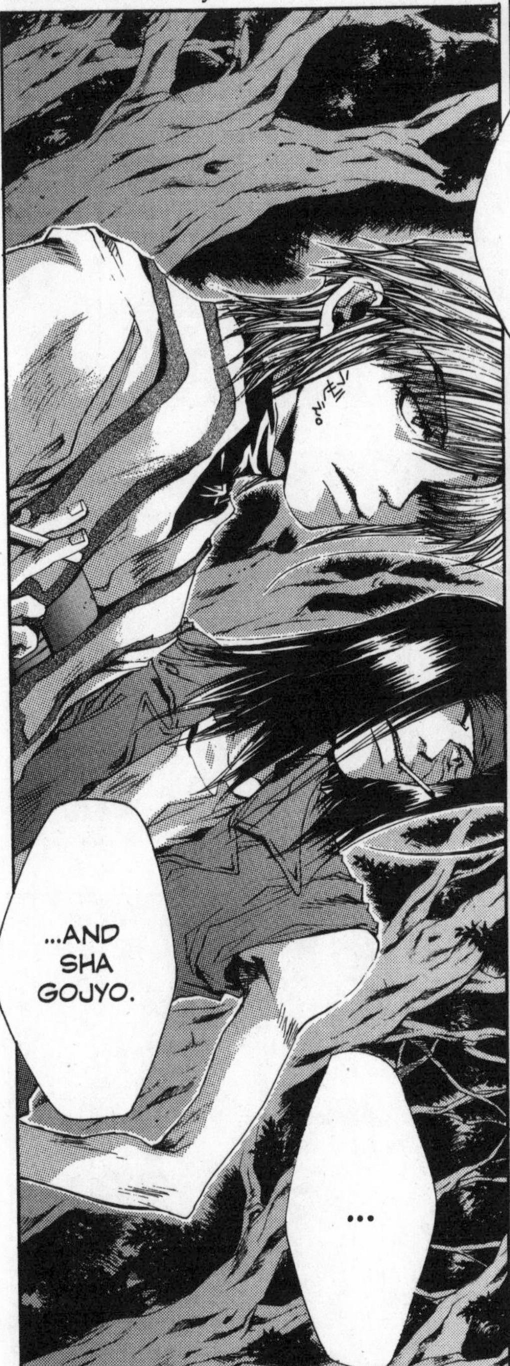
...AND SHA GOJYO.
...

SANZO'S CHEEK: So annoying.

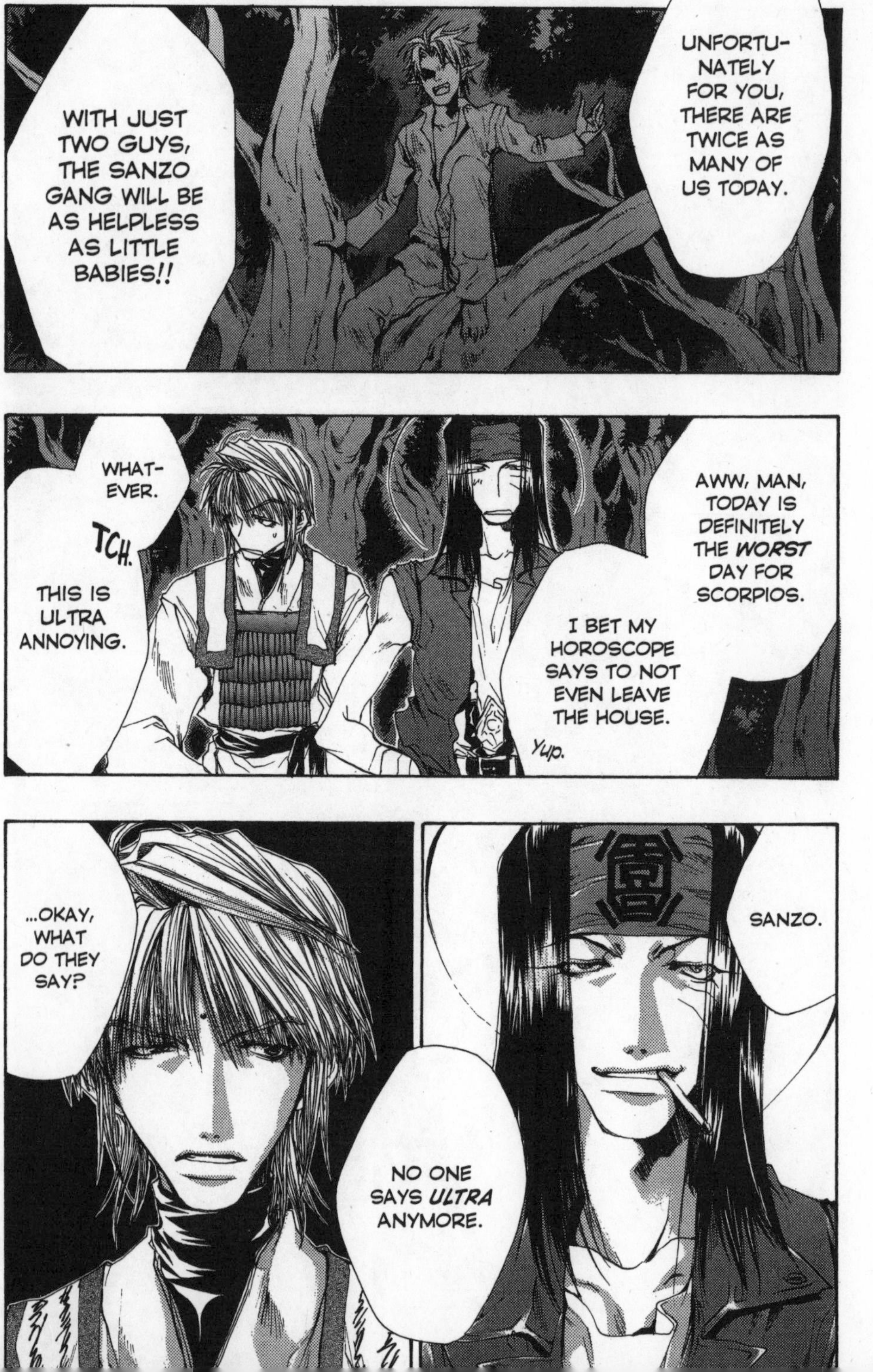

UNFORTUNATELY FOR YOU, THERE ARE TWICE AS MANY OF US TODAY.
WITH JUST TWO GUYS, THE SANZO GANG WILL BE AS HELPLESS AS LITTLE BABIES!!
AWW, MAN, TODAY IS DEFINITELY THE *WORST* DAY FOR SCORPIOS.
I BET MY HOROSCOPE SAYS TO NOT EVEN LEAVE THE HOUSE.
Yup.
WHATEVER.
TCH.
THIS IS ULTRA ANNOYING.
SANZO.
NO ONE SAYS *ULTRA* ANYMORE.
...OKAY, WHAT DO THEY SAY?

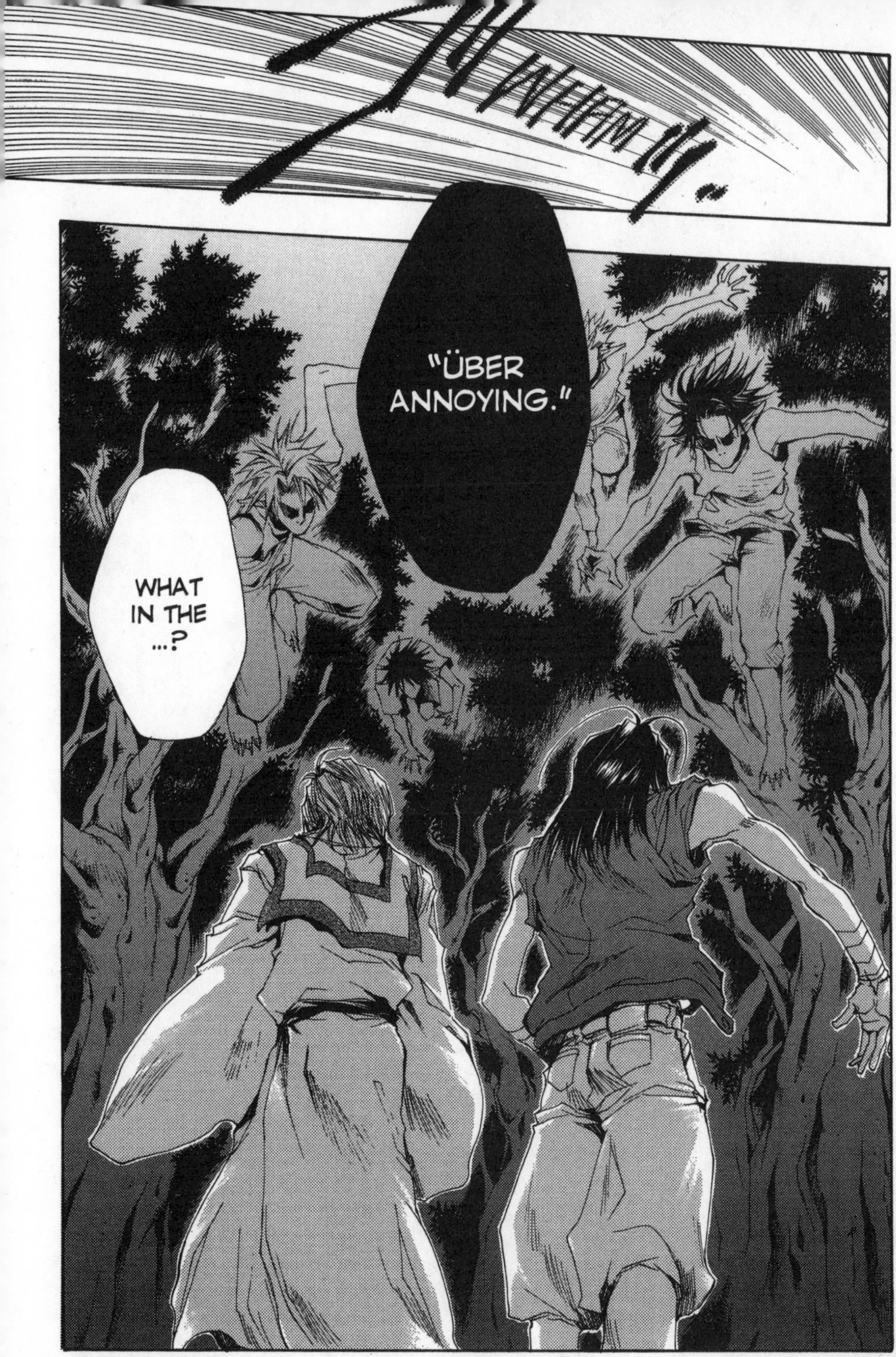
"ÜBER ANNOYING."
WHAT IN THE ...?

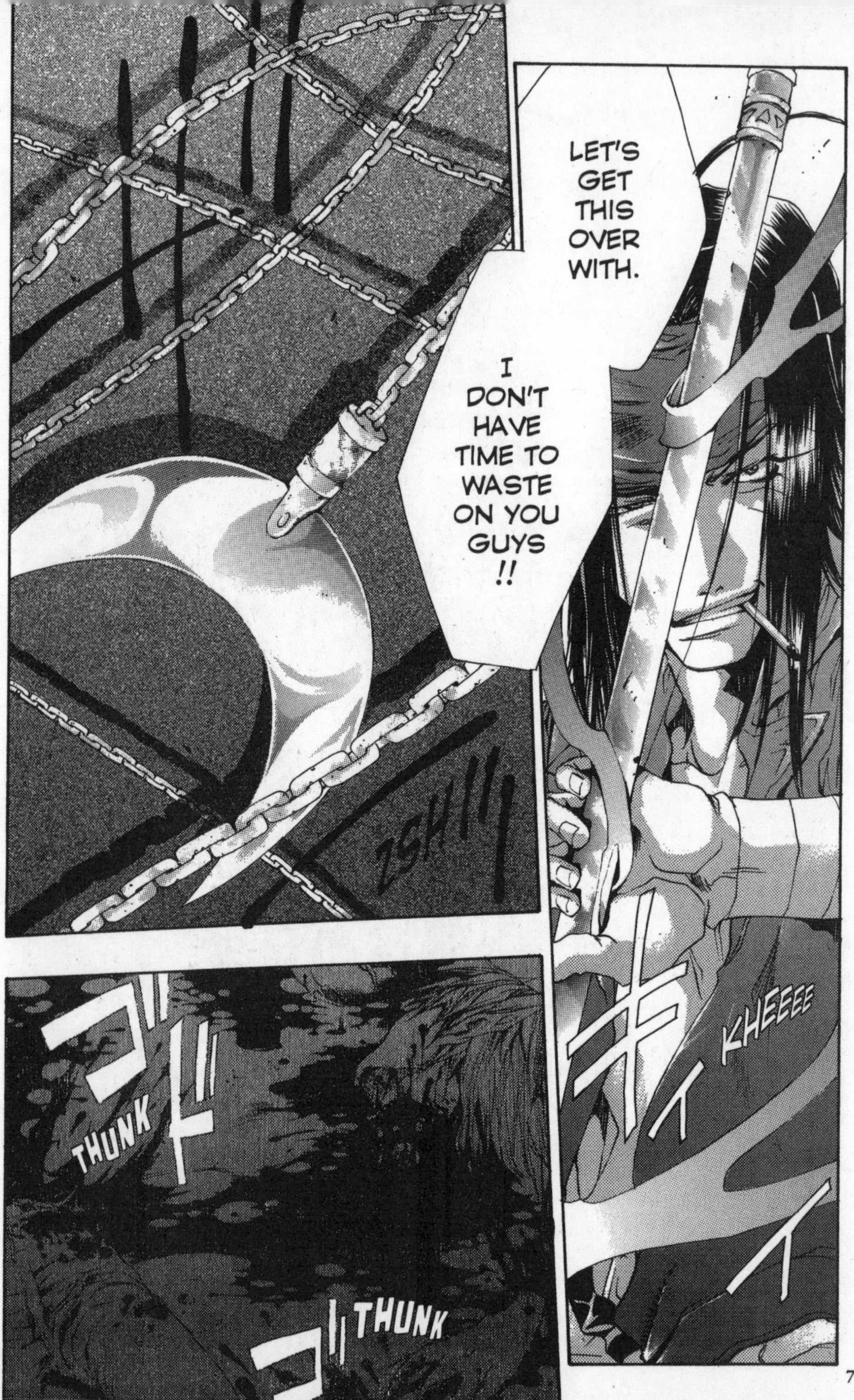
LET'S GET THIS OVER WITH.
I DON'T HAVE TIME TO WASTE ON YOU GUYS !!
KHEEEE
ZSH
THUNK
THUNK

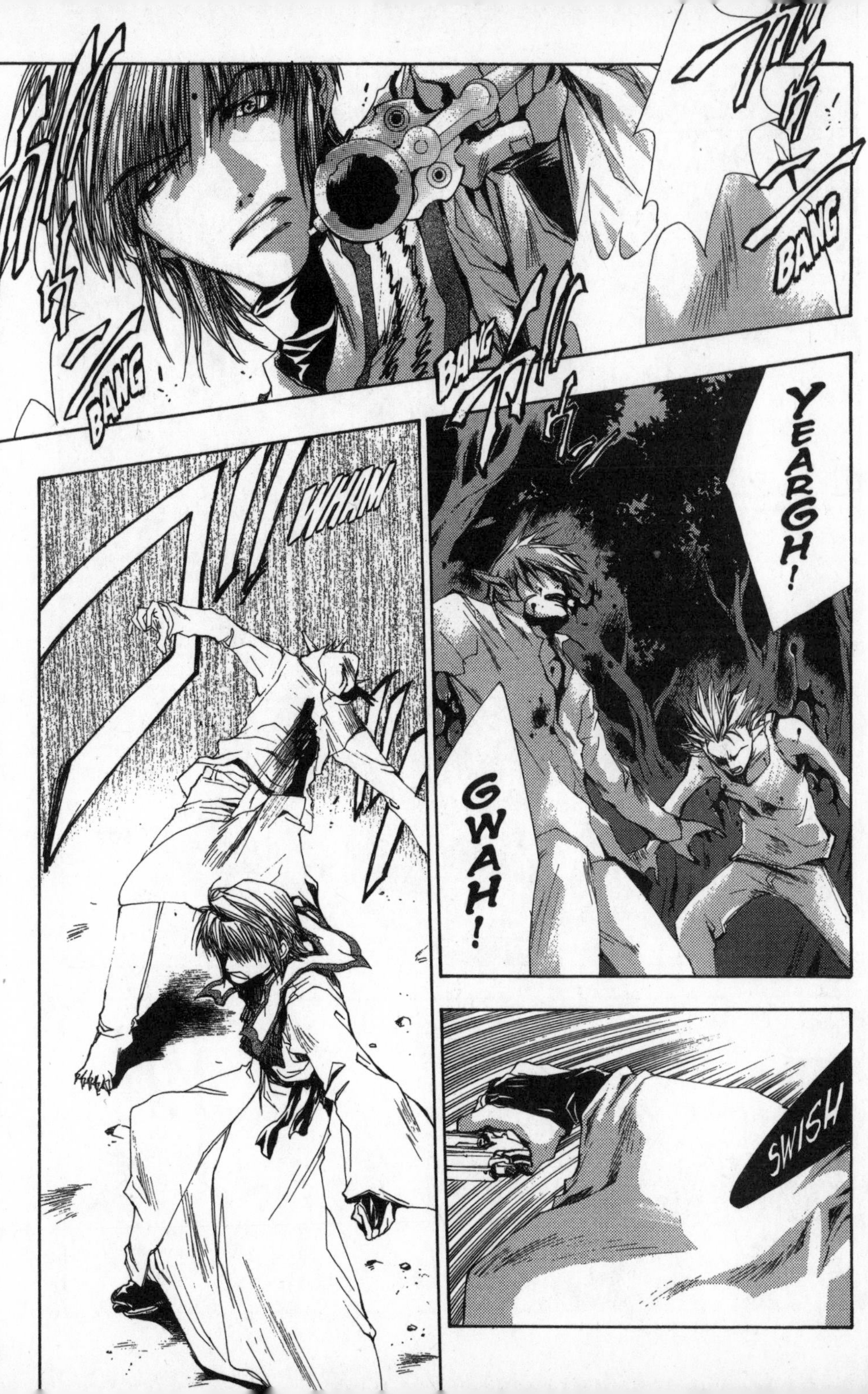
BANG
BANG
BANG
YEARGH!
GWAH!
SWISH
WHAM

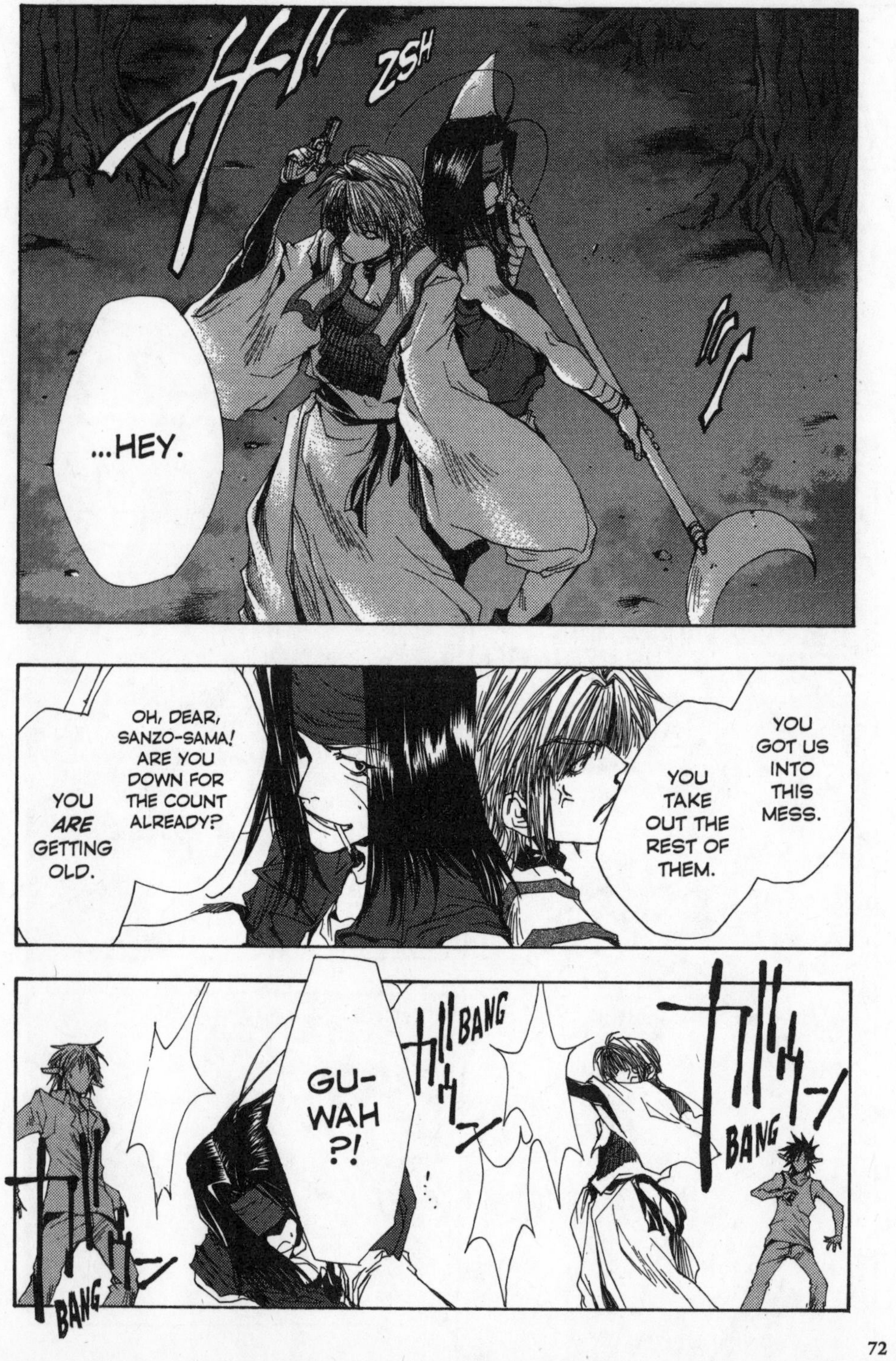
ZSH
...HEY.
YOU GOT US INTO THIS MESS.
YOU TAKE OUT THE REST OF THEM.
OH, DEAR, SANZO-SAMA! ARE YOU DOWN FOR THE COUNT ALREADY?
YOU *ARE* GETTING OLD.
BANG
!
BANG
GU-WAH?!
BANG

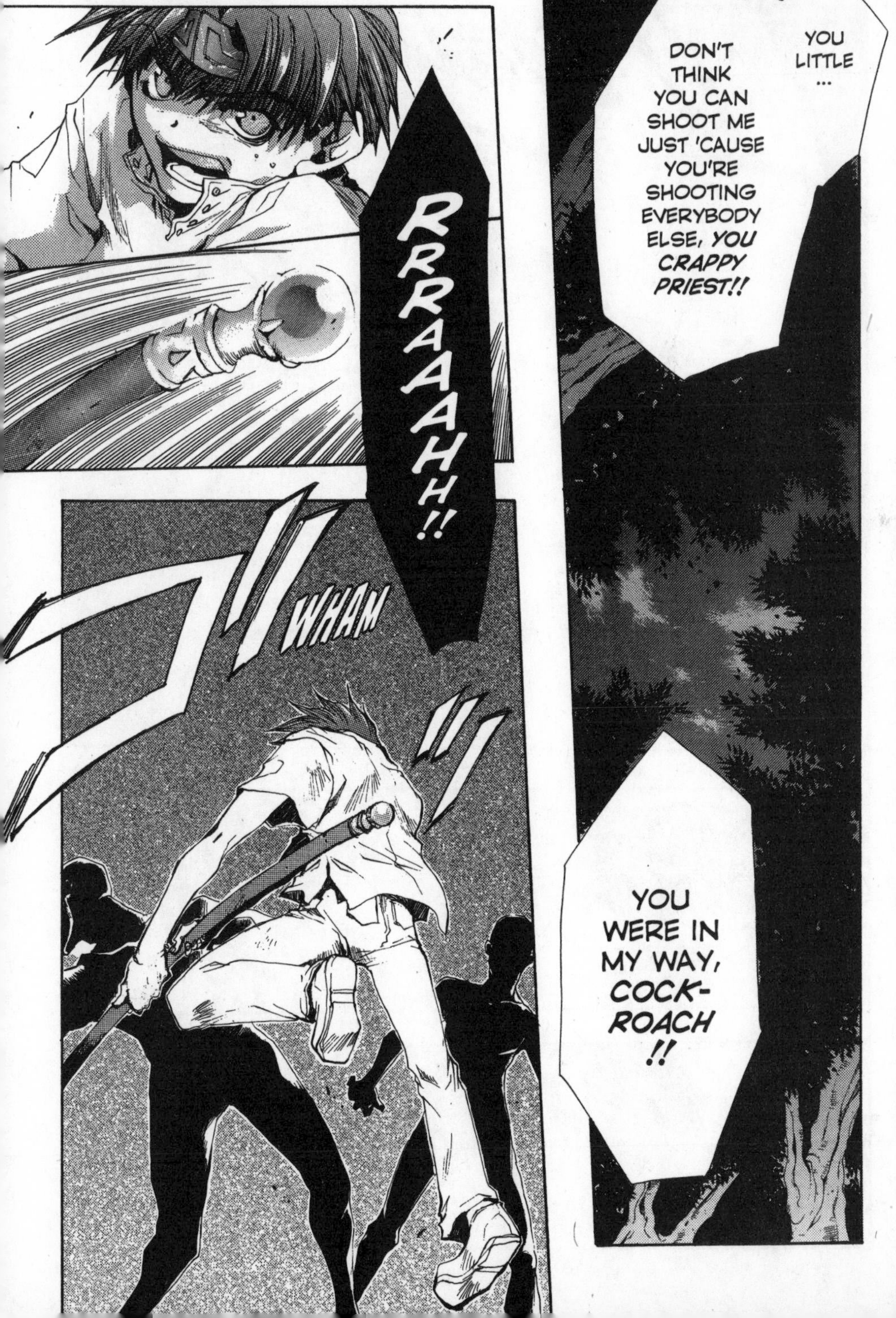
YOU LITTLE ...
DON'T THINK YOU CAN SHOOT ME JUST 'CAUSE YOU'RE SHOOTING EVERYBODY ELSE, *YOU CRAPPY PRIEST!!*
YOU WERE IN MY WAY, *COCK-ROACH!!*
RRRAAAHH!!
WHAM

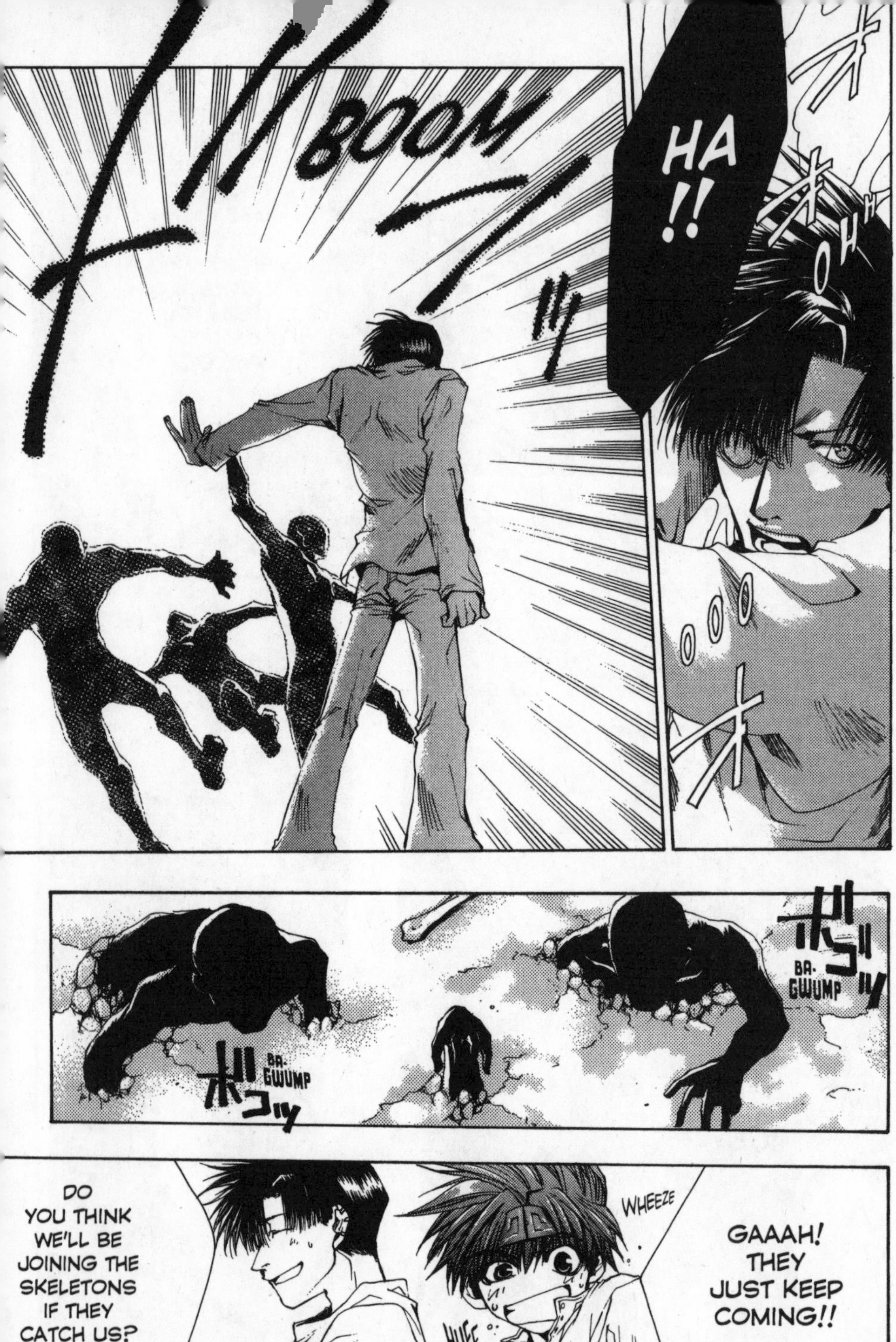
HA!!
BOOM
BA-GWUMP
BA-GWUMP
GAAAH! THEY JUST KEEP COMING!!
WHEEZE
HUFF
DO YOU THINK WE'LL BE JOINING THE SKELETONS IF THEY CATCH US?

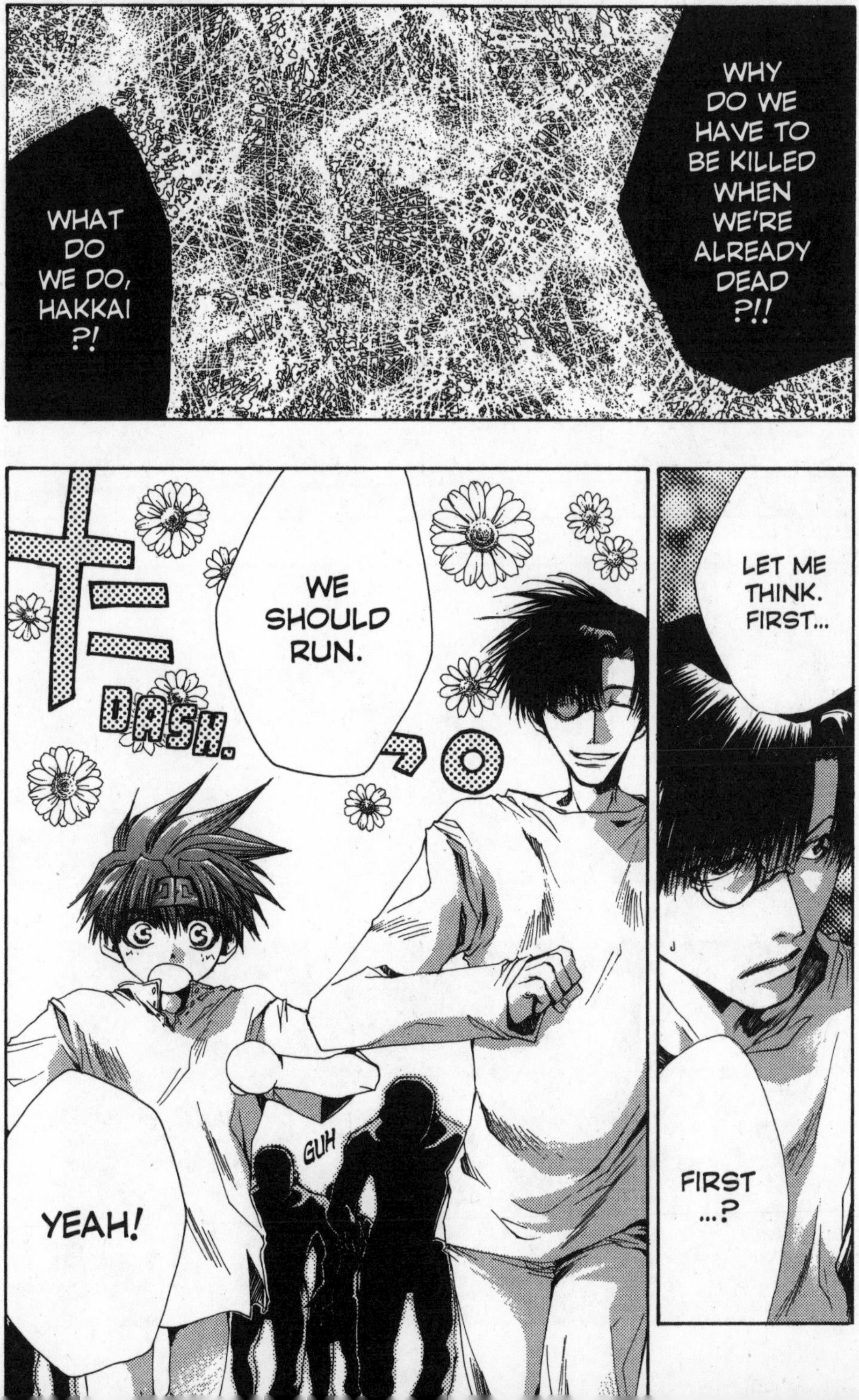
WHY DO WE HAVE TO BE KILLED WHEN WE'RE ALREADY DEAD?!!
WHAT DO WE DO, HAKKAI?!
LET ME THINK. FIRST...
FIRST...?
WE SHOULD RUN.
DASH.
YEAH!
GUH

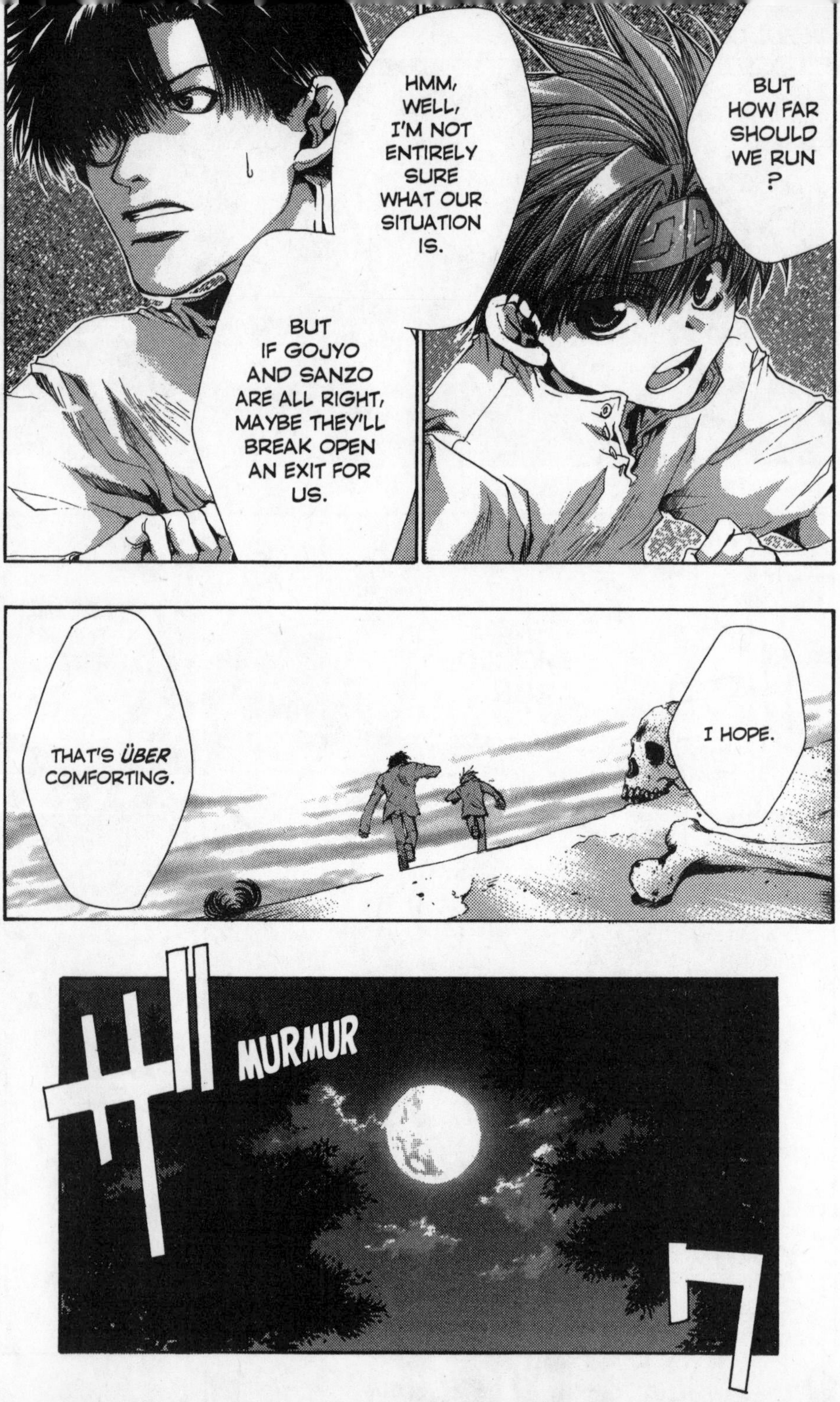
BUT HOW FAR SHOULD WE RUN?
HMM, WELL, I'M NOT ENTIRELY SURE WHAT OUR SITUATION IS.
BUT IF GOJYO AND SANZO ARE ALL RIGHT, MAYBE THEY'LL BREAK OPEN AN EXIT FOR US.
I HOPE.
THAT'S *ÜBER* COMFORTING.
MURMUR

CHAPTER 39: Critical Day

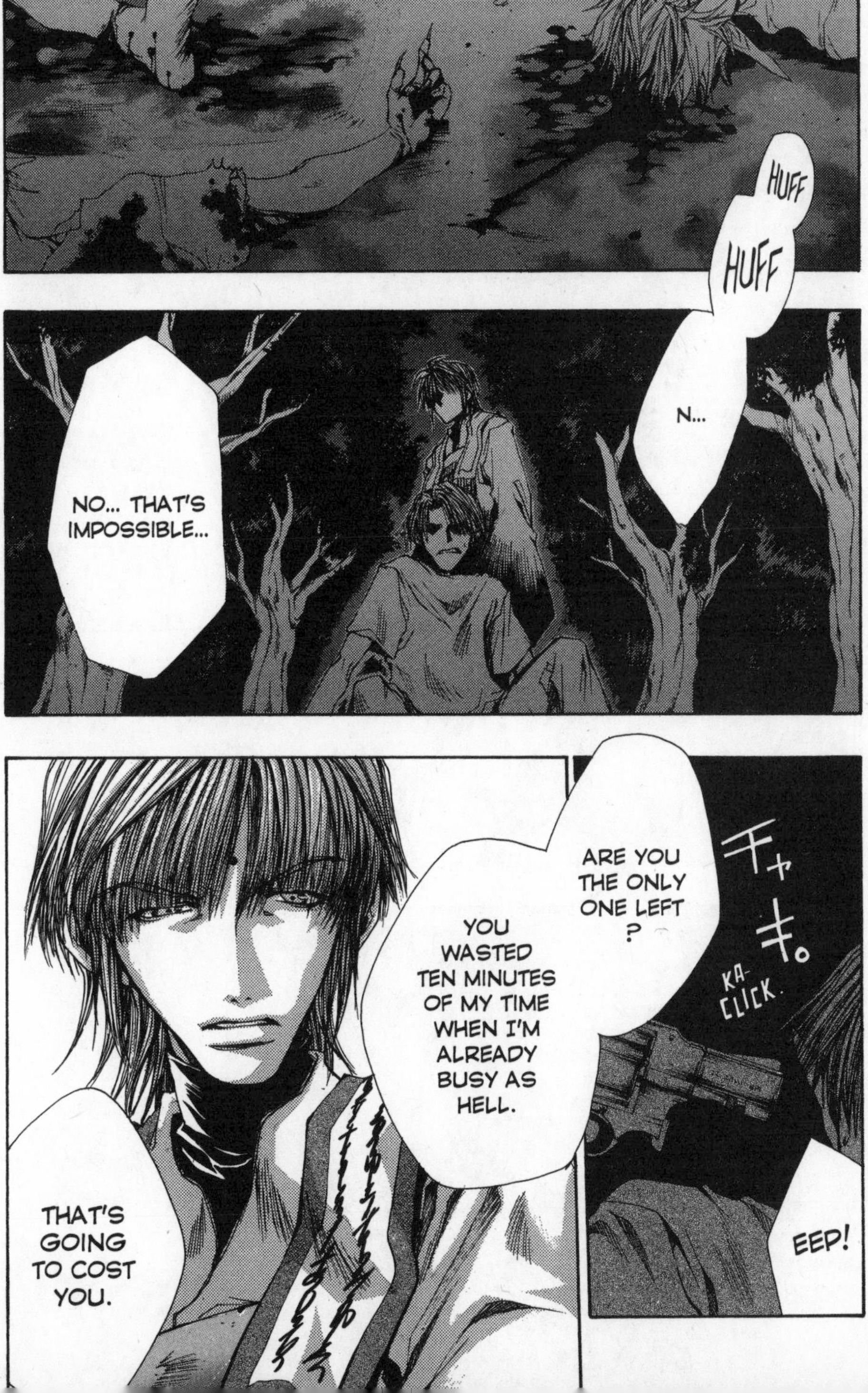
HUFF
HUFF
N...
NO... THAT'S IMPOSSIBLE...
ARE YOU THE ONLY ONE LEFT?
チャキ。
KA-CLICK.
EEP!
YOU WASTED TEN MINUTES OF MY TIME WHEN I'M ALREADY BUSY AS HELL.
THAT'S GOING TO COST YOU.

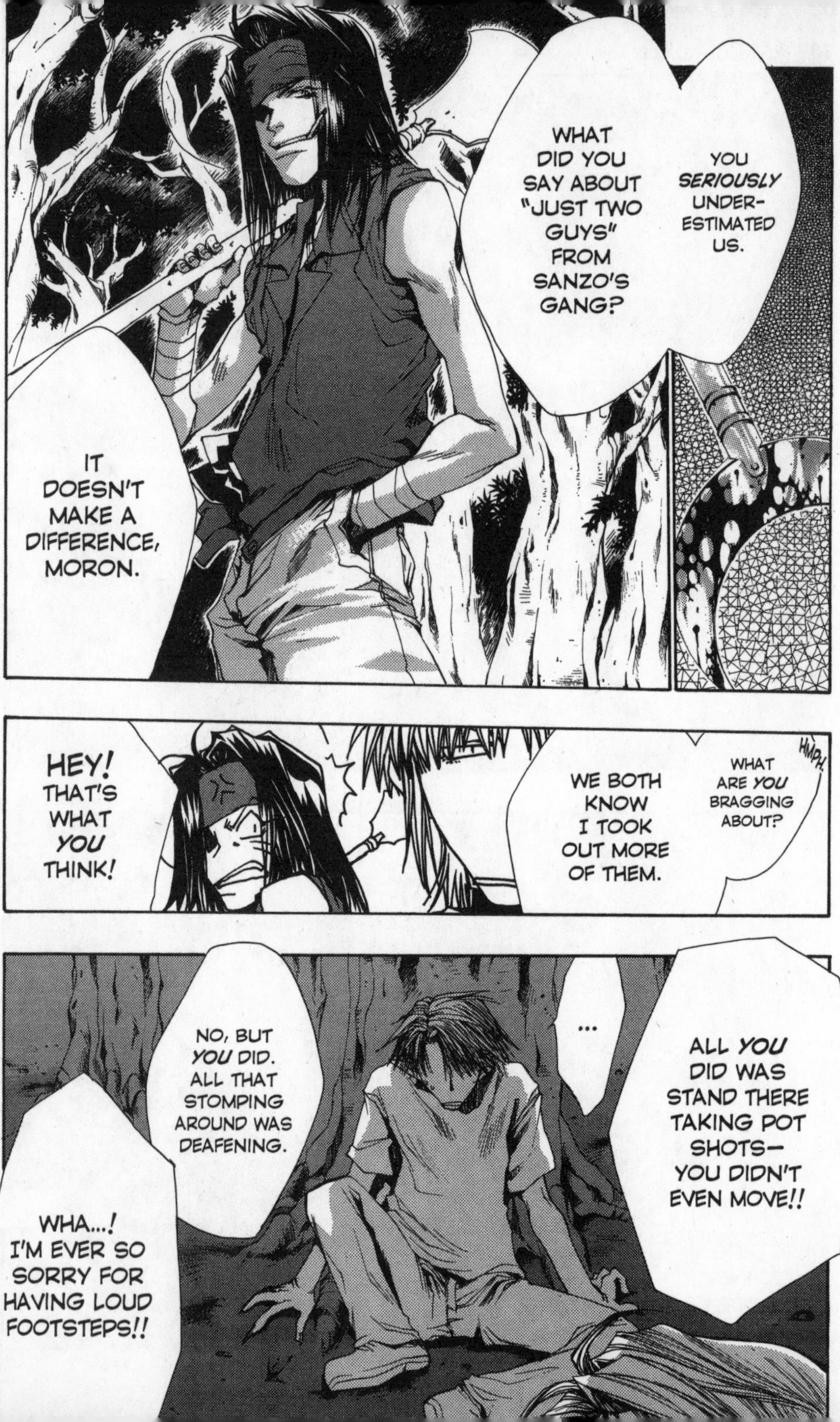

YOU *SERIOUSLY* UNDER-ESTIMATED US.
WHAT DID YOU SAY ABOUT "JUST TWO GUYS" FROM SANZO'S GANG?
IT DOESN'T MAKE A DIFFERENCE, MORON.
HMPH.
WHAT ARE *YOU* BRAGGING ABOUT?
WE BOTH KNOW I TOOK OUT MORE OF THEM.
HEY! THAT'S WHAT *YOU* THINK!
ALL *YOU* DID WAS STAND THERE TAKING POT SHOTS— YOU DIDN'T EVEN MOVE!!
...
NO, BUT *YOU* DID. ALL THAT STOMPING AROUND WAS DEAFENING.
WHA...! I'M EVER SO SORRY FOR HAVING LOUD FOOTSTEPS!!

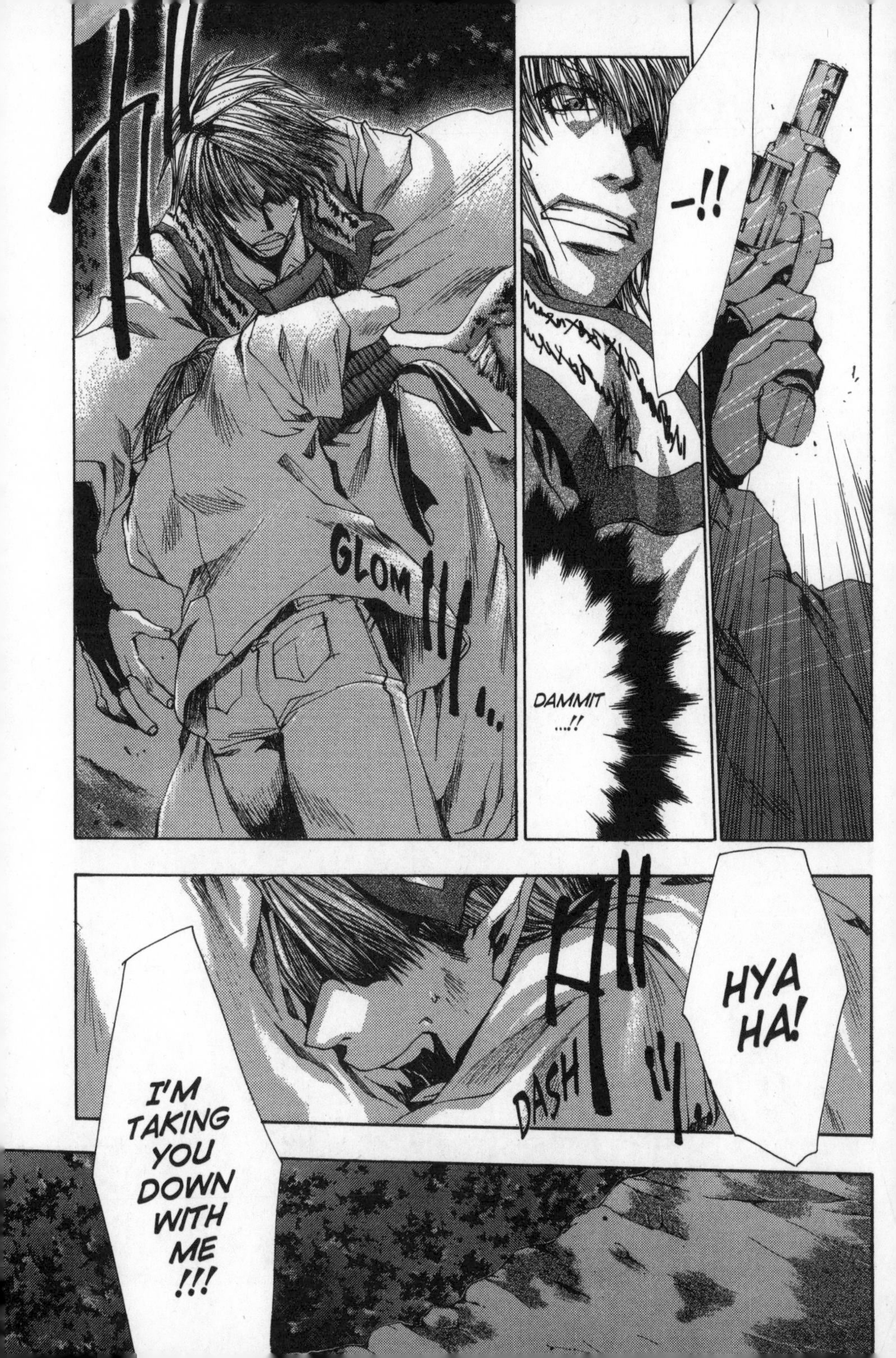
—!!
DAMMIT ...!!
GLOM
HYA HA!
DASH
I'M TAKING YOU DOWN WITH ME !!!

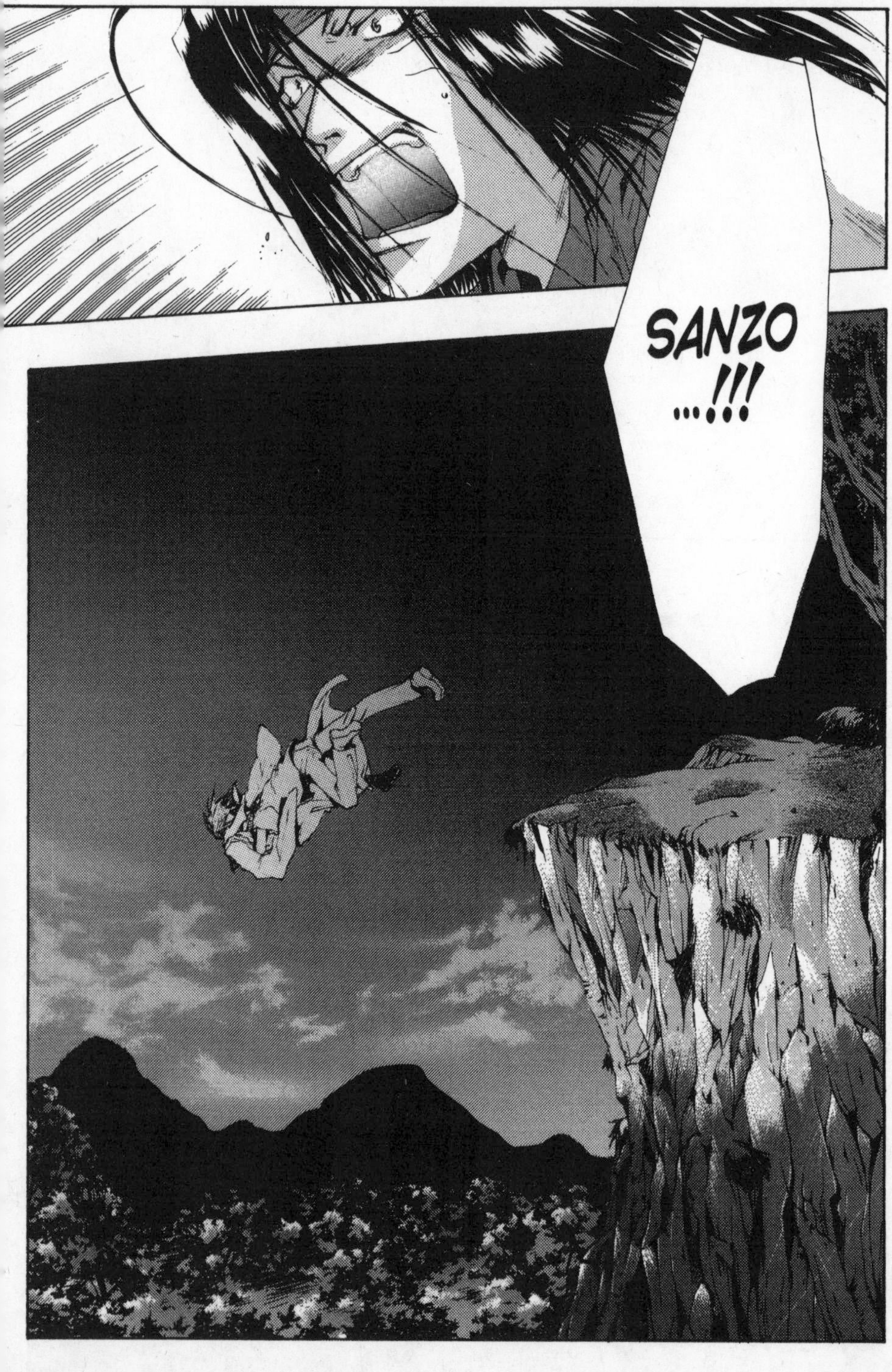
SANZO
...!!!

CHAPTER 39: Critical Day

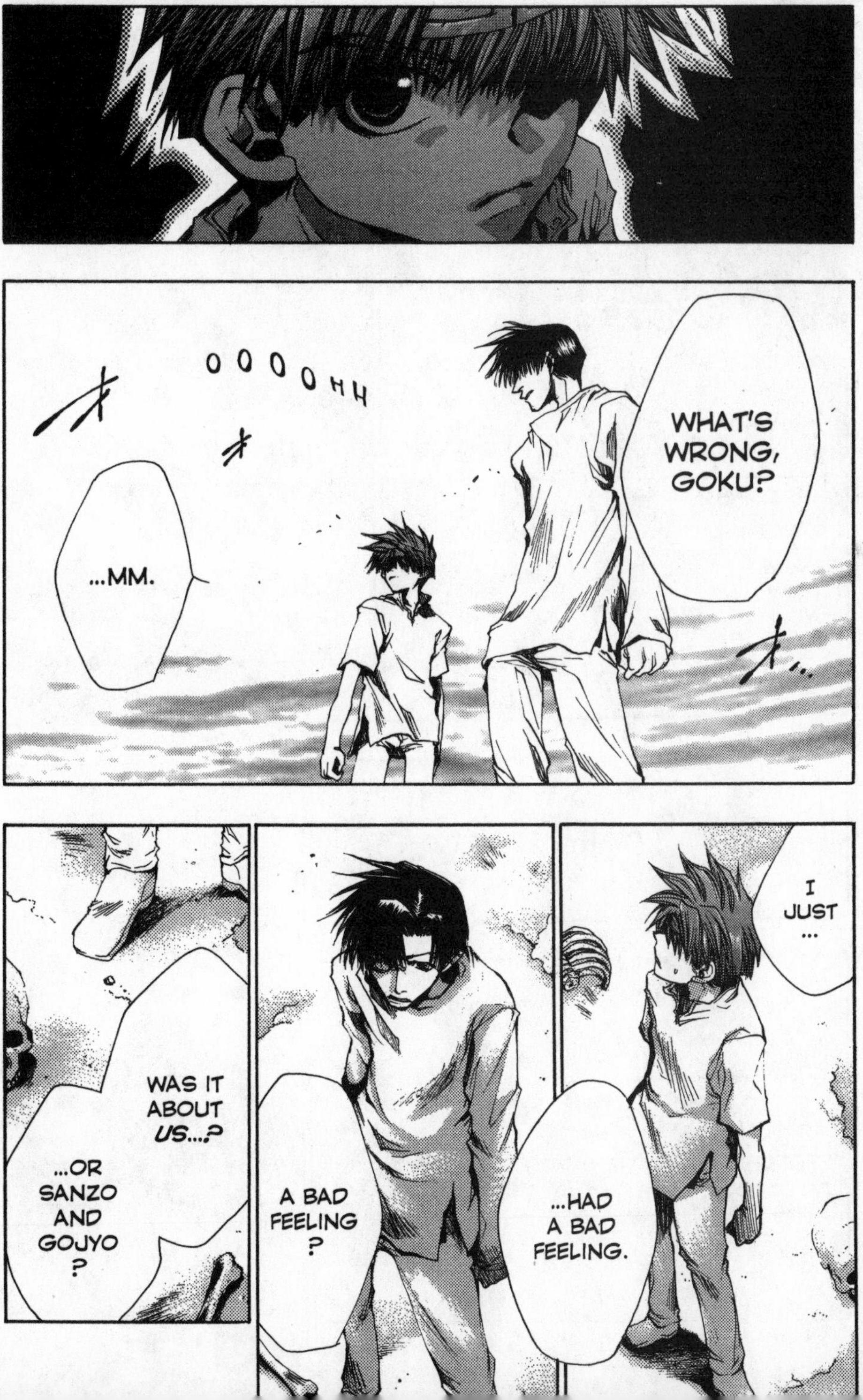

WHAT'S WRONG, GOKU?
OOOOHH
...MM.
I JUST ...
...HAD A BAD FEELING.
A BAD FEELING?
WAS IT ABOUT US...?
...OR SANZO AND GOJYO?

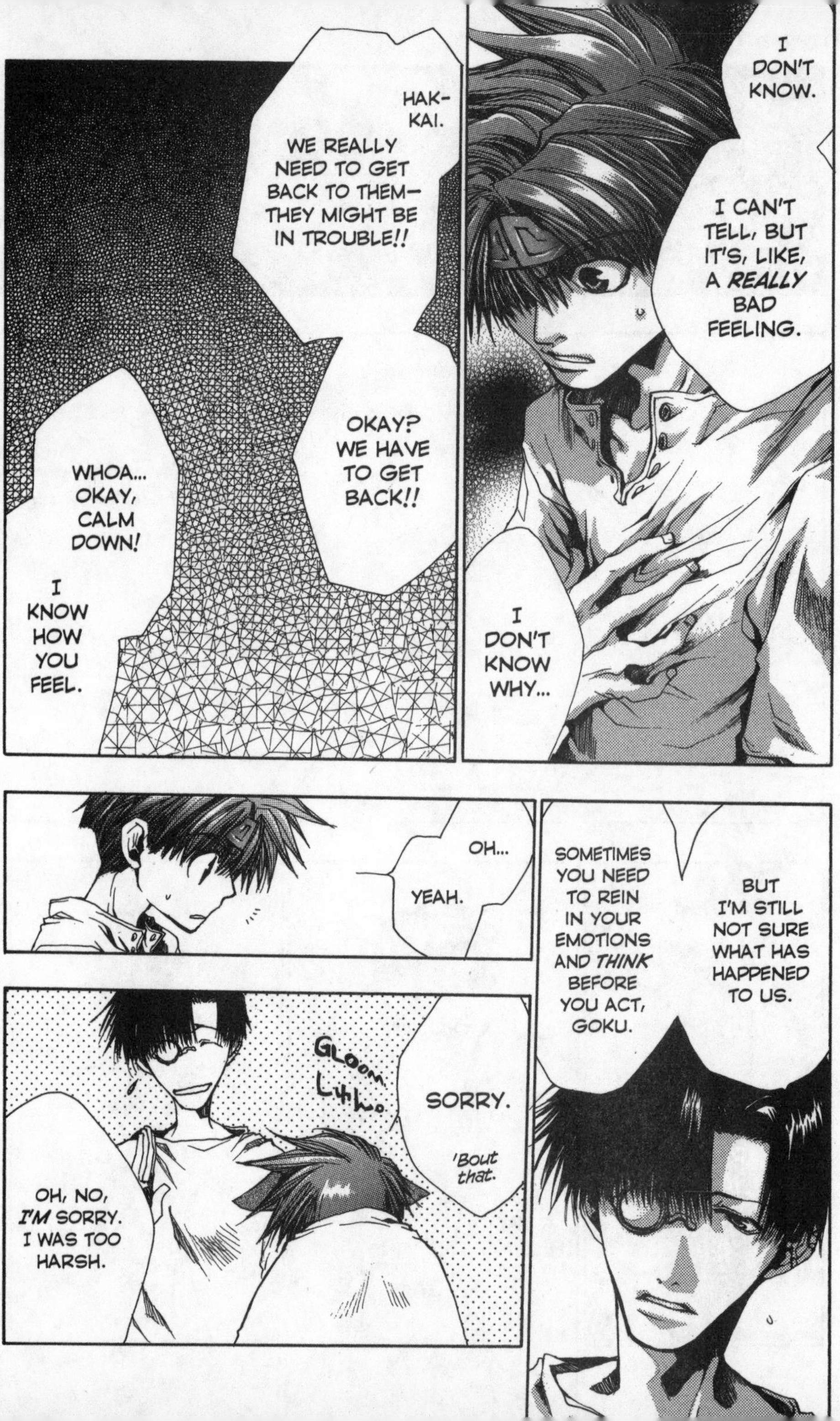

I DON'T KNOW.
I CAN'T TELL, BUT IT'S, LIKE, A *REALLY* BAD FEELING.
I DON'T KNOW WHY...
HAK-KAI.
WE REALLY NEED TO GET BACK TO THEM—THEY MIGHT BE IN TROUBLE!!
OKAY? WE HAVE TO GET BACK!!
WHOA... OKAY, CALM DOWN!
I KNOW HOW YOU FEEL.
BUT I'M STILL NOT SURE WHAT HAS HAPPENED TO US.
SOMETIMES YOU NEED TO REIN IN YOUR EMOTIONS AND *THINK* BEFORE YOU ACT, GOKU.
OH...
YEAH.
GLOOM
SORRY.
'Bout that.
OH, NO, *I'M* SORRY. I WAS TOO HARSH.

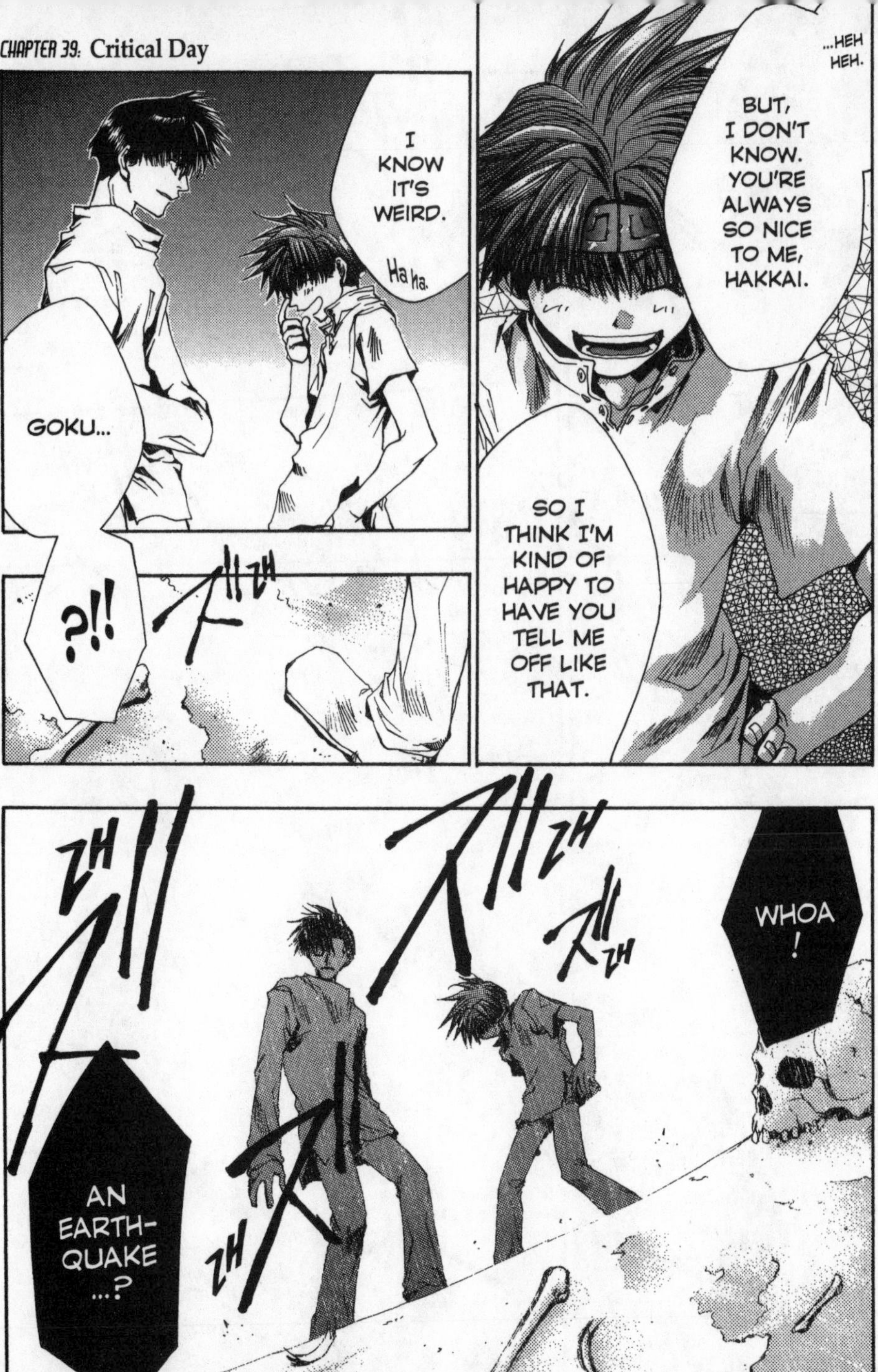
...HEH HEH.
BUT, I DON'T KNOW. YOU'RE ALWAYS SO NICE TO ME, HAKKAI.
SO I THINK I'M KIND OF HAPPY TO HAVE YOU TELL ME OFF LIKE THAT.
I KNOW IT'S WEIRD.
Ha ha.
GOKU...
?!!
WHOA!
AN EARTH-QUAKE...?

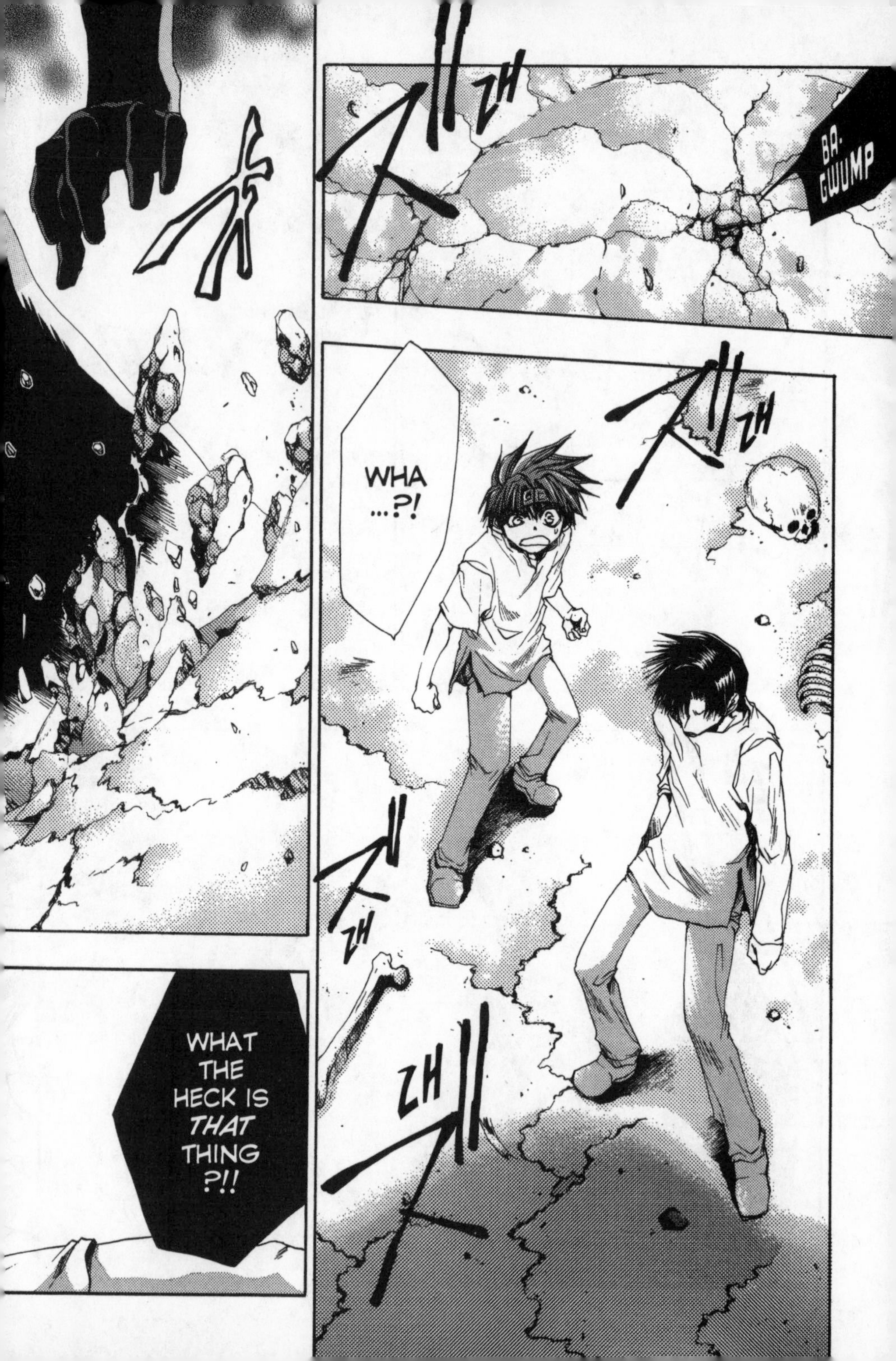
BA-
GWUUMP
WHA ...?!
WHAT THE HECK IS *THAT* THING ?!!

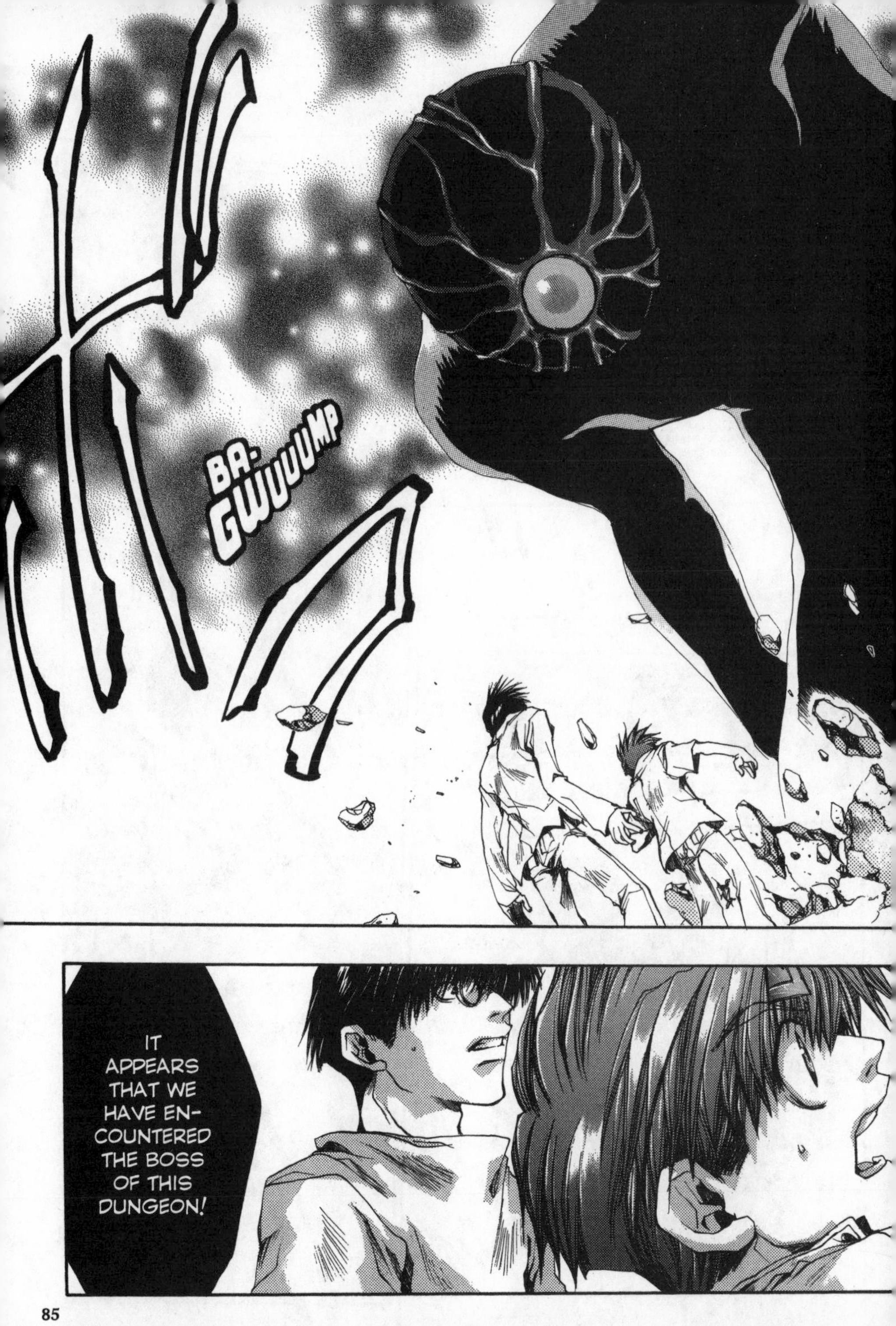
BA-GWUUUMP
IT APPEARS THAT WE HAVE EN-COUNTERED THE BOSS OF THIS DUNGEON!

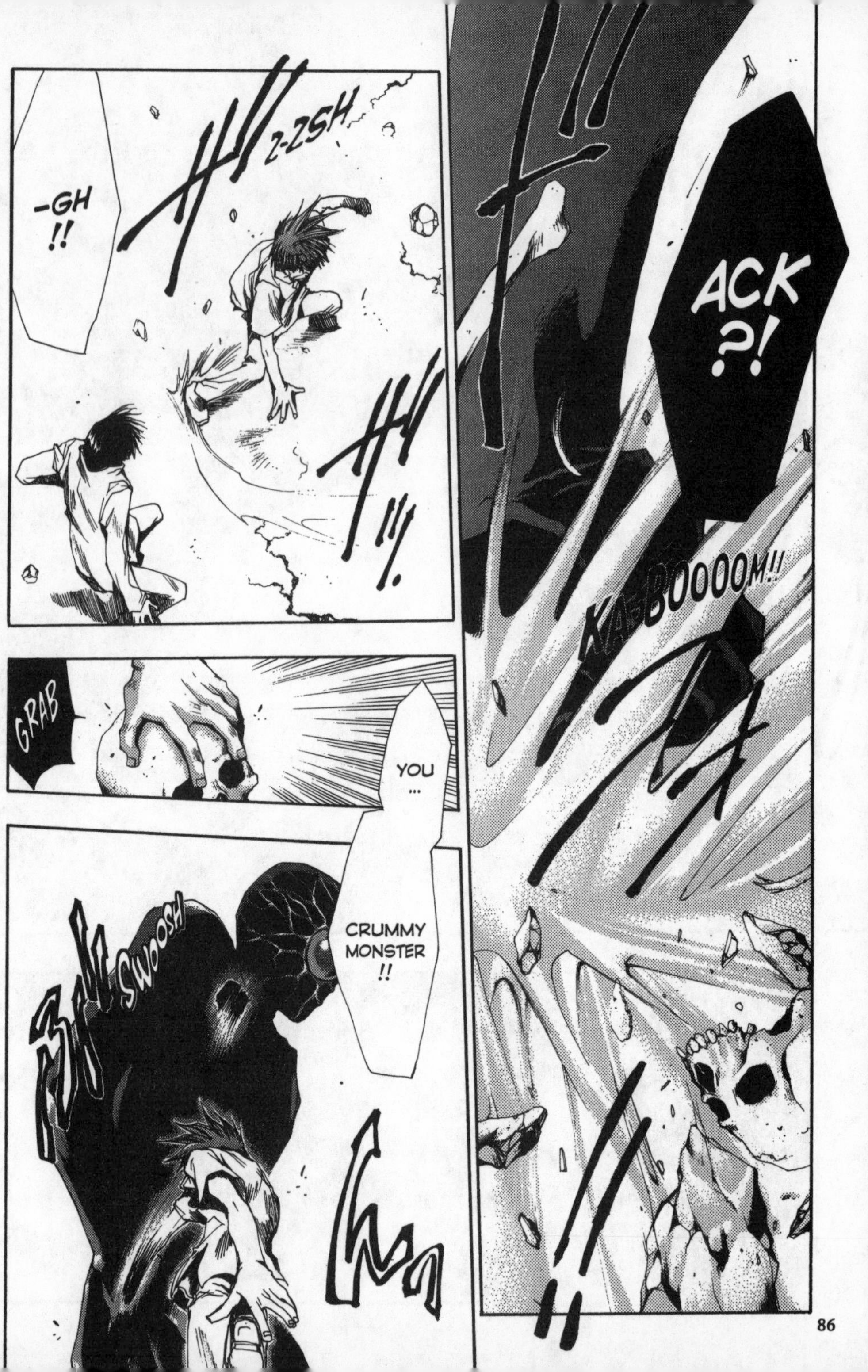
ACK ?!
KA-BOOOOM!!
Z-ZSH
-GH !!
GRAB
YOU ...
CRUMMY MONSTER !!
SWOOSH

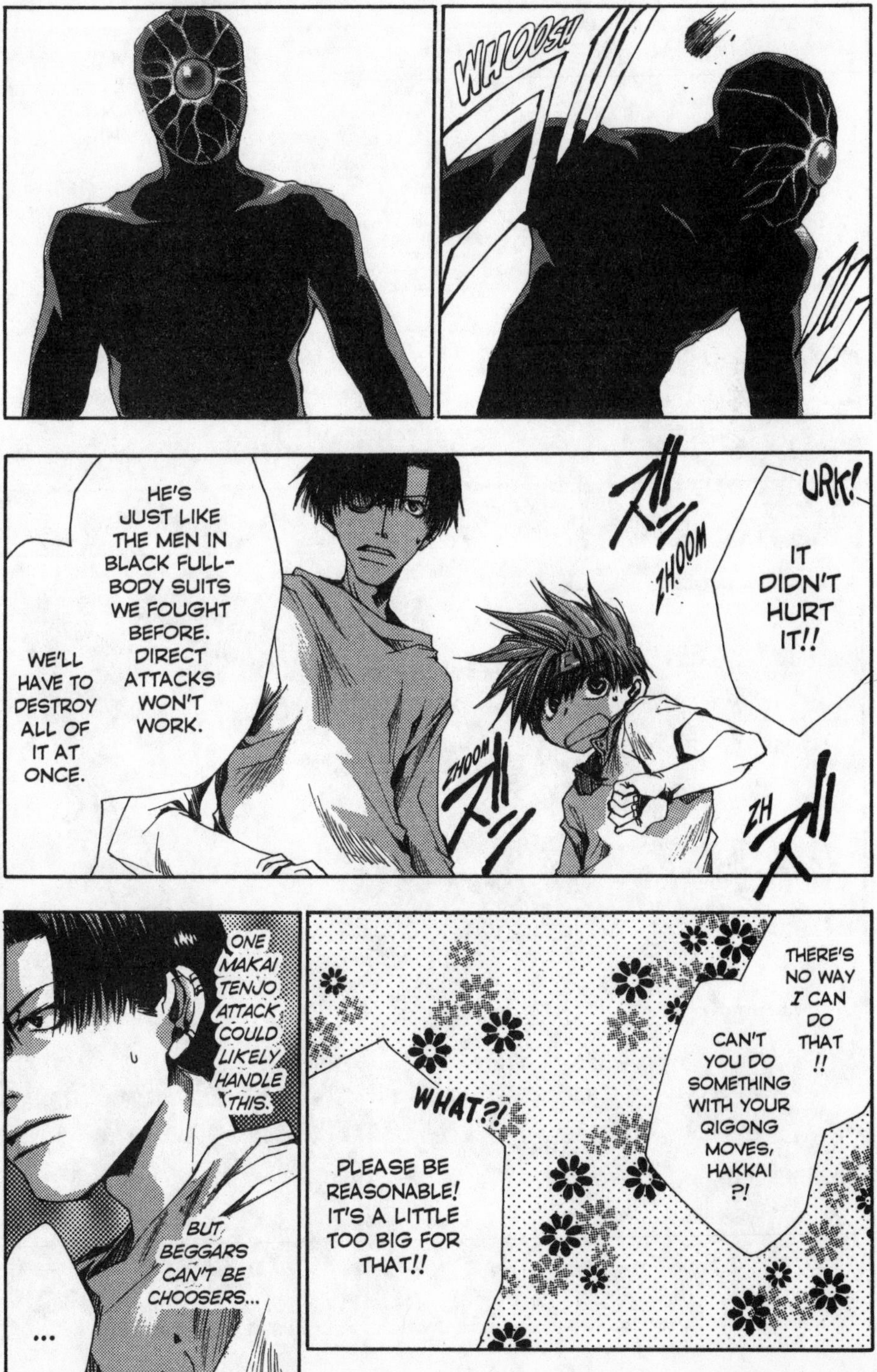
WHOOSH!!
URK!
IT DIDN'T HURT IT!!
ZHOOM
ZHOOM
ZH
HE'S JUST LIKE THE MEN IN BLACK FULL-BODY SUITS WE FOUGHT BEFORE. DIRECT ATTACKS WON'T WORK.
WE'LL HAVE TO DESTROY ALL OF IT AT ONCE.
THERE'S NO WAY I CAN DO THAT!!
CAN'T YOU DO SOMETHING WITH YOUR QIGONG MOVES, HAKKAI?!
WHAT?!
PLEASE BE REASONABLE! IT'S A LITTLE TOO BIG FOR THAT!!
ONE MAKAI TENJO ATTACK COULD LIKELY HANDLE THIS.
BUT BEGGARS CAN'T BE CHOOSERS...
...

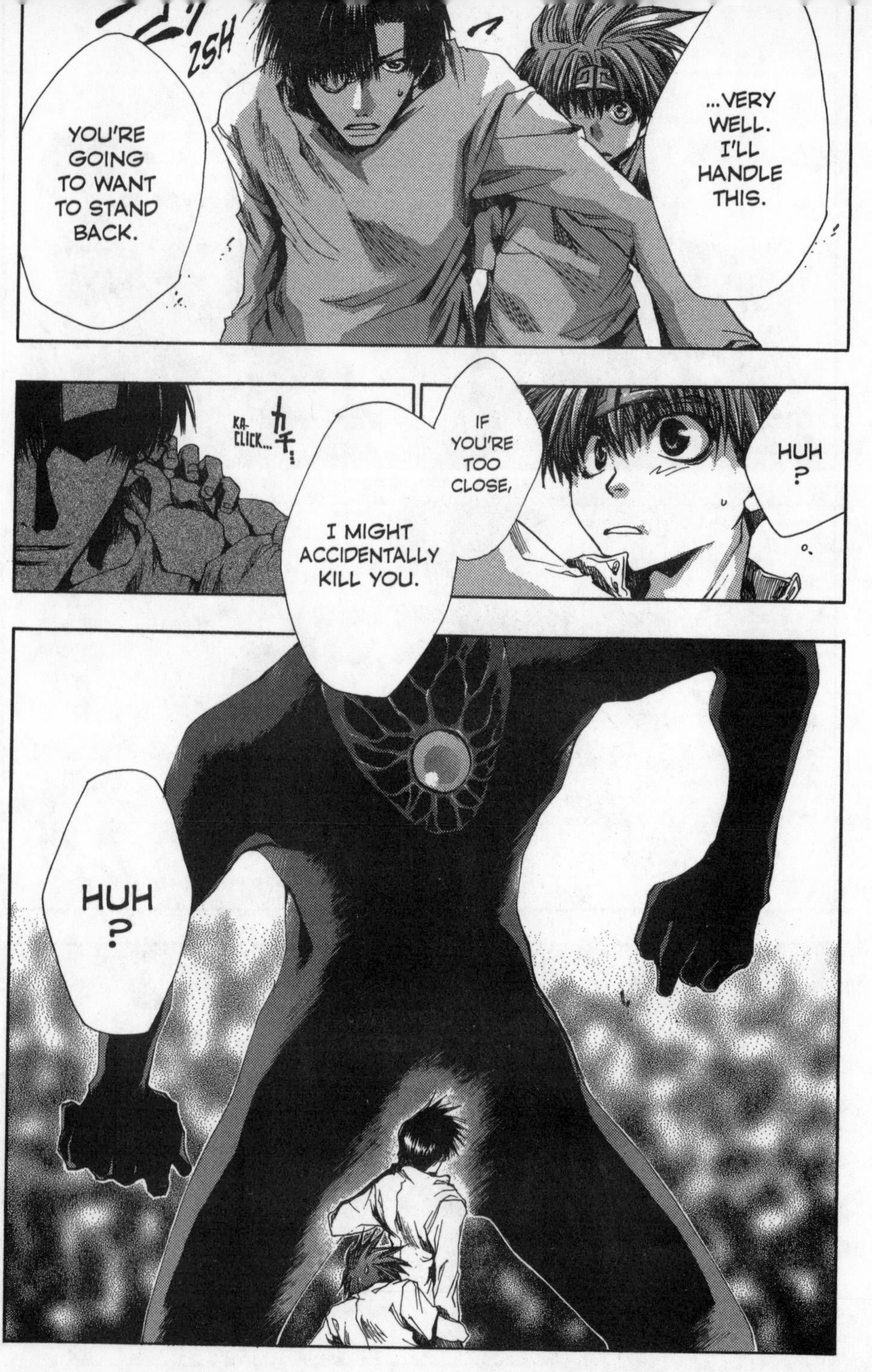
...VERY WELL. I'LL HANDLE THIS.
ZSH
YOU'RE GOING TO WANT TO STAND BACK.
HUH?
IF YOU'RE TOO CLOSE,
I MIGHT ACCIDENTALLY KILL YOU.
KA-CLICK...
HUH?

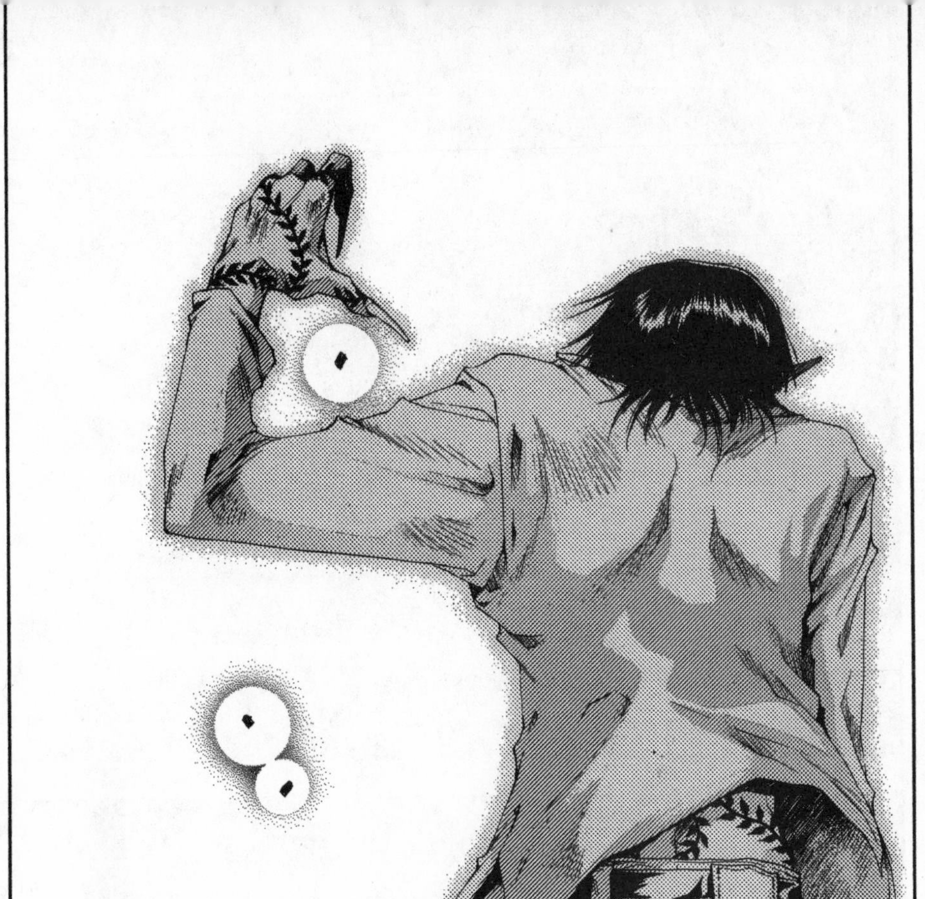

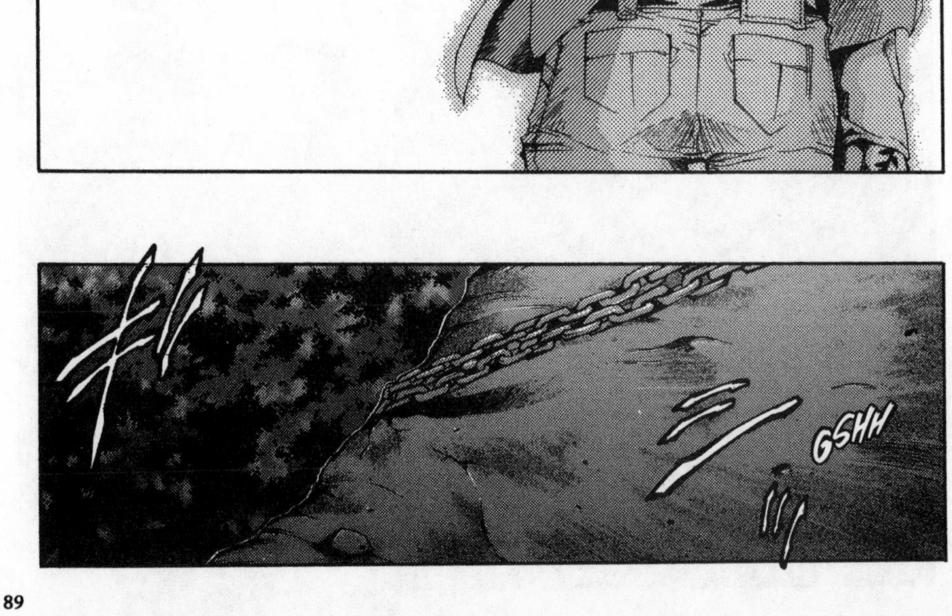
GSHH

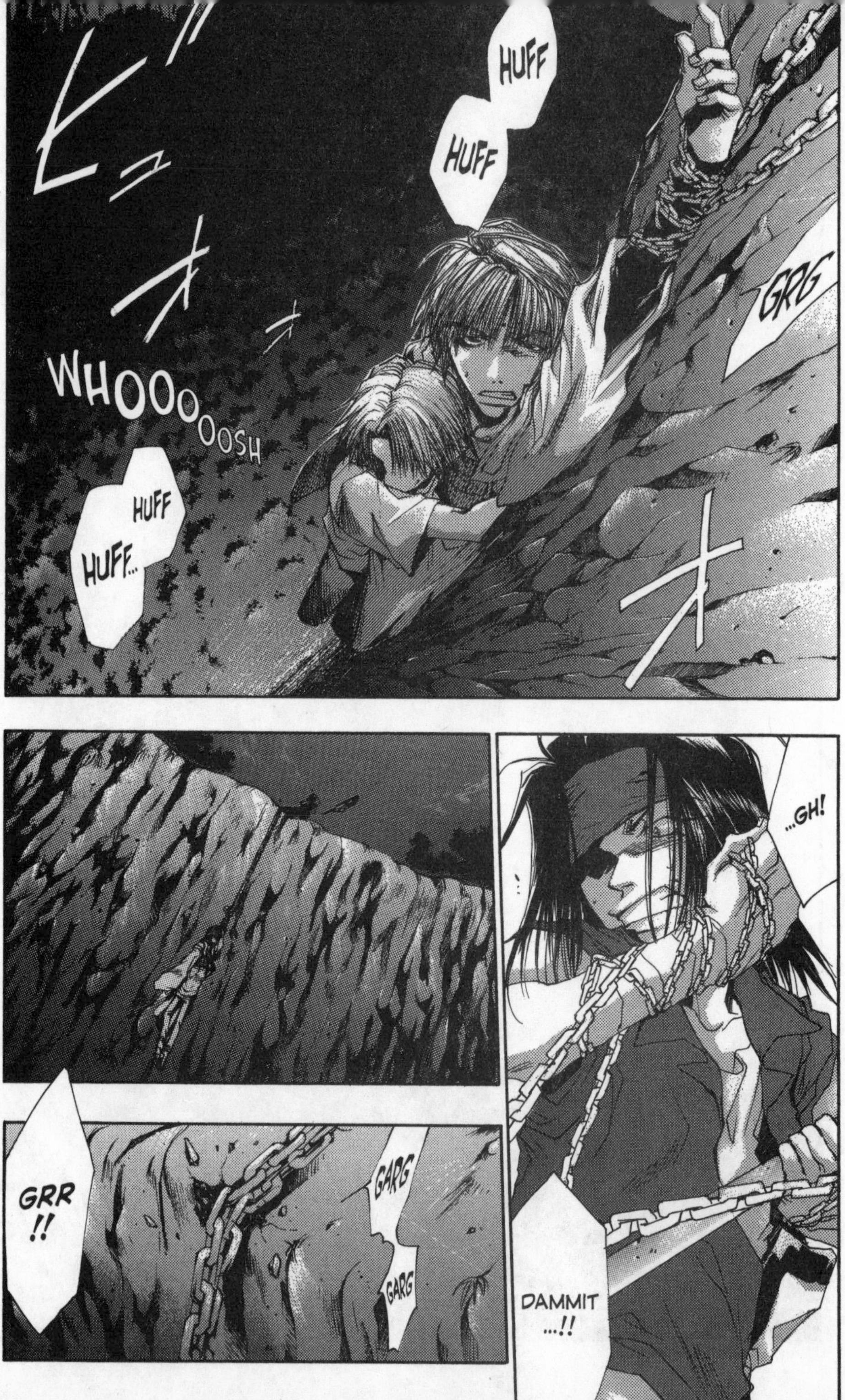
HUFF
HUFF
GRG
ビュオォオ
WHOOOOOOSH
HUFF
HUFF...
...GH!
DAMMIT ...!!
GARG
GARG
GRR !!

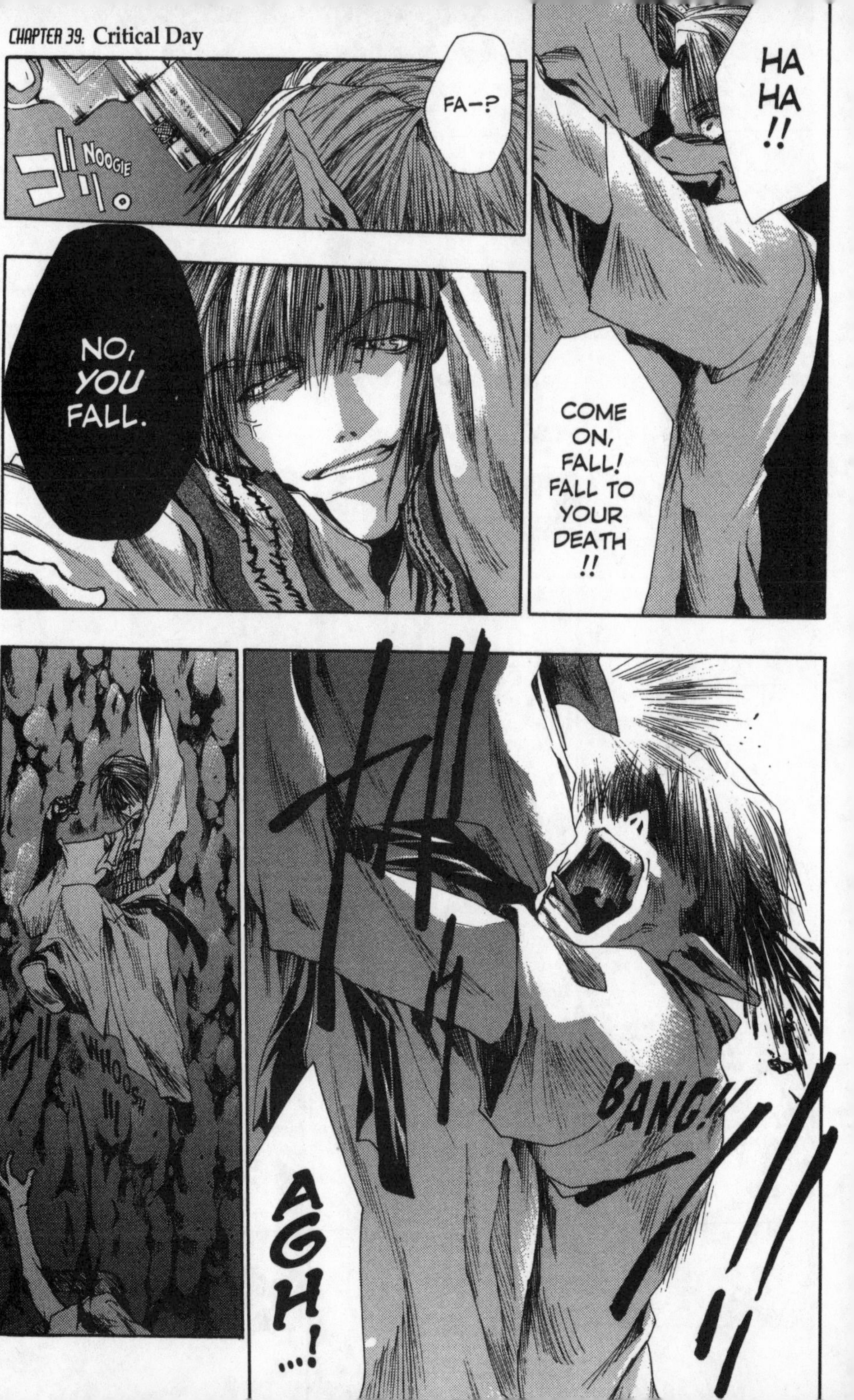
HA HA!!
COME ON, FALL! FALL TO YOUR DEATH!!
FA—?
NOOGIE
NO, YOU FALL.
BANG!!
AGH!...
WHOOSH!!

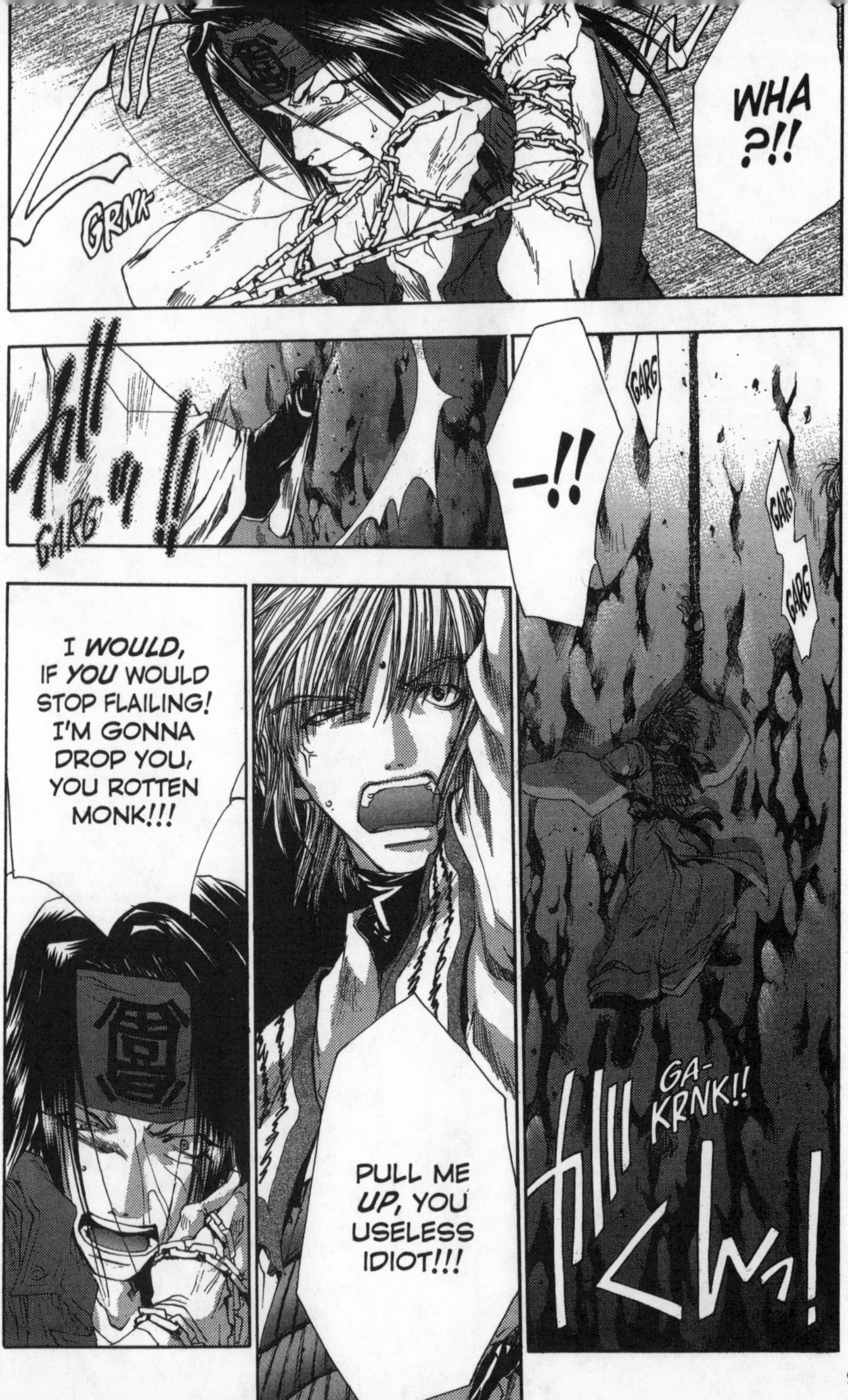
WHA ?!!
GRNK
—!!
GARG
GARG
GARG
GA-KRNK!!
GARG
PULL ME *UP*, YOU USELESS IDIOT!!!
I *WOULD*, IF *YOU* WOULD STOP FLAILING! I'M GONNA DROP YOU, YOU ROTTEN MONK!!!

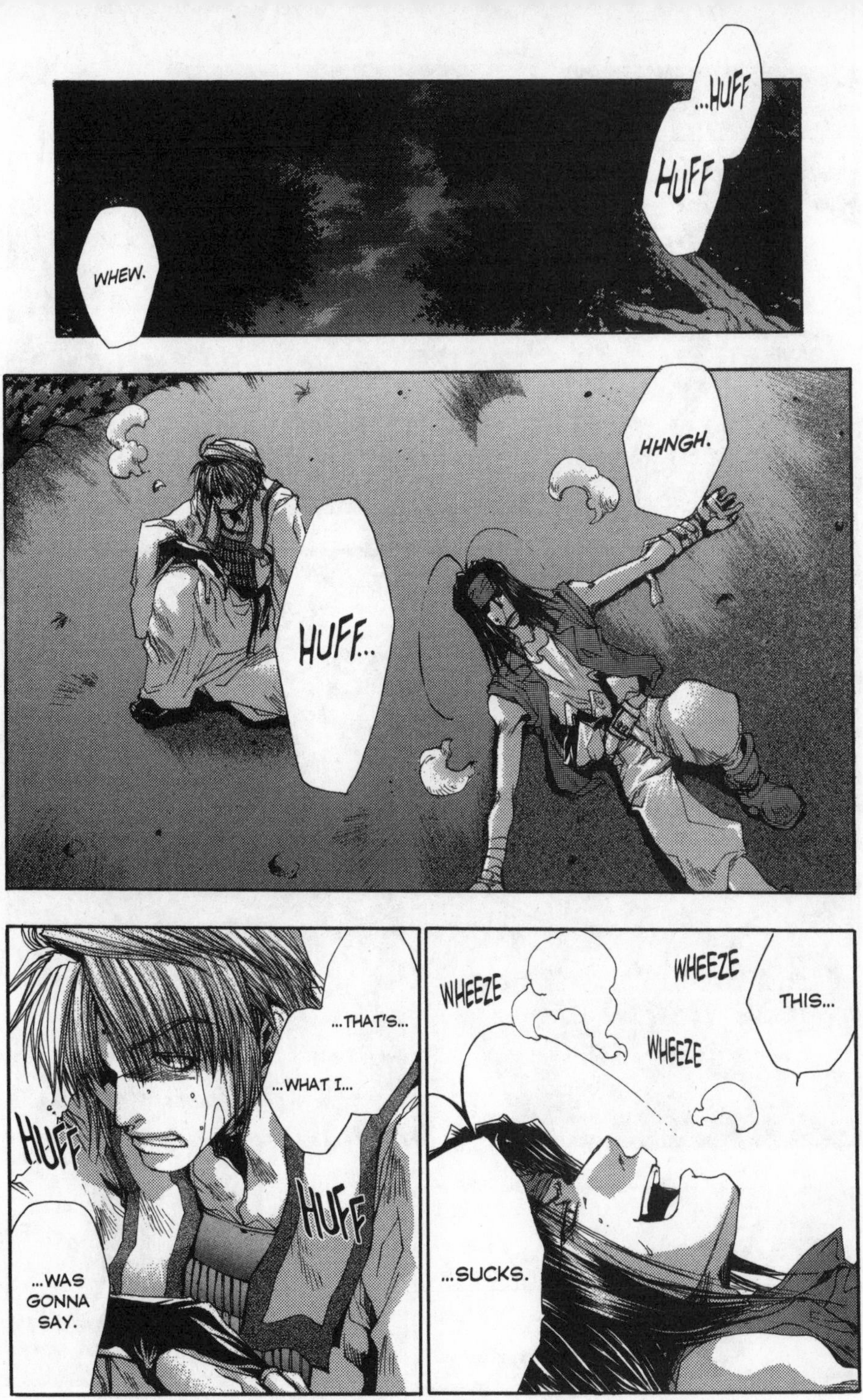
...HUFF
HUFF
WHEW.
HHNGH.
HUFF...
THIS...
WHEEZE
WHEEZE
WHEEZE
...SUCKS.
...THAT'S...
...WHAT I...
HUFF
HUFF
...WAS GONNA SAY.

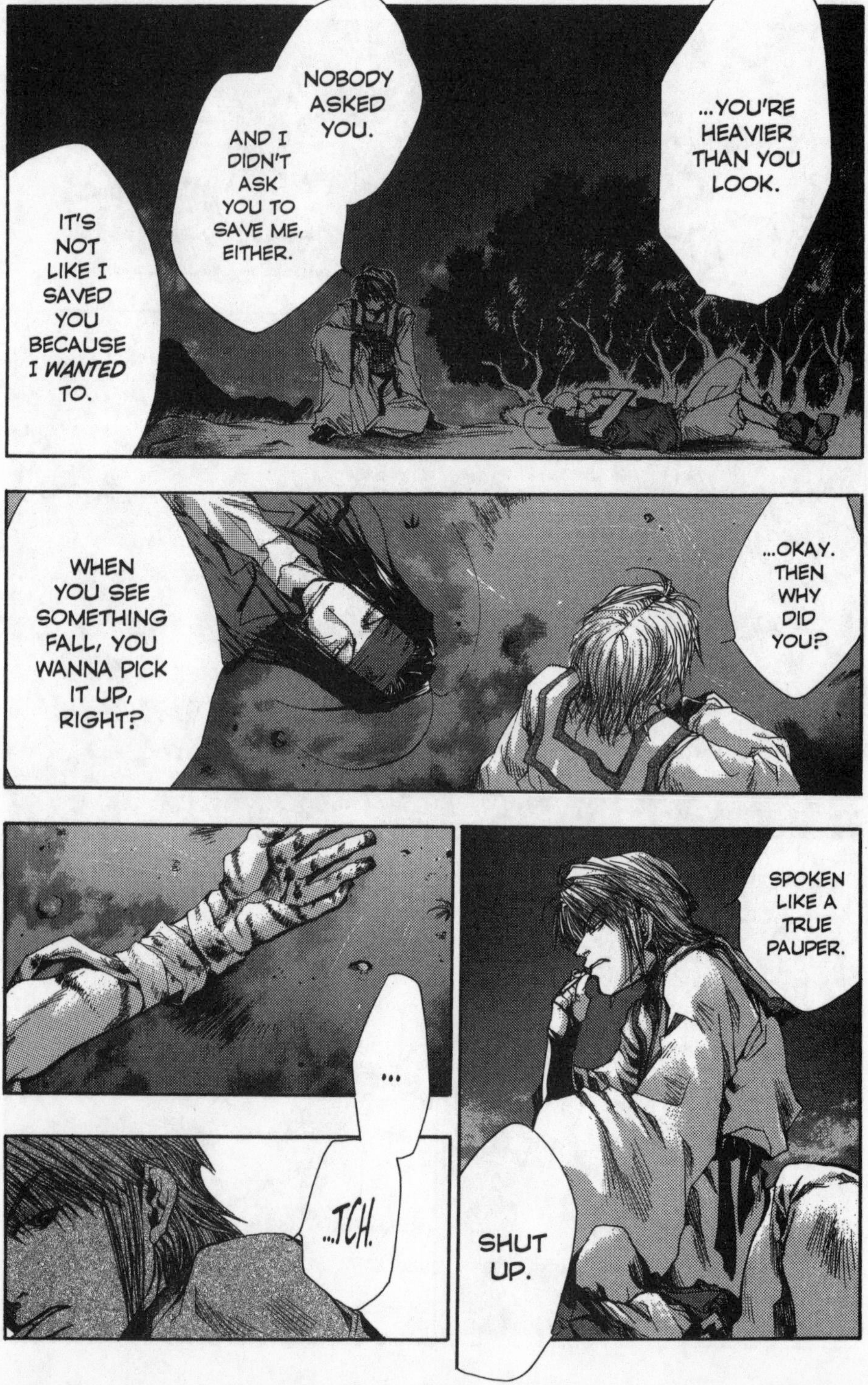
...YOU'RE HEAVIER THAN YOU LOOK.
NOBODY ASKED YOU.
AND I DIDN'T ASK YOU TO SAVE ME, EITHER.
IT'S NOT LIKE I SAVED YOU BECAUSE I *WANTED* TO.
...OKAY. THEN WHY DID YOU?
WHEN YOU SEE SOMETHING FALL, YOU WANNA PICK IT UP, RIGHT?
SPOKEN LIKE A TRUE PAUPER.
SHUT UP.
...
...TCH.

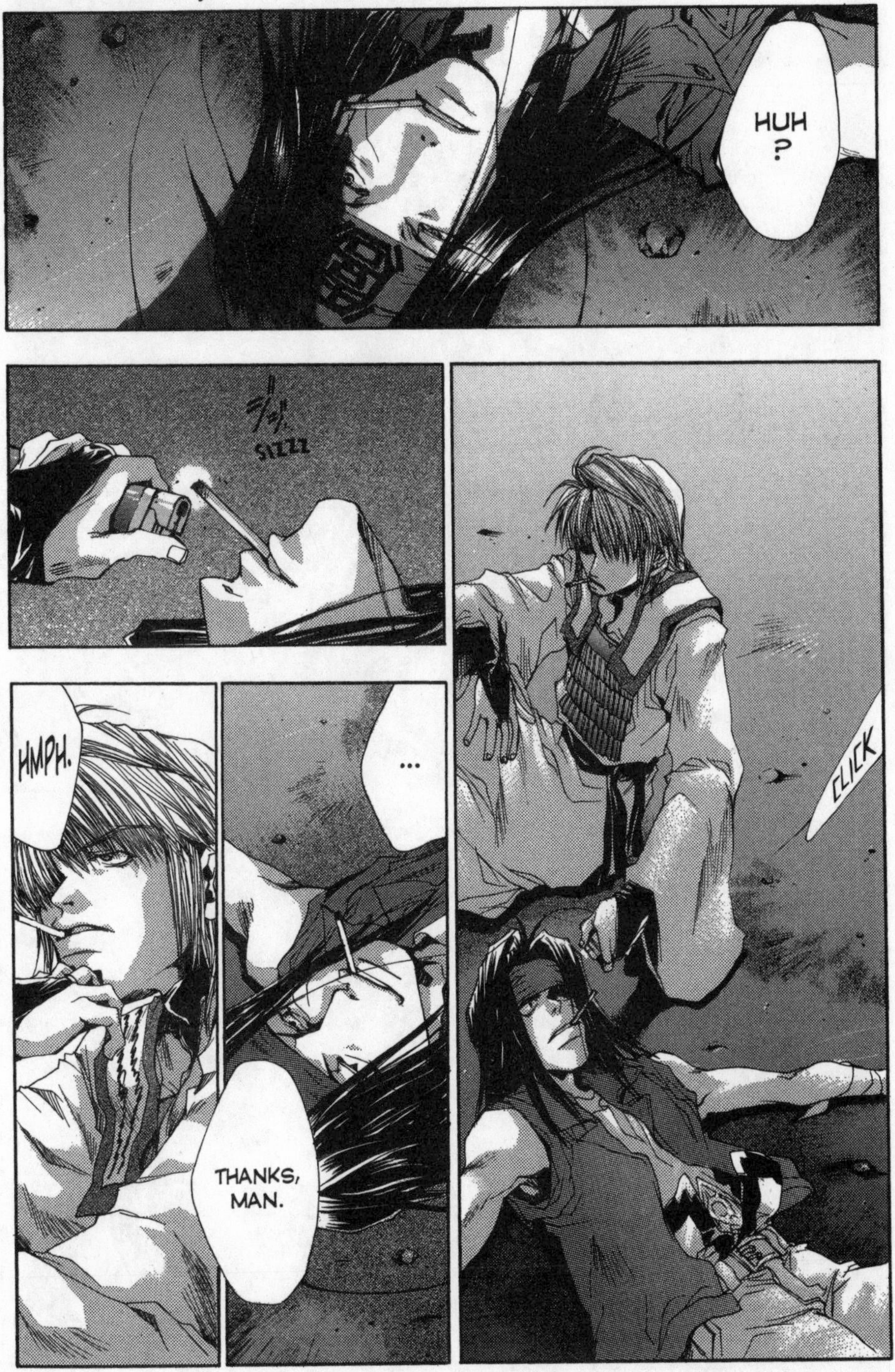
HUH ?
CLICK
SIZZZ
...
THANKS, MAN.
HMPH.

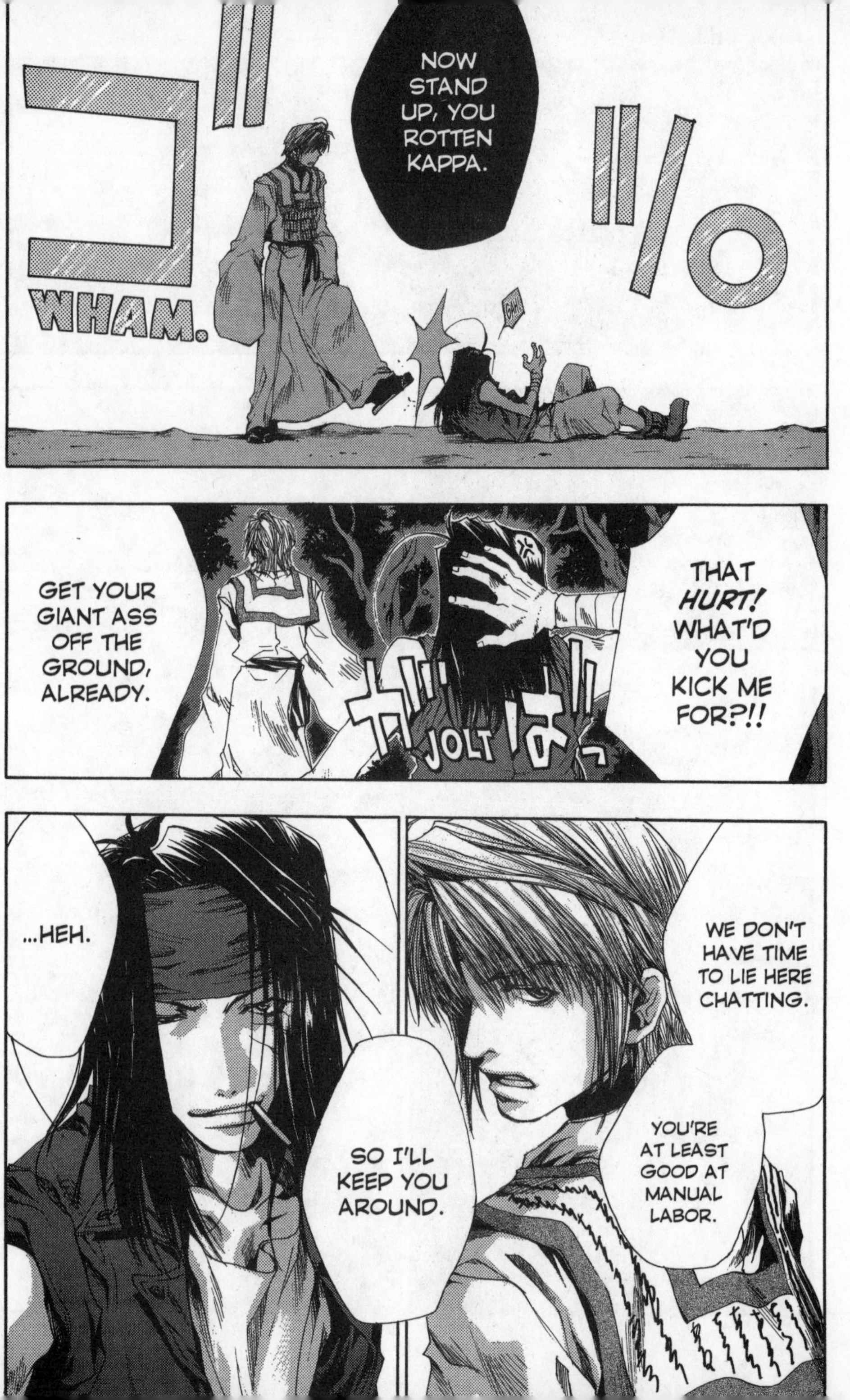
NOW STAND UP, YOU ROTTEN KAPPA.
WHAM.
GAH!
THAT HURT! WHAT'D YOU KICK ME FOR?!!
JOLT
GET YOUR GIANT ASS OFF THE GROUND, ALREADY.
WE DON'T HAVE TIME TO LIE HERE CHATTING.
YOU'RE AT LEAST GOOD AT MANUAL LABOR.
SO I'LL KEEP YOU AROUND.
...HEH.

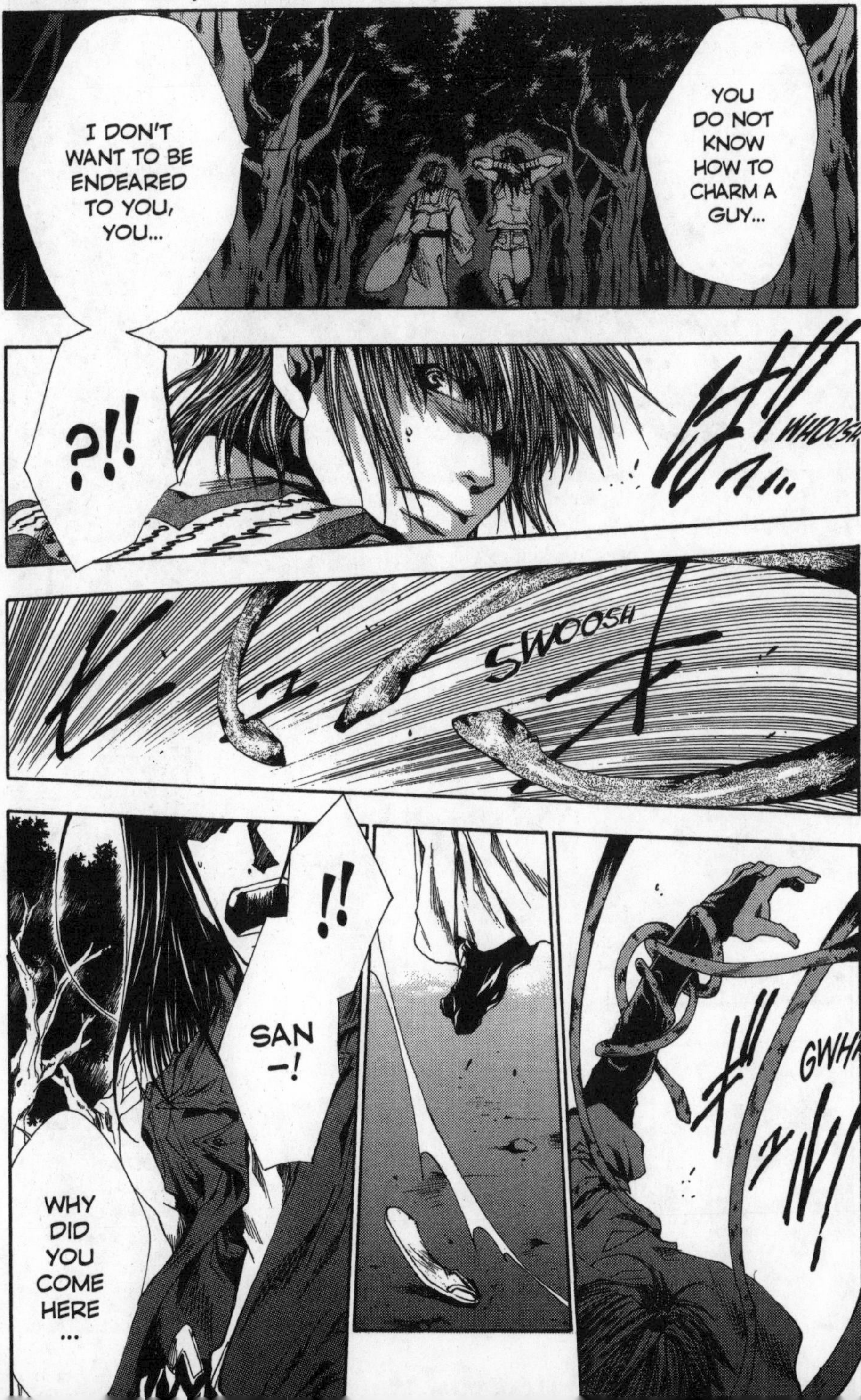
YOU DO NOT KNOW HOW TO CHARM A GUY...
I DON'T WANT TO BE ENDEARED TO YOU, YOU...
WHOOSH
?!!
SWOOSH
GWHRR
!!
SAN—!
WHY DID YOU COME HERE ...

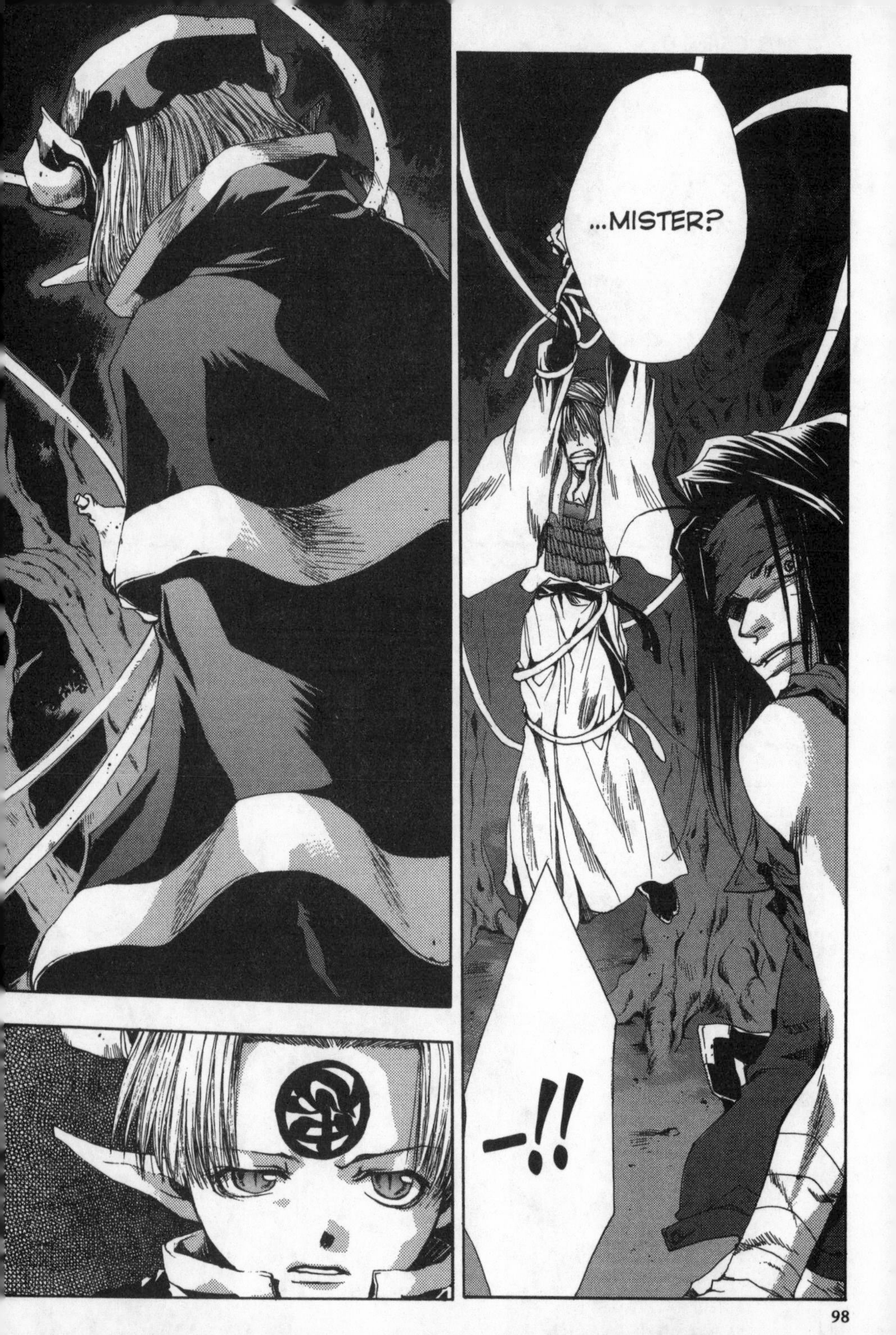
...MISTER?
—!!

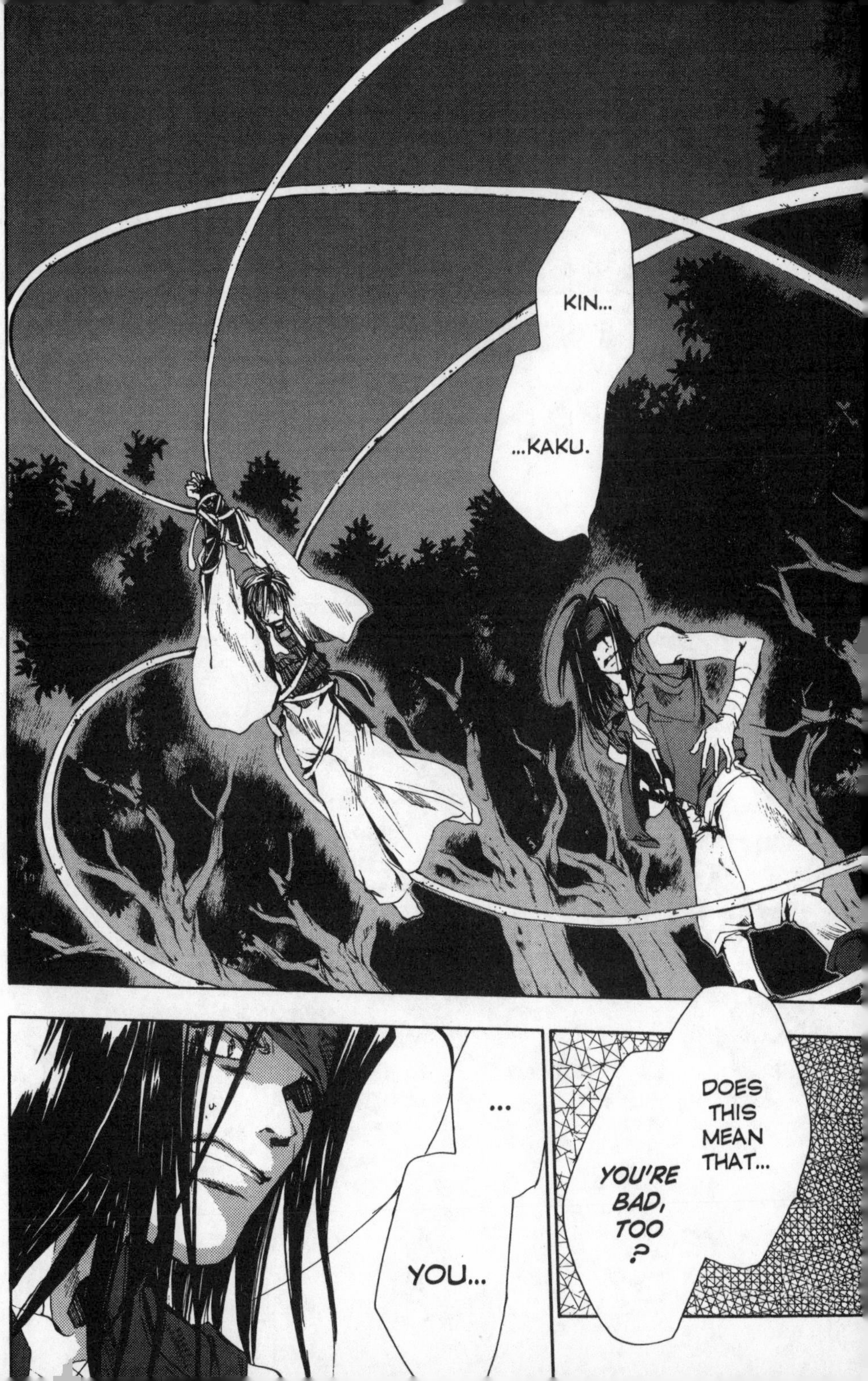
KIN...
...KAKU.
DOES THIS MEAN THAT...
YOU'RE BAD, TOO?
...
YOU...

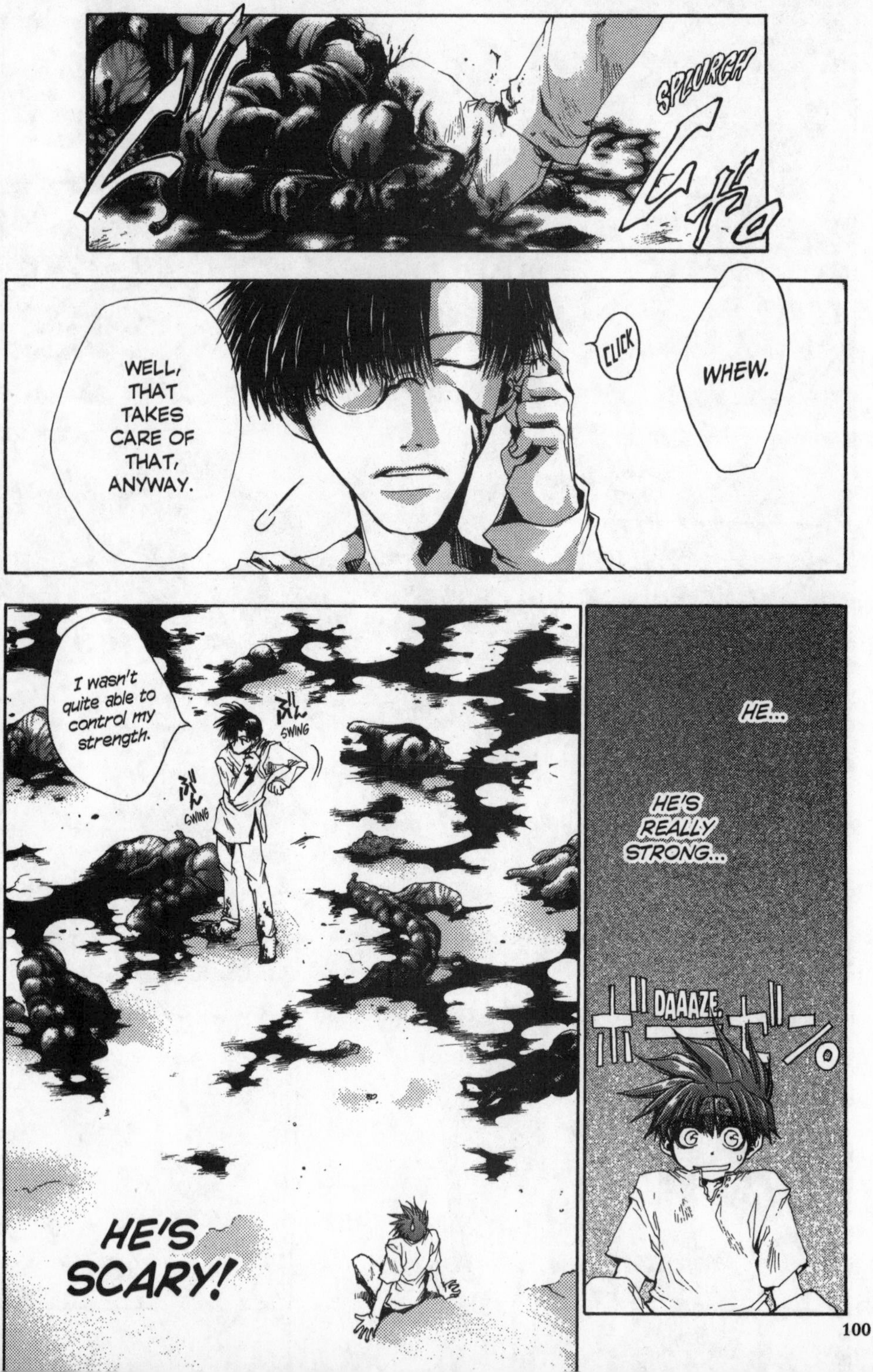
SPLURCH
WHEW.
CLICK
WELL, THAT TAKES CARE OF THAT, ANYWAY.
HE...
HE'S REALLY STRONG...
DAAAZE.
I wasn't quite able to control my strength.
SWING
SWING
HE'S SCARY!

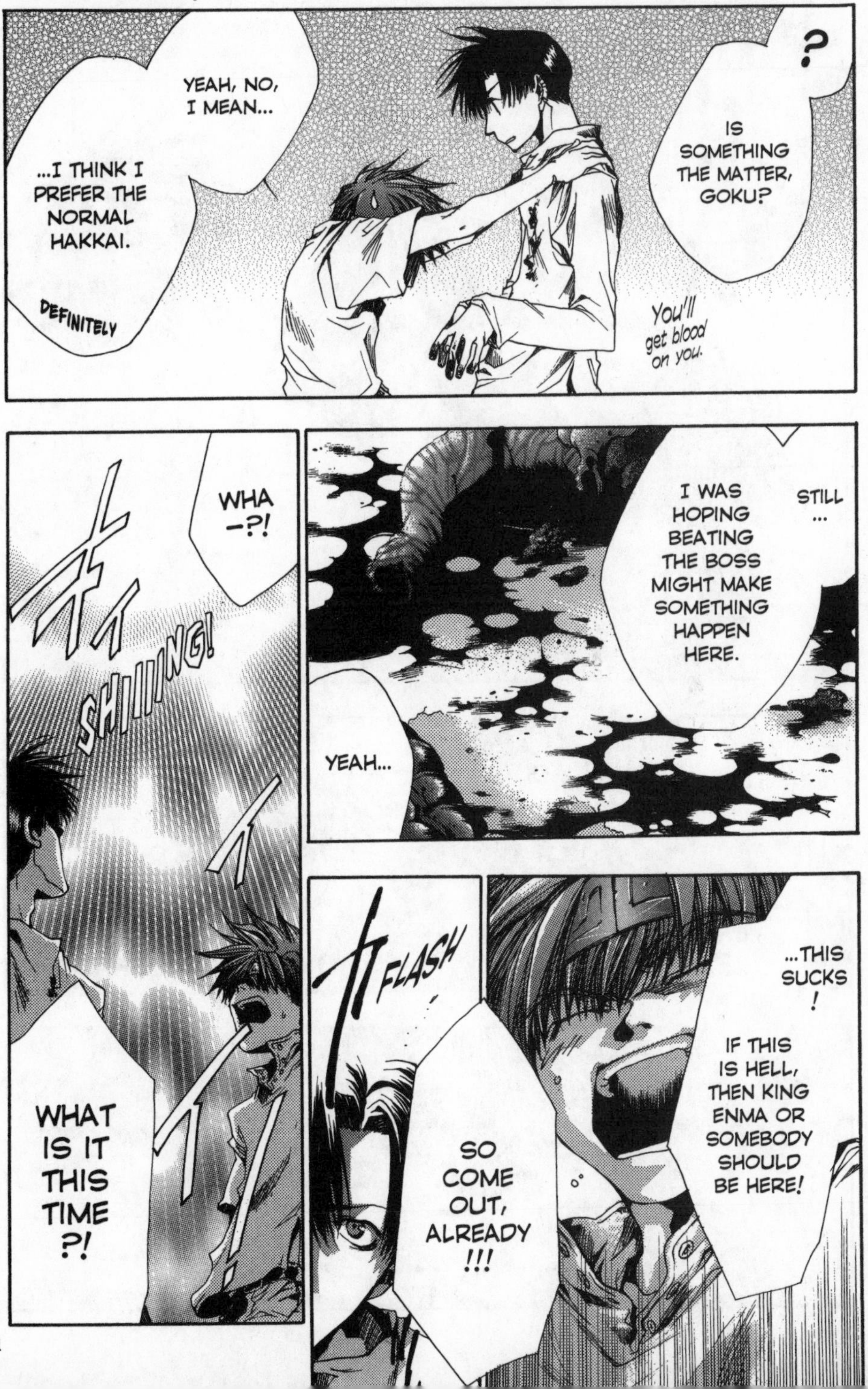
?
IS SOMETHING THE MATTER, GOKU?
You'll get blood on you.
YEAH, NO, I MEAN...
...I THINK I PREFER THE NORMAL HAKKAI.
DEFINITELY
STILL ...
I WAS HOPING BEATING THE BOSS MIGHT MAKE SOMETHING HAPPEN HERE.
YEAH...
...THIS SUCKS!
IF THIS IS HELL, THEN KING ENMA OR SOMEBODY SHOULD BE HERE!
SO COME OUT, ALREADY!!!
FLASH
WHA-?!
SHIIIING!
WHAT IS IT THIS TIME?!

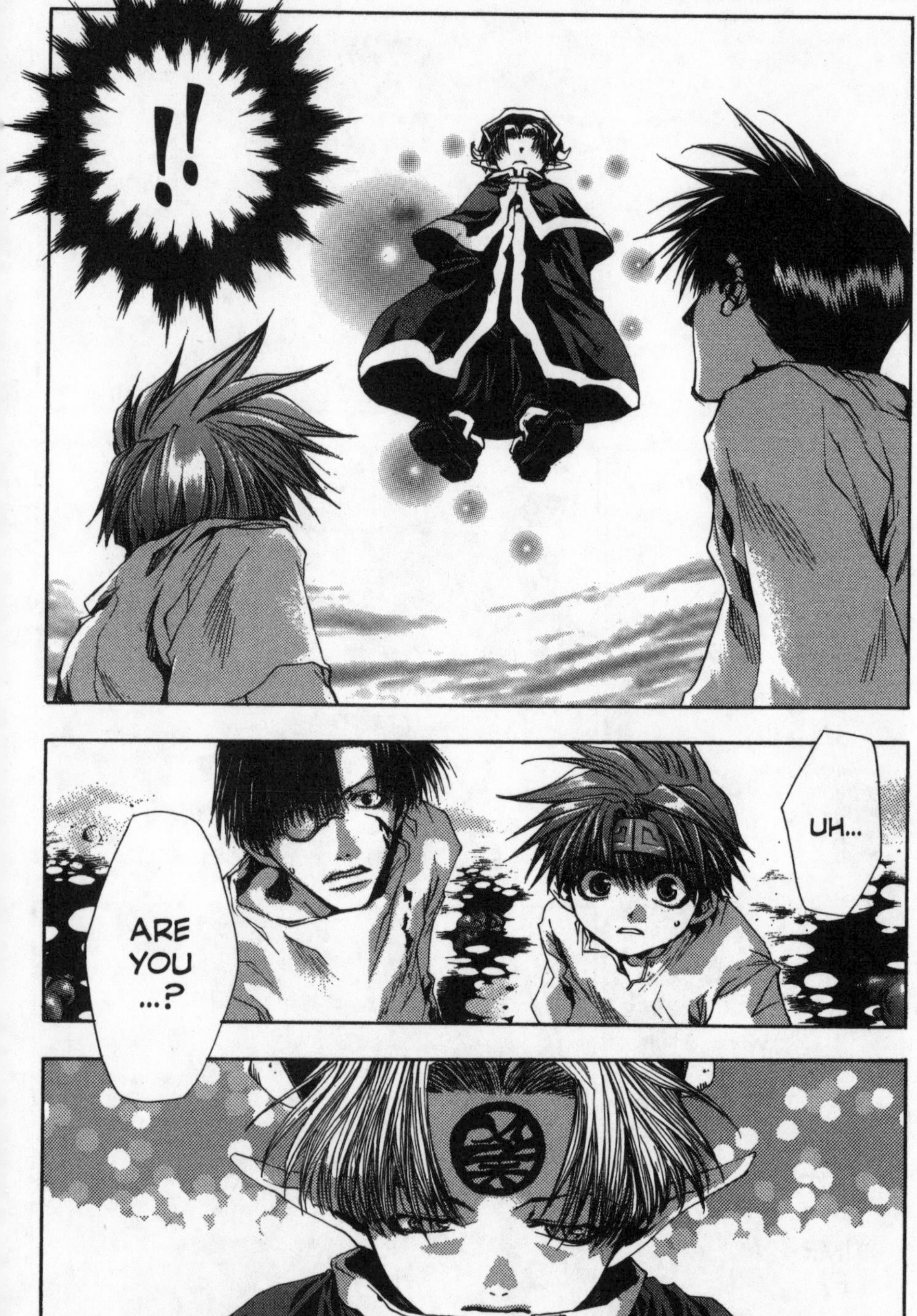
!!
UH...
ARE YOU ...?

CHAPTER 40: Blind Faith

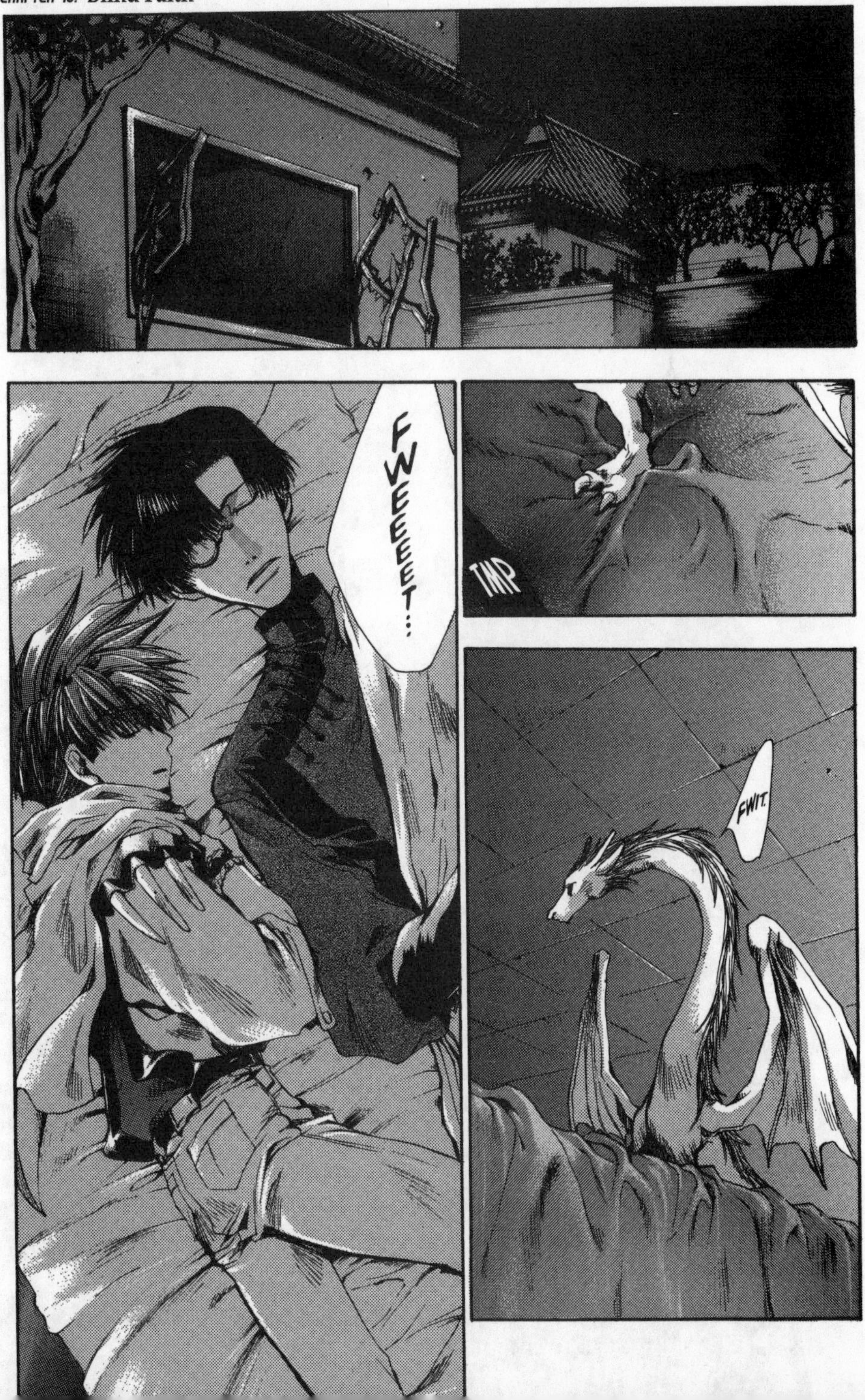
TMP
FWIT.
FWEEEET...

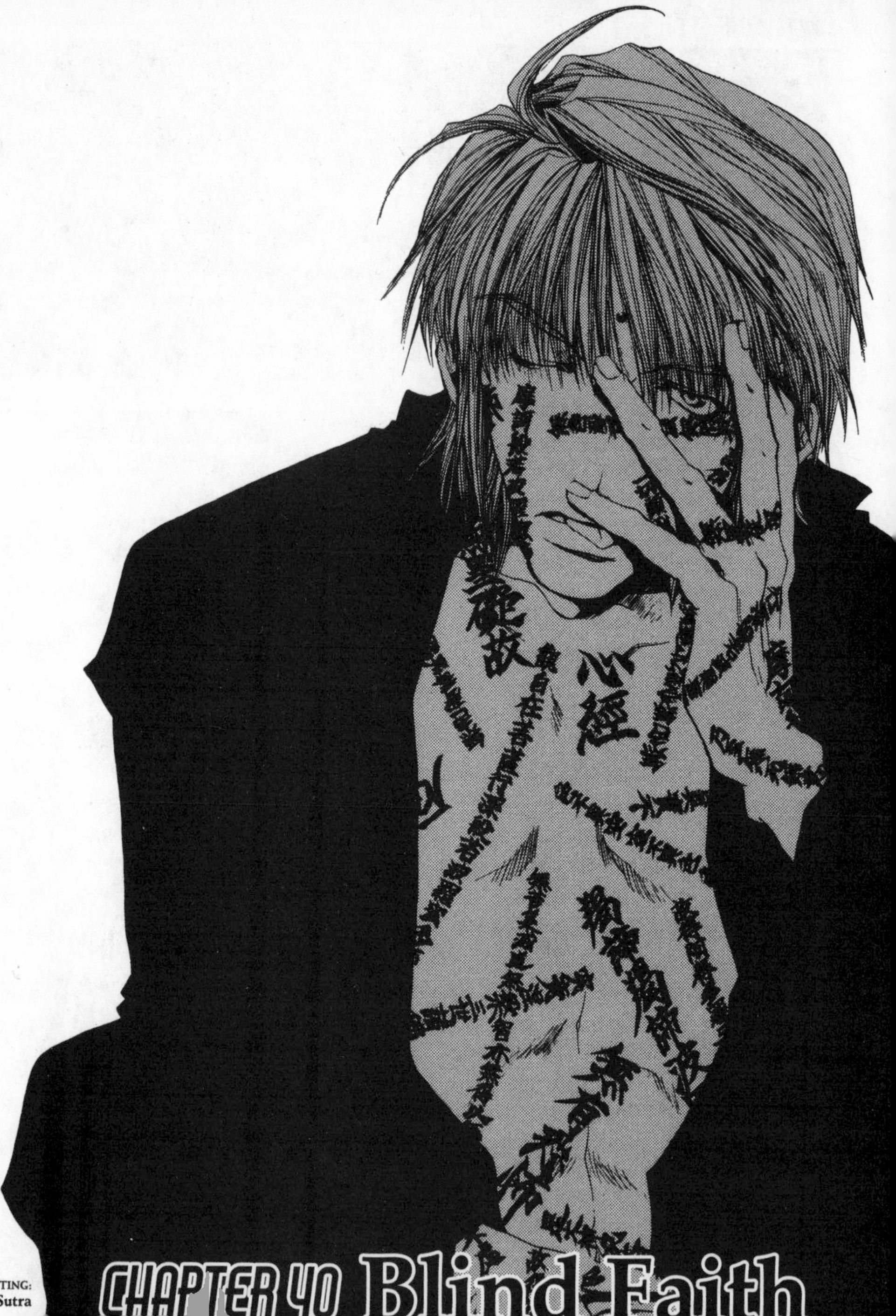
心經

CHAPTER 40 Blind Faith

WRITING:
Heart Sutra

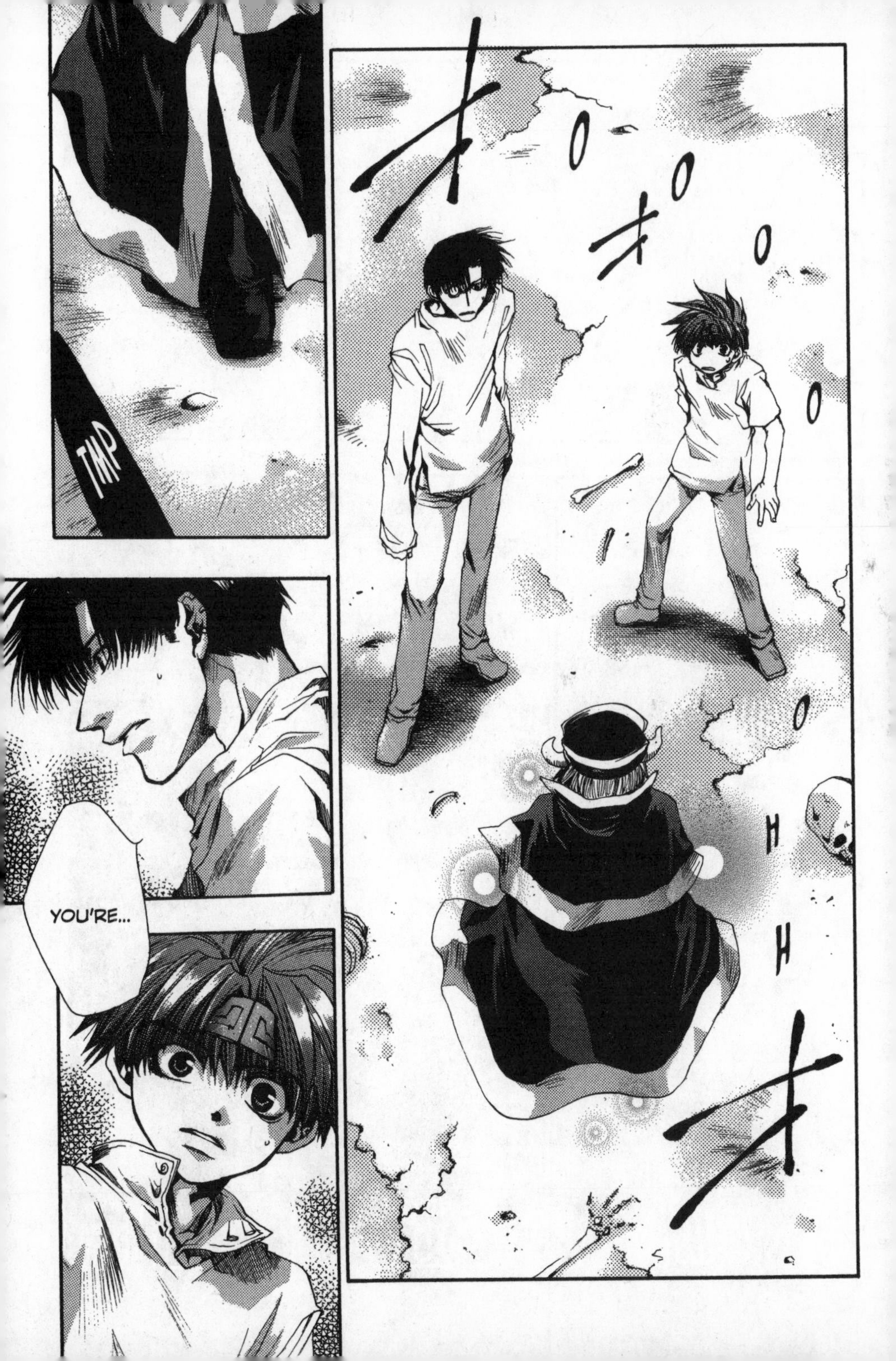

オOオOOOOHHHオ
TMP
YOU'RE...

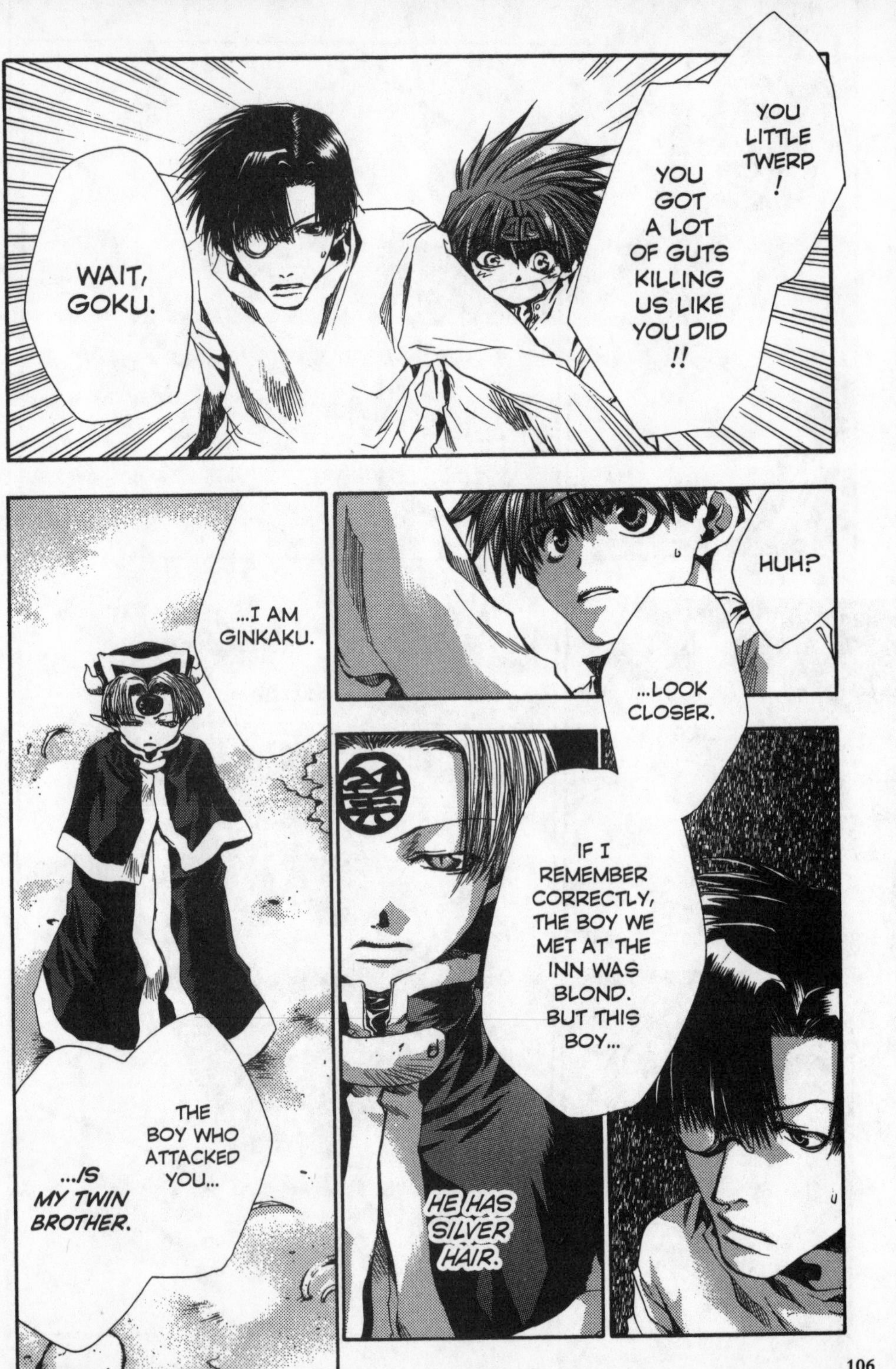
YOU LITTLE TWERP!
YOU GOT A LOT OF GUTS KILLING US LIKE YOU DID!!
WAIT, GOKU.
HUH?
...LOOK CLOSER.
IF I REMEMBER CORRECTLY, THE BOY WE MET AT THE INN WAS BLOND. BUT THIS BOY...
HE HAS SILVER HAIR.
...I AM GINKAKU.
THE BOY WHO ATTACKED YOU...
...IS MY TWIN BROTHER.

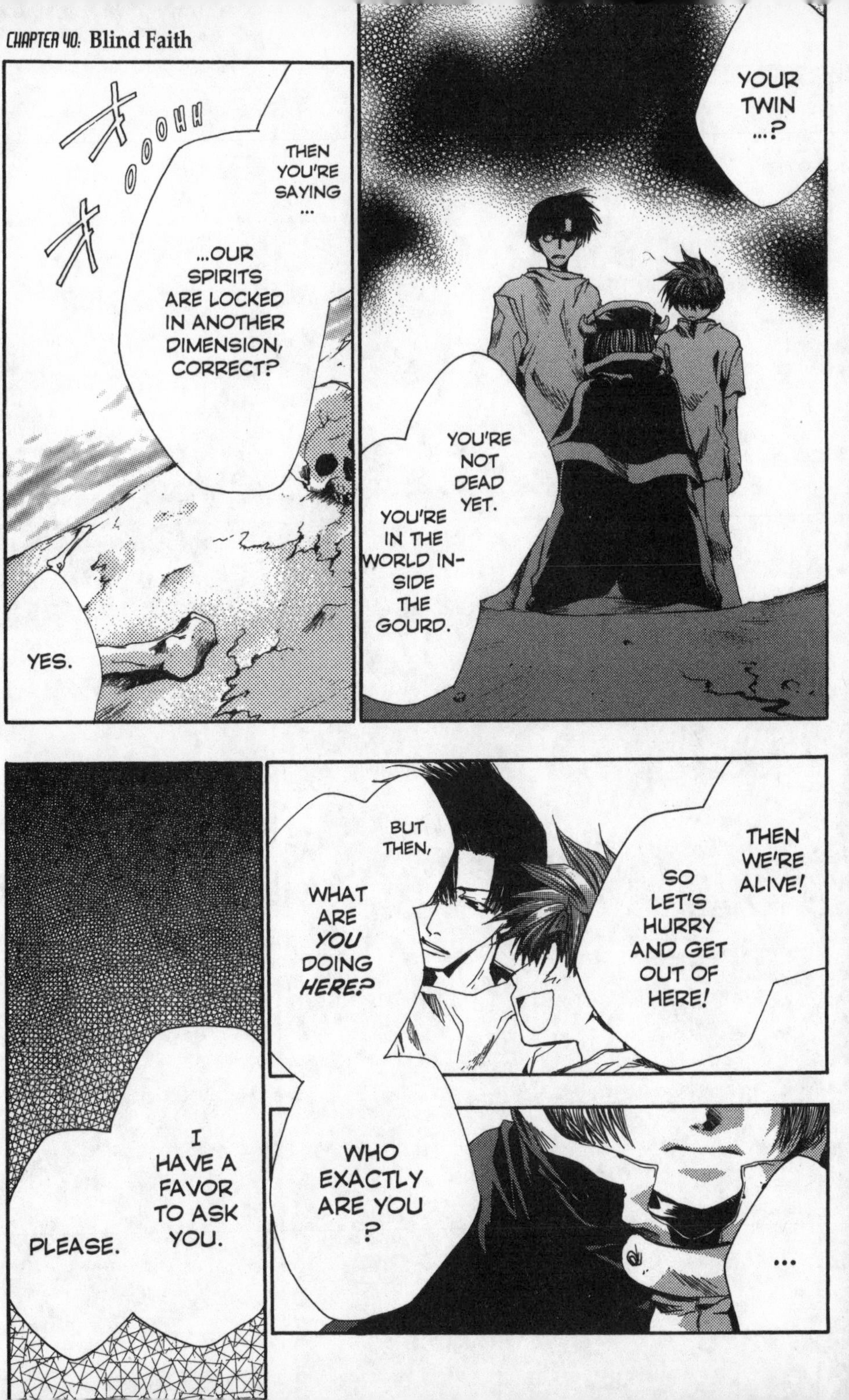
YOUR TWIN ...?
YOU'RE NOT DEAD YET.
YOU'RE IN THE WORLD INSIDE THE GOURD.
THEN YOU'RE SAYING ...
...OUR SPIRITS ARE LOCKED IN ANOTHER DIMENSION, CORRECT?
OOOHH
YES.
THEN WE'RE ALIVE!
SO LET'S HURRY AND GET OUT OF HERE!
BUT THEN,
WHAT ARE *YOU* DOING *HERE?*
...
WHO EXACTLY ARE YOU ?
I HAVE A FAVOR TO ASK YOU.
PLEASE.

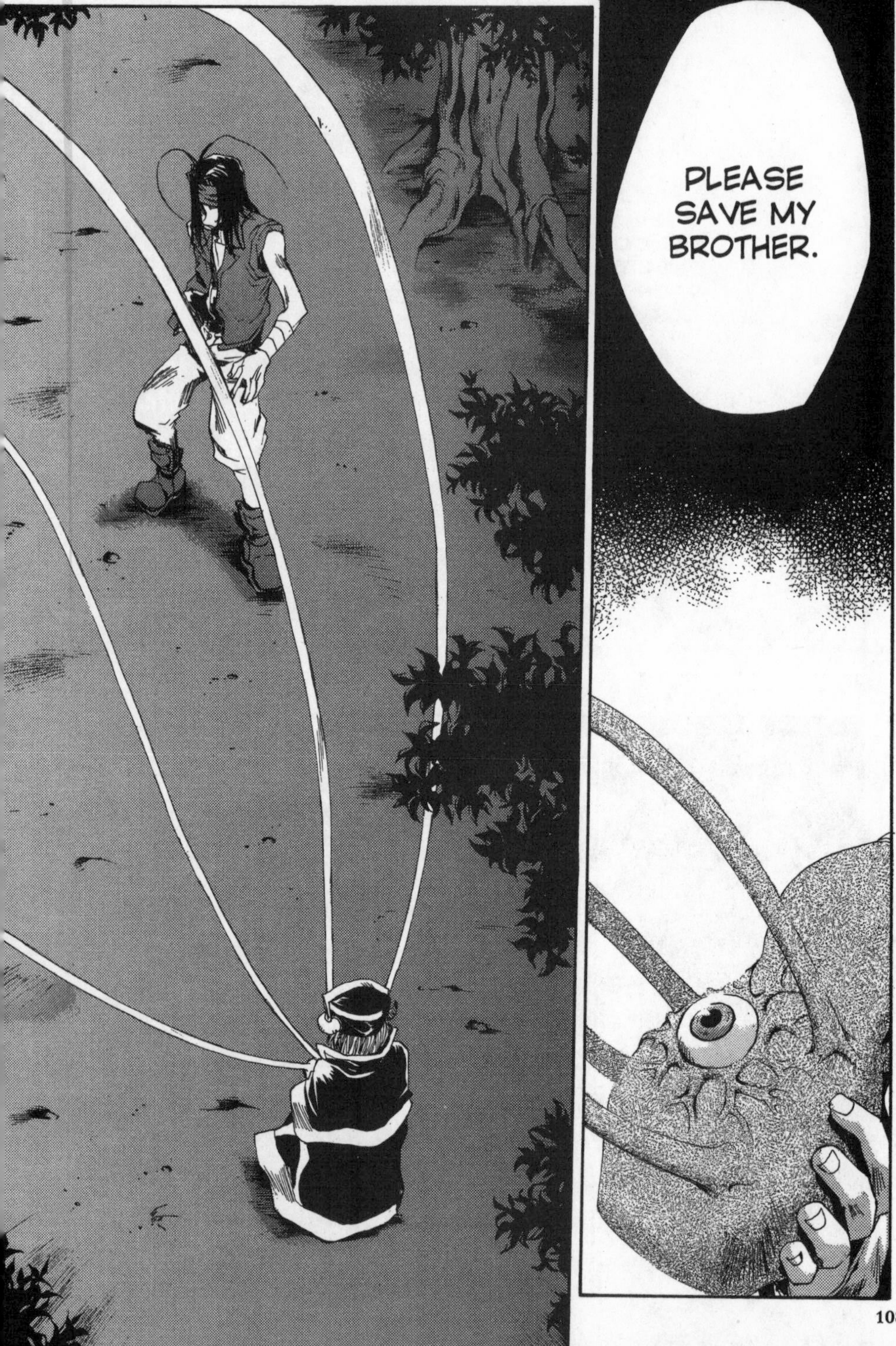
PLEASE SAVE MY BROTHER.

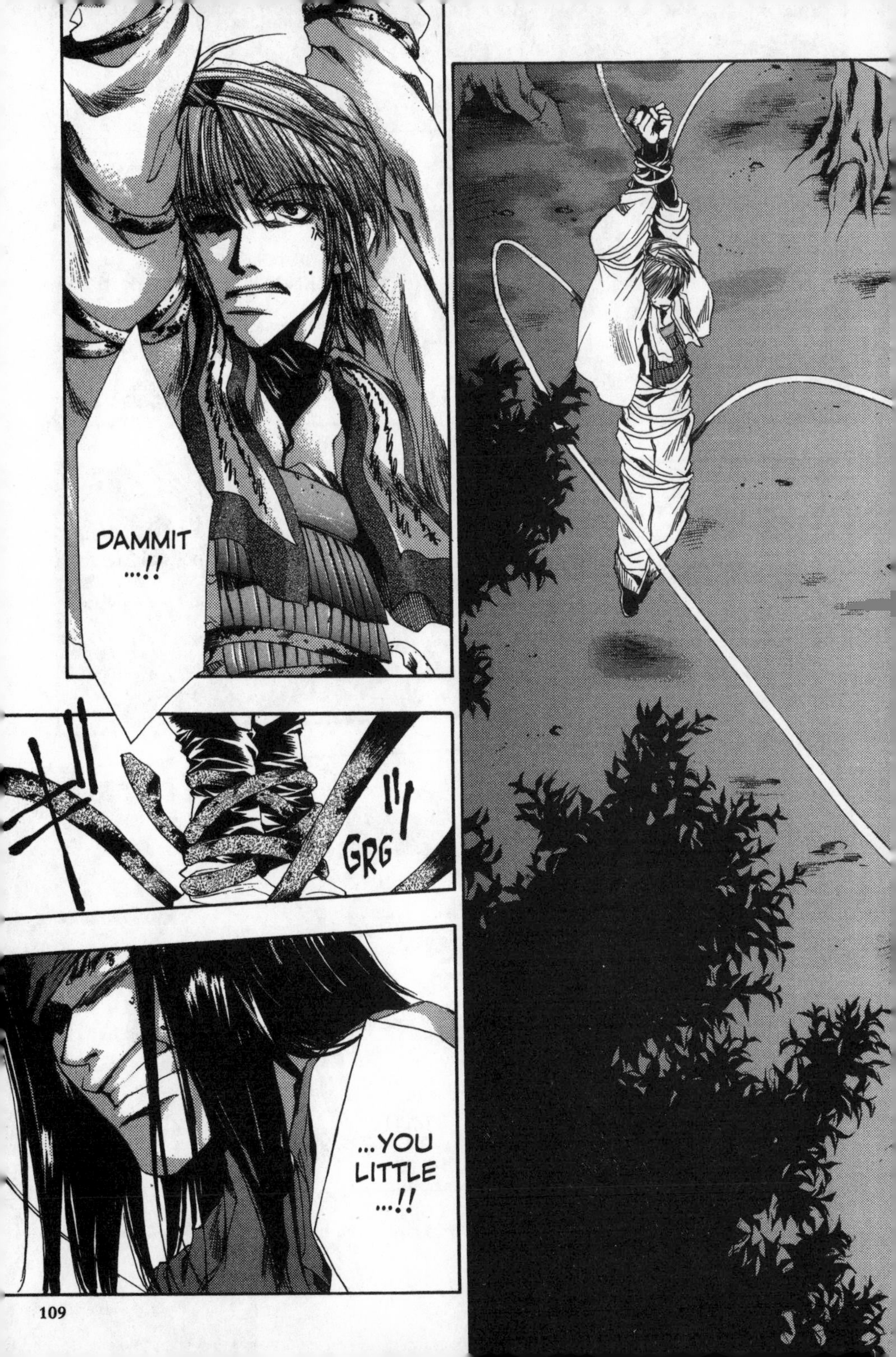
DAMMIT ...!!
GRG
...YOU LITTLE ...!!

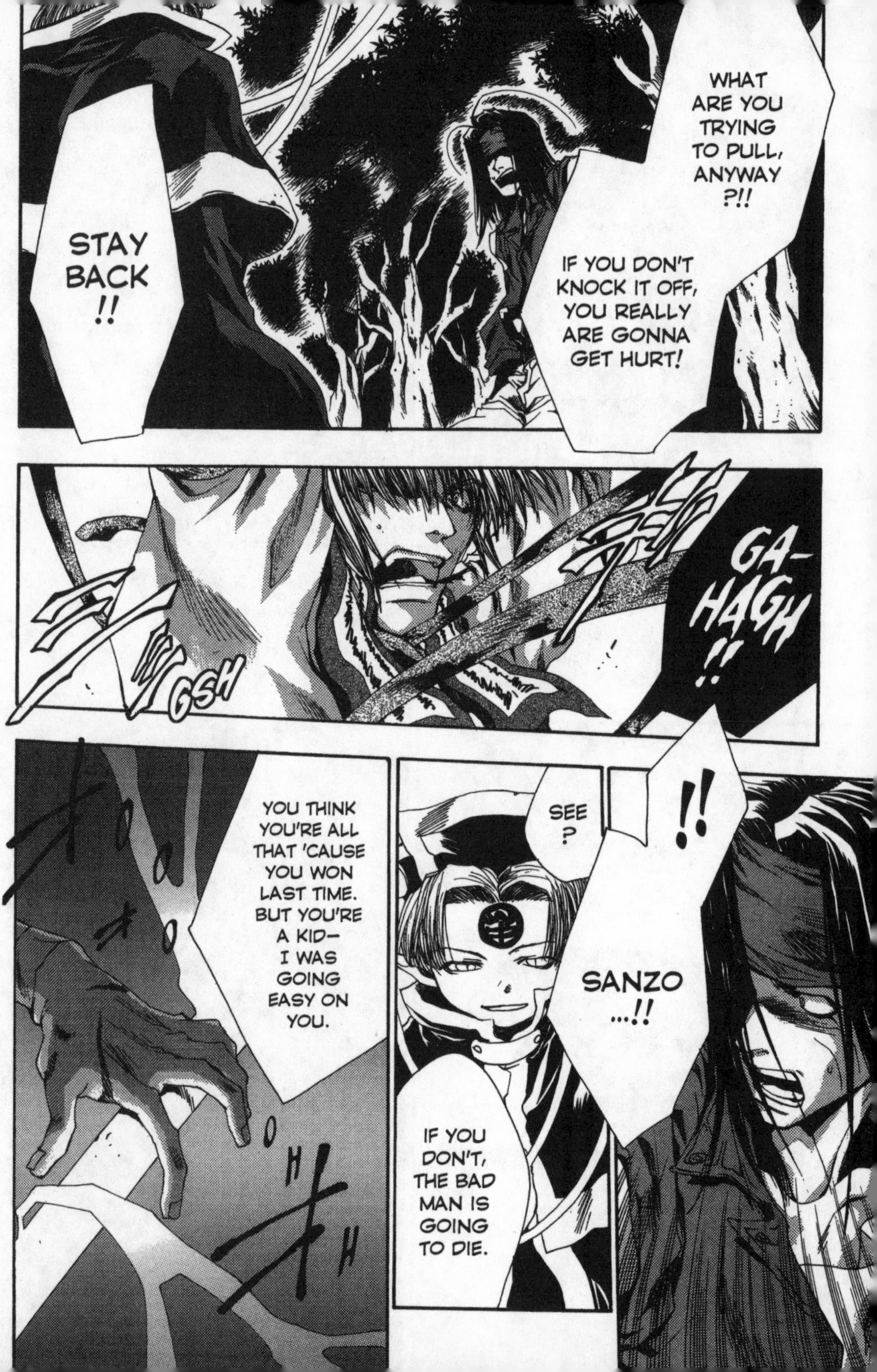
WHAT ARE YOU TRYING TO PULL, ANYWAY?!!
IF YOU DON'T KNOCK IT OFF, YOU REALLY ARE GONNA GET HURT!
STAY BACK!!
GA-HAGH!!
GSH
!!
SANZO...!!
SEE?
IF YOU DON'T, THE BAD MAN IS GOING TO DIE.
YOU THINK YOU'RE ALL THAT 'CAUSE YOU WON LAST TIME. BUT YOU'RE A KID— I WAS GOING EASY ON YOU.

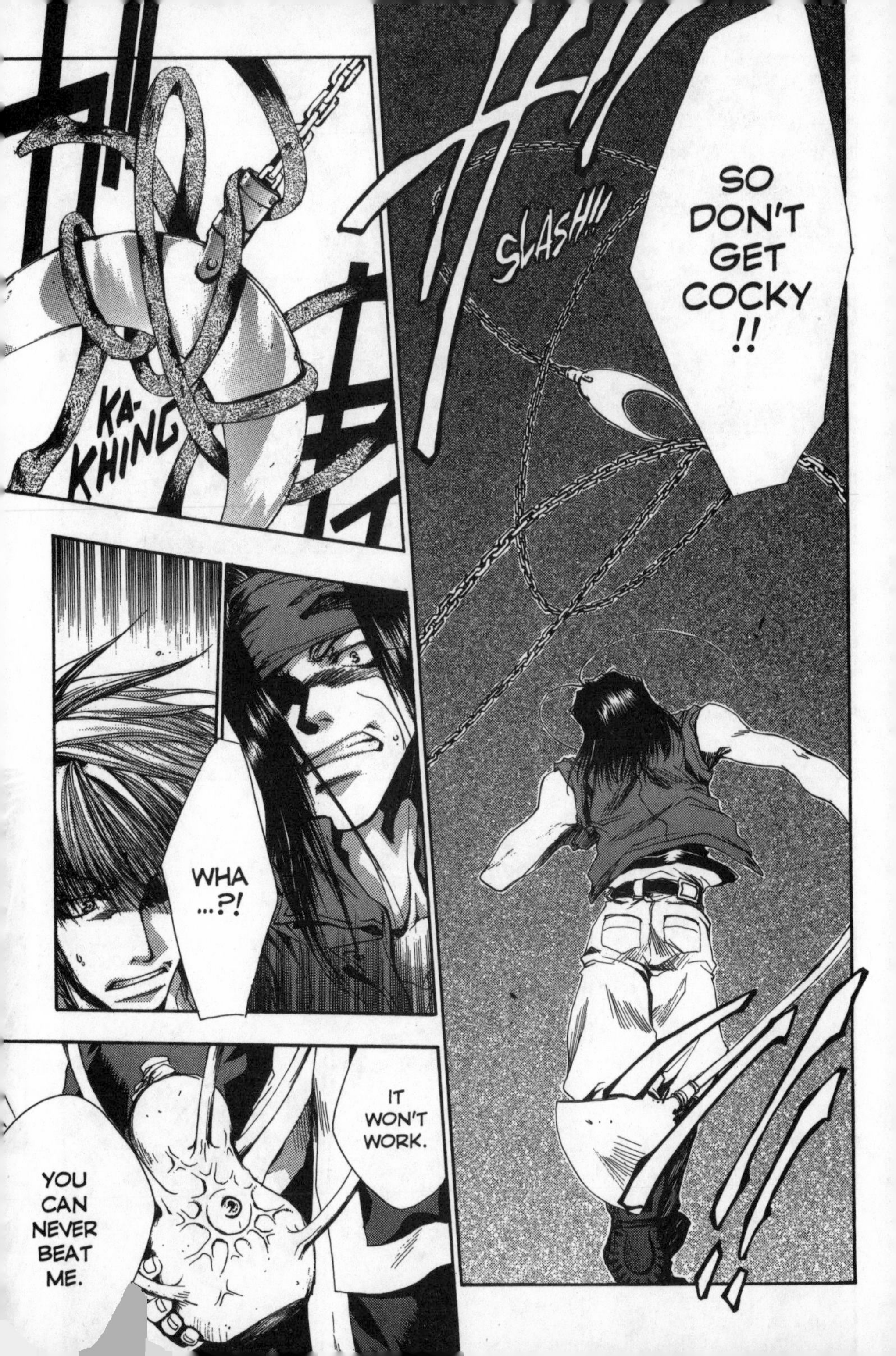
SO DON'T GET COCKY !!
SLASH!!
KA-KHING
WHA ...?!
IT WON'T WORK.
YOU CAN NEVER BEAT ME.

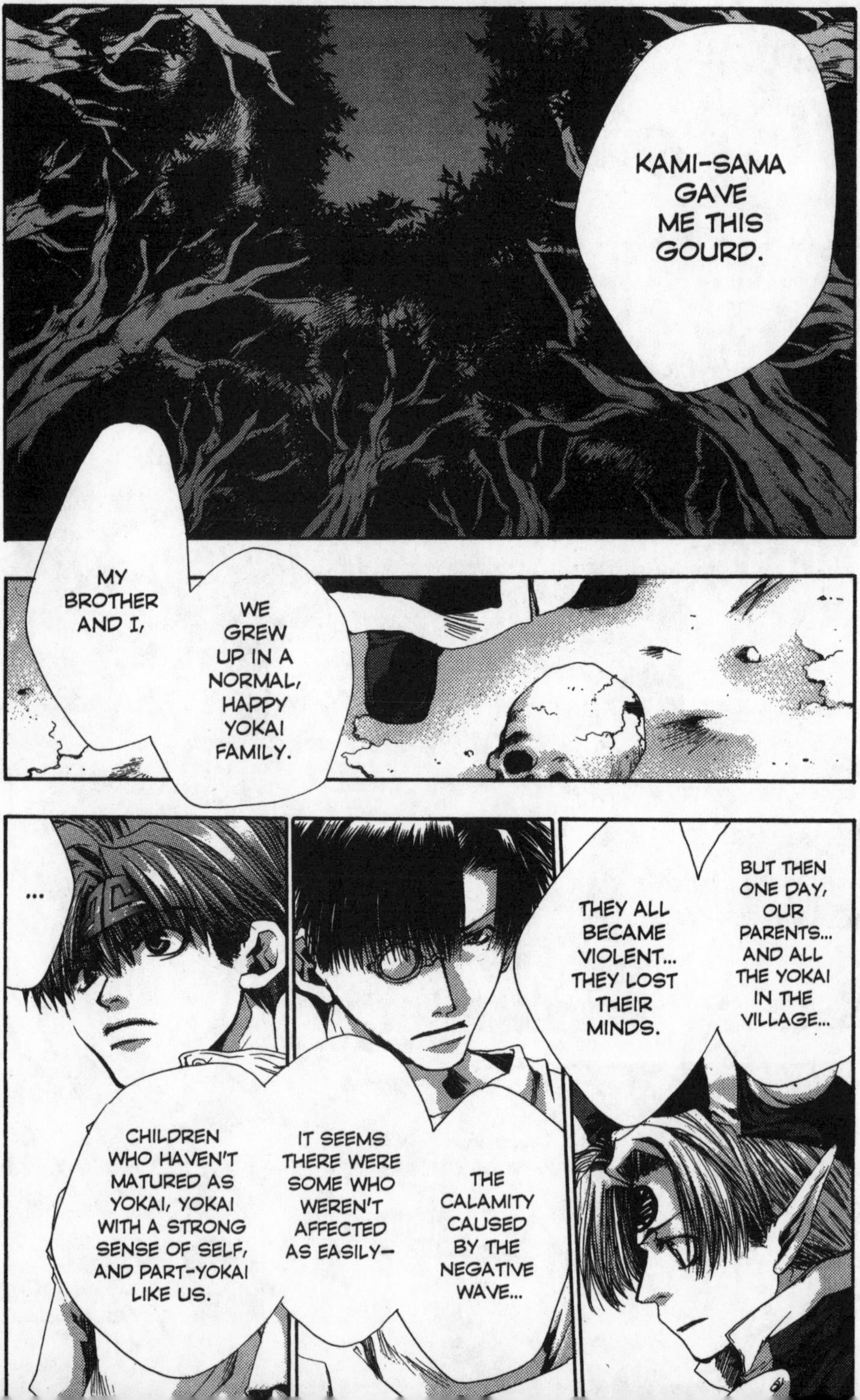
KAMI-SAMA GAVE ME THIS GOURD.
MY BROTHER AND I,
WE GREW UP IN A NORMAL, HAPPY YOKAI FAMILY.
BUT THEN ONE DAY, OUR PARENTS... AND ALL THE YOKAI IN THE VILLAGE...
THEY ALL BECAME VIOLENT... THEY LOST THEIR MINDS.
THE CALAMITY CAUSED BY THE NEGATIVE WAVE...
IT SEEMS THERE WERE SOME WHO WEREN'T AFFECTED AS EASILY—
CHILDREN WHO HAVEN'T MATURED AS YOKAI, YOKAI WITH A STRONG SENSE OF SELF, AND PART-YOKAI LIKE US.
...

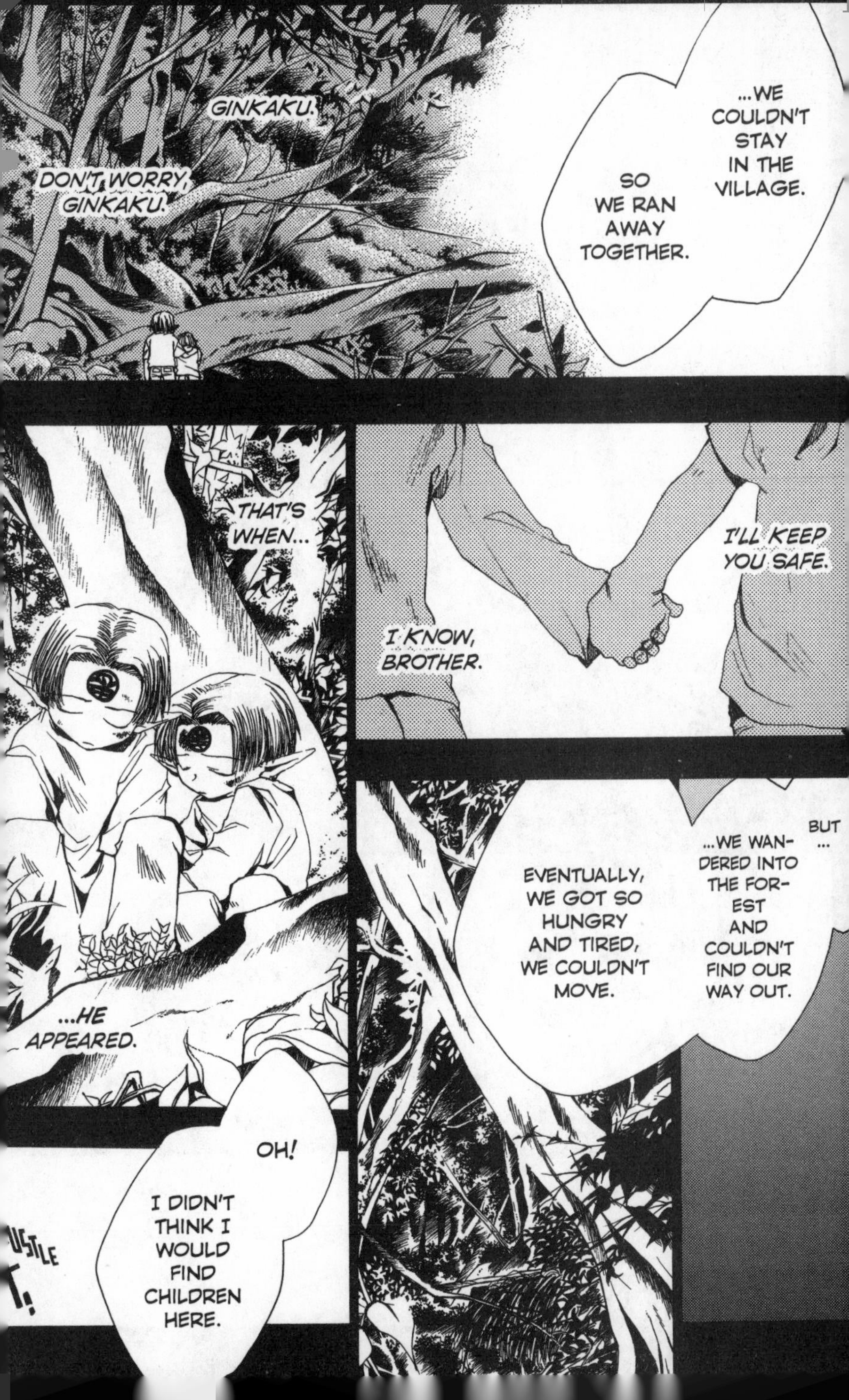

...WE COULDN'T STAY IN THE VILLAGE.
SO WE RAN AWAY TOGETHER.
GINKAKU.
DON'T WORRY, GINKAKU.
I'LL KEEP YOU SAFE.
I KNOW, BROTHER.
BUT ...
...WE WAN-DERED INTO THE FOR-EST AND COULDN'T FIND OUR WAY OUT.
EVENTUALLY, WE GOT SO HUNGRY AND TIRED, WE COULDN'T MOVE.
THAT'S WHEN...
...HE APPEARED.
OH!
I DIDN'T THINK I WOULD FIND CHILDREN HERE.

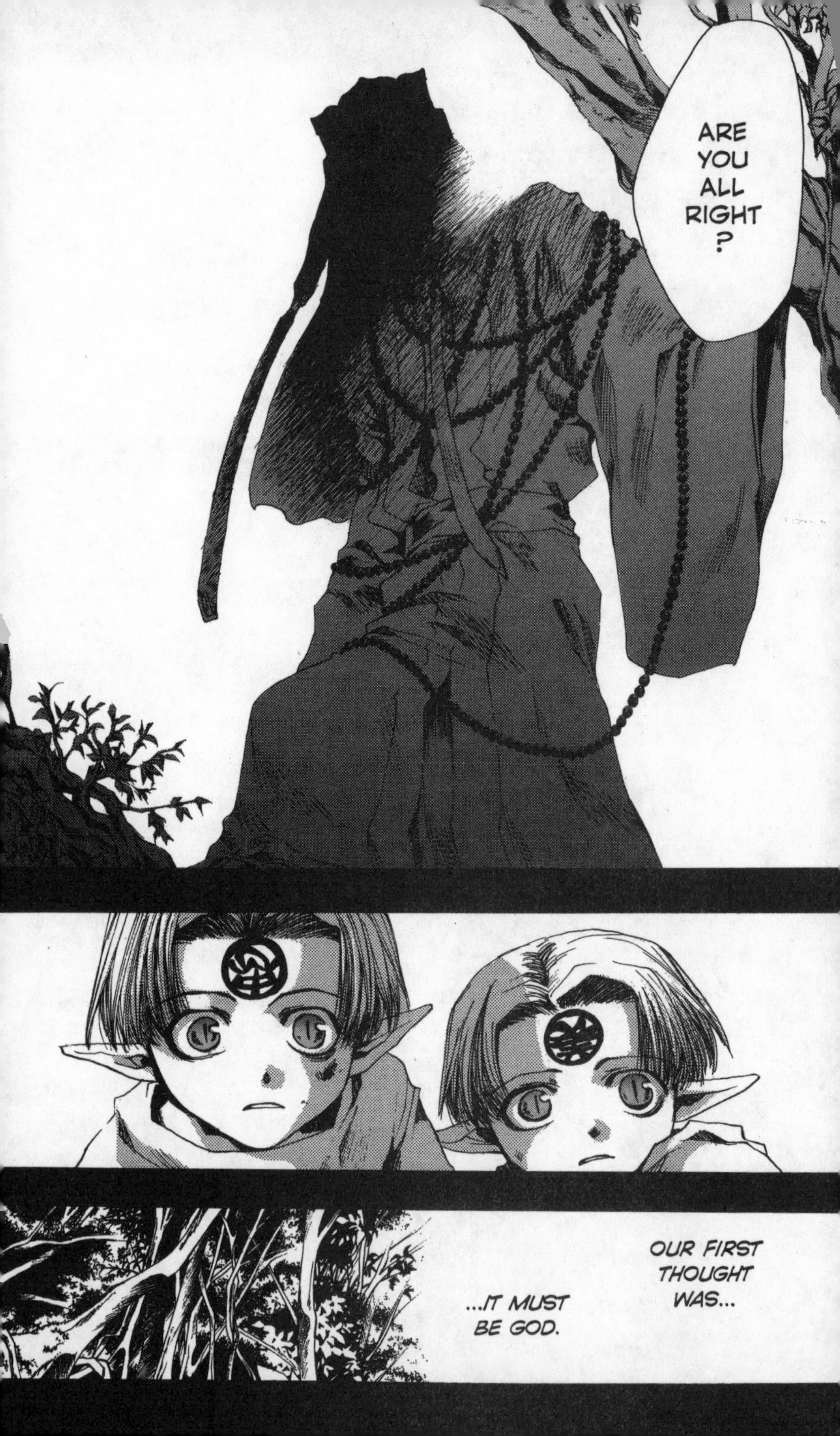
ARE YOU ALL RIGHT?
OUR FIRST THOUGHT WAS...
...IT MUST BE GOD.

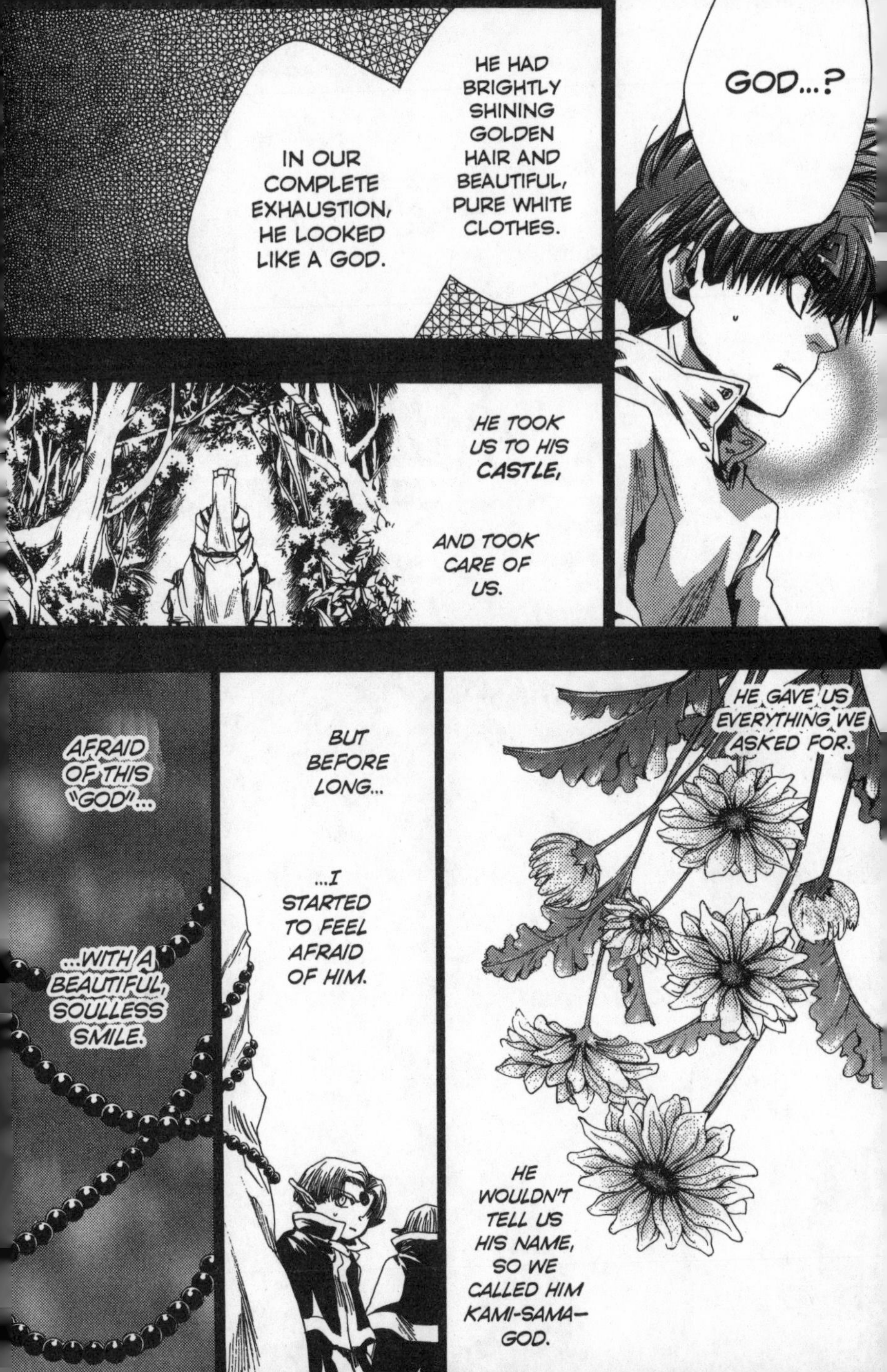
GOD...?
HE HAD BRIGHTLY SHINING GOLDEN HAIR AND BEAUTIFUL, PURE WHITE CLOTHES.
IN OUR COMPLETE EXHAUSTION, HE LOOKED LIKE A GOD.
HE TOOK US TO HIS CASTLE,
AND TOOK CARE OF US.
HE GAVE US EVERYTHING WE ASKED FOR.
HE WOULDN'T TELL US HIS NAME, SO WE CALLED HIM KAMI-SAMA—GOD.
BUT BEFORE LONG...
...I STARTED TO FEEL AFRAID OF HIM.
AFRAID OF THIS "GOD"...
...WITH A BEAUTIFUL, SOULLESS SMILE.

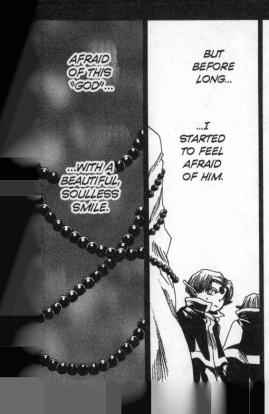

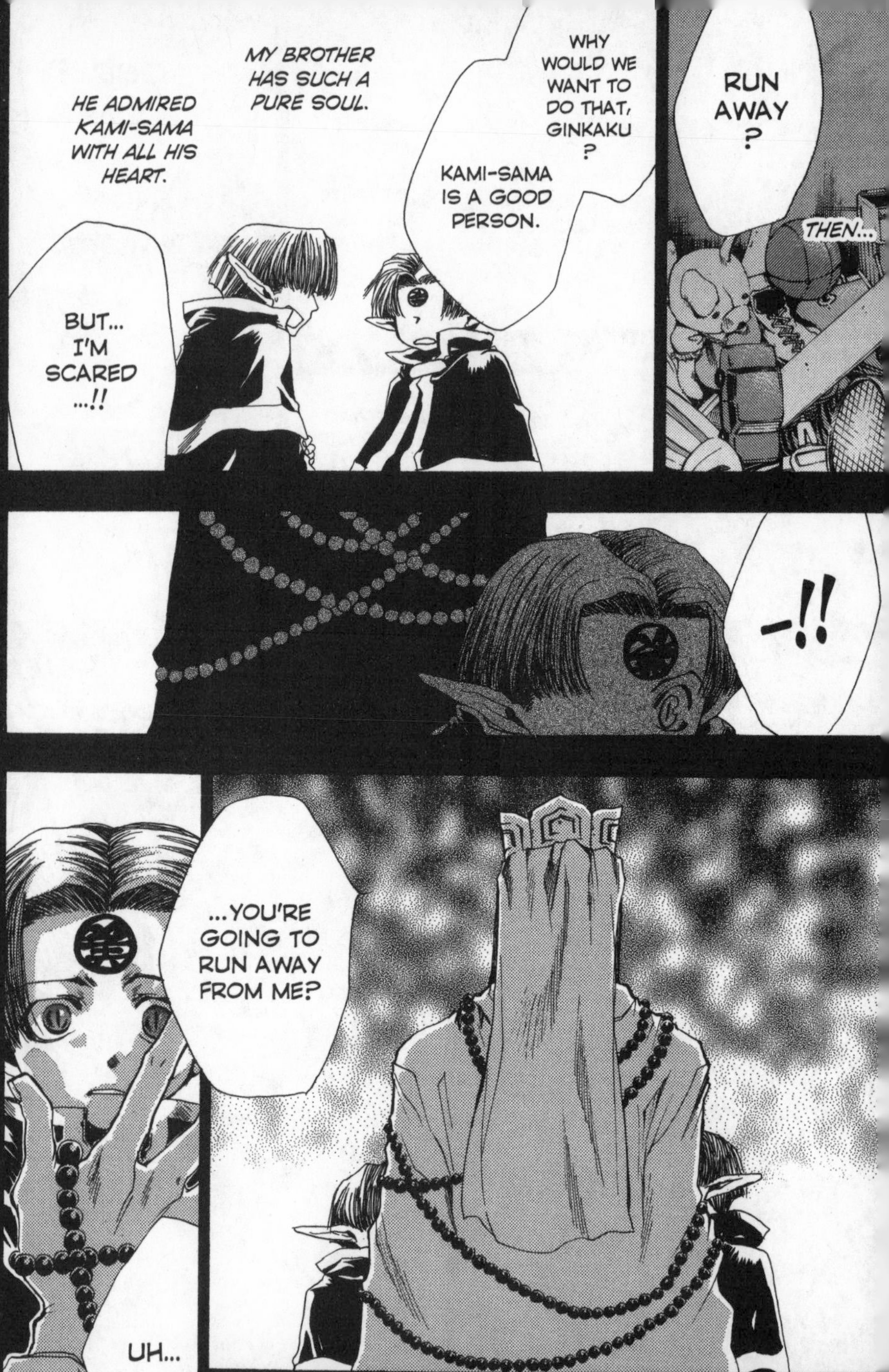
RUN AWAY ?
THEN...
WHY WOULD WE WANT TO DO THAT, GINKAKU ?
KAMI-SAMA IS A GOOD PERSON.
MY BROTHER HAS SUCH A PURE SOUL.
HE ADMIRED KAMI-SAMA WITH ALL HIS HEART.
BUT... I'M SCARED ...!!
—!!
...YOU'RE GOING TO RUN AWAY FROM ME?
UH...

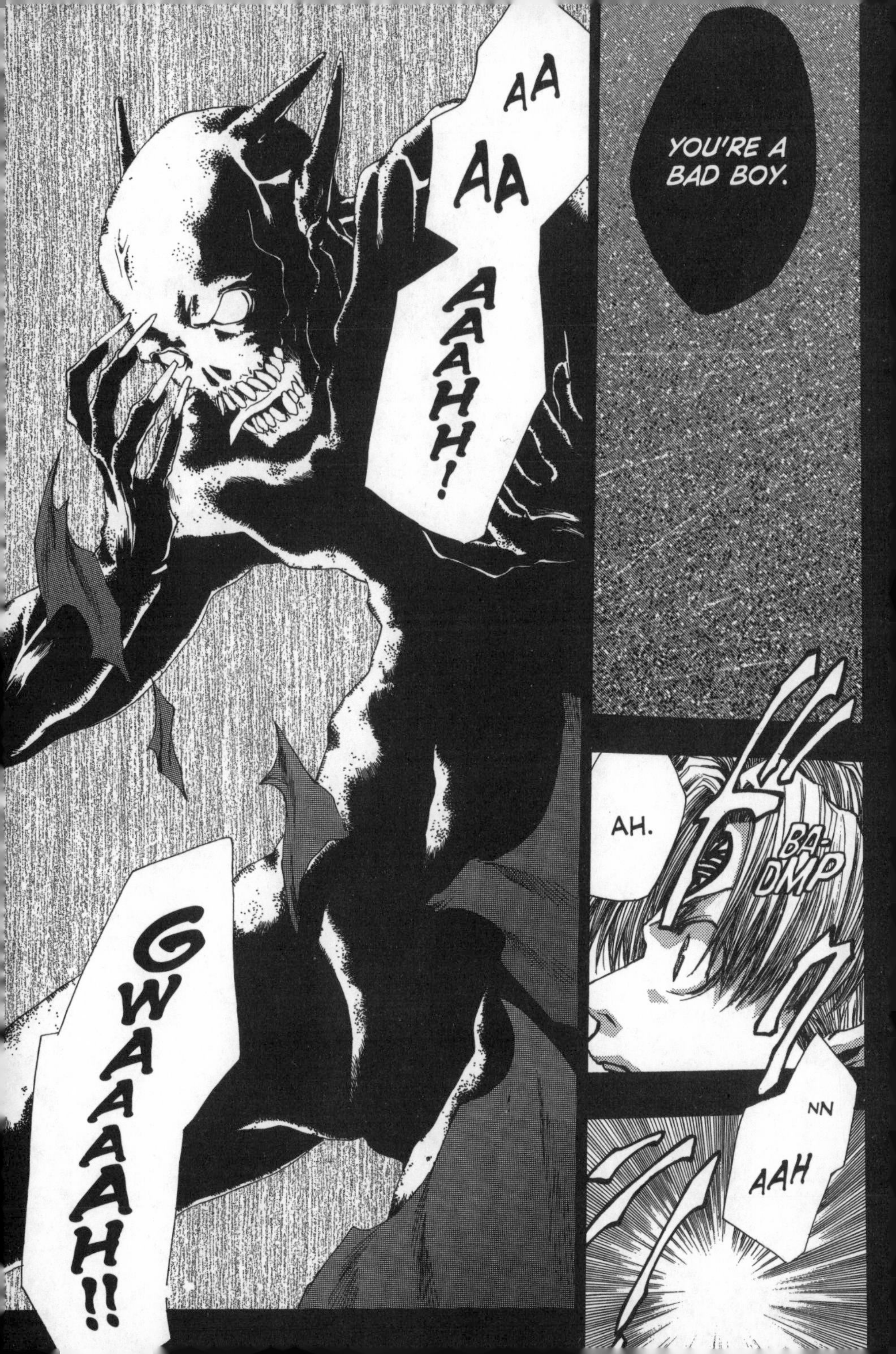
YOU'RE A BAD BOY.
AH.
BA-DMP
NN
AAH
AA AA AAAHH!
GWAAAAAH!!

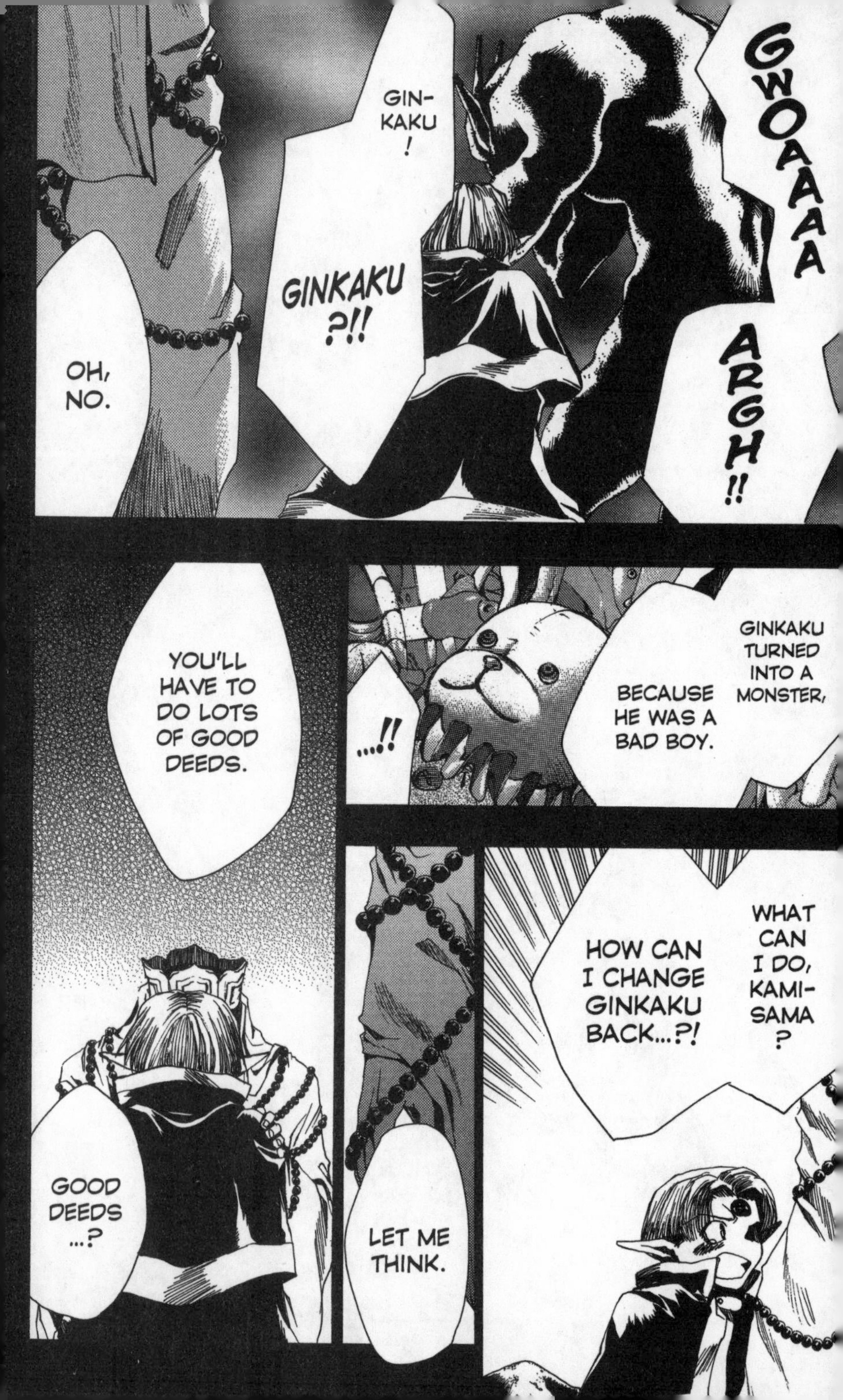

GWOAAAA
ARGH!!
GIN-KAKU!
GINKAKU?!!
OH, NO.
GINKAKU TURNED INTO A MONSTER,
BECAUSE HE WAS A BAD BOY.
...!!
WHAT CAN I DO, KAMI-SAMA?
HOW CAN I CHANGE GINKAKU BACK...?!
LET ME THINK.
YOU'LL HAVE TO DO LOTS OF GOOD DEEDS.
GOOD DEEDS...?

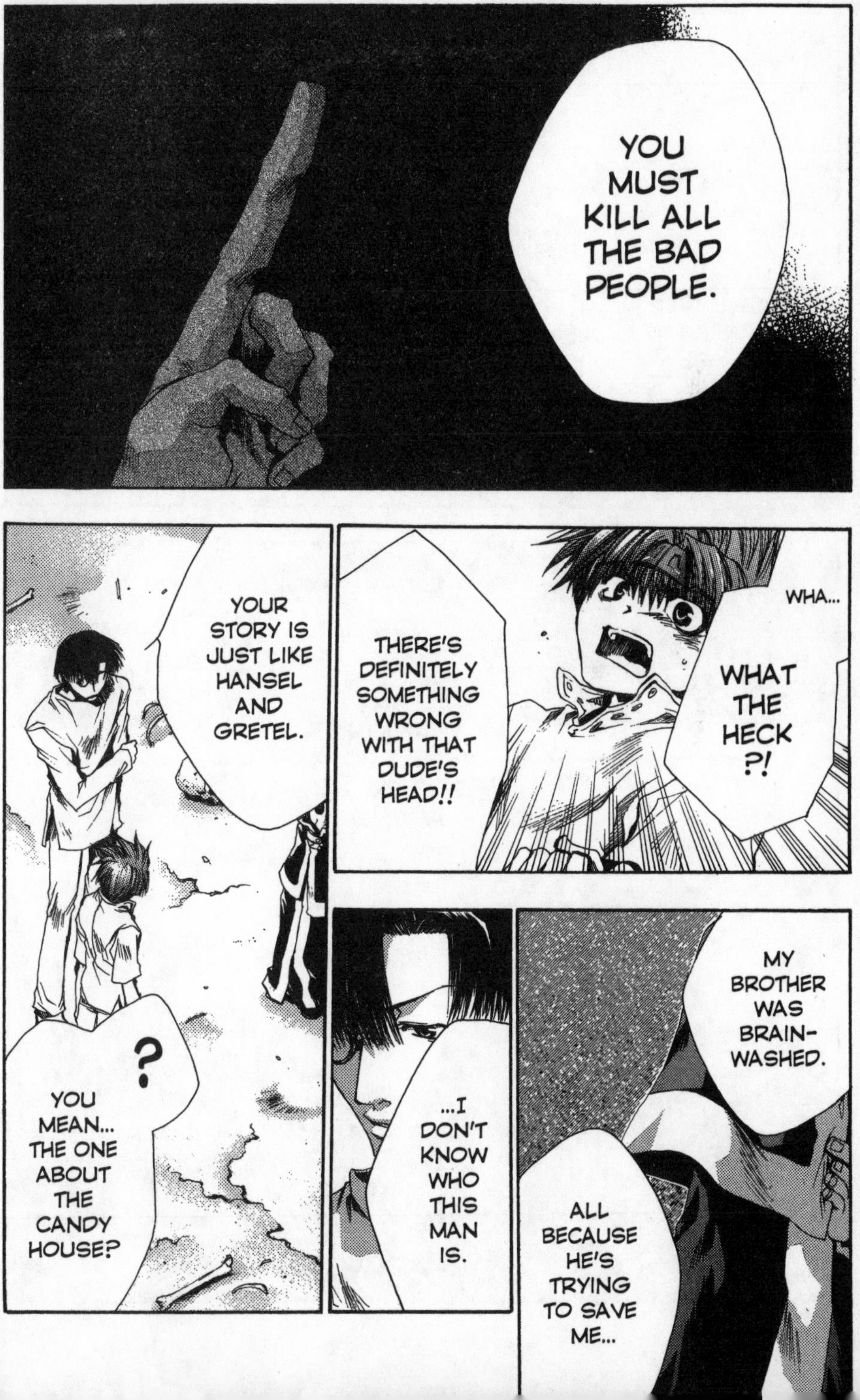
YOU MUST KILL ALL THE BAD PEOPLE.
WHA...
WHAT THE HECK?!
THERE'S DEFINITELY SOMETHING WRONG WITH THAT DUDE'S HEAD!!
MY BROTHER WAS BRAIN-WASHED.
ALL BECAUSE HE'S TRYING TO SAVE ME...
...I DON'T KNOW WHO THIS MAN IS.
YOUR STORY IS JUST LIKE HANSEL AND GRETEL.
?
YOU MEAN... THE ONE ABOUT THE CANDY HOUSE?

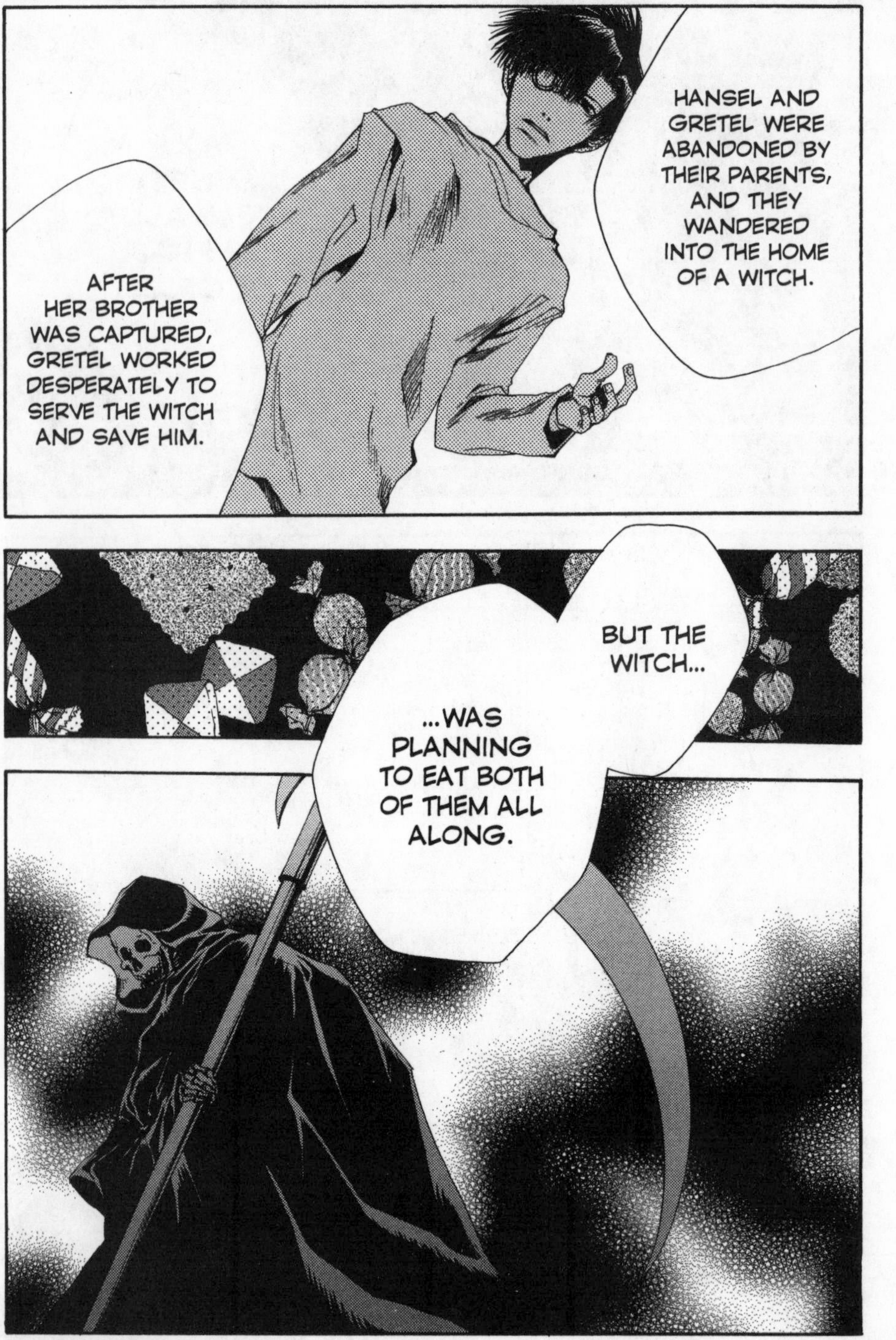
HANSEL AND GRETEL WERE ABANDONED BY THEIR PARENTS, AND THEY WANDERED INTO THE HOME OF A WITCH.
AFTER HER BROTHER WAS CAPTURED, GRETEL WORKED DESPERATELY TO SERVE THE WITCH AND SAVE HIM.
BUT THE WITCH...
...WAS PLANNING TO EAT BOTH OF THEM ALL ALONG.

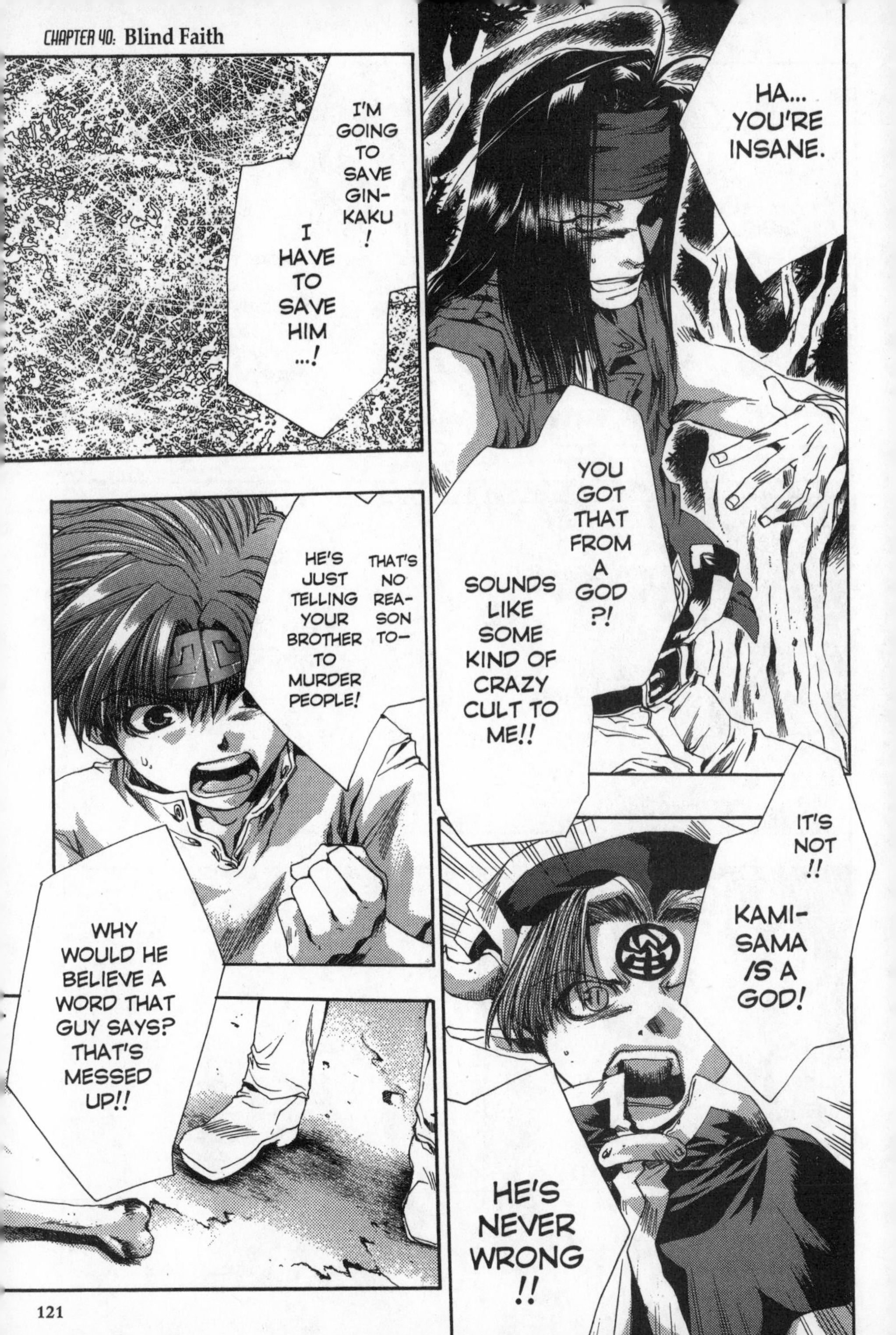
HA... YOU'RE INSANE.
YOU GOT THAT FROM A GOD?!
SOUNDS LIKE SOME KIND OF CRAZY CULT TO ME!!
I'M GOING TO SAVE GIN-KAKU!
I HAVE TO SAVE HIM...!
THAT'S NO REA-SON TO—
HE'S JUST TELLING YOUR BROTHER TO MURDER PEOPLE!
IT'S NOT!!
KAMI-SAMA IS A GOD!
HE'S NEVER WRONG!!
WHY WOULD HE BELIEVE A WORD THAT GUY SAYS? THAT'S MESSED UP!!

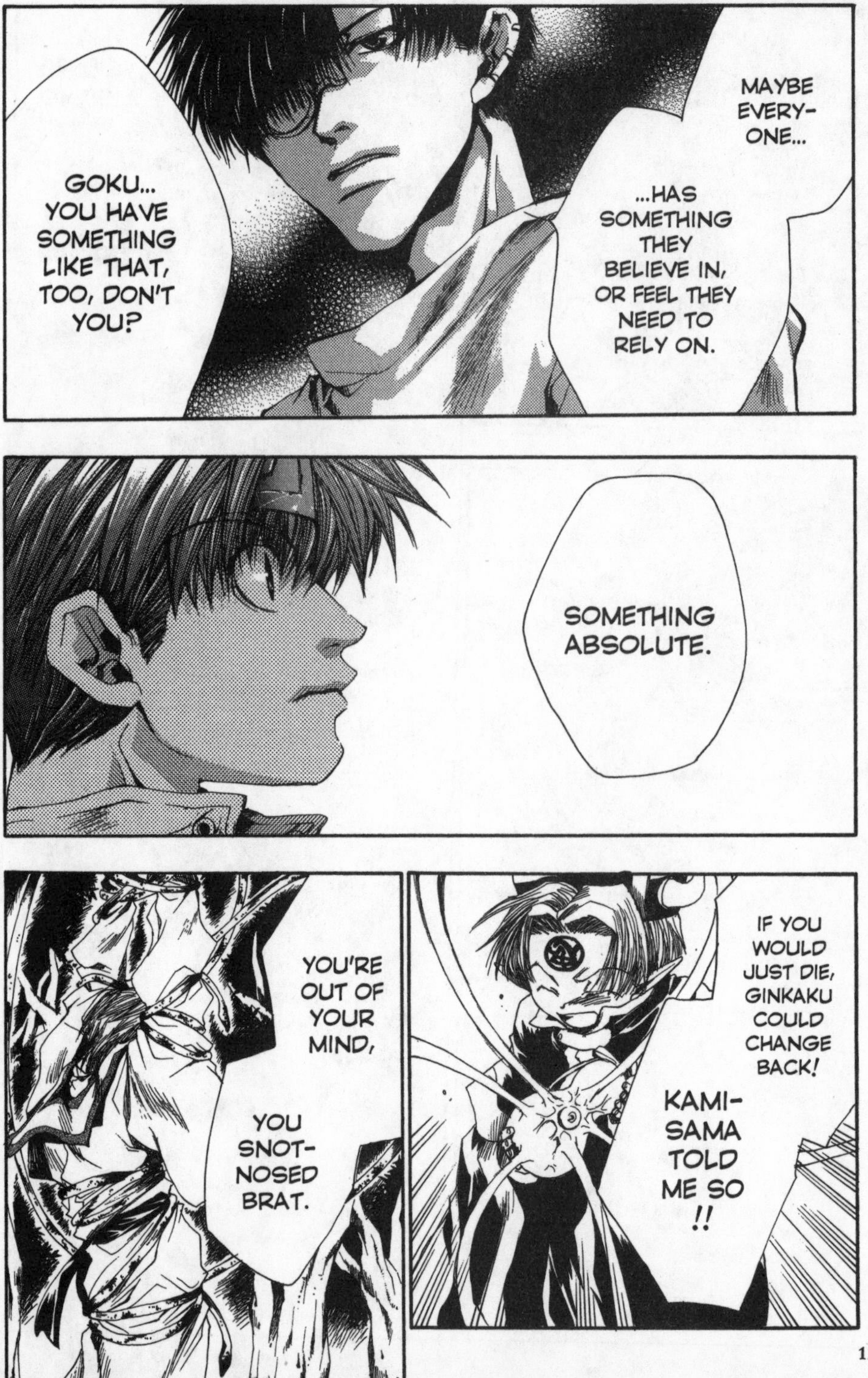
MAYBE EVERY-ONE...
...HAS SOMETHING THEY BELIEVE IN, OR FEEL THEY NEED TO RELY ON.
GOKU... YOU HAVE SOMETHING LIKE THAT, TOO, DON'T YOU?
SOMETHING ABSOLUTE.
IF YOU WOULD JUST DIE, GINKAKU COULD CHANGE BACK!
KAMI-SAMA TOLD ME SO !!
YOU'RE OUT OF YOUR MIND,
YOU SNOT-NOSED BRAT.

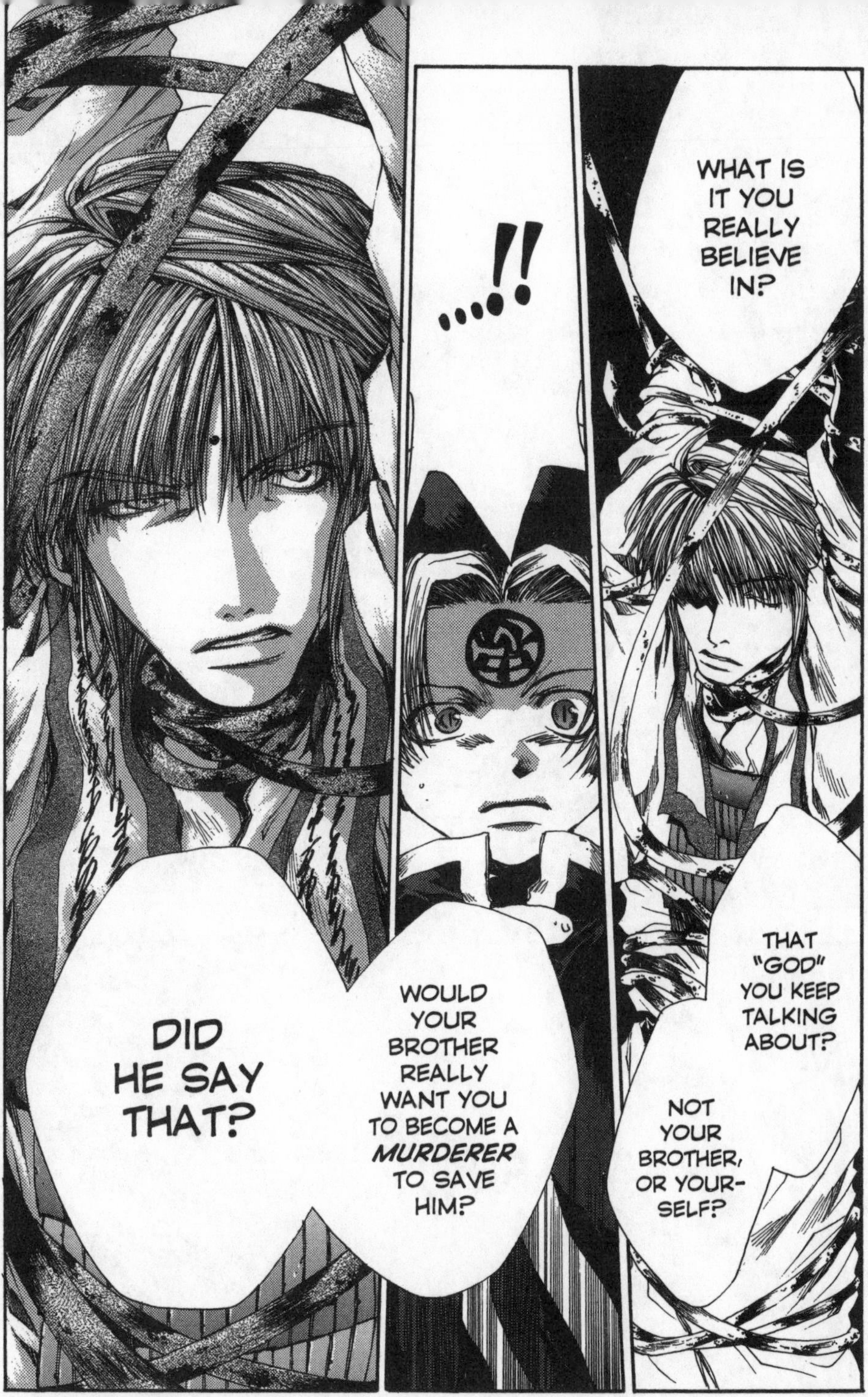
WHAT IS IT YOU REALLY BELIEVE IN?
THAT "GOD" YOU KEEP TALKING ABOUT?
NOT YOUR BROTHER, OR YOUR-SELF?
...!!
WOULD YOUR BROTHER REALLY WANT YOU TO BECOME A *MURDERER* TO SAVE HIM?
DID HE SAY THAT?

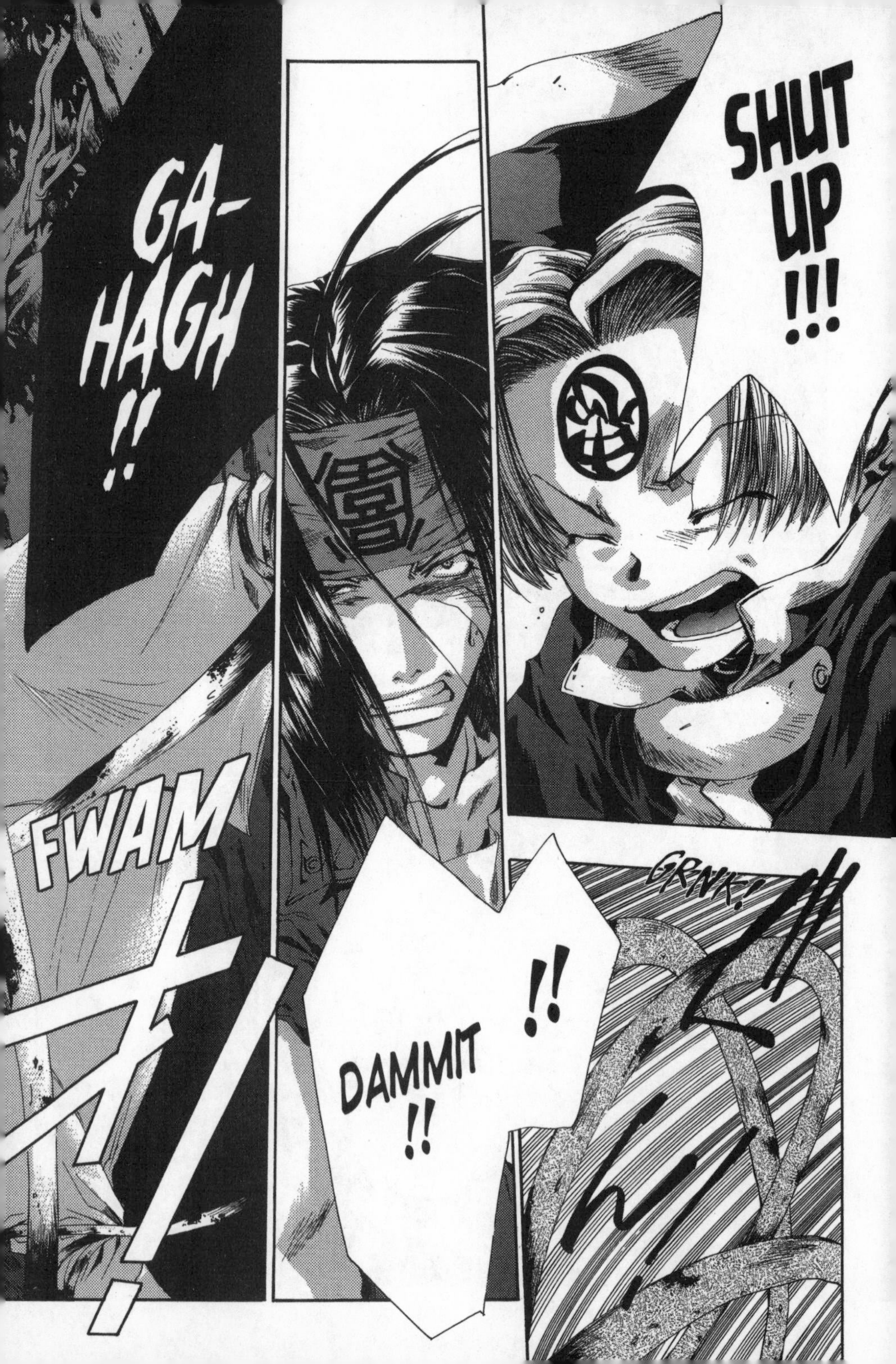
SHUT UP!!!
GRNK!
!! DAMMIT !!
GA-HAGH!!
FWAM!

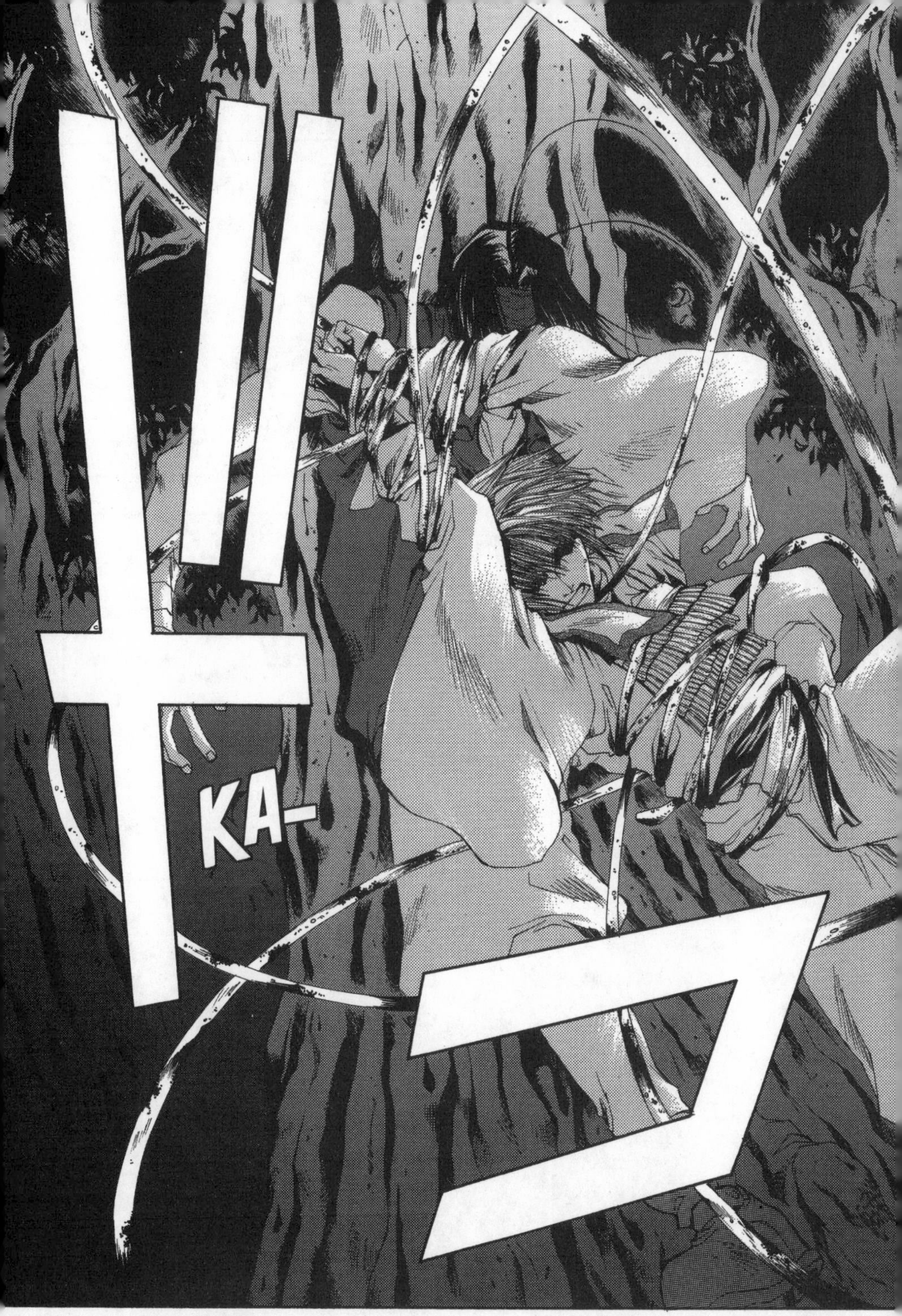
KA-

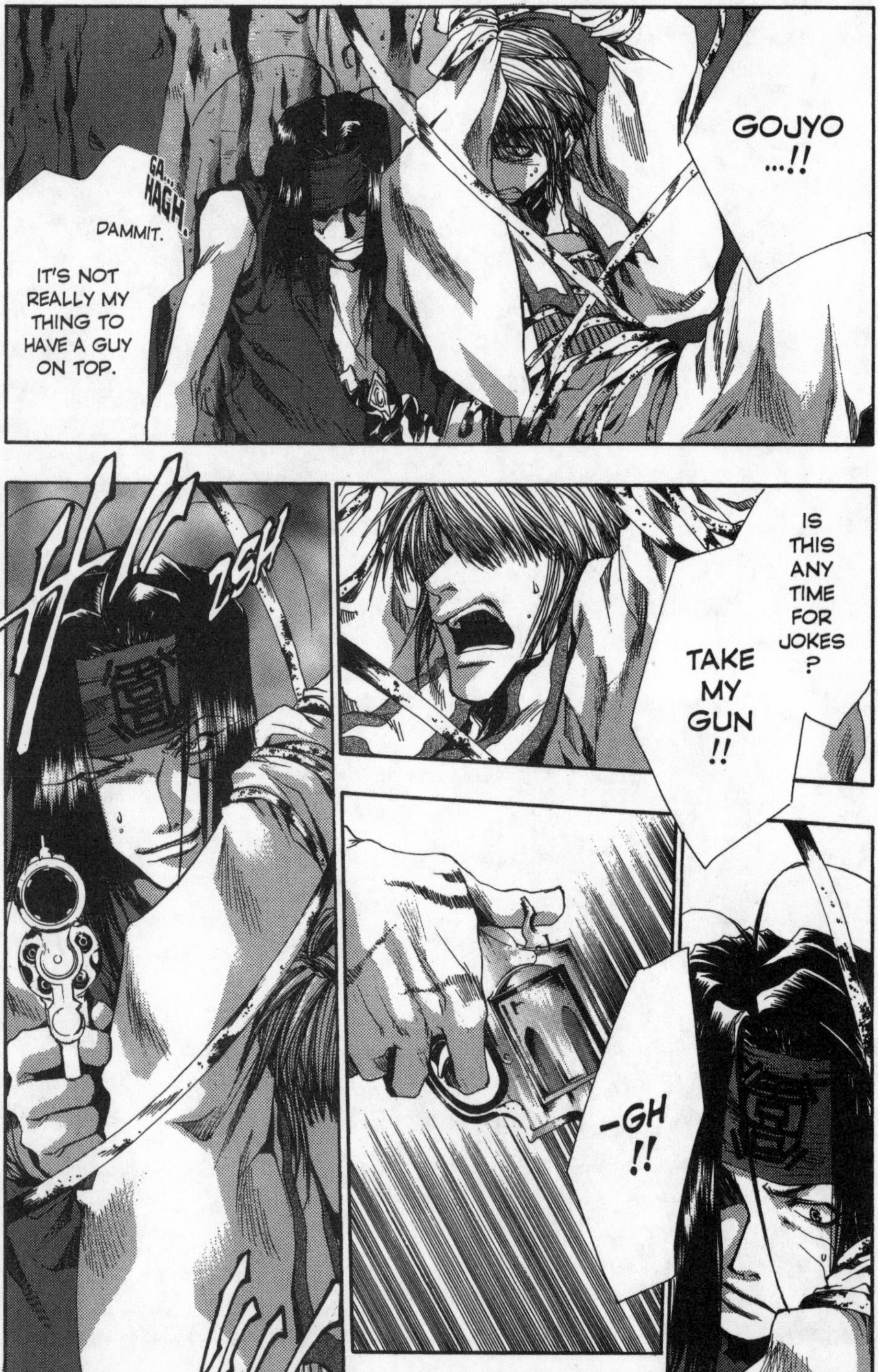
GOJYO ...!!
GA... HAGH.
DAMMIT.
IT'S NOT REALLY MY THING TO HAVE A GUY ON TOP.
IS THIS ANY TIME FOR JOKES ?
TAKE MY GUN !!
-GH !!
ZSH

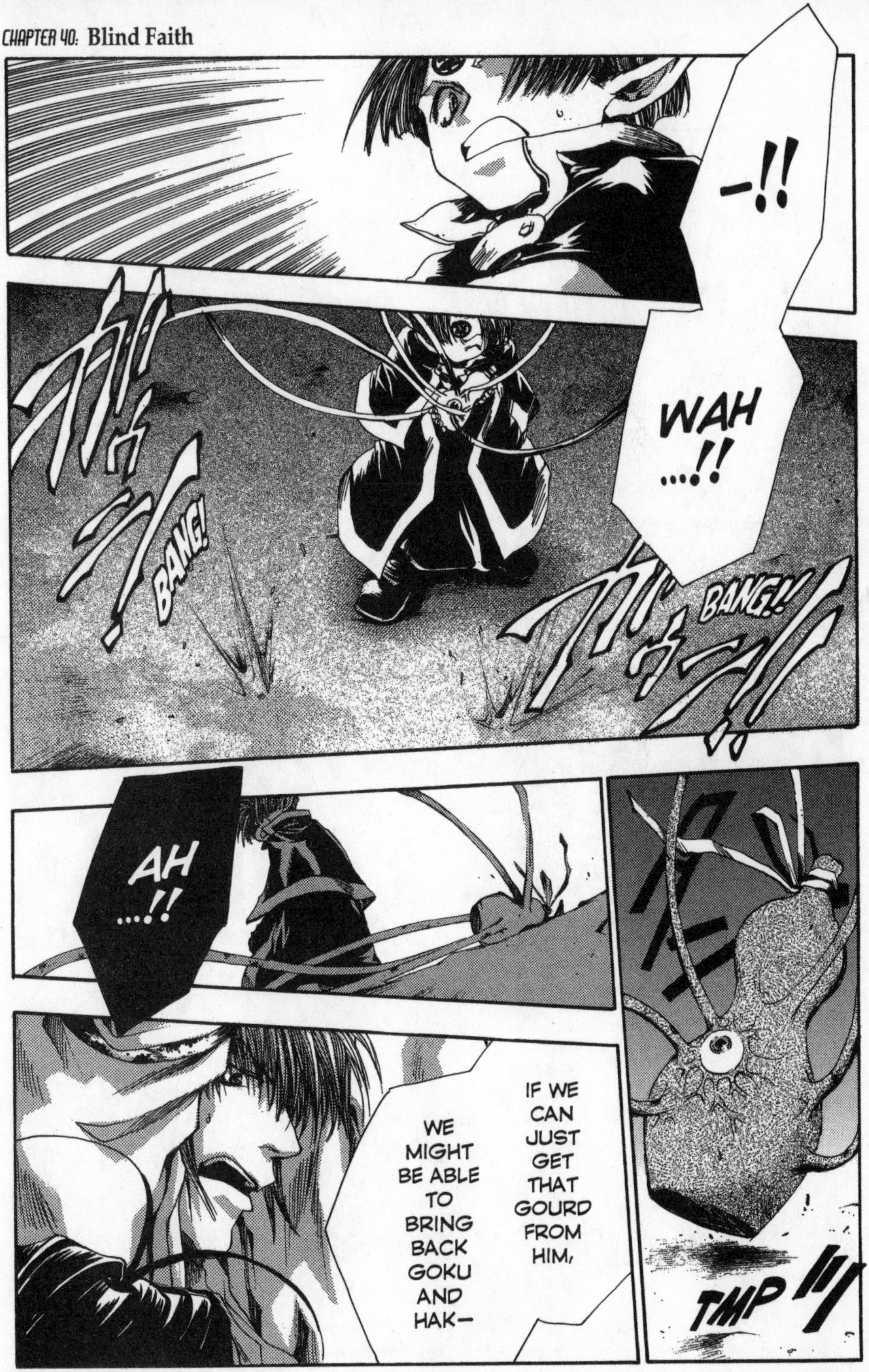
—!!
WAH ...!!
BANG!!
BANG!
TMP
AH ...!!
IF WE CAN JUST GET THAT GOURD FROM HIM,
WE MIGHT BE ABLE TO BRING BACK GOKU AND HAK—

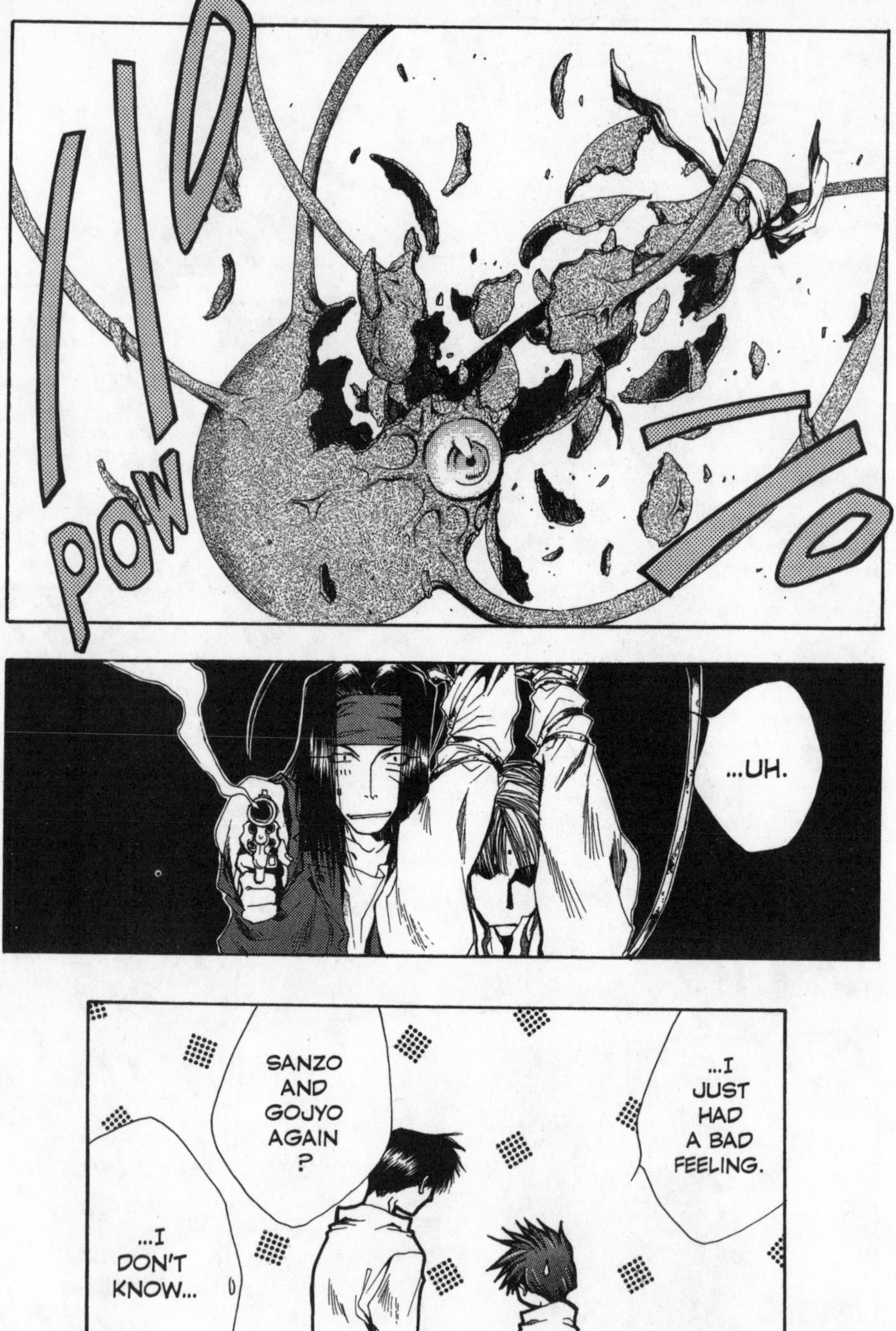
POW
...UH.
...I JUST HAD A BAD FEELING.
SANZO AND GOJYO AGAIN?
...I DON'T KNOW...

CHAPTER 41 Farewell.

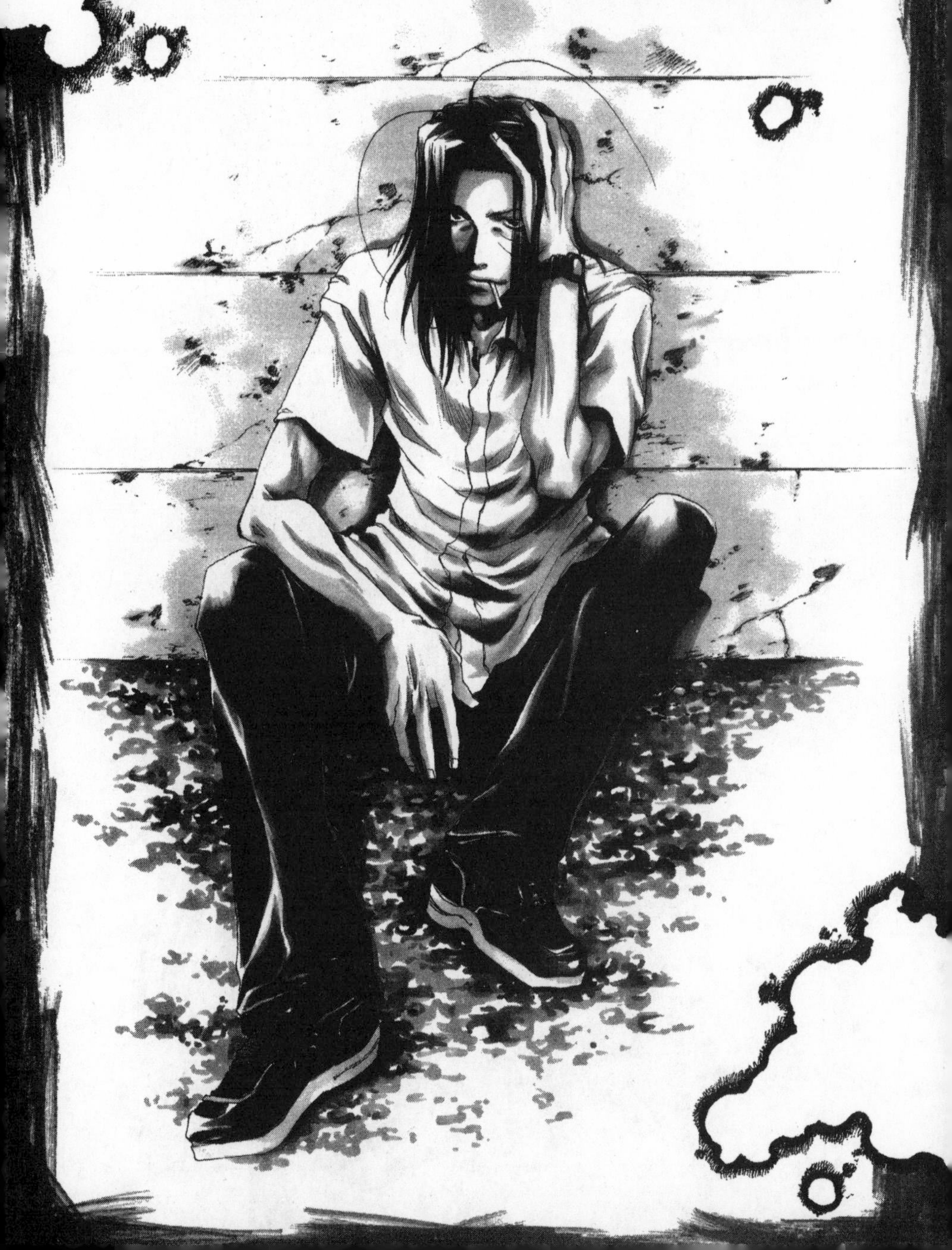

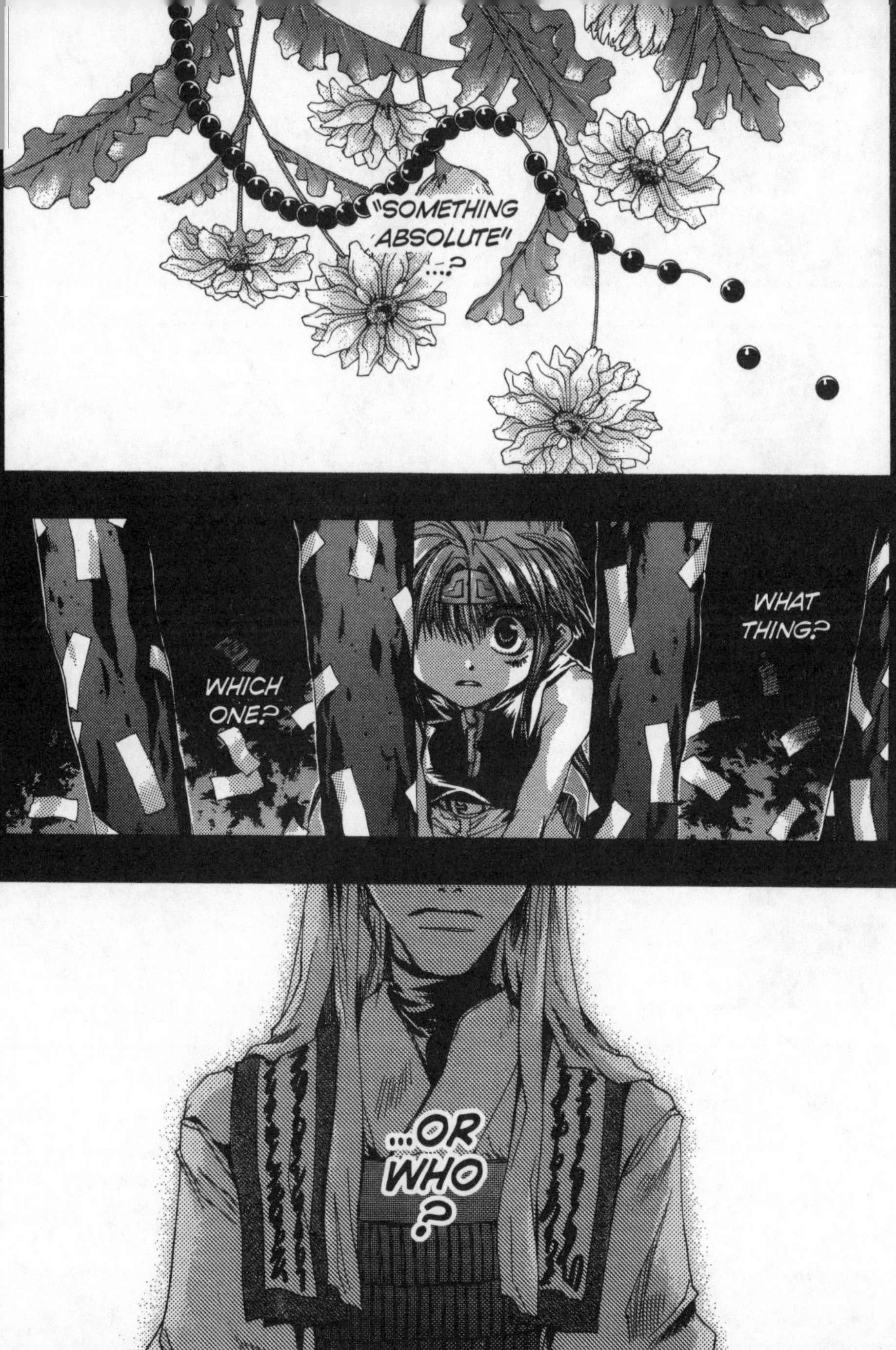
"SOMETHING ABSOLUTE"
...?
WHAT THING?
WHICH ONE?
...OR WHO?

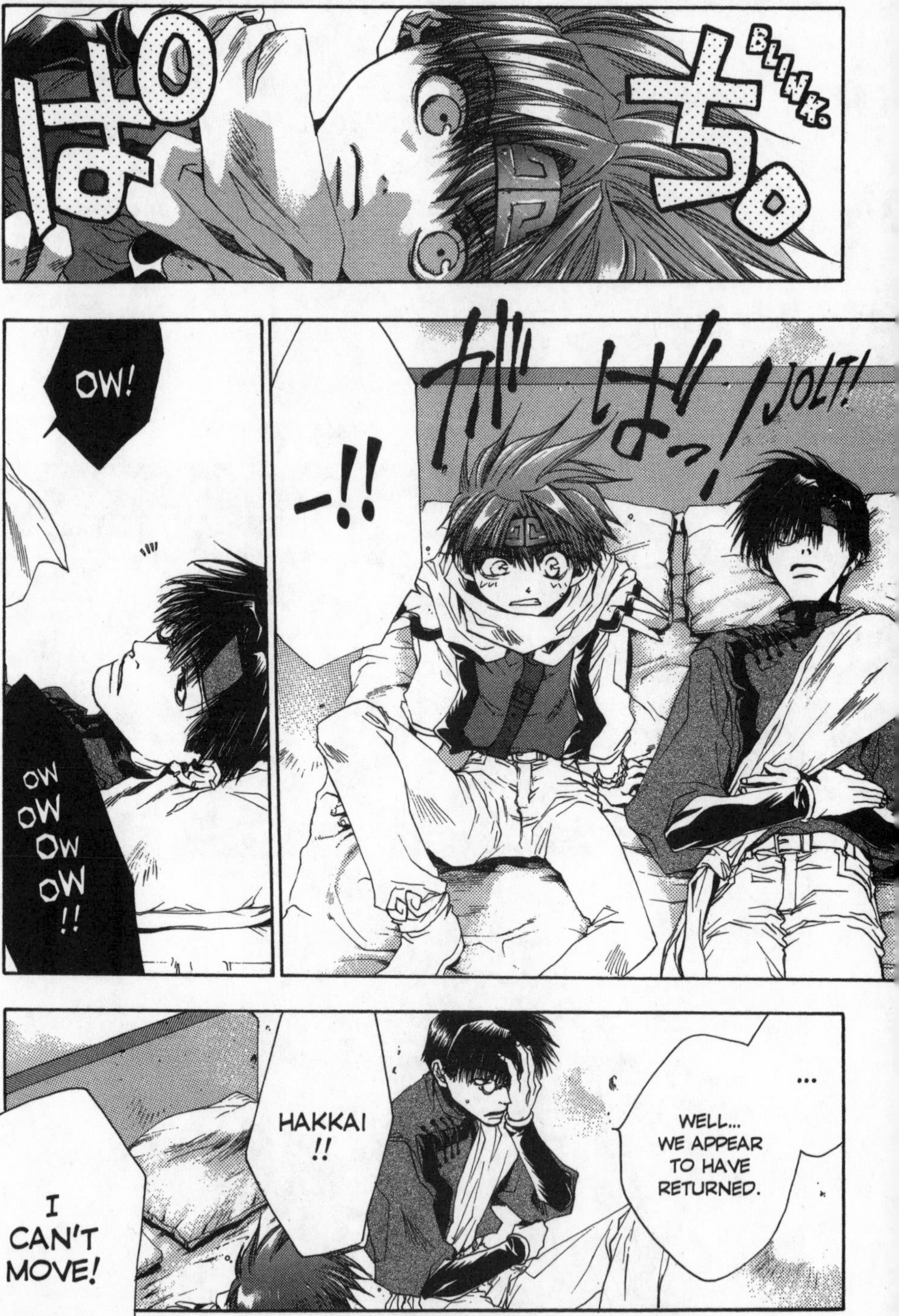

ぱち。
BLINK.
がばっ!!
JOLT!
ー!!
OW!
OW OW OW OW!!
...
WELL... WE APPEAR TO HAVE RETURNED.
HAKKAI!!
I CAN'T MOVE!

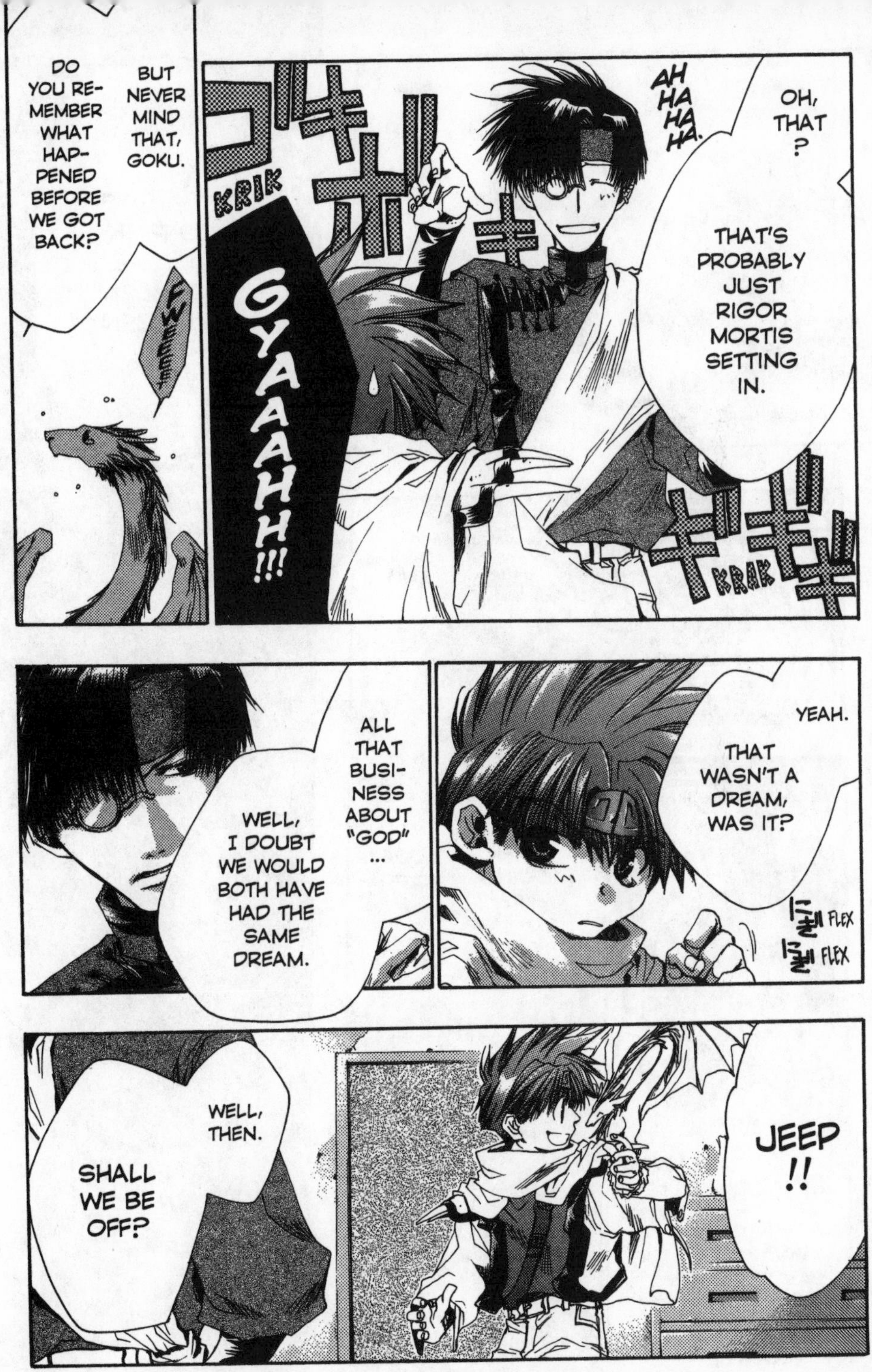

AH HA HA HA.
OH, THAT?
THAT'S PROBABLY JUST RIGOR MORTIS SETTING IN.
KRIK
GYAAAAHH!!!
KRIK
BUT NEVER MIND THAT, GOKU.
DO YOU RE-MEMBER WHAT HAP-PENED BEFORE WE GOT BACK?
FWEEE
YEAH.
THAT WASN'T A DREAM, WAS IT?
FLEX
FLEX
ALL THAT BUSI-NESS ABOUT "GOD" ...
WELL, I DOUBT WE WOULD BOTH HAVE HAD THE SAME DREAM.
JEEP !!
WELL, THEN.
SHALL WE BE OFF?

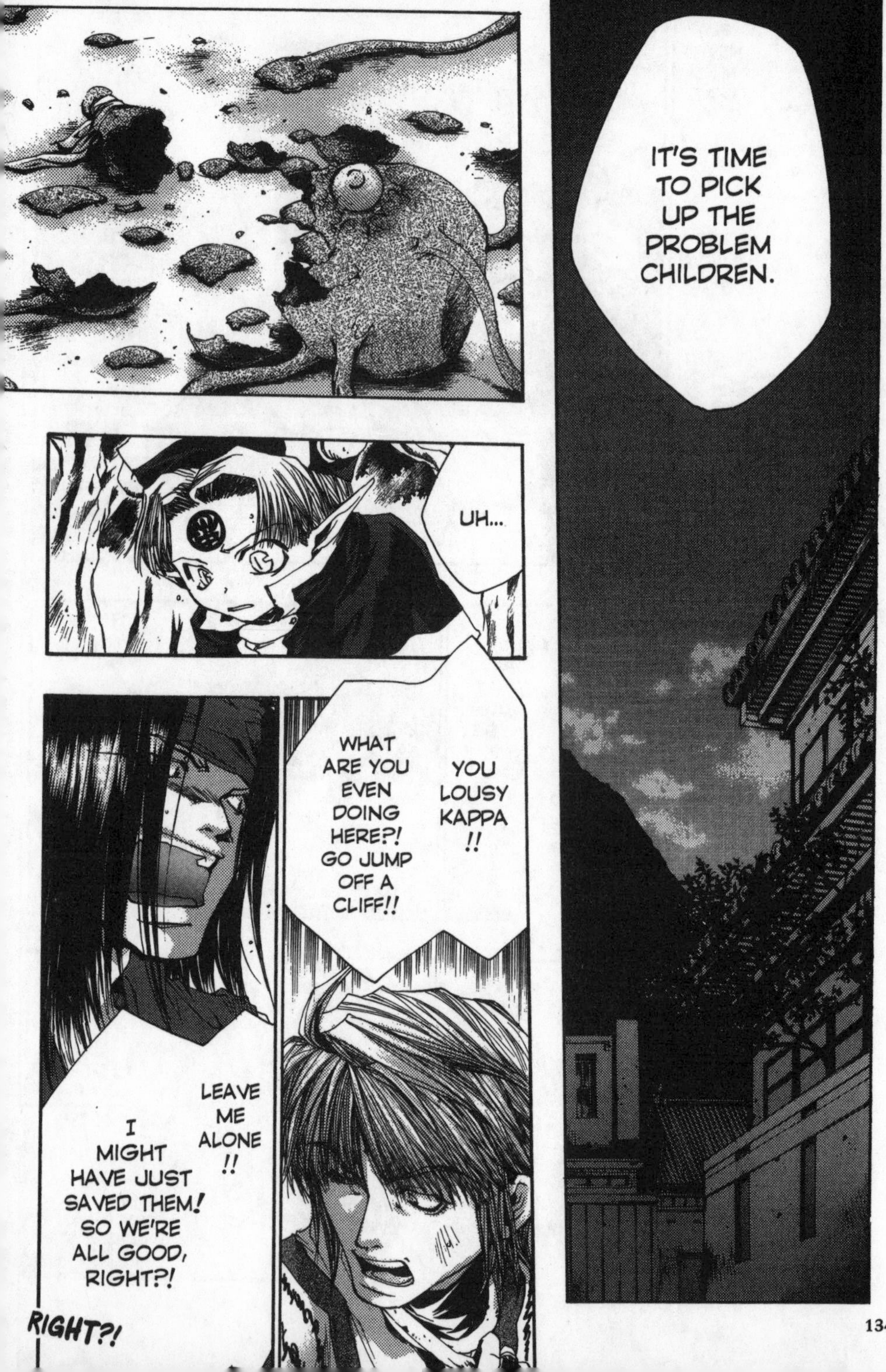
IT'S TIME TO PICK UP THE PROBLEM CHILDREN.
UH...
YOU LOUSY KAPPA!!
WHAT ARE YOU EVEN DOING HERE?! GO JUMP OFF A CLIFF!!
LEAVE ME ALONE!!
I MIGHT HAVE JUST SAVED THEM! SO WE'RE ALL GOOD, RIGHT?!
RIGHT?!

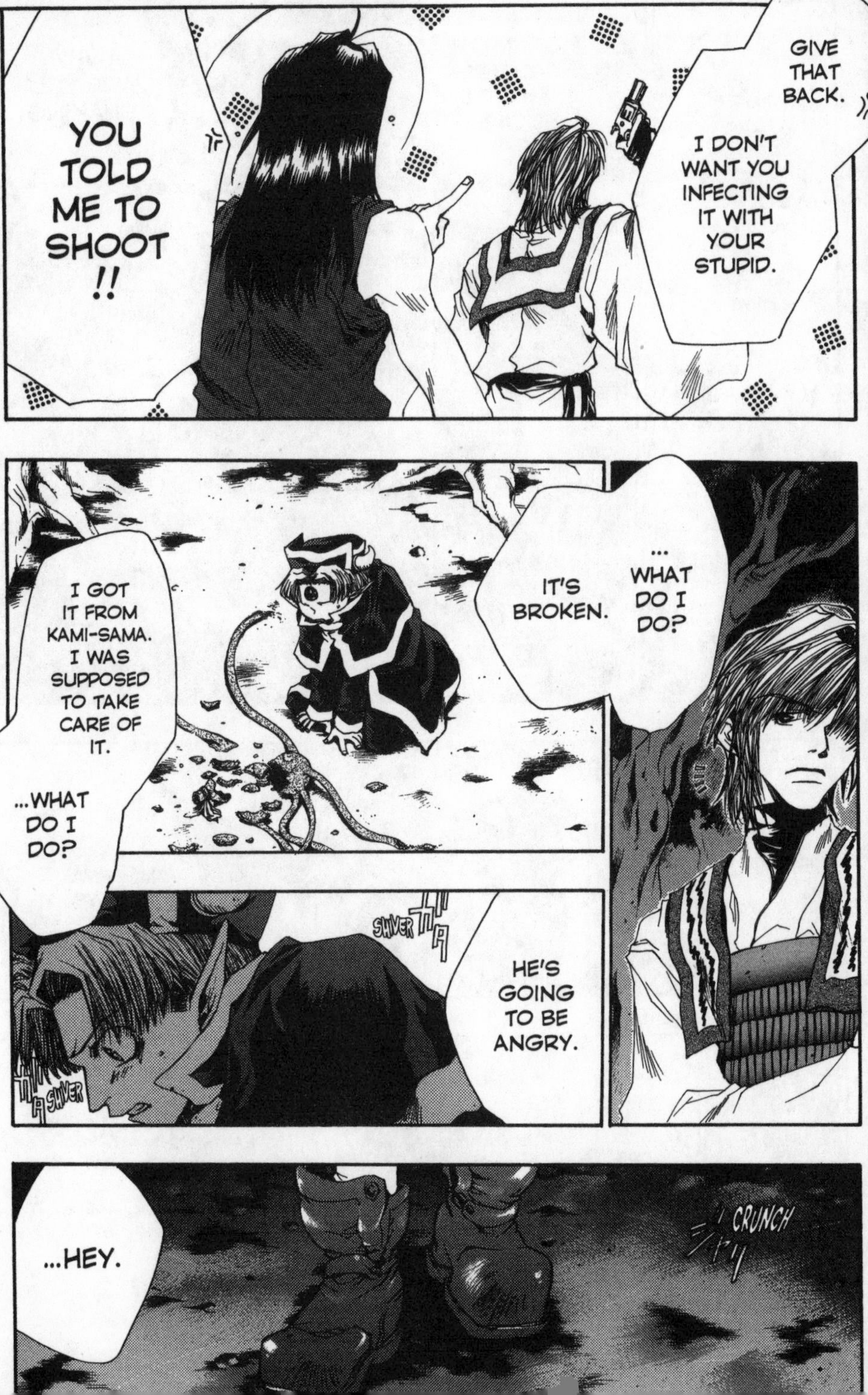
GIVE THAT BACK.
I DON'T WANT YOU INFECTING IT WITH YOUR STUPID.
YOU TOLD ME TO SHOOT!!
... WHAT DO I DO?
IT'S BROKEN.
I GOT IT FROM KAMI-SAMA. I WAS SUPPOSED TO TAKE CARE OF IT.
...WHAT DO I DO?
SHIVER
HE'S GOING TO BE ANGRY.
SHIVER
CRUNCH
...HEY.

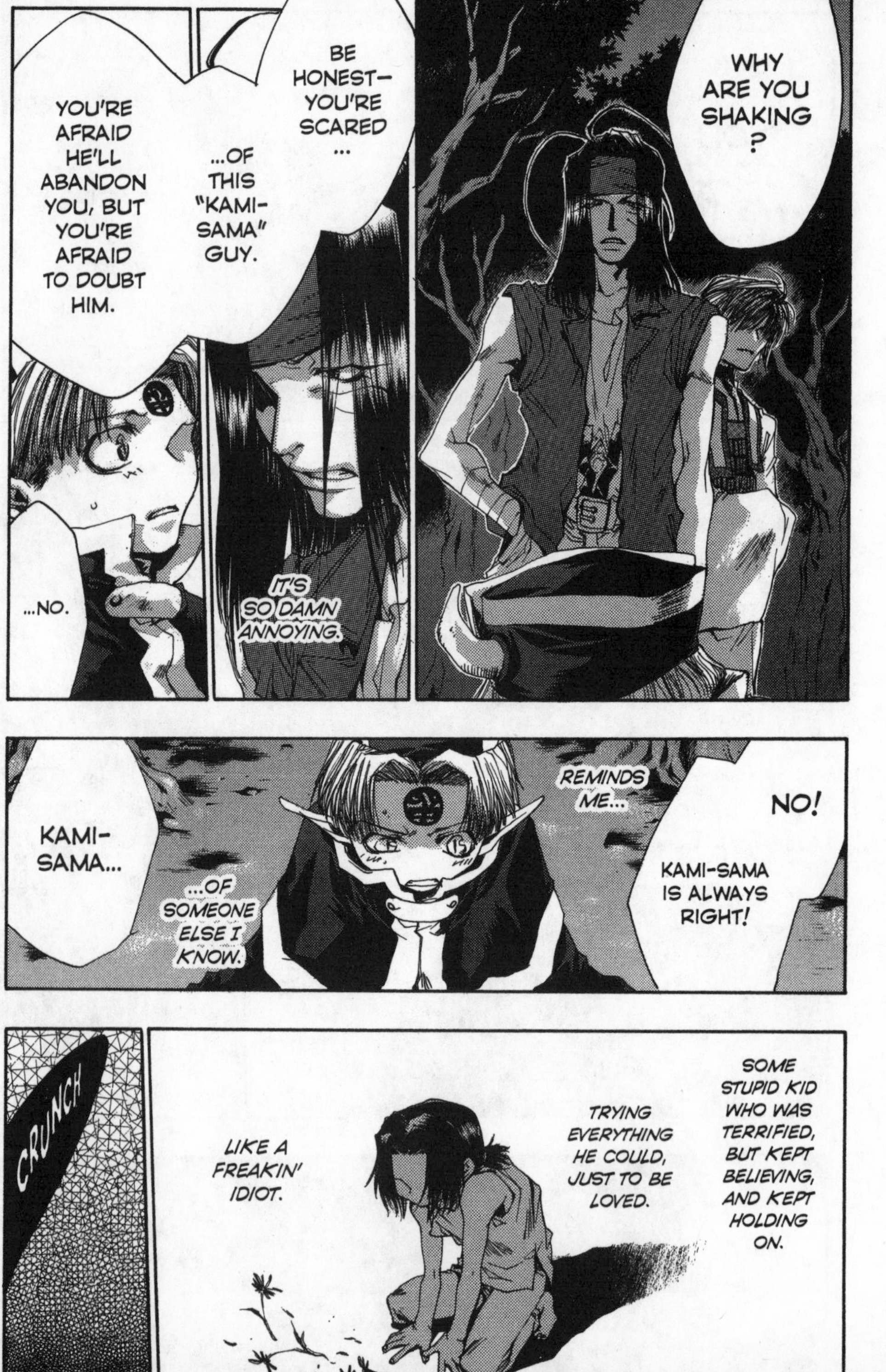
WHY ARE YOU SHAKING?
BE HONEST— YOU'RE SCARED ...
...OF THIS "KAMI-SAMA" GUY.
IT'S SO DAMN ANNOYING.
YOU'RE AFRAID HE'LL ABANDON YOU, BUT YOU'RE AFRAID TO DOUBT HIM.
...NO.
NO!
KAMI-SAMA IS ALWAYS RIGHT!
REMINDS ME...
...OF SOMEONE ELSE I KNOW.
KAMI-SAMA...
SOME STUPID KID WHO WAS TERRIFIED, BUT KEPT BELIEVING, AND KEPT HOLDING ON.
TRYING EVERYTHING HE COULD, JUST TO BE LOVED.
LIKE A FREAKIN' IDIOT.
CRUNCH

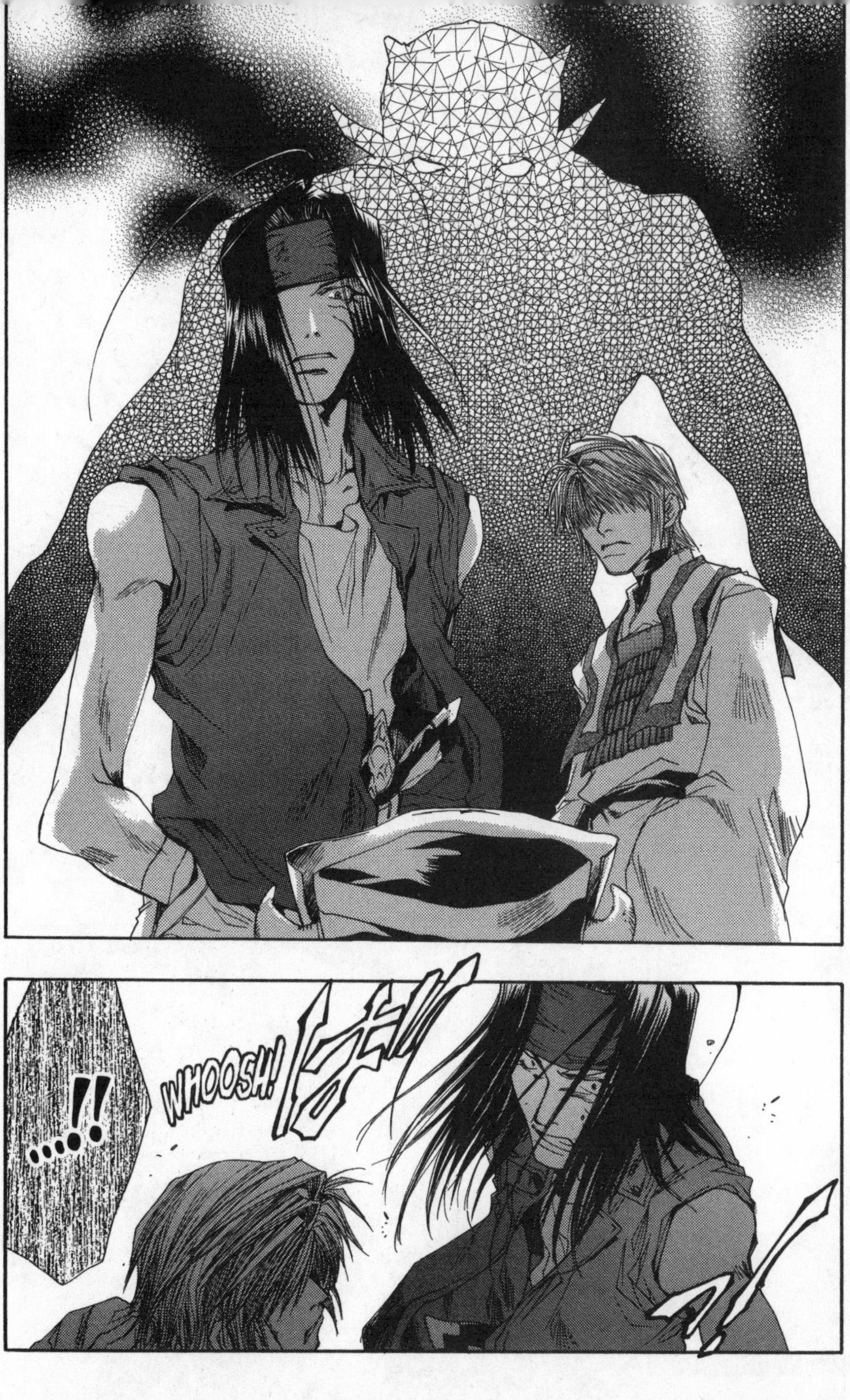
WHOOSH!
...!!

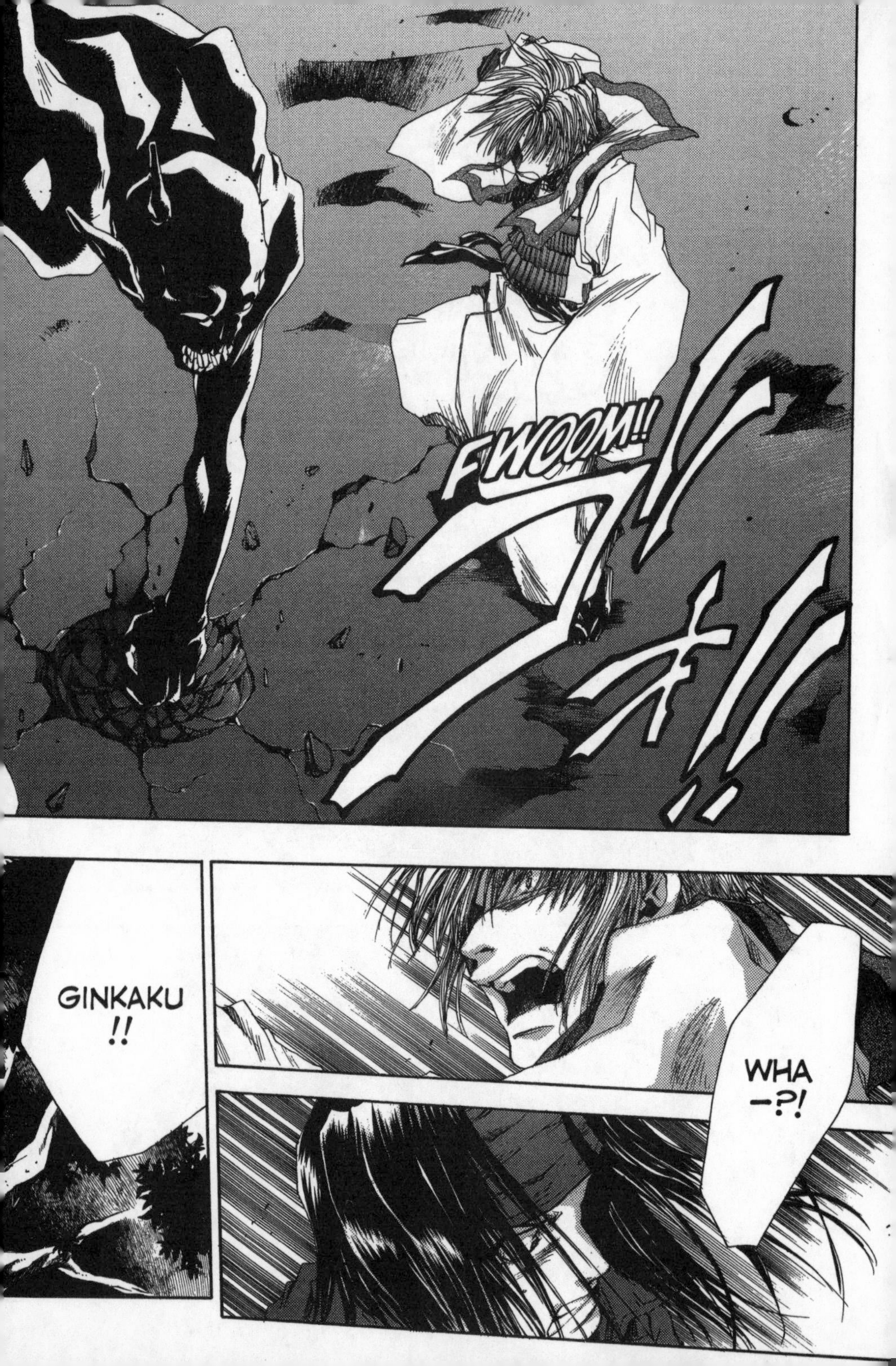
FWOOM!!
WHA
—?!
GINKAKU
!!

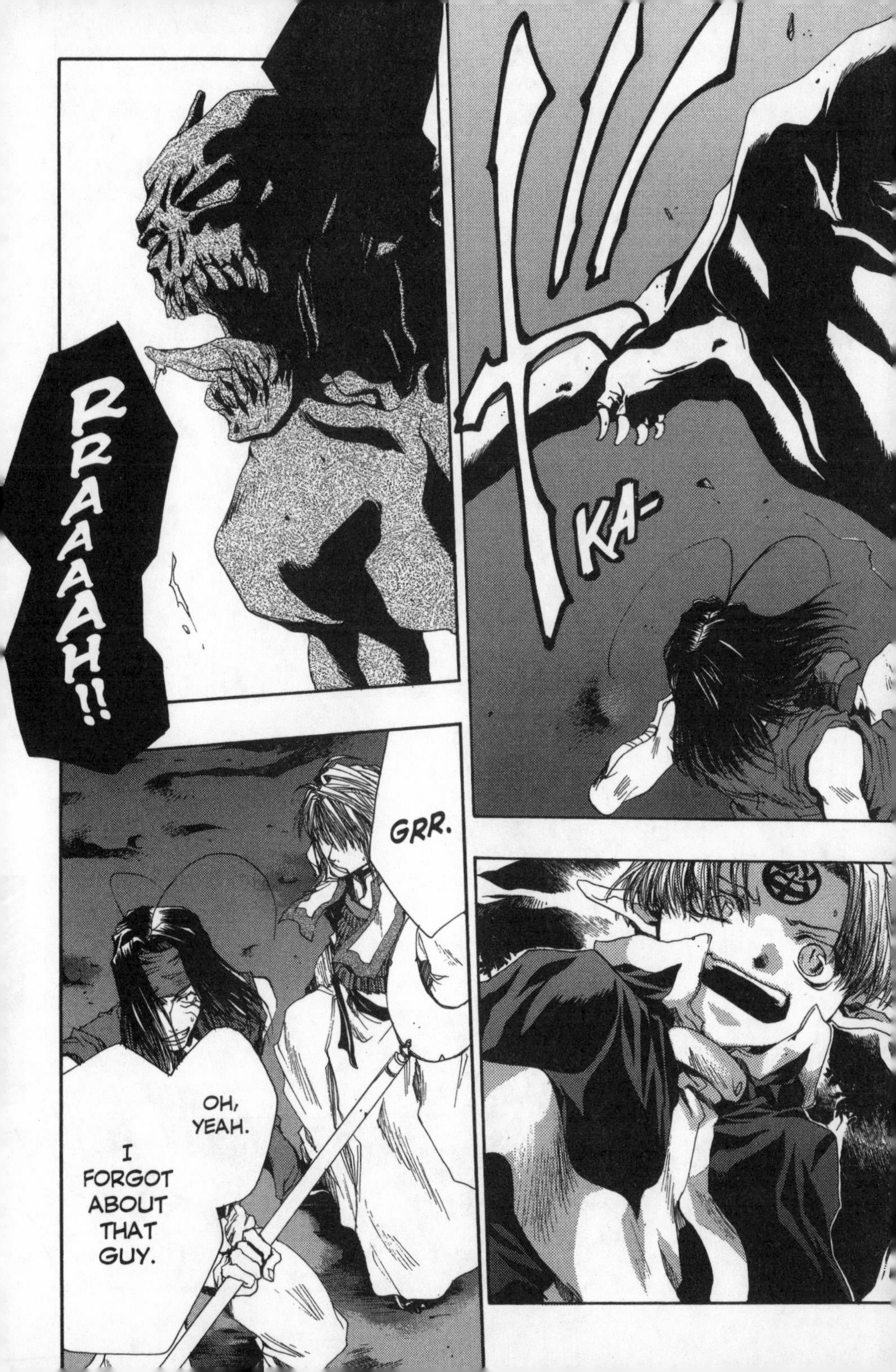
KA-
RRAAAAH!!
GRR.
OH, YEAH.
I FORGOT ABOUT THAT GUY.

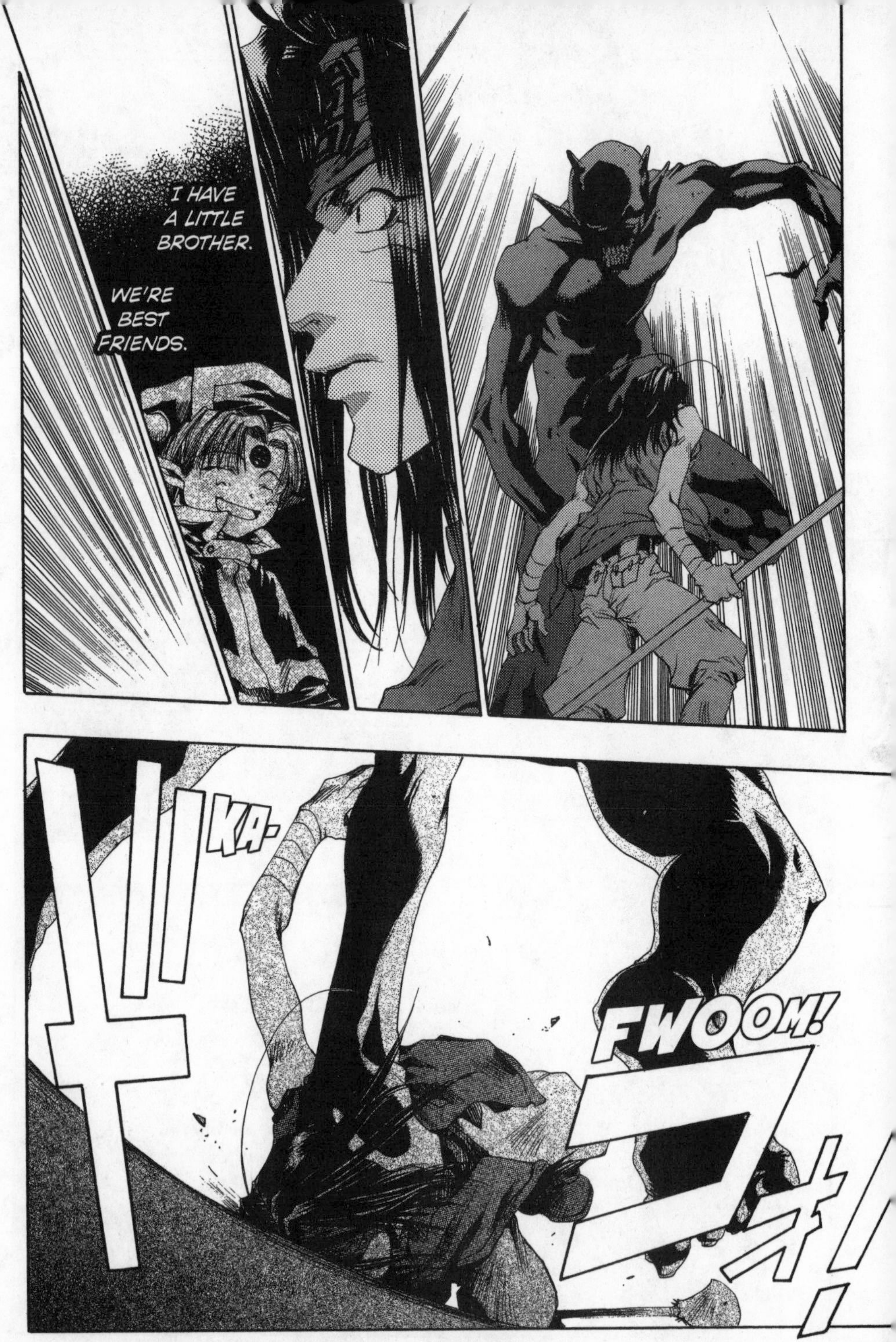
I HAVE A LITTLE BROTHER.
WE'RE BEST FRIENDS.
KA-
FWOOM!

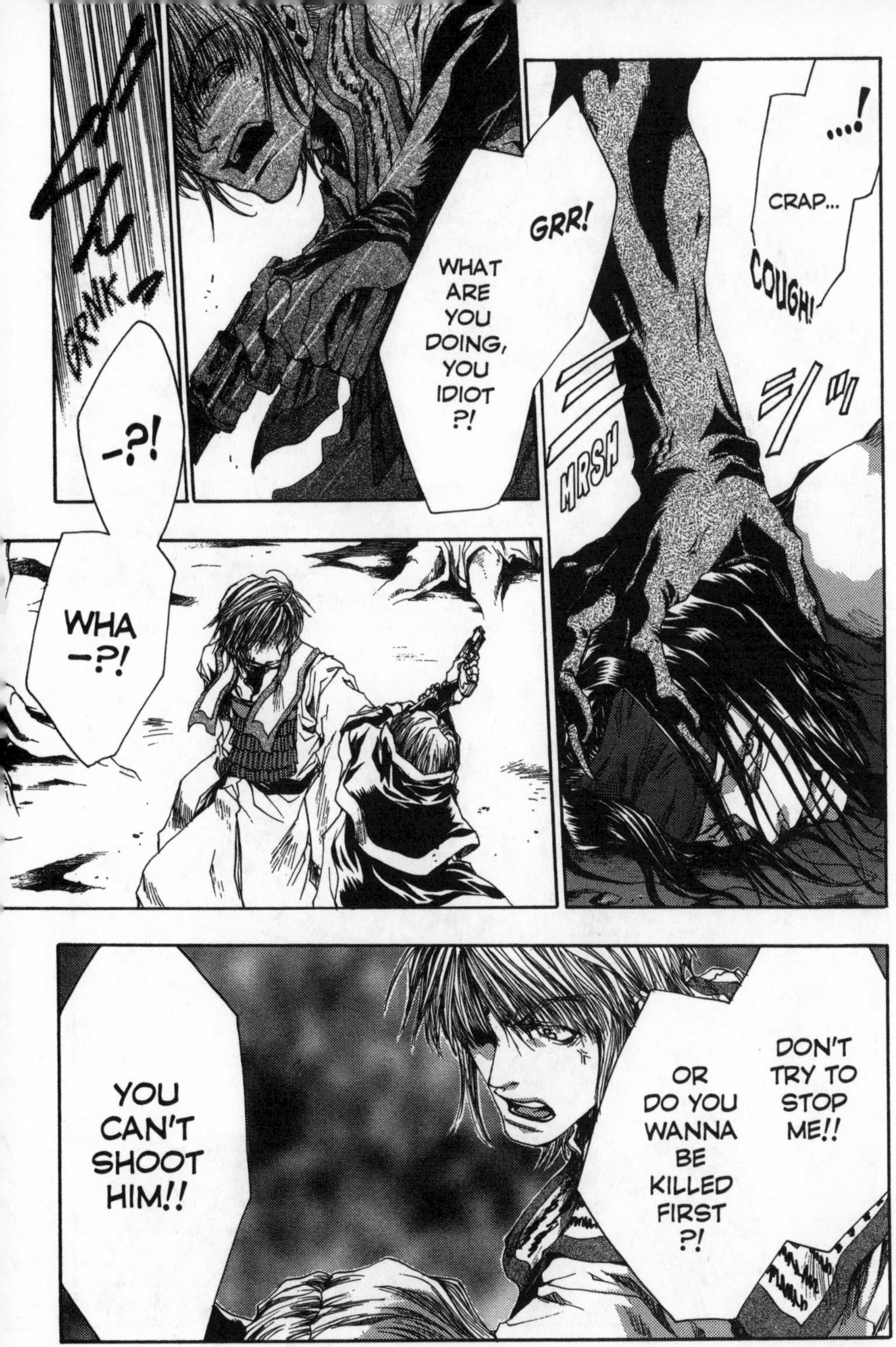
...!
CRAP...
COUGH!
MRSH
GRR!
WHAT ARE YOU DOING, YOU IDIOT?!
GRNK
-?!
WHA-?!
DON'T TRY TO STOP ME!!
OR DO YOU WANNA BE KILLED FIRST?!
YOU CAN'T SHOOT HIM!!

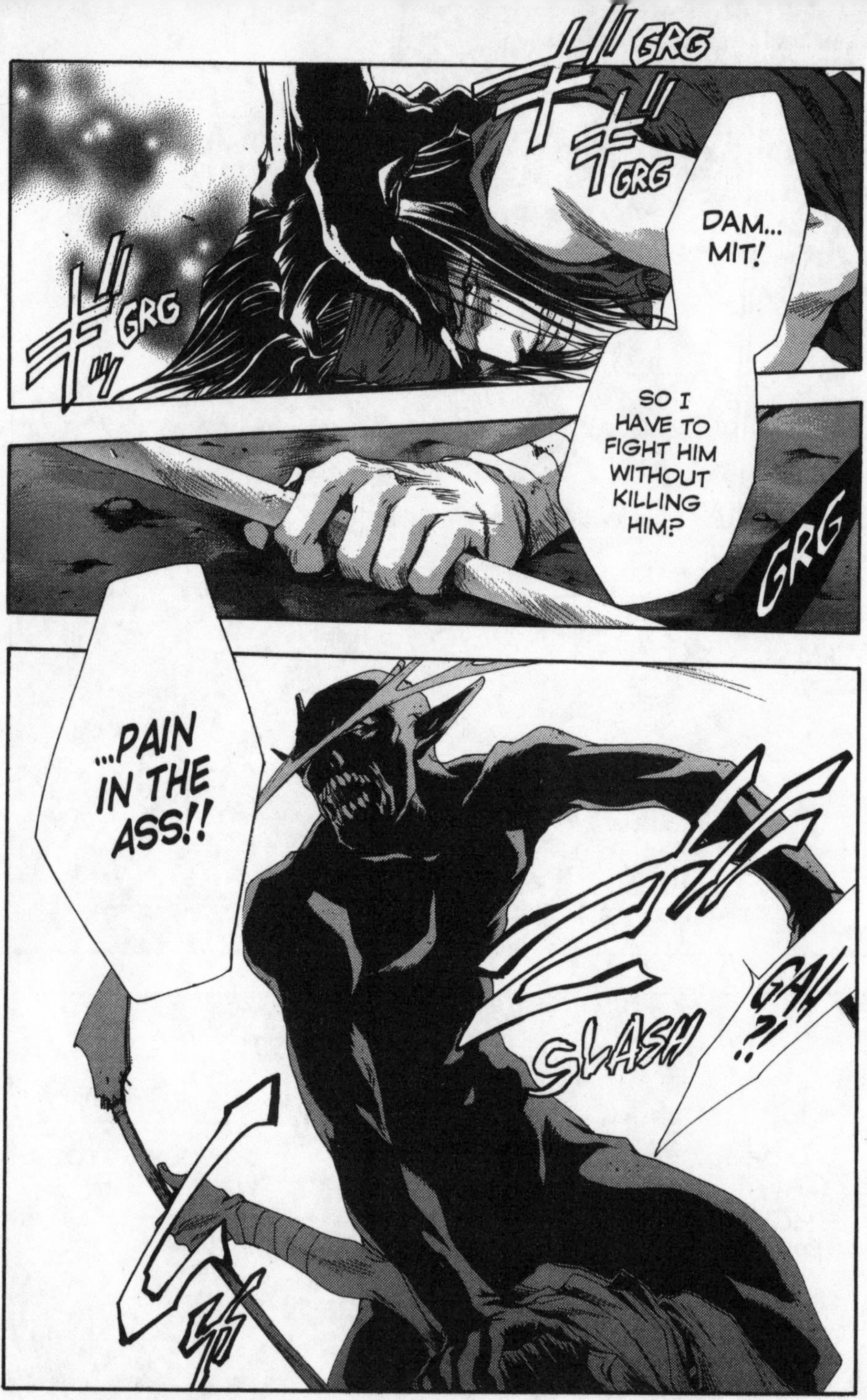
GRG
GRG
DAM... MIT!
GRG
SO I HAVE TO FIGHT HIM WITHOUT KILLING HIM?
GRG
...PAIN IN THE ASS!!
GAH?!
SLASH

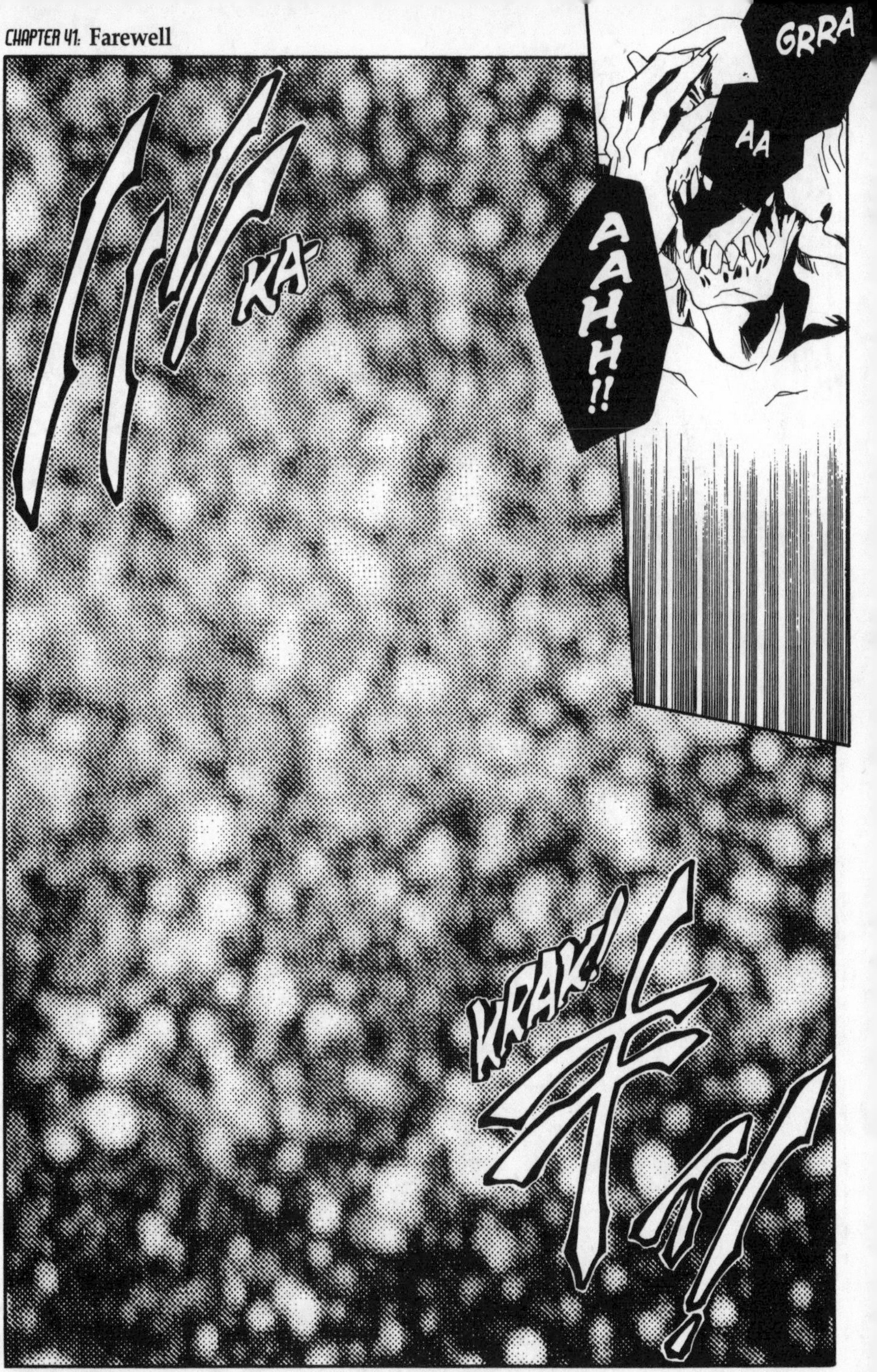
GRRA
AA
AAHH!!
KA-
KRAK!

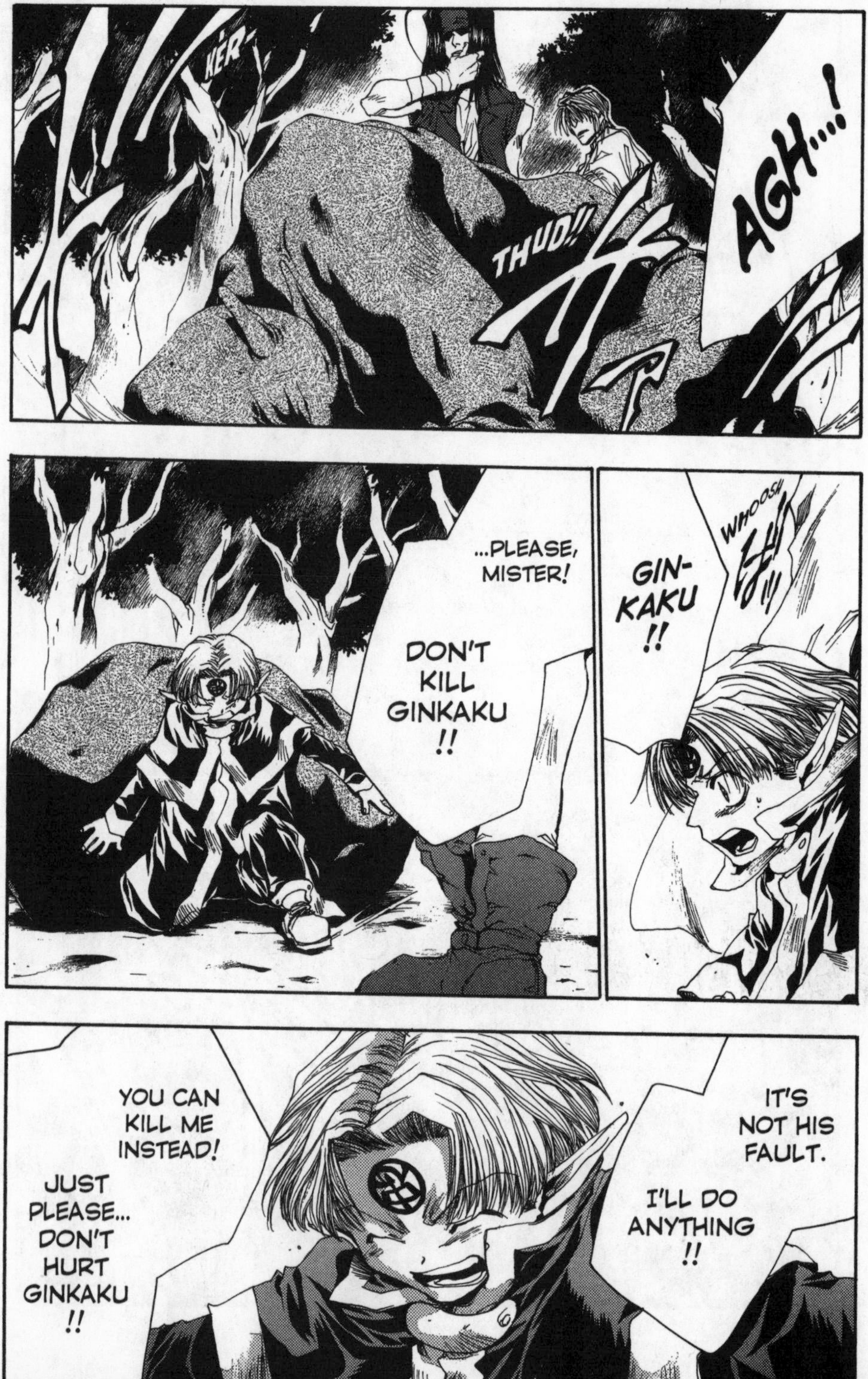
AGH...!
THUD!!
KER-
WHOOSH
GIN-KAKU!!
...PLEASE, MISTER!
DON'T KILL GINKAKU!!
IT'S NOT HIS FAULT.
I'LL DO ANYTHING!!
YOU CAN KILL ME INSTEAD!
JUST PLEASE... DON'T HURT GINKAKU!!

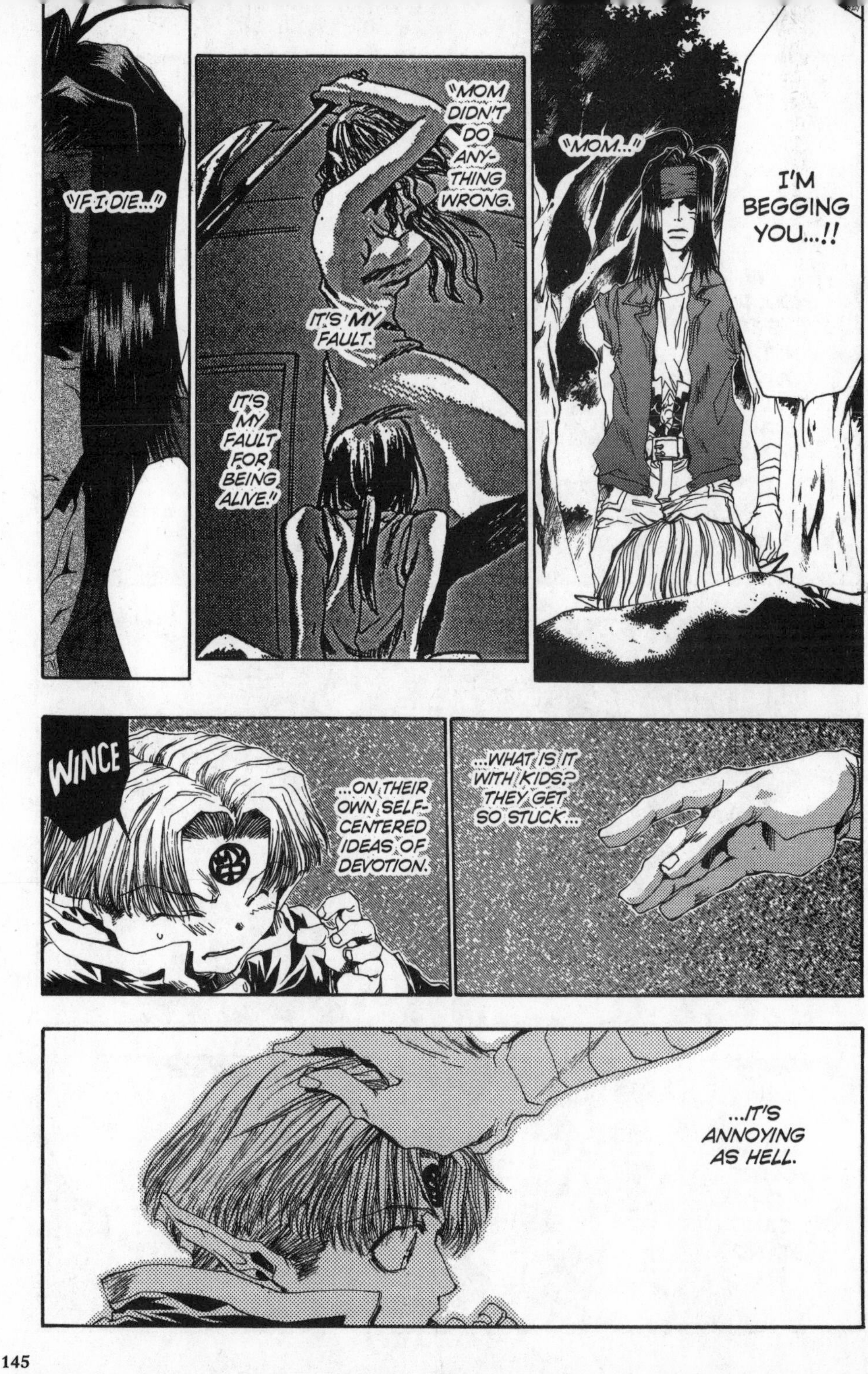
I'M BEGGING YOU...!!
"MOM..."
"MOM DIDN'T DO ANYTHING WRONG.
IT'S MY FAULT.
IT'S MY FAULT FOR BEING ALIVE."
"IF I DIE..."
...WHAT IS IT WITH KIDS? THEY GET SO STUCK...
...ON THEIR OWN SELF-CENTERED IDEAS OF DEVOTION.
WINCE
...IT'S ANNOYING AS HELL.

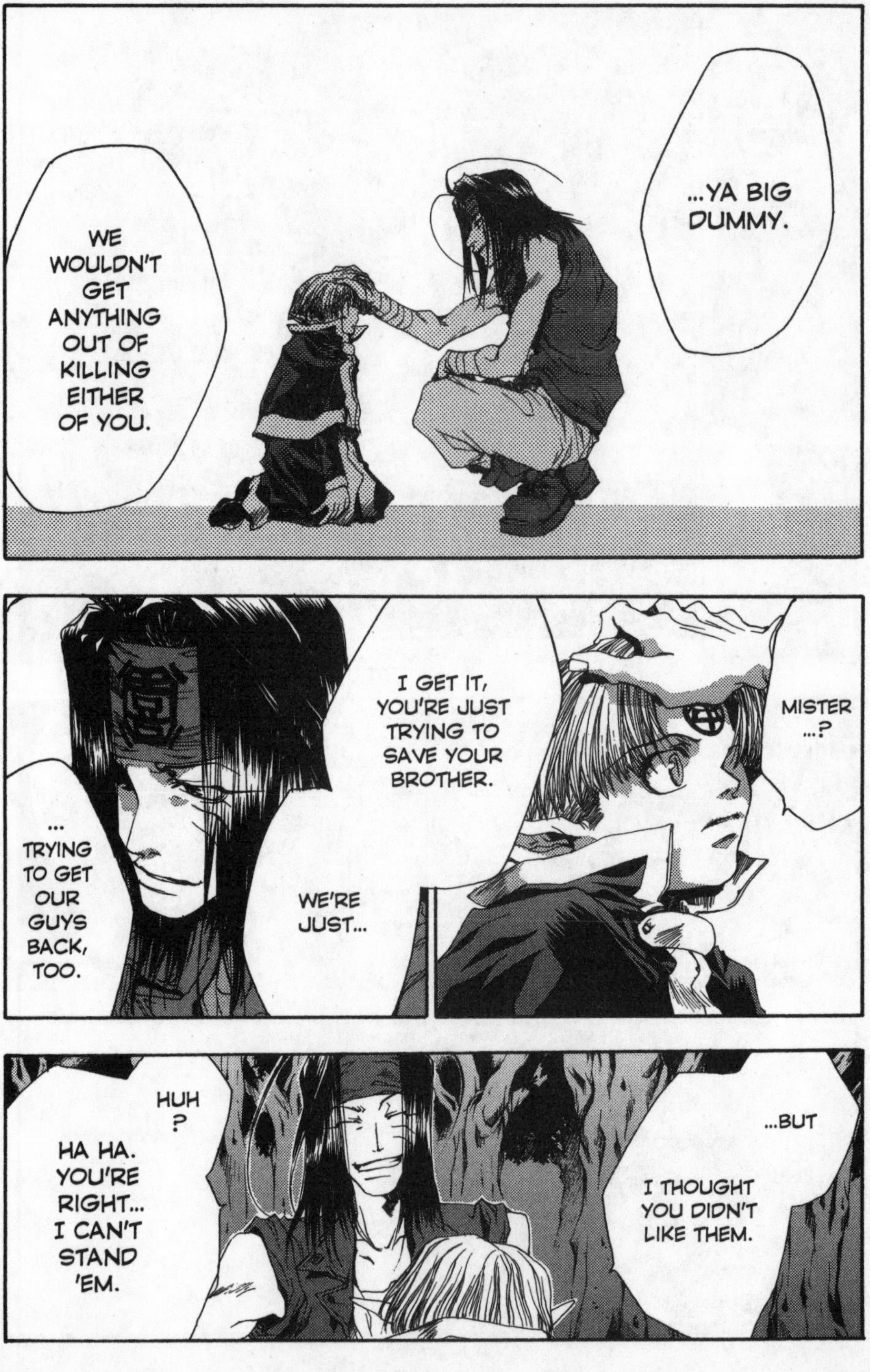
...YA BIG DUMMY.
WE WOULDN'T GET ANYTHING OUT OF KILLING EITHER OF YOU.
MISTER ...?
I GET IT, YOU'RE JUST TRYING TO SAVE YOUR BROTHER.
WE'RE JUST...
... TRYING TO GET OUR GUYS BACK, TOO.
...BUT
I THOUGHT YOU DIDN'T LIKE THEM.
HUH ?
HA HA. YOU'RE RIGHT... I CAN'T STAND 'EM.

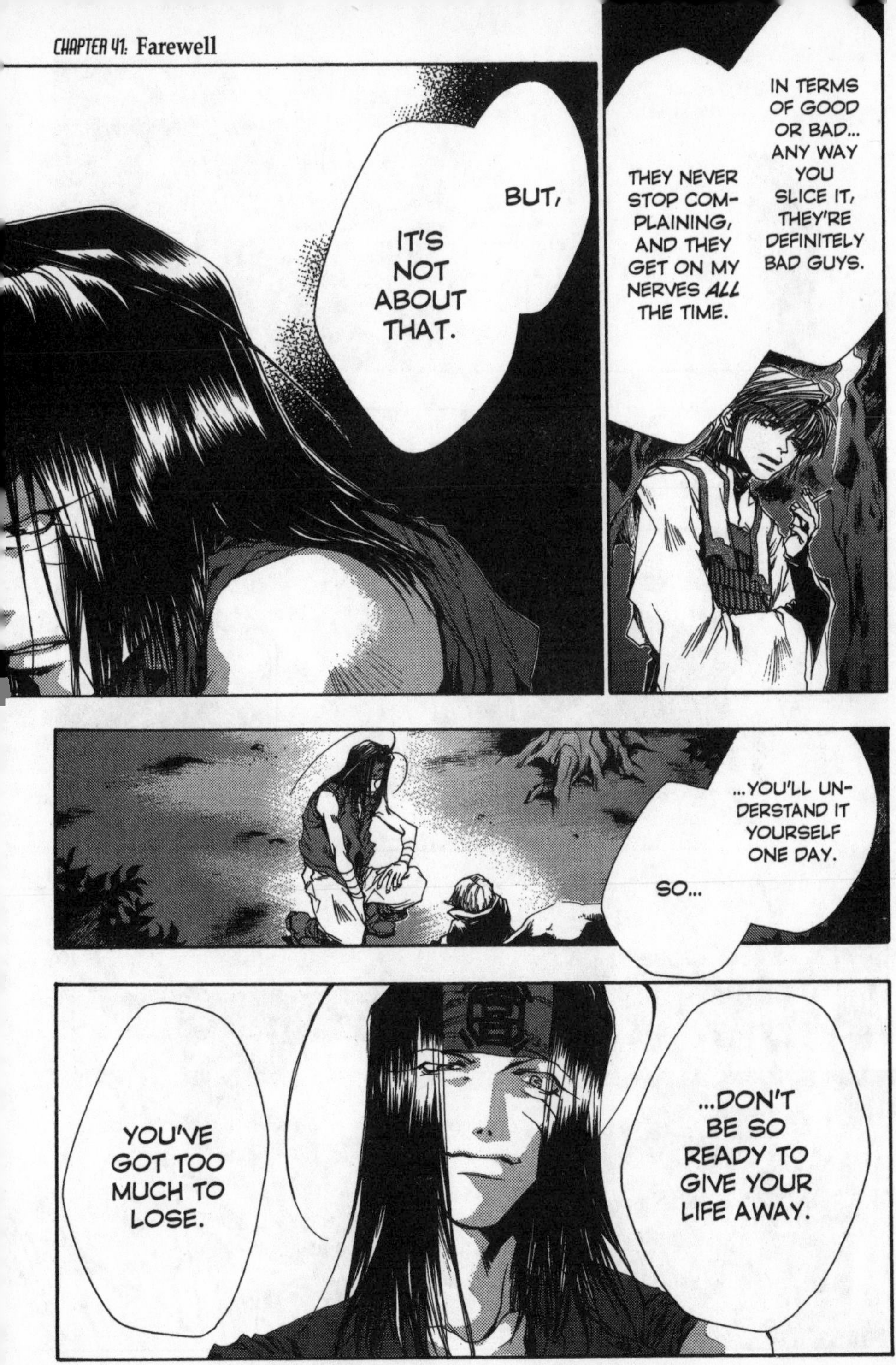
IN TERMS OF GOOD OR BAD... ANY WAY YOU SLICE IT, THEY'RE DEFINITELY BAD GUYS.
THEY NEVER STOP COM-PLAINING, AND THEY GET ON MY NERVES *ALL* THE TIME.
BUT,
IT'S NOT ABOUT THAT.
...YOU'LL UN-DERSTAND IT YOURSELF ONE DAY.
SO...
...DON'T BE SO READY TO GIVE YOUR LIFE AWAY.
YOU'VE GOT TOO MUCH TO LOSE.

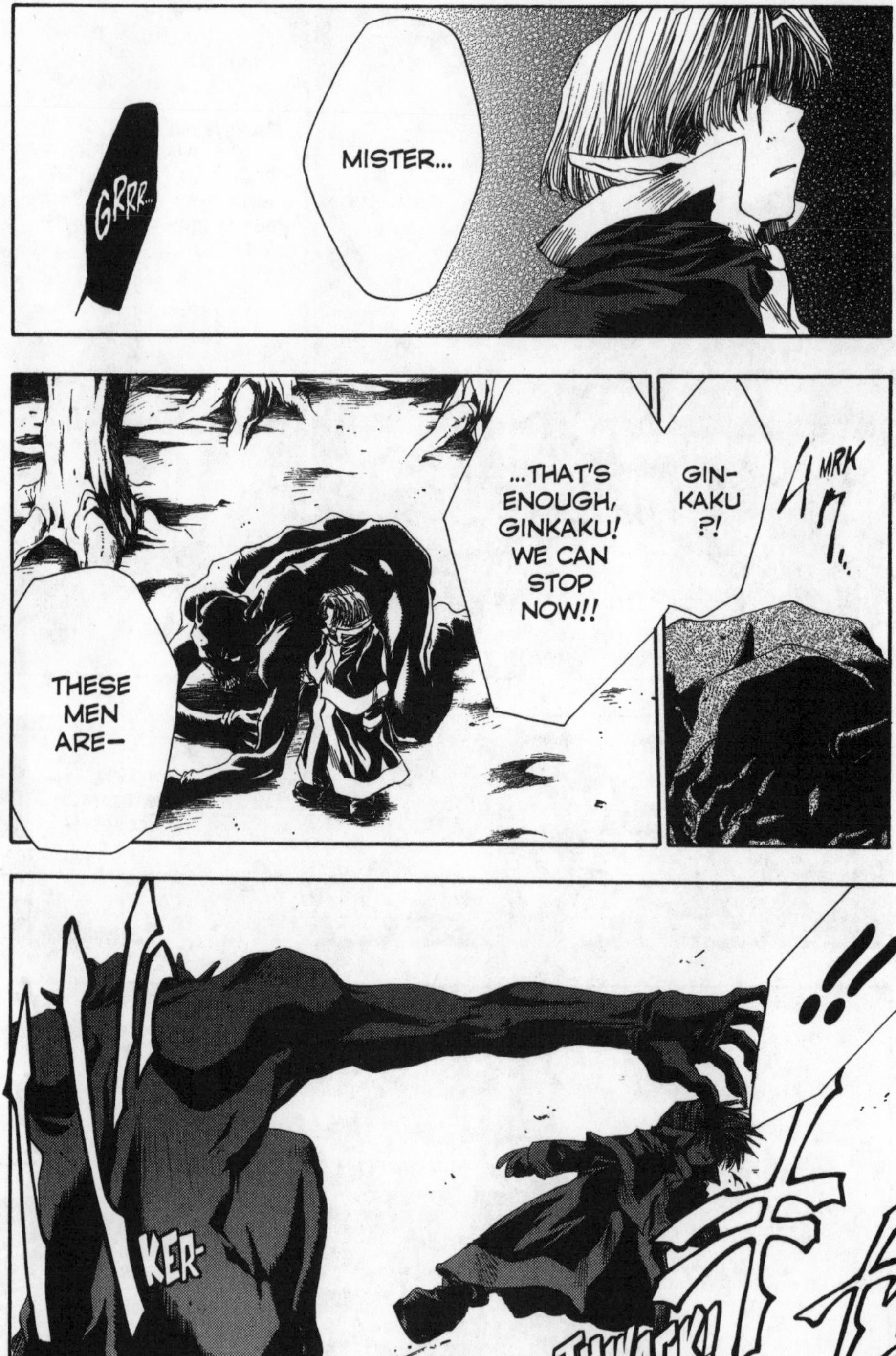
MISTER...
GRRR...
MRK
GIN-KAKU?!
...THAT'S ENOUGH, GINKAKU! WE CAN STOP NOW!!
THESE MEN ARE—
!!
THWACK!
KER-

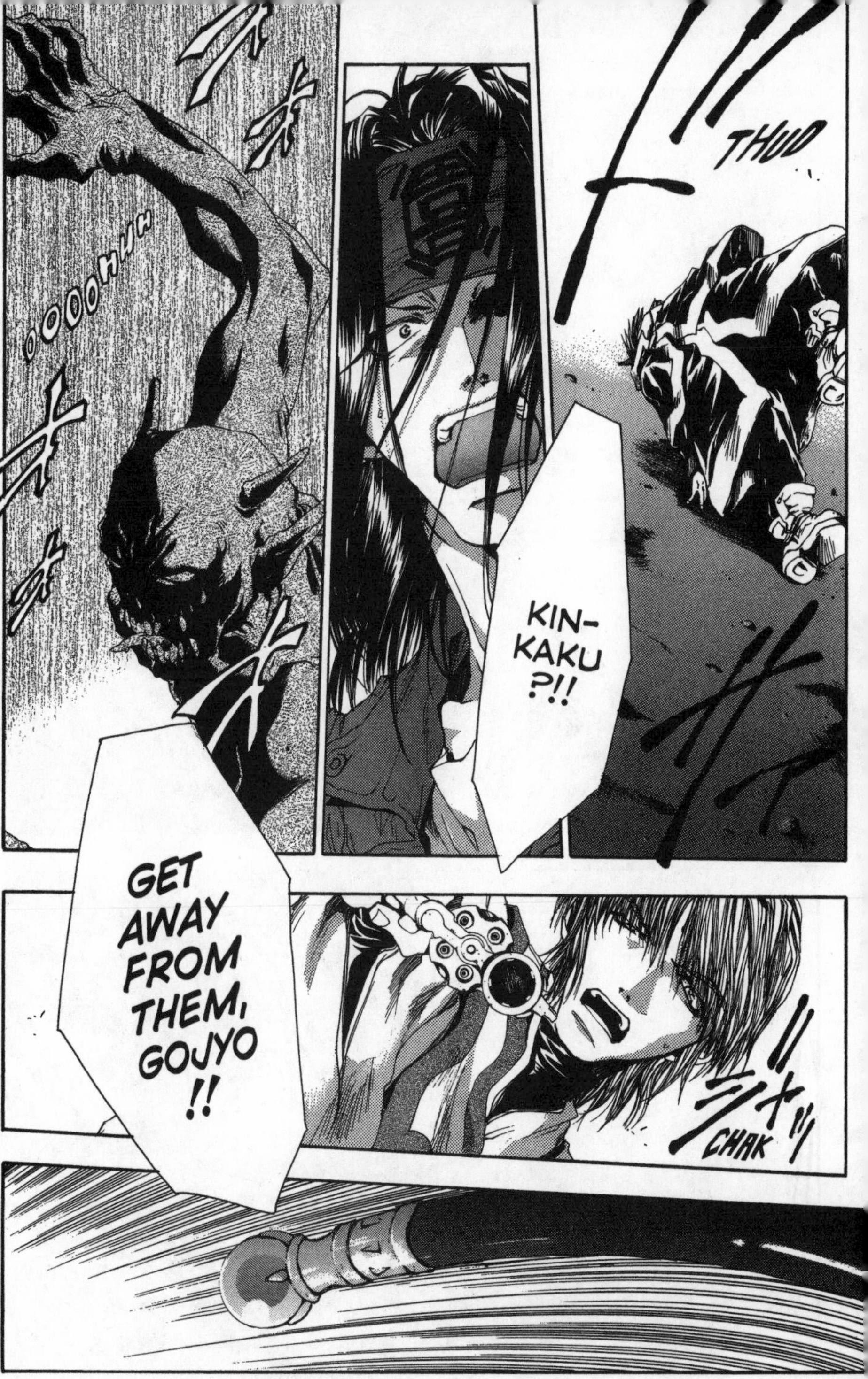
THUD
KIN-KAKU?!!
OOOOOHHH
CHAK
GET AWAY FROM THEM, GOJYO!!

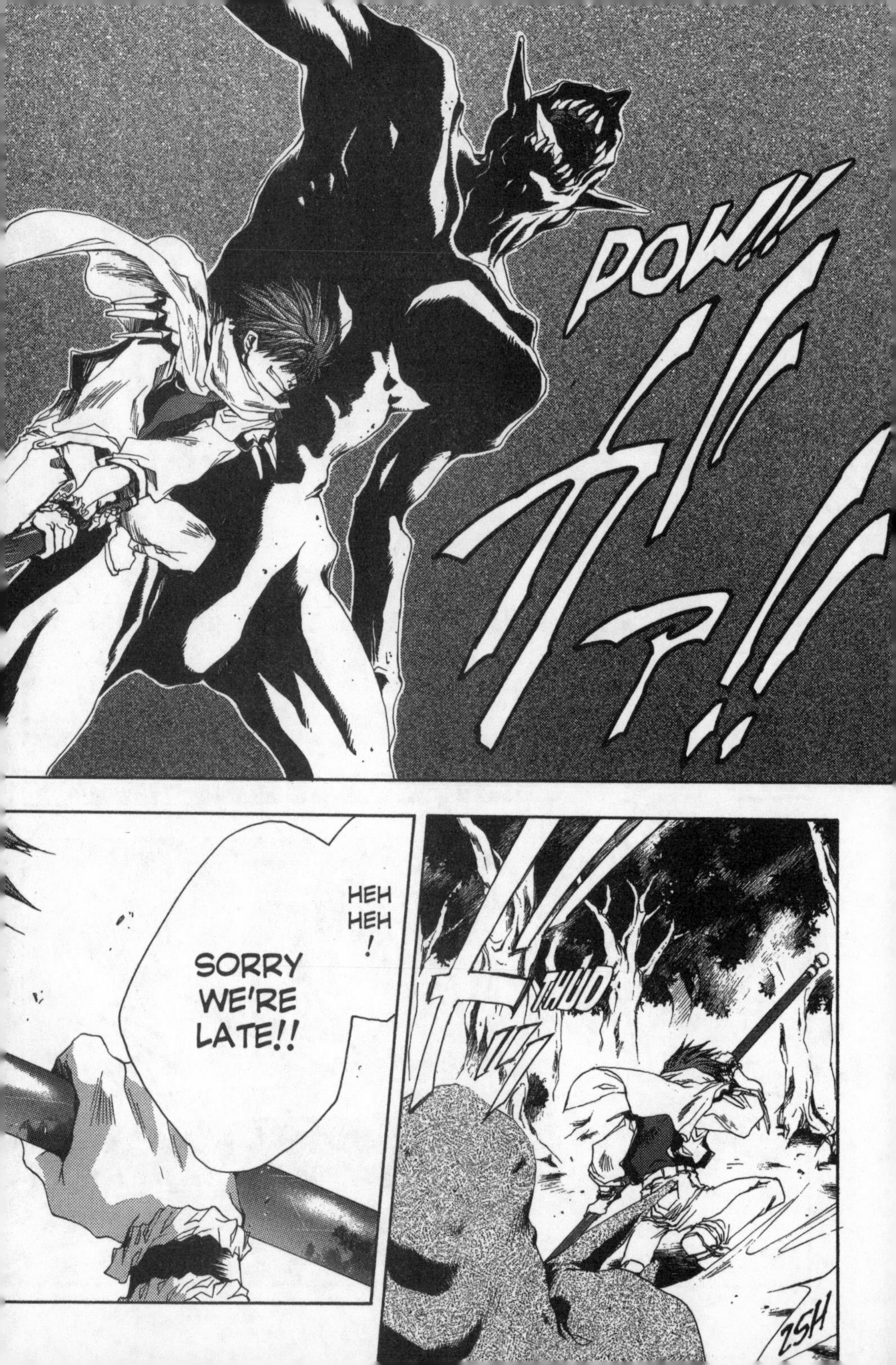
POW!!
THUD
ZSH
HEH HEH!
SORRY WE'RE LATE!!

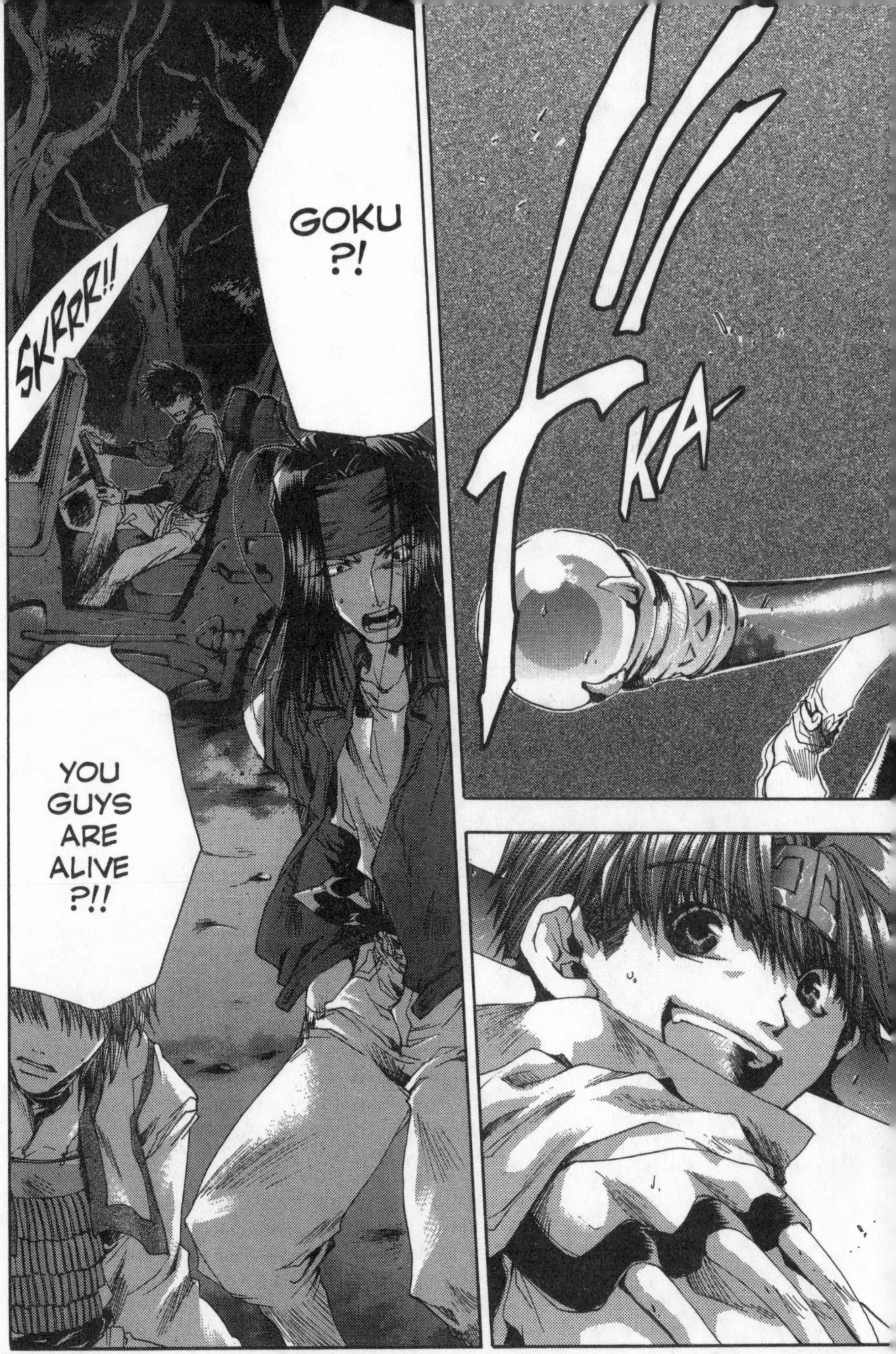
KA-
GOKU ?!
SKRRR!!
YOU GUYS ARE ALIVE ?!!

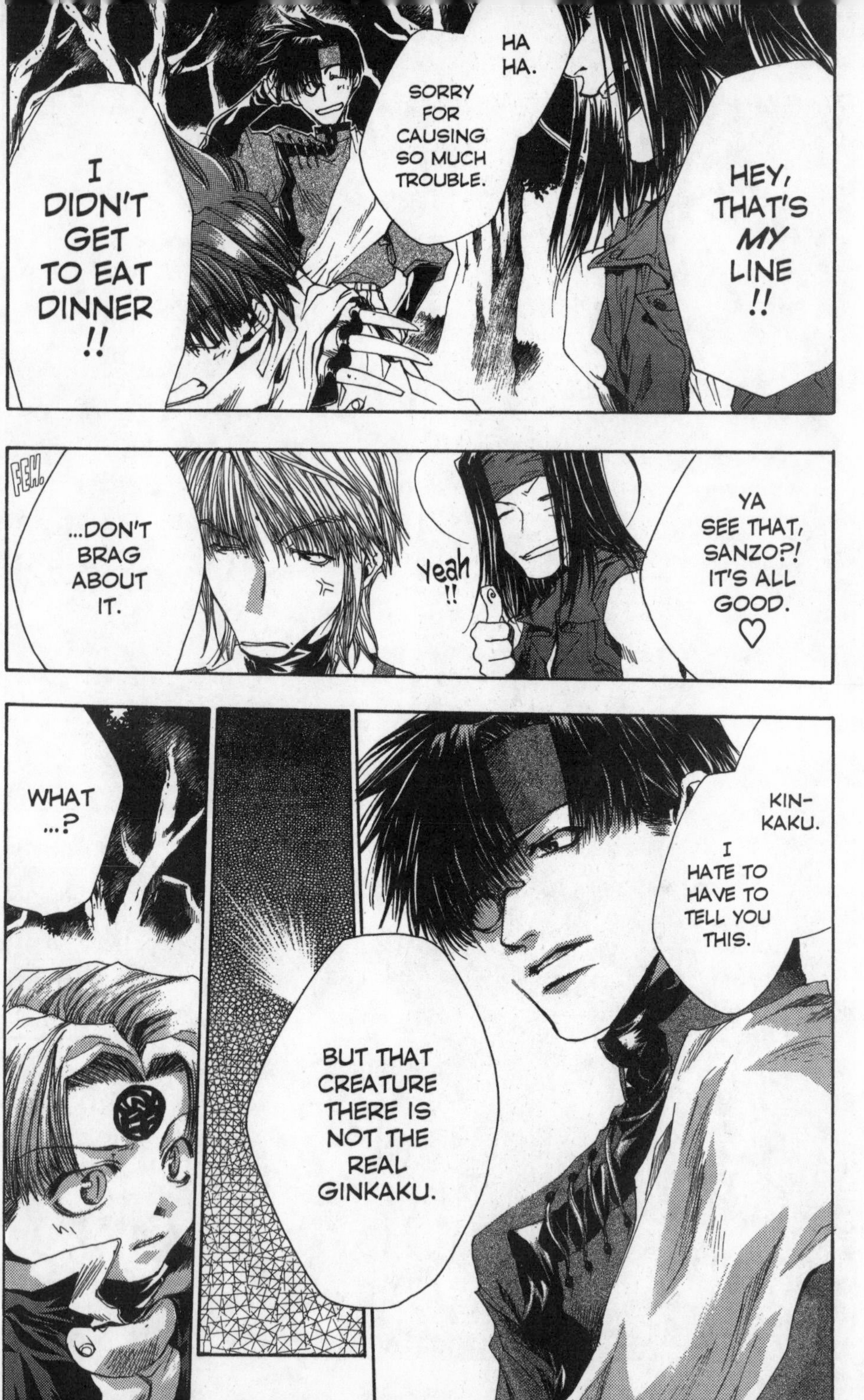
HEY, THAT'S *MY* LINE!!
HA HA. SORRY FOR CAUSING SO MUCH TROUBLE.
I DIDN'T GET TO EAT DINNER!!
YA SEE THAT, SANZO?! IT'S ALL GOOD. ♡
Yeah!!
FEH.
...DON'T BRAG ABOUT IT.
KIN-KAKU.
I HATE TO HAVE TO TELL YOU THIS.
BUT THAT CREATURE THERE IS NOT THE REAL GINKAKU.
WHAT ...?

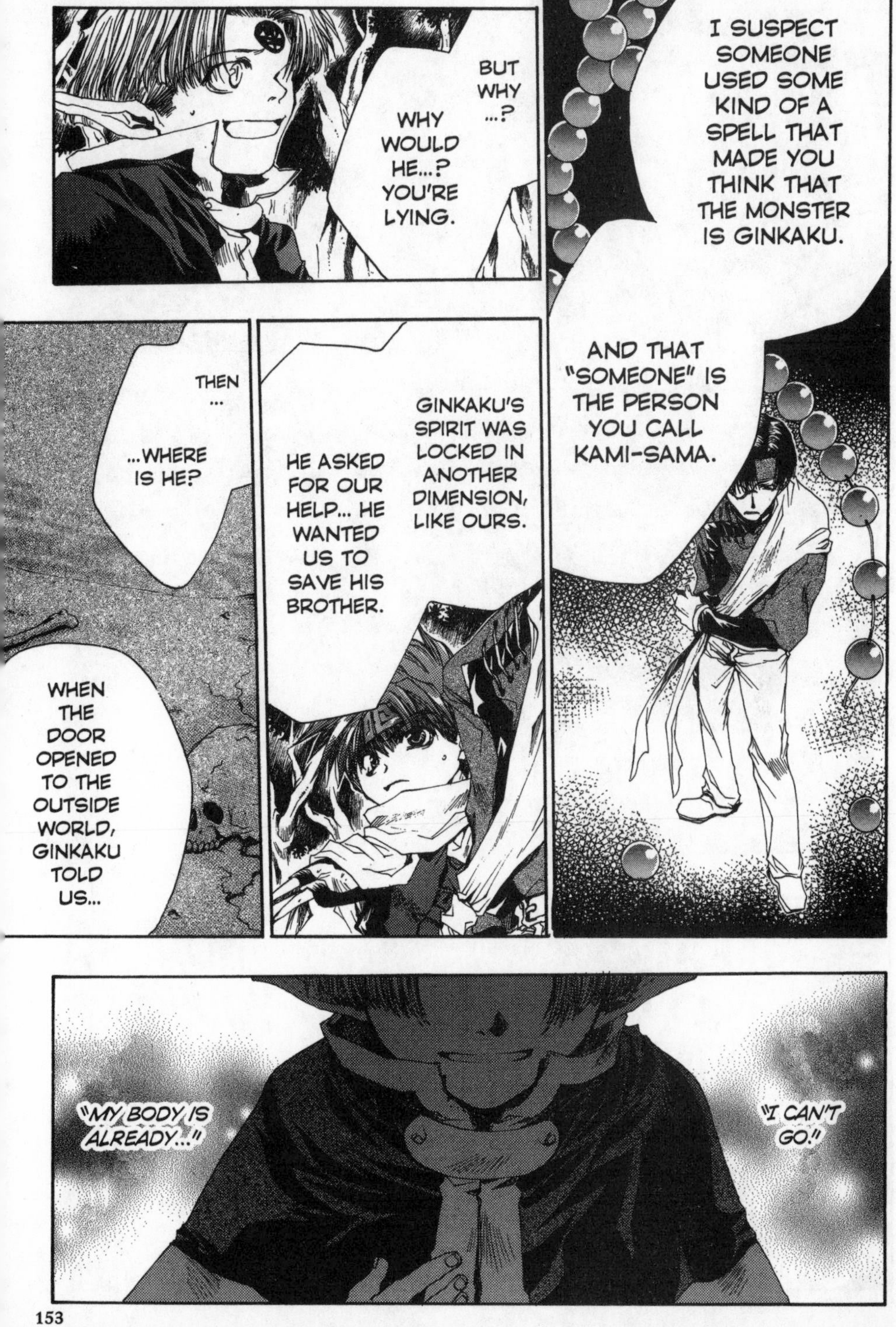
I SUSPECT SOMEONE USED SOME KIND OF A SPELL THAT MADE YOU THINK THAT THE MONSTER IS GINKAKU.
BUT WHY ...?
WHY WOULD HE...? YOU'RE LYING.
AND THAT "SOMEONE" IS THE PERSON YOU CALL KAMI-SAMA.
GINKAKU'S SPIRIT WAS LOCKED IN ANOTHER DIMENSION, LIKE OURS.
HE ASKED FOR OUR HELP... HE WANTED US TO SAVE HIS BROTHER.
THEN ...
...WHERE IS HE?
WHEN THE DOOR OPENED TO THE OUTSIDE WORLD, GINKAKU TOLD US...
"I CAN'T GO."
"MY BODY IS ALREADY..."

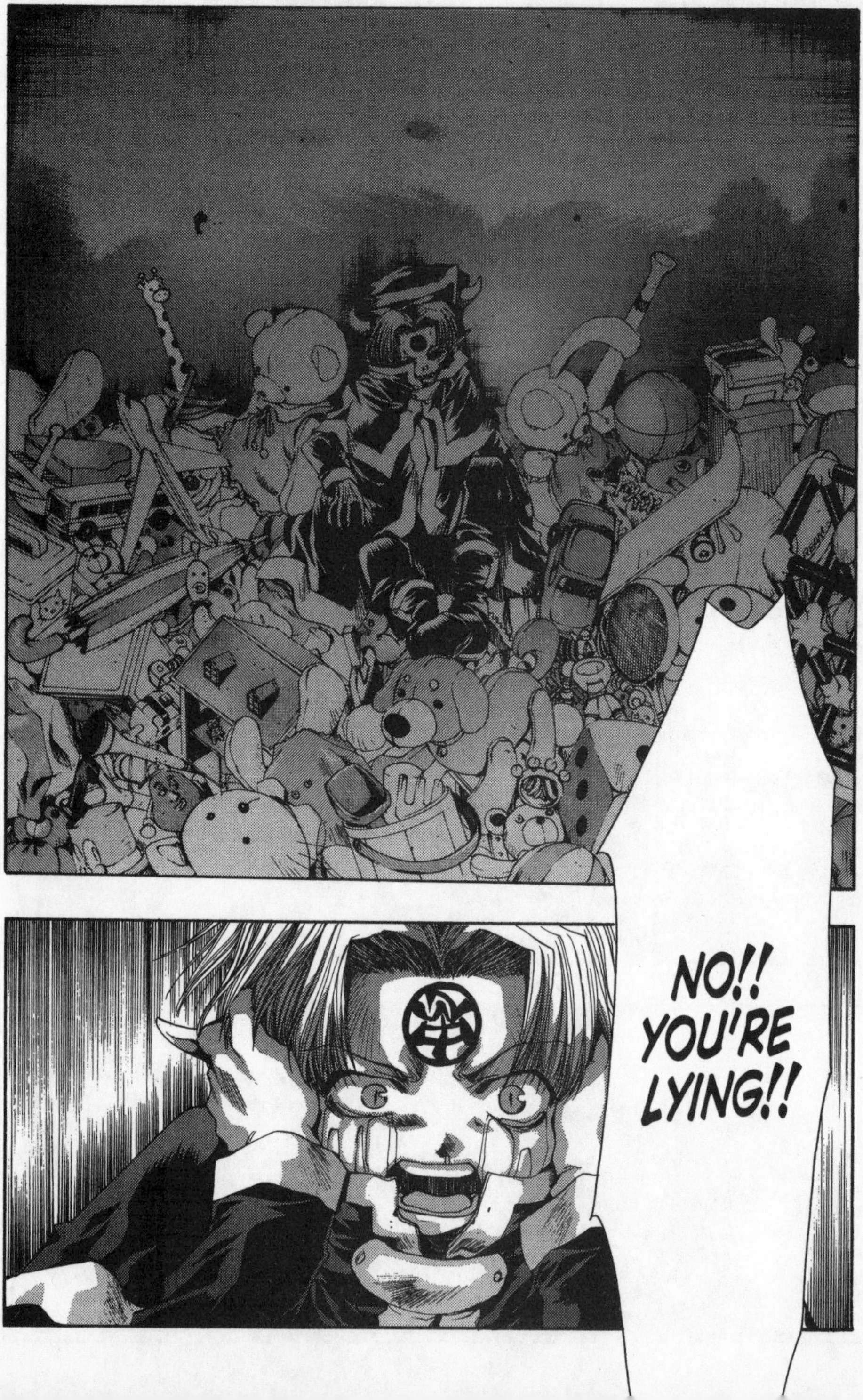
NO!! YOU'RE LYING!!

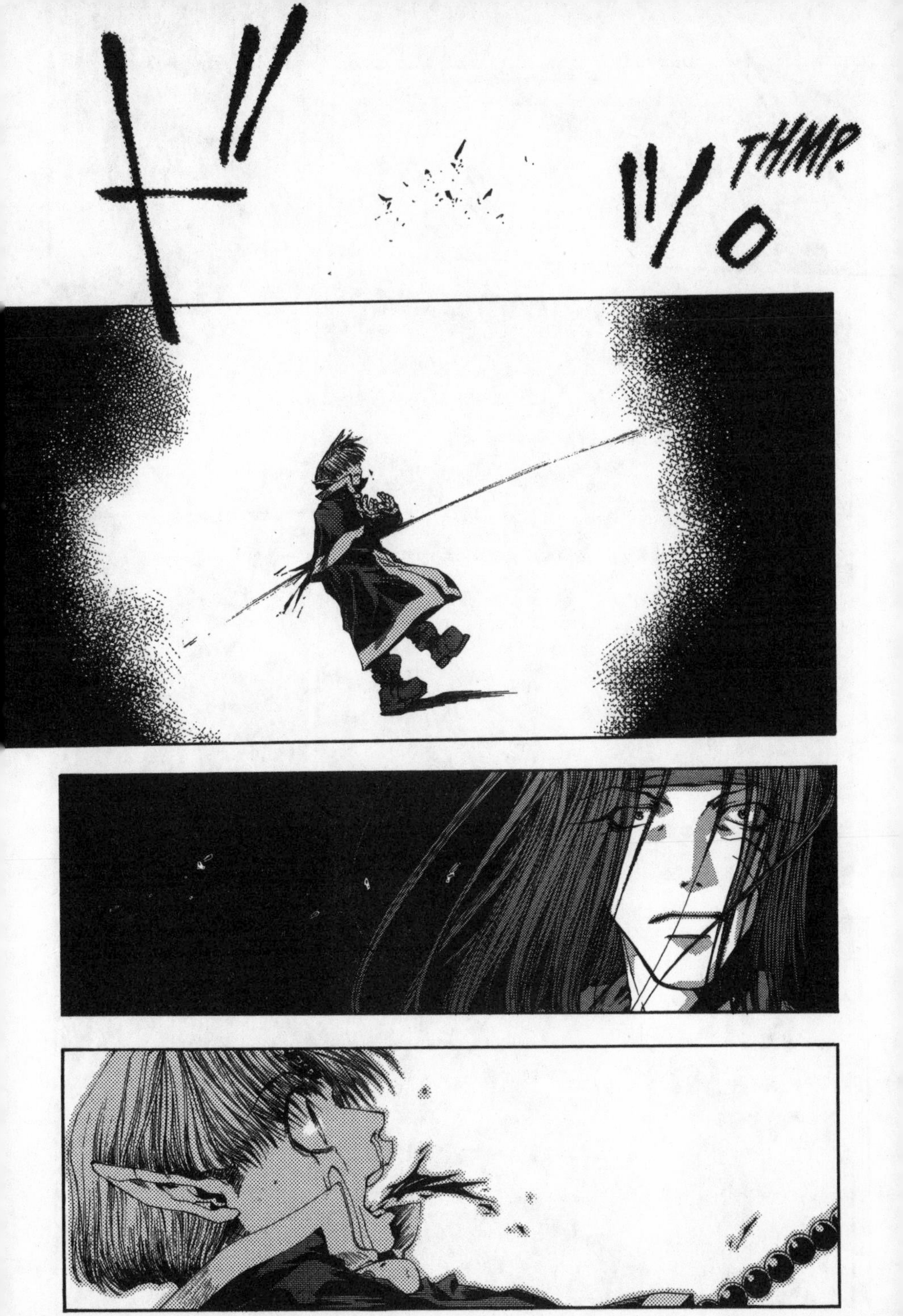
THMP.

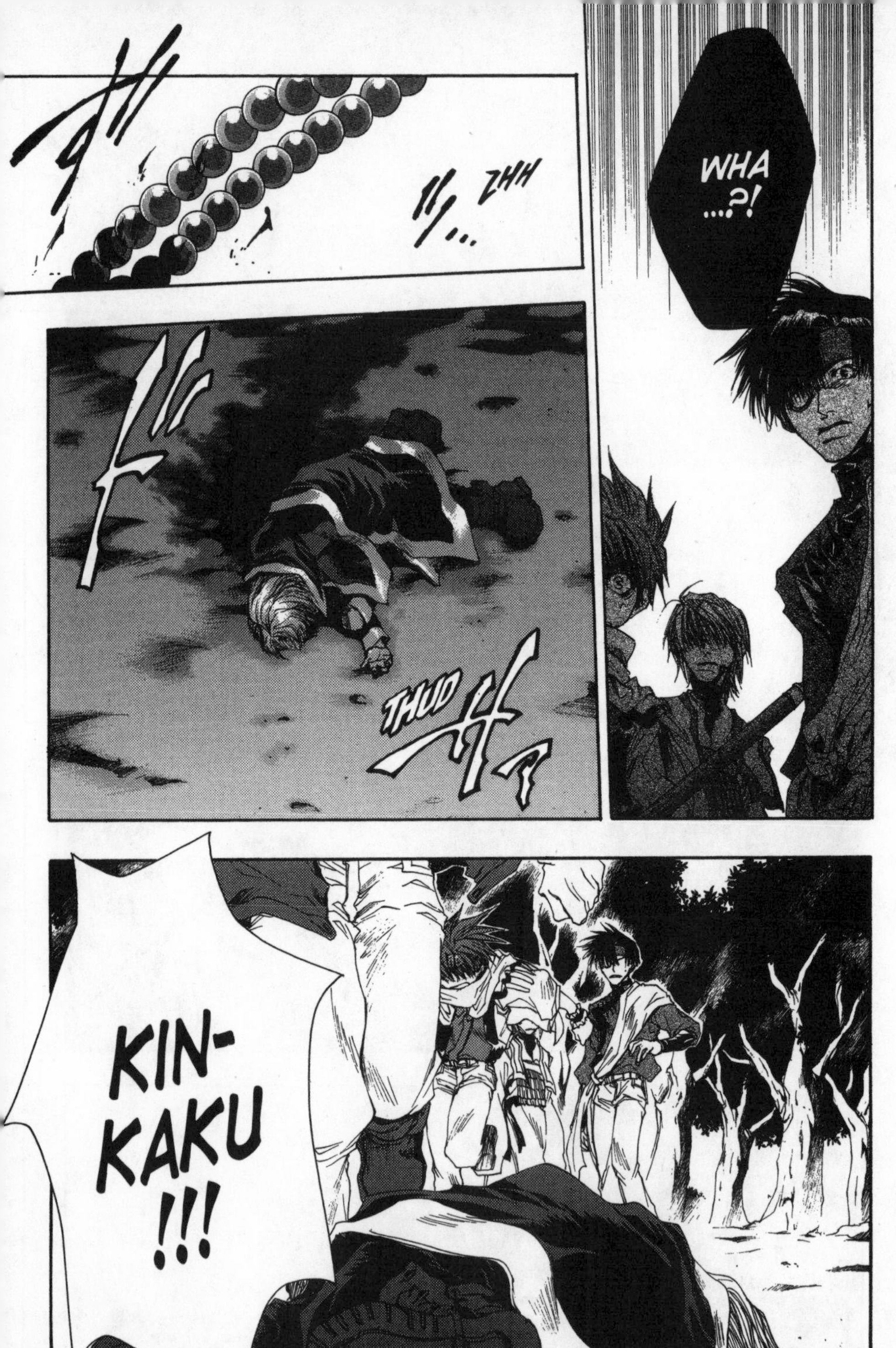
WHA ...?!
ZHH
THUD
KIN-KAKU!!!

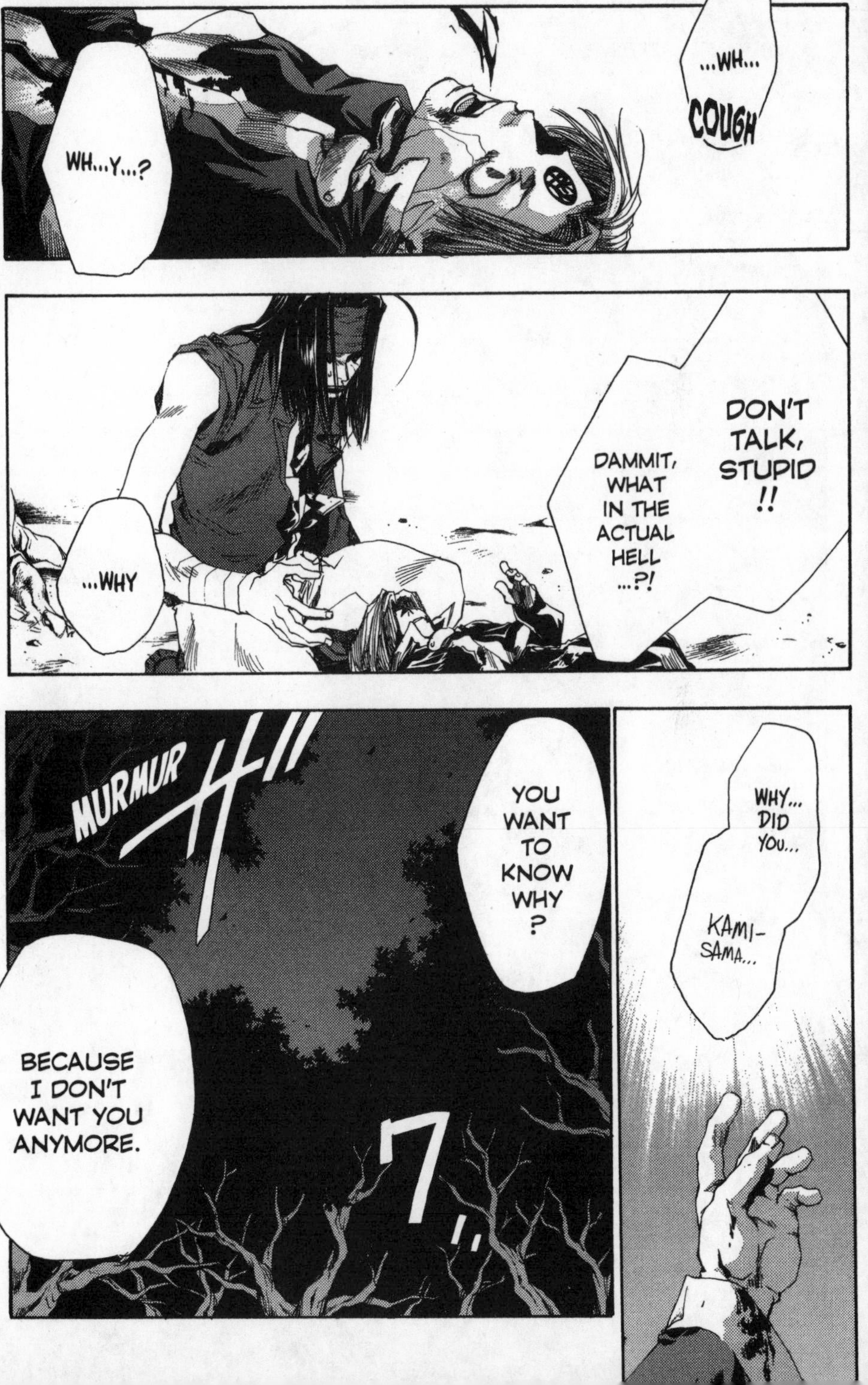
...WH...
COUGH
WH...Y...?
DON'T TALK, STUPID!!
DAMMIT, WHAT IN THE ACTUAL HELL...?!
...WHY
WHY... DID YOU...
KAMI-SAMA...
YOU WANT TO KNOW WHY?
MURMUR
BECAUSE I DON'T WANT YOU ANYMORE.

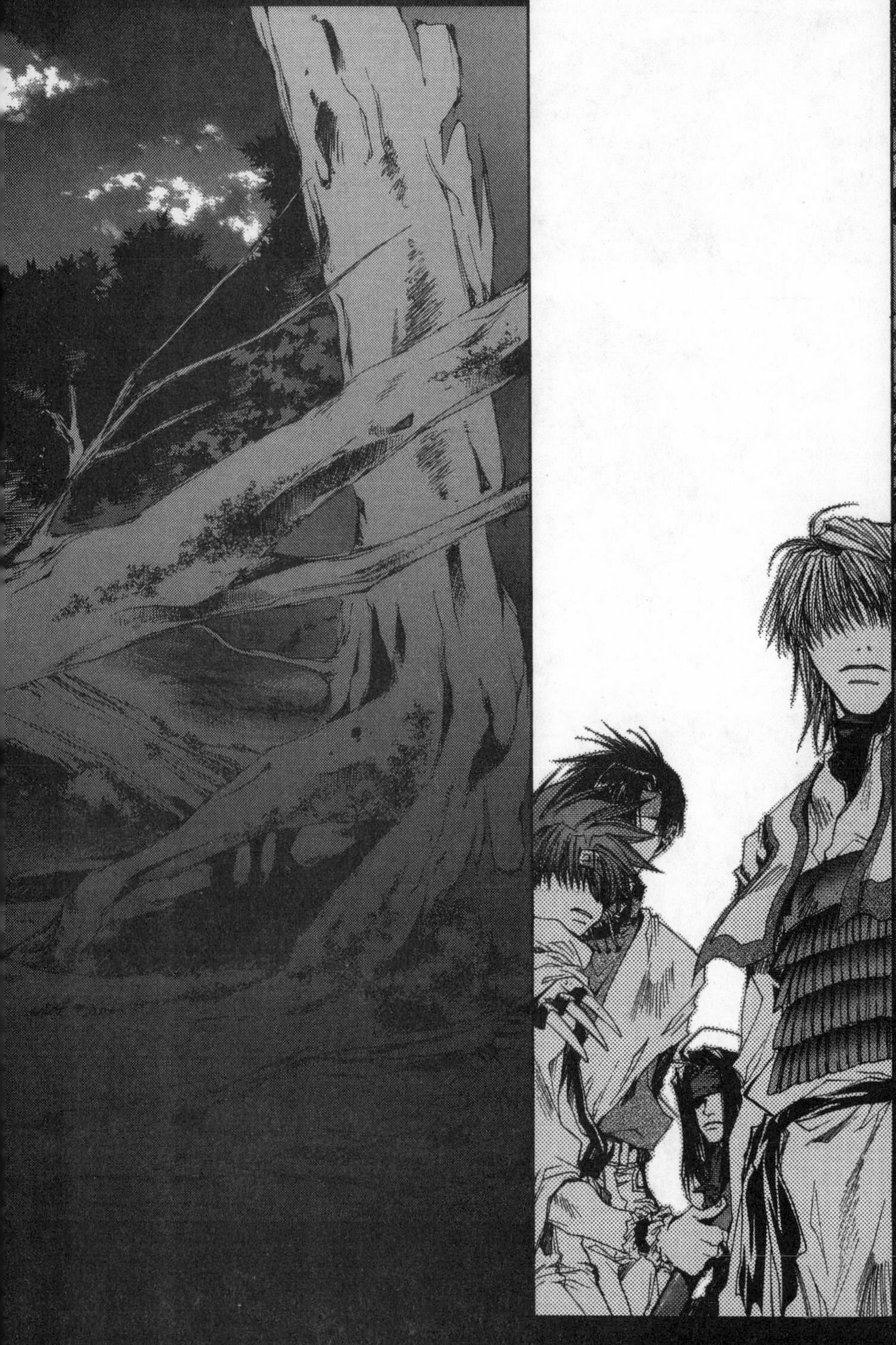

CHAPTER 41: Farewell

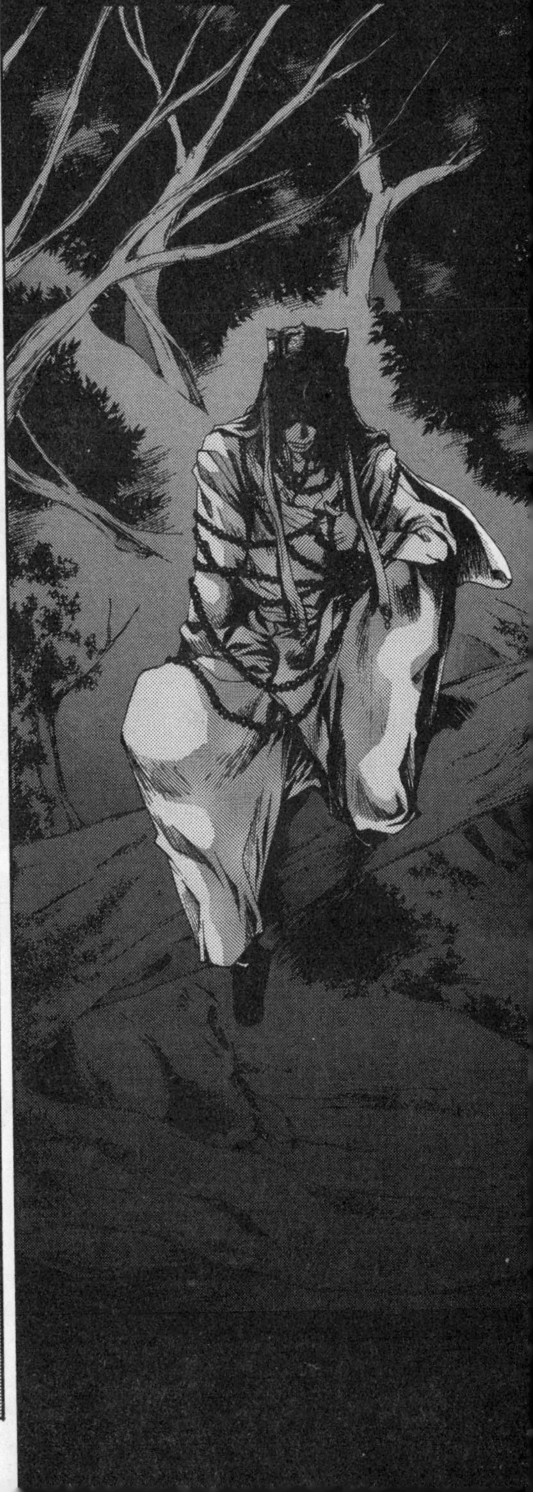

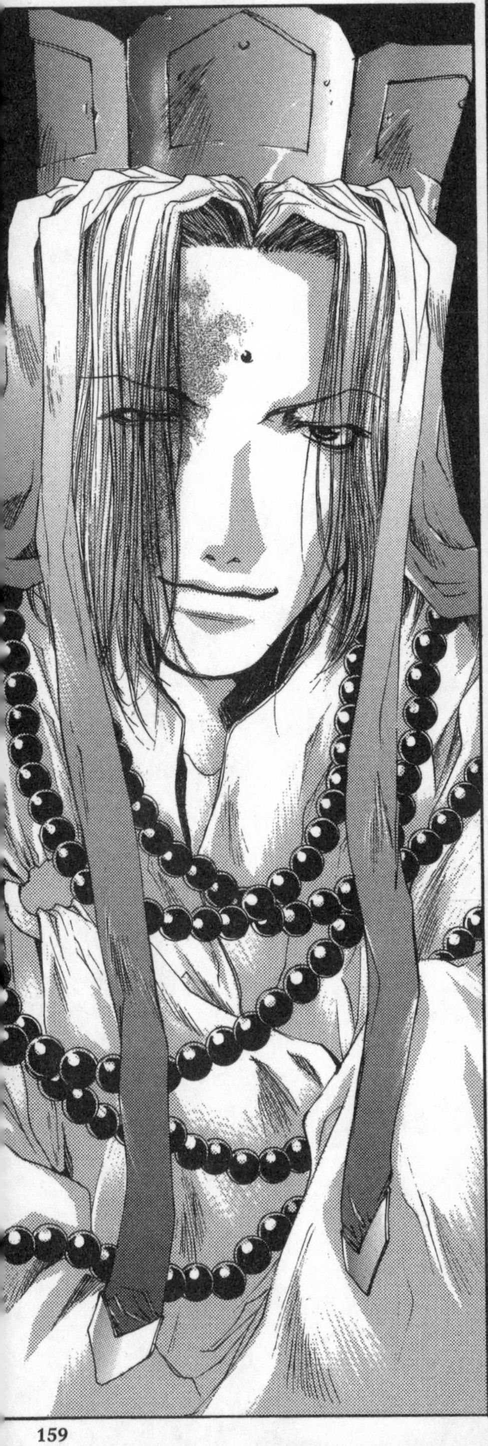

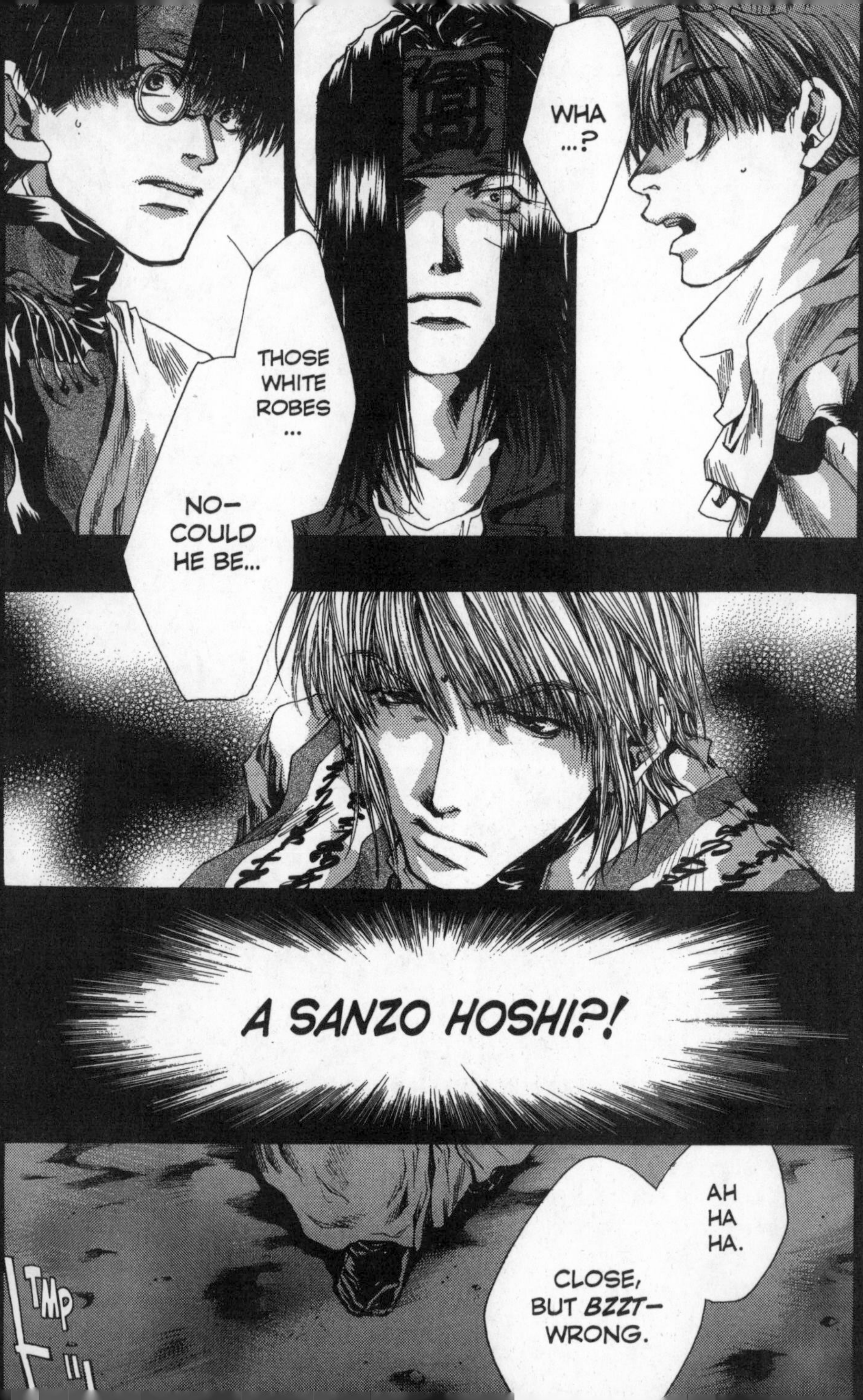

WHA ...?
THOSE WHITE ROBES ...
NO— COULD HE BE...
A SANZO HOSHI?!
AH HA HA.
CLOSE, BUT *BZZT*— WRONG.
TMP

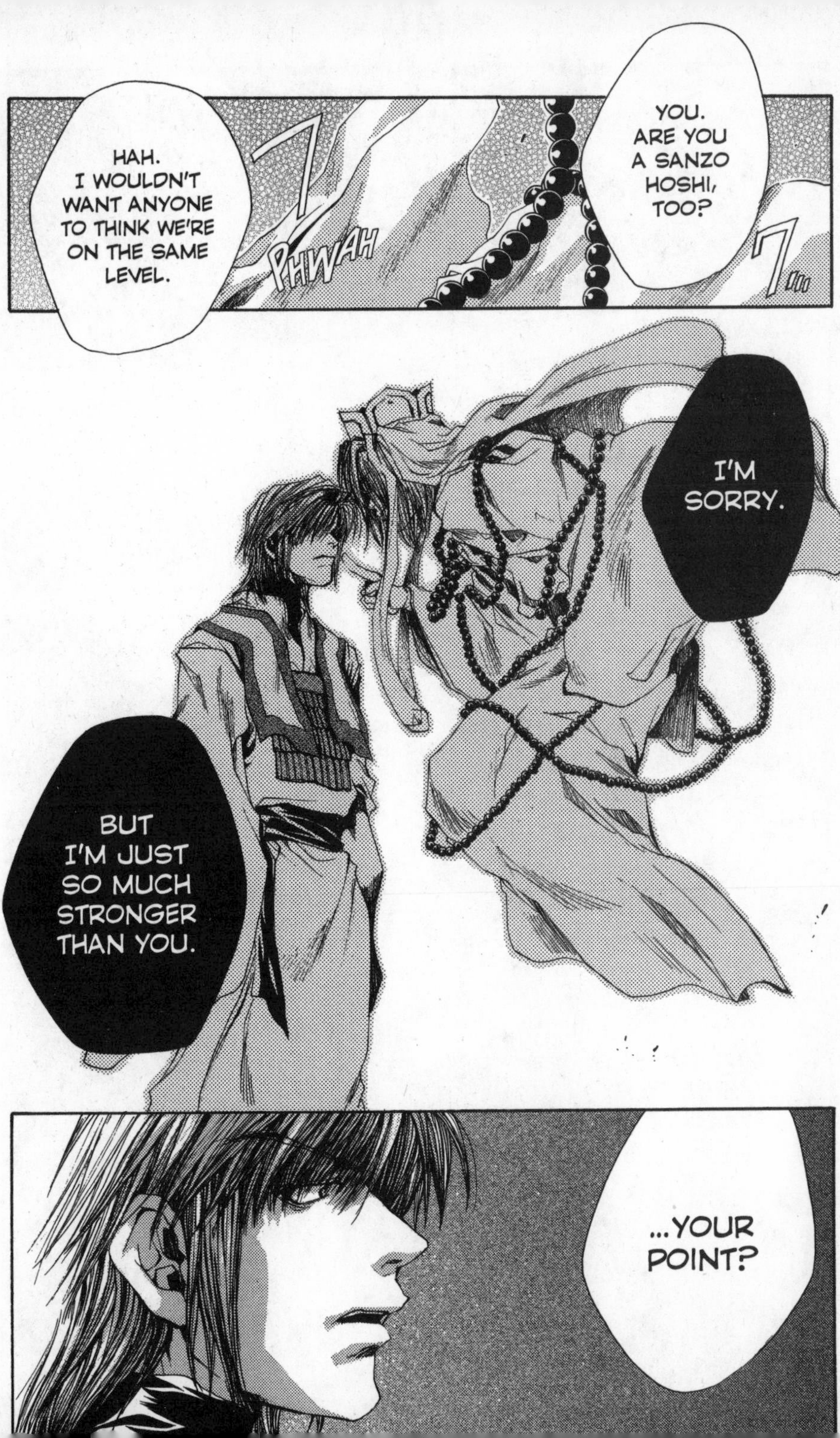
YOU. ARE YOU A SANZO HOSHI, TOO?
PHWAH
HAH. I WOULDN'T WANT ANYONE TO THINK WE'RE ON THE SAME LEVEL.
I'M SORRY.
BUT I'M JUST SO MUCH STRONGER THAN YOU.
...YOUR POINT?

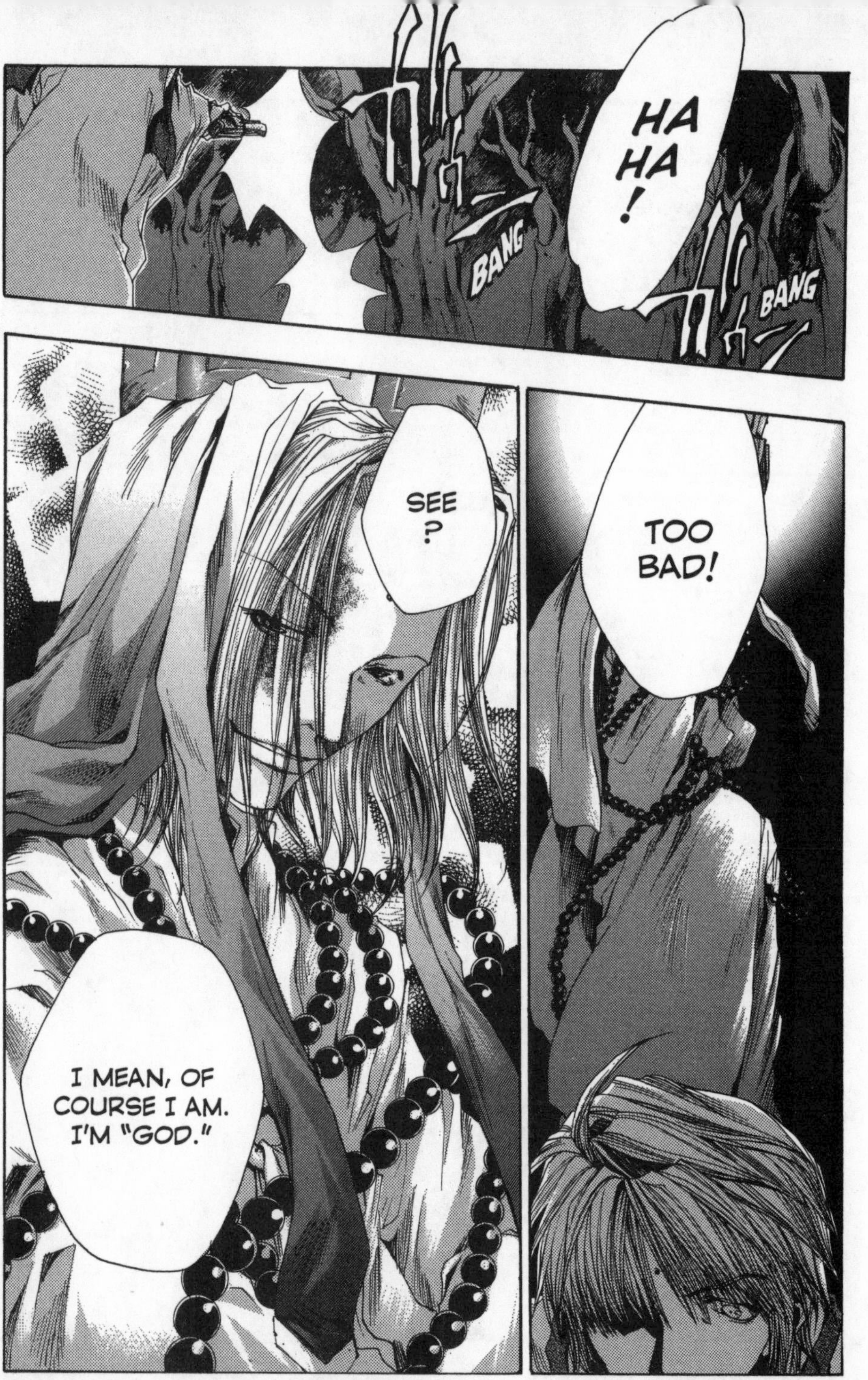
HA HA!
BANG
BANG
TOO BAD!
SEE?
I MEAN, OF COURSE I AM. I'M "GOD."

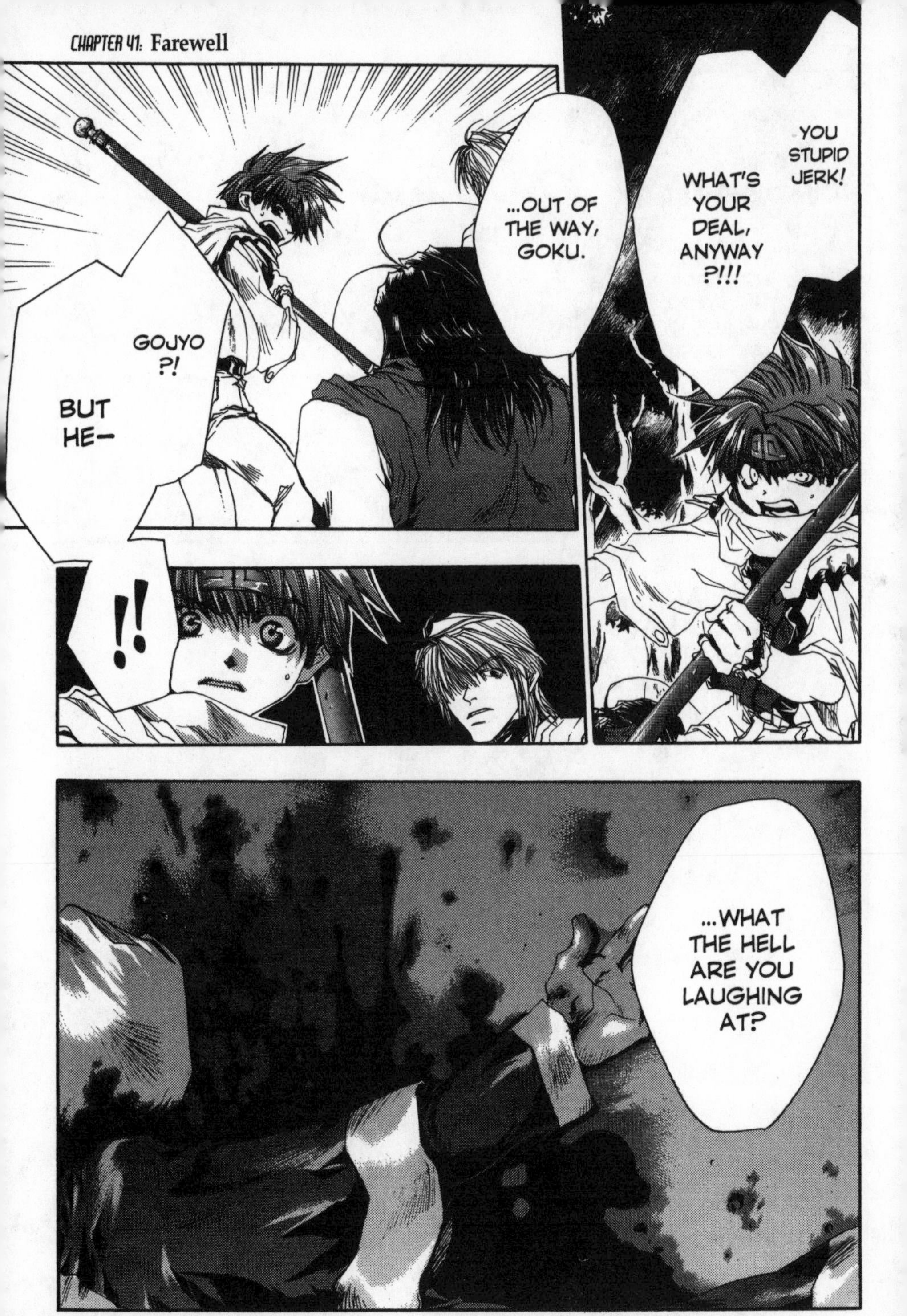
YOU STUPID JERK!
WHAT'S YOUR DEAL, ANYWAY ?!!!
...OUT OF THE WAY, GOKU.
GOJYO ?!
BUT HE—
!!
...WHAT THE HELL ARE YOU LAUGHING AT?

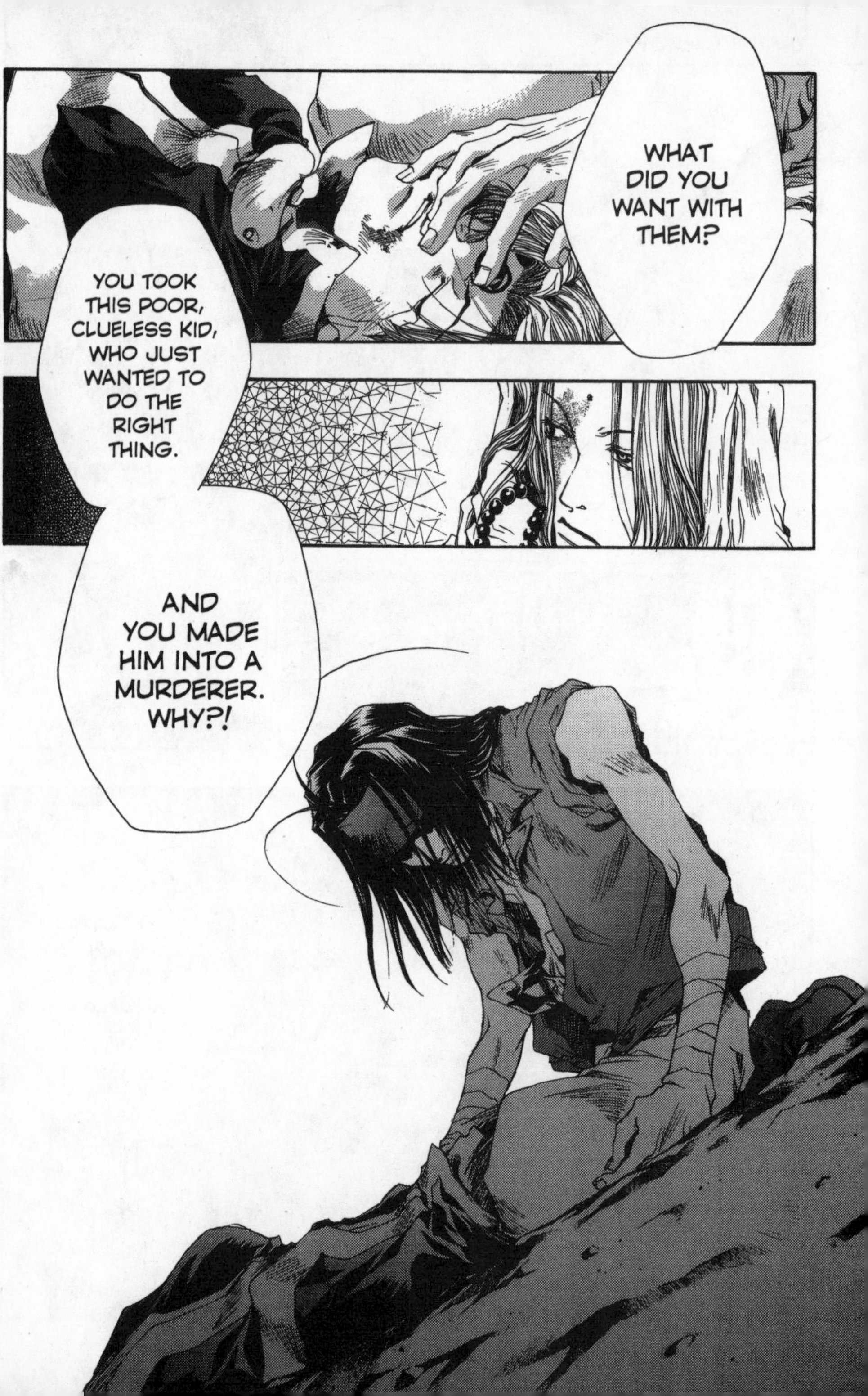
WHAT DID YOU WANT WITH THEM?
YOU TOOK THIS POOR, CLUELESS KID, WHO JUST WANTED TO DO THE RIGHT THING.
AND YOU MADE HIM INTO A MURDERER. WHY?!

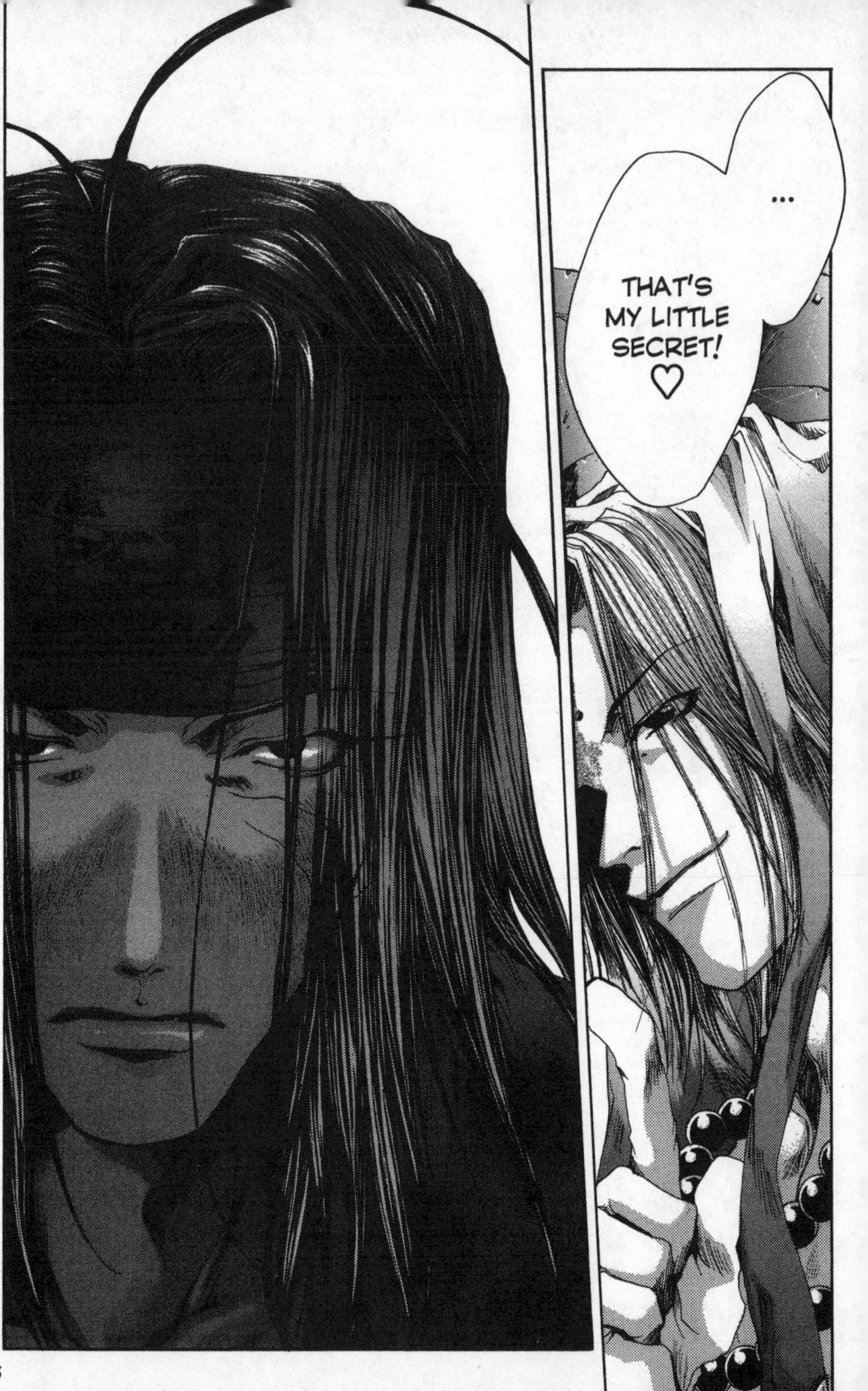
...
THAT'S MY LITTLE SECRET! ♡

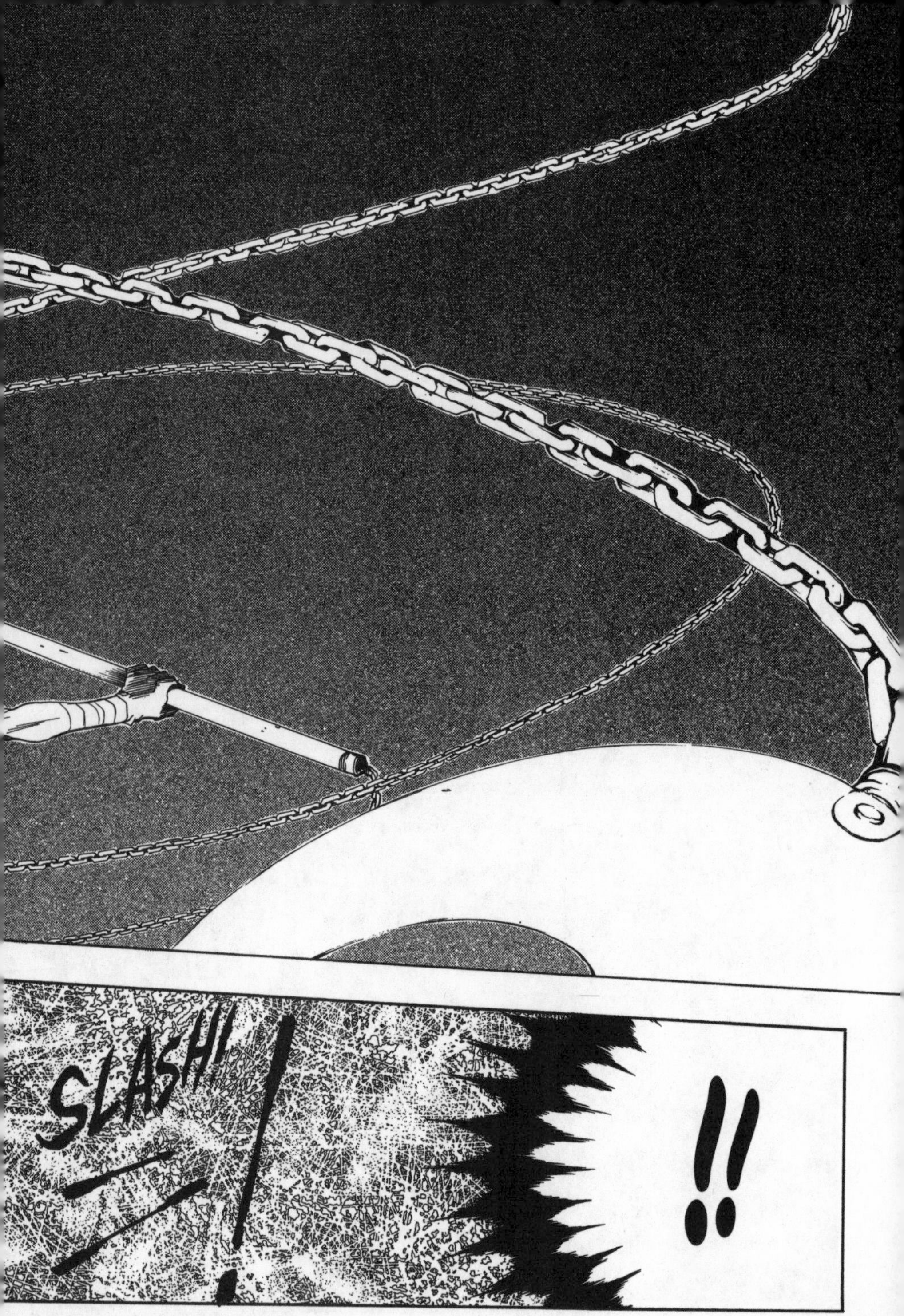
SLASH!
!!

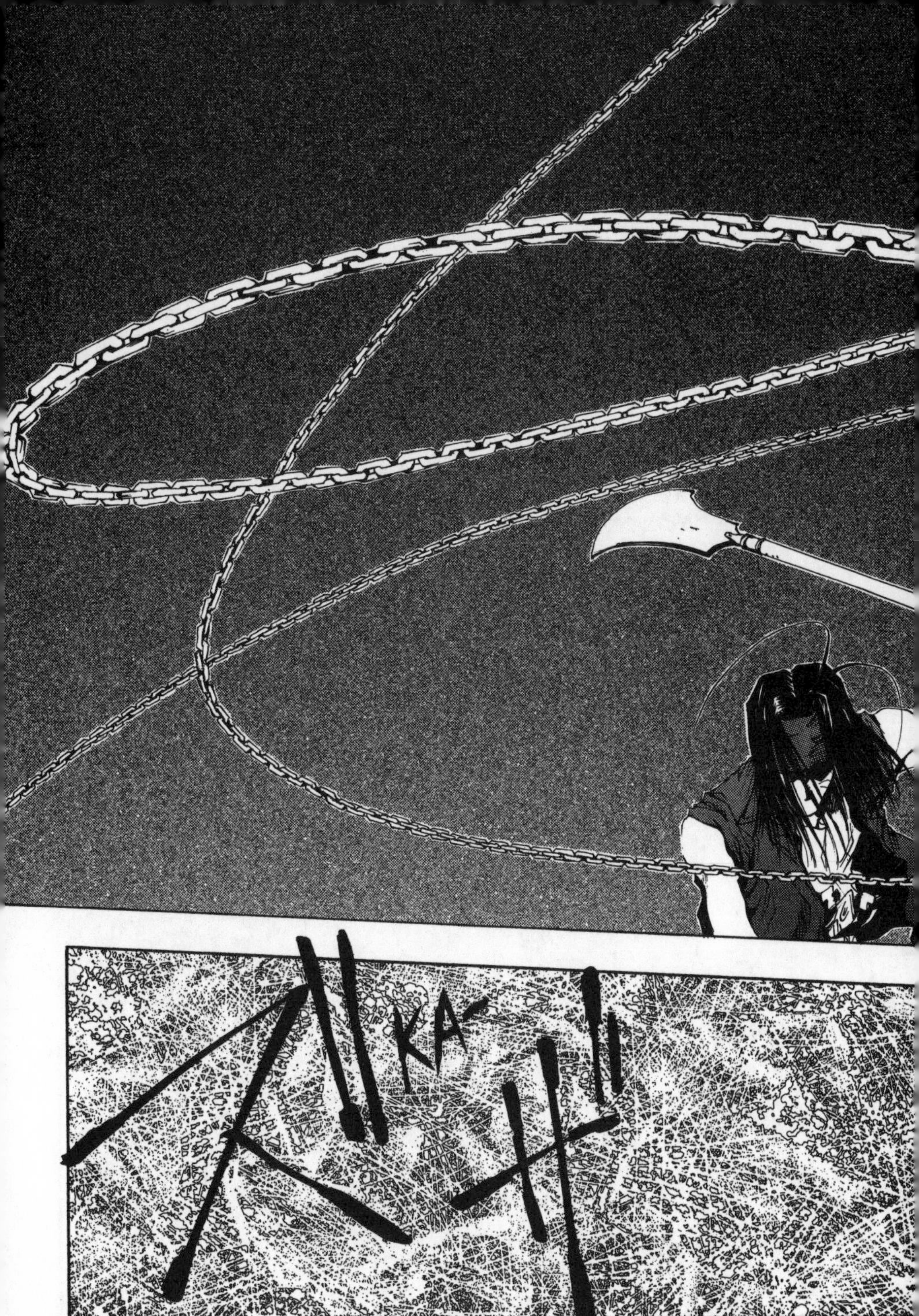
KA-

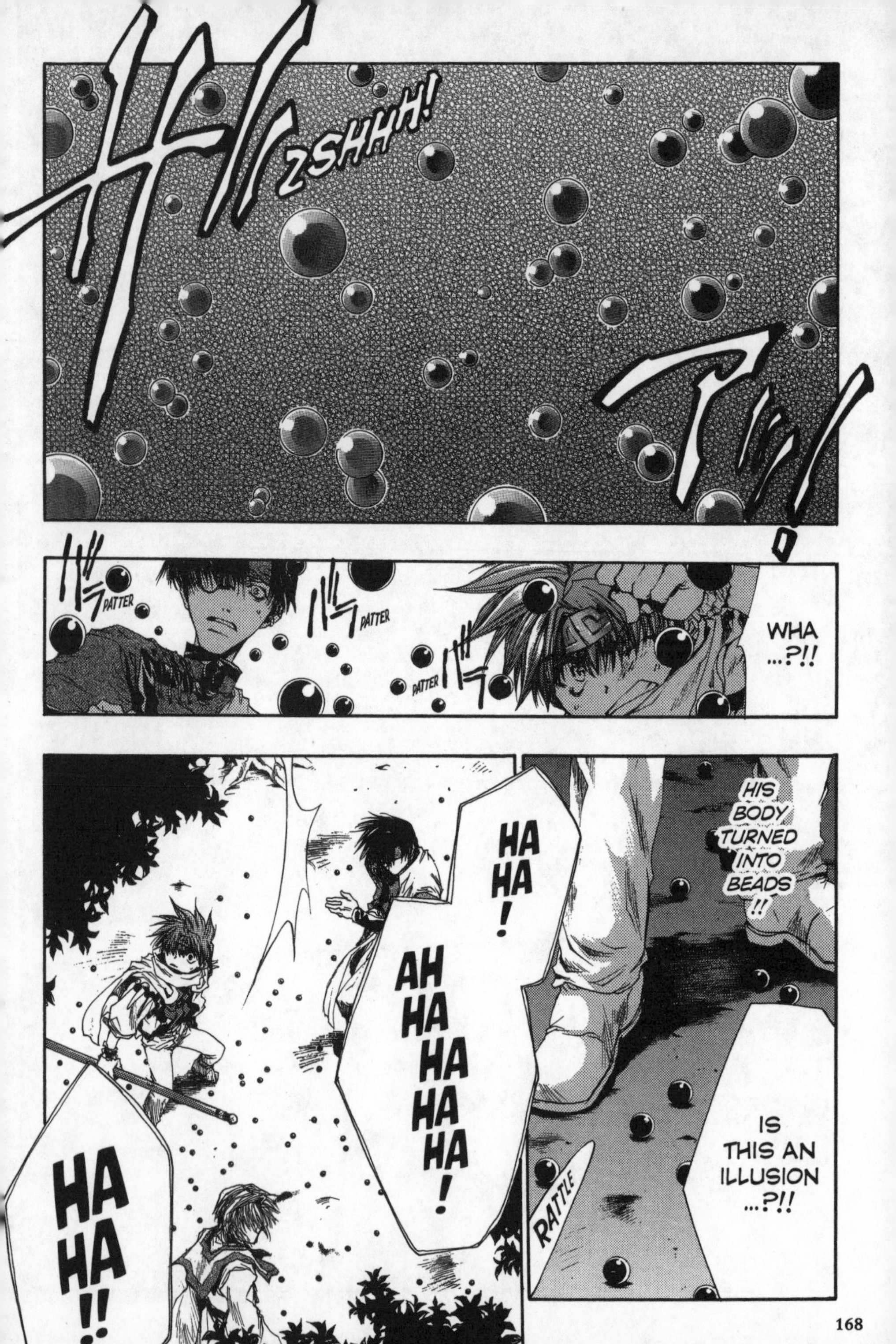
ZSHHH!
WHA ...?!!
PATTER
PATTER
PATTER
HIS BODY TURNED INTO BEADS !!
IS THIS AN ILLUSION ...?!!
RATTLE
HA HA!
AH HA HA HA HA HA!
HA HA!!

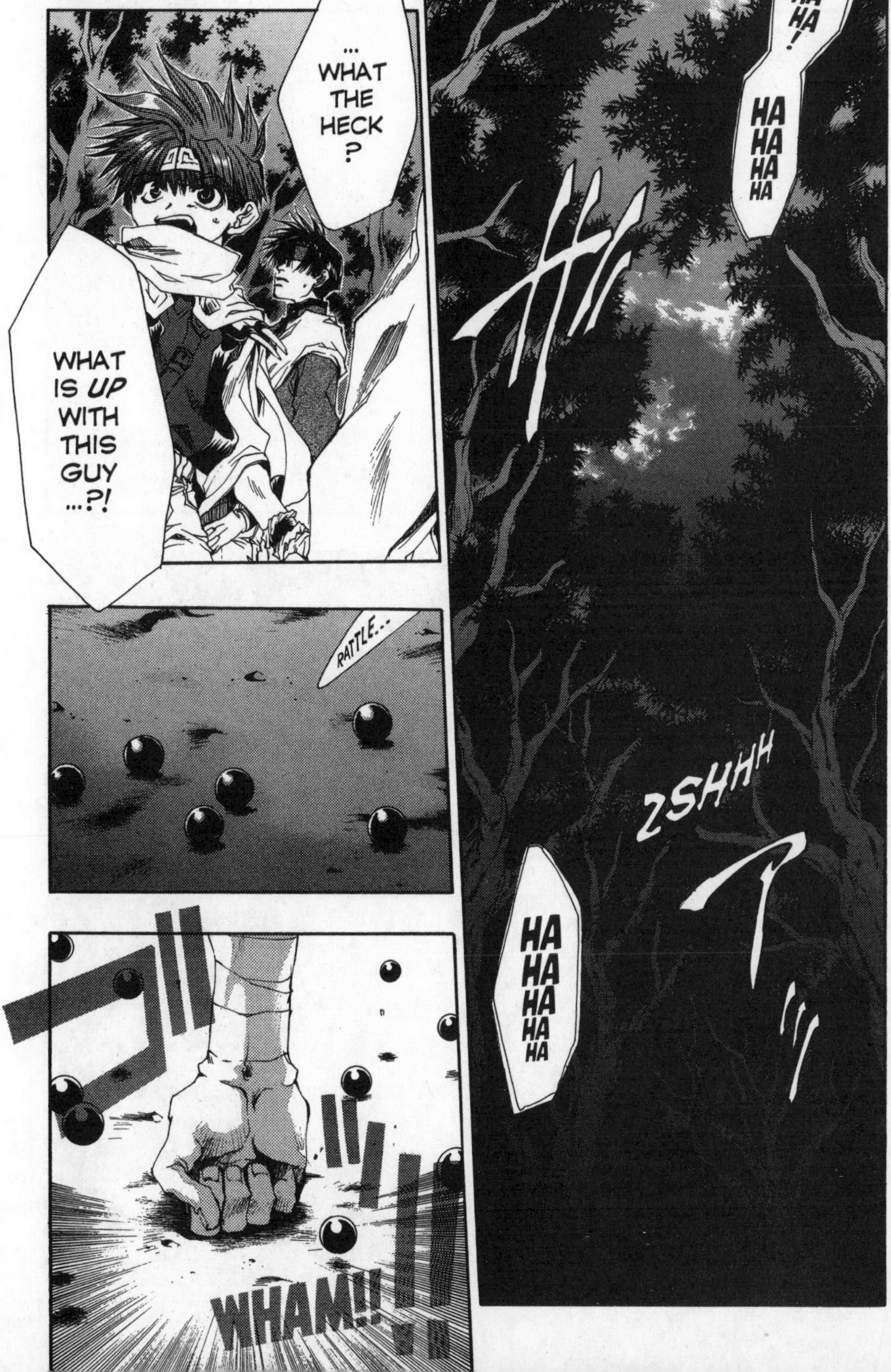
HA HA HA!
HA HA HA HA HA
ZSHHH
HA HA HA HA HA HA
... WHAT THE HECK?
WHAT IS *UP* WITH THIS GUY ...?!
RATTLE...
WHAM!!

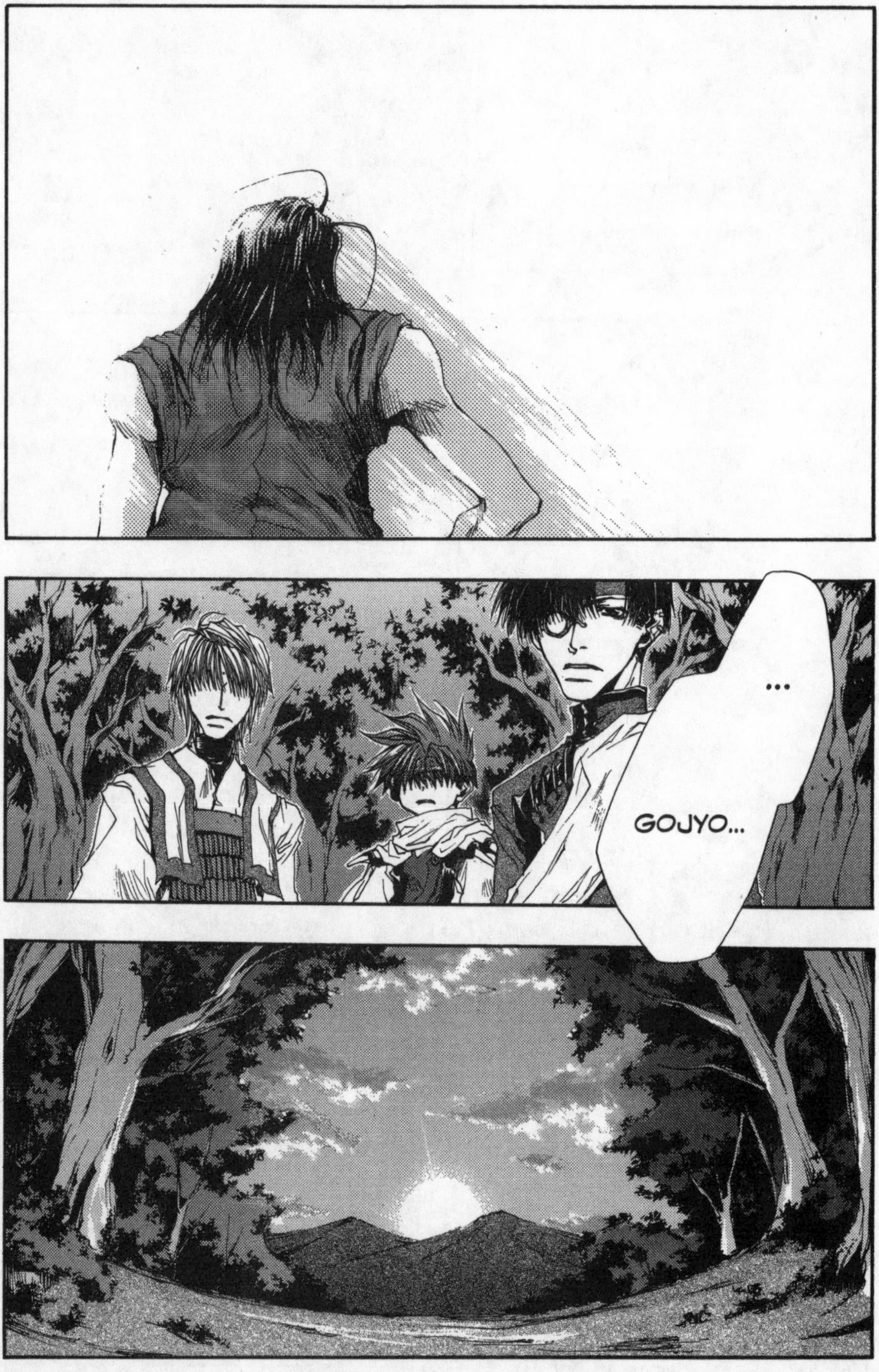
...
GOJYO...

CHAPTER 41: Farewell

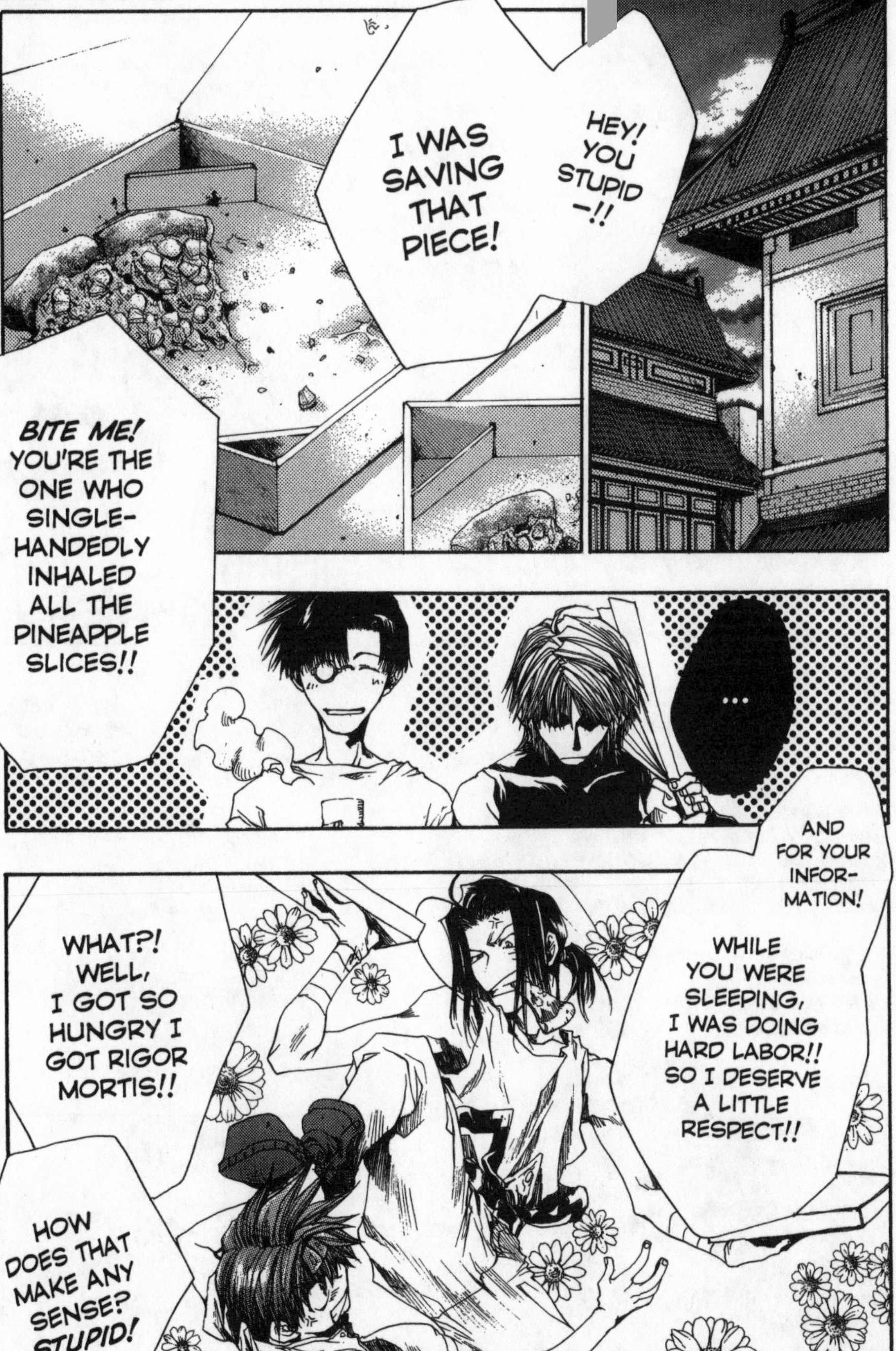
HEY! YOU STUPID—!!
I WAS SAVING THAT PIECE!
BITE ME! YOU'RE THE ONE WHO SINGLE-HANDEDLY INHALED ALL THE PINEAPPLE SLICES!!
...
AND FOR YOUR INFORMATION!
WHILE YOU WERE SLEEPING, I WAS DOING HARD LABOR!! SO I DESERVE A LITTLE RESPECT!!
WHAT?! WELL, I GOT SO HUNGRY I GOT RIGOR MORTIS!!
HOW DOES THAT MAKE ANY SENSE? STUPID!

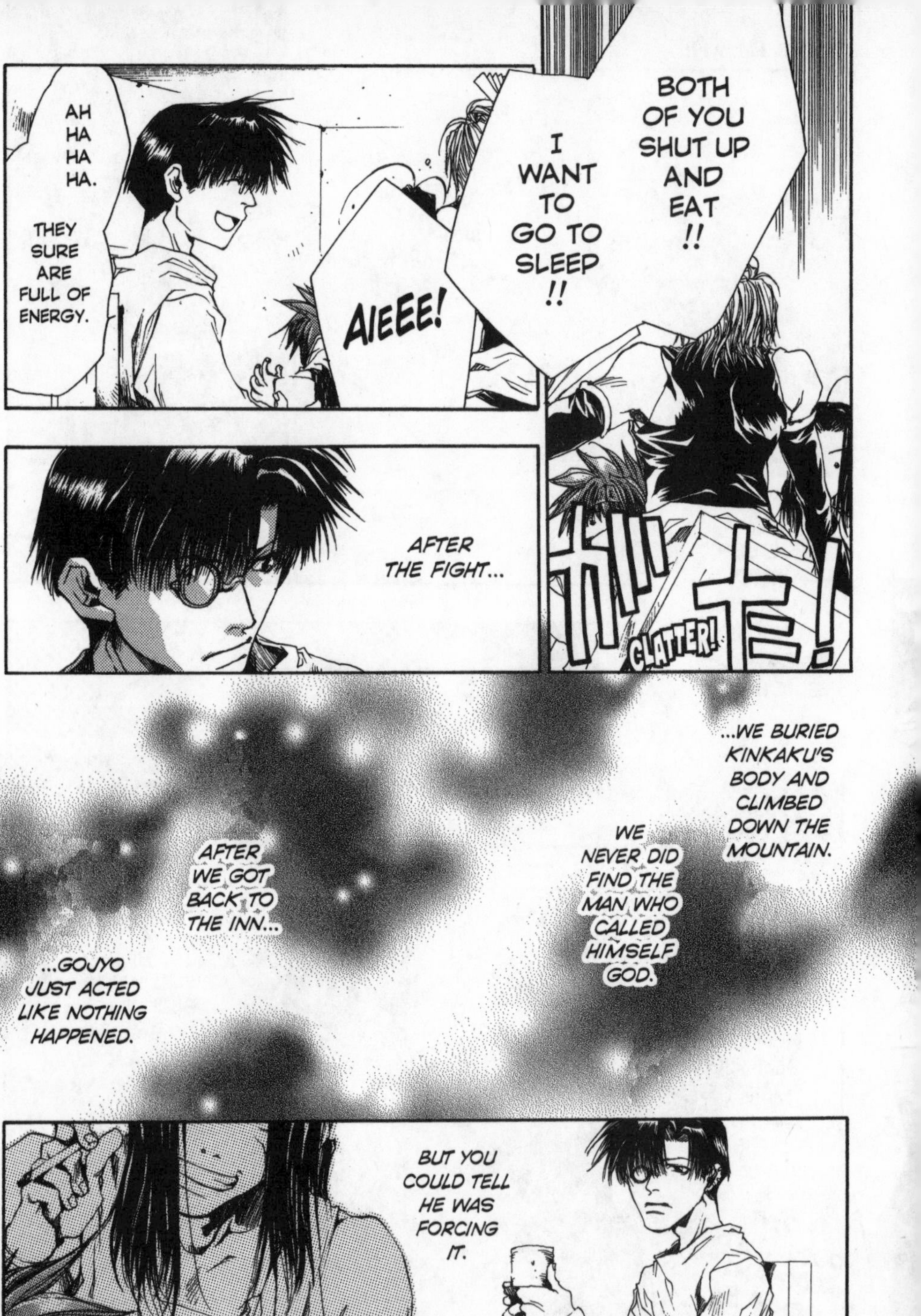
BOTH OF YOU SHUT UP AND EAT !!
CLATTER!
I WANT TO GO TO SLEEP !!
AIEEE!
AH HA HA HA.
THEY SURE ARE FULL OF ENERGY.
AFTER THE FIGHT...
...WE BURIED KINKAKU'S BODY AND CLIMBED DOWN THE MOUNTAIN.
WE NEVER DID FIND THE MAN WHO CALLED HIMSELF GOD.
AFTER WE GOT BACK TO THE INN...
...GOJYO JUST ACTED LIKE NOTHING HAPPENED.
BUT YOU COULD TELL HE WAS FORCING IT.

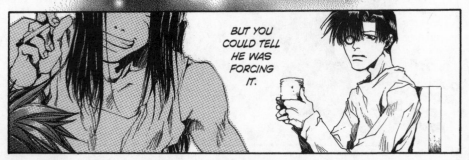

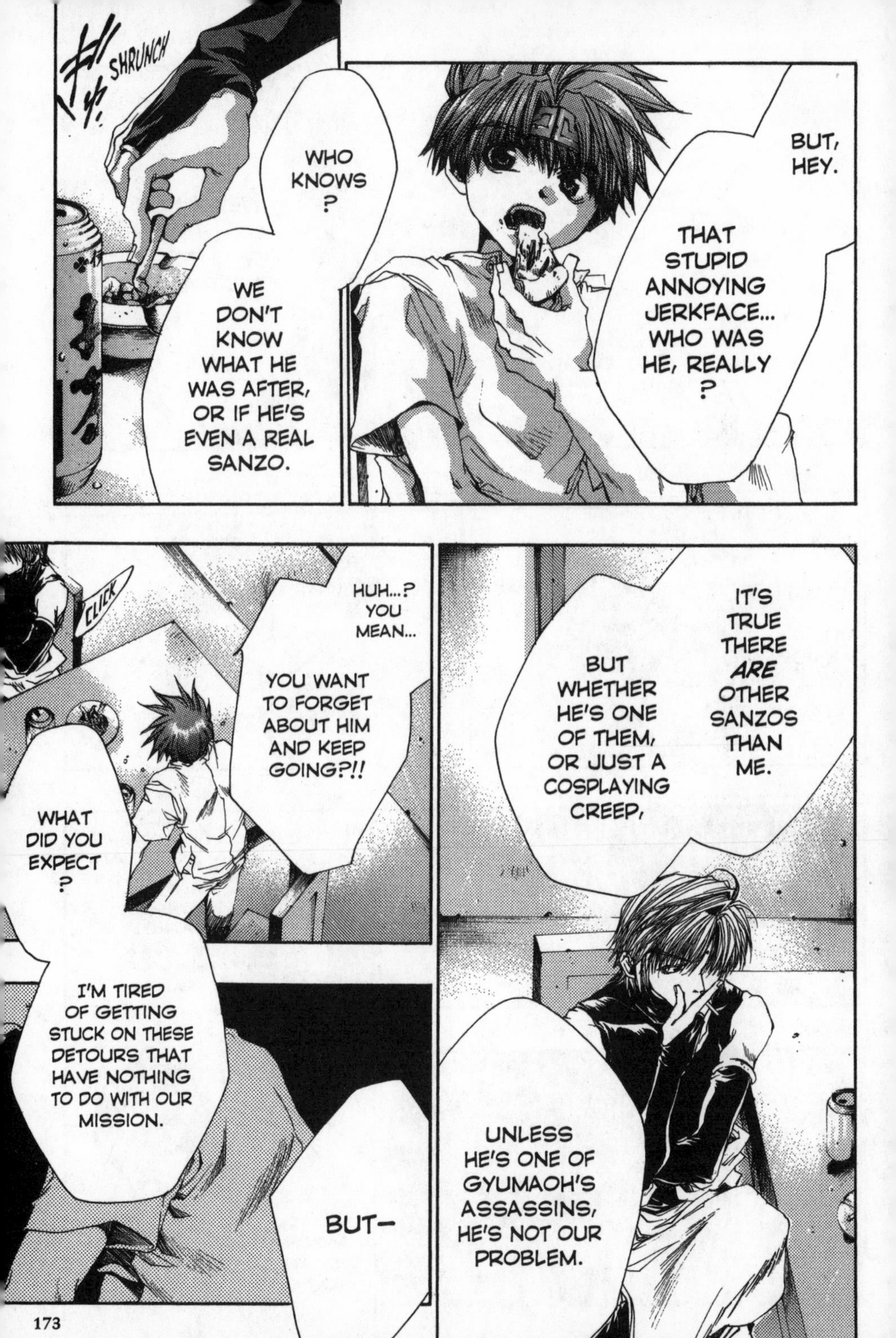
BUT, HEY.
THAT STUPID ANNOYING JERKFACE... WHO WAS HE, REALLY?
SHRUNCH
WHO KNOWS?
WE DON'T KNOW WHAT HE WAS AFTER, OR IF HE'S EVEN A REAL SANZO.
IT'S TRUE THERE *ARE* OTHER SANZOS THAN ME.
BUT WHETHER HE'S ONE OF THEM, OR JUST A COSPLAYING CREEP,
UNLESS HE'S ONE OF GYUMAOH'S ASSASSINS, HE'S NOT OUR PROBLEM.
HUH...? YOU MEAN...
YOU WANT TO FORGET ABOUT HIM AND KEEP GOING?!!
CLICK
WHAT DID YOU EXPECT?
I'M TIRED OF GETTING STUCK ON THESE DETOURS THAT HAVE NOTHING TO DO WITH OUR MISSION.
BUT–

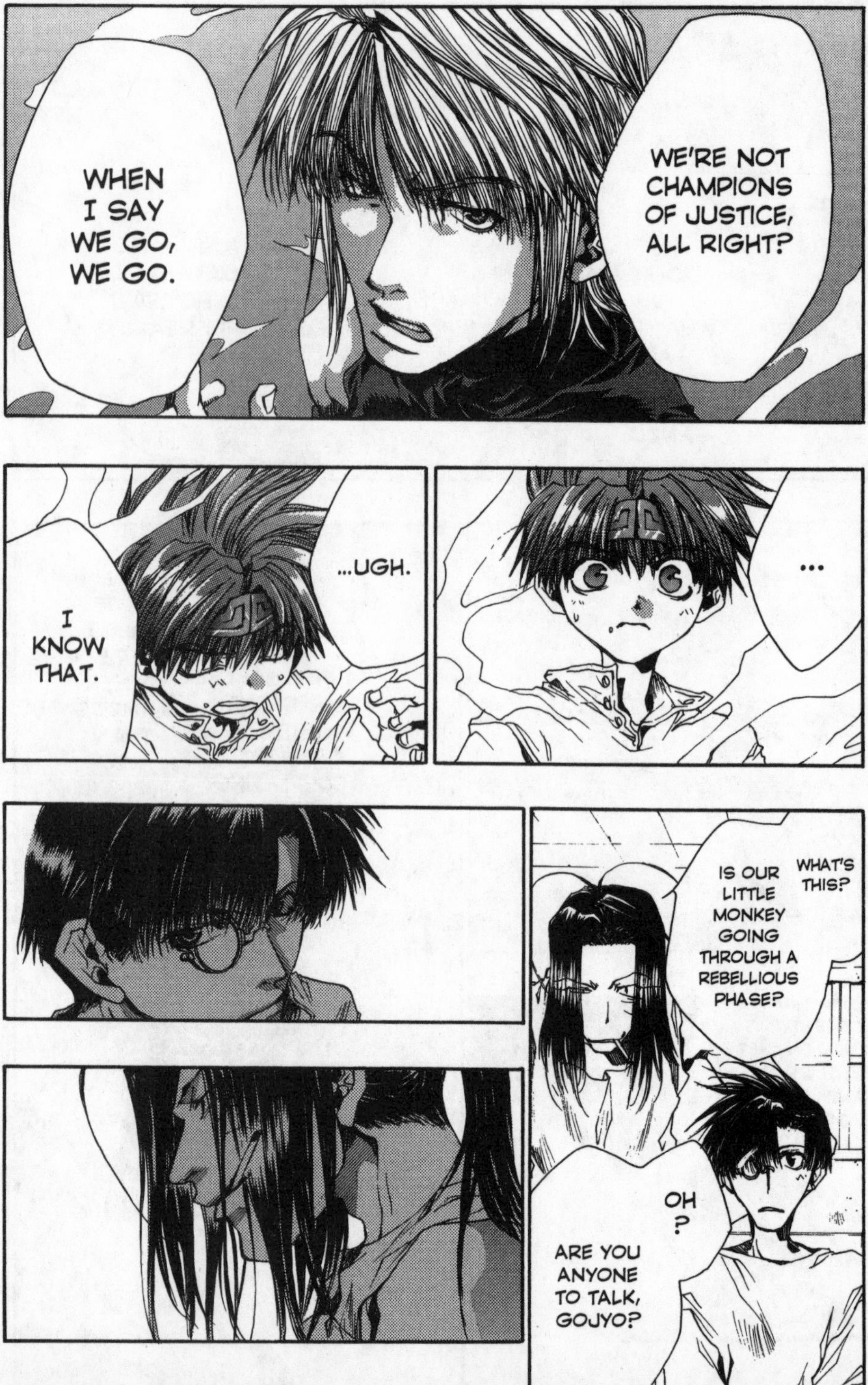
WE'RE NOT CHAMPIONS OF JUSTICE, ALL RIGHT?
WHEN I SAY WE GO, WE GO.
...
...UGH.
I KNOW THAT.
WHAT'S THIS?
IS OUR LITTLE MONKEY GOING THROUGH A REBELLIOUS PHASE?
OH?
ARE YOU ANYONE TO TALK, GOJYO?

CHAPTER 41: Farewell

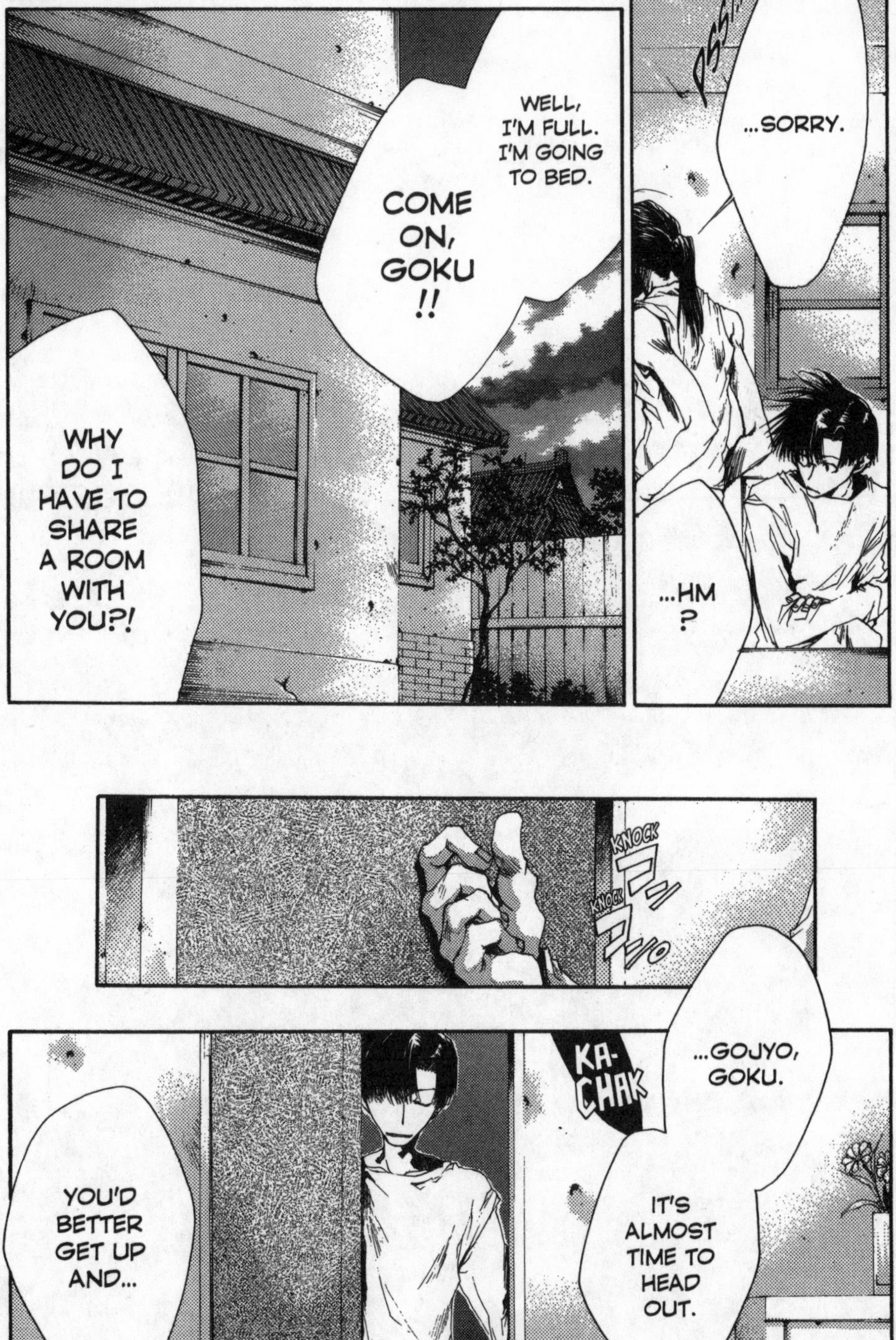

PSST...
...SORRY.
...HM?
WELL, I'M FULL. I'M GOING TO BED.
COME ON, GOKU!!
WHY DO I HAVE TO SHARE A ROOM WITH YOU?!
KNOCK
KNOCK
...GOJYO, GOKU.
KA-CHAK
IT'S ALMOST TIME TO HEAD OUT.
YOU'D BETTER GET UP AND...

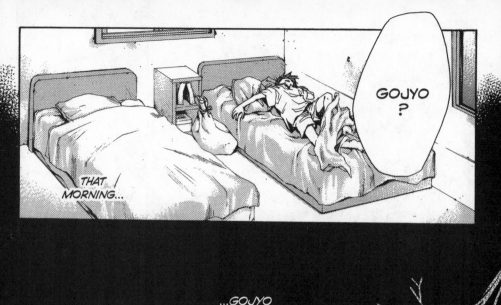

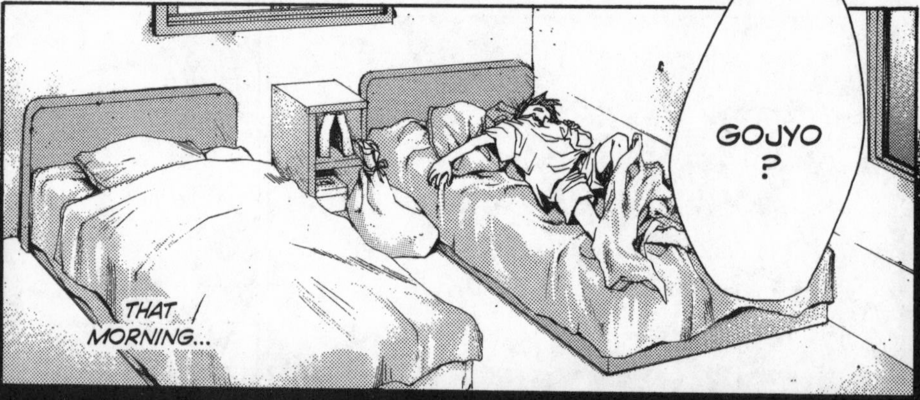
GOJYO ?
THAT MORNING...

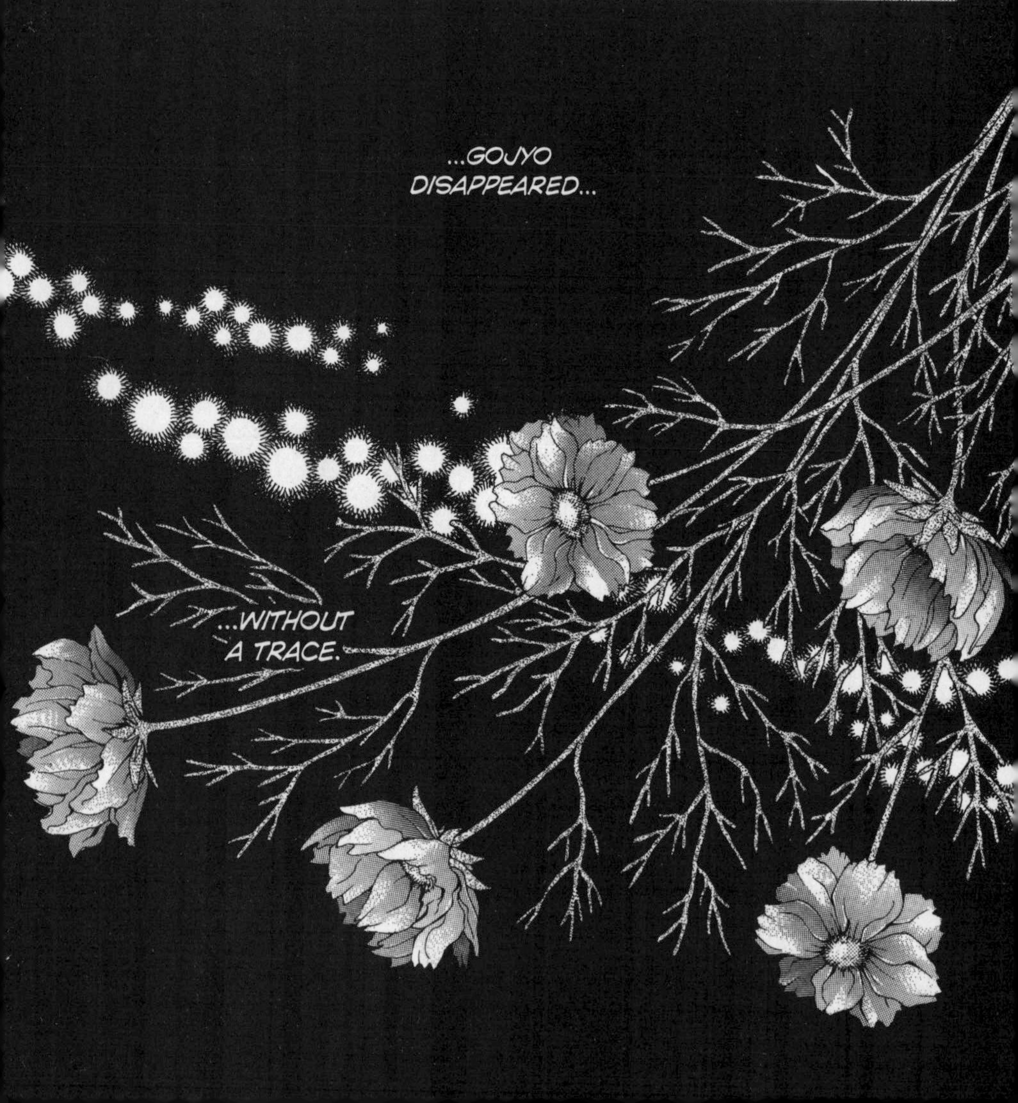
...GOJYO DISAPPEARED...
...WITHOUT A TRACE.

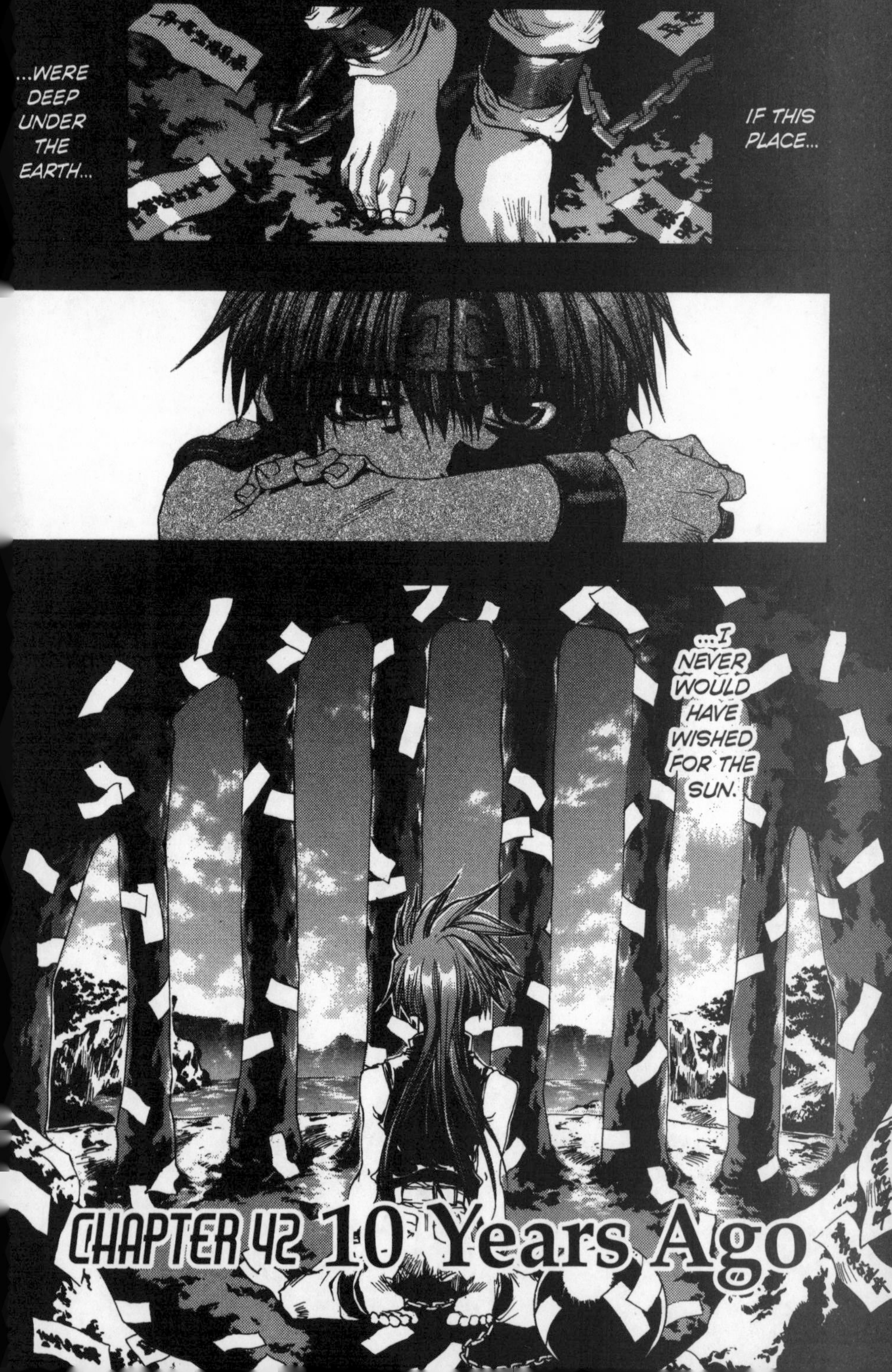
IF THIS PLACE...
...WERE DEEP UNDER THE EARTH...
...I NEVER WOULD HAVE WISHED FOR THE SUN.
CHAPTER 42 10 Years Ago

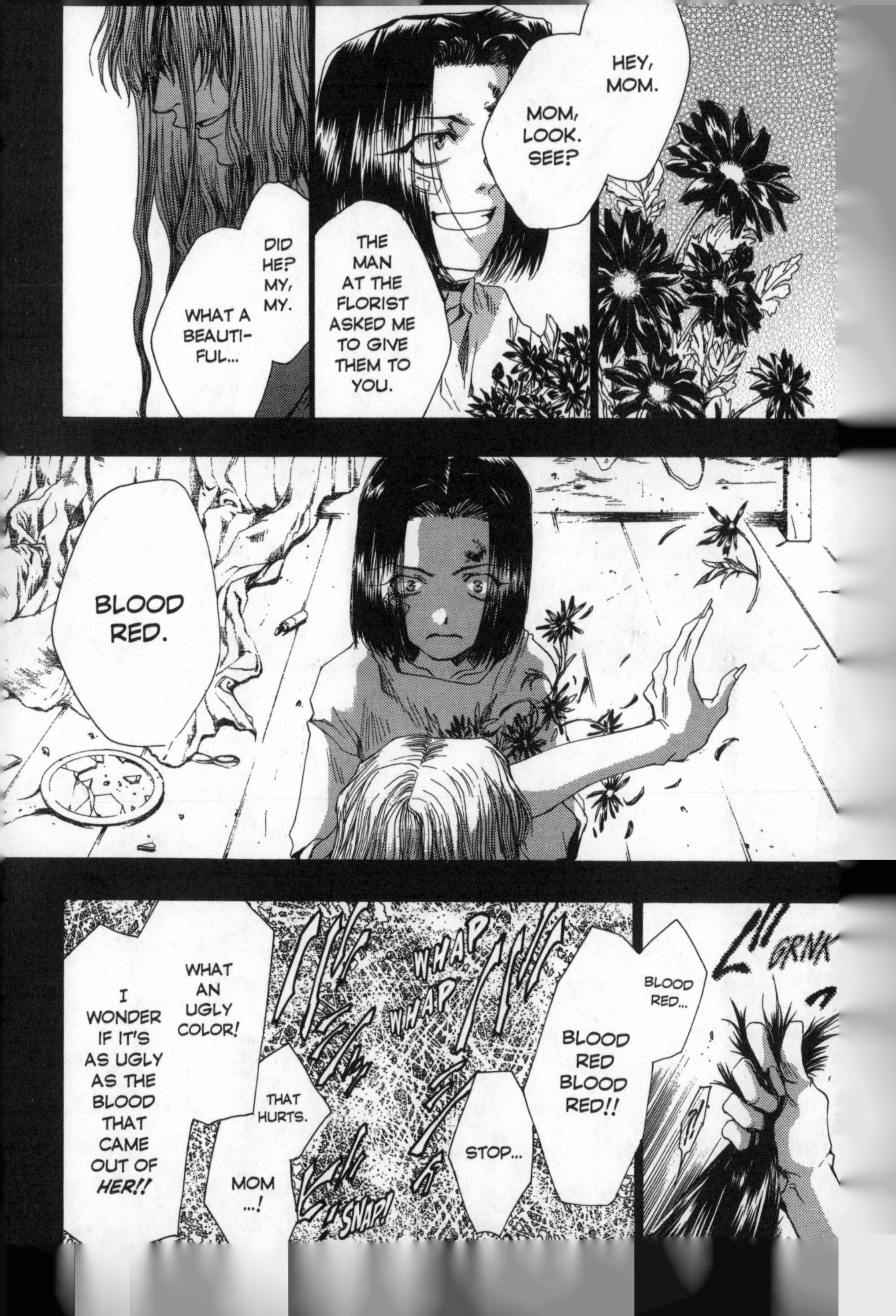
HEY, MOM.
MOM, LOOK. SEE?
THE MAN AT THE FLORIST ASKED ME TO GIVE THEM TO YOU.
DID HE? MY, MY.
WHAT A BEAUTI-FUL...
BLOOD RED.
GRNK
BLOOD RED...
BLOOD RED BLOOD RED!!
WHAP
WHAP
STOP...
WHAT AN UGLY COLOR!
THAT HURTS.
I WONDER IF IT'S AS UGLY AS THE BLOOD THAT CAME OUT OF *HER!!*
MOM ...!
SNAP!

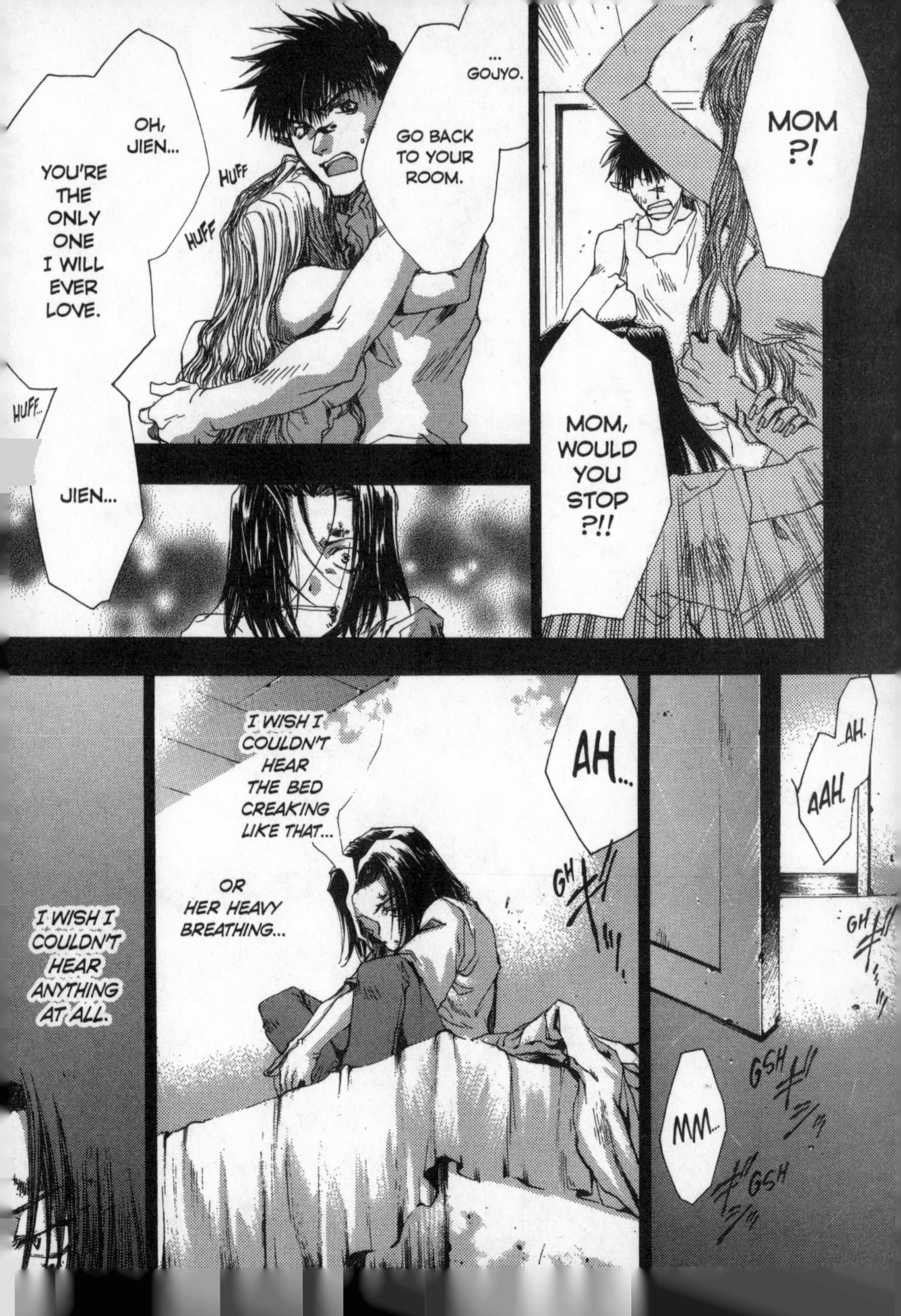
MOM ?!
MOM, WOULD YOU STOP ?!!
... GOJYO.
GO BACK TO YOUR ROOM.
HUFF
HUFF
OH, JIEN...
YOU'RE THE ONLY ONE I WILL EVER LOVE.
HUFF...
JIEN...
...AH.
AAH.
GH
GSH
MM...
GSH
AH...
GH
I WISH I COULDN'T HEAR THE BED CREAKING LIKE THAT...
OR HER HEAVY BREATHING...
I WISH I COULDN'T HEAR ANYTHING AT ALL.

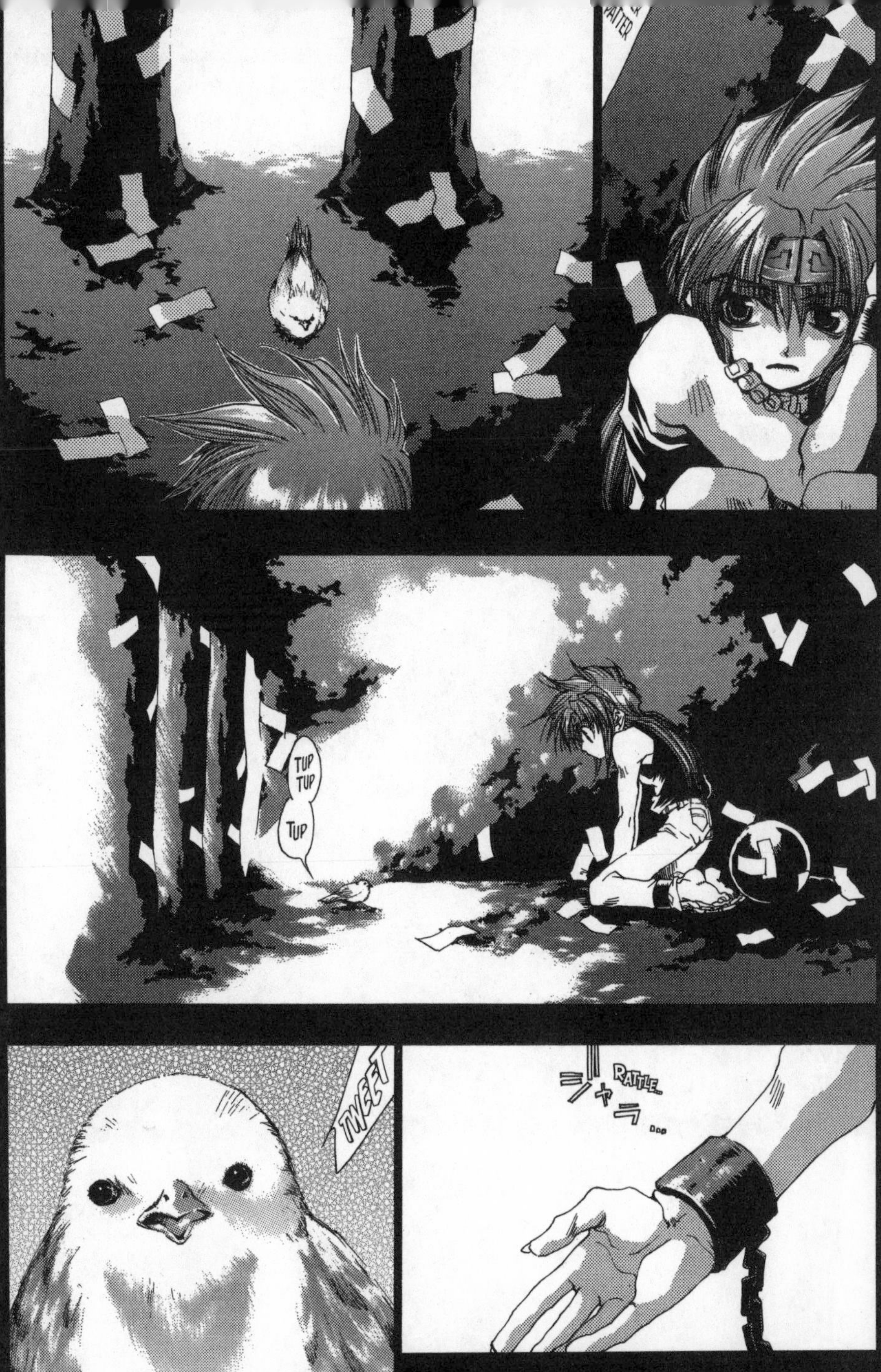
PATTER
TUP TUP
TUP
RATTLE...
TWEET

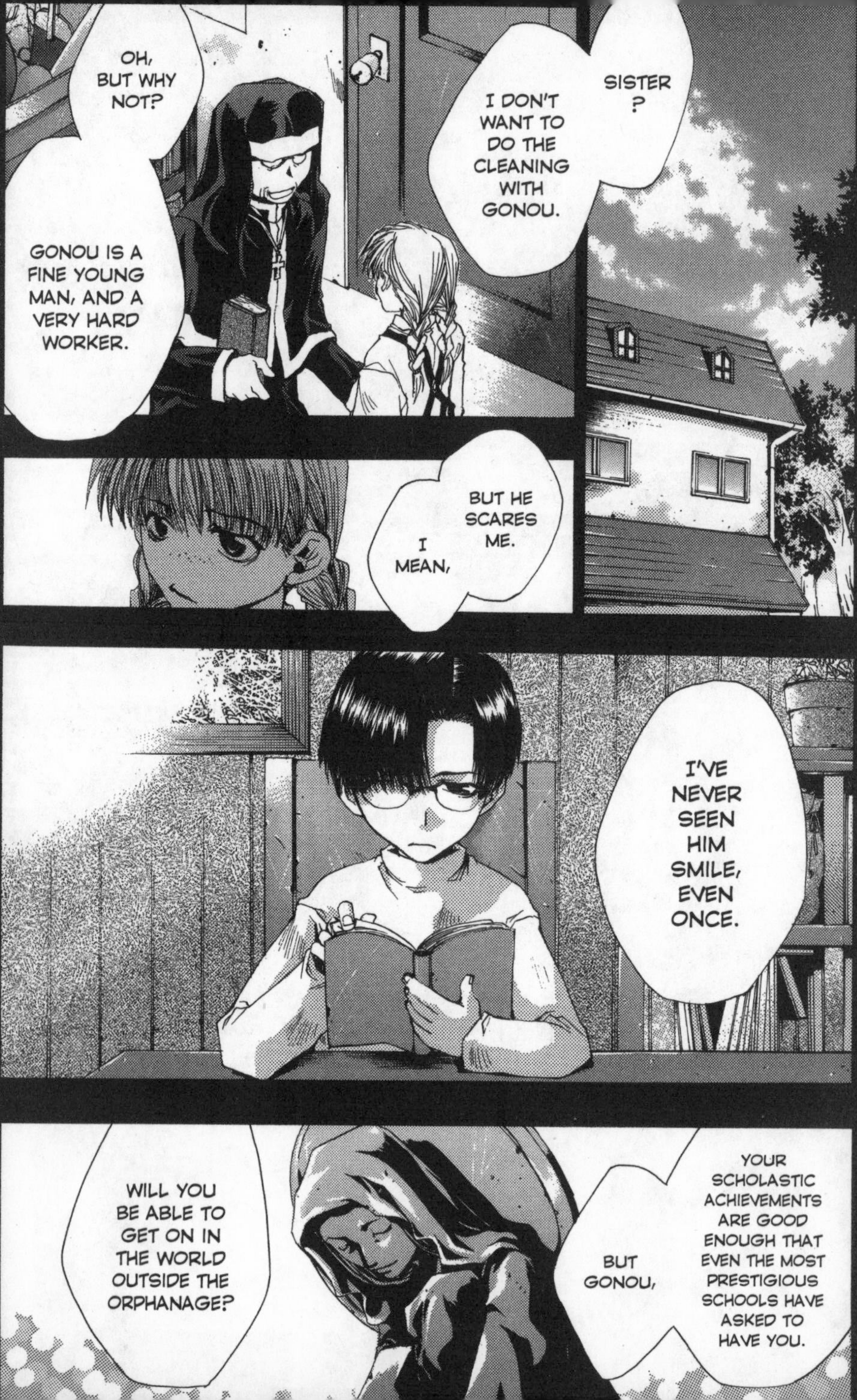
SISTER ?
I DON'T WANT TO DO THE CLEANING WITH GONOU.
OH, BUT WHY NOT?
GONOU IS A FINE YOUNG MAN, AND A VERY HARD WORKER.
I MEAN, BUT HE SCARES ME.
I'VE NEVER SEEN HIM SMILE, EVEN ONCE.
YOUR SCHOLASTIC ACHIEVEMENTS ARE GOOD ENOUGH THAT EVEN THE MOST PRESTIGIOUS SCHOOLS HAVE ASKED TO HAVE YOU.
BUT GONOU,
WILL YOU BE ABLE TO GET ON IN THE WORLD OUTSIDE THE ORPHANAGE?

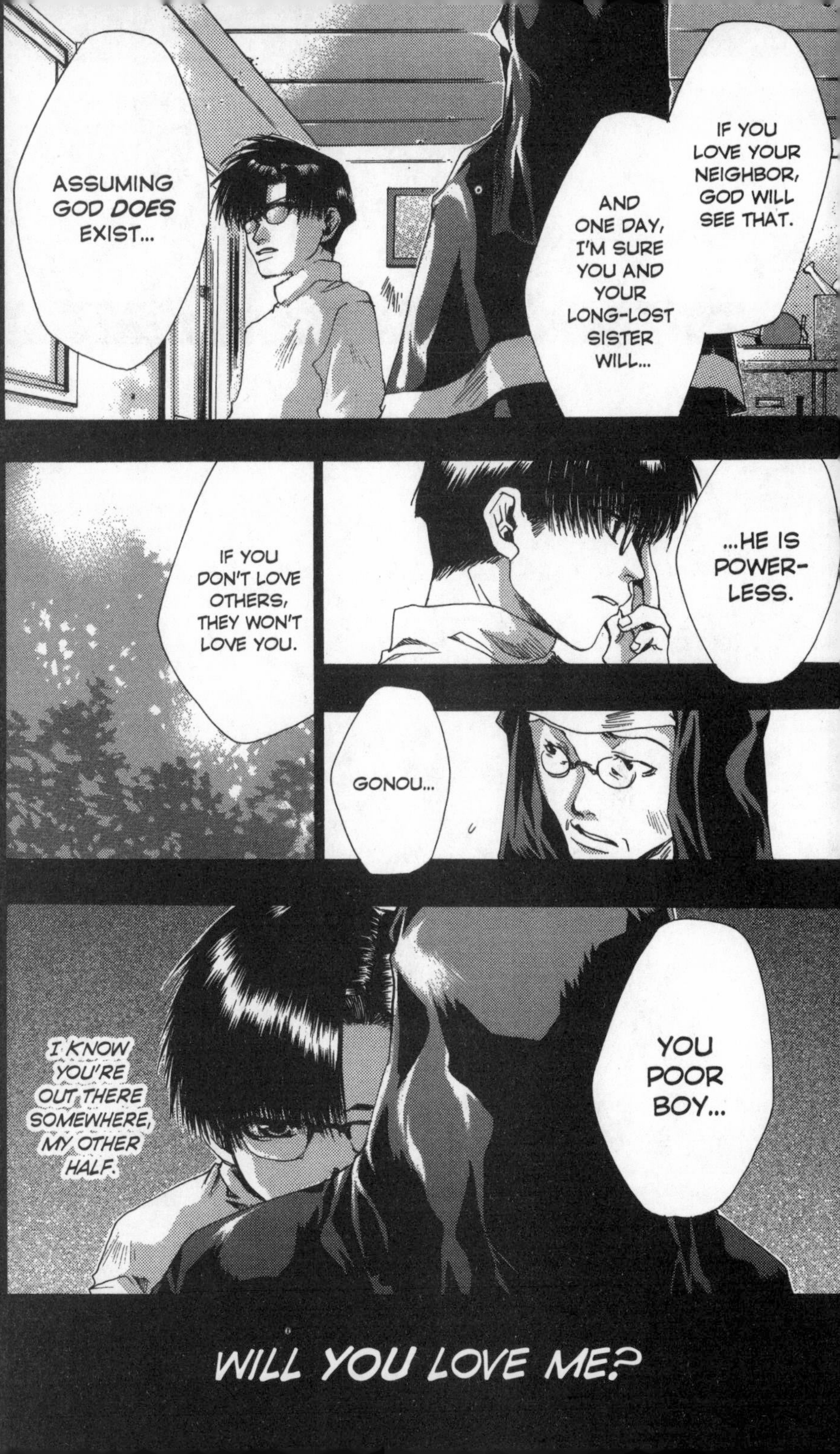
IF YOU LOVE YOUR NEIGHBOR, GOD WILL SEE THAT.
AND ONE DAY, I'M SURE YOU AND YOUR LONG-LOST SISTER WILL...
ASSUMING GOD *DOES* EXIST...
...HE IS POWER-LESS.
GONOU...
IF YOU DON'T LOVE OTHERS, THEY WON'T LOVE YOU.
YOU POOR BOY...
I KNOW YOU'RE OUT THERE SOMEWHERE, MY OTHER HALF.
WILL YOU LOVE ME?

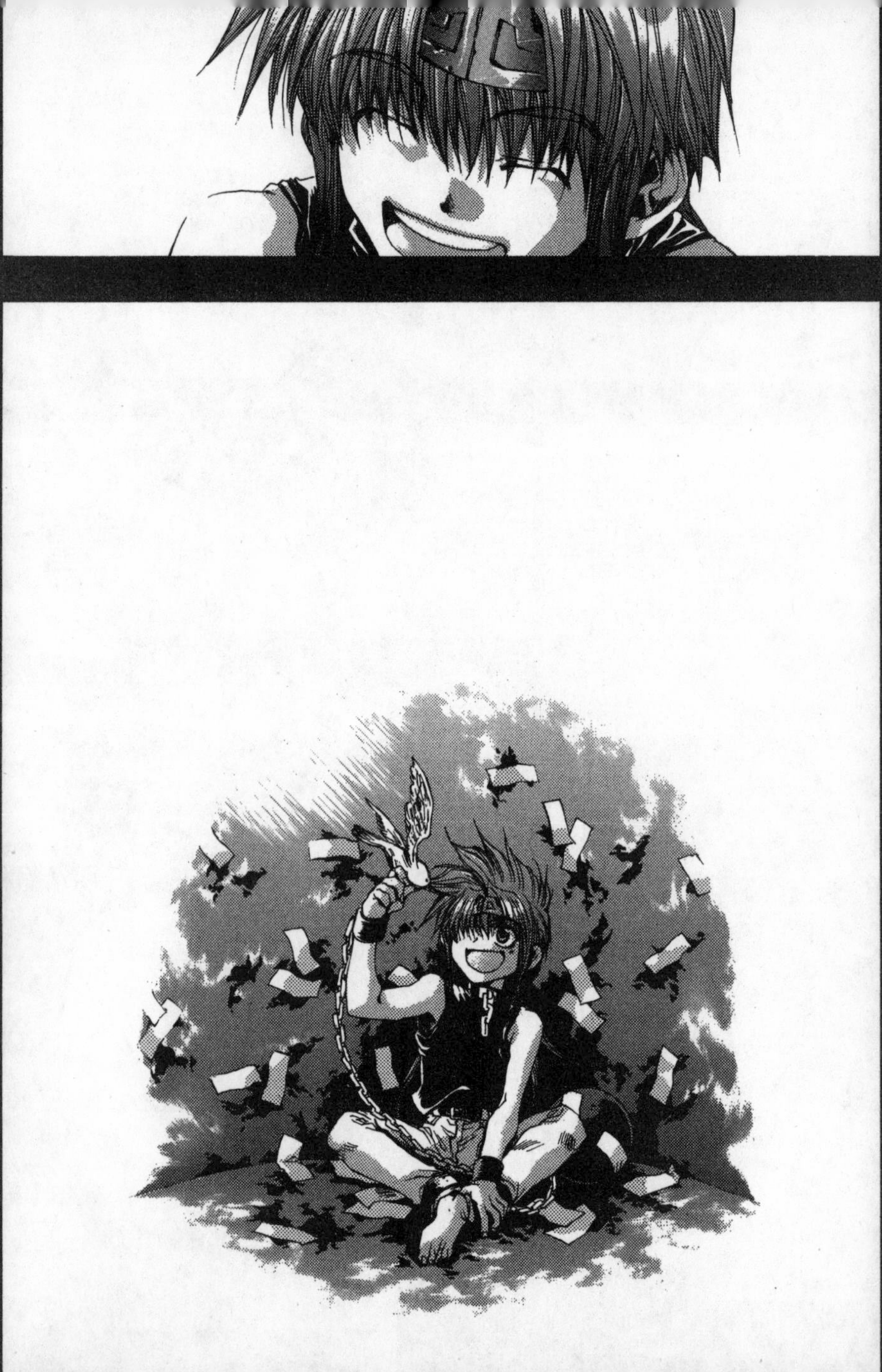

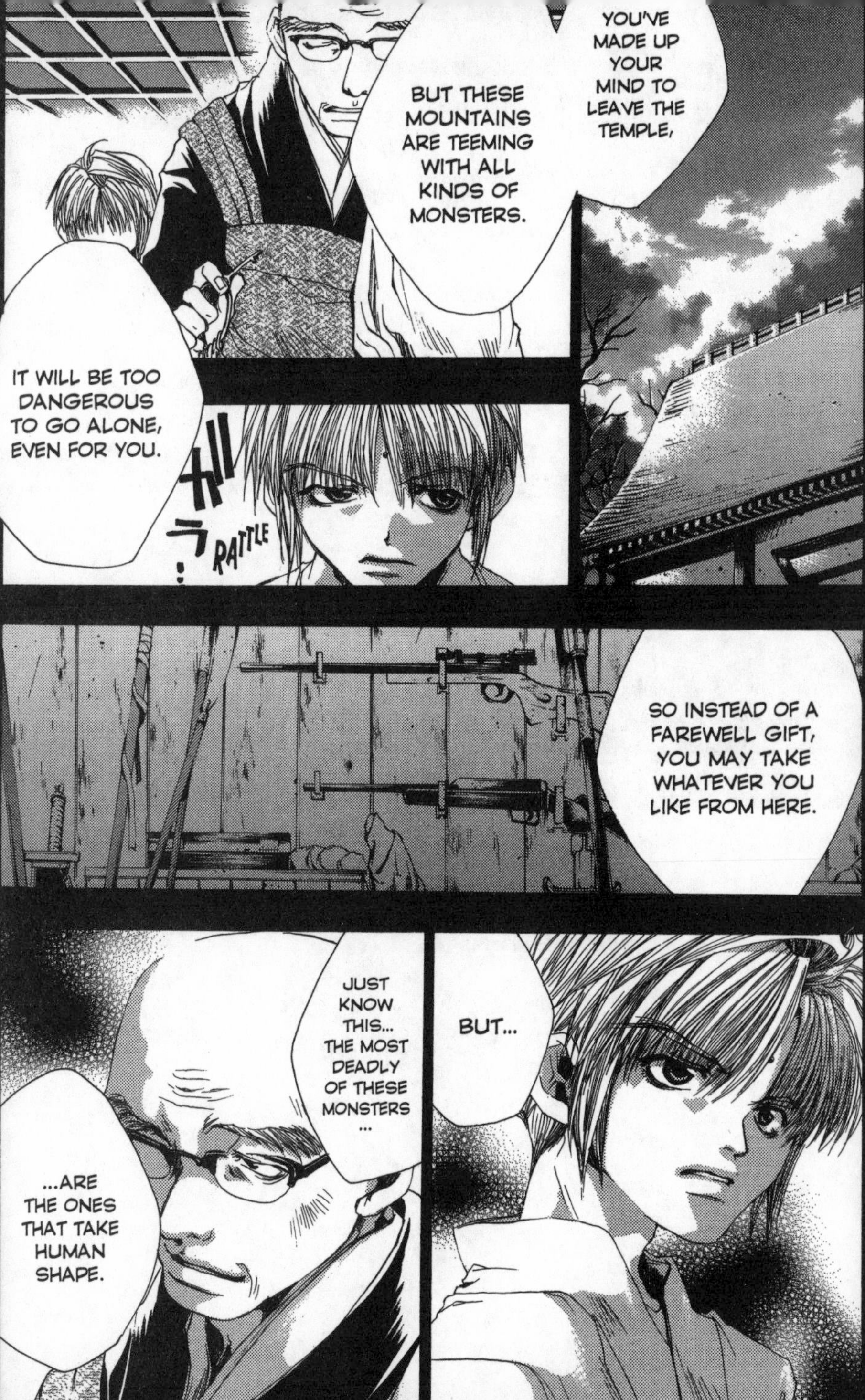
YOU'VE MADE UP YOUR MIND TO LEAVE THE TEMPLE,
BUT THESE MOUNTAINS ARE TEEMING WITH ALL KINDS OF MONSTERS.
IT WILL BE TOO DANGEROUS TO GO ALONE, EVEN FOR YOU.
ガラ
RATTLE
SO INSTEAD OF A FAREWELL GIFT, YOU MAY TAKE WHATEVER YOU LIKE FROM HERE.
BUT...
JUST KNOW THIS... THE MOST DEADLY OF THESE MONSTERS ...
...ARE THE ONES THAT TAKE HUMAN SHAPE.

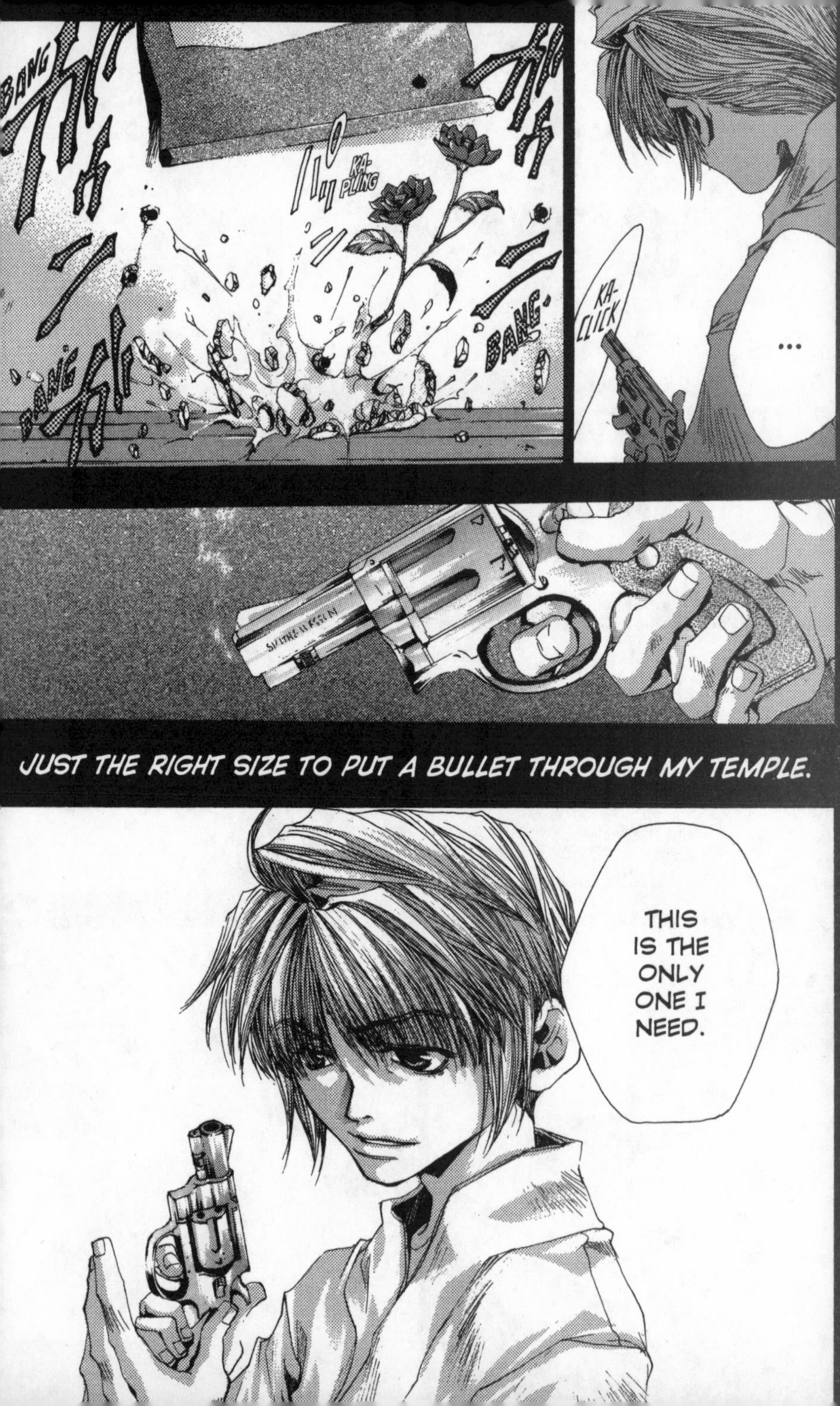
KA-CLICK
...
BANG-
KA-PLING
BANG
BANG
JUST THE RIGHT SIZE TO PUT A BULLET THROUGH MY TEMPLE.
THIS IS THE ONLY ONE I NEED.

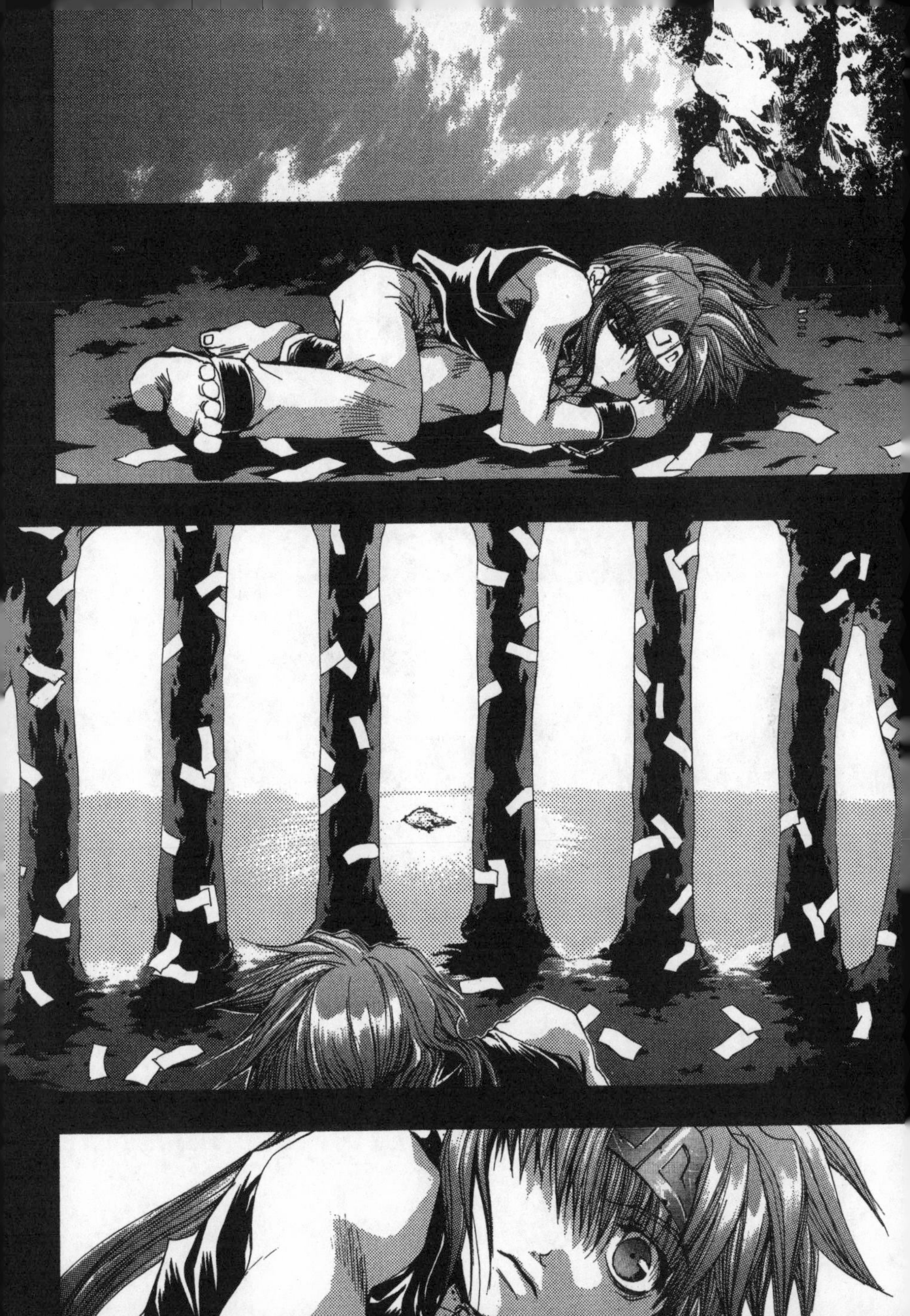

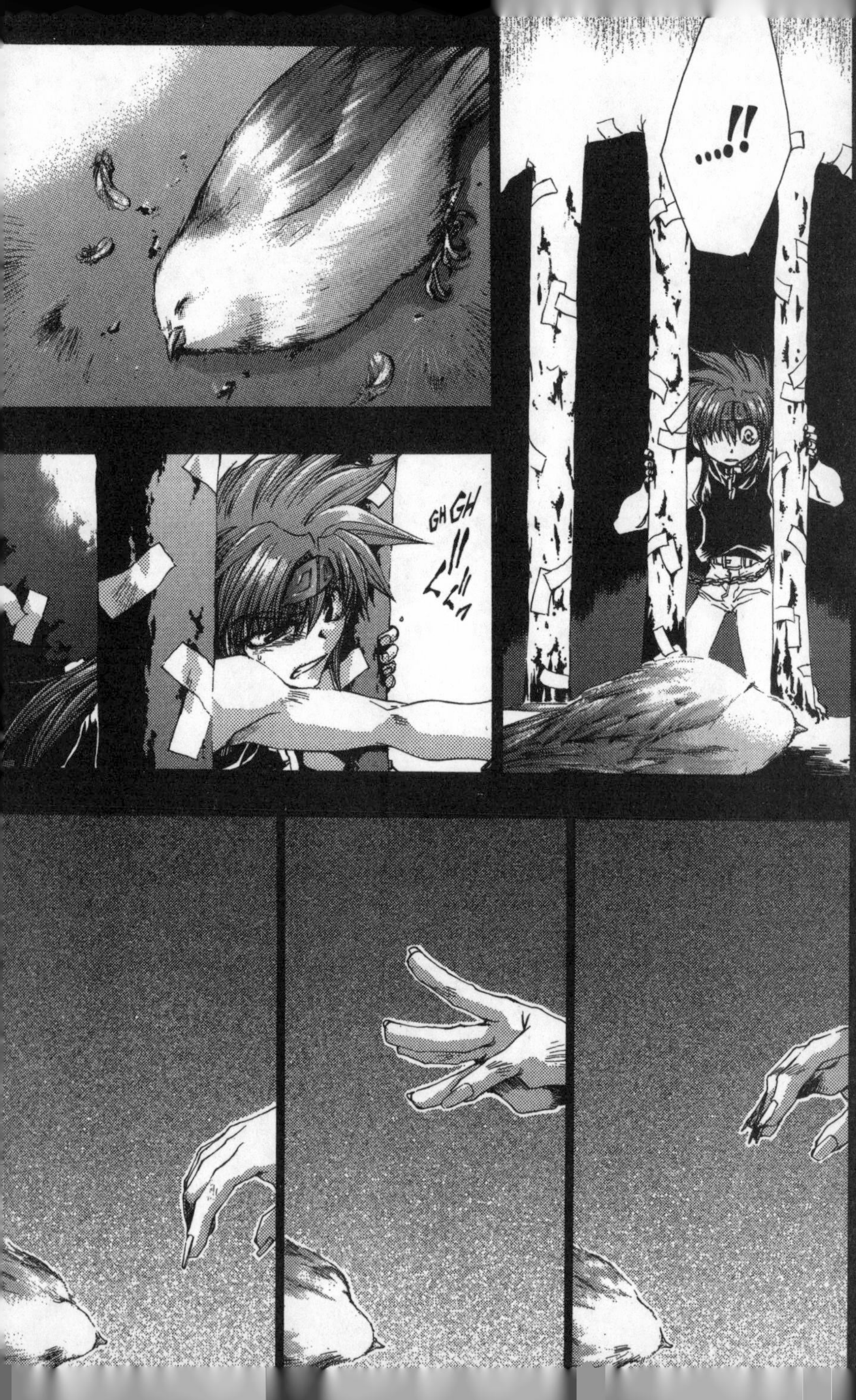
...!!
GH GH !!
くぐぃ

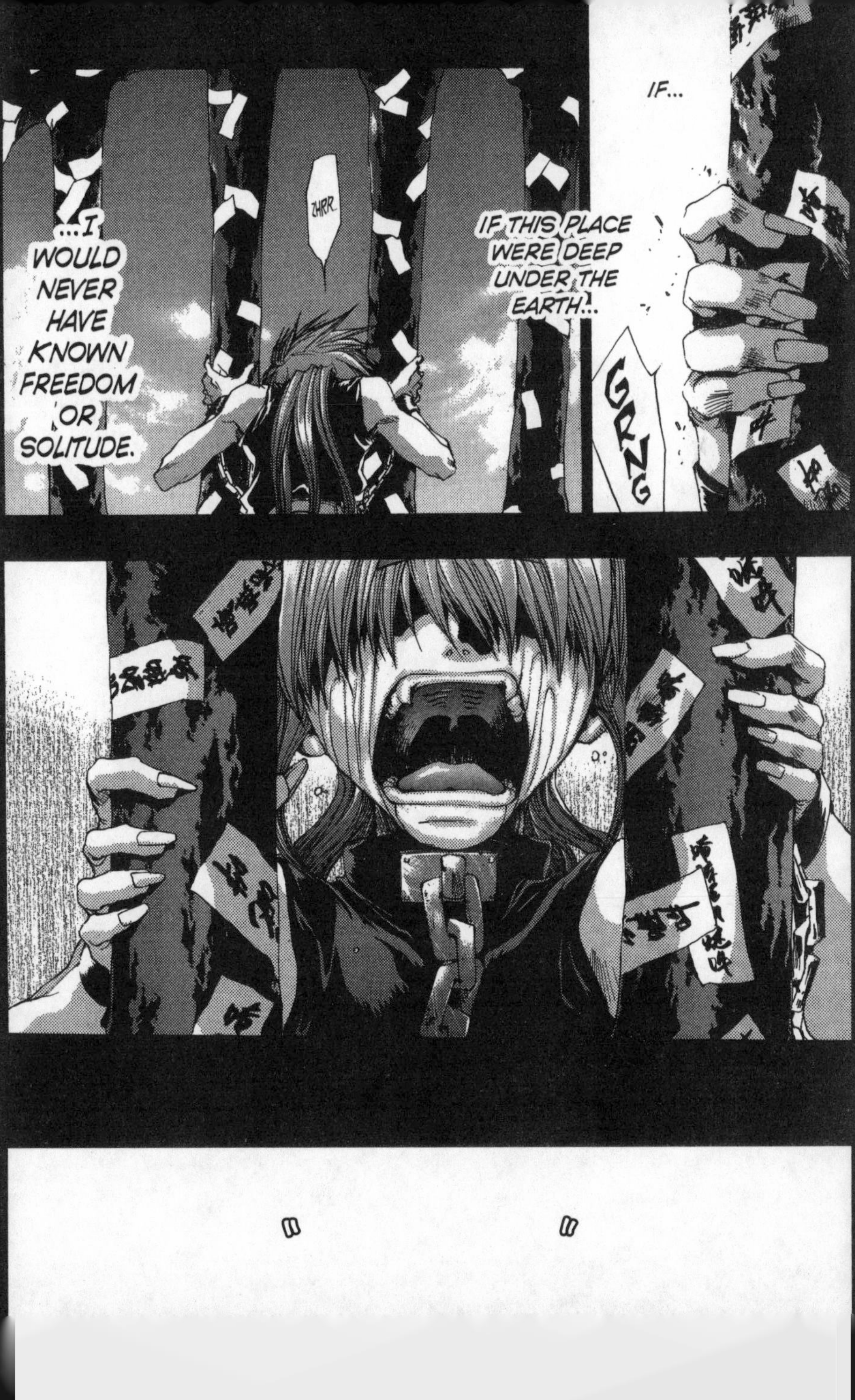
IF...
IF THIS PLACE WERE DEEP UNDER THE EARTH...
GRNG
ZHRR...
...I WOULD NEVER HAVE KNOWN FREEDOM OR SOLITUDE.

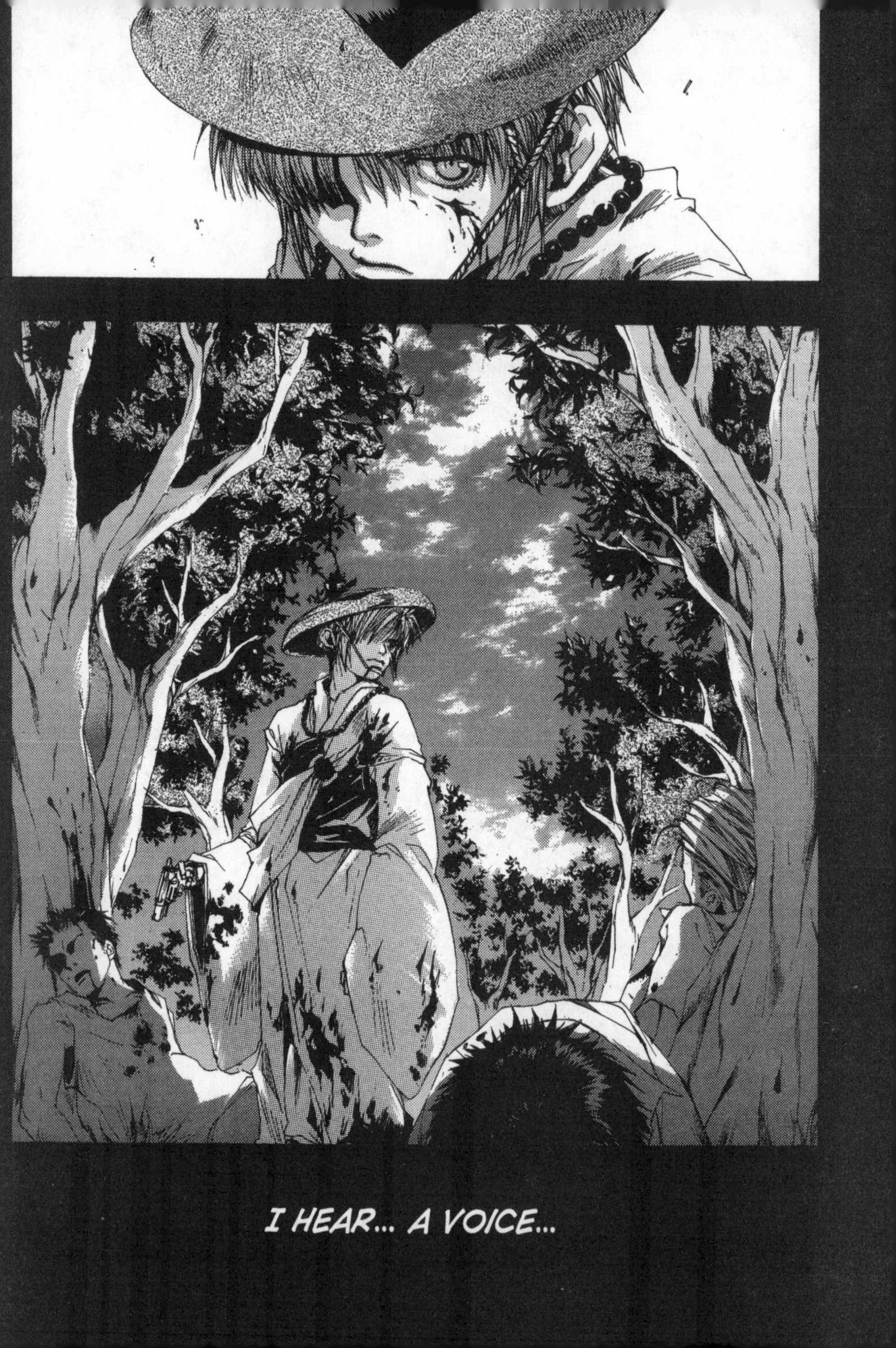
I HEAR... A VOICE...

STAFF

ORIGINAL WORKS
Kazuya Minekura

ASSISTANTS
Azuma Asu
Jiro Suzuki

Yuzu Mizutani
Katsuya Seino

EDITOR
Yousuke Sugino

IT'S NOT LIKE I HELD ON TO THE PAIN
JUST SO WE COULD LICK EACH OTHER'S WOUNDS.

WE'VE MADE IT TO VOLUME SEVEN AT LAST. ...I SAY "AT LAST," BUT WE'RE FAR FROM THE END.

THIS KINKAKU/GINKAKU STORY IS THE BEGINNING OF THE LONGEST ARC SAIYUKI HAS HAD SO FAR. WHO IS THIS KAMI-SAMA? WHERE ARE YOU GOING, GOJYO? WHAT HAPPENED TO KOUGAIJI (HA HA)? THE SPOTLIGHT WAS ON GOJYO THIS TIME, BUT I DON'T WANT TO ONLY FOCUS ON HIM—I WANT TO DRAW EACH MEMBER OF SANZO'S GANG. THEIR INDIVIDUAL PERSPECTIVES, OR OPINIONS... HOW THEY CHANGE, HOW THEY GROW, HOW THEY REGRESS (WHICH IS IT?).

ANYWAY, THERE REALLY IS NO FEMALE PRESENCE IN THIS VOLUME, IS THERE? I WAS FLIPPING THROUGH IT, LIKE, "ARE THERE **ANY** WOMEN IN HERE?" AND THERE WAS! KANNON, IN A FEW PANELS. WELL, IN THE CASE OF KANNON, I'M NOT SURE...

...WELL, THEN, MINEKURA HERE, PROMISING TO BURN MY LIFE FORCE TO CREATE THE NEXT VOLUME. IF I LOOK LIKE I'M ABOUT TO GO OUT, PLEASE GENTLY RELIGHT ME.

KAZUYA MINEKURA, OCTOBER 2000

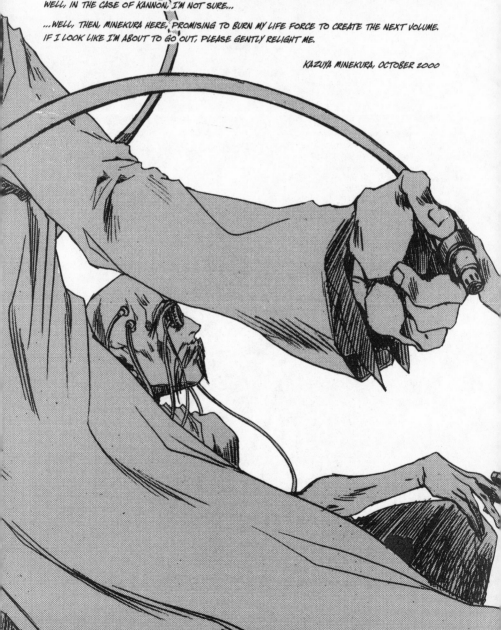

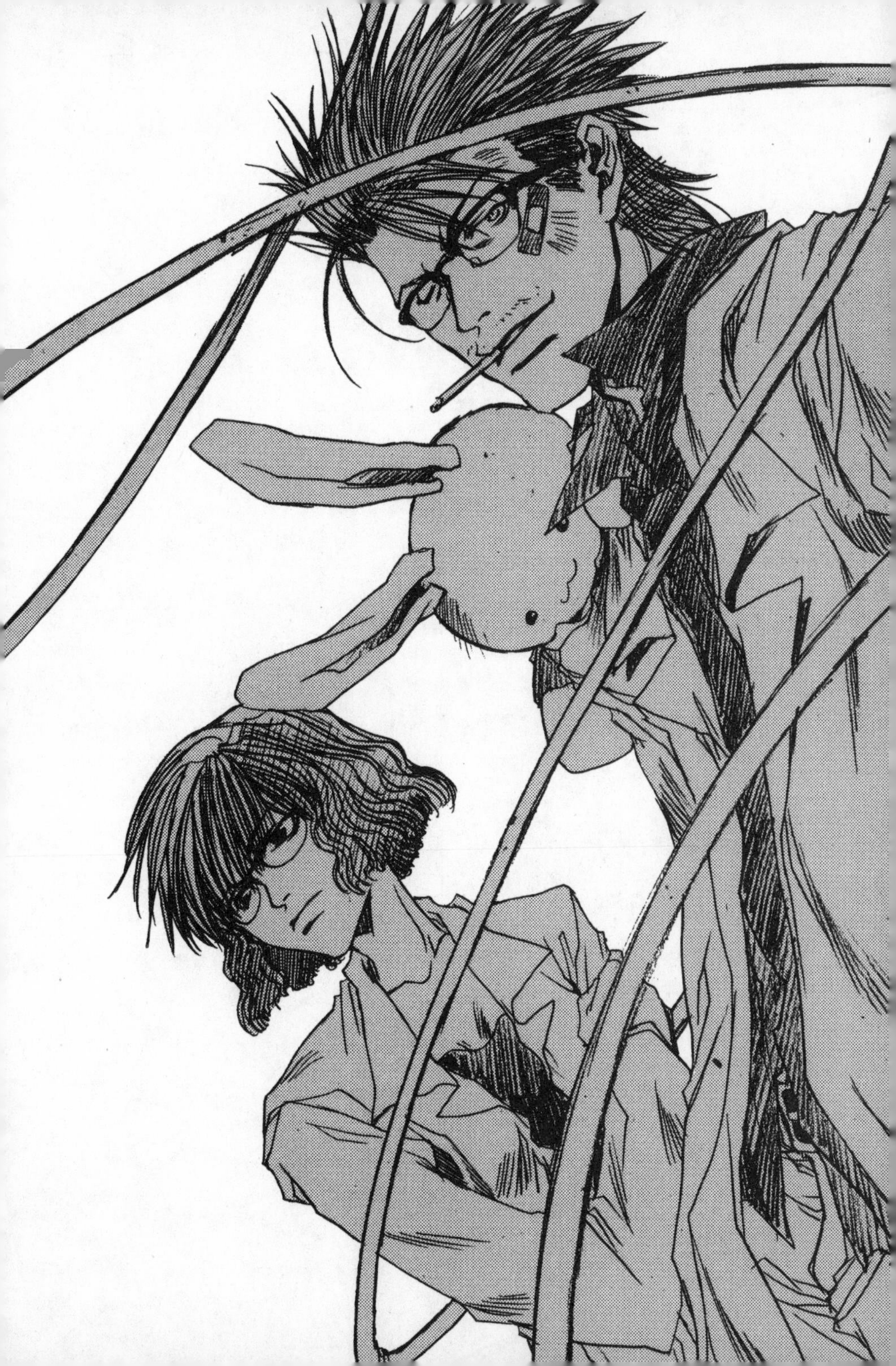

A note from the author

KAZUYA MINEKURA

She... she jumped!!

SAIYUKI

KAZUYA MINEKURA

— VOLUME VII SYNOPSIS —

A Negative Wave has spread across the fount of culture and faith, Togenkyo. Four lawless desperados set out on a journey to the West to stop the experiments to revive the great yokai Gyumaoh—experiments believed to be the cause of this calamity.

Gojyo goes out alone to do the shopping, and he comes across a strange boy. When he returns to the inn later, he is met with the sight of his friends collapsed on the floor, and the boy—Kinkaku—sitting on the shoulders of a monster.

Sanzo and Gojyo set out after the boy to find a way to rouse Goku and Hakkai from unconsciousness.

Meanwhile, Goku and Hakkai awaken in a strange world. There they meet Kinkaku's younger twin brother Ginkaku, who explains to them what has happened.

There was a man who deceived Kinkaku and killed him. He called himself Kami-sama—God—and disappeared. Our four antiheroes are vexed by this turn of events, but Sanzo chooses to ignore the self-proclaimed deity and press onward in their journey.

The next day, Gojyo is nowhere to be found...

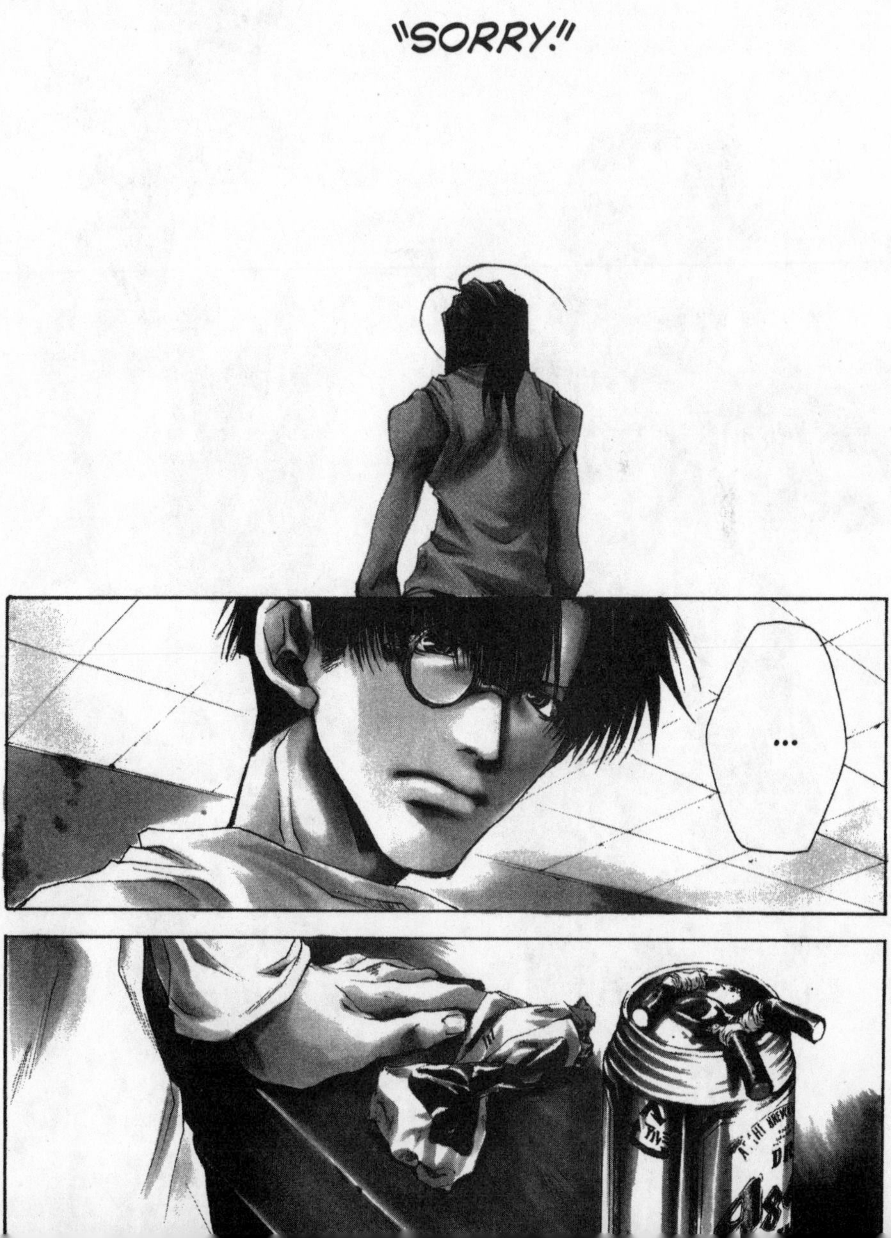
"SORRY!"
...

CAN: Aluminum Draft

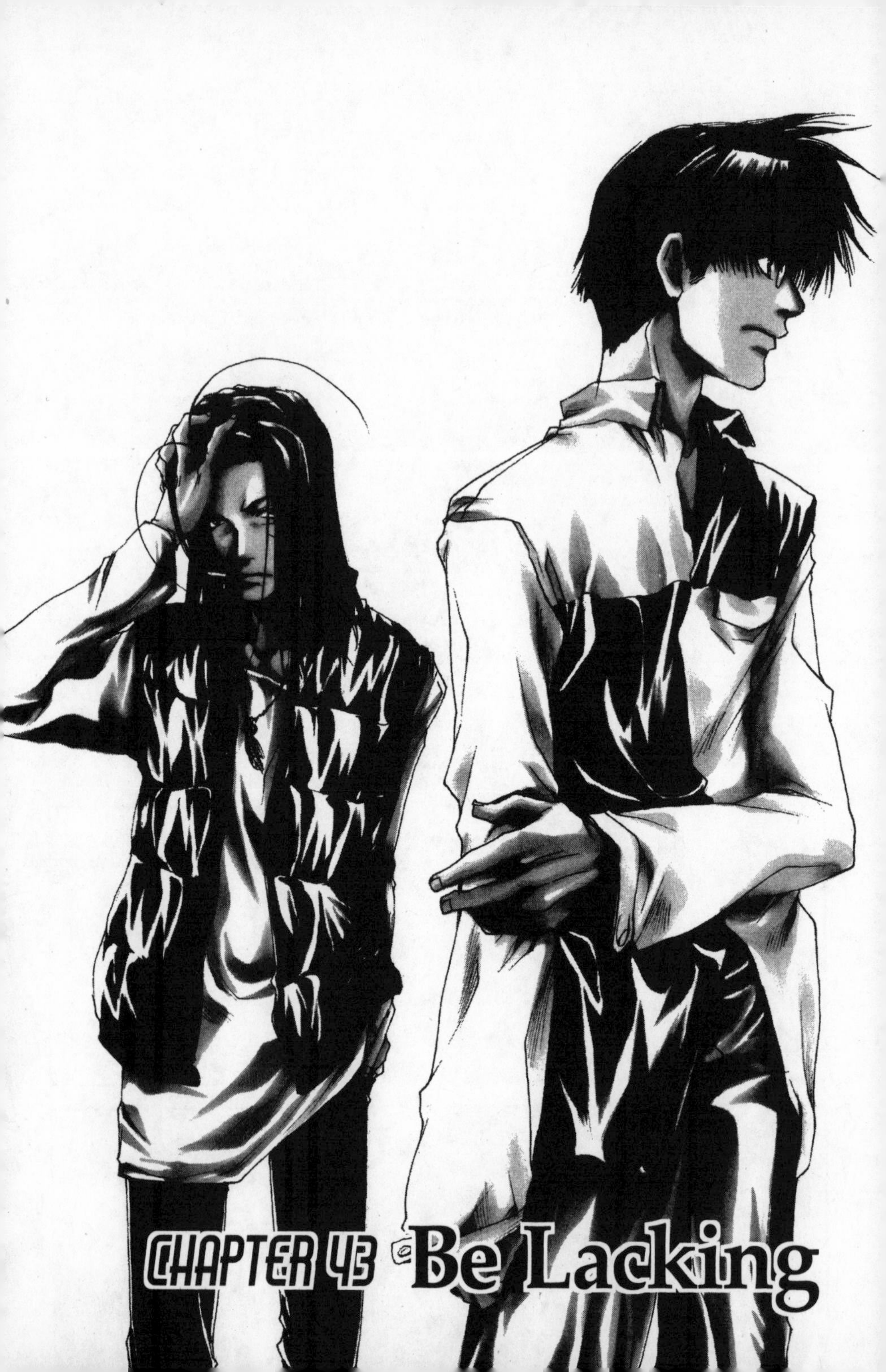
CHAPTER 43 Be Lacking

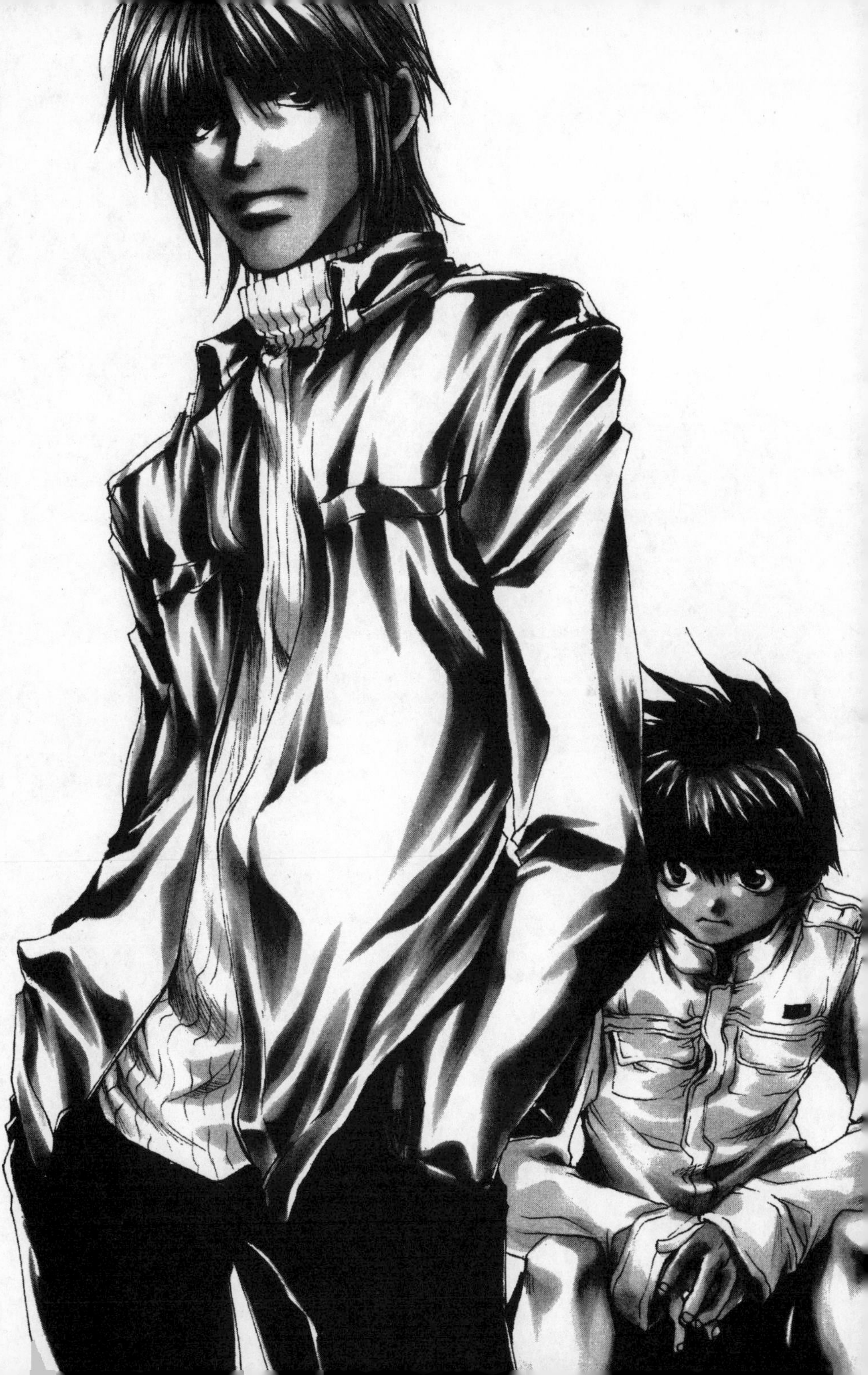

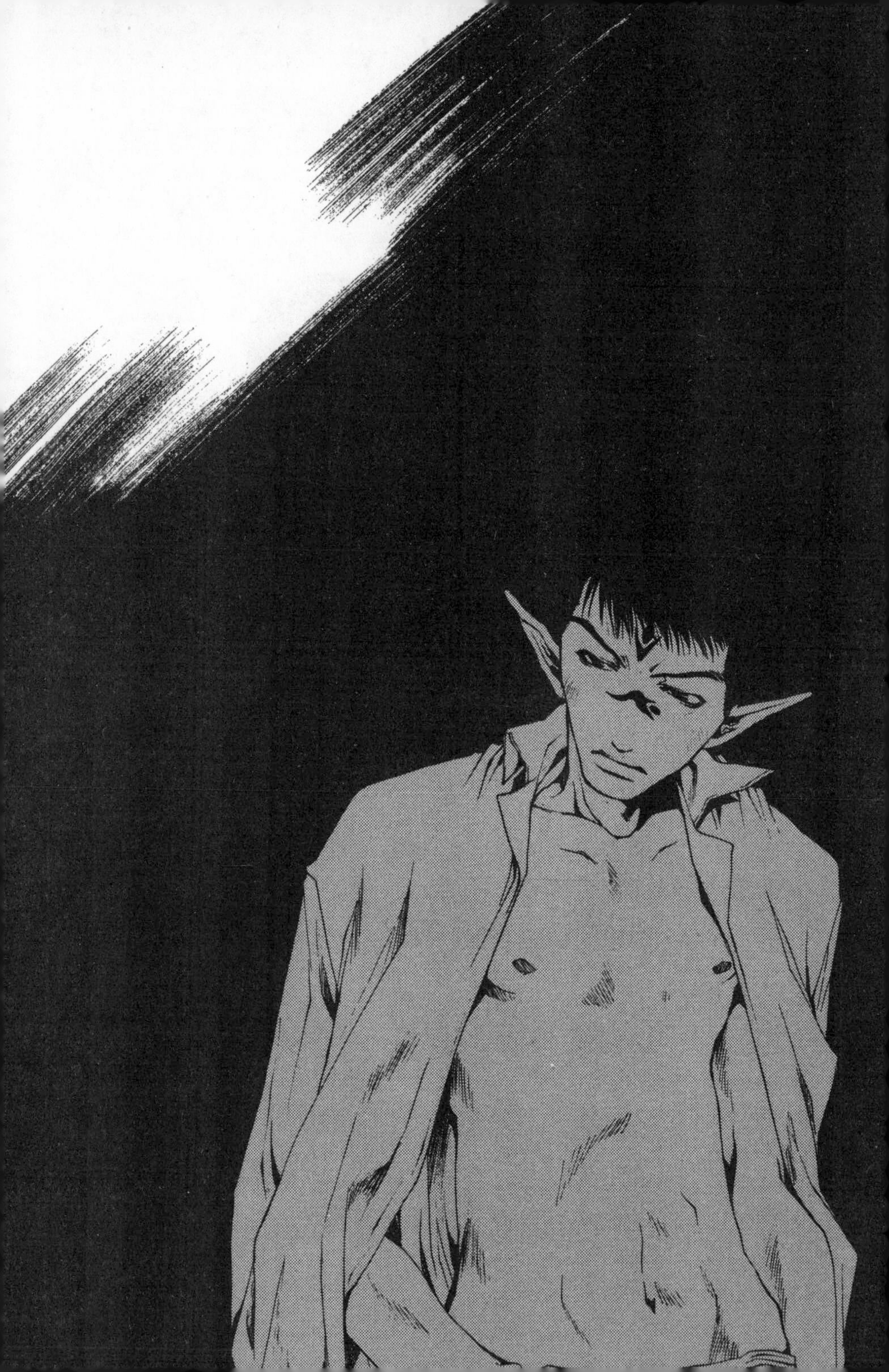

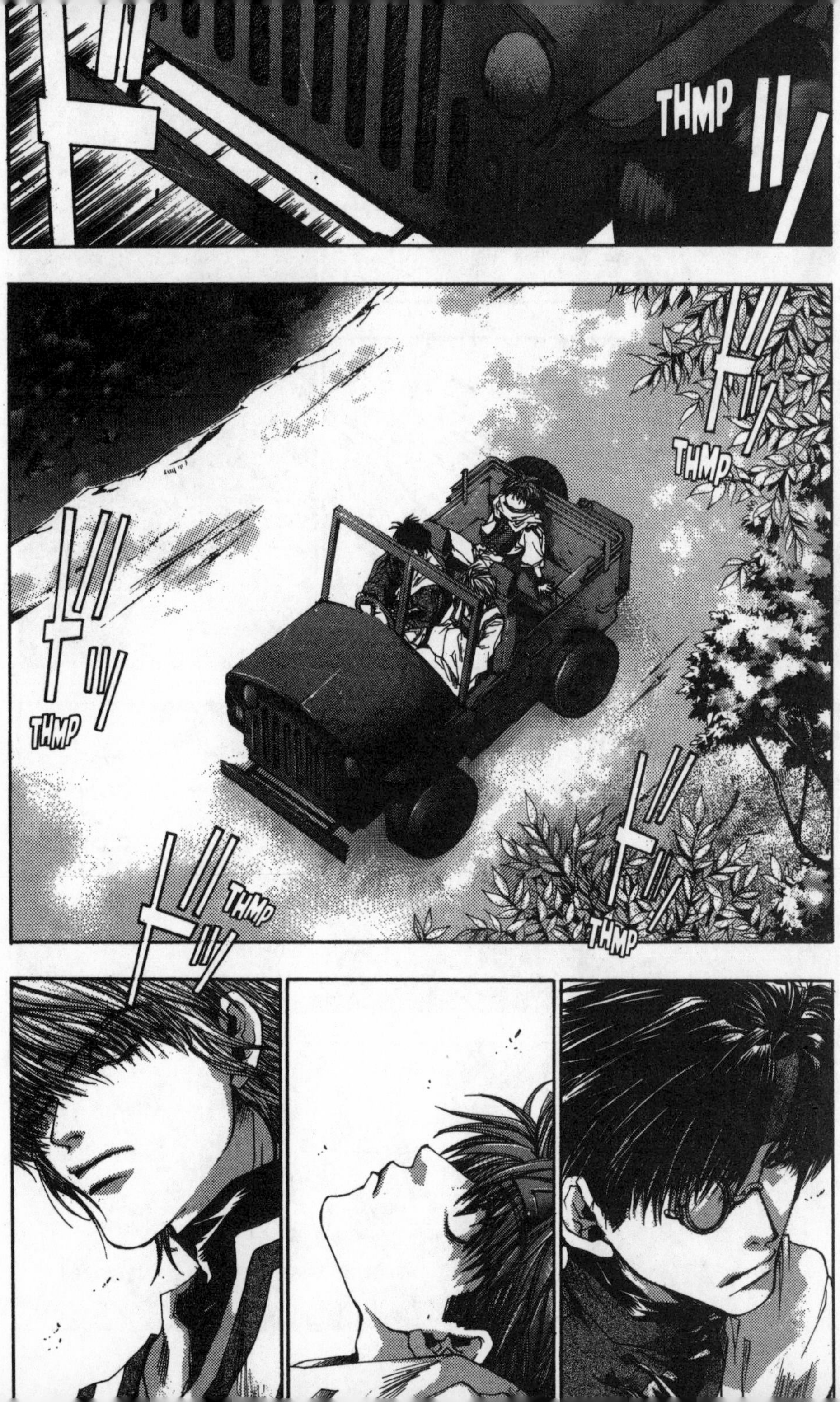
THMP
THMP
THMP
THMP
THMP

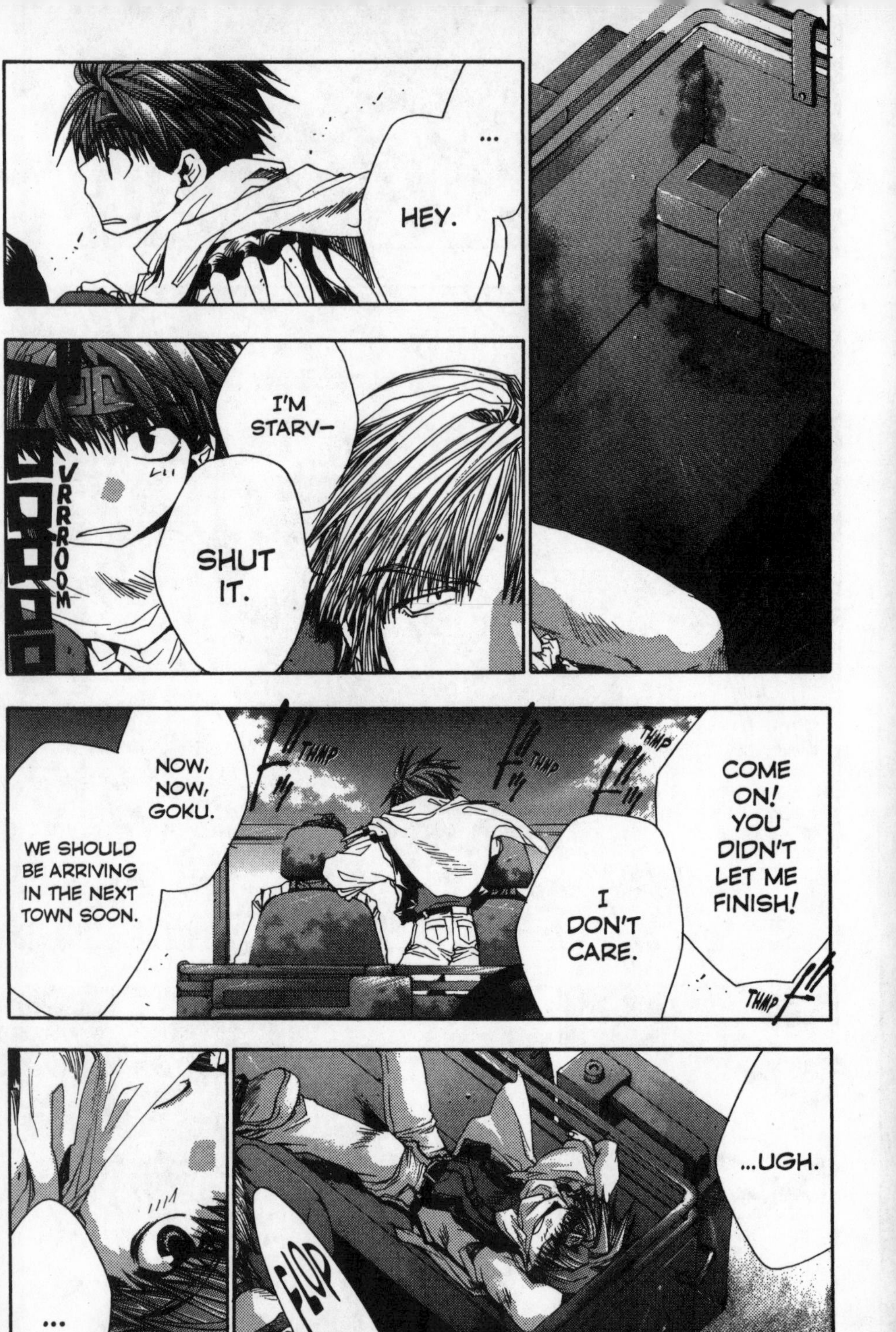
...
HEY.
I'M STARV–
SHUT IT.
VRRROOM
COME ON! YOU DIDN'T LET ME FINISH!
THMP
THMP
THMP
THMP
I DON'T CARE.
NOW, NOW, GOKU.
WE SHOULD BE ARRIVING IN THE NEXT TOWN SOON.
...UGH.
FLOP
...

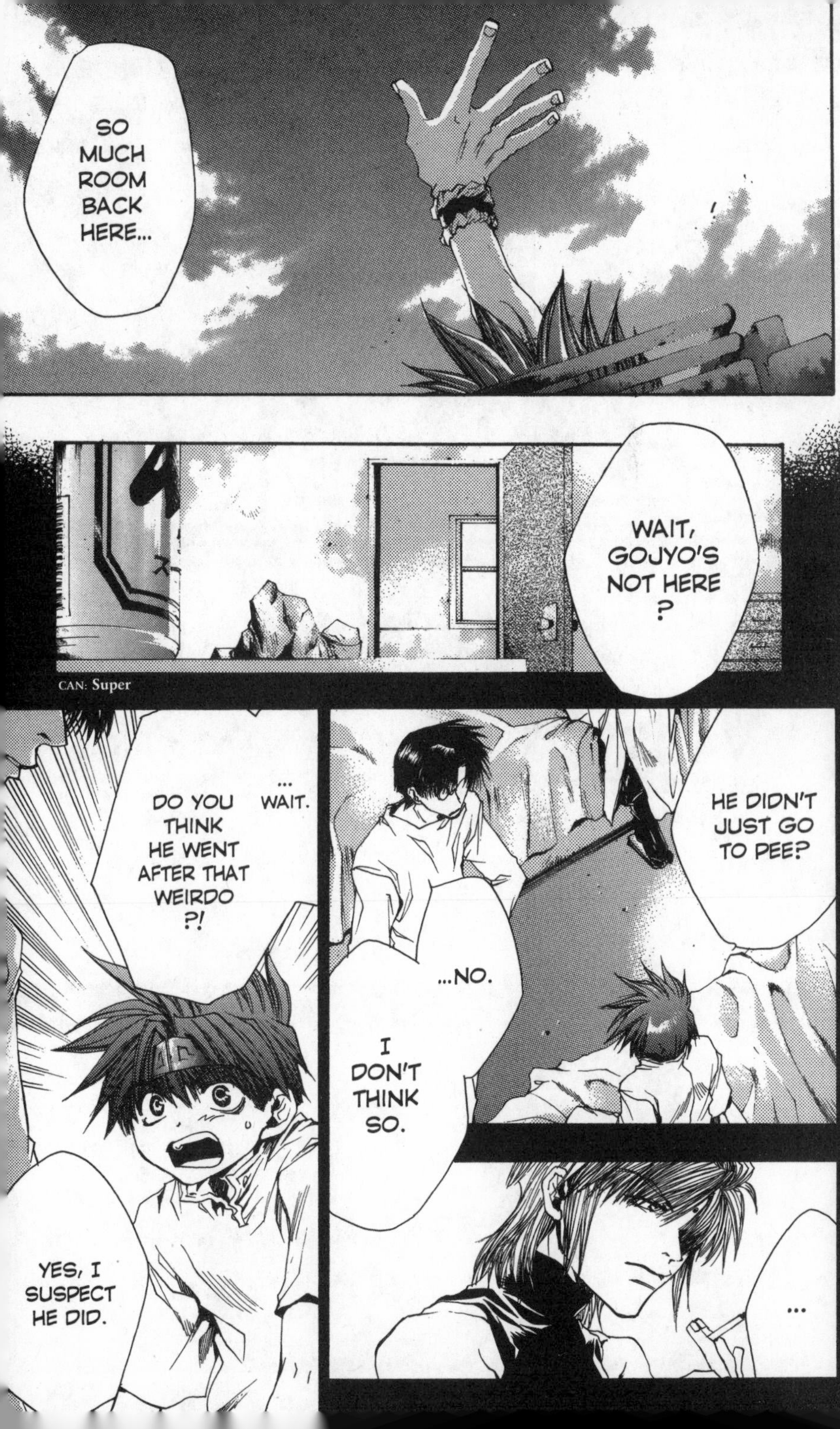
SO MUCH ROOM BACK HERE...
WAIT, GOJYO'S NOT HERE?
CAN: Super
HE DIDN'T JUST GO TO PEE?
...NO.
I DON'T THINK SO.
...
...WAIT.
DO YOU THINK HE WENT AFTER THAT WEIRDO?!
YES, I SUSPECT HE DID.

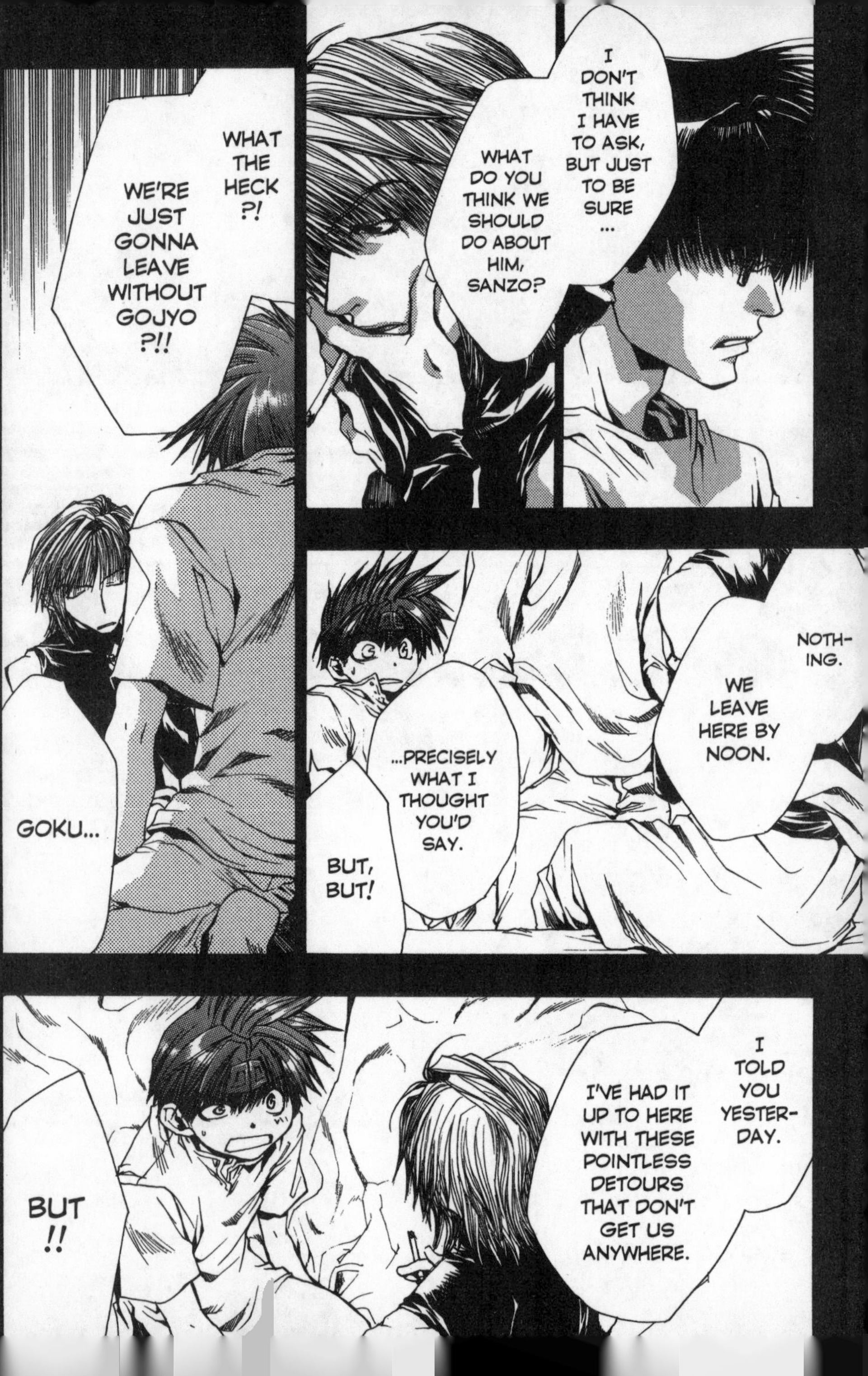
I DON'T THINK I HAVE TO ASK, BUT JUST TO BE SURE ...
WHAT DO YOU THINK WE SHOULD DO ABOUT HIM, SANZO?
NOTHING.
WE LEAVE HERE BY NOON.
...PRECISELY WHAT I THOUGHT YOU'D SAY.
BUT, BUT!
WHAT THE HECK ?!
WE'RE JUST GONNA LEAVE WITHOUT GOJYO ?!!
GOKU...
I TOLD YOU YESTERDAY.
I'VE HAD IT UP TO HERE WITH THESE POINTLESS DETOURS THAT DON'T GET US ANYWHERE.
BUT !!

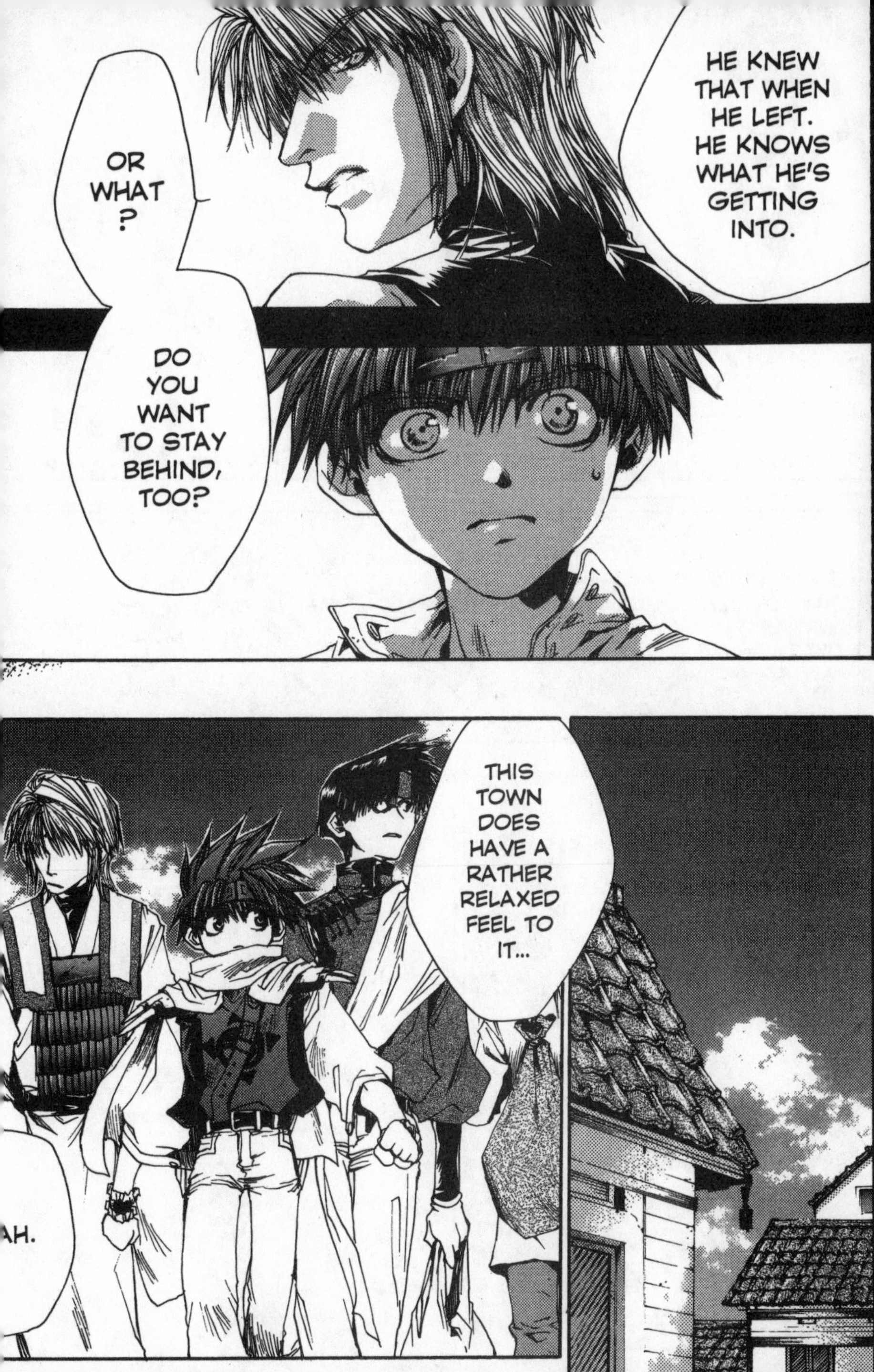
HE KNEW THAT WHEN HE LEFT. HE KNOWS WHAT HE'S GETTING INTO.
OR WHAT ?
DO YOU WANT TO STAY BEHIND, TOO?
THIS TOWN DOES HAVE A RATHER RELAXED FEEL TO IT...

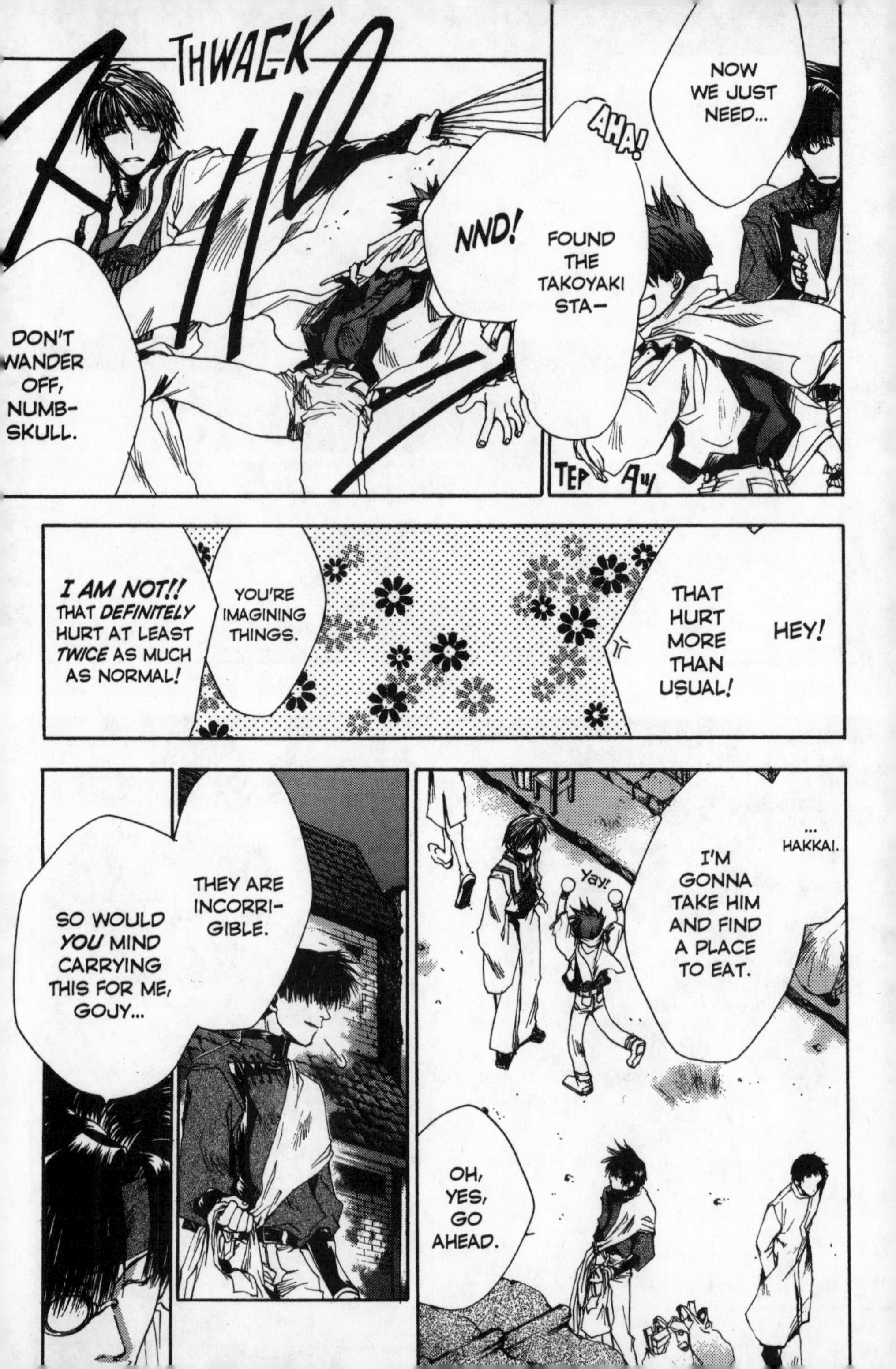
NOW WE JUST NEED...
AHA!
NND! FOUND THE TAKOYAKI STA—
TEP
THWACK
DON'T WANDER OFF, NUMBSKULL.
HEY!
THAT HURT MORE THAN USUAL!
YOU'RE IMAGINING THINGS.
I AM NOT!! THAT DEFINITELY HURT AT LEAST TWICE AS MUCH AS NORMAL!
... HAKKAI.
I'M GONNA TAKE HIM AND FIND A PLACE TO EAT.
Yay!
OH, YES, GO AHEAD.
THEY ARE INCORRIGIBLE.
SO WOULD YOU MIND CARRYING THIS FOR ME, GOJY...

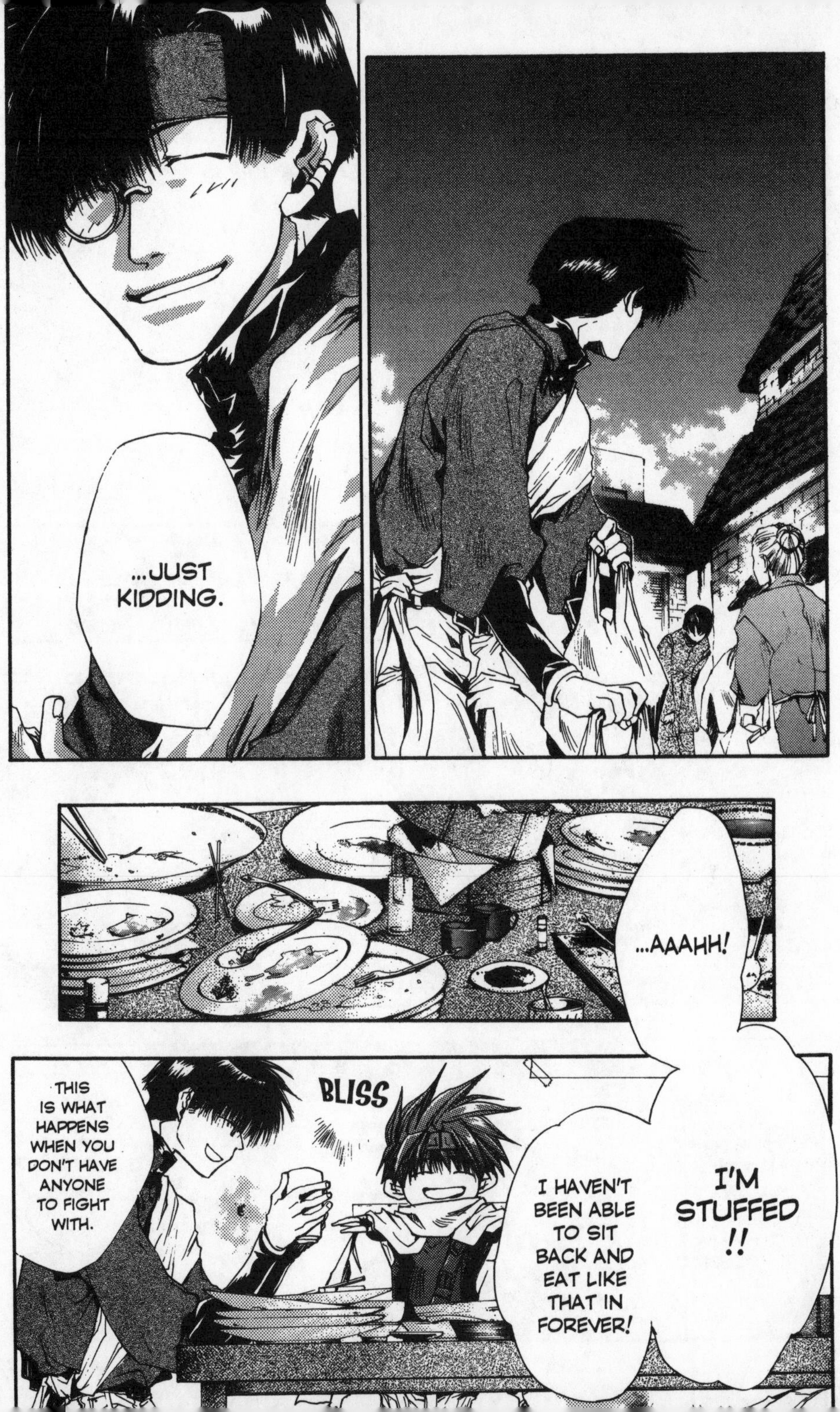
...JUST KIDDING.
...AAAHH!
I'M STUFFED!!
I HAVEN'T BEEN ABLE TO SIT BACK AND EAT LIKE THAT IN FOREVER!
BLISS
THIS IS WHAT HAPPENS WHEN YOU DON'T HAVE ANYONE TO FIGHT WITH.

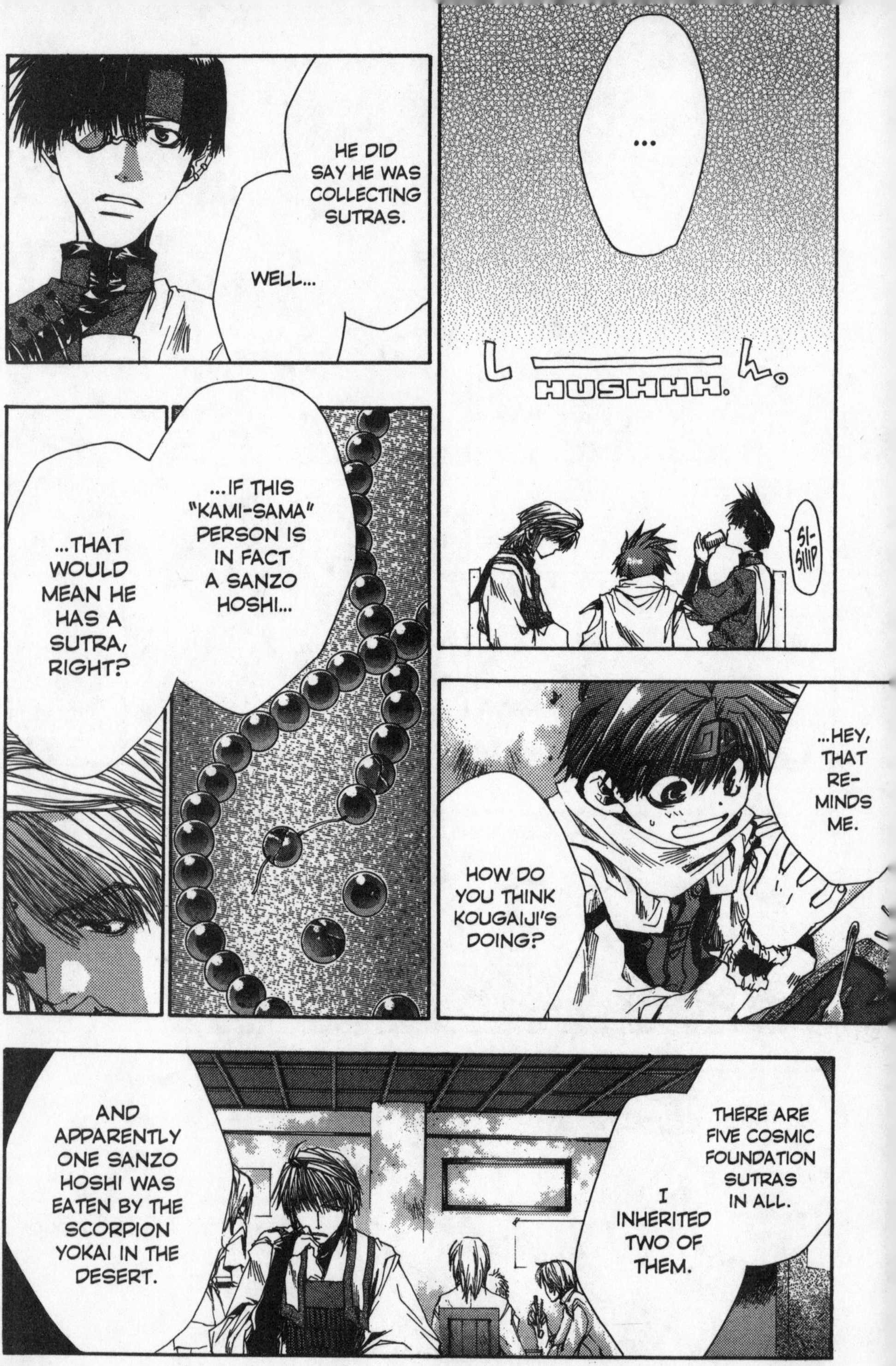
...
L——h.
HUSHHH.
SI-SIIP
HE DID SAY HE WAS COLLECTING SUTRAS.
WELL...
...IF THIS "KAMI-SAMA" PERSON IS IN FACT A SANZO HOSHI...
...THAT WOULD MEAN HE HAS A SUTRA, RIGHT?
...HEY, THAT RE-MINDS ME.
HOW DO YOU THINK KOUGAIJI'S DOING?
THERE ARE FIVE COSMIC FOUNDATION SUTRAS IN ALL.
I INHERITED TWO OF THEM.
AND APPARENTLY ONE SANZO HOSHI WAS EATEN BY THE SCORPION YOKAI IN THE DESERT.

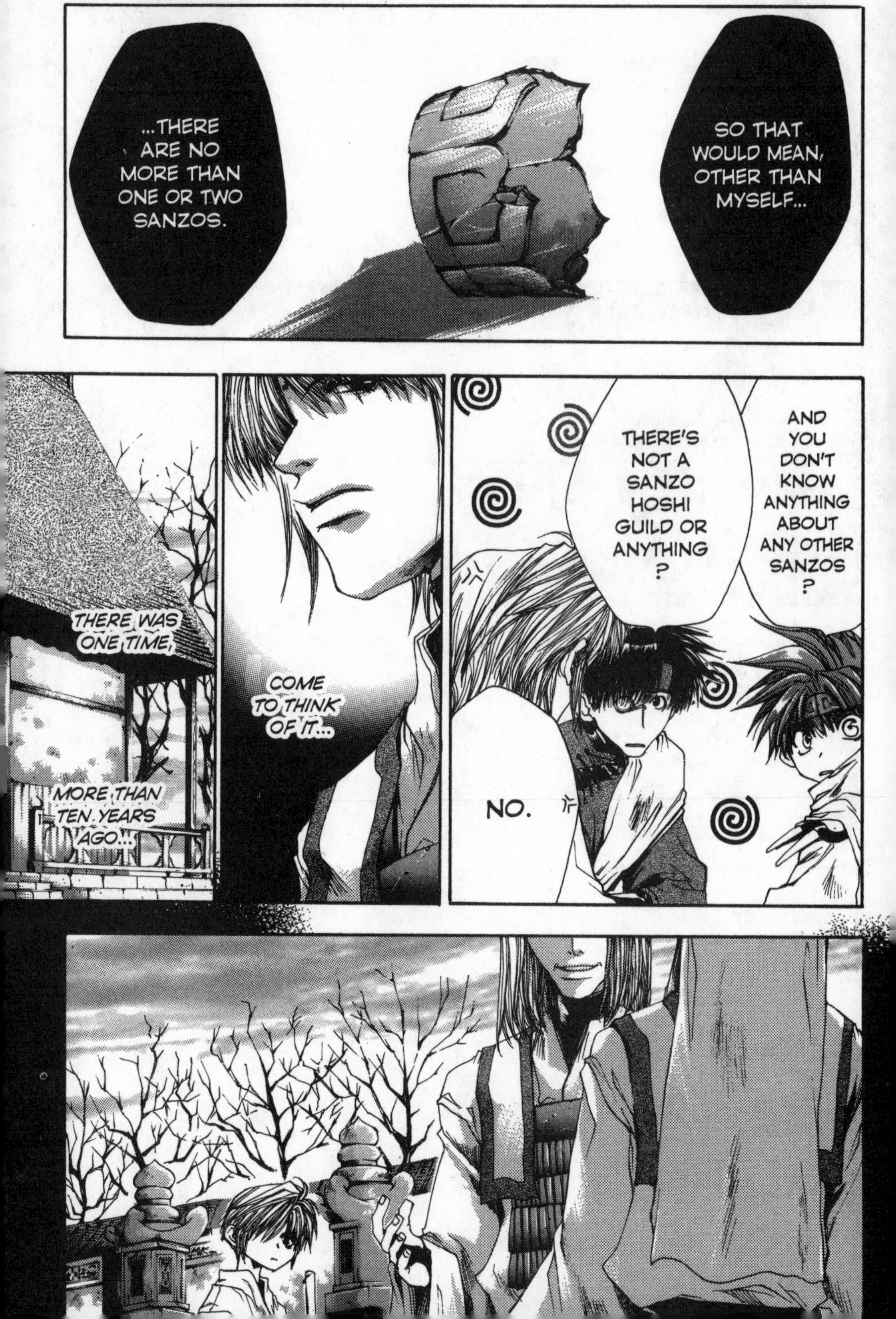
SO THAT WOULD MEAN, OTHER THAN MYSELF...
...THERE ARE NO MORE THAN ONE OR TWO SANZOS.
AND YOU DON'T KNOW ANYTHING ABOUT ANY OTHER SANZOS?
THERE'S NOT A SANZO HOSHI GUILD OR ANYTHING?
NO.
COME TO THINK OF IT...
THERE WAS ONE TIME,
MORE THAN TEN YEARS AGO...

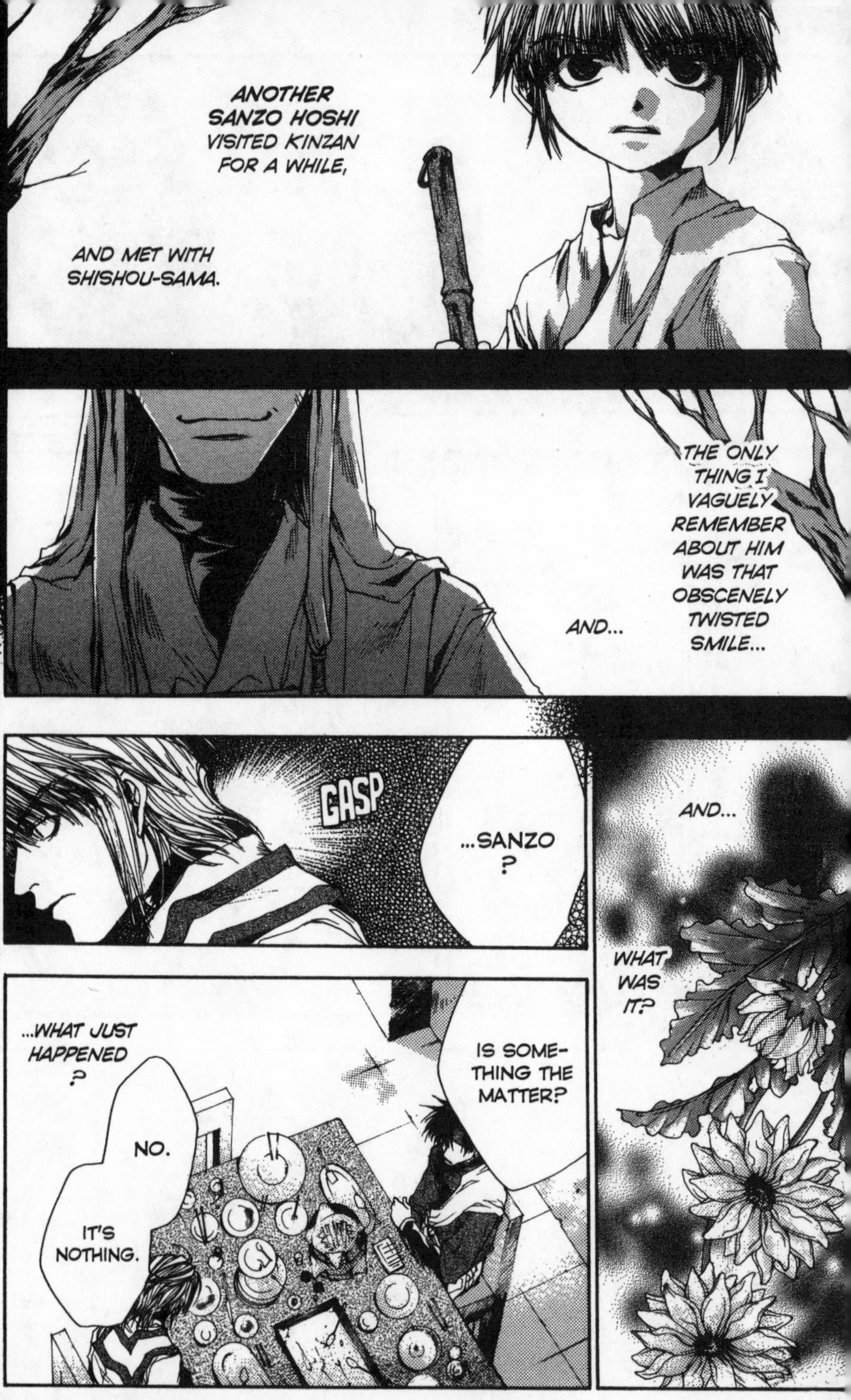
ANOTHER SANZO HOSHI VISITED KINZAN FOR A WHILE,
AND MET WITH SHISHOU-SAMA.
THE ONLY THING I VAGUELY REMEMBER ABOUT HIM WAS THAT OBSCENELY TWISTED SMILE...
AND...
AND...
WHAT WAS IT?
GASP
...SANZO ?
IS SOME-THING THE MATTER?
...WHAT JUST HAPPENED ?
NO.
IT'S NOTHING.

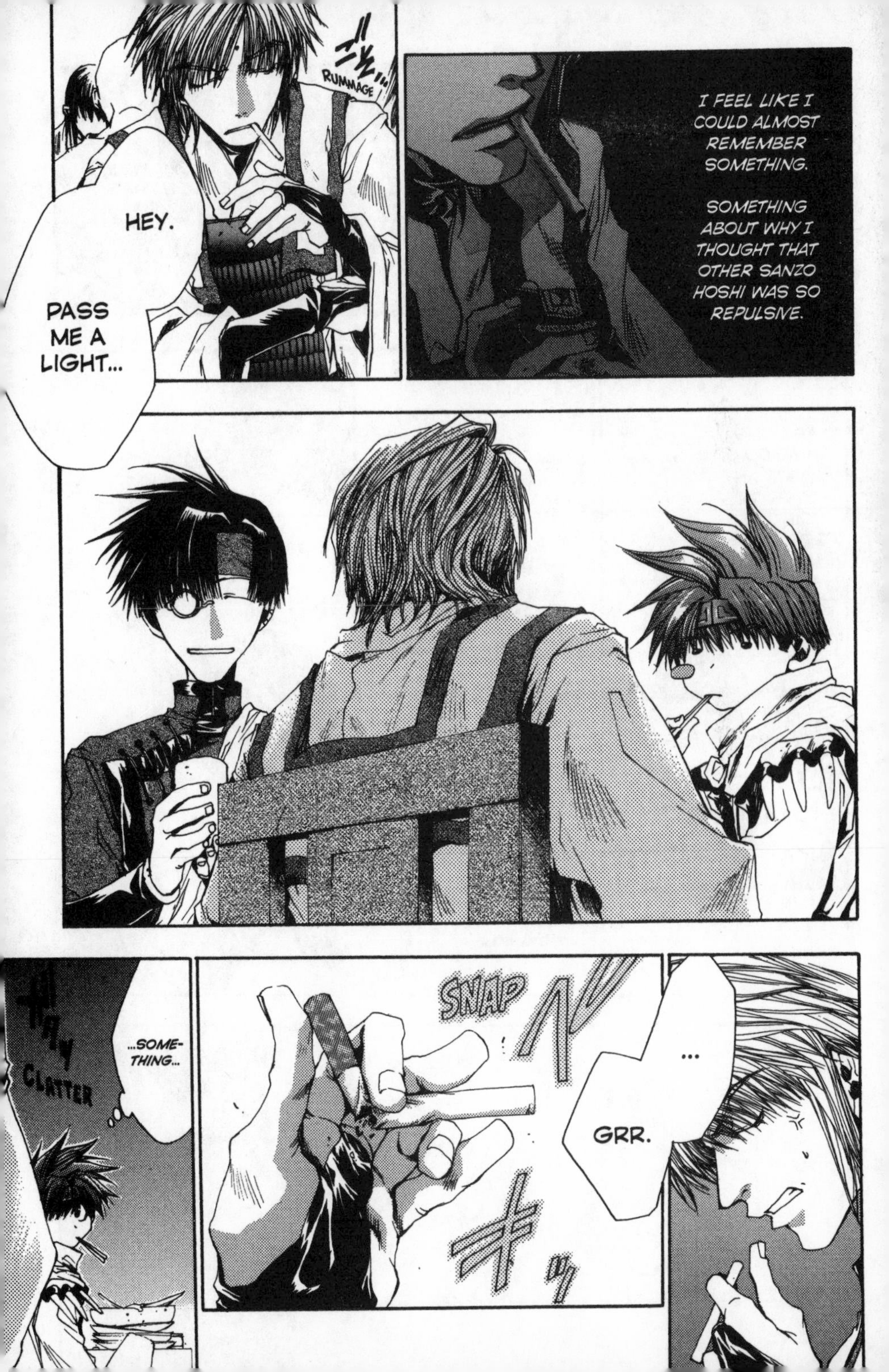
I FEEL LIKE I COULD ALMOST REMEMBER SOMETHING.
SOMETHING ABOUT WHY I THOUGHT THAT OTHER SANZO HOSHI WAS SO REPULSIVE.
RUMMAGE
HEY.
PASS ME A LIGHT...
...
GRR.
SNAP
...SOME-THING...
CLATTER

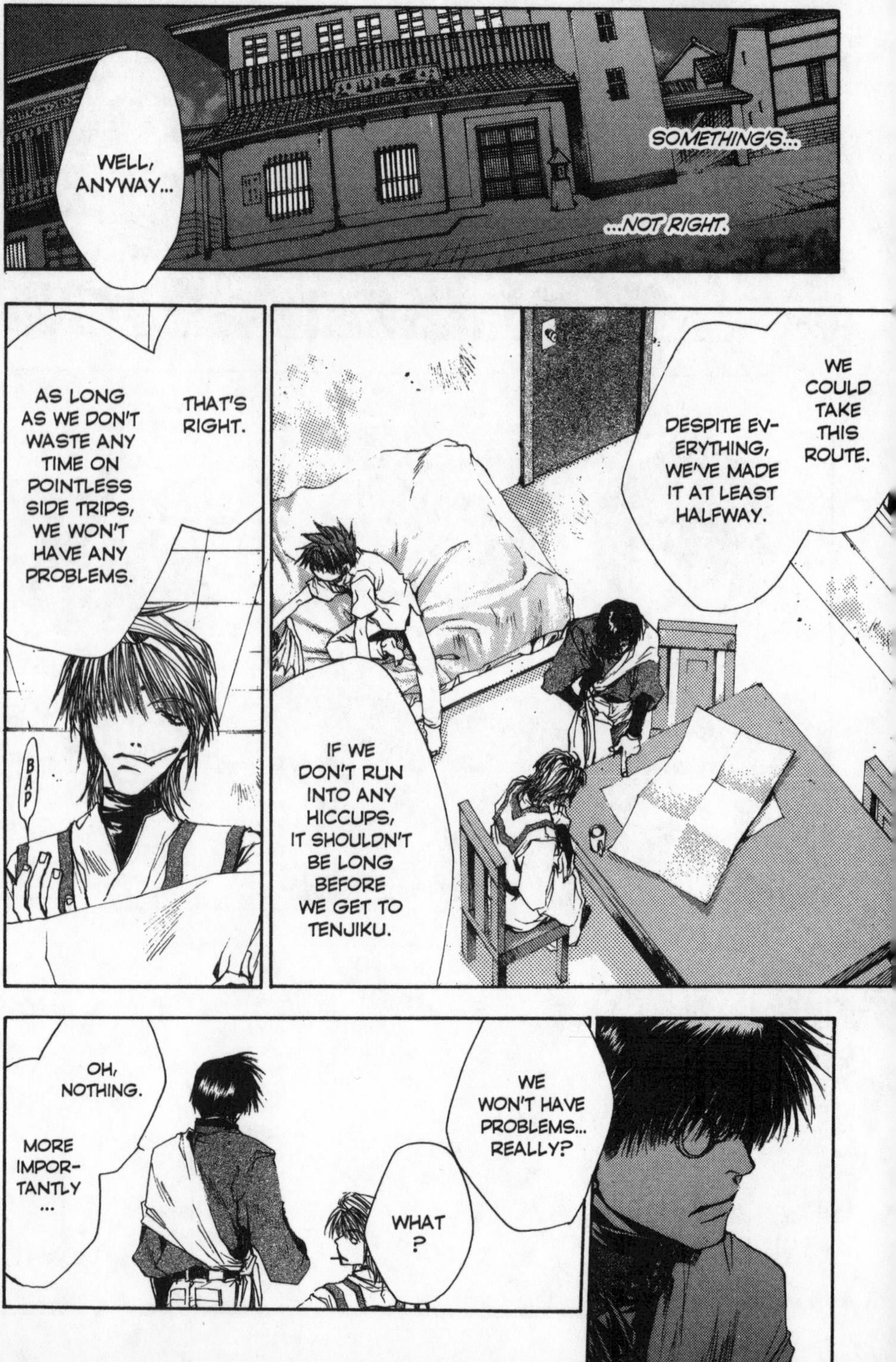
SOMETHING'S...
...NOT RIGHT.
WELL, ANYWAY...
WE COULD TAKE THIS ROUTE.
DESPITE EV-ERYTHING, WE'VE MADE IT AT LEAST HALFWAY.
IF WE DON'T RUN INTO ANY HICCUPS, IT SHOULDN'T BE LONG BEFORE WE GET TO TENJIKU.
THAT'S RIGHT.
AS LONG AS WE DON'T WASTE ANY TIME ON POINTLESS SIDE TRIPS, WE WON'T HAVE ANY PROBLEMS.
BAP
WE WON'T HAVE PROBLEMS... REALLY?
WHAT?
OH, NOTHING.
MORE IMPOR-TANTLY...

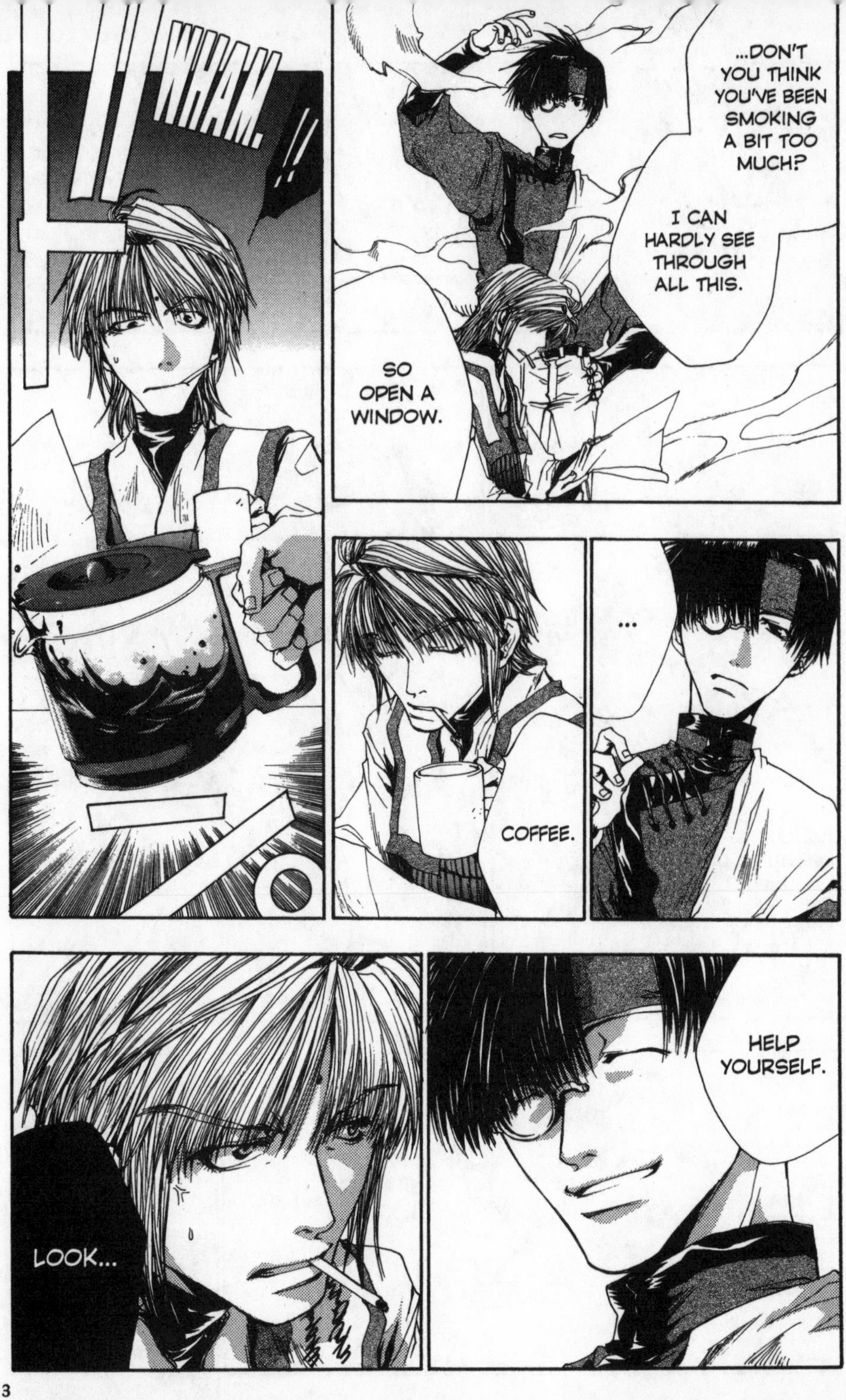
...DON'T YOU THINK YOU'VE BEEN SMOKING A BIT TOO MUCH?
I CAN HARDLY SEE THROUGH ALL THIS.
SO OPEN A WINDOW.
...
COFFEE.
WHAM.!!
HELP YOURSELF.
LOOK...

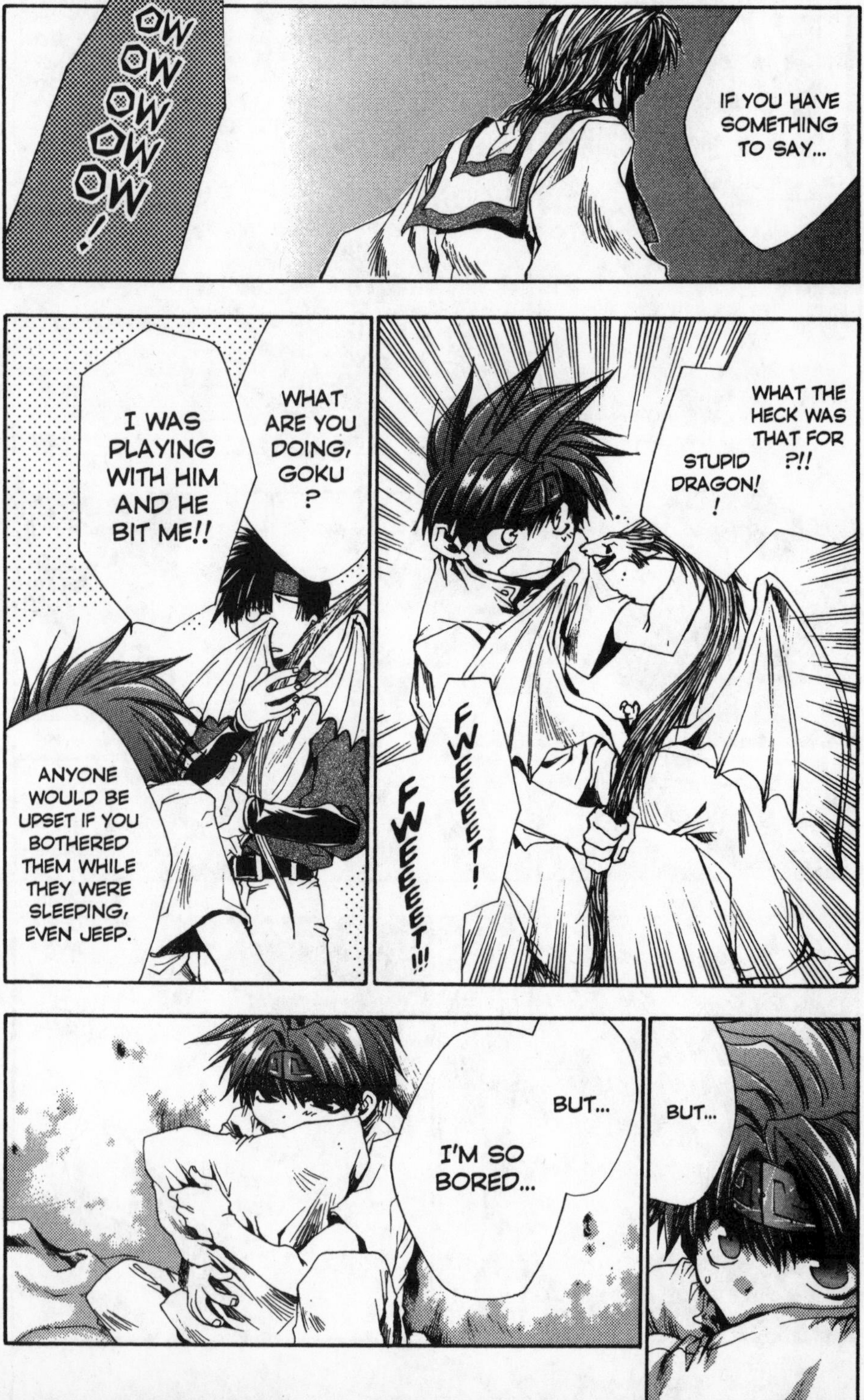
IF YOU HAVE SOMETHING TO SAY...
OWOWOWOWOW!
WHAT THE HECK WAS THAT FOR?!!
STUPID DRAGON!!
FWEEET!
FWEEEEET!!!
WHAT ARE YOU DOING, GOKU?
I WAS PLAYING WITH HIM AND HE BIT ME!!
ANYONE WOULD BE UPSET IF YOU BOTHERED THEM WHILE THEY WERE SLEEPING, EVEN JEEP.
BUT...
BUT...
I'M SO BORED...

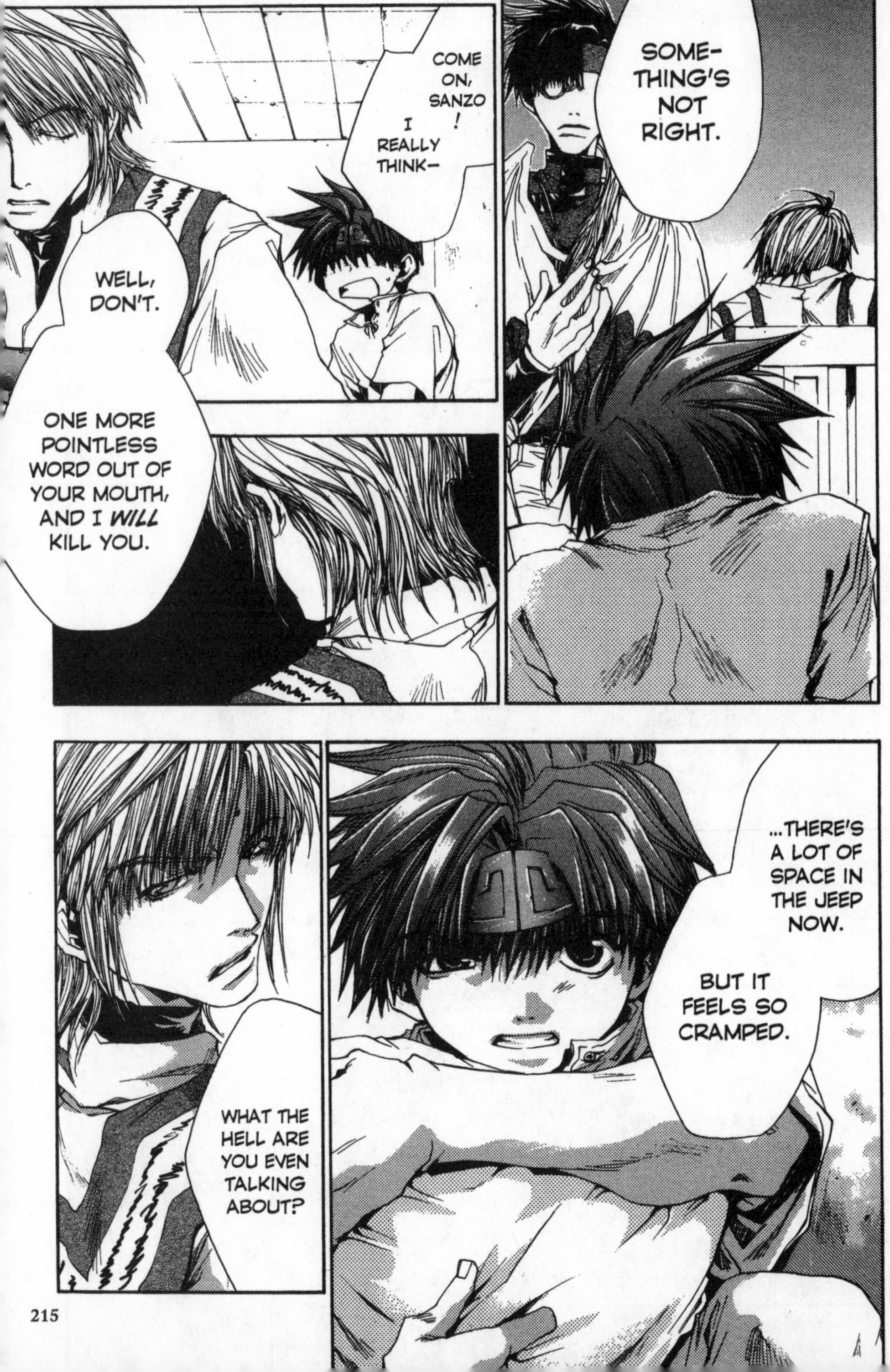
SOME-THING'S NOT RIGHT.
COME ON, SANZO!
I REALLY THINK—
WELL, DON'T.
ONE MORE POINTLESS WORD OUT OF YOUR MOUTH, AND I *WILL* KILL YOU.
...THERE'S A LOT OF SPACE IN THE JEEP NOW.
BUT IT FEELS SO CRAMPED.
WHAT THE HELL ARE YOU EVEN TALKING ABOUT?

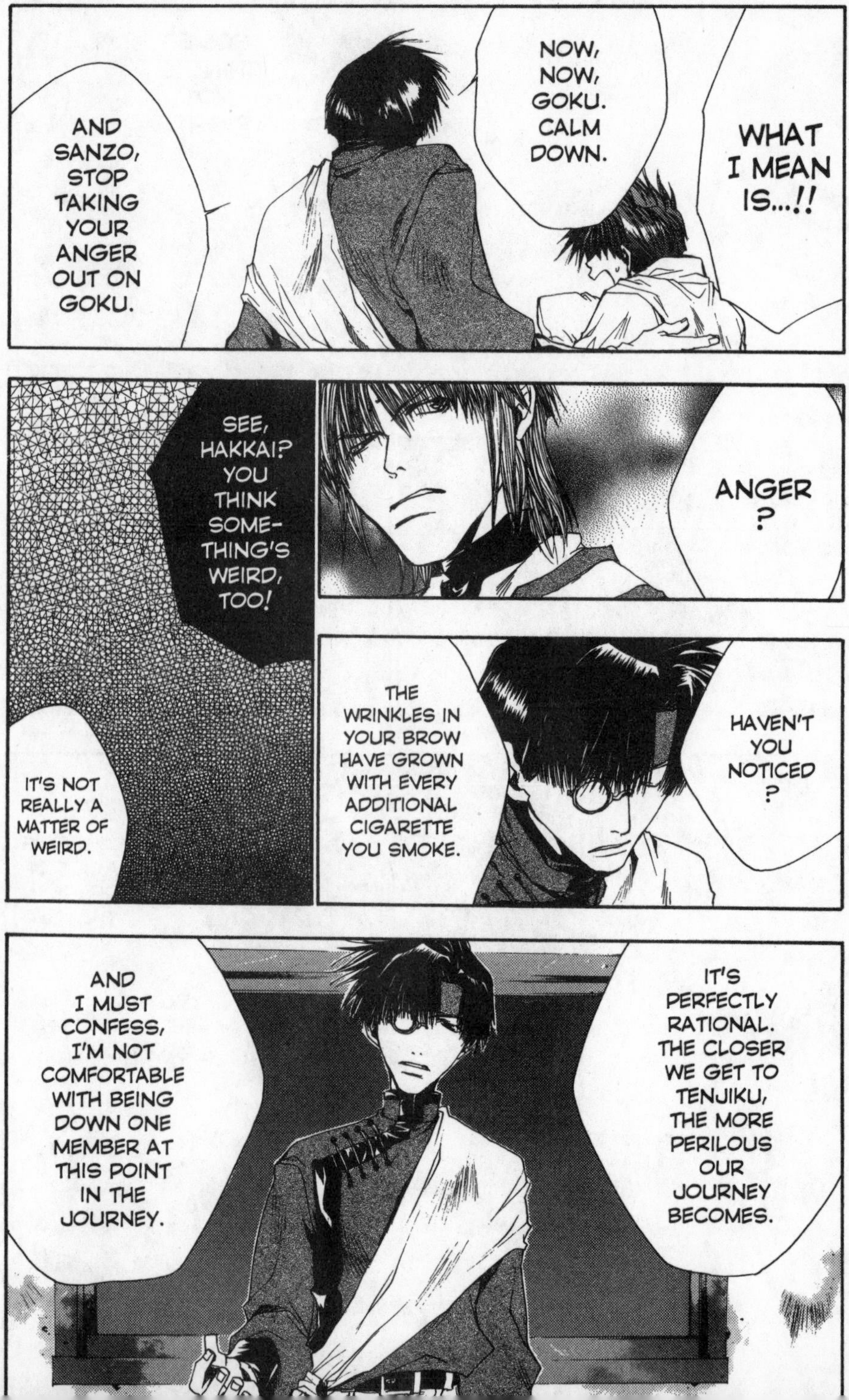
WHAT I MEAN IS...!!
NOW, NOW, GOKU. CALM DOWN.
AND SANZO, STOP TAKING YOUR ANGER OUT ON GOKU.
ANGER ?
HAVEN'T YOU NOTICED ?
THE WRINKLES IN YOUR BROW HAVE GROWN WITH EVERY ADDITIONAL CIGARETTE YOU SMOKE.
SEE, HAKKAI? YOU THINK SOME-THING'S WEIRD, TOO!
IT'S NOT REALLY A MATTER OF WEIRD.
IT'S PERFECTLY RATIONAL. THE CLOSER WE GET TO TENJIKU, THE MORE PERILOUS OUR JOURNEY BECOMES.
AND I MUST CONFESS, I'M NOT COMFORTABLE WITH BEING DOWN ONE MEMBER AT THIS POINT IN THE JOURNEY.

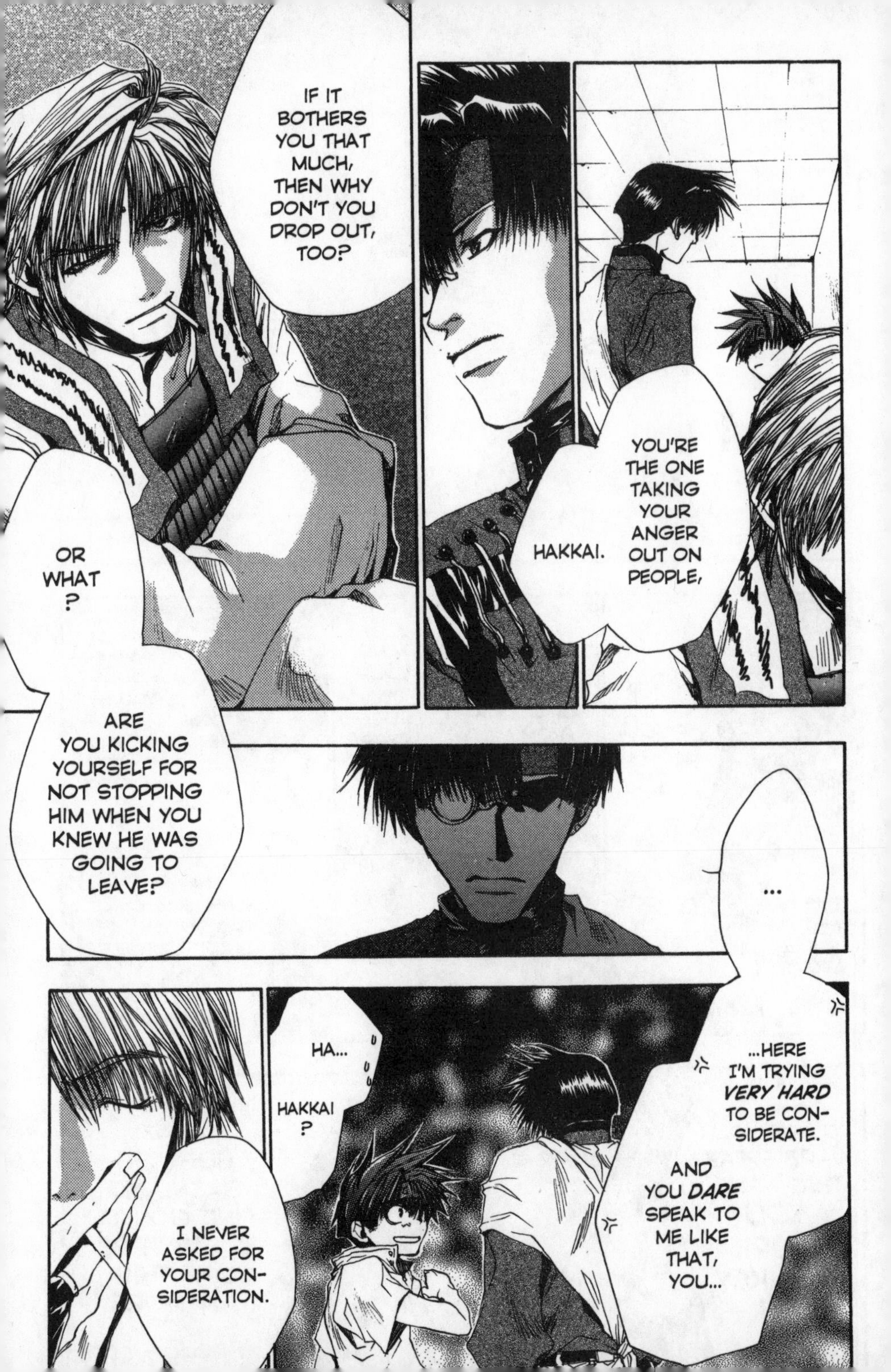
YOU'RE THE ONE TAKING YOUR ANGER OUT ON PEOPLE,
HAKKAI.
IF IT BOTHERS YOU THAT MUCH, THEN WHY DON'T YOU DROP OUT, TOO?
OR WHAT?
ARE YOU KICKING YOURSELF FOR NOT STOPPING HIM WHEN YOU KNEW HE WAS GOING TO LEAVE?
...
...HERE I'M TRYING *VERY HARD* TO BE CON-SIDERATE.
AND YOU *DARE* SPEAK TO ME LIKE THAT, YOU...
HA...
HAKKAI?
I NEVER ASKED FOR YOUR CON-SIDERATION.

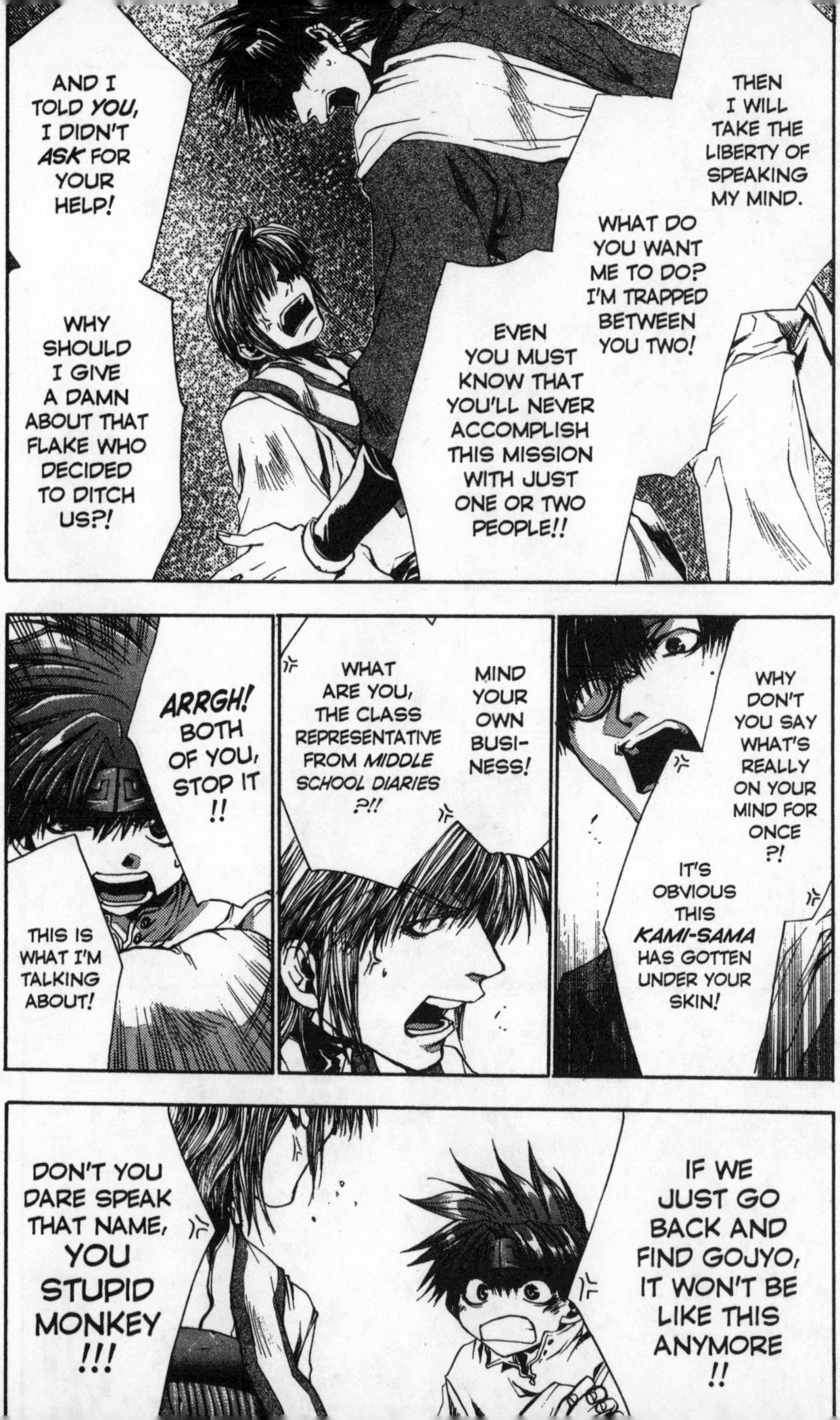

THEN I WILL TAKE THE LIBERTY OF SPEAKING MY MIND.
WHAT DO YOU WANT ME TO DO? I'M TRAPPED BETWEEN YOU TWO!
EVEN YOU MUST KNOW THAT YOU'LL NEVER ACCOMPLISH THIS MISSION WITH JUST ONE OR TWO PEOPLE!!
AND I TOLD *YOU*, I DIDN'T *ASK* FOR YOUR HELP!
WHY SHOULD I GIVE A DAMN ABOUT THAT FLAKE WHO DECIDED TO DITCH US?!
WHY DON'T YOU SAY WHAT'S REALLY ON YOUR MIND FOR ONCE ?!
IT'S OBVIOUS THIS *KAMI-SAMA* HAS GOTTEN UNDER YOUR SKIN!
MIND YOUR OWN BUSI-NESS!
WHAT ARE YOU, THE CLASS REPRESENTATIVE FROM *MIDDLE SCHOOL DIARIES* ?!!
ARRGH! BOTH OF YOU, STOP IT !!
THIS IS WHAT I'M TALKING ABOUT!
IF WE JUST GO BACK AND FIND GOJYO, IT WON'T BE LIKE THIS ANYMORE !!
DON'T YOU DARE SPEAK THAT NAME, **YOU STUPID MONKEY** !!!

CHAPTER 43: Be Lacking

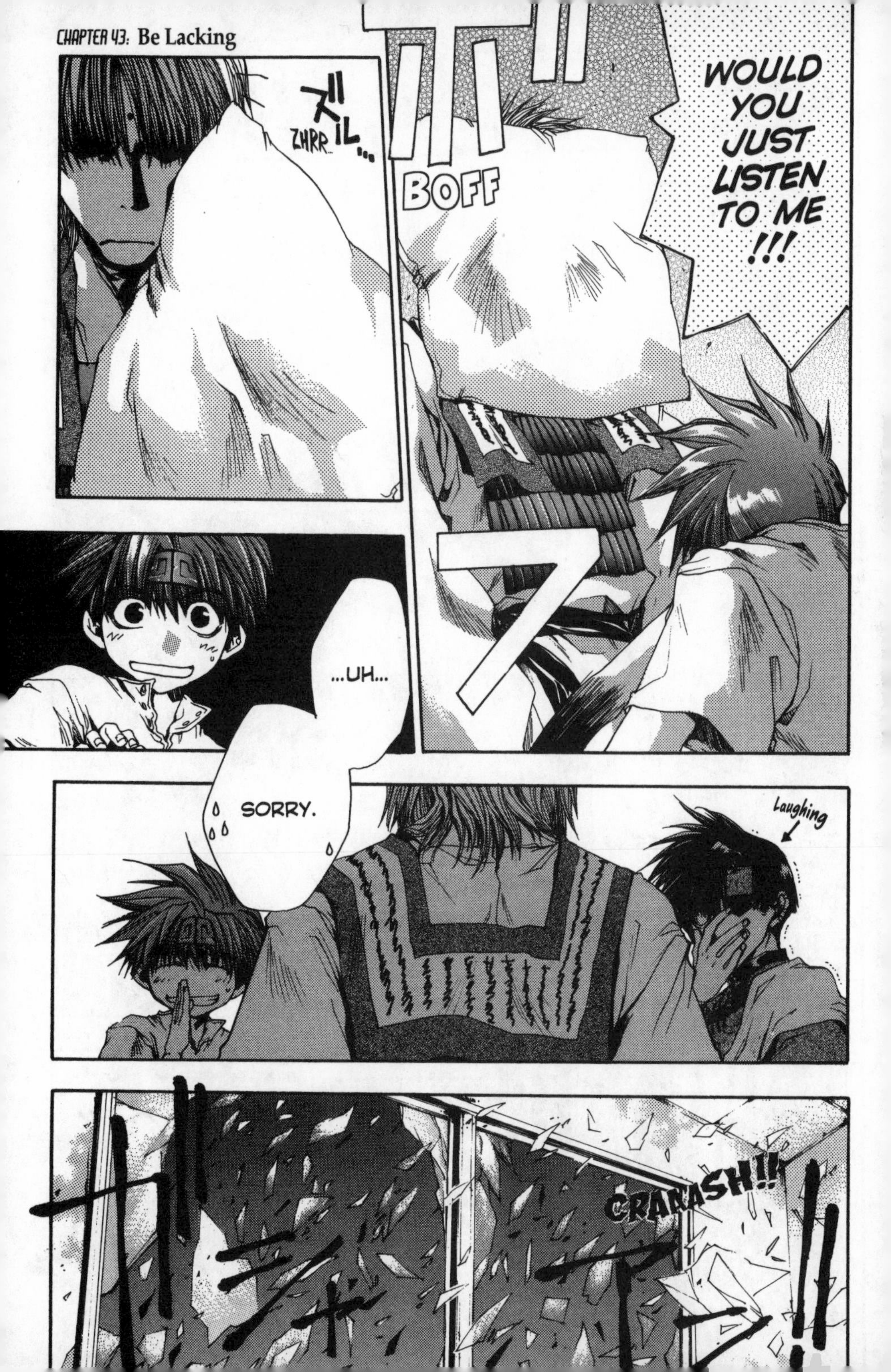
WOULD YOU JUST LISTEN TO ME!!!
BOFF
ズル
ZHRR...
...UH...
SORRY.
Laughing
CRAAASH!!

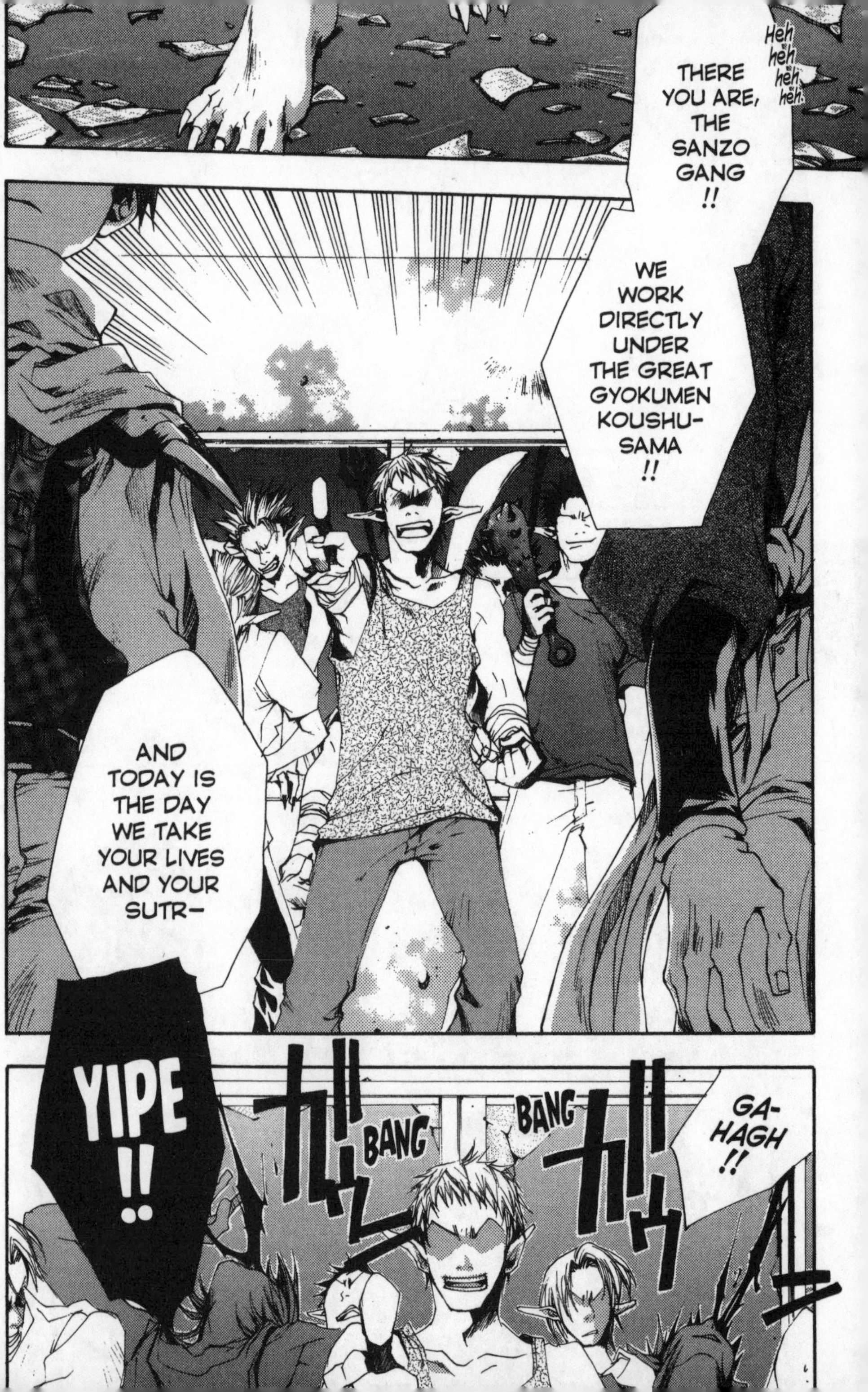
THERE YOU ARE, THE SANZO GANG!!
Heh heh heh heh
WE WORK DIRECTLY UNDER THE GREAT GYOKUMEN KOUSHU-SAMA!!
AND TODAY IS THE DAY WE TAKE YOUR LIVES AND YOUR SUTR–
GA-HAGH!!
BANG
BANG
YIPE!!

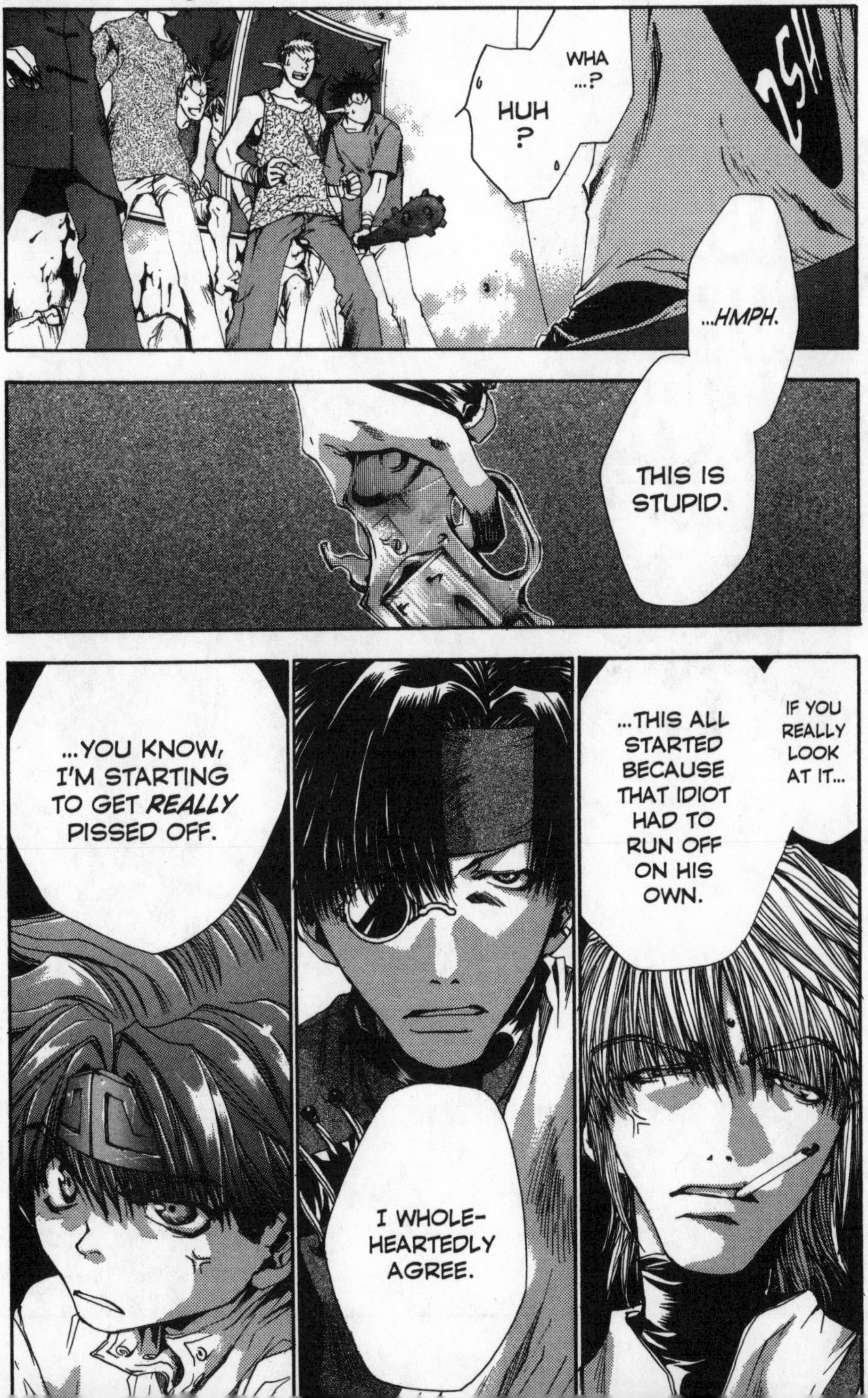
WHA ...? HUH ?
...HMPH.
THIS IS STUPID.
IF YOU REALLY LOOK AT IT...
...THIS ALL STARTED BECAUSE THAT IDIOT HAD TO RUN OFF ON HIS OWN.
I WHOLE-HEARTEDLY AGREE.
...YOU KNOW, I'M STARTING TO GET *REALLY* PISSED OFF.

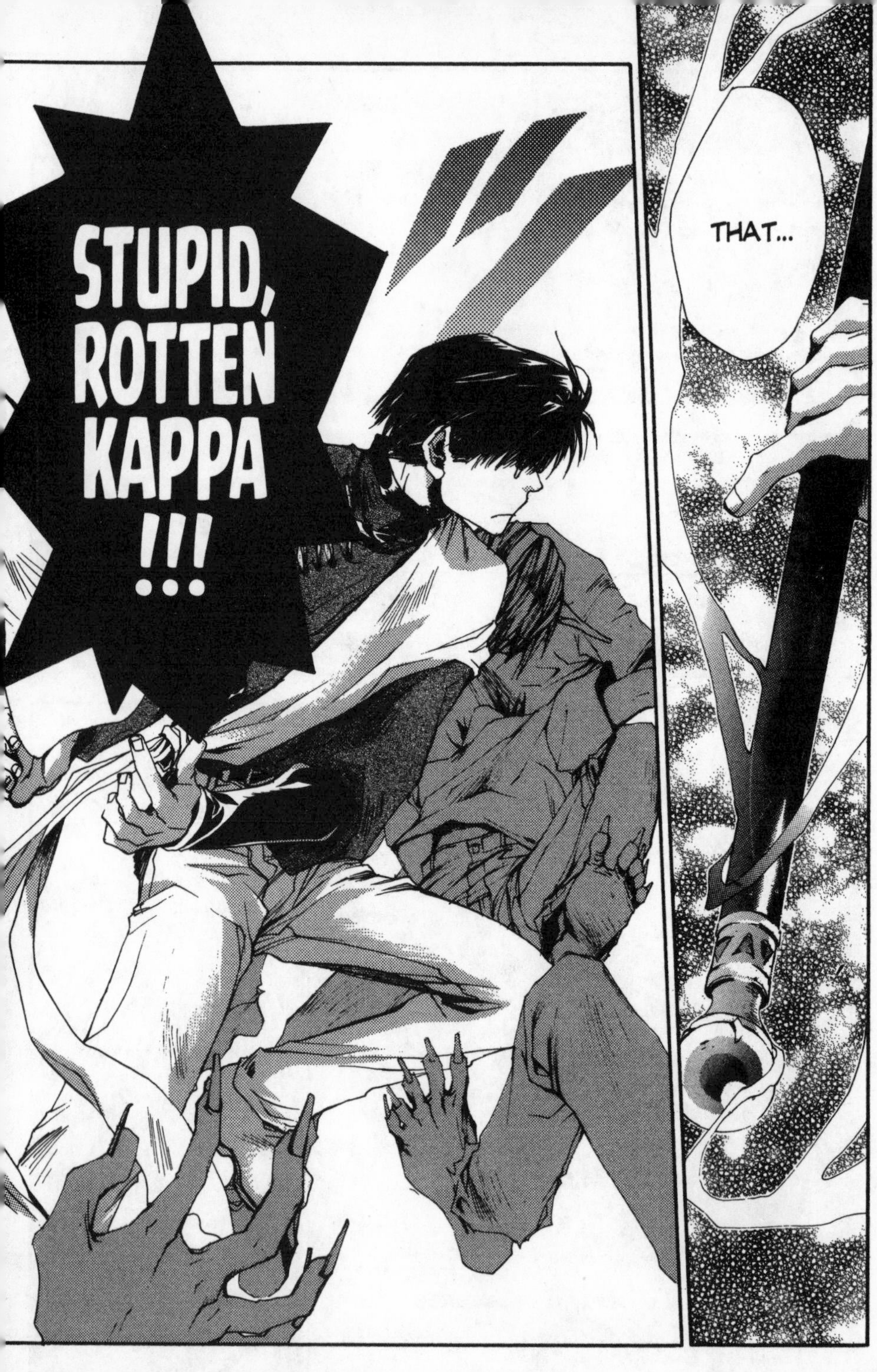
THAT...
STUPID, ROTTEN KAPPA !!!

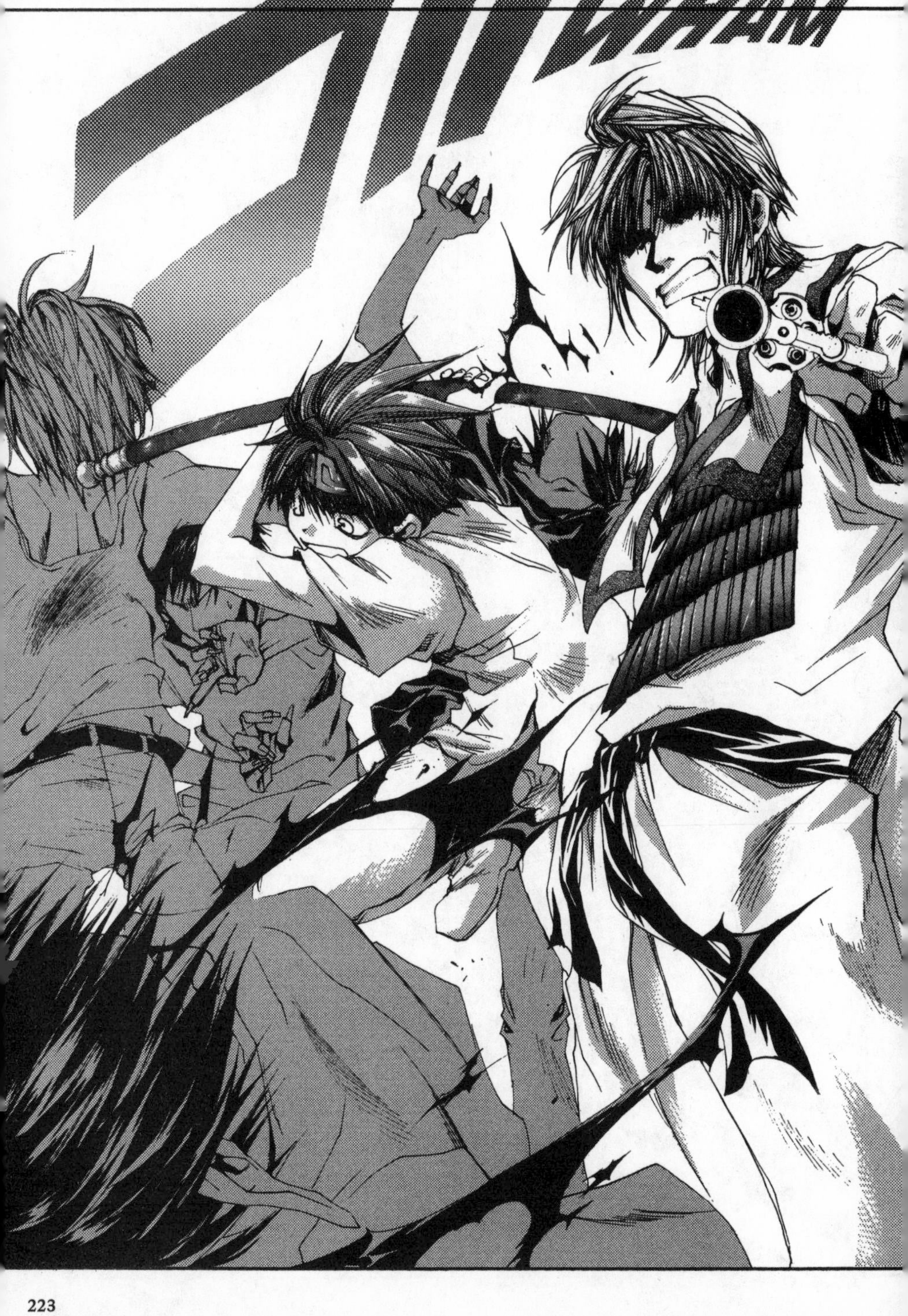
WHAM

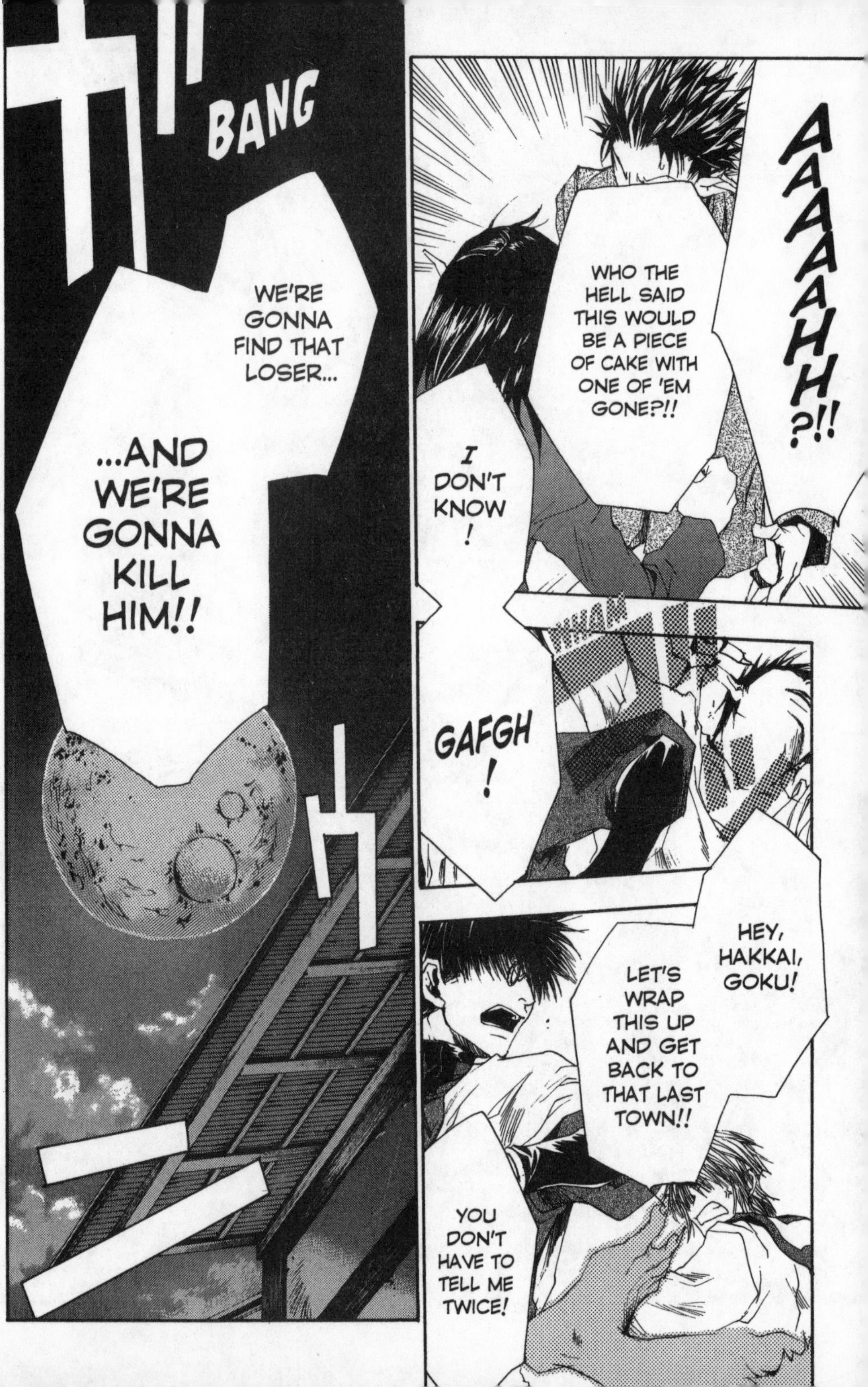
AAAAAHH?!!
WHO THE HELL SAID THIS WOULD BE A PIECE OF CAKE WITH ONE OF 'EM GONE?!!
I DON'T KNOW!
GAFGH!
HEY, HAKKAI, GOKU!
LET'S WRAP THIS UP AND GET BACK TO THAT LAST TOWN!!
YOU DON'T HAVE TO TELL ME TWICE!
BANG
WE'RE GONNA FIND THAT LOSER...
...AND WE'RE GONNA KILL HIM!!

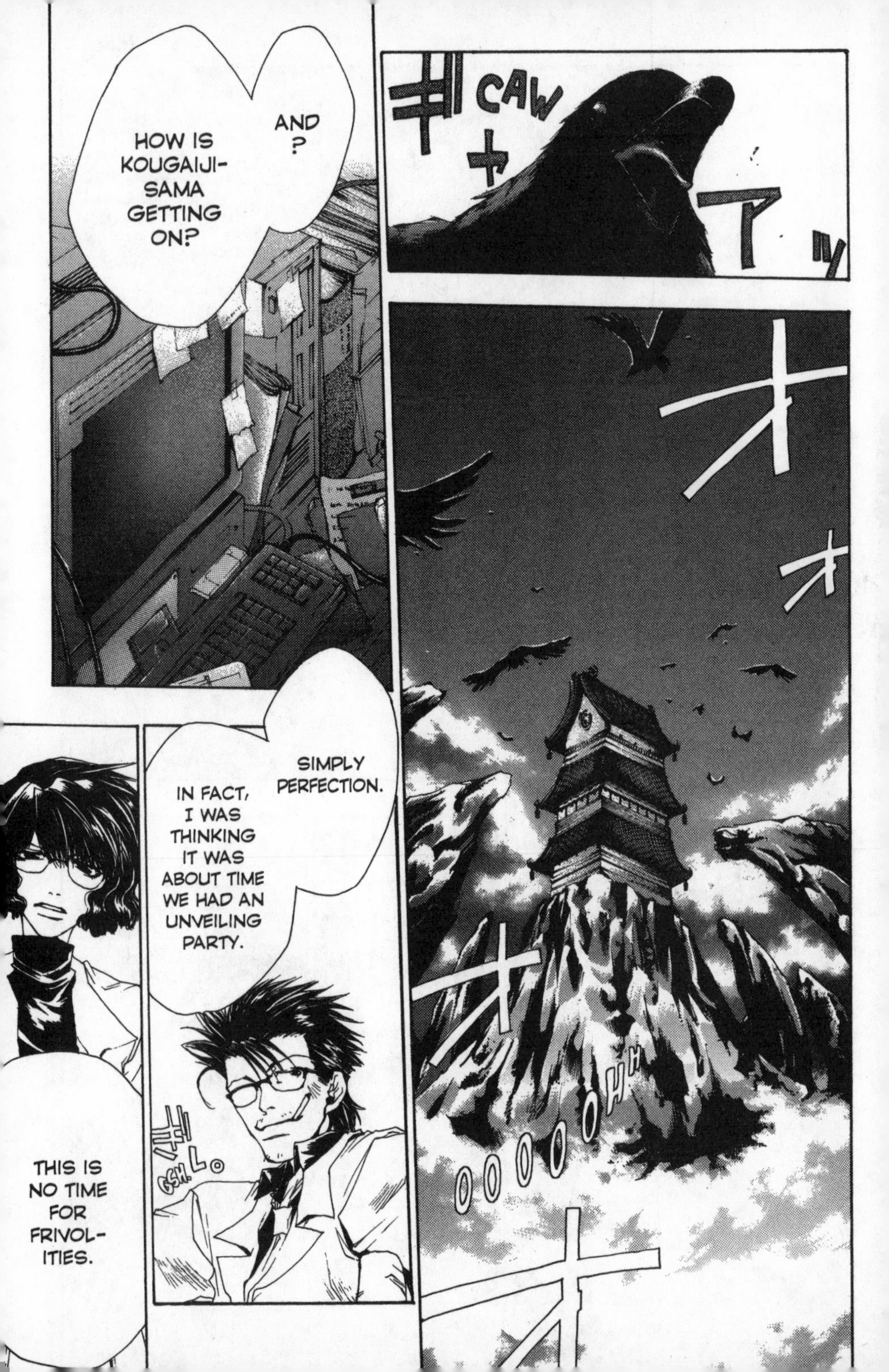
CAW
OOOOOOHH
AND?
HOW IS KOUGAIJI-SAMA GETTING ON?
SIMPLY PERFECTION.
IN FACT, I WAS THINKING IT WAS ABOUT TIME WE HAD AN UNVEILING PARTY.
GSH.
THIS IS NO TIME FOR FRIVOL-ITIES.

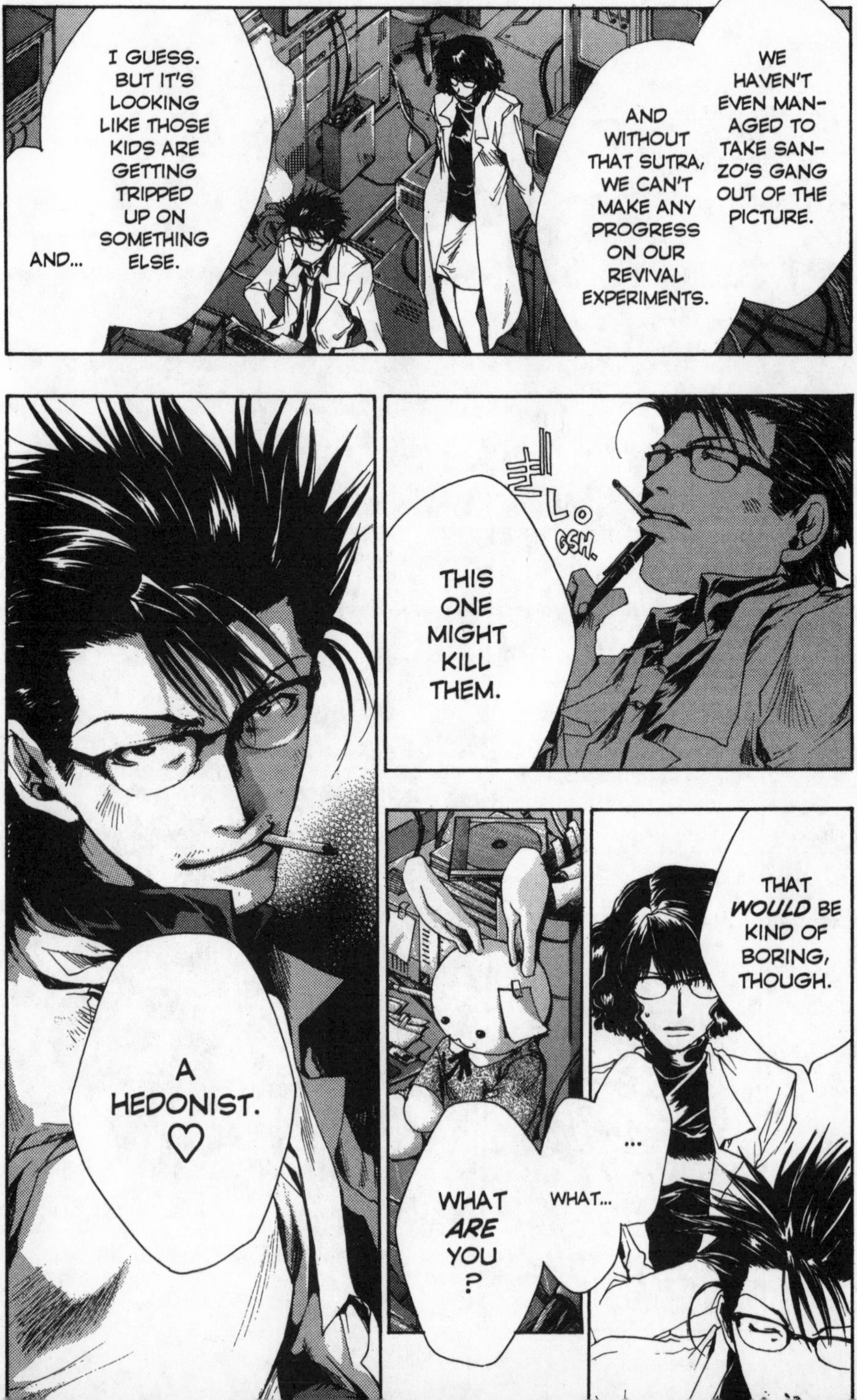
WE HAVEN'T EVEN MAN-AGED TO TAKE SAN-ZO'S GANG OUT OF THE PICTURE.
AND WITHOUT THAT SUTRA, WE CAN'T MAKE ANY PROGRESS ON OUR REVIVAL EXPERIMENTS.
I GUESS. BUT IT'S LOOKING LIKE THOSE KIDS ARE GETTING TRIPPED UP ON SOMETHING ELSE.
AND...
GSH.
THIS ONE MIGHT KILL THEM.
THAT *WOULD* BE KIND OF BORING, THOUGH.
...
WHAT...
WHAT *ARE* YOU ?
A HEDONIST. ♡

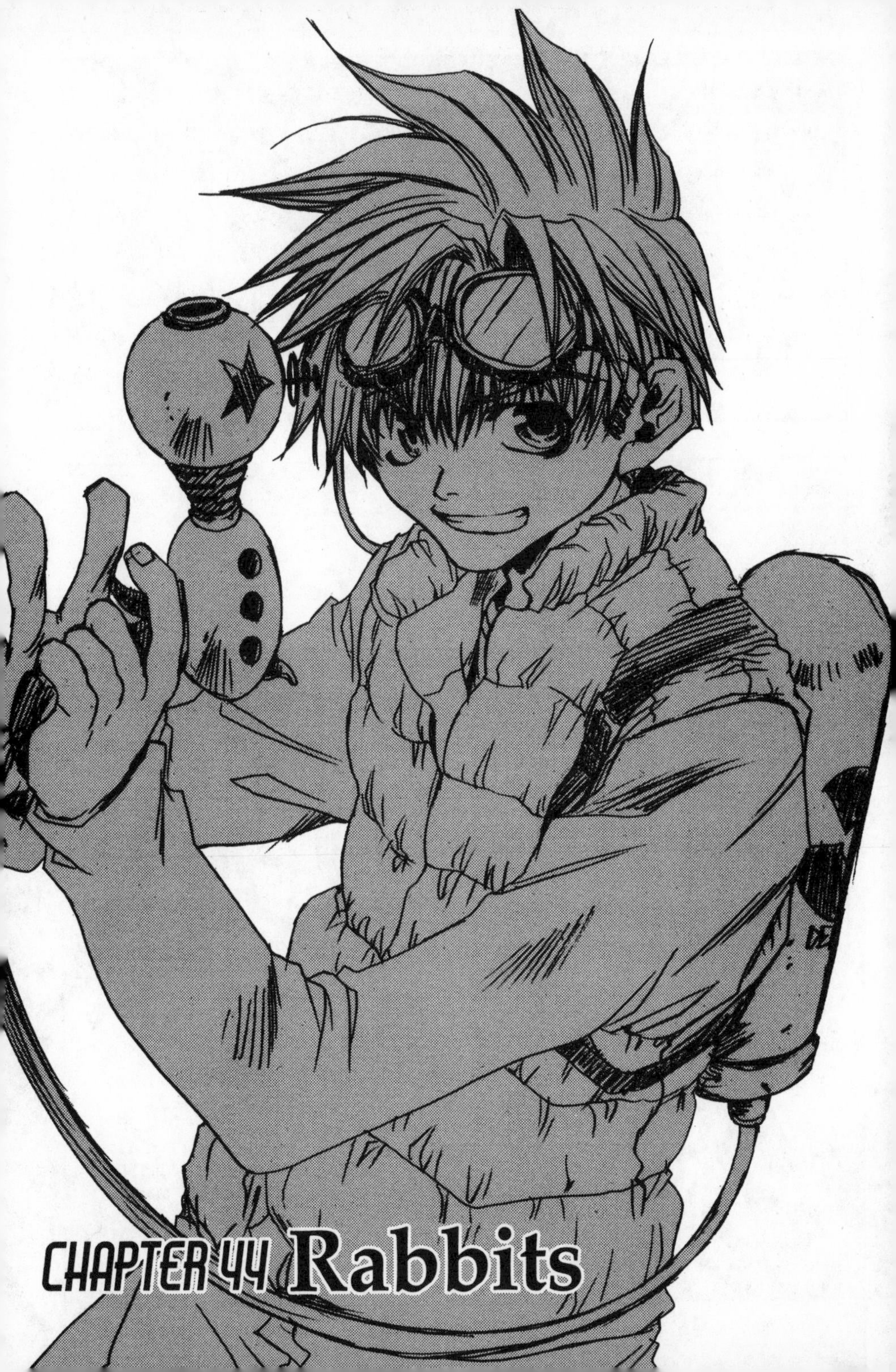

CHAPTER 44 Rabbits

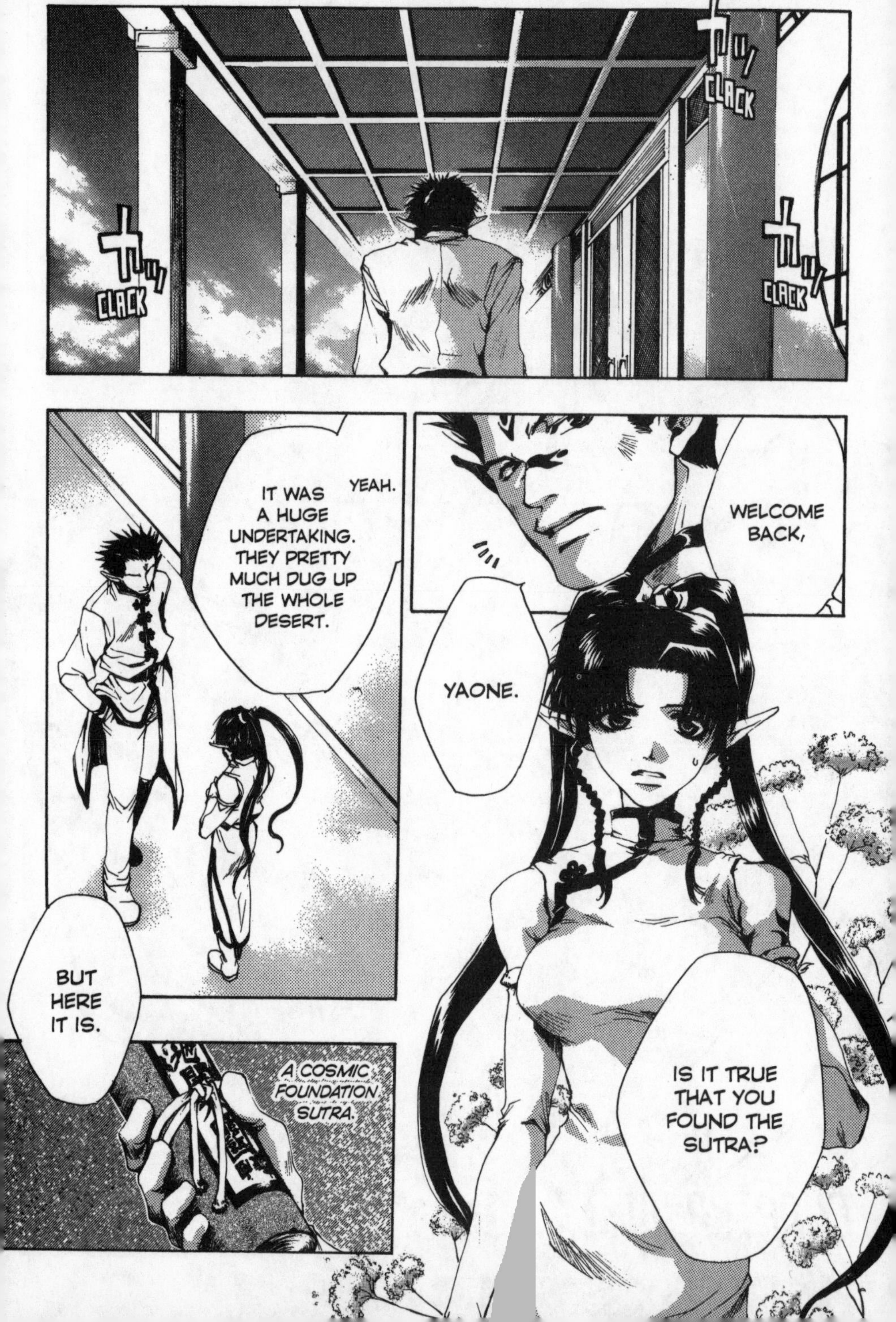

CLACK
CLACK
CLACK
WELCOME BACK,
YAONE.
IS IT TRUE THAT YOU FOUND THE SUTRA?
YEAH.
IT WAS A HUGE UNDERTAKING. THEY PRETTY MUCH DUG UP THE WHOLE DESERT.
BUT HERE IT IS.
A COSMIC FOUNDATION SUTRA.

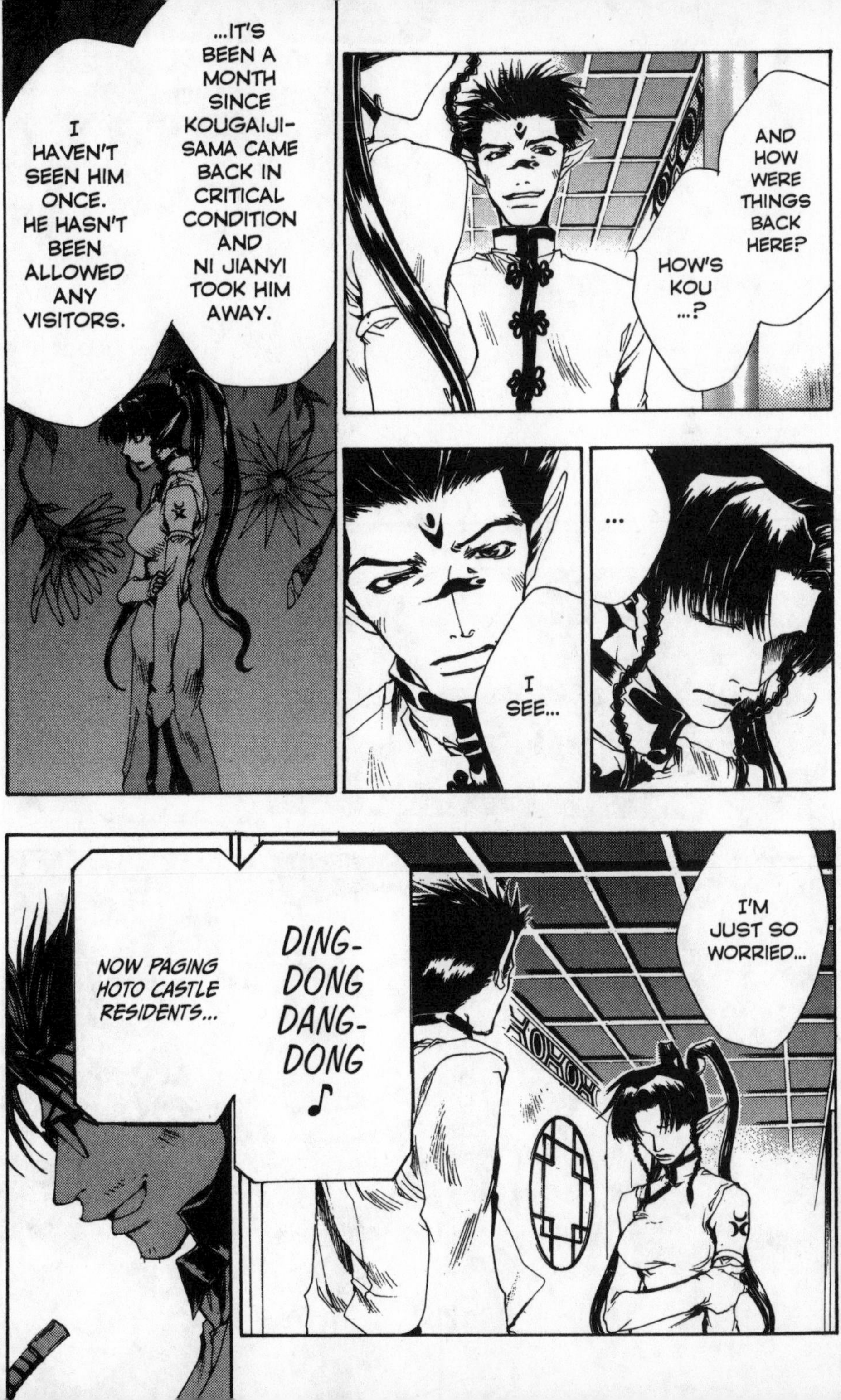
AND HOW WERE THINGS BACK HERE?
HOW'S KOU ...?
...
I SEE...
...IT'S BEEN A MONTH SINCE KOUGAIJI-SAMA CAME BACK IN CRITICAL CONDITION AND NI JIANYI TOOK HIM AWAY.
I HAVEN'T SEEN HIM ONCE. HE HASN'T BEEN ALLOWED ANY VISITORS.
I'M JUST SO WORRIED...
DING-DONG DANG-DONG ♪
NOW PAGING HOTO CASTLE RESIDENTS...

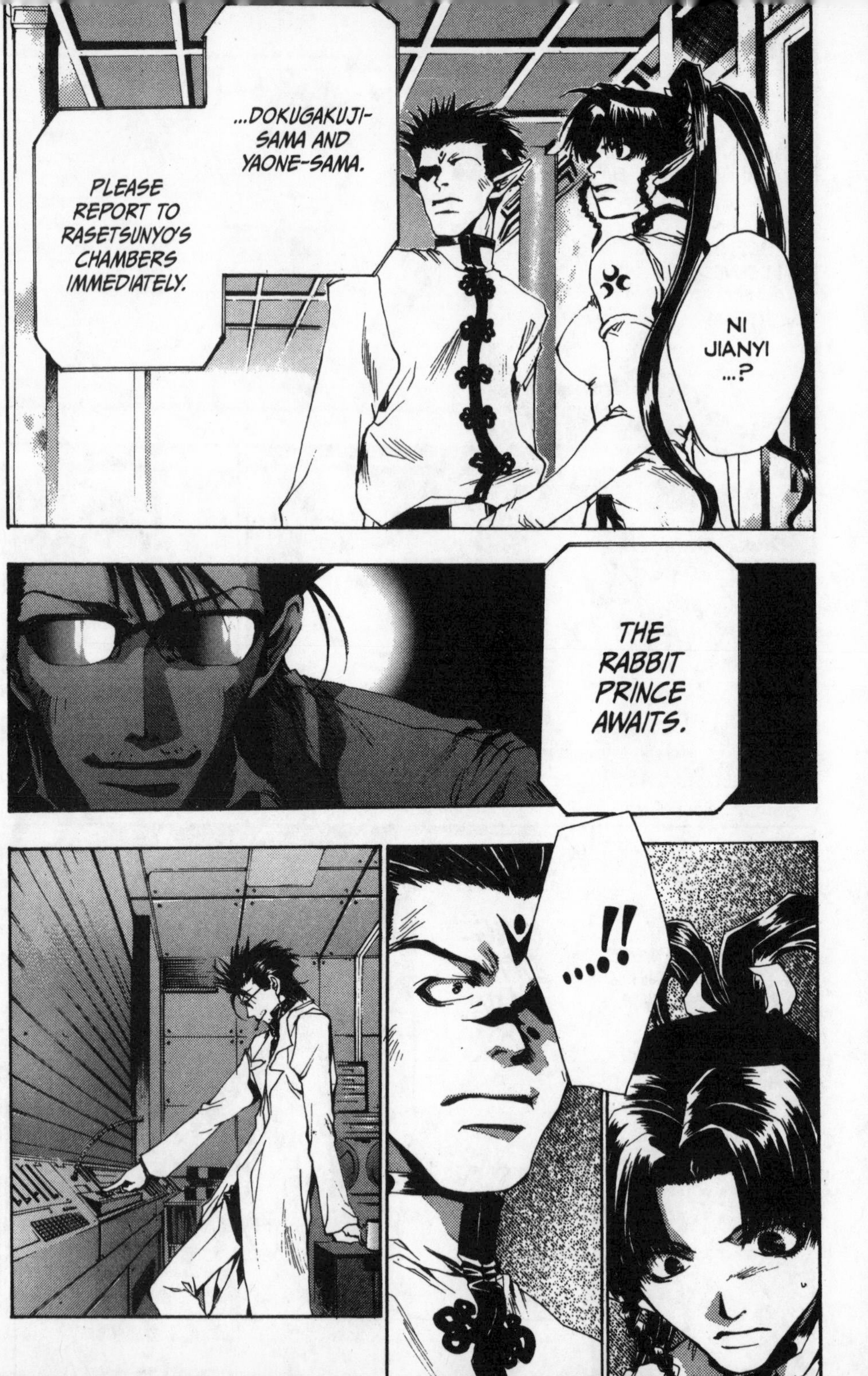
NI JIANYI ...?
...DOKUGAKUJI-SAMA AND YAONE-SAMA.
PLEASE REPORT TO RASETSUNYO'S CHAMBERS IMMEDIATELY.
THE RABBIT PRINCE AWAITS.
...!!

CHAPTER 44: Rabbits

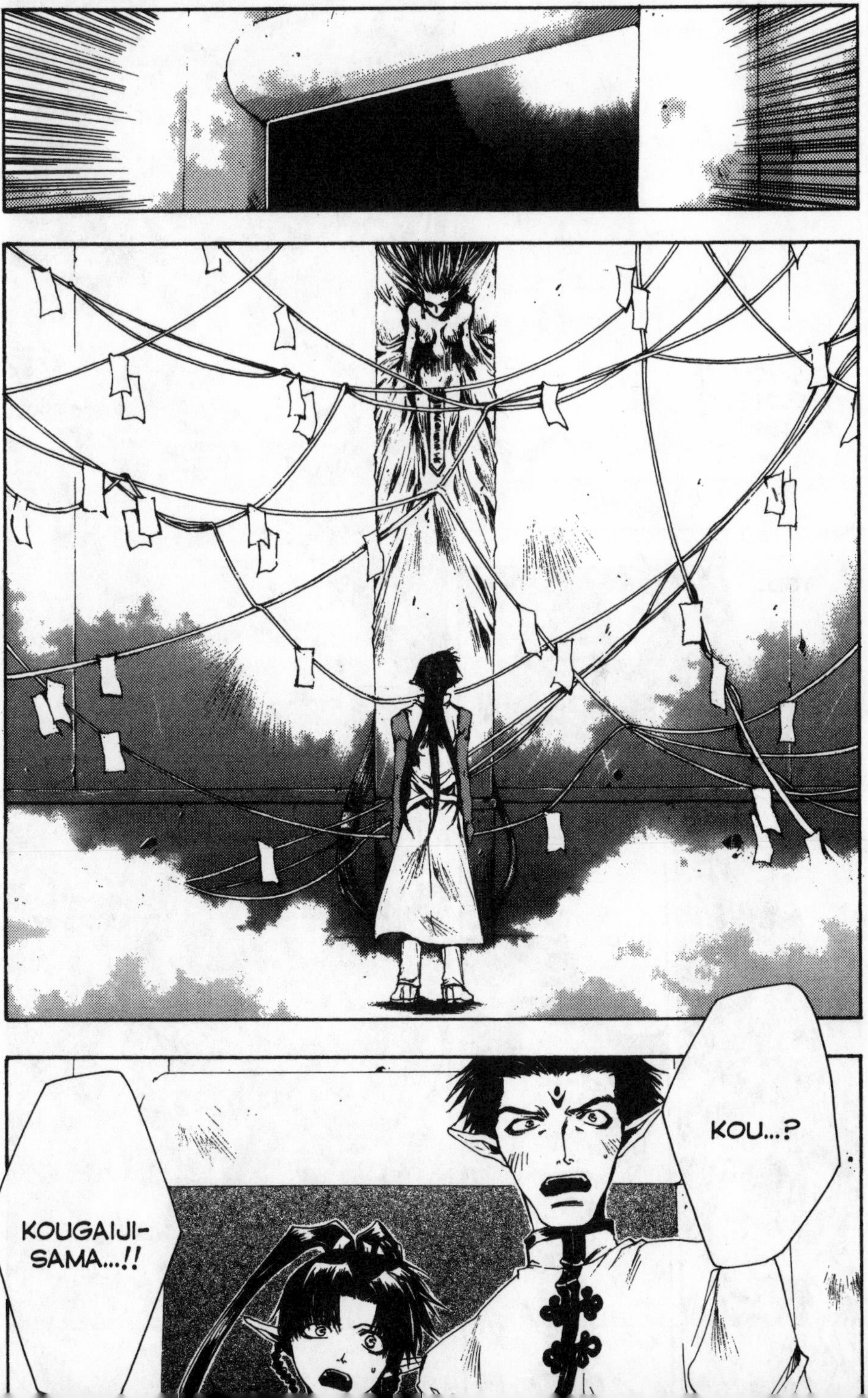
KOU...?
KOUGAIJI-SAMA...!!

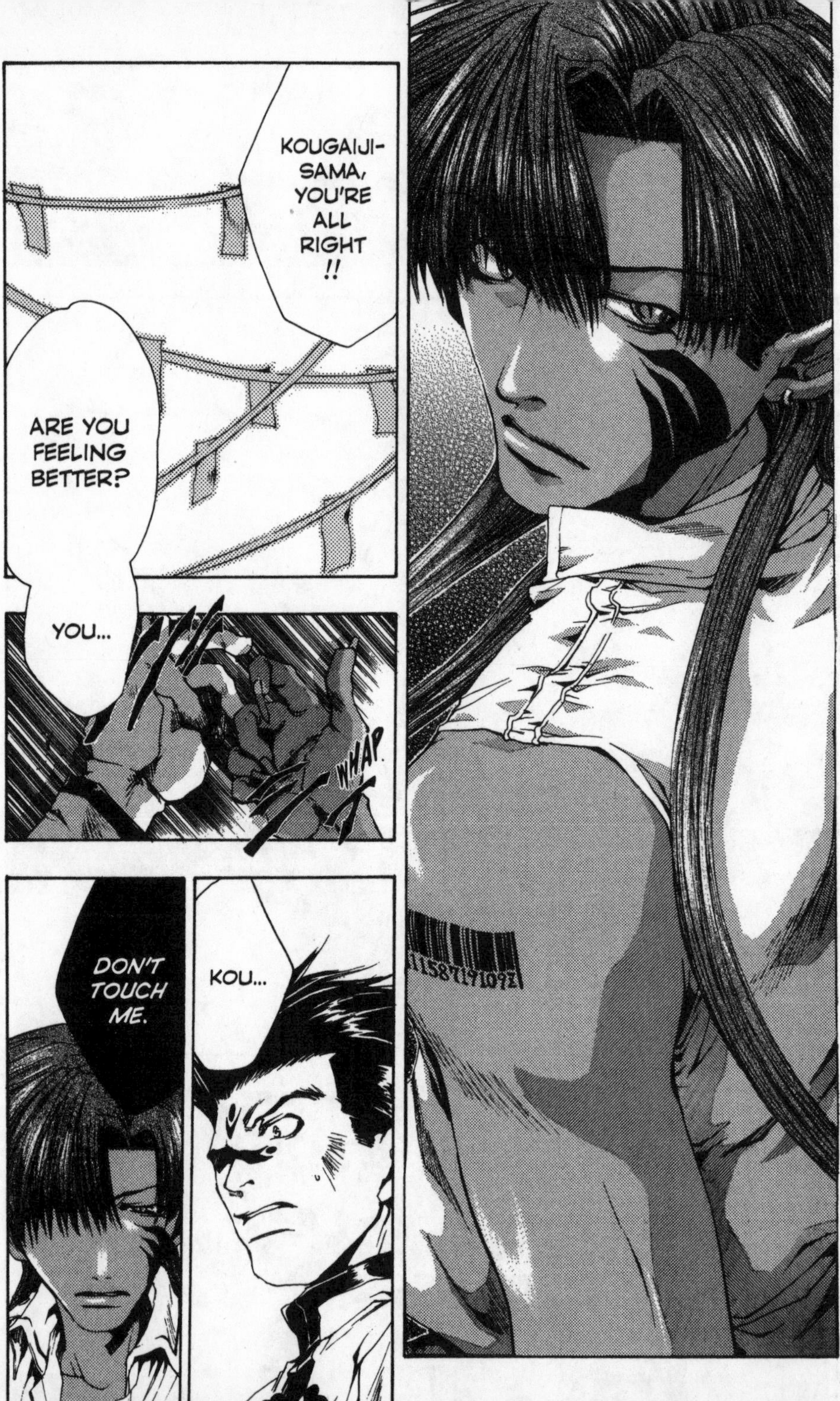
KOUGAIJI-SAMA, YOU'RE ALL RIGHT!!
ARE YOU FEELING BETTER?
YOU...
WHAP
KOU...
DON'T TOUCH ME.

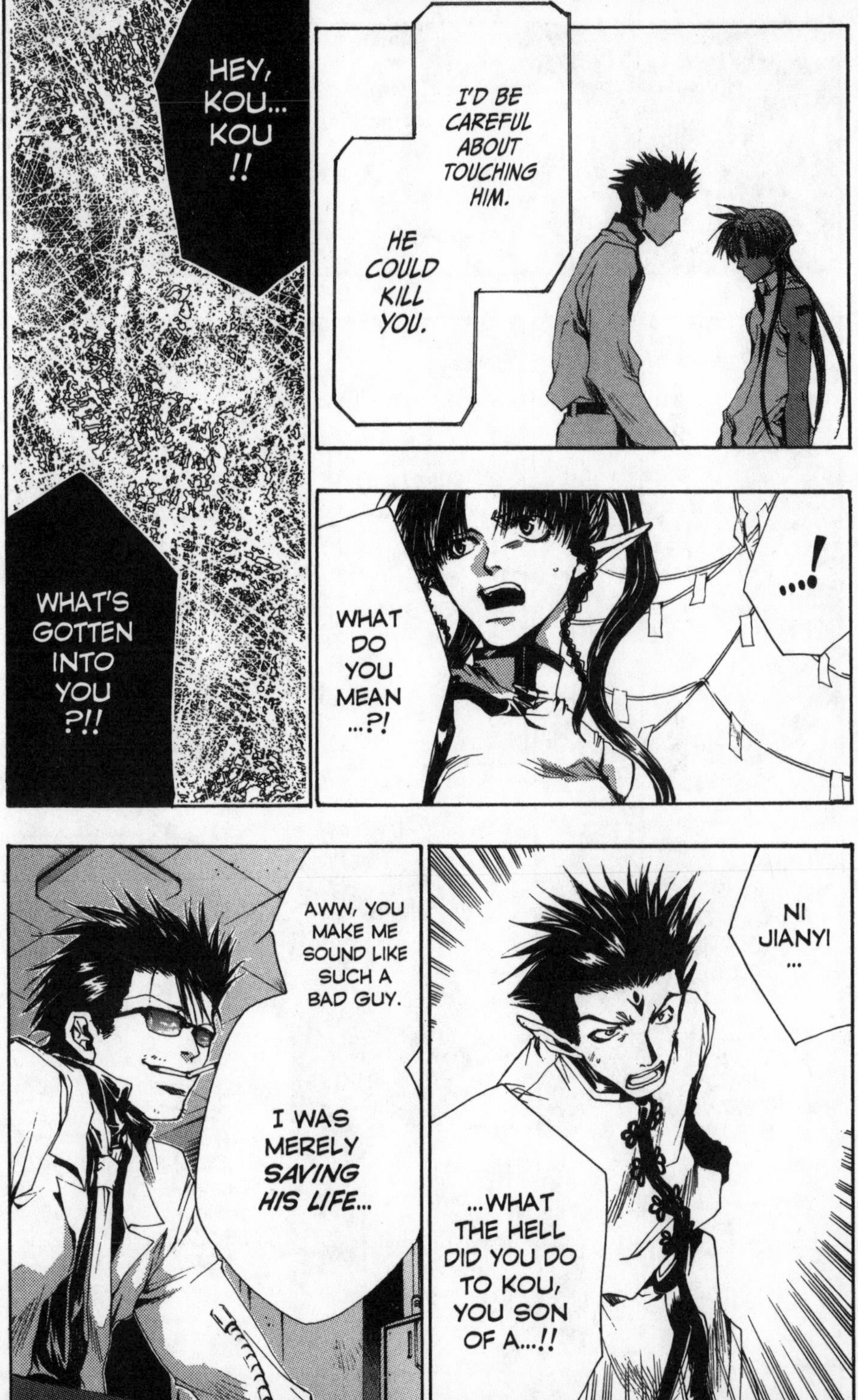
I'D BE CAREFUL ABOUT TOUCHING HIM.
HE COULD KILL YOU.
...!
WHAT DO YOU MEAN ...?!
HEY, KOU... KOU !!
WHAT'S GOTTEN INTO YOU ?!!
NI JIANYI ...
...WHAT THE HELL DID YOU DO TO KOU, YOU SON OF A...!!
AWW, YOU MAKE ME SOUND LIKE SUCH A BAD GUY.
I WAS MERELY *SAVING HIS LIFE*...

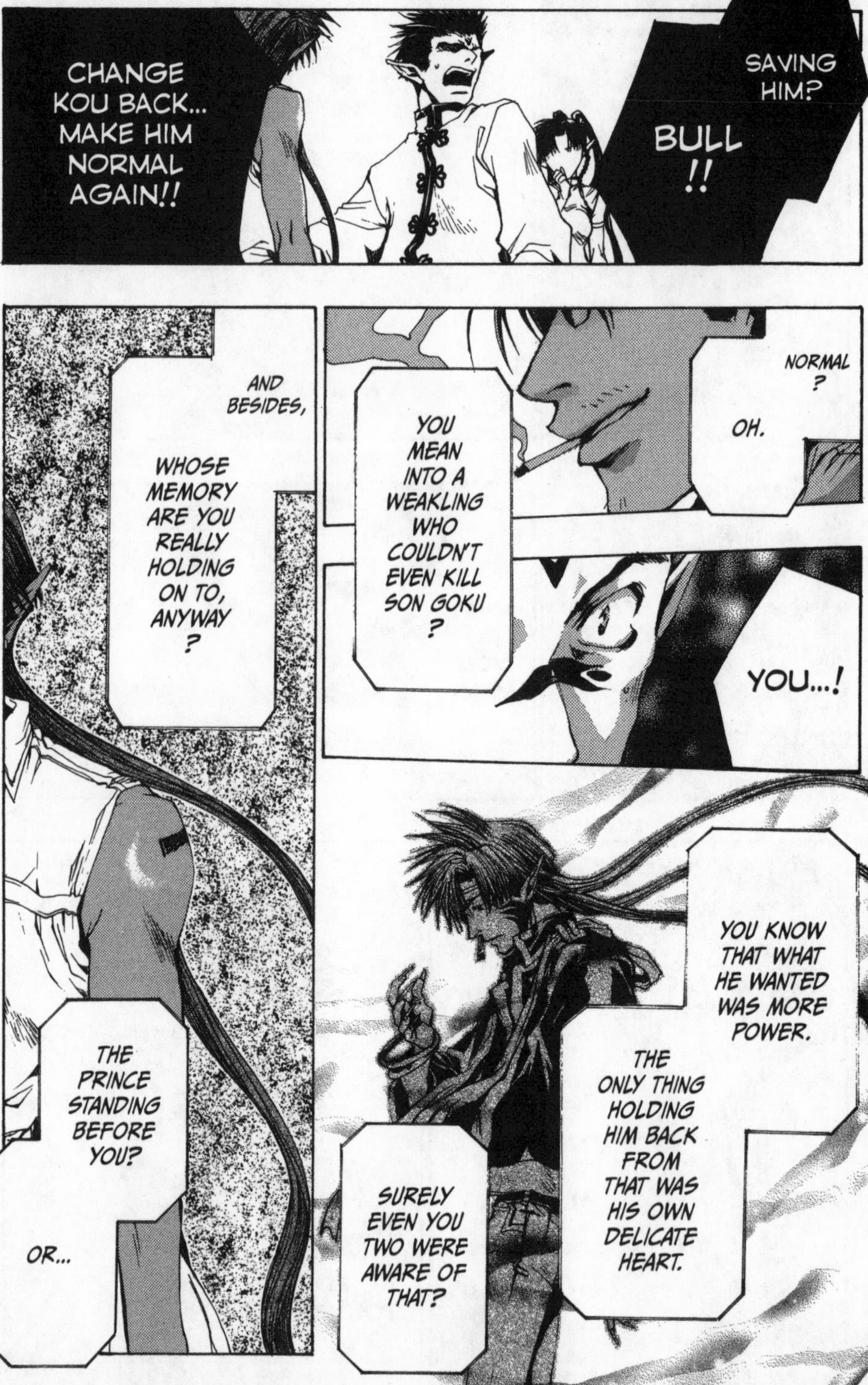
SAVING HIM?
BULL!!
CHANGE KOU BACK... MAKE HIM NORMAL AGAIN!!
NORMAL?
OH.
YOU MEAN INTO A WEAKLING WHO COULDN'T EVEN KILL SON GOKU?
YOU...!
YOU KNOW THAT WHAT HE WANTED WAS MORE POWER.
THE ONLY THING HOLDING HIM BACK FROM THAT WAS HIS OWN DELICATE HEART.
SURELY EVEN YOU TWO WERE AWARE OF THAT?
AND BESIDES,
WHOSE MEMORY ARE YOU REALLY HOLDING ON TO, ANYWAY?
THE PRINCE STANDING BEFORE YOU?
OR...

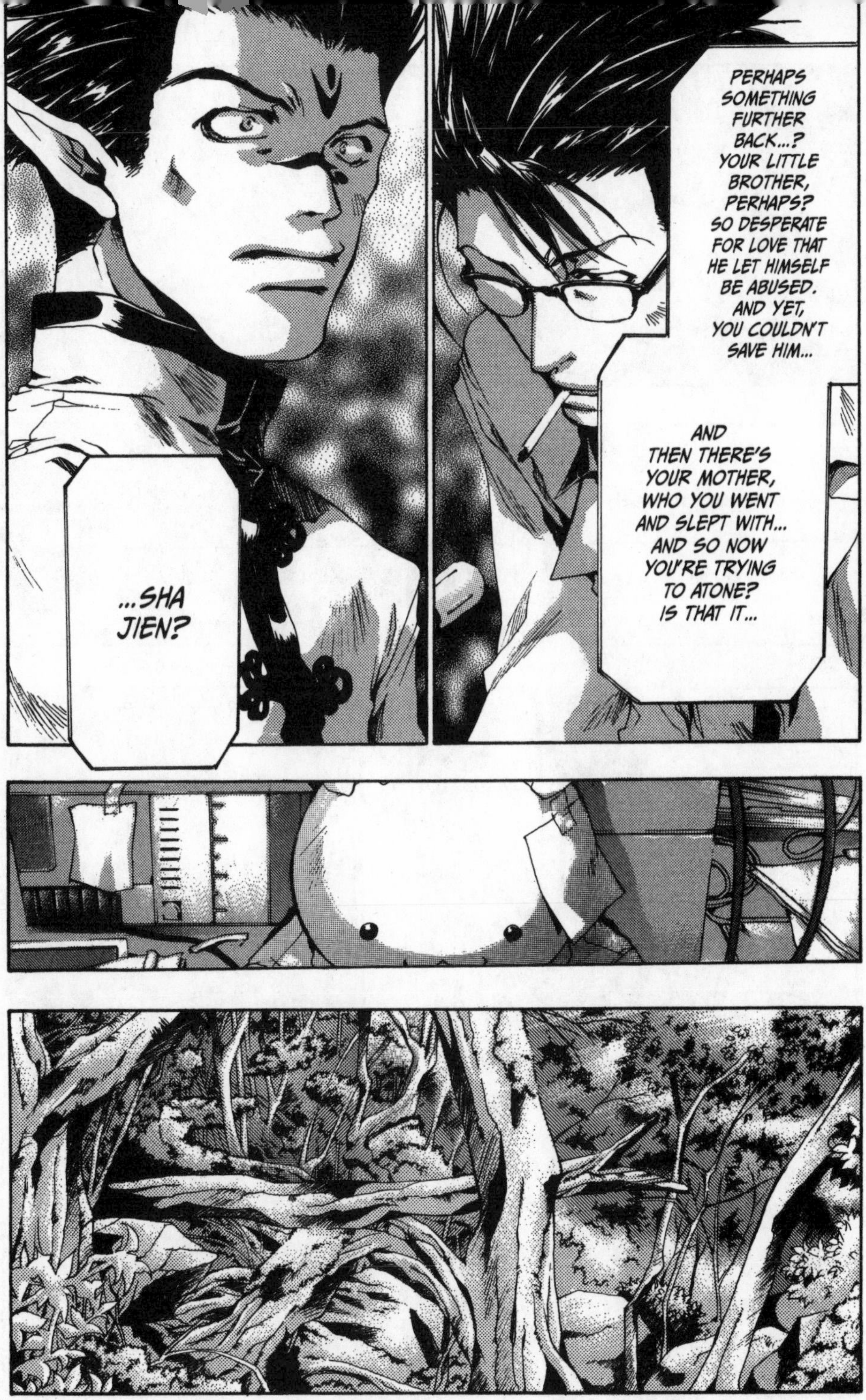
PERHAPS SOMETHING FURTHER BACK...? YOUR LITTLE BROTHER, PERHAPS? SO DESPERATE FOR LOVE THAT HE LET HIMSELF BE ABUSED. AND YET, YOU COULDN'T SAVE HIM...
AND THEN THERE'S YOUR MOTHER, WHO YOU WENT AND SLEPT WITH... AND SO NOW YOU'RE TRYING TO ATONE? IS THAT IT...
...SHA JIEN?

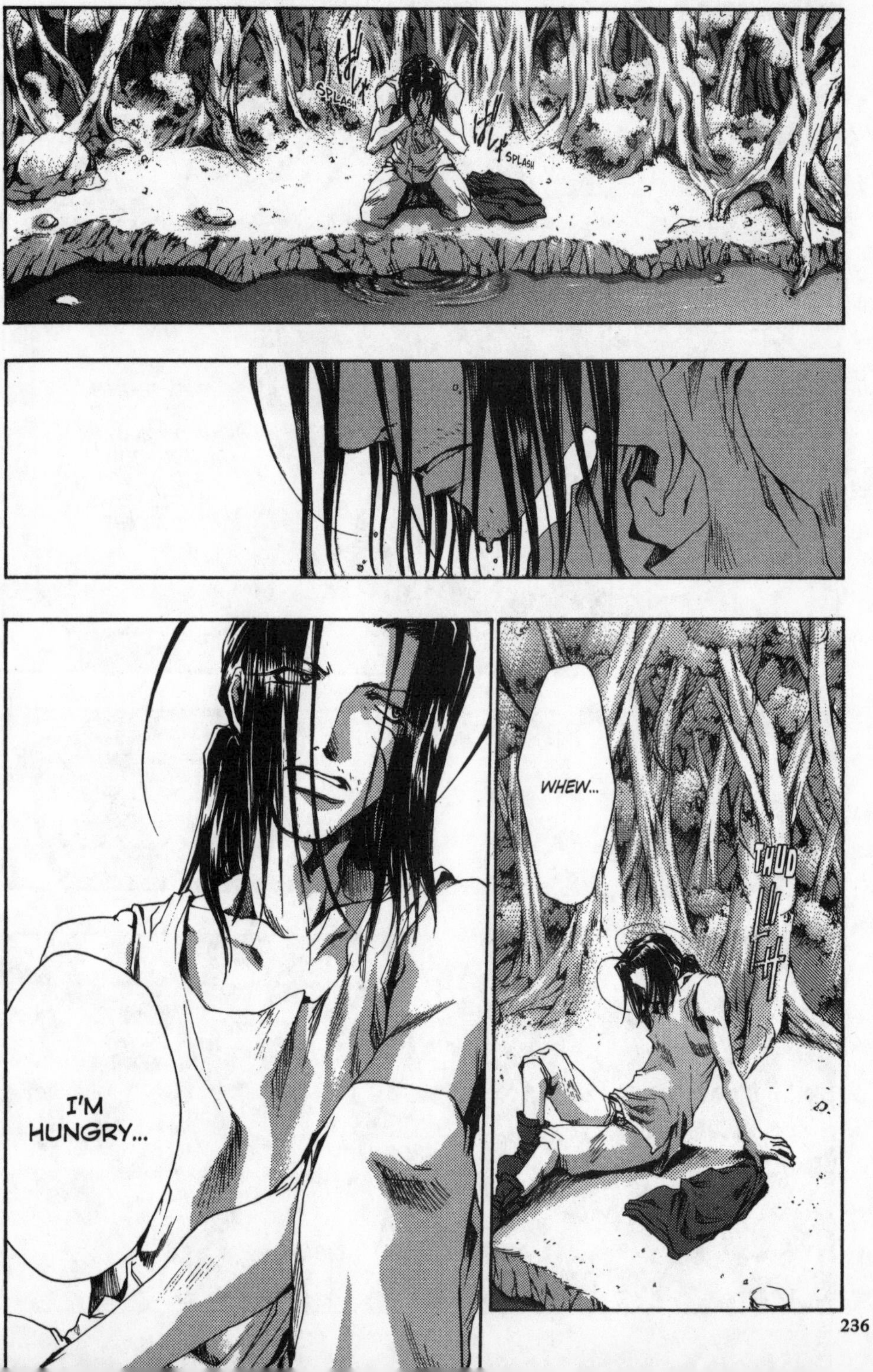
SPLASH
SPLASH
WHEW...
THUD
I'M HUNGRY...

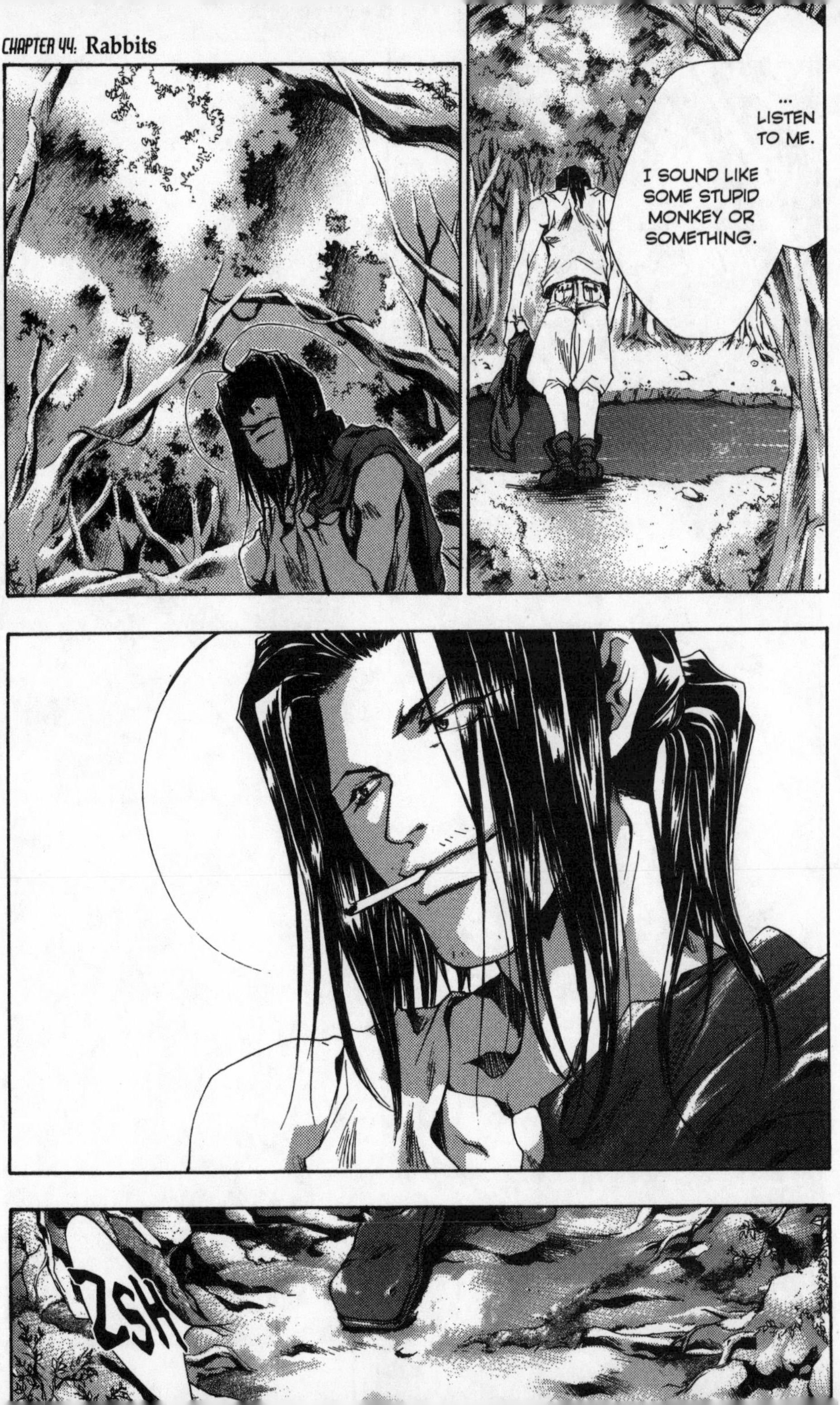
... LISTEN TO ME.
I SOUND LIKE SOME STUPID MONKEY OR SOMETHING.
ZSH

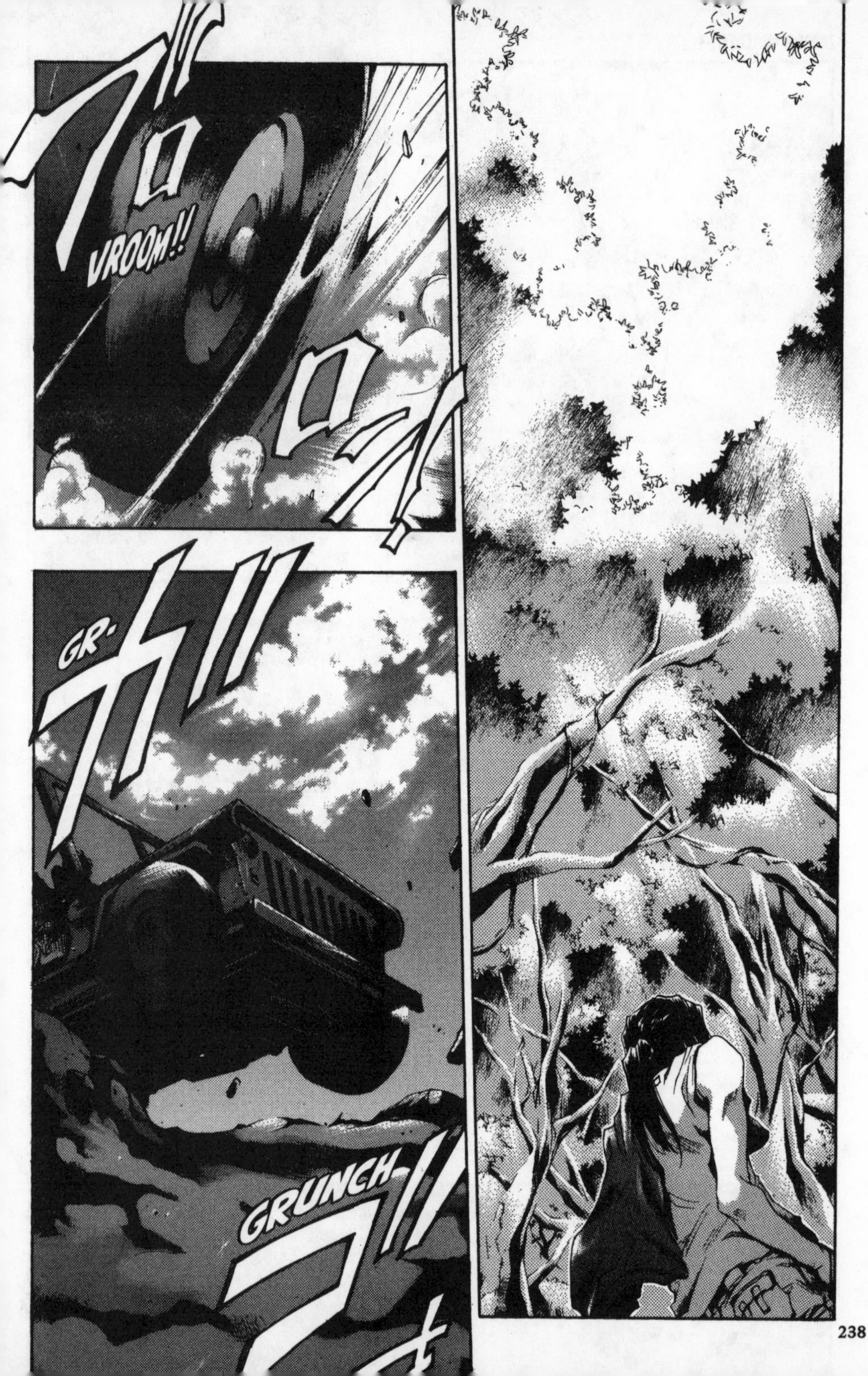
VROOM!!
GR-
GRUNCH-

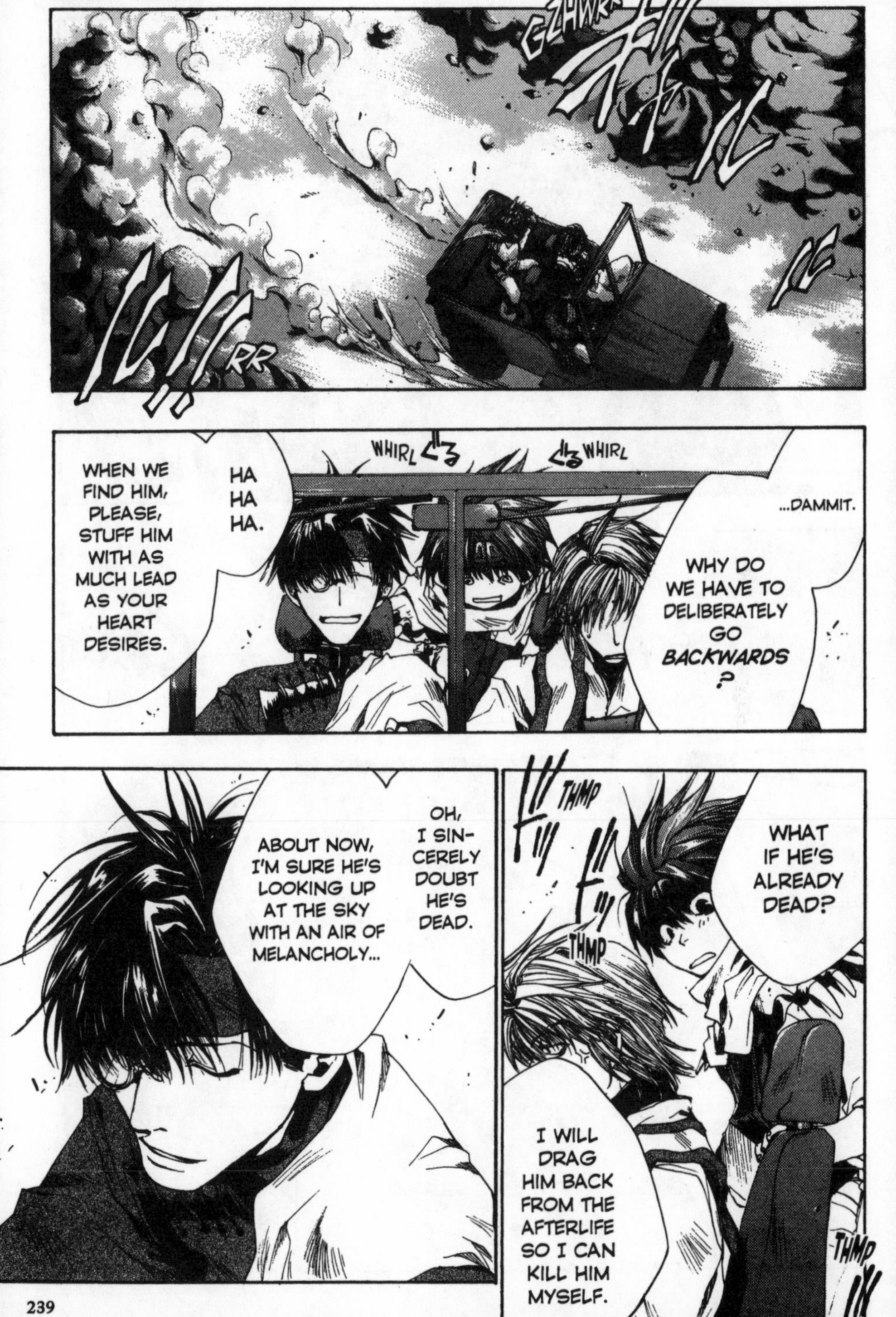
GZHWRR
RR
...DAMMIT.
WHY DO WE HAVE TO DELIBERATELY GO *BACKWARDS*?
WHIRL
WHIRL
HA HA HA.
WHEN WE FIND HIM, PLEASE, STUFF HIM WITH AS MUCH LEAD AS YOUR HEART DESIRES.
WHAT IF HE'S ALREADY DEAD?
THMP
THMP
I WILL DRAG HIM BACK FROM THE AFTERLIFE SO I CAN KILL HIM MYSELF.
THMP
OH, I SIN-CERELY DOUBT HE'S DEAD.
ABOUT NOW, I'M SURE HE'S LOOKING UP AT THE SKY WITH AN AIR OF MELANCHOLY...

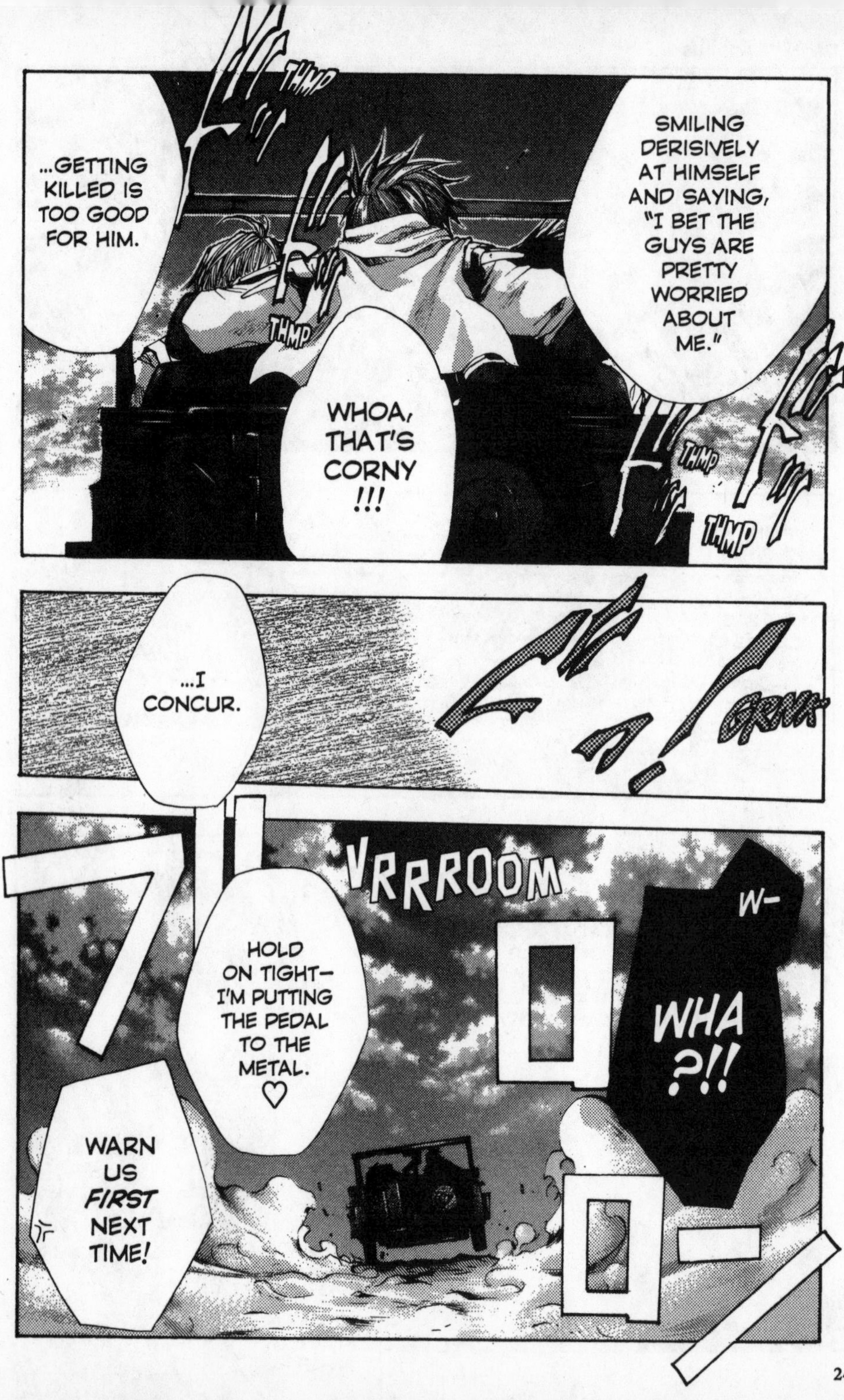
THMP
SMILING DERISIVELY AT HIMSELF AND SAYING, "I BET THE GUYS ARE PRETTY WORRIED ABOUT ME."
...GETTING KILLED IS TOO GOOD FOR HIM.
THMP
WHOA, THAT'S CORNY!!!
THMP
THMP
GRNK
...I CONCUR.
VRRROOM
W-
WHA?!!
HOLD ON TIGHT—I'M PUTTING THE PEDAL TO THE METAL. ♡
WARN US *FIRST* NEXT TIME!

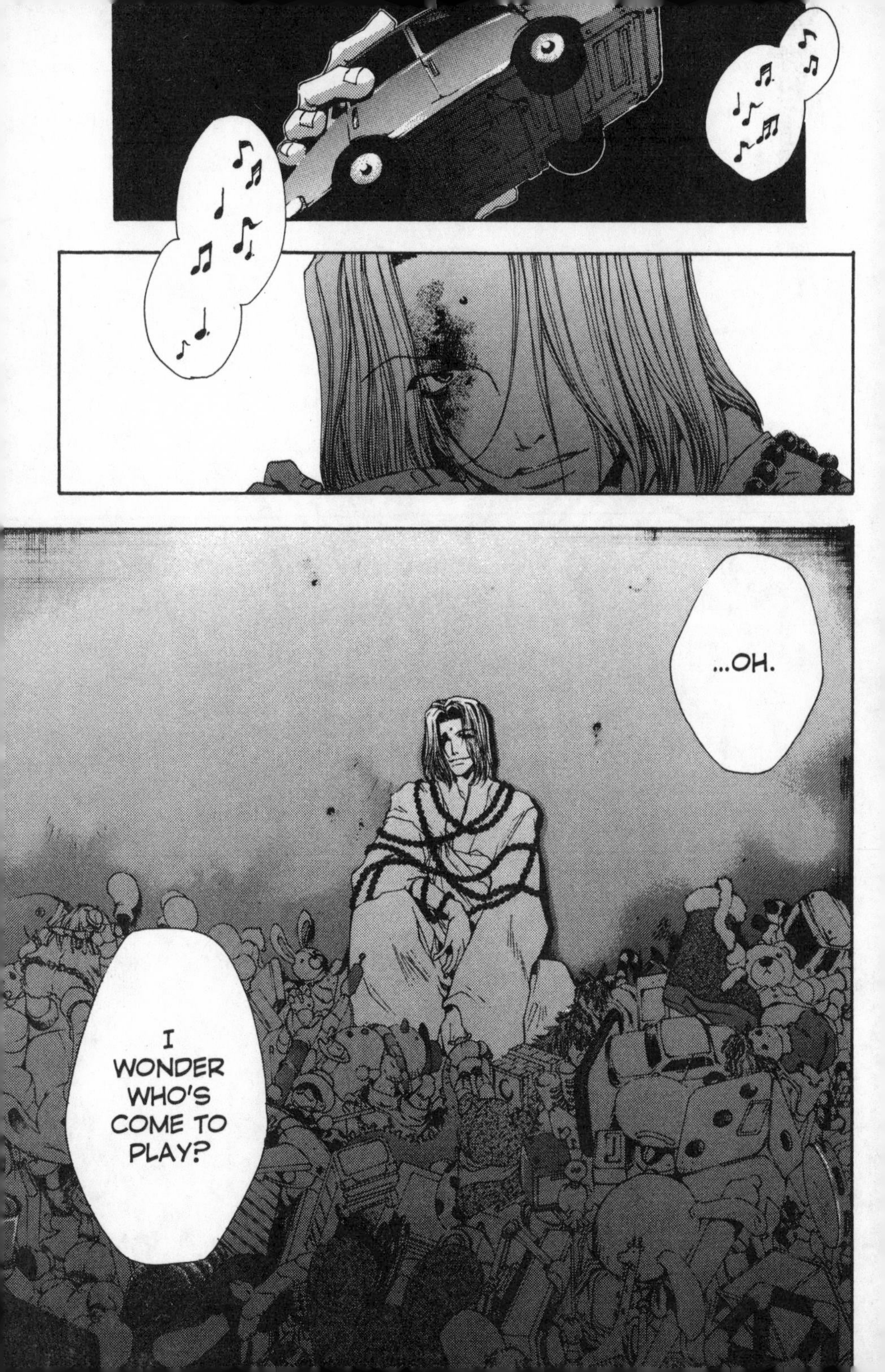
...OH.
I WONDER WHO'S COME TO PLAY?

CHAPTER 45 Chase

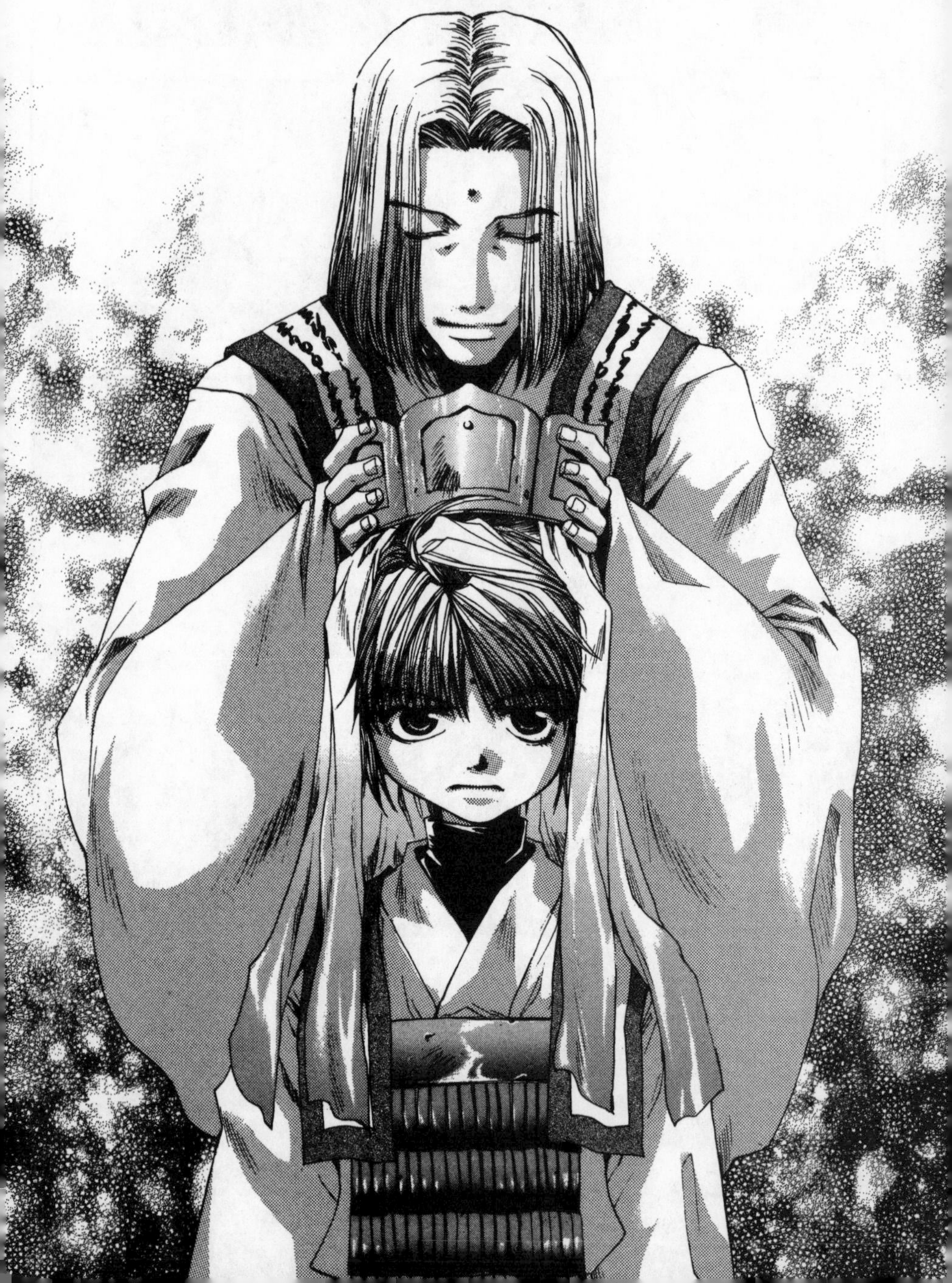

CHAPTER 45: Chase

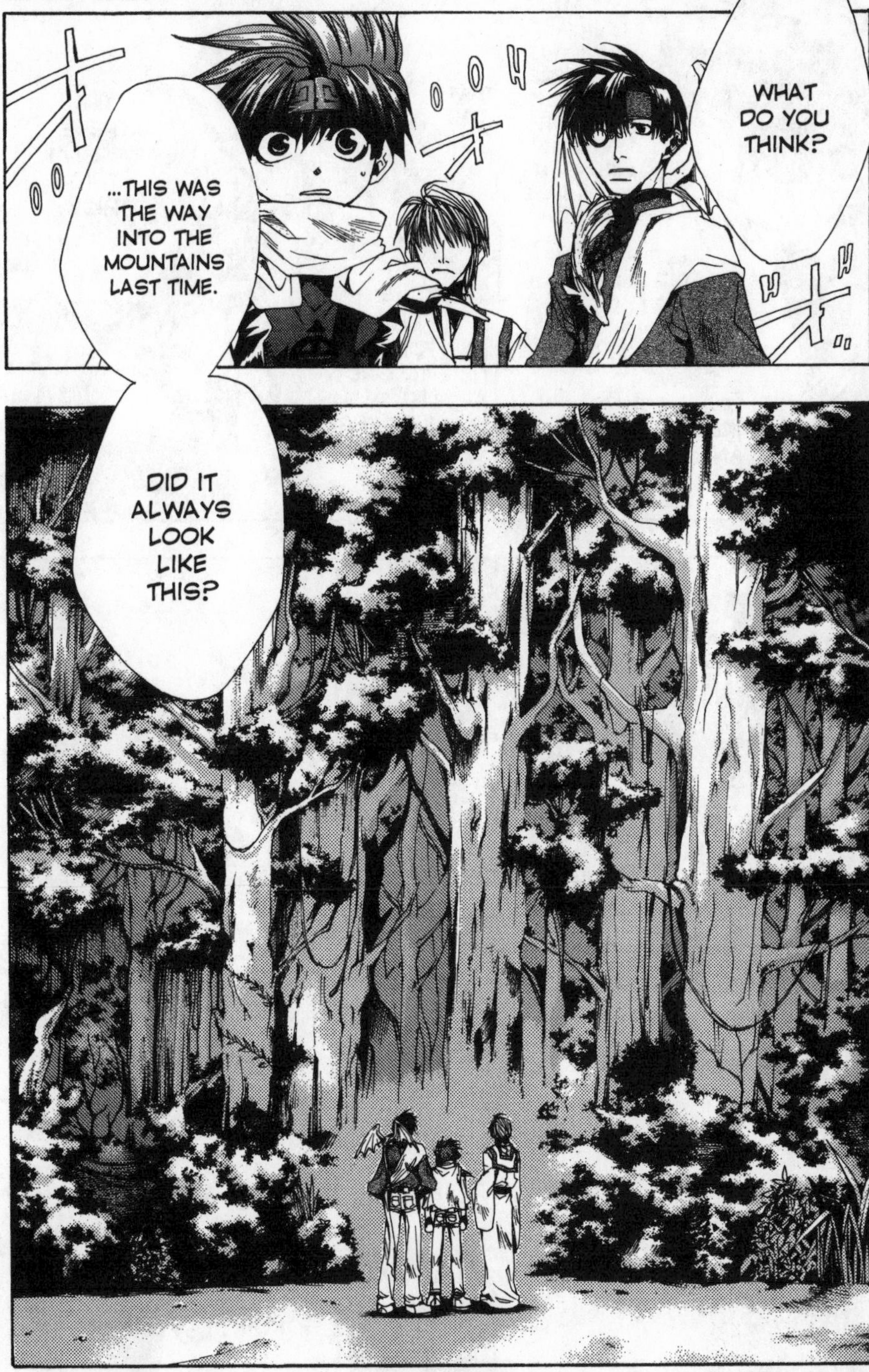
WHAT DO YOU THINK?
...THIS WAS THE WAY INTO THE MOUNTAINS LAST TIME.
DID IT ALWAYS LOOK LIKE THIS?

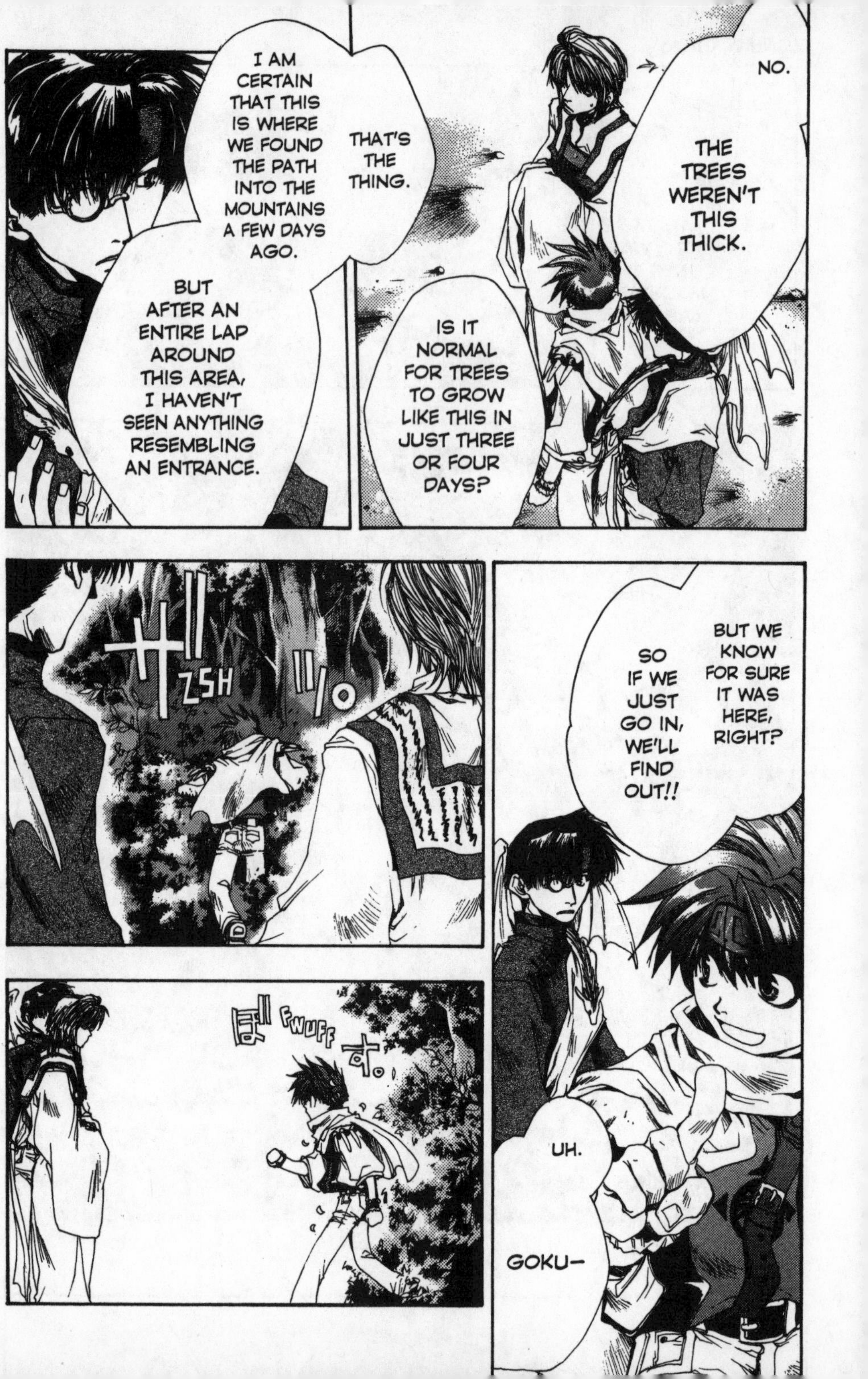
NO.
THE TREES WEREN'T THIS THICK.
IS IT NORMAL FOR TREES TO GROW LIKE THIS IN JUST THREE OR FOUR DAYS?
THAT'S THE THING.
I AM CERTAIN THAT THIS IS WHERE WE FOUND THE PATH INTO THE MOUNTAINS A FEW DAYS AGO.
BUT AFTER AN ENTIRE LAP AROUND THIS AREA, I HAVEN'T SEEN ANYTHING RESEMBLING AN ENTRANCE.
BUT WE KNOW FOR SURE IT WAS HERE, RIGHT?
SO IF WE JUST GO IN, WE'LL FIND OUT!!
UH.
GOKU—
ZSH
FWUFF

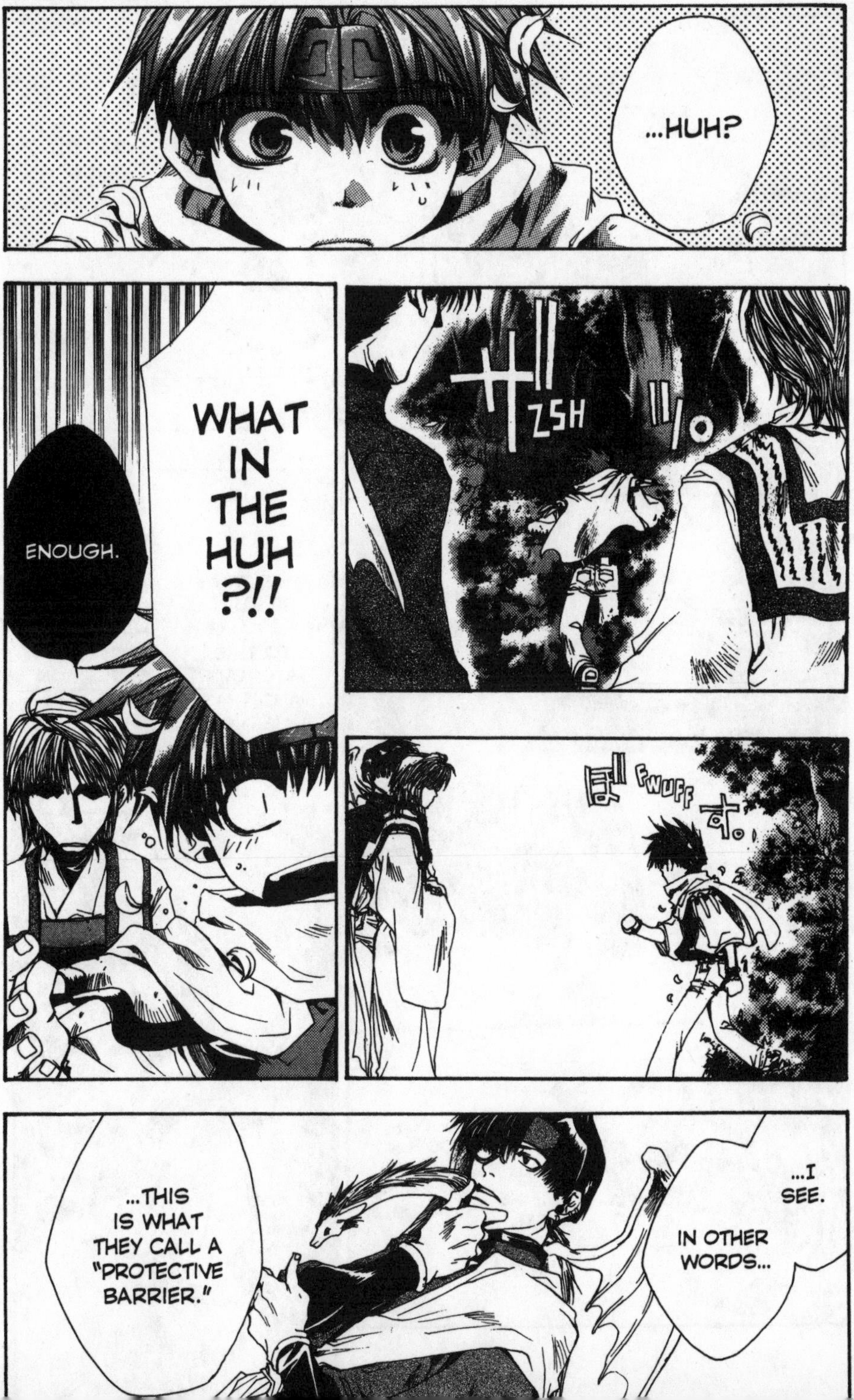
...HUH?
ZSH
FWUFF
WHAT IN THE HUH ?!!
ENOUGH.
...I SEE.
IN OTHER WORDS...
...THIS IS WHAT THEY CALL A "PROTECTIVE BARRIER."

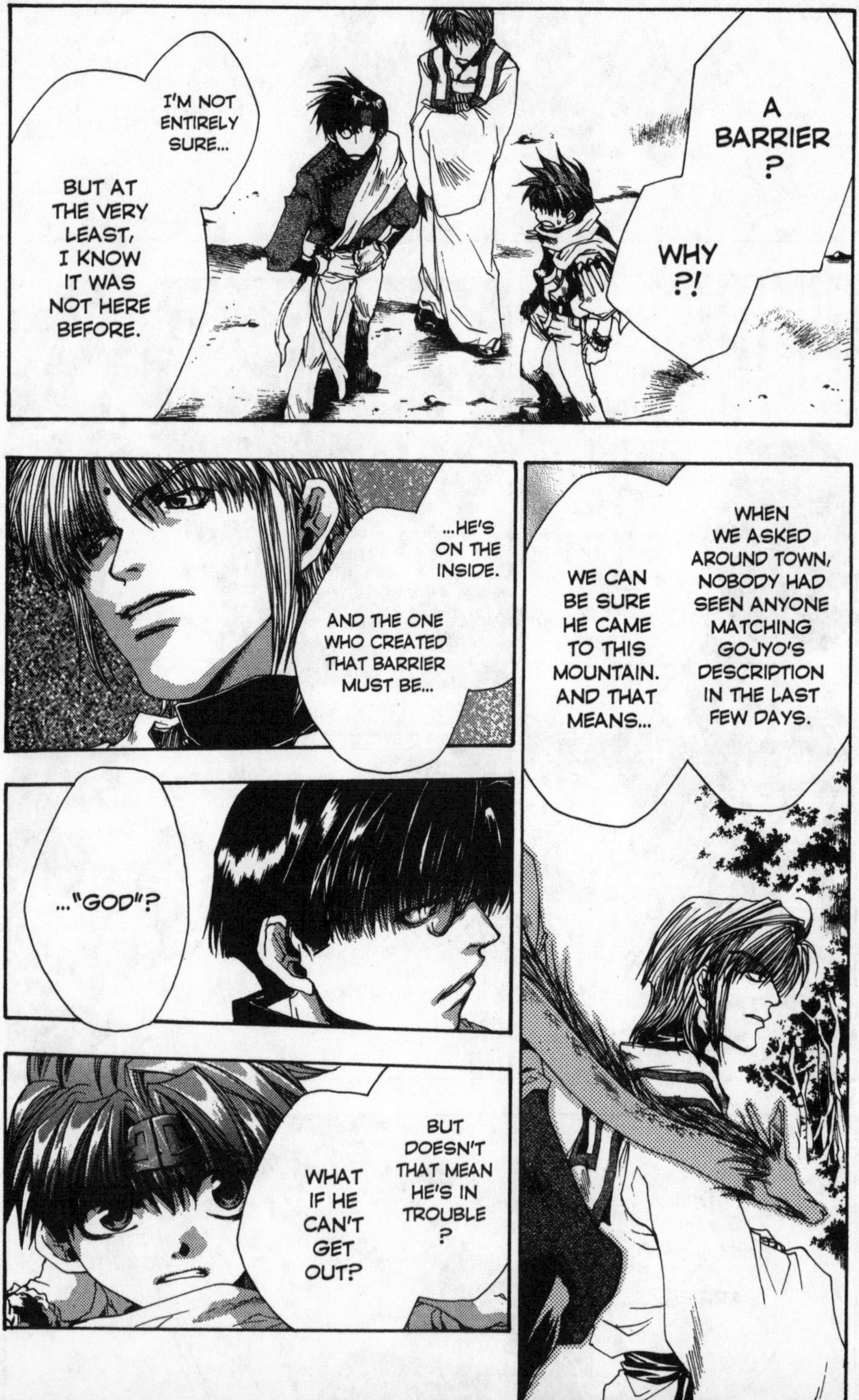
A BARRIER?
WHY?!
I'M NOT ENTIRELY SURE...
BUT AT THE VERY LEAST, I KNOW IT WAS NOT HERE BEFORE.
WHEN WE ASKED AROUND TOWN, NOBODY HAD SEEN ANYONE MATCHING GOJYO'S DESCRIPTION IN THE LAST FEW DAYS.
WE CAN BE SURE HE CAME TO THIS MOUNTAIN. AND THAT MEANS...
...HE'S ON THE INSIDE.
AND THE ONE WHO CREATED THAT BARRIER MUST BE...
..."GOD"?
BUT DOESN'T THAT MEAN HE'S IN TROUBLE?
WHAT IF HE CAN'T GET OUT?

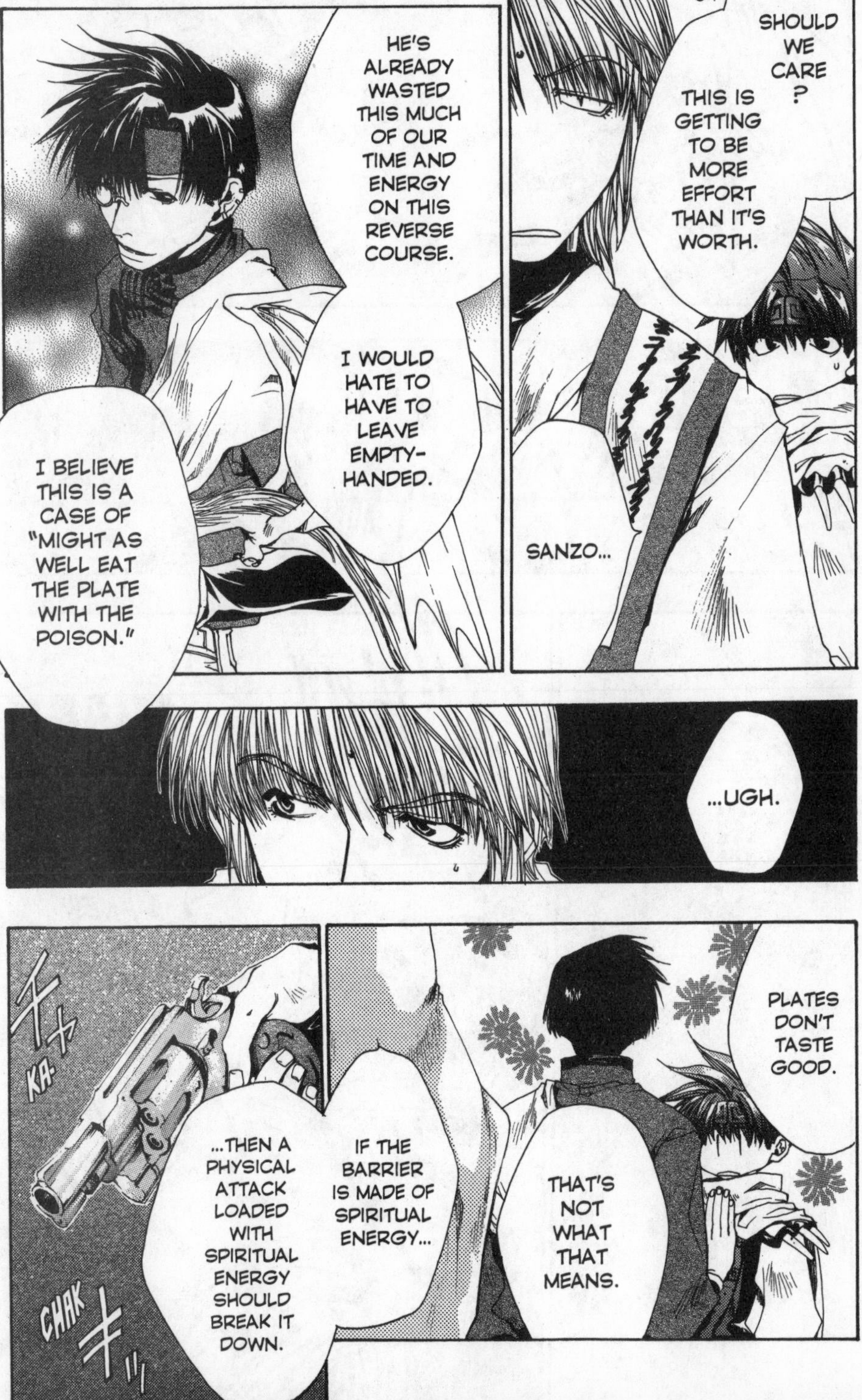
SIGH
SHOULD WE CARE ?
THIS IS GETTING TO BE MORE EFFORT THAN IT'S WORTH.
SANZO...
HE'S ALREADY WASTED THIS MUCH OF OUR TIME AND ENERGY ON THIS REVERSE COURSE.
I WOULD HATE TO HAVE TO LEAVE EMPTY-HANDED.
I BELIEVE THIS IS A CASE OF "MIGHT AS WELL EAT THE PLATE WITH THE POISON."
...UGH.
PLATES DON'T TASTE GOOD.
THAT'S NOT WHAT THAT MEANS.
IF THE BARRIER IS MADE OF SPIRITUAL ENERGY...
...THEN A PHYSICAL ATTACK LOADED WITH SPIRITUAL ENERGY SHOULD BREAK IT DOWN.
KA-
CHAK

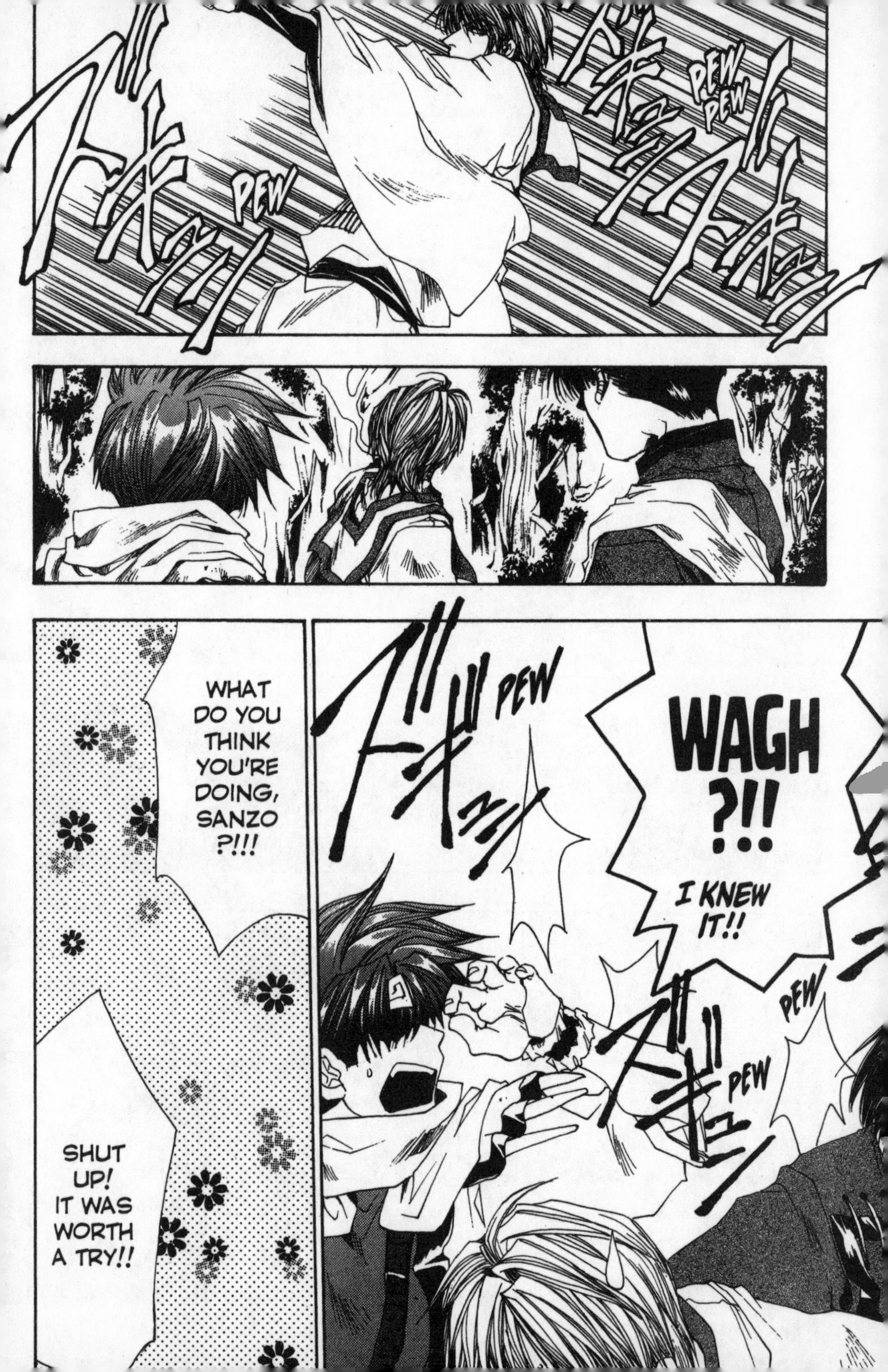
PEW PEW
PEW
WAGH?!!
I KNEW IT!!
PEW
PEW
PEW
WHAT DO YOU THINK YOU'RE DOING, SANZO?!!!
SHUT UP! IT WAS WORTH A TRY!!

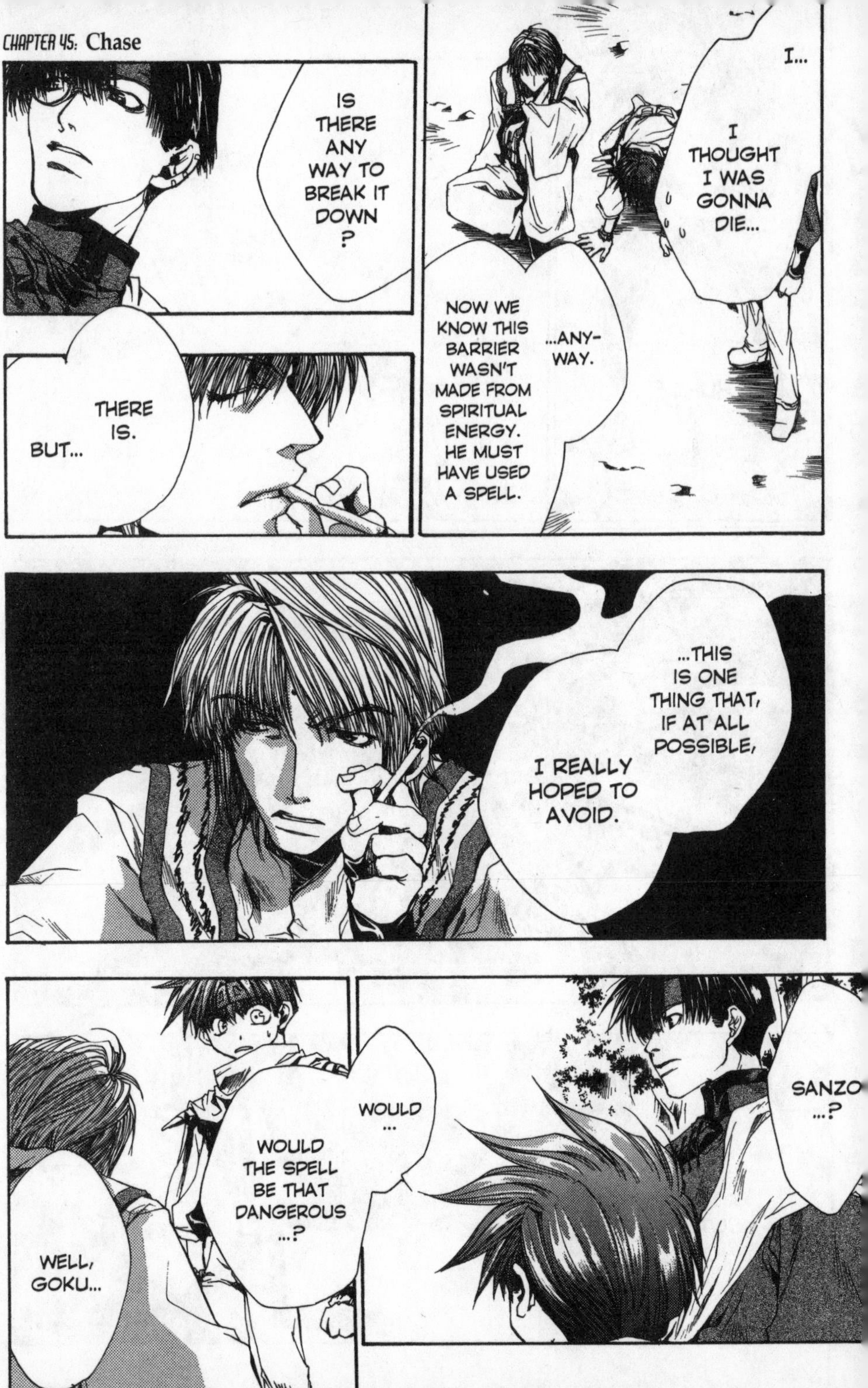
I...
I THOUGHT I WAS GONNA DIE...
...ANY-WAY.
NOW WE KNOW THIS BARRIER WASN'T MADE FROM SPIRITUAL ENERGY. HE MUST HAVE USED A SPELL.
IS THERE ANY WAY TO BREAK IT DOWN?
THERE IS.
BUT...
...THIS IS ONE THING THAT, IF AT ALL POSSIBLE,
I REALLY HOPED TO AVOID.
SANZO...?
WOULD...
WOULD THE SPELL BE THAT DANGEROUS...?
WELL, GOKU...

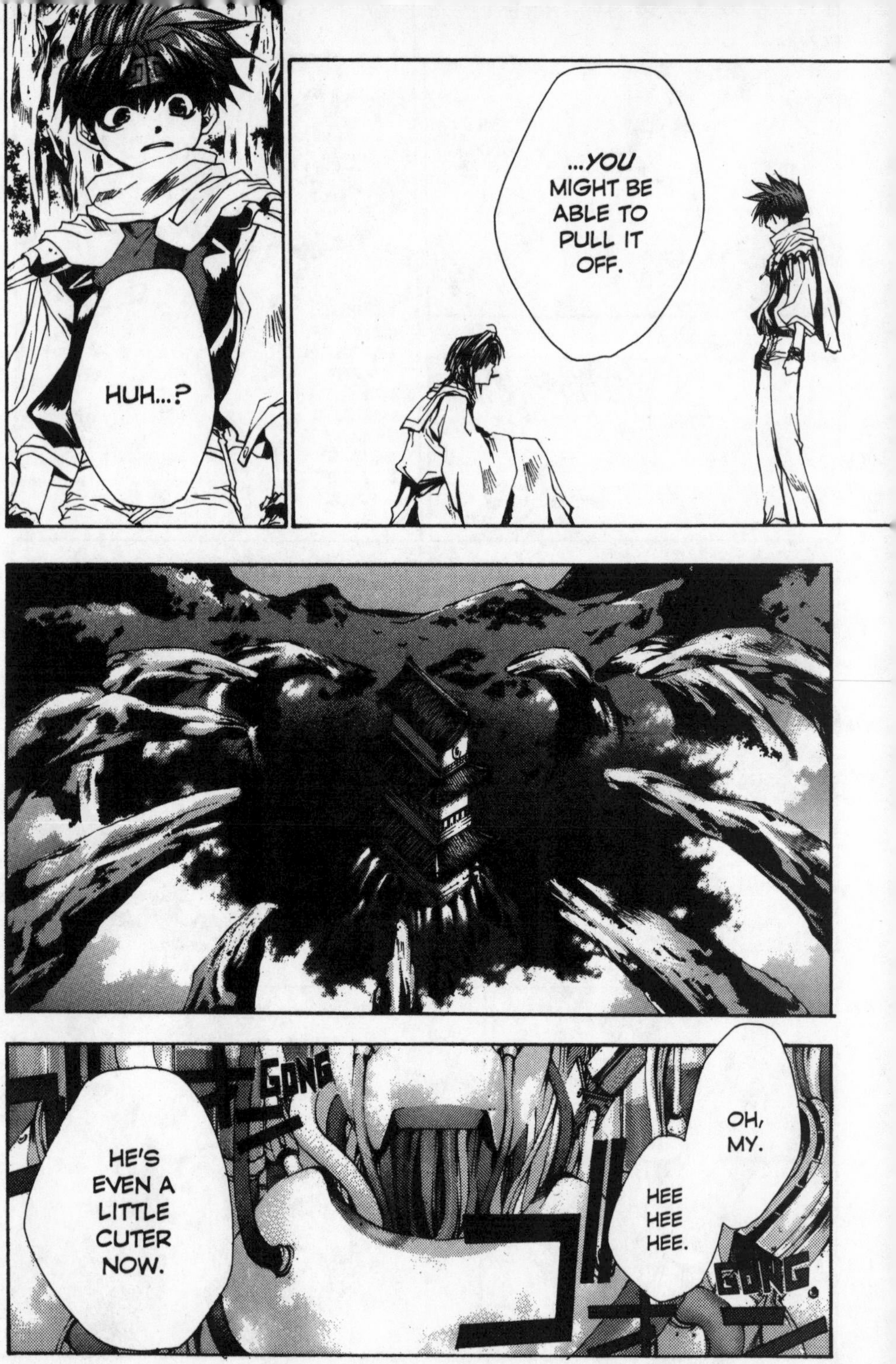
...YOU MIGHT BE ABLE TO PULL IT OFF.
HUH...?
OH, MY.
HEE HEE HEE.
GONG
HE'S EVEN A LITTLE CUTER NOW.
GONG.

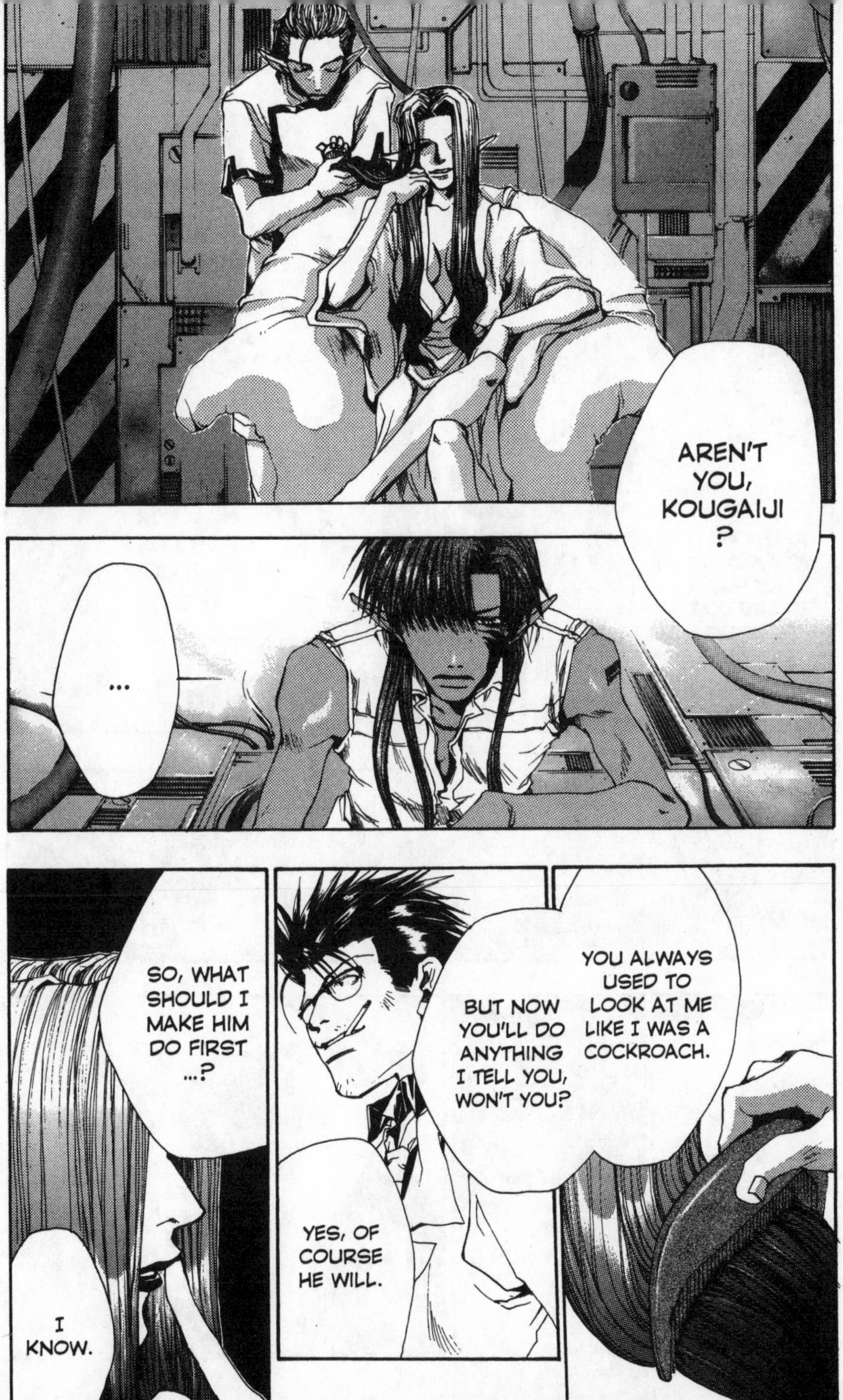
AREN'T YOU, KOUGAIJI ?
...
YOU ALWAYS USED TO LOOK AT ME LIKE I WAS A COCKROACH.
BUT NOW YOU'LL DO ANYTHING I TELL YOU, WON'T YOU?
YES, OF COURSE HE WILL.
SO, WHAT SHOULD I MAKE HIM DO FIRST ...?
I KNOW.

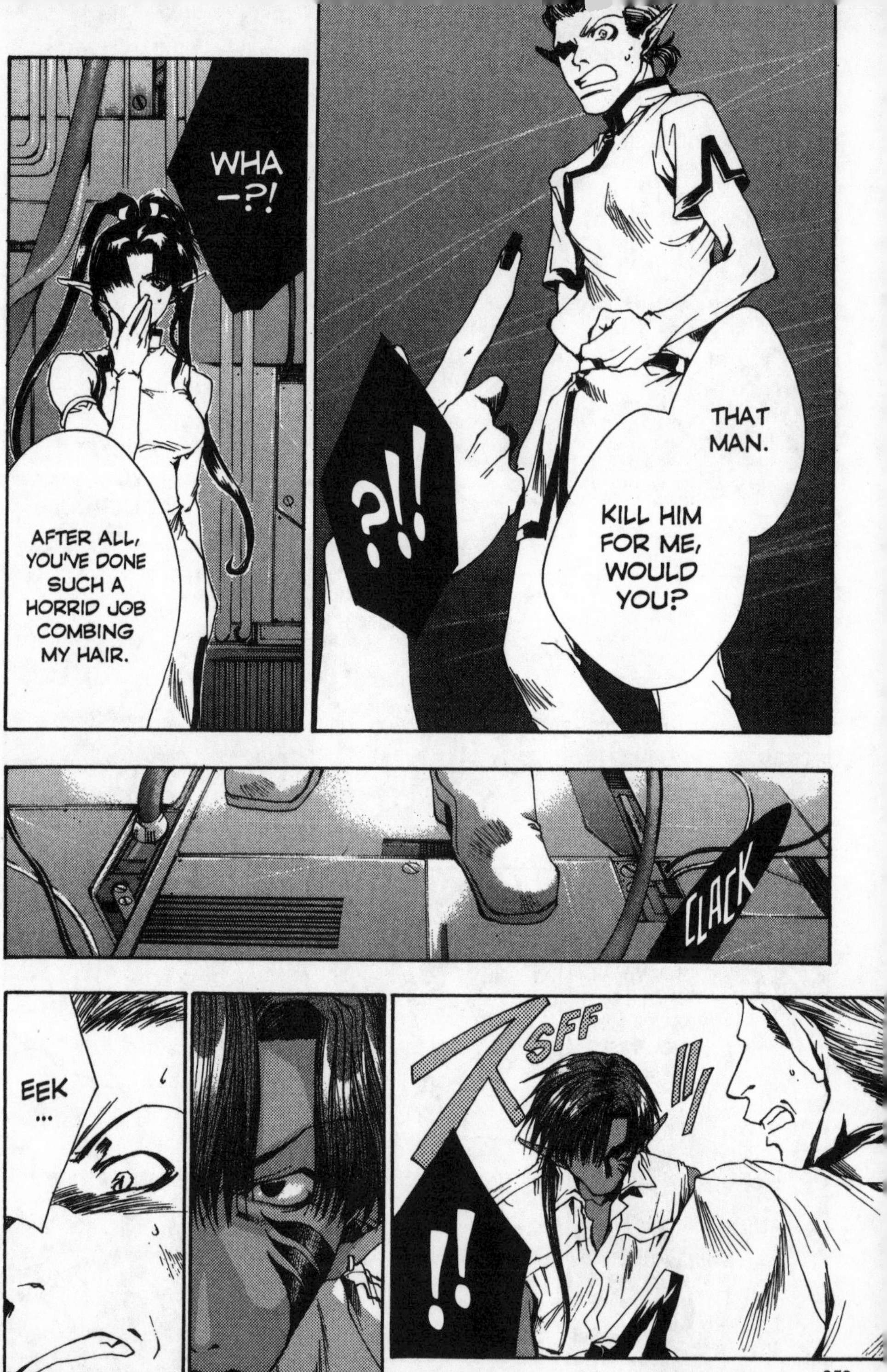
THAT MAN.
KILL HIM FOR ME, WOULD YOU?
?!!
WHA –?!
AFTER ALL, YOU'VE DONE SUCH A HORRID JOB COMBING MY HAIR.
CLACK
SFF
!!
EEK ...

CHAPTER 45: Chase

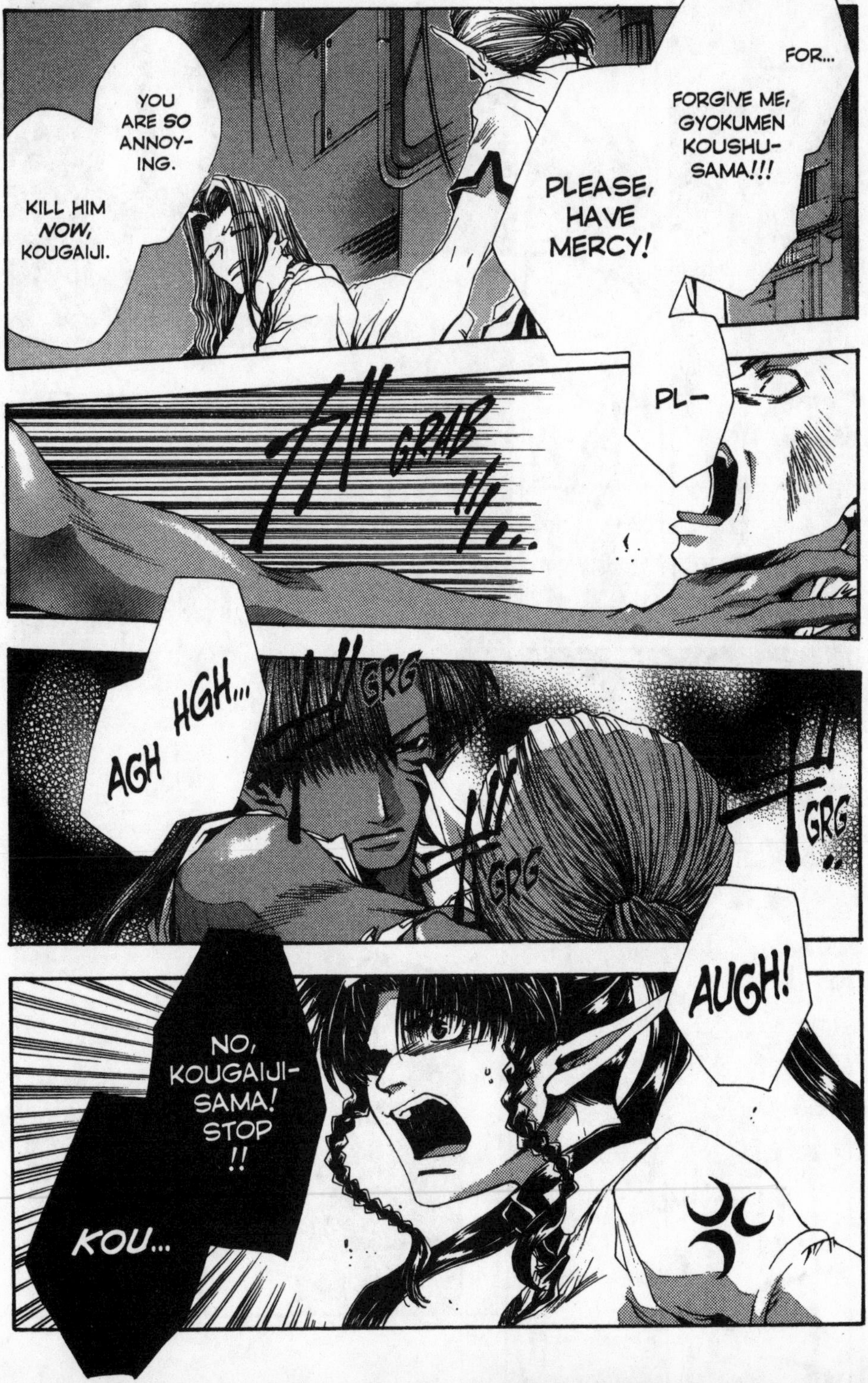
FOR...
FORGIVE ME, GYOKUMEN KOUSHU-SAMA!!!
PLEASE, HAVE MERCY!
YOU ARE SO ANNOY-ING.
KILL HIM NOW, KOUGAIJI.
PL—
GRAB
GRG
GRG
GRG
AGH HGH...
AUGH!
NO, KOUGAIJI-SAMA! STOP !!
KOU...

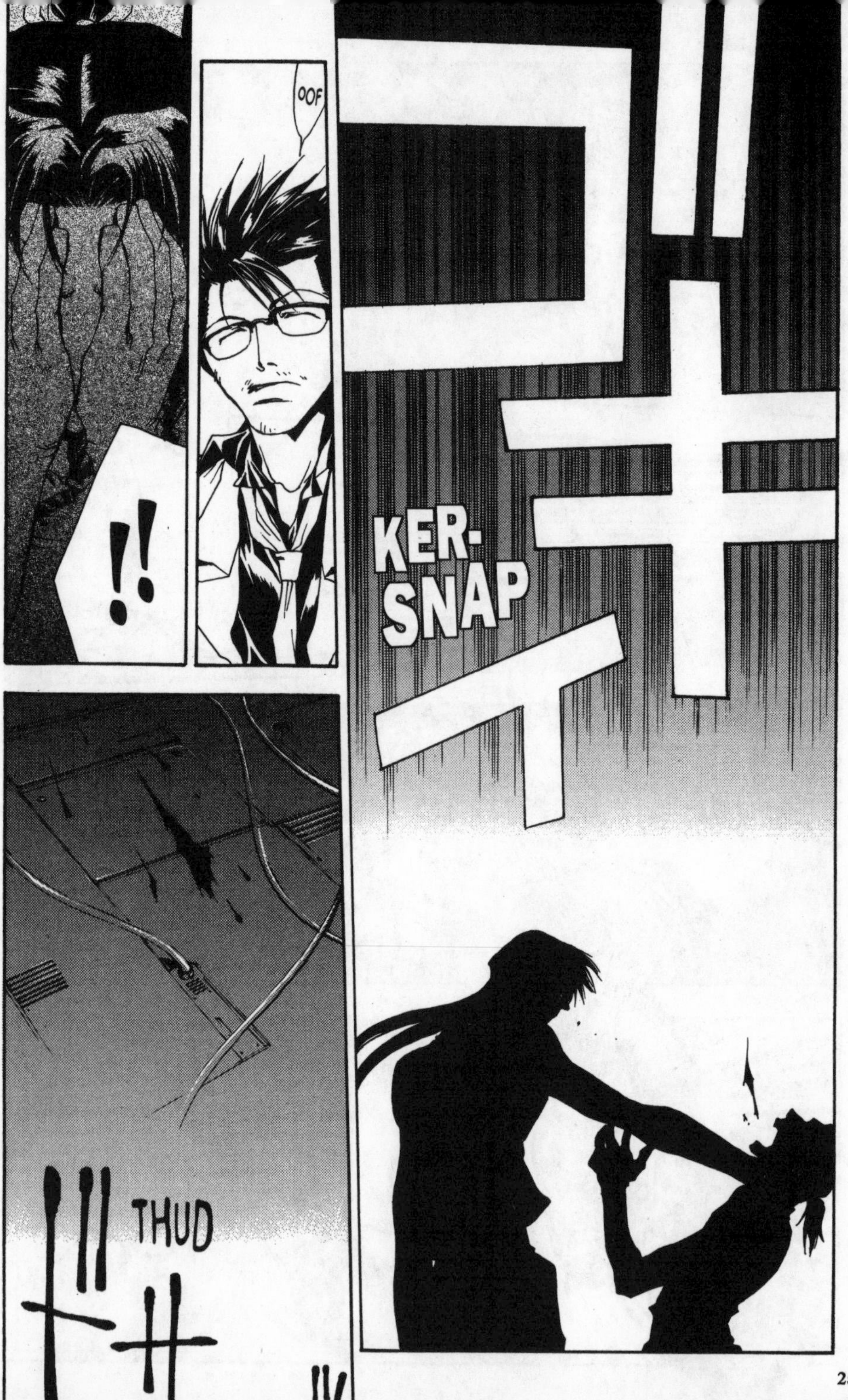
KER-
SNAP
OOF
!!
THUD

CHAPTER 45: Chase

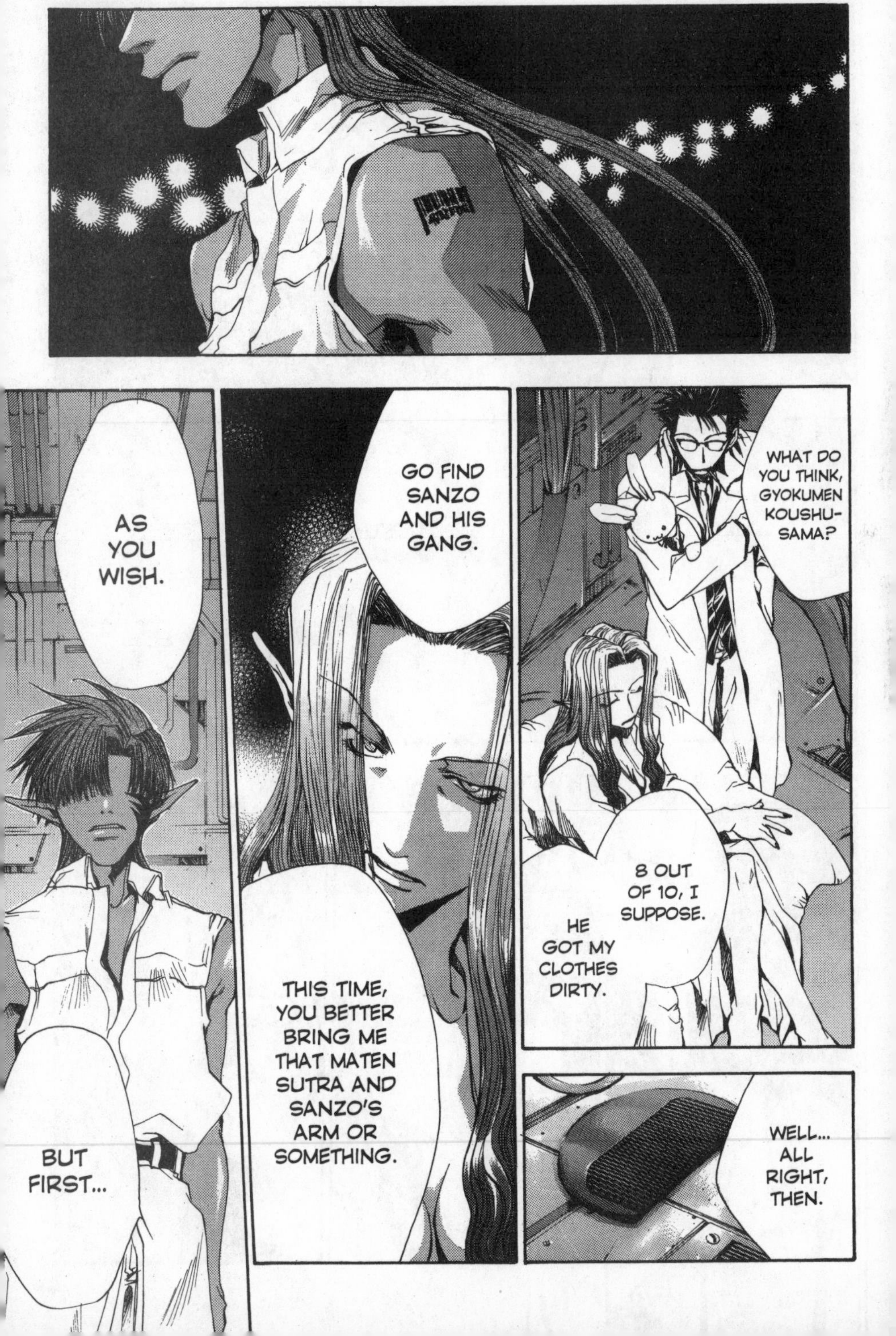
WHAT DO YOU THINK, GYOKUMEN KOUSHU-SAMA?
8 OUT OF 10, I SUPPOSE.
HE GOT MY CLOTHES DIRTY.
WELL... ALL RIGHT, THEN.
GO FIND SANZO AND HIS GANG.
THIS TIME, YOU BETTER BRING ME THAT MATEN SUTRA AND SANZO'S ARM OR SOMETHING.
AS YOU WISH.
BUT FIRST...

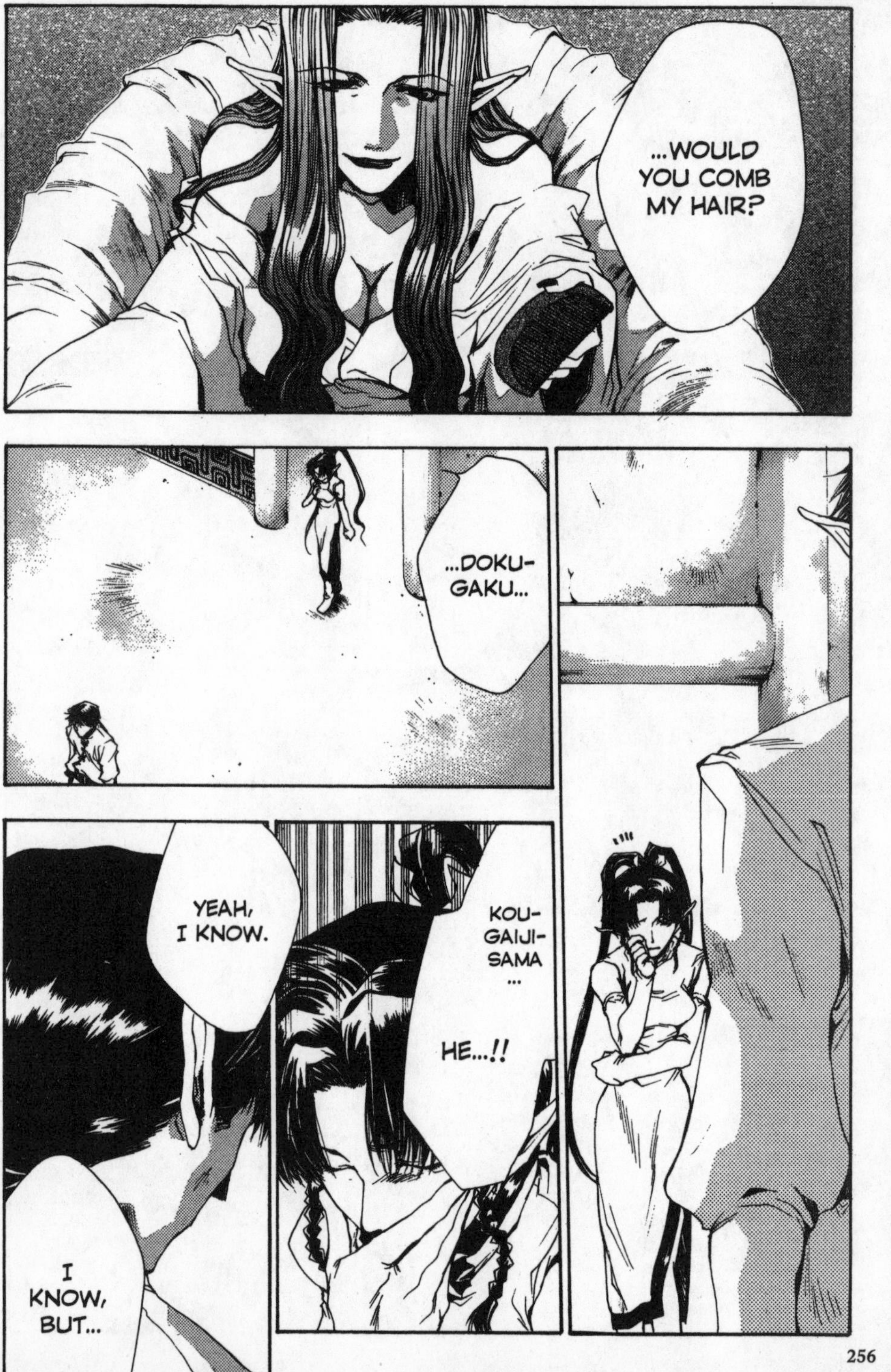
...WOULD YOU COMB MY HAIR?
...DOKU-GAKU...
KOU-GAIJI-SAMA ...
HE...!!
YEAH, I KNOW.
I KNOW, BUT...

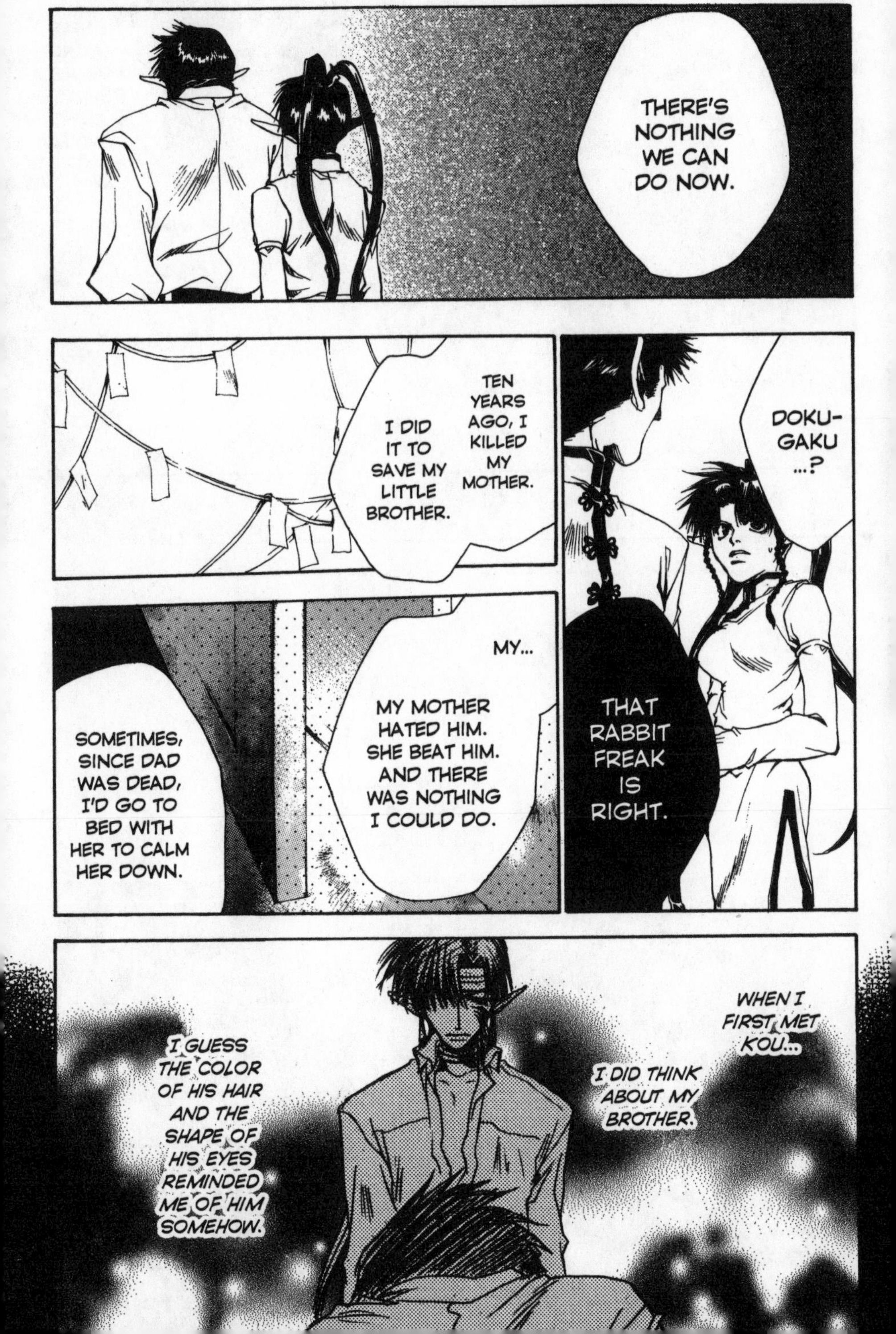
THERE'S NOTHING WE CAN DO NOW.
DOKU-GAKU ...?
THAT RABBIT FREAK IS RIGHT.
TEN YEARS AGO, I KILLED MY MOTHER.
I DID IT TO SAVE MY LITTLE BROTHER.
MY...
MY MOTHER HATED HIM. SHE BEAT HIM. AND THERE WAS NOTHING I COULD DO.
SOMETIMES, SINCE DAD WAS DEAD, I'D GO TO BED WITH HER TO CALM HER DOWN.
WHEN I FIRST MET KOU...
I DID THINK ABOUT MY BROTHER.
I GUESS THE COLOR OF HIS HAIR AND THE SHAPE OF HIS EYES REMINDED ME OF HIM SOMEHOW.

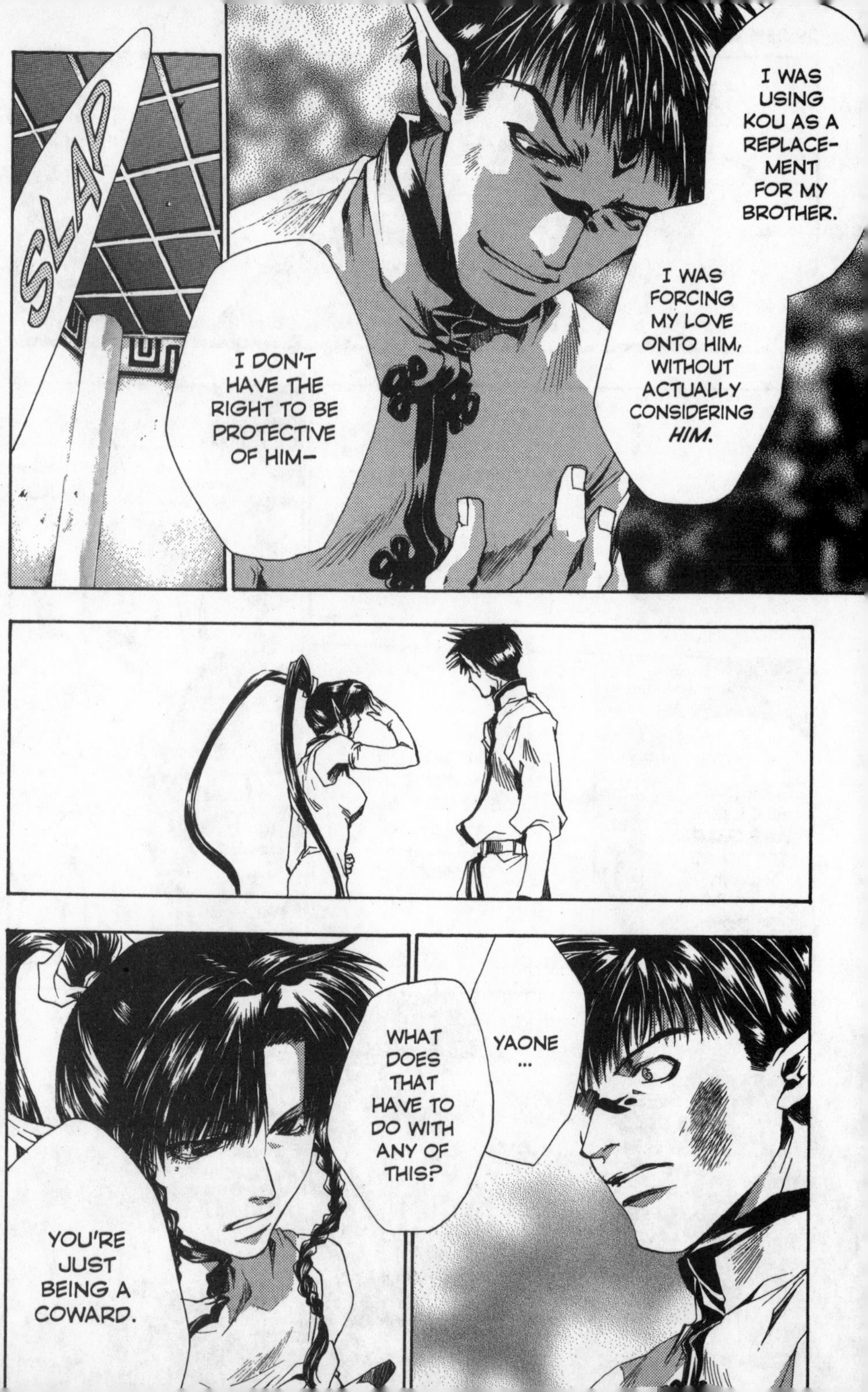
I WAS USING KOU AS A REPLACEMENT FOR MY BROTHER.
I WAS FORCING MY LOVE ONTO HIM, WITHOUT ACTUALLY CONSIDERING *HIM*.
I DON'T HAVE THE RIGHT TO BE PROTECTIVE OF HIM—
SLAP
YAONE ...
WHAT DOES THAT HAVE TO DO WITH ANY OF THIS?
YOU'RE JUST BEING A COWARD.

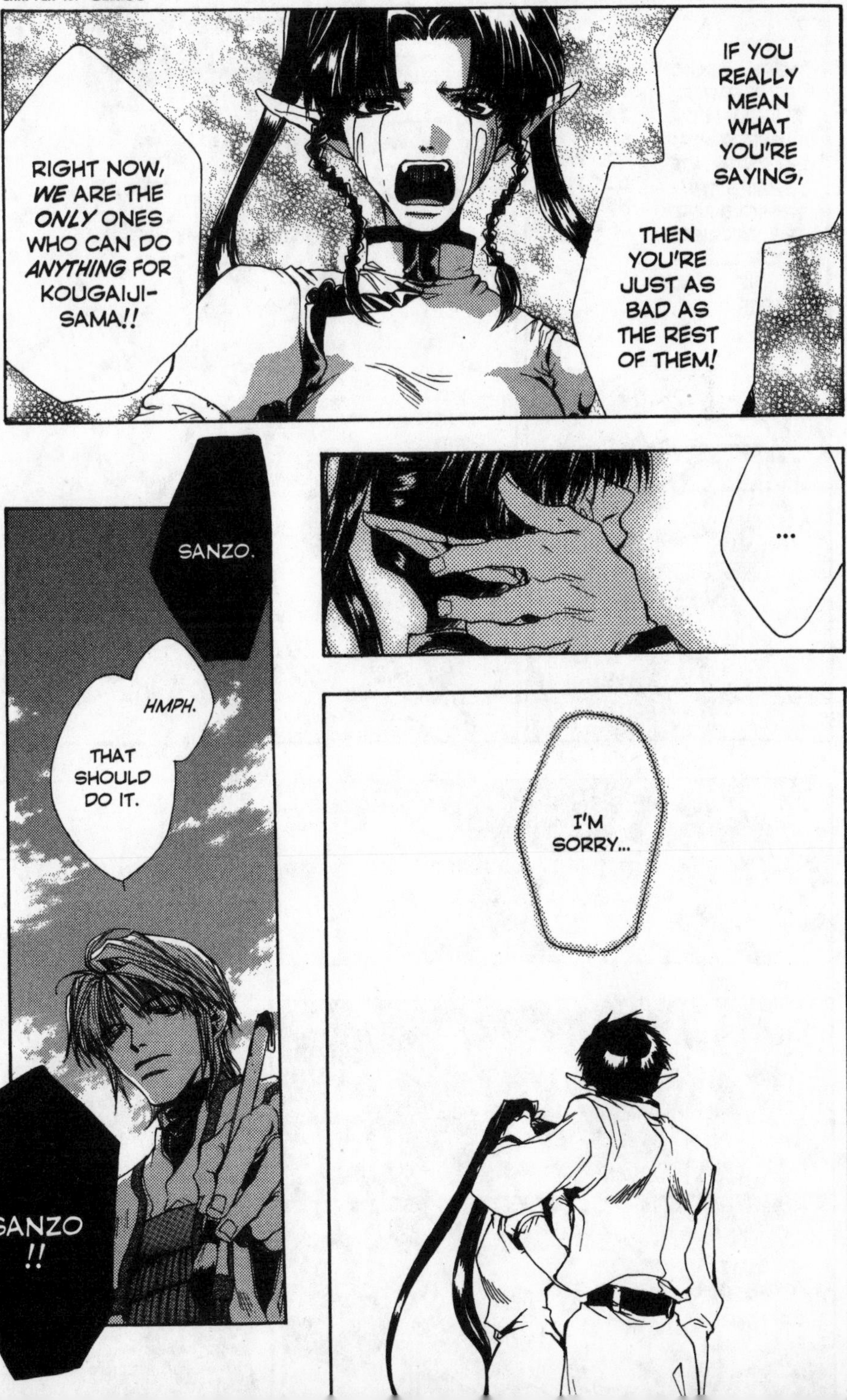
IF YOU REALLY MEAN WHAT YOU'RE SAYING,
THEN YOU'RE JUST AS BAD AS THE REST OF THEM!
RIGHT NOW, *WE* ARE THE *ONLY* ONES WHO CAN DO *ANYTHING* FOR KOUGAIJI-SAMA!!
...
I'M SORRY...
SANZO.
HMPH.
THAT SHOULD DO IT.
SANZO !!

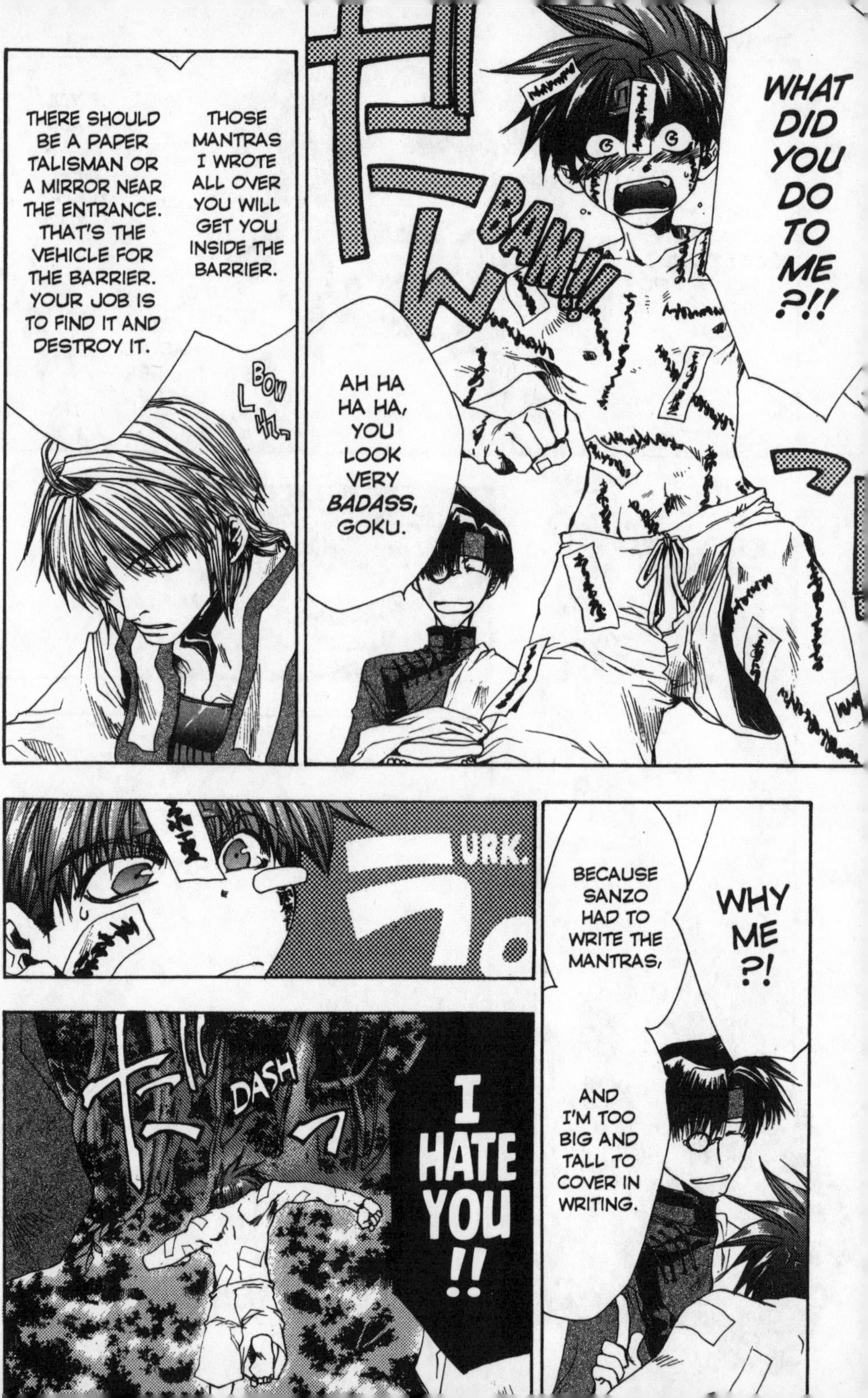
WHAT DID YOU DO TO ME?!!
BAM!!
AH HA HA HA, YOU LOOK VERY *BADASS,* GOKU.
THOSE MANTRAS I WROTE ALL OVER YOU WILL GET YOU INSIDE THE BARRIER.
THERE SHOULD BE A PAPER TALISMAN OR A MIRROR NEAR THE ENTRANCE. THAT'S THE VEHICLE FOR THE BARRIER. YOUR JOB IS TO FIND IT AND DESTROY IT.
WHY ME?!
BECAUSE SANZO HAD TO WRITE THE MANTRAS,
AND I'M TOO BIG AND TALL TO COVER IN WRITING.
URK.
DASH
I HATE YOU!!

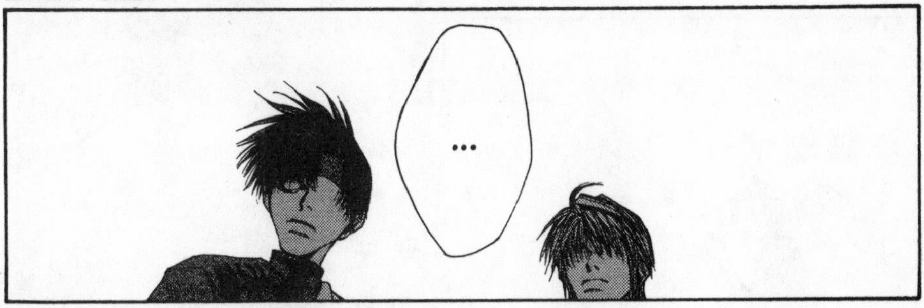
...

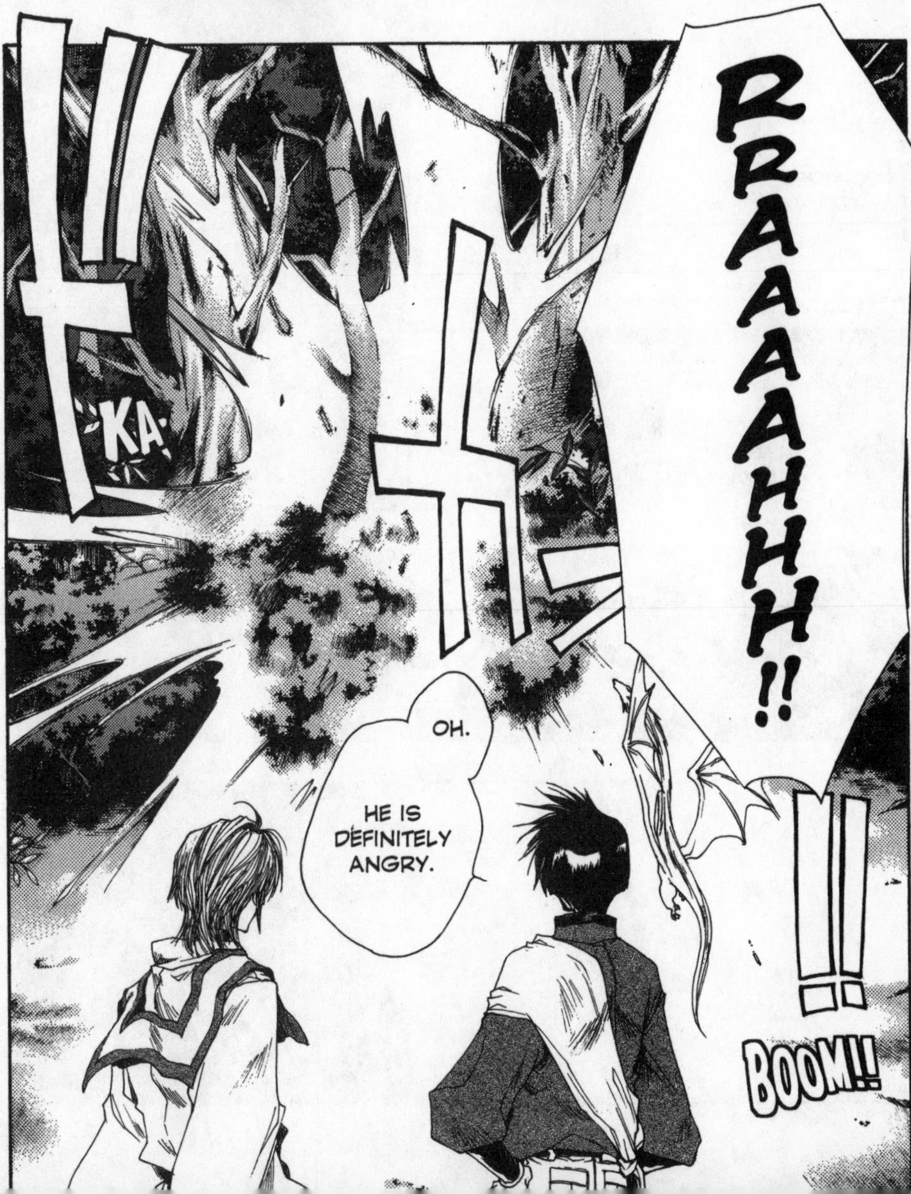
RRAAAAHHH!!
KA
OH.
HE IS DEFINITELY ANGRY.
BOOM!!

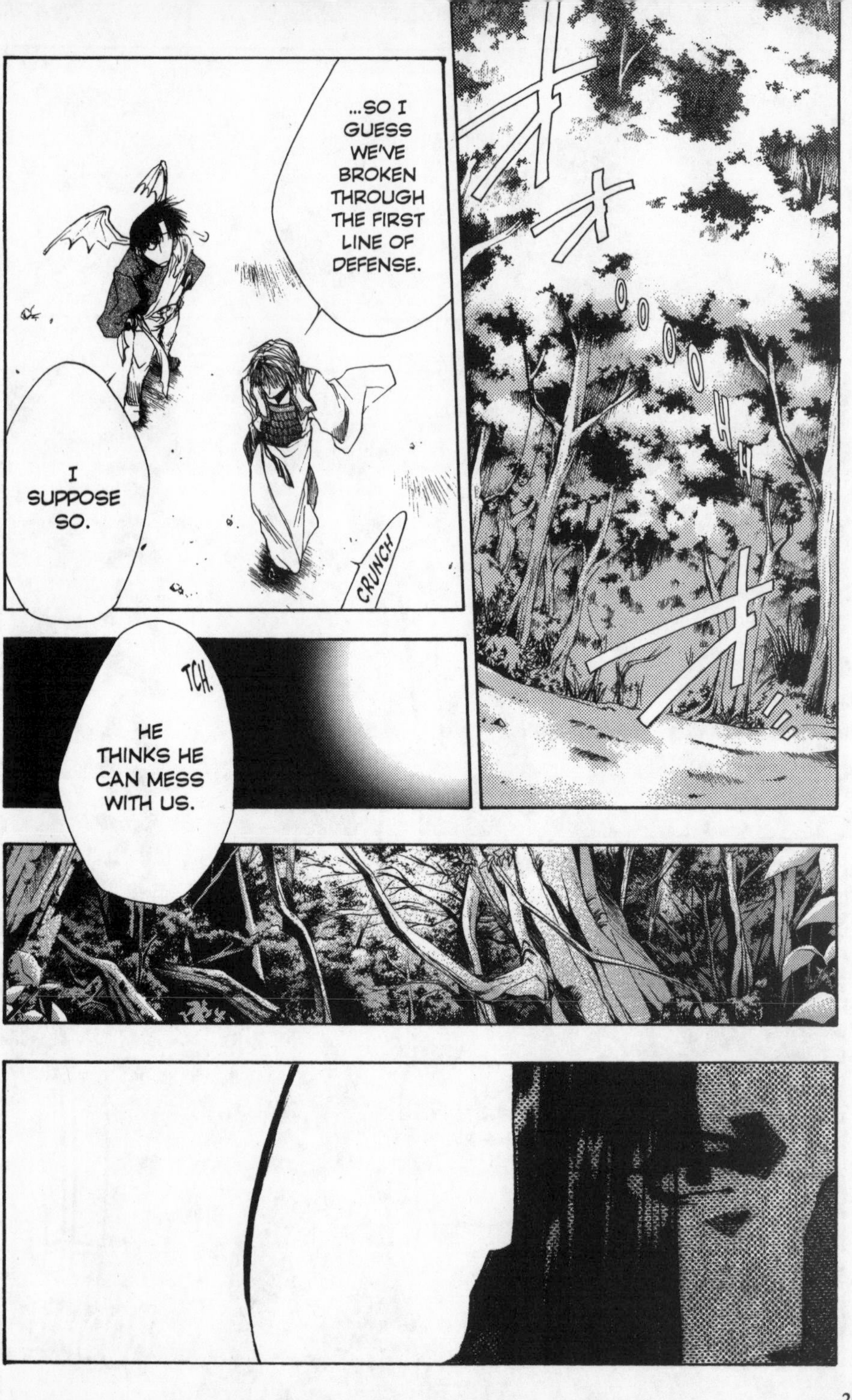
...SO I GUESS WE'VE BROKEN THROUGH THE FIRST LINE OF DEFENSE.
CRUNCH
I SUPPOSE SO.
TCH.
HE THINKS HE CAN MESS WITH US.

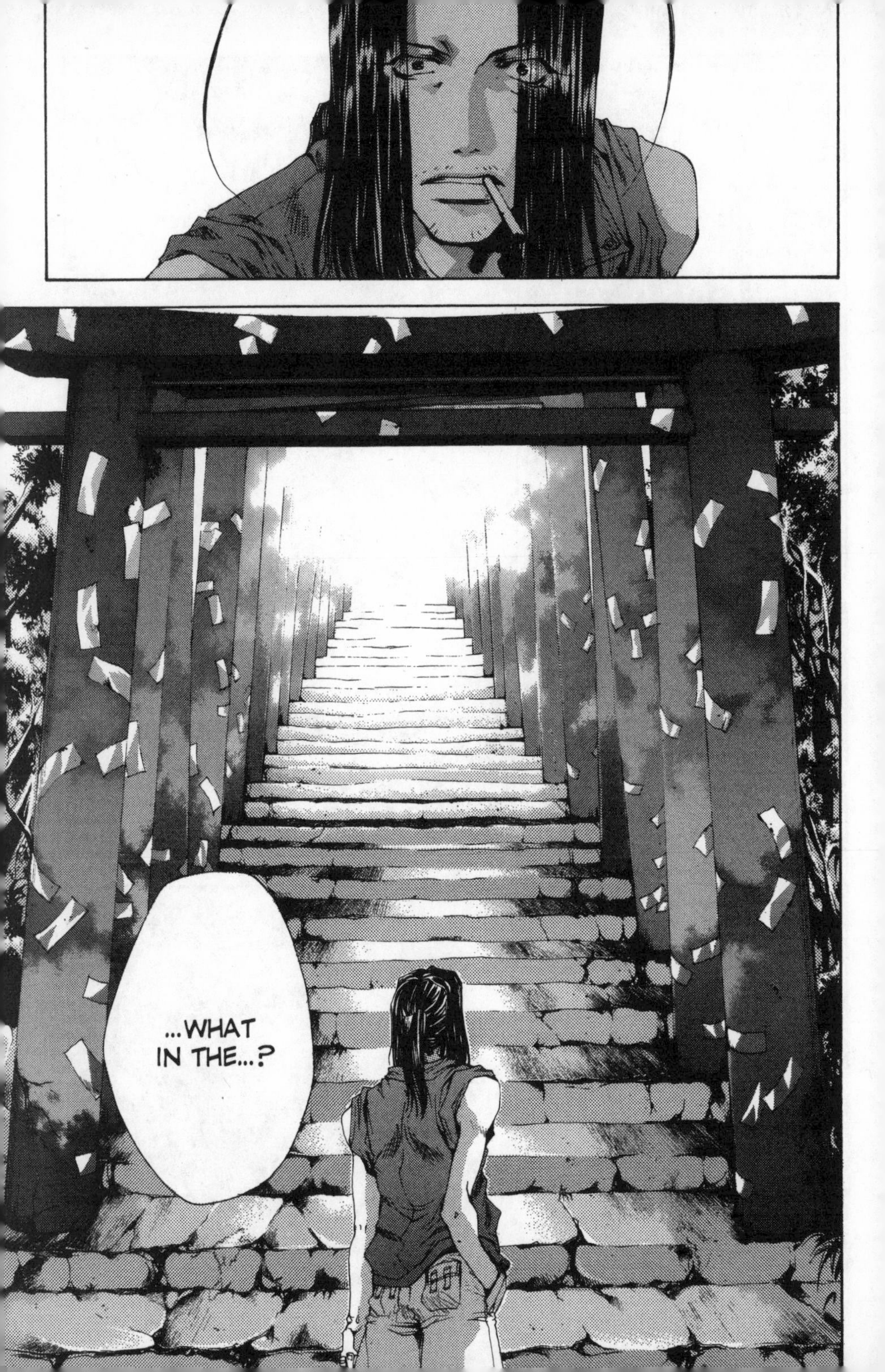
...WHAT IN THE...?

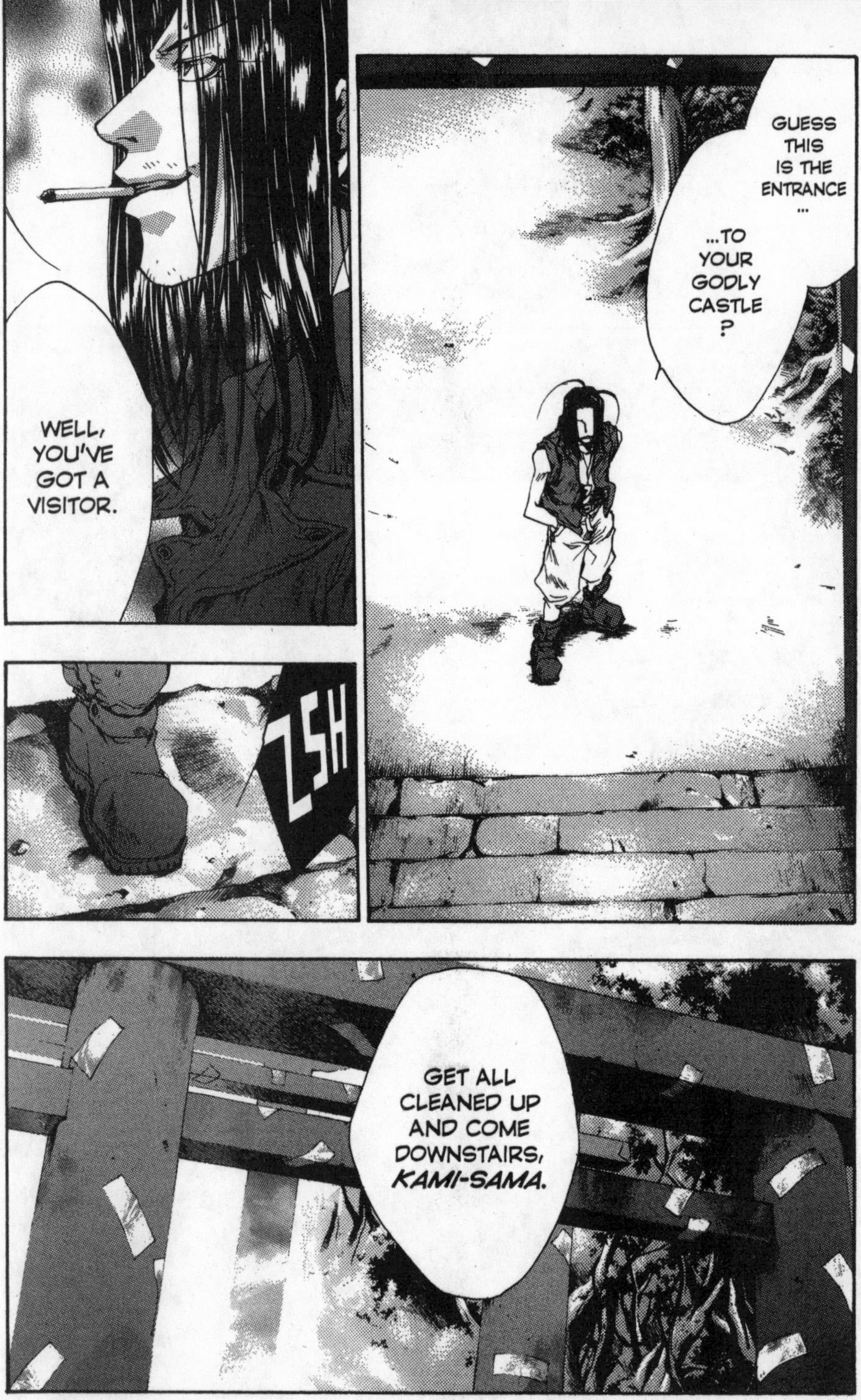
GUESS THIS IS THE ENTRANCE ...
...TO YOUR GODLY CASTLE ?
WELL, YOU'VE GOT A VISITOR.
ZSH
GET ALL CLEANED UP AND COME DOWNSTAIRS, *KAMI-SAMA*.

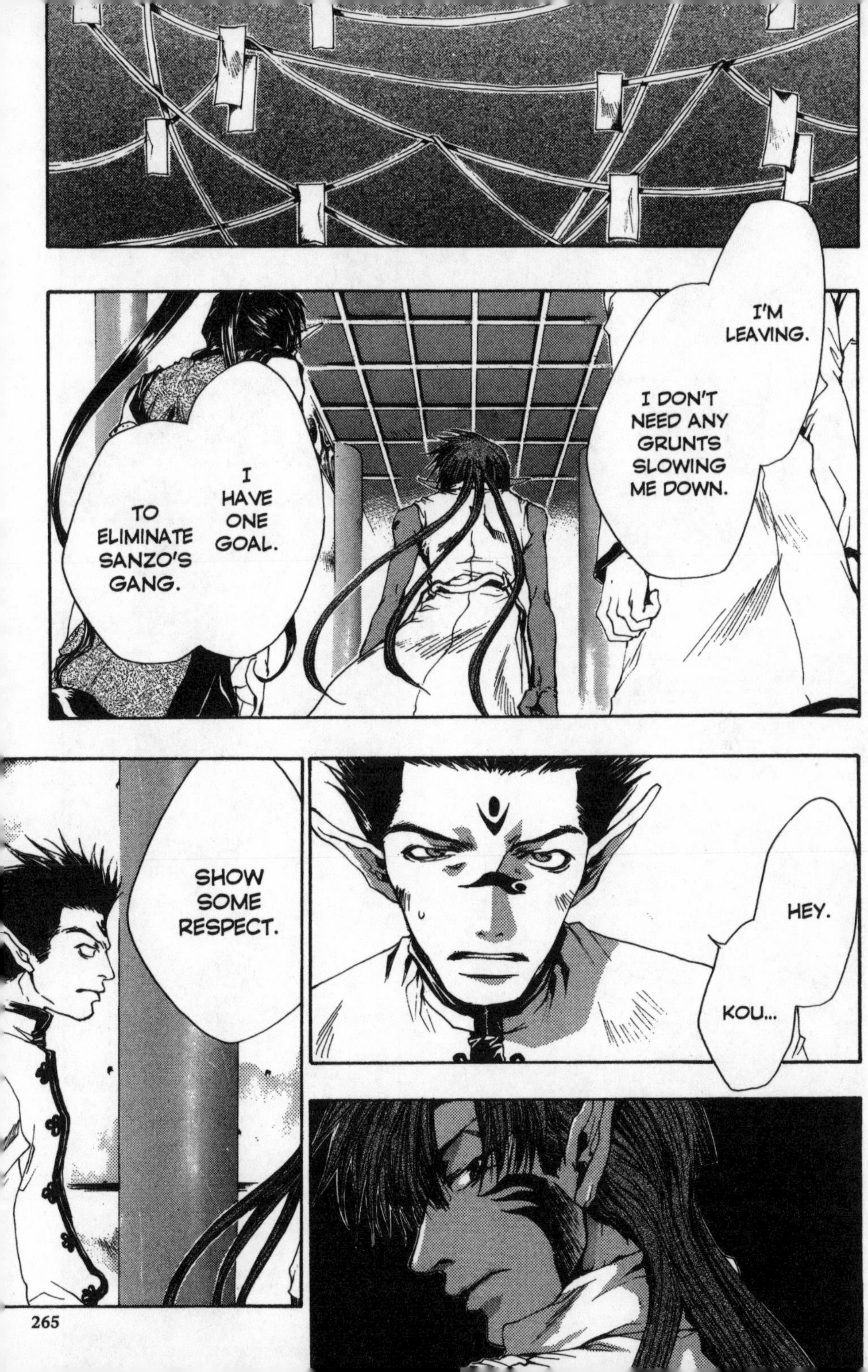

I'M LEAVING.
I DON'T NEED ANY GRUNTS SLOWING ME DOWN.
I HAVE ONE GOAL.
TO ELIMINATE SANZO'S GANG.
HEY.
KOU...
SHOW SOME RESPECT.

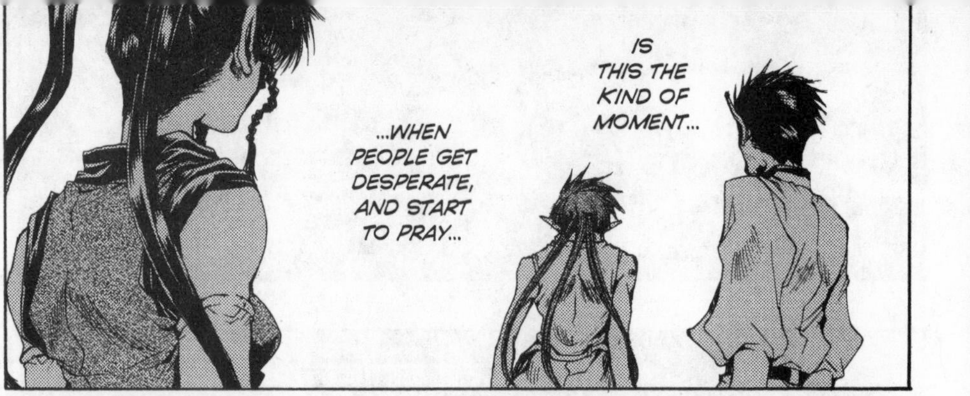
IS THIS THE KIND OF MOMENT...
...WHEN PEOPLE GET DESPERATE, AND START TO PRAY...

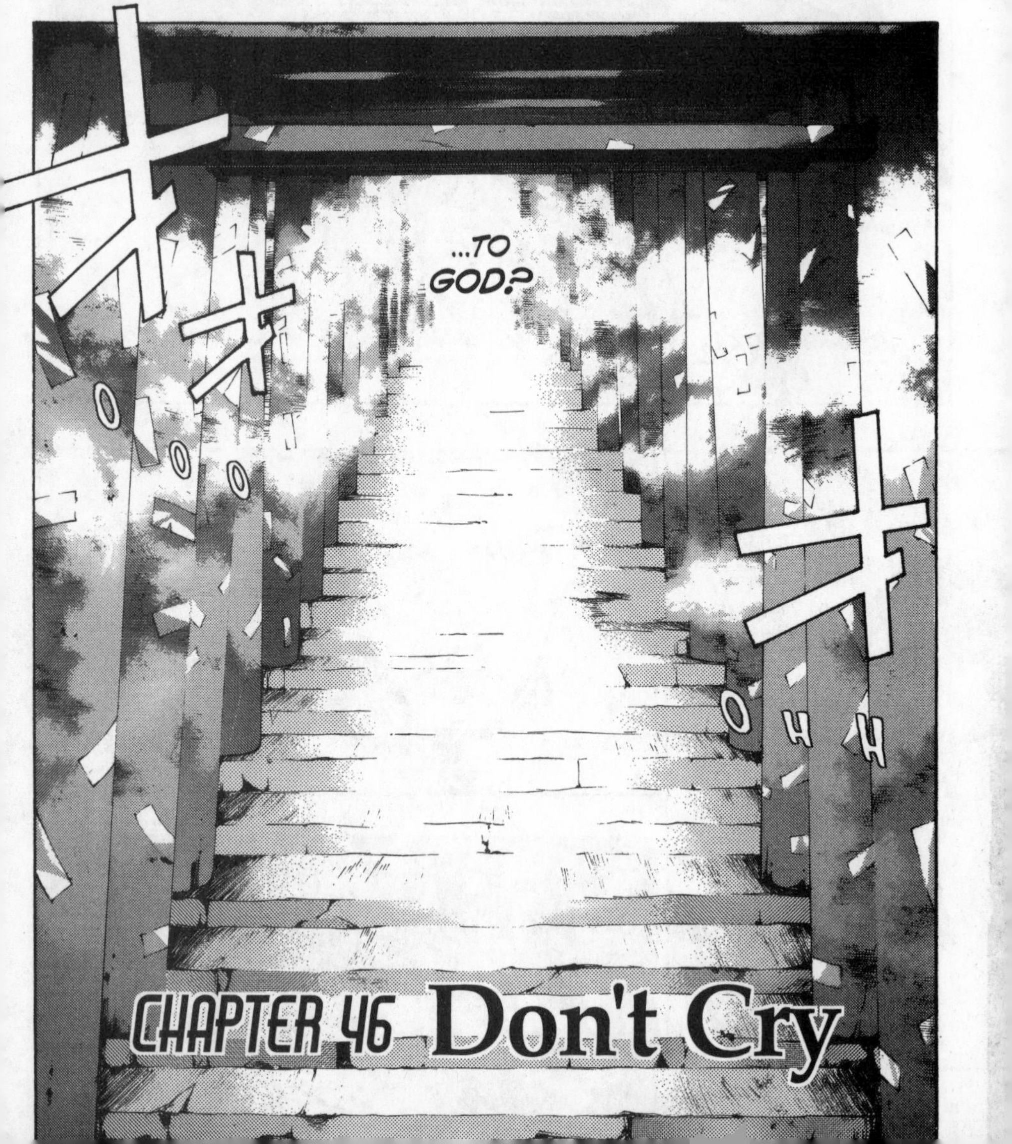
...TO GOD?
OOOOHH

CHAPTER 46 Don't Cry

CHAPTER 46: Don't Cry

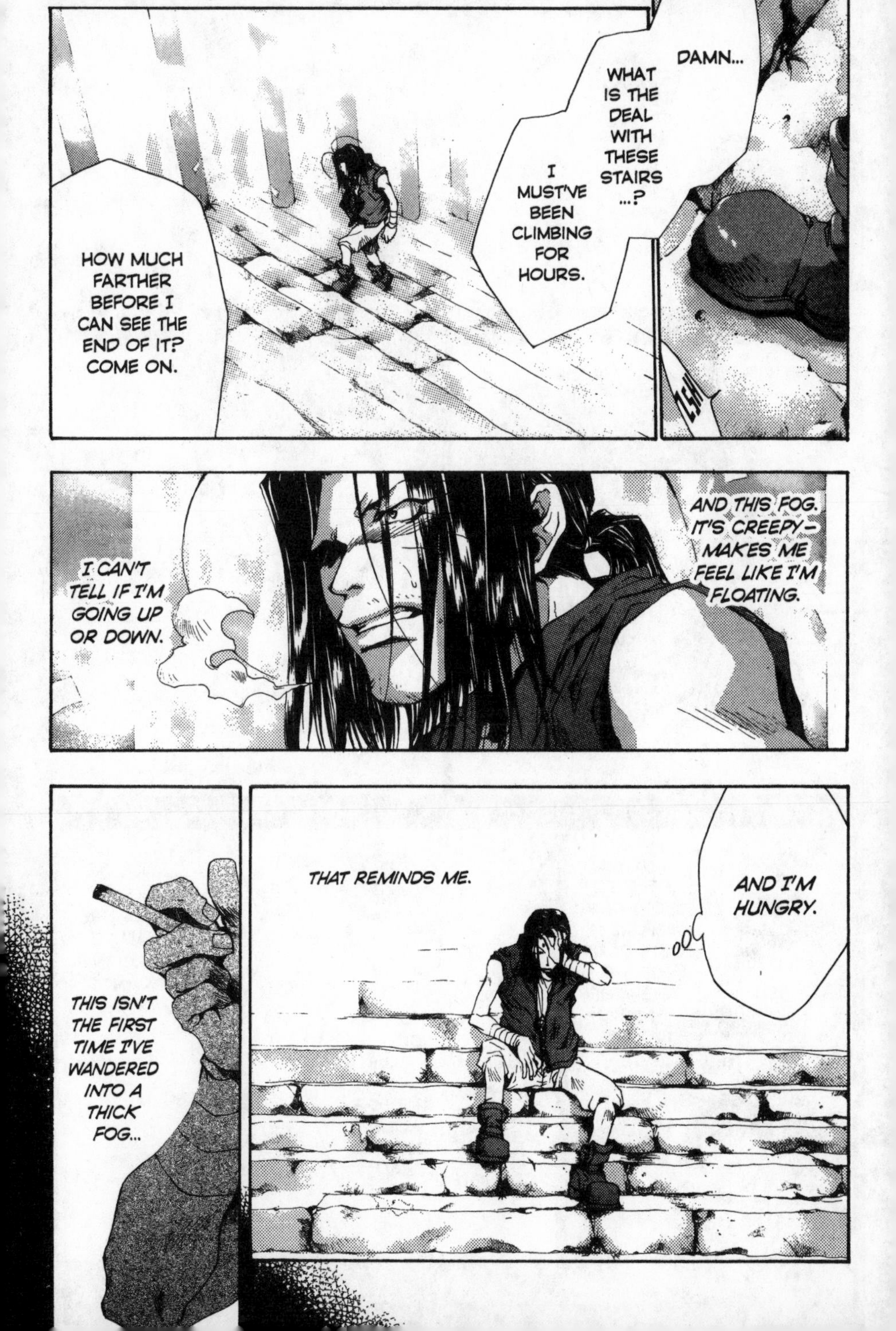
DAMN...
WHAT IS THE DEAL WITH THESE STAIRS ...?
I MUST'VE BEEN CLIMBING FOR HOURS.
HOW MUCH FARTHER BEFORE I CAN SEE THE END OF IT? COME ON.
AND THIS FOG. IT'S CREEPY— MAKES ME FEEL LIKE I'M FLOATING.
I CAN'T TELL IF I'M GOING UP OR DOWN.
AND I'M HUNGRY.
THAT REMINDS ME.
THIS ISN'T THE FIRST TIME I'VE WANDERED INTO A THICK FOG...

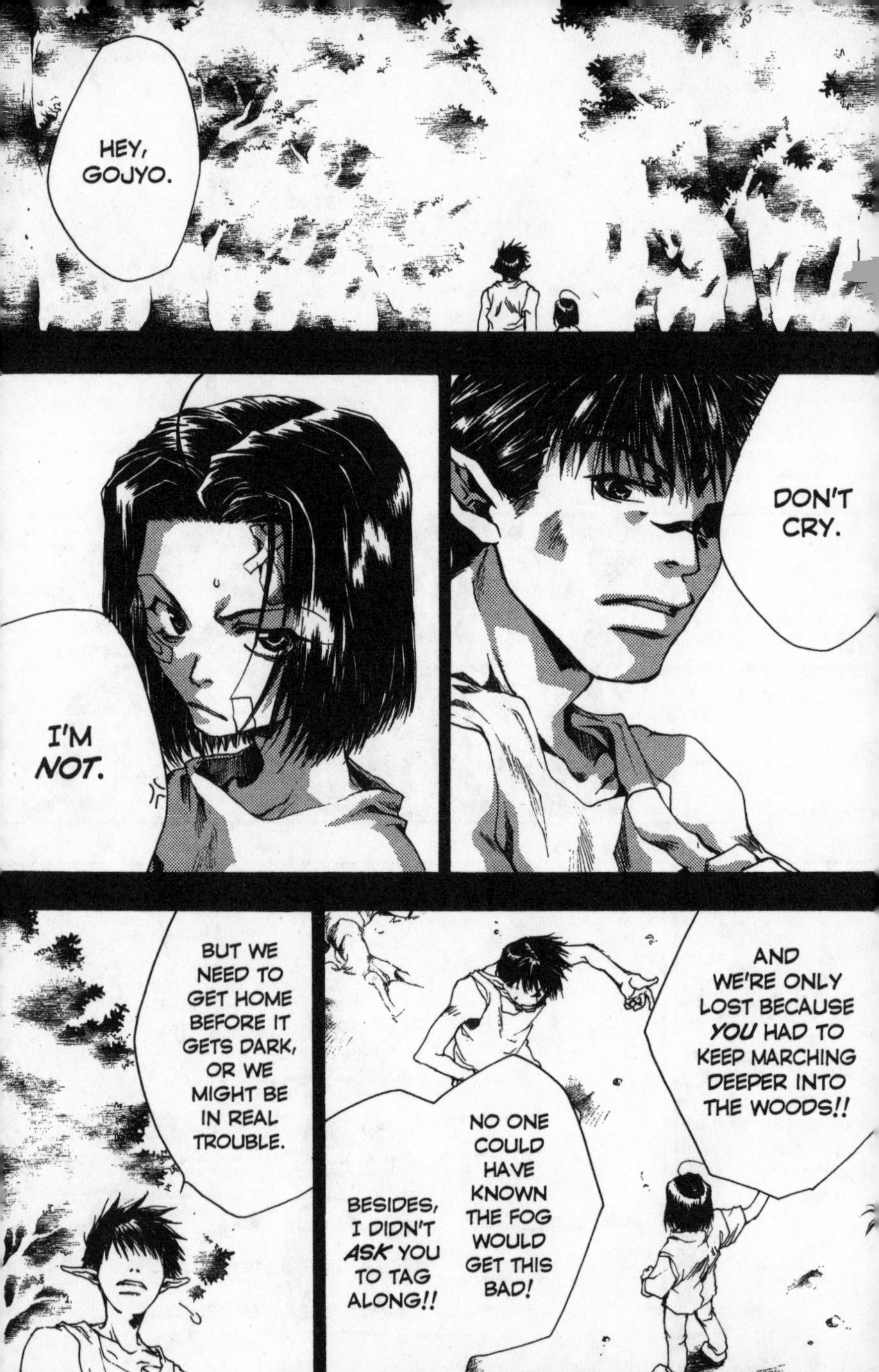
HEY, GOJYO.
DON'T CRY.
I'M *NOT*.
AND WE'RE ONLY LOST BECAUSE *YOU* HAD TO KEEP MARCHING DEEPER INTO THE WOODS!!
NO ONE COULD HAVE KNOWN THE FOG WOULD GET THIS BAD!
BESIDES, I DIDN'T *ASK* YOU TO TAG ALONG!!
BUT WE NEED TO GET HOME BEFORE IT GETS DARK, OR WE MIGHT BE IN REAL TROUBLE.

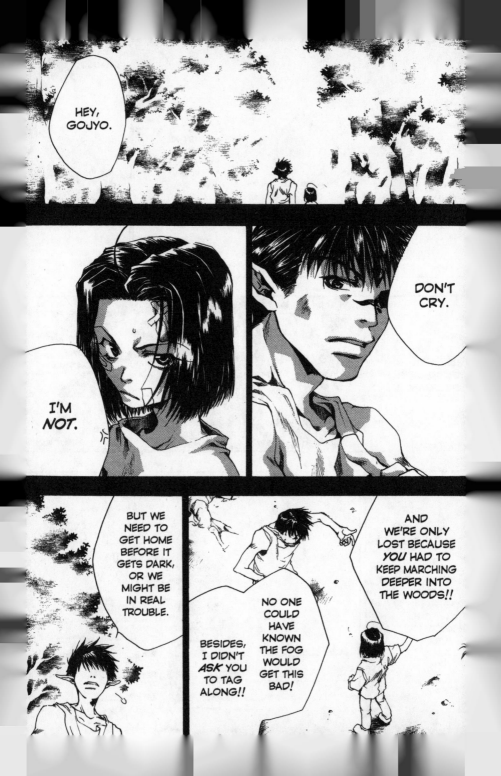

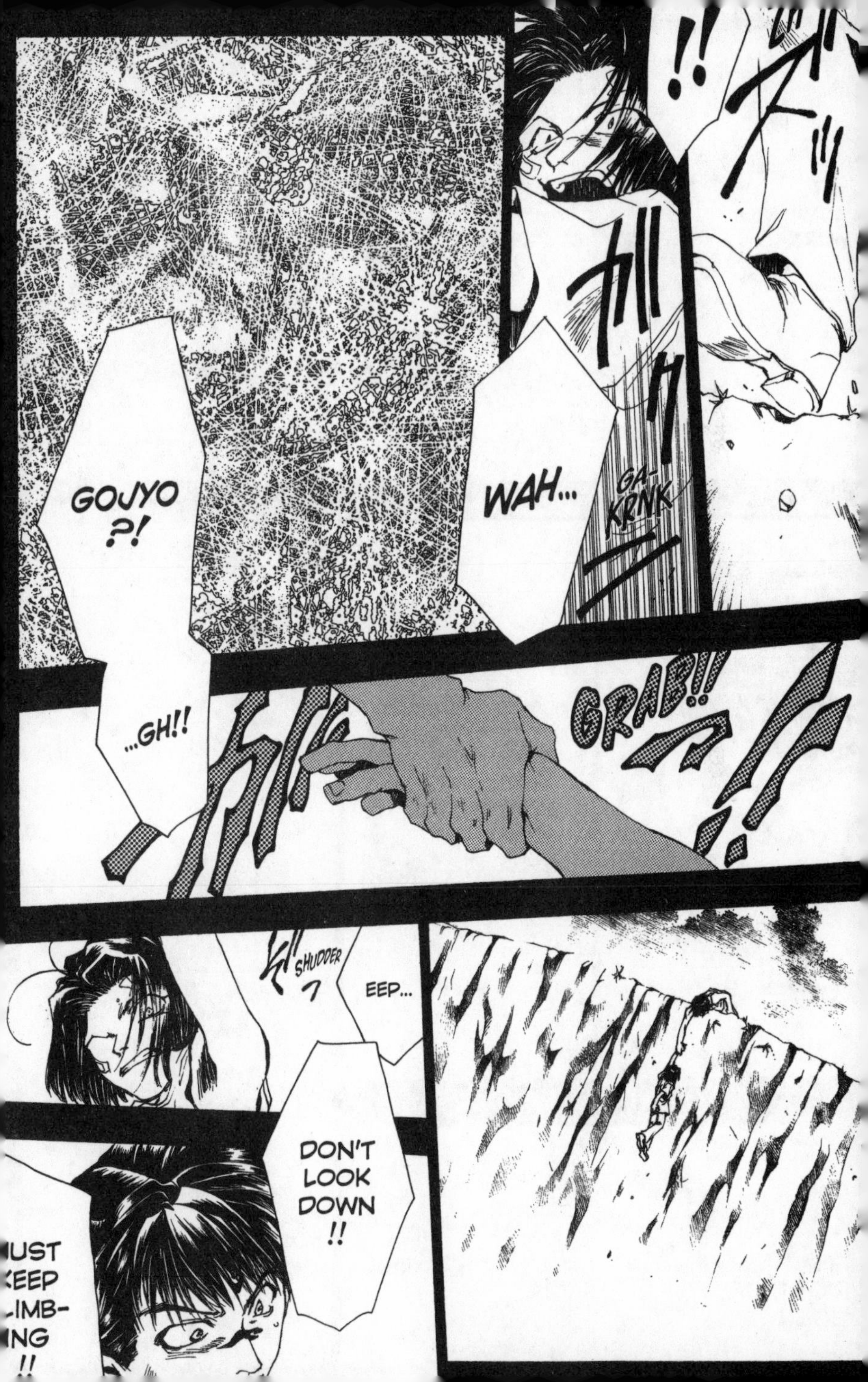
WAH...
GA-KRNK
GOJYO ?!
...GH!!
GRAB!!
SHUDDER
EEP...
DON'T LOOK DOWN !!
UST EEP LIMB- NG !!

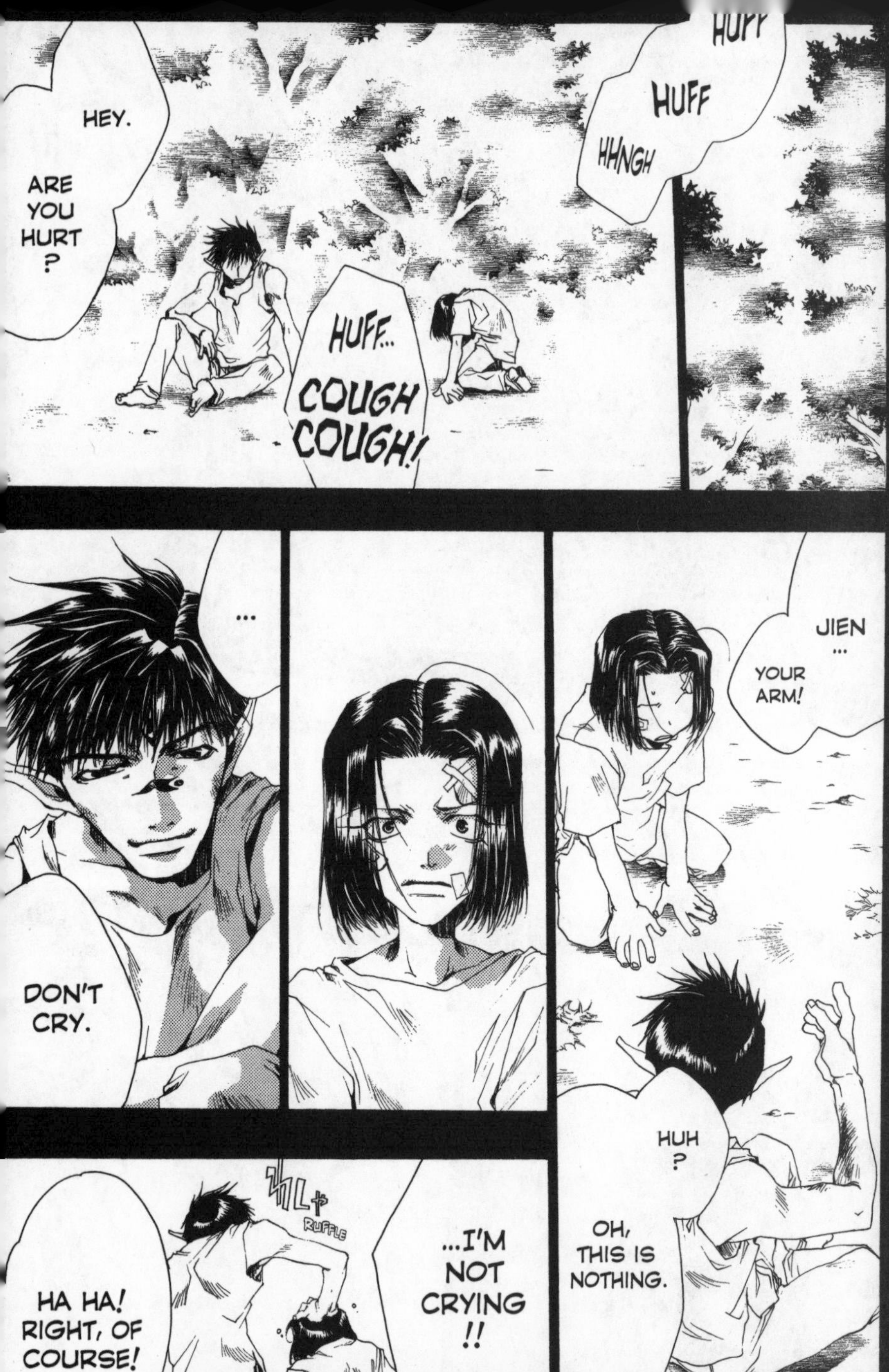
HUFF
HUFF
HHNGH
HUFF... COUGH COUGH!
HEY.
ARE YOU HURT?
JIEN...
YOUR ARM!
HUH?
OH, THIS IS NOTHING.
...
DON'T CRY.
...I'M NOT CRYING!!
RUFFLE
HA HA! RIGHT, OF COURSE!

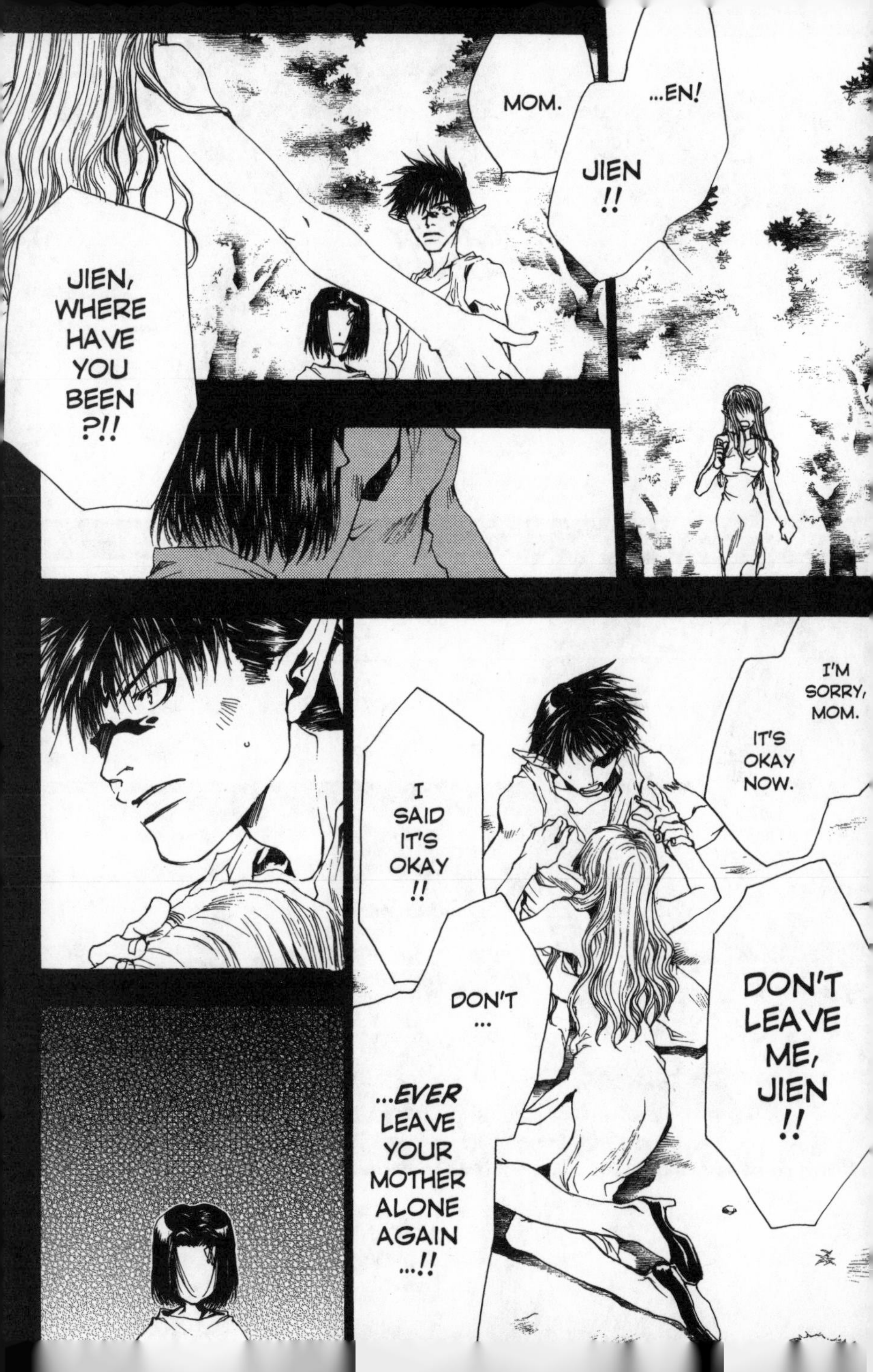
...EN!
JIEN!!
MOM.
JIEN, WHERE HAVE YOU BEEN?!!
I'M SORRY, MOM.
IT'S OKAY NOW.
I SAID IT'S OKAY!!
DON'T LEAVE ME, JIEN!!
DON'T...
...EVER LEAVE YOUR MOTHER ALONE AGAIN...!!

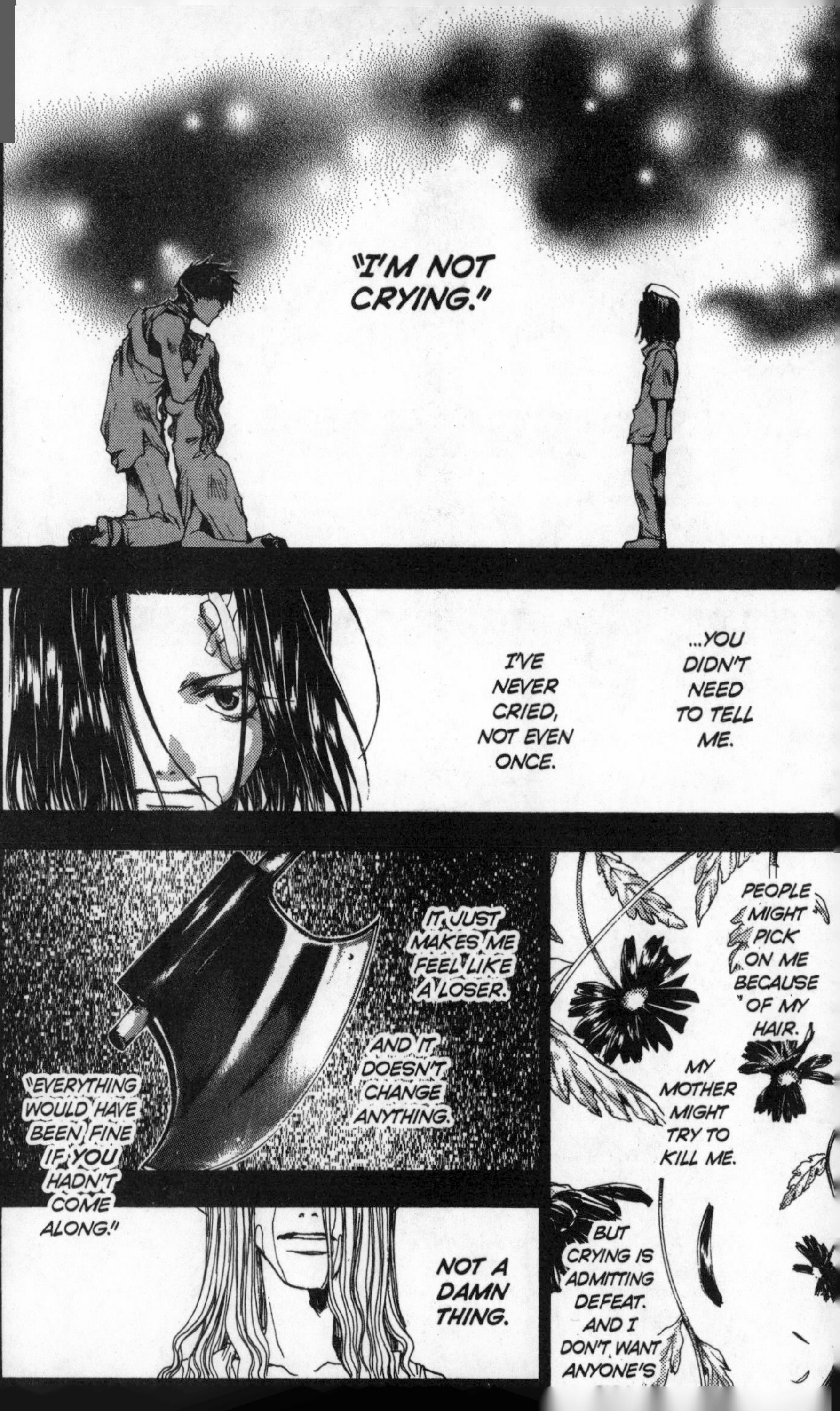
"I'M NOT CRYING."
...YOU DIDN'T NEED TO TELL ME.
I'VE NEVER CRIED, NOT EVEN ONCE.
PEOPLE MIGHT PICK ON ME BECAUSE OF MY HAIR.
MY MOTHER MIGHT TRY TO KILL ME.
BUT CRYING IS ADMITTING DEFEAT. AND I DON'T WANT ANYONE'S
IT JUST MAKES ME FEEL LIKE A LOSER.
AND IT DOESN'T CHANGE ANYTHING.
"EVERYTHING WOULD HAVE BEEN FINE IF YOU HADN'T COME ALONG."
NOT A DAMN THING.

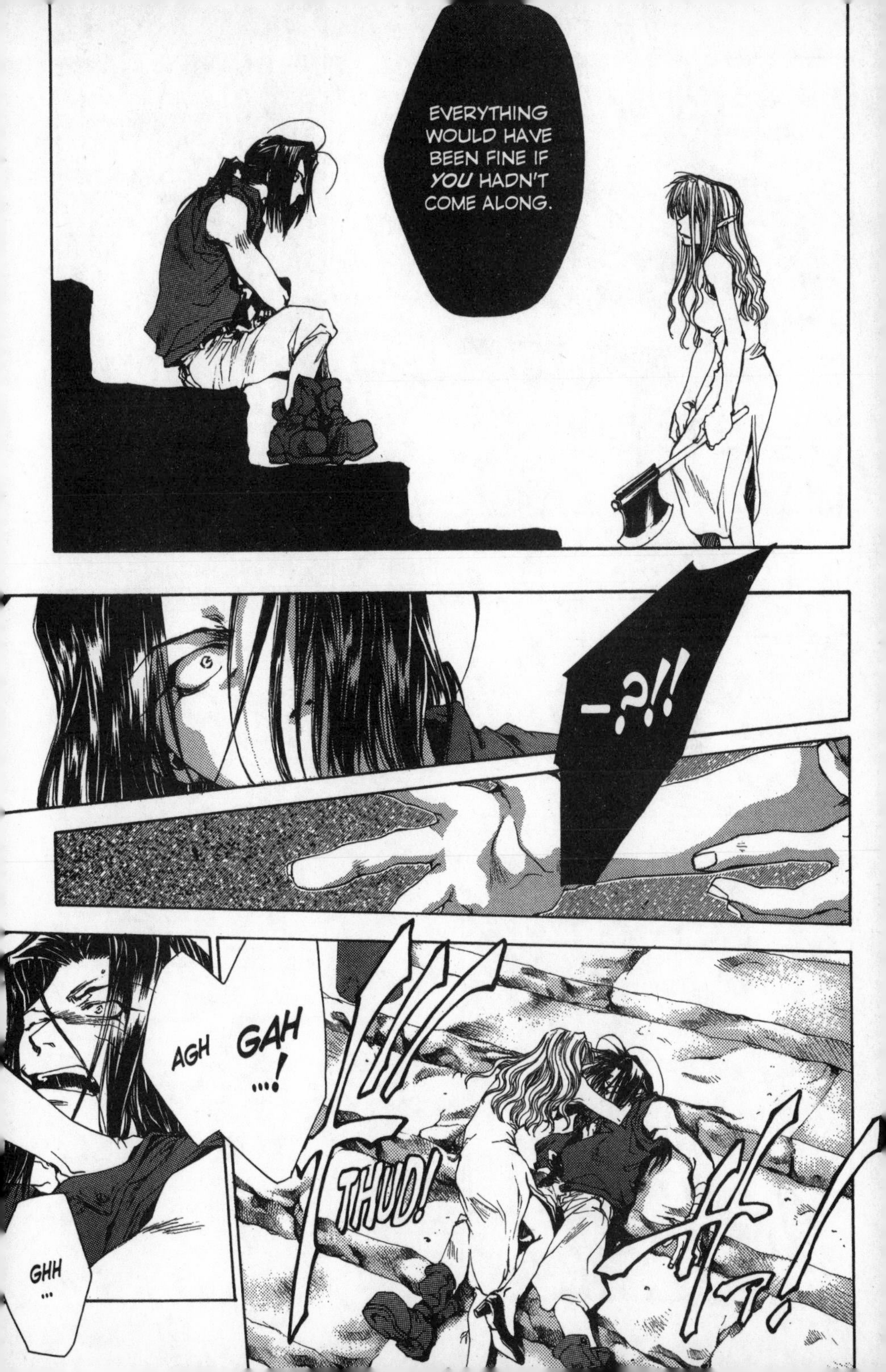
EVERYTHING WOULD HAVE BEEN FINE IF *YOU* HADN'T COME ALONG.
–?!!
GAH ...!
AGH
THUD!
GHH ...

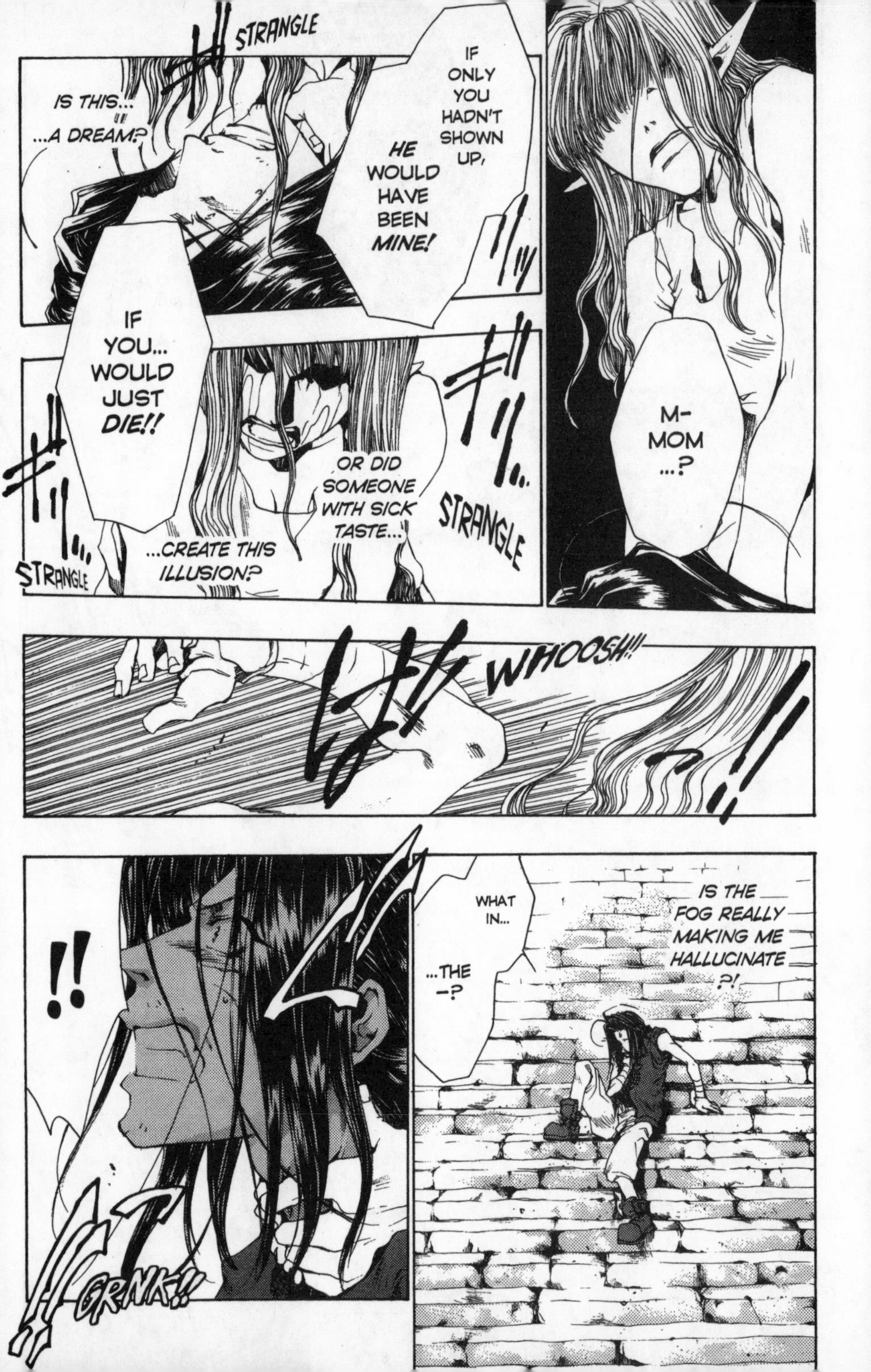
M-MOM ...?
IF ONLY YOU HADN'T SHOWN UP, HE WOULD HAVE BEEN MINE!
STRANGLE
IS THIS... ...A DREAM?
IF YOU... WOULD JUST DIE!!
STRANGLE
OR DID SOMEONE WITH SICK TASTE...
...CREATE THIS ILLUSION?
STRANGLE
WHOOSH!!
WHAT IN... ...THE —?
IS THE FOG REALLY MAKING ME HALLUCINATE ?!
GRNK!!

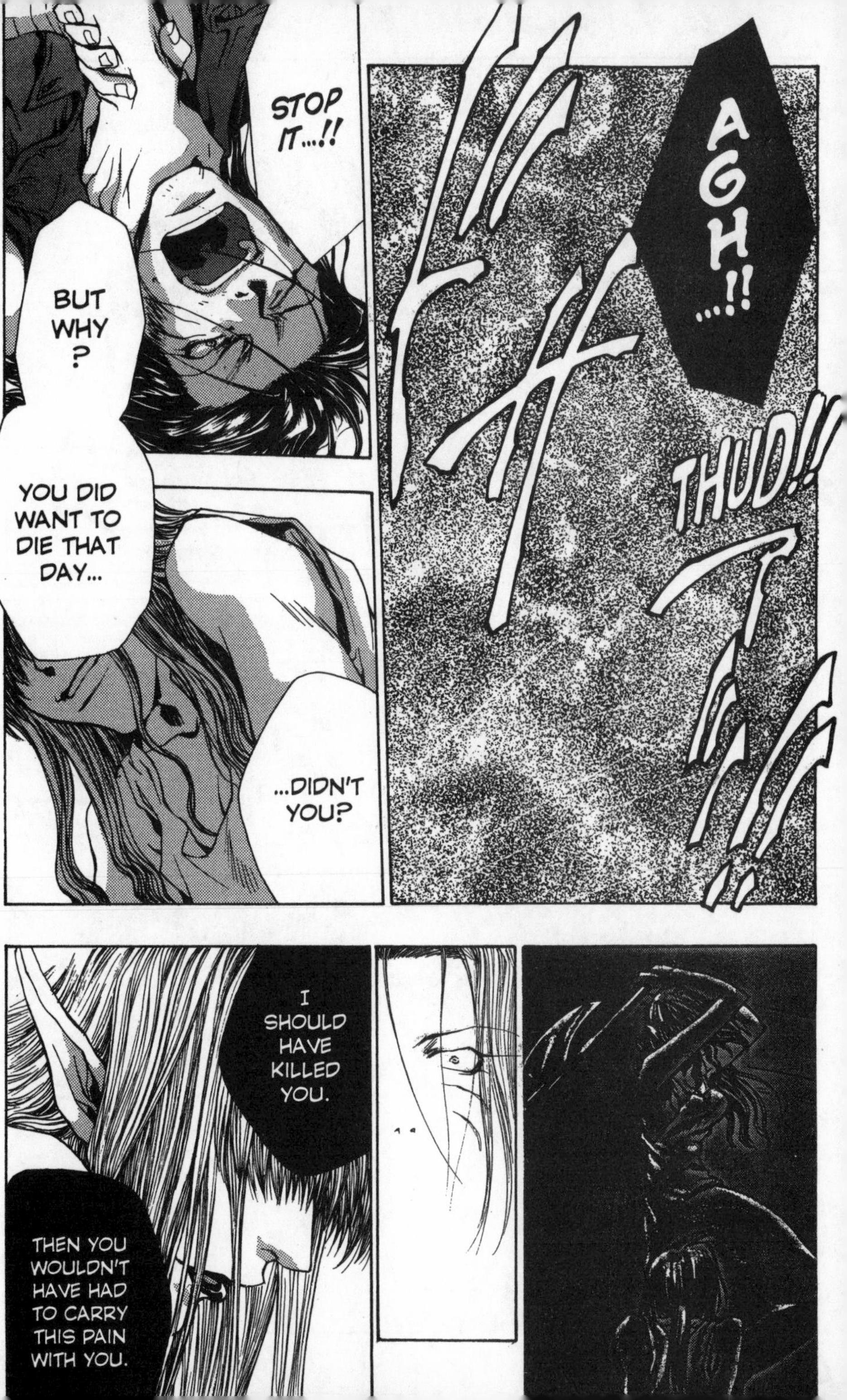
AGH...!!
THUD!!
STOP IT...!!
BUT WHY?
YOU DID WANT TO DIE THAT DAY...
...DIDN'T YOU?
I SHOULD HAVE KILLED YOU.
THEN YOU WOULDN'T HAVE HAD TO CARRY THIS PAIN WITH YOU.

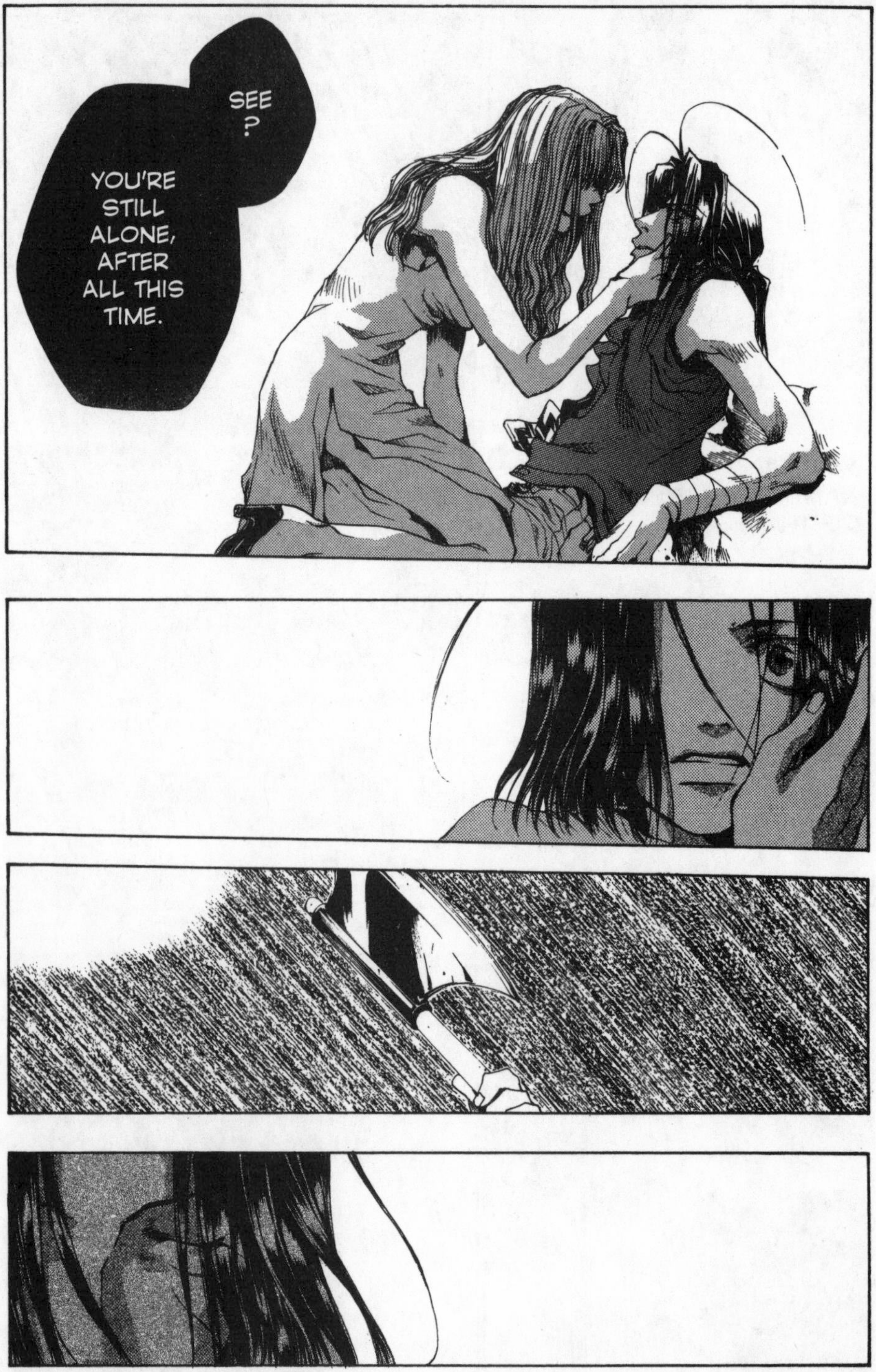
SEE?
YOU'RE STILL ALONE, AFTER ALL THIS TIME.

CHAPTER 46: Don't Cry

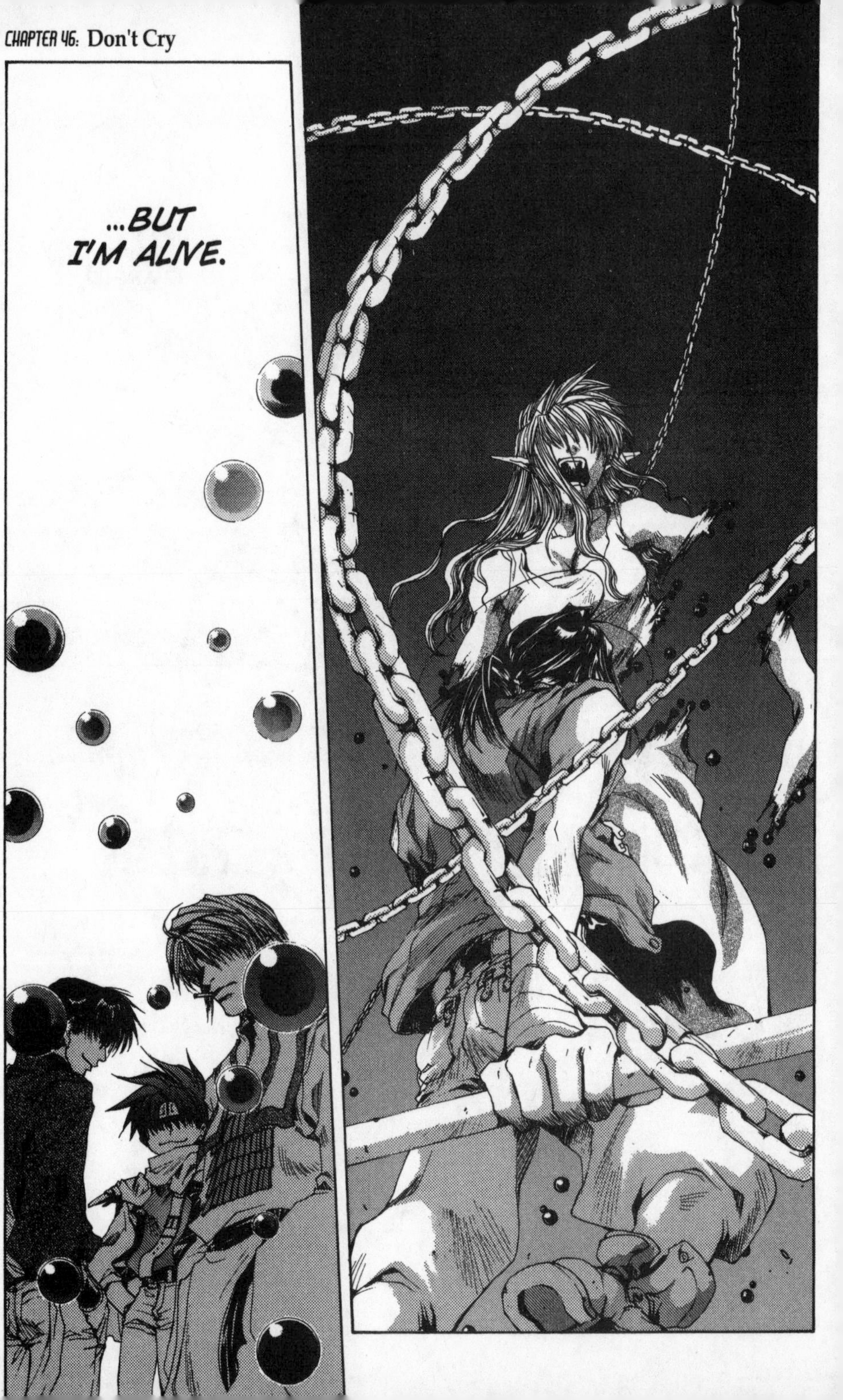
...BUT
I'M ALIVE.

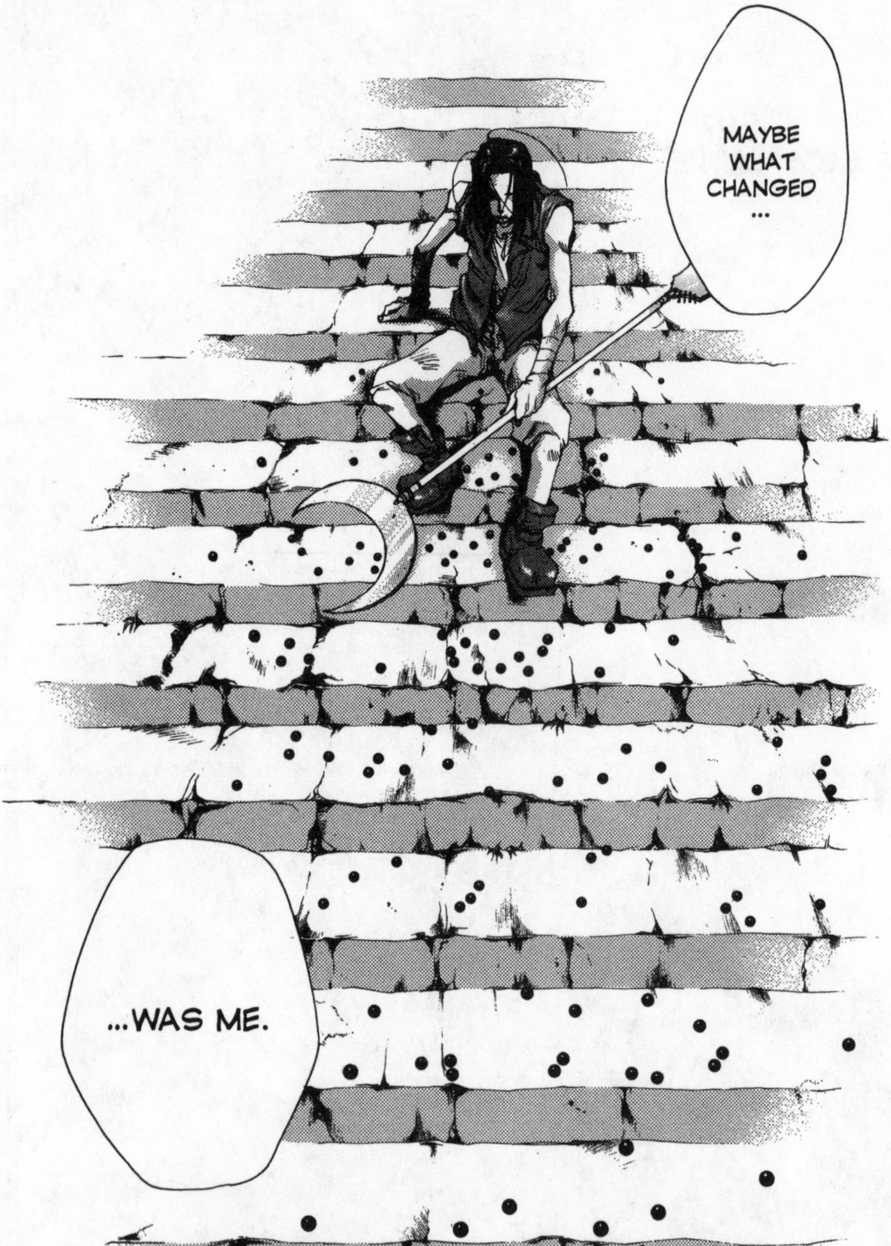
MAYBE WHAT CHANGED ...
...WAS ME.

CHAPTER 46: Don't Cry

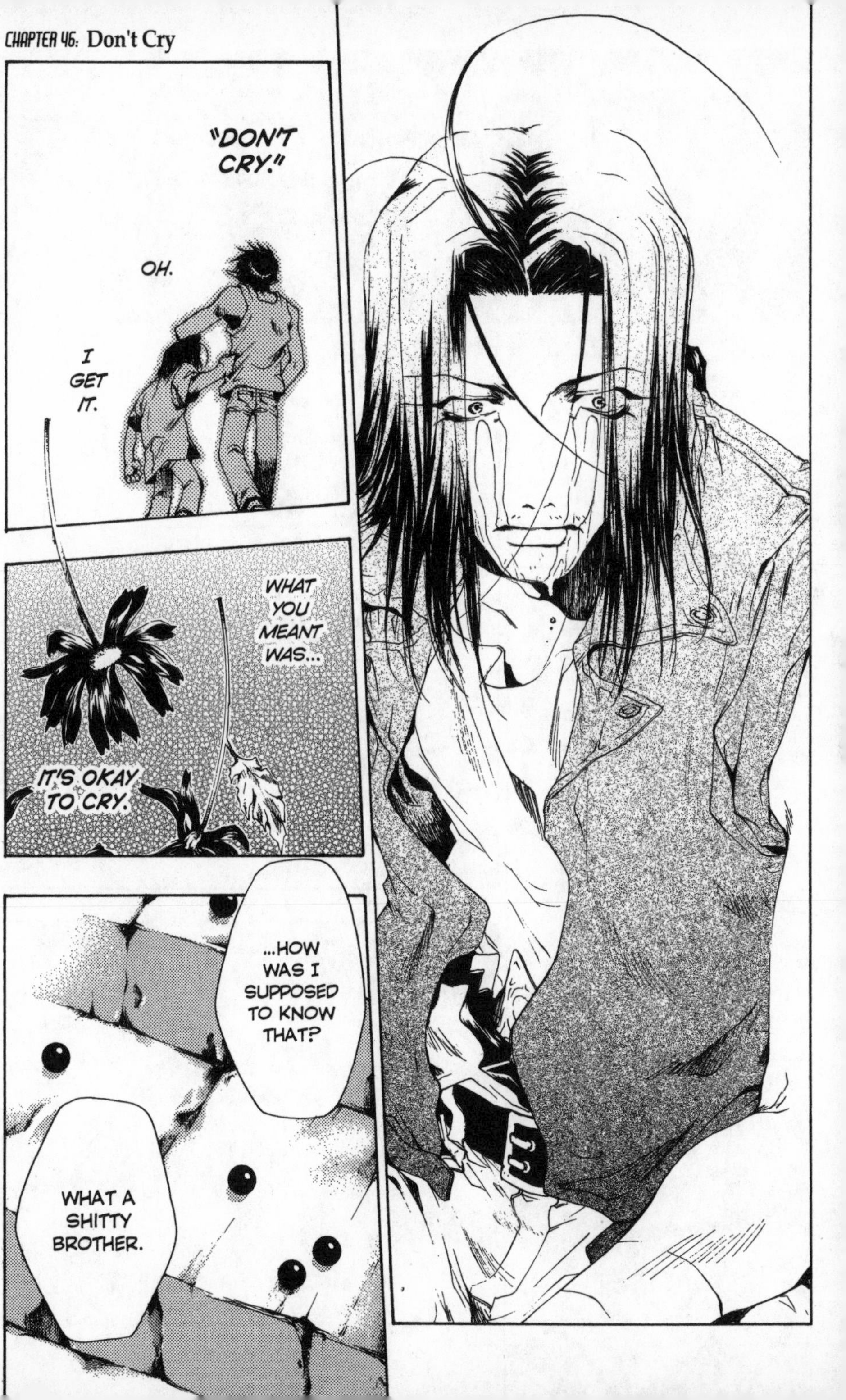
"DON'T CRY."
OH.
I GET IT.
WHAT YOU MEANT WAS...
IT'S OKAY TO CRY.
...HOW WAS I SUPPOSED TO KNOW THAT?
WHAT A SHITTY BROTHER.

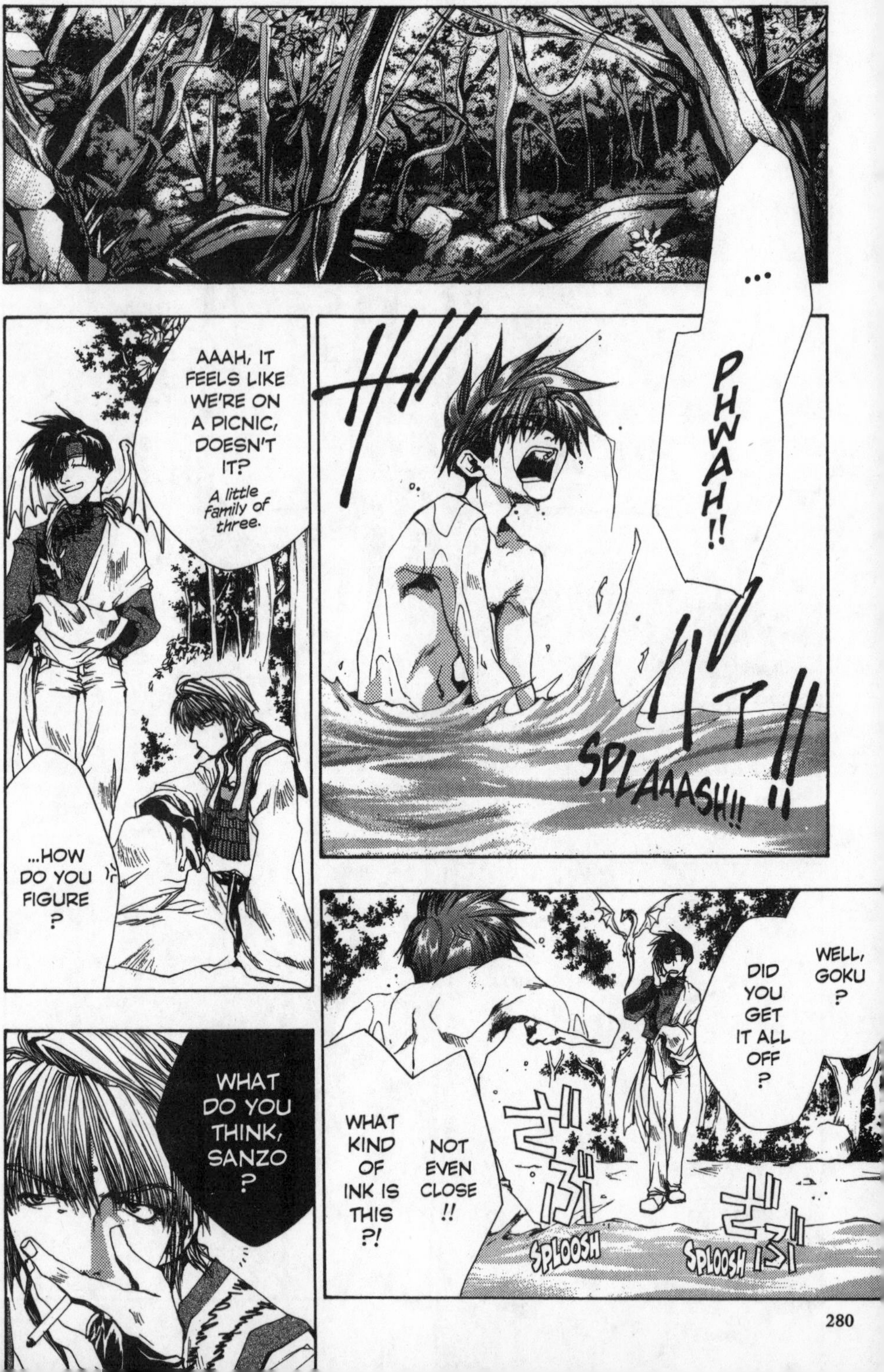
...
PHWAH!!
SPLAAASH!!
AAAH, IT FEELS LIKE WE'RE ON A PICNIC, DOESN'T IT?
A little family of three.
...HOW DO YOU FIGURE?
WELL, GOKU?
DID YOU GET IT ALL OFF?
NOT EVEN CLOSE!!
WHAT KIND OF INK IS THIS?!
SPLOOSH
SPLOOSH
WHAT DO YOU THINK, SANZO?

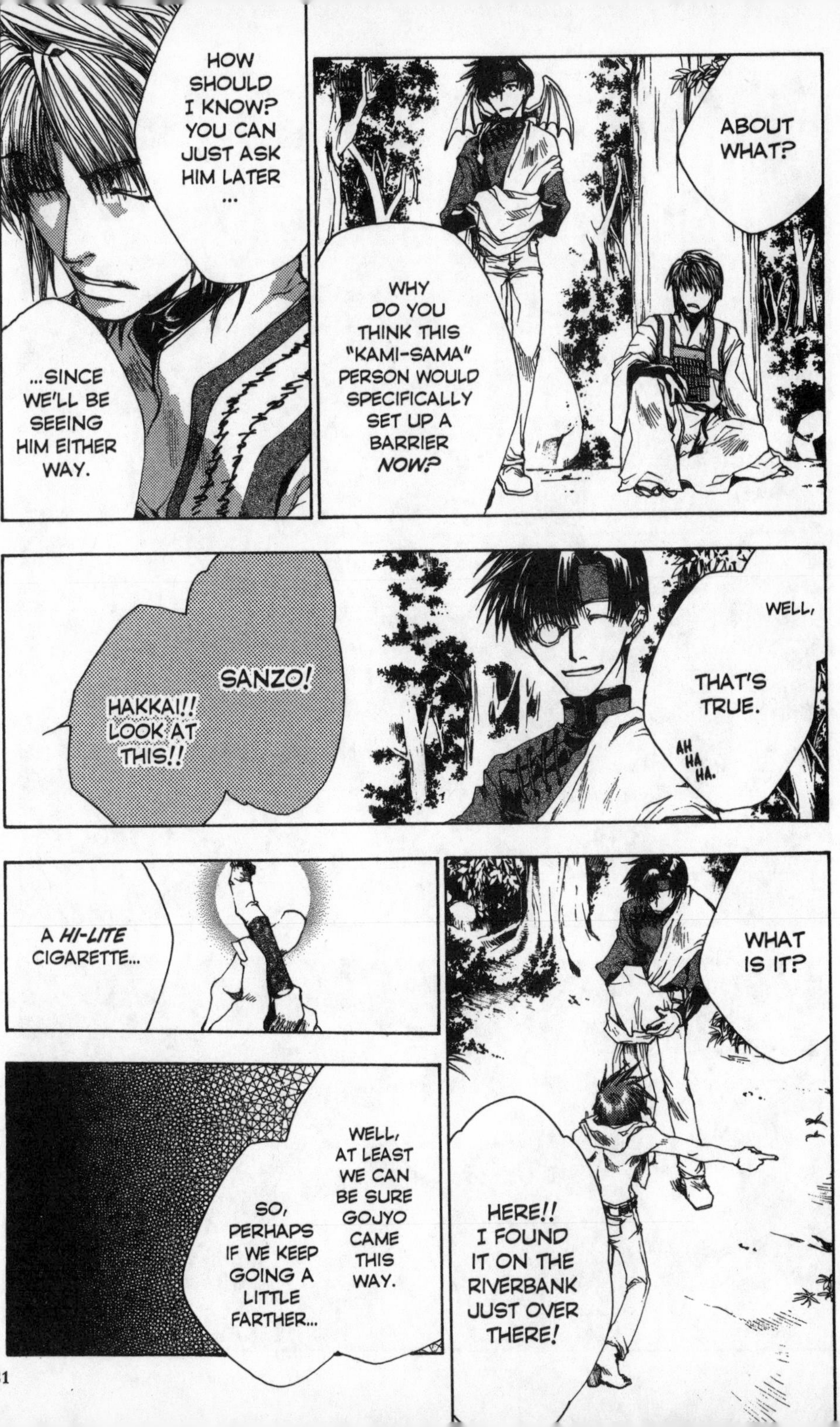
ABOUT WHAT?
WHY DO YOU THINK THIS "KAMI-SAMA" PERSON WOULD SPECIFICALLY SET UP A BARRIER *NOW?*
HOW SHOULD I KNOW? YOU CAN JUST ASK HIM LATER ...
...SINCE WE'LL BE SEEING HIM EITHER WAY.
WELL, THAT'S TRUE.
AH HA HA.
SANZO!
HAKKAI!! LOOK AT THIS!!
WHAT IS IT?
HERE!! I FOUND IT ON THE RIVERBANK JUST OVER THERE!
A *HI-LITE* CIGARETTE...
WELL, AT LEAST WE CAN BE SURE GOJYO CAME THIS WAY.
SO, PERHAPS IF WE KEEP GOING A LITTLE FARTHER...

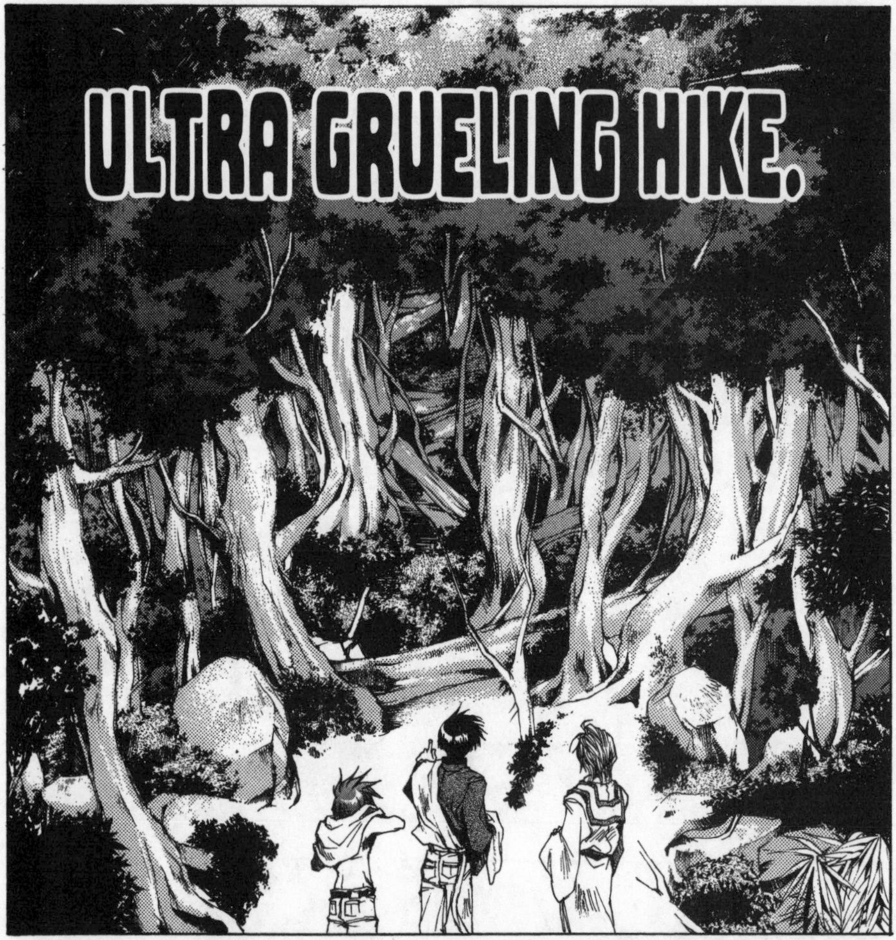
ULTRA GRUELING HIKE.
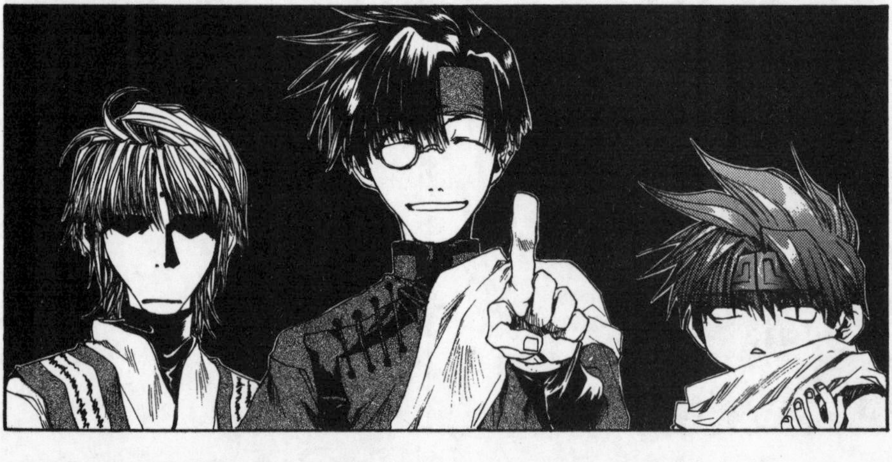

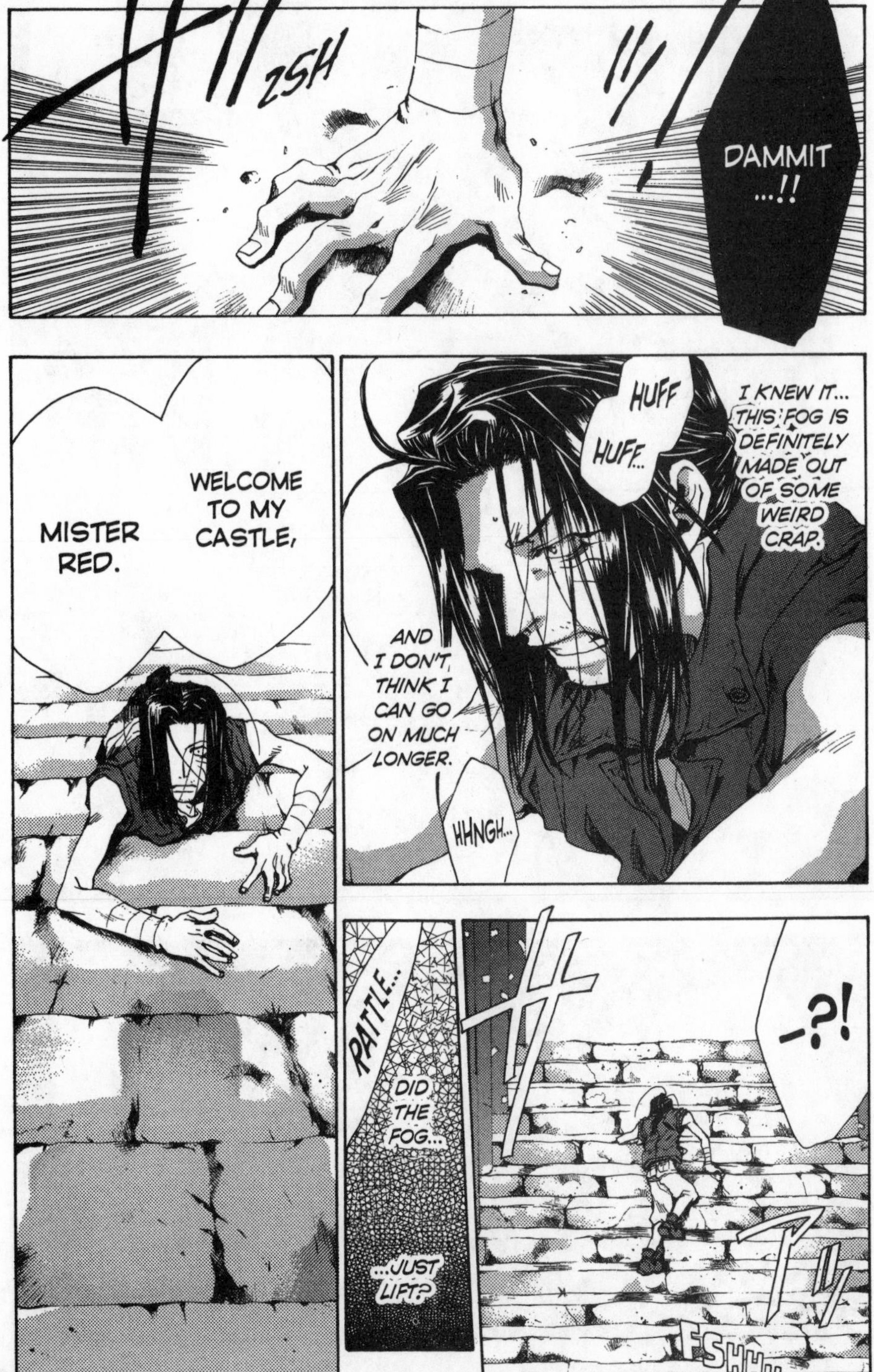
DAMMIT ...!!
ZSH
I KNEW IT... THIS FOG IS DEFINITELY MADE OUT OF SOME WEIRD CRAP.
HUFF
HUFF...
AND I DON'T THINK I CAN GO ON MUCH LONGER.
HHNGH...
-?!
RATTLE...
DID THE FOG...
...JUST LIFT?
FSHHH
WELCOME TO MY CASTLE,
MISTER RED.

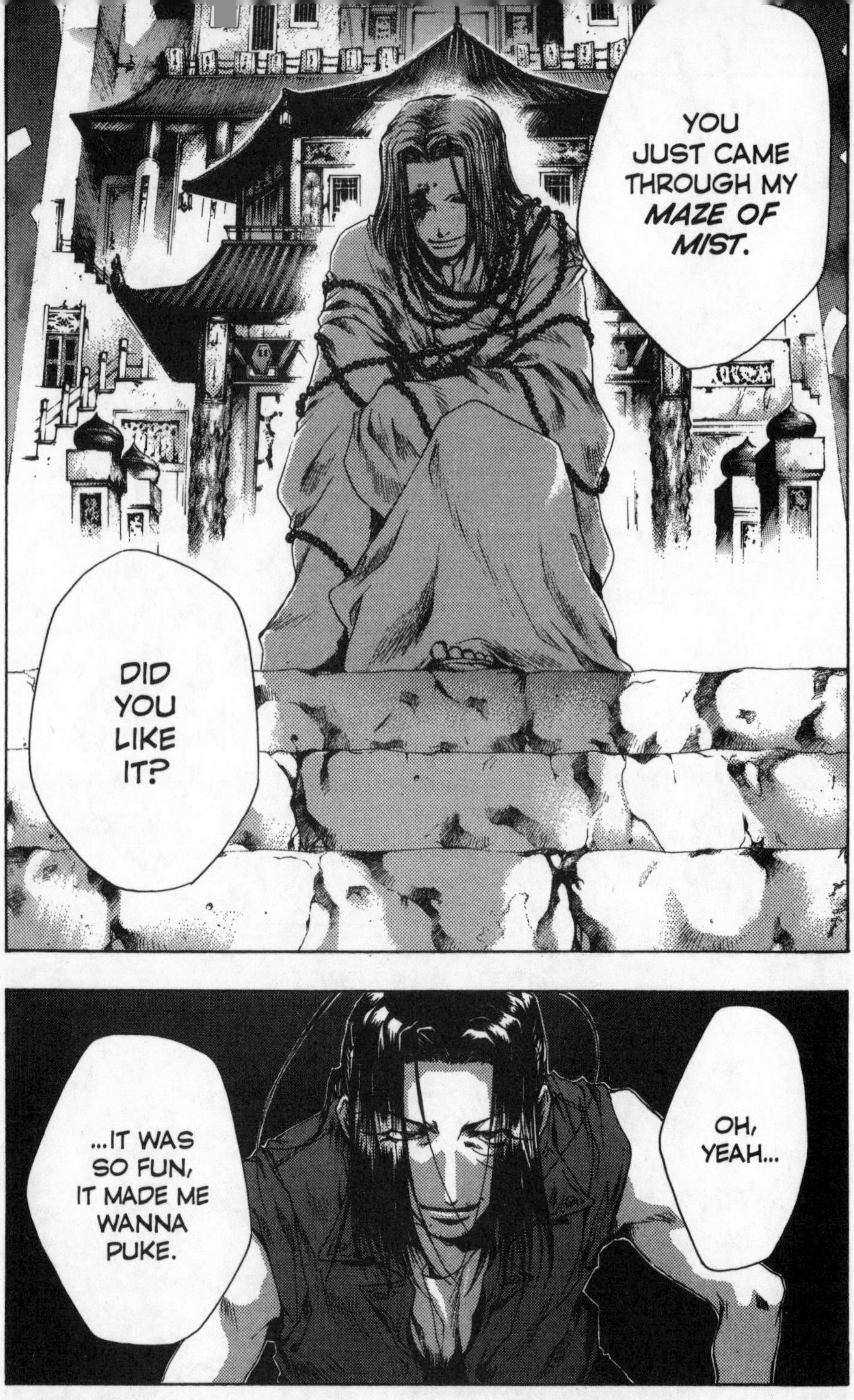
YOU JUST CAME THROUGH MY *MAZE OF MIST*.
DID YOU LIKE IT?
OH, YEAH...
...IT WAS SO FUN, IT MADE ME WANNA PUKE.

CHAPTER 47: Recreation

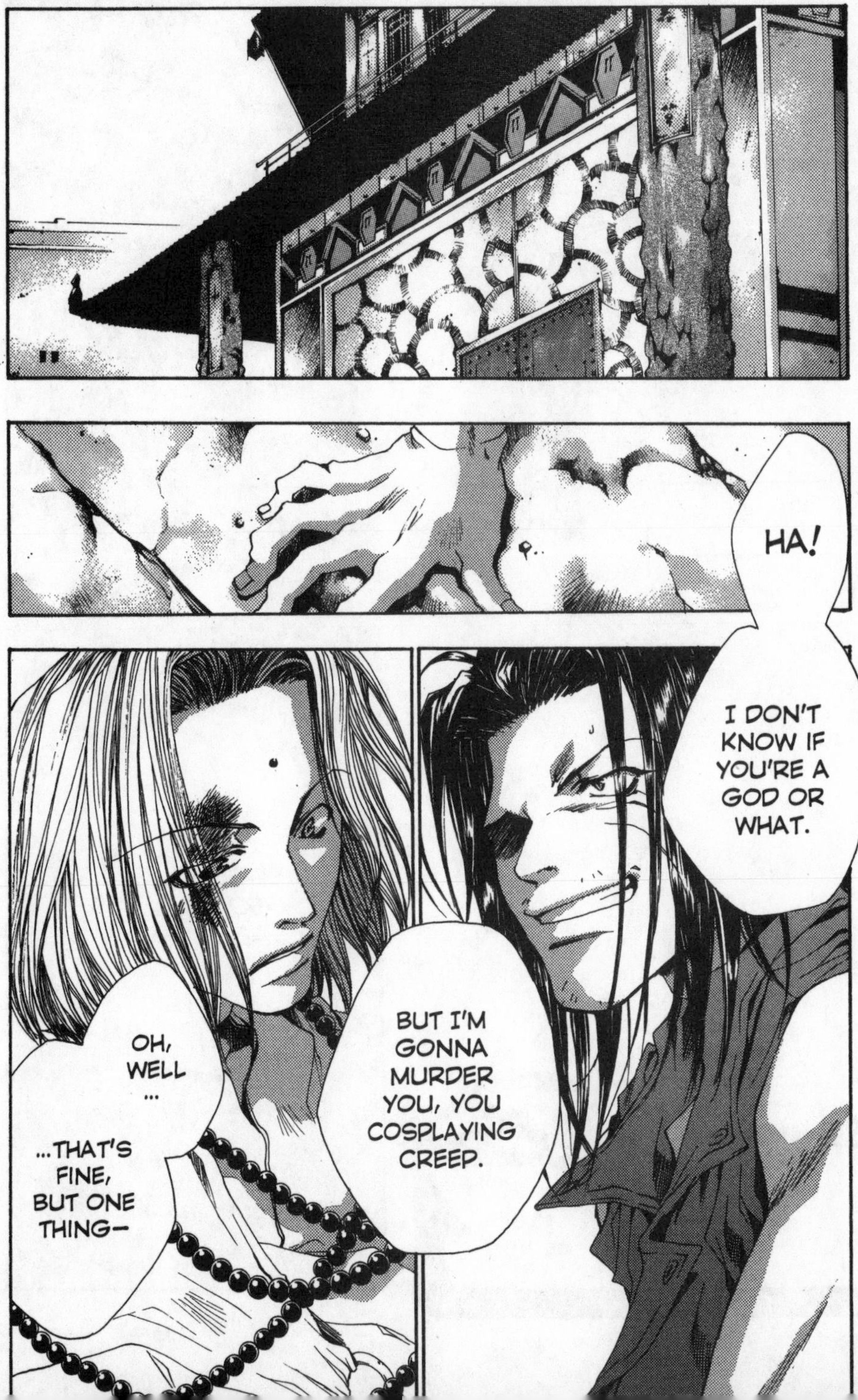
HA!
I DON'T KNOW IF YOU'RE A GOD OR WHAT.
BUT I'M GONNA MURDER YOU, YOU COSPLAYING CREEP.
OH, WELL ...
...THAT'S FINE, BUT ONE THING—

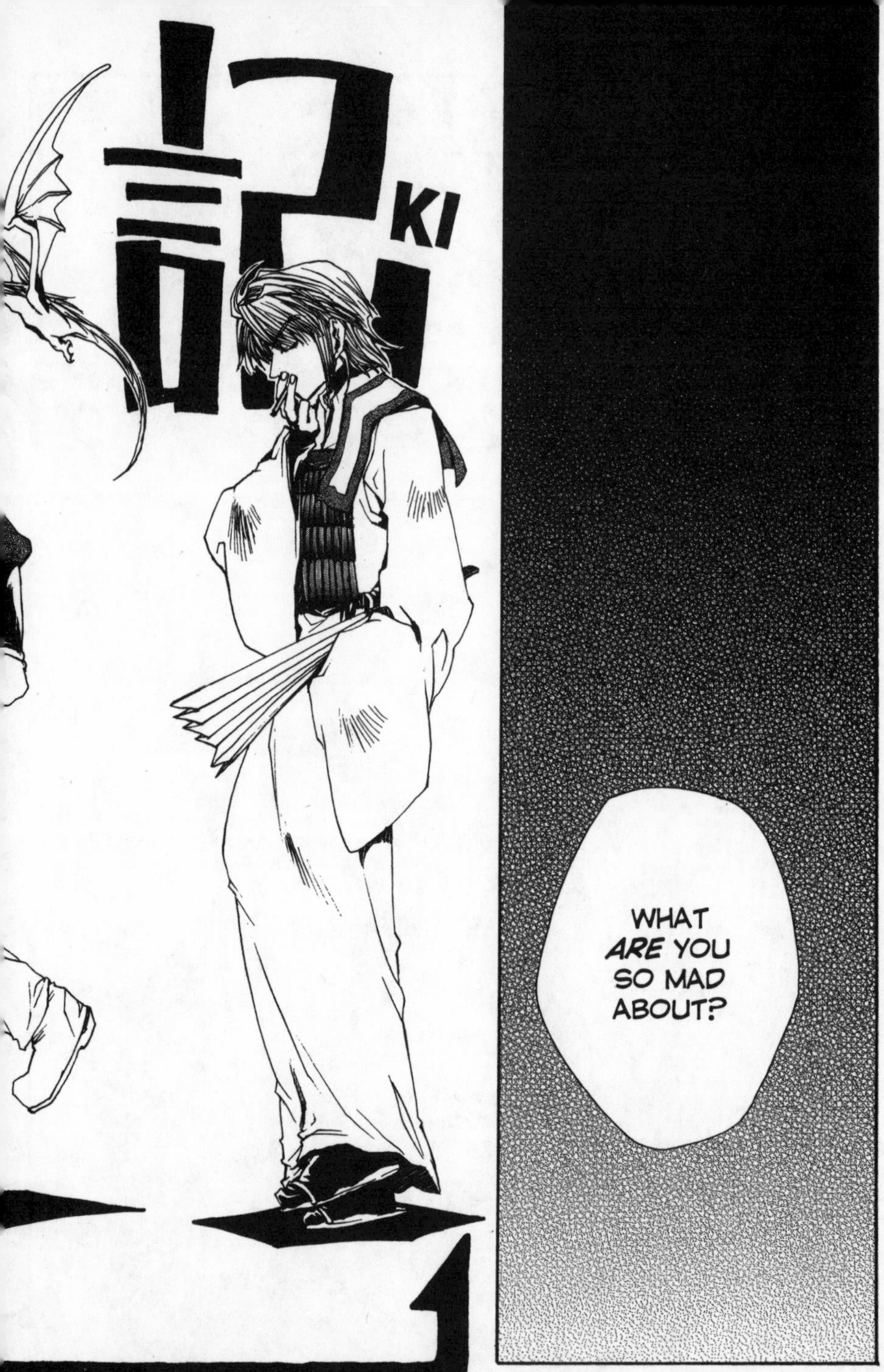
WHAT
ARE YOU
SO MAD
ABOUT?
KI

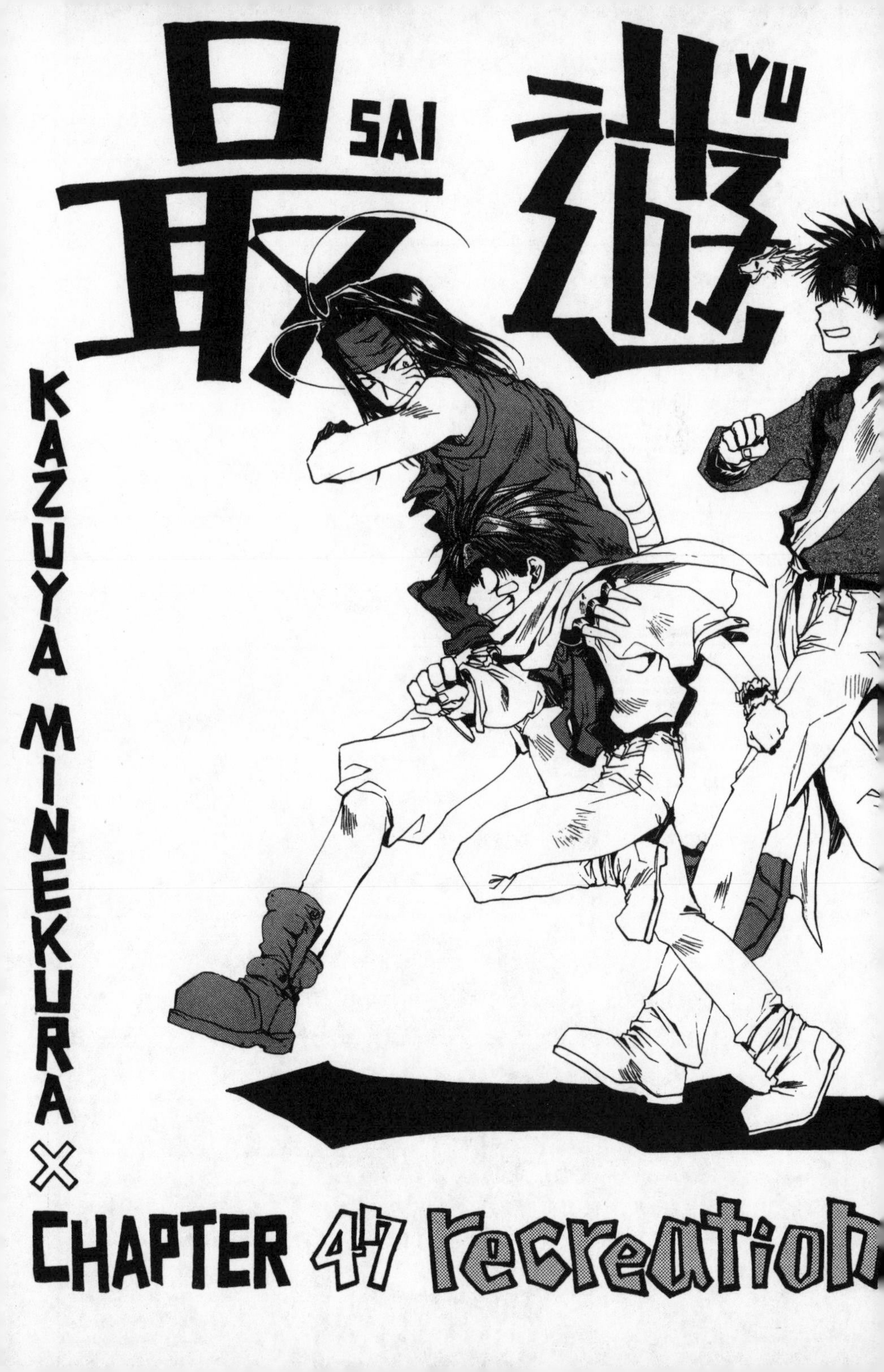
最遊
SAI YU
KAZUYA MINEKURA ×
CHAPTER 47 recreation

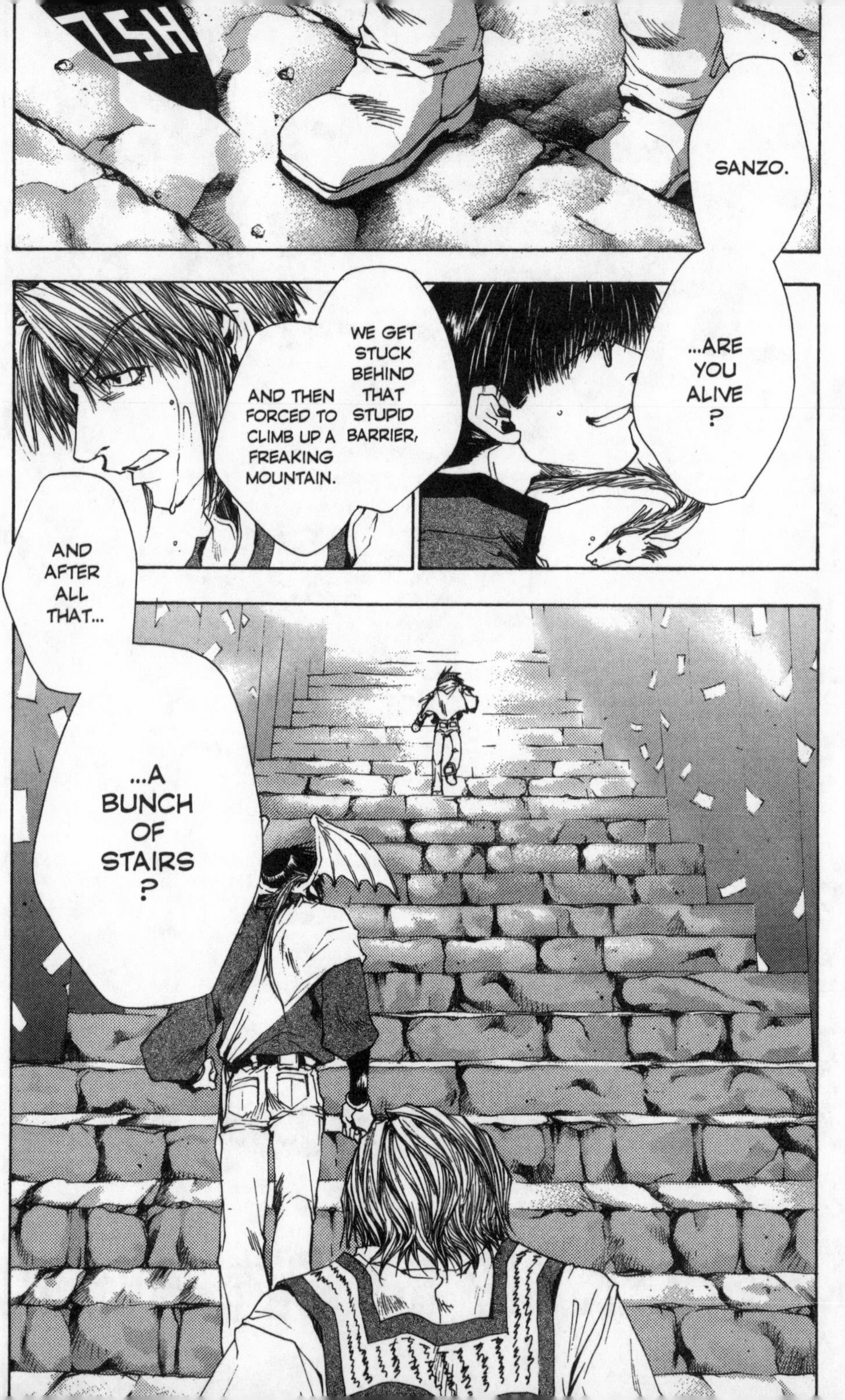
SANZO.
...ARE YOU ALIVE?
WE GET STUCK BEHIND THAT STUPID BARRIER,
AND THEN FORCED TO CLIMB UP A FREAKING MOUNTAIN.
AND AFTER ALL THAT...
...A BUNCH OF STAIRS?

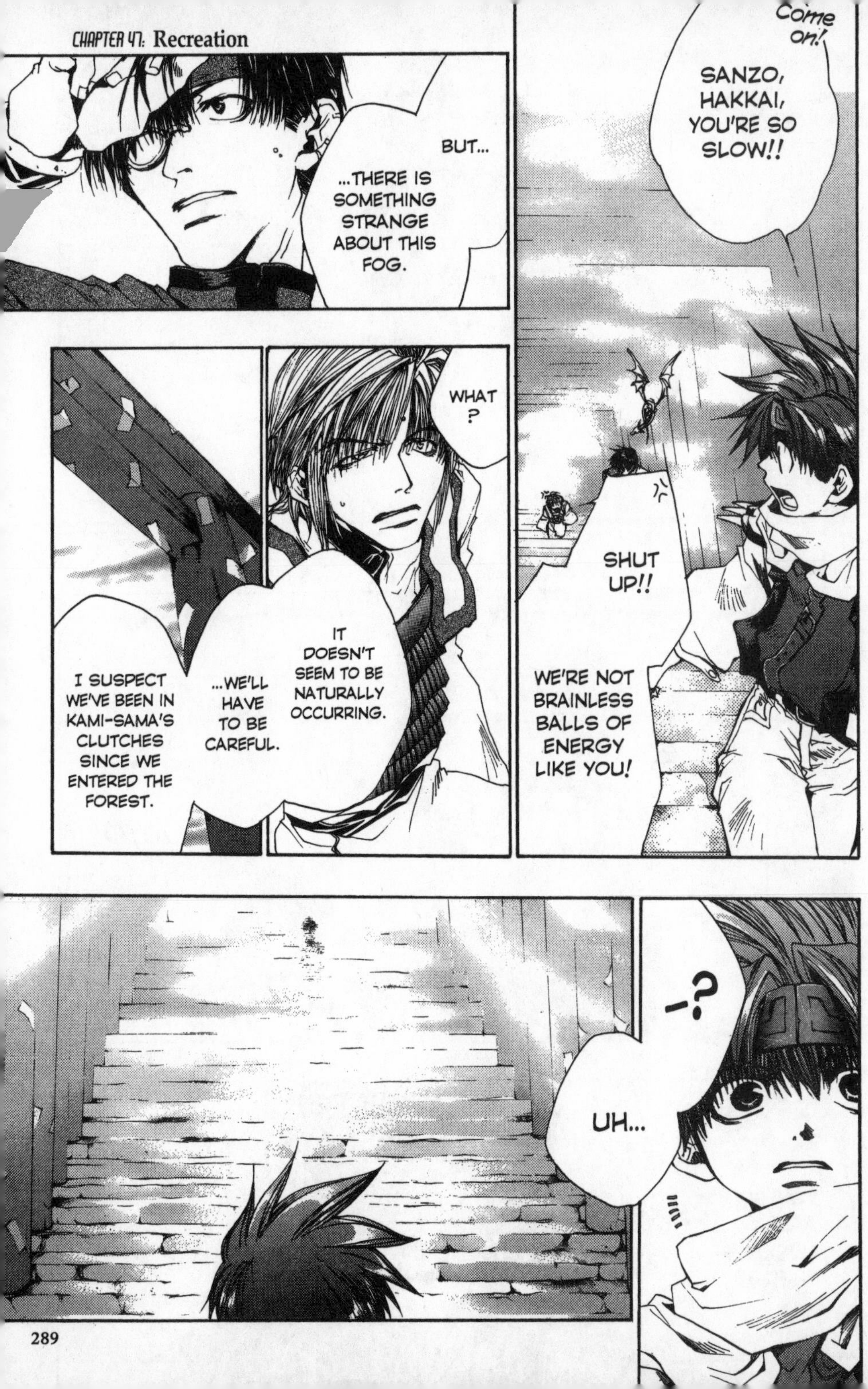
Come on!
SANZO, HAKKAI, YOU'RE SO SLOW!!
SHUT UP!!
WE'RE NOT BRAINLESS BALLS OF ENERGY LIKE YOU!
BUT...
...THERE IS SOMETHING STRANGE ABOUT THIS FOG.
WHAT?
IT DOESN'T SEEM TO BE NATURALLY OCCURRING.
...WE'LL HAVE TO BE CAREFUL.
I SUSPECT WE'VE BEEN IN KAMI-SAMA'S CLUTCHES SINCE WE ENTERED THE FOREST.
-?
UH...

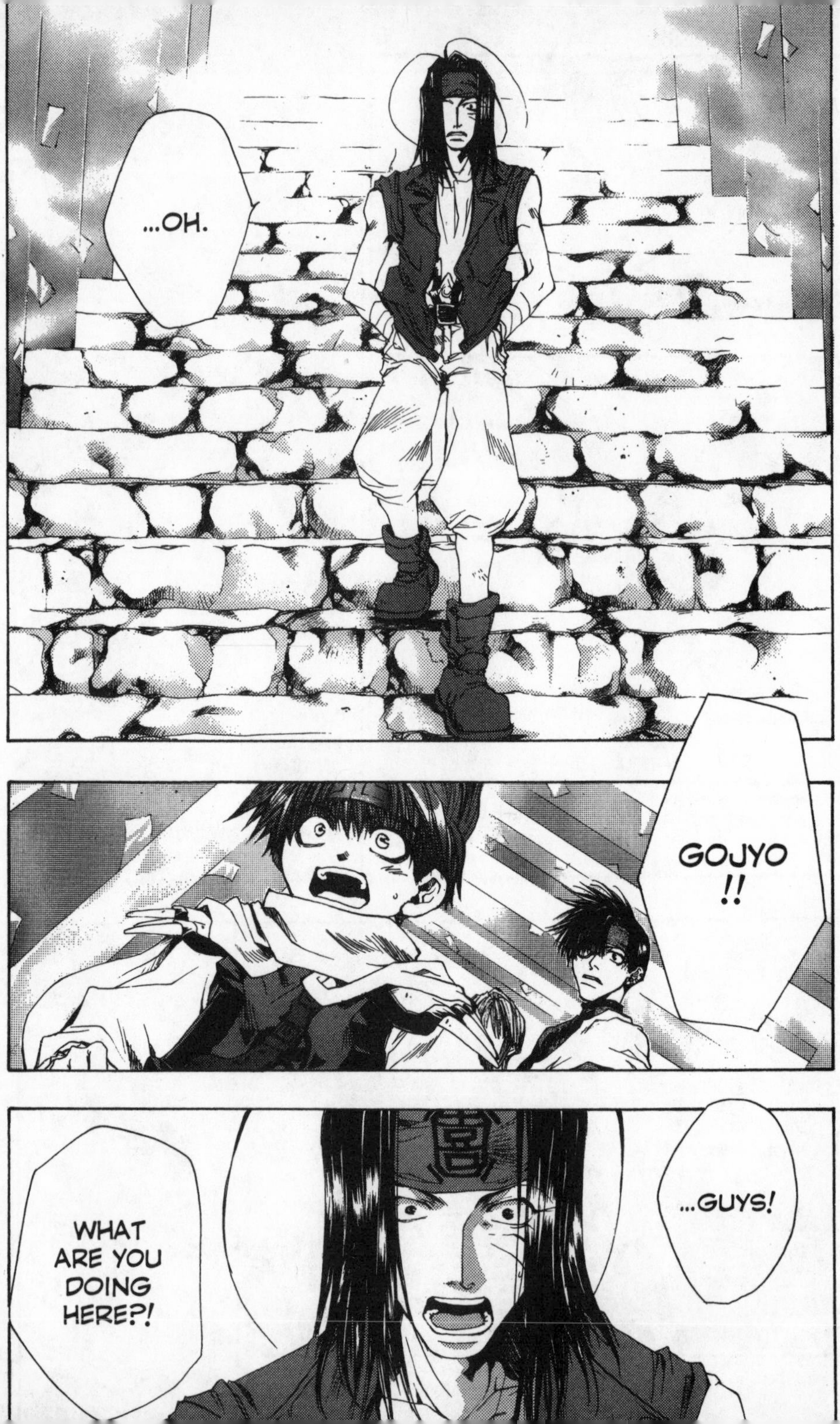
...OH.
GOJYO !!
...GUYS!
WHAT ARE YOU DOING HERE?!

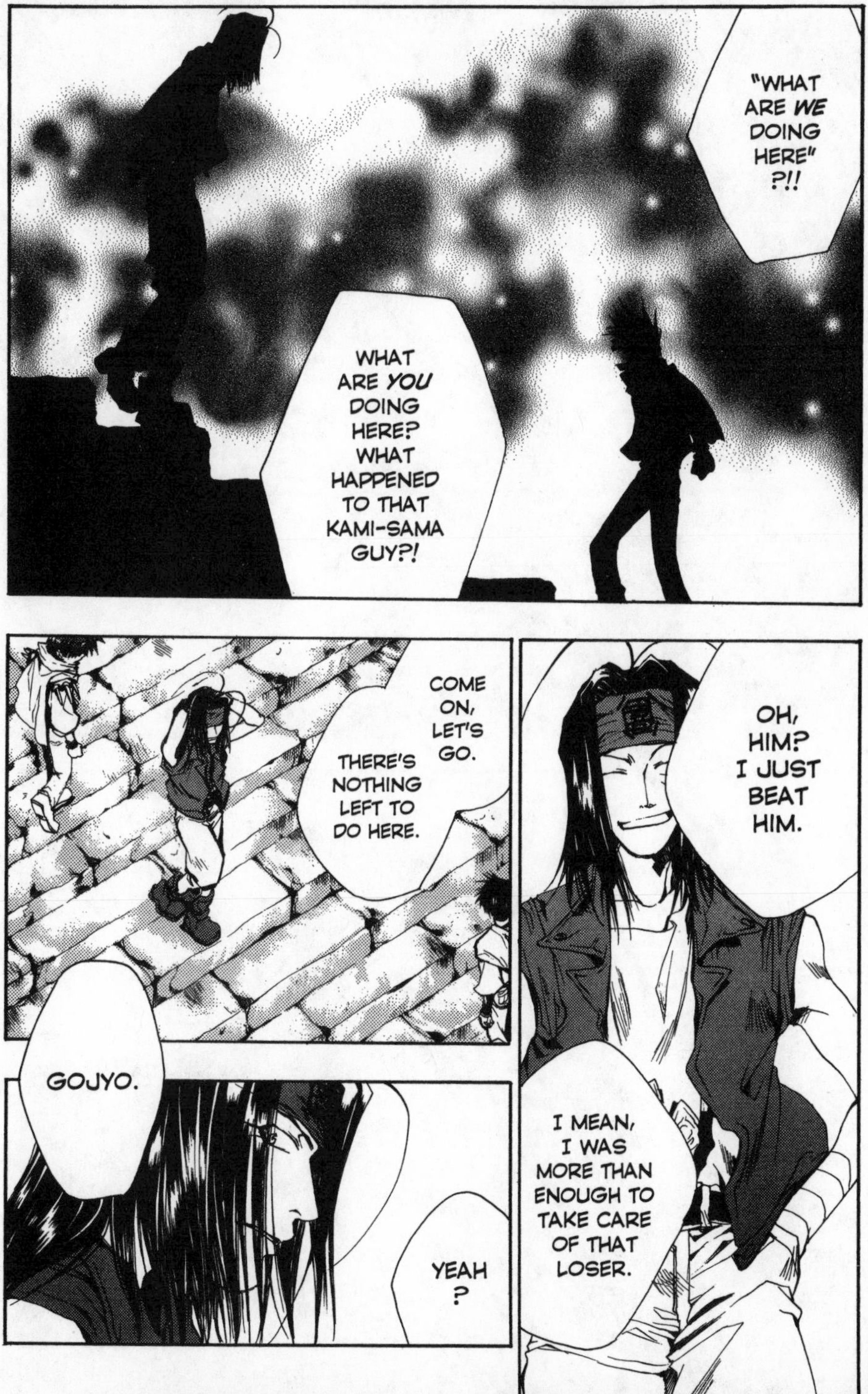
"WHAT ARE *WE* DOING HERE" ?!!
WHAT ARE *YOU* DOING HERE? WHAT HAPPENED TO THAT KAMI-SAMA GUY?!
OH, HIM? I JUST BEAT HIM.
I MEAN, I WAS MORE THAN ENOUGH TO TAKE CARE OF THAT LOSER.
COME ON, LET'S GO.
THERE'S NOTHING LEFT TO DO HERE.
GOJYO.
YEAH ?

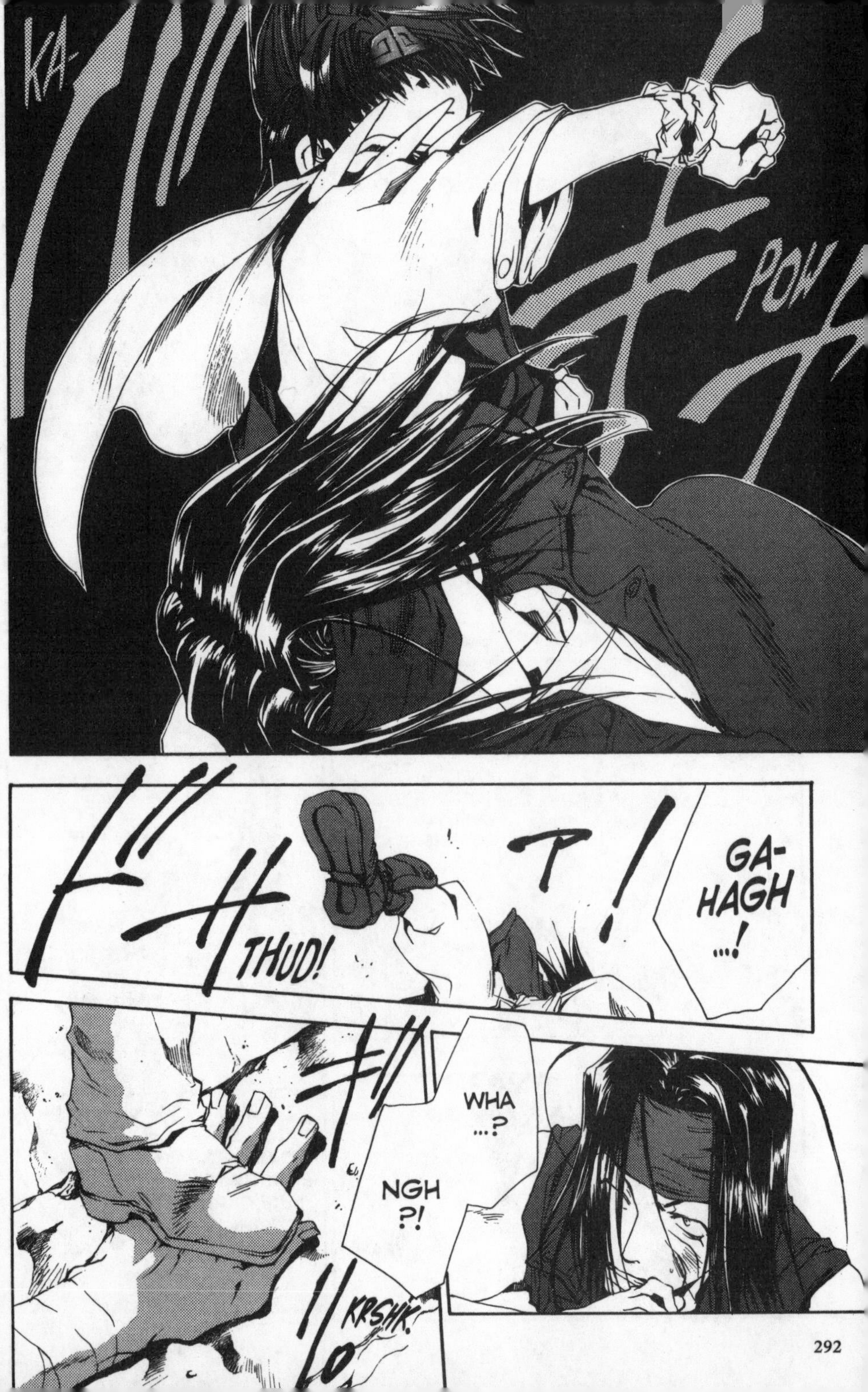
KA-
POW
GA-HAGH ...!
THUD!
WHA ...?
NGH ?!
KRSHK.

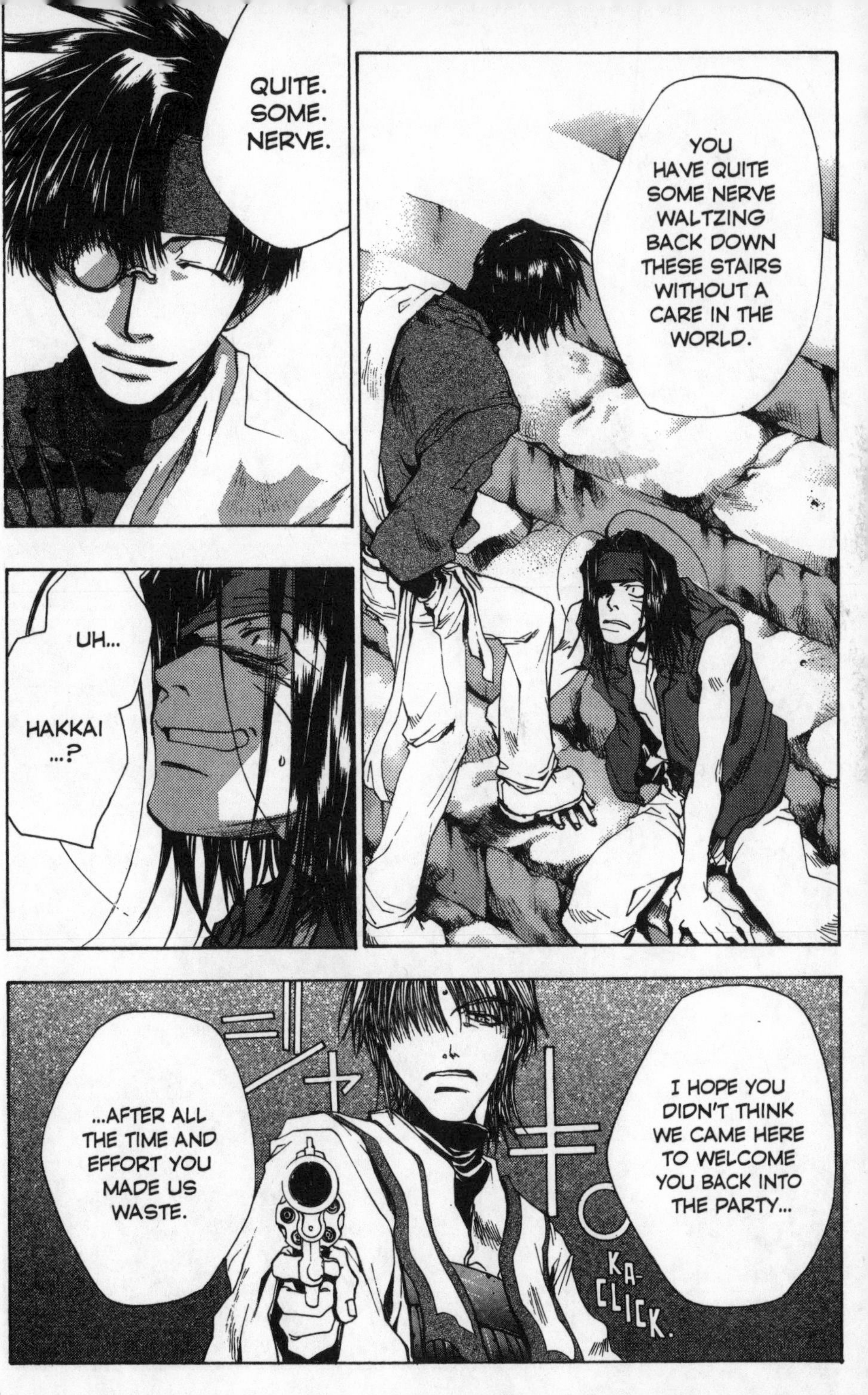
YOU HAVE QUITE SOME NERVE WALTZING BACK DOWN THESE STAIRS WITHOUT A CARE IN THE WORLD.
QUITE. SOME. NERVE.
UH...
HAKKAI ...?
I HOPE YOU DIDN'T THINK WE CAME HERE TO WELCOME YOU BACK INTO THE PARTY...
KA-CLICK.
...AFTER ALL THE TIME AND EFFORT YOU MADE US WASTE.

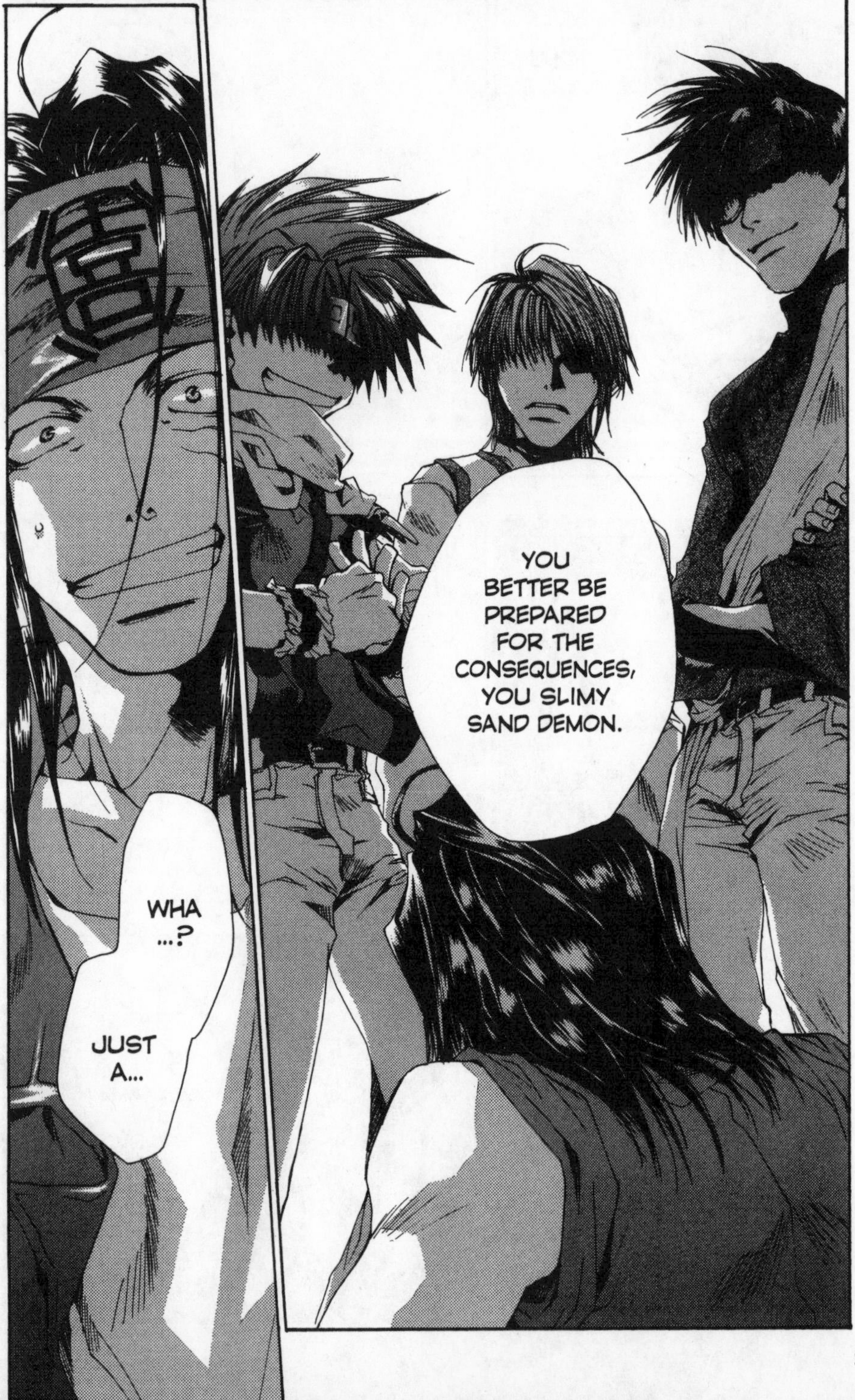
YOU BETTER BE PREPARED FOR THE CONSEQUENCES, YOU SLIMY SAND DEMON.
WHA ...?
JUST A...

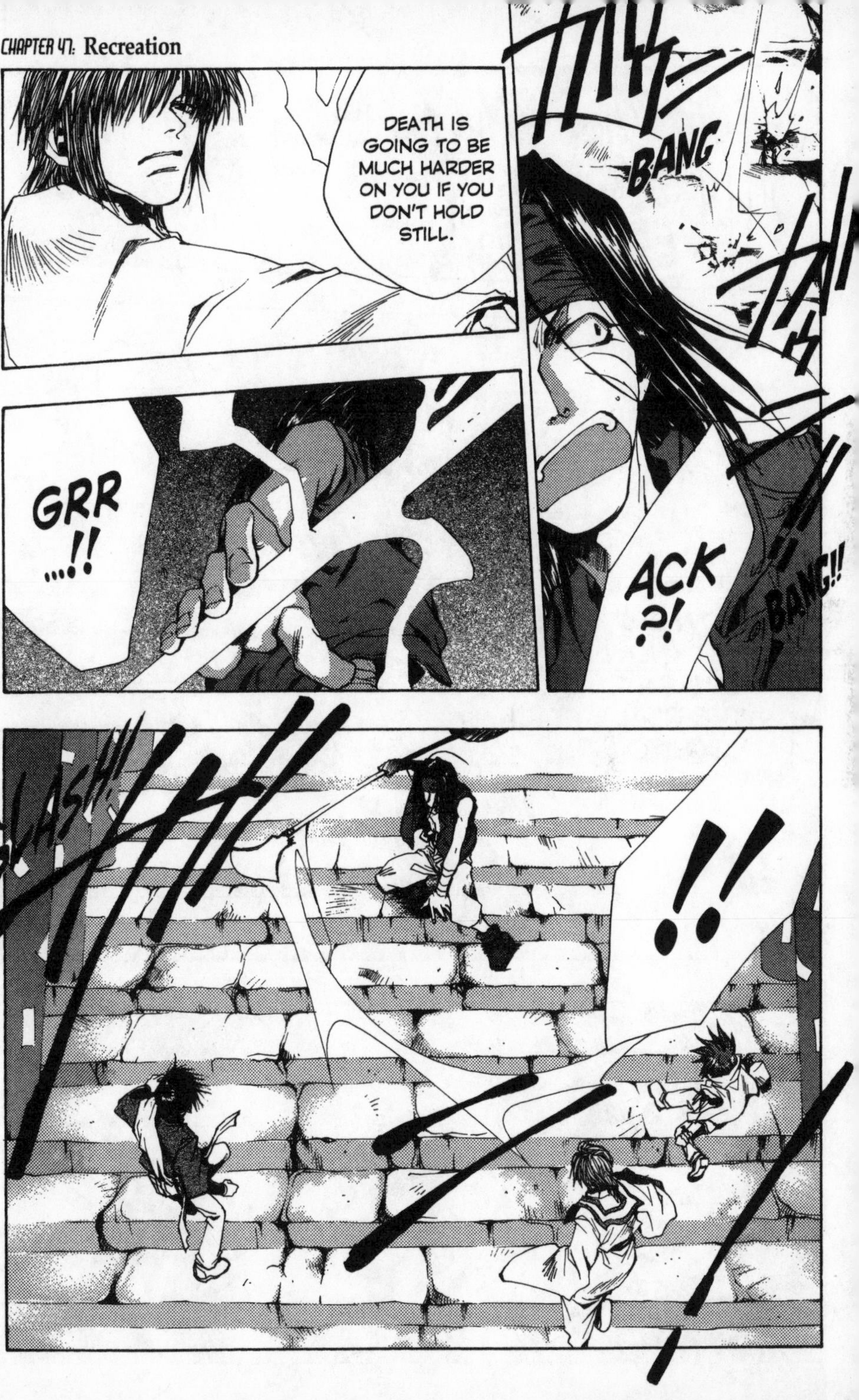
BANG
ACK ?!
BANG!!
DEATH IS GOING TO BE MUCH HARDER ON YOU IF YOU DON'T HOLD STILL.
GRR ...!!
SLASH!!
!!

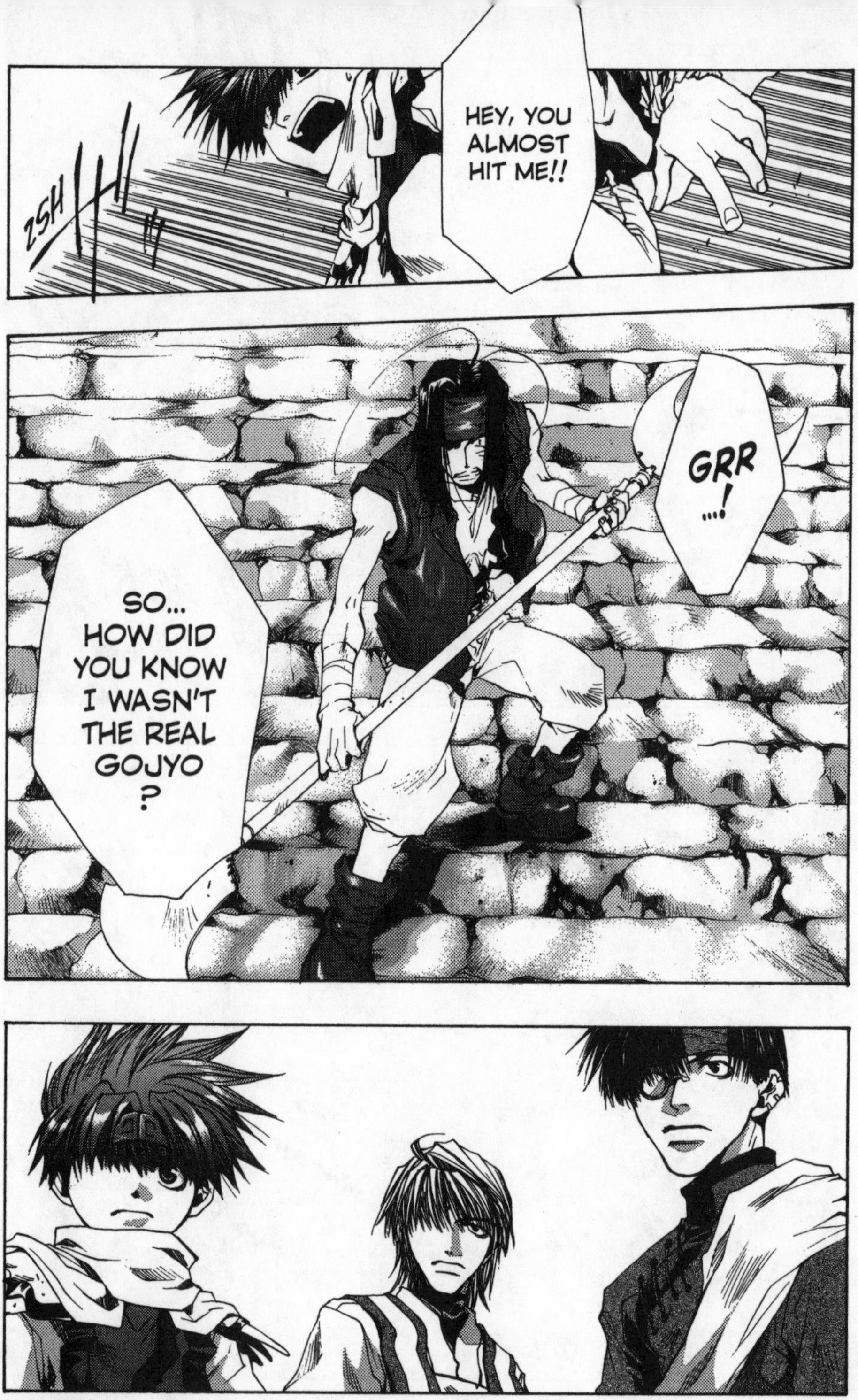
HEY, YOU ALMOST HIT ME!!
ZSH
GRR ...!
SO... HOW DID YOU KNOW I WASN'T THE REAL GOJYO ?

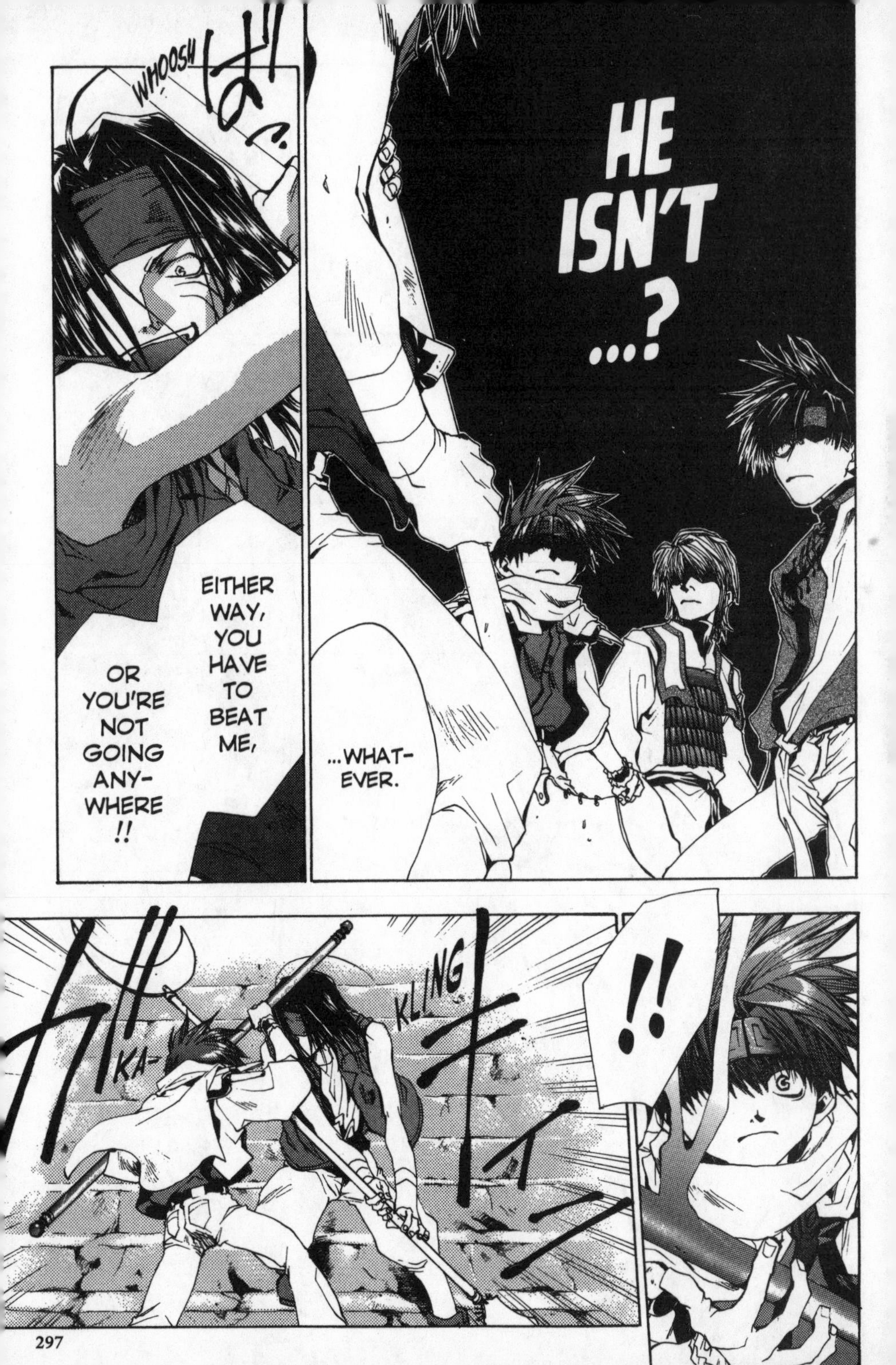
HE ISN'T ...?
...WHAT-EVER.
WHOOSH
EITHER WAY, YOU HAVE TO BEAT ME,
OR YOU'RE NOT GOING ANY-WHERE !!
!!
KA-KLING

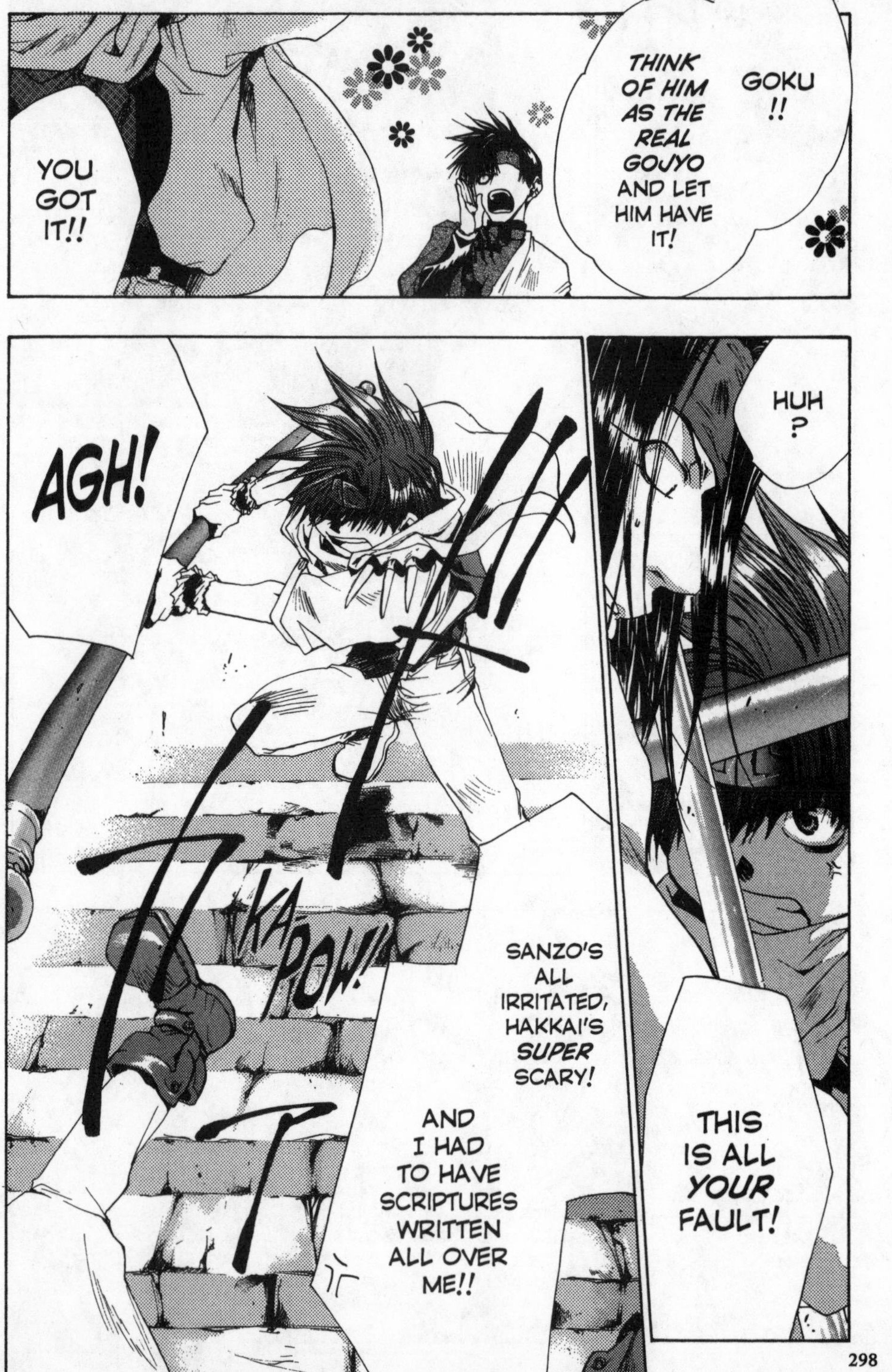
GOKU!!
THINK OF HIM AS THE REAL GOJYO AND LET HIM HAVE IT!
YOU GOT IT!!
HUH?
AGH!
KA-POW!!
SANZO'S ALL IRRITATED, HAKKAI'S SUPER SCARY!
AND I HAD TO HAVE SCRIPTURES WRITTEN ALL OVER ME!!
THIS IS ALL YOUR FAULT!

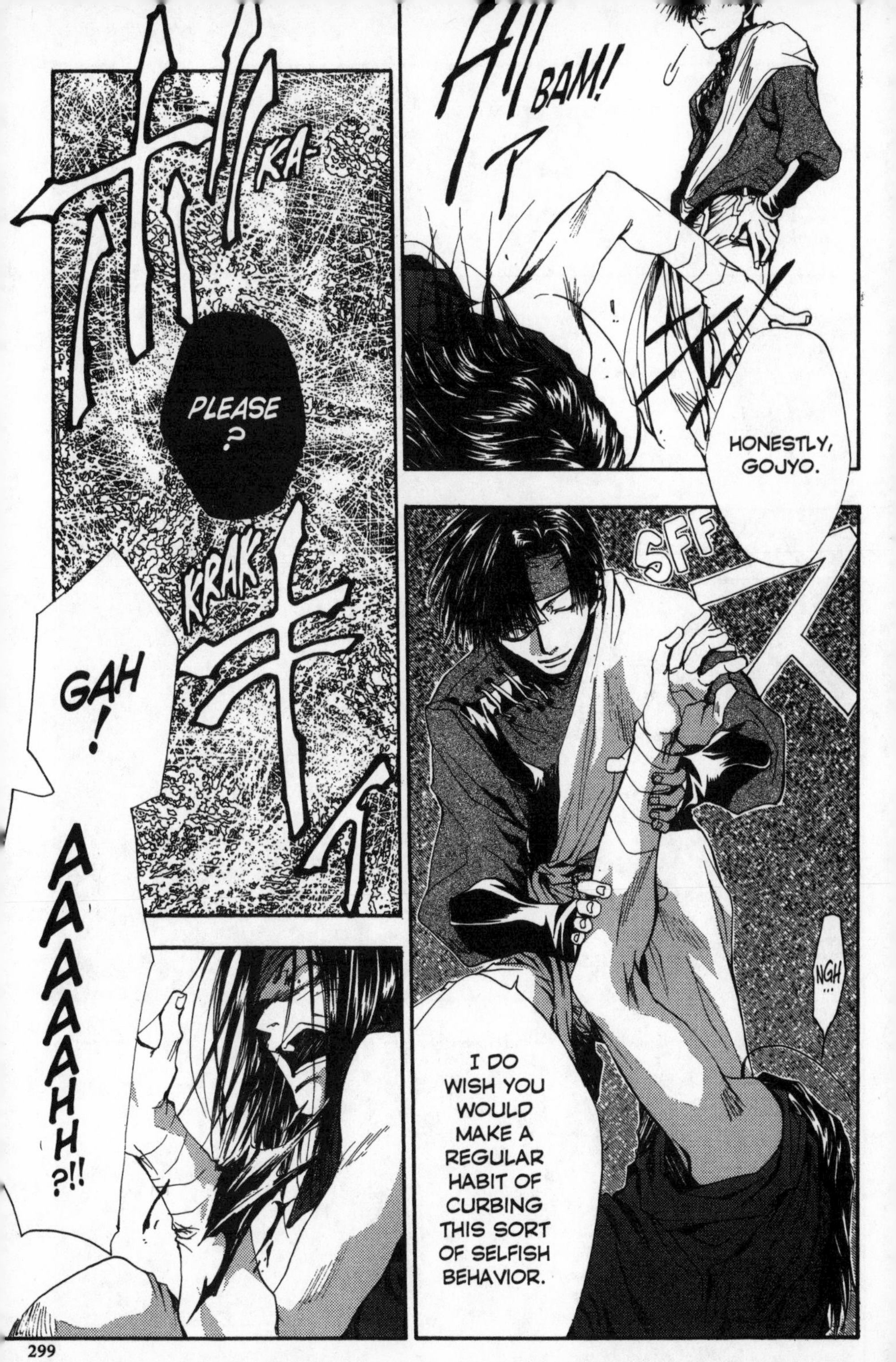
BAM!
HONESTLY, GOJYO.
KA-
PLEASE ?
KRAK
SFF
NGH ...
I DO WISH YOU WOULD MAKE A REGULAR HABIT OF CURBING THIS SORT OF SELFISH BEHAVIOR.
GAH!
AAAAAAHH?!!

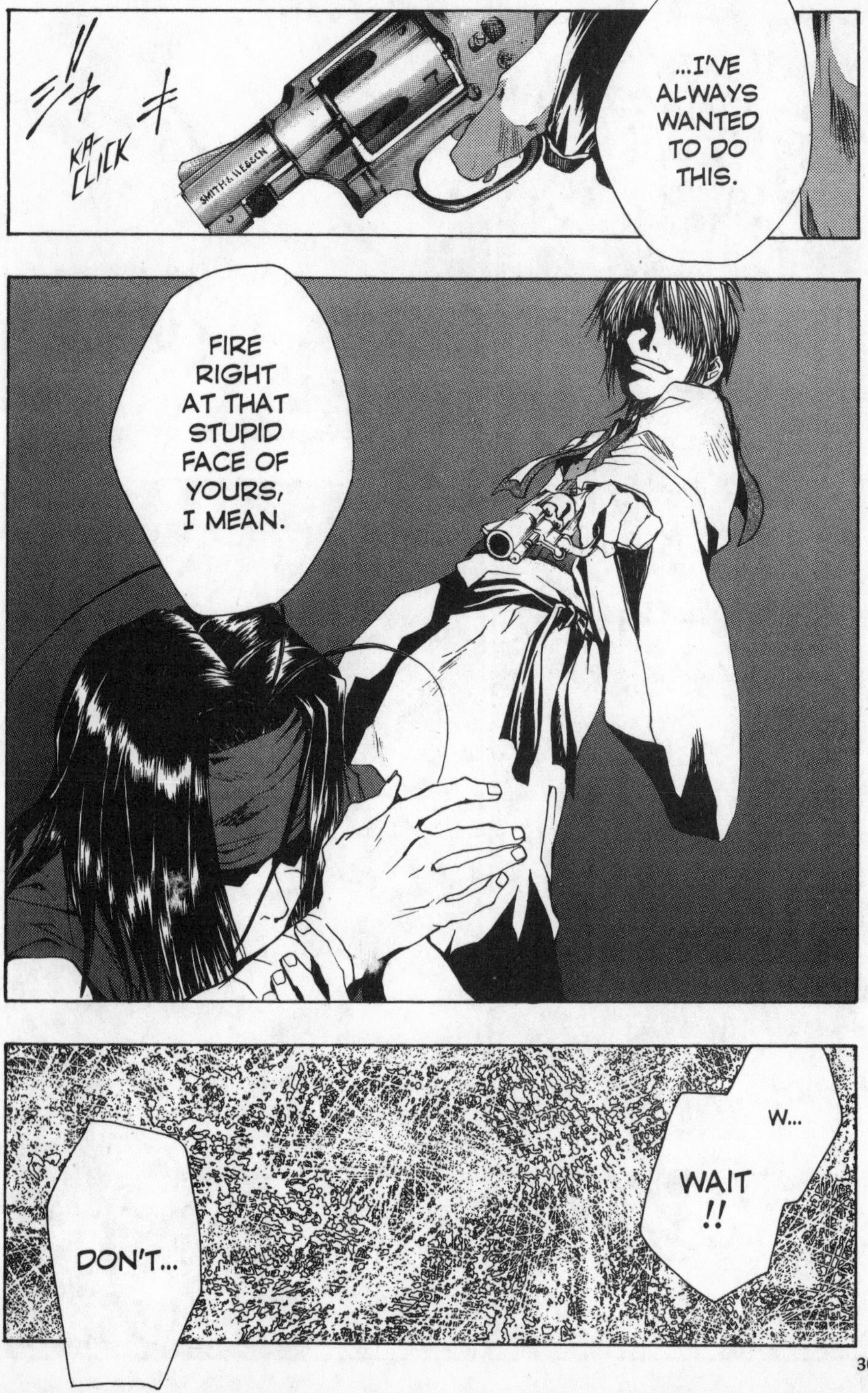
...I'VE ALWAYS WANTED TO DO THIS.
ジャキ
KA-CLICK
SMITH & WESSON
FIRE RIGHT AT THAT STUPID FACE OF YOURS, I MEAN.
W...
WAIT !!
DON'T...

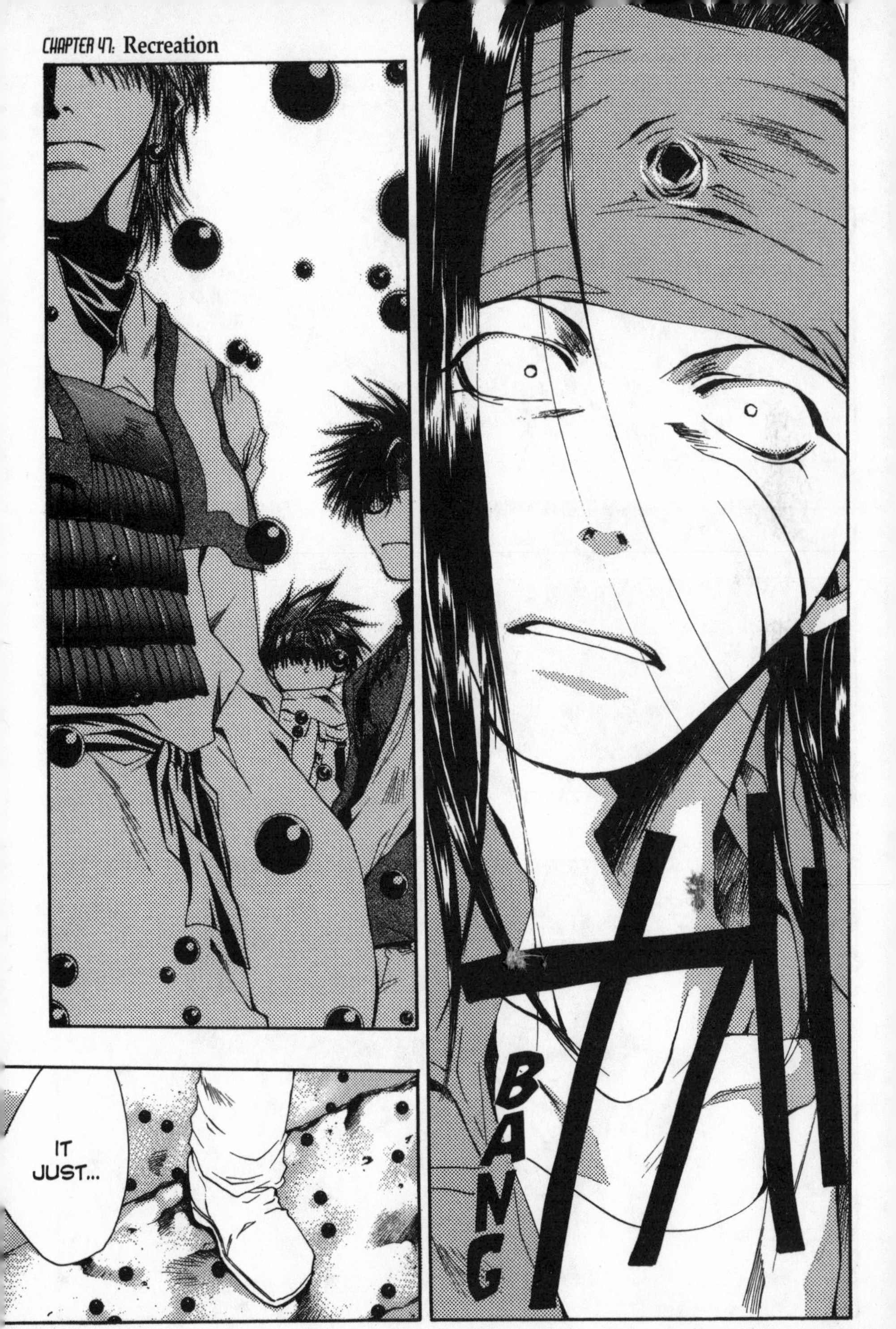
BANG
IT JUST...

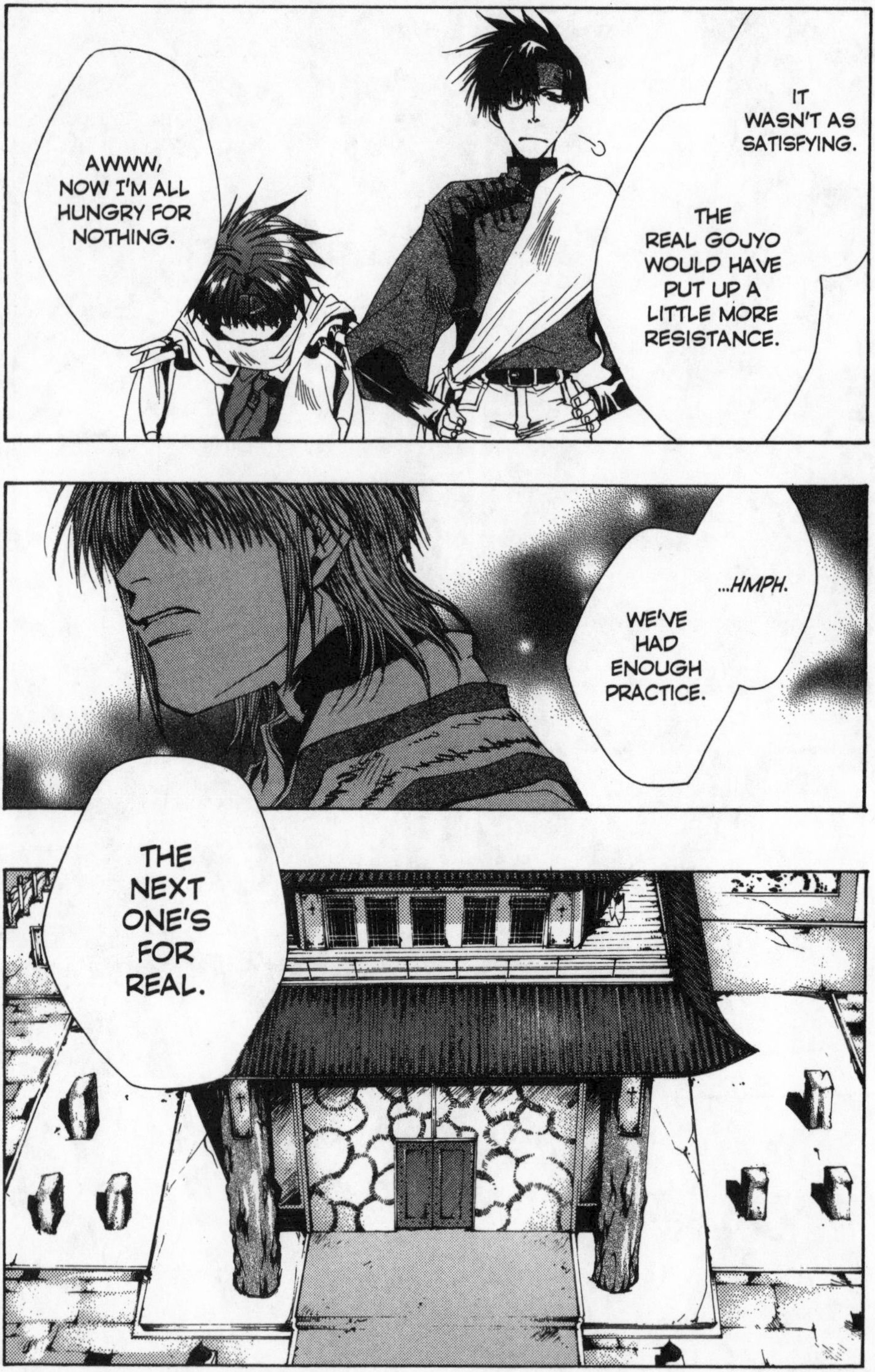

IT WASN'T AS SATISFYING.
THE REAL GOJYO WOULD HAVE PUT UP A LITTLE MORE RESISTANCE.
AWWW, NOW I'M ALL HUNGRY FOR NOTHING.
...HMPH.
WE'VE HAD ENOUGH PRACTICE.
THE NEXT ONE'S FOR REAL.

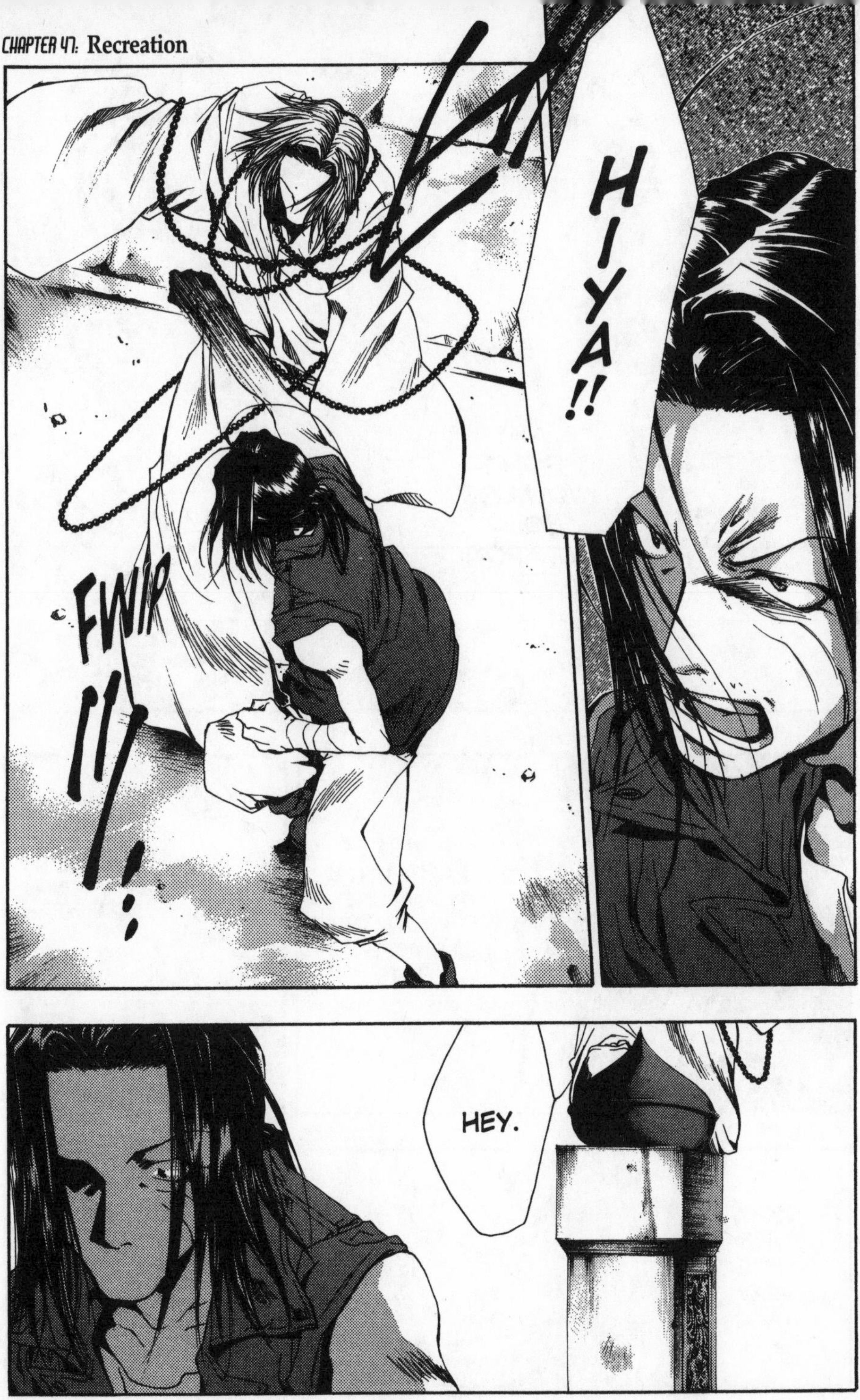
HIYA!!
FWIP
!!
HEY.

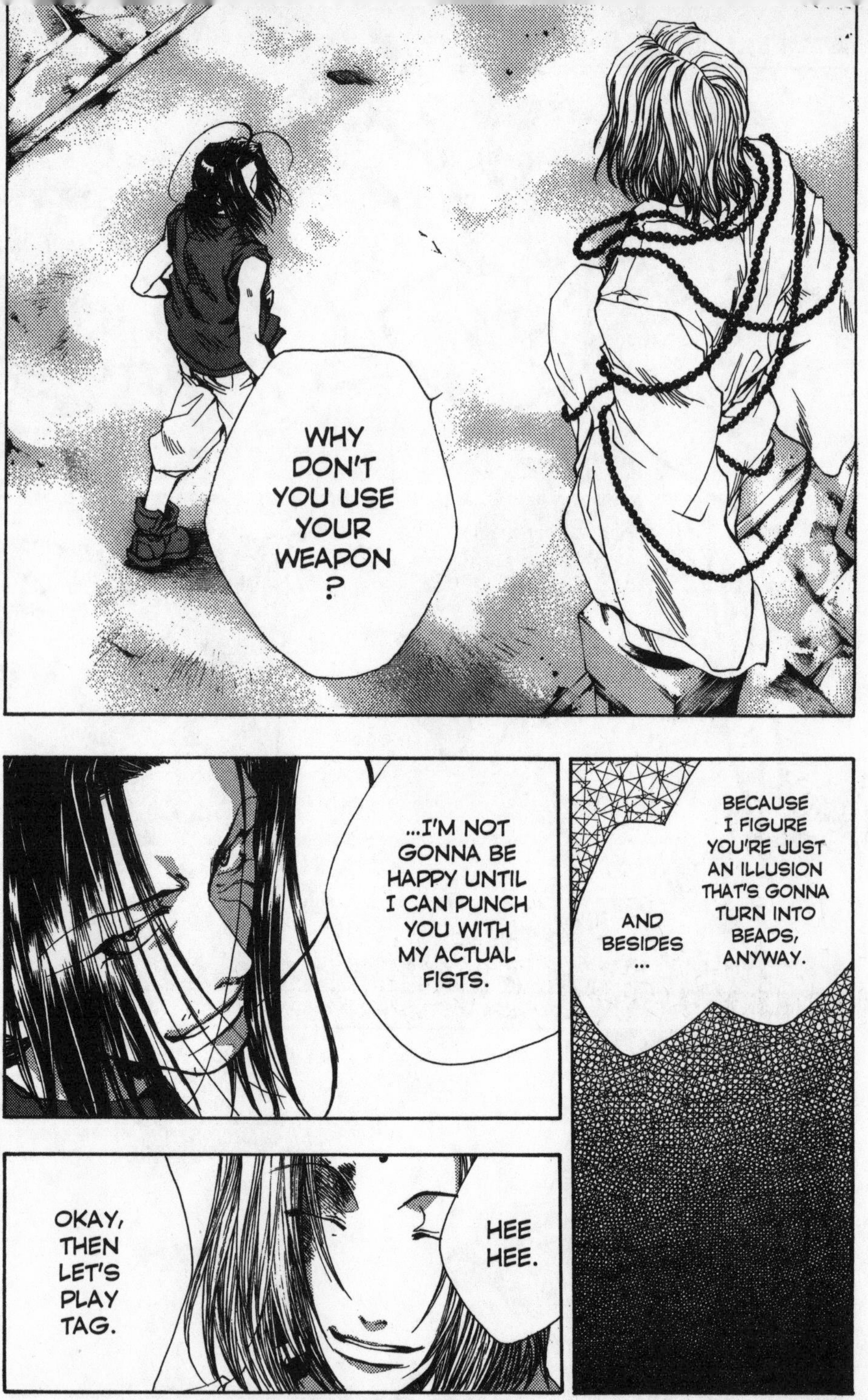
WHY DON'T YOU USE YOUR WEAPON?
BECAUSE I FIGURE YOU'RE JUST AN ILLUSION THAT'S GONNA TURN INTO BEADS, ANYWAY.
AND BESIDES...
...I'M NOT GONNA BE HAPPY UNTIL I CAN PUNCH YOU WITH MY ACTUAL FISTS.
HEE HEE.
OKAY, THEN LET'S PLAY TAG.

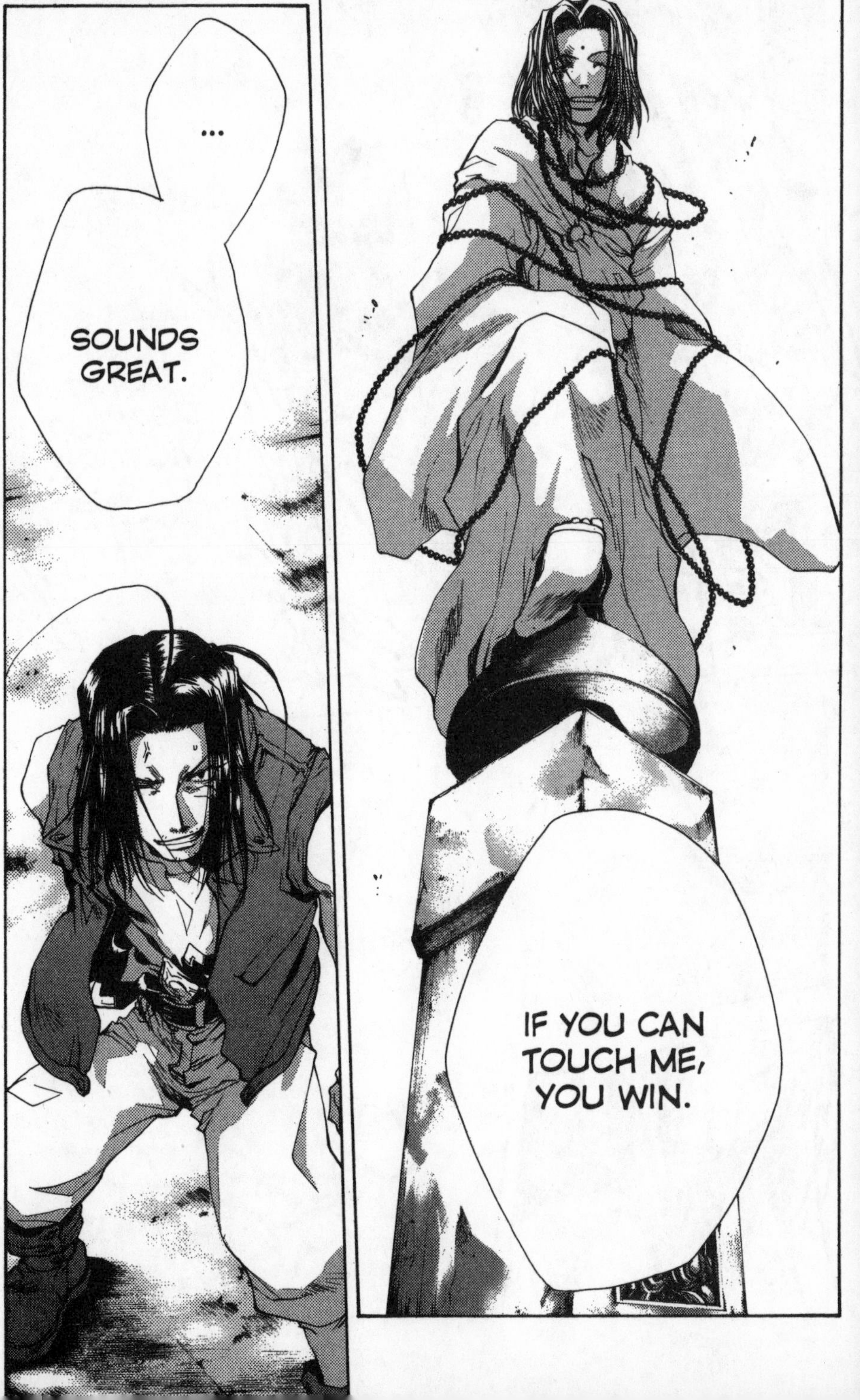
IF YOU CAN TOUCH ME, YOU WIN.
...
SOUNDS GREAT.

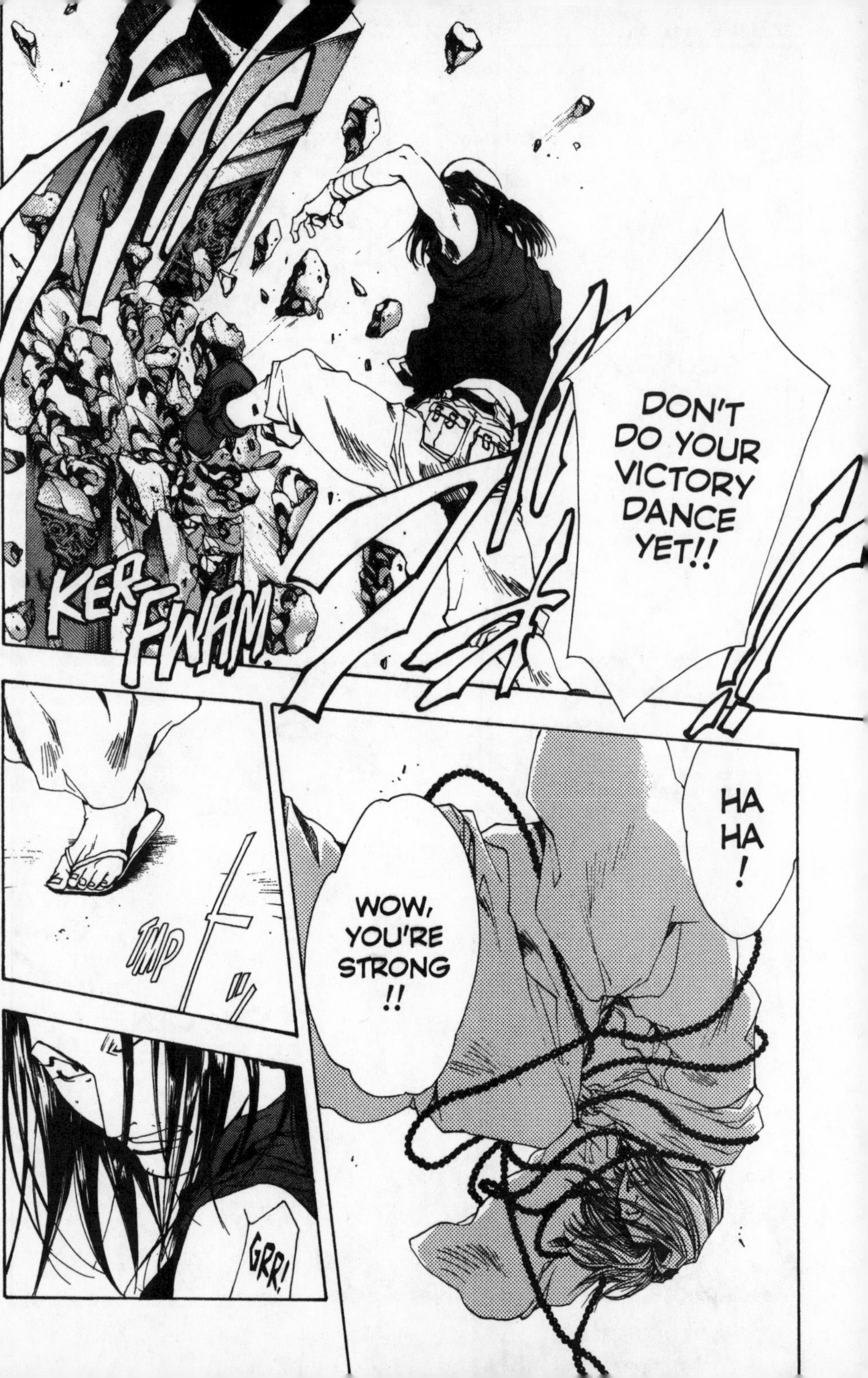
DON'T DO YOUR VICTORY DANCE YET!!
KER-FWAM
HA HA!
WOW, YOU'RE STRONG!!
TMP
GRR!

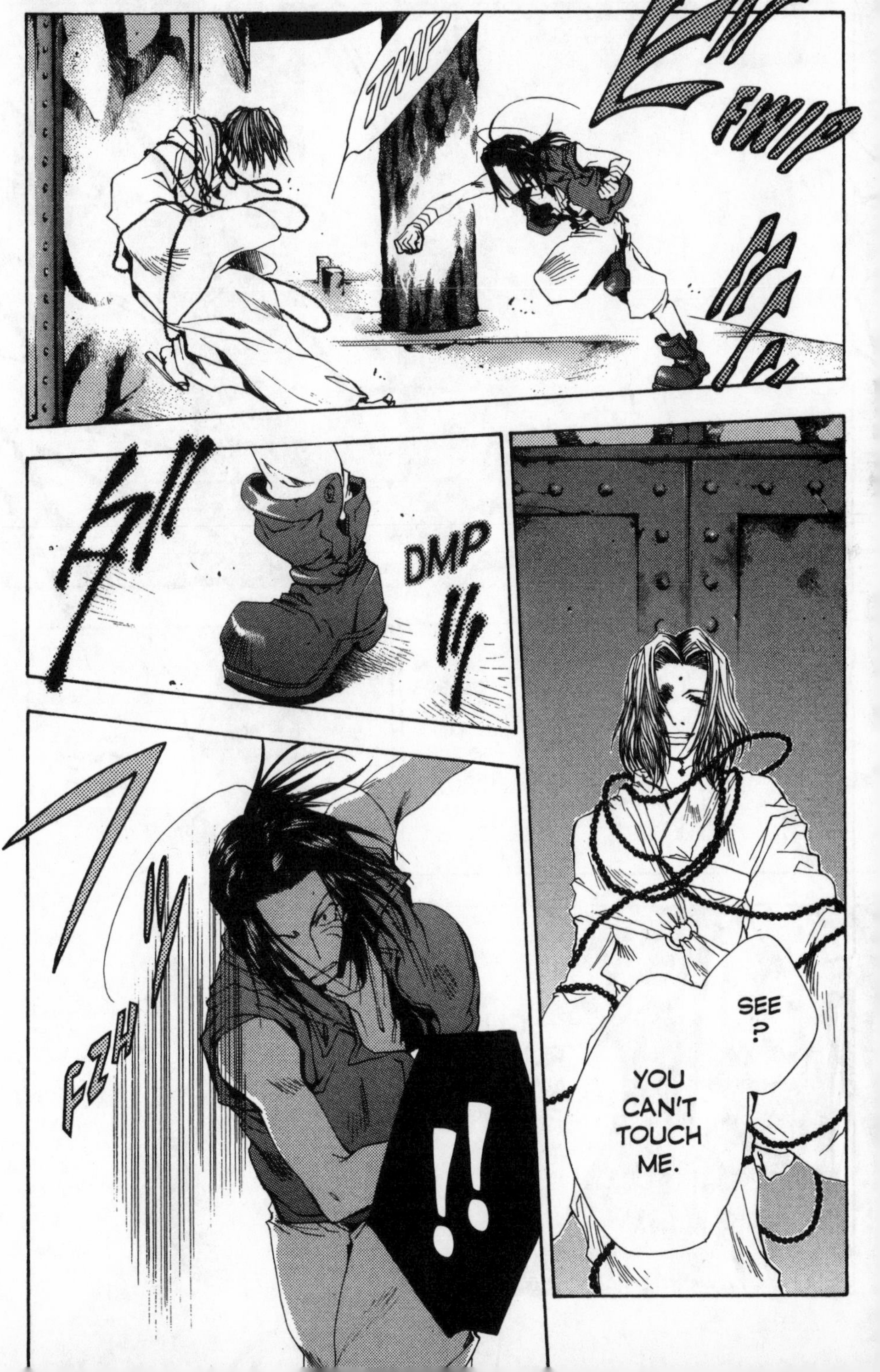
FWIP
TMP
SEE?
YOU CAN'T TOUCH ME.
DMP
FZH
!!

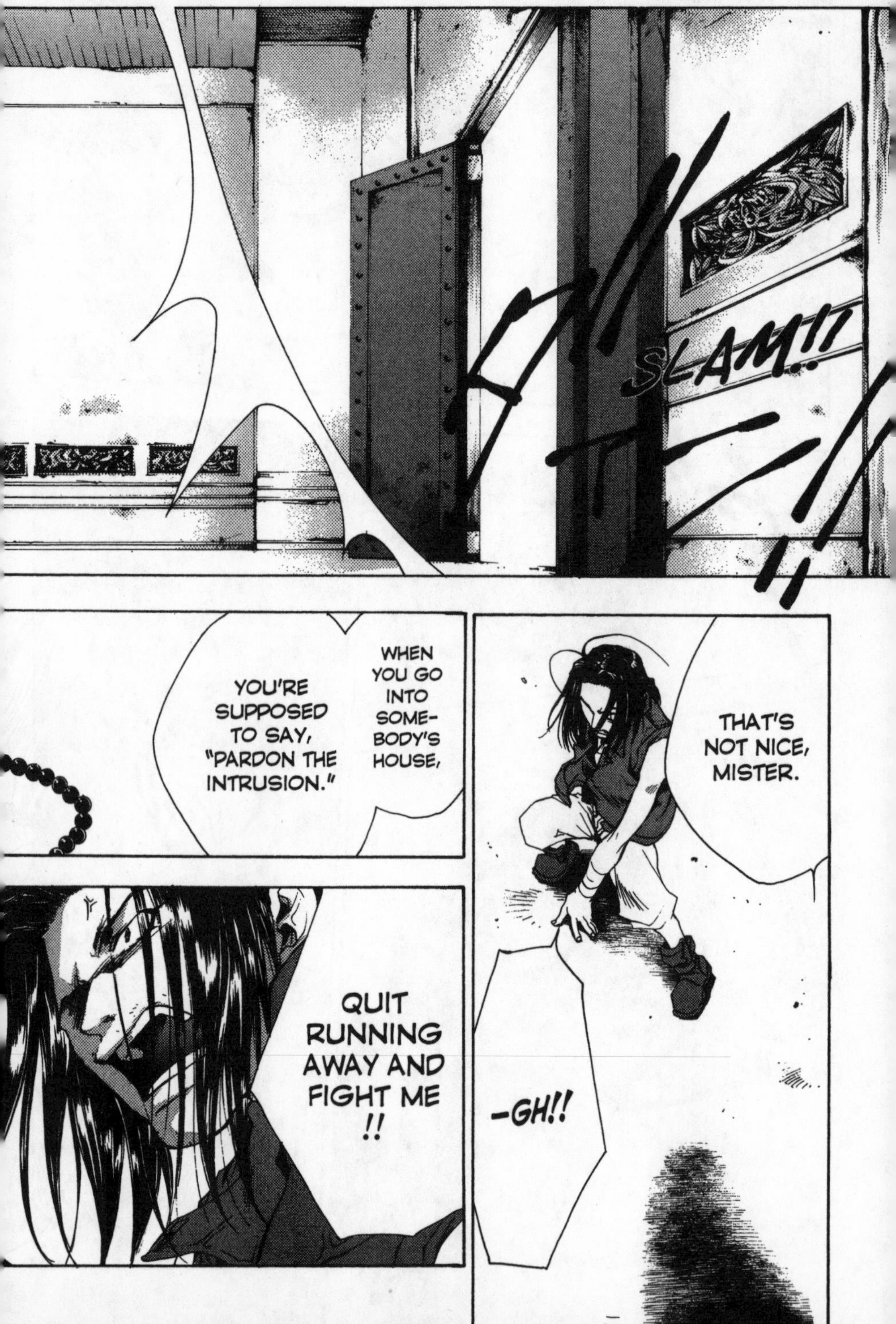
SLAM!!
THAT'S NOT NICE, MISTER.
-GH!!
WHEN YOU GO INTO SOME-BODY'S HOUSE,
YOU'RE SUPPOSED TO SAY, "PARDON THE INTRUSION."
QUIT RUNNING AWAY AND FIGHT ME !!

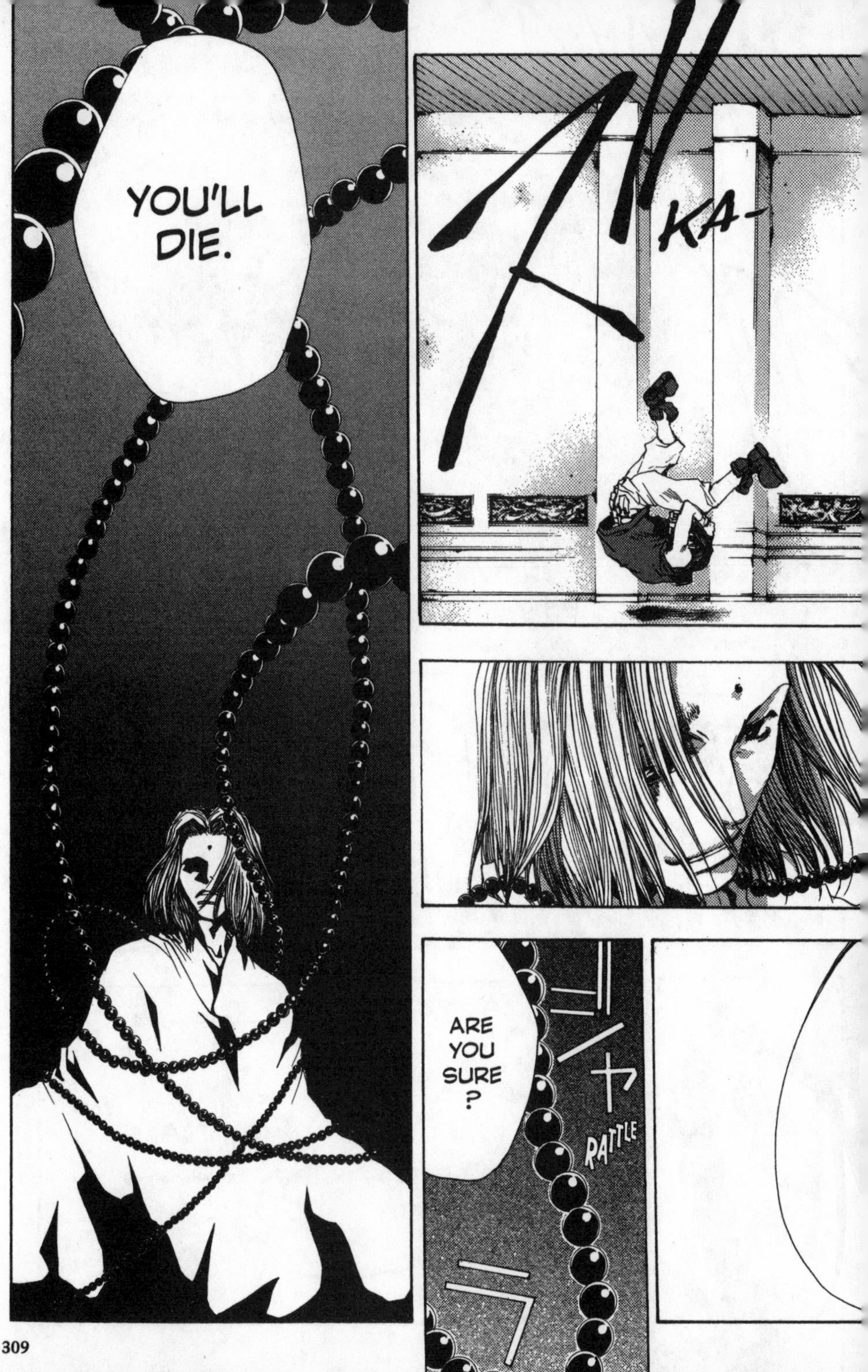
KA-
ARE YOU SURE?
RATTLE
YOU'LL DIE.

ZAM!!

...GH!!

GA-HAGH

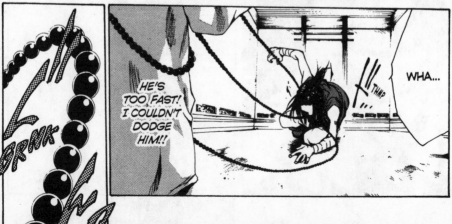

GRNK

HE'S TOO FAST! I COULDN'T DODGE HIM!!

THMP

WHA...

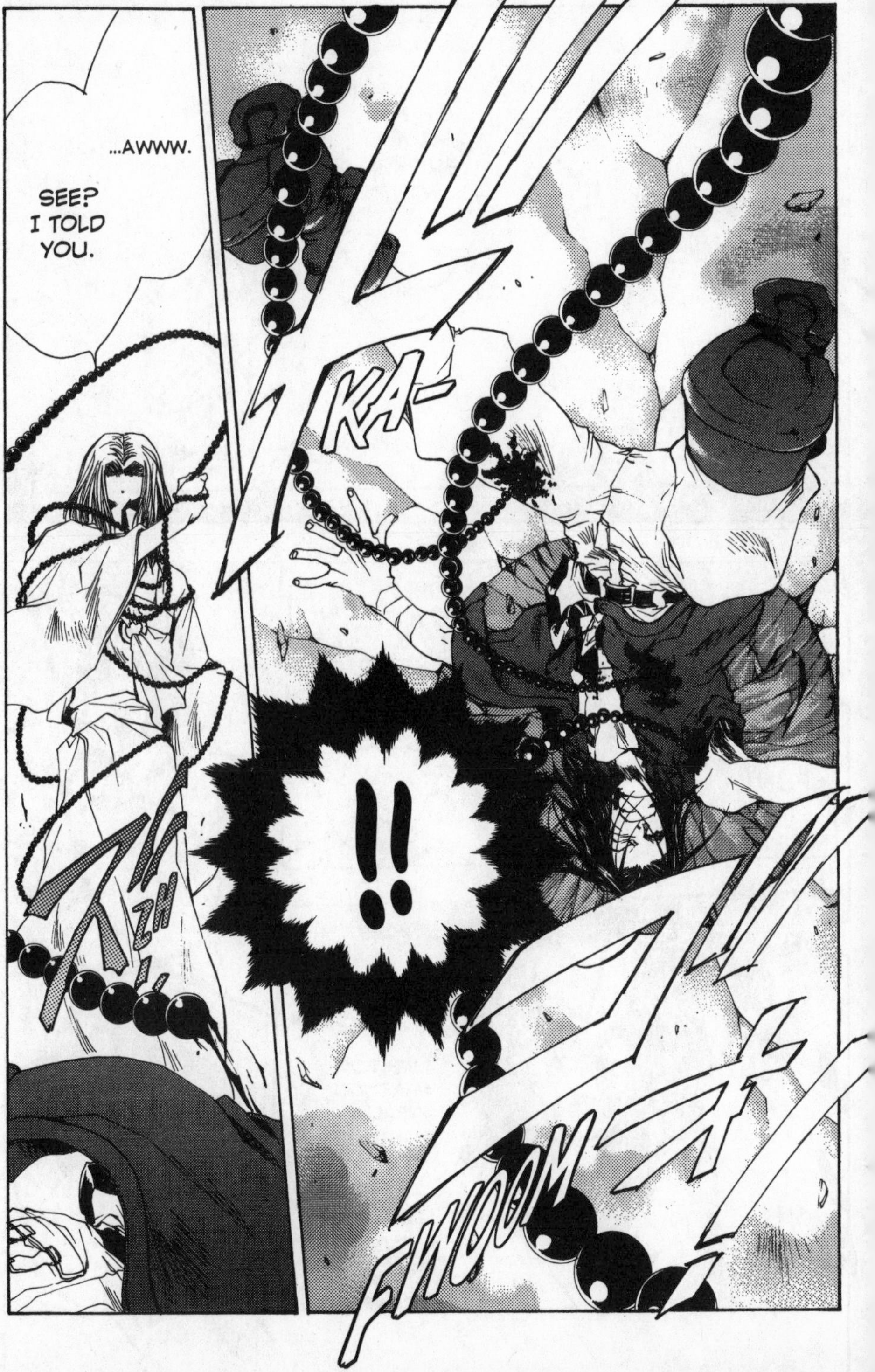
KA-
!!
FWOOM
...AWWW.
SEE? I TOLD YOU.
ZH

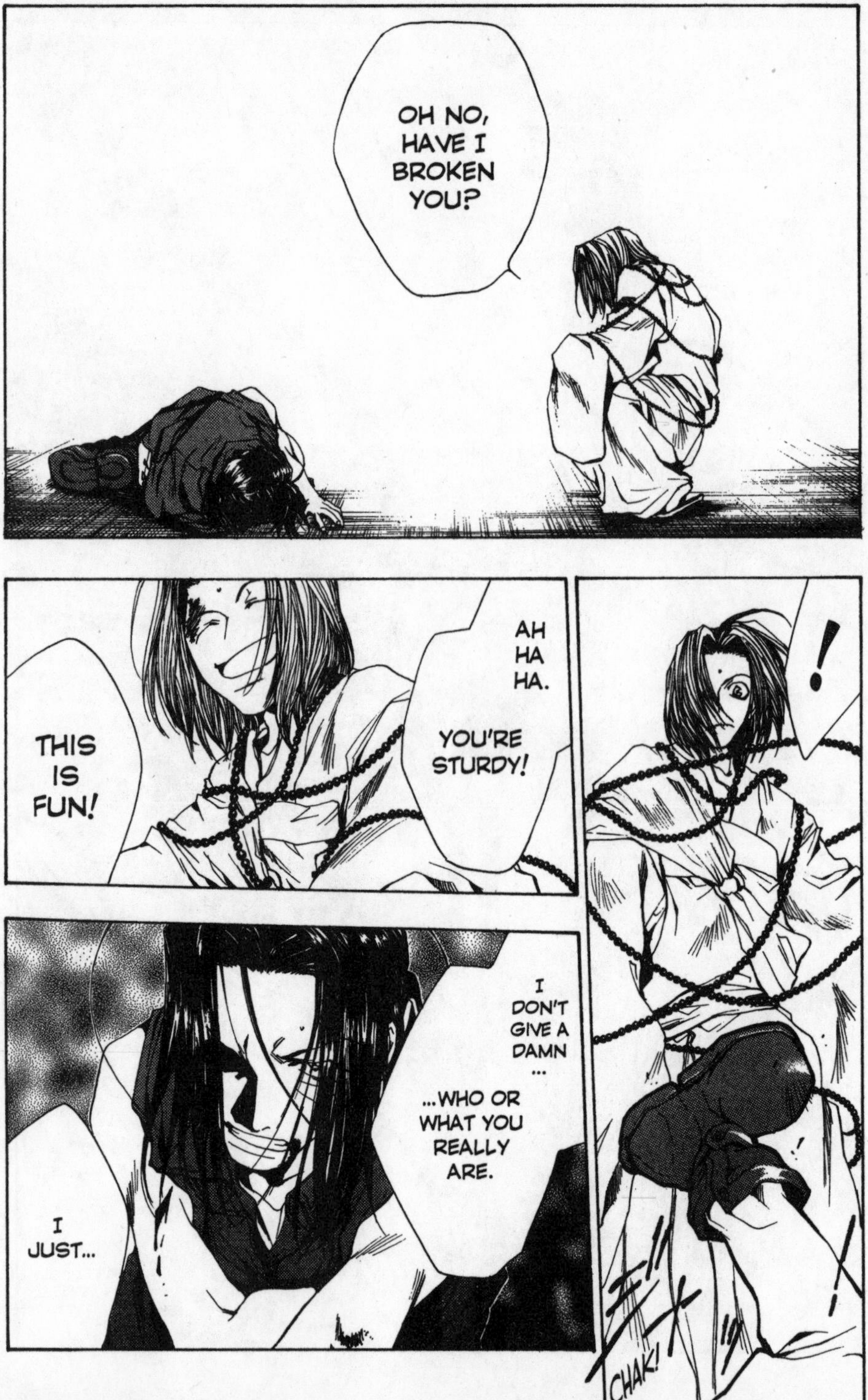
OH NO, HAVE I BROKEN YOU?
!
CHAK!
AH HA HA.
YOU'RE STURDY!
THIS IS FUN!
I DON'T GIVE A DAMN ...
...WHO OR WHAT YOU REALLY ARE.
I JUST...

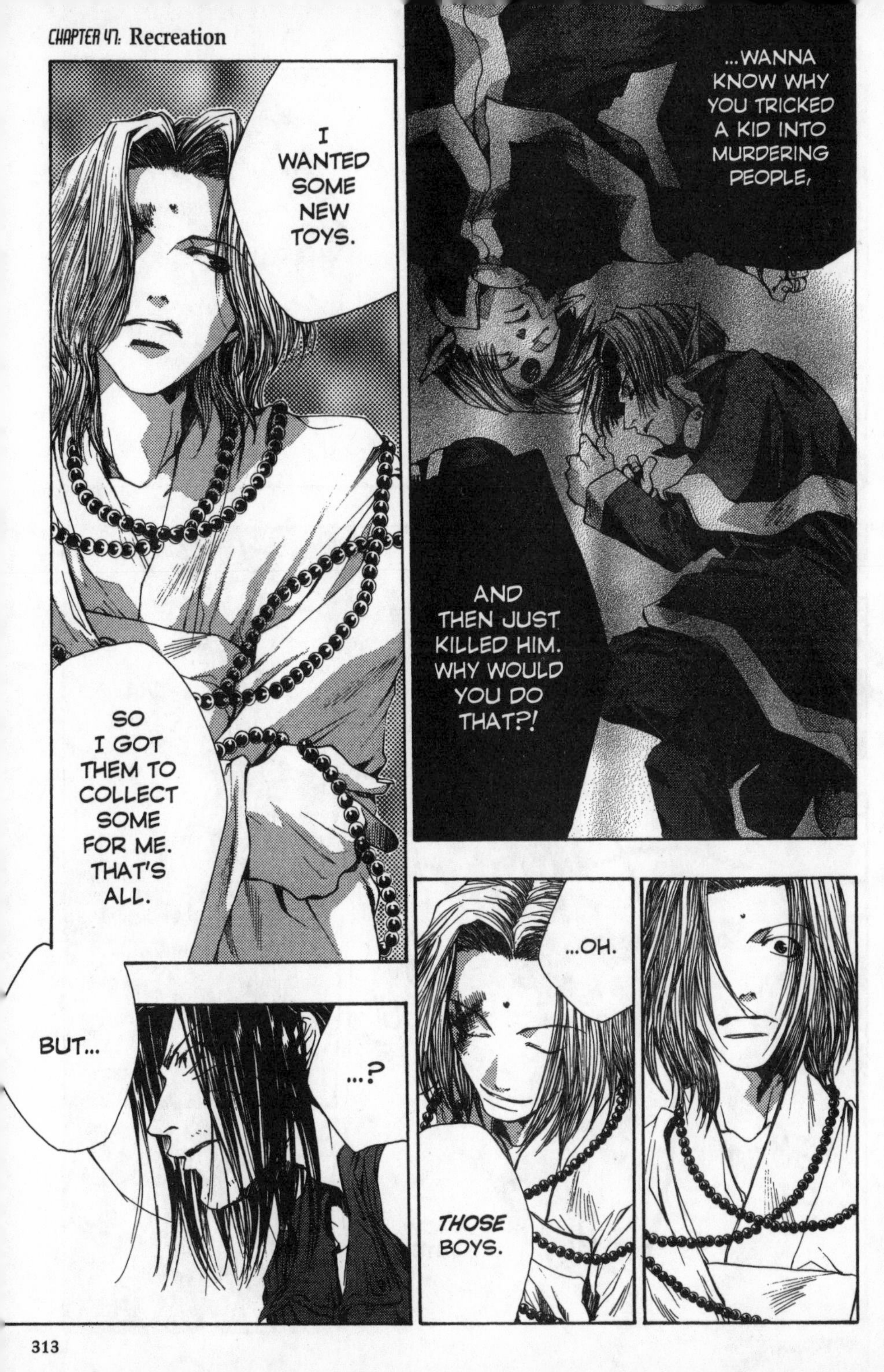
...WANNA KNOW WHY YOU TRICKED A KID INTO MURDERING PEOPLE,
AND THEN JUST KILLED HIM. WHY WOULD YOU DO THAT?!
I WANTED SOME NEW TOYS.
SO I GOT THEM TO COLLECT SOME FOR ME. THAT'S ALL.
...OH.
THOSE BOYS.
BUT...
...?

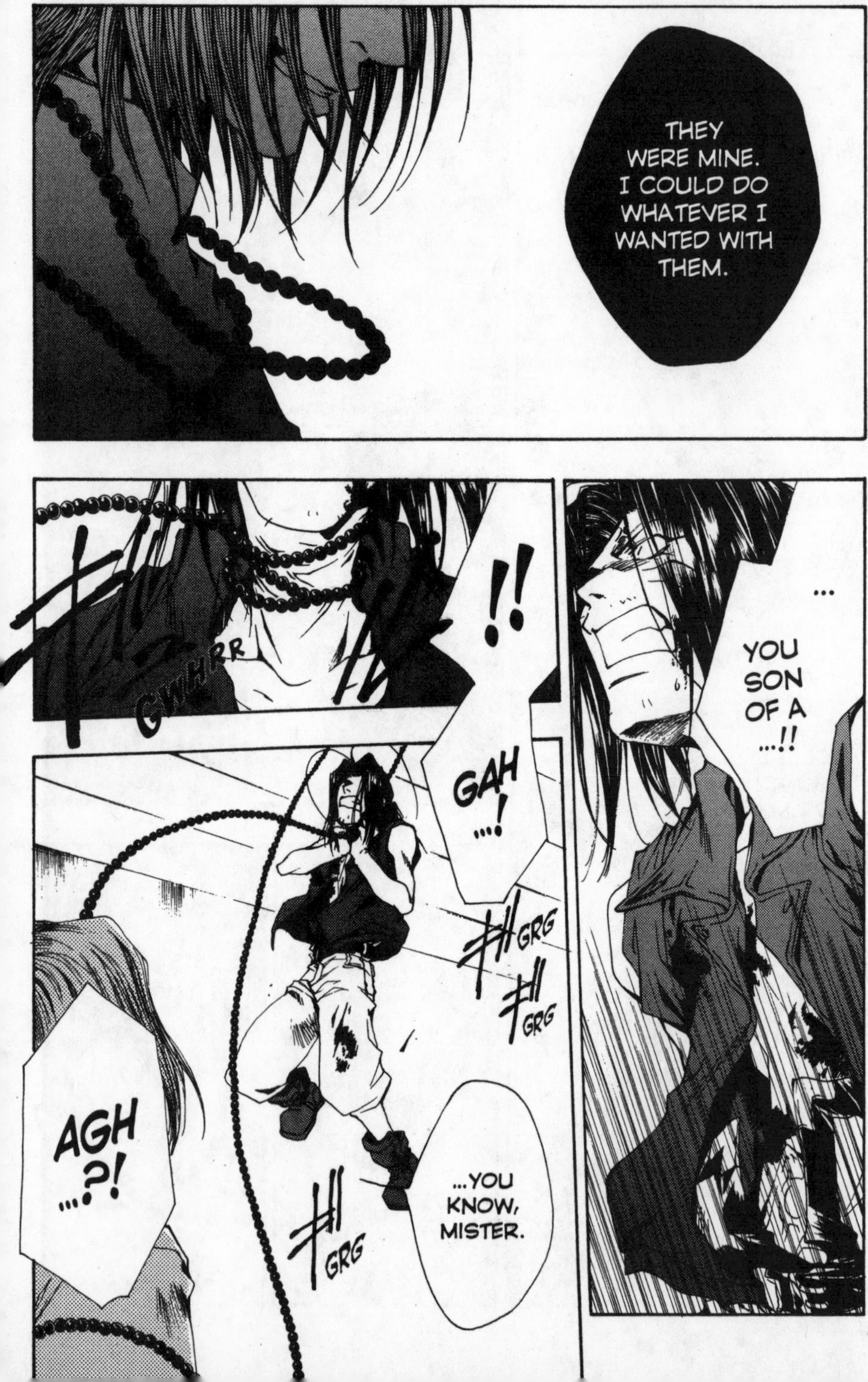
THEY WERE MINE. I COULD DO WHATEVER I WANTED WITH THEM.
...
YOU SON OF A ...!!
GWHRR
!!
GAH ...!
GRG
GRG
...YOU KNOW, MISTER.
GRG
AGH ...?!

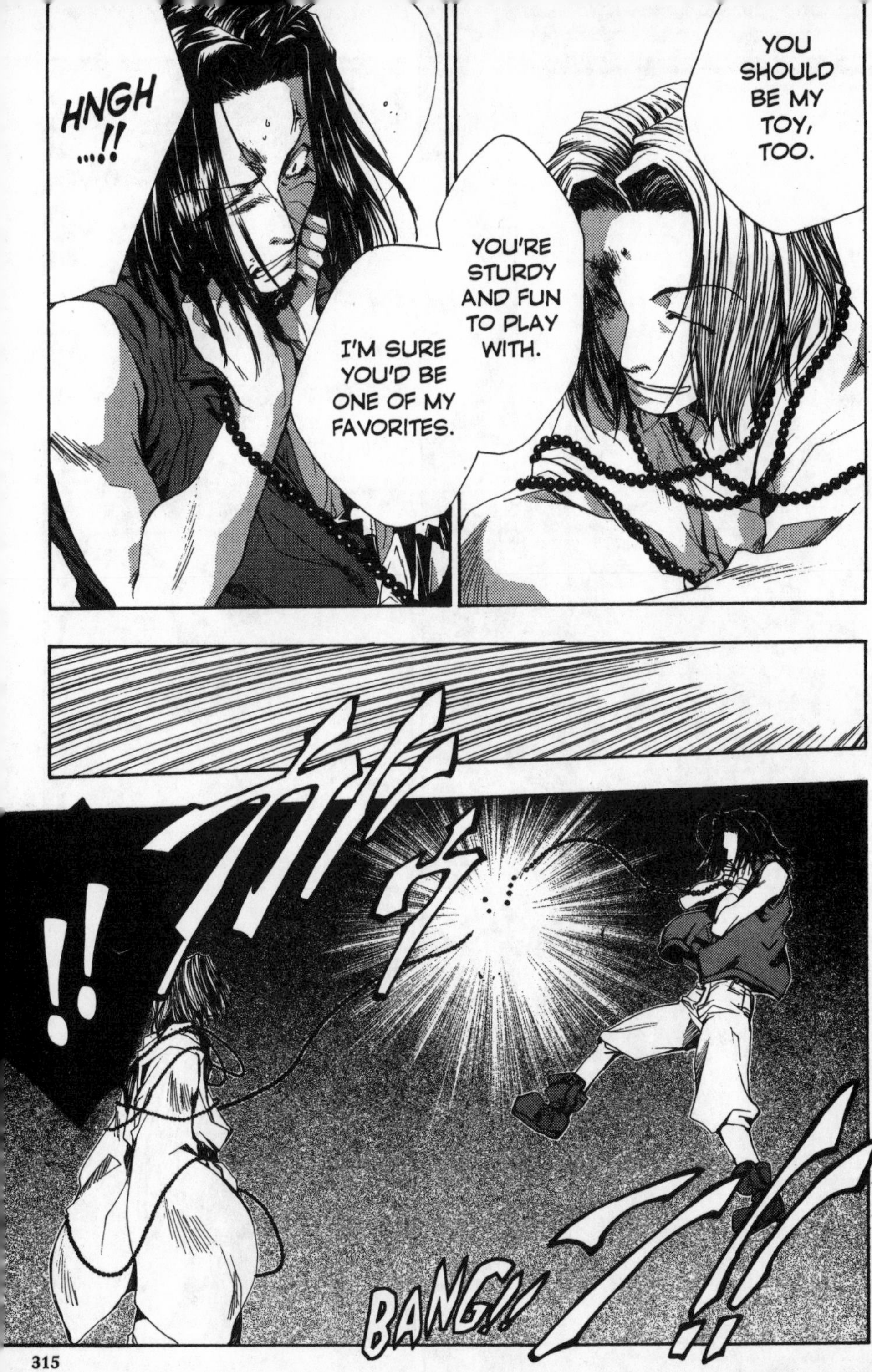
YOU SHOULD BE MY TOY, TOO.
YOU'RE STURDY AND FUN TO PLAY WITH.
I'M SURE YOU'D BE ONE OF MY FAVORITES.
HNGH ...!!
BANG!!
!!

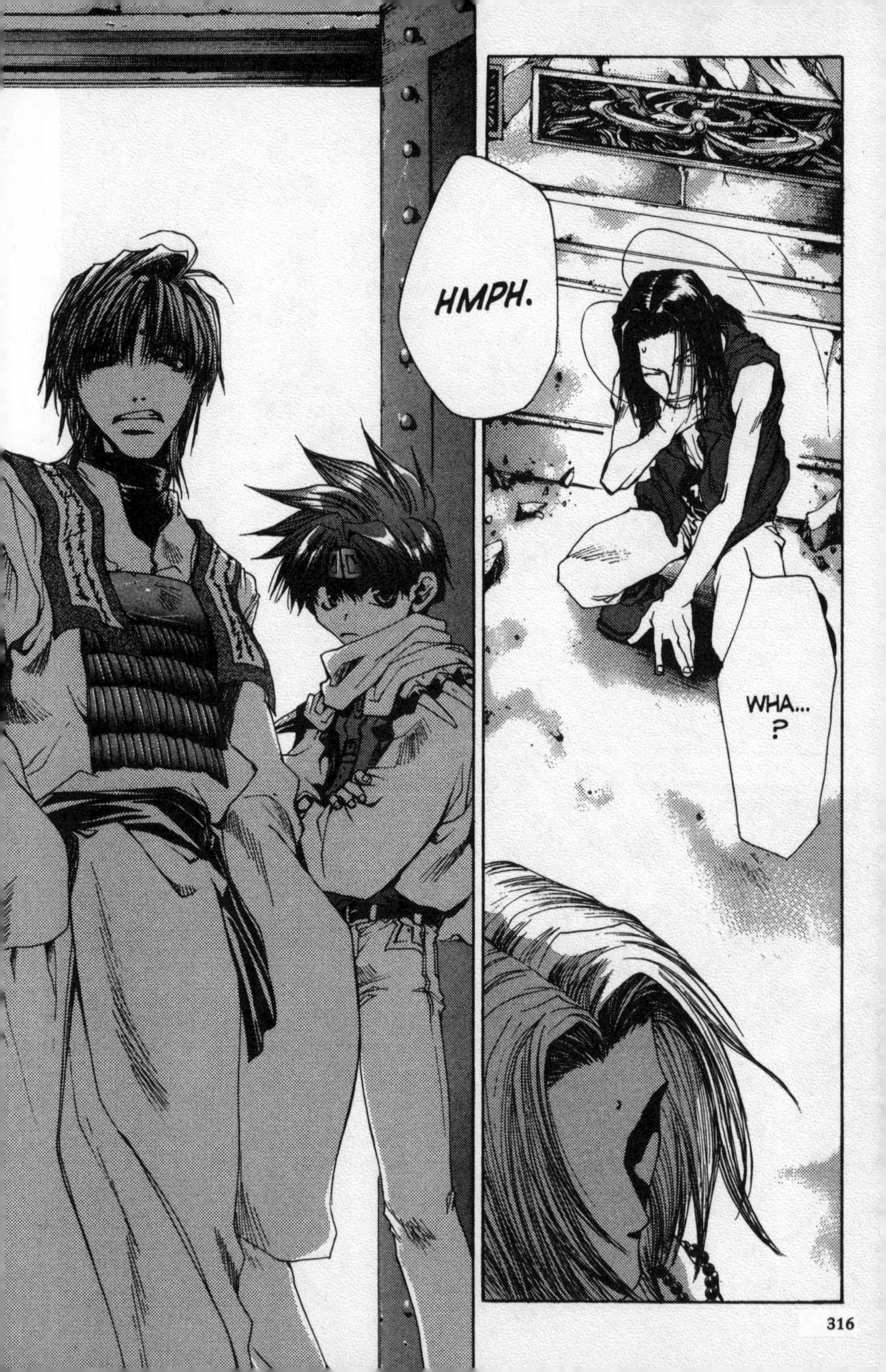
HMPH.
WHA... ?

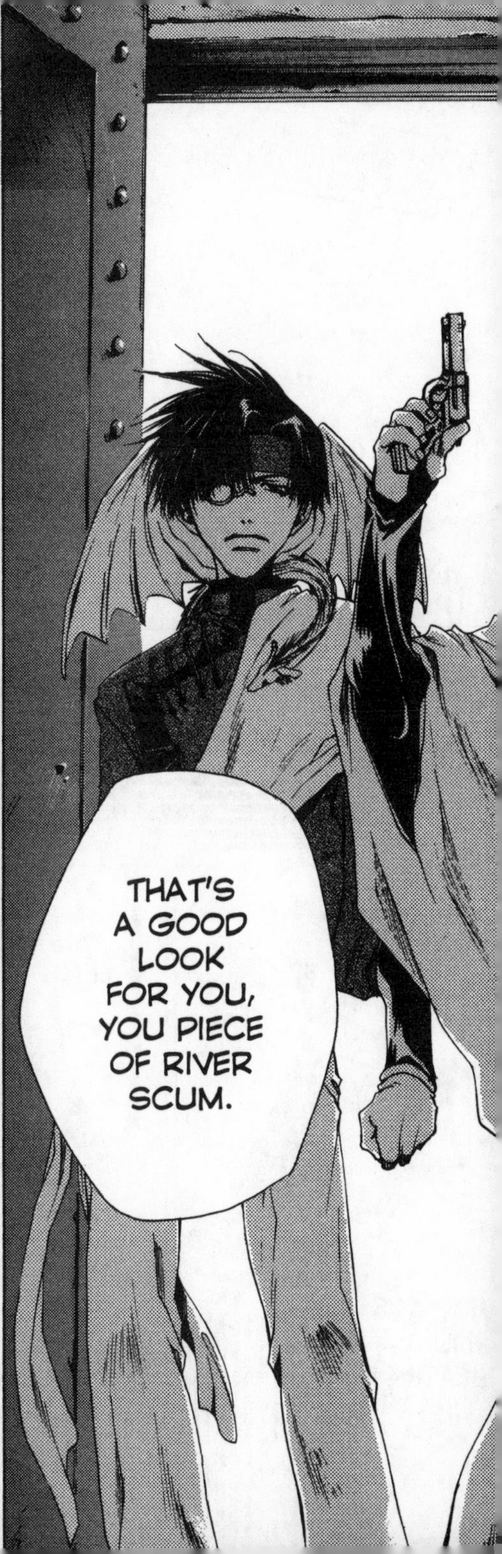
THAT'S A GOOD LOOK FOR YOU, YOU PIECE OF RIVER SCUM.

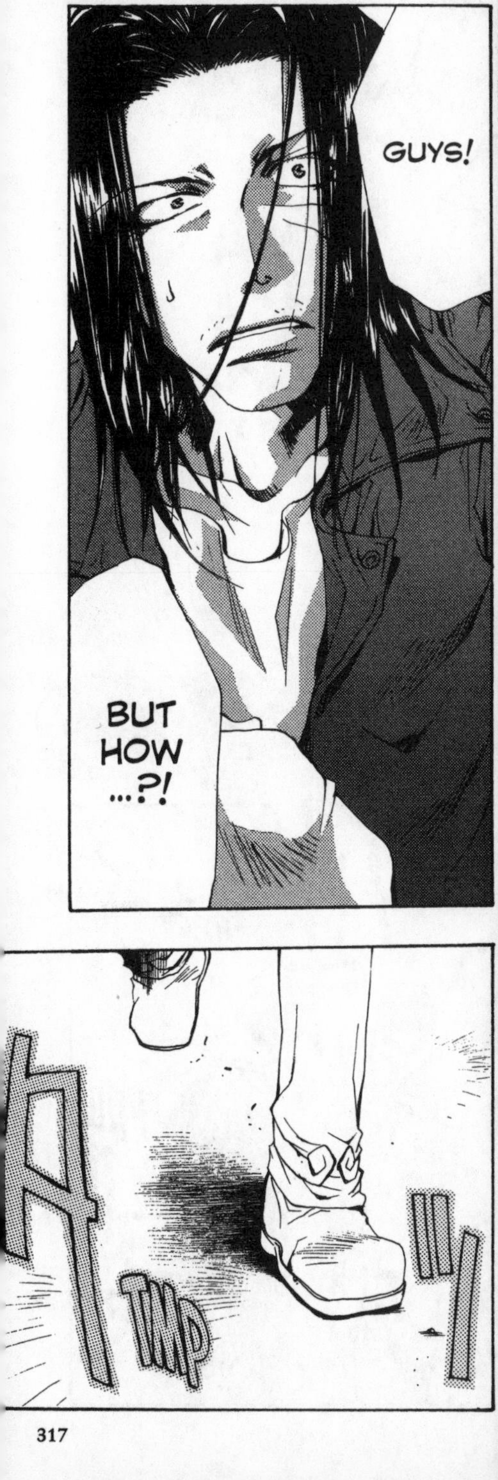
GUYS!
BUT HOW ...?!
TMP

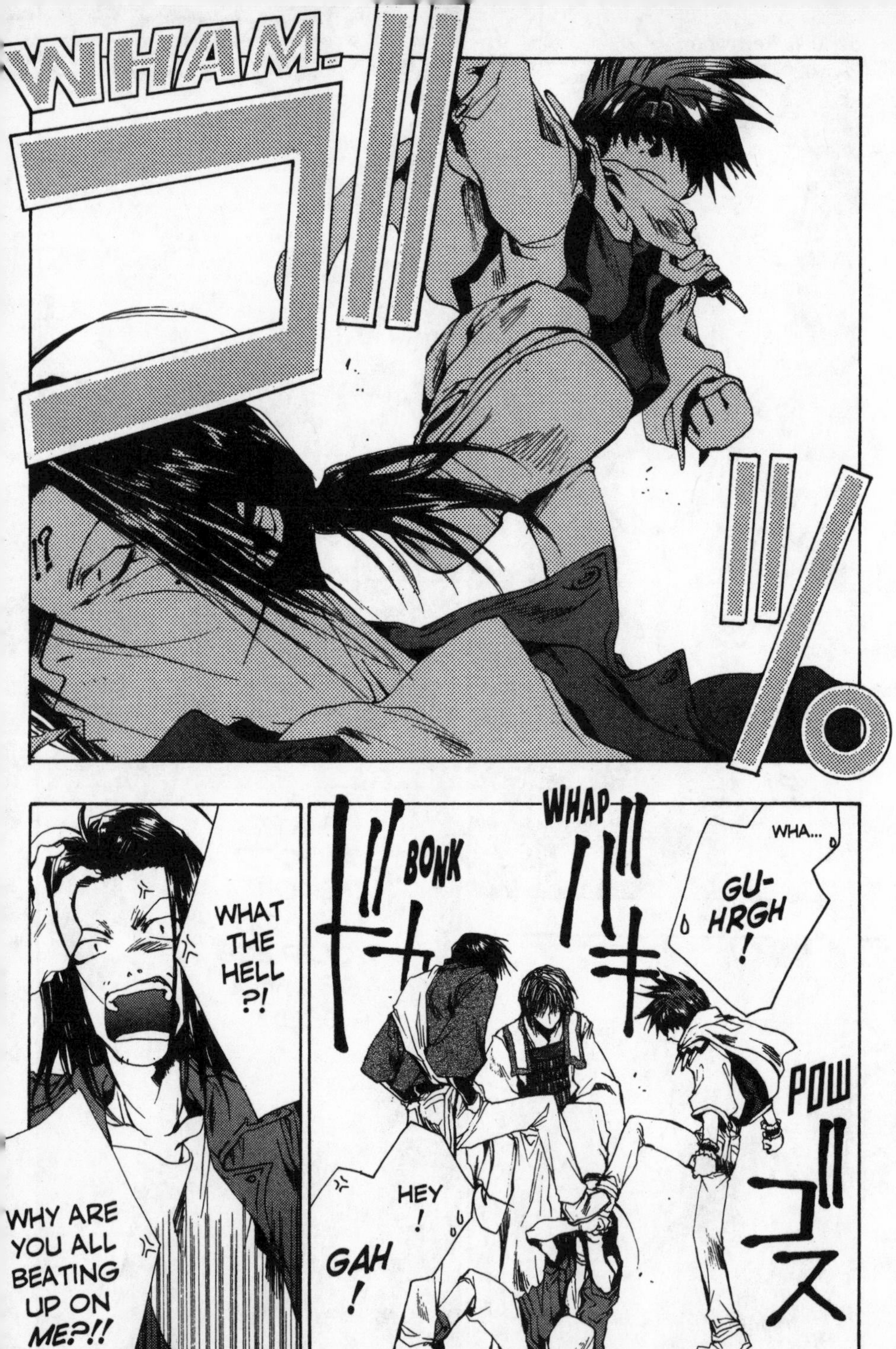
WHAM.
!?
WHA...
GU-HRGH!
POW
ゴス
WHAP
バキ
BONK
HEY!
GAH!
WHAT THE HELL?!
WHY ARE YOU ALL BEATING UP ON ME?!!

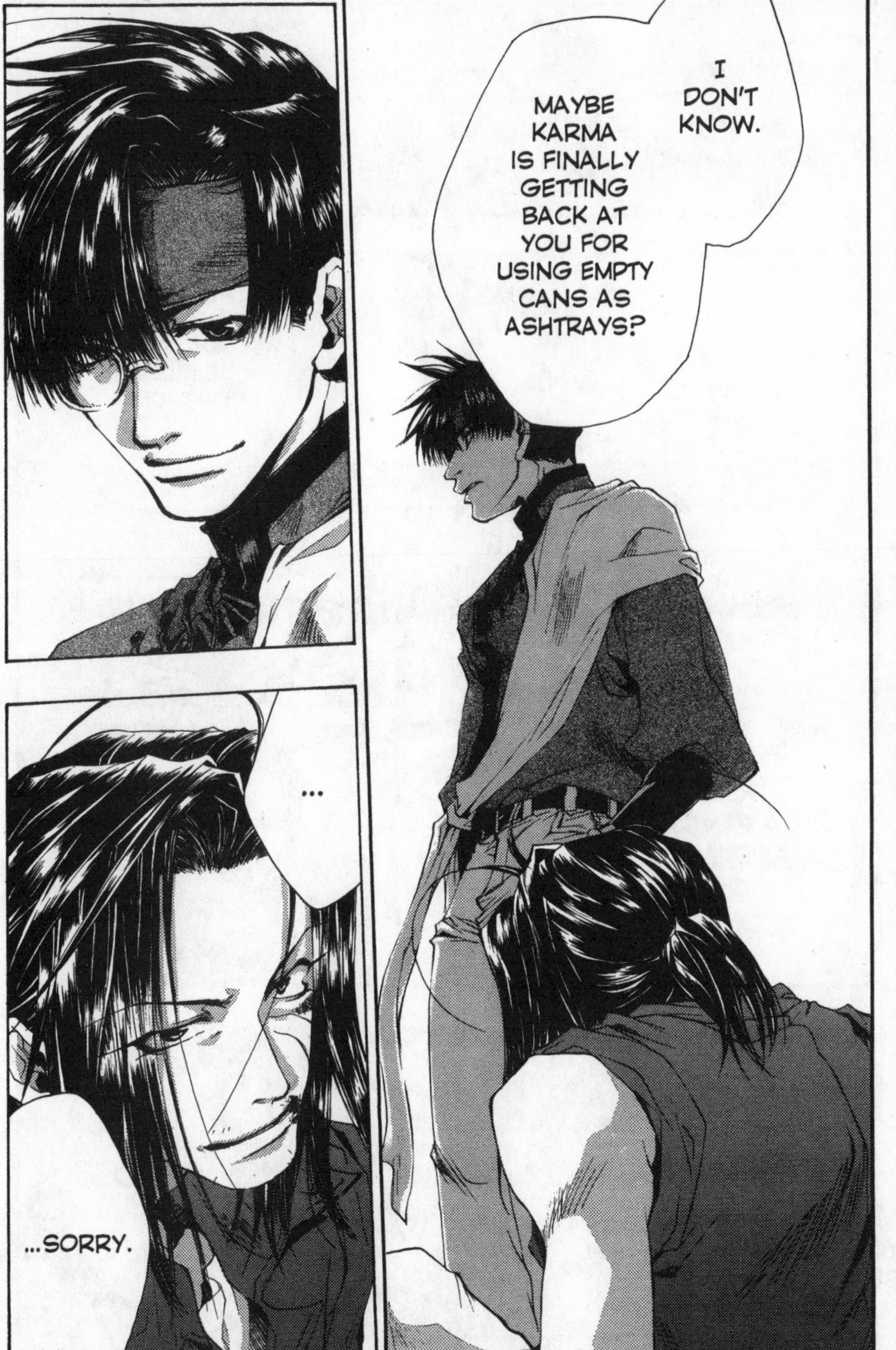
I DON'T KNOW.
MAYBE KARMA IS FINALLY GETTING BACK AT YOU FOR USING EMPTY CANS AS ASHTRAYS?
...
...SORRY.

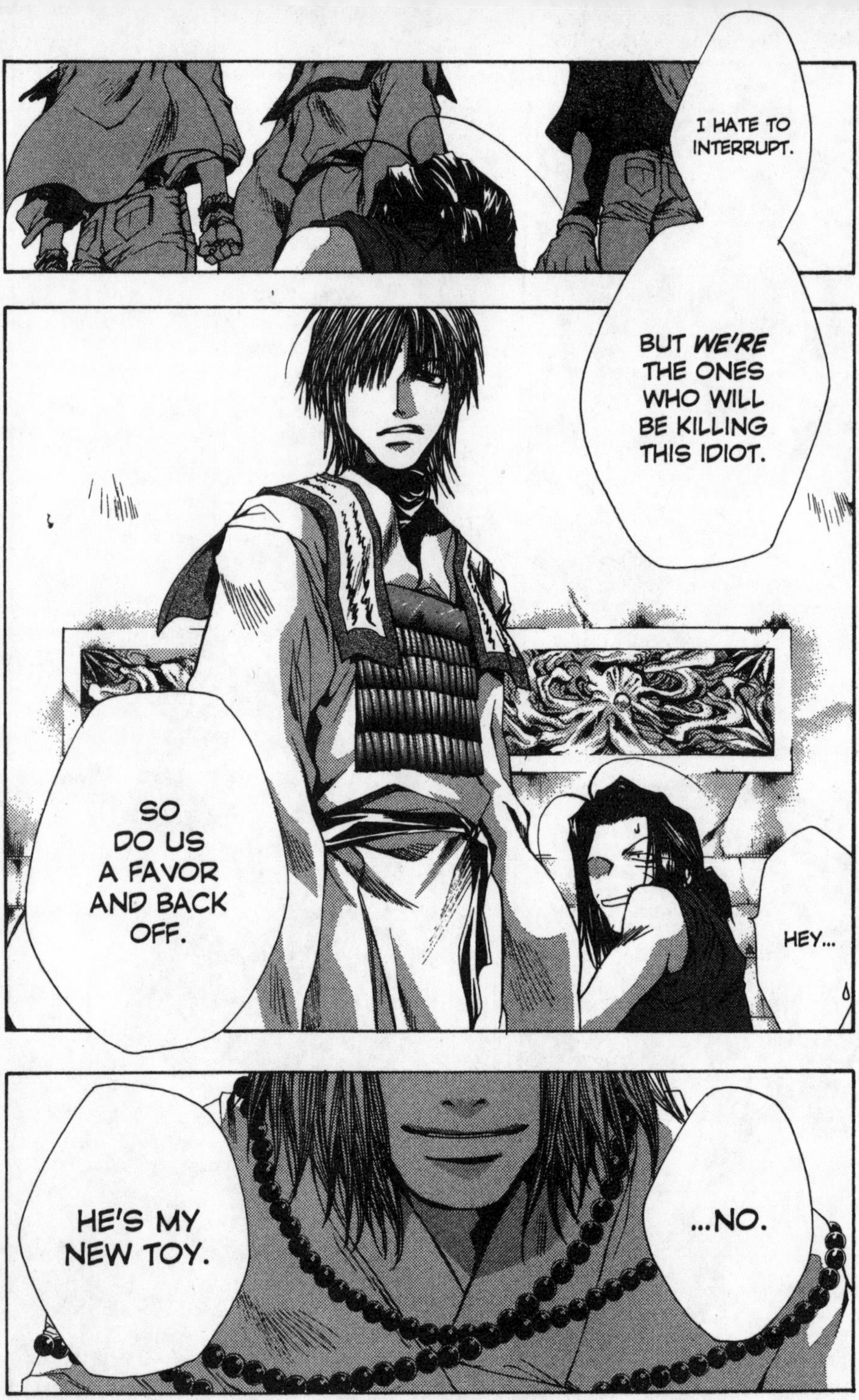
I HATE TO INTERRUPT.
BUT *WE'RE* THE ONES WHO WILL BE KILLING THIS IDIOT.
SO DO US A FAVOR AND BACK OFF.
HEY...
...NO.
HE'S MY NEW TOY.

CHAPTER 48 Lose

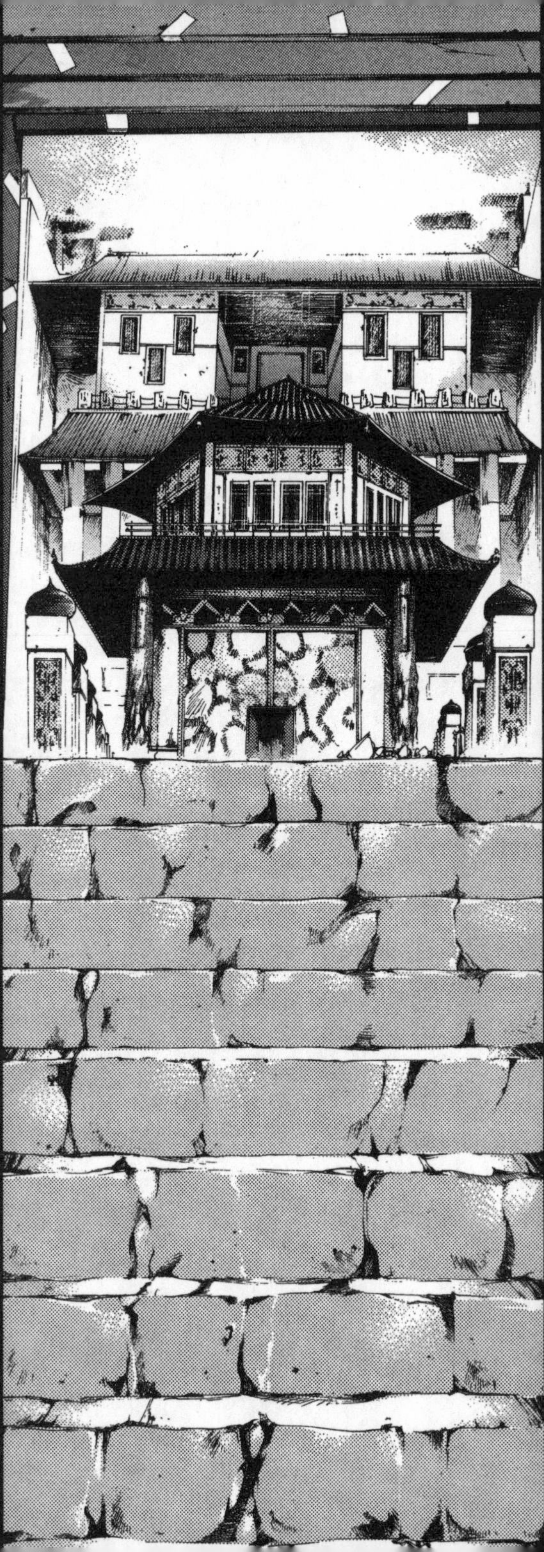

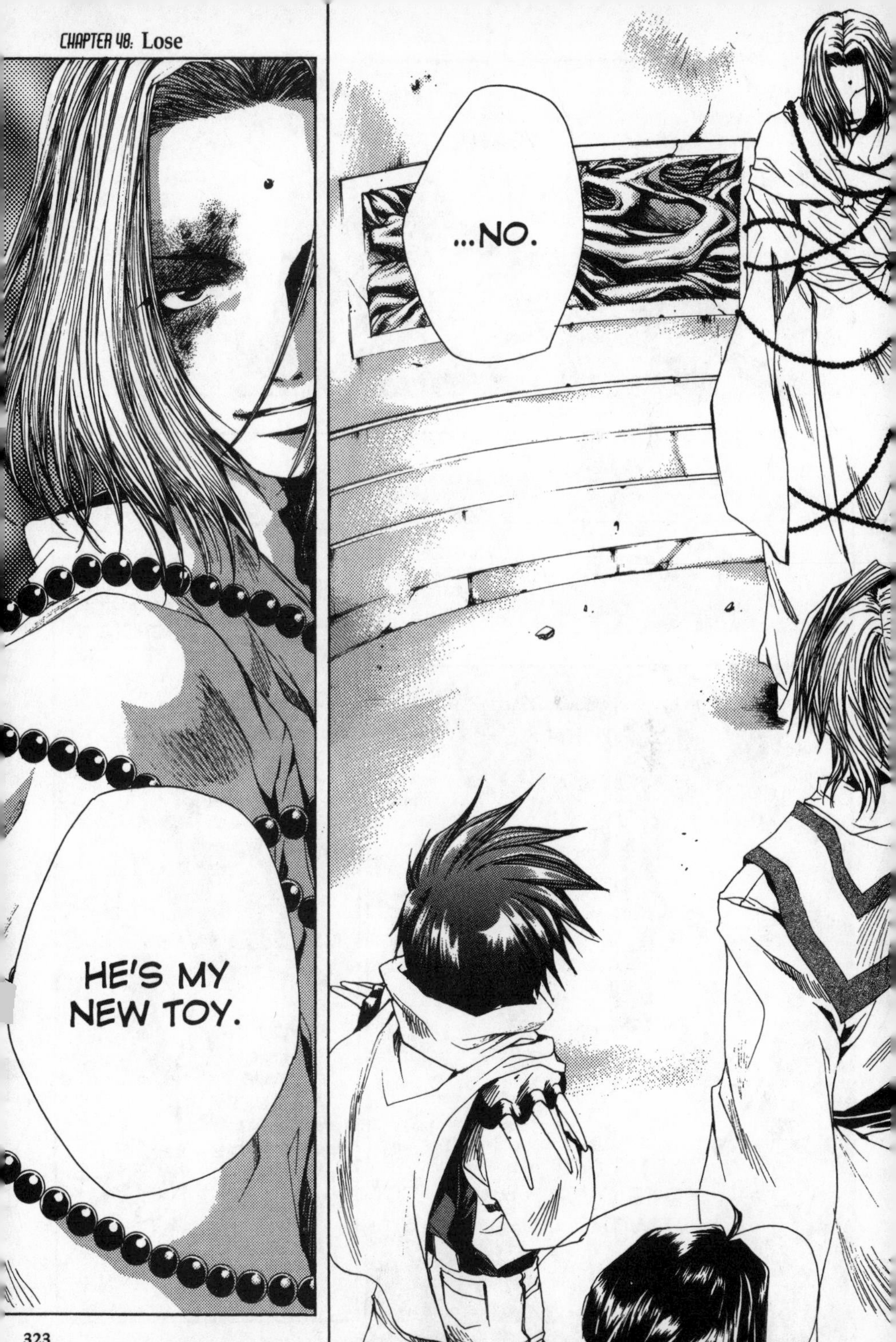
...NO.
HE'S MY NEW TOY.

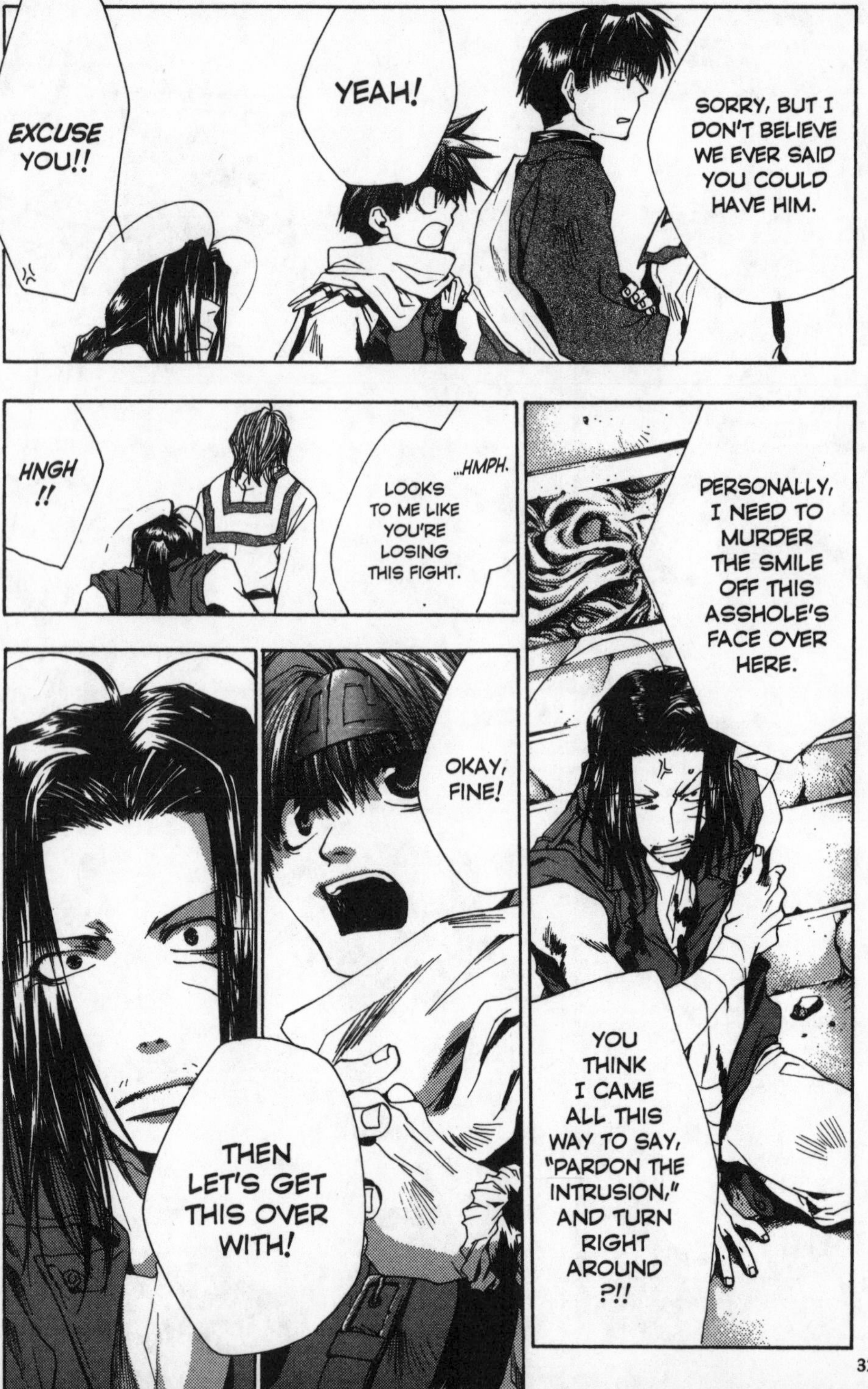
SORRY, BUT I DON'T BELIEVE WE EVER SAID YOU COULD HAVE HIM.
YEAH!
EXCUSE YOU!!
PERSONALLY, I NEED TO MURDER THE SMILE OFF THIS ASSHOLE'S FACE OVER HERE.
YOU THINK I CAME ALL THIS WAY TO SAY, "PARDON THE INTRUSION," AND TURN RIGHT AROUND ?!!
...HMPH.
LOOKS TO ME LIKE YOU'RE LOSING THIS FIGHT.
HNGH !!
OKAY, FINE!
THEN LET'S GET THIS OVER WITH!

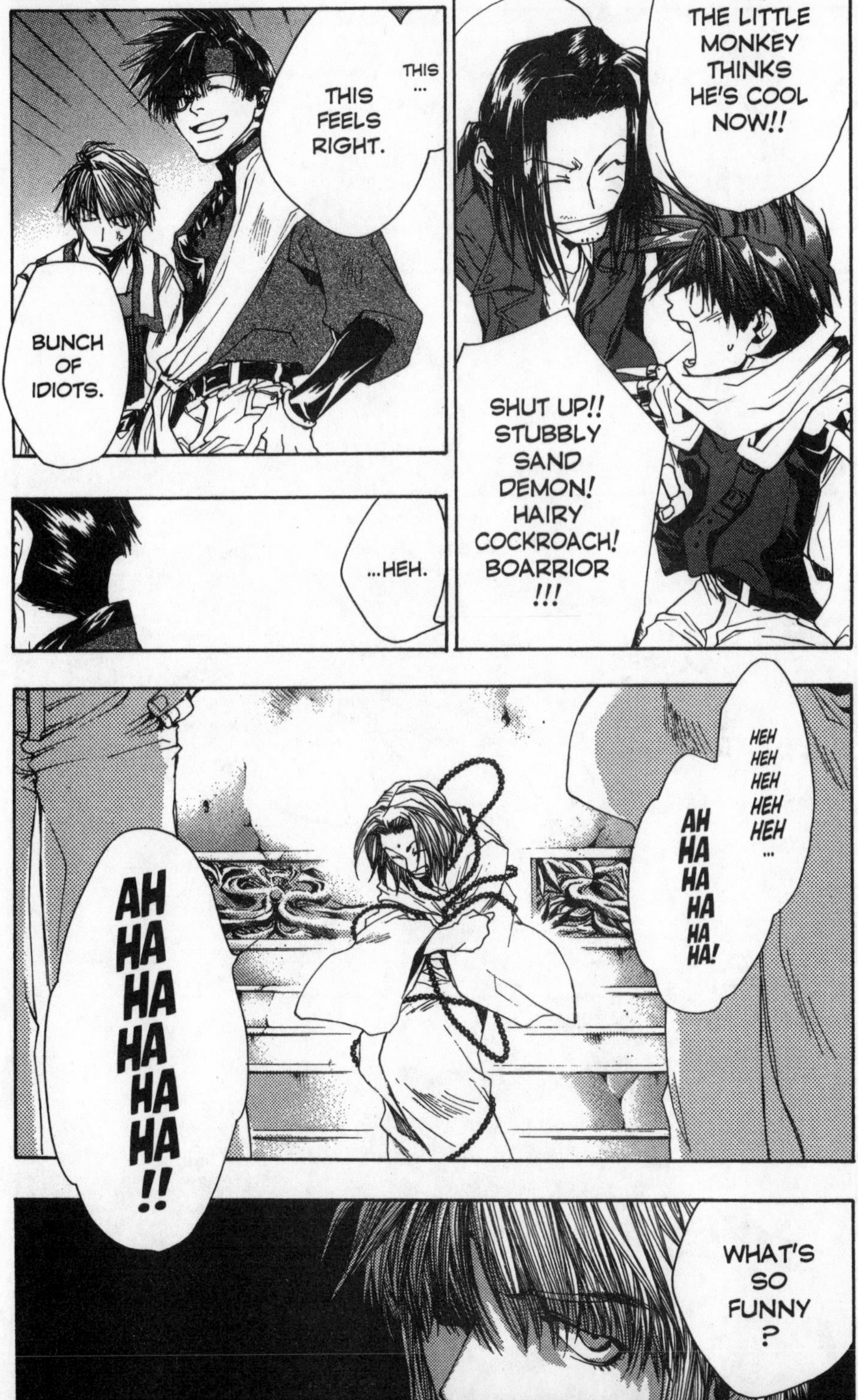
OH, THE LITTLE MONKEY THINKS HE'S COOL NOW!!
SHUT UP!! STUBBLY SAND DEMON! HAIRY COCKROACH! BOARRIOR !!!
THIS ...
THIS FEELS RIGHT.
BUNCH OF IDIOTS.
...HEH.
HEH HEH HEH HEH HEH ...
AH HA HA HA HA HA HA!
AH HA HA HA HA HA HA!!
WHAT'S SO FUNNY ?

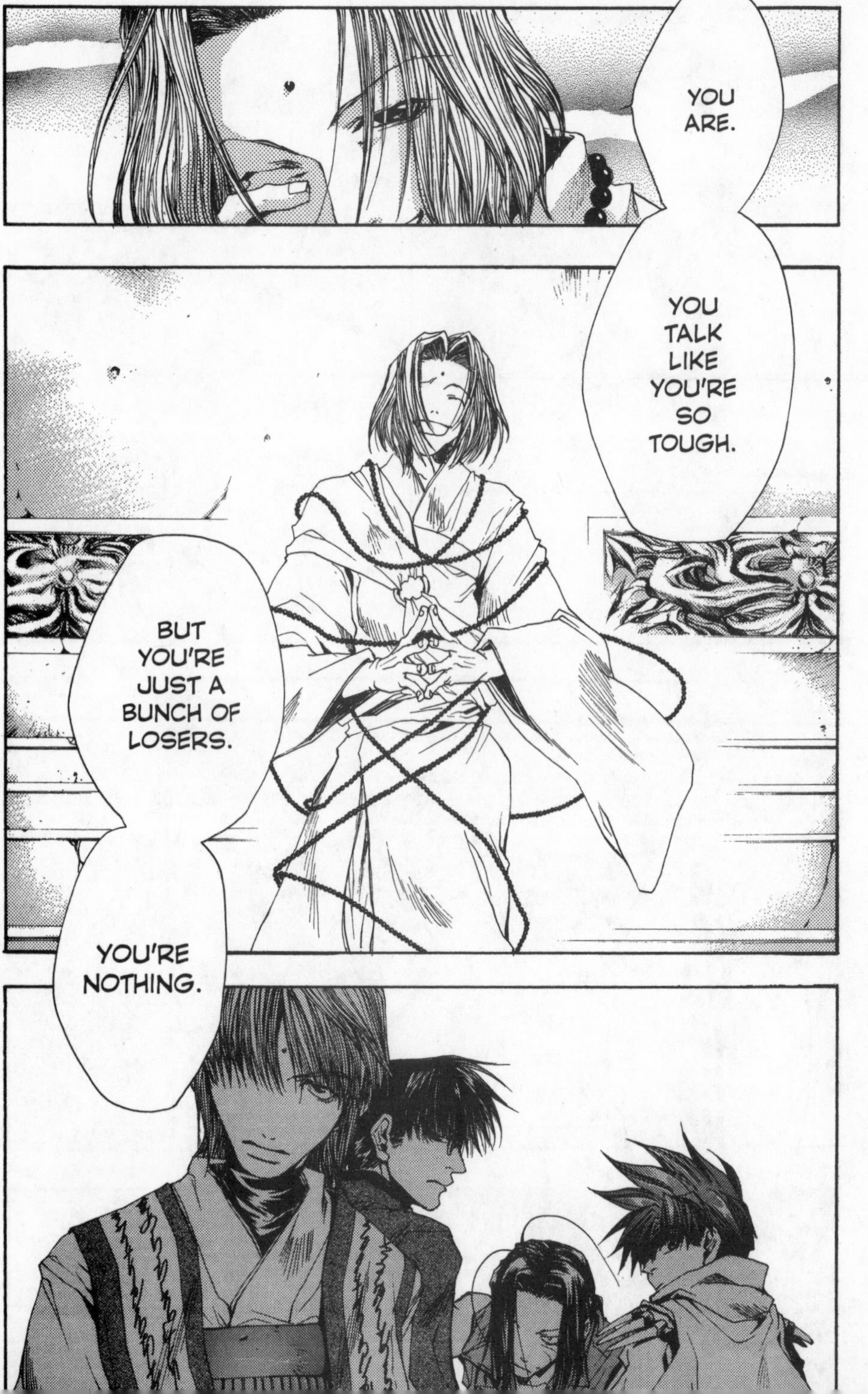
YOU ARE.
YOU TALK LIKE YOU'RE SO TOUGH.
BUT YOU'RE JUST A BUNCH OF LOSERS.
YOU'RE NOTHING.

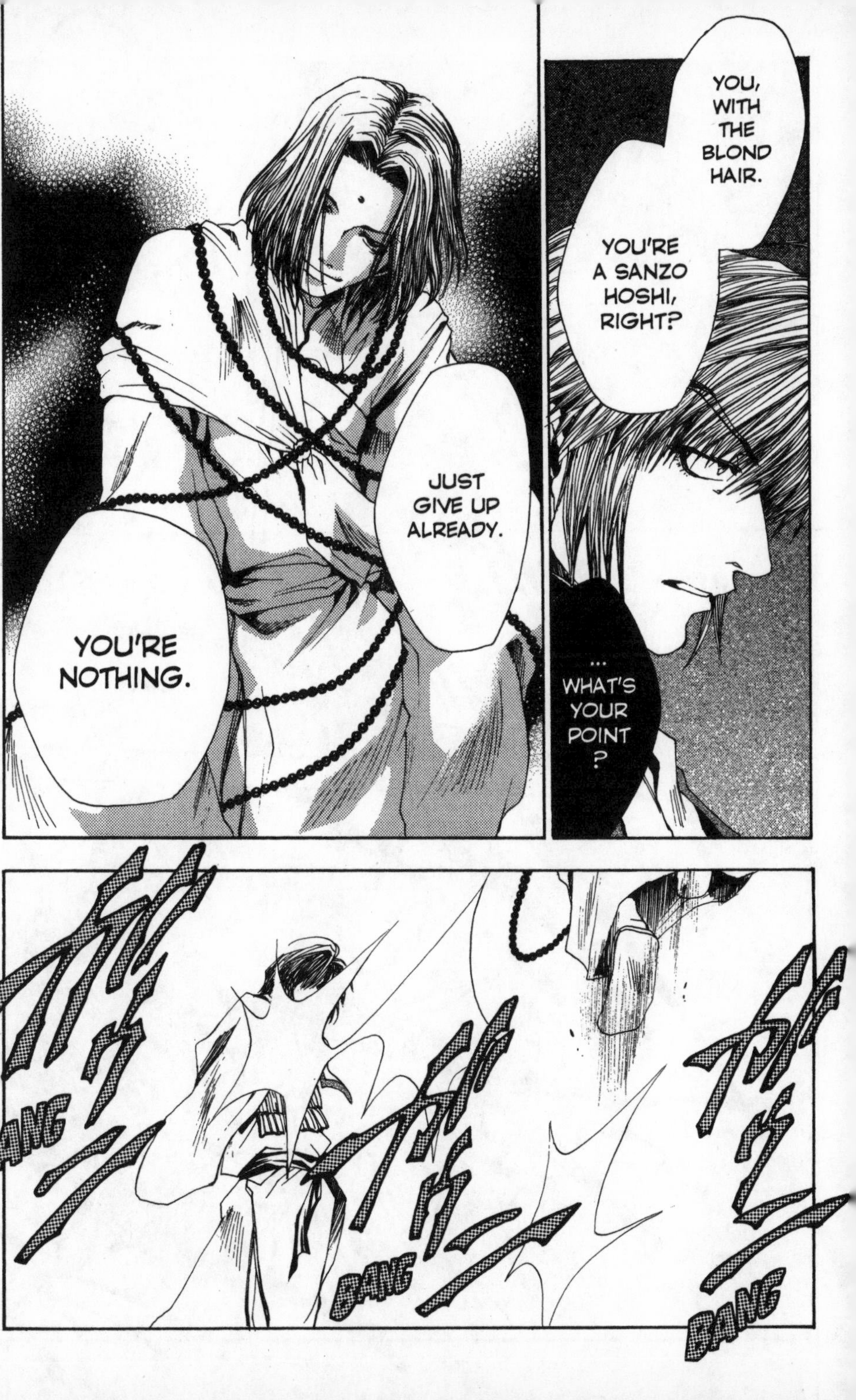
YOU, WITH THE BLOND HAIR.
YOU'RE A SANZO HOSHI, RIGHT?
... WHAT'S YOUR POINT?
JUST GIVE UP ALREADY.
YOU'RE NOTHING.
BANG
BANG
BANG

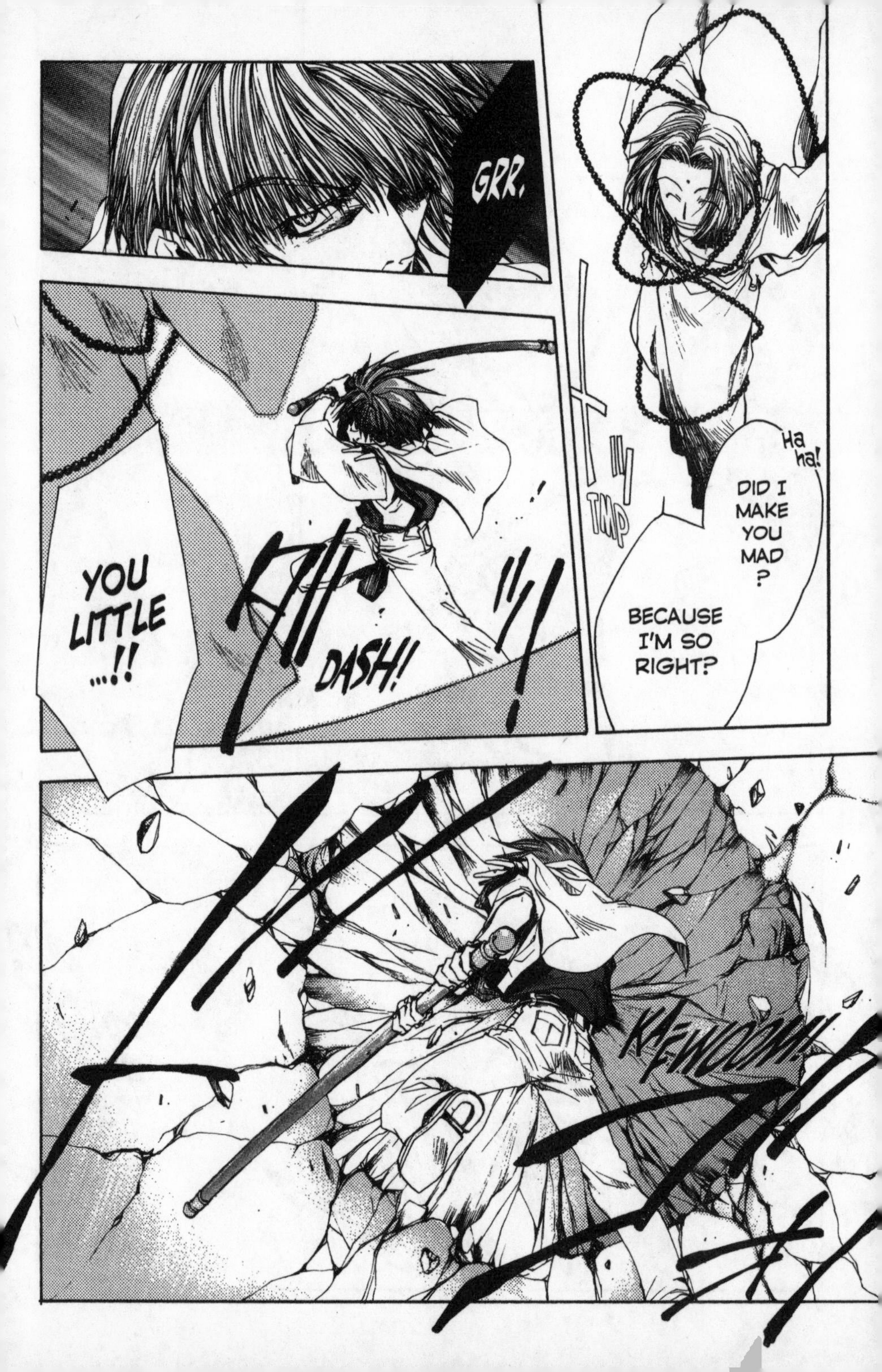
Ha ha!
DID I MAKE YOU MAD?
BECAUSE I'M SO RIGHT?
TMP
GRR.
YOU LITTLE ...!!
DASH!
KA-BWOOM!!

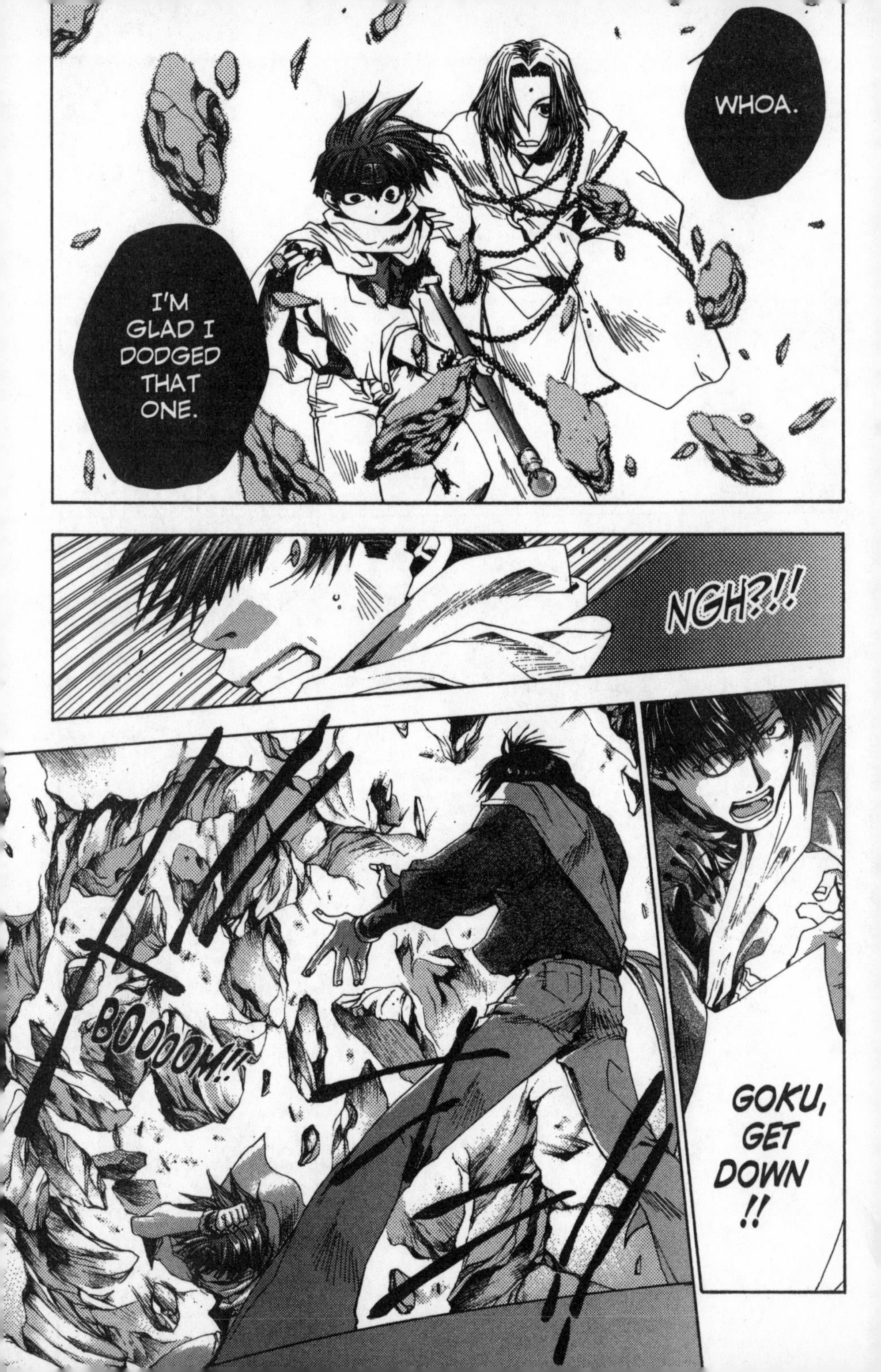
WHOA.
I'M GLAD I DODGED THAT ONE.
NGH?!!
GOKU, GET DOWN!!
BOOOOM!!

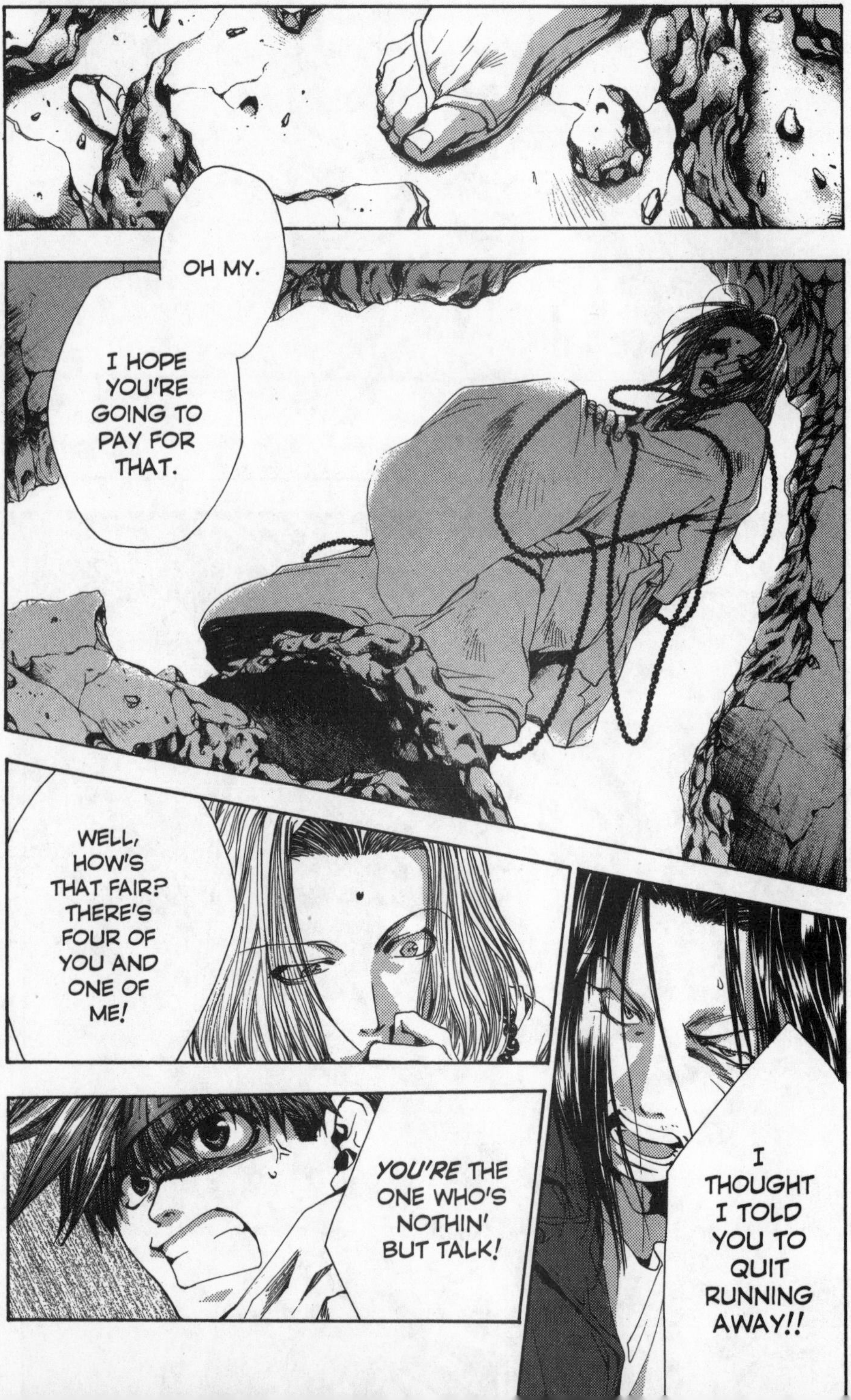
OH MY.
I HOPE YOU'RE GOING TO PAY FOR THAT.
I THOUGHT I TOLD YOU TO QUIT RUNNING AWAY!!
WELL, HOW'S THAT FAIR? THERE'S FOUR OF YOU AND ONE OF ME!
YOU'RE THE ONE WHO'S NOTHIN' BUT TALK!

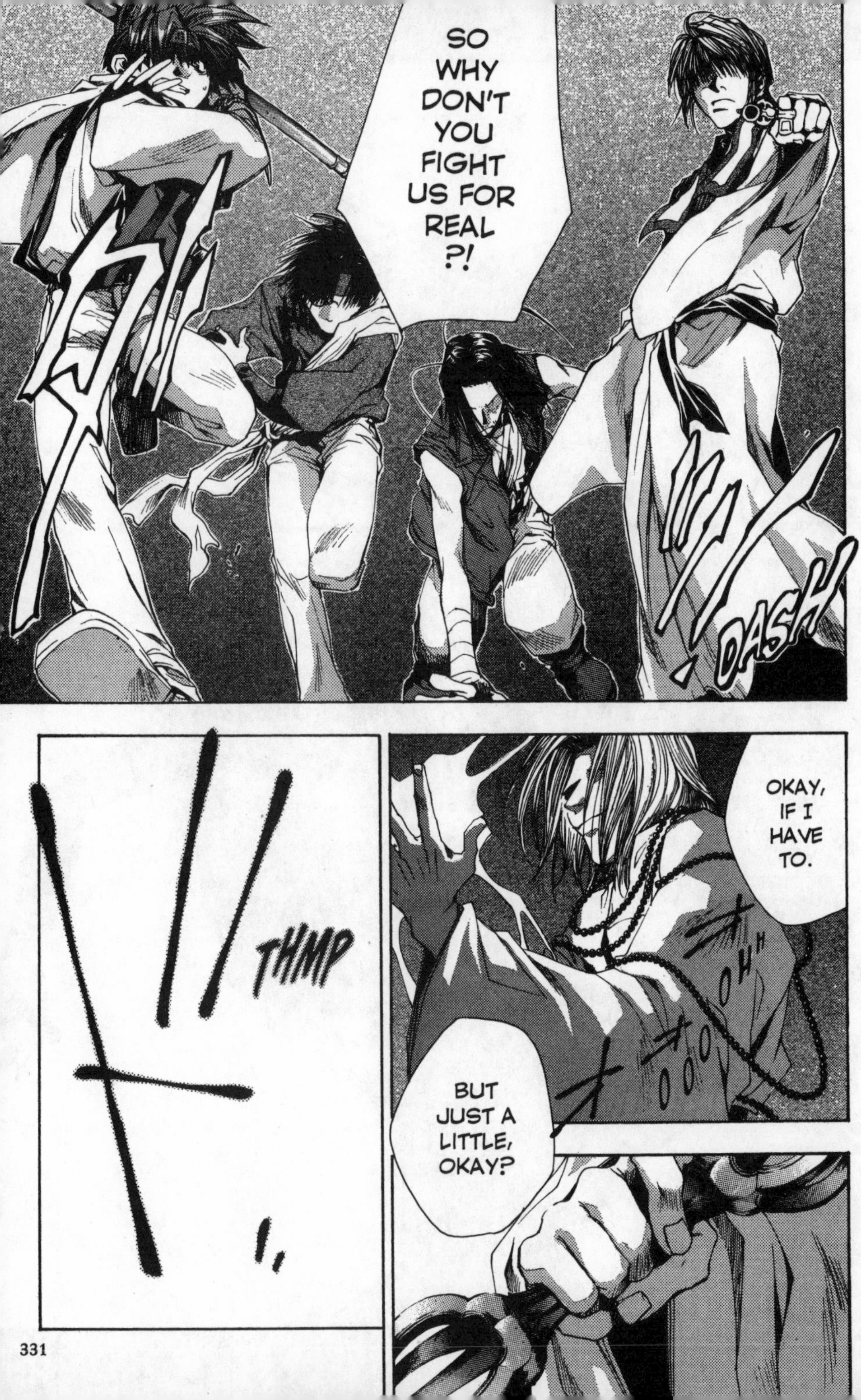
SO WHY DON'T YOU FIGHT US FOR REAL ?!
DASH
OKAY, IF I HAVE TO.
BUT JUST A LITTLE, OKAY?
THMP

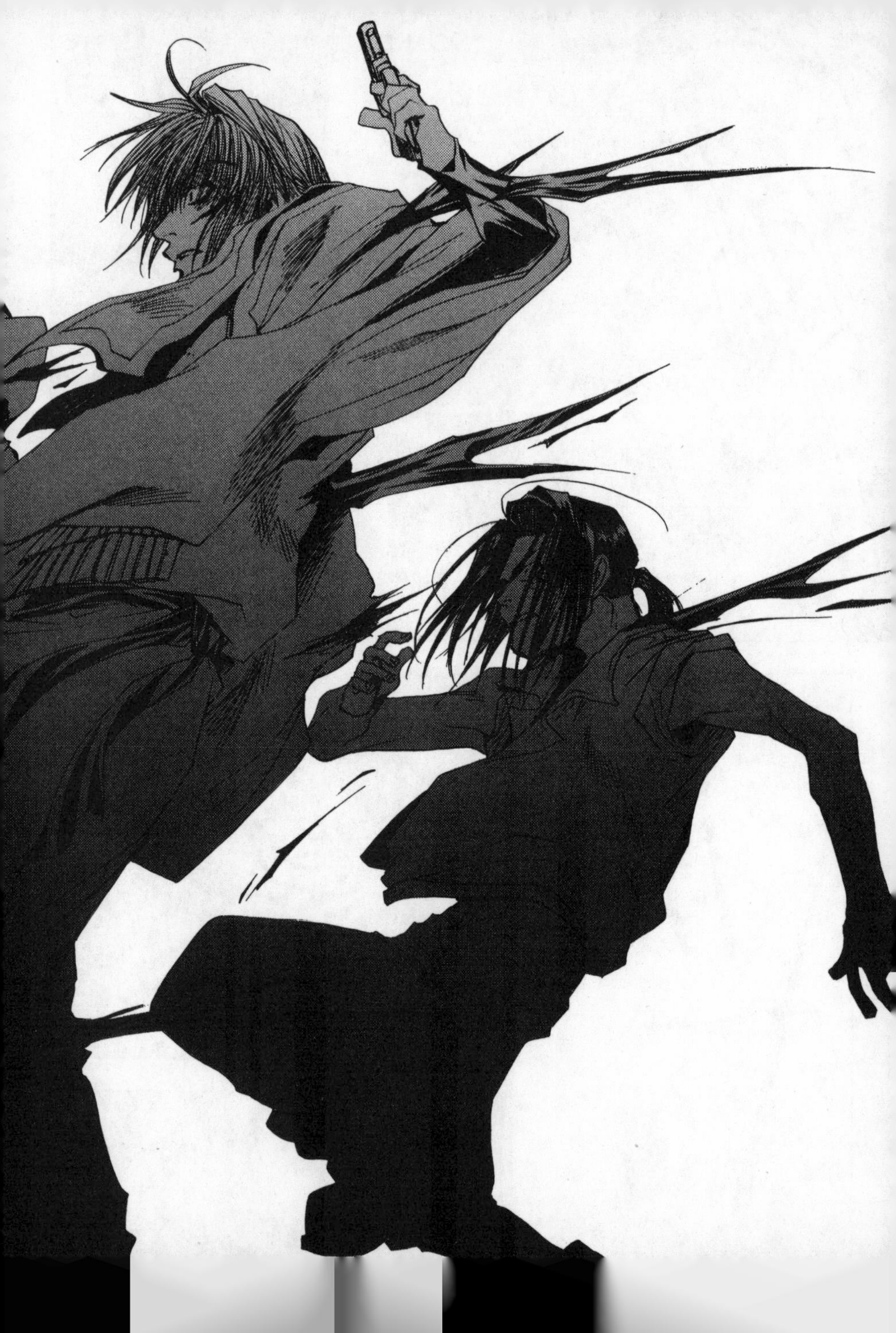

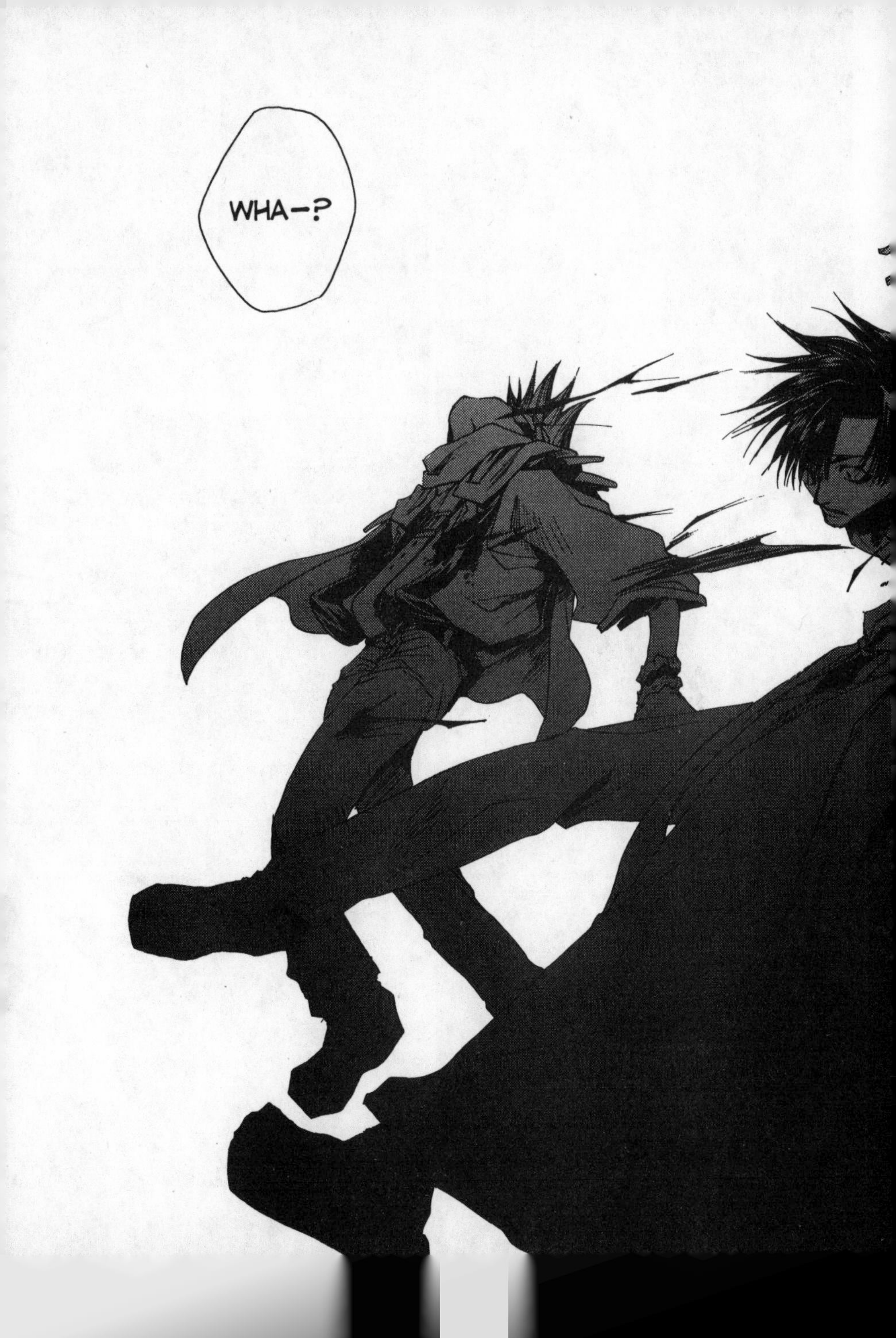
WHA-?

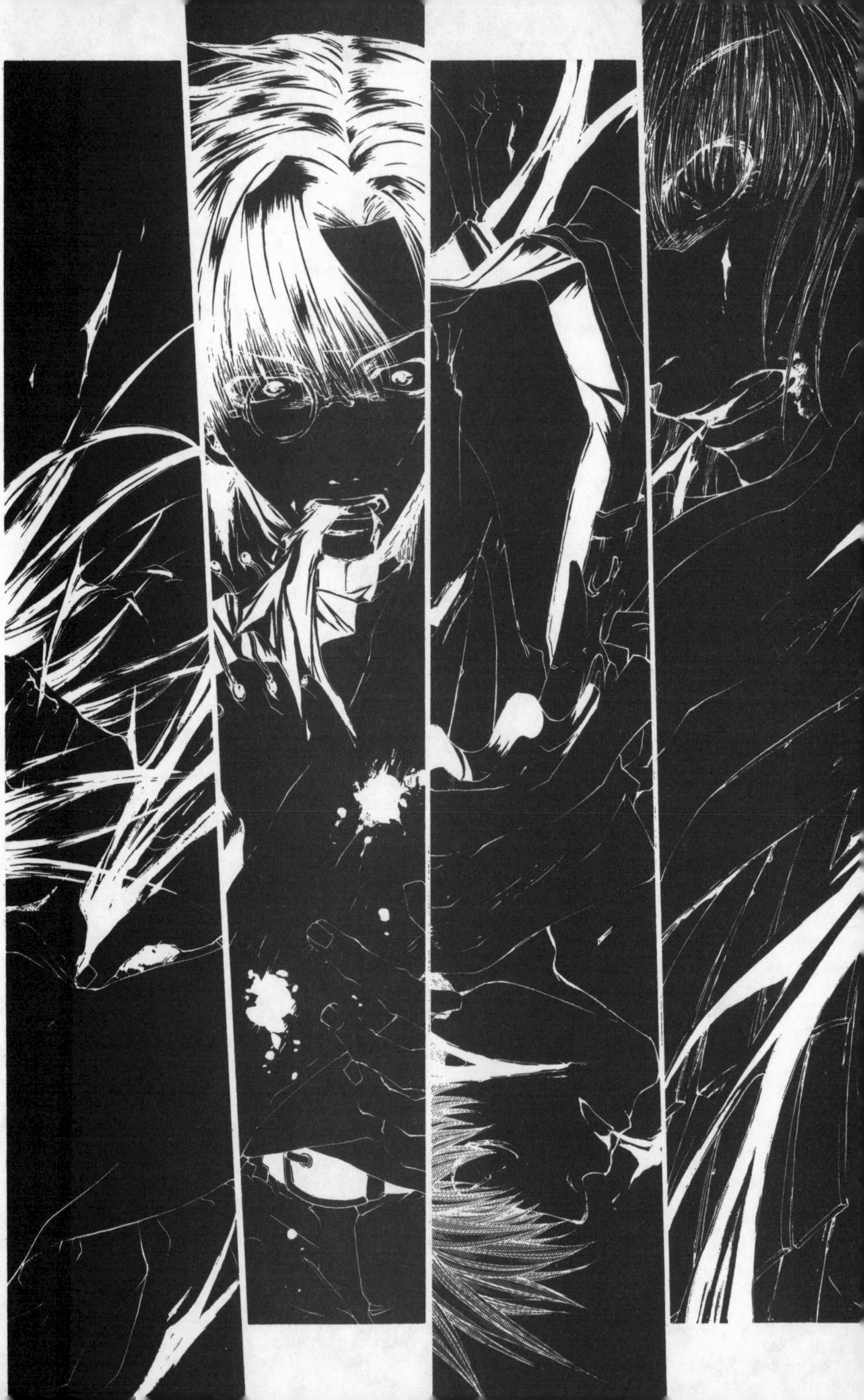

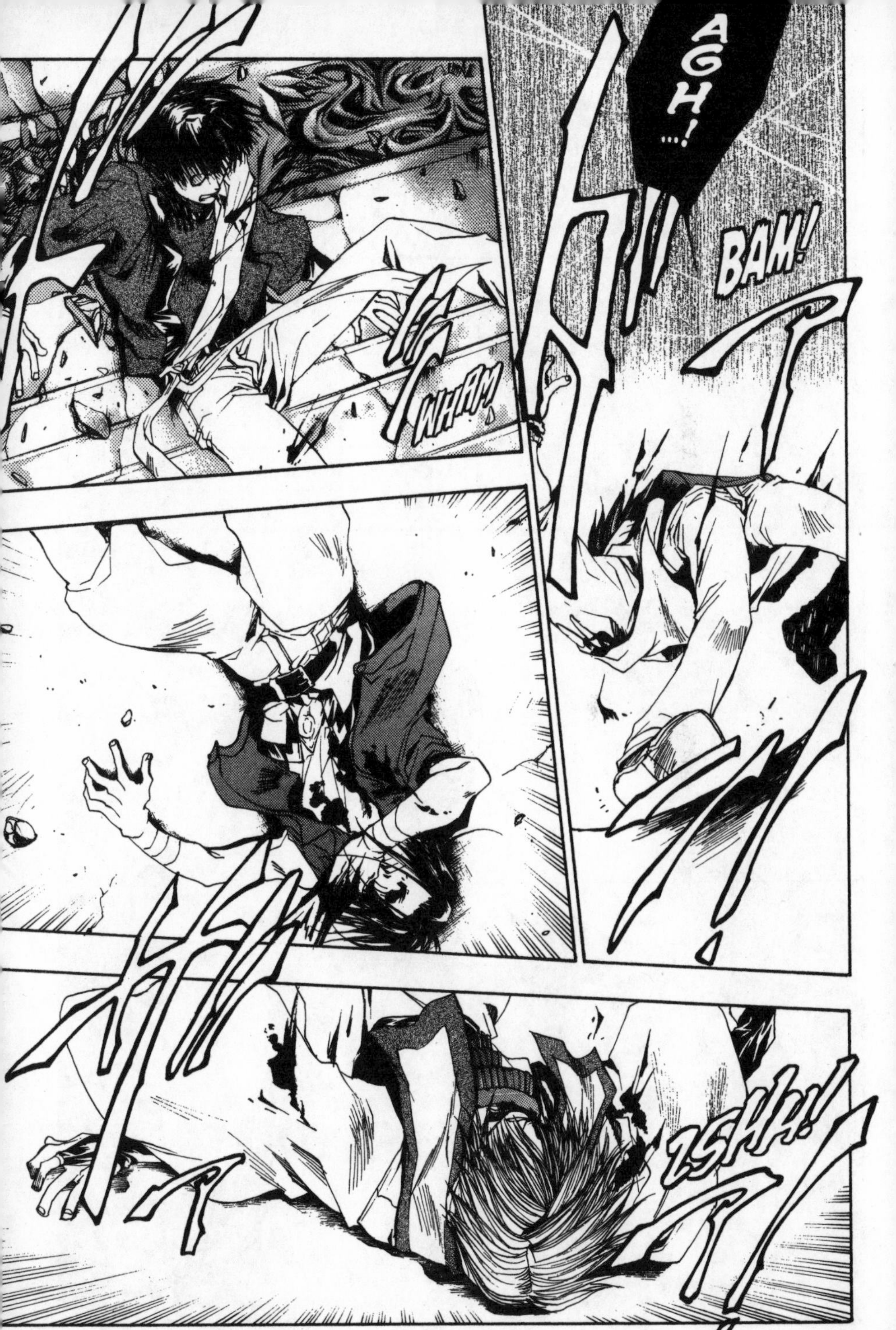
AGH...!
BAM!
WHAM!
ZSHH!

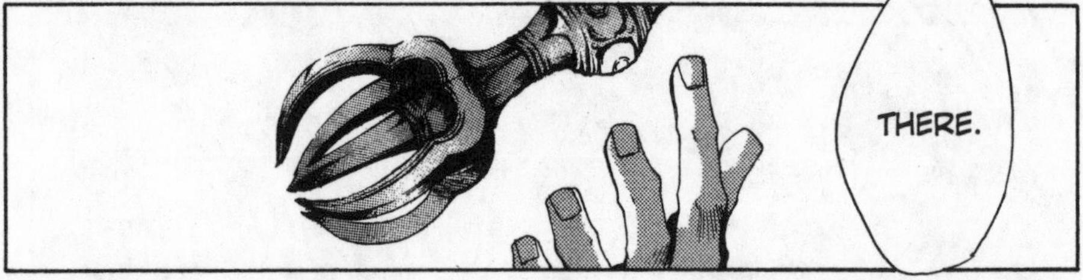
THERE.

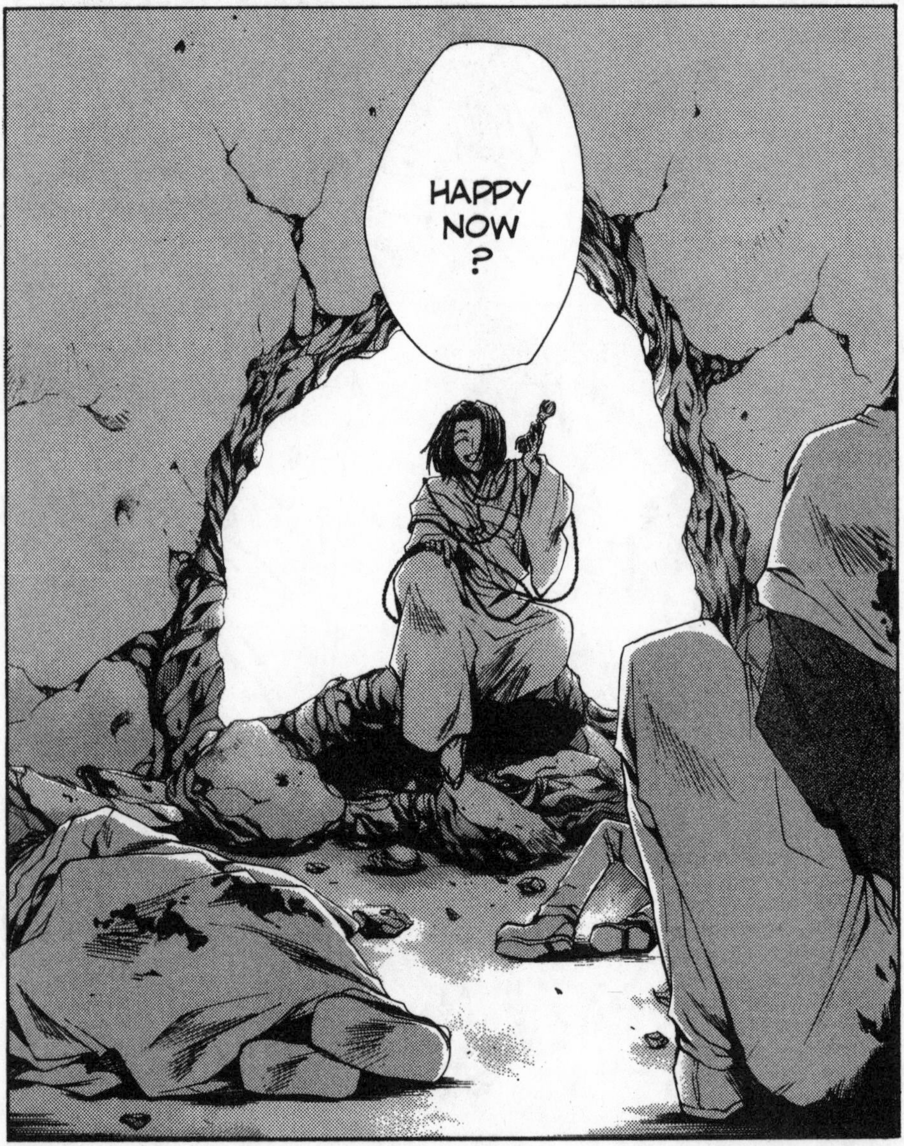
HAPPY NOW ?

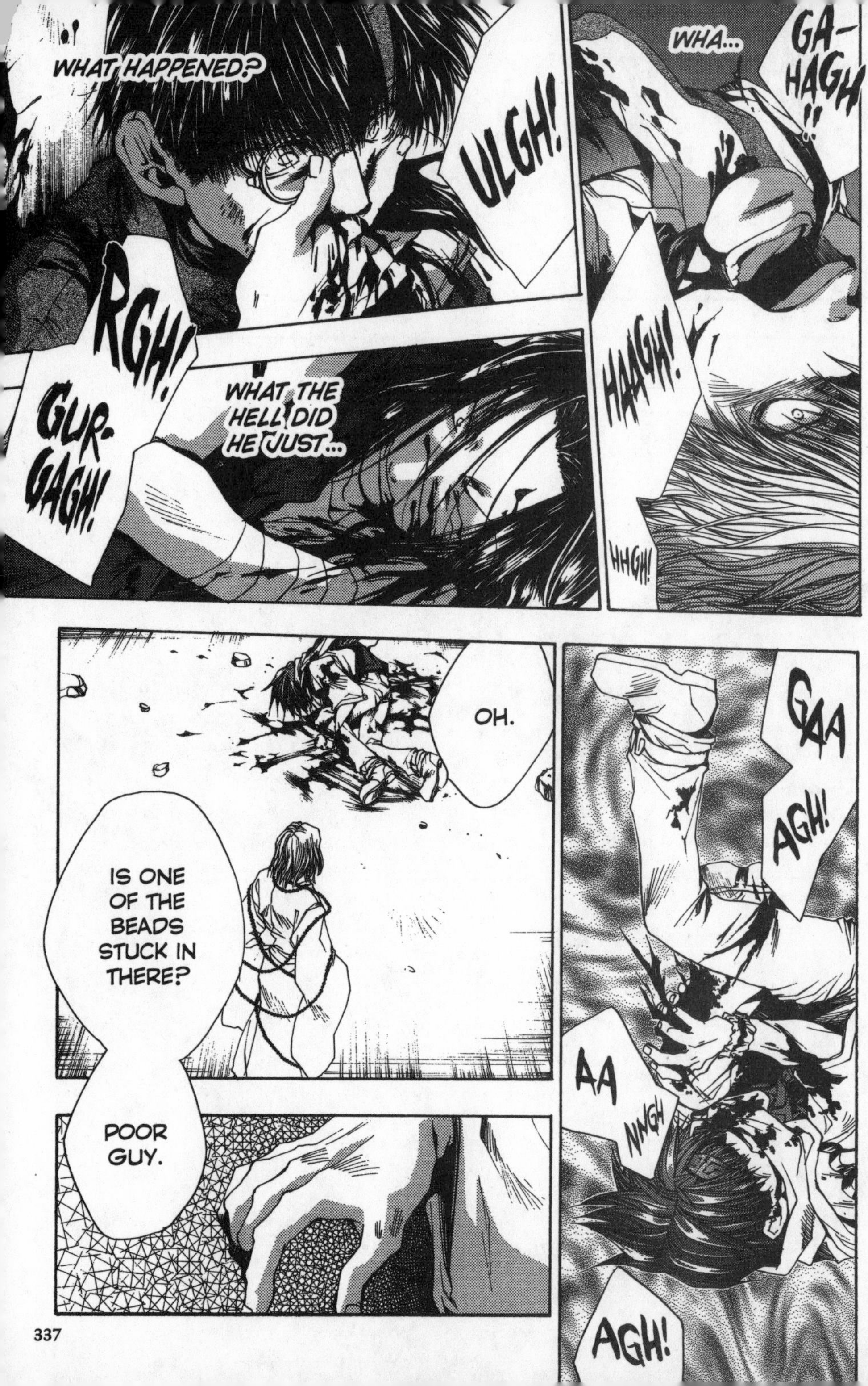
GA-HAGH!!
WHA...
HAAGH!
HHGH!
WHAT HAPPENED?
ULGH!
RGH!
GUR-GAGH!
WHAT THE HELL DID HE JUST...
GAAAGH!
AA NNGH
AGH!
OH.
IS ONE OF THE BEADS STUCK IN THERE?
POOR GUY.

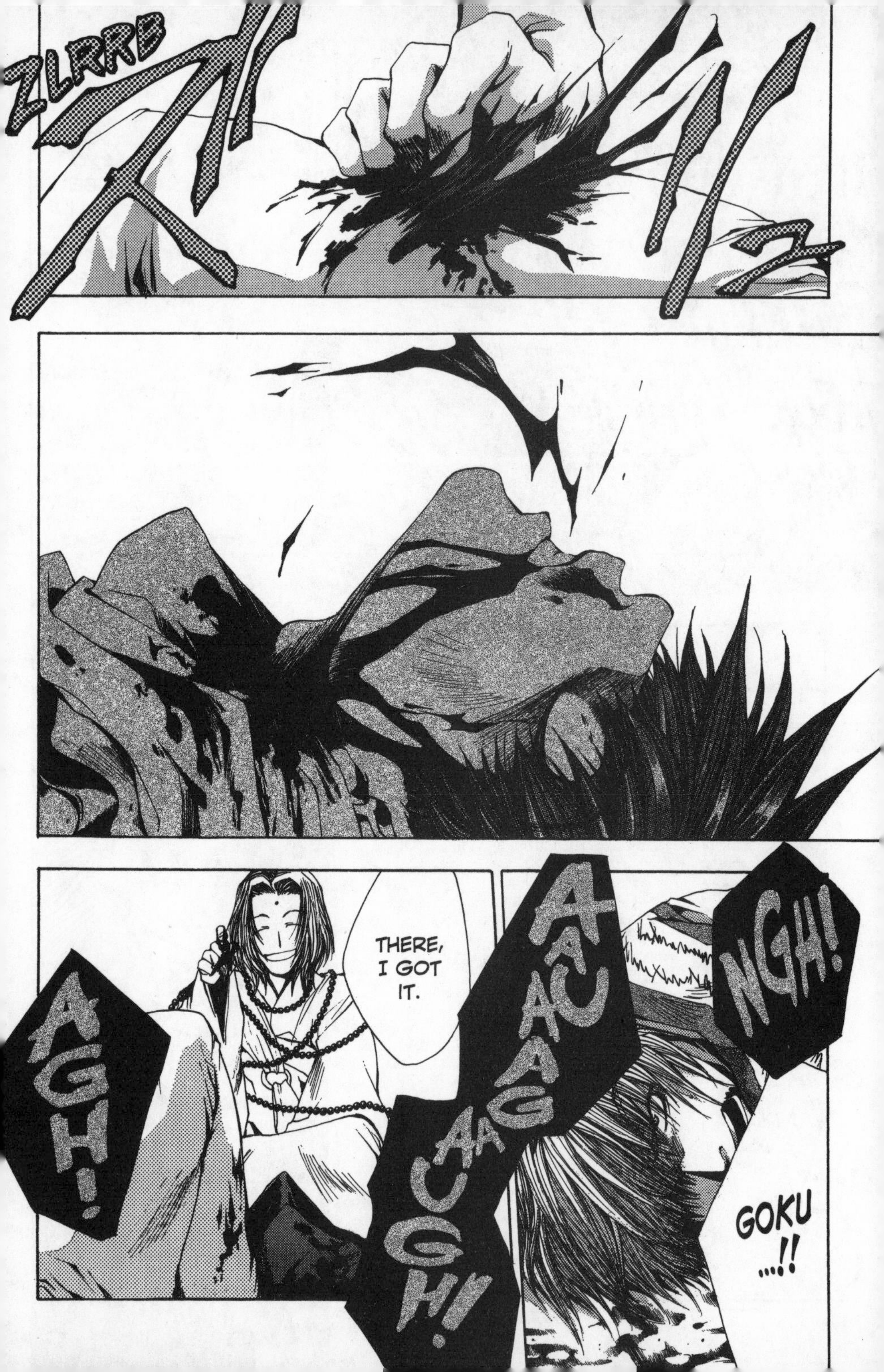
ZLRRB
NGH!
AAUAAGAAUGH!
GOKU ...!!
THERE, I GOT IT.
AGH!

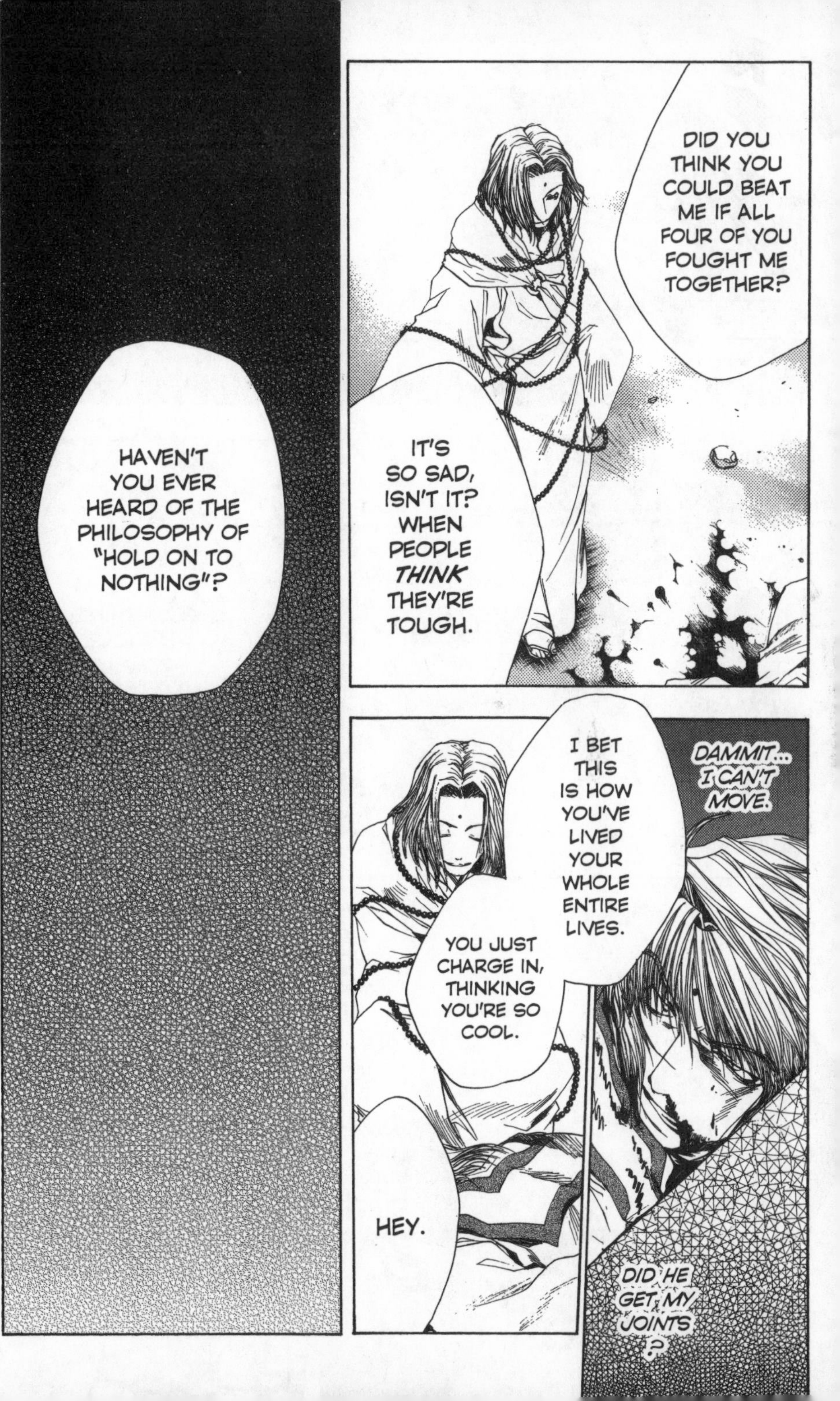
DID YOU THINK YOU COULD BEAT ME IF ALL FOUR OF YOU FOUGHT ME TOGETHER?
IT'S SO SAD, ISN'T IT? WHEN PEOPLE THINK THEY'RE TOUGH.
DAMMIT... I CAN'T MOVE.
I BET THIS IS HOW YOU'VE LIVED YOUR WHOLE ENTIRE LIVES.
YOU JUST CHARGE IN, THINKING YOU'RE SO COOL.
DID HE GET MY JOINTS?
HEY.
HAVEN'T YOU EVER HEARD OF THE PHILOSOPHY OF "HOLD ON TO NOTHING"?

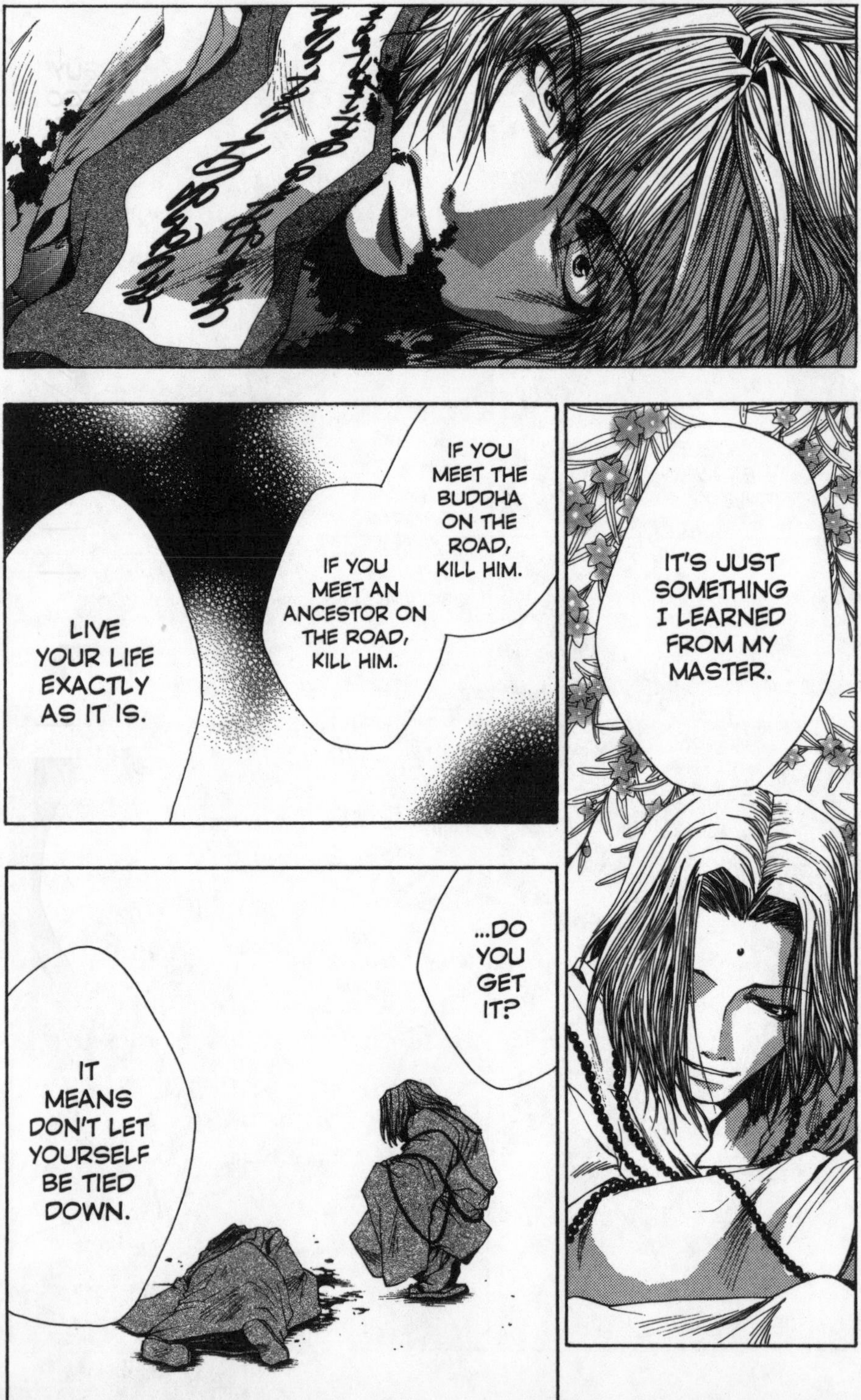
IT'S JUST SOMETHING I LEARNED FROM MY MASTER.
IF YOU MEET THE BUDDHA ON THE ROAD, KILL HIM.
IF YOU MEET AN ANCESTOR ON THE ROAD, KILL HIM.
LIVE YOUR LIFE EXACTLY AS IT IS.
...DO YOU GET IT?
IT MEANS DON'T LET YOURSELF BE TIED DOWN.

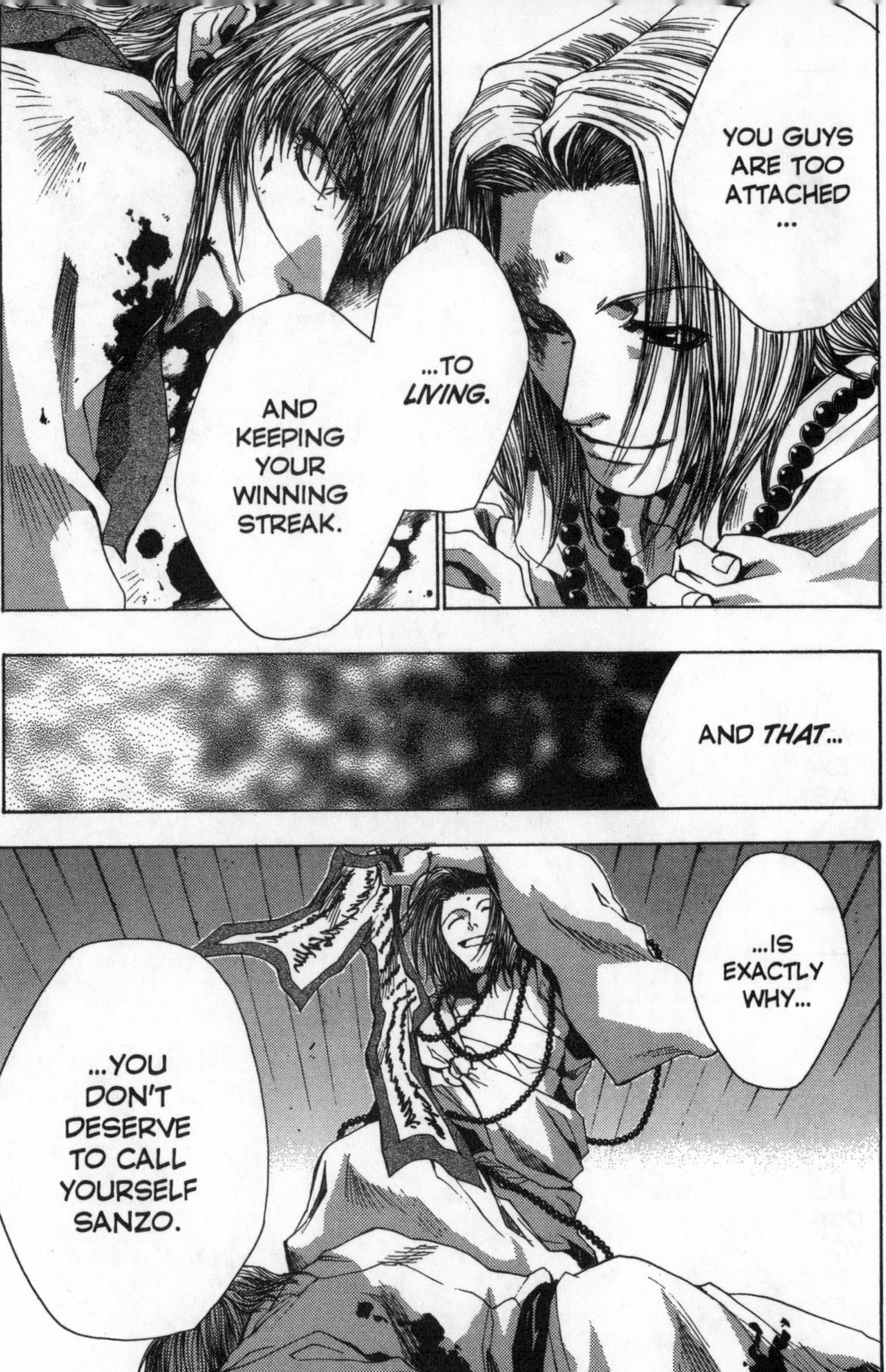
YOU GUYS ARE TOO ATTACHED ...
...TO *LIVING*.
AND KEEPING YOUR WINNING STREAK.
AND *THAT*...
...IS EXACTLY WHY...
...YOU DON'T DESERVE TO CALL YOURSELF SANZO.

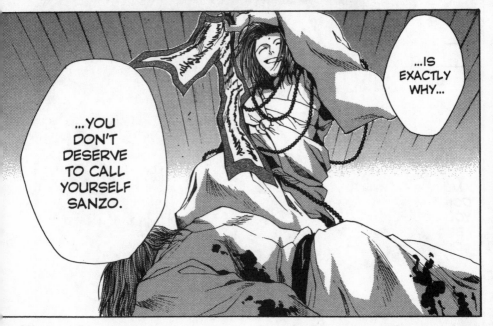

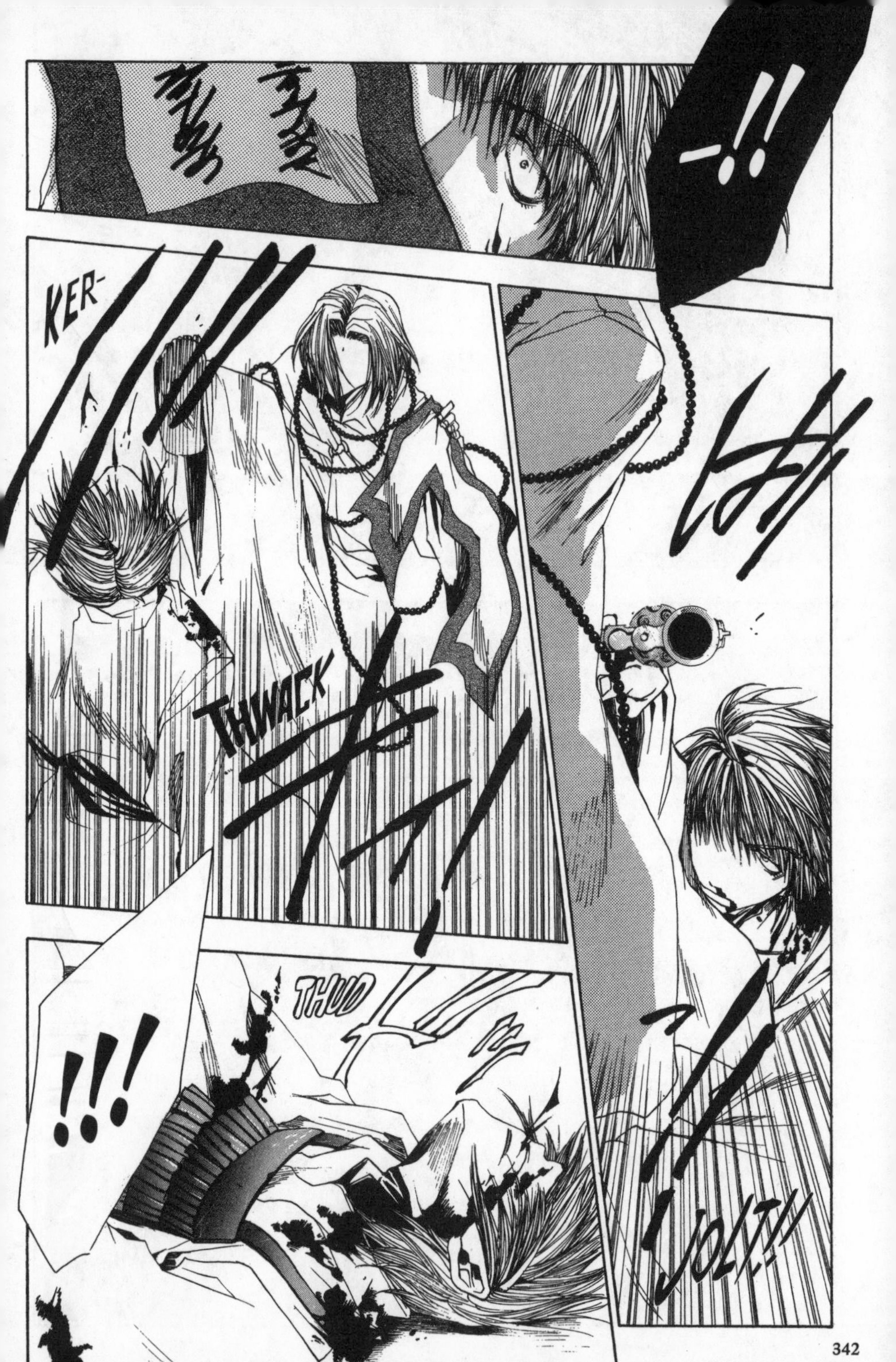
!!
KER-
THWACK
JOLT!!
THUD
!!!

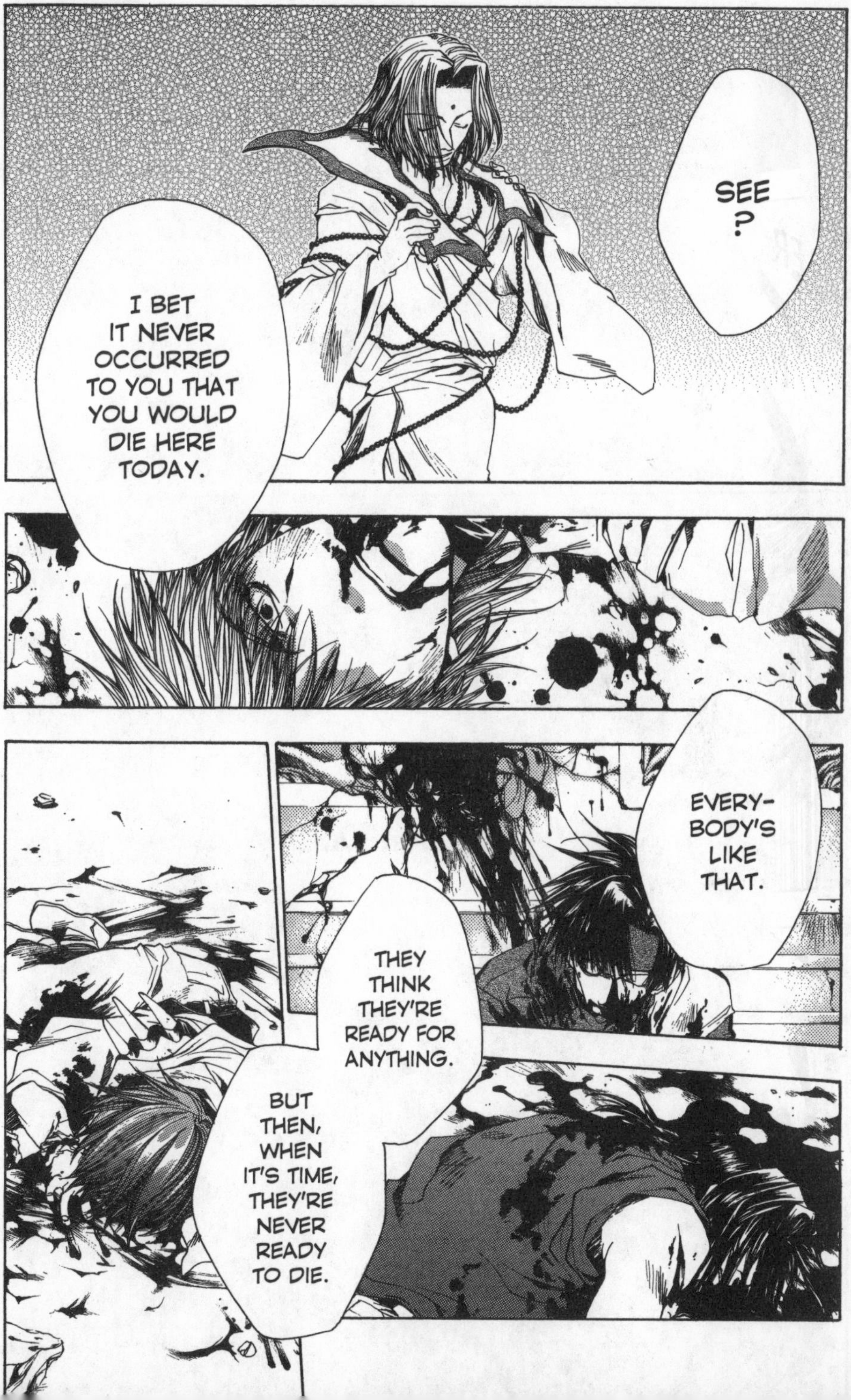
SEE?
I BET IT NEVER OCCURRED TO YOU THAT YOU WOULD DIE HERE TODAY.
EVERY-BODY'S LIKE THAT.
THEY THINK THEY'RE READY FOR ANYTHING.
BUT THEN, WHEN IT'S TIME, THEY'RE NEVER READY TO DIE.

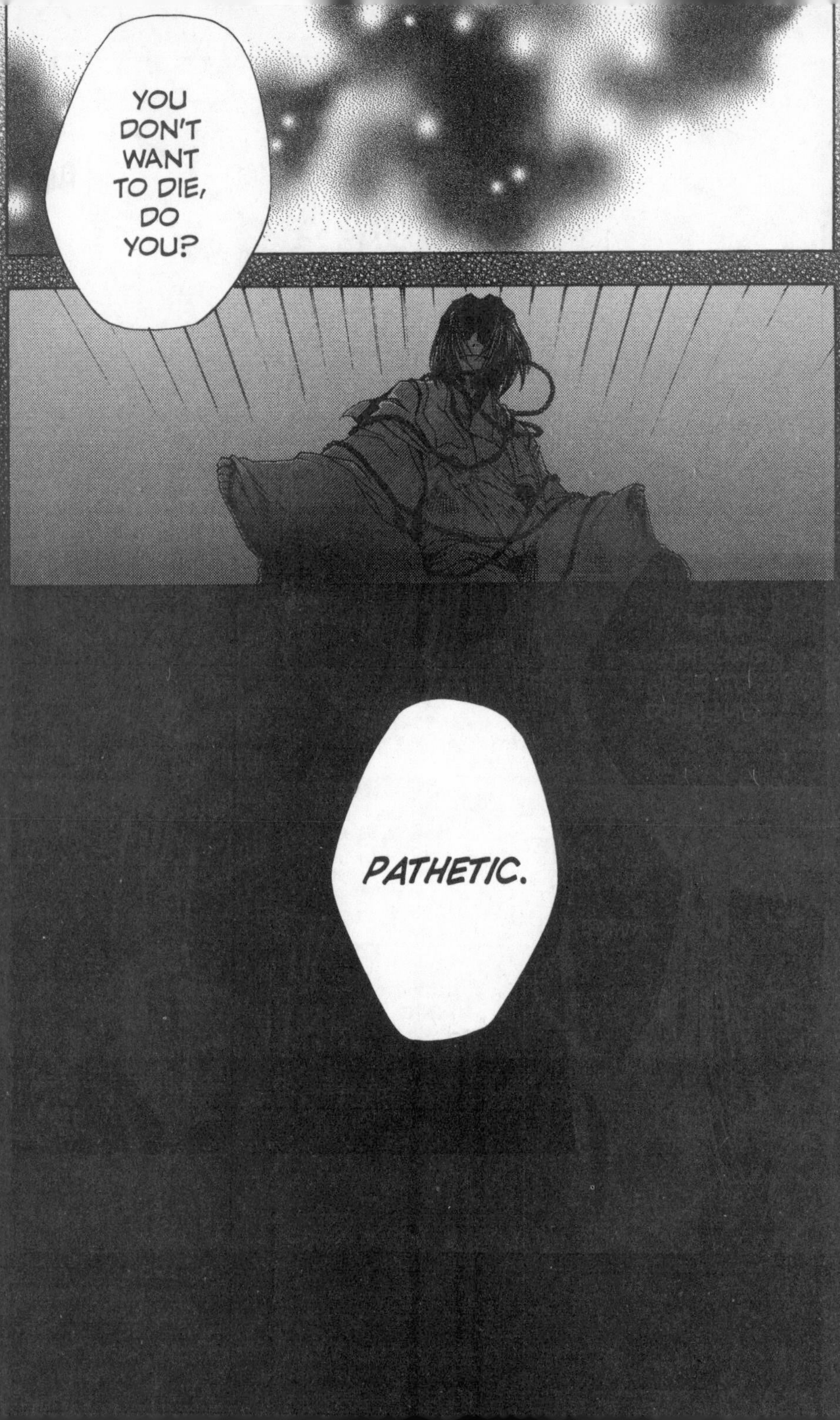
YOU DON'T WANT TO DIE, DO YOU?
PATHETIC.

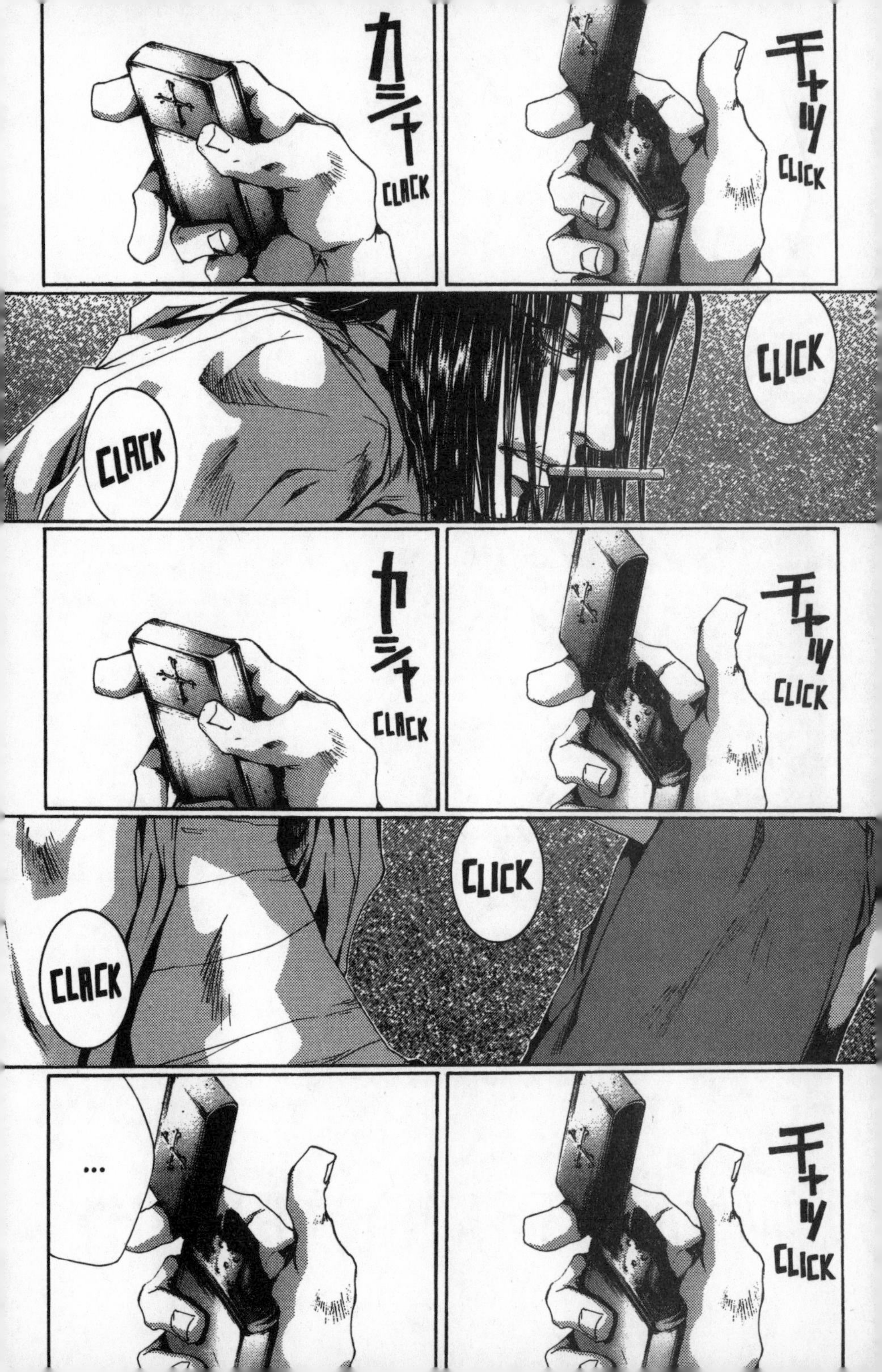
チャッ
CLICK
カシャ
CLACK
CLICK
CLACK
チャッ
CLICK
カシャ
CLACK
CLICK
CLACK
チャッ
CLICK
...

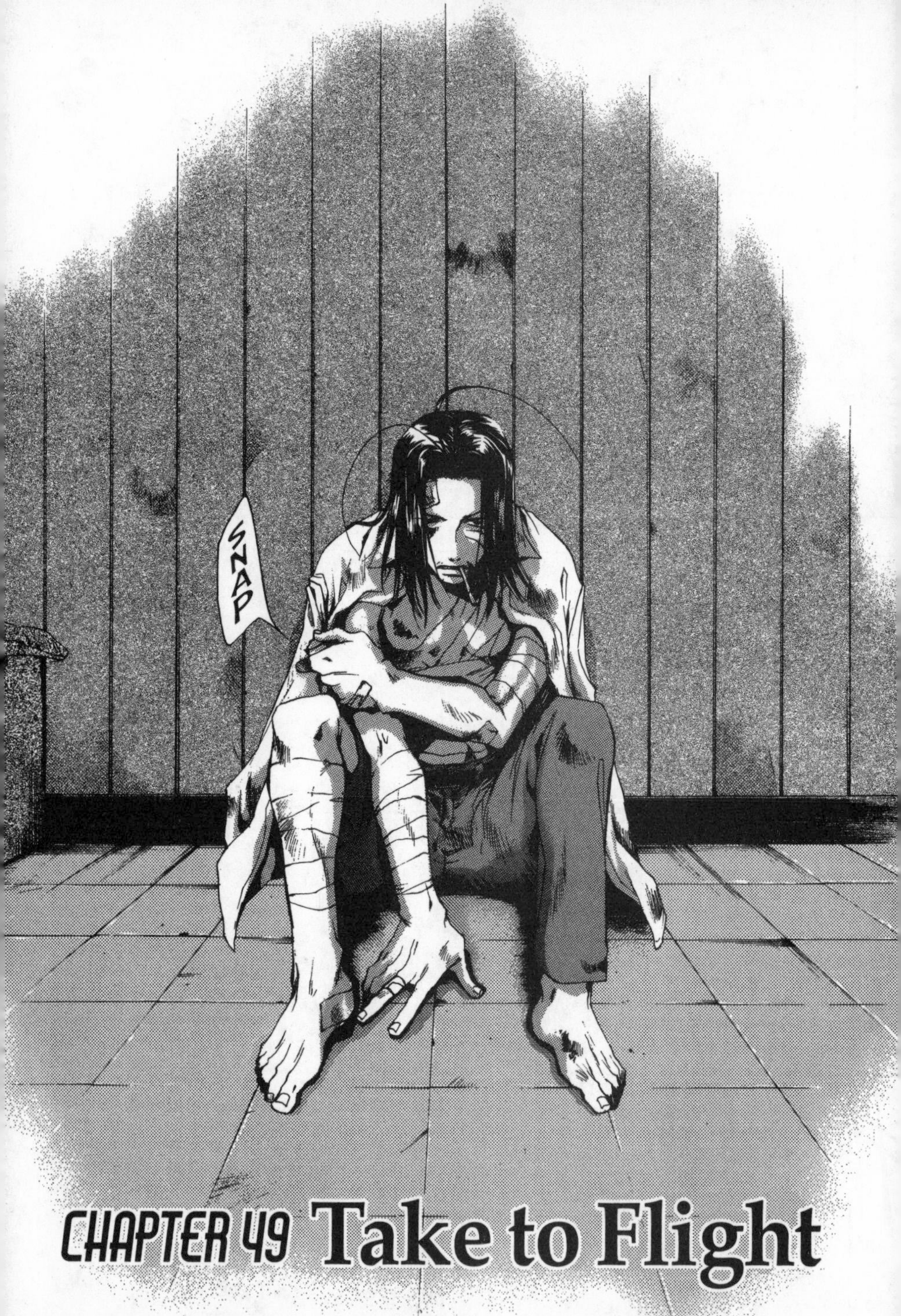
SNAP

CHAPTER 49 Take to Flight

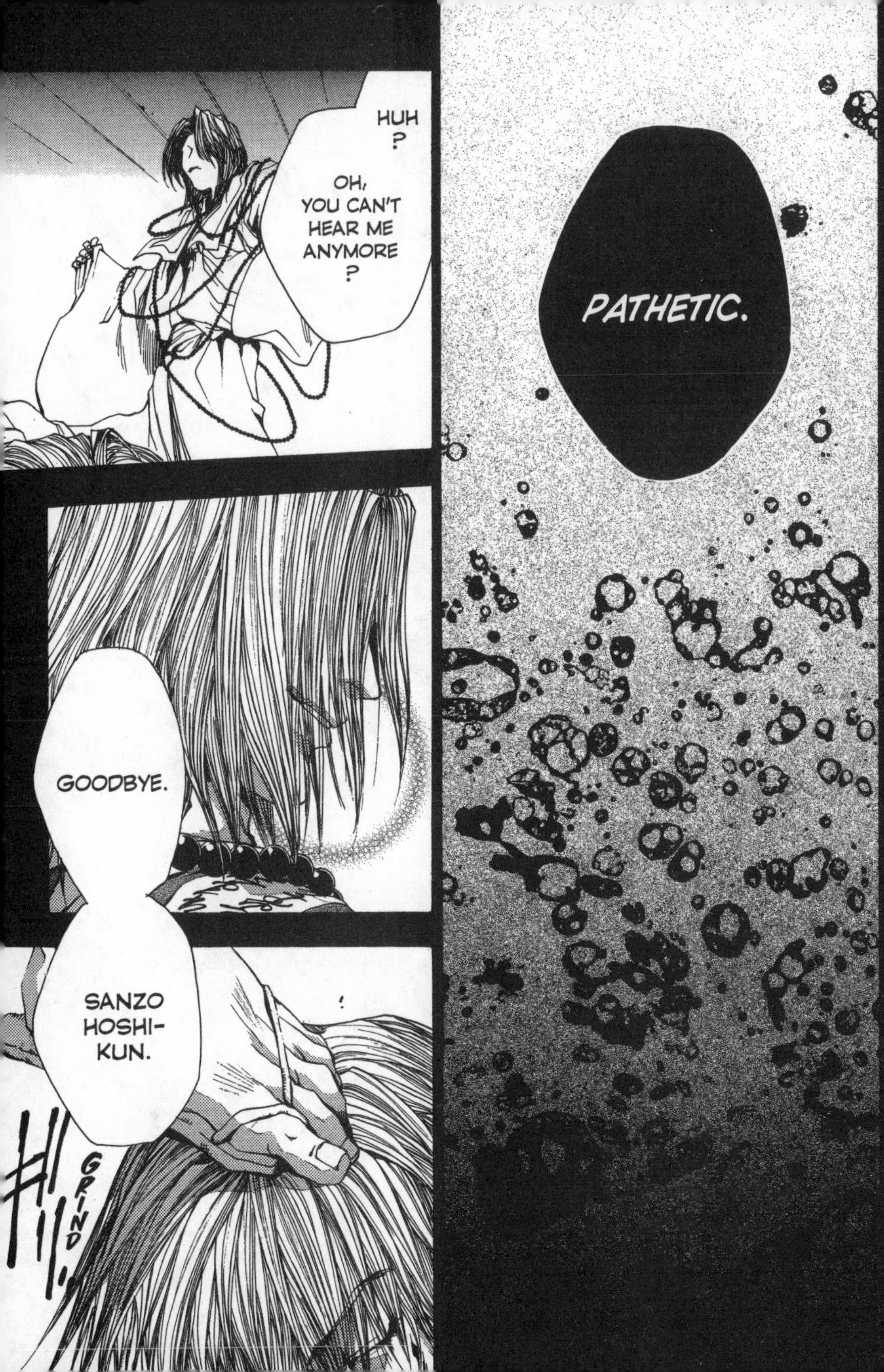
PATHETIC.
HUH?
OH, YOU CAN'T HEAR ME ANYMORE?
GOODBYE.
SANZO HOSHI-KUN.
!
GRIND

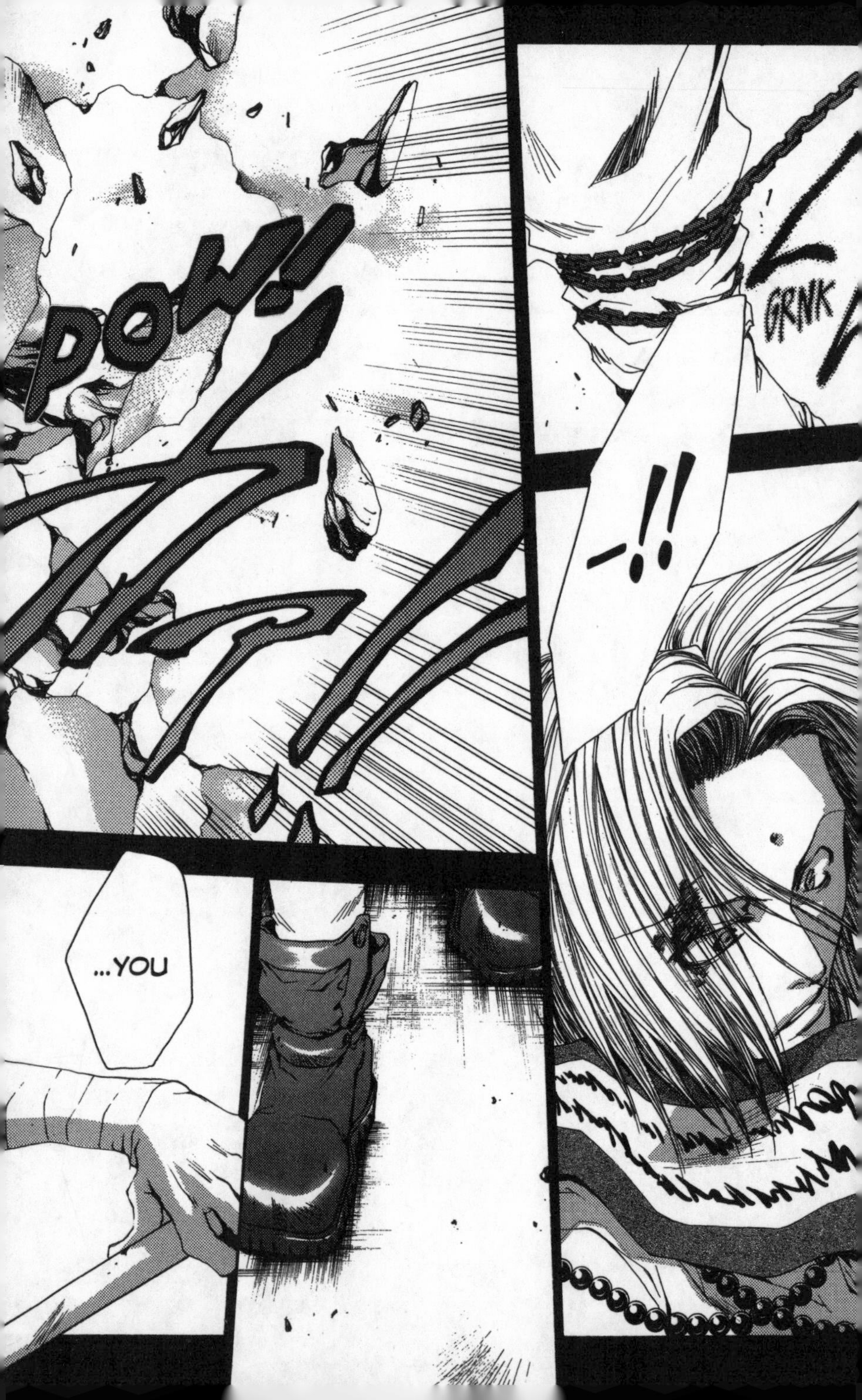
GRNK
—!!
POW!!
...YOU

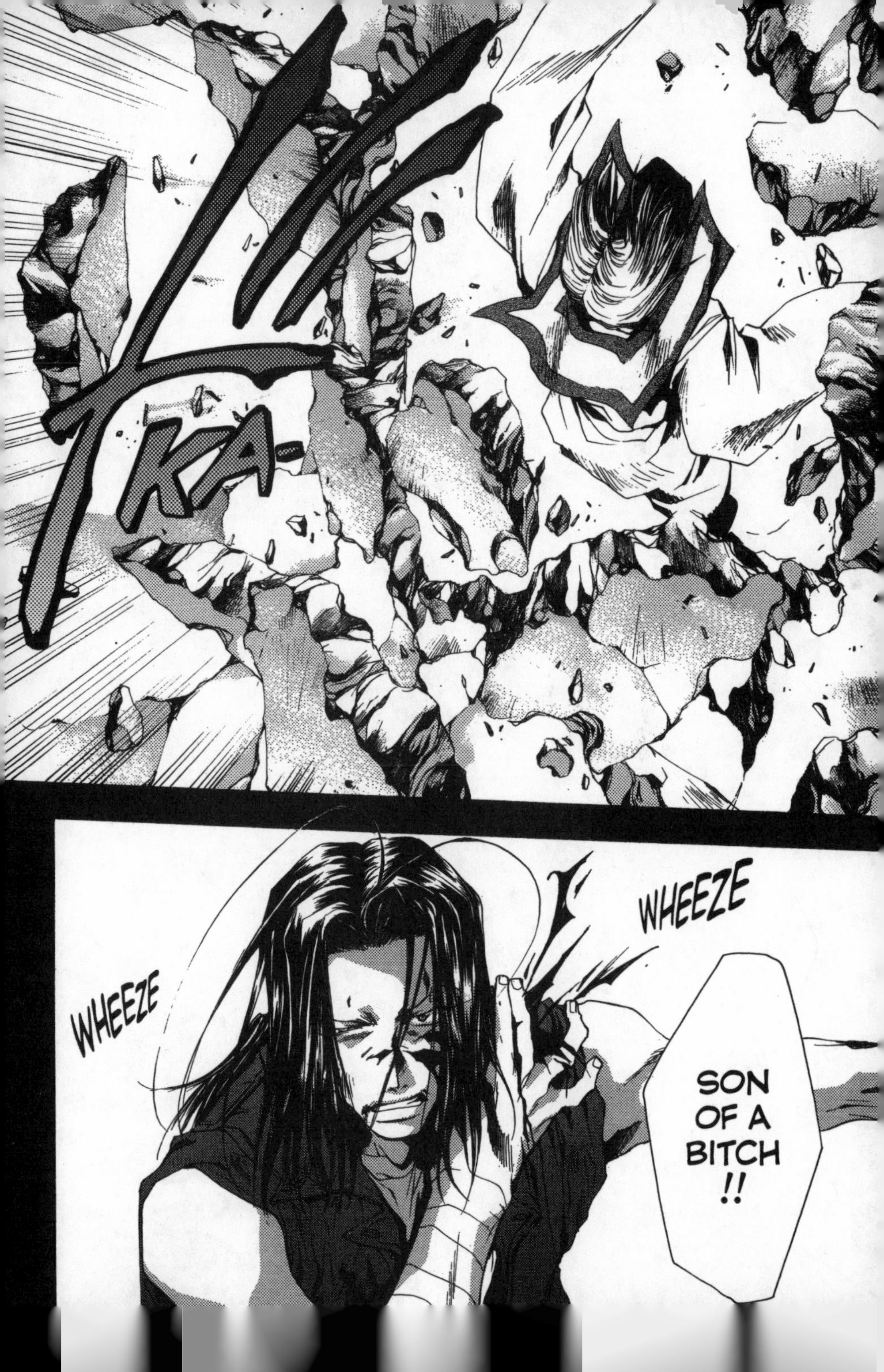
KA-
WHEEZE
SON OF A BITCH!!
WHEEZE

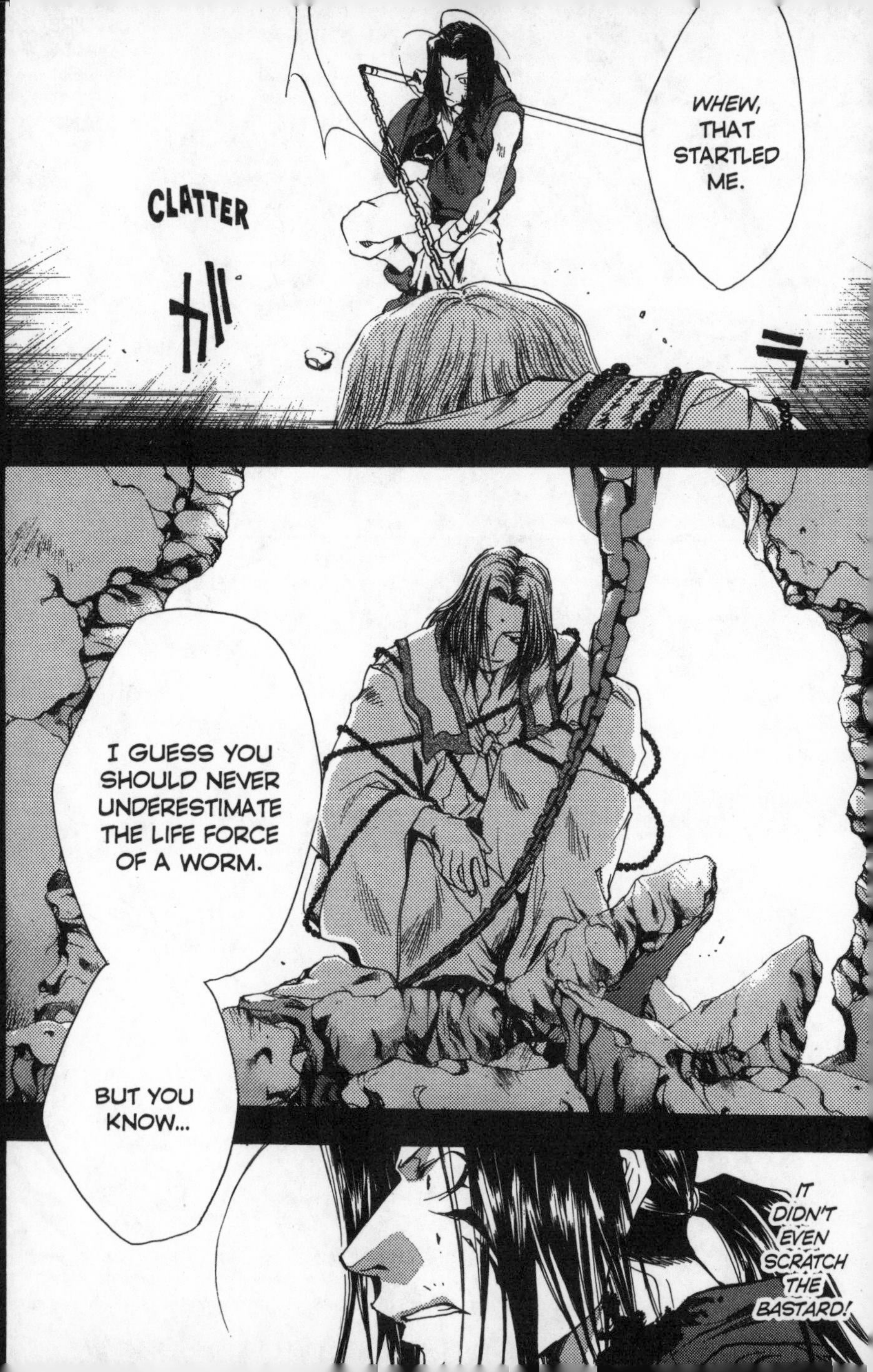
WHEW, THAT STARTLED ME.
CLATTER
ガ
ラ
I GUESS YOU SHOULD NEVER UNDERESTIMATE THE LIFE FORCE OF A WORM.
BUT YOU KNOW...
IT DIDN'T EVEN SCRATCH THE BASTARD!

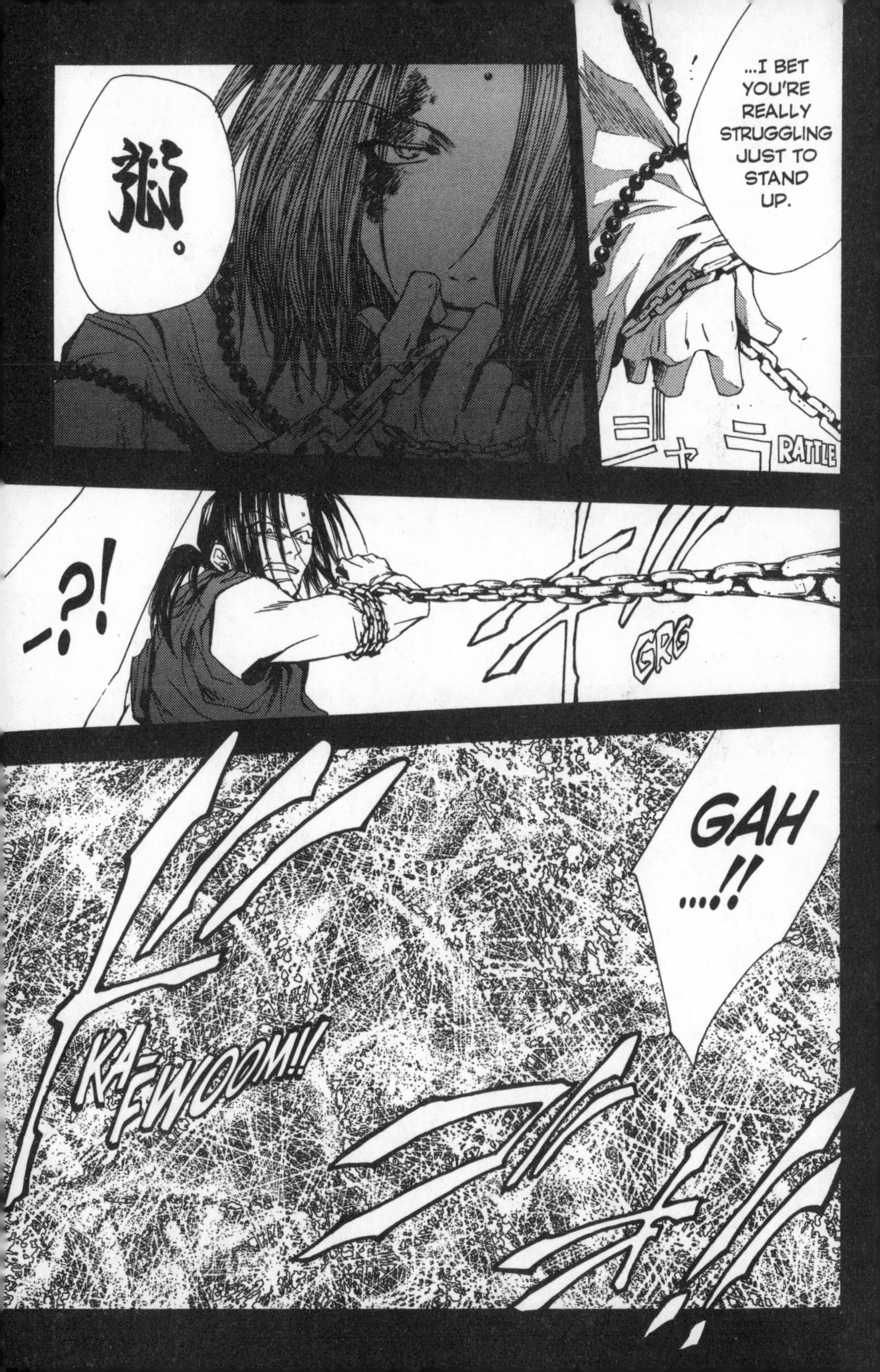
...I BET YOU'RE REALLY STRUGGLING JUST TO STAND UP.
RATTLE
-?!
GRG
GAH
....!!
KA-FWOOM!!

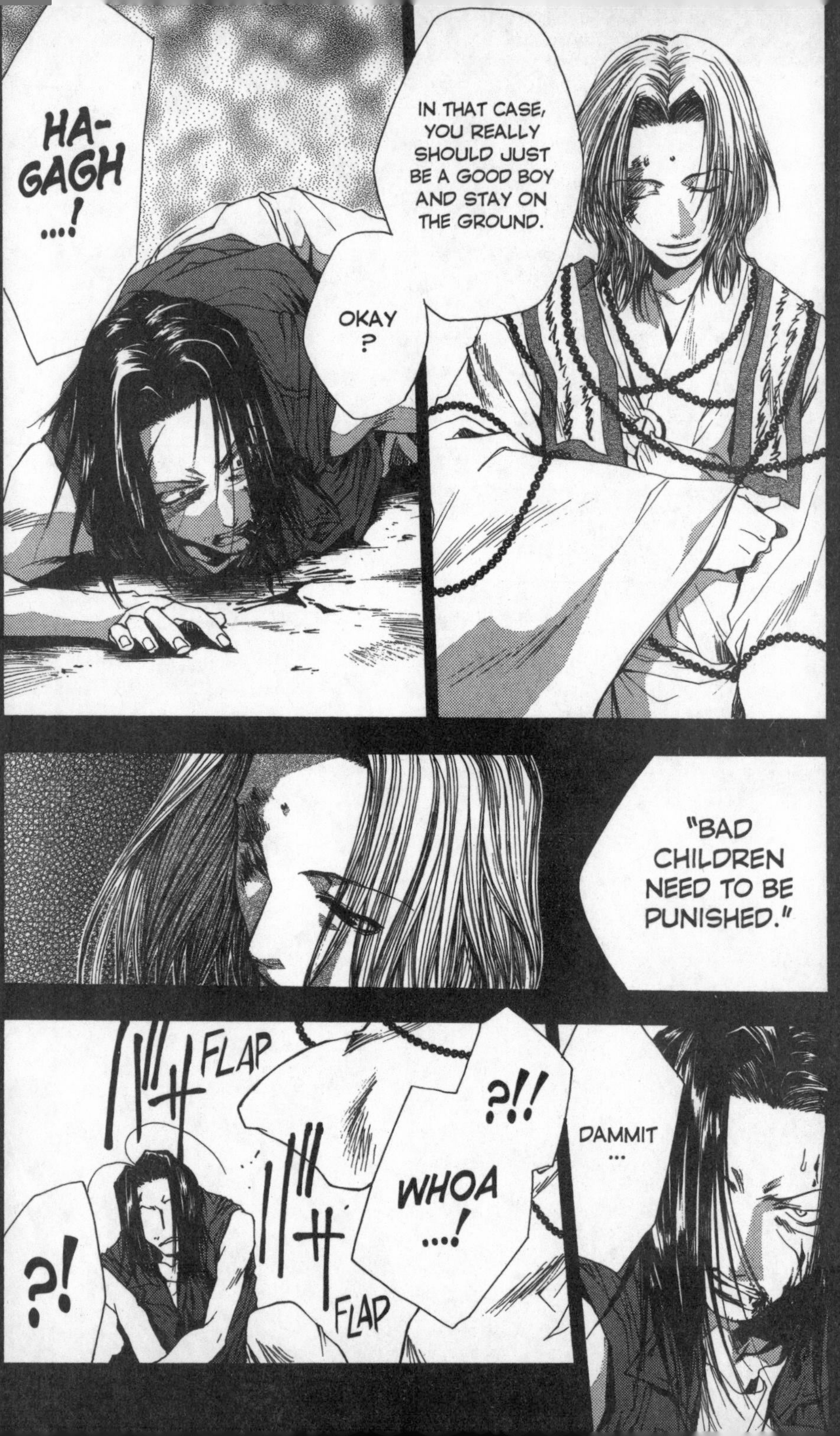
IN THAT CASE, YOU REALLY SHOULD JUST BE A GOOD BOY AND STAY ON THE GROUND.
OKAY ?
HA-GAGH ...!
"BAD CHILDREN NEED TO BE PUNISHED."
DAMMIT ...
?!!
FLAP
WHOA ...!
?!
FLAP

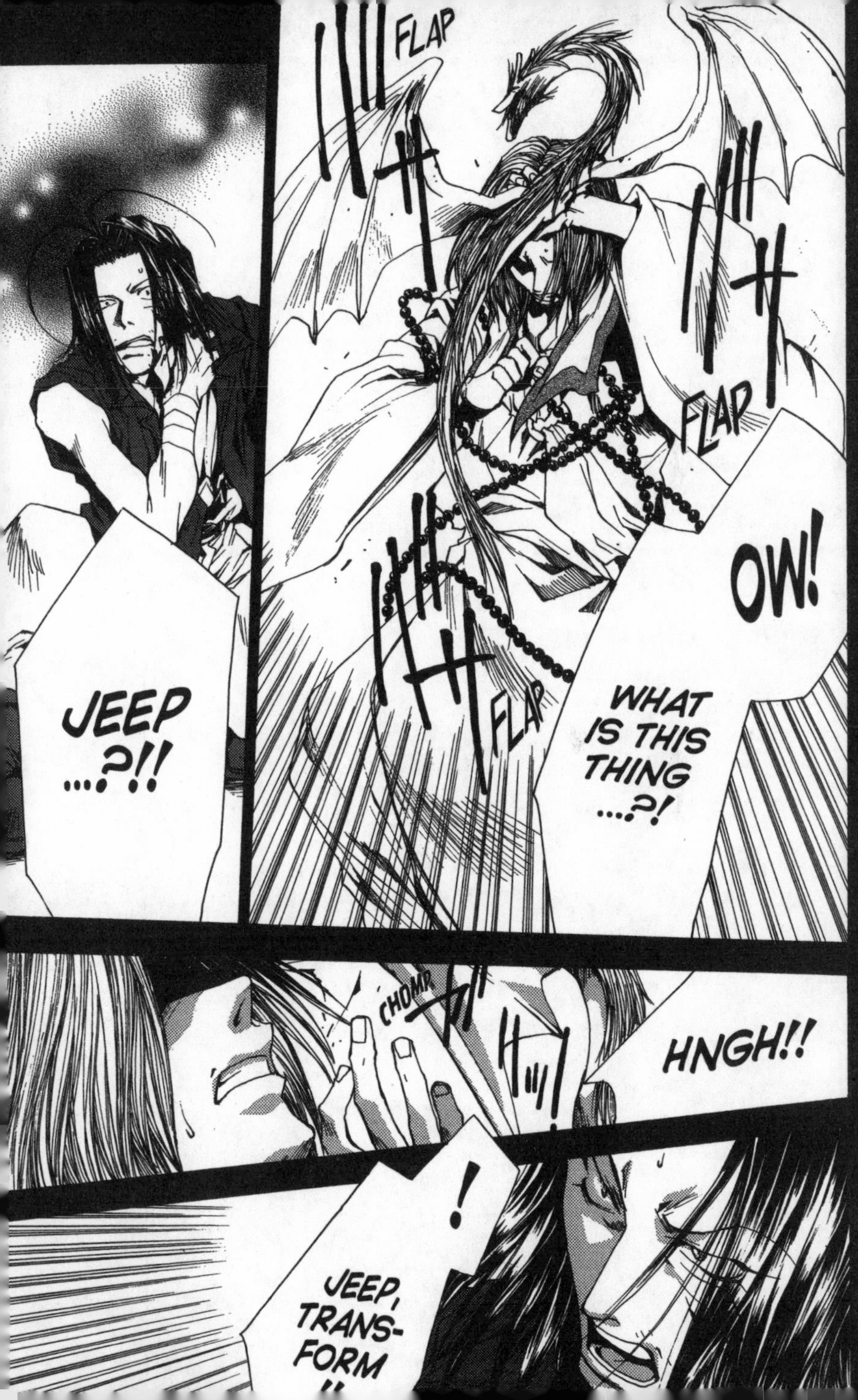
FLAP
FLAP
OW!
FLAP
WHAT IS THIS THING ...?!
JEEP ...?!!
HNGH!!
CHOMP
!
JEEP, TRANS-FORM

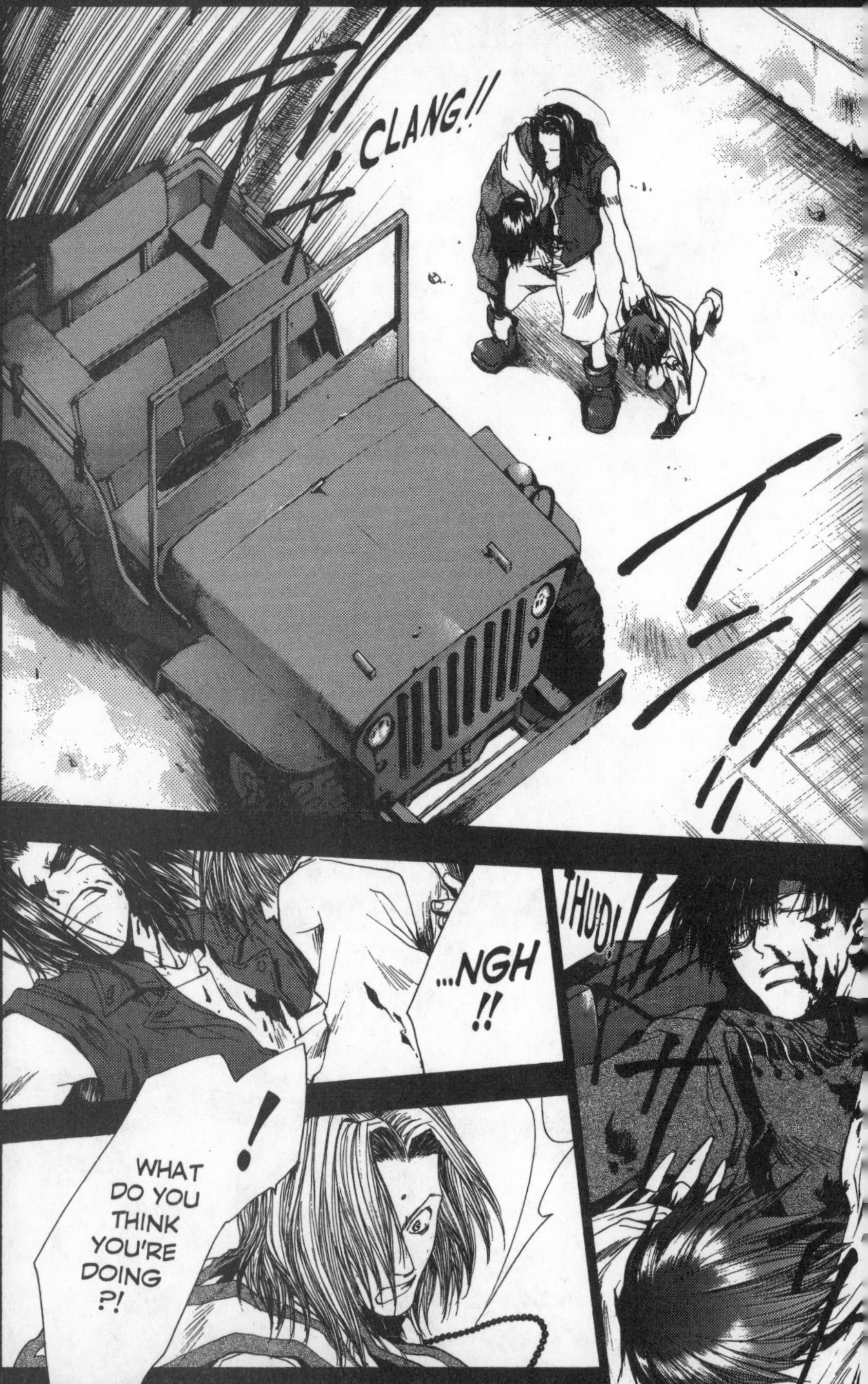
CLANG!!
THUD!
...NGH !!
!
WHAT DO YOU THINK YOU'RE DOING ?!

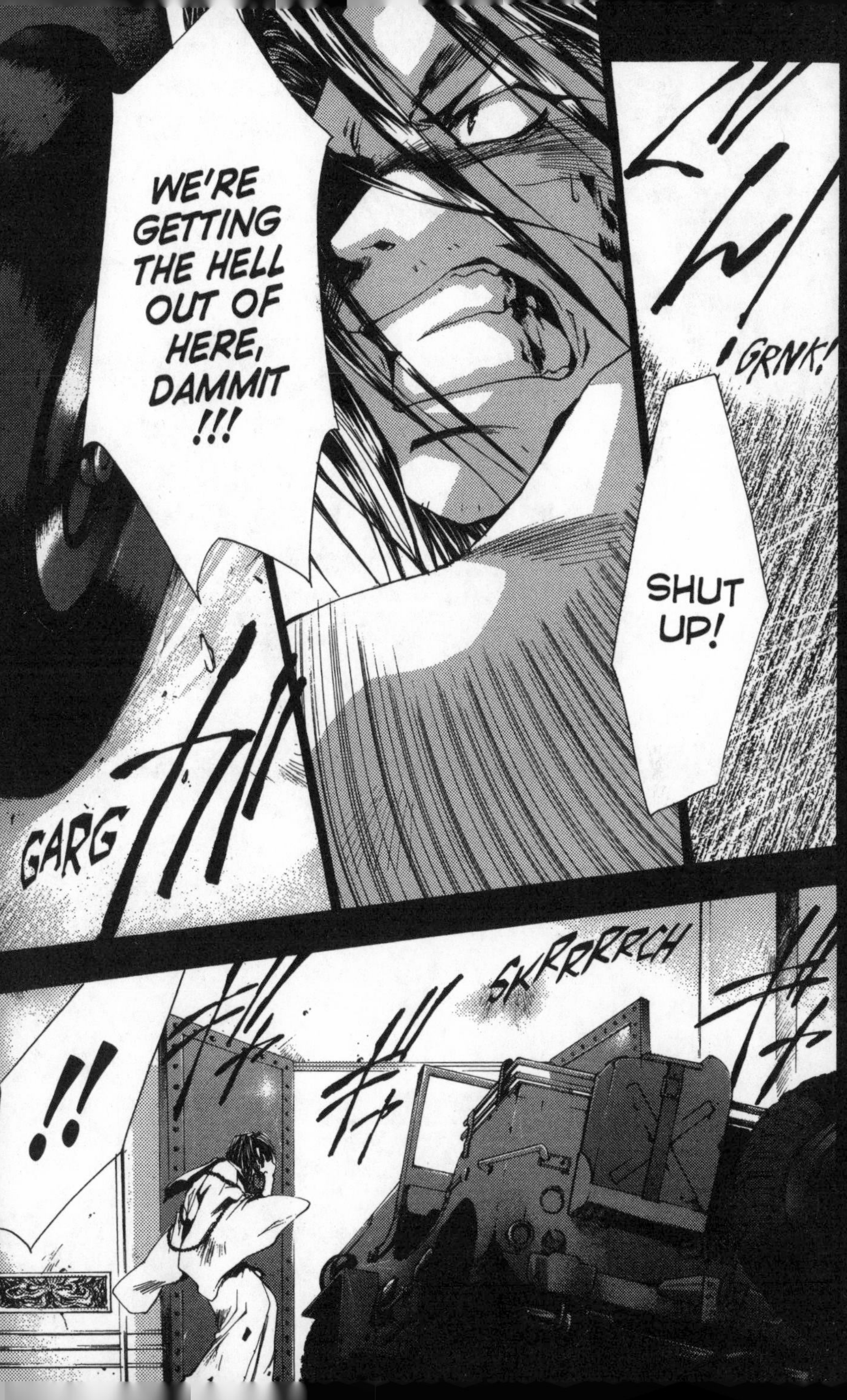
GRNK!
SHUT UP!
WE'RE GETTING THE HELL OUT OF HERE, DAMMIT !!!
GARG
SKRRRRCH
!!

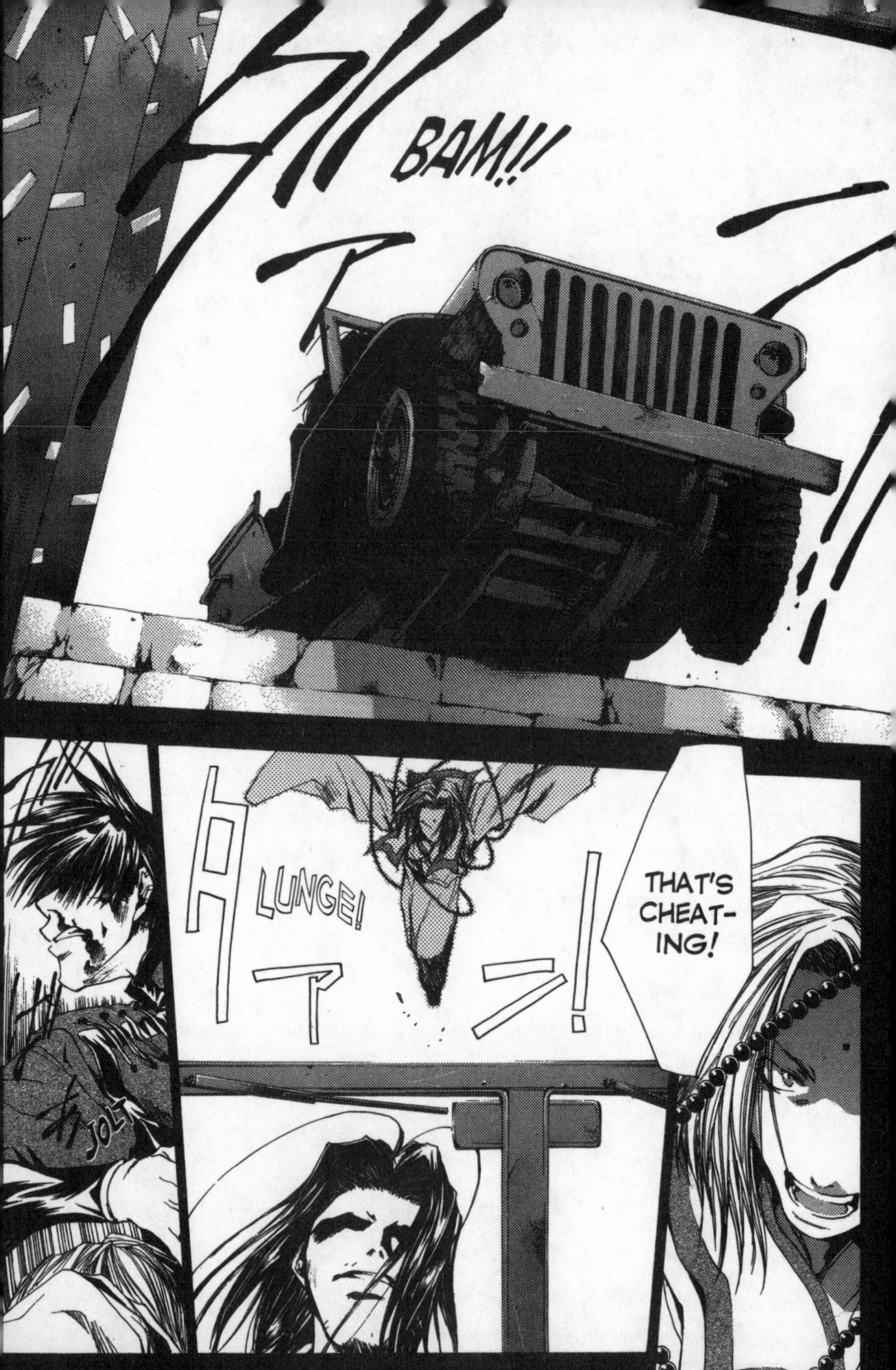
BAM!!
THAT'S CHEAT-ING!
LUNGE!
JOLT

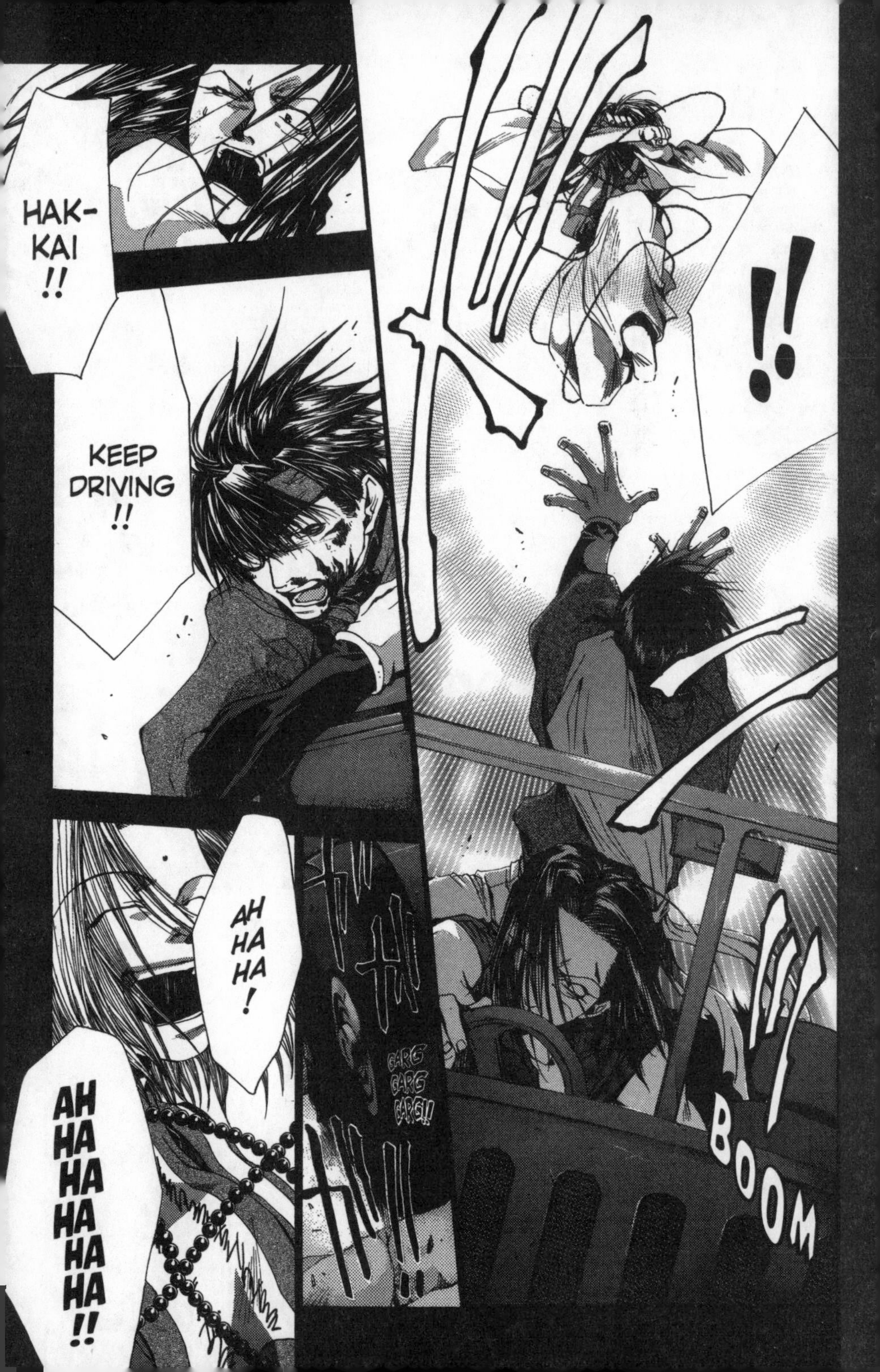
!!
HAK-KAI!!
KEEP DRIVING!!
BOOM
GARG GARG GARG!!
AH HA HA!
AH HA HA HA HA HA!!

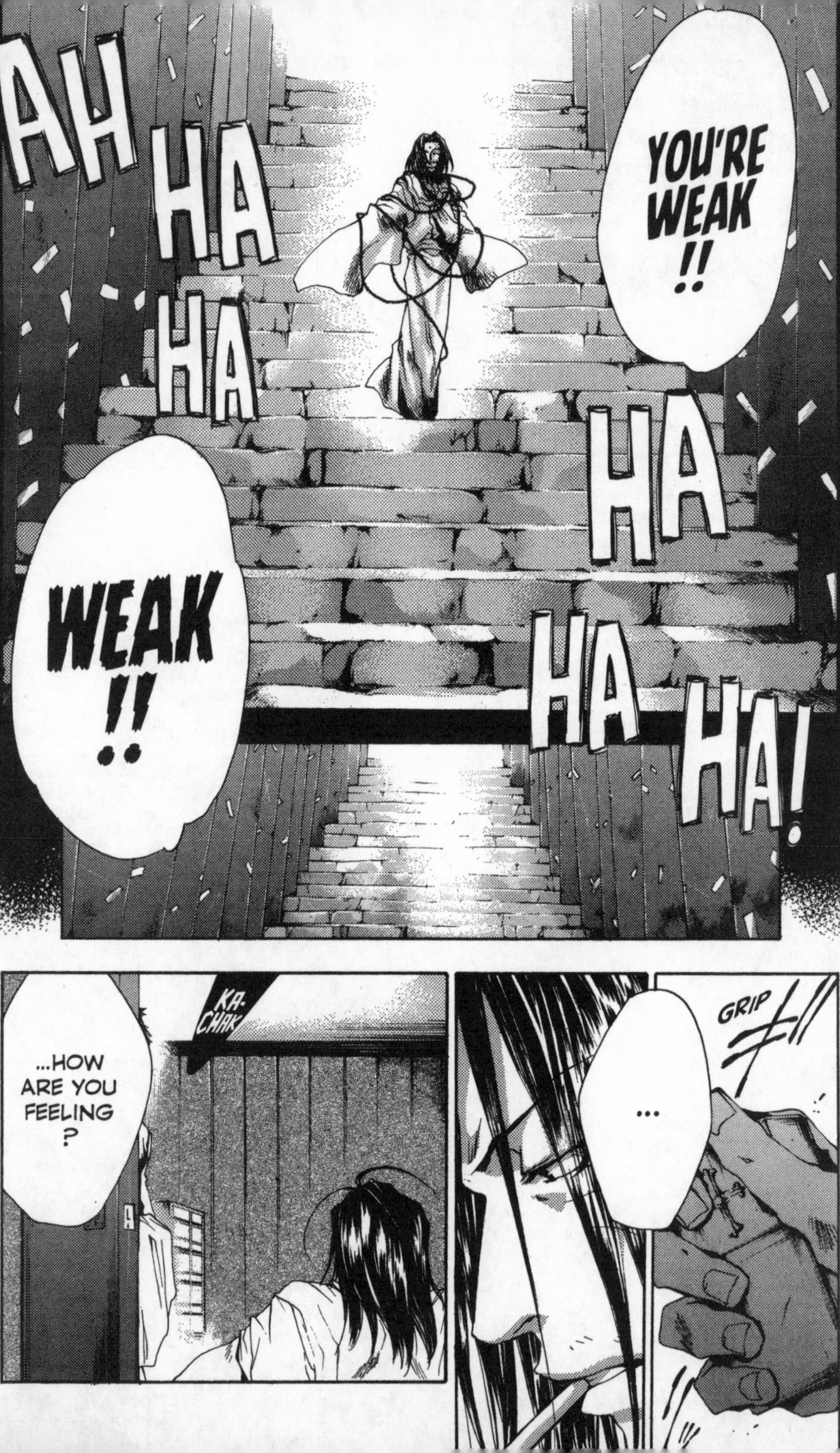
YOU'RE WEAK!!
AH HA HA HA
HA HA HA HA!
WEAK!!
GRIP
...
KA-CHAK
...HOW ARE YOU FEELING?

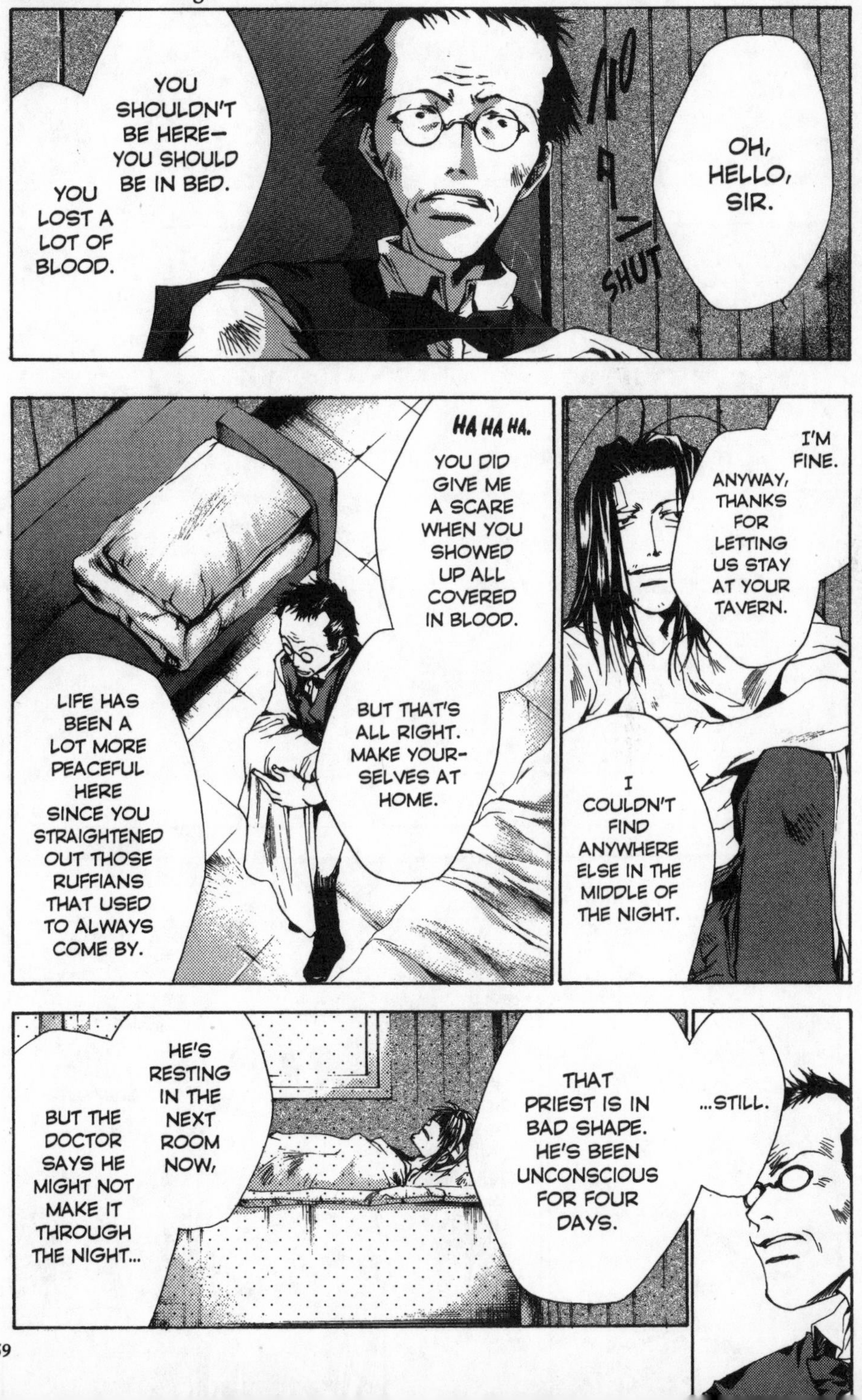
OH, HELLO, SIR.
SHUT
YOU SHOULDN'T BE HERE— YOU SHOULD BE IN BED.
YOU LOST A LOT OF BLOOD.
I'M FINE.
ANYWAY, THANKS FOR LETTING US STAY AT YOUR TAVERN.
I COULDN'T FIND ANYWHERE ELSE IN THE MIDDLE OF THE NIGHT.
HA HA HA.
YOU DID GIVE ME A SCARE WHEN YOU SHOWED UP ALL COVERED IN BLOOD.
BUT THAT'S ALL RIGHT. MAKE YOUR-SELVES AT HOME.
LIFE HAS BEEN A LOT MORE PEACEFUL HERE SINCE YOU STRAIGHTENED OUT THOSE RUFFIANS THAT USED TO ALWAYS COME BY.
...STILL.
THAT PRIEST IS IN BAD SHAPE. HE'S BEEN UNCONSCIOUS FOR FOUR DAYS.
HE'S RESTING IN THE NEXT ROOM NOW,
BUT THE DOCTOR SAYS HE MIGHT NOT MAKE IT THROUGH THE NIGHT...

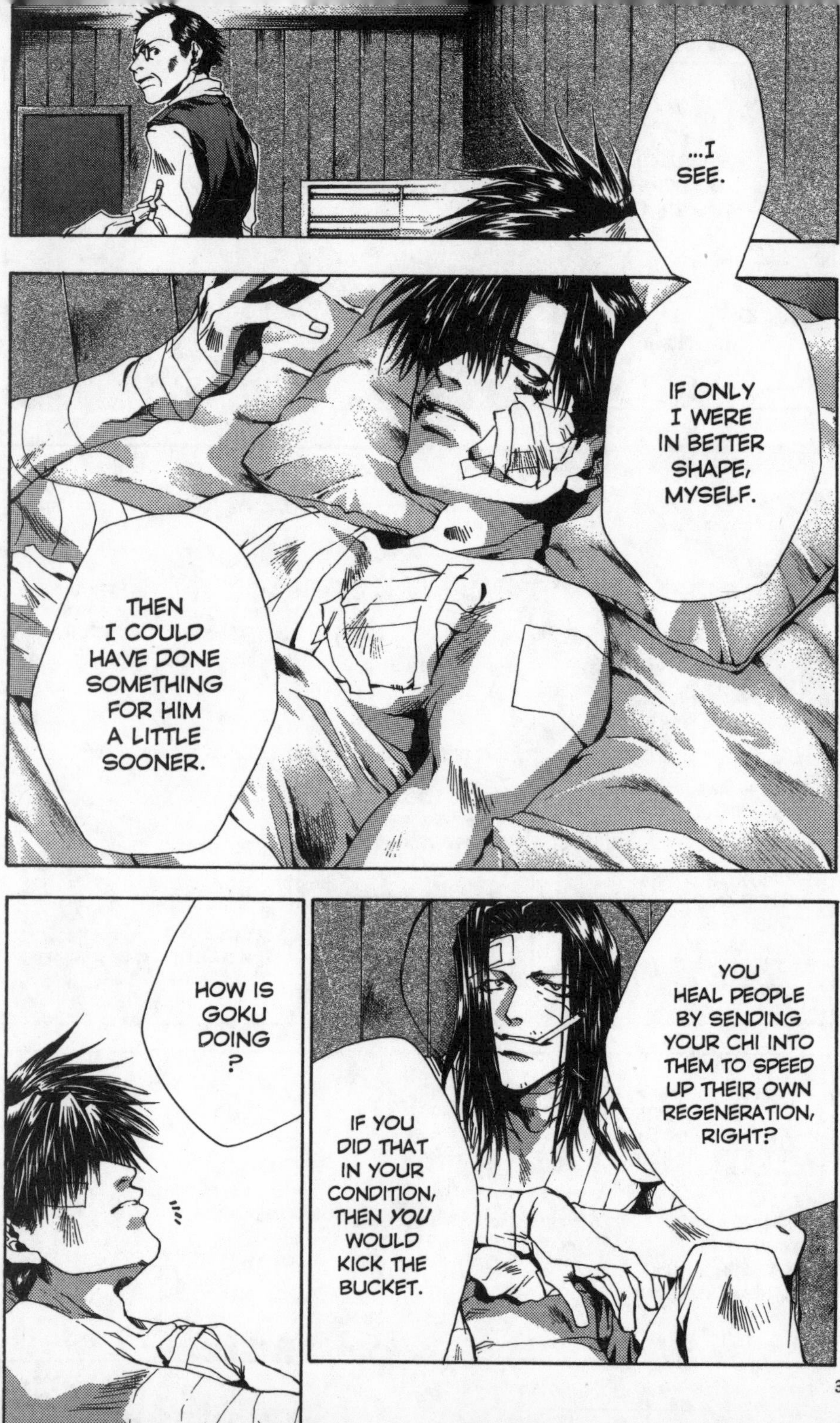
...I SEE.
IF ONLY I WERE IN BETTER SHAPE, MYSELF.
THEN I COULD HAVE DONE SOMETHING FOR HIM A LITTLE SOONER.
YOU HEAL PEOPLE BY SENDING YOUR CHI INTO THEM TO SPEED UP THEIR OWN REGENERATION, RIGHT?
IF YOU DID THAT IN YOUR CONDITION, THEN *YOU* WOULD KICK THE BUCKET.
HOW IS GOKU DOING?

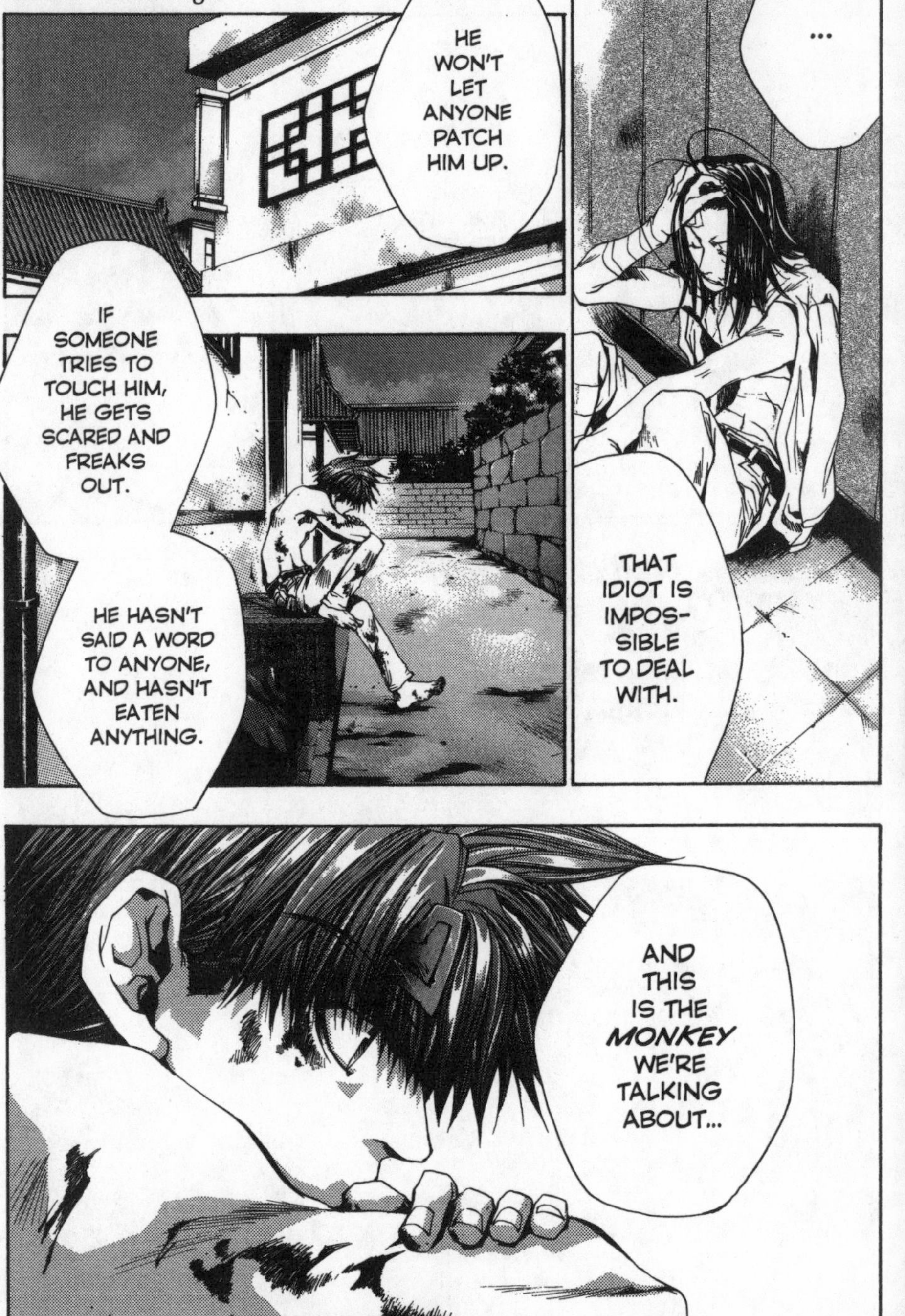
...
THAT IDIOT IS IMPOSSIBLE TO DEAL WITH.
HE WON'T LET ANYONE PATCH HIM UP.
IF SOMEONE TRIES TO TOUCH HIM, HE GETS SCARED AND FREAKS OUT.
HE HASN'T SAID A WORD TO ANYONE, AND HASN'T EATEN ANYTHING.
AND THIS IS THE *MONKEY* WE'RE TALKING ABOUT...

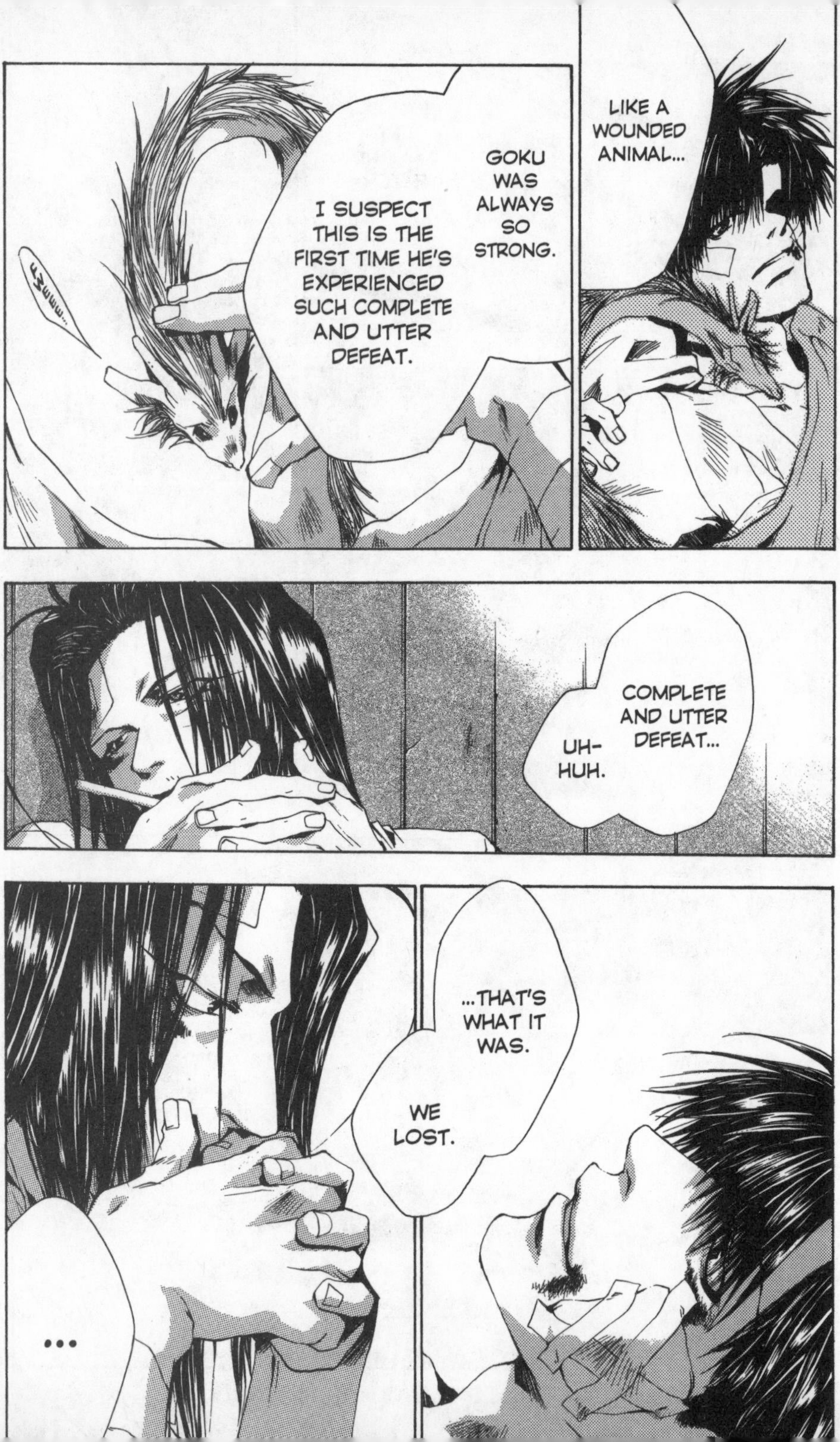
LIKE A WOUNDED ANIMAL...
GOKU WAS ALWAYS SO STRONG.
I SUSPECT THIS IS THE FIRST TIME HE'S EXPERIENCED SUCH COMPLETE AND UTTER DEFEAT.
COMPLETE AND UTTER DEFEAT...
UH-HUH.
...THAT'S WHAT IT WAS.
WE LOST.
...

CHAPTER 49: Take to Flight

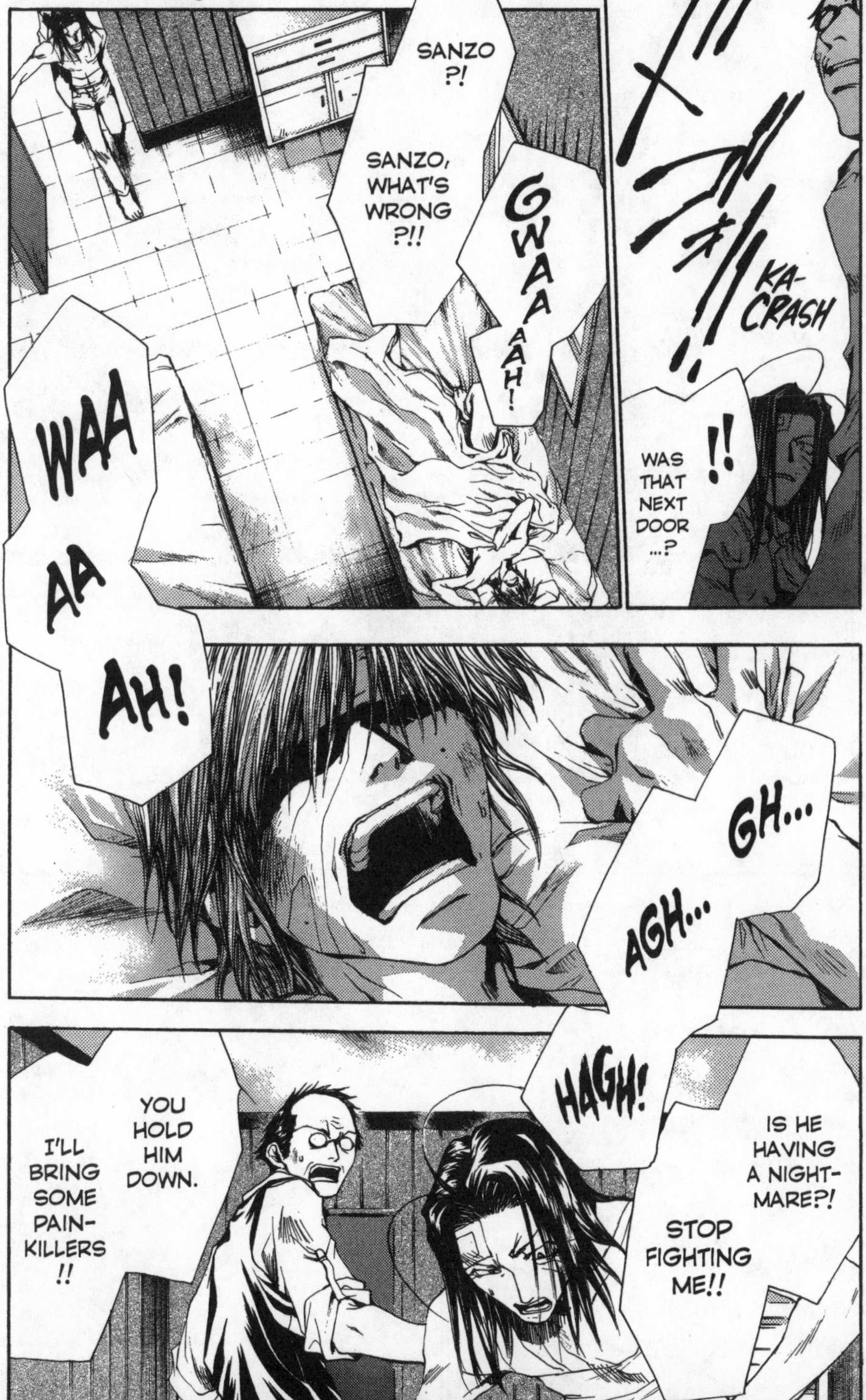
KA-CRASH
!!
WAS THAT NEXT DOOR ...?
SANZO ?!
SANZO, WHAT'S WRONG ?!!
GWAAAAH!
WAAAAAH!
GH...
AGH...
HAGH!
IS HE HAVING A NIGHT-MARE?!
STOP FIGHTING ME!!
YOU HOLD HIM DOWN.
I'LL BRING SOME PAIN-KILLERS !!

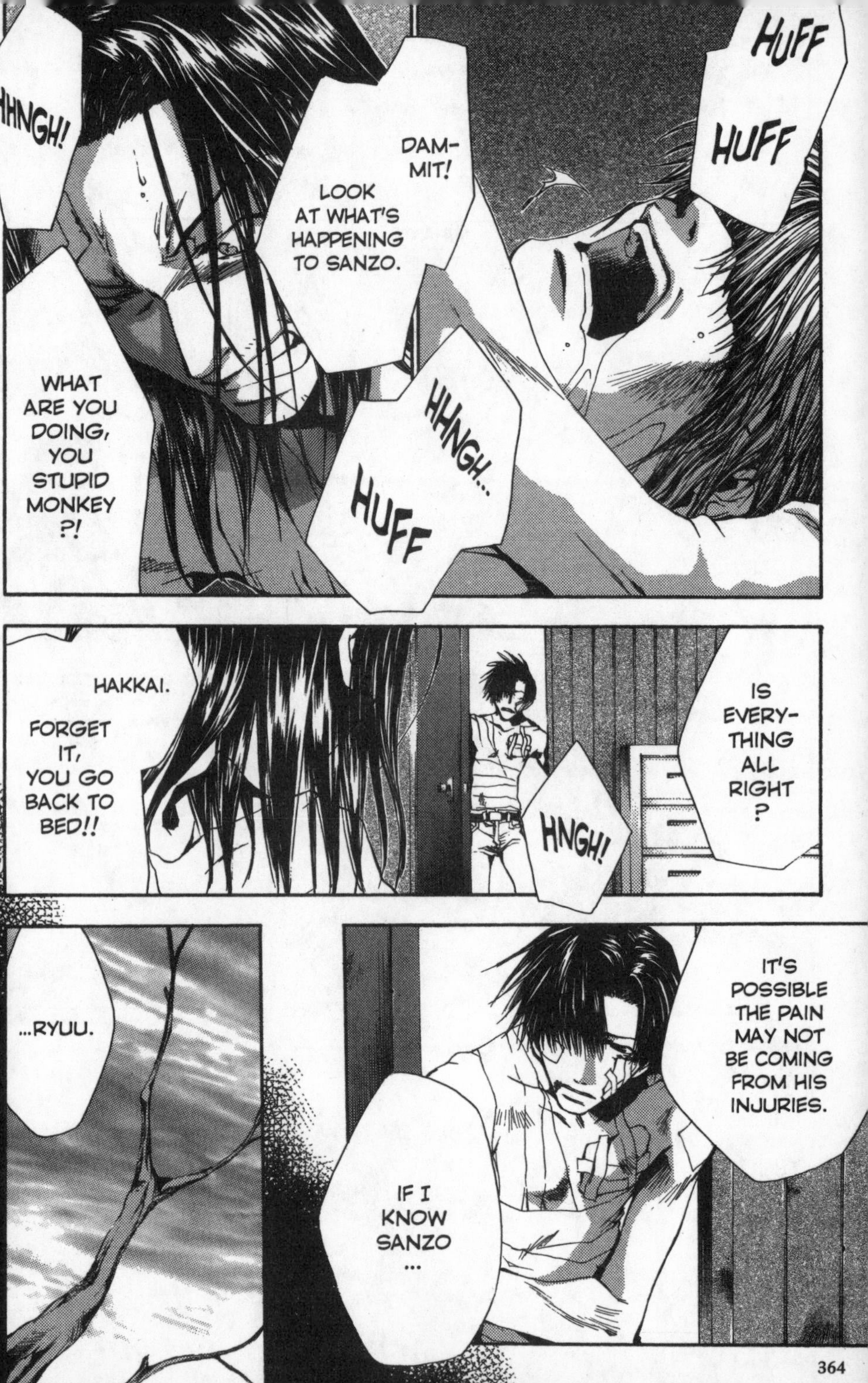
HUFF
HUFF
DAM-MIT!
LOOK AT WHAT'S HAPPENING TO SANZO.
HHNGH!
HHNGH...
HUFF
WHAT ARE YOU DOING, YOU STUPID MONKEY ?!
IS EVERY-THING ALL RIGHT ?
HNGH!
HAKKAI.
FORGET IT, YOU GO BACK TO BED!!
IT'S POSSIBLE THE PAIN MAY NOT BE COMING FROM HIS INJURIES.
IF I KNOW SANZO ...
...RYUU.

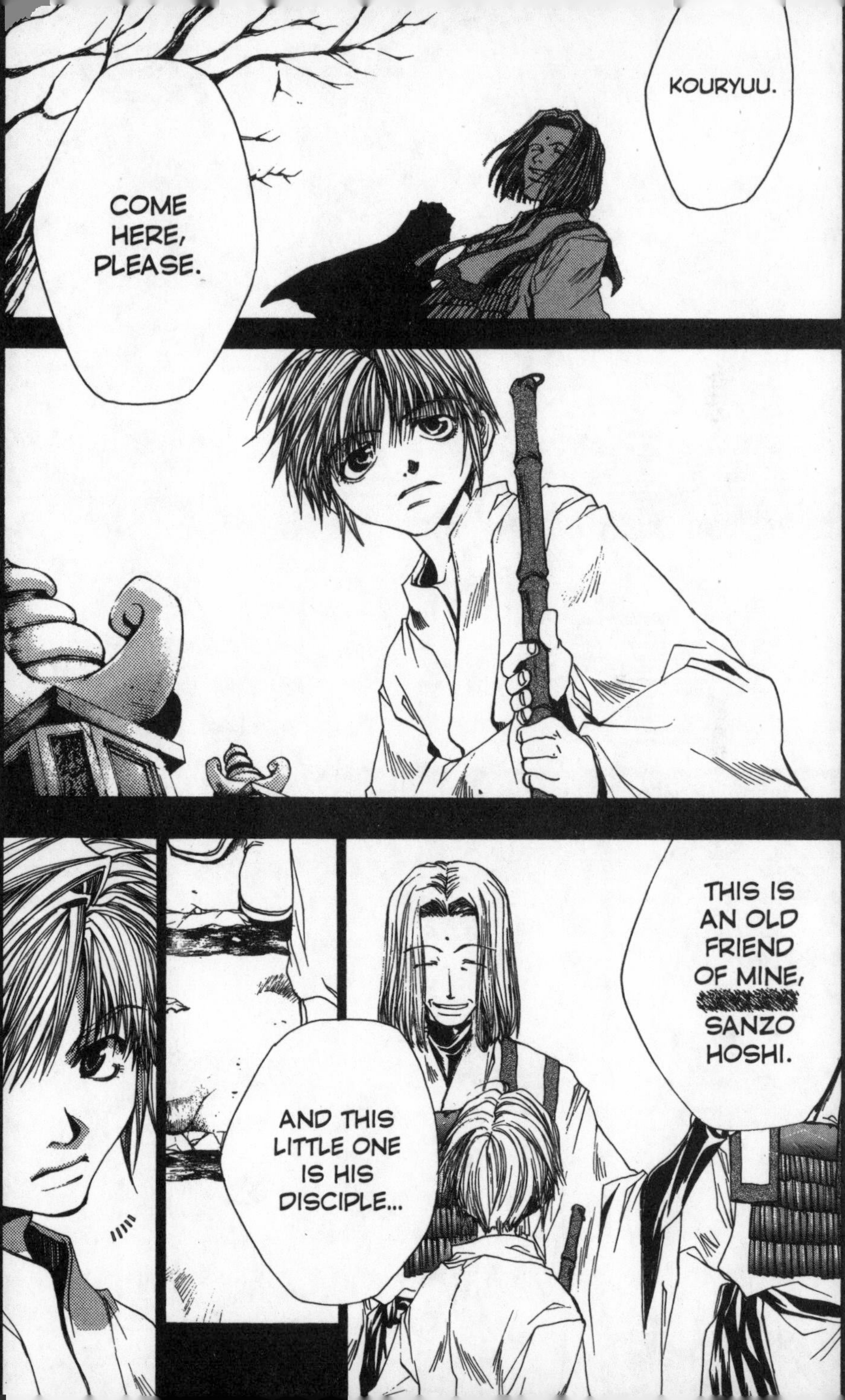
KOURYUU.
COME HERE, PLEASE.
THIS IS AN OLD FRIEND OF MINE, [redacted] SANZO HOSHI.
AND THIS LITTLE ONE IS HIS DISCIPLE...

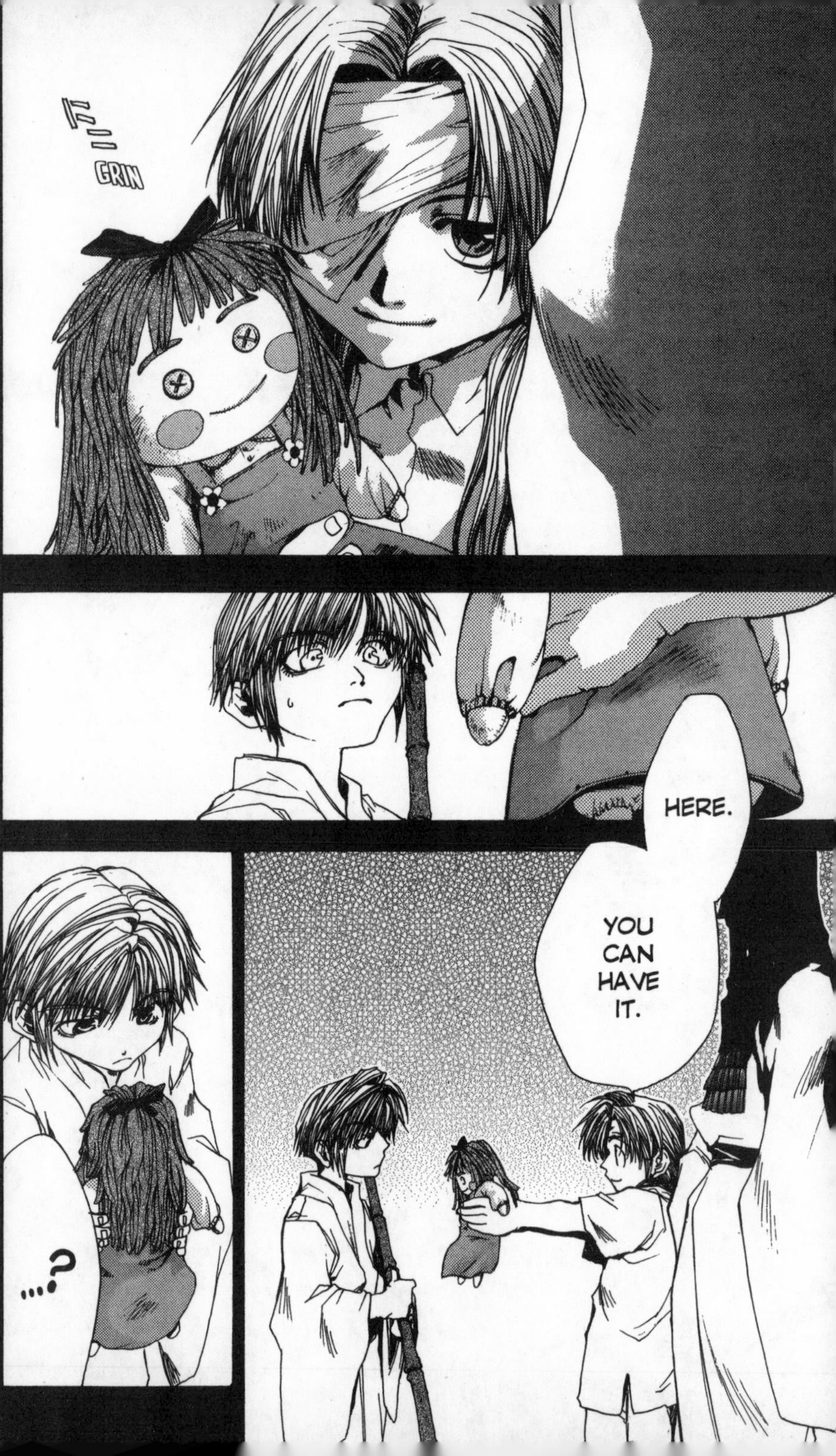
GRIN
HERE.
YOU CAN HAVE IT.
...?

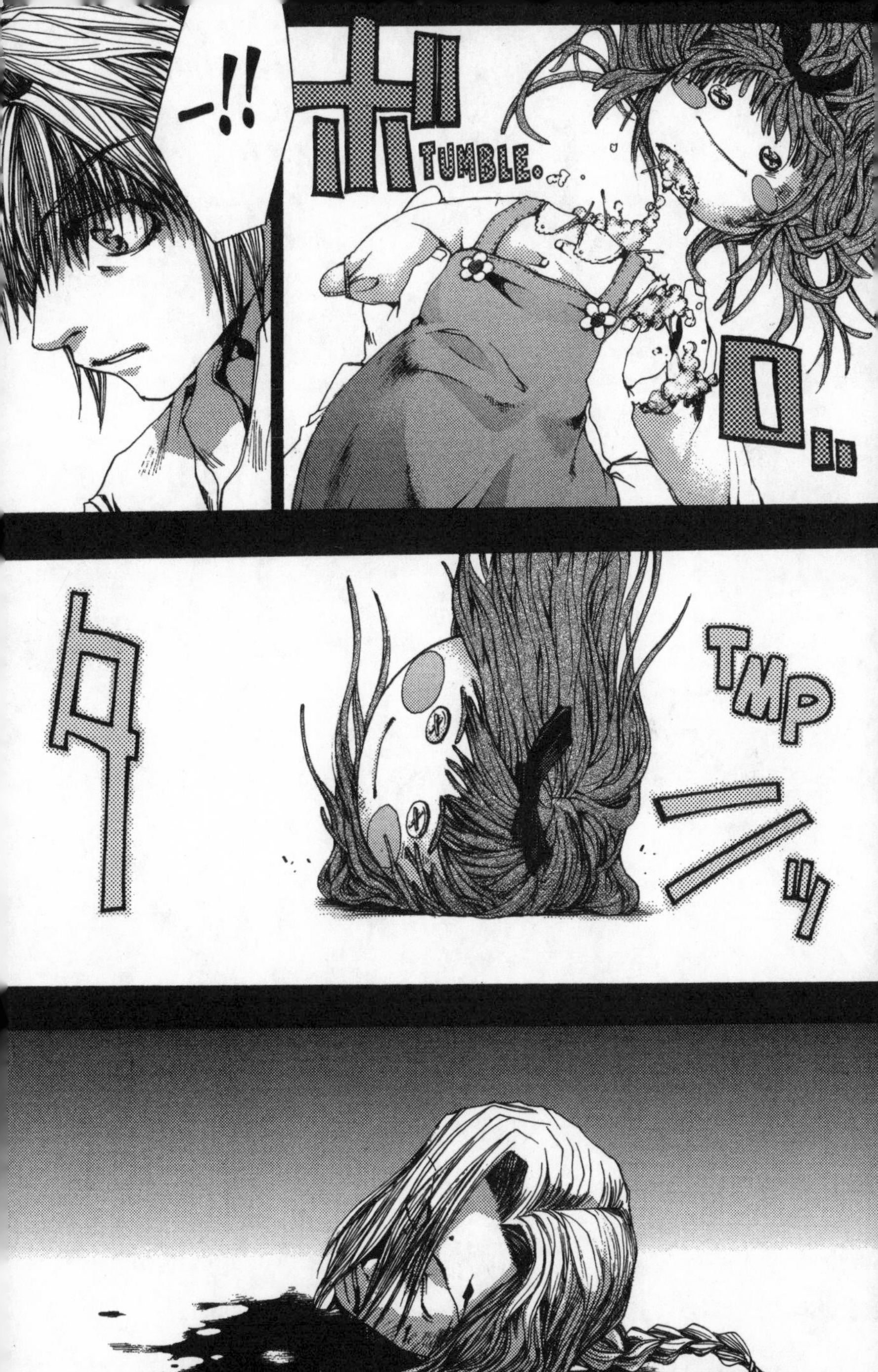

TUMBLE.
—!!
TMP

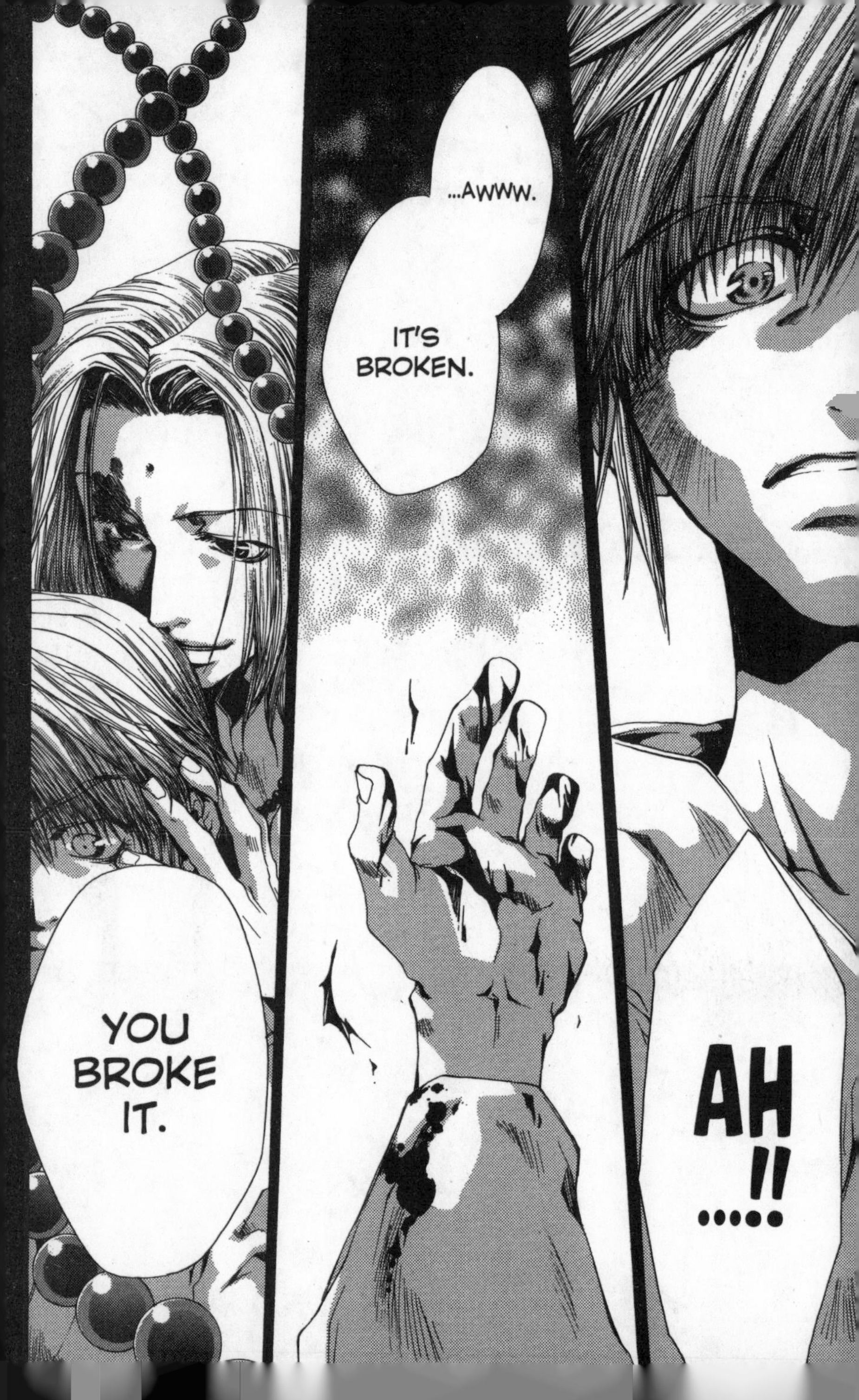
AH.....!!
...AWWW.
IT'S BROKEN.
YOU BROKE IT.

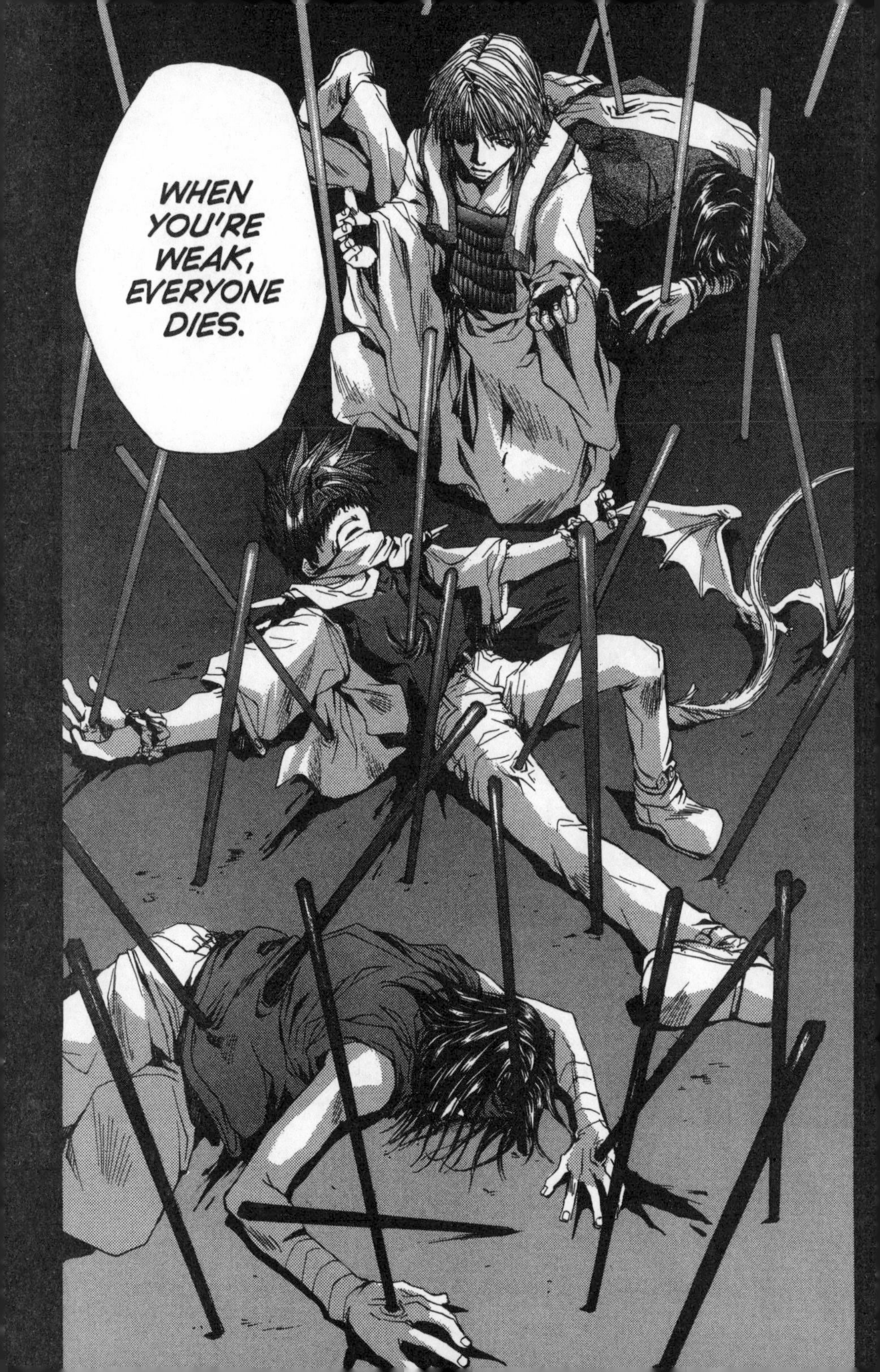
WHEN YOU'RE WEAK, EVERYONE DIES.

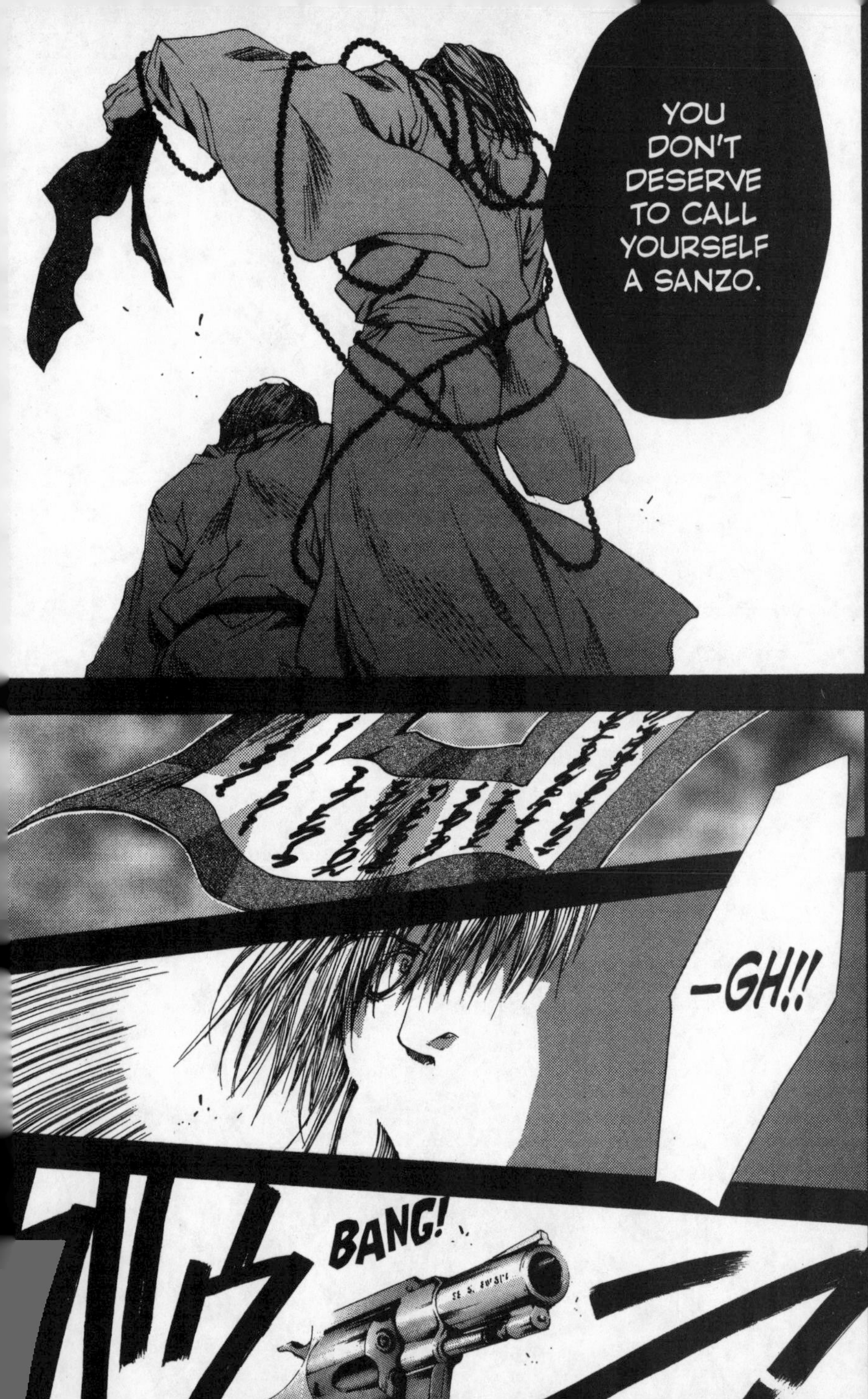
YOU DON'T DESERVE TO CALL YOURSELF A SANZO.
—GH!!
BANG!

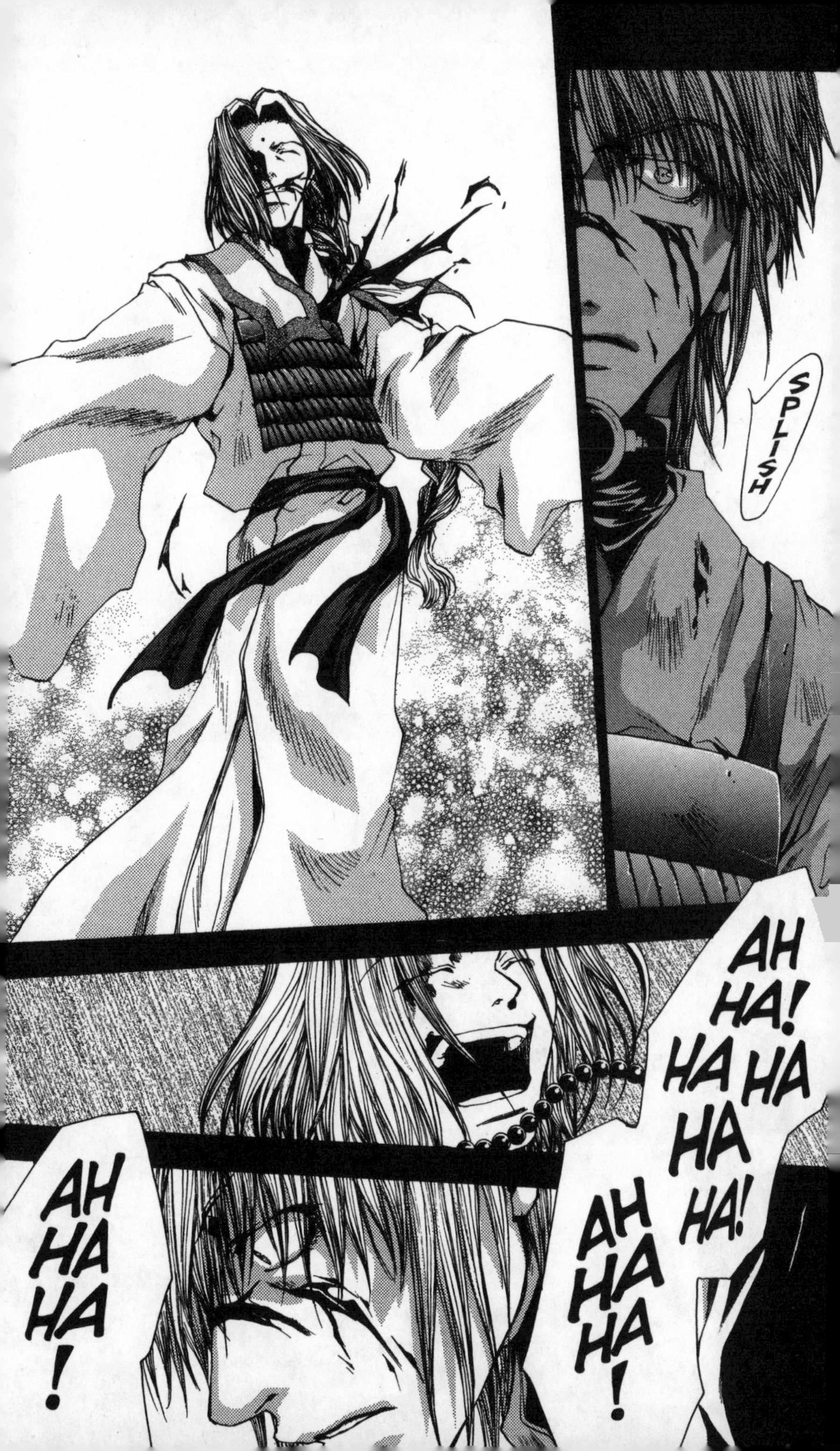
SPLISH
AH HA! HA HA HA HA HA!
AH HA HA HA!
AH HA HA HA!

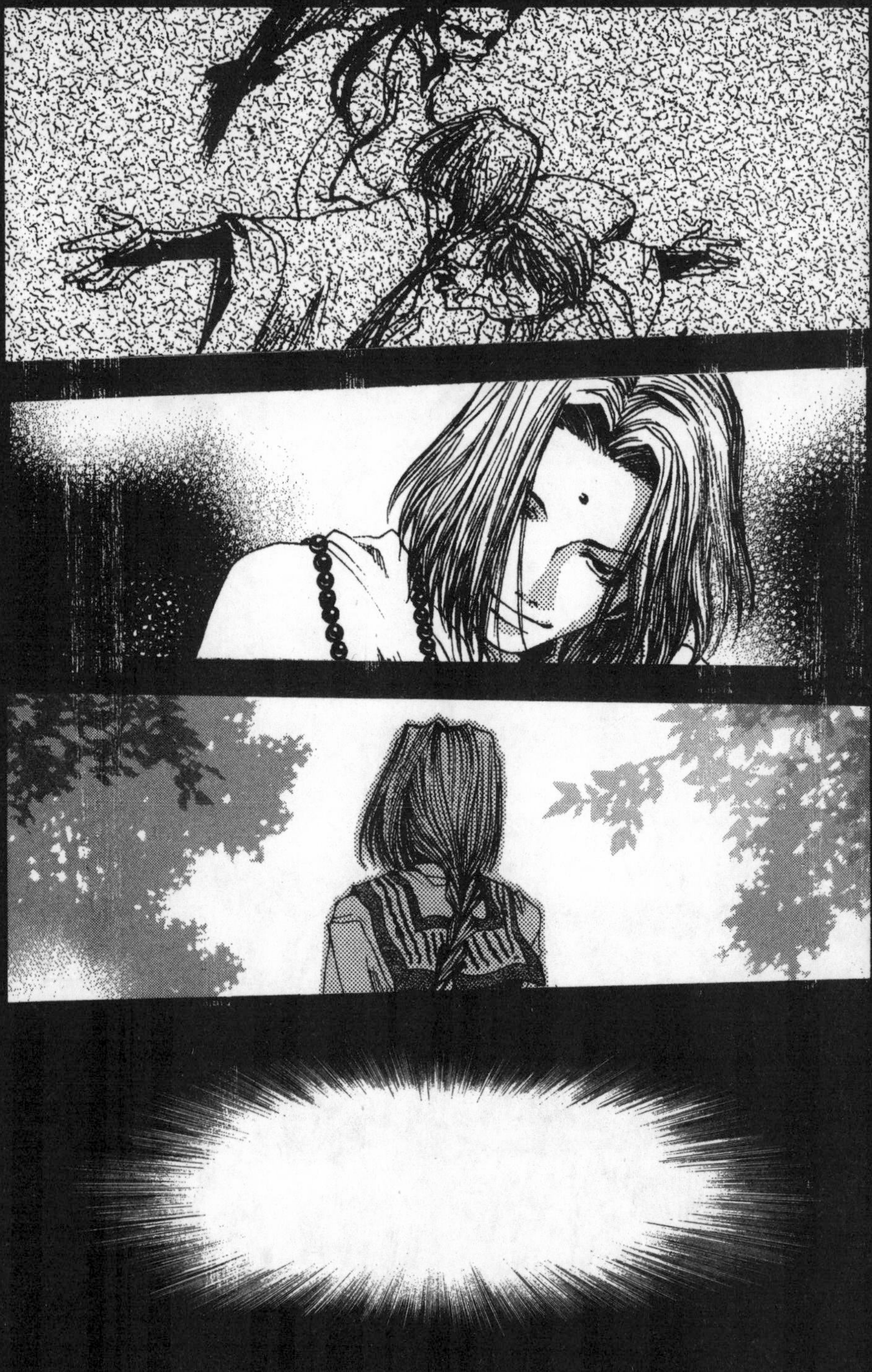

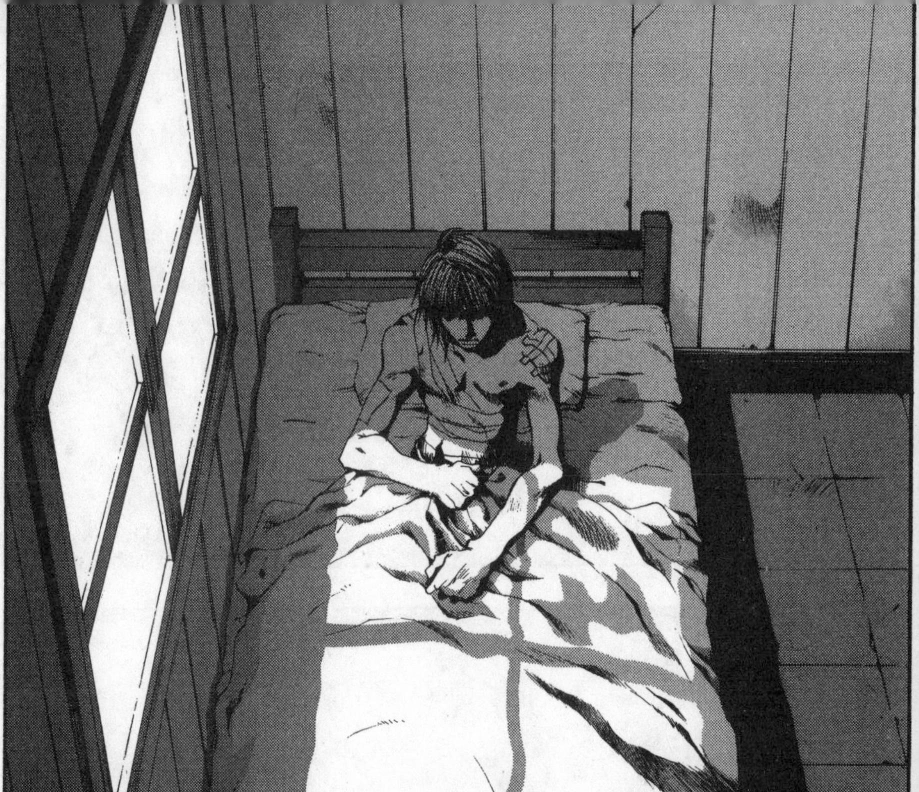
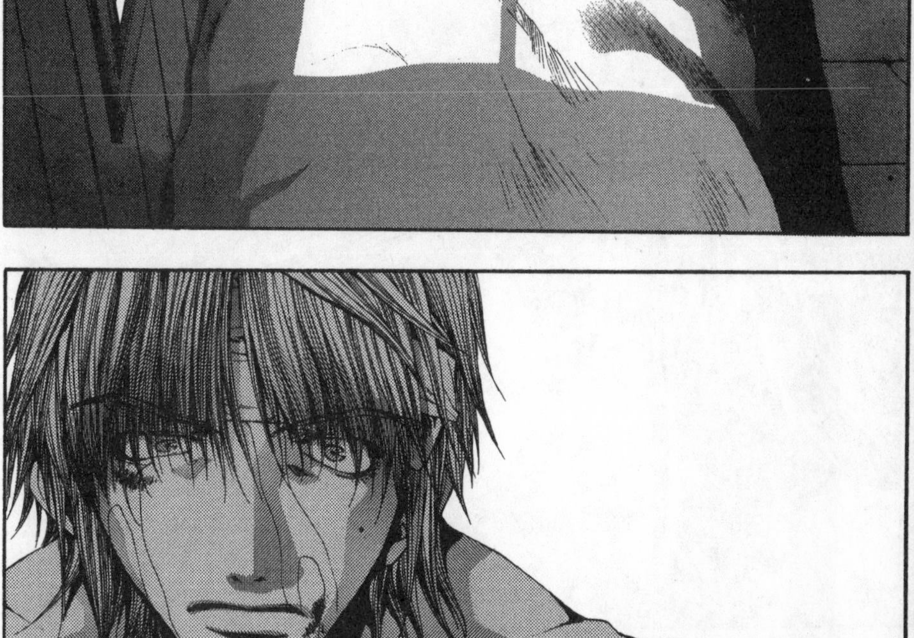

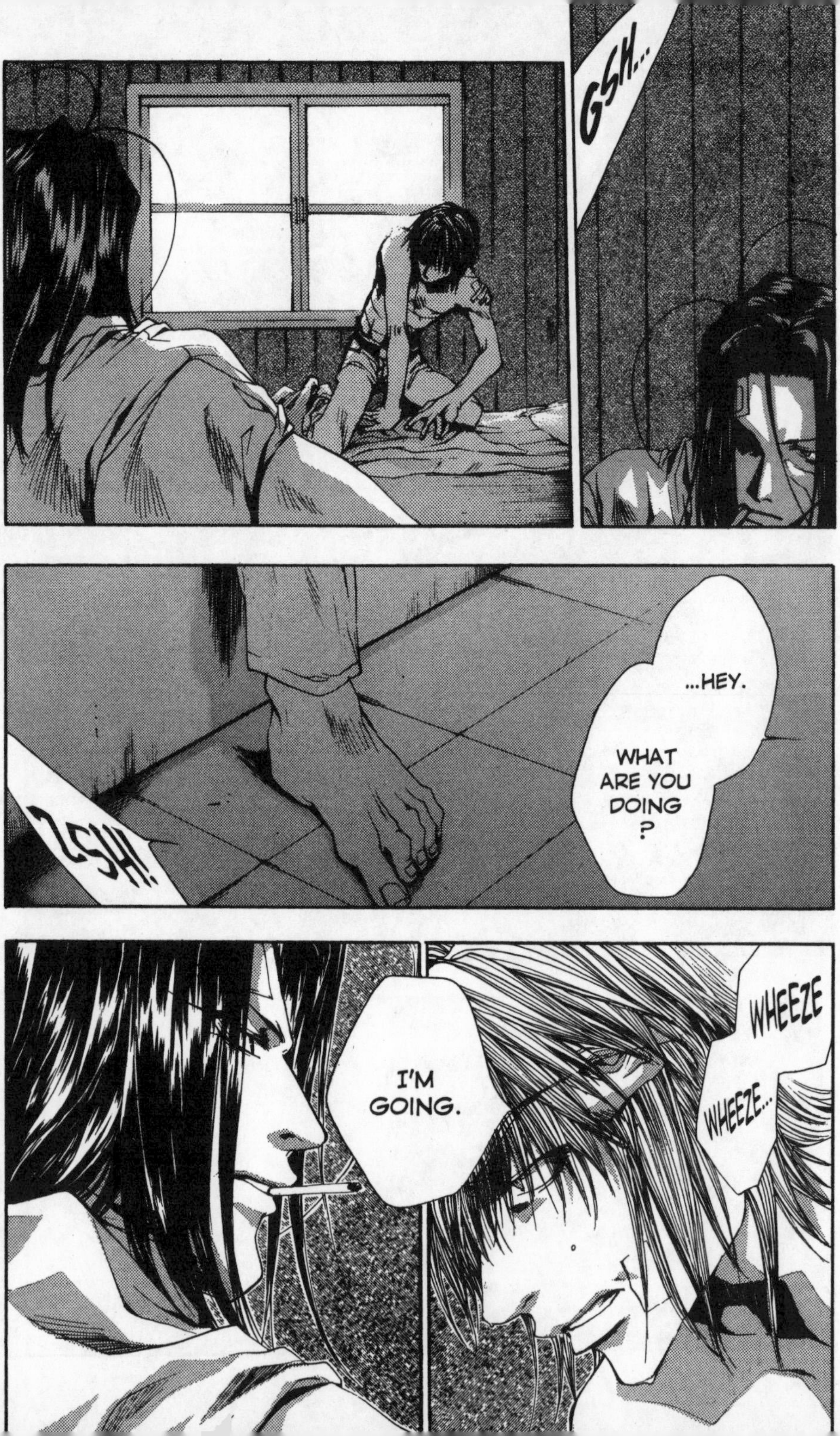
GSH...
...HEY.
WHAT ARE YOU DOING?
ZSH!
WHEEZE
WHEEZE...
I'M GOING.

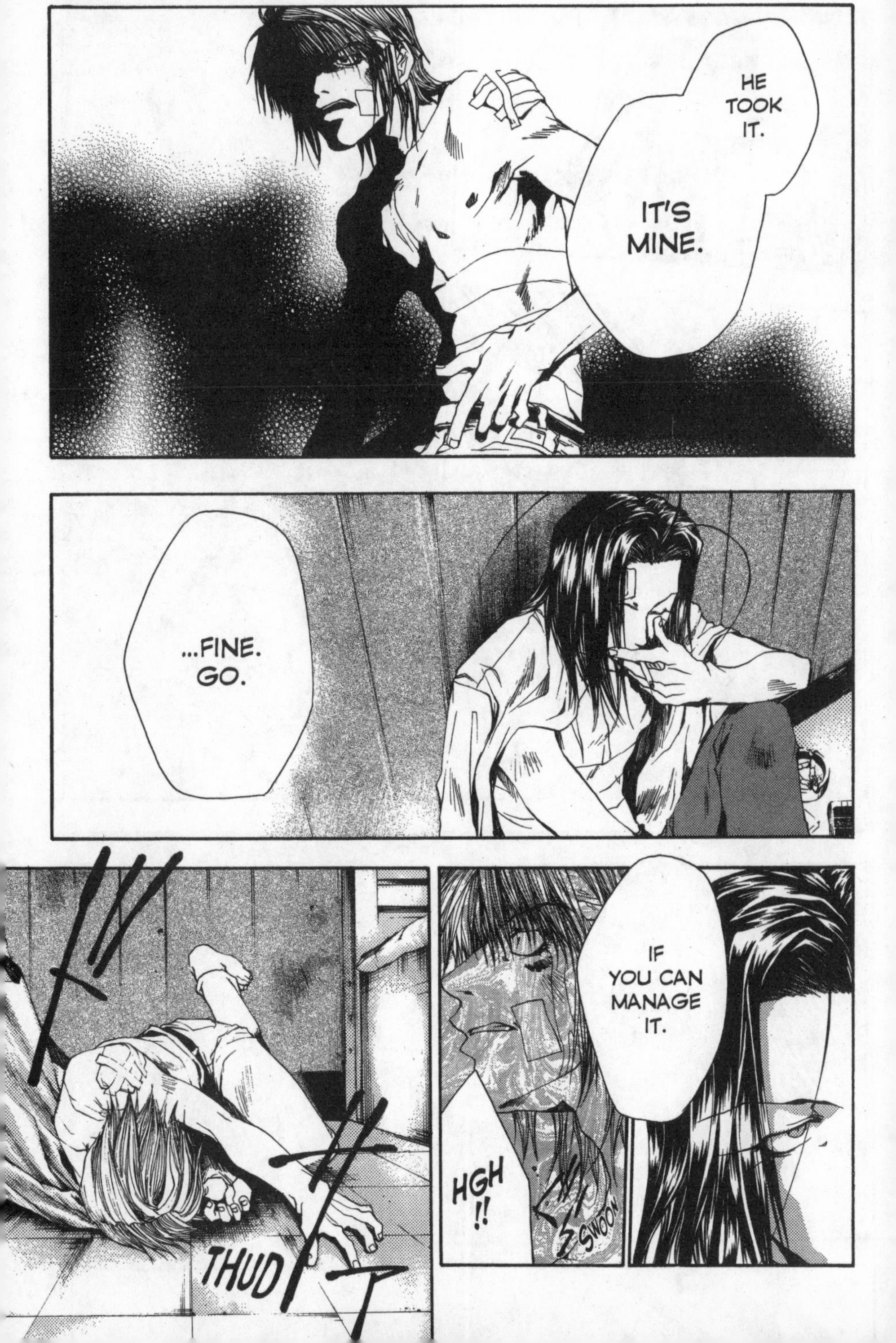
HE TOOK IT.
IT'S MINE.
...FINE. GO.
IF YOU CAN MANAGE IT.
HGH !!
SWOON
THUD

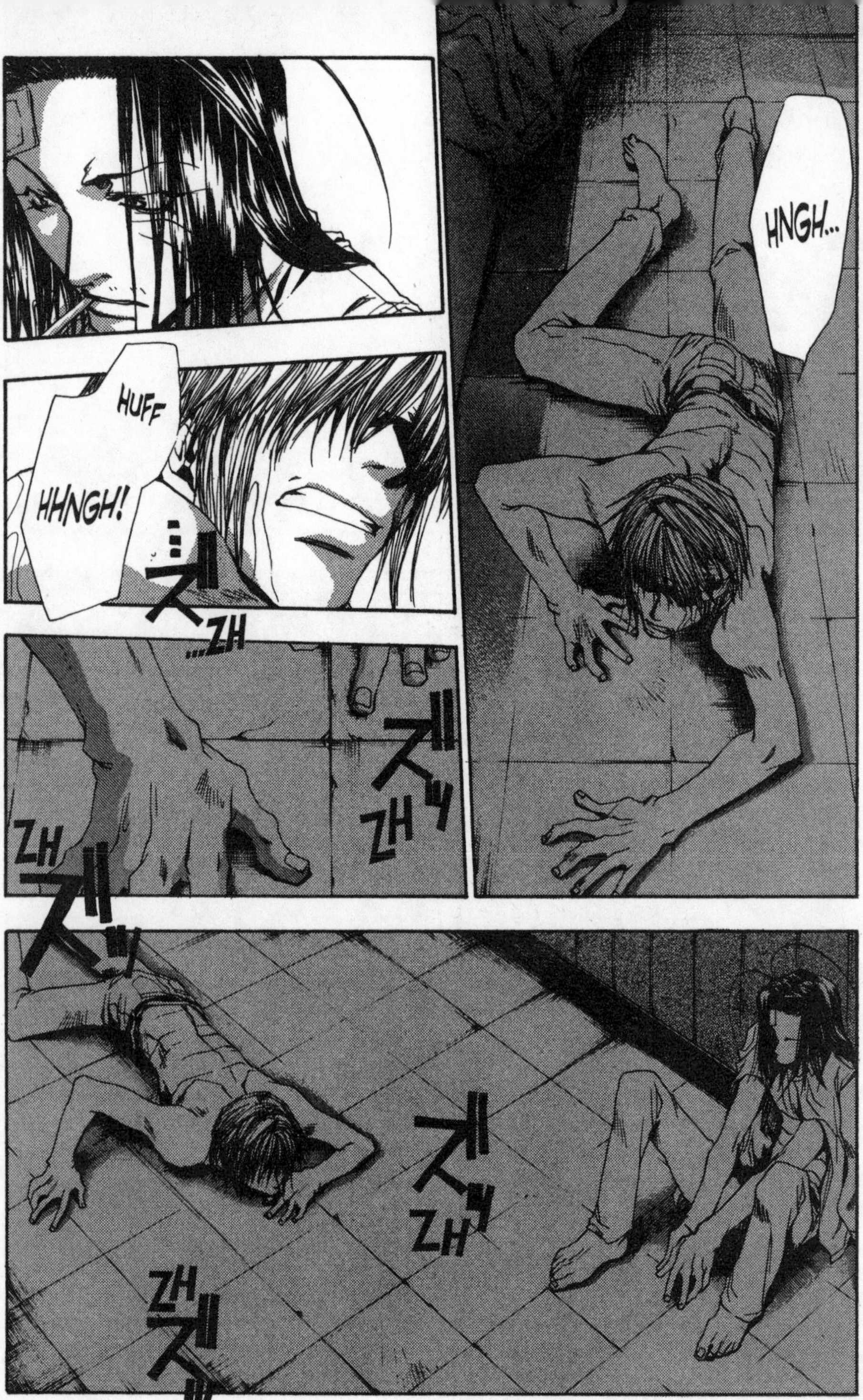
HNGH...
HUFF
HHNGH!
...
...ZH
ZH
ZH
ZH
ZH

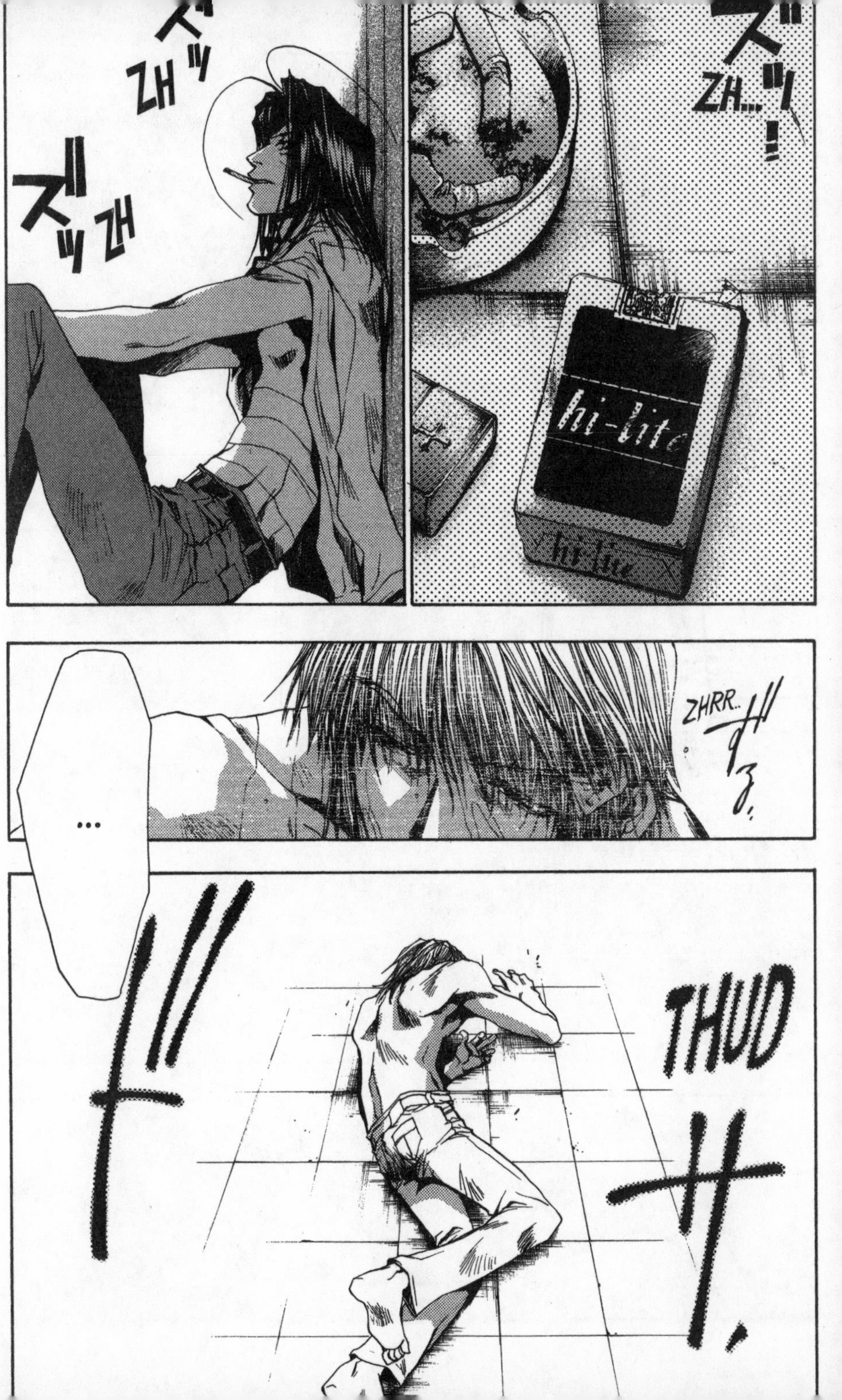
ZH...
hi-lite
hi-lite
ZH
ZH
ZHRR..
...
THUD

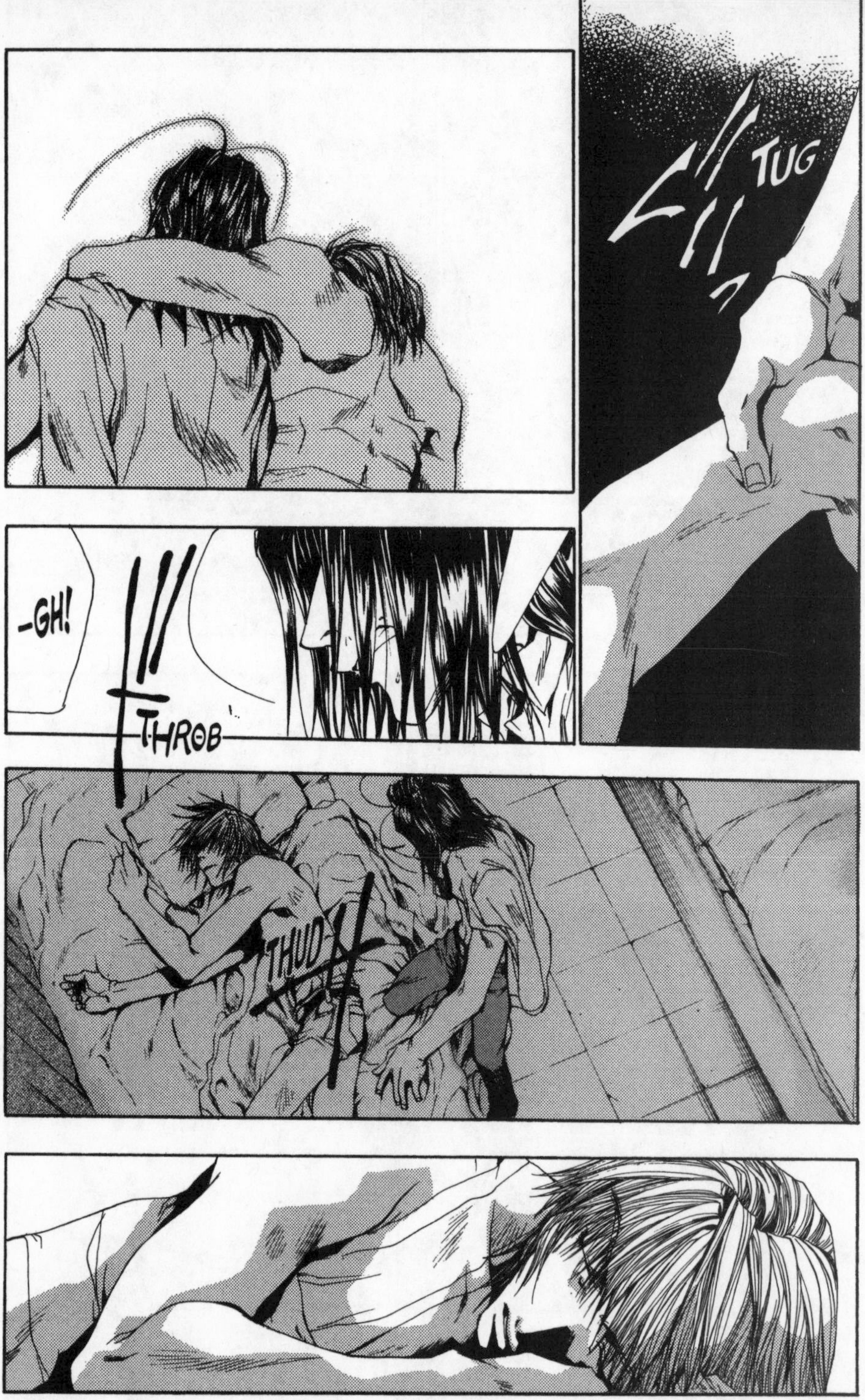
TUG
-GH!
T-THROB
THUD

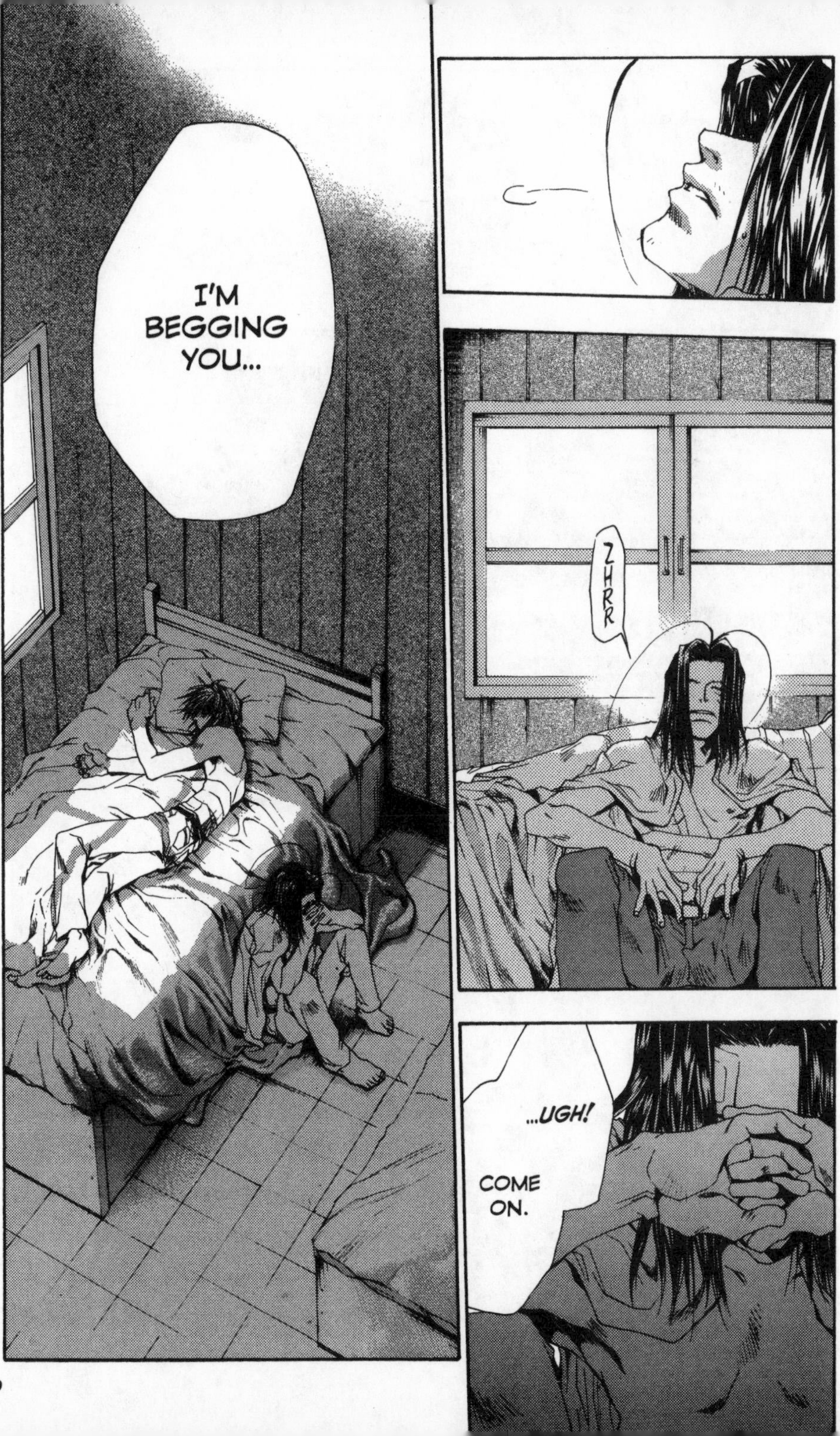
ZHRR
...UGH!
COME ON.
I'M BEGGING YOU...

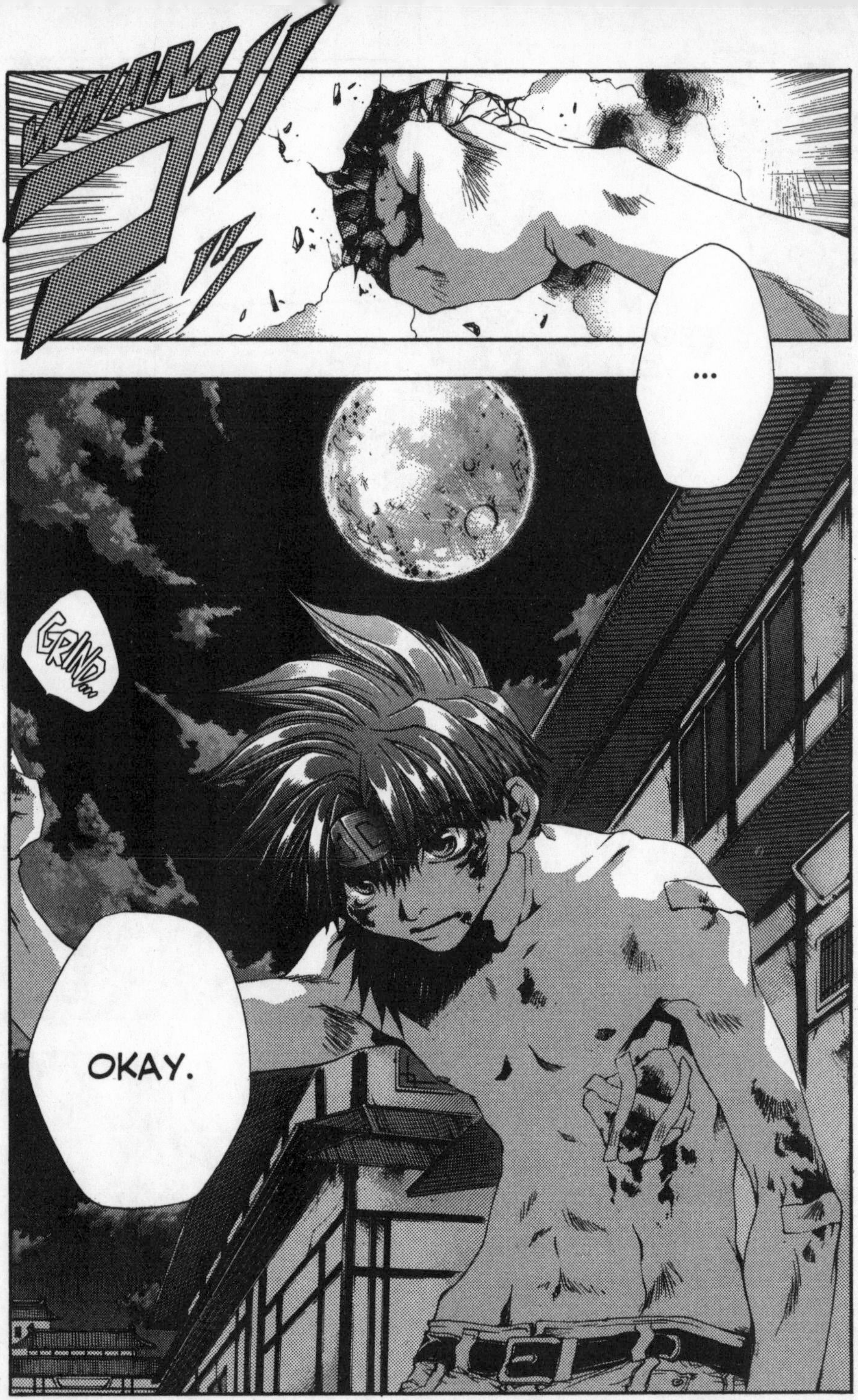
...
GRIND...
OKAY.

To be continued...

STAFF

original works...
KAZUYA MINEKURA

assistant works...
JIRO SUZUKI
KATSUYA SEINO
YUZU MIZUTANI

editor...
YOUSUKE SUGINO

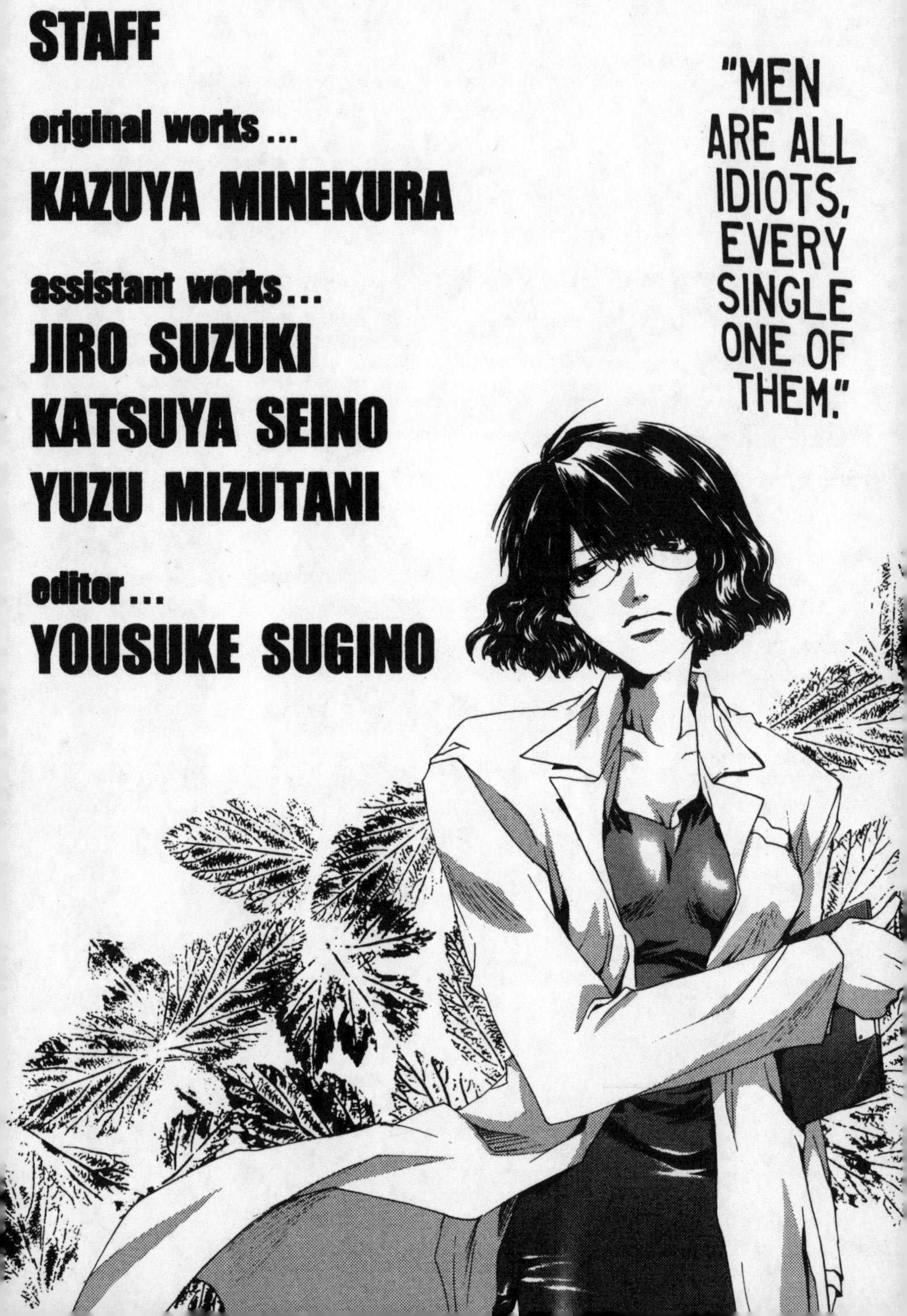
"MEN ARE ALL IDIOTS, EVERY SINGLE ONE OF THEM."

A note from the author

KAZUYA MINEKURA

On to the next one!!

SAIYUKI

9

KAZUYA MINEKURA

— VOLUME VIII SYNOPSIS —

"Sorry."

With one final word, Gojyo leaves the party. As he wanders off in search of "Kami-sama," the self-proclaimed god who killed Kinkaku, he comes across an endless series of gates and stone stairs...

At Hoto Castle, Kougaiji has undergone biological engineering at the hands of Ni Jianyi, giving him immense power. He then cuts down one of Gyokumen Koushu's servants at her whim, and Yaone and Do- kugakuji are left stunned at how he has changed...

Inside the Maze of Mist, Gojyo sees an illusion of his mother. He fights her off and moves onward, finally confronting Kami-sama himself. Gojyo challenges him to a fight, but he is no match for this "god"'s overwhelming power. Sanzo, Goku, and Hakkai join the fray, but one attack from Kami-sama knocks them all to the ground.

As the gang gets in Jeep and drives away, Kami-sama calls derisively after them, "You're weak!" They had suffered their first "complete and utter defeat"...

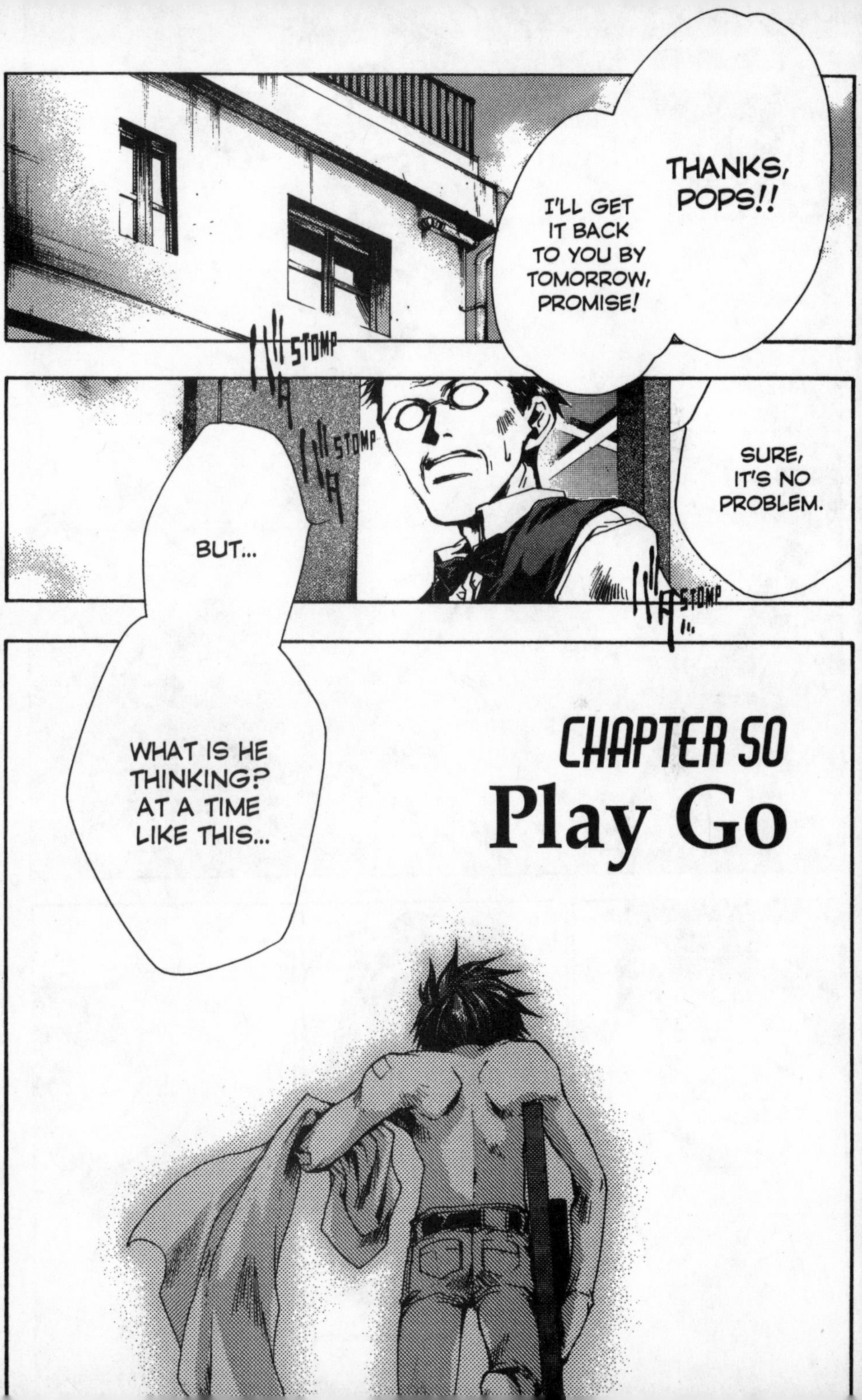
THANKS, POPS!!
I'LL GET IT BACK TO YOU BY TOMORROW, PROMISE!
STOMP
STOMP
SURE, IT'S NO PROBLEM.
STOMP
BUT...
WHAT IS HE THINKING? AT A TIME LIKE THIS...
CHAPTER 50
Play Go

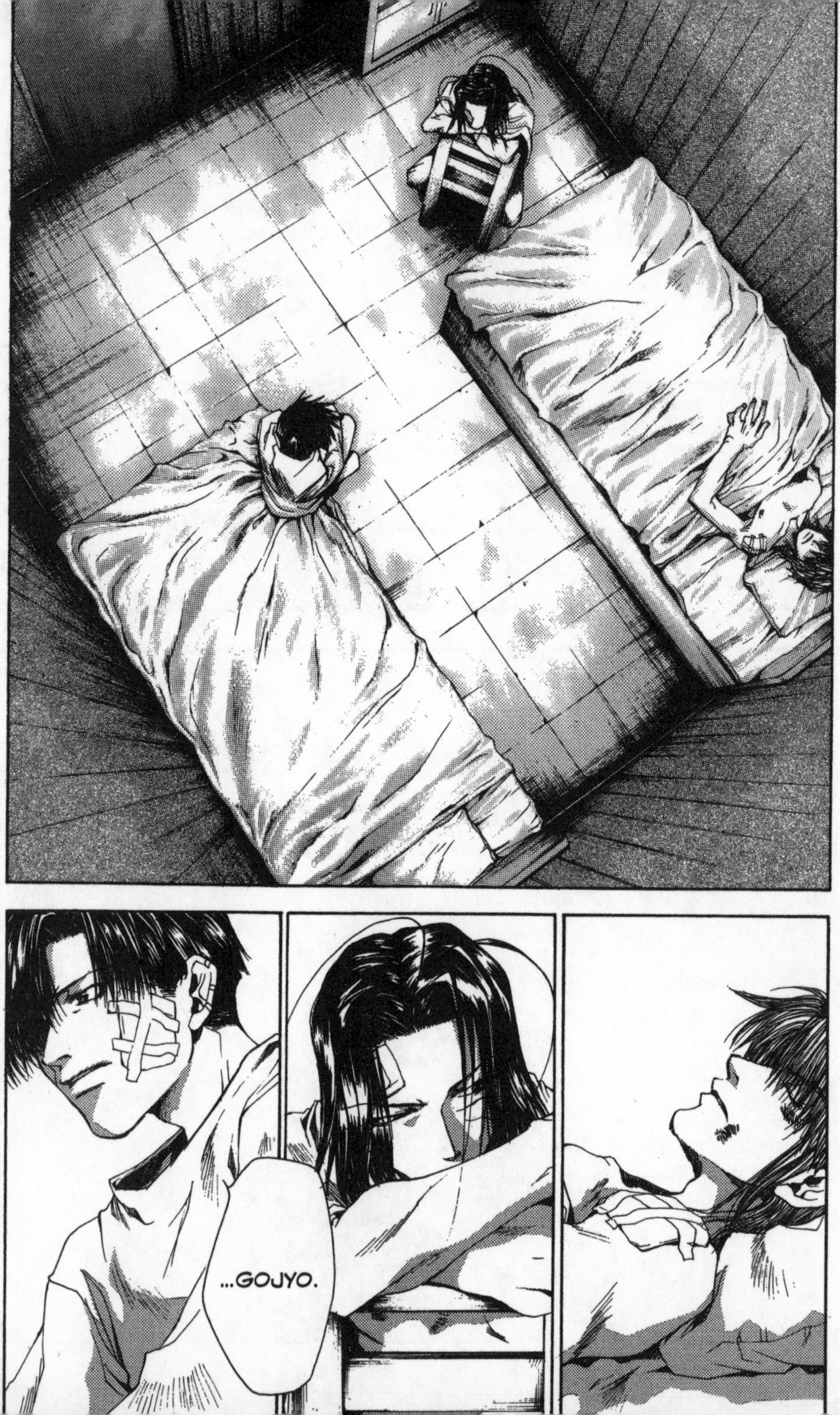
...GOJYO.

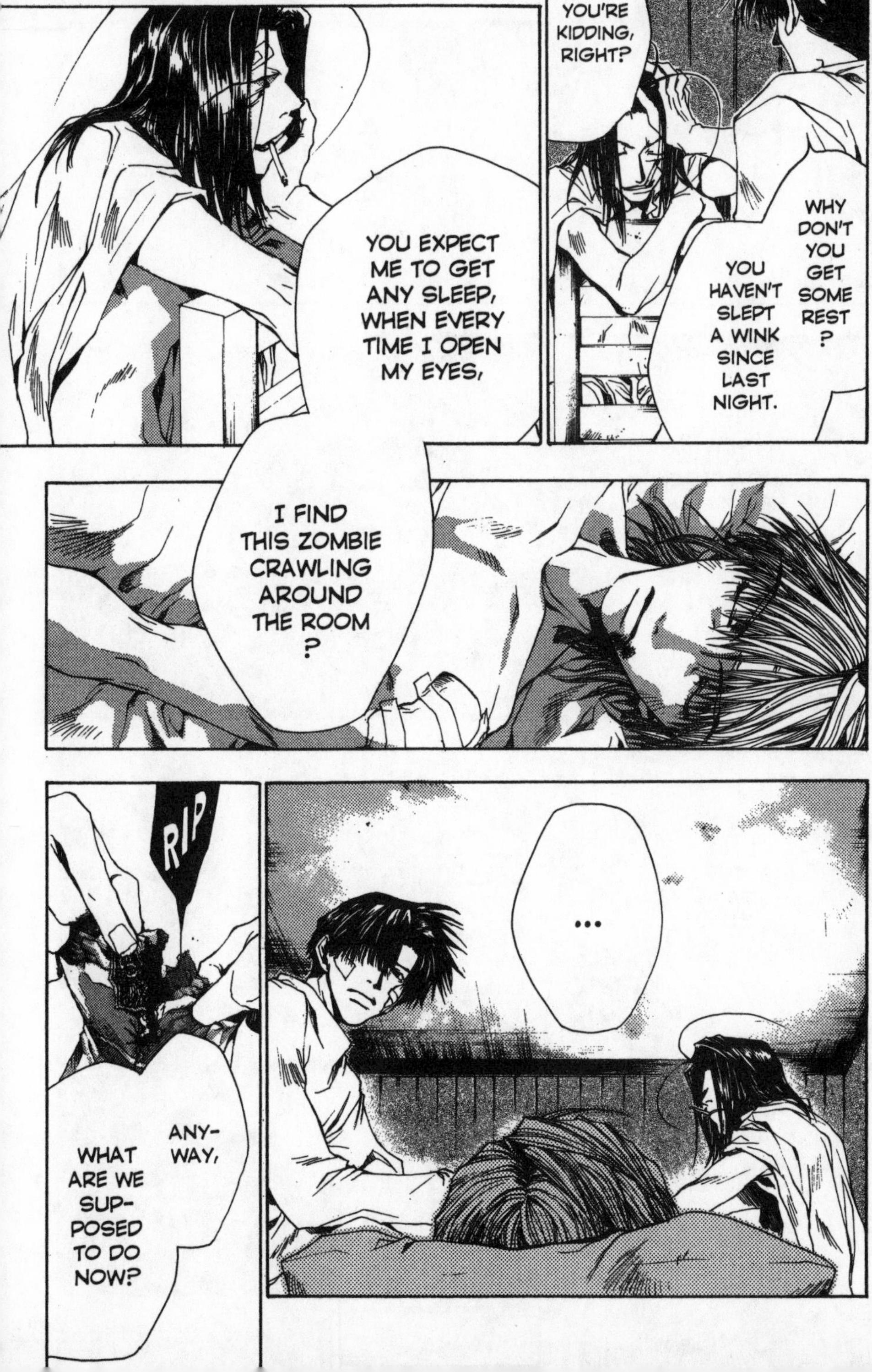
WHY DON'T YOU GET SOME REST?
YOU HAVEN'T SLEPT A WINK SINCE LAST NIGHT.
YOU'RE KIDDING, RIGHT?
YOU EXPECT ME TO GET ANY SLEEP, WHEN EVERY TIME I OPEN MY EYES,
I FIND THIS ZOMBIE CRAWLING AROUND THE ROOM?
...
RIP
ANY-WAY,
WHAT ARE WE SUP-POSED TO DO NOW?

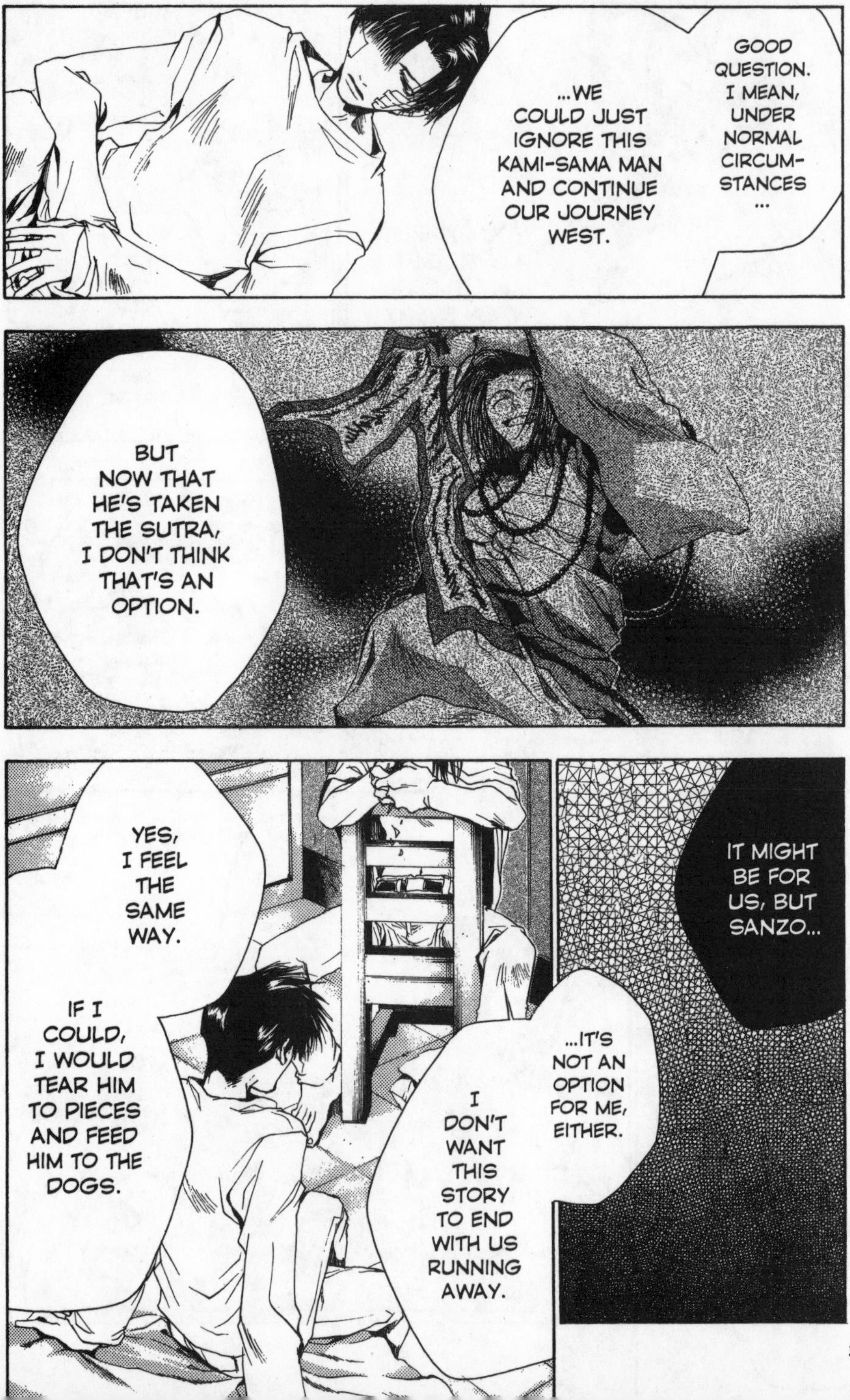
GOOD QUESTION. I MEAN, UNDER NORMAL CIRCUM-STANCES ...
...WE COULD JUST IGNORE THIS KAMI-SAMA MAN AND CONTINUE OUR JOURNEY WEST.
BUT NOW THAT HE'S TAKEN THE SUTRA, I DON'T THINK THAT'S AN OPTION.
IT MIGHT BE FOR US, BUT SANZO...
...IT'S NOT AN OPTION FOR ME, EITHER.
I DON'T WANT THIS STORY TO END WITH US RUNNING AWAY.
YES, I FEEL THE SAME WAY.
IF I COULD, I WOULD TEAR HIM TO PIECES AND FEED HIM TO THE DOGS.

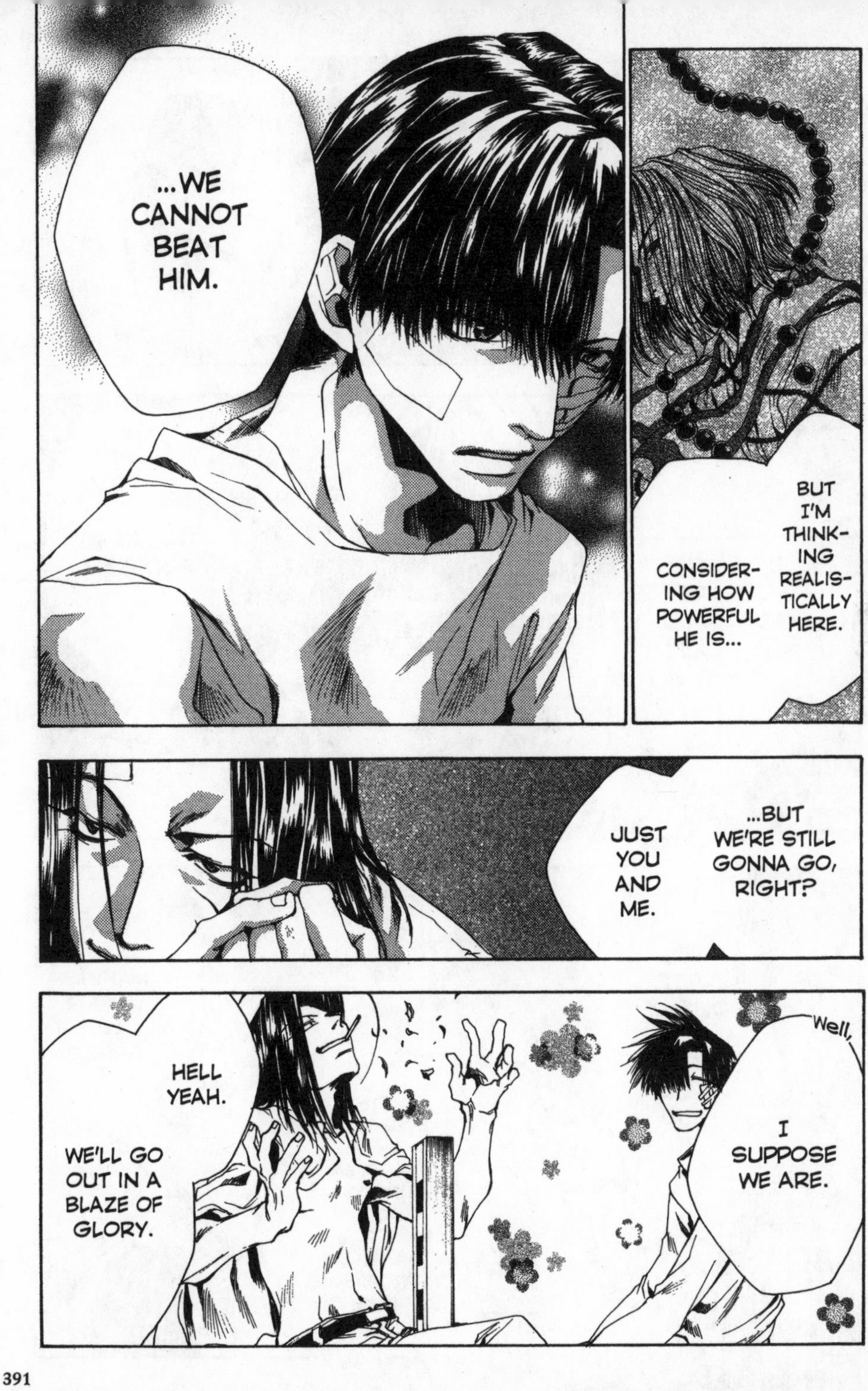
BUT I'M THINKING REALISTICALLY HERE.
CONSIDERING HOW POWERFUL HE IS...
...WE CANNOT BEAT HIM.
...BUT WE'RE STILL GONNA GO, RIGHT?
JUST YOU AND ME.
Well, I SUPPOSE WE ARE.
HELL YEAH.
WE'LL GO OUT IN A BLAZE OF GLORY.

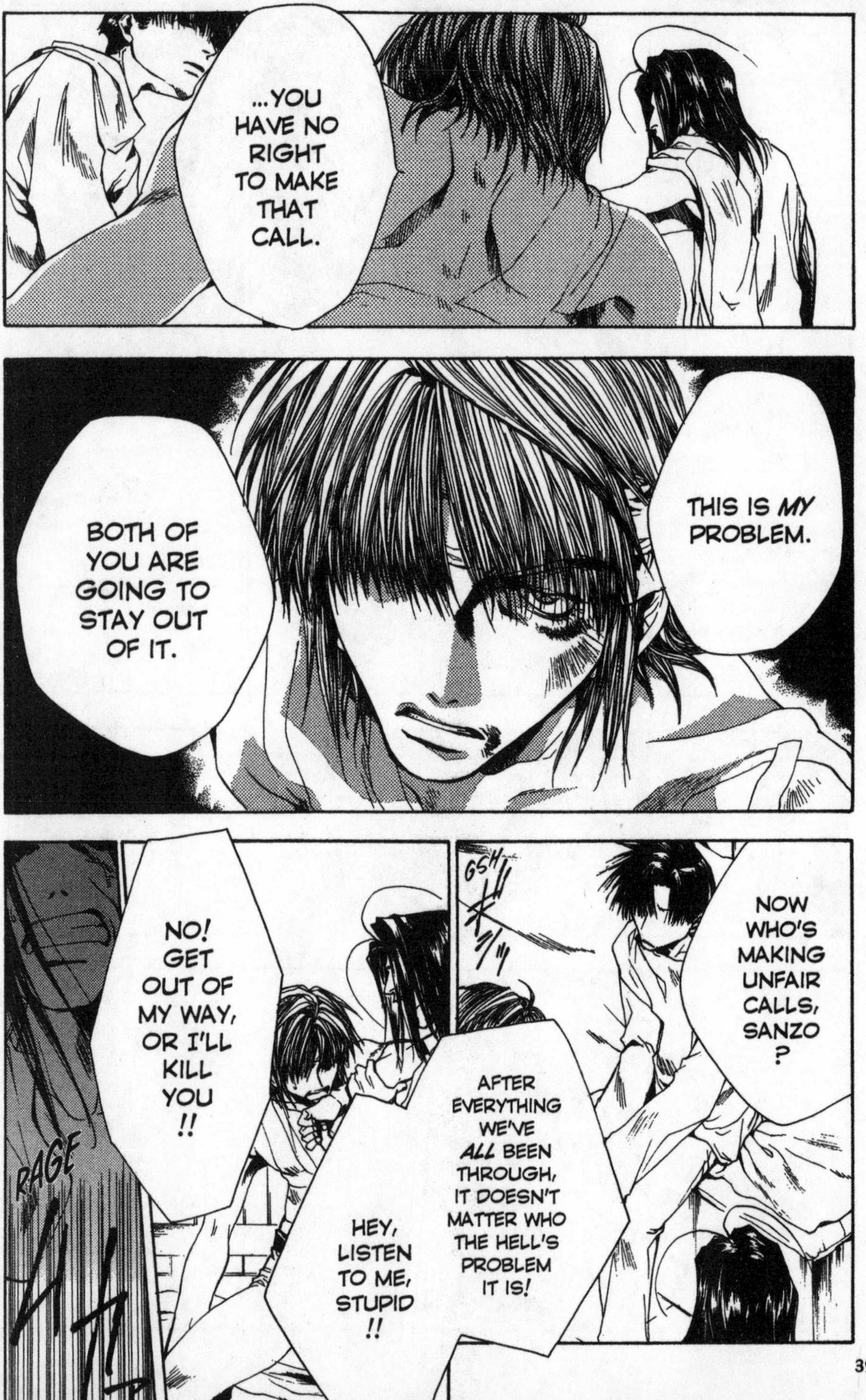
...YOU HAVE NO RIGHT TO MAKE THAT CALL.
THIS IS *MY* PROBLEM.
BOTH OF YOU ARE GOING TO STAY OUT OF IT.
GSH
NOW WHO'S MAKING UNFAIR CALLS, SANZO?
NO! GET OUT OF MY WAY, OR I'LL KILL YOU!!
RAGE
AFTER EVERYTHING WE'VE *ALL* BEEN THROUGH, IT DOESN'T MATTER WHO THE HELL'S PROBLEM IT IS!
HEY, LISTEN TO ME, STUPID!!

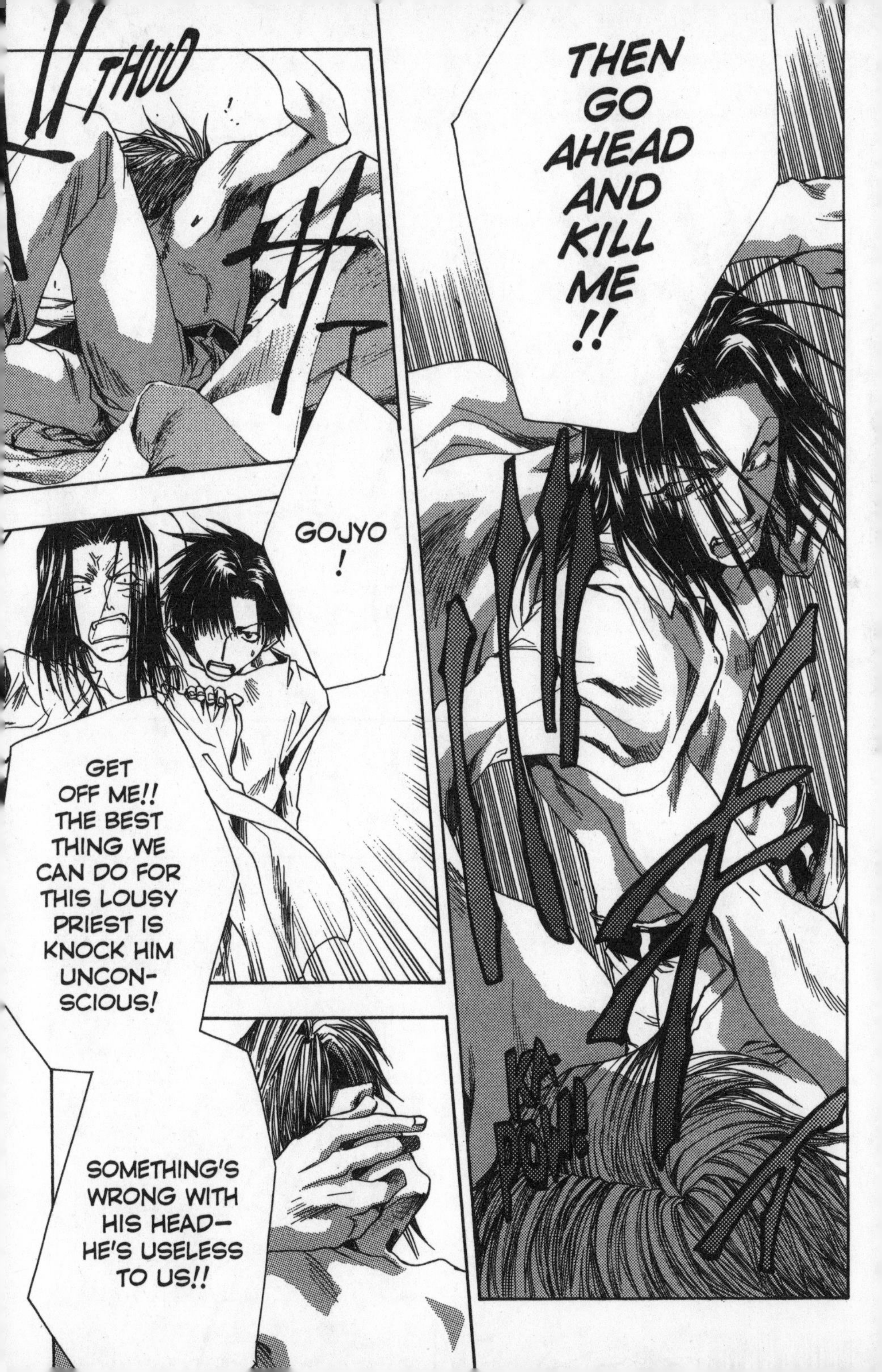
THEN GO AHEAD AND KILL ME!!
THUD
GOJYO!
GET OFF ME!! THE BEST THING WE CAN DO FOR THIS LOUSY PRIEST IS KNOCK HIM UNCONSCIOUS!
SOMETHING'S WRONG WITH HIS HEAD— HE'S USELESS TO US!!

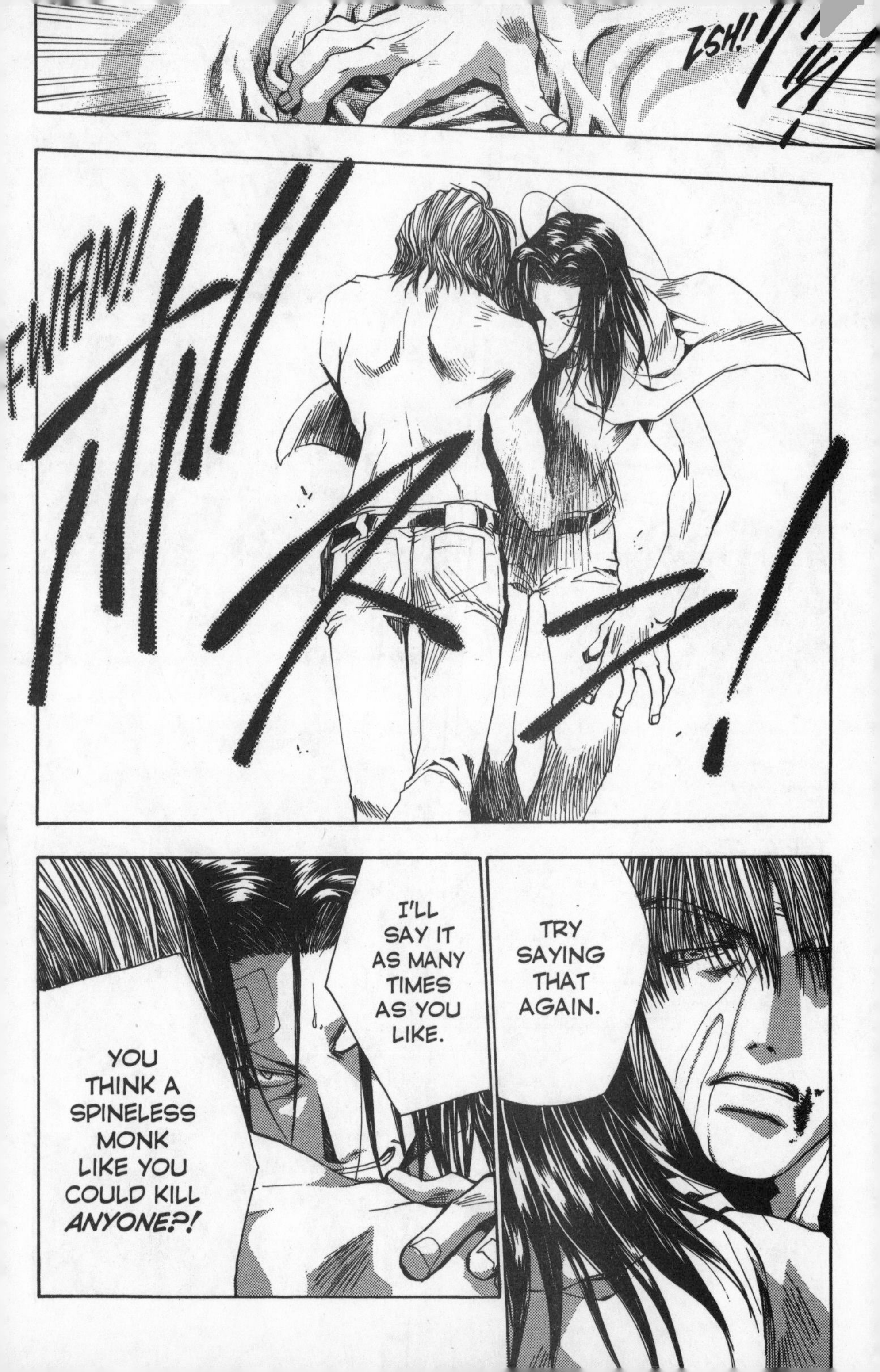
ZSH!
FWAM!
TRY SAYING THAT AGAIN.
I'LL SAY IT AS MANY TIMES AS YOU LIKE.
YOU THINK A SPINELESS MONK LIKE YOU COULD KILL *ANYONE?!*

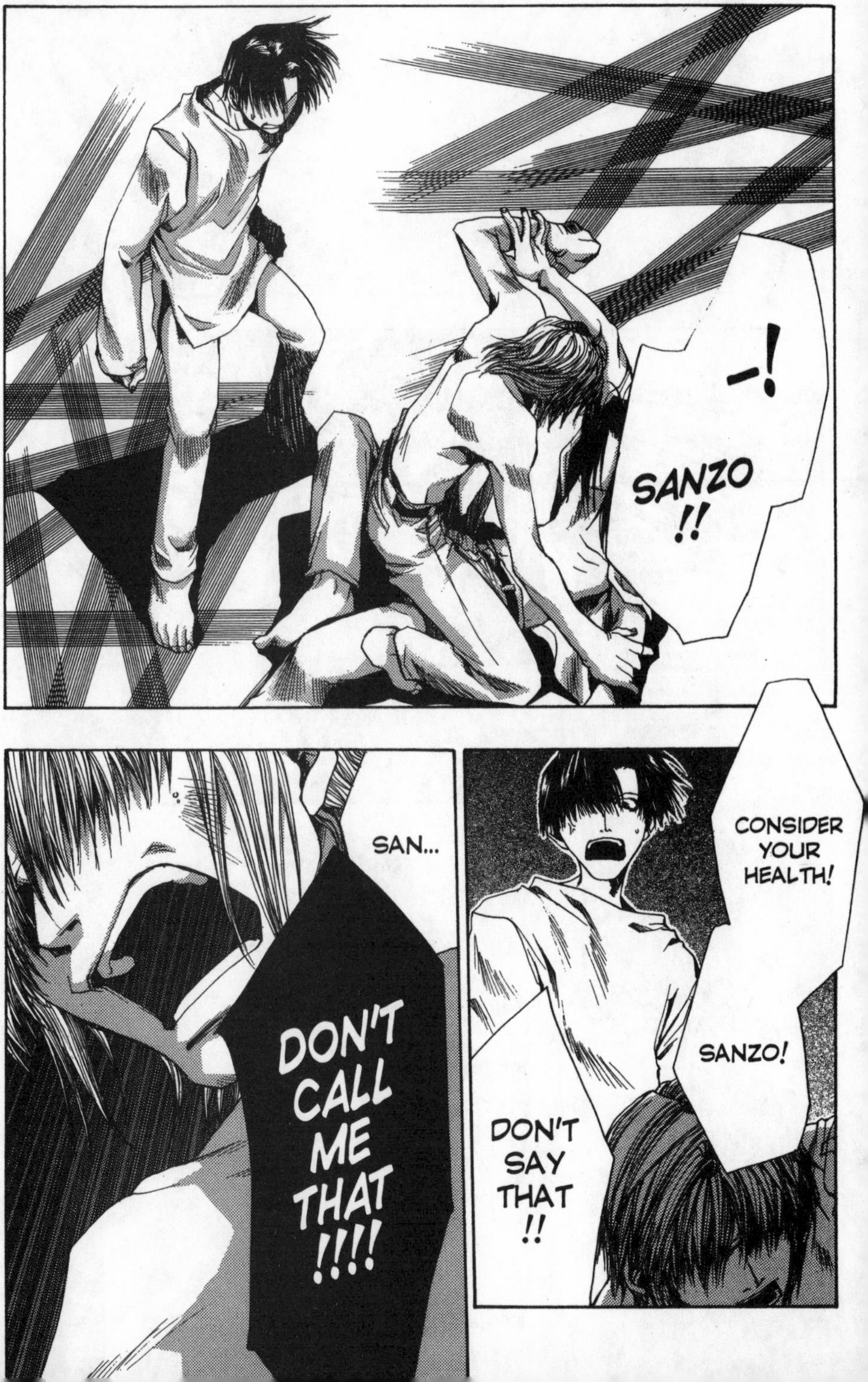
—!
SANZO!!
CONSIDER YOUR HEALTH!
SANZO!
DON'T SAY THAT!!
SAN...
DON'T CALL ME THAT!!!!

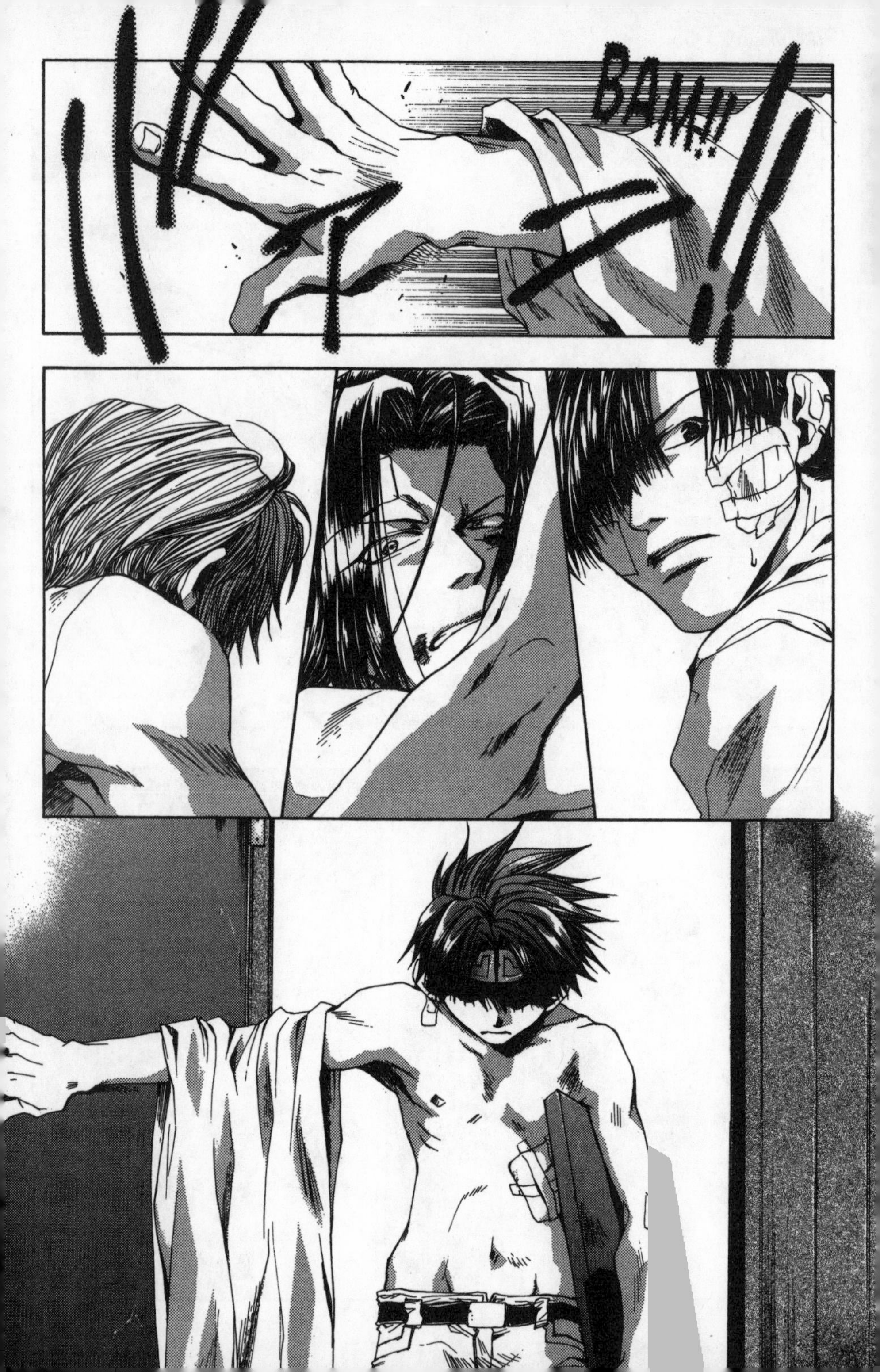
BAM!!

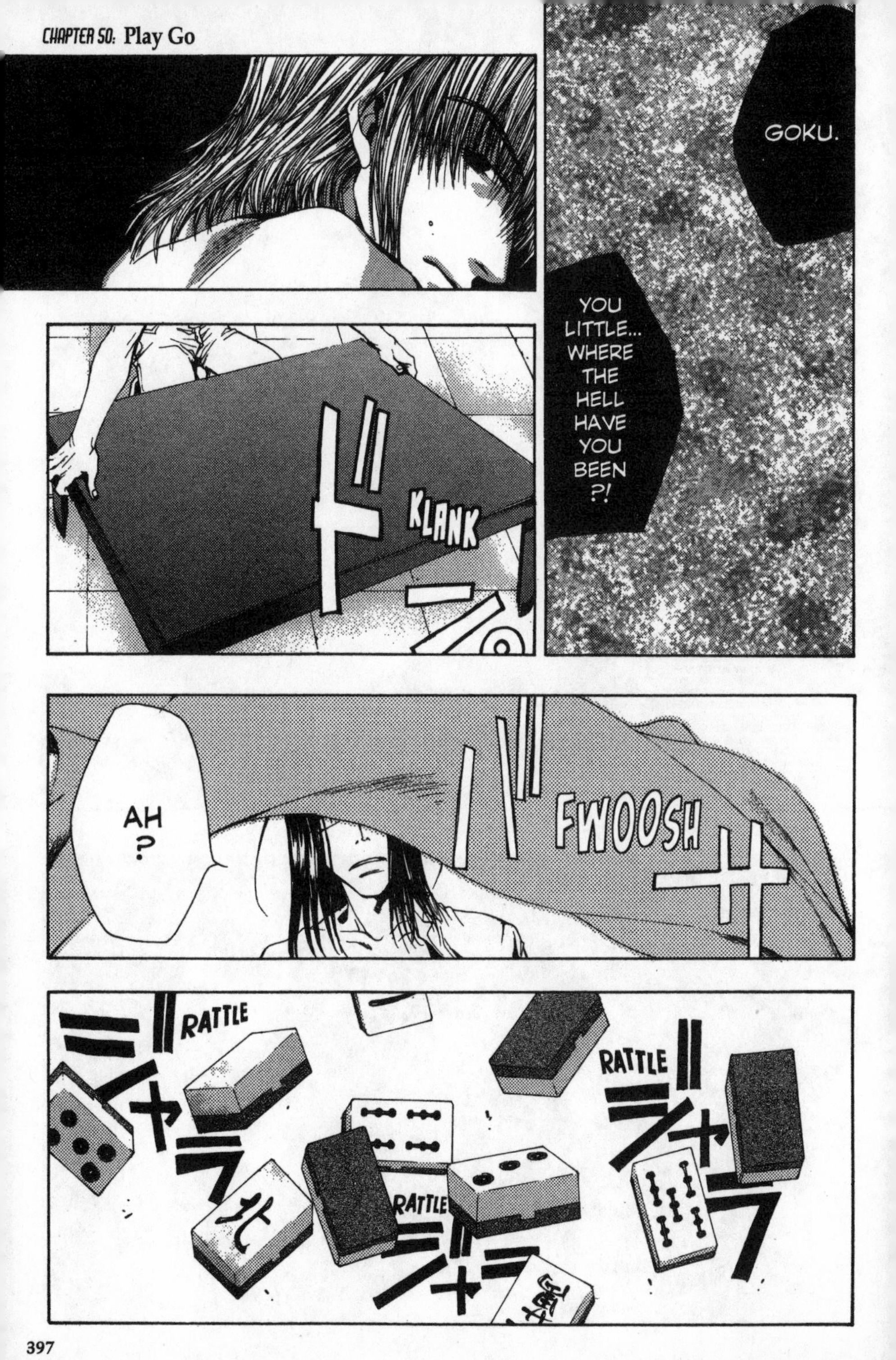
GOKU.
YOU LITTLE... WHERE THE HELL HAVE YOU BEEN ?!
KLANK
FWOOSH
AH ?
RATTLE
RATTLE
RATTLE

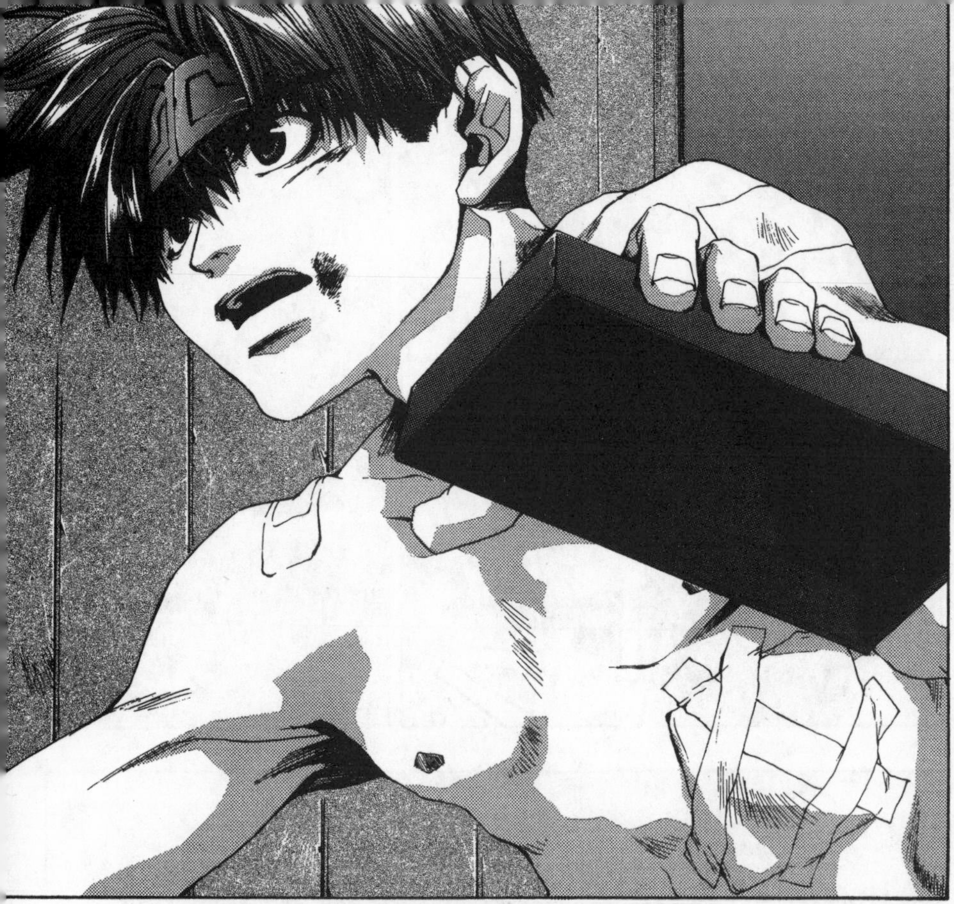

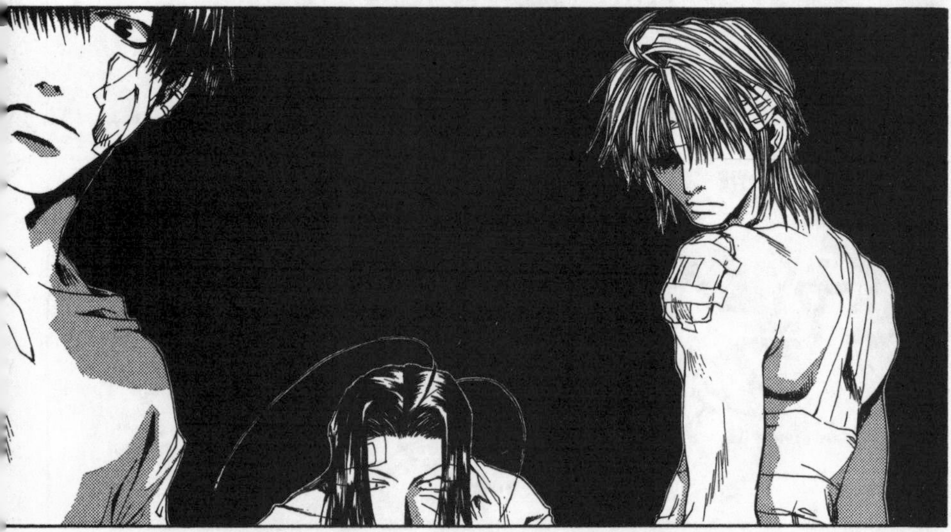

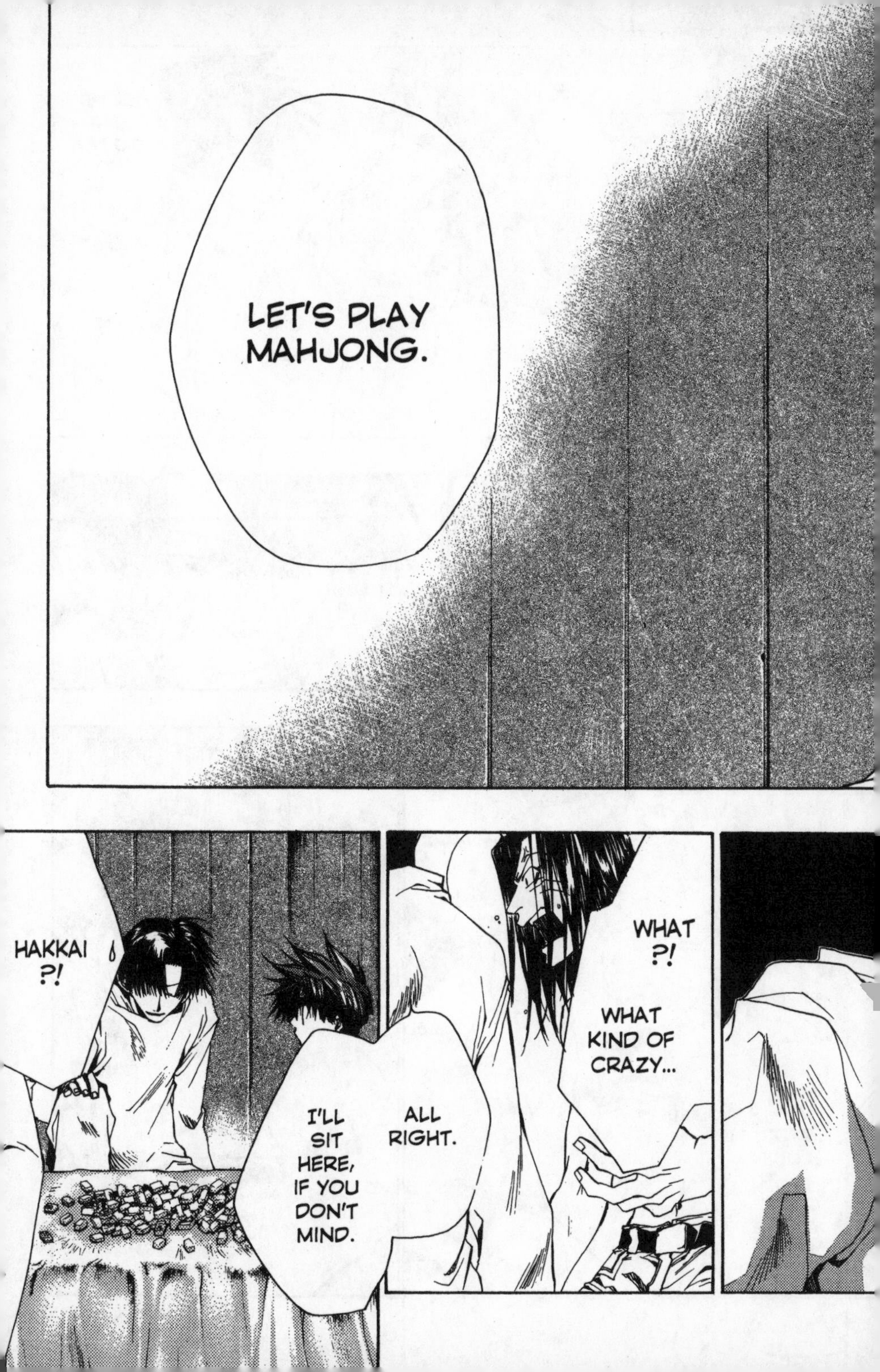
LET'S PLAY MAHJONG.
WHAT ?!
WHAT KIND OF CRAZY...
ALL RIGHT.
I'LL SIT HERE, IF YOU DON'T MIND.
HAKKAI ?!

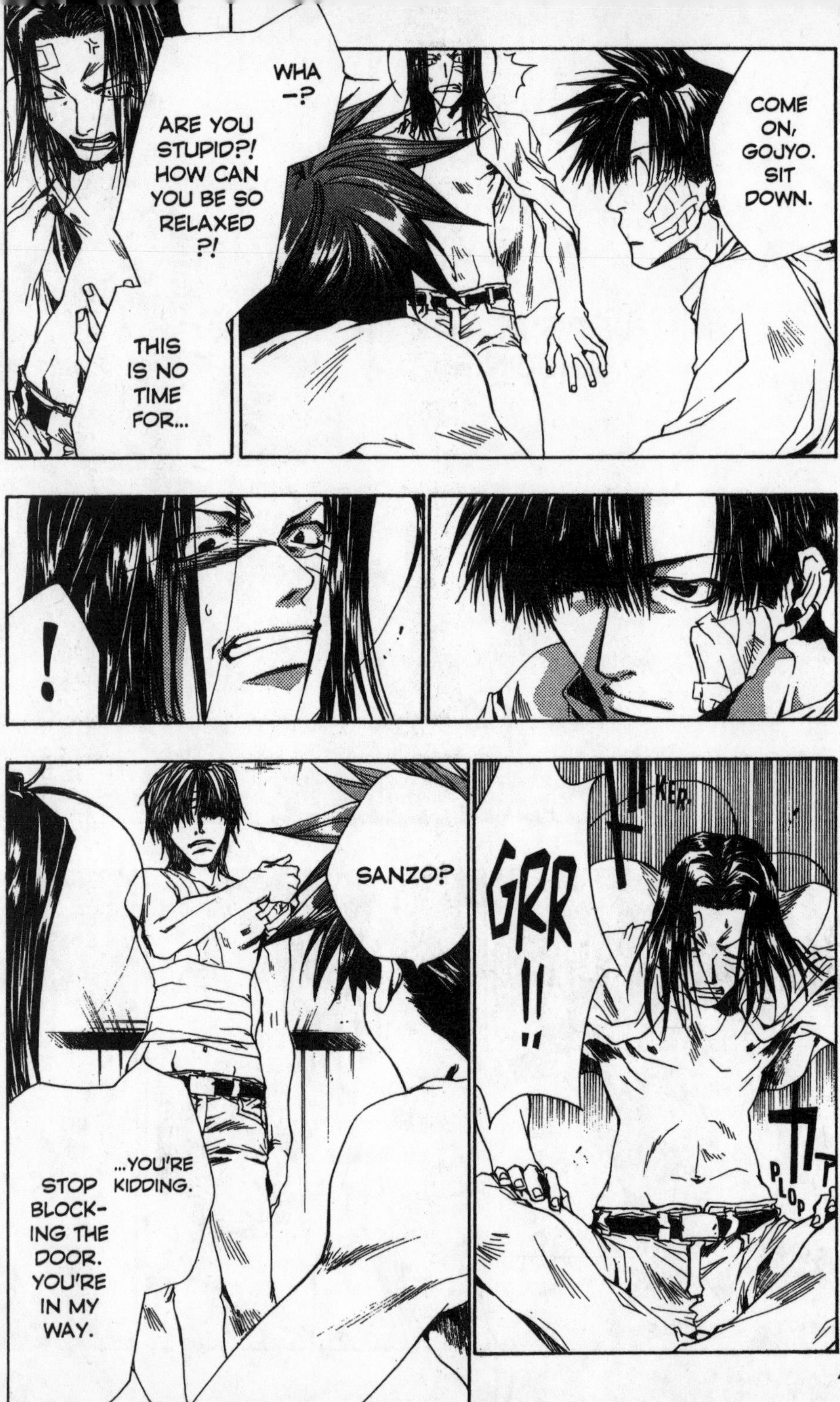
COME ON, GOJYO. SIT DOWN.
WHA —?
ARE YOU STUPID?! HOW CAN YOU BE SO RELAXED ?!
THIS IS NO TIME FOR...
!
KER-
GRR !!
PLOP
SANZO?
...YOU'RE KIDDING.
STOP BLOCKING THE DOOR. YOU'RE IN MY WAY.

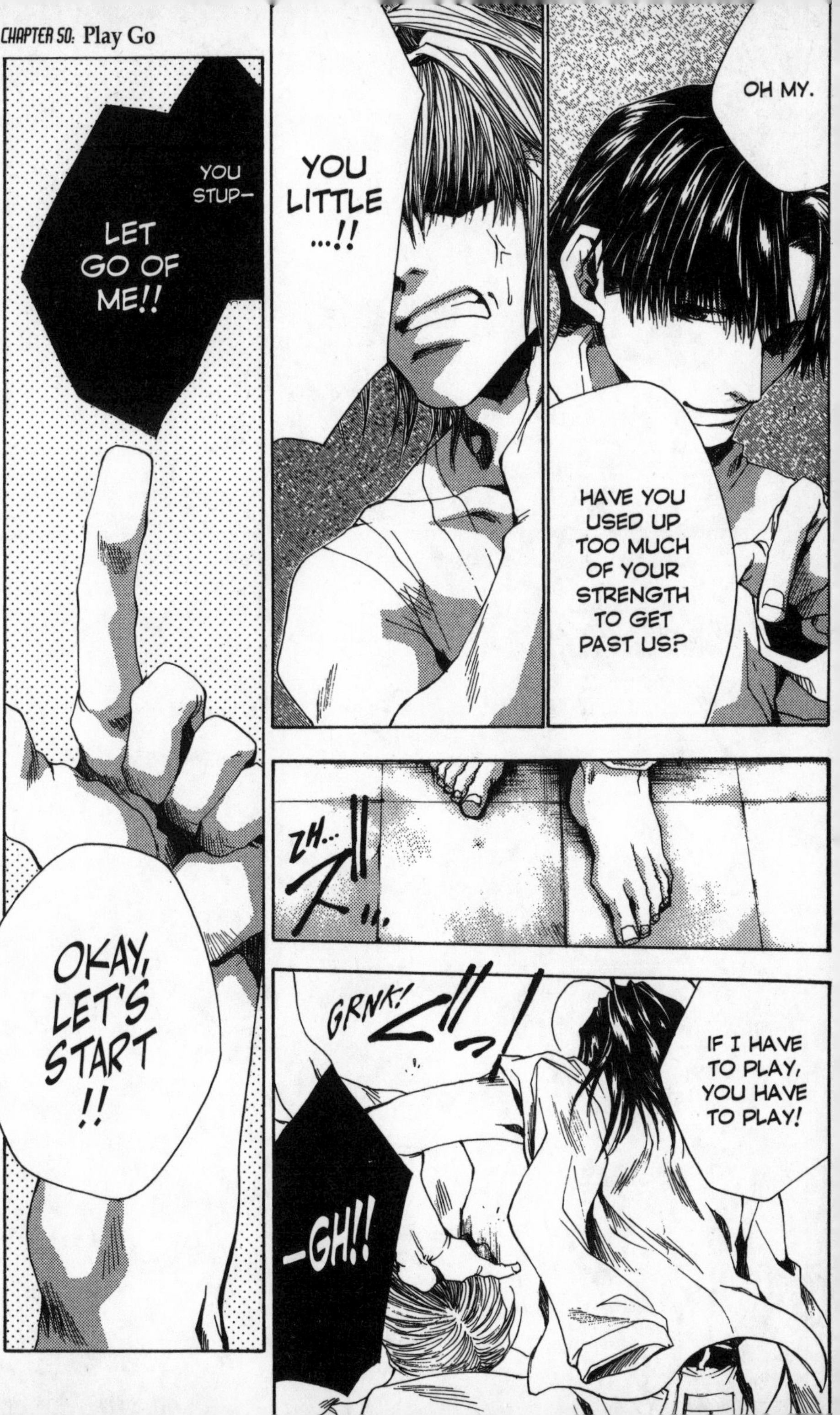
OH MY.
HAVE YOU USED UP TOO MUCH OF YOUR STRENGTH TO GET PAST US?
YOU LITTLE ...!!
ZH...
GRNK!
IF I HAVE TO PLAY, YOU HAVE TO PLAY!
-GH!!
YOU STUP-
LET GO OF ME!!
OKAY, LET'S START!!

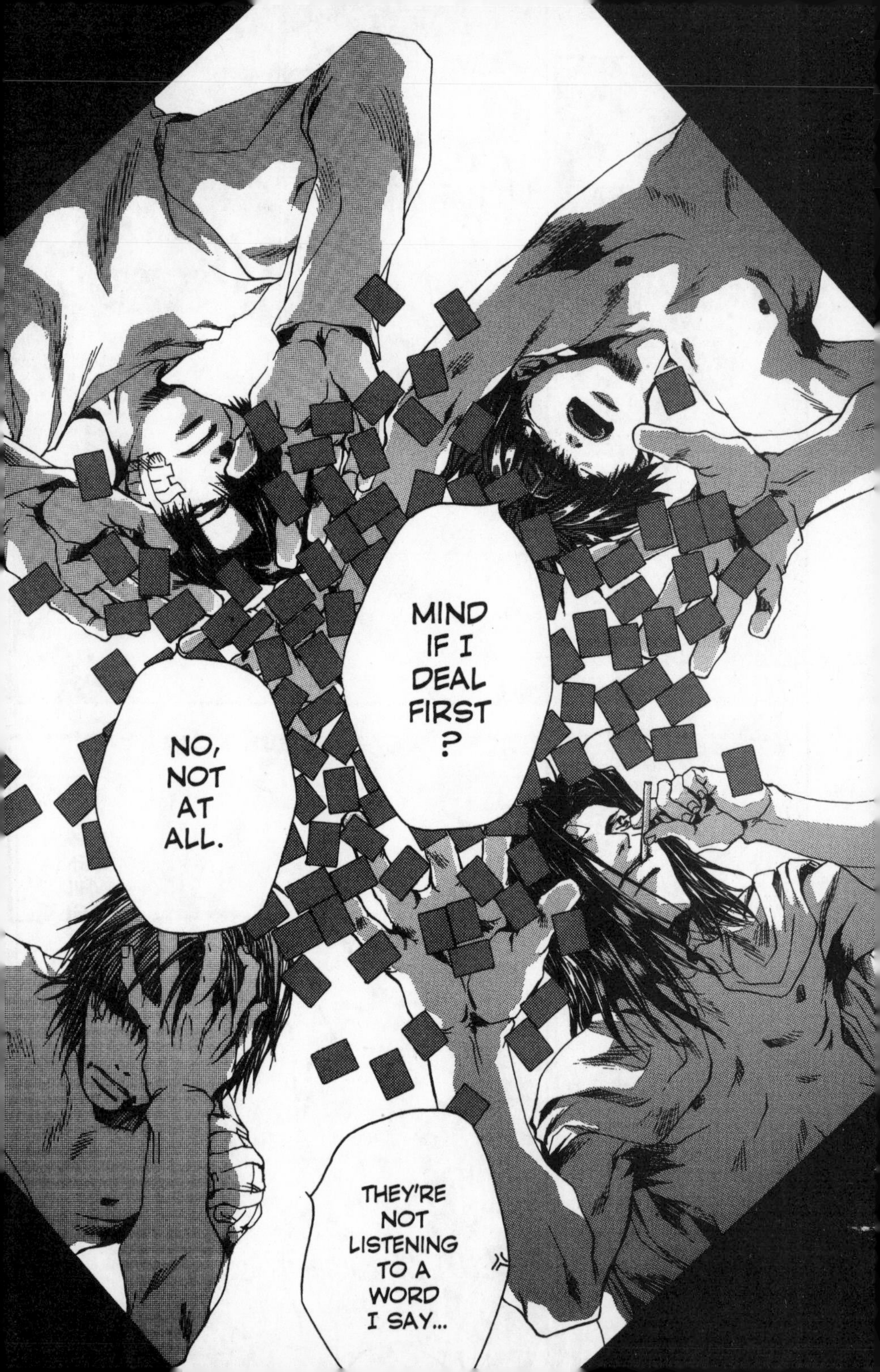
MIND IF I DEAL FIRST?
NO, NOT AT ALL.
THEY'RE NOT LISTENING TO A WORD I SAY...

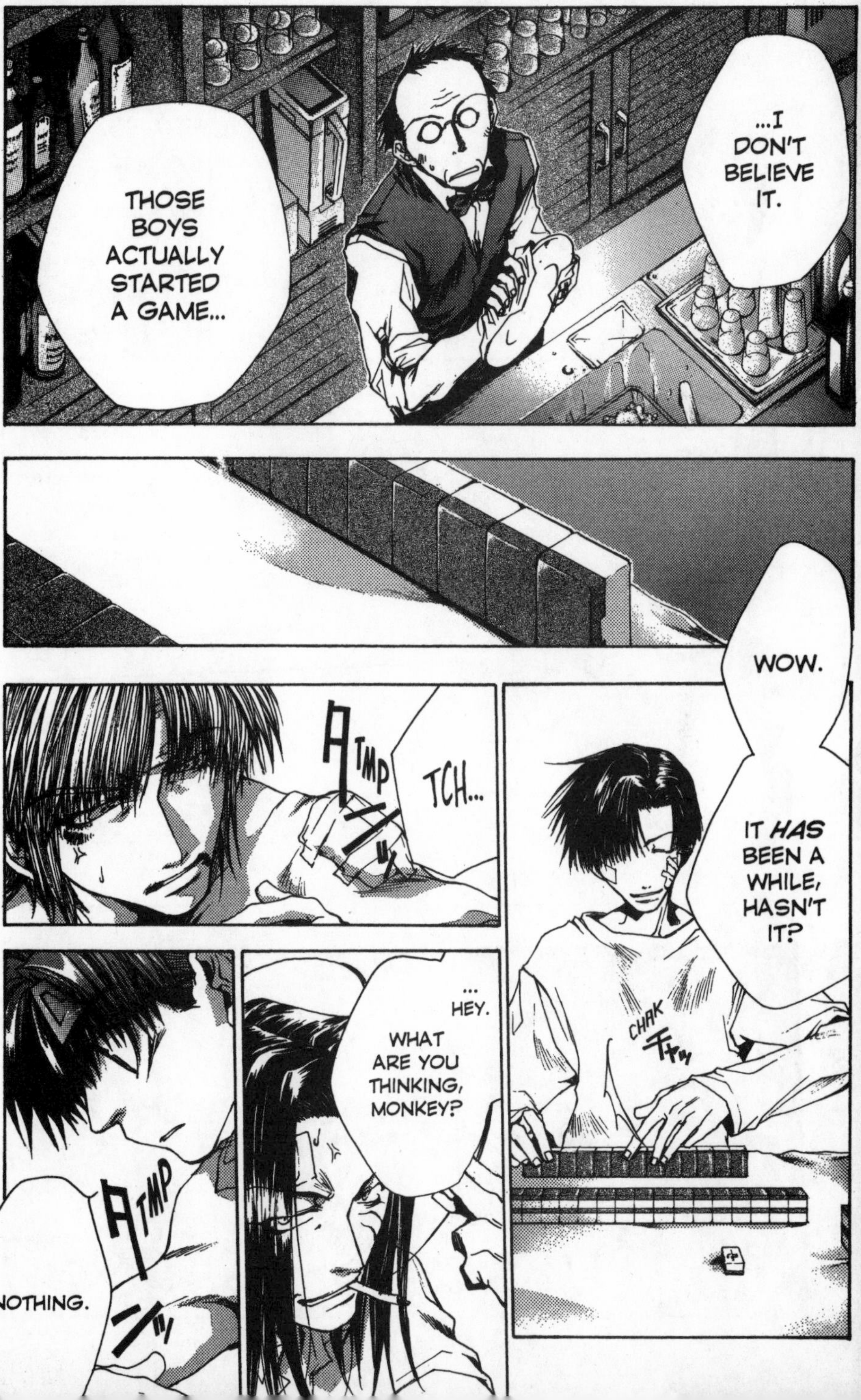
...I DON'T BELIEVE IT.
THOSE BOYS ACTUALLY STARTED A GAME...
WOW.
IT HAS BEEN A WHILE, HASN'T IT?
CHAK
TCH...
TMP
...HEY.
WHAT ARE YOU THINKING, MONKEY?
TMP
NOTHING.

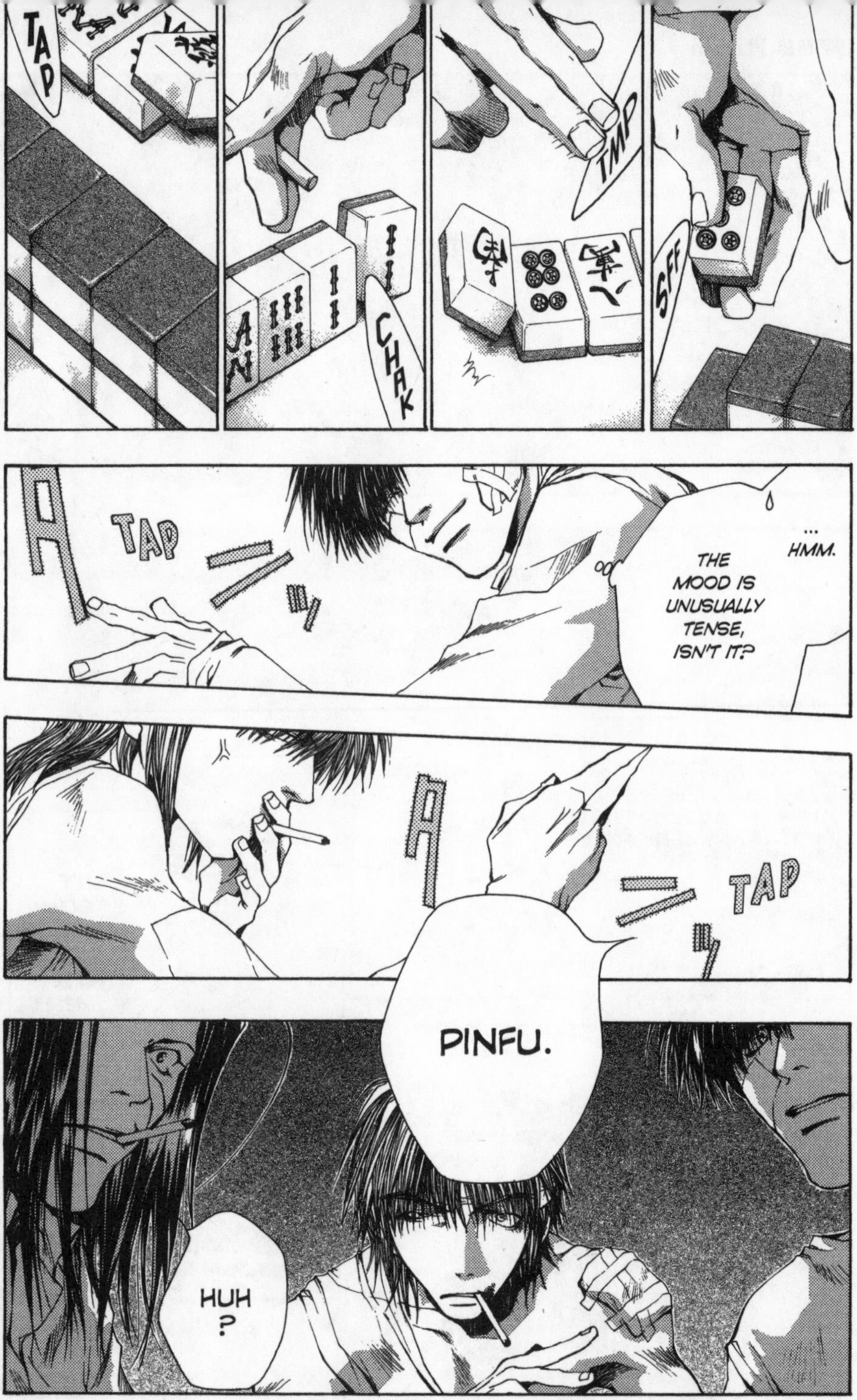
SFF
TMP
CHAK
TAP
... HMM.
THE MOOD IS UNUSUALLY TENSE, ISN'T IT?
TAP
TAP
PINFU.
HUH ?

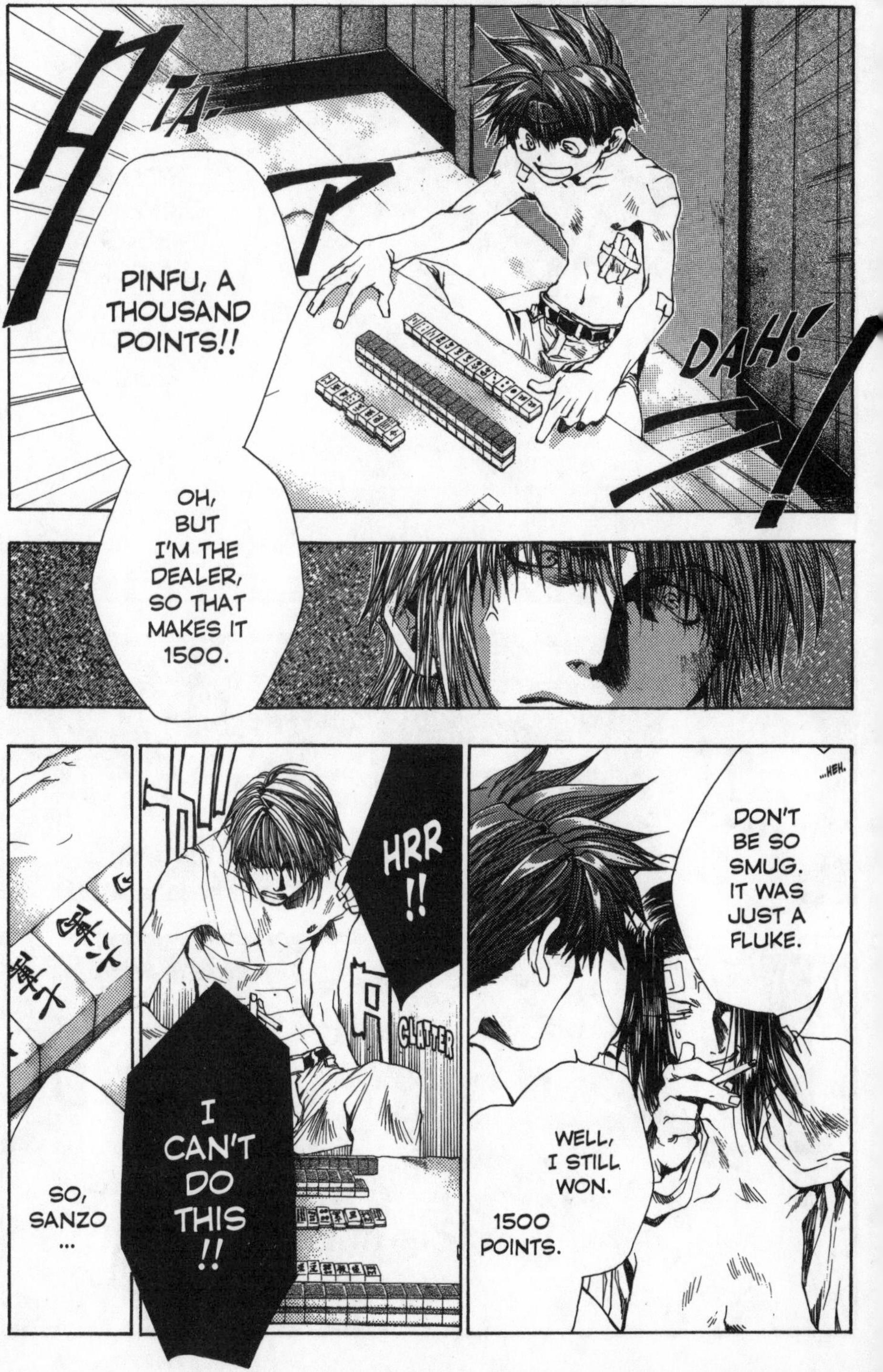
TA-
DAH!
PINFU, A THOUSAND POINTS!!
OH, BUT I'M THE DEALER, SO THAT MAKES IT 1500.
...HEH.
DON'T BE SO SMUG. IT WAS JUST A FLUKE.
WELL, I STILL WON.
1500 POINTS.
HRR!!
CLATTER
I CAN'T DO THIS!!
SO, SANZO ...

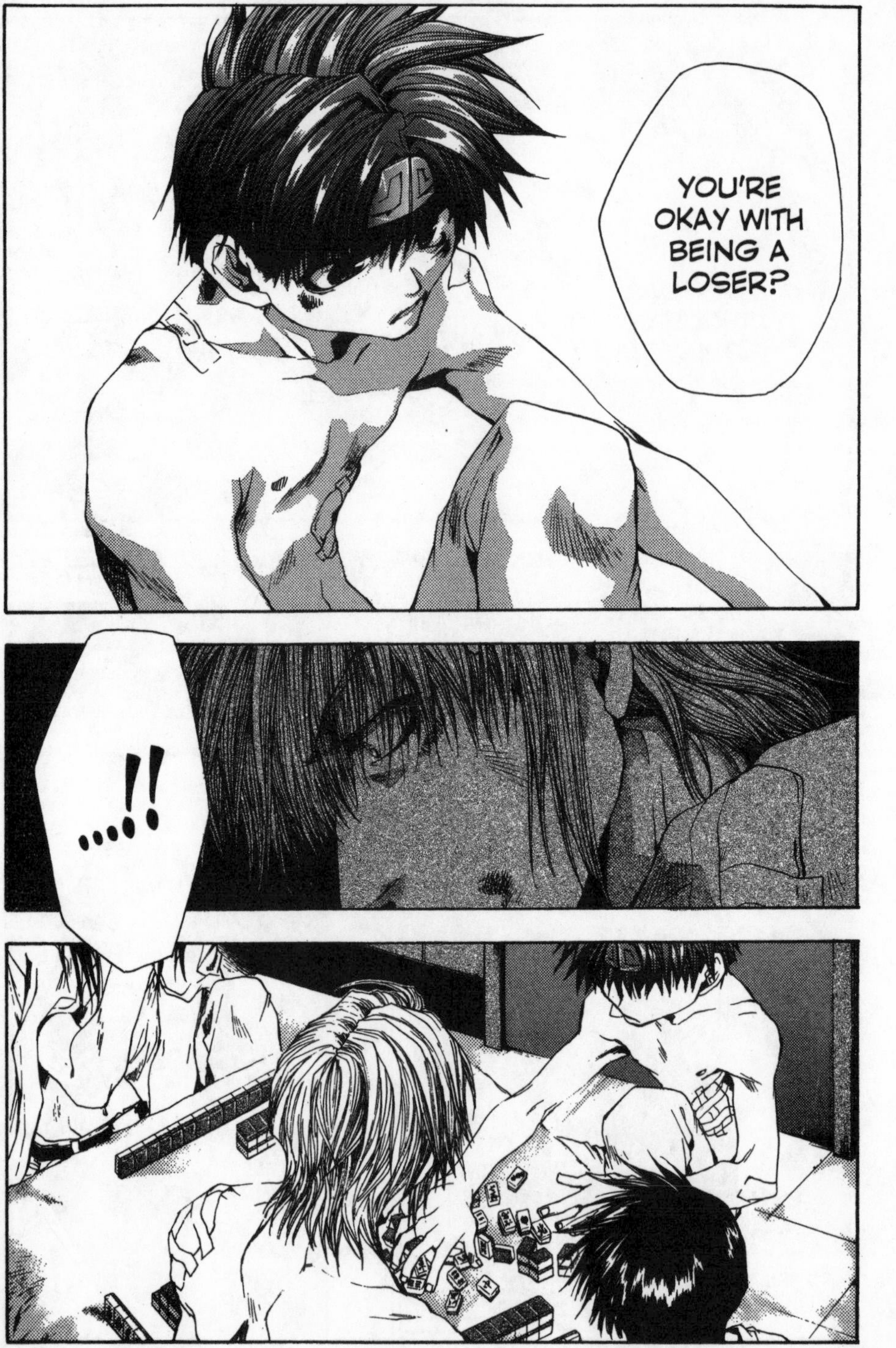
YOU'RE OKAY WITH BEING A LOSER?
...!!

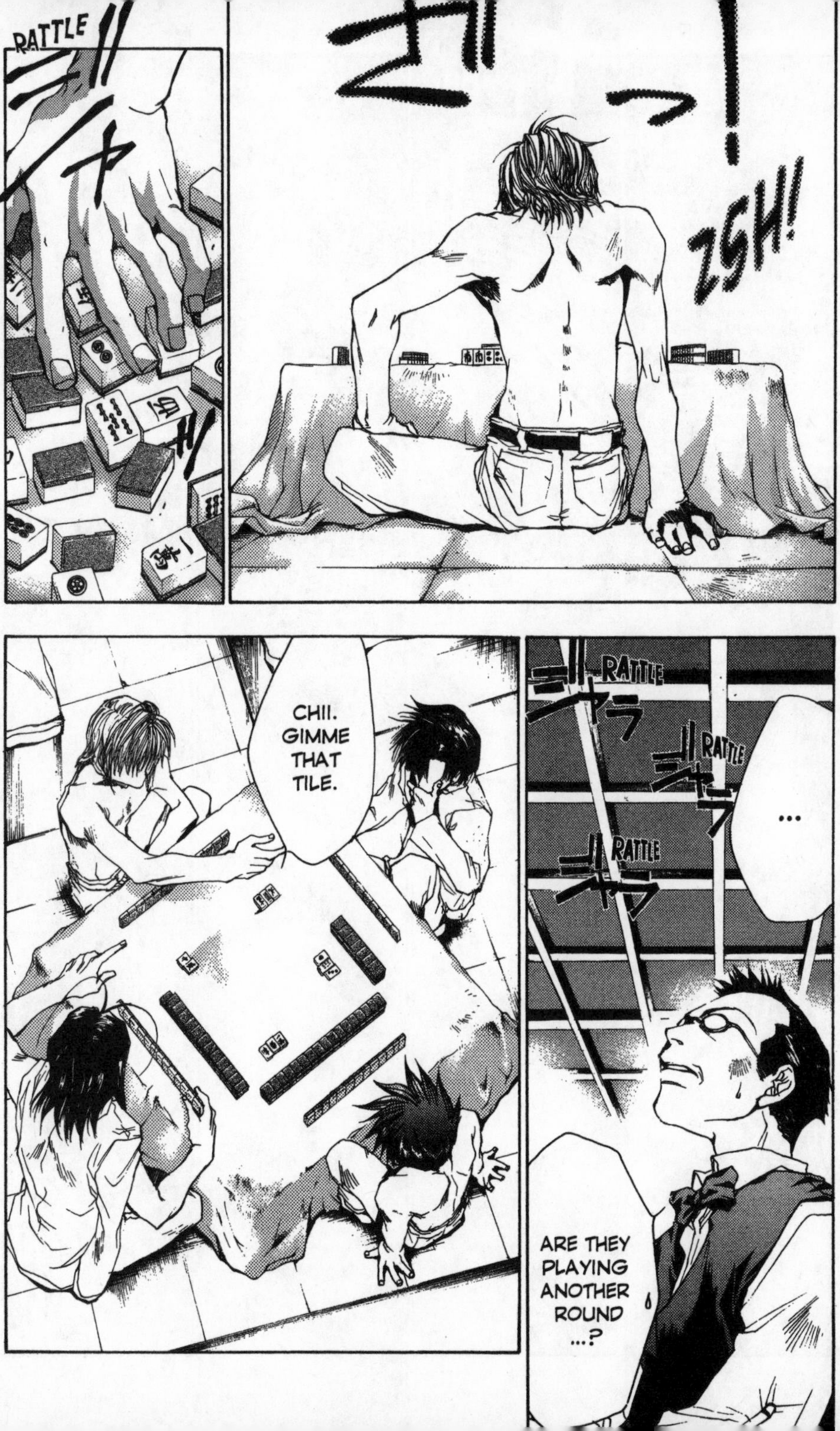
ざっ!
ZSH!!
RATTLE
RATTLE
ジャラ
RATTLE
ジャラ
RATTLE
ジャラ
...
ARE THEY PLAYING ANOTHER ROUND ...?
CHII. GIMME THAT TILE.

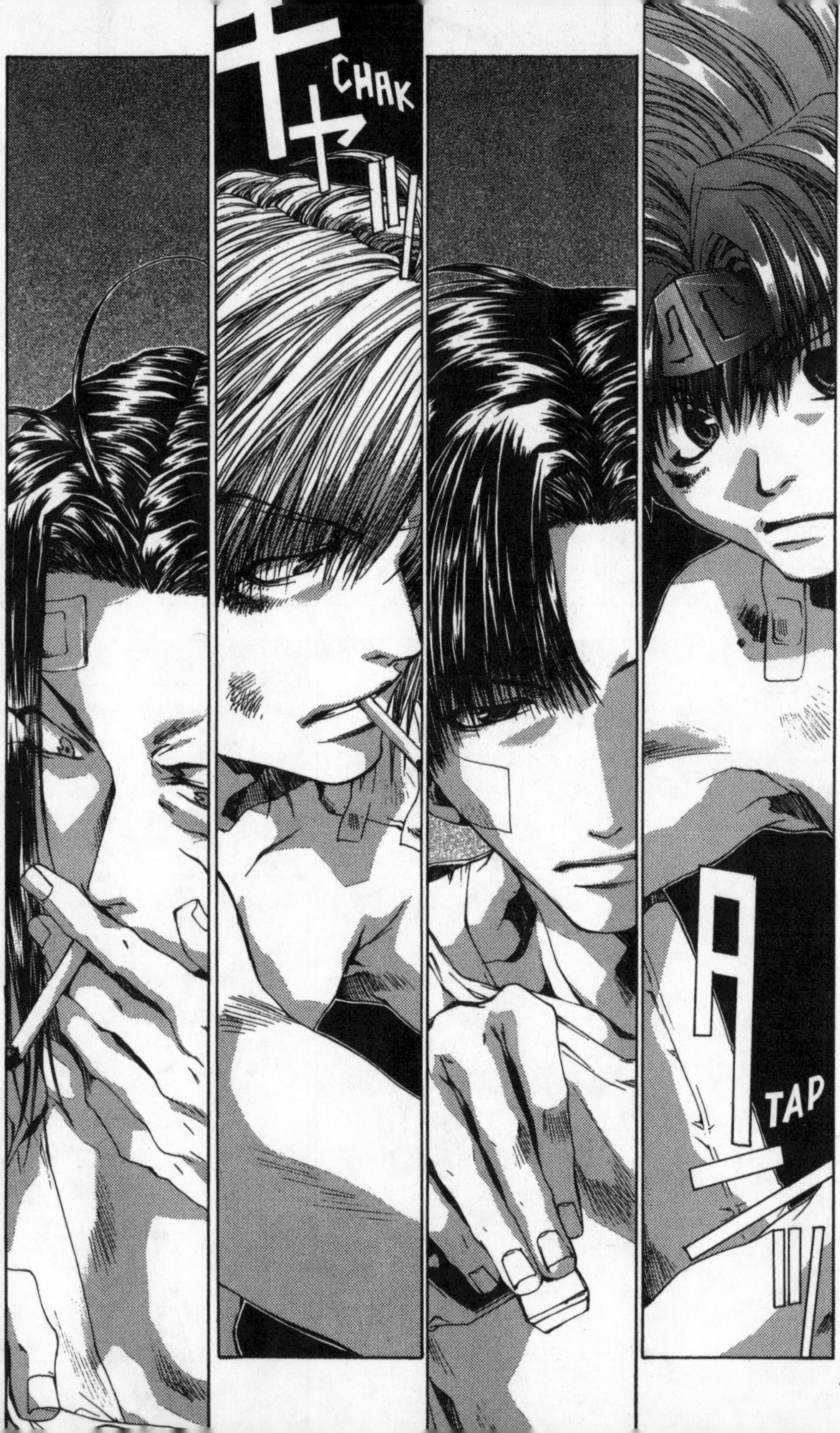
TAP
CHAK

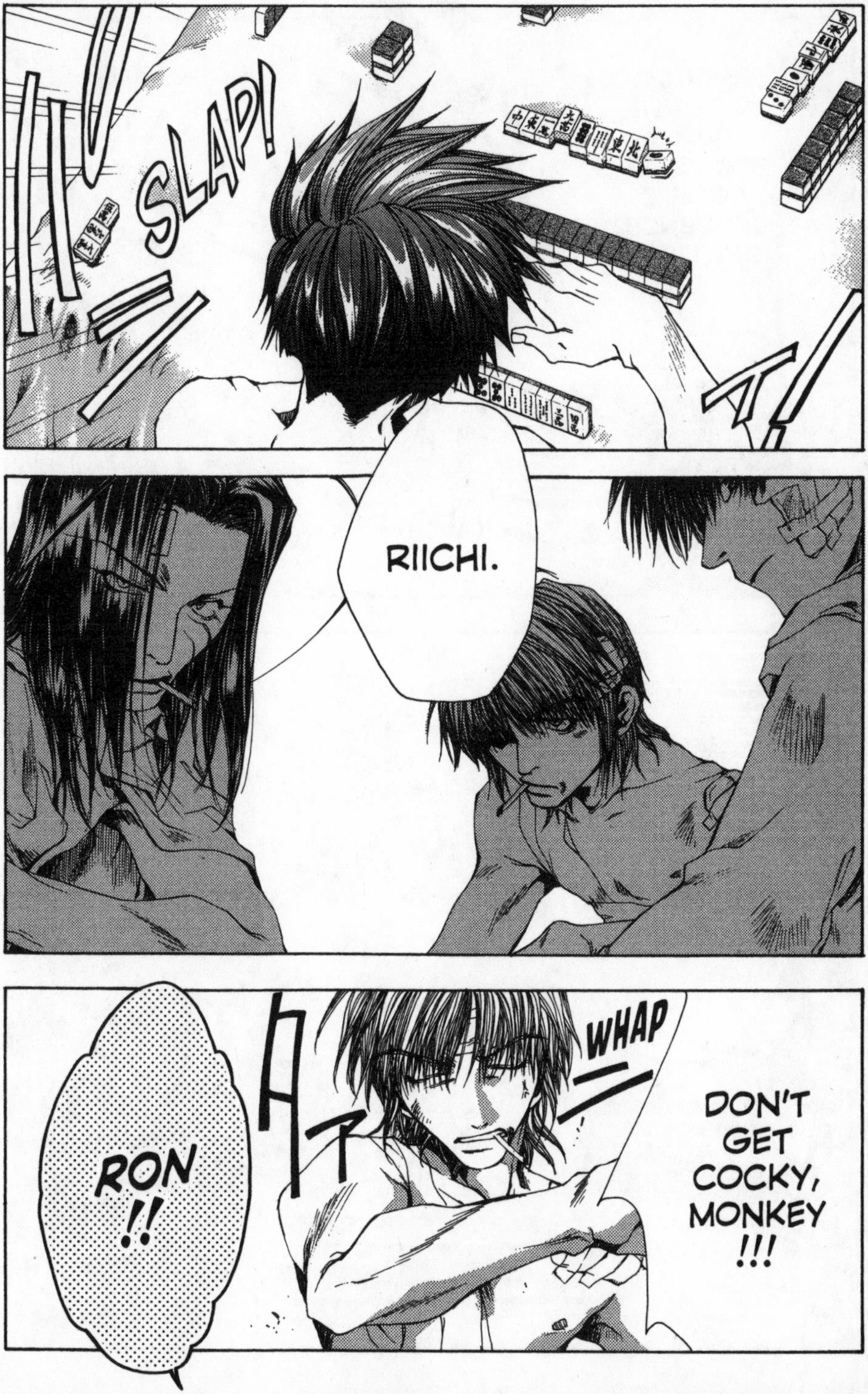
SLAP!
RIICHI.
WHAP
DON'T GET COCKY, MONKEY!!!
RON!!

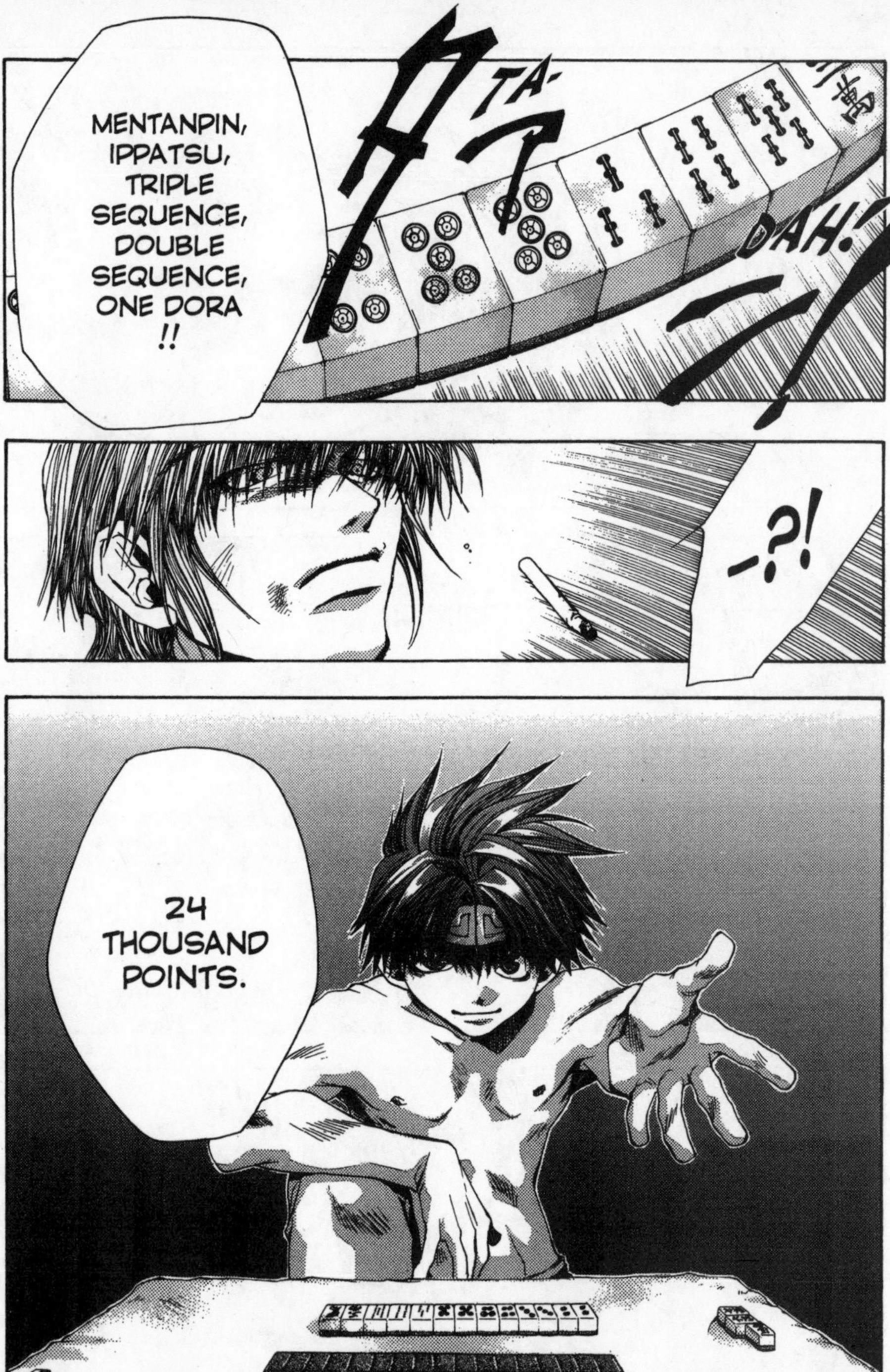
TA-
DAH!
MENTANPIN, IPPATSU, TRIPLE SEQUENCE, DOUBLE SEQUENCE, ONE DORA !!
-?!
24 THOUSAND POINTS.

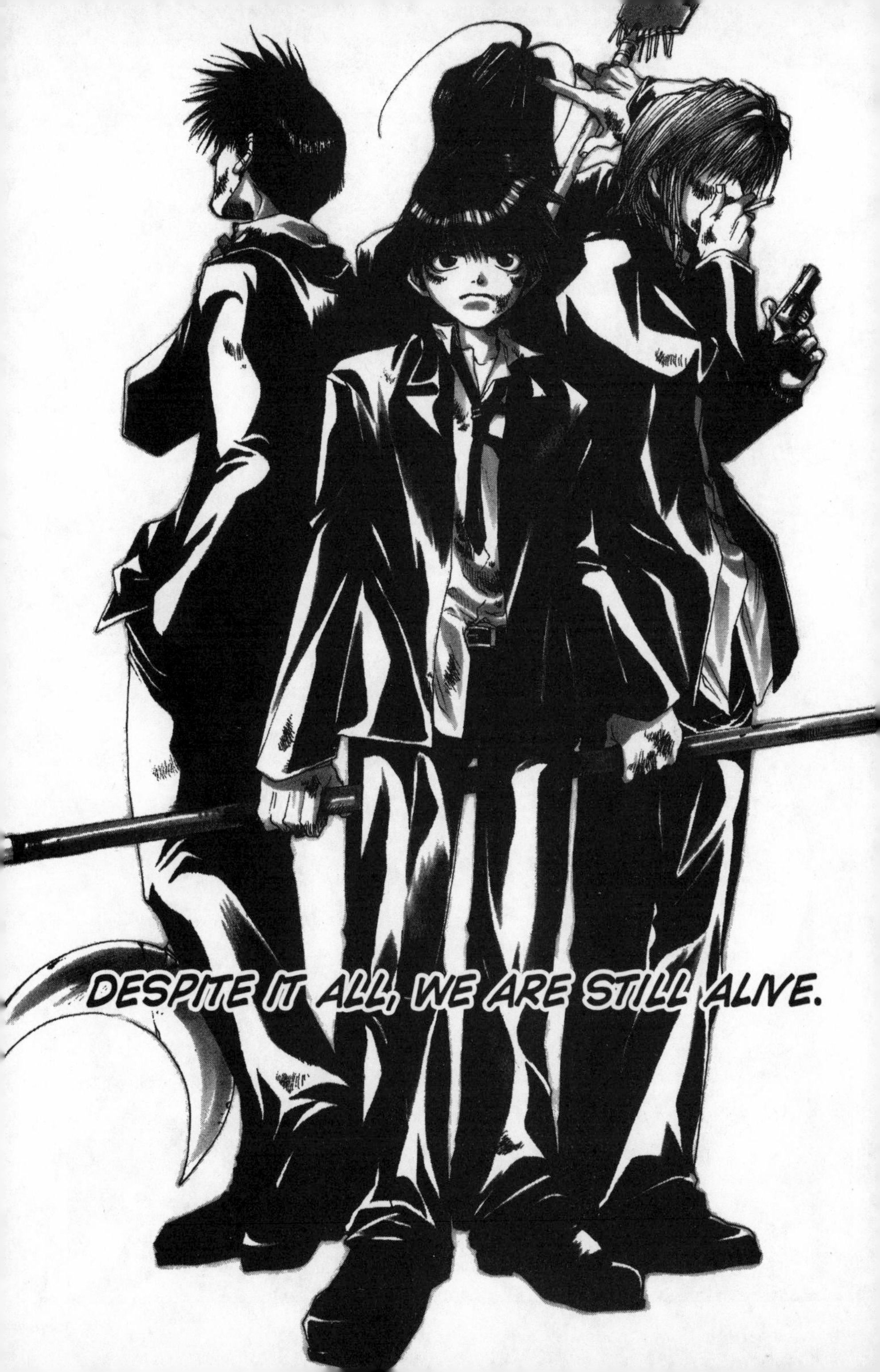
DESPITE IT ALL, WE ARE STILL ALIVE.

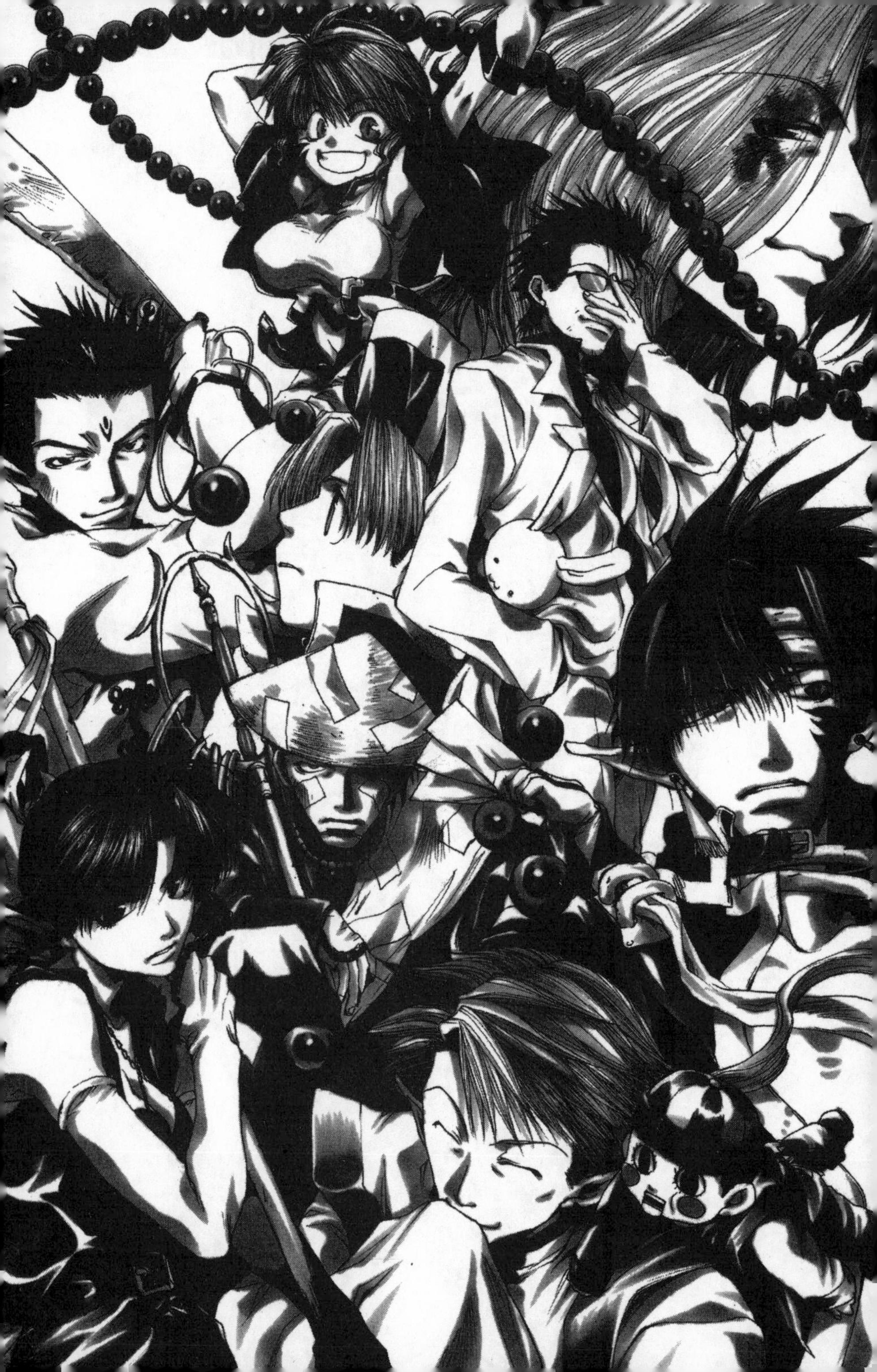

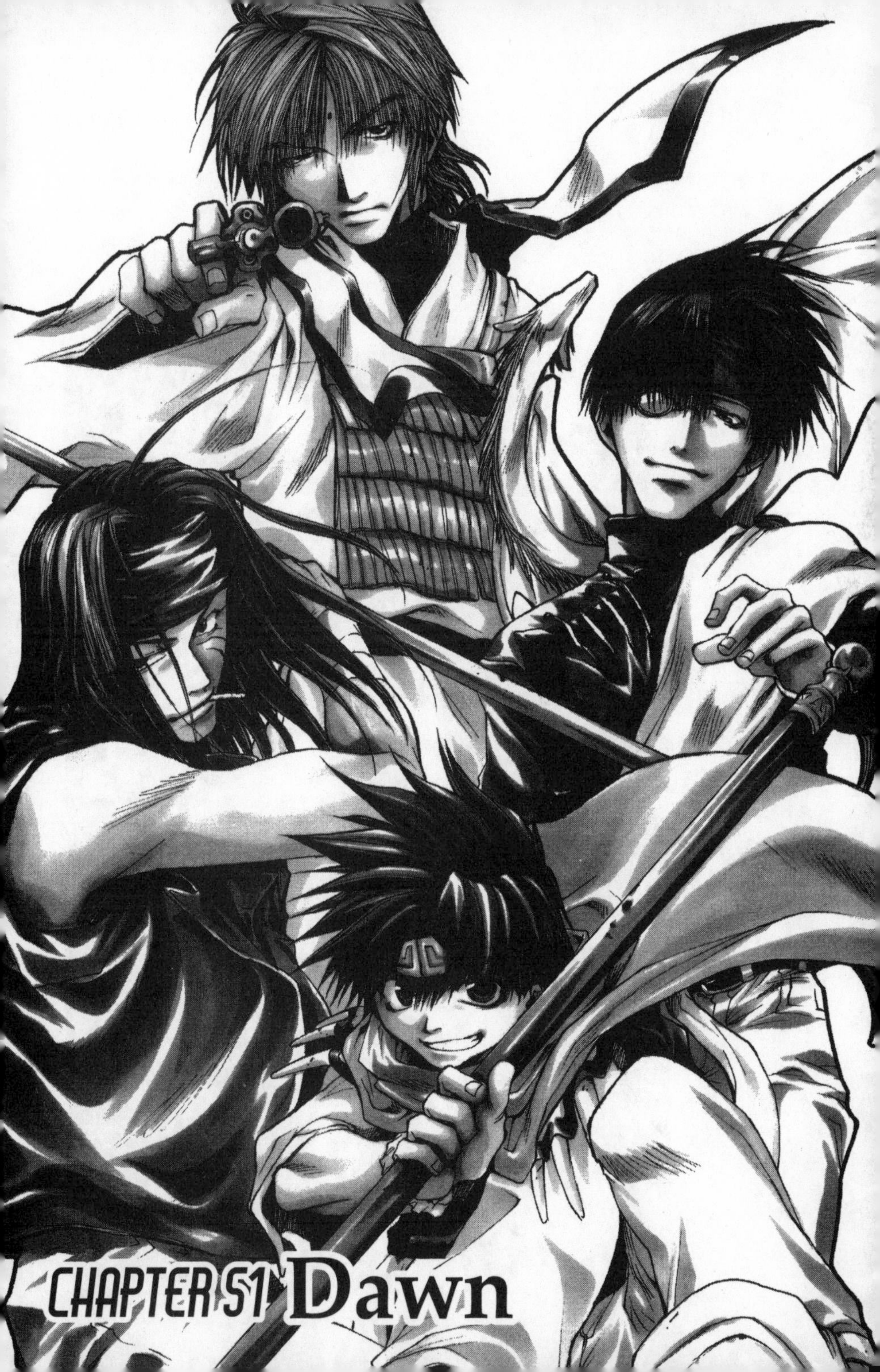

CHAPTER 51 Dawn

CHAPTER 51: Dawn

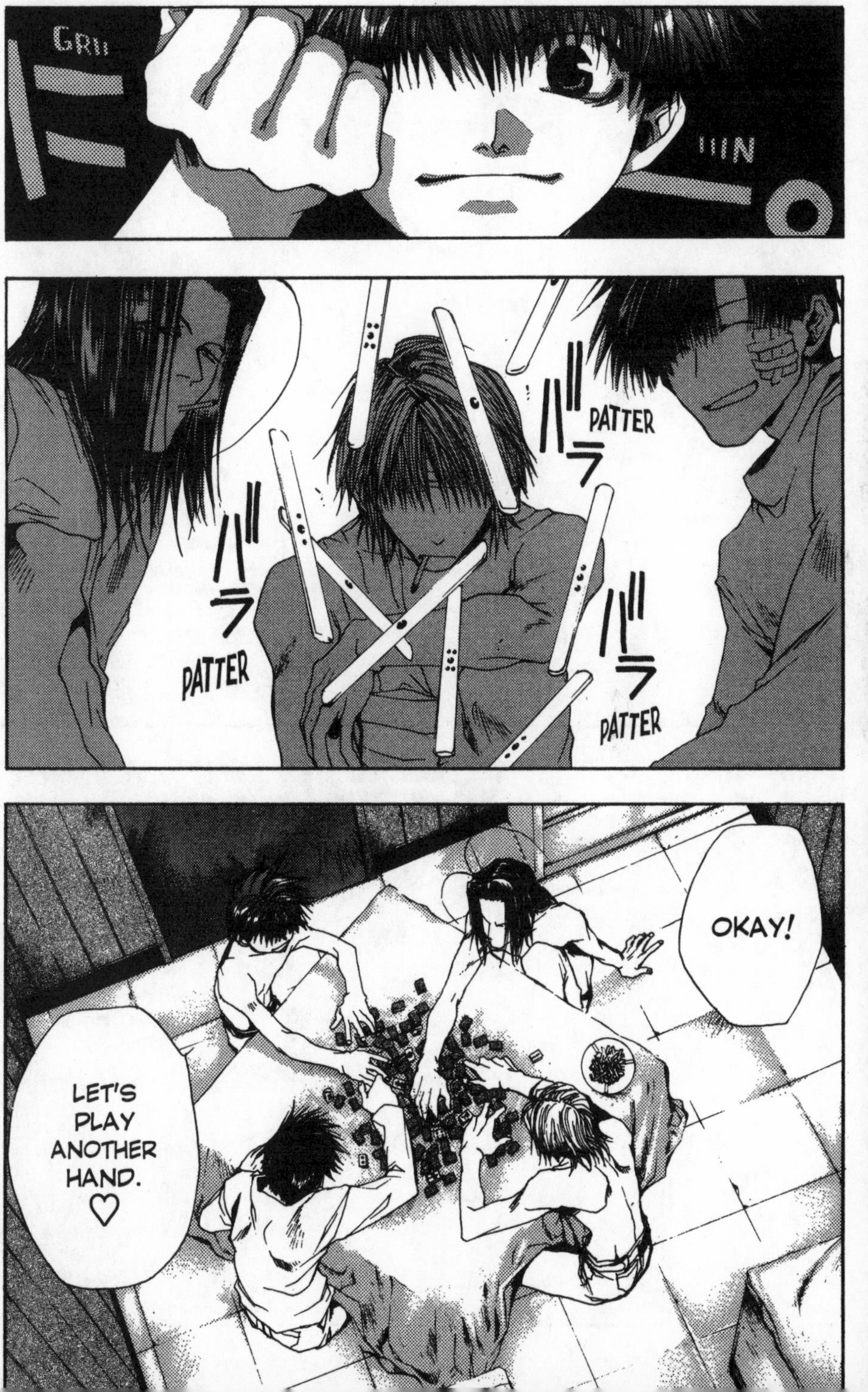
GRII
IIIN
バラ
PATTER
バラ
PATTER
バラ
PATTER
OKAY!
LET'S PLAY ANOTHER HAND. ♡

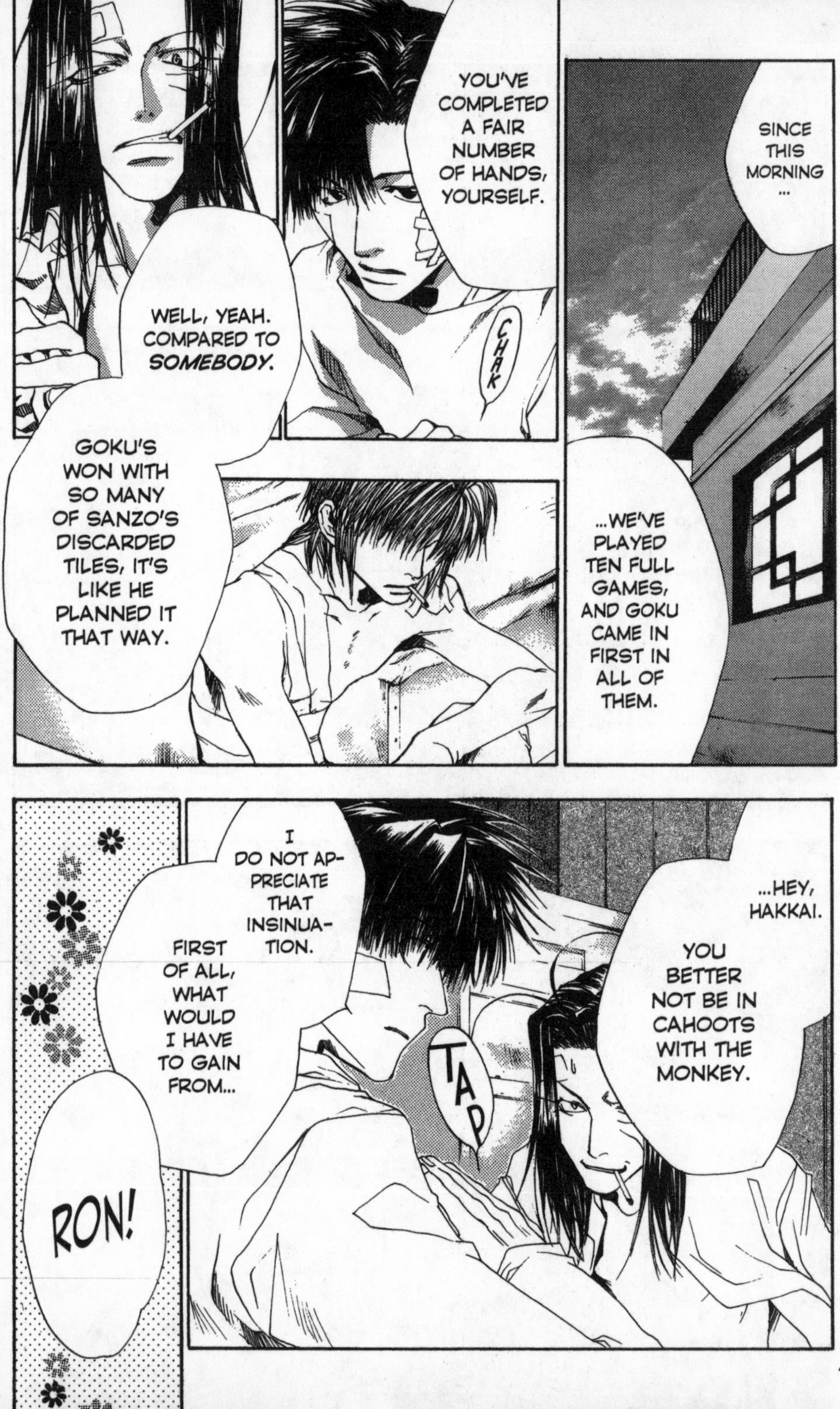
SINCE THIS MORNING ...
...WE'VE PLAYED TEN FULL GAMES, AND GOKU CAME IN FIRST IN ALL OF THEM.
YOU'VE COMPLETED A FAIR NUMBER OF HANDS, YOURSELF.
CHAK
WELL, YEAH. COMPARED TO *SOMEBODY*.
GOKU'S WON WITH SO MANY OF SANZO'S DISCARDED TILES, IT'S LIKE HE PLANNED IT THAT WAY.
...HEY, HAKKAI.
YOU BETTER NOT BE IN CAHOOTS WITH THE MONKEY.
I DO NOT AP-PRECIATE THAT INSINUA-TION.
FIRST OF ALL, WHAT WOULD I HAVE TO GAIN FROM...
TAP
RON!

SEVEN PAIRS, TWO DORA!
64 HUNDRED POINTS.
AH HA HA HA.
GOKU CERTAINLY IS ON A ROLL.
PATTER PATTER PATTER
HE IS MAD.
DEFINITELY NOT IN CAHOOTS.
TCH.
CHAK!

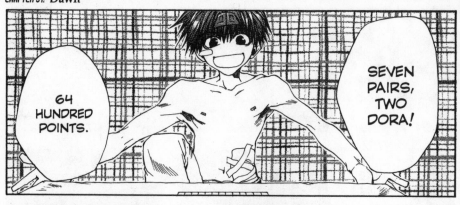

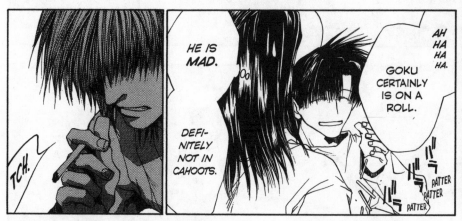

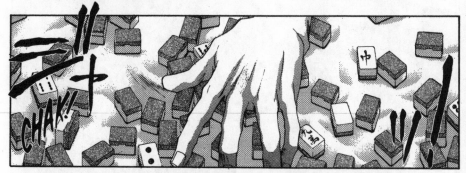

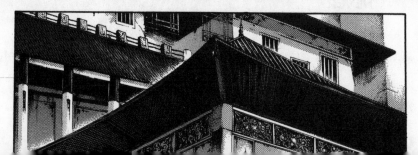

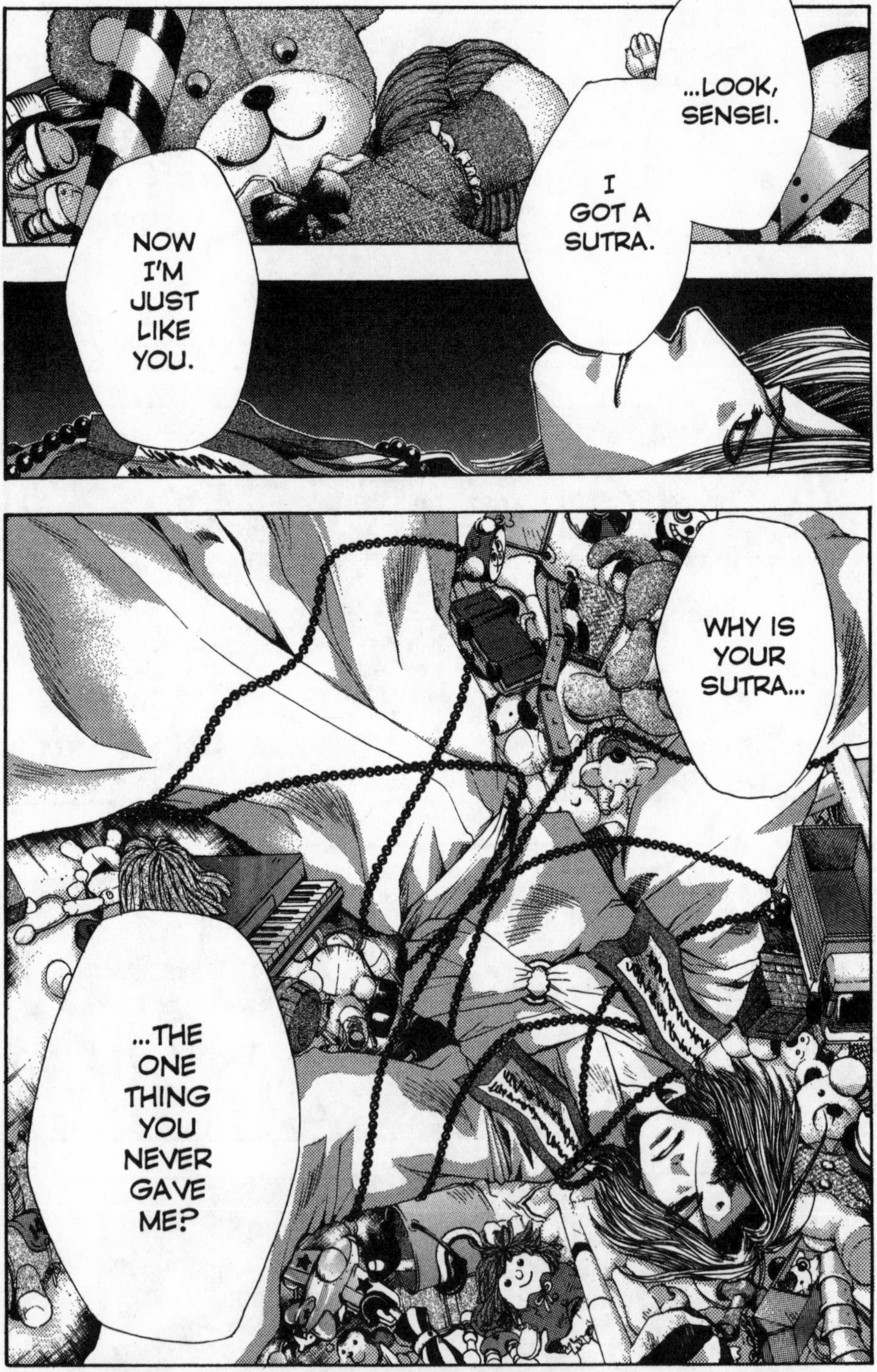
...LOOK, SENSEI.
I GOT A SUTRA.
NOW I'M JUST LIKE YOU.
WHY IS YOUR SUTRA...
...THE ONE THING YOU NEVER GAVE ME?

CHAPTER 51: Dawn

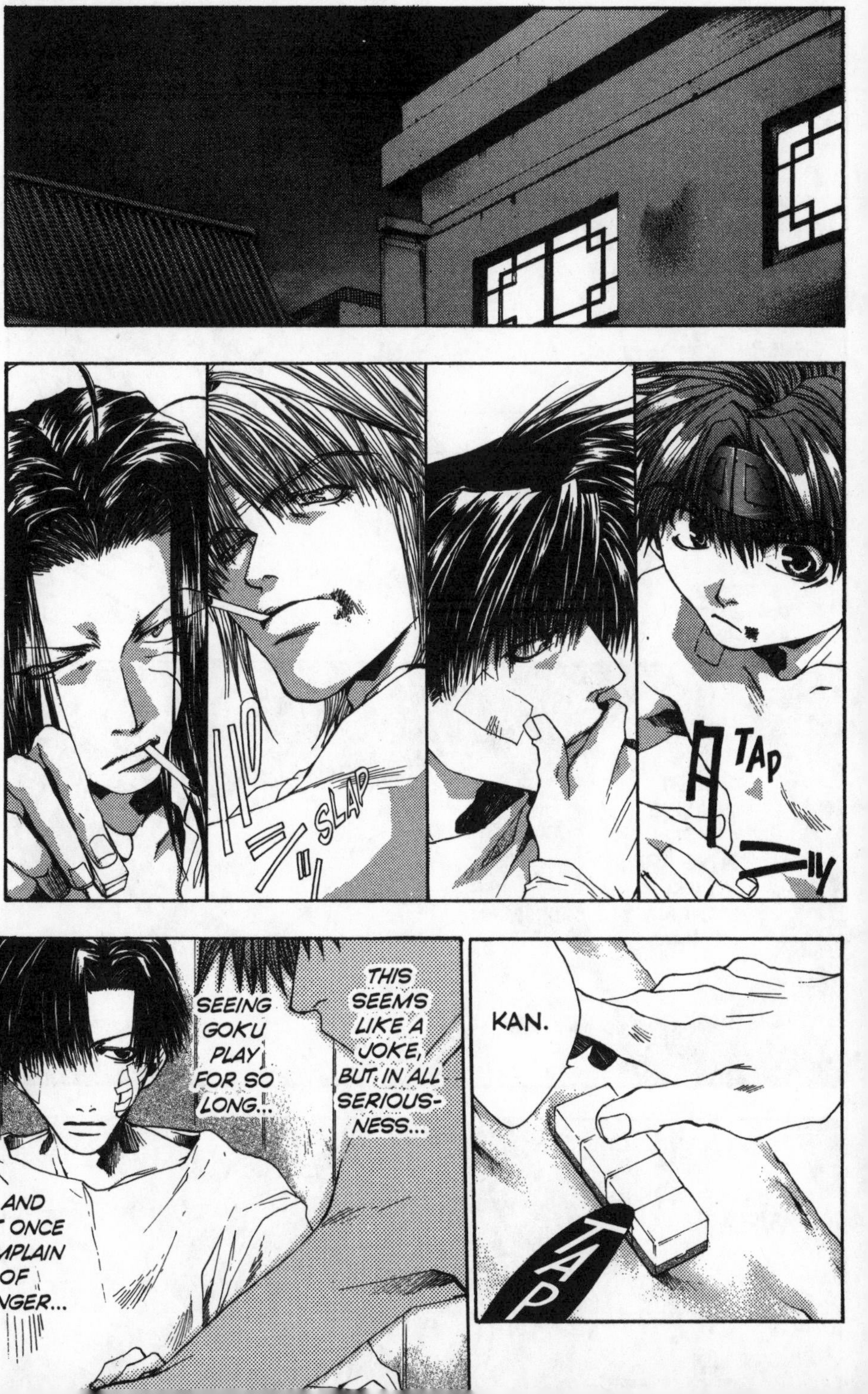
TAP
SLAP
KAN.
TAP
THIS SEEMS LIKE A JOKE, BUT IN ALL SERIOUSNESS...
SEEING GOKU PLAY FOR SO LONG...
...AND NOT ONCE COMPLAIN OF HUNGER...

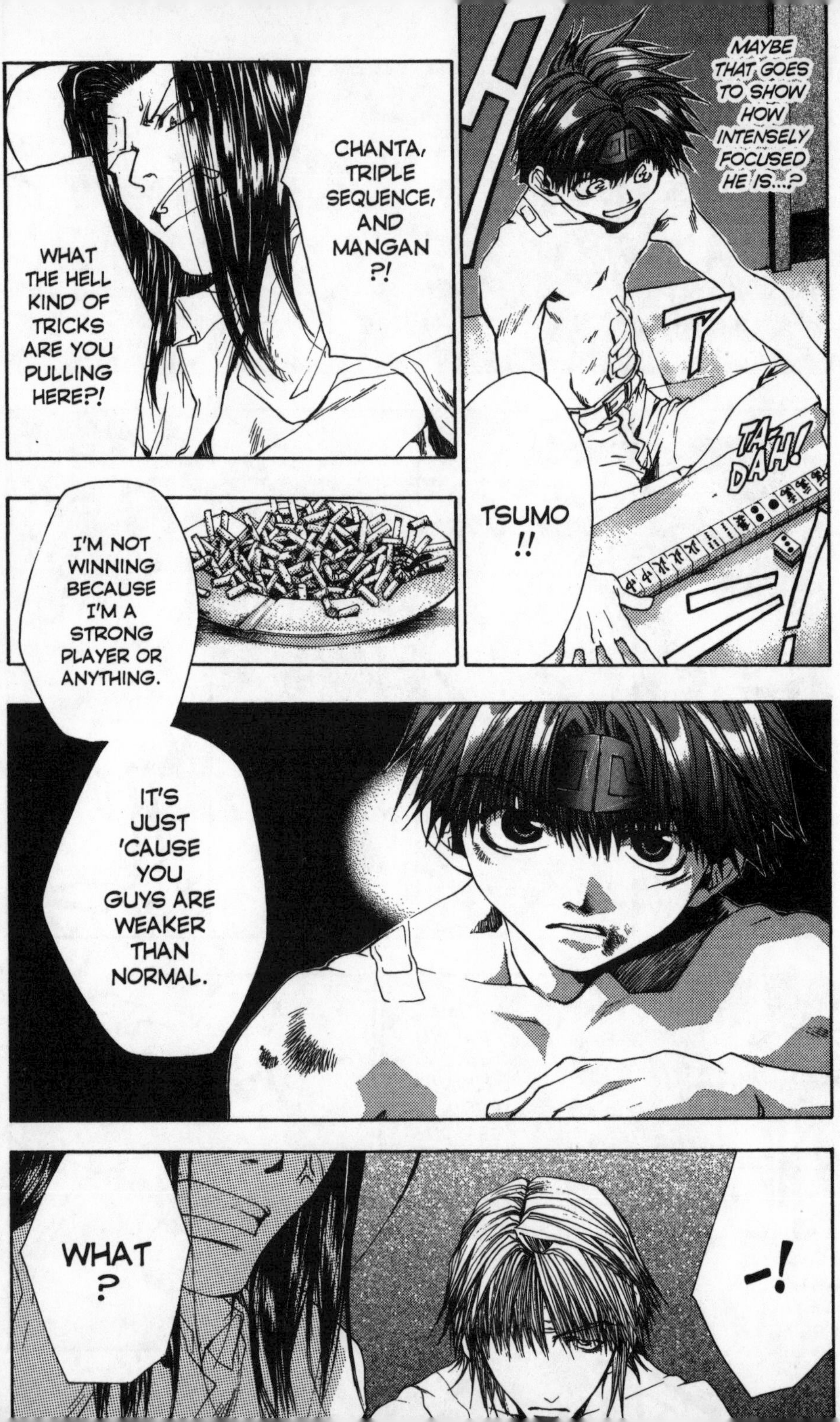
MAYBE THAT GOES TO SHOW HOW INTENSELY FOCUSED HE IS...?
TA-DAH!
TSUMO!!
CHANTA, TRIPLE SEQUENCE, AND MANGAN?!
WHAT THE HELL KIND OF TRICKS ARE YOU PULLING HERE?!
I'M NOT WINNING BECAUSE I'M A STRONG PLAYER OR ANYTHING.
IT'S JUST 'CAUSE YOU GUYS ARE WEAKER THAN NORMAL.
–!
WHAT?

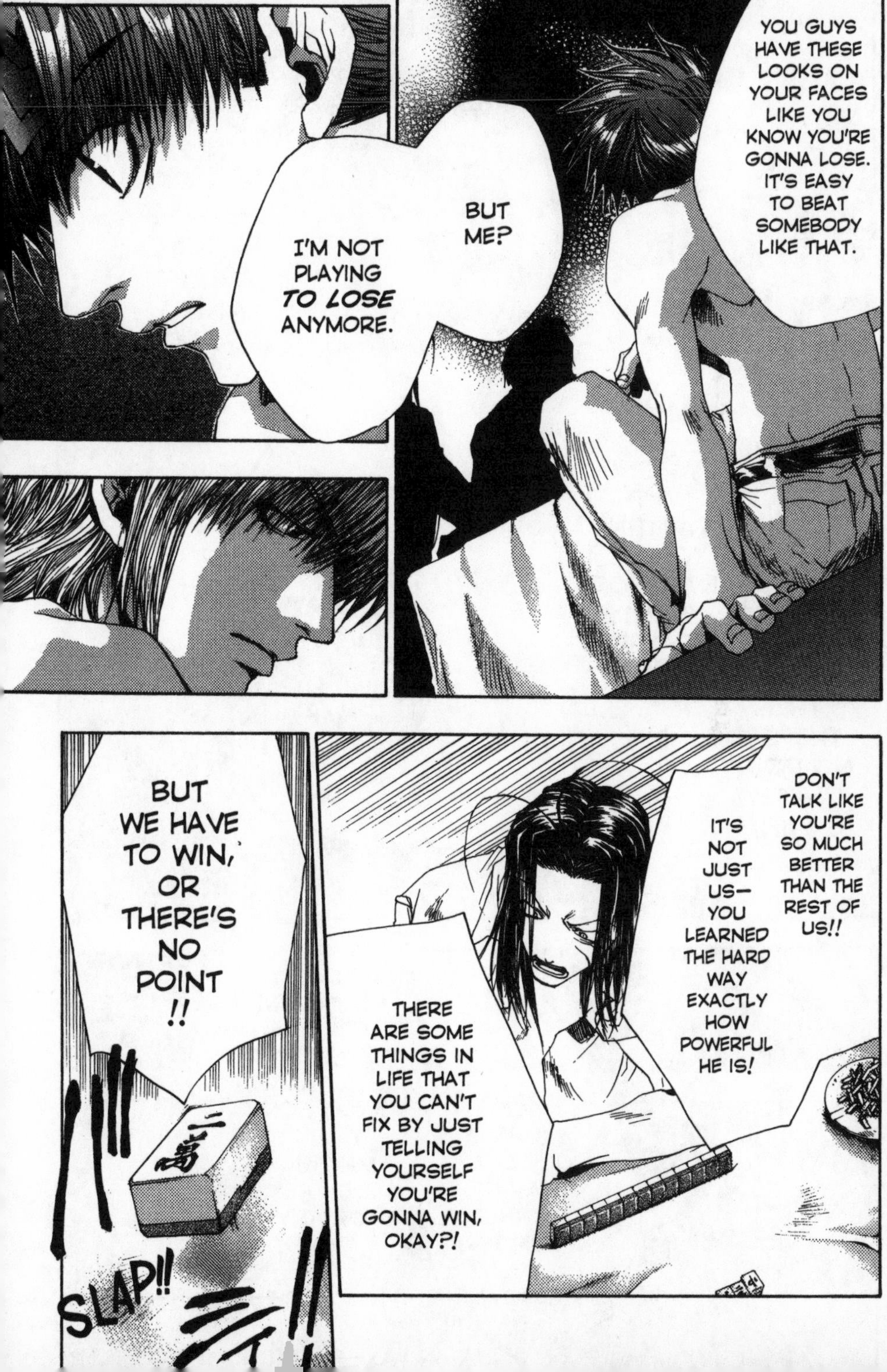
YOU GUYS HAVE THESE LOOKS ON YOUR FACES LIKE YOU KNOW YOU'RE GONNA LOSE. IT'S EASY TO BEAT SOMEBODY LIKE THAT.
BUT ME?
I'M NOT PLAYING *TO LOSE* ANYMORE.
DON'T TALK LIKE YOU'RE SO MUCH BETTER THAN THE REST OF US!!
IT'S NOT JUST US— YOU LEARNED THE HARD WAY EXACTLY HOW POWERFUL HE IS!
THERE ARE SOME THINGS IN LIFE THAT YOU CAN'T FIX BY JUST TELLING YOURSELF YOU'RE GONNA WIN, OKAY?!
BUT WE HAVE TO WIN, OR THERE'S NO POINT!!
SLAP!!

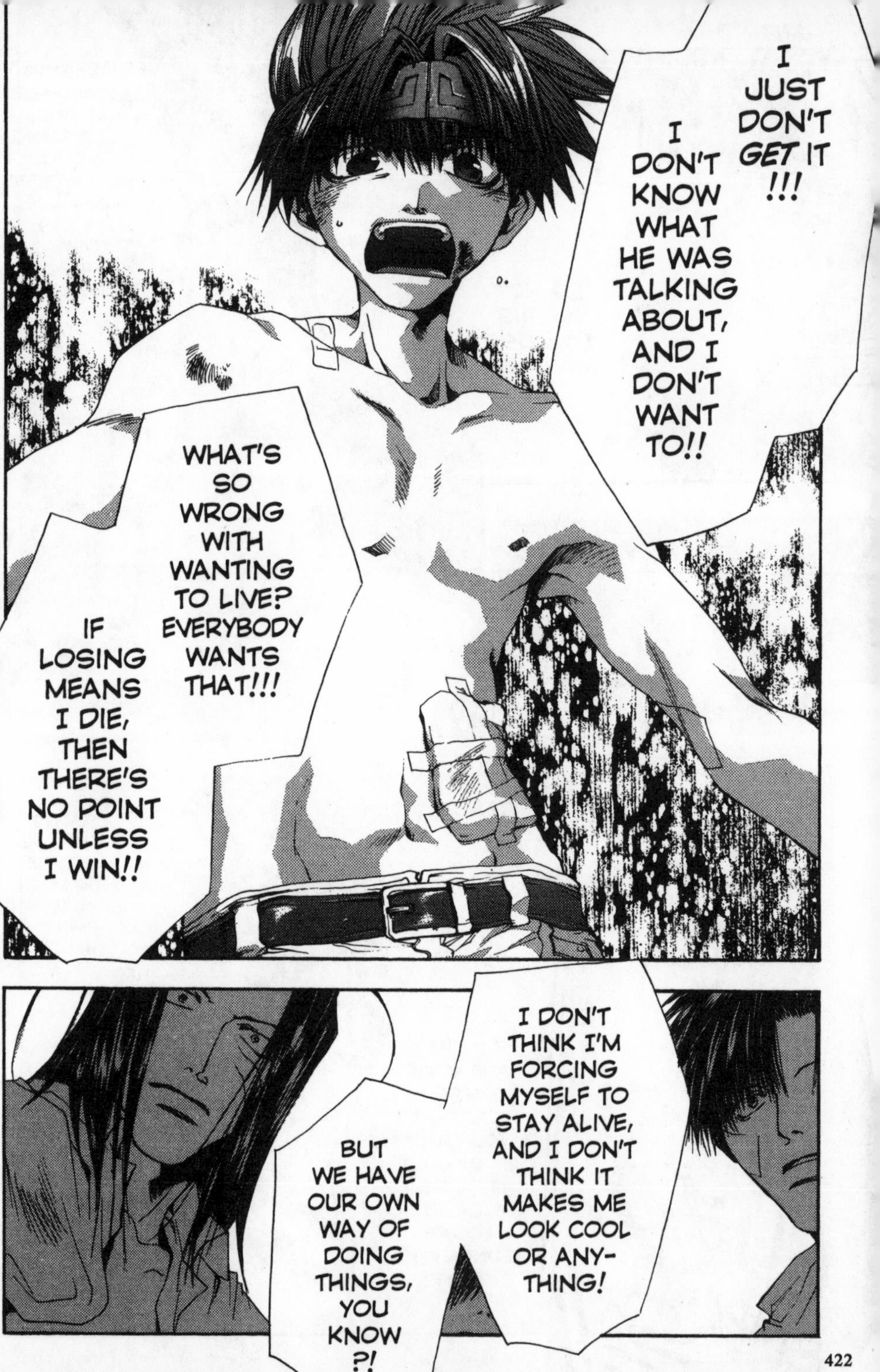
I JUST DON'T *GET* IT!!!
I DON'T KNOW WHAT HE WAS TALKING ABOUT, AND I DON'T WANT TO!!
WHAT'S SO WRONG WITH WANTING TO LIVE? EVERYBODY WANTS THAT!!!
IF LOSING MEANS I DIE, THEN THERE'S NO POINT UNLESS I WIN!!
I DON'T THINK I'M FORCING MYSELF TO STAY ALIVE, AND I DON'T THINK IT MAKES ME LOOK COOL OR ANY-THING!
BUT WE HAVE OUR OWN WAY OF DOING THINGS, YOU KNOW?!

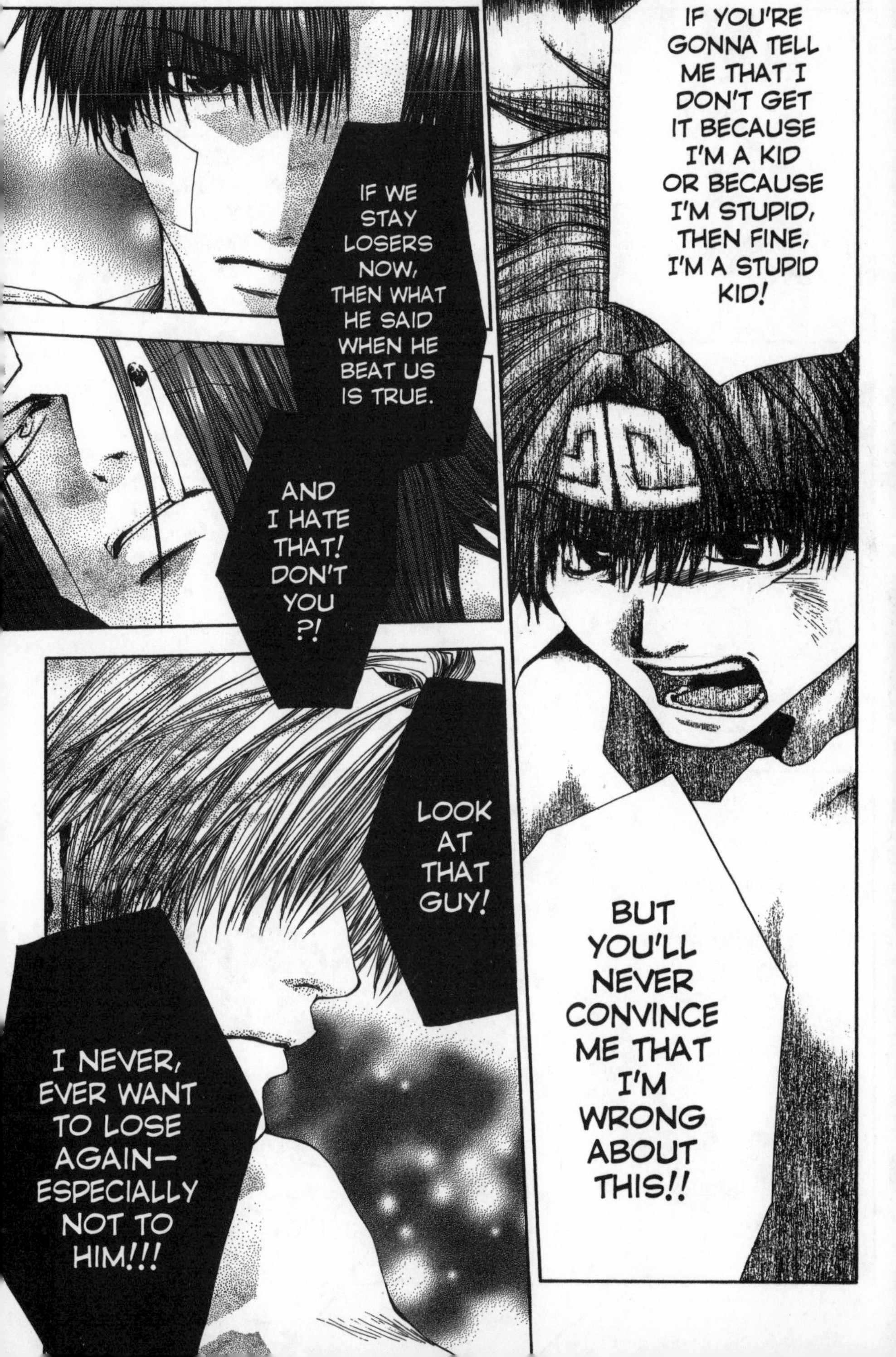
IF YOU'RE GONNA TELL ME THAT I DON'T GET IT BECAUSE I'M A KID OR BECAUSE I'M STUPID, THEN FINE, I'M A STUPID KID!
BUT YOU'LL NEVER CONVINCE ME THAT I'M WRONG ABOUT THIS!!
IF WE STAY LOSERS NOW, THEN WHAT HE SAID WHEN HE BEAT US IS TRUE.
AND I HATE THAT! DON'T YOU ?!
LOOK AT THAT GUY!
I NEVER, EVER WANT TO LOSE AGAIN— ESPECIALLY NOT TO HIM!!!

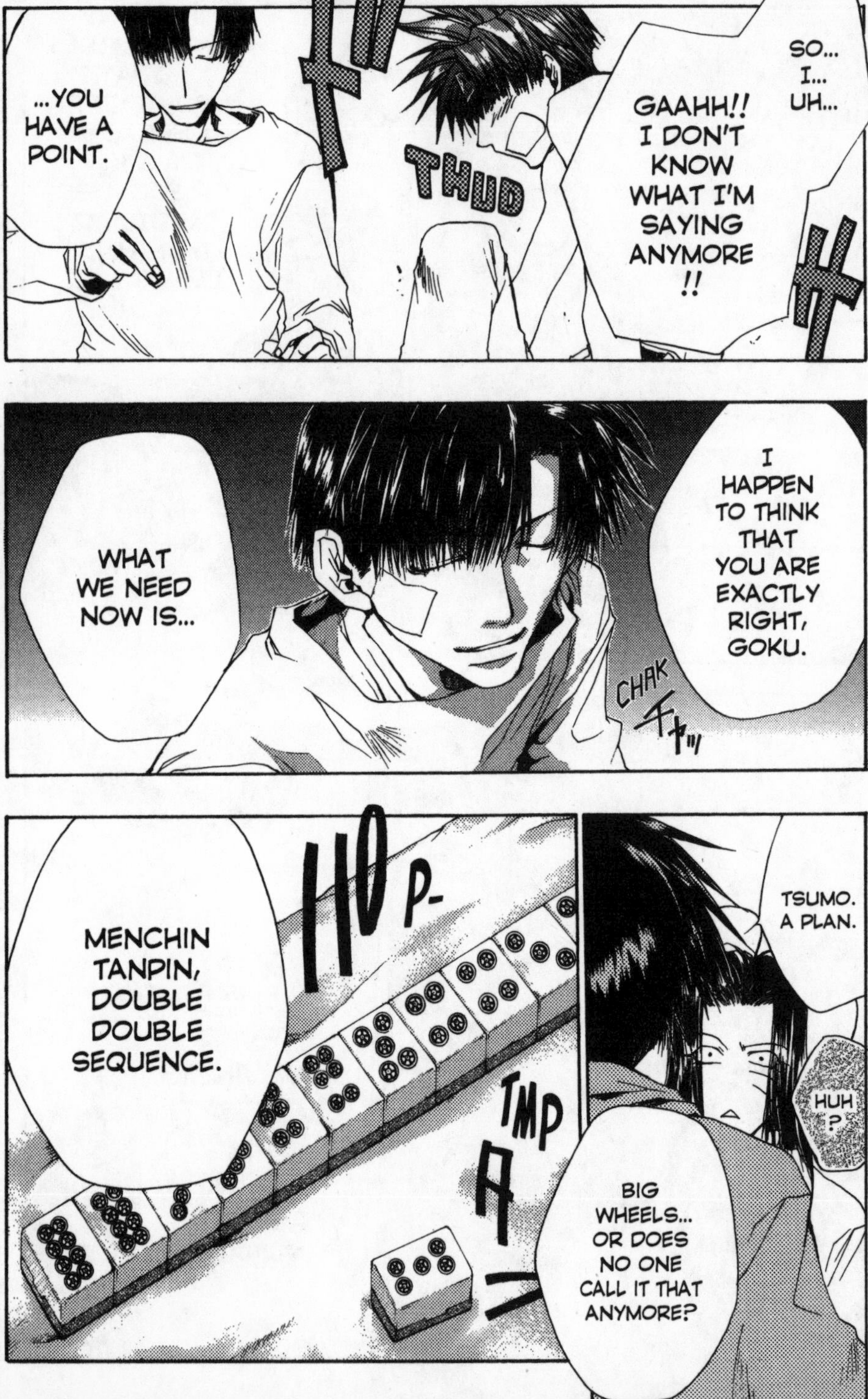
SO... I... UH...
GAAHH!! I DON'T KNOW WHAT I'M SAYING ANYMORE!!
THUD
...YOU HAVE A POINT.
I HAPPEN TO THINK THAT YOU ARE EXACTLY RIGHT, GOKU.
CHAK
WHAT WE NEED NOW IS...
TSUMO. A PLAN.
HUH?
BIG WHEELS... OR DOES NO ONE CALL IT THAT ANYMORE?
MENCHIN TANPIN, DOUBLE DOUBLE SEQUENCE.
TMP

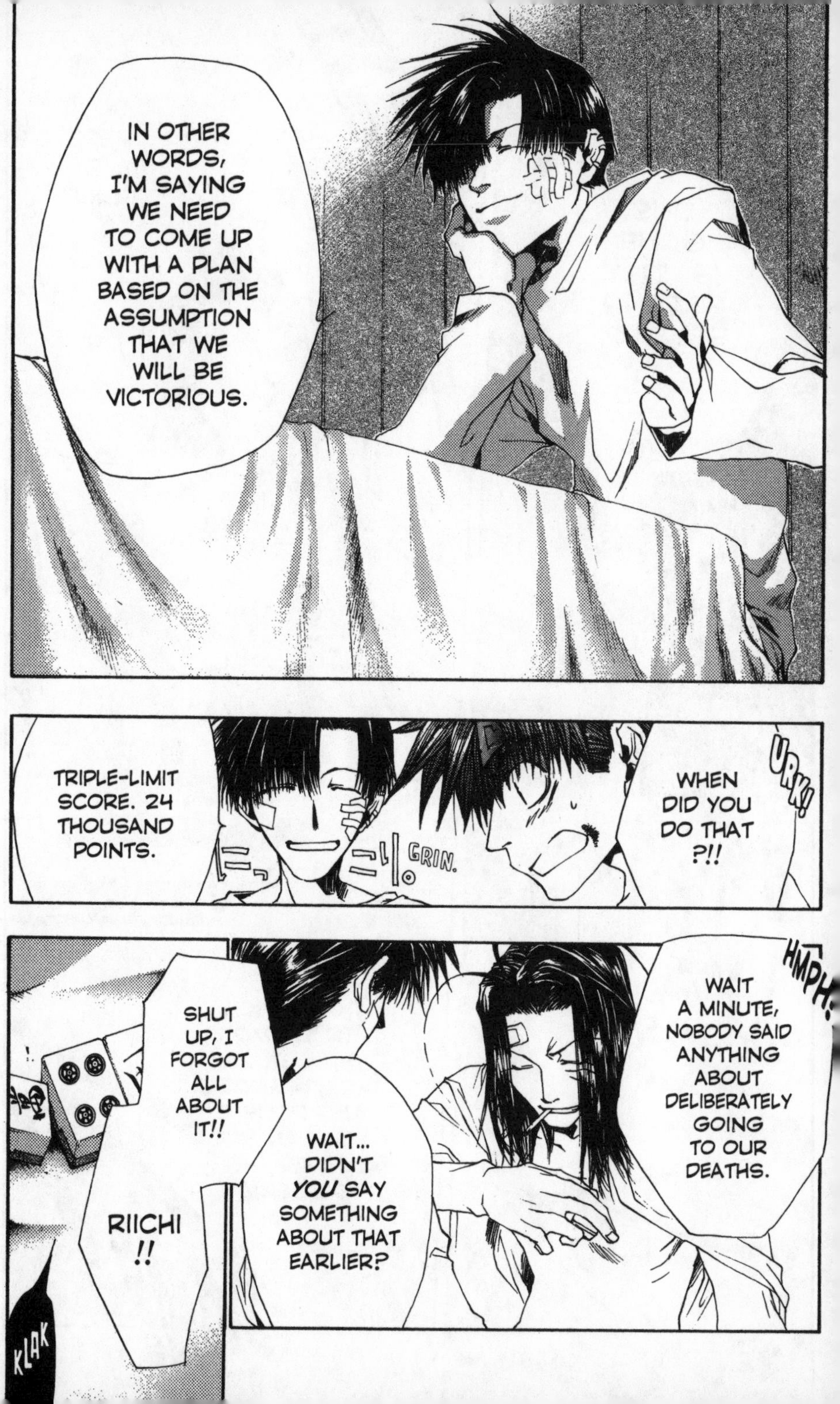
IN OTHER WORDS, I'M SAYING WE NEED TO COME UP WITH A PLAN BASED ON THE ASSUMPTION THAT WE WILL BE VICTORIOUS.
URK!!
WHEN DID YOU DO THAT ?!!
GRIN.
TRIPLE-LIMIT SCORE. 24 THOUSAND POINTS.
HMPH!
WAIT A MINUTE, NOBODY SAID ANYTHING ABOUT DELIBERATELY GOING TO OUR DEATHS.
WAIT... DIDN'T *YOU* SAY SOMETHING ABOUT THAT EARLIER?
SHUT UP, I FORGOT ALL ABOUT IT!!
RIICHI !!
KLAK

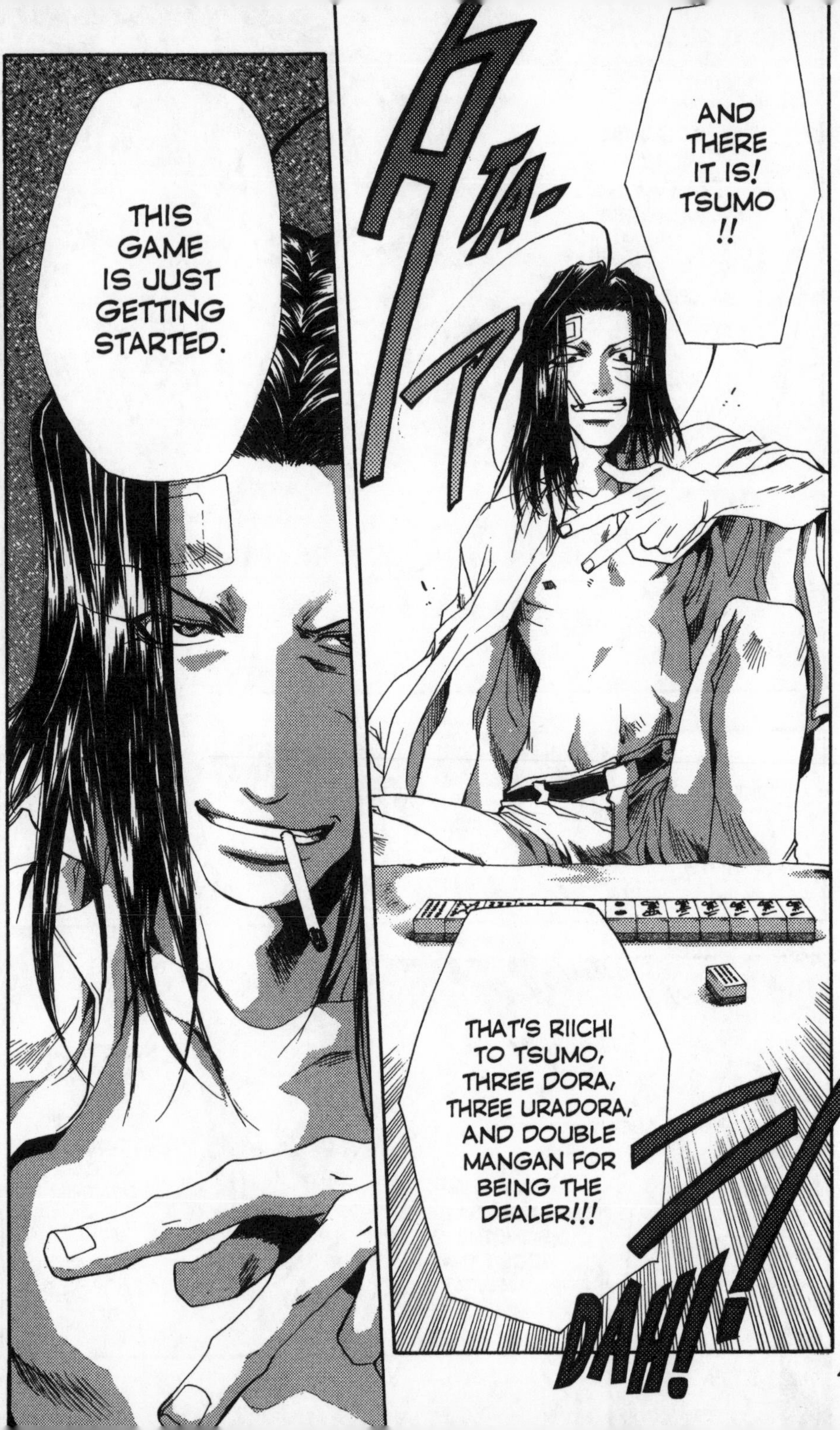
ATA-A
AND THERE IT IS! TSUMO!!
THAT'S RIICHI TO TSUMO, THREE DORA, THREE URADORA, AND DOUBLE MANGAN FOR BEING THE DEALER!!!
DAH!
THIS GAME IS JUST GETTING STARTED.

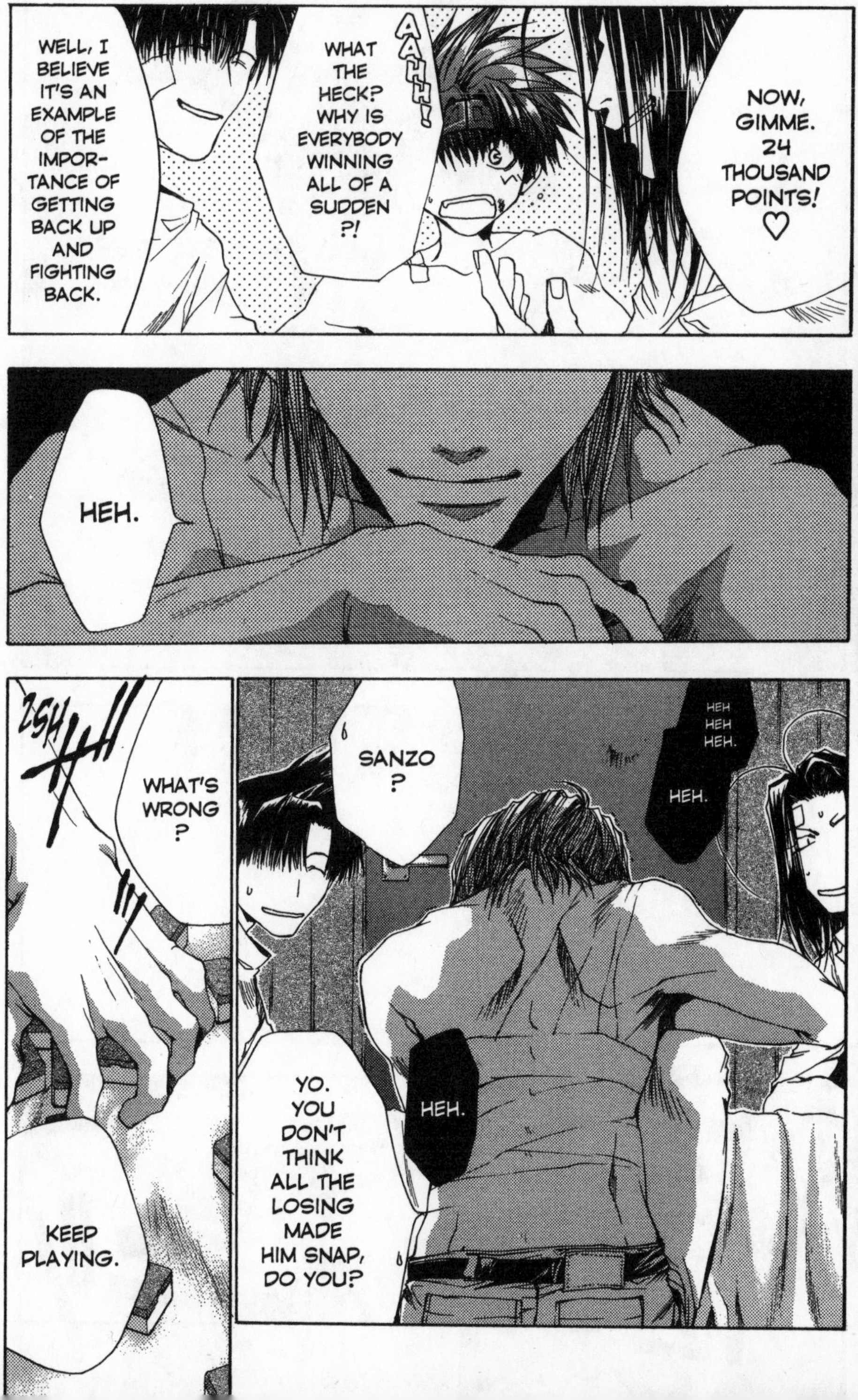
NOW, GIMME. 24 THOUSAND POINTS! ♡
AAHH!
WHAT THE HECK? WHY IS EVERYBODY WINNING ALL OF A SUDDEN?!
WELL, I BELIEVE IT'S AN EXAMPLE OF THE IMPORTANCE OF GETTING BACK UP AND FIGHTING BACK.
HEH.
HEH HEH HEH.
HEH.
SANZO?
HEH.
YO. YOU DON'T THINK ALL THE LOSING MADE HIM SNAP, DO YOU?
ZSH
WHAT'S WRONG?
KEEP PLAYING.

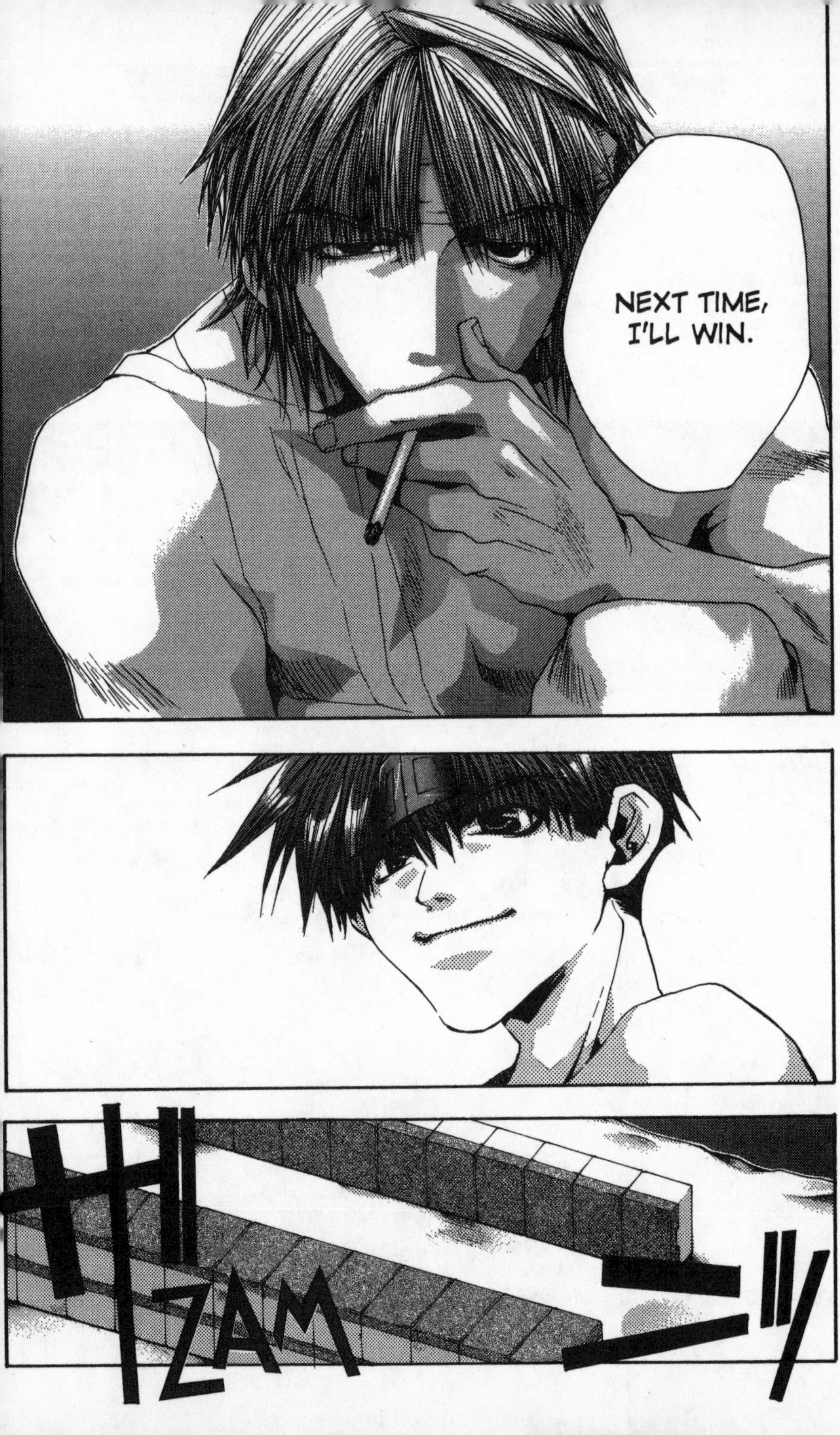
NEXT TIME, I'LL WIN.
ZAM

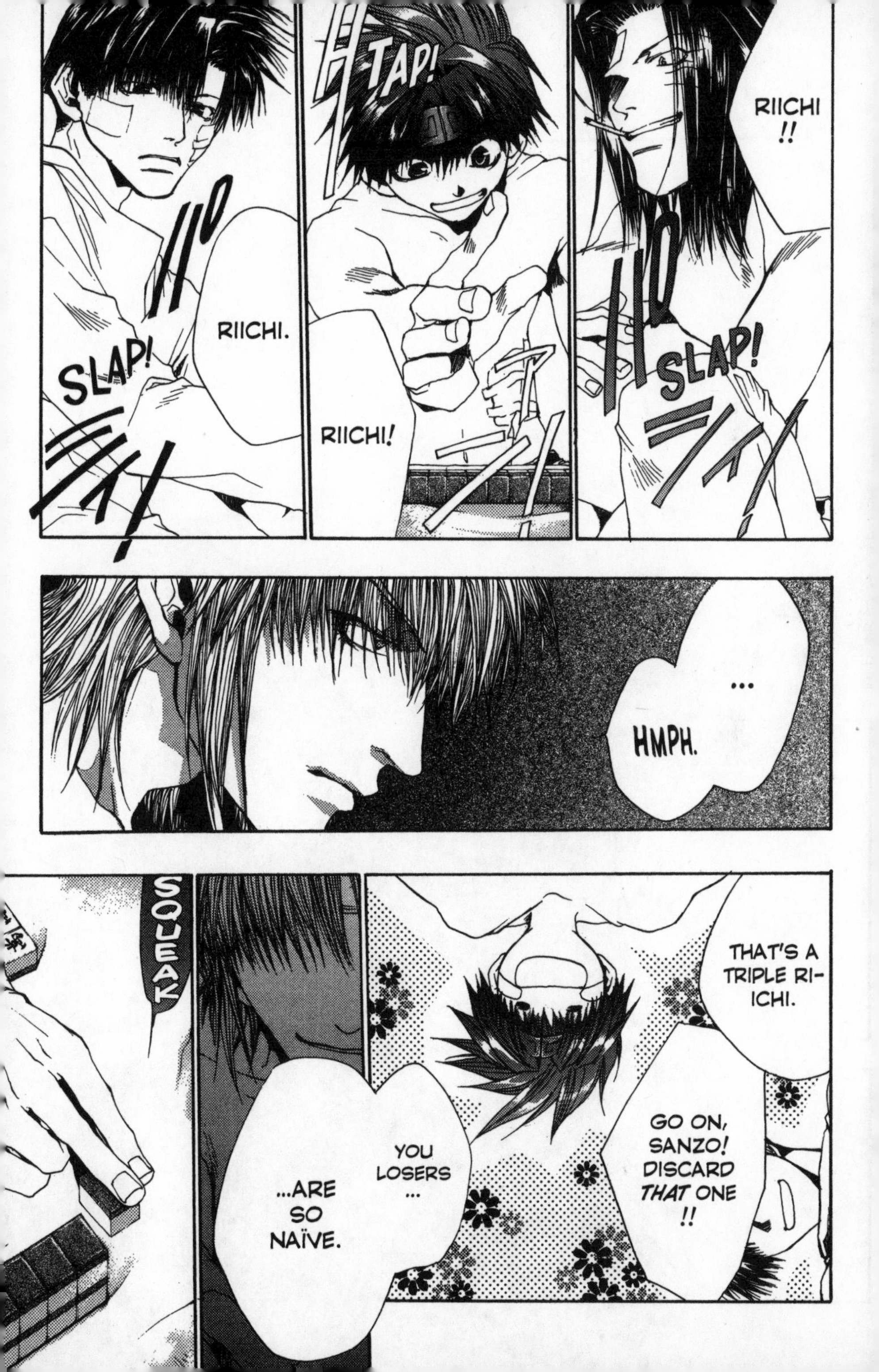
RIICHI !!
SLAP!
TAP!
RIICHI!
RIICHI.
SLAP!
...
HMPH.
THAT'S A TRIPLE RI-ICHI.
GO ON, SANZO! DISCARD *THAT* ONE !!
YOU LOSERS ...
...ARE SO NAÏVE.
SQUEAK

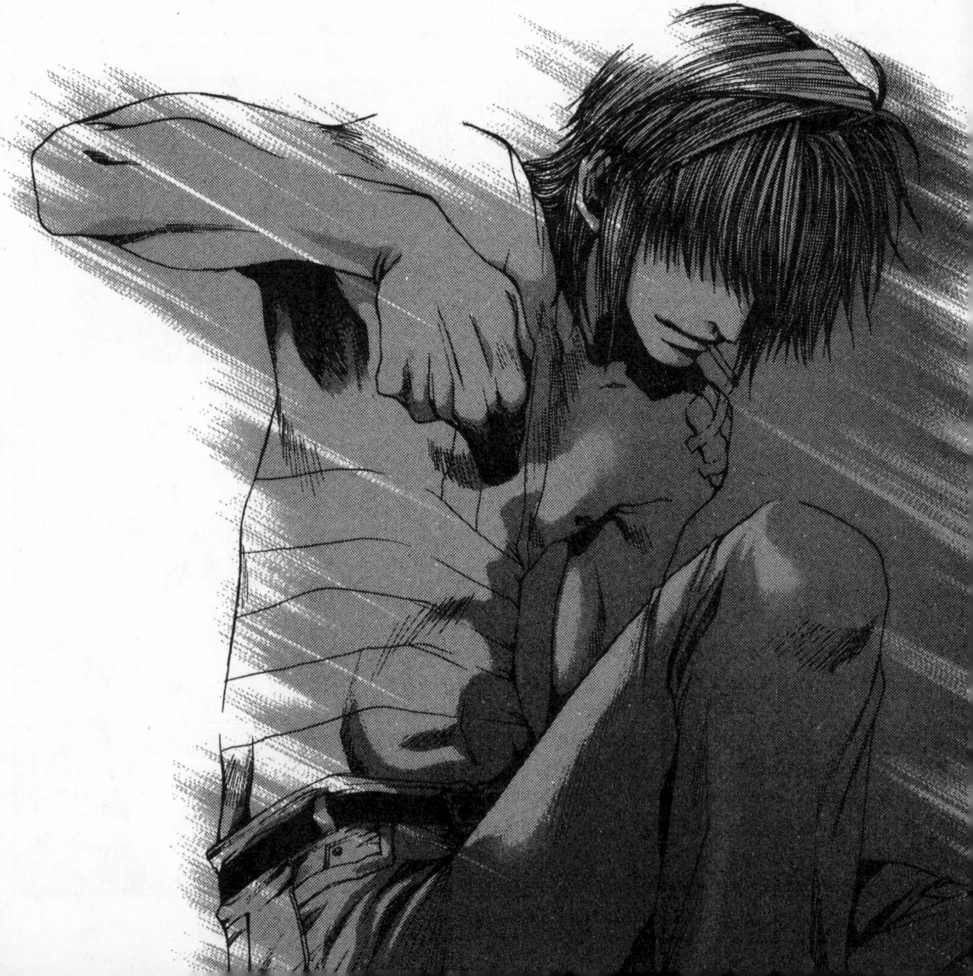

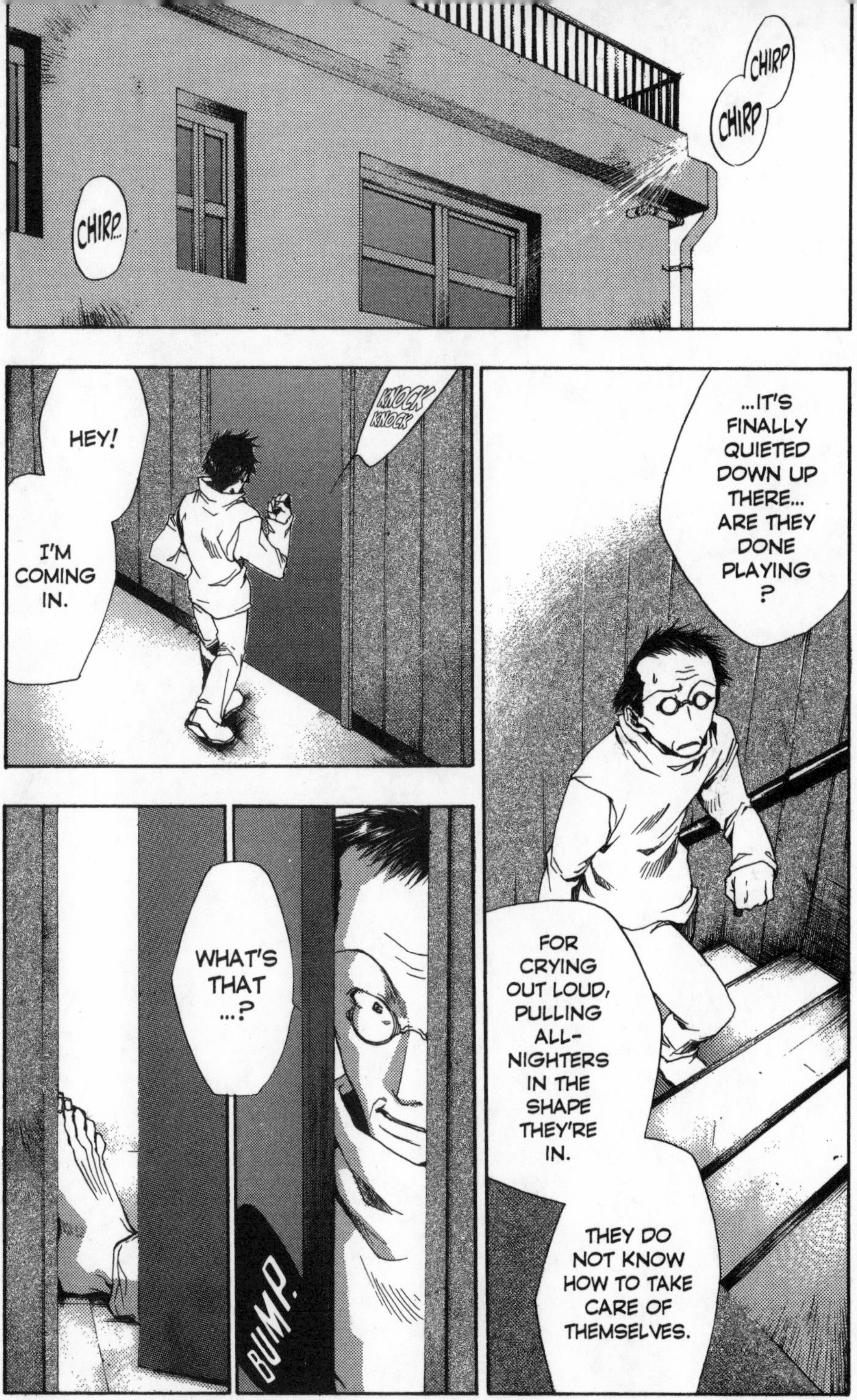
CHIRP
CHIRP
CHIRP...
...IT'S FINALLY QUIETED DOWN UP THERE... ARE THEY DONE PLAYING?
FOR CRYING OUT LOUD, PULLING ALL-NIGHTERS IN THE SHAPE THEY'RE IN.
THEY DO NOT KNOW HOW TO TAKE CARE OF THEMSELVES.
KNOCK KNOCK
HEY!
I'M COMING IN.
WHAT'S THAT ...?
BUMP.

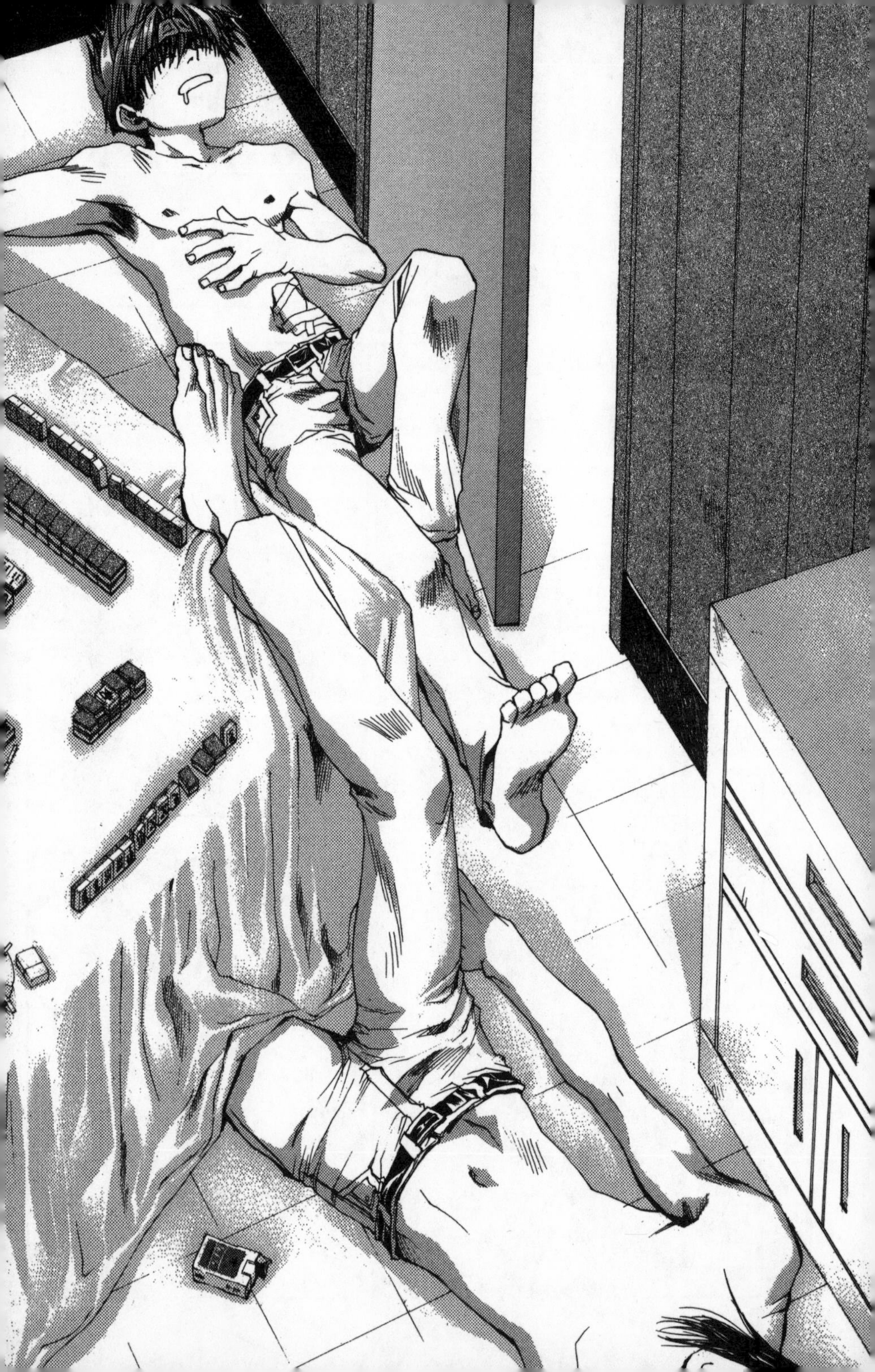

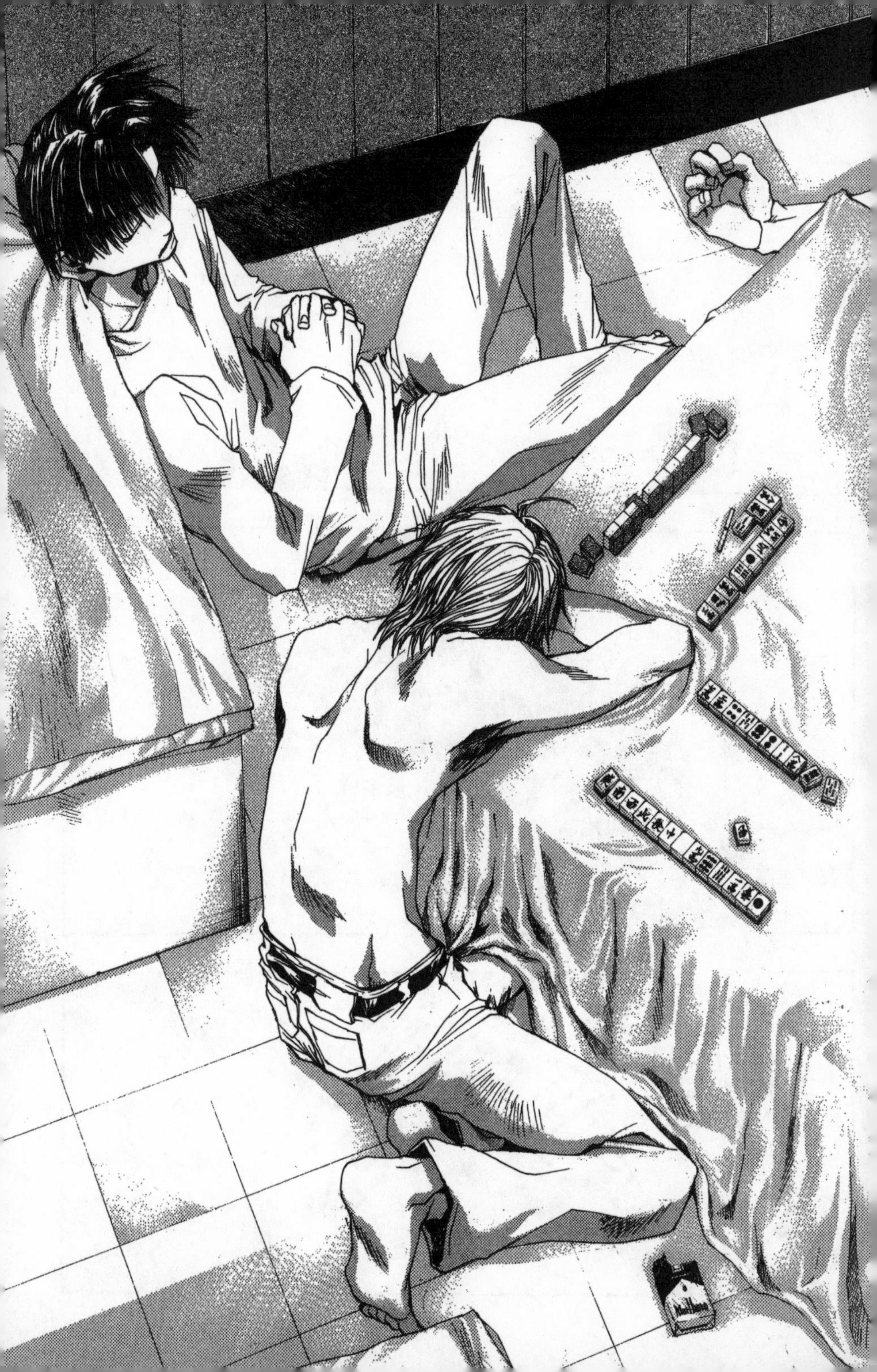

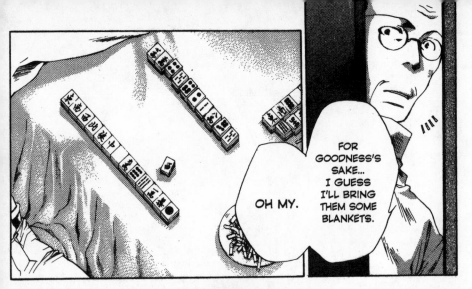

OH MY.

FOR GOODNESS'S SAKE... I GUESS I'LL BRING THEM SOME BLANKETS.

THAT'S A KOKUSHI MUSOU...

TILE: West

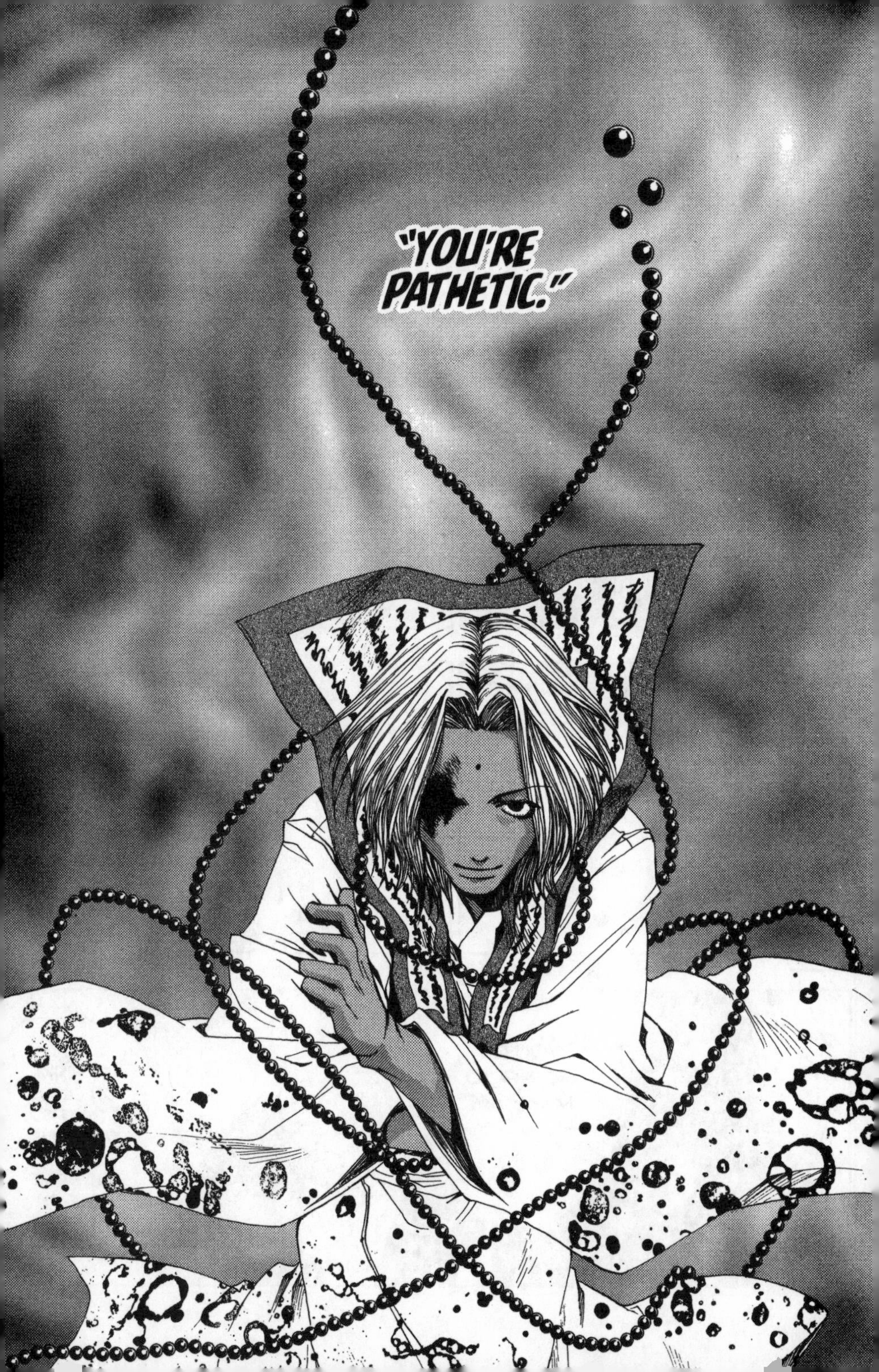
"YOU'RE PATHETIC."

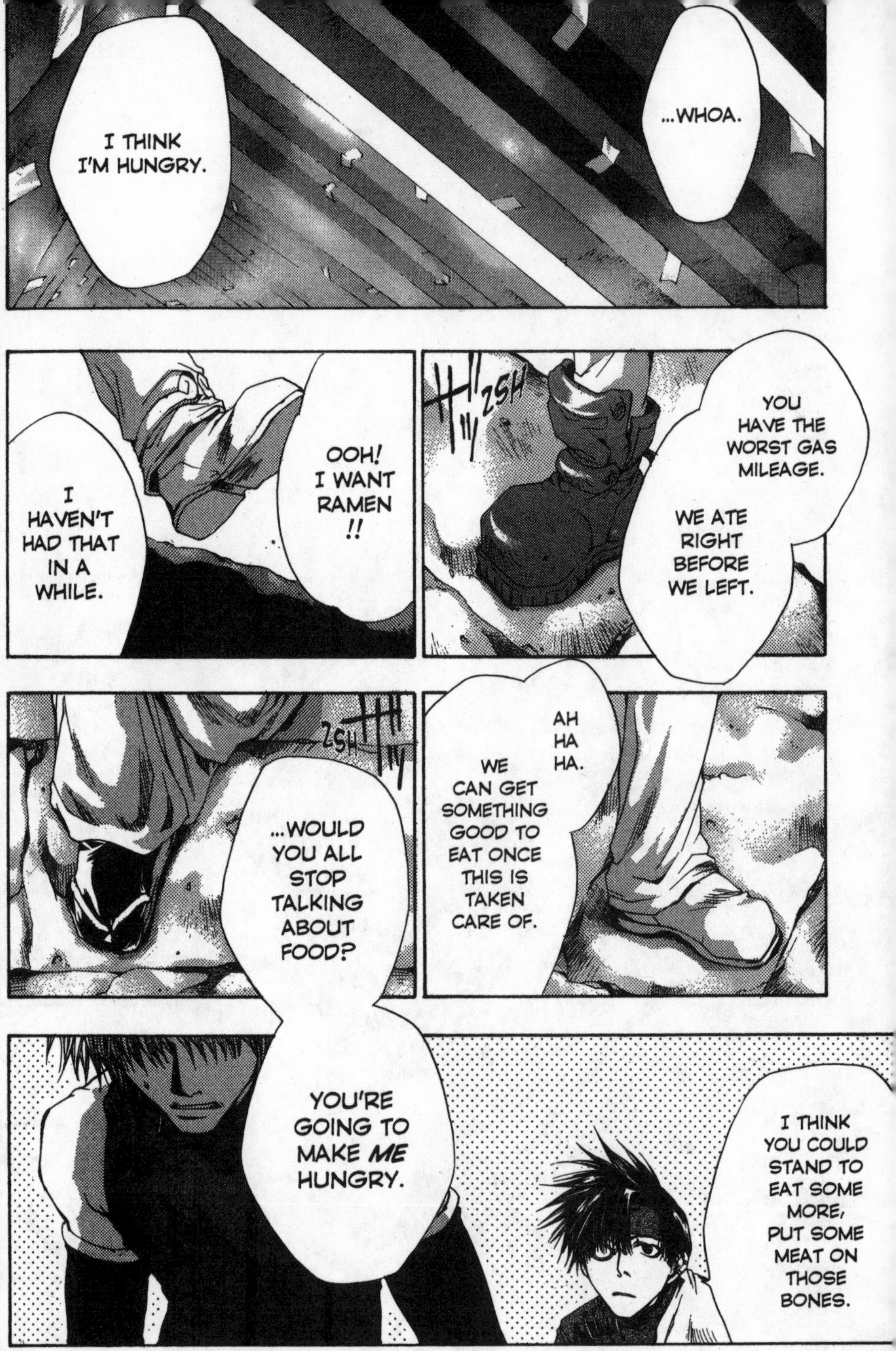
...WHOA.
I THINK I'M HUNGRY.
ZSH
YOU HAVE THE WORST GAS MILEAGE.
WE ATE RIGHT BEFORE WE LEFT.
OOH! I WANT RAMEN!!
I HAVEN'T HAD THAT IN A WHILE.
AH HA HA.
WE CAN GET SOMETHING GOOD TO EAT ONCE THIS IS TAKEN CARE OF.
ZSH
...WOULD YOU ALL STOP TALKING ABOUT FOOD?
YOU'RE GOING TO MAKE *ME* HUNGRY.
I THINK YOU COULD STAND TO EAT SOME MORE, PUT SOME MEAT ON THOSE BONES.

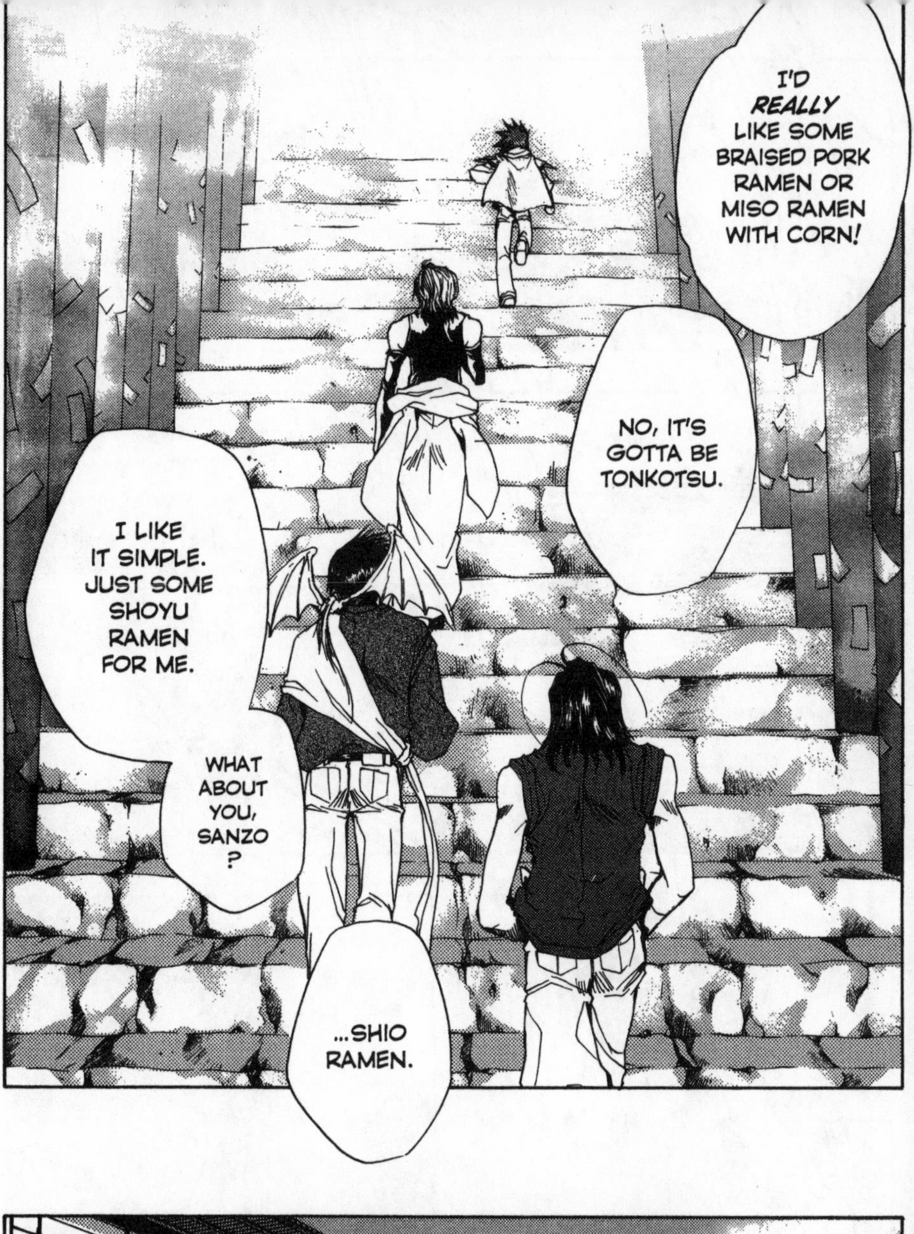
I'D *REALLY* LIKE SOME BRAISED PORK RAMEN OR MISO RAMEN WITH CORN!
NO, IT'S GOTTA BE TONKOTSU.
I LIKE IT SIMPLE. JUST SOME SHOYU RAMEN FOR ME.
WHAT ABOUT YOU, SANZO?
...SHIO RAMEN.

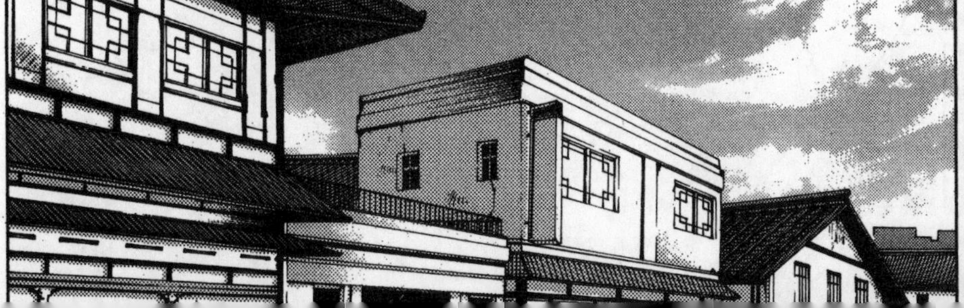

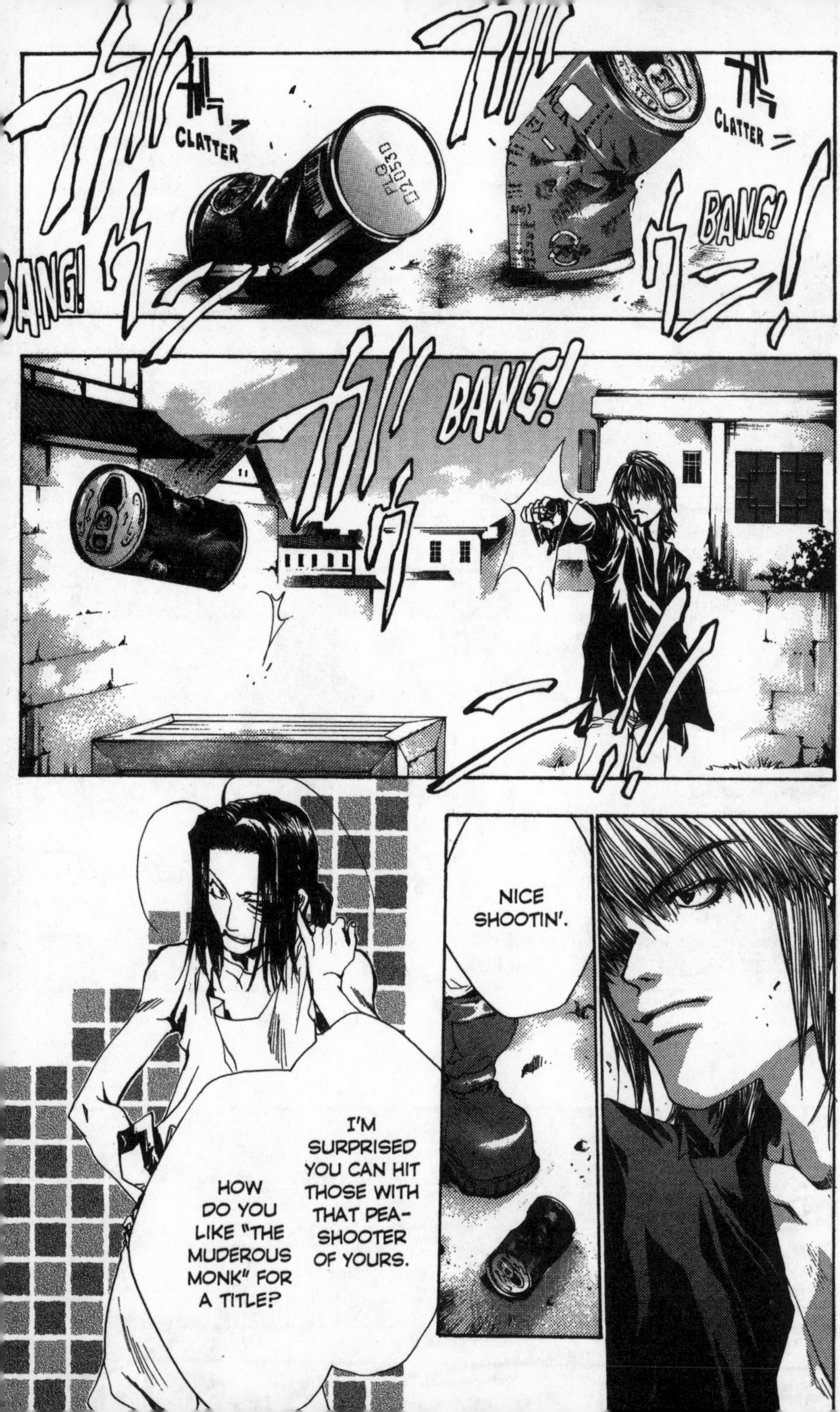
CLATTER
BANG!
CLATTER
BANG!
BANG!
NICE SHOOTIN'.
I'M SURPRISED YOU CAN HIT THOSE WITH THAT PEA-SHOOTER OF YOURS.
HOW DO YOU LIKE "THE MUDEROUS MONK" FOR A TITLE?

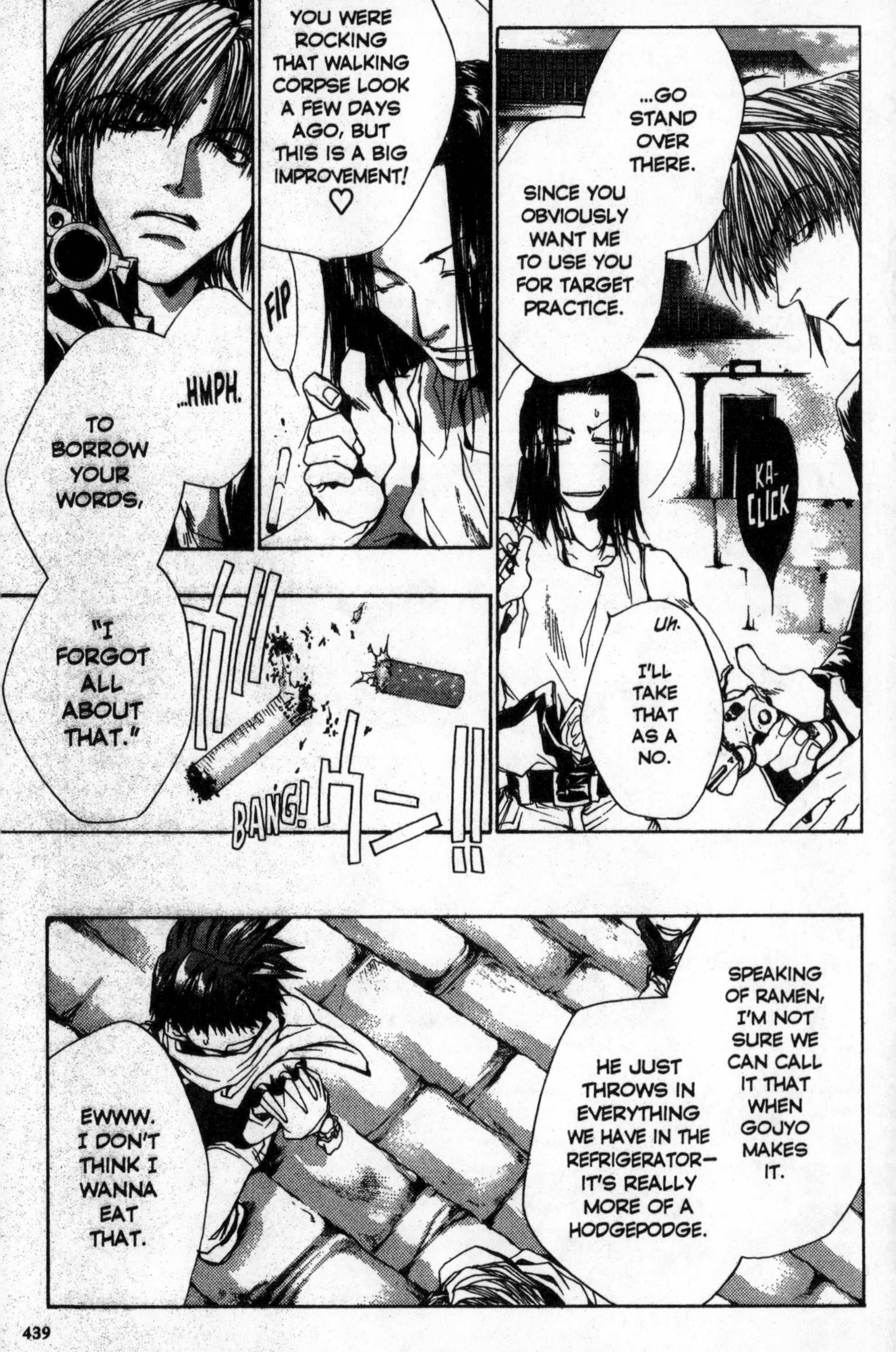
...GO STAND OVER THERE.
SINCE YOU OBVIOUSLY WANT ME TO USE YOU FOR TARGET PRACTICE.
KA-CLICK
UH.
I'LL TAKE THAT AS A NO.
YOU WERE ROCKING THAT WALKING CORPSE LOOK A FEW DAYS AGO, BUT THIS IS A BIG IMPROVEMENT! ♡
FIP
...HMPH.
TO BORROW YOUR WORDS,
"I FORGOT ALL ABOUT THAT."
BANG!
SPEAKING OF RAMEN, I'M NOT SURE WE CAN CALL IT THAT WHEN GOJYO MAKES IT.
HE JUST THROWS IN EVERYTHING WE HAVE IN THE REFRIGERATOR— IT'S REALLY MORE OF A HODGEPODGE.
EWWW. I DON'T THINK I WANNA EAT THAT.

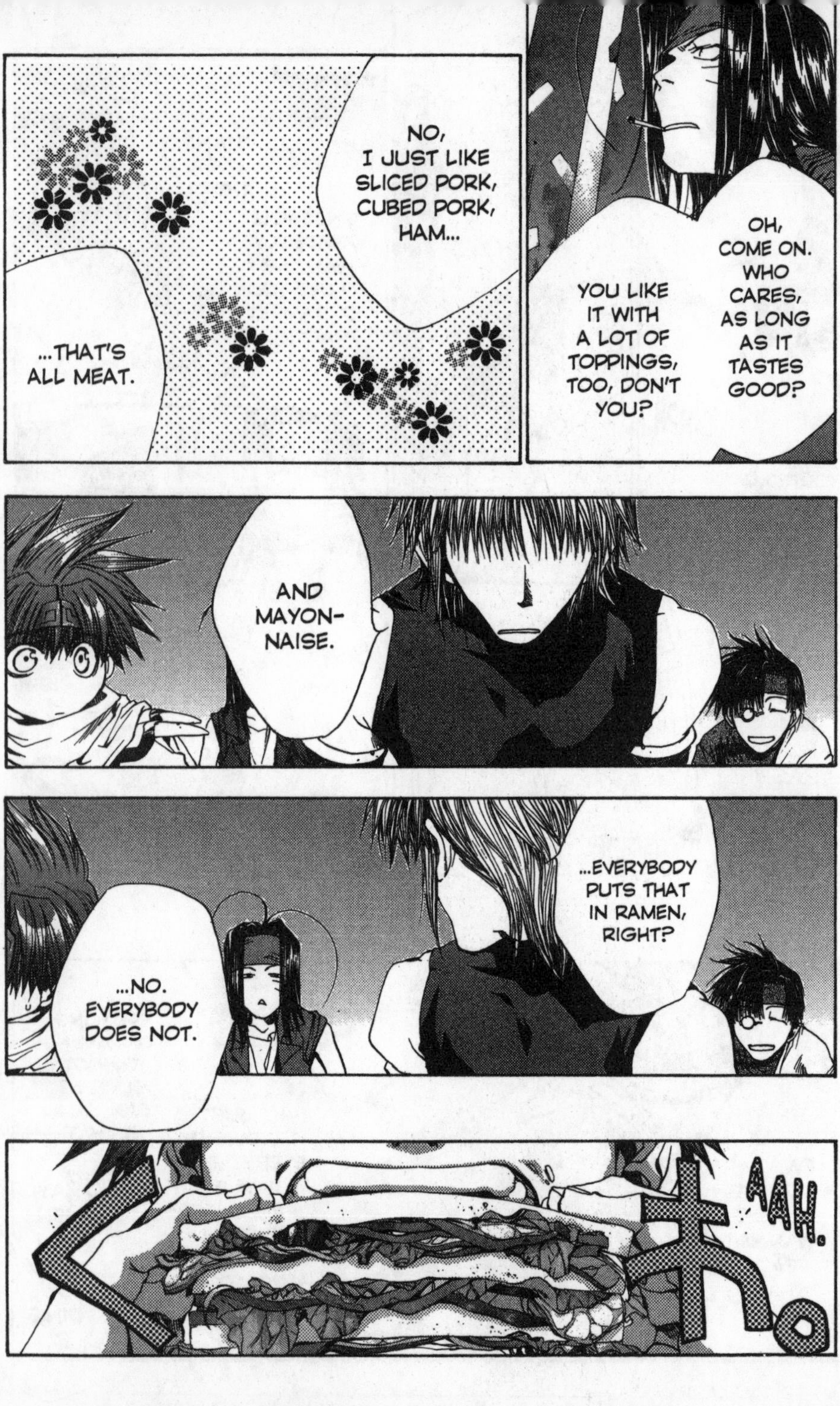
OH, COME ON. WHO CARES, AS LONG AS IT TASTES GOOD?
YOU LIKE IT WITH A LOT OF TOPPINGS, TOO, DON'T YOU?
NO, I JUST LIKE SLICED PORK, CUBED PORK, HAM...
...THAT'S ALL MEAT.
AND MAYON-NAISE.
...EVERYBODY PUTS THAT IN RAMEN, RIGHT?
...NO. EVERYBODY DOES NOT.
AAH.

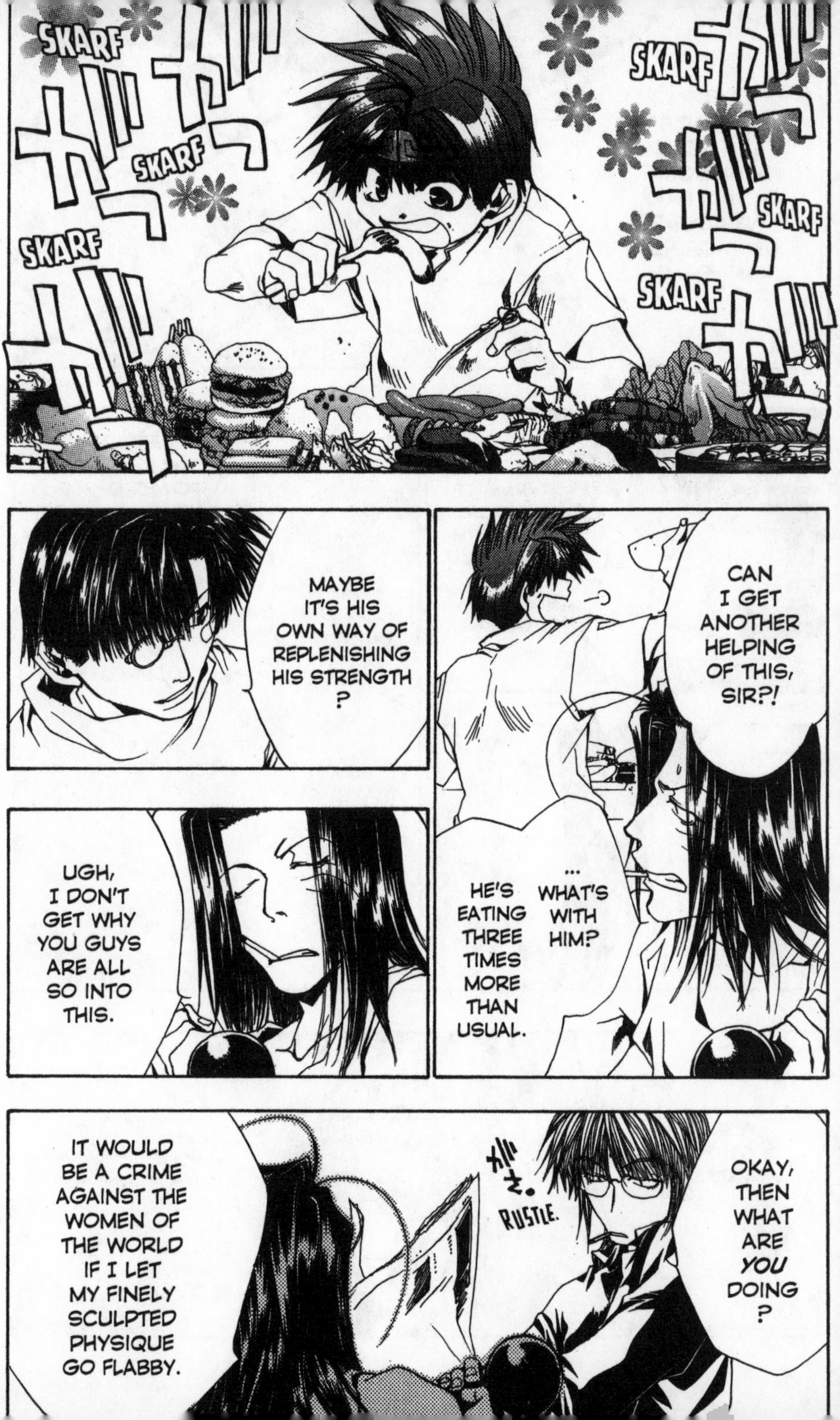
SKARF
SKARF
SKARF
SKARF
SKARF
SKARF
CAN I GET ANOTHER HELPING OF THIS, SIR?!
... WHAT'S WITH HIM?
HE'S EATING THREE TIMES MORE THAN USUAL.
MAYBE IT'S HIS OWN WAY OF REPLENISHING HIS STRENGTH?
UGH, I DON'T GET WHY YOU GUYS ARE ALL SO INTO THIS.
OKAY, THEN WHAT ARE *YOU* DOING?
RUSTLE.
IT WOULD BE A CRIME AGAINST THE WOMEN OF THE WORLD IF I LET MY FINELY SCULPTED PHYSIQUE GO FLABBY.

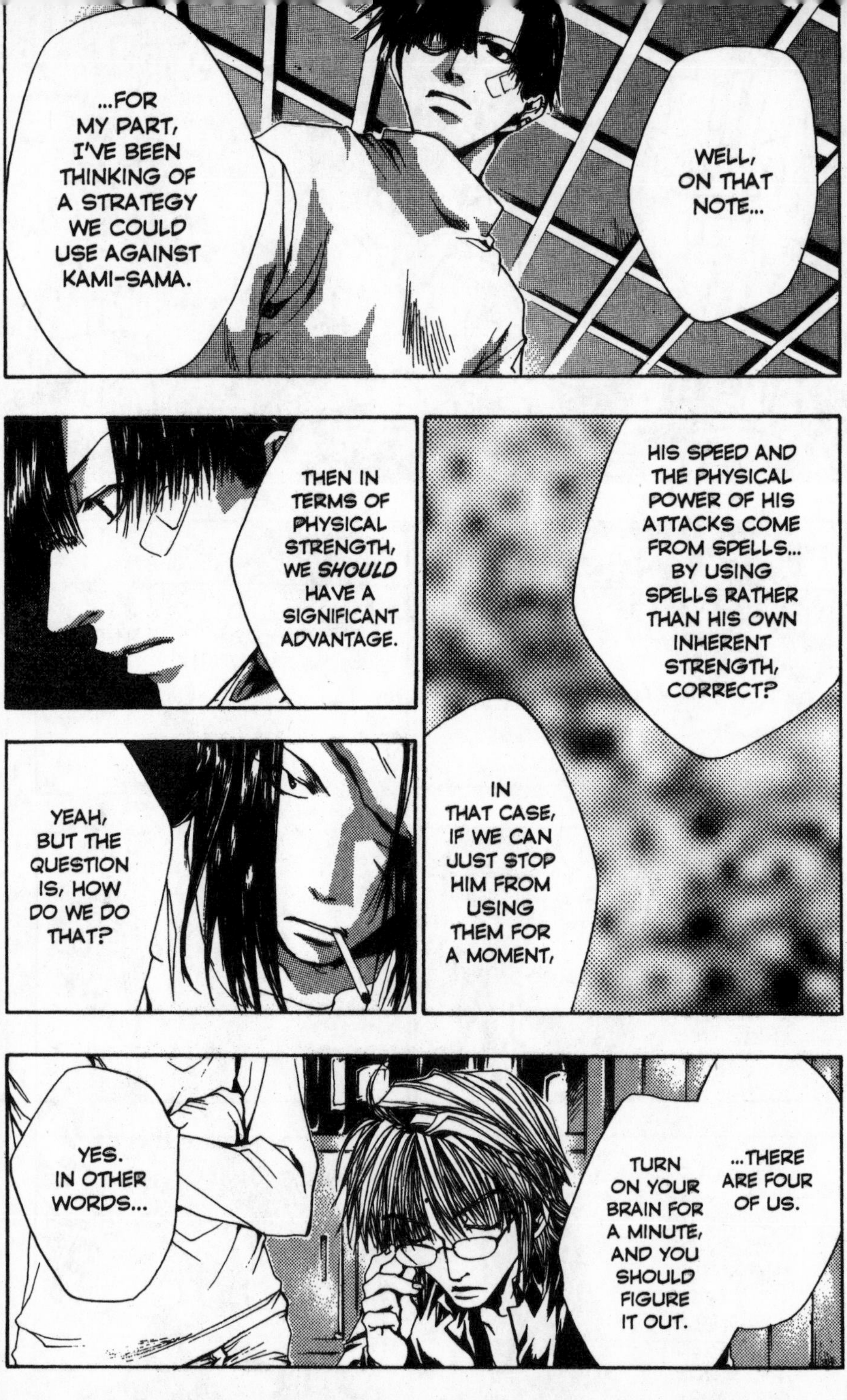
WELL, ON THAT NOTE...
...FOR MY PART, I'VE BEEN THINKING OF A STRATEGY WE COULD USE AGAINST KAMI-SAMA.
HIS SPEED AND THE PHYSICAL POWER OF HIS ATTACKS COME FROM SPELLS... BY USING SPELLS RATHER THAN HIS OWN INHERENT STRENGTH, CORRECT?
IN THAT CASE, IF WE CAN JUST STOP HIM FROM USING THEM FOR A MOMENT,
THEN IN TERMS OF PHYSICAL STRENGTH, WE *SHOULD* HAVE A SIGNIFICANT ADVANTAGE.
YEAH, BUT THE QUESTION IS, HOW DO WE DO THAT?
...THERE ARE FOUR OF US.
TURN ON YOUR BRAIN FOR A MINUTE, AND YOU SHOULD FIGURE IT OUT.
YES. IN OTHER WORDS...

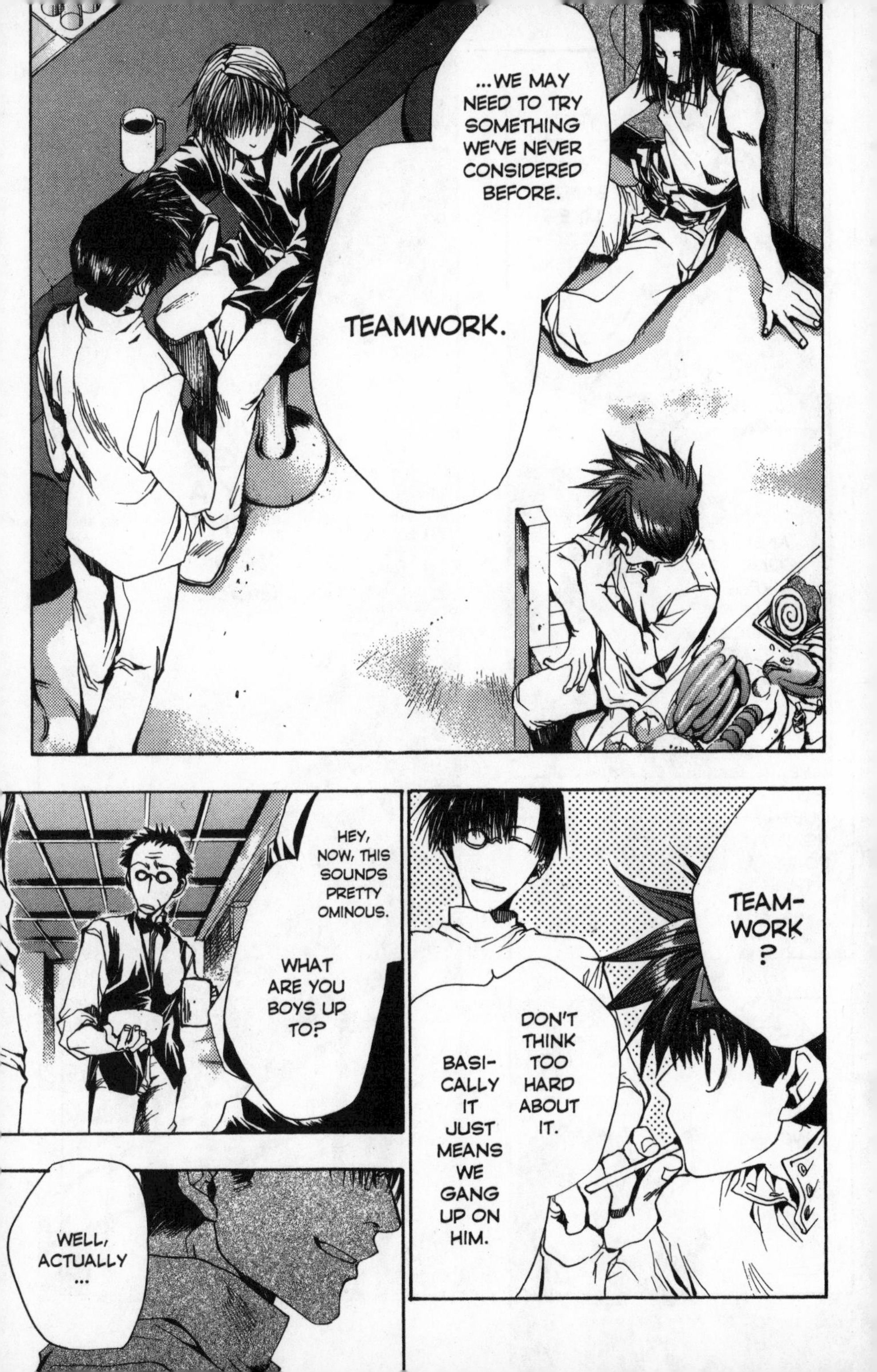
...WE MAY NEED TO TRY SOMETHING WE'VE NEVER CONSIDERED BEFORE.
TEAMWORK.
TEAM-WORK?
DON'T THINK TOO HARD ABOUT IT.
BASI-CALLY IT JUST MEANS WE GANG UP ON HIM.
HEY, NOW, THIS SOUNDS PRETTY OMINOUS.
WHAT ARE YOU BOYS UP TO?
WELL, ACTUALLY ...

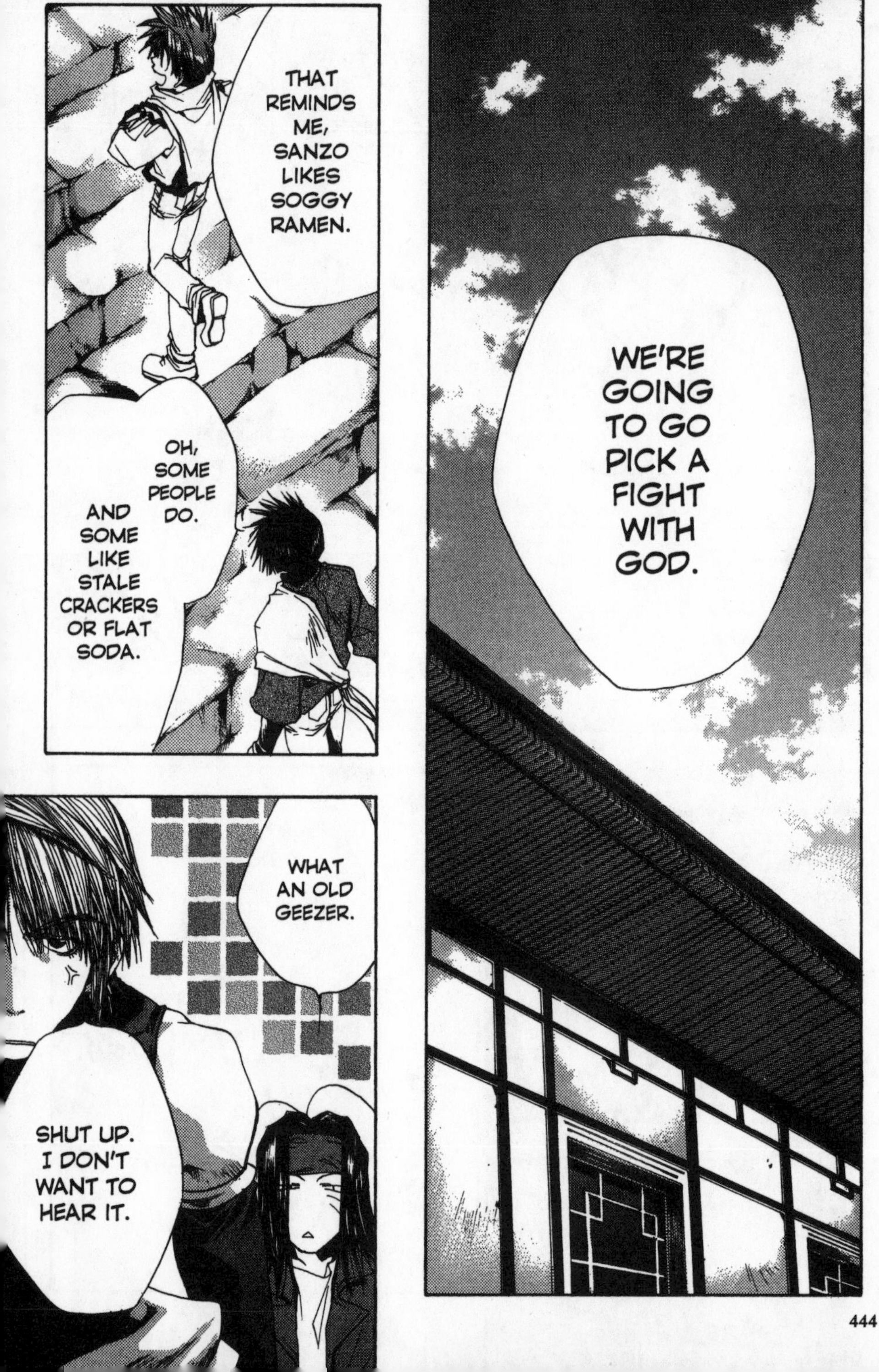
WE'RE GOING TO GO PICK A FIGHT WITH GOD.
THAT REMINDS ME, SANZO LIKES SOGGY RAMEN.
OH, SOME PEOPLE DO.
AND SOME LIKE STALE CRACKERS OR FLAT SODA.
WHAT AN OLD GEEZER.
SHUT UP. I DON'T WANT TO HEAR IT.

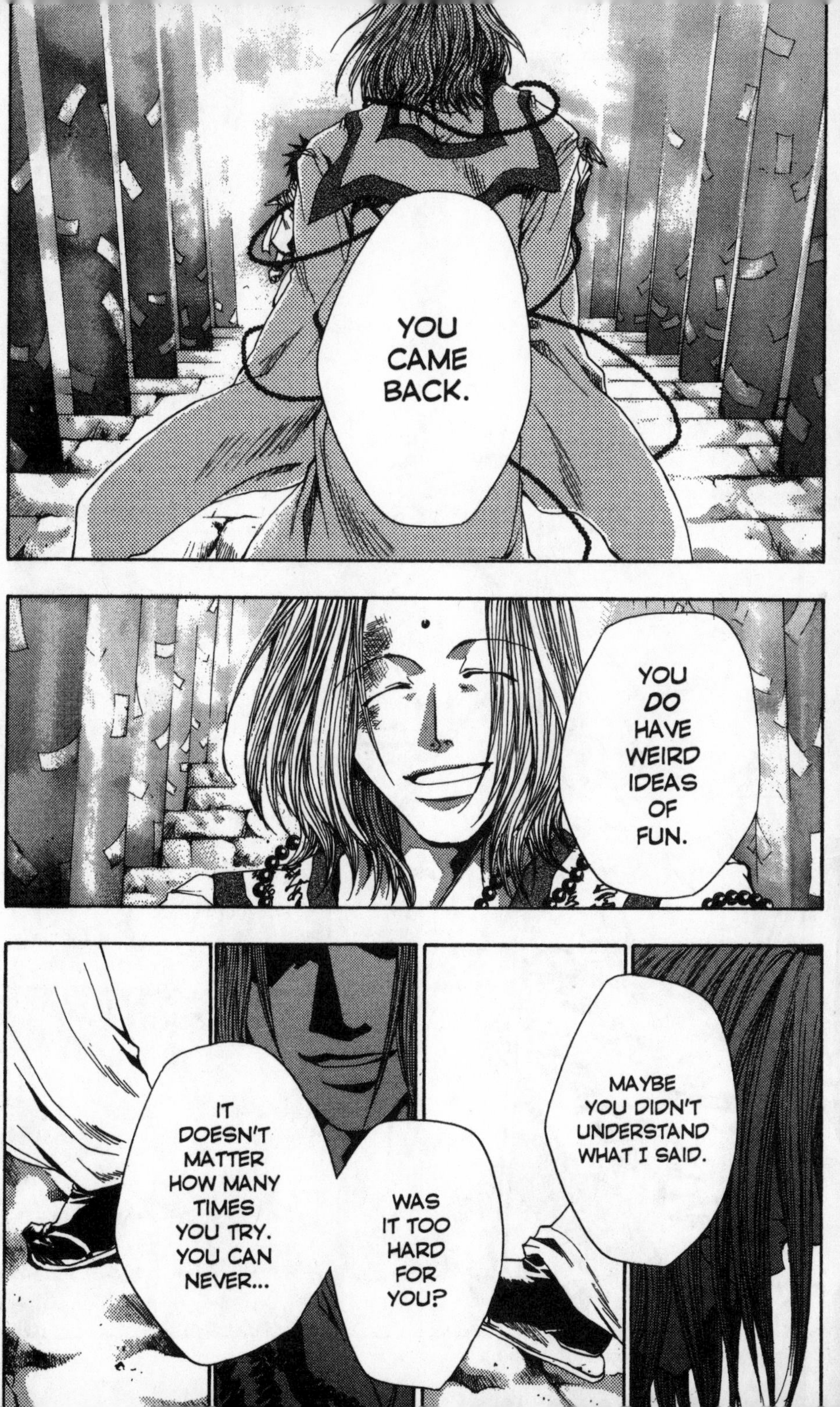
YOU CAME BACK.
YOU DO HAVE WEIRD IDEAS OF FUN.
MAYBE YOU DIDN'T UNDERSTAND WHAT I SAID.
WAS IT TOO HARD FOR YOU?
IT DOESN'T MATTER HOW MANY TIMES YOU TRY. YOU CAN NEVER...

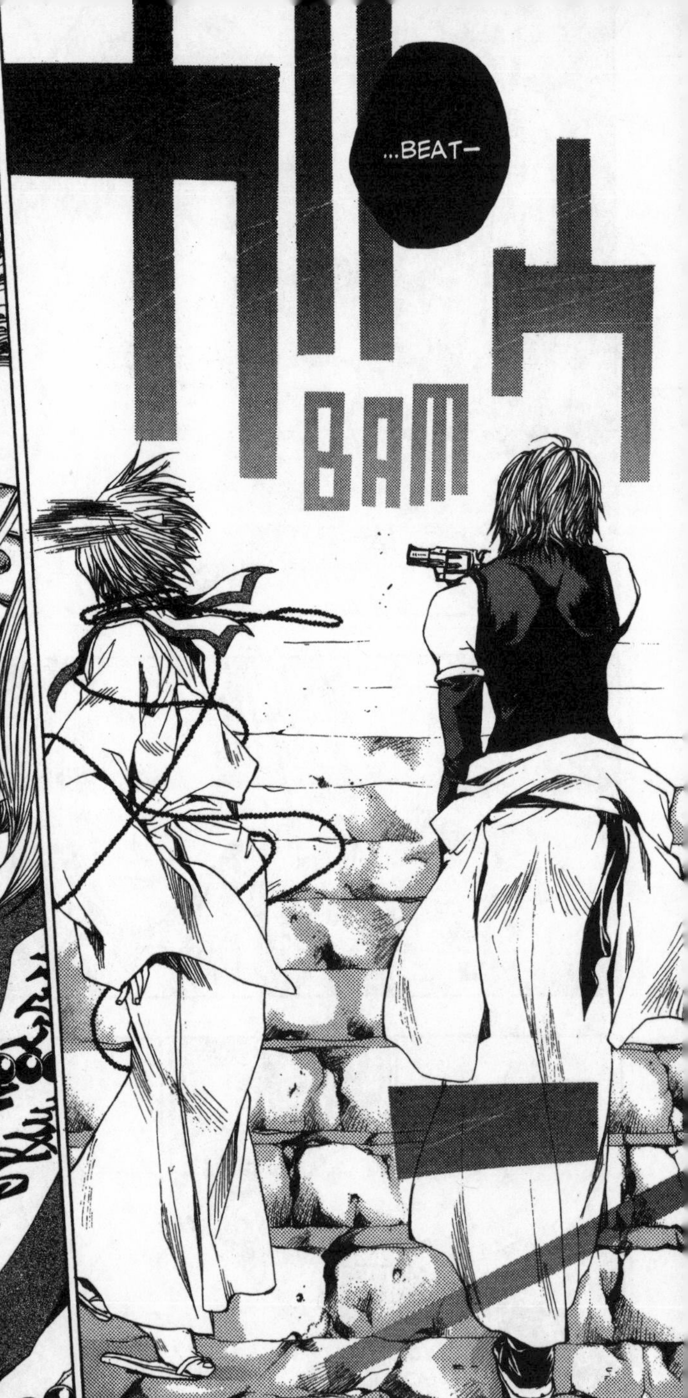
...BEAT—
BAM
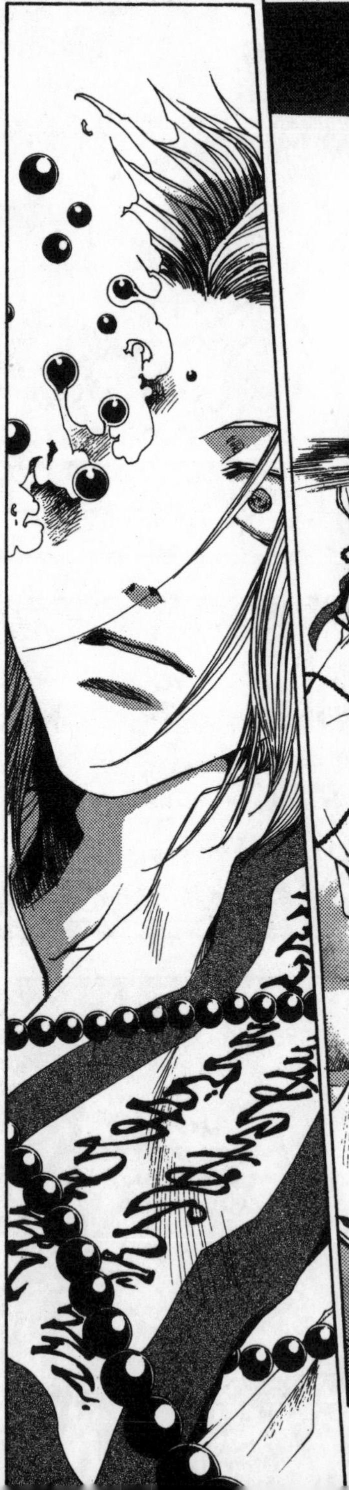

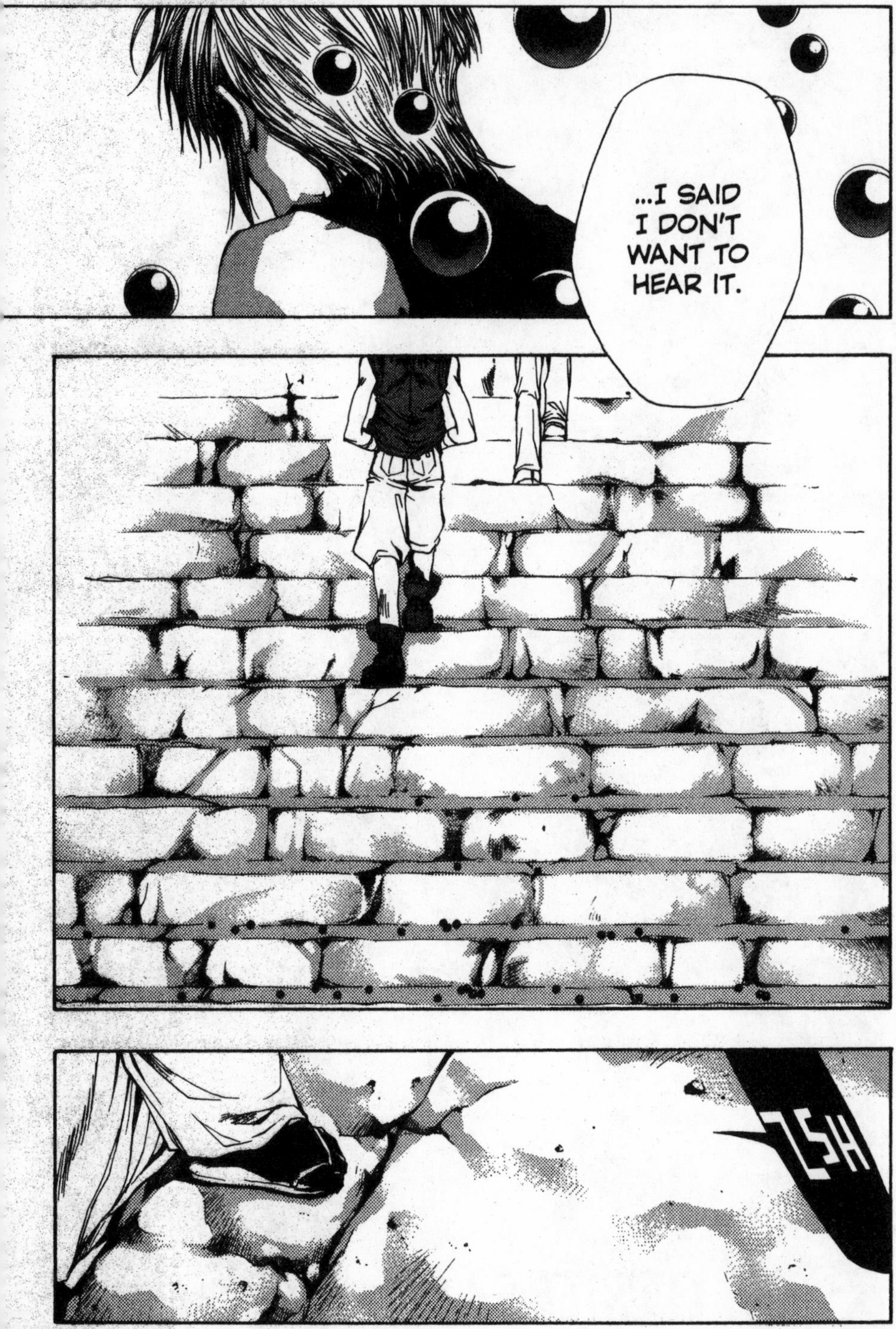
...I SAID I DON'T WANT TO HEAR IT.

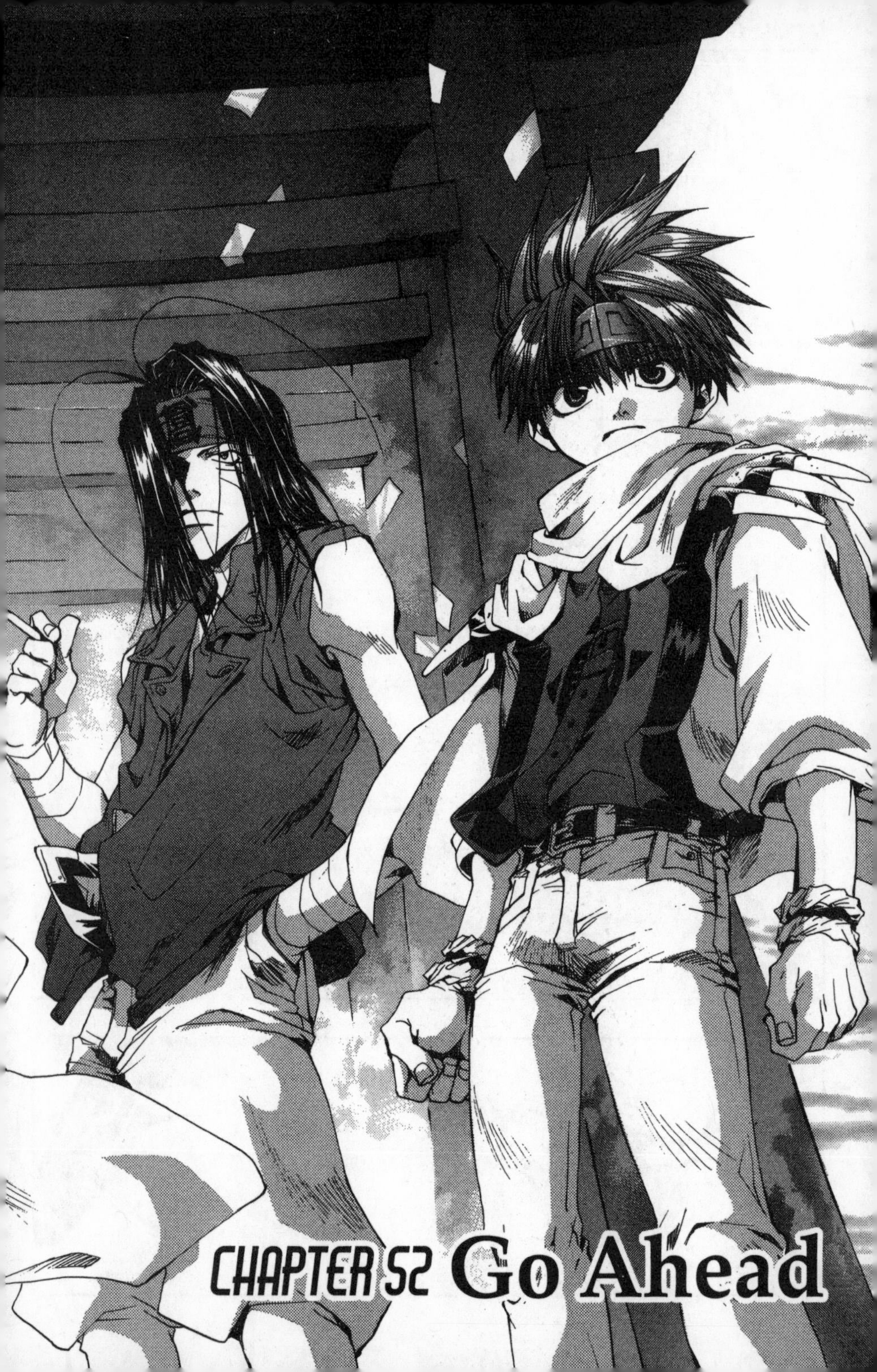
CHAPTER 52 Go Ahead

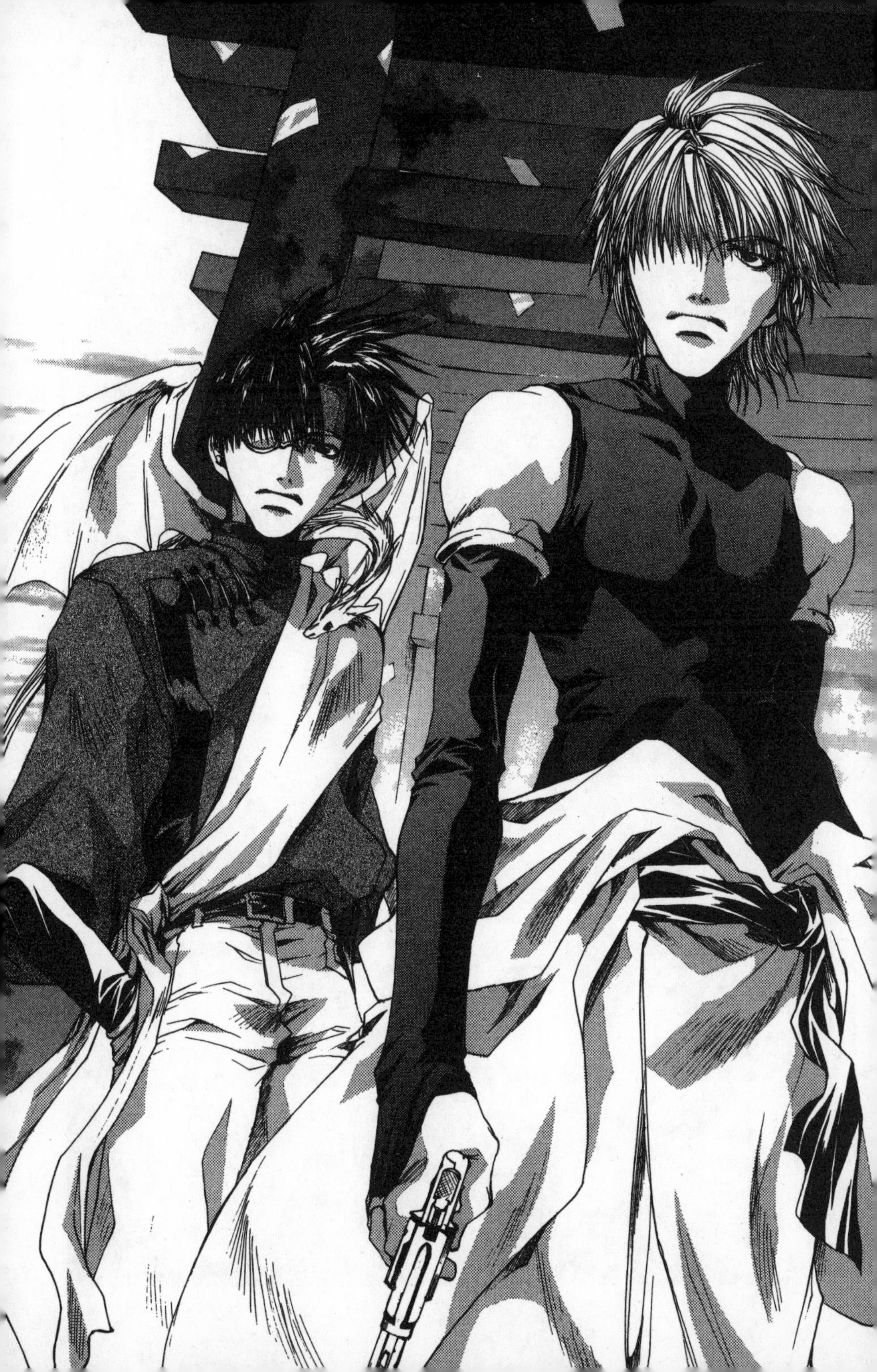

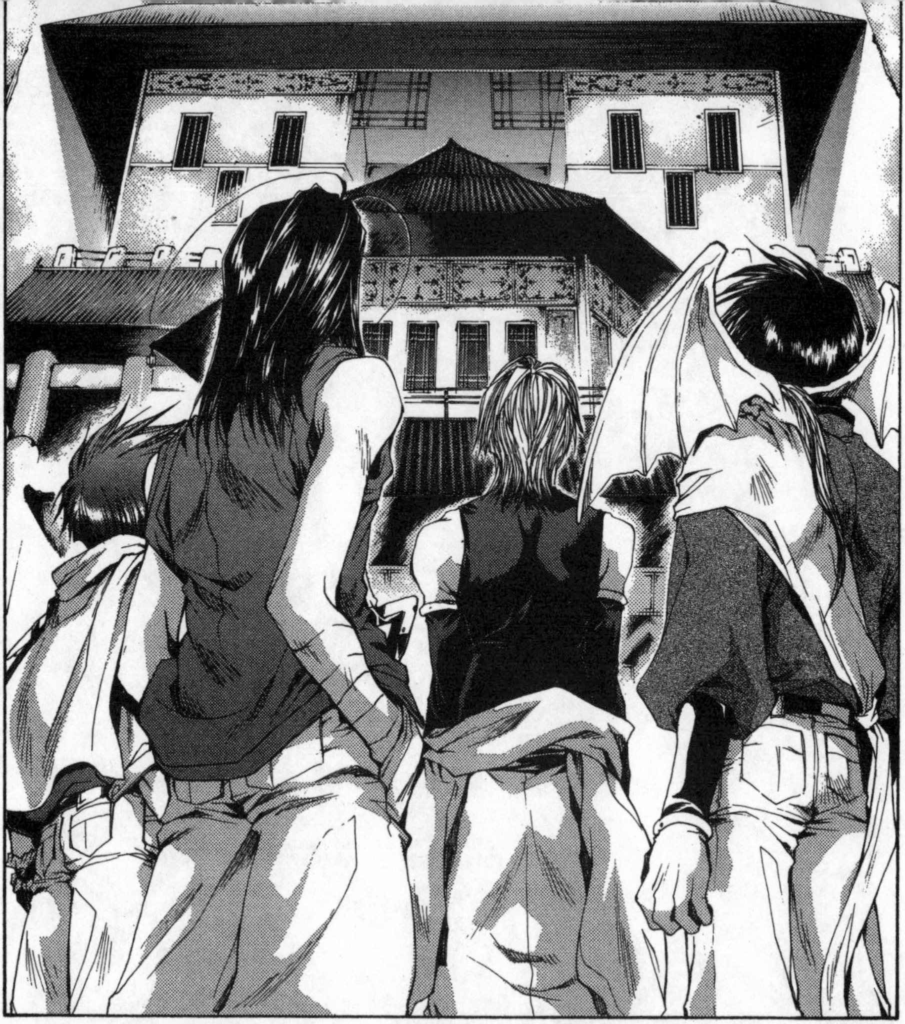

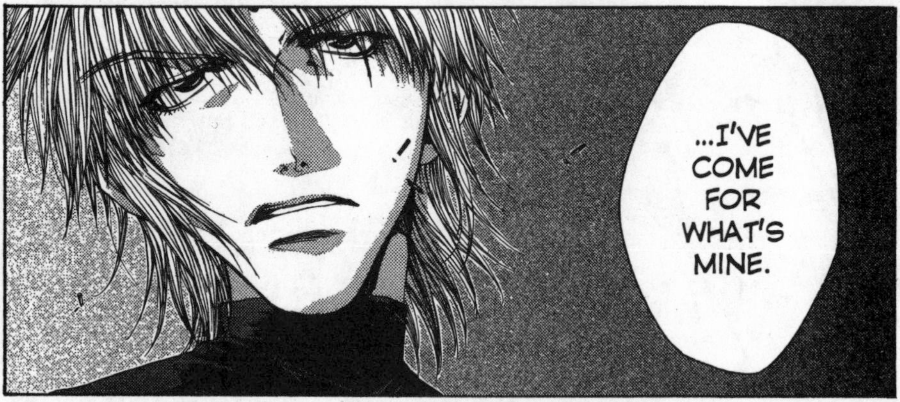
...I'VE COME FOR WHAT'S MINE.

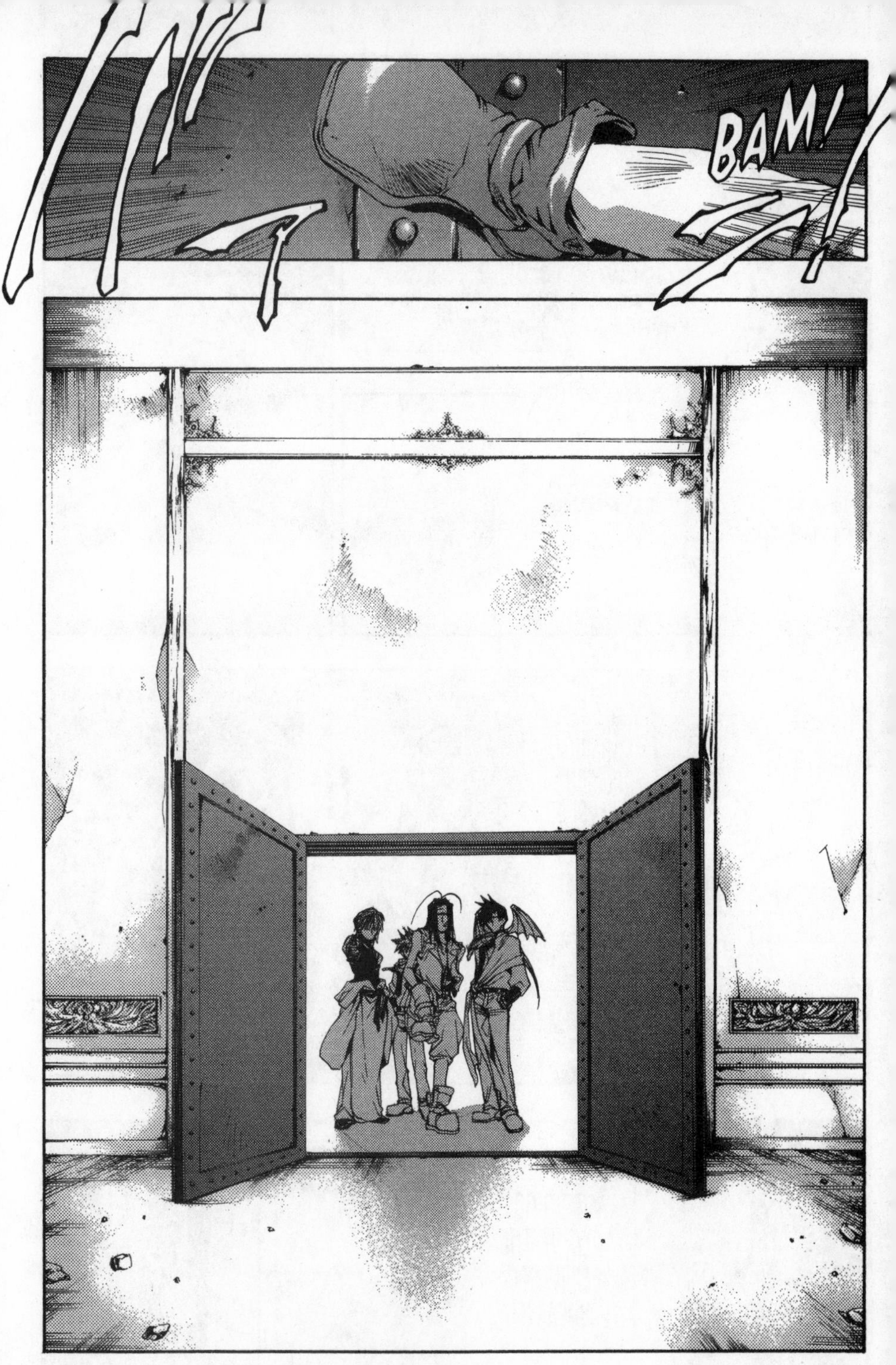
BAM!

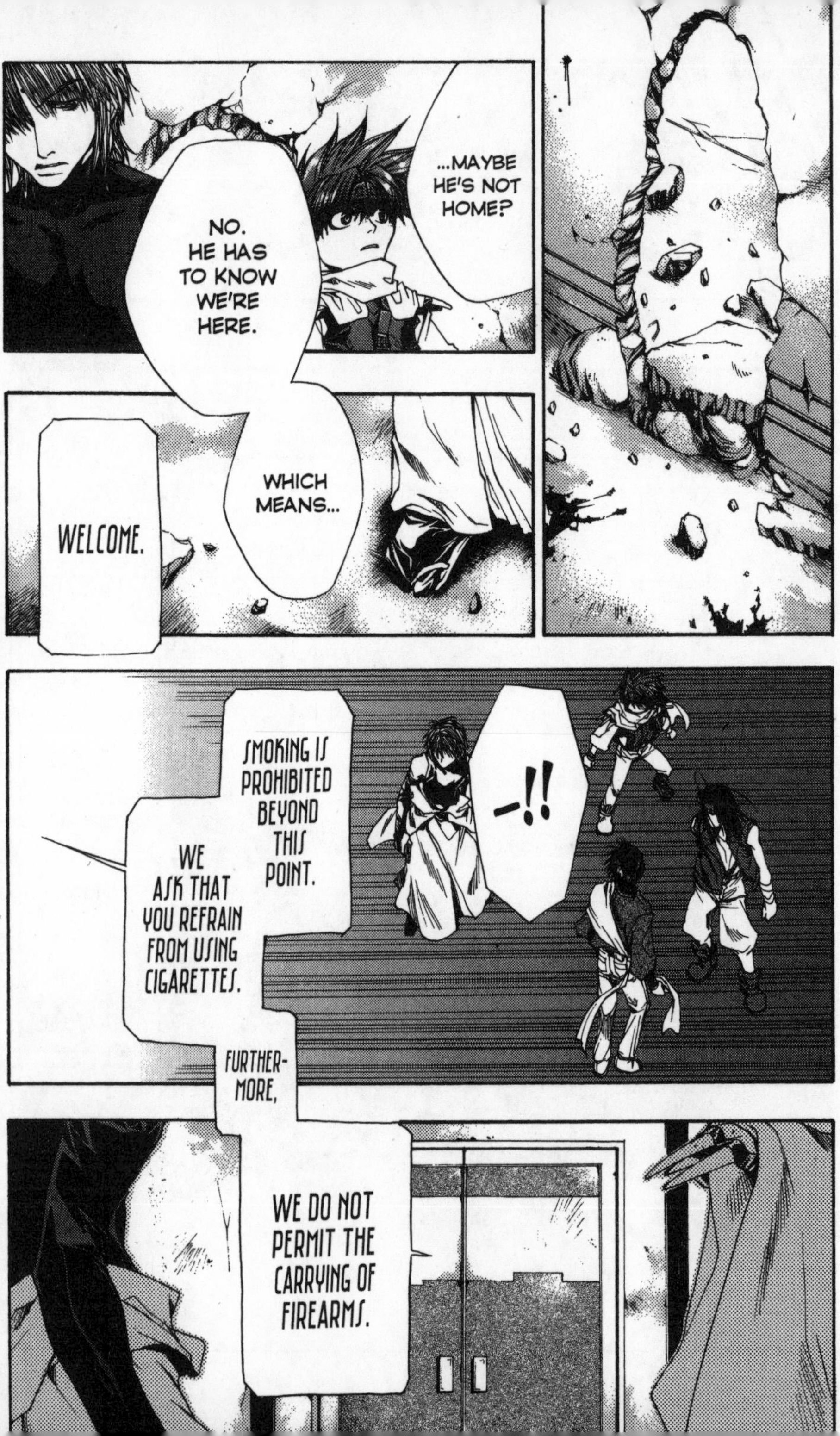

...MAYBE HE'S NOT HOME?
NO. HE HAS TO KNOW WE'RE HERE.
WHICH MEANS...
WELCOME.
—!!
SMOKING IS PROHIBITED BEYOND THIS POINT.
WE ASK THAT YOU REFRAIN FROM USING CIGARETTES.
FURTHERMORE,
WE DO NOT PERMIT THE CARRYING OF FIREARMS.

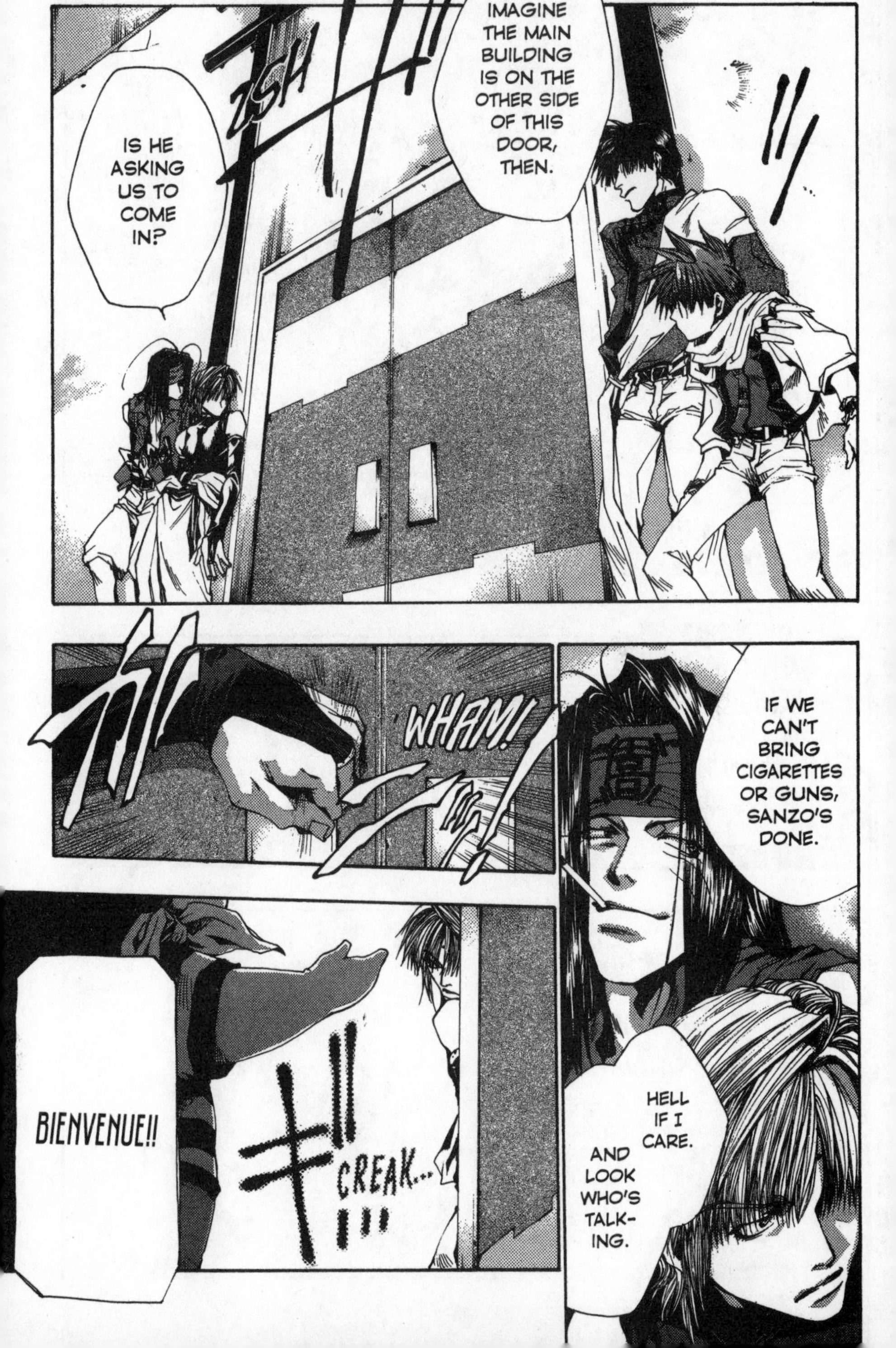
I IMAGINE THE MAIN BUILDING IS ON THE OTHER SIDE OF THIS DOOR, THEN.
ZSH
IS HE ASKING US TO COME IN?
IF WE CAN'T BRING CIGARETTES OR GUNS, SANZO'S DONE.
HELL IF I CARE.
AND LOOK WHO'S TALKING.
WHAM!
BIENVENUE!!
CREAK...

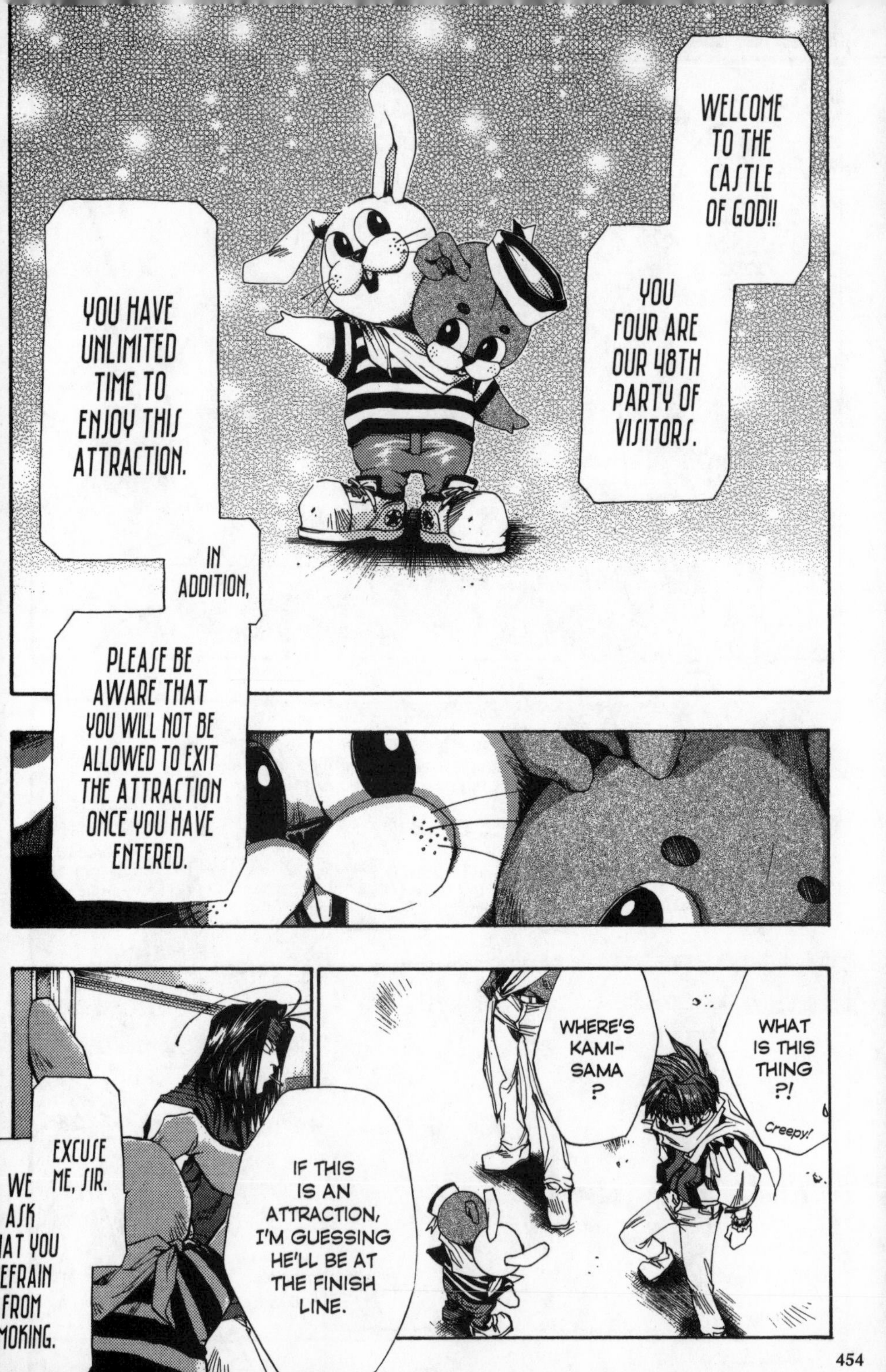

WELCOME TO THE CASTLE OF GOD!!
YOU FOUR ARE OUR 48TH PARTY OF VISITORS.
YOU HAVE UNLIMITED TIME TO ENJOY THIS ATTRACTION.
IN ADDITION,
PLEASE BE AWARE THAT YOU WILL NOT BE ALLOWED TO EXIT THE ATTRACTION ONCE YOU HAVE ENTERED.
WHAT IS THIS THING ?!
Creepy!
WHERE'S KAMI-SAMA ?
IF THIS IS AN ATTRACTION, I'M GUESSING HE'LL BE AT THE FINISH LINE.
EXCUSE ME, SIR.
WE ASK AT YOU EFRAIN FROM MOKING.

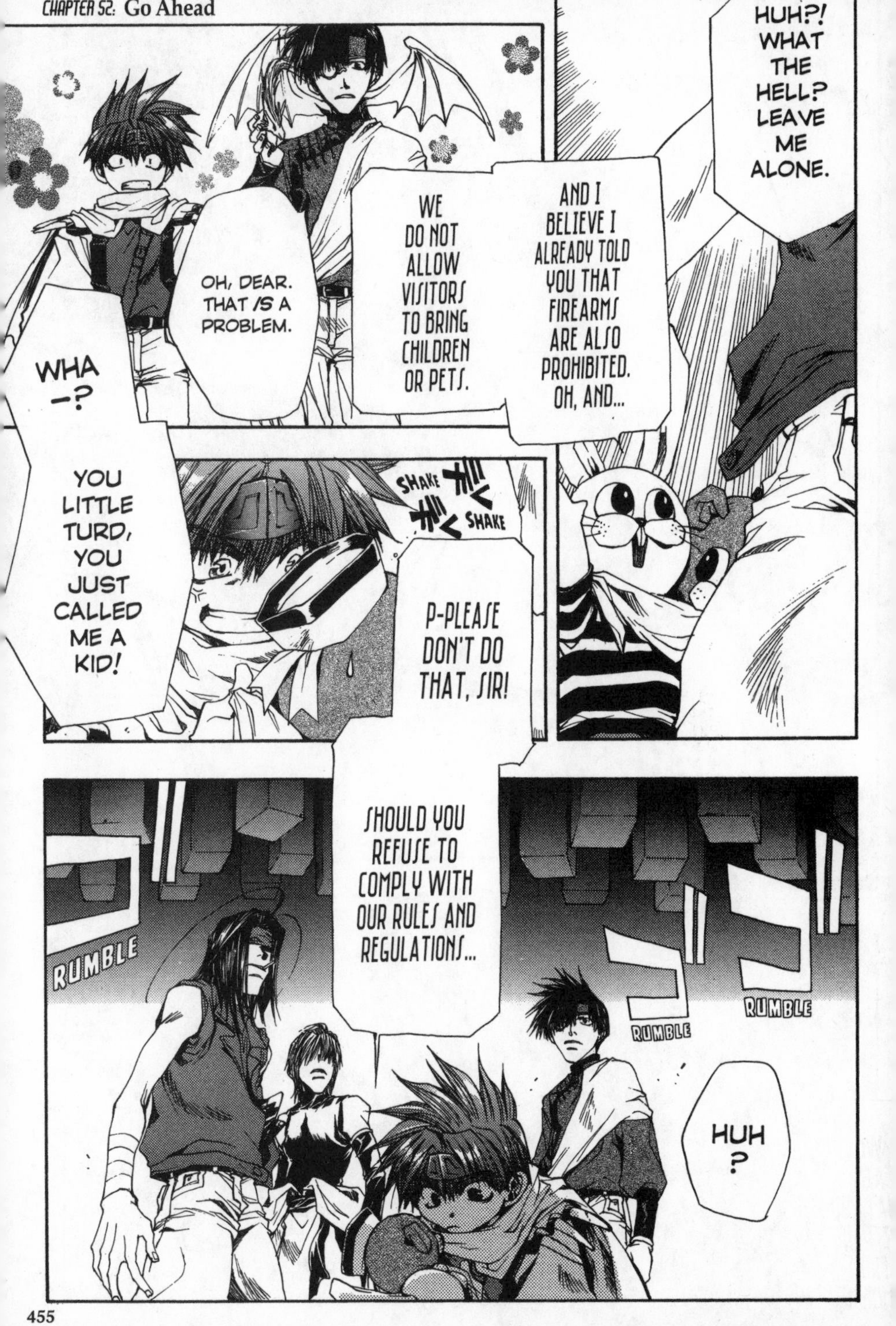
HUH?! WHAT THE HELL? LEAVE ME ALONE.
WE DO NOT ALLOW VISITORS TO BRING CHILDREN OR PETS.
AND I BELIEVE I ALREADY TOLD YOU THAT FIREARMS ARE ALSO PROHIBITED. OH, AND...
OH, DEAR. THAT IS A PROBLEM.
WHA-?
YOU LITTLE TURD, YOU JUST CALLED ME A KID!
SHAKE
SHAKE
P-PLEASE DON'T DO THAT, SIR!
SHOULD YOU REFUSE TO COMPLY WITH OUR RULES AND REGULATIONS...
RUMBLE
RUMBLE
HUH?
RUMBLE

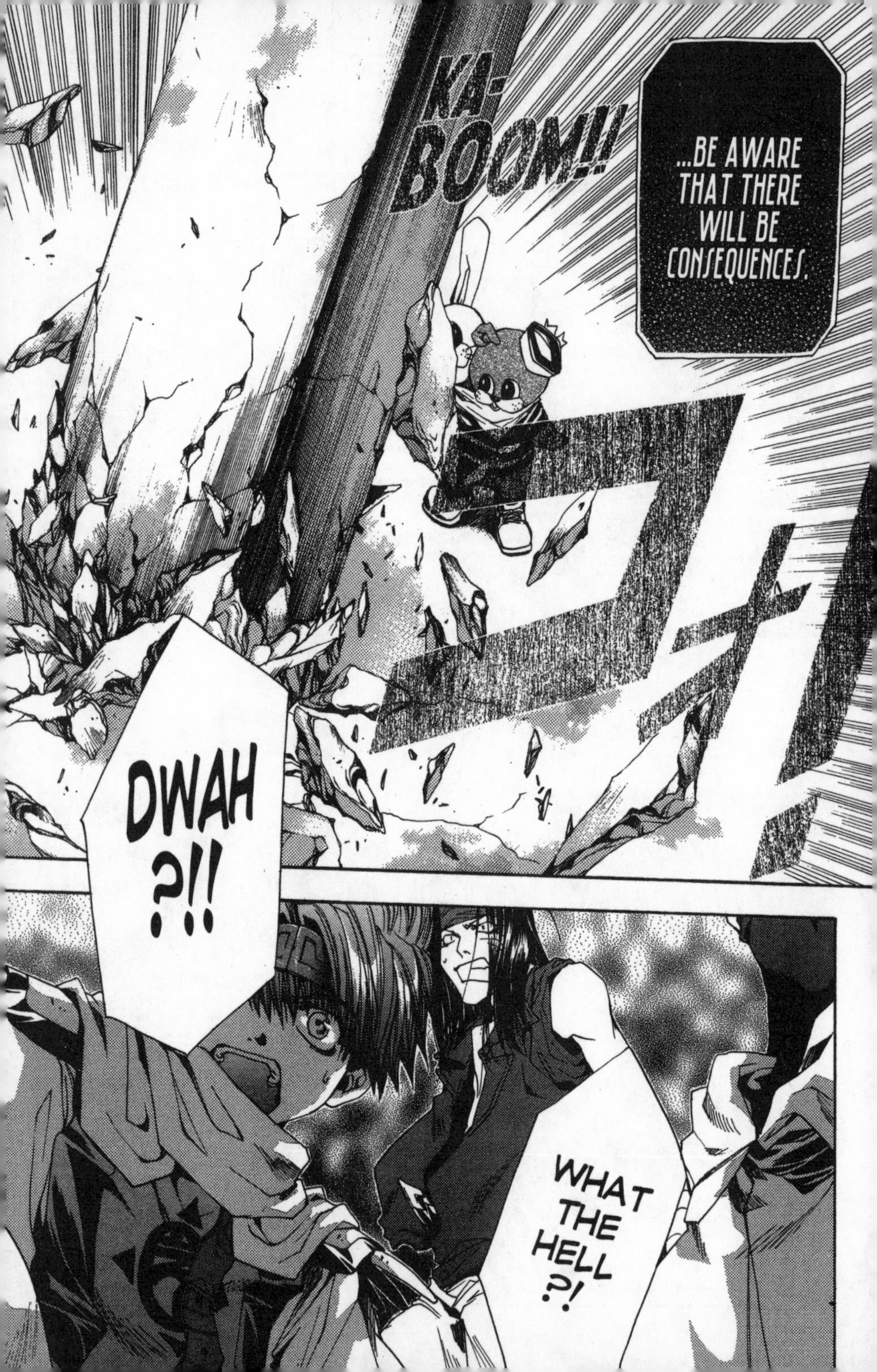
...BE AWARE THAT THERE WILL BE CONSEQUENCES.
KA-BOOM!!
DWAH ?!!
WHAT THE HELL ?!

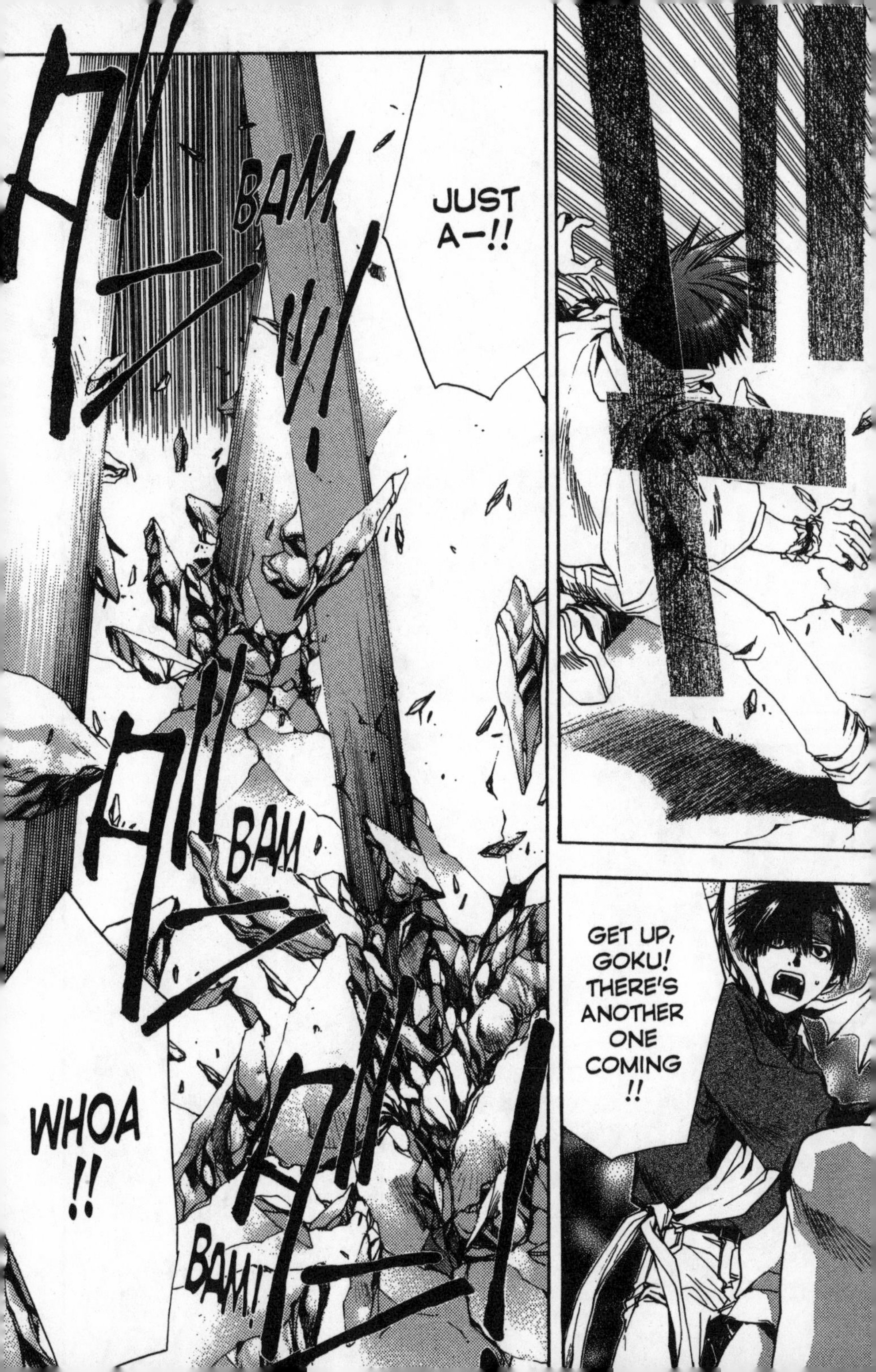
GET UP, GOKU! THERE'S ANOTHER ONE COMING !!
JUST A—!!
BAM
BAM
WHOA !!
BAM!

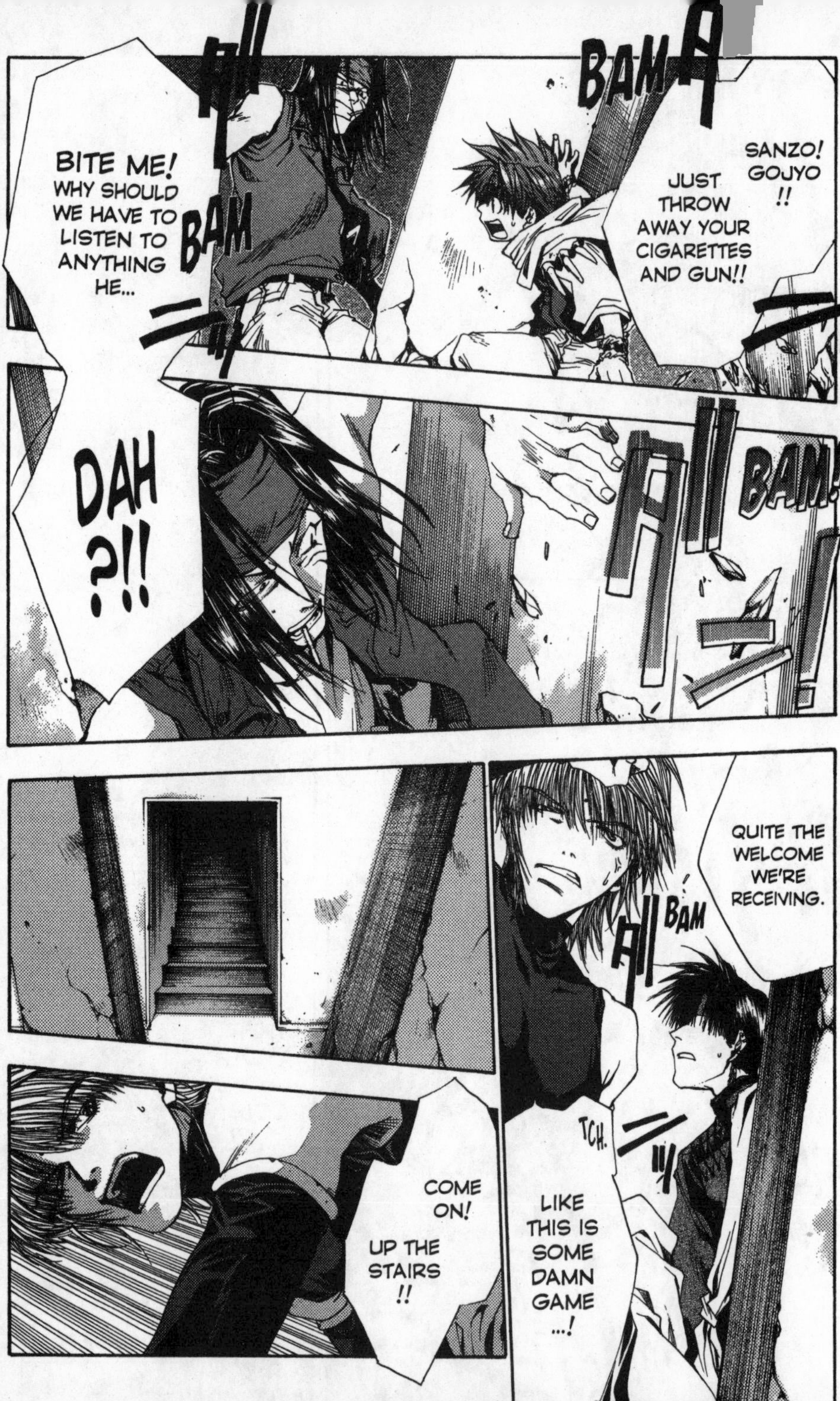
SANZO! GOJYO !!
JUST THROW AWAY YOUR CIGARETTES AND GUN!!
BAMA
BAM
BITE ME! WHY SHOULD WE HAVE TO LISTEN TO ANYTHING HE...
BAM!
DAH ?!!
QUITE THE WELCOME WE'RE RECEIVING.
BAM
TCH.
LIKE THIS IS SOME DAMN GAME ...!
COME ON!
UP THE STAIRS !!

CHAPTER 52: Go Ahead

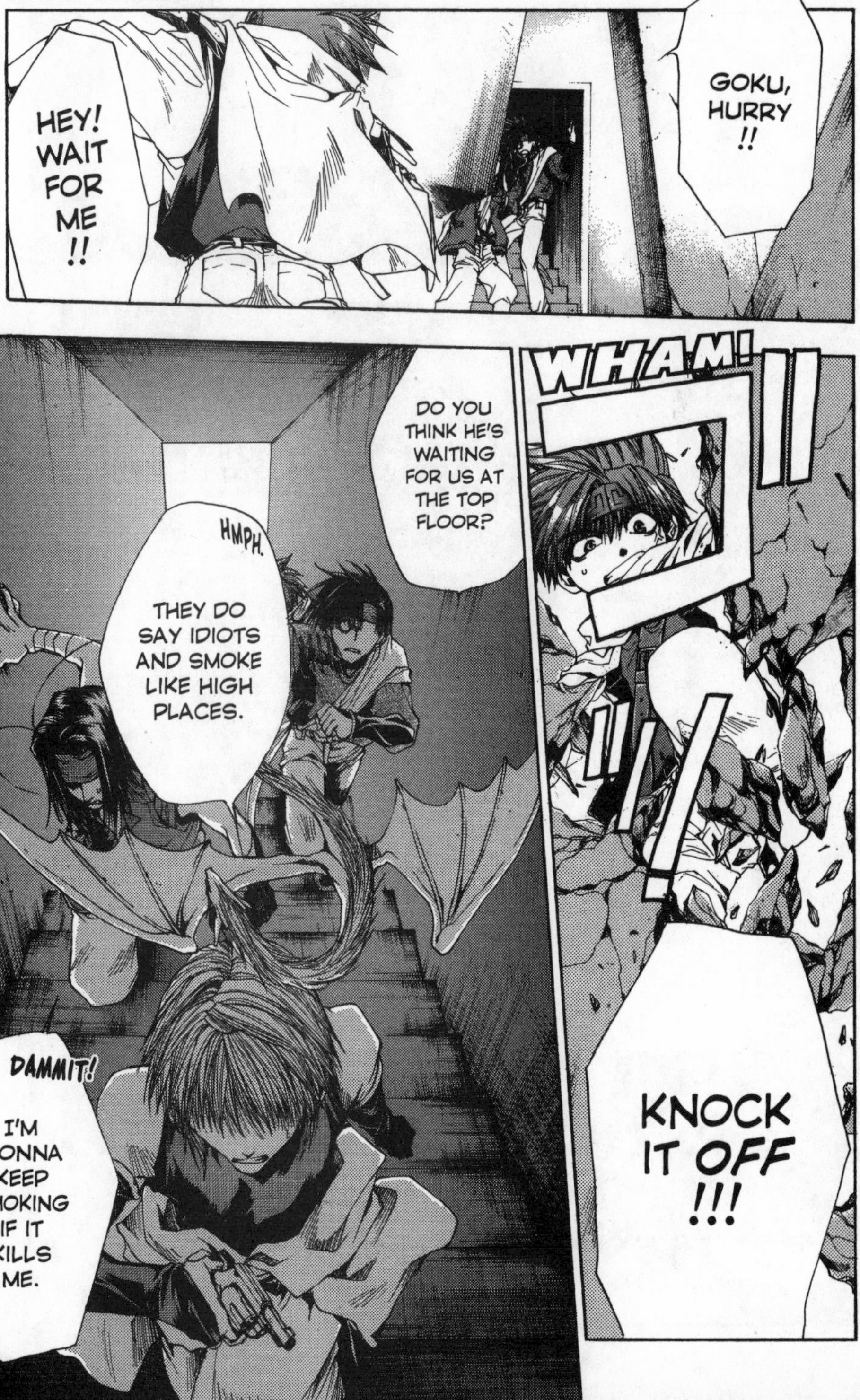
GOKU, HURRY !!
HEY! WAIT FOR ME !!
WHAM!
KNOCK IT OFF !!!
DO YOU THINK HE'S WAITING FOR US AT THE TOP FLOOR?
HMPH.
THEY DO SAY IDIOTS AND SMOKE LIKE HIGH PLACES.
DAMMIT!
I'M GONNA KEEP SMOKING IF IT KILLS ME.

↑2F/13F

...

PLEASE TAKE YOUR TIME.

AND HAVE FUN.

CHAPTER 53
Bet

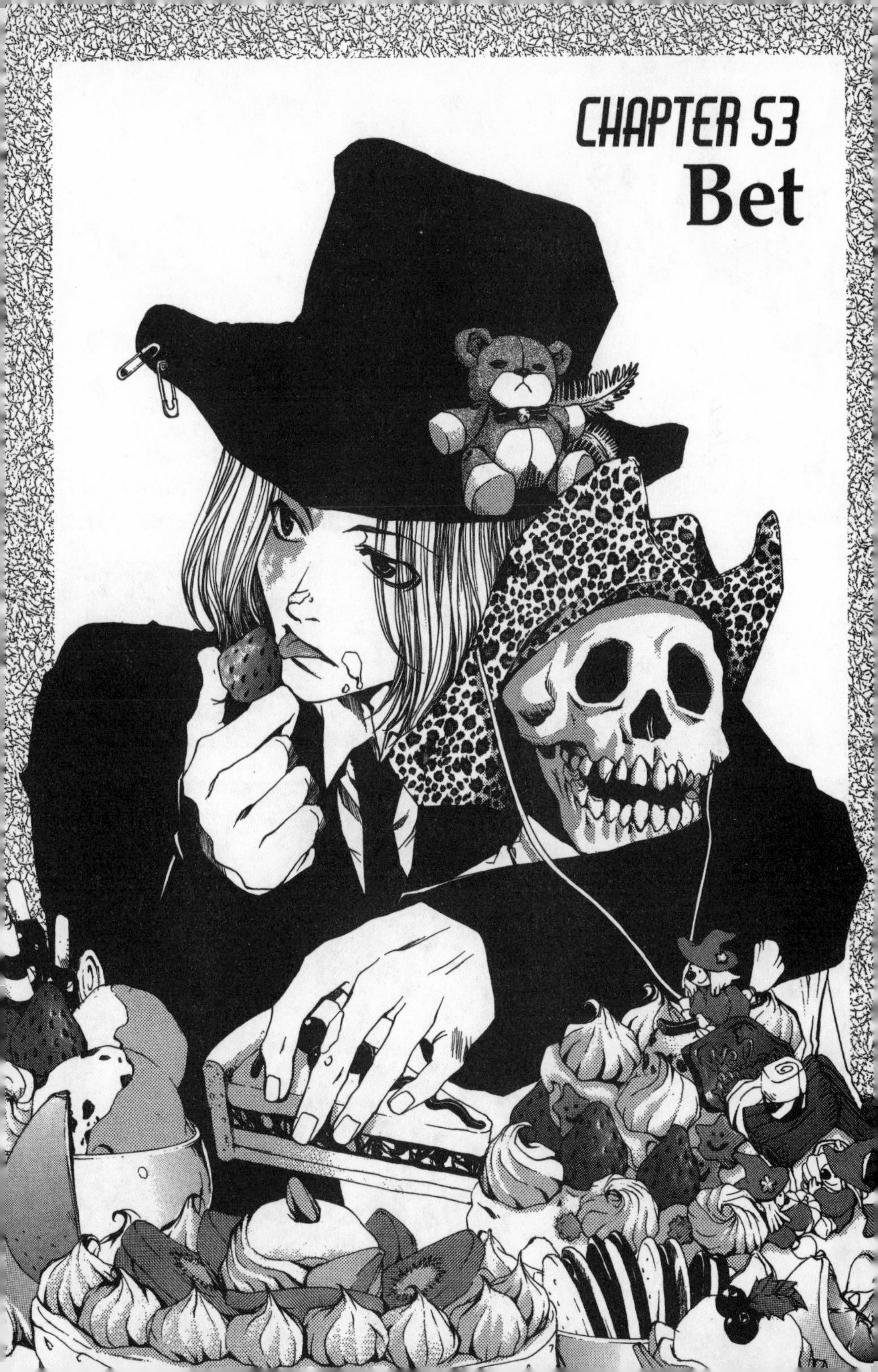

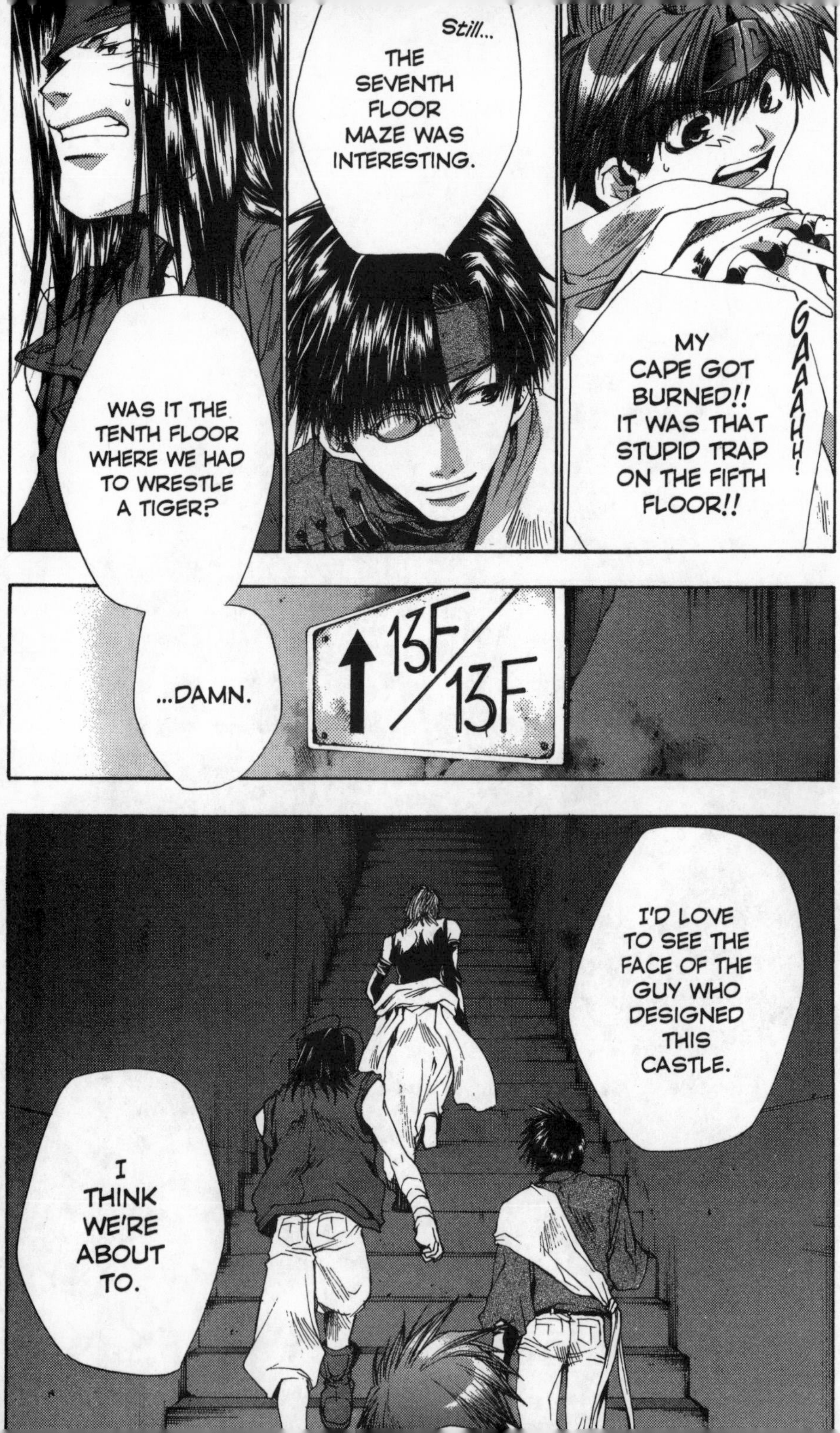
GAAAAHH!
MY CAPE GOT BURNED!! IT WAS THAT STUPID TRAP ON THE FIFTH FLOOR!!
Still... THE SEVENTH FLOOR MAZE WAS INTERESTING.
WAS IT THE TENTH FLOOR WHERE WE HAD TO WRESTLE A TIGER?
13F/13F
...DAMN.
I'D LOVE TO SEE THE FACE OF THE GUY WHO DESIGNED THIS CASTLE.
I THINK WE'RE ABOUT TO.

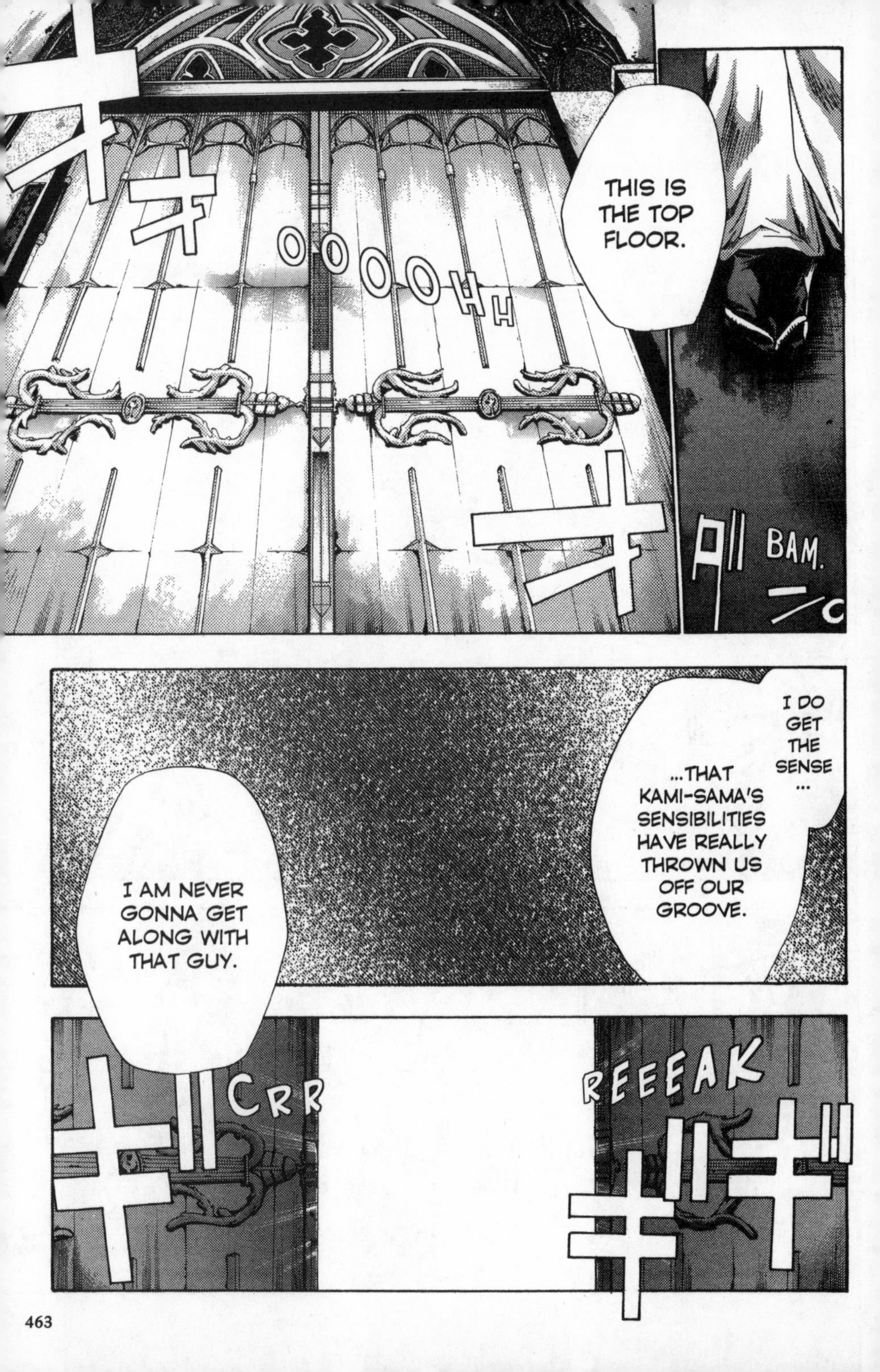
THIS IS THE TOP FLOOR.
OOOOHH
BAM.
I DO GET THE SENSE ...
...THAT KAMI-SAMA'S SENSIBILITIES HAVE REALLY THROWN US OFF OUR GROOVE.
I AM NEVER GONNA GET ALONG WITH THAT GUY.
REEEAK
CRR

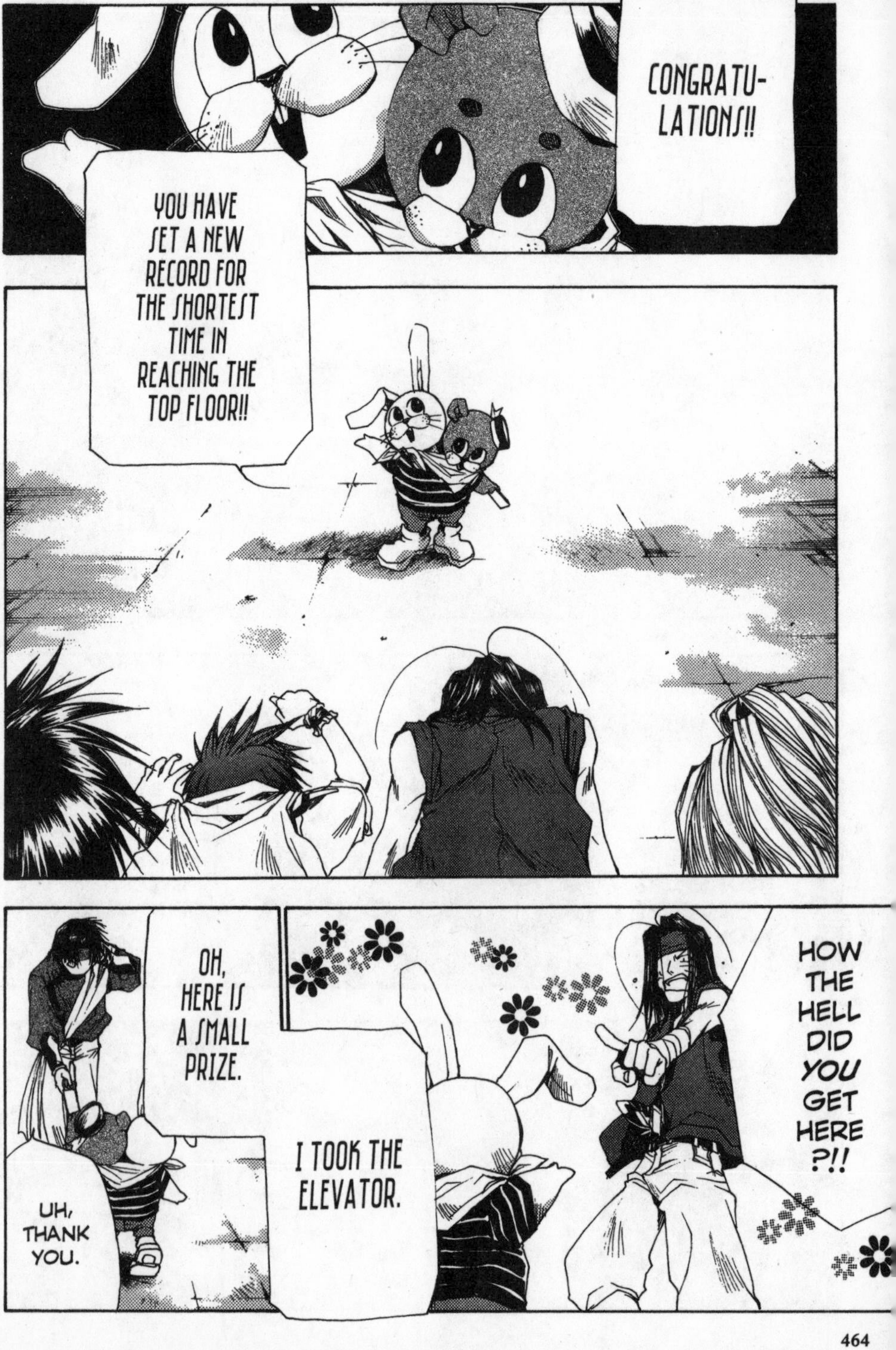
CONGRATU-LATIONS!!
YOU HAVE SET A NEW RECORD FOR THE SHORTEST TIME IN REACHING THE TOP FLOOR!!
HOW THE HELL DID *YOU* GET HERE?!!
I TOOK THE ELEVATOR.
OH, HERE IS A SMALL PRIZE.
UH, THANK YOU.

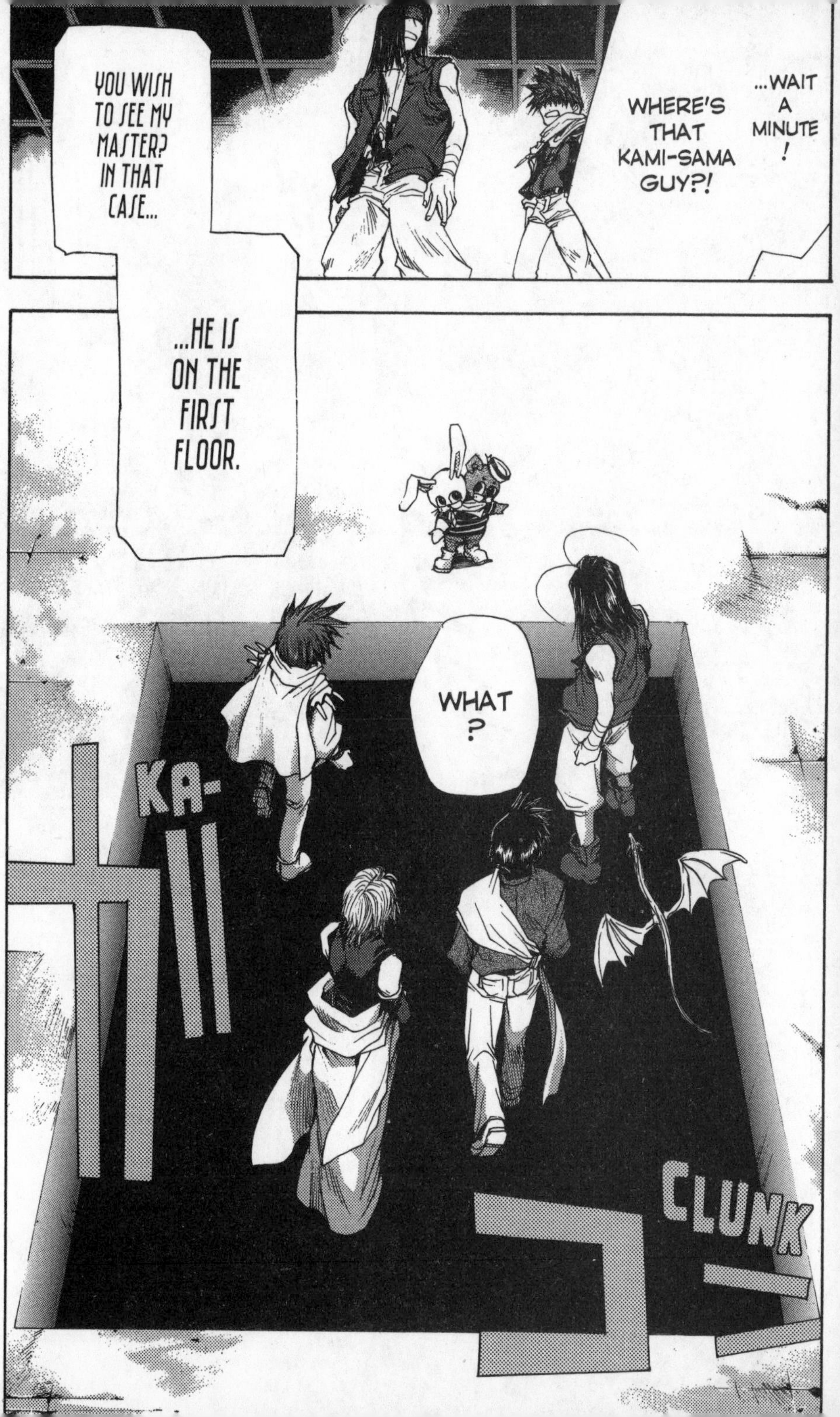
...WAIT A MINUTE!
WHERE'S THAT KAMI-SAMA GUY?!
YOU WISH TO SEE MY MASTER? IN THAT CASE...
...HE IS ON THE FIRST FLOOR.
WHAT?
KA-
CLUNK

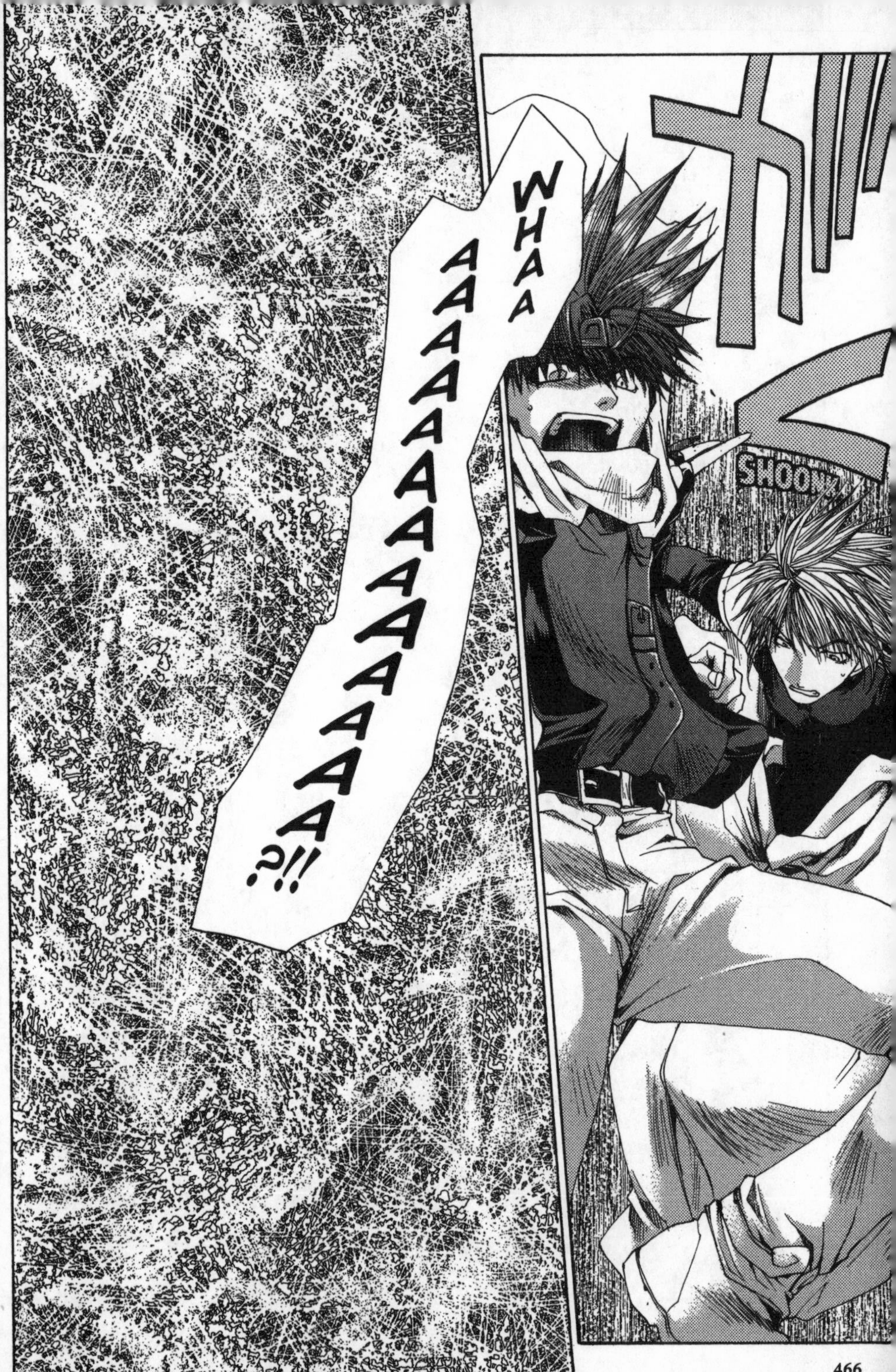
WHAAAAAAAAAAAAAAAAA?!!
SHOON

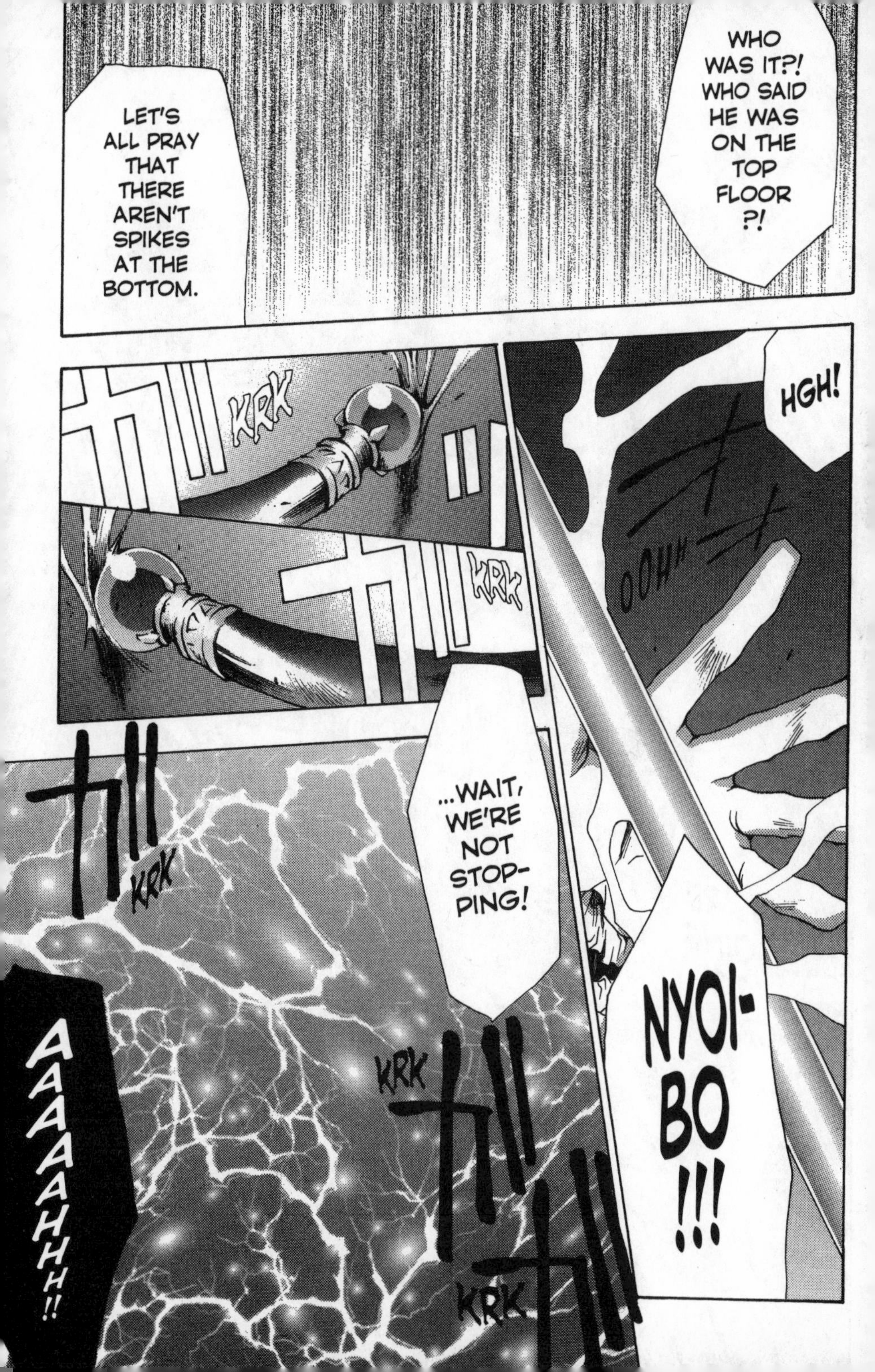
WHO WAS IT?! WHO SAID HE WAS ON THE TOP FLOOR ?!
LET'S ALL PRAY THAT THERE AREN'T SPIKES AT THE BOTTOM.
HGH!
OOHH
KRK
KRK
...WAIT, WE'RE NOT STOP-PING!
NYOI-BO !!!
KRK
KRK
KRK
AAAAAAHHH!!

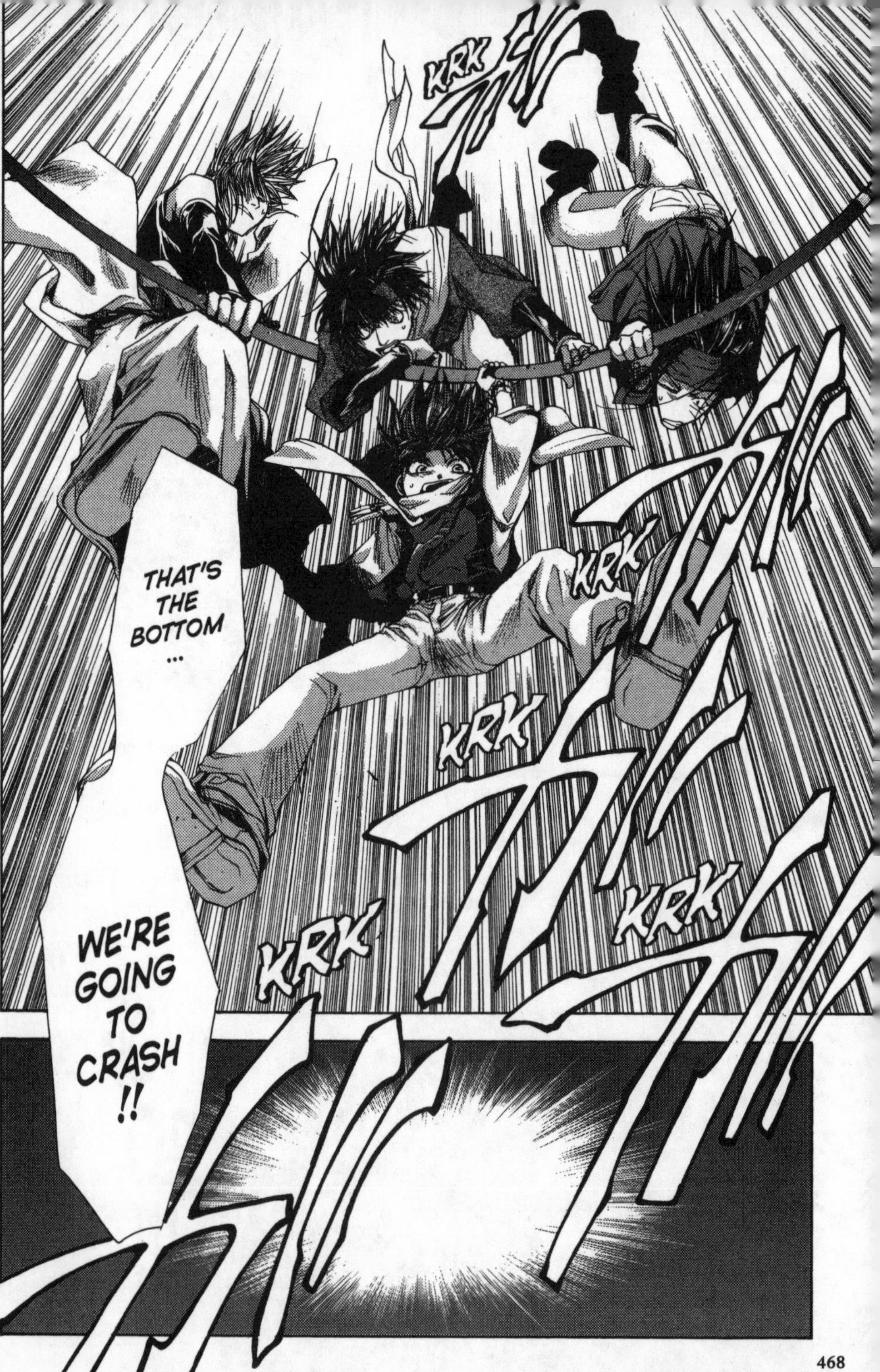
KRK
KRK
THAT'S THE BOTTOM ...
KRK
KRK
KRK
WE'RE GOING TO CRASH !!

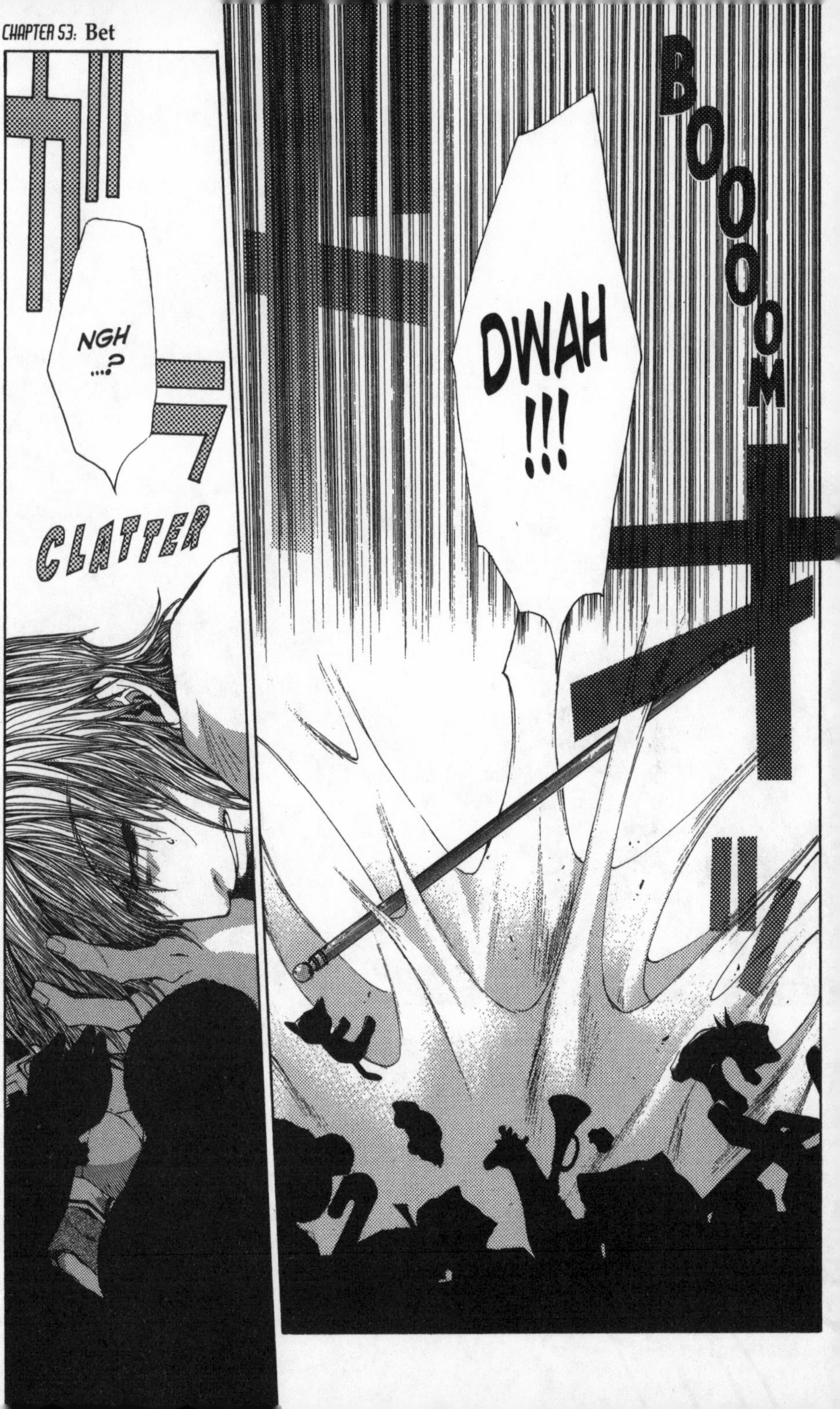
BOOOOOM
DWAH !!!
NGH ...?
CLATTER

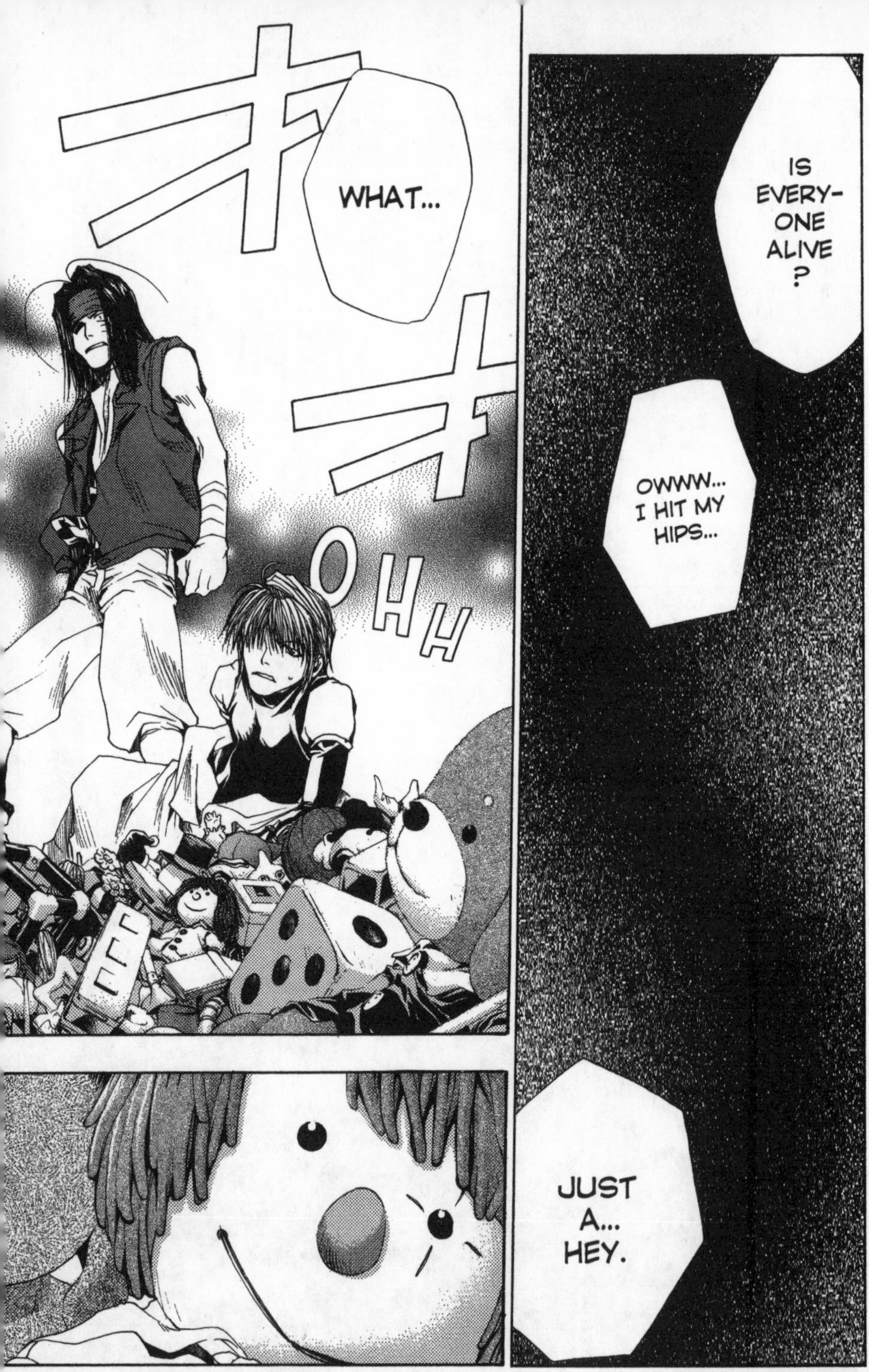
IS EVERY-ONE ALIVE?
OWWW... I HIT MY HIPS...
JUST A... HEY.
WHAT...
OHH

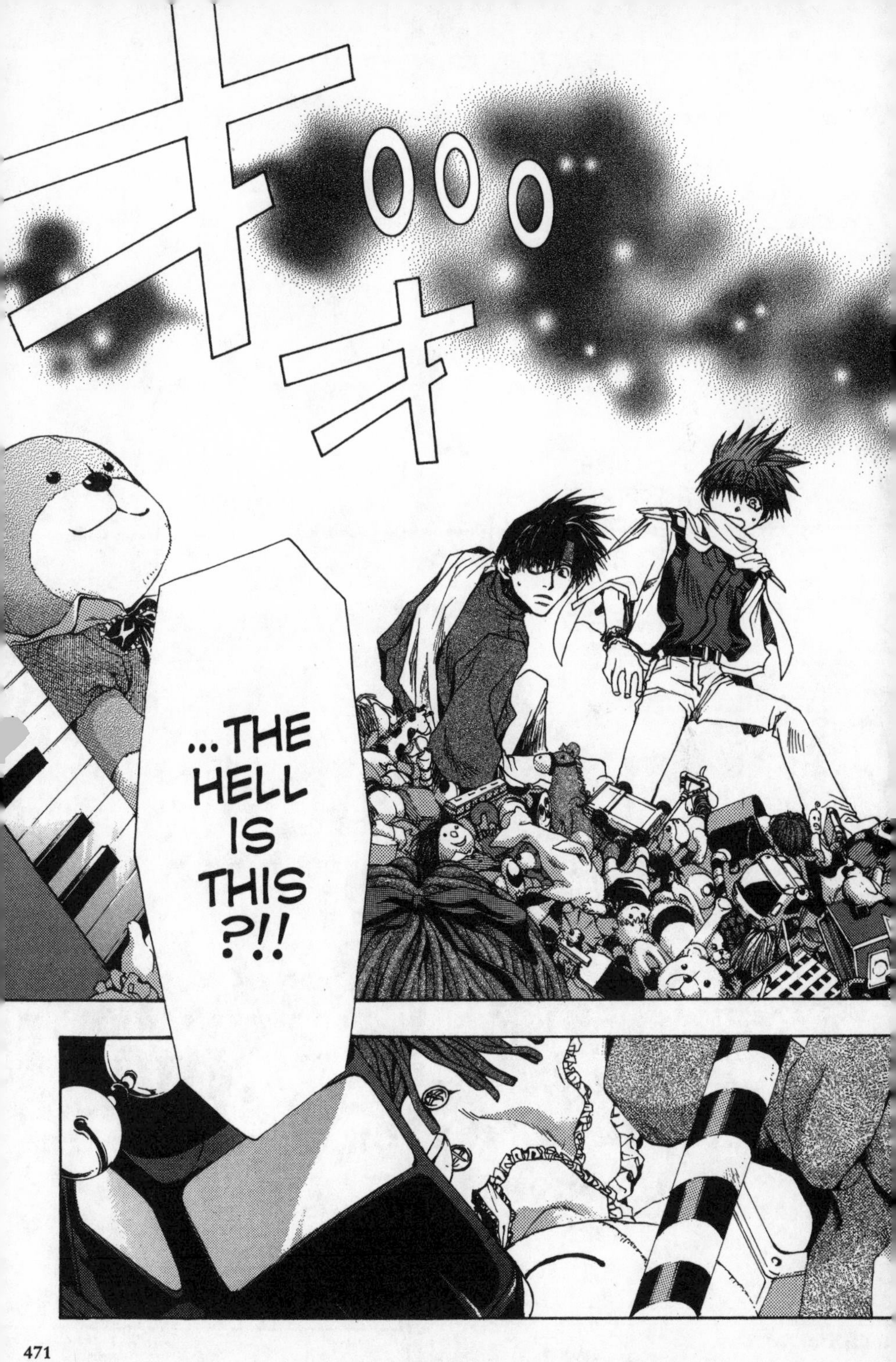
...THE HELL IS THIS ?!!

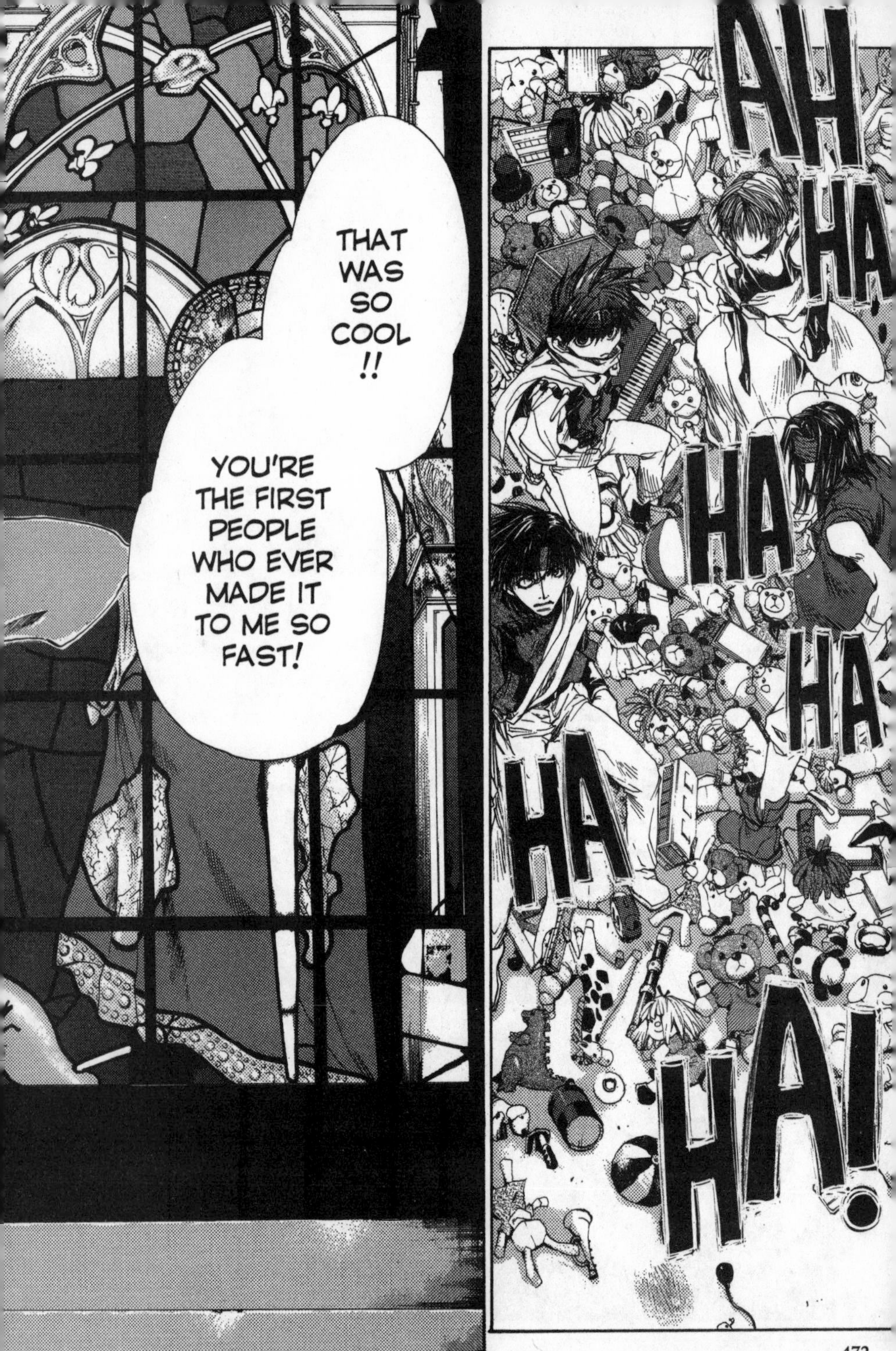
AH HA HA HA HA HA HA!
THAT WAS SO COOL!!
YOU'RE THE FIRST PEOPLE WHO EVER MADE IT TO ME SO FAST!

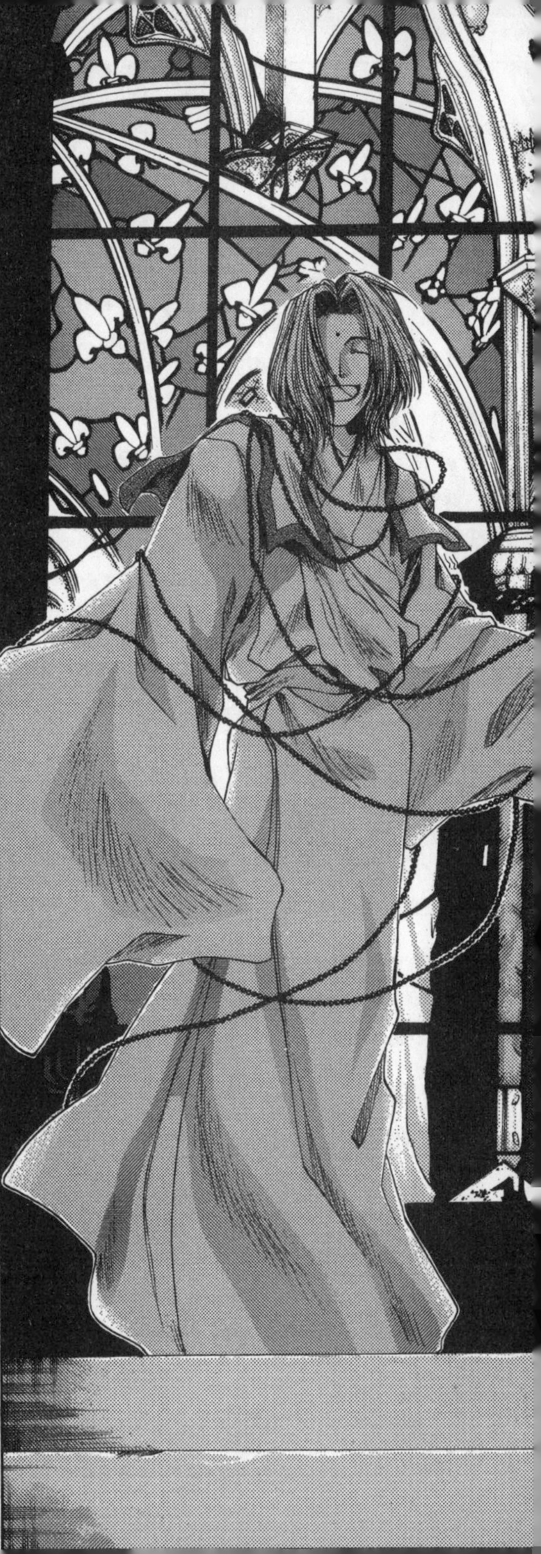

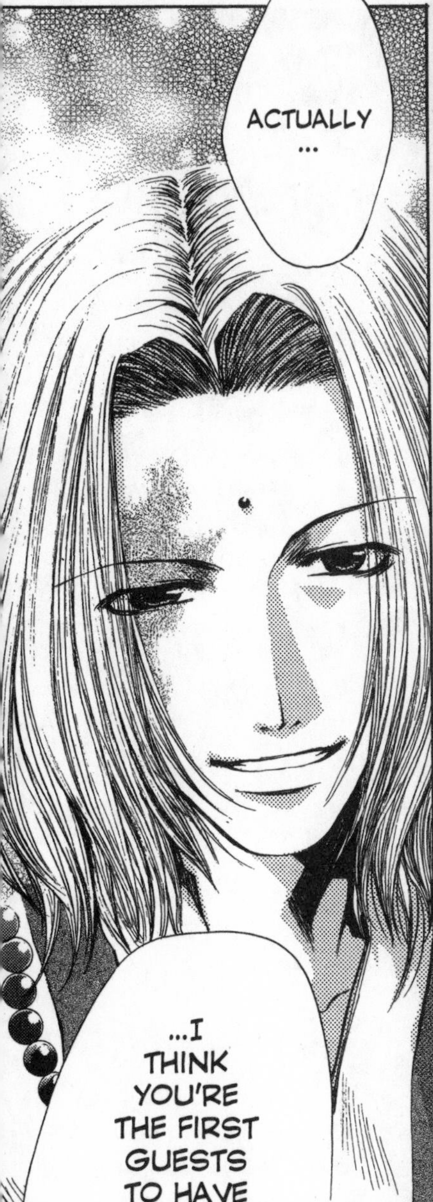
ACTUALLY ...
...I THINK YOU'RE THE FIRST GUESTS TO HAVE EVER MADE IT TO MY TOY BOX.

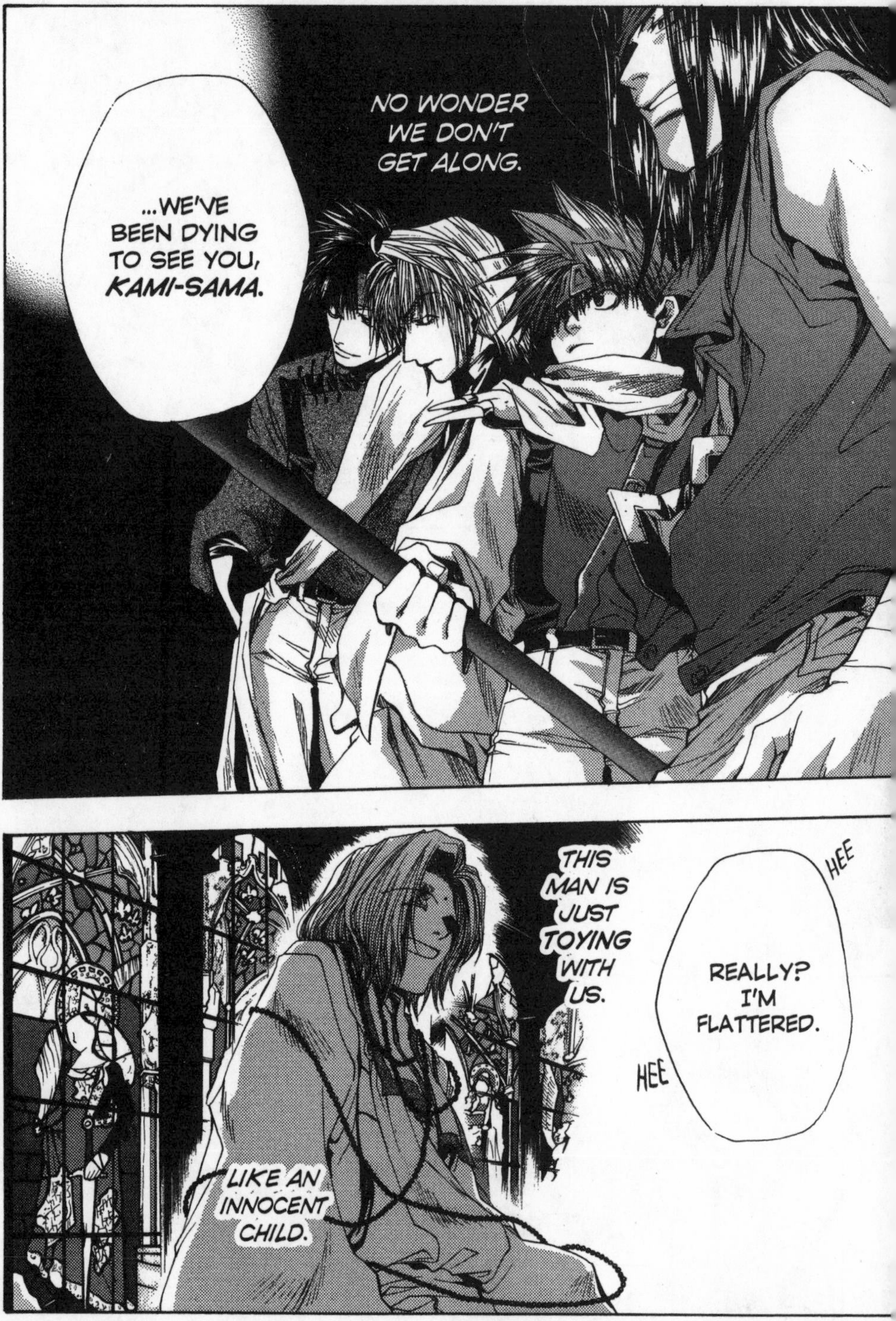
NO WONDER WE DON'T GET ALONG.
...WE'VE BEEN DYING TO SEE YOU, *KAMI-SAMA*.
HEE
REALLY? I'M FLATTERED.
HEE
THIS MAN IS JUST TOYING WITH US.
LIKE AN INNOCENT CHILD.

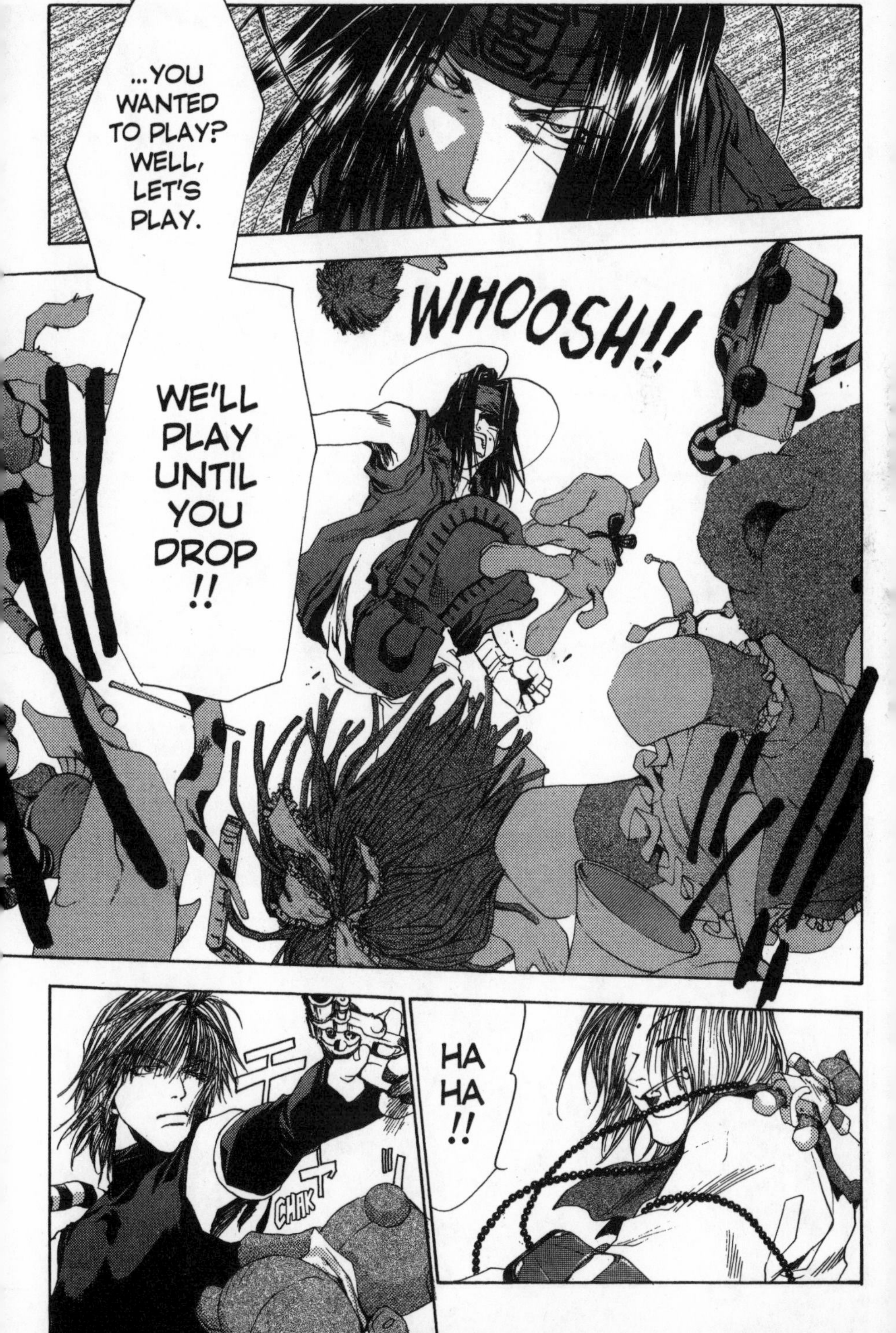
...YOU WANTED TO PLAY? WELL, LET'S PLAY.
WHOOSH!!
WE'LL PLAY UNTIL YOU DROP!!
HA HA!!
CHAK

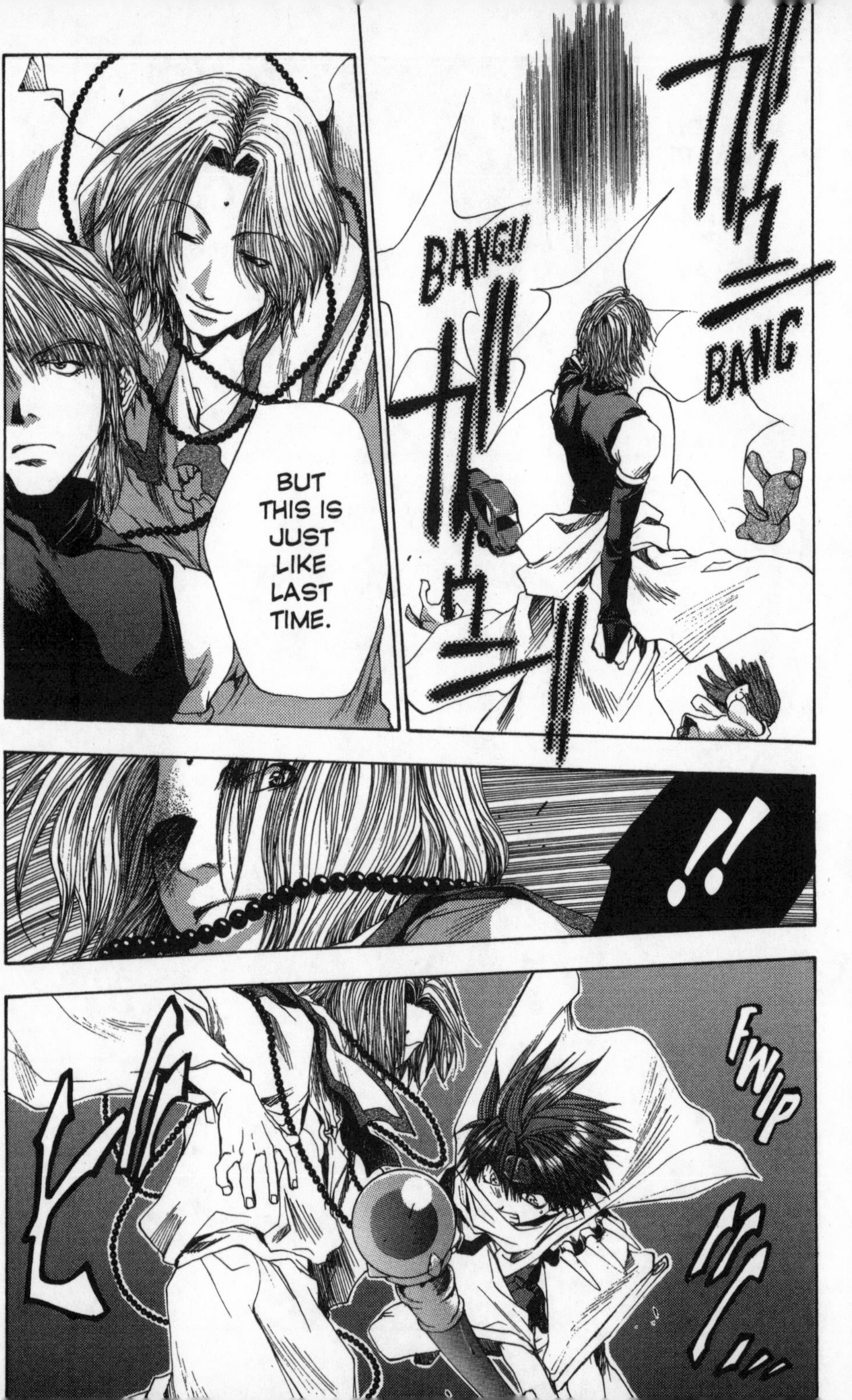

BANG!!
BANG
BUT THIS IS JUST LIKE LAST TIME.
!!
FWIP

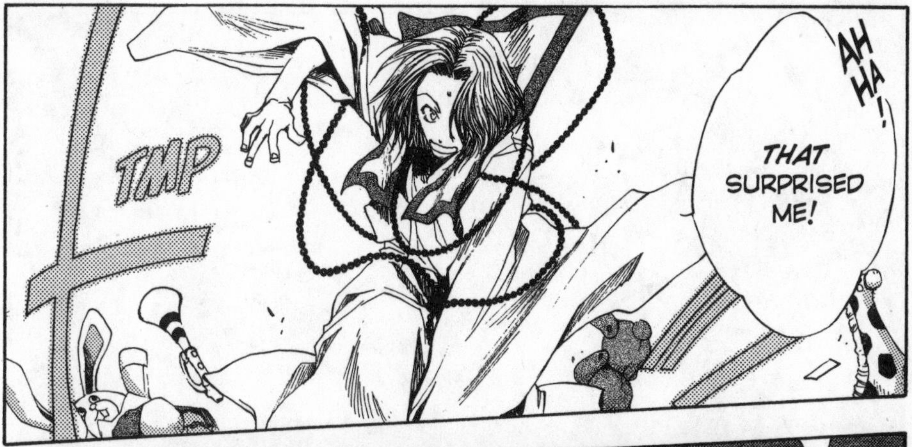
AH HA!
THAT SURPRISED ME!
TMP

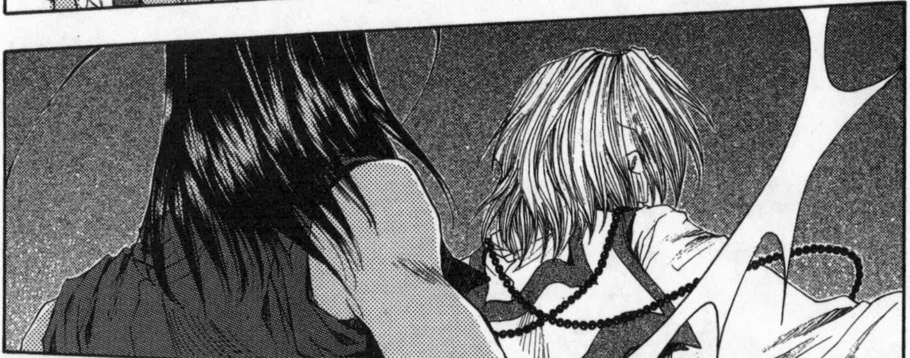

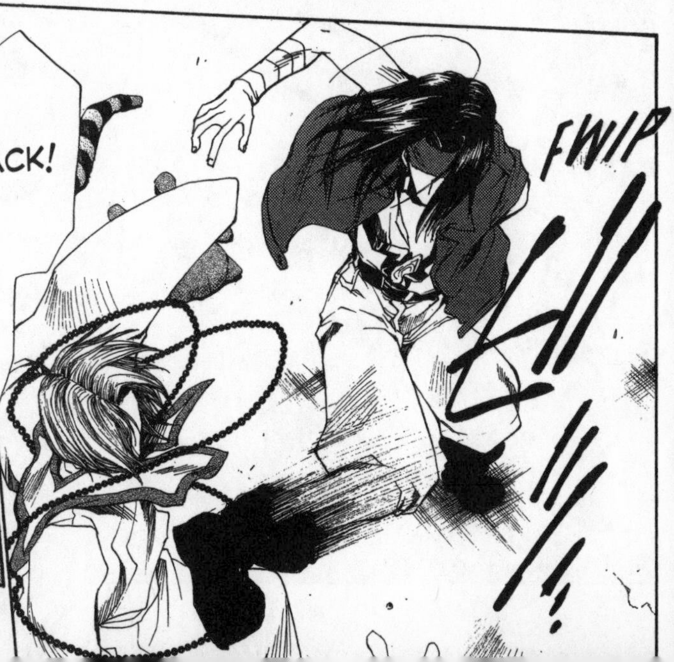
FWIP
ACK!
YOU ...!!

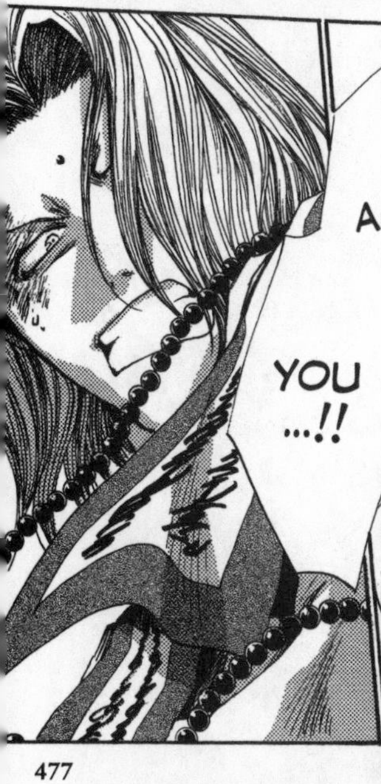

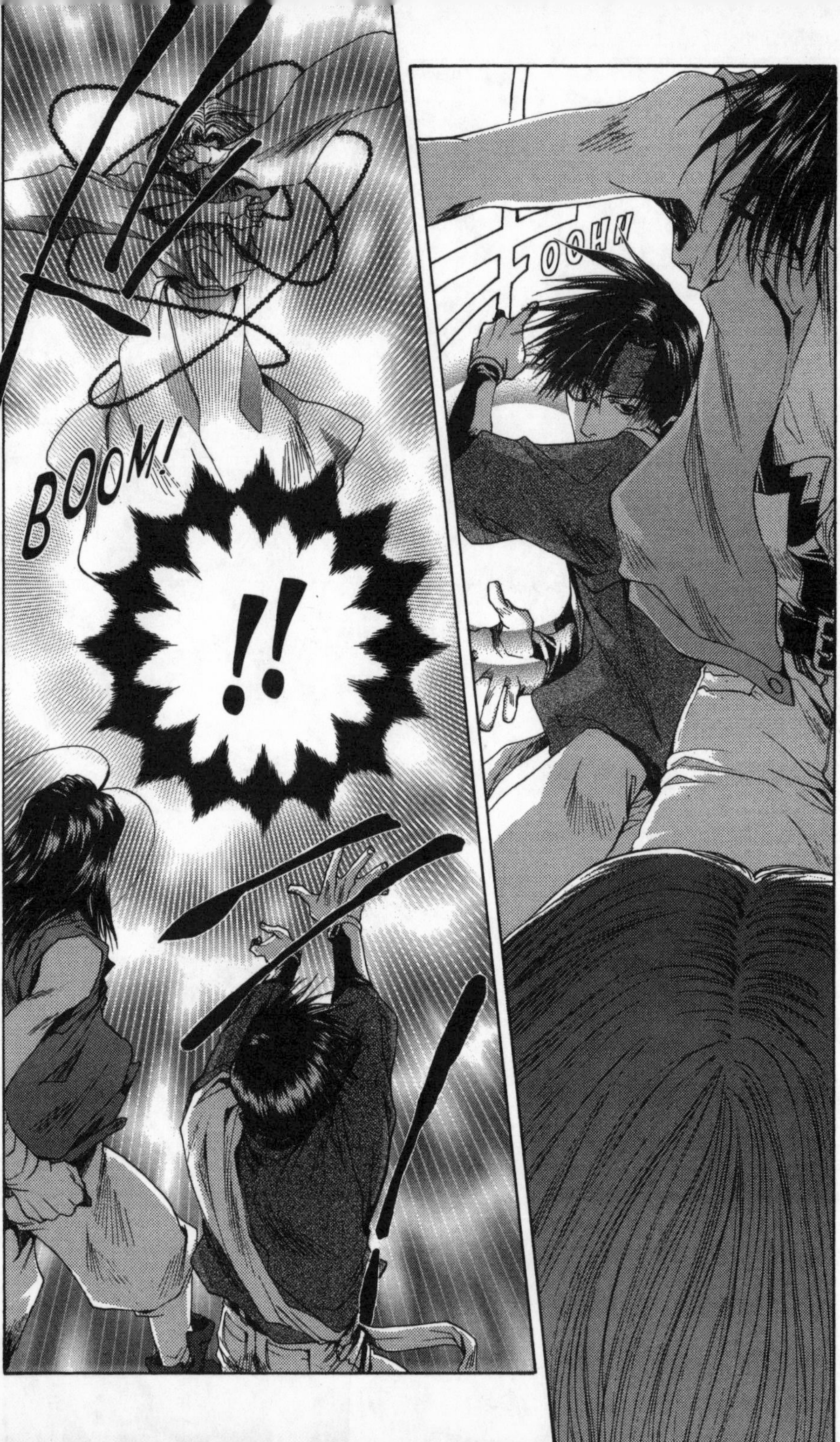
FOOHN
BOOM!
!!

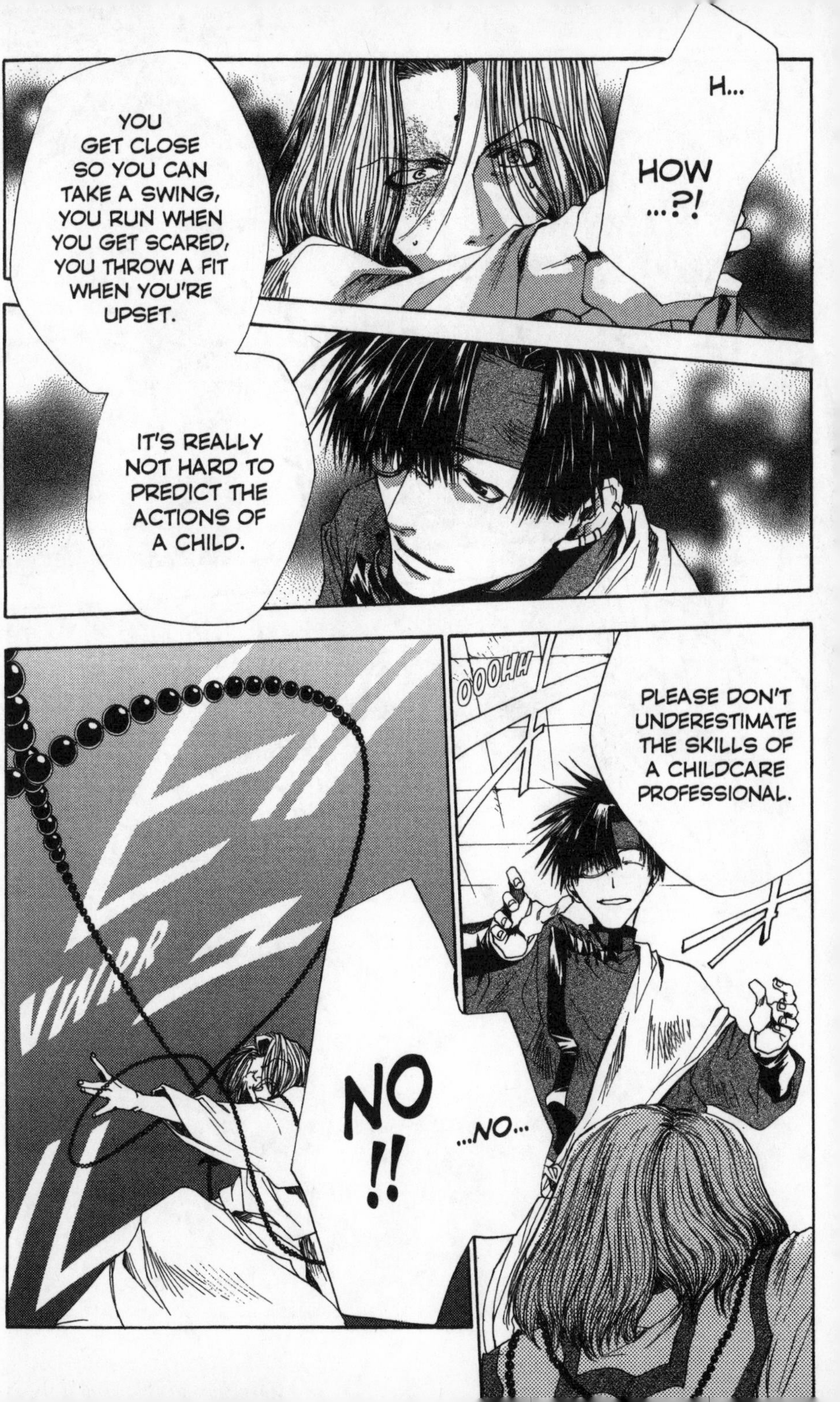
H... HOW ...?!
YOU GET CLOSE SO YOU CAN TAKE A SWING, YOU RUN WHEN YOU GET SCARED, YOU THROW A FIT WHEN YOU'RE UPSET.
IT'S REALLY NOT HARD TO PREDICT THE ACTIONS OF A CHILD.
OOOHH
PLEASE DON'T UNDERESTIMATE THE SKILLS OF A CHILDCARE PROFESSIONAL.
...NO...
NO !!
VWRR

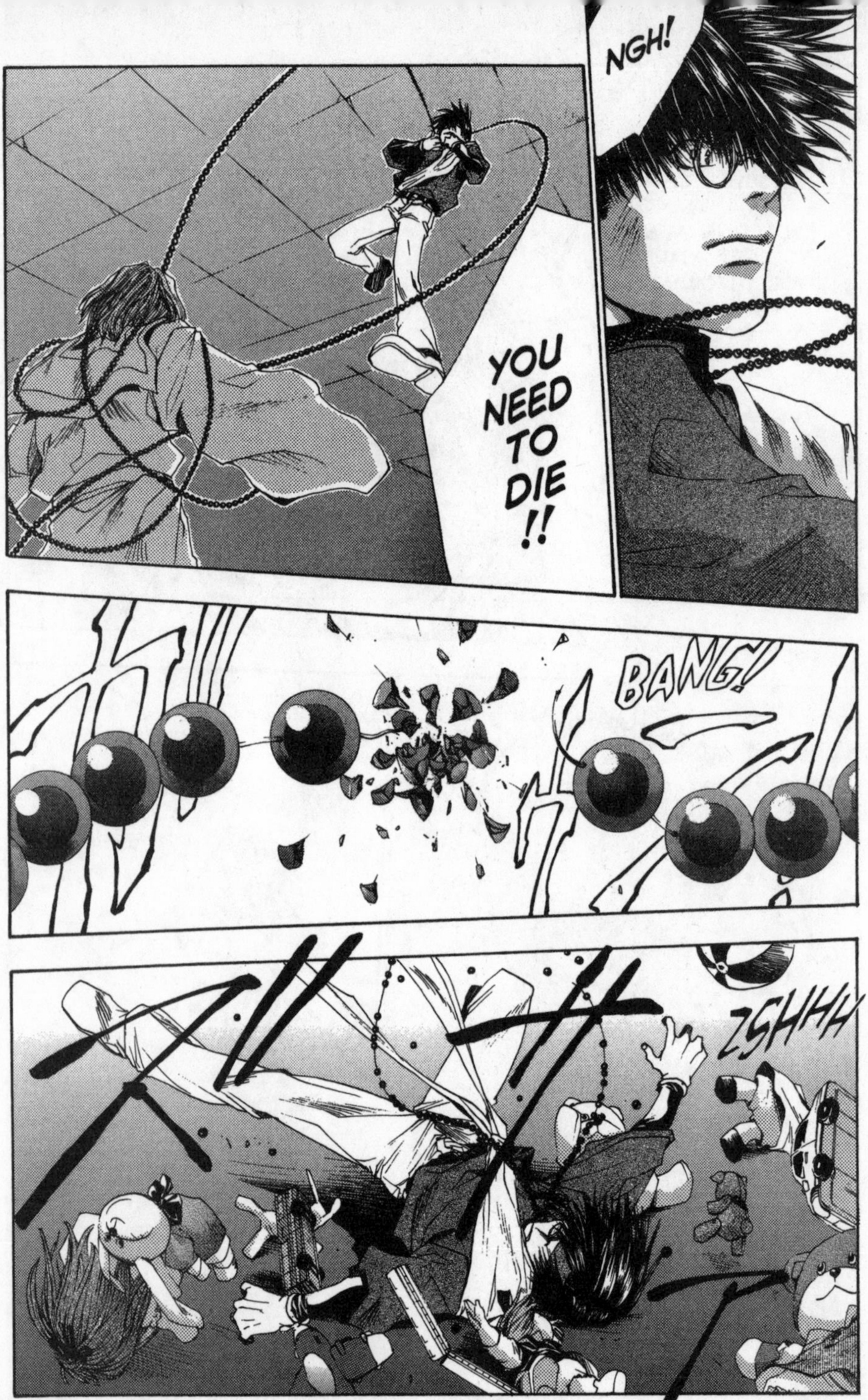
NGH!
YOU NEED TO DIE!!
BANG!
ZSHHH

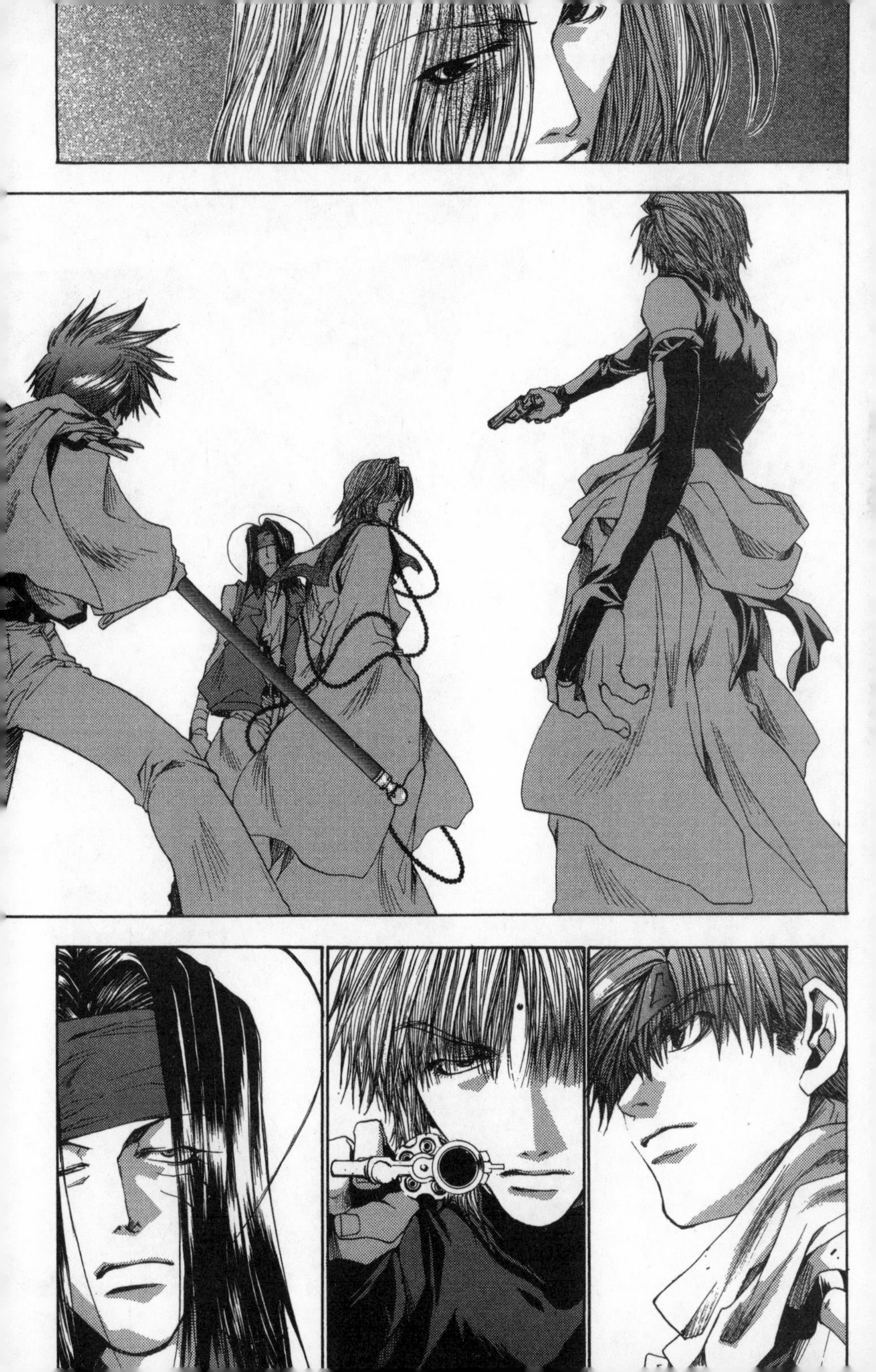

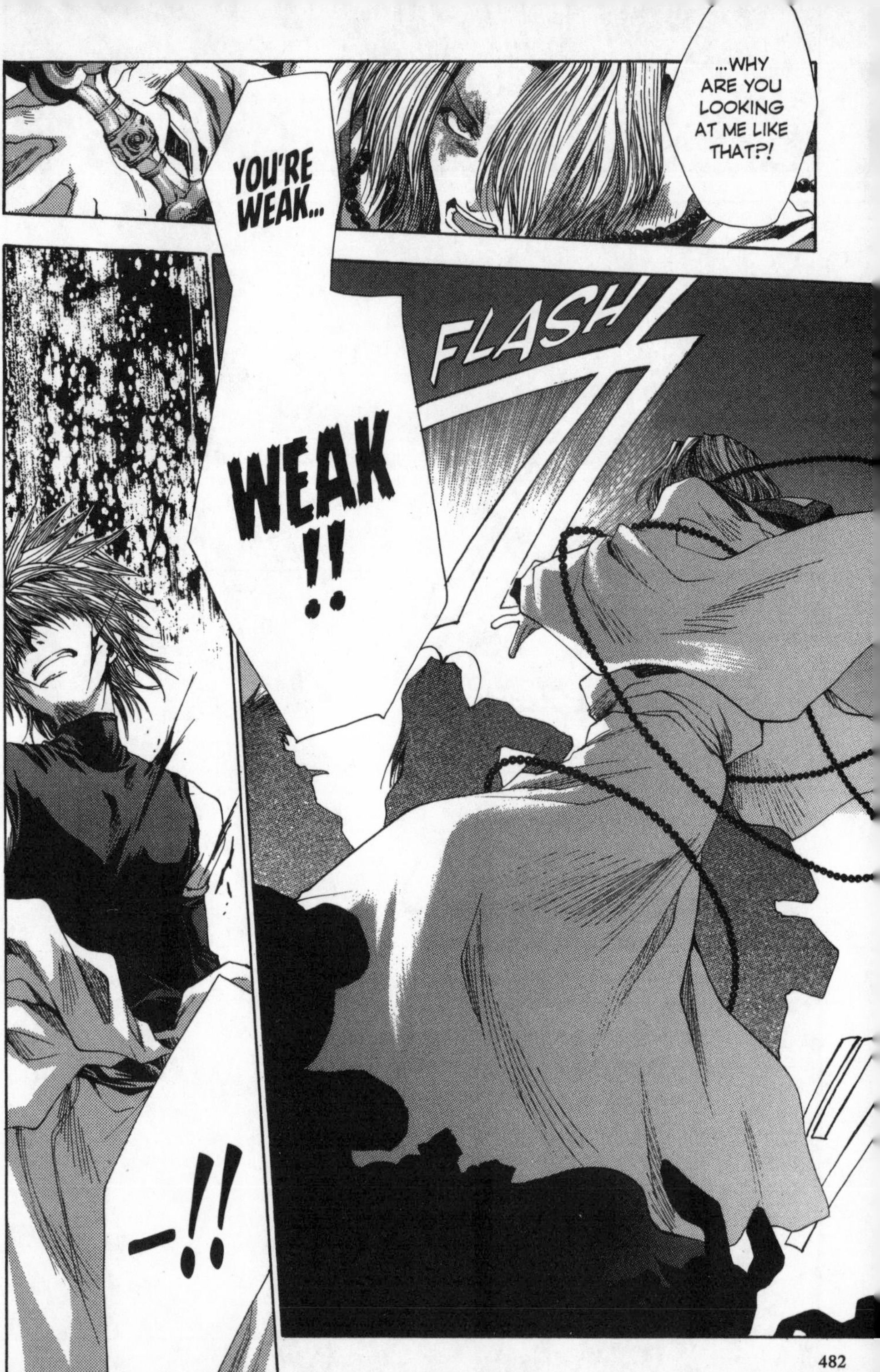

...WHY ARE YOU LOOKING AT ME LIKE THAT?!
YOU'RE WEAK...
WEAK!!
FLASH
—!!

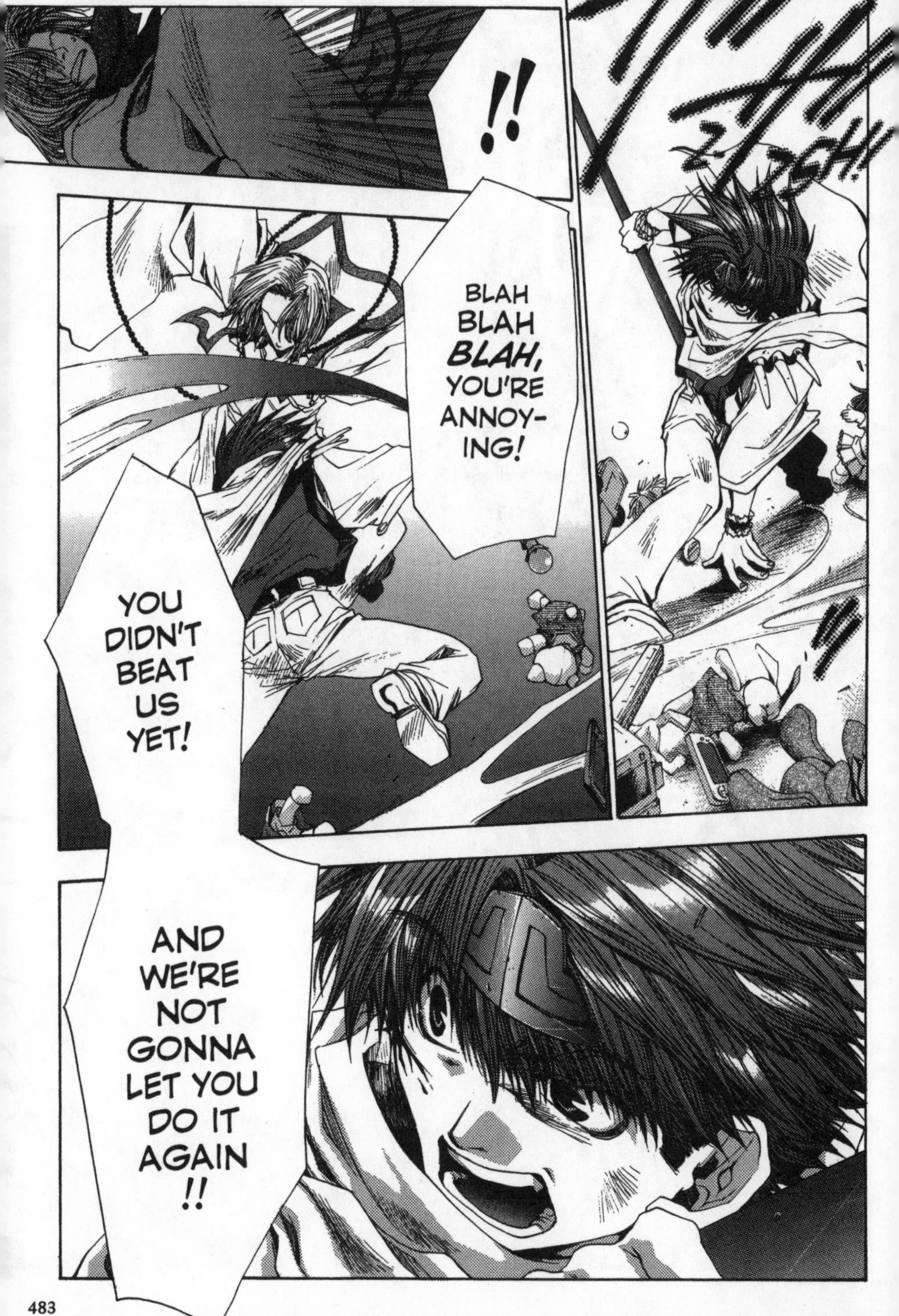
!!
BLAH BLAH *BLAH*, YOU'RE ANNOY-ING!
YOU DIDN'T BEAT US YET!
AND WE'RE NOT GONNA LET YOU DO IT AGAIN !!

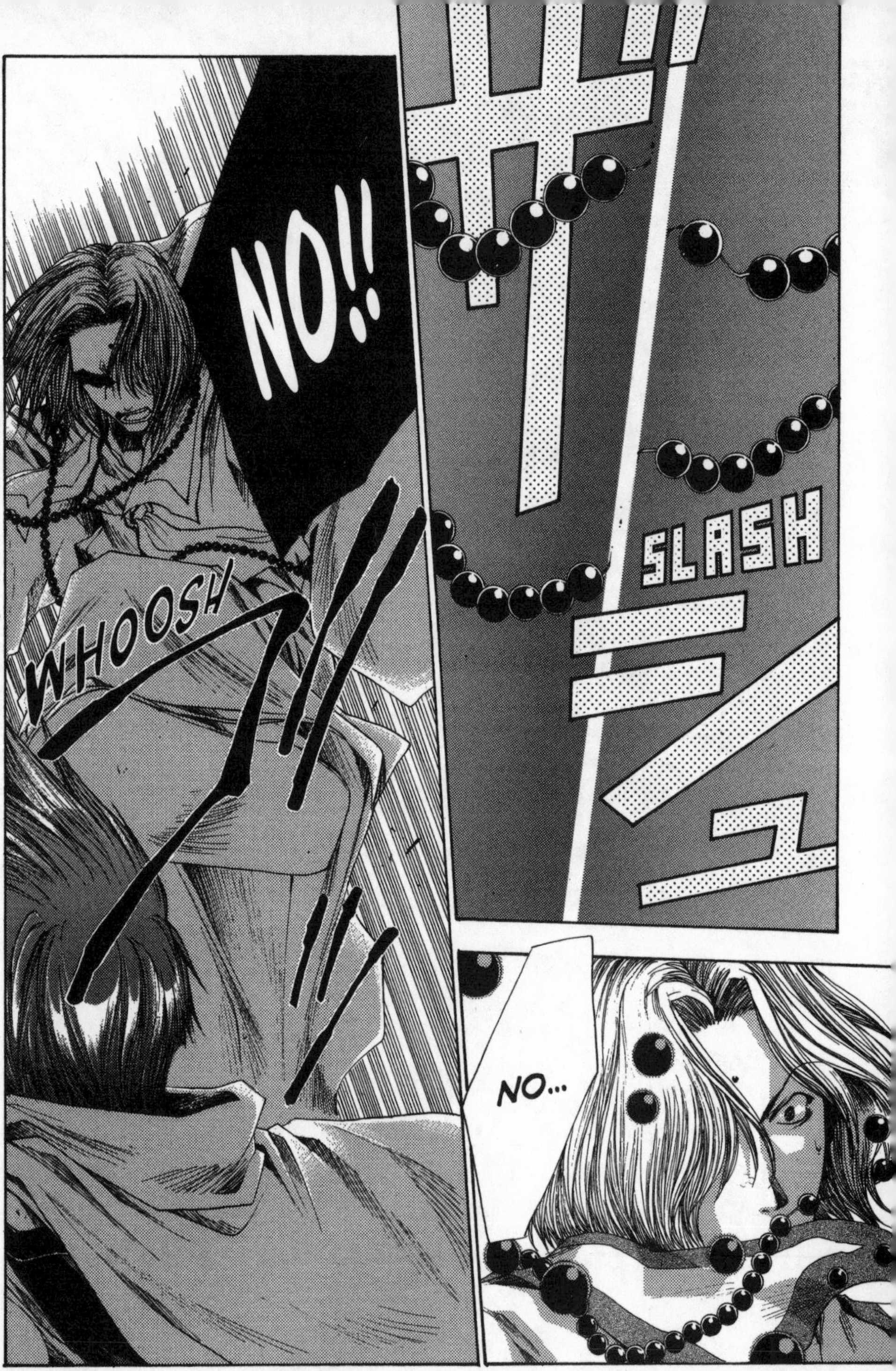
SLASH
NO...
NO!!
WHOOSH

CHAPTER 53: Bet

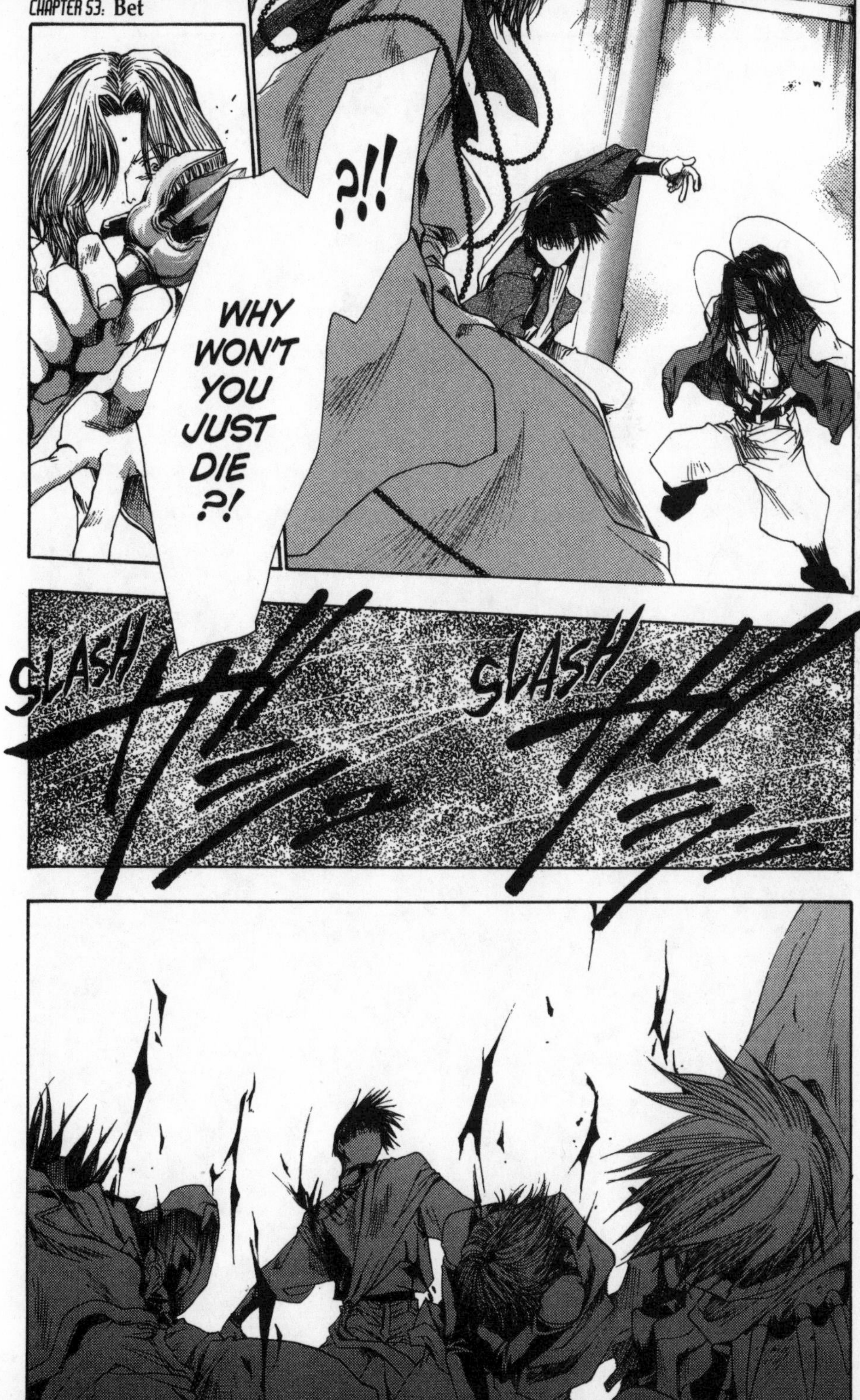
?!!
WHY WON'T YOU JUST DIE?!
SLASH
SLASH

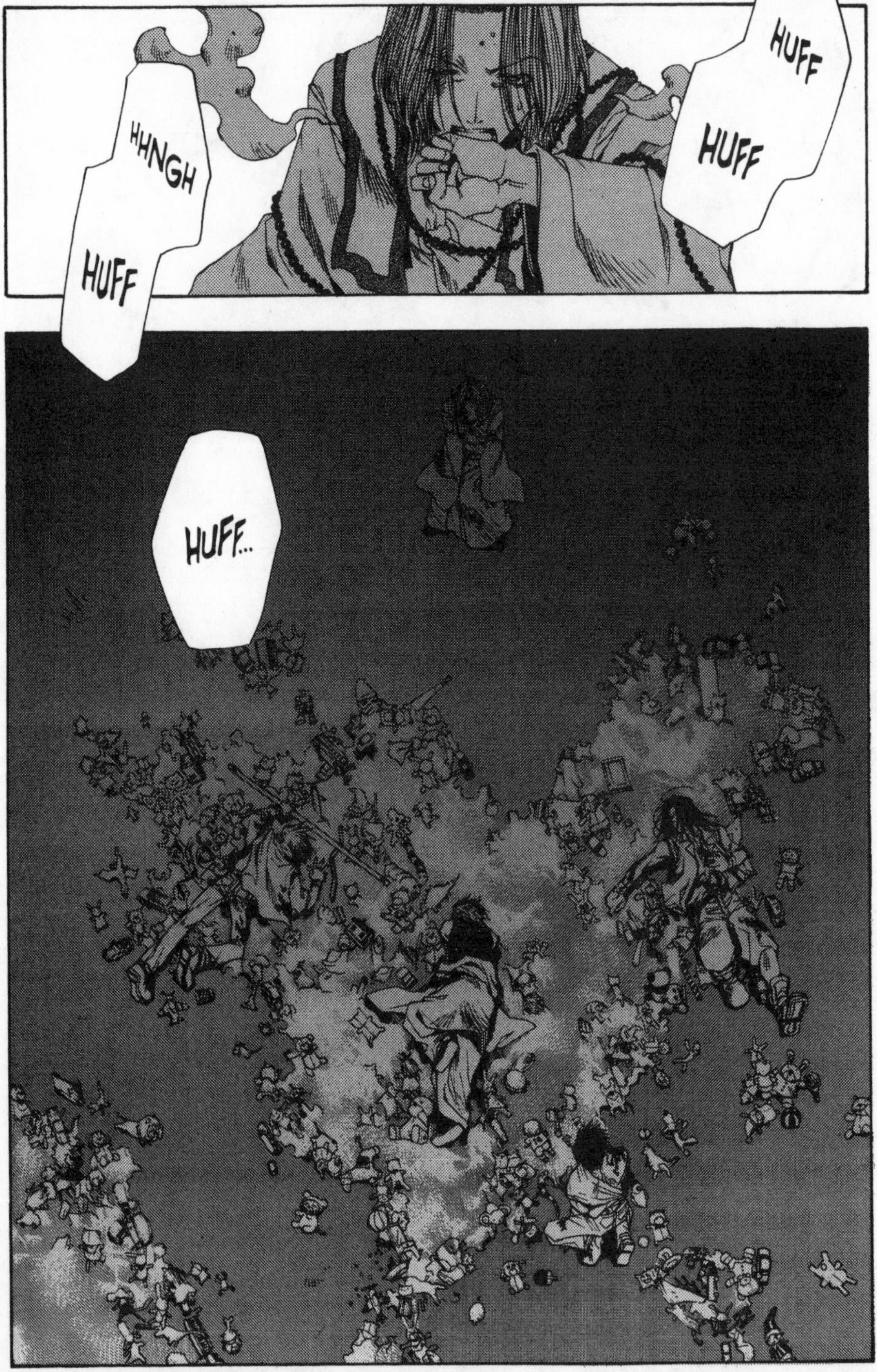
HUFF HUFF
HHNGH HUFF
HUFF...

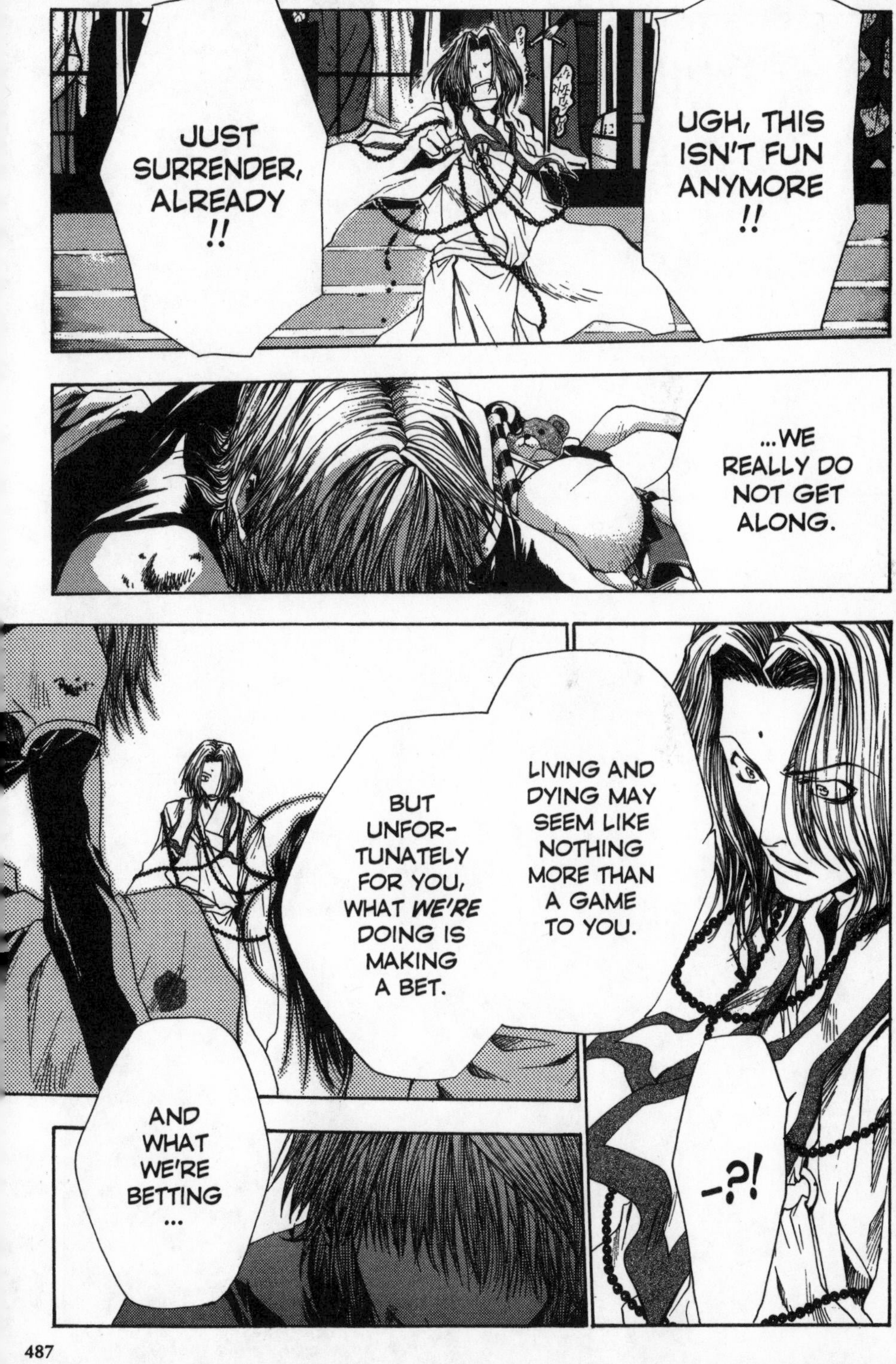
UGH, THIS ISN'T FUN ANYMORE!!
JUST SURRENDER, ALREADY!!
...WE REALLY DO NOT GET ALONG.
LIVING AND DYING MAY SEEM LIKE NOTHING MORE THAN A GAME TO YOU.
BUT UNFORTUNATELY FOR YOU, WHAT *WE'RE* DOING IS MAKING A BET.
-?!
AND WHAT WE'RE BETTING...

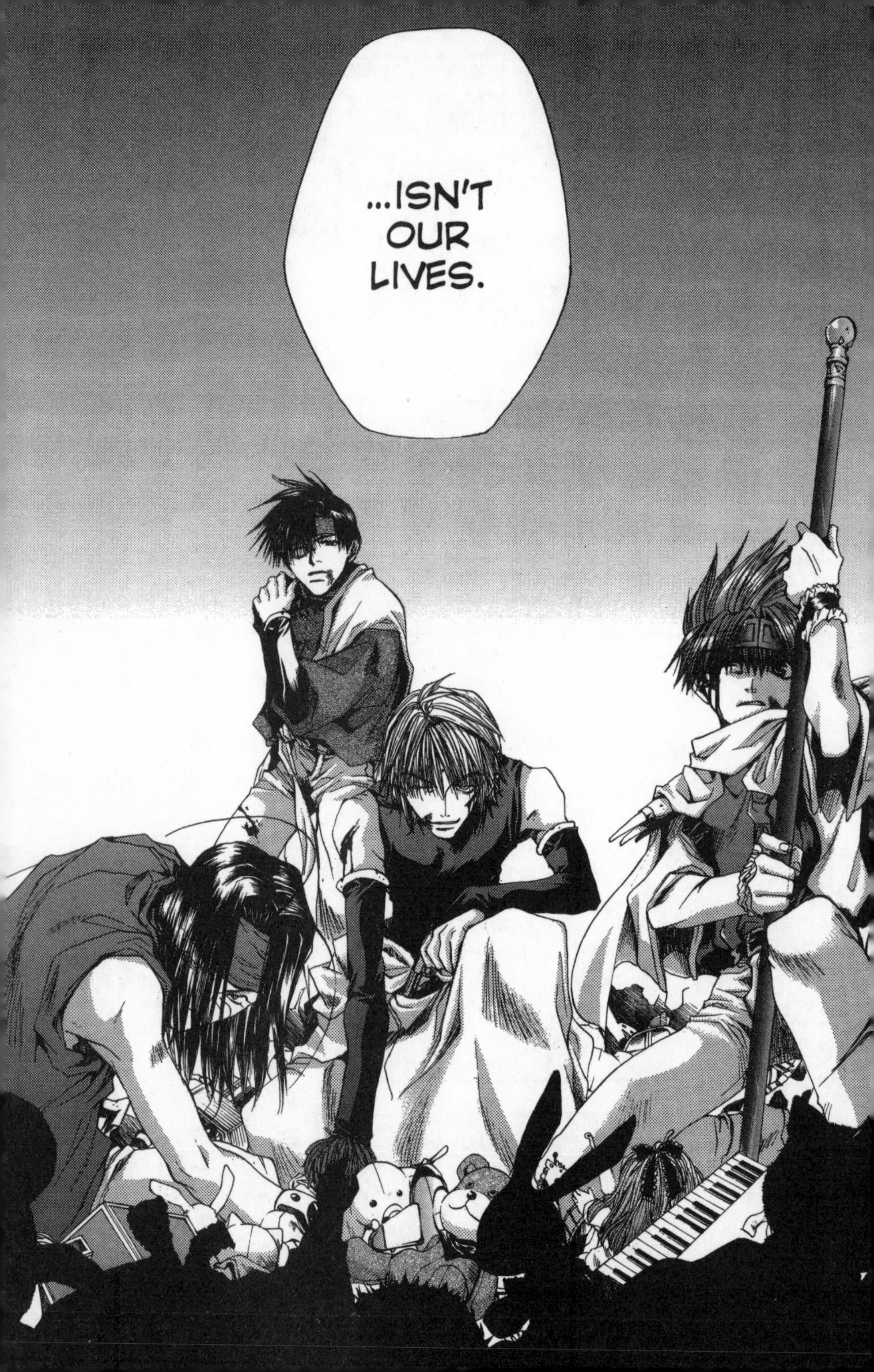
...ISN'T OUR LIVES.

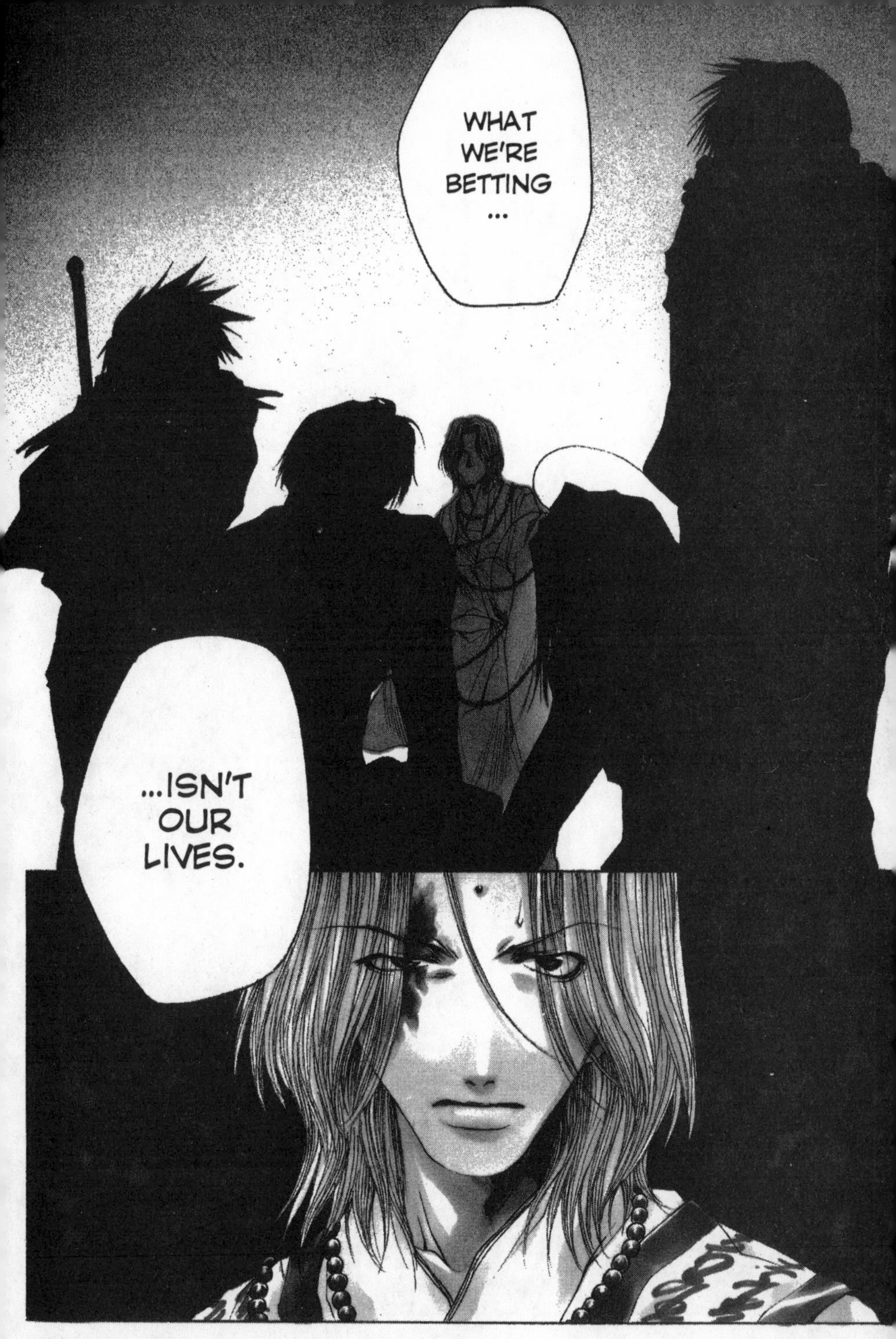
WHAT WE'RE BETTING ...
...ISN'T OUR LIVES.

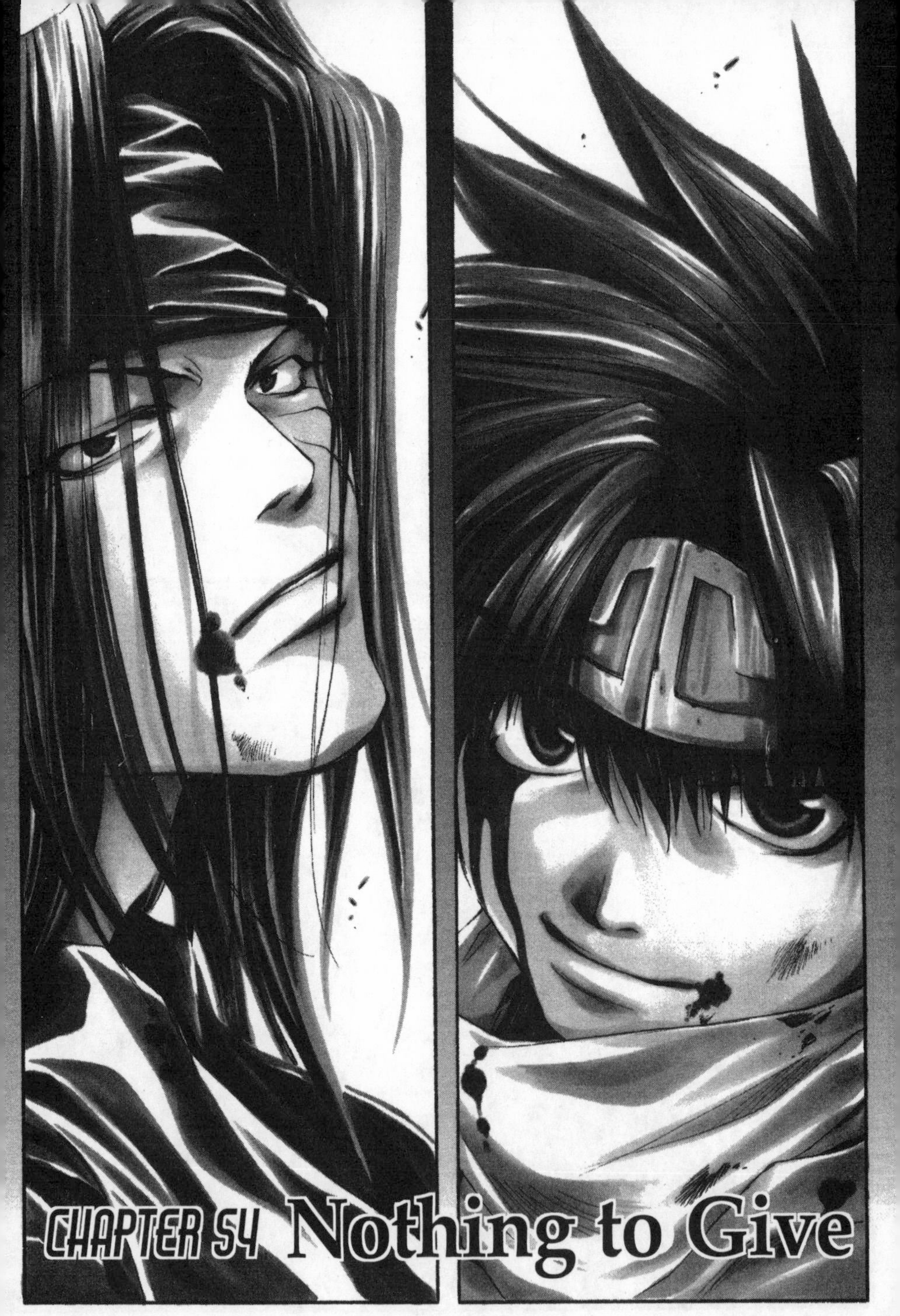
CHAPTER 54 Nothing to Give

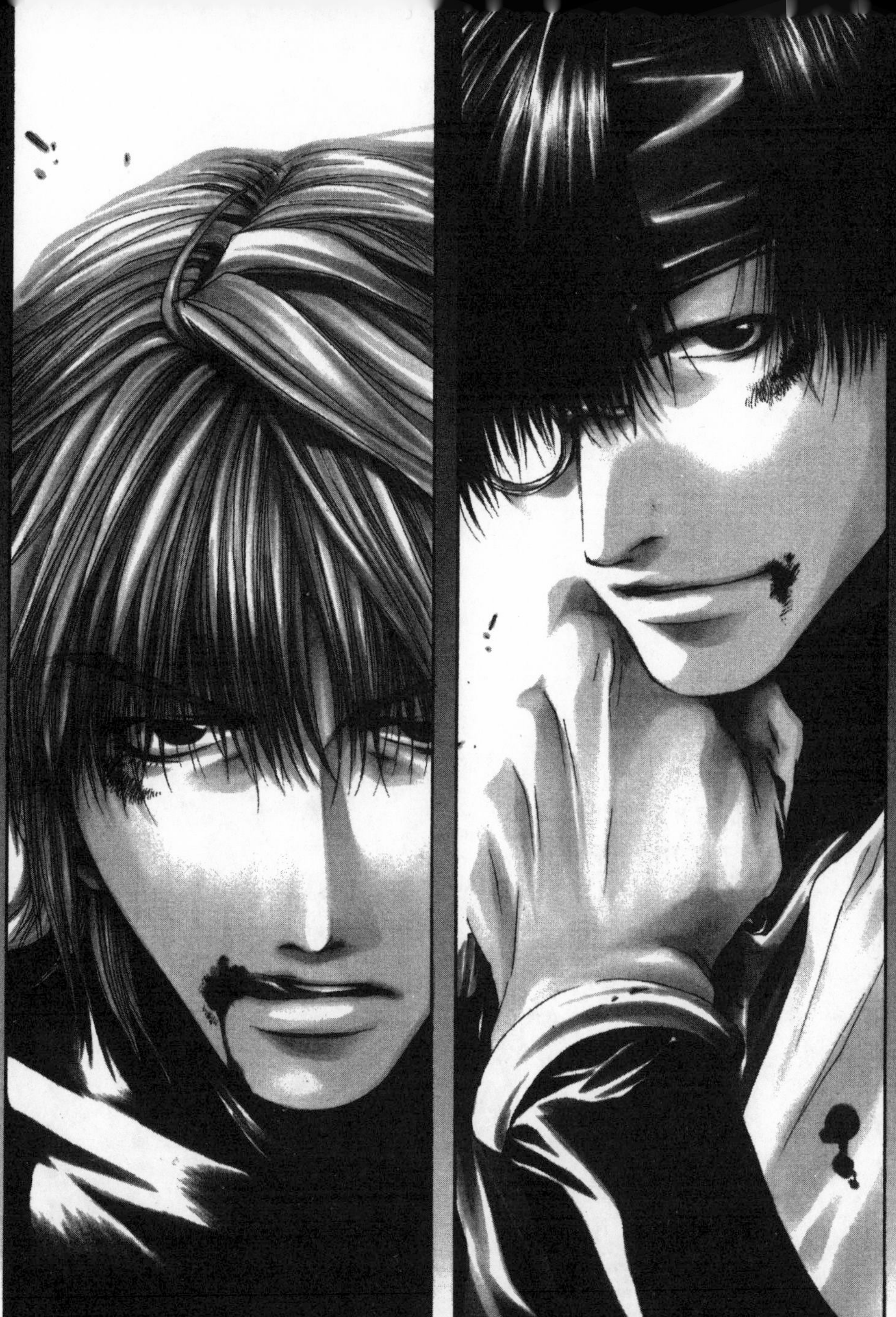

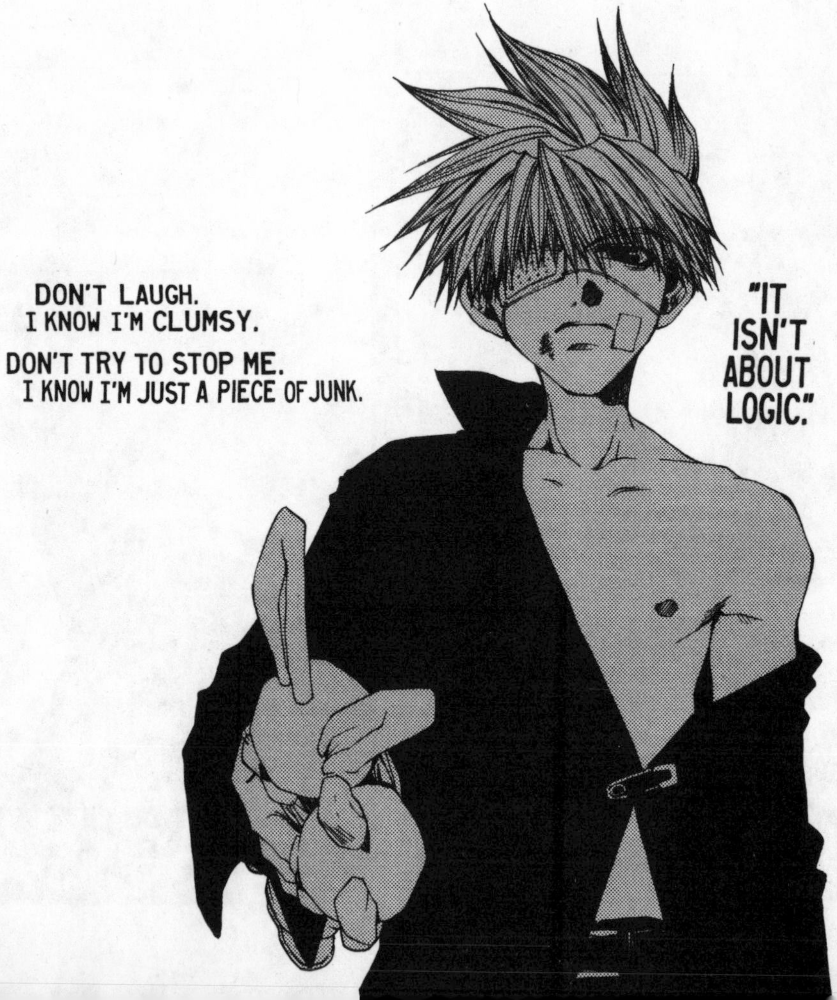
"IT ISN'T ABOUT LOGIC."
DON'T LAUGH.
I KNOW I'M CLUMSY.
DON'T TRY TO STOP ME.
I KNOW I'M JUST A PIECE OF JUNK.

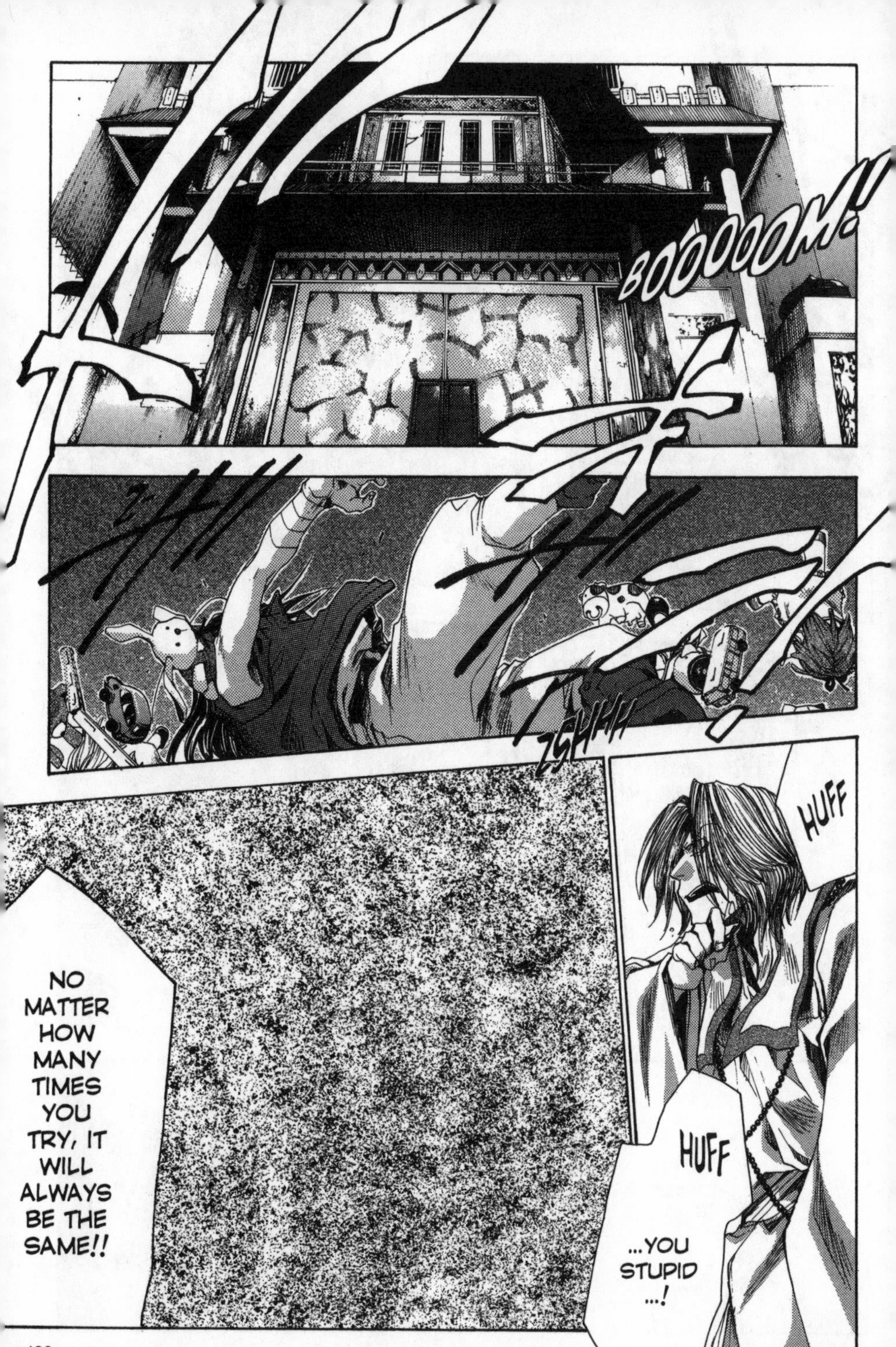
BOOOOOM!!
ZSHHH
HUFF
HUFF
...YOU STUPID ...!
NO MATTER HOW MANY TIMES YOU TRY, IT WILL ALWAYS BE THE SAME!!

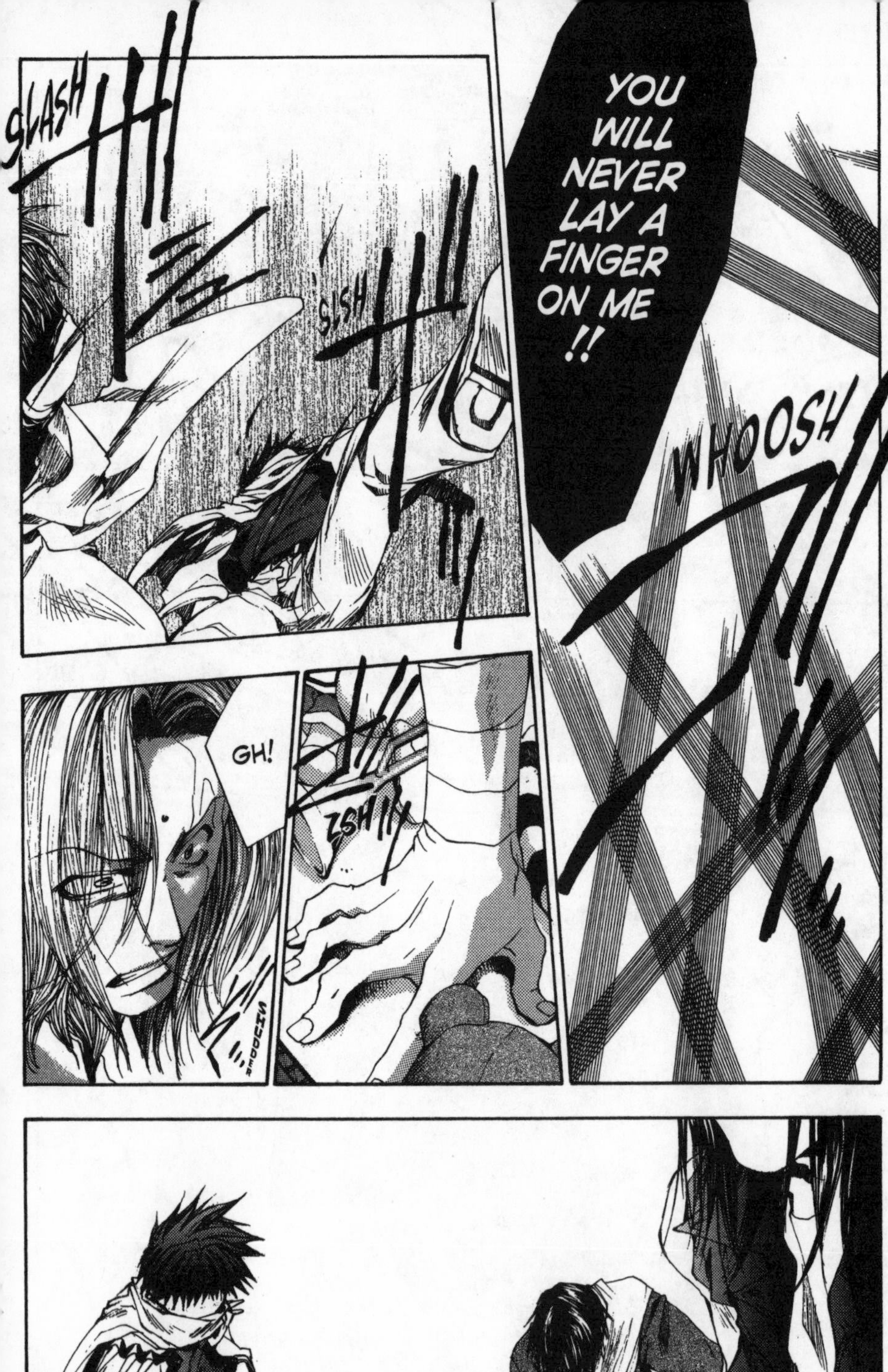
YOU WILL NEVER LAY A FINGER ON ME !!
WHOOSH
SLASH
SLSH
ZSH !!
GH!
SHUDDER

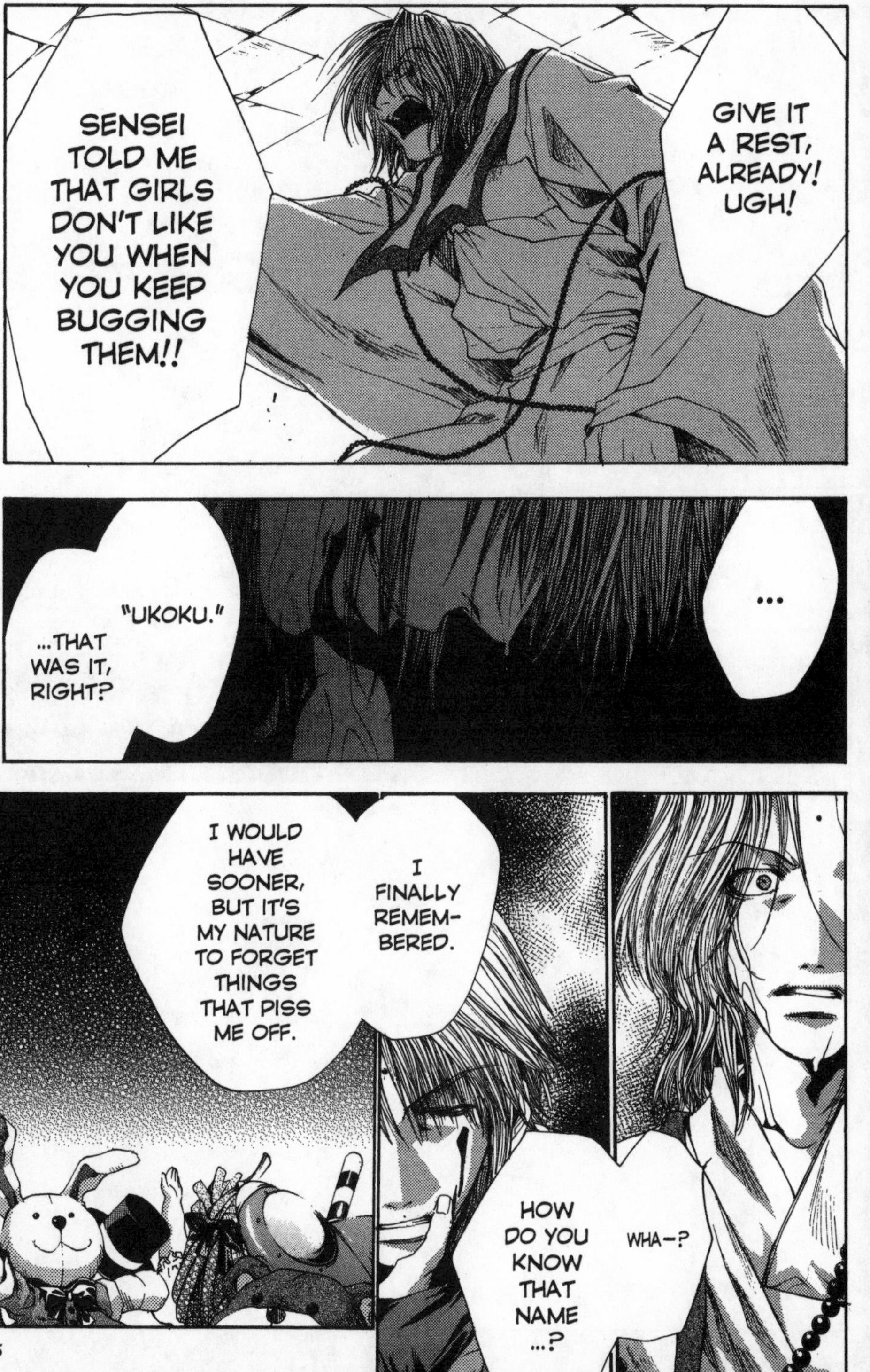
GIVE IT A REST, ALREADY! UGH!
SENSEI TOLD ME THAT GIRLS DON'T LIKE YOU WHEN YOU KEEP BUGGING THEM!!
...
"UKOKU." ...THAT WAS IT, RIGHT?
WHA-?
I FINALLY REMEMBERED.
I WOULD HAVE SOONER, BUT IT'S MY NATURE TO FORGET THINGS THAT PISS ME OFF.
HOW DO YOU KNOW THAT NAME ...?

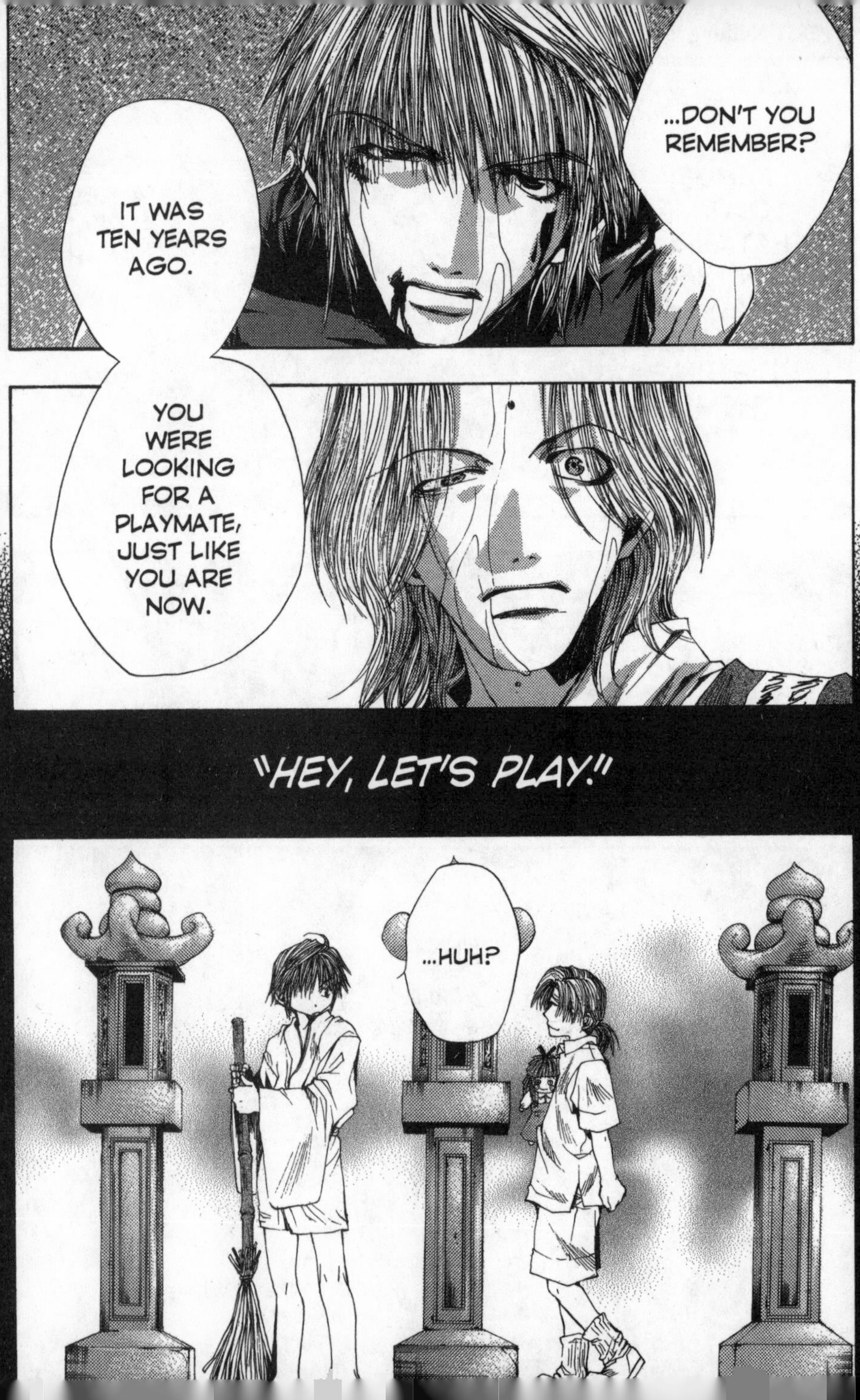
...DON'T YOU REMEMBER?
IT WAS TEN YEARS AGO.
YOU WERE LOOKING FOR A PLAYMATE, JUST LIKE YOU ARE NOW.
"HEY, LET'S PLAY!"
...HUH?

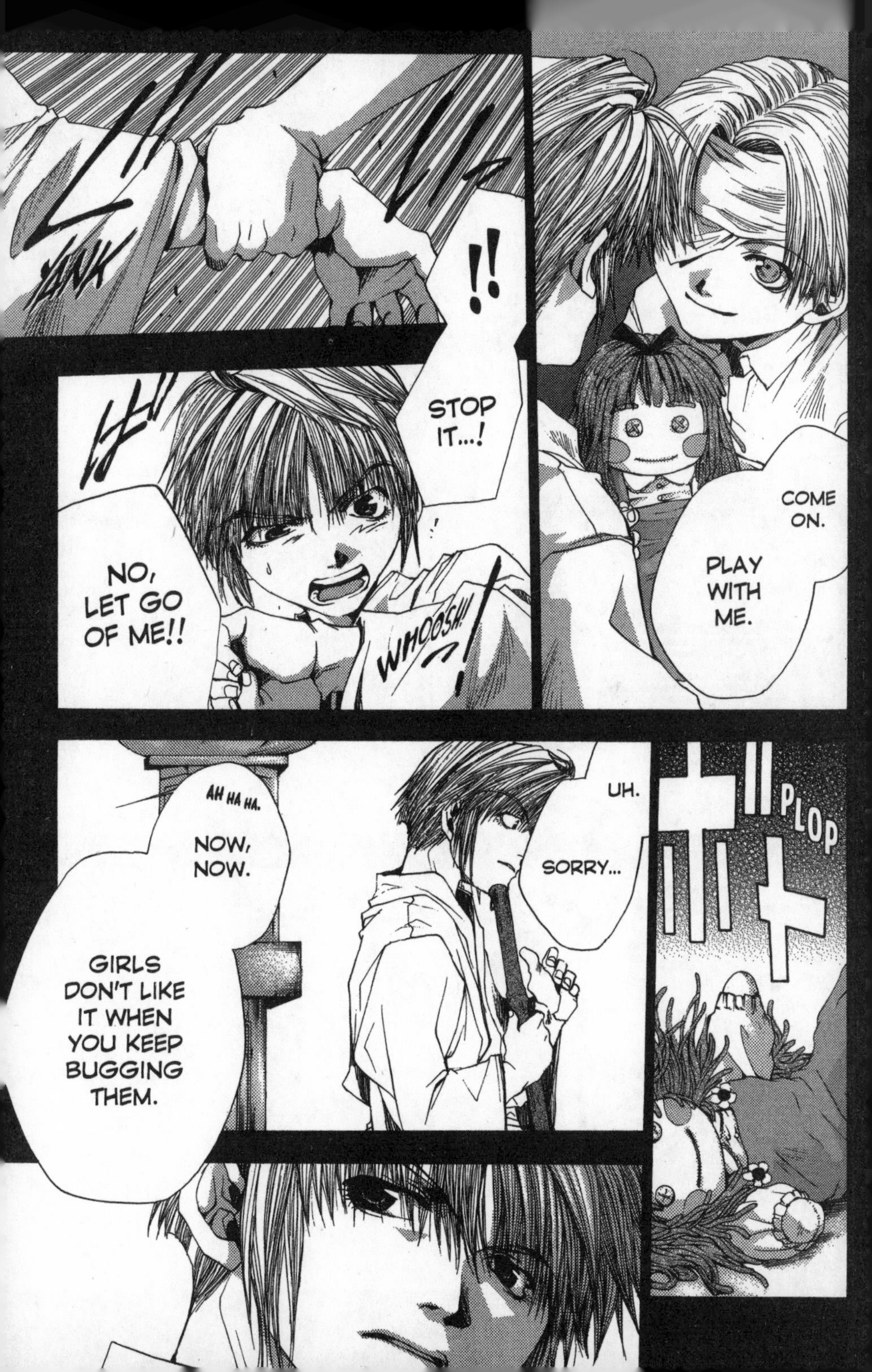
COME ON.
PLAY WITH ME.
YANK
!!
STOP IT...!
NO, LET GO OF ME!!
WHOOSH!!
PLOP
UH.
SORRY...
AH HA HA.
NOW, NOW.
GIRLS DON'T LIKE IT WHEN YOU KEEP BUGGING THEM.

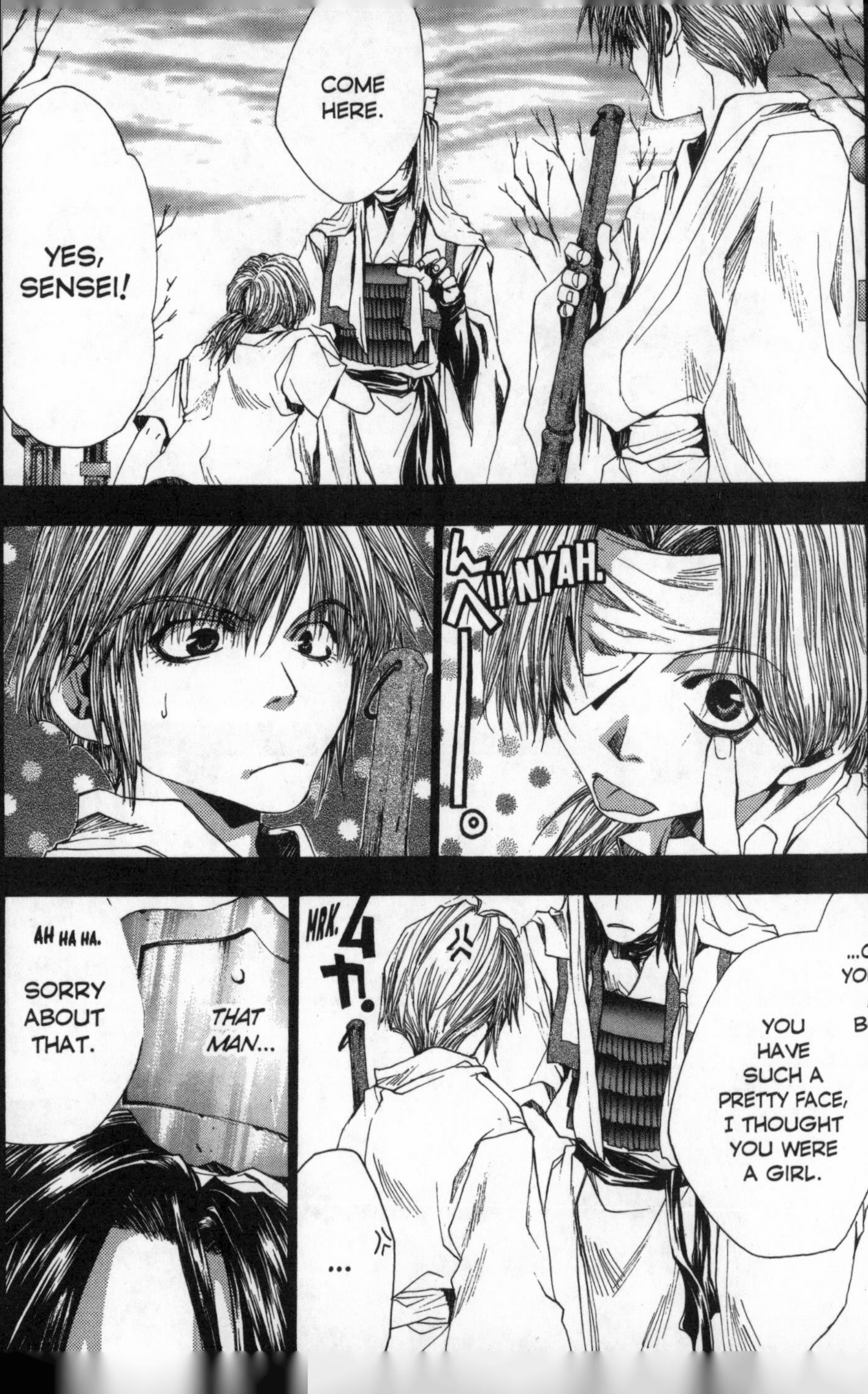
COME HERE.
YES, SENSEI!
んべーっ。
NYAH.
...OH? YOU'RE A BOY?
YOU HAVE SUCH A PRETTY FACE, I THOUGHT YOU WERE A GIRL.
MRK.
ムカッ
...
AH HA HA.
SORRY ABOUT THAT.
THAT MAN...

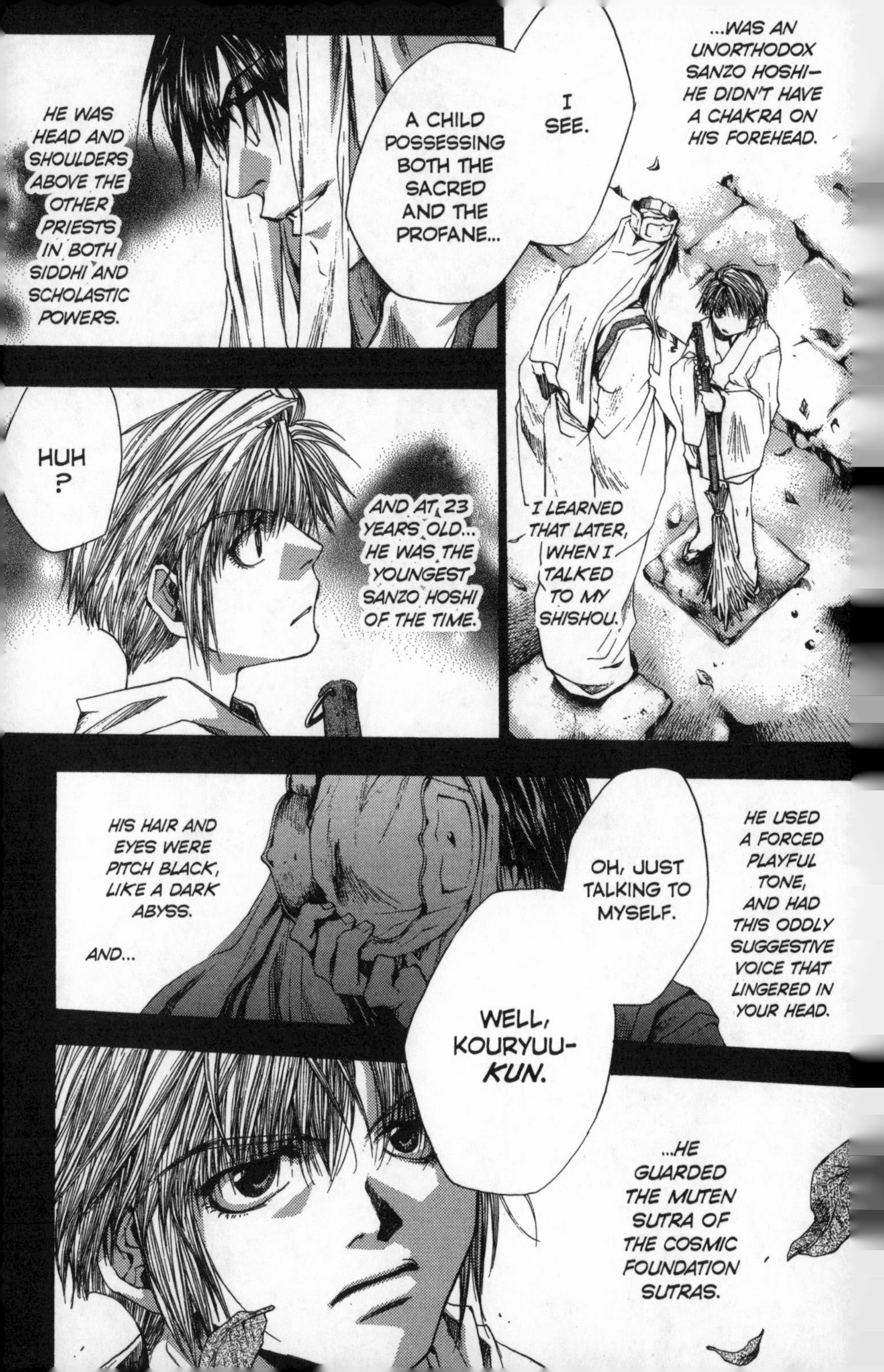
...WAS AN UNORTHODOX SANZO HOSHI—HE DIDN'T HAVE A CHAKRA ON HIS FOREHEAD.
I SEE.
I LEARNED THAT LATER, WHEN I TALKED TO MY SHISHOU.
A CHILD POSSESSING BOTH THE SACRED AND THE PROFANE...
HE WAS HEAD AND SHOULDERS ABOVE THE OTHER PRIESTS IN BOTH SIDDHI AND SCHOLASTIC POWERS.
AND AT 23 YEARS OLD... HE WAS THE YOUNGEST SANZO HOSHI OF THE TIME.
HUH?
HE USED A FORCED PLAYFUL TONE, AND HAD THIS ODDLY SUGGESTIVE VOICE THAT LINGERED IN YOUR HEAD.
OH, JUST TALKING TO MYSELF.
HIS HAIR AND EYES WERE PITCH BLACK, LIKE A DARK ABYSS.
AND...
WELL, KOURYUU-*KUN*.
...HE GUARDED THE MUTEN SUTRA OF THE COSMIC FOUNDATION SUTRAS.

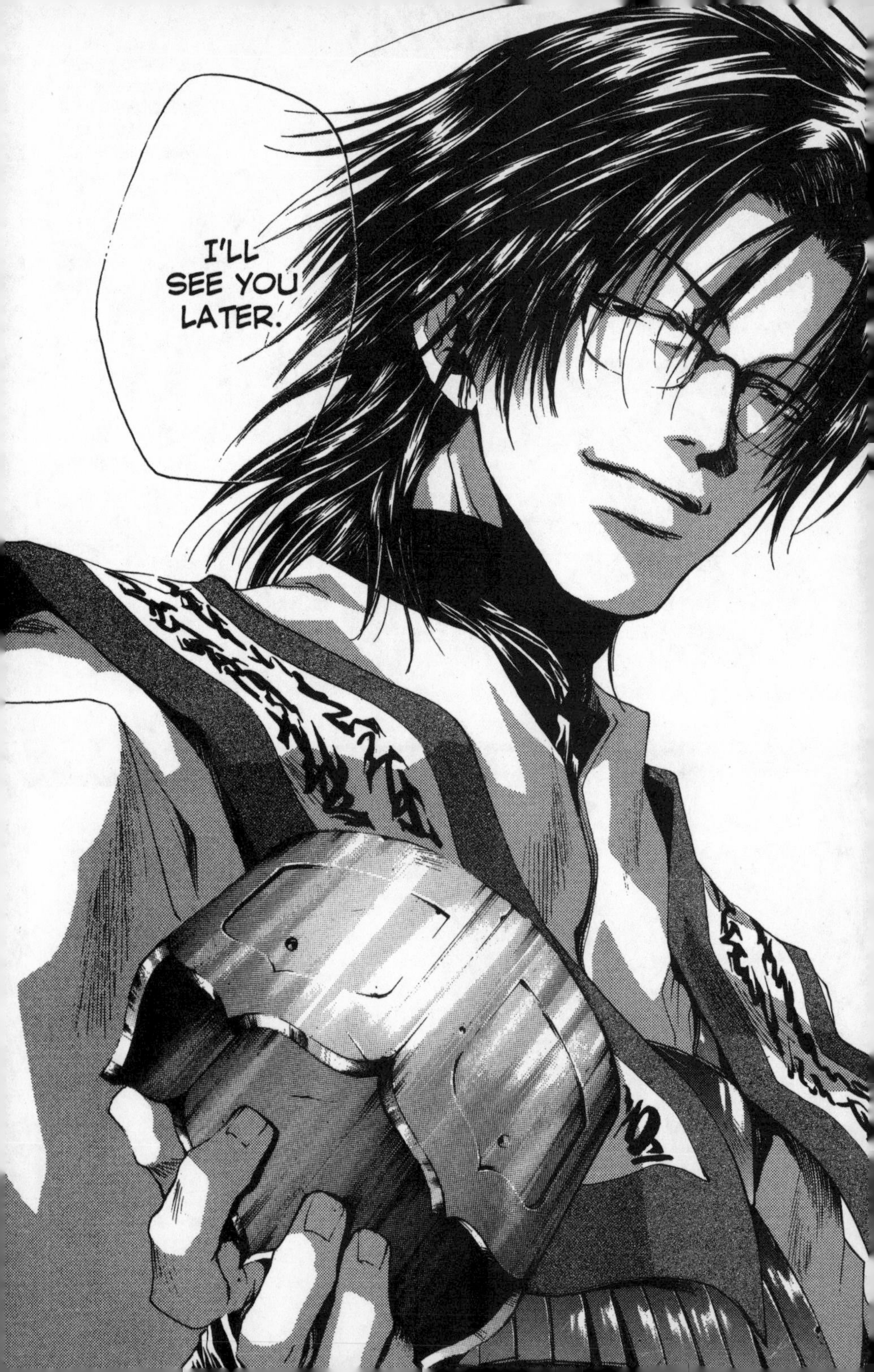
I'LL SEE YOU LATER.

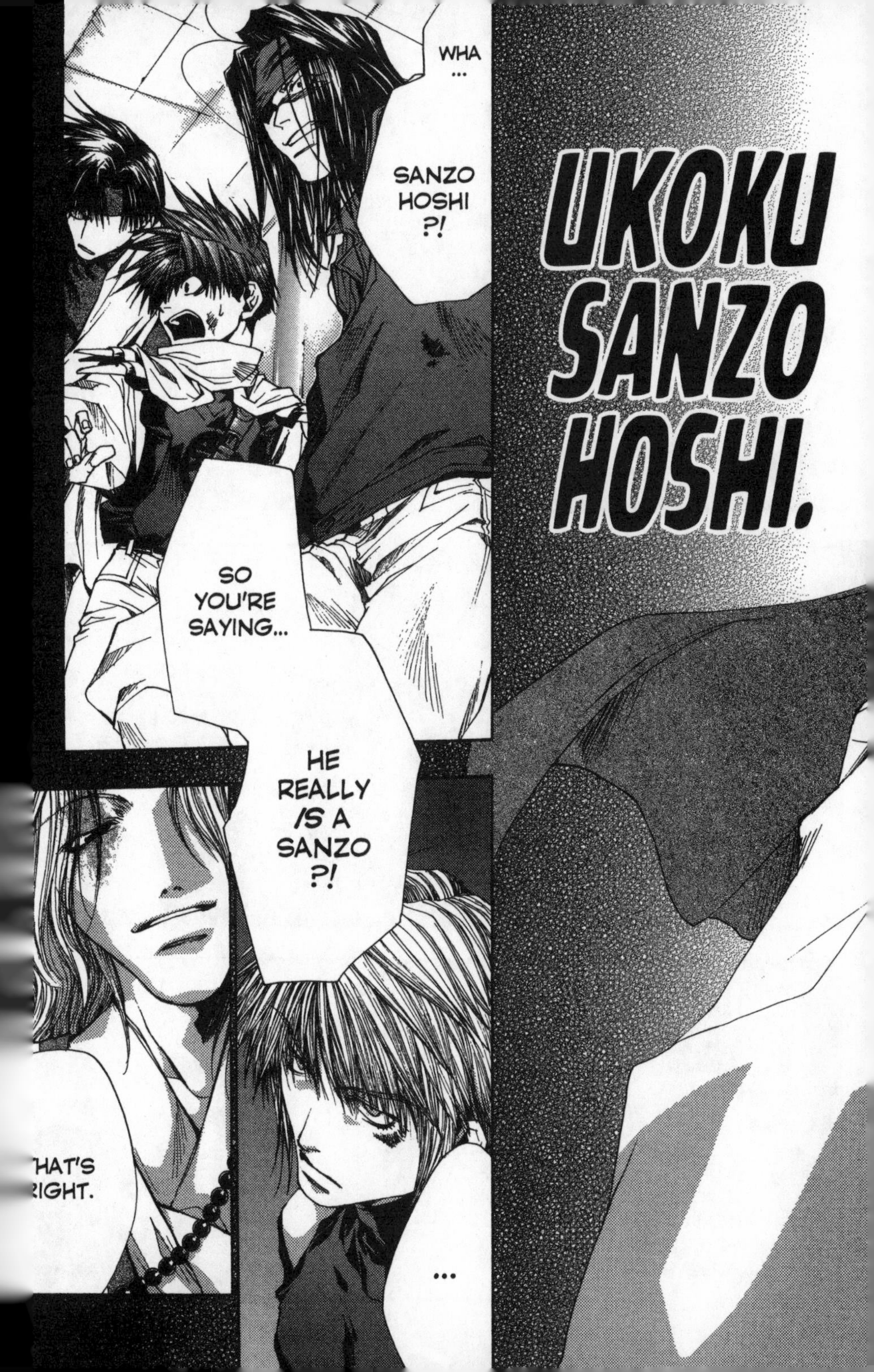
UKOKU SANZO HOSHI.
WHA ...
SANZO HOSHI ?!
SO YOU'RE SAYING...
HE REALLY IS A SANZO ?!
...
HAT'S RIGHT.

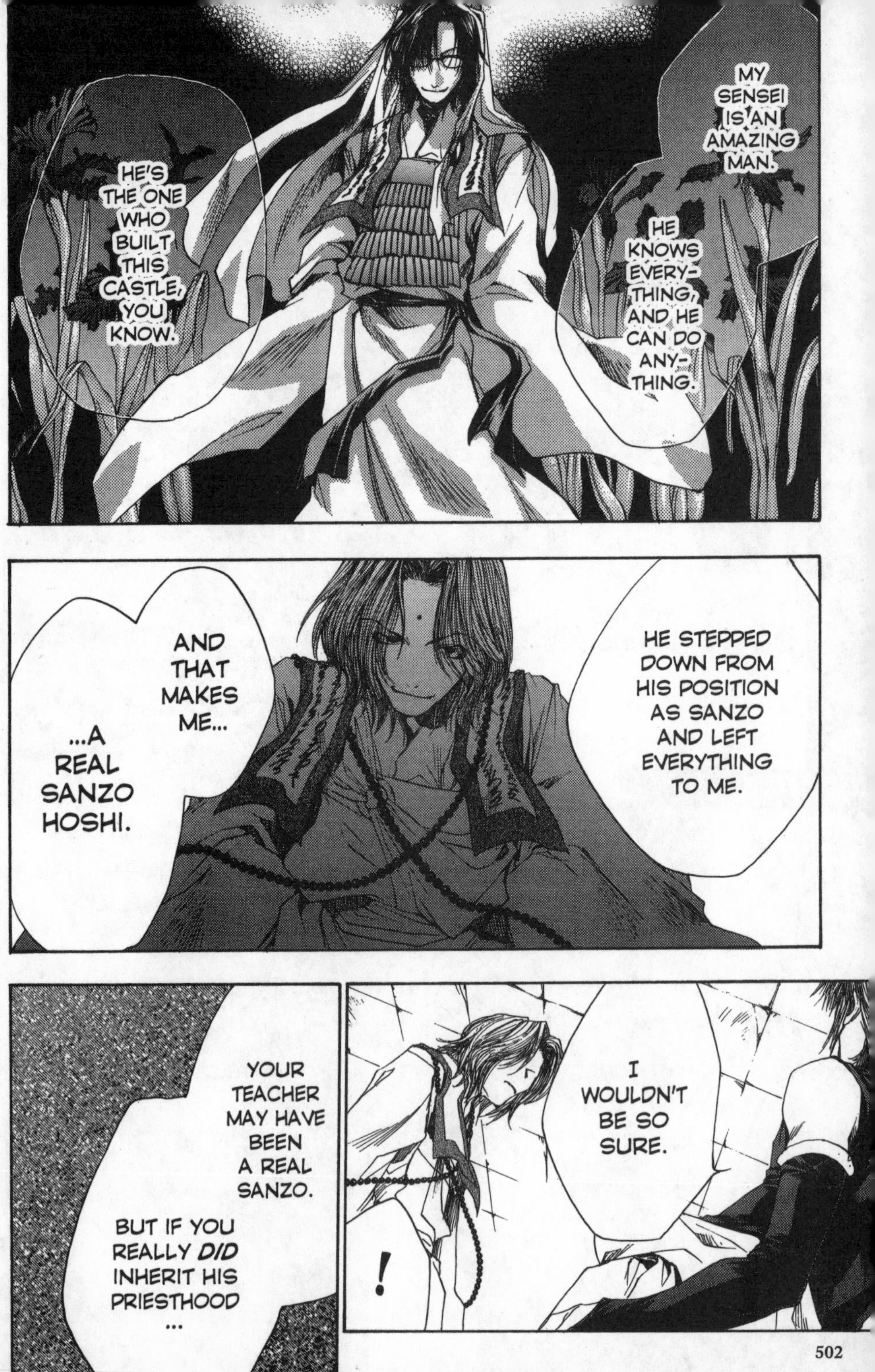
MY SENSEI IS AN AMAZING MAN.
HE KNOWS EVERY-THING, AND HE CAN DO ANY-THING.
HE'S THE ONE WHO BUILT THIS CASTLE, YOU KNOW.
HE STEPPED DOWN FROM HIS POSITION AS SANZO AND LEFT EVERYTHING TO ME.
AND THAT MAKES ME...
...A REAL SANZO HOSHI.
I WOULDN'T BE SO SURE.
!
YOUR TEACHER MAY HAVE BEEN A REAL SANZO.
BUT IF YOU REALLY *DID* INHERIT HIS PRIESTHOOD ...

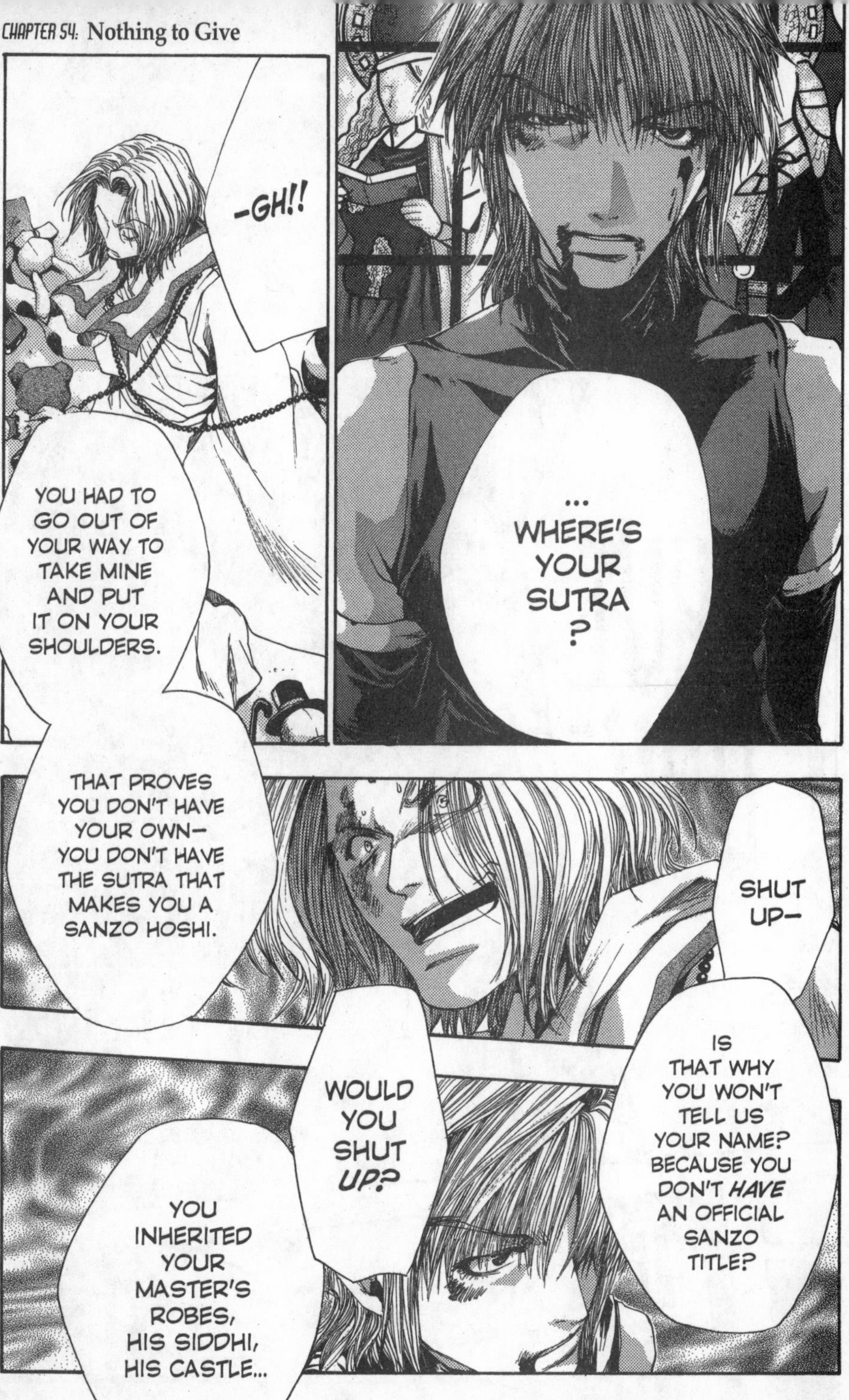
... WHERE'S YOUR SUTRA ?
-GH!!
YOU HAD TO GO OUT OF YOUR WAY TO TAKE MINE AND PUT IT ON YOUR SHOULDERS.
THAT PROVES YOU DON'T HAVE YOUR OWN— YOU DON'T HAVE THE SUTRA THAT MAKES YOU A SANZO HOSHI.
SHUT UP—
IS THAT WHY YOU WON'T TELL US YOUR NAME? BECAUSE YOU DON'T *HAVE* AN OFFICIAL SANZO TITLE?
WOULD YOU SHUT *UP*?
YOU INHERITED YOUR MASTER'S ROBES, HIS SIDDHI, HIS CASTLE...

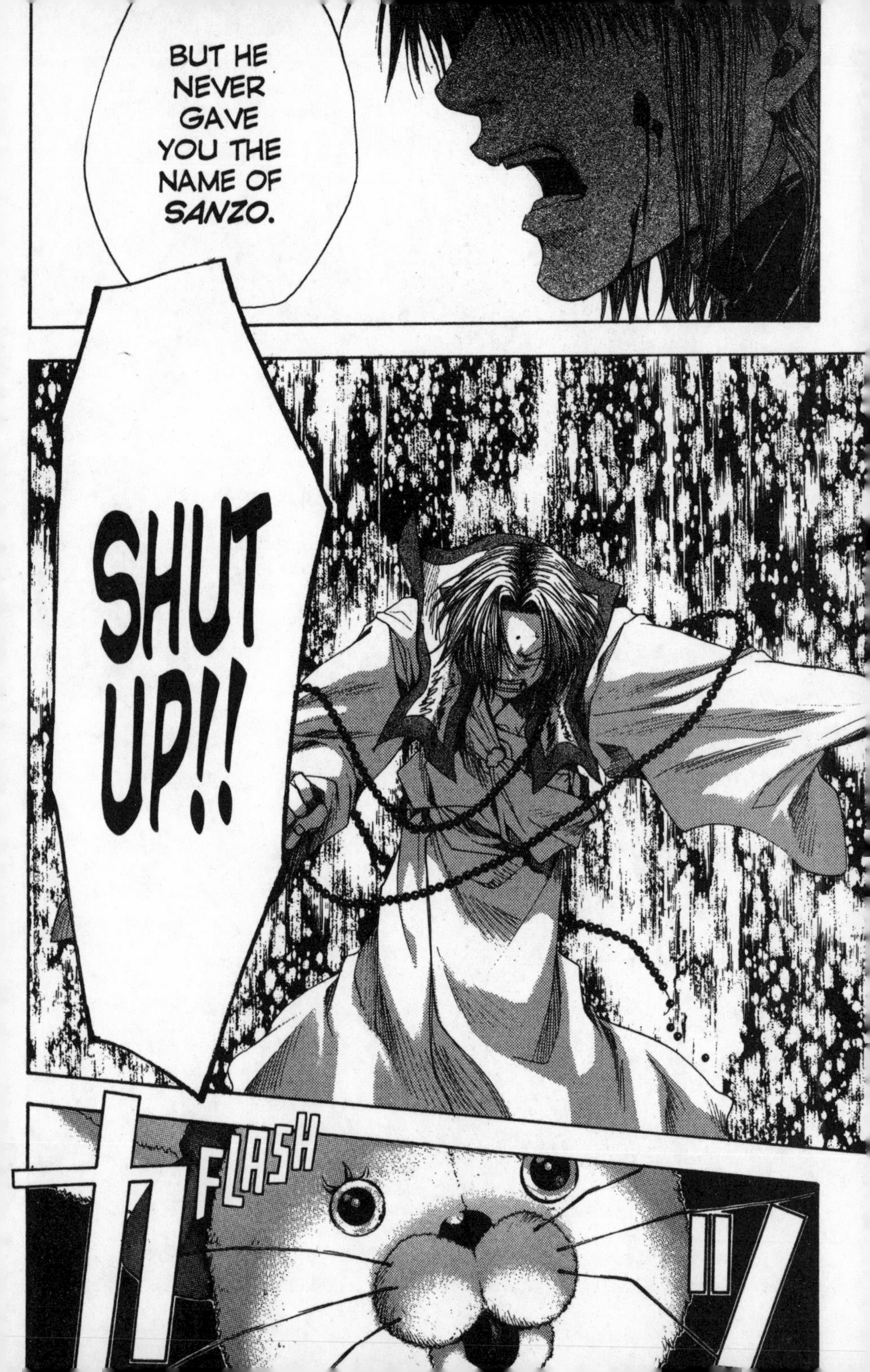
BUT HE NEVER GAVE YOU THE NAME OF SANZO.
SHUT UP!!
FLASH

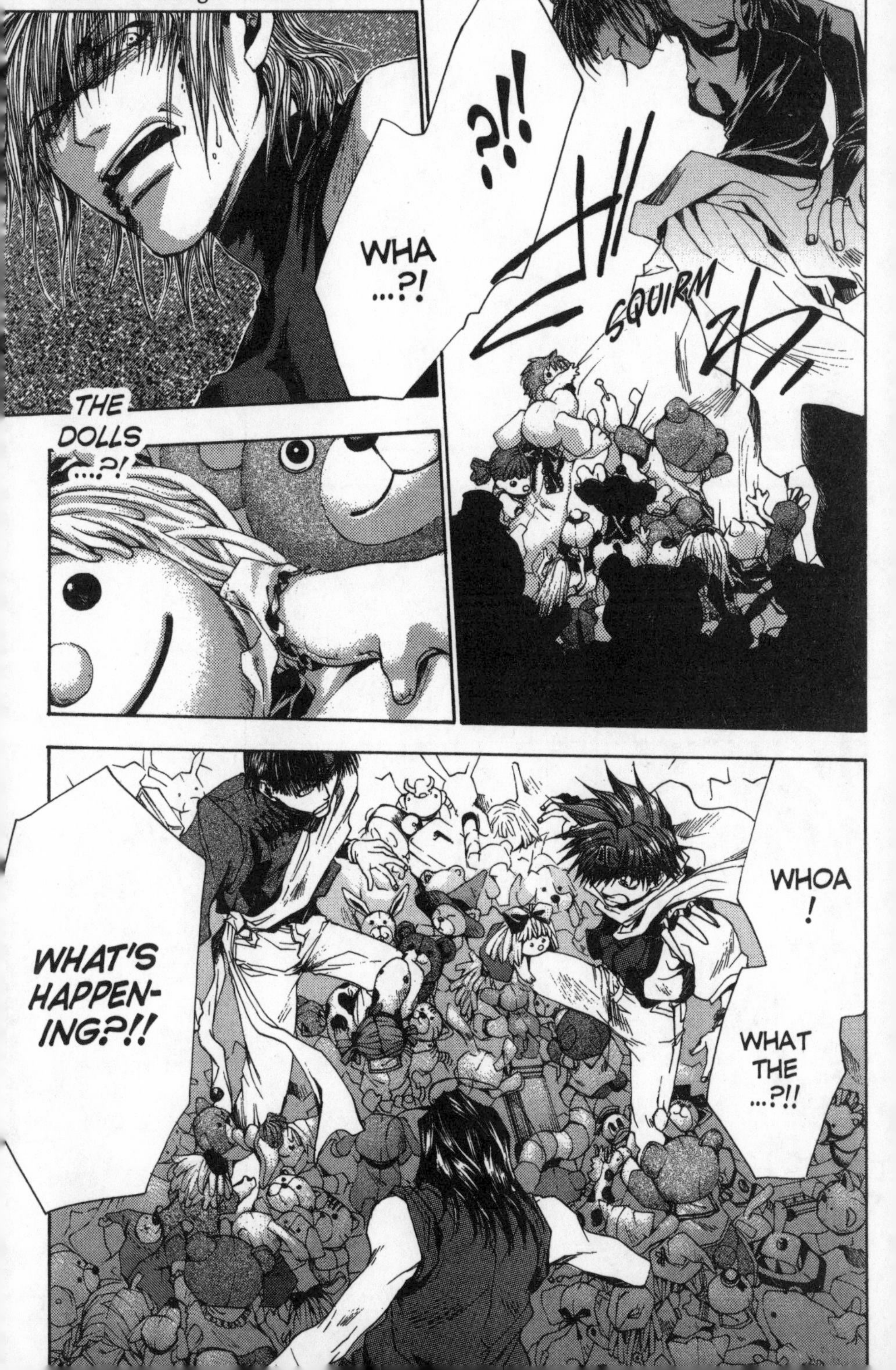
?!!
WHA ...?!
SQUIRM
THE DOLLS ...?!
WHOA!
WHAT THE ...?!!
WHAT'S HAPPEN-ING?!!

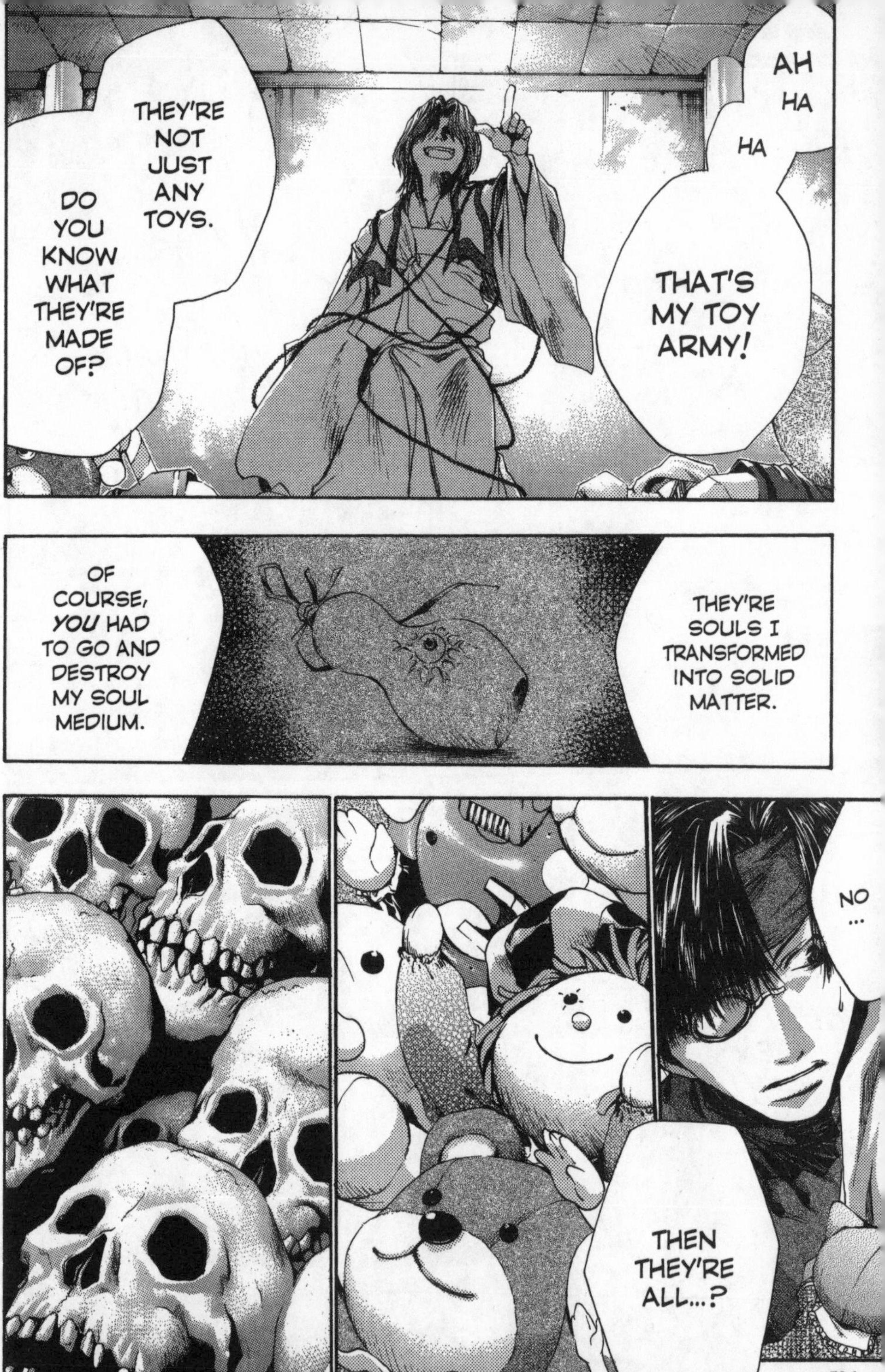
AH HA HA
THAT'S MY TOY ARMY!
THEY'RE NOT JUST ANY TOYS.
DO YOU KNOW WHAT THEY'RE MADE OF?
THEY'RE SOULS I TRANSFORMED INTO SOLID MATTER.
OF COURSE, *YOU* HAD TO GO AND DESTROY MY SOUL MEDIUM.
NO ...
THEN THEY'RE ALL...?

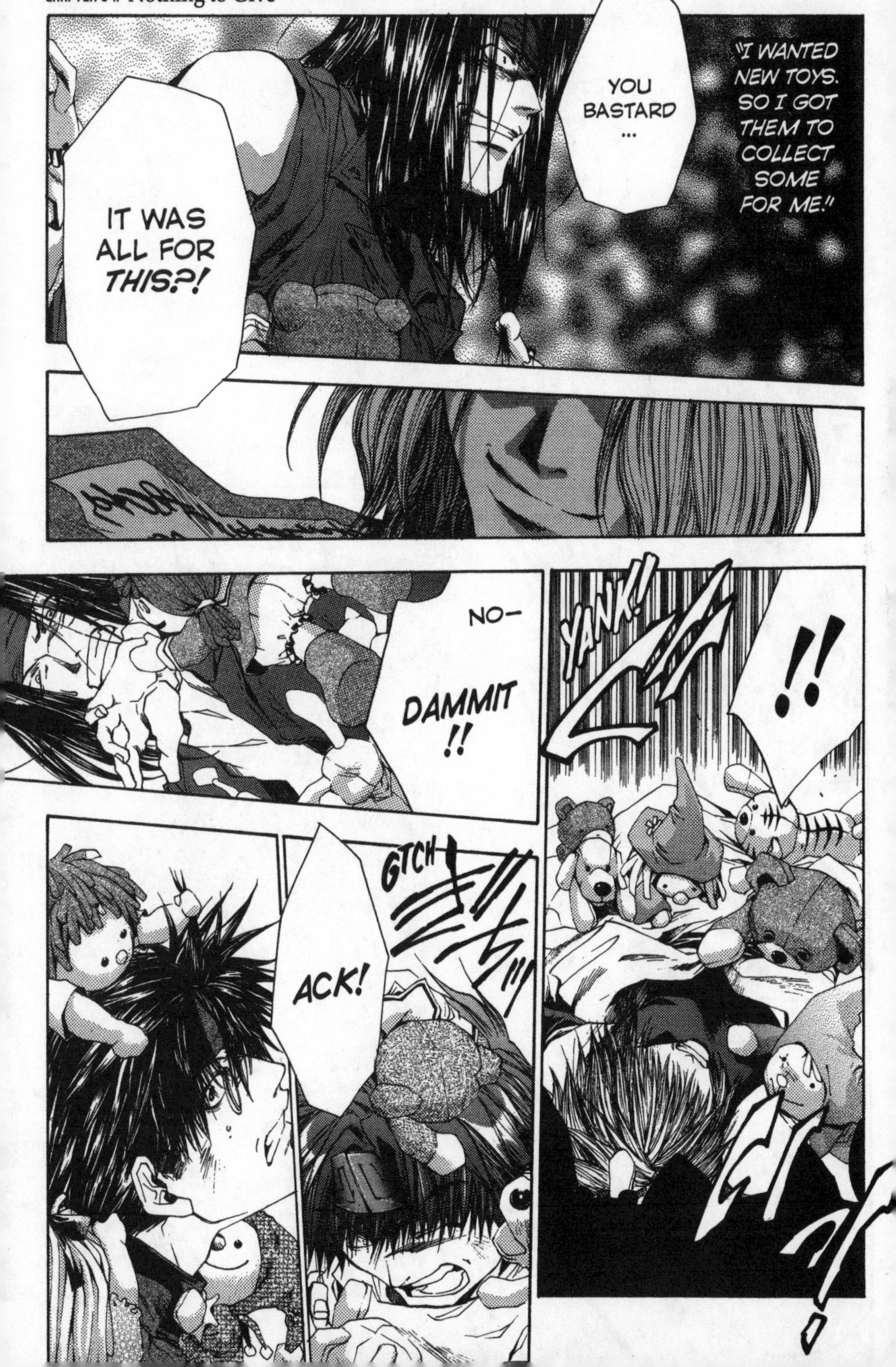
"I WANTED NEW TOYS. SO I GOT THEM TO COLLECT SOME FOR ME."
YOU BASTARD ...
IT WAS ALL FOR THIS?!
YANK!!
!!
NO—
DAMMIT !!
GTCH
ACK!

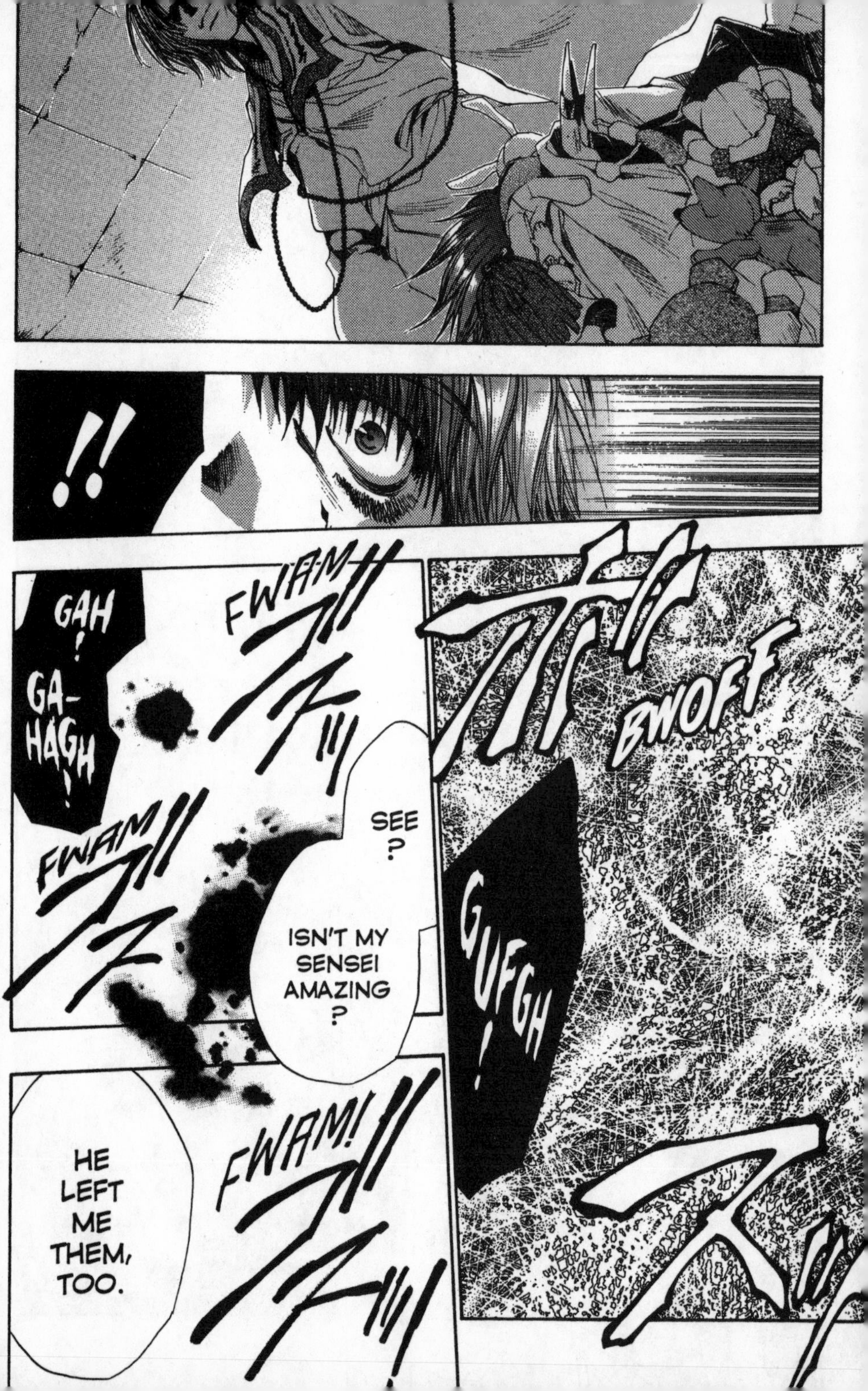
!!
BWOFF
GUFGH!
FWAM
SEE? ISN'T MY SENSEI AMAZING?
GAH! GA-HAGH!
FWAM
FWAM!
HE LEFT ME THEM, TOO.

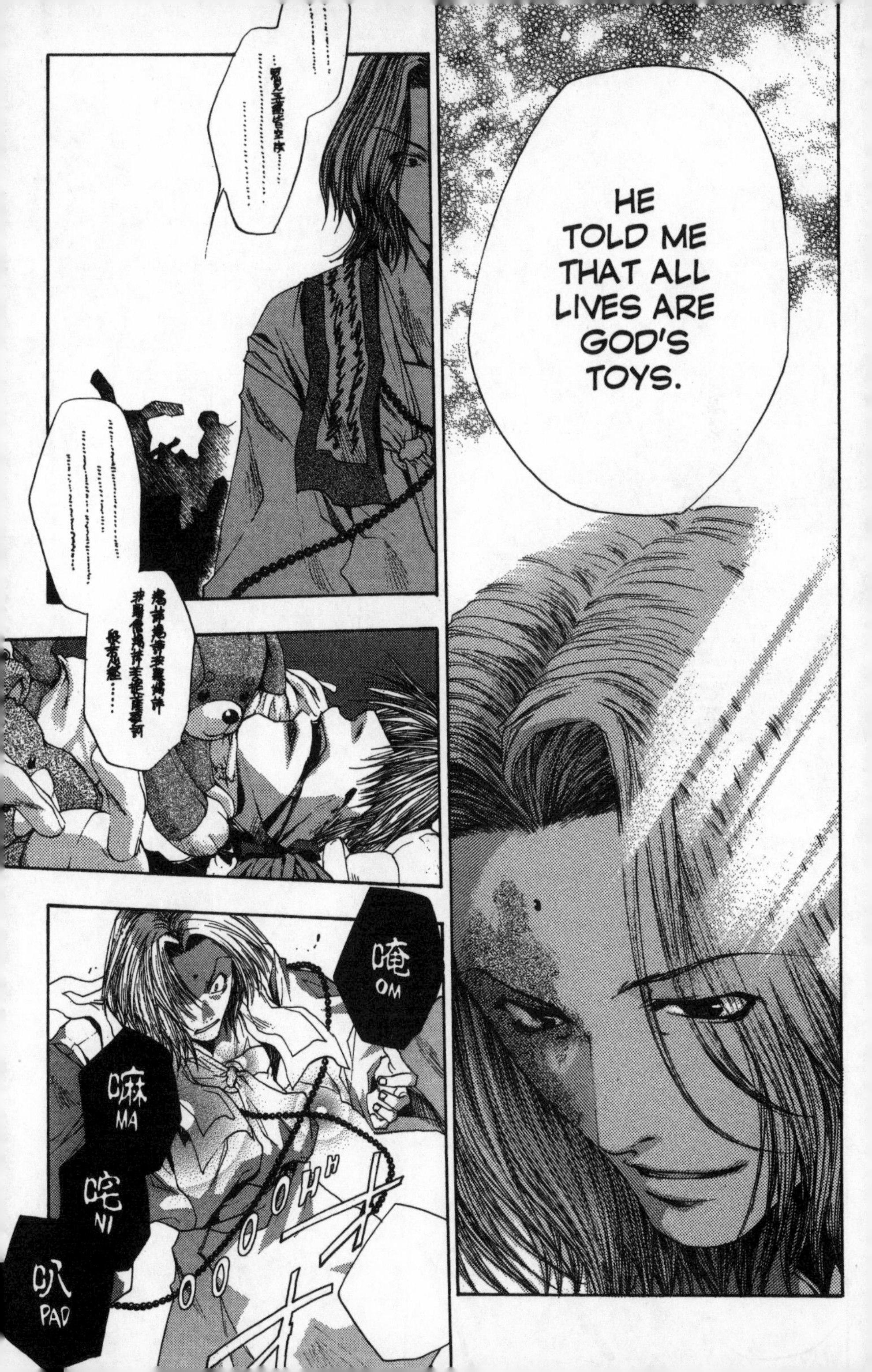

HE TOLD ME THAT ALL LIVES ARE GOD'S TOYS.
唵
OM
嘛
MA
呢
NI
叭
PAD

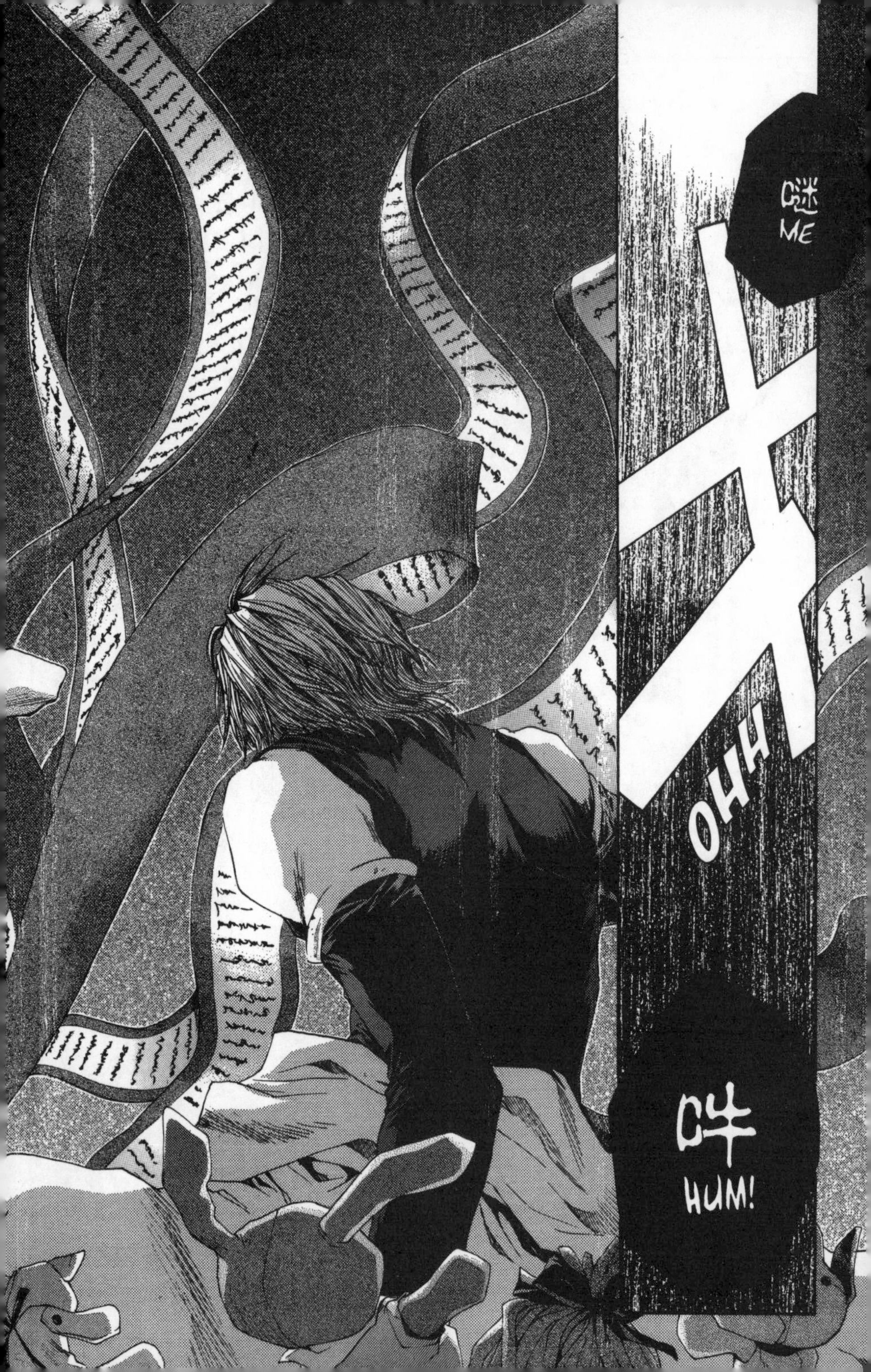
ME
OHH
吽
HUM!

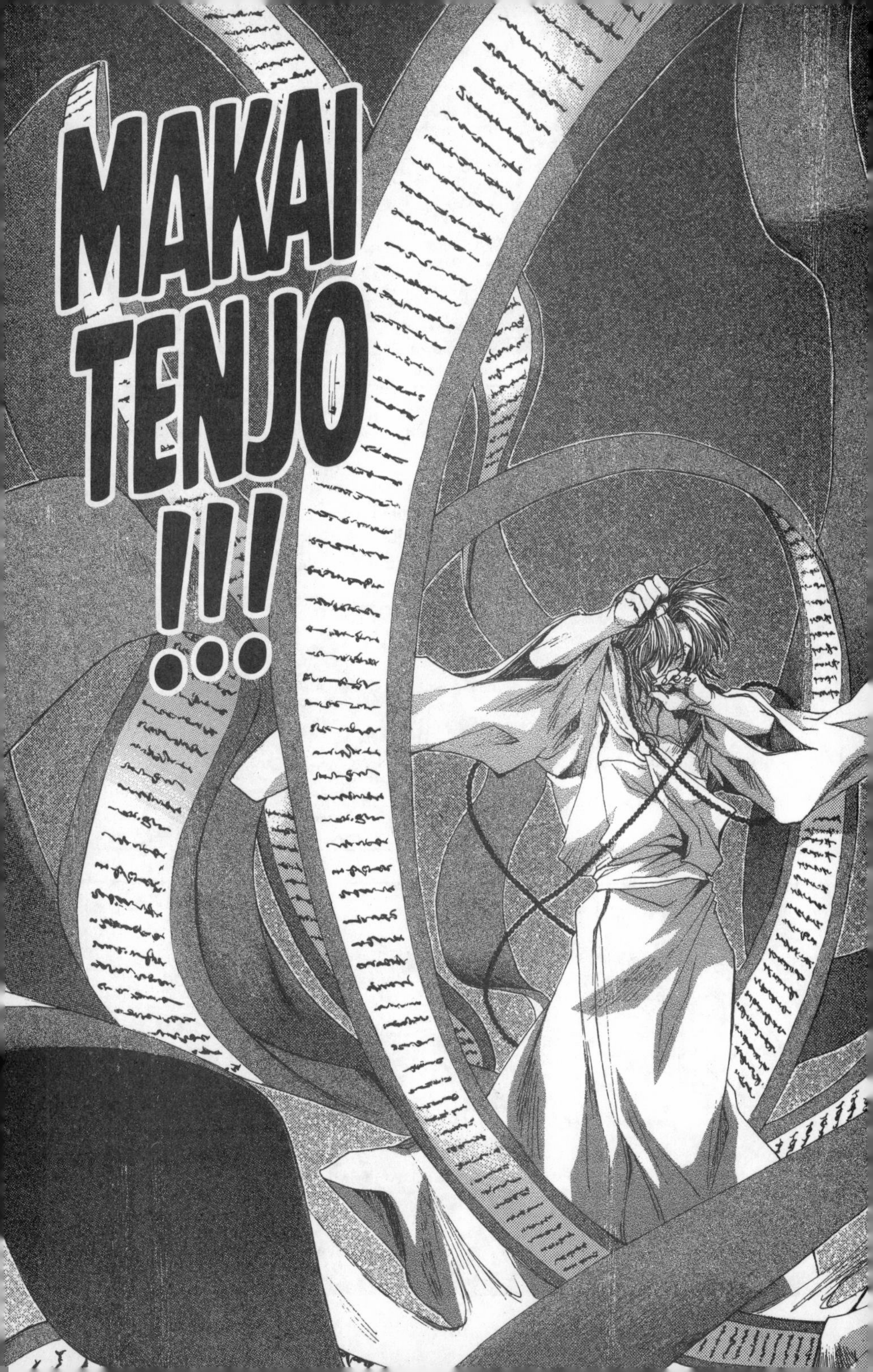
MAKAI TENJO!!!...

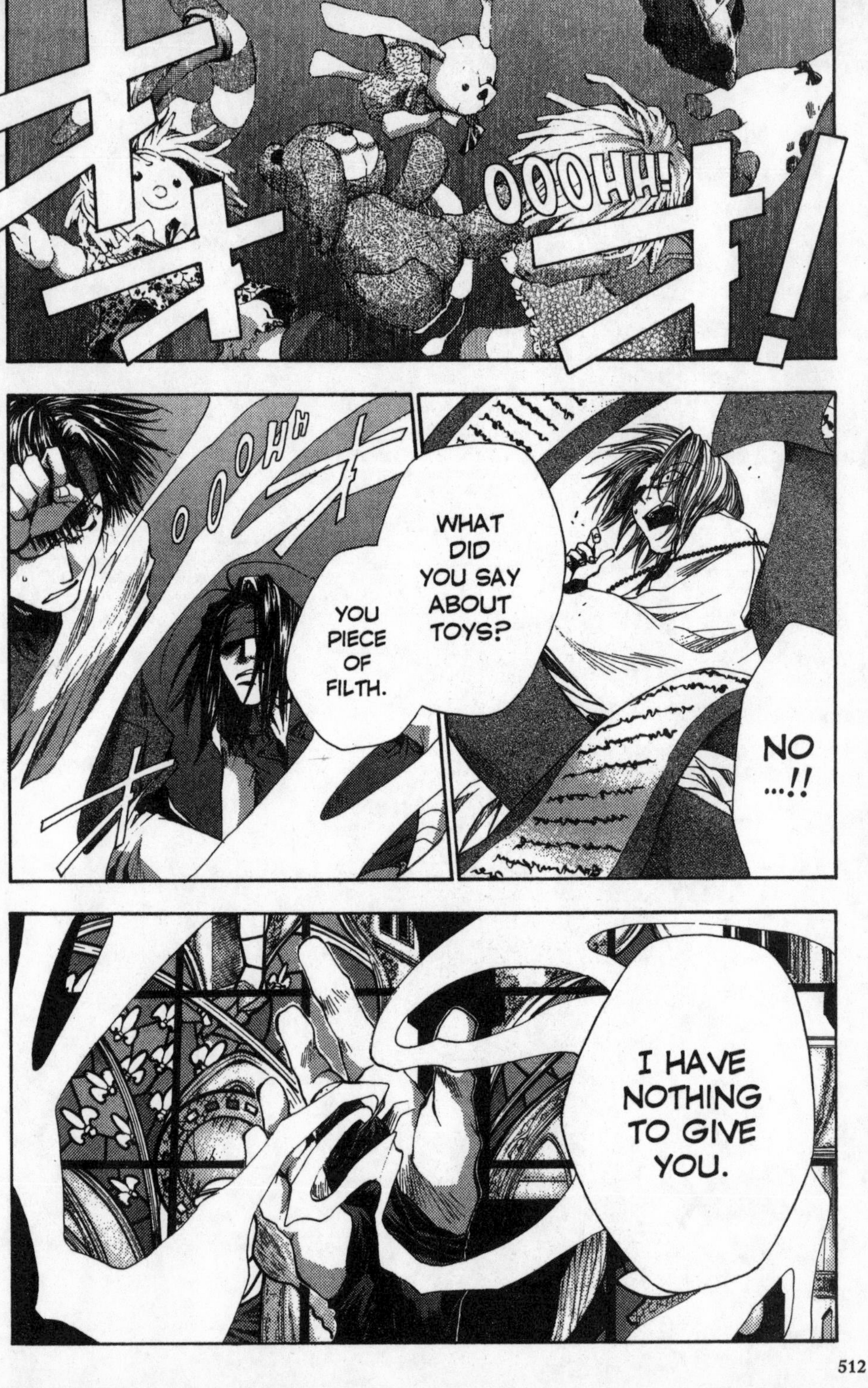
OOOHH!
NO ...!!
WHAT DID YOU SAY ABOUT TOYS?
YOU PIECE OF FILTH.
OOOOHH
I HAVE NOTHING TO GIVE YOU.

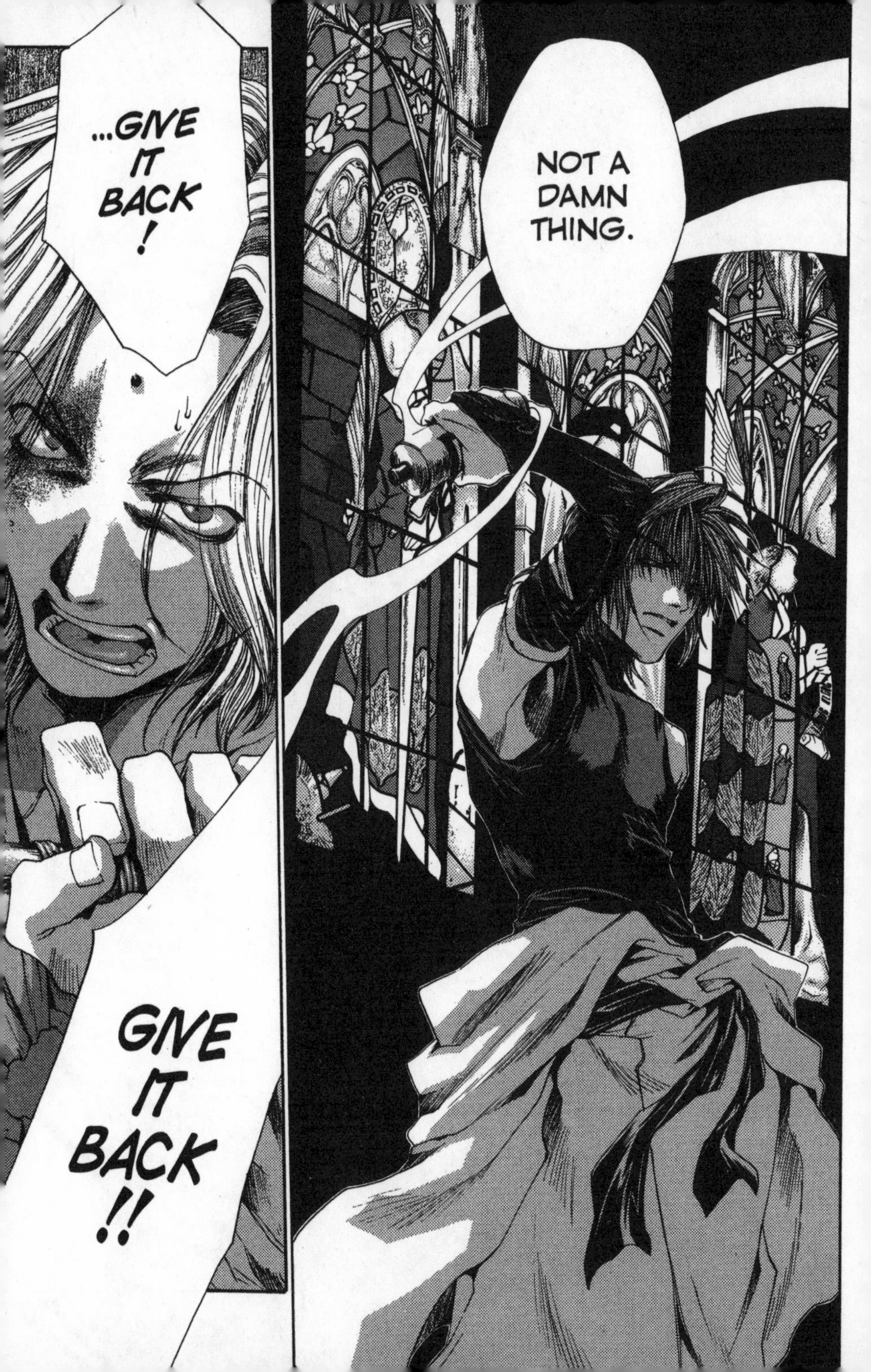
NOT A DAMN THING.
...GIVE IT BACK!
GIVE IT BACK!!

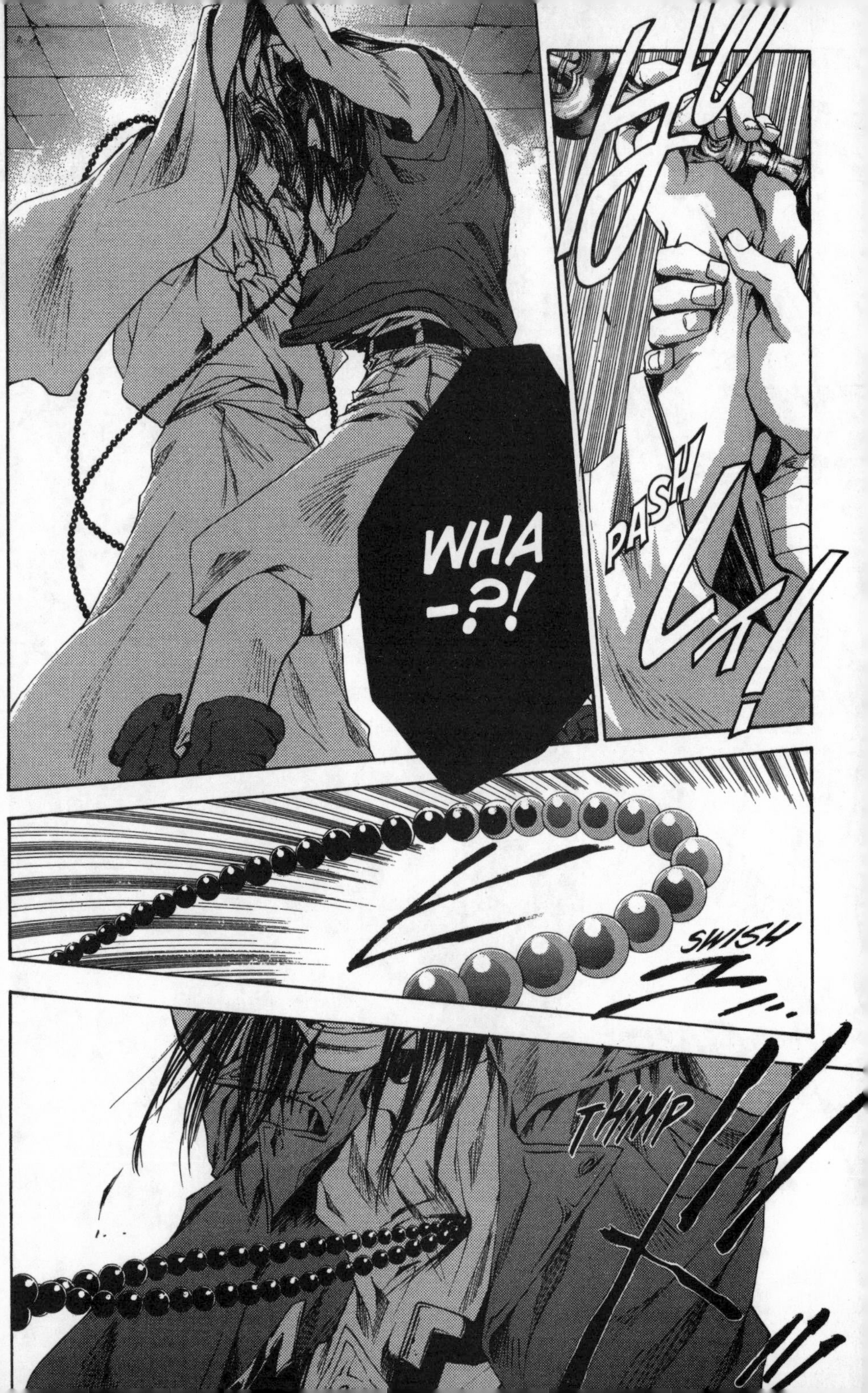
PASH
WHA -?!
SWISH
THMP

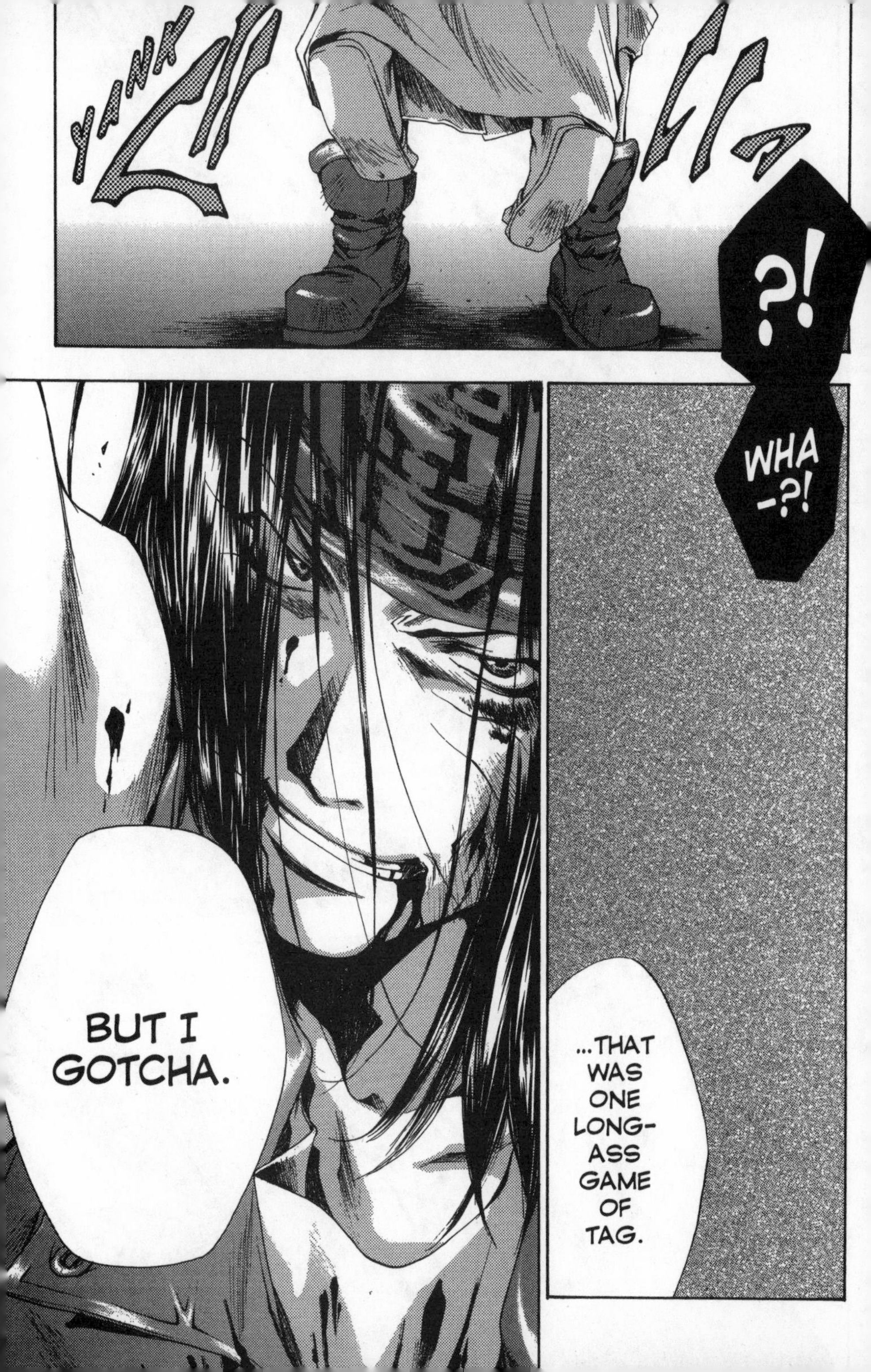
YANK
?!
WHA-?!
...THAT WAS ONE LONG-ASS GAME OF TAG.
BUT I GOTCHA.

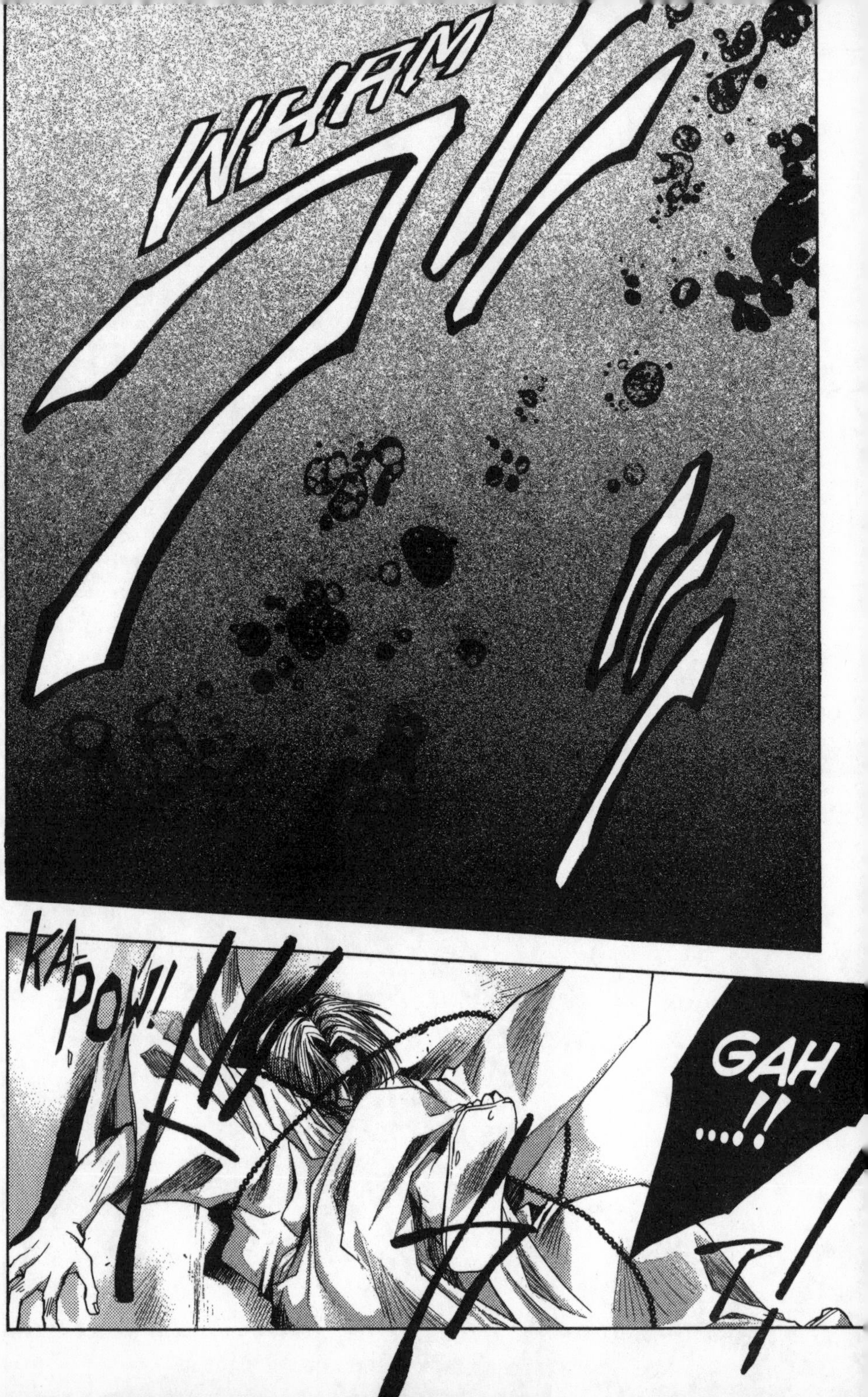
WHAM
GAH ....!!
KAPOW!

CHAPTER 54: Nothing to Give

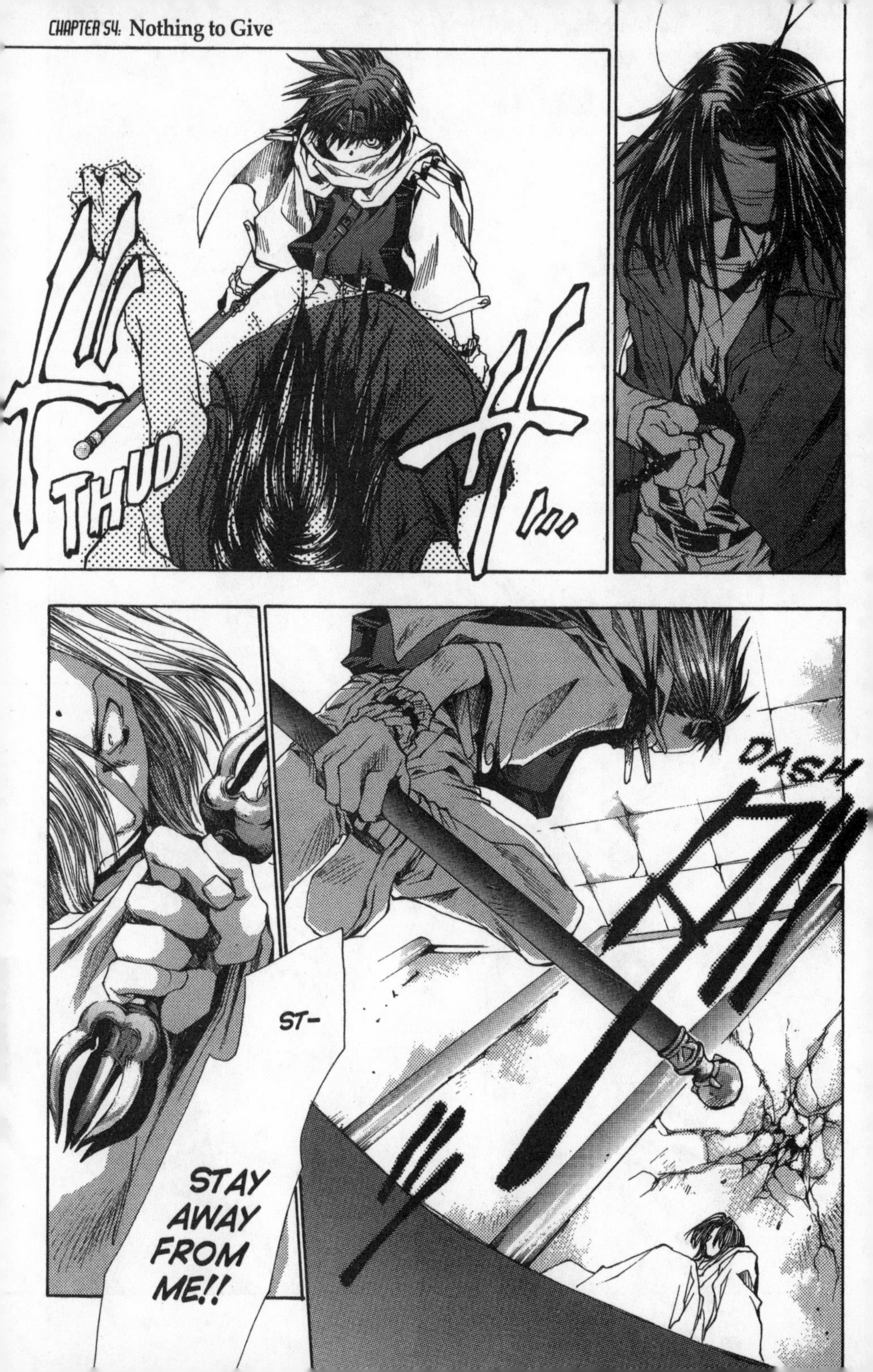
THUD
DASH
ST-
STAY AWAY FROM ME!!

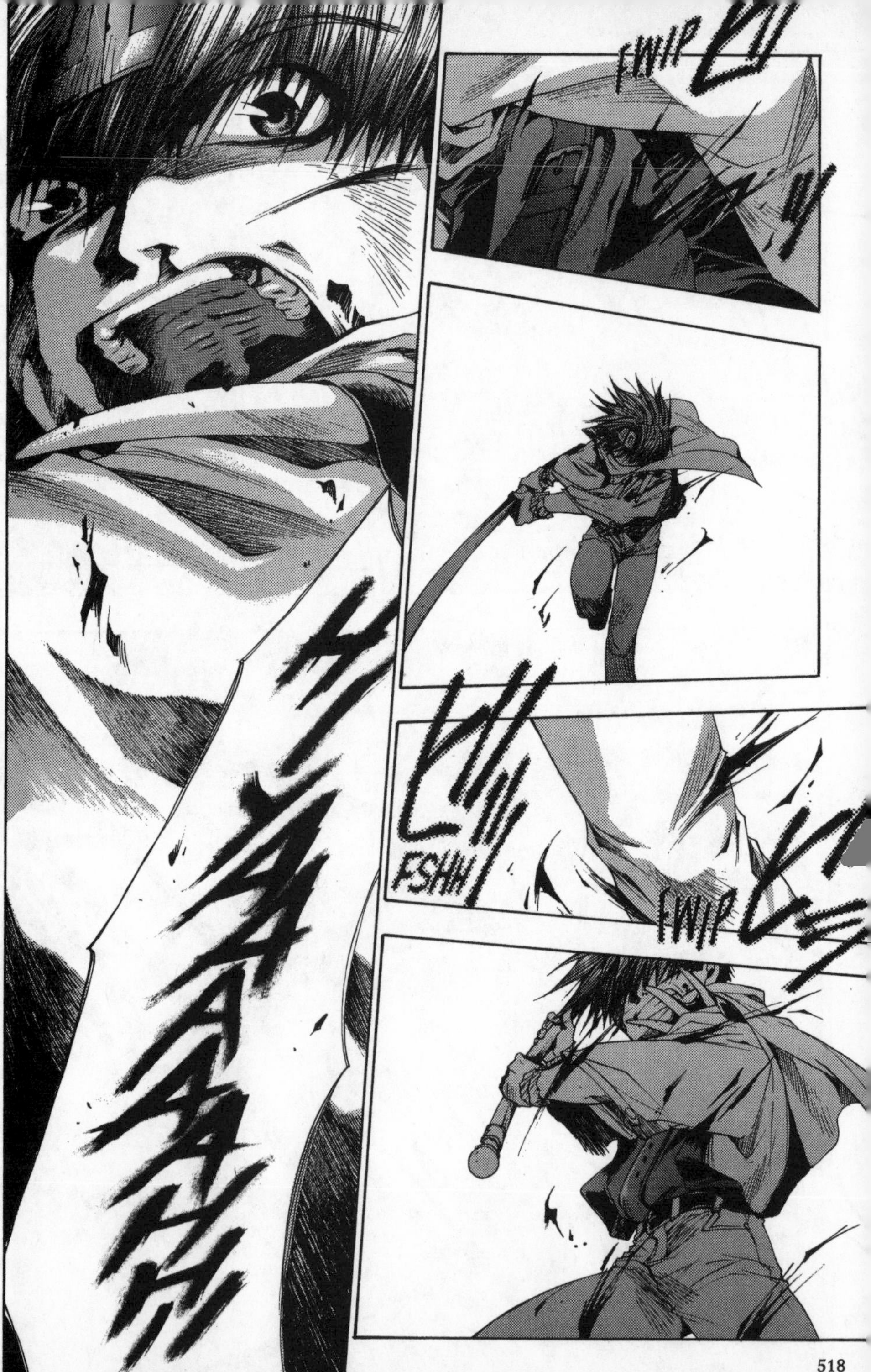
FWIP
FSHH
FWIP
HIYAAAAAH!!

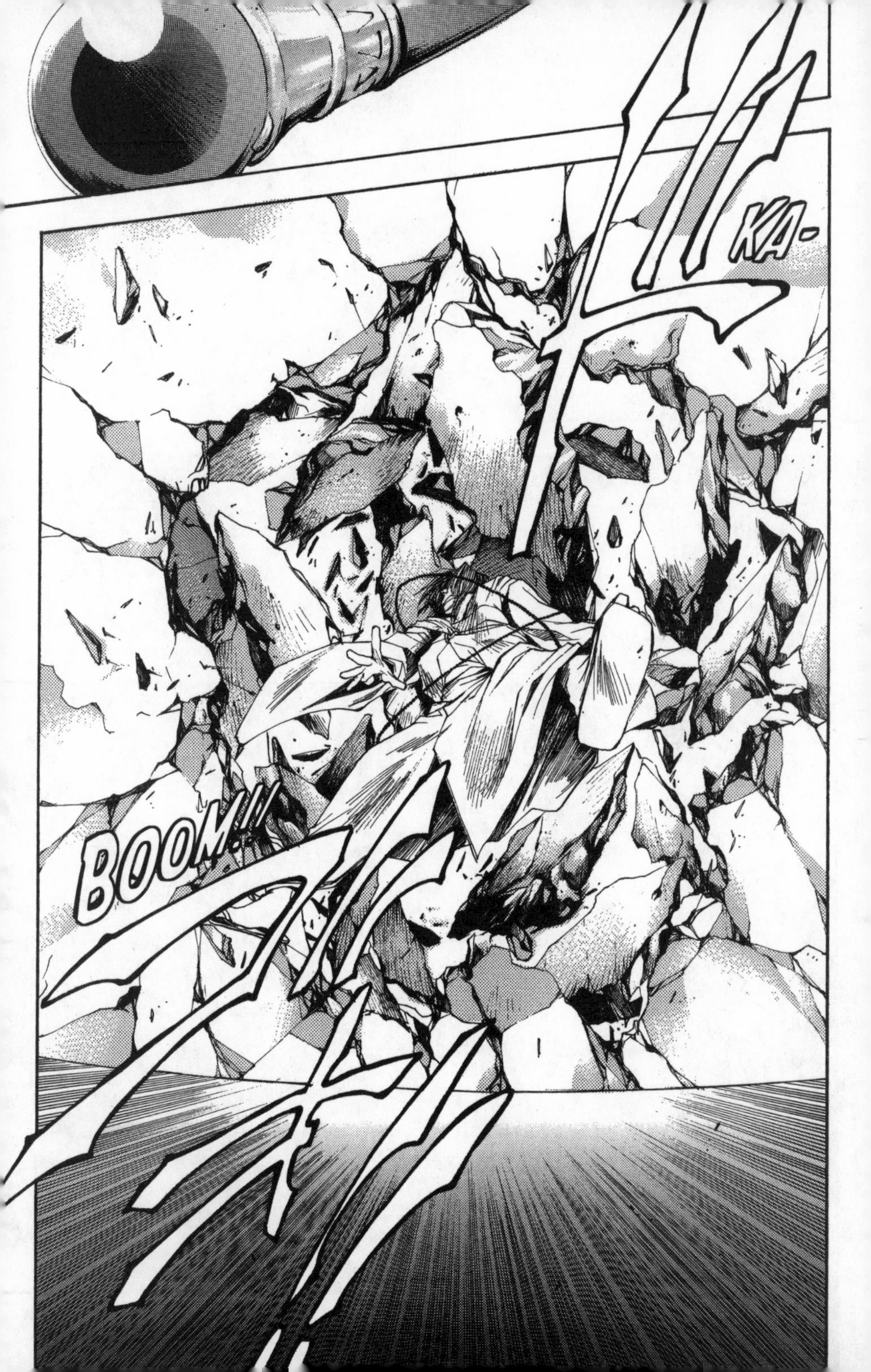
KA-
BOOM!!

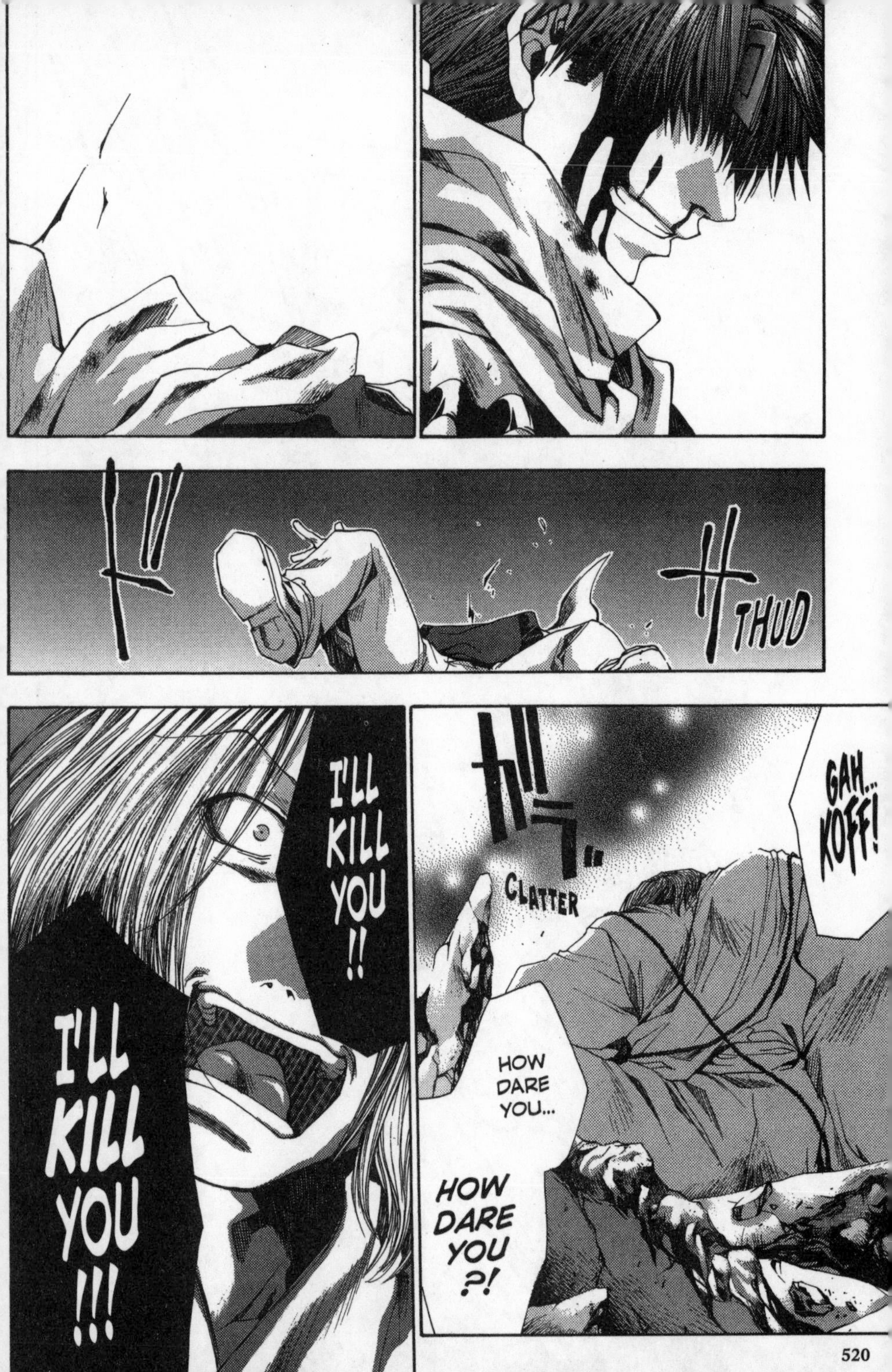
THUD
GAH... KOFF!
CLATTER
HOW DARE YOU...
HOW DARE YOU ?!
I'LL KILL YOU !!
I'LL KILL YOU !!!

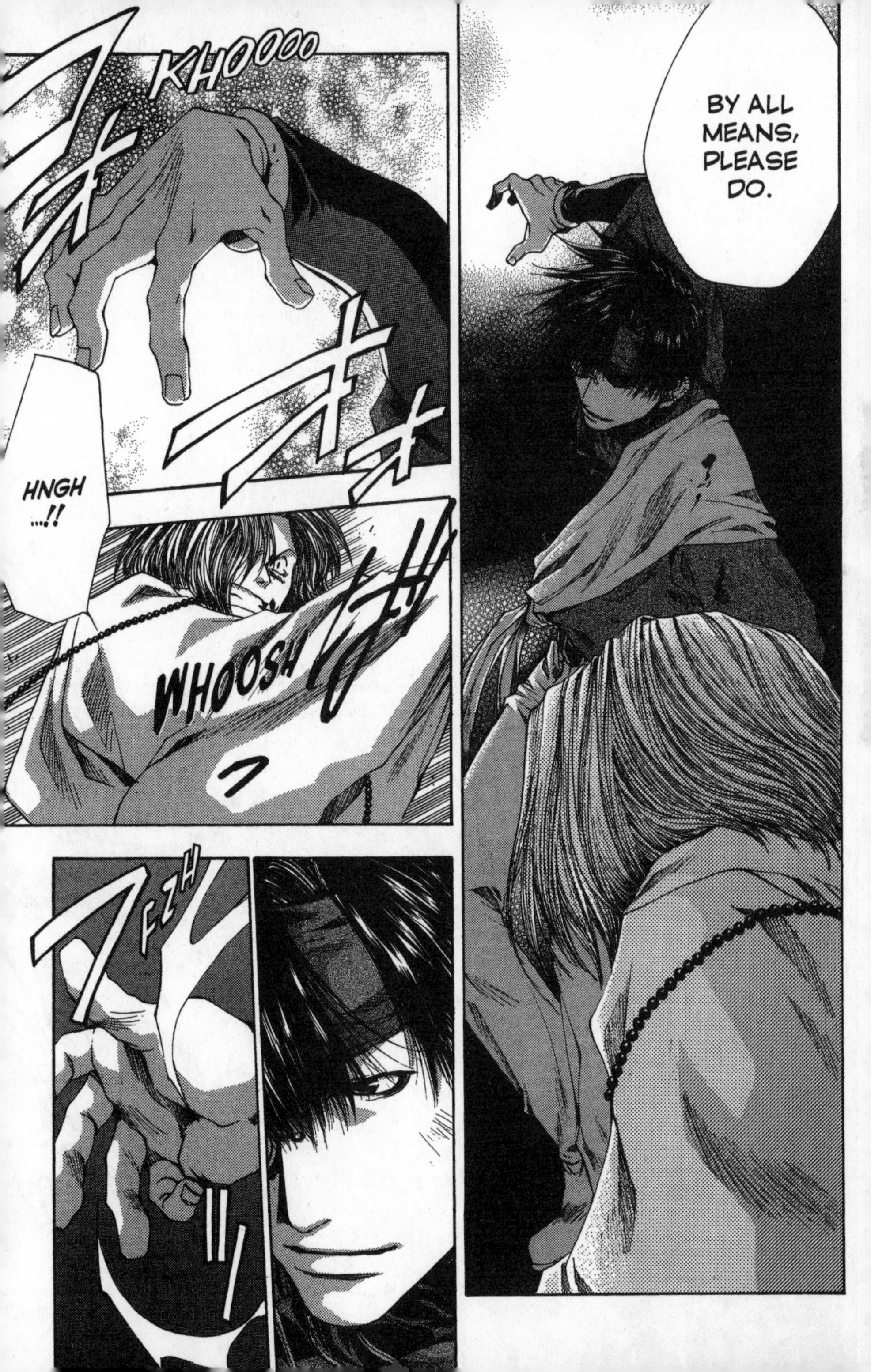
BY ALL MEANS, PLEASE DO.
KHOOOO
HNGH ...!!
WHOOSH
FZH

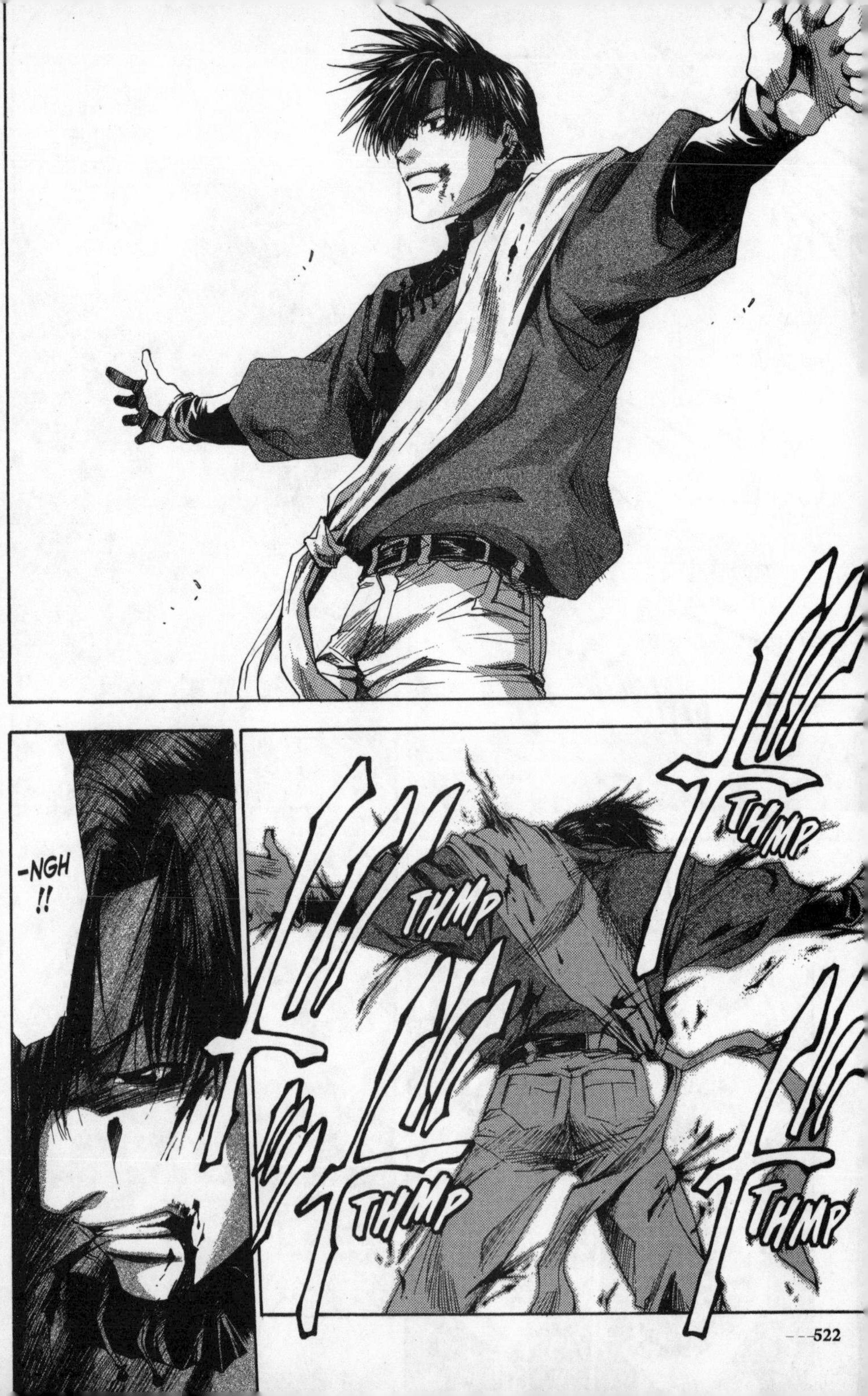
THMP
THMP
THMP
THMP
-NGH
!!

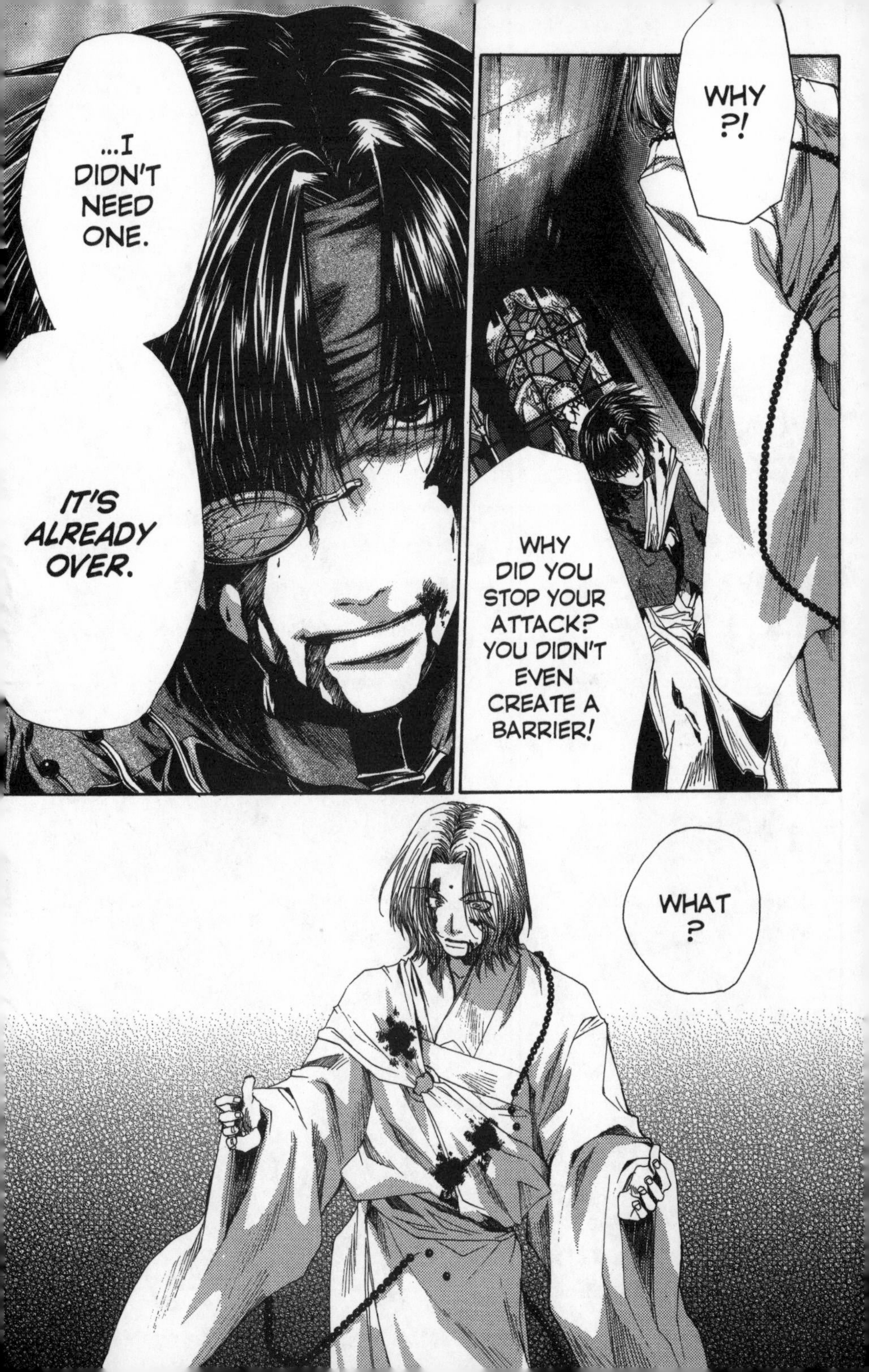
WHY ?!
WHY DID YOU STOP YOUR ATTACK? YOU DIDN'T EVEN CREATE A BARRIER!
...I DIDN'T NEED ONE.
IT'S ALREADY OVER.
WHAT ?

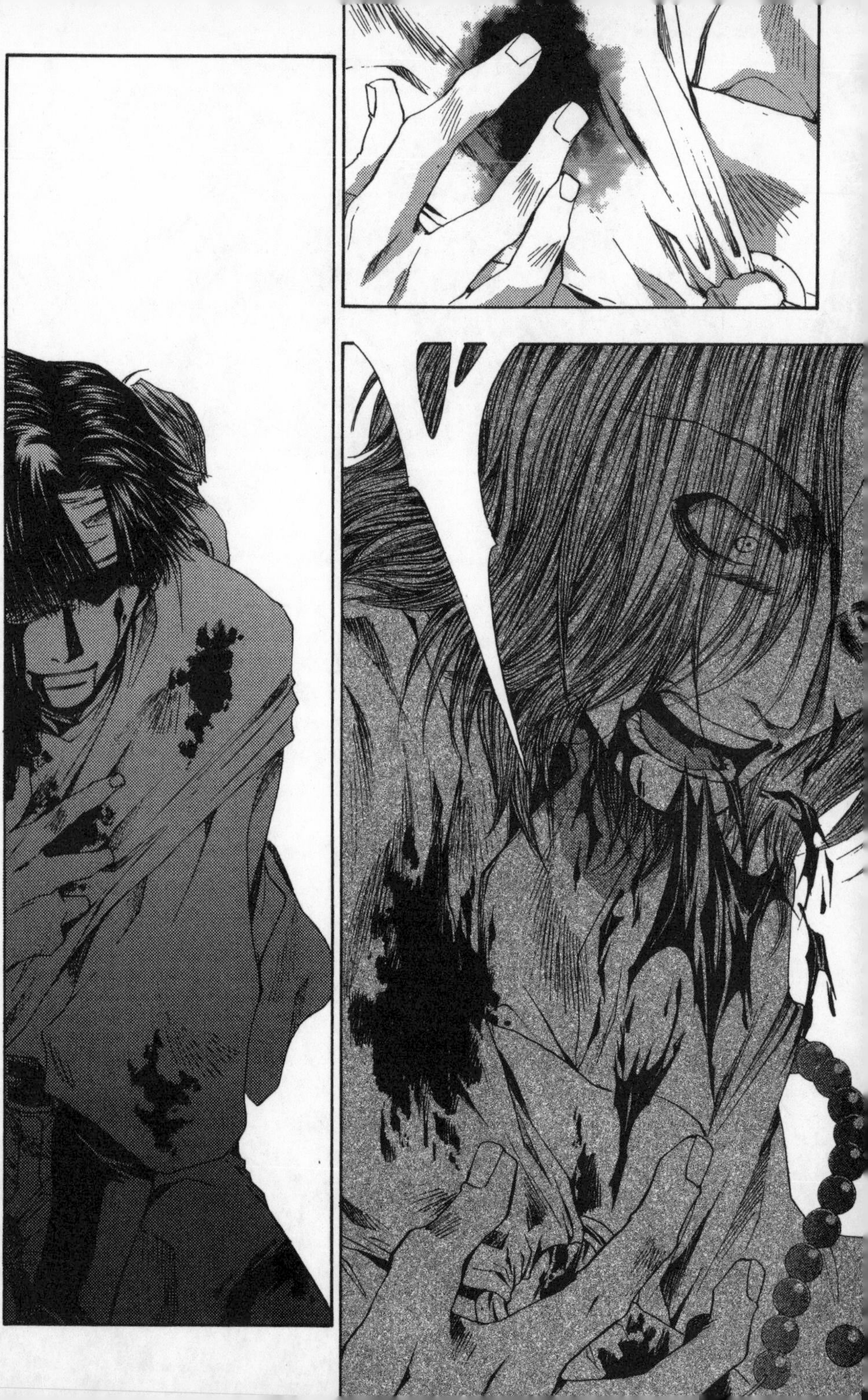

CHAPTER 54: Nothing to Give

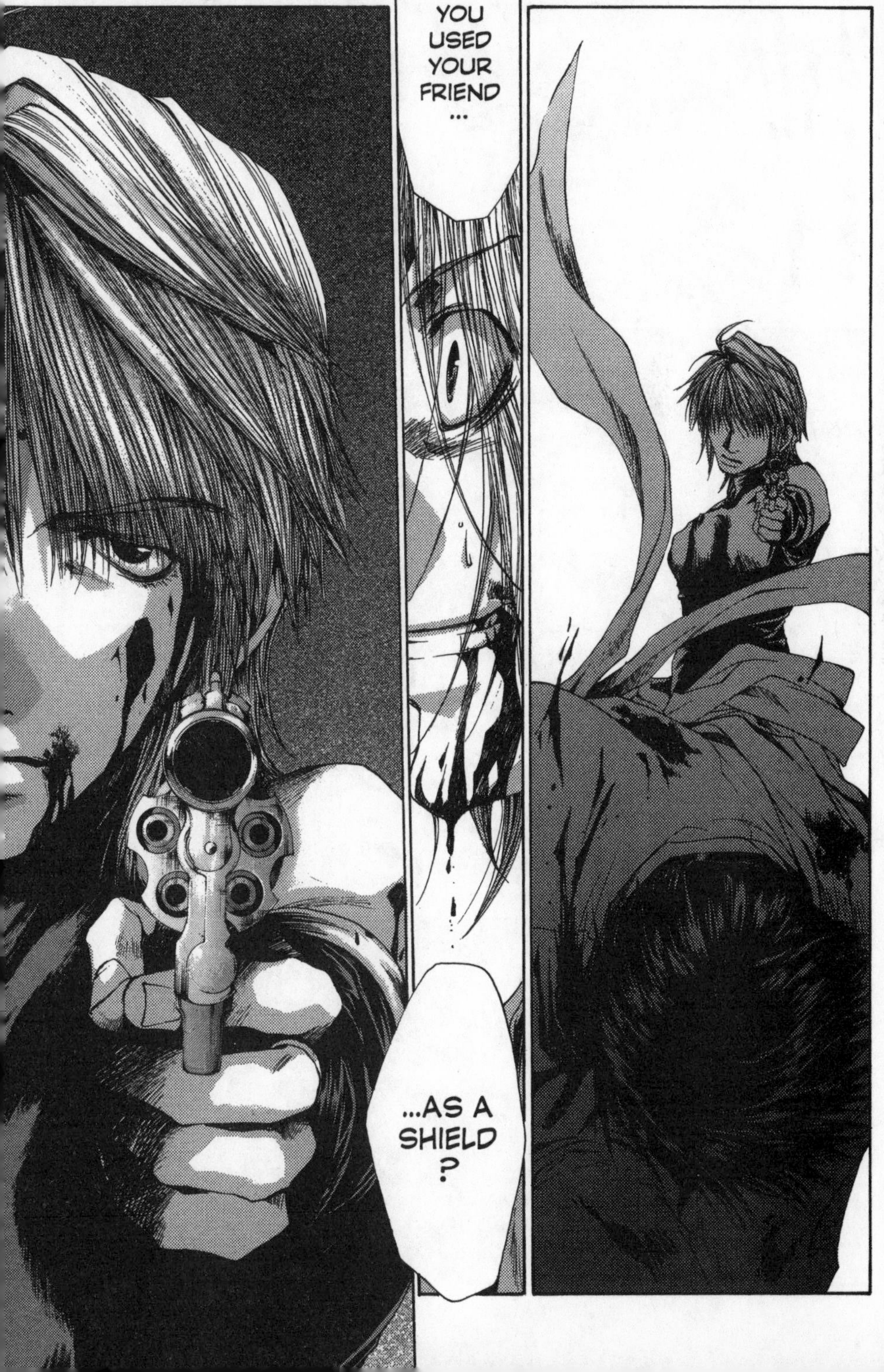
YOU USED YOUR FRIEND ...
...AS A SHIELD ?

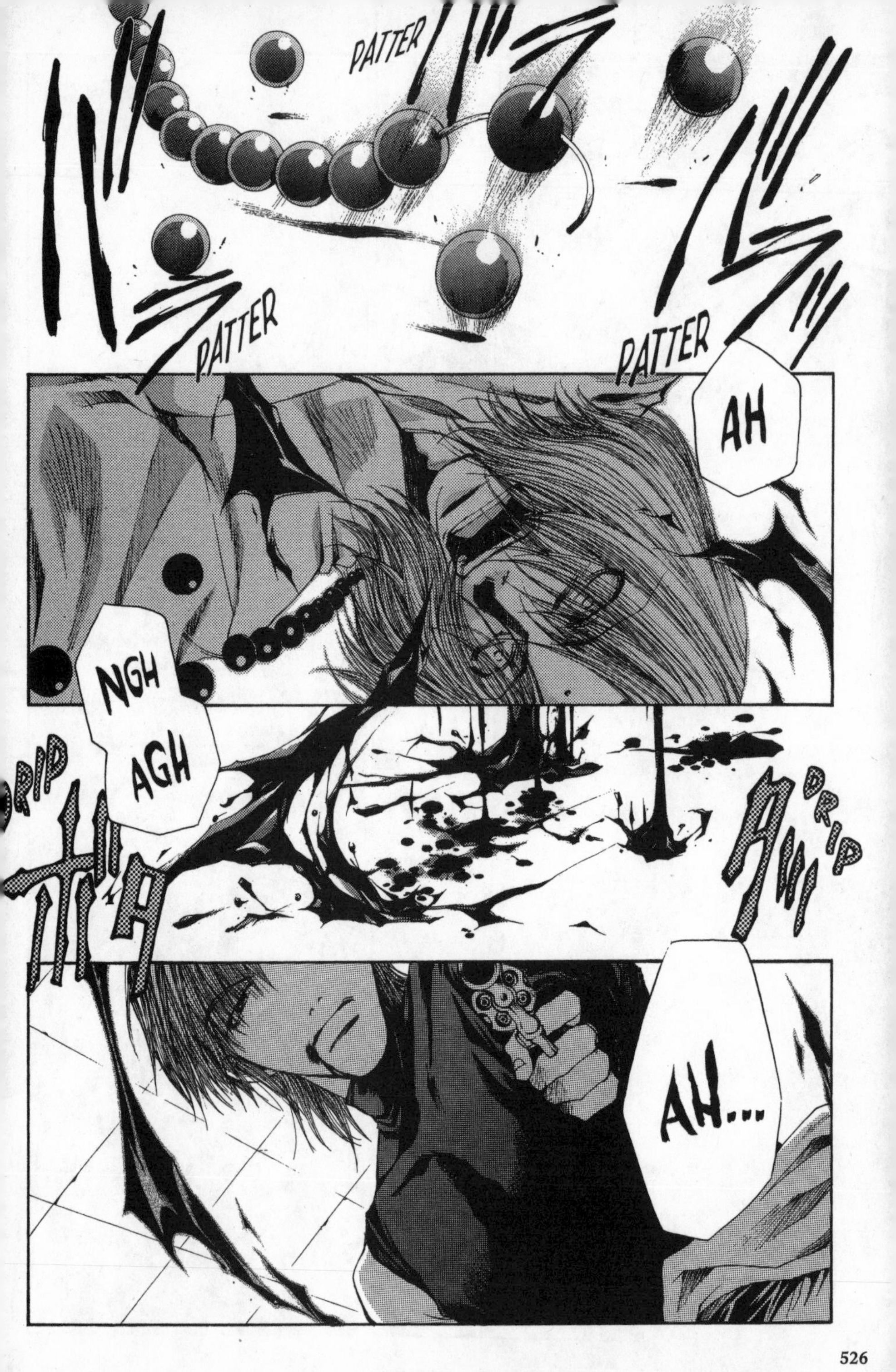
PATTER
PATTER
PATTER
AH
NGH AGH
DRIP
DRIP
AH...

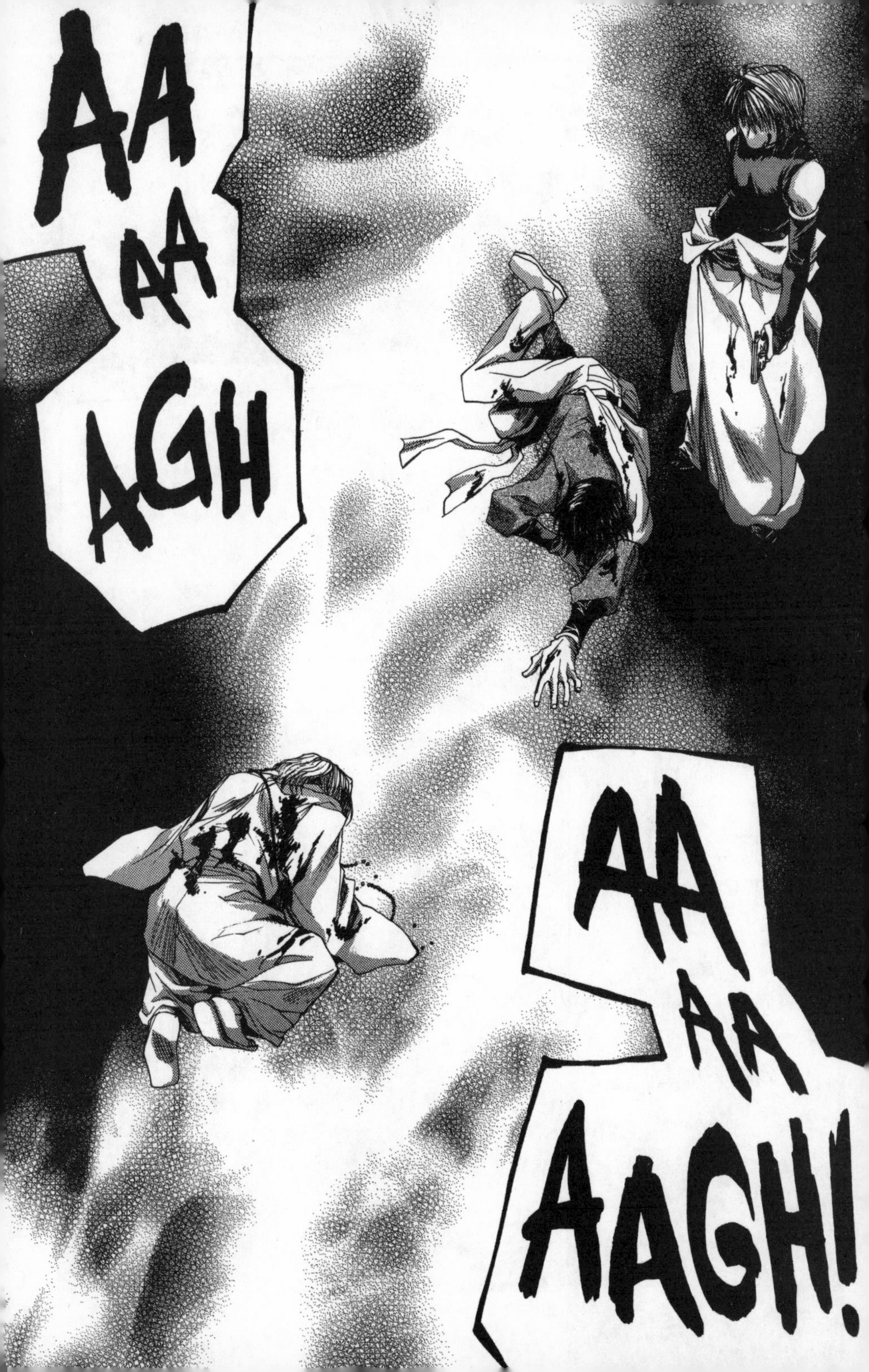
AAAAAGH
AAAAAAGH!

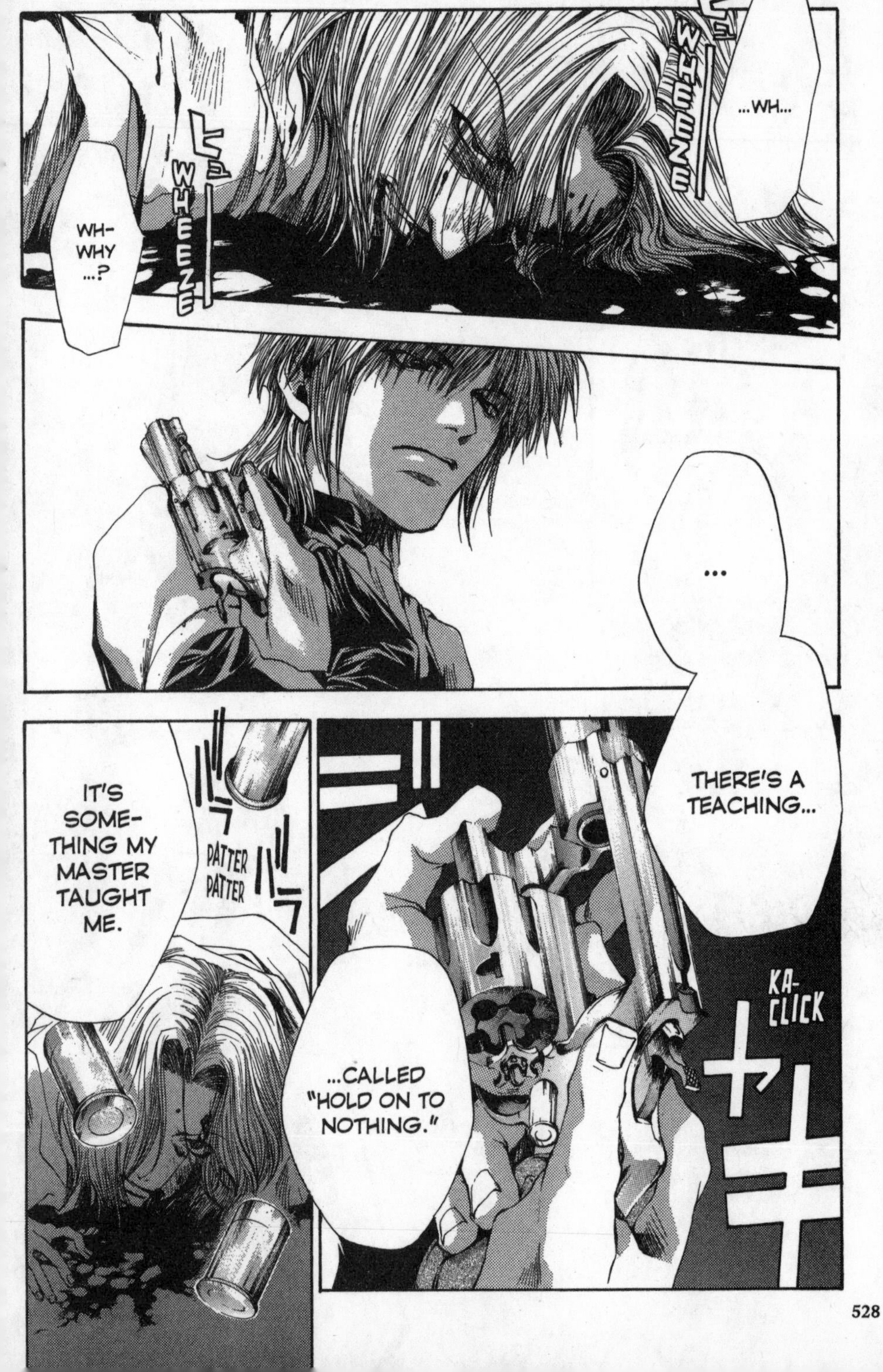
...WH...
WHEEZE
WH- WHY ...?
WHEEZE
...
THERE'S A TEACHING...
KA-CLICK
...CALLED "HOLD ON TO NOTHING."
IT'S SOME- THING MY MASTER TAUGHT ME.
PATTER PATTER

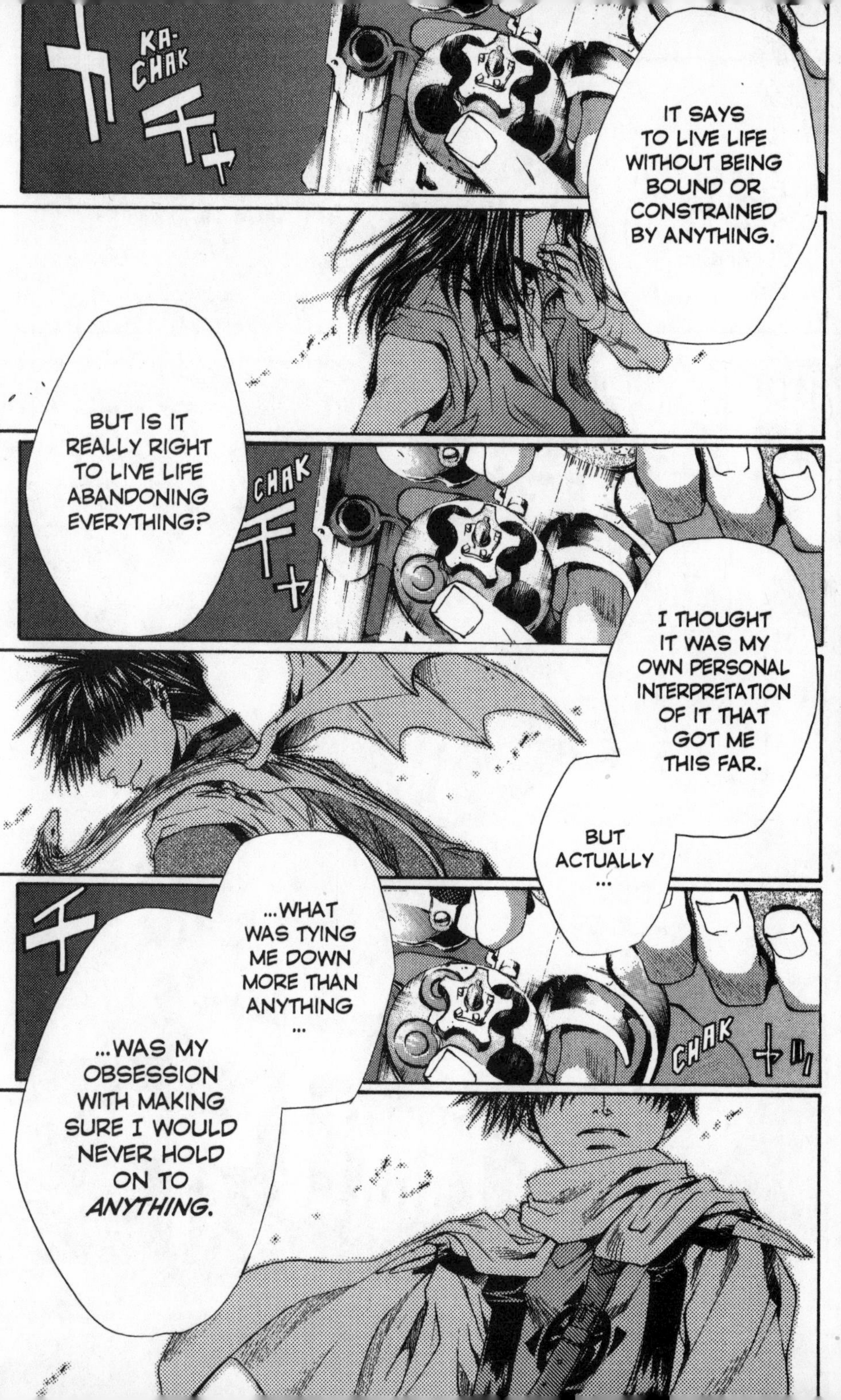
IT SAYS TO LIVE LIFE WITHOUT BEING BOUND OR CONSTRAINED BY ANYTHING.
KA-CHAK
カチャ
BUT IS IT REALLY RIGHT TO LIVE LIFE ABANDONING EVERYTHING?
CHAK
チャ
I THOUGHT IT WAS MY OWN PERSONAL INTERPRETATION OF IT THAT GOT ME THIS FAR.
BUT ACTUALLY ...
...WHAT WAS TYING ME DOWN MORE THAN ANYTHING ...
CHAK
...WAS MY OBSESSION WITH MAKING SURE I WOULD NEVER HOLD ON TO *ANYTHING*.

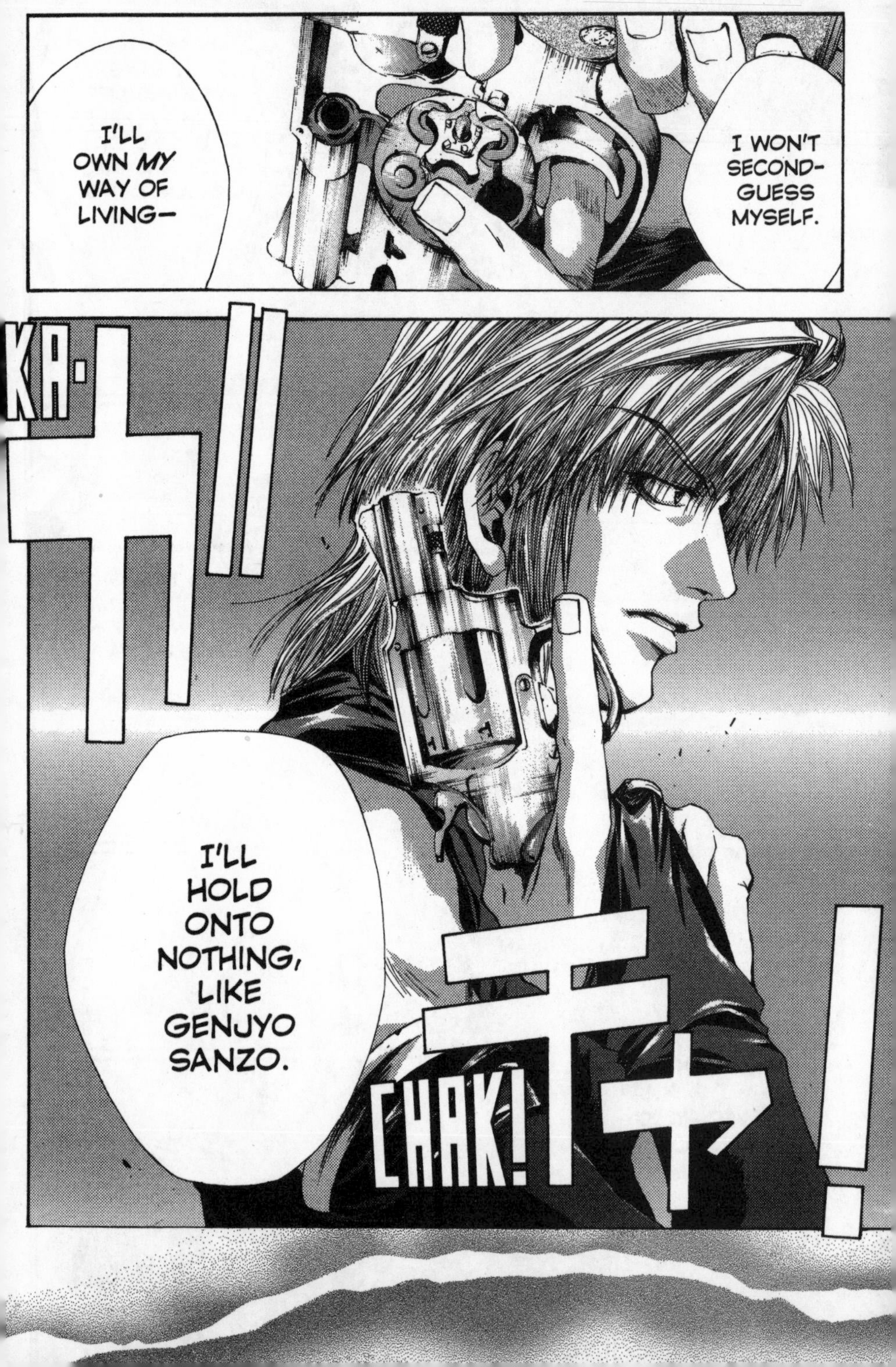
I'LL OWN *MY* WAY OF LIVING—
I WON'T SECOND-GUESS MYSELF.
KA-
I'LL HOLD ONTO NOTHING, LIKE GENJYO SANZO.
CHAK!

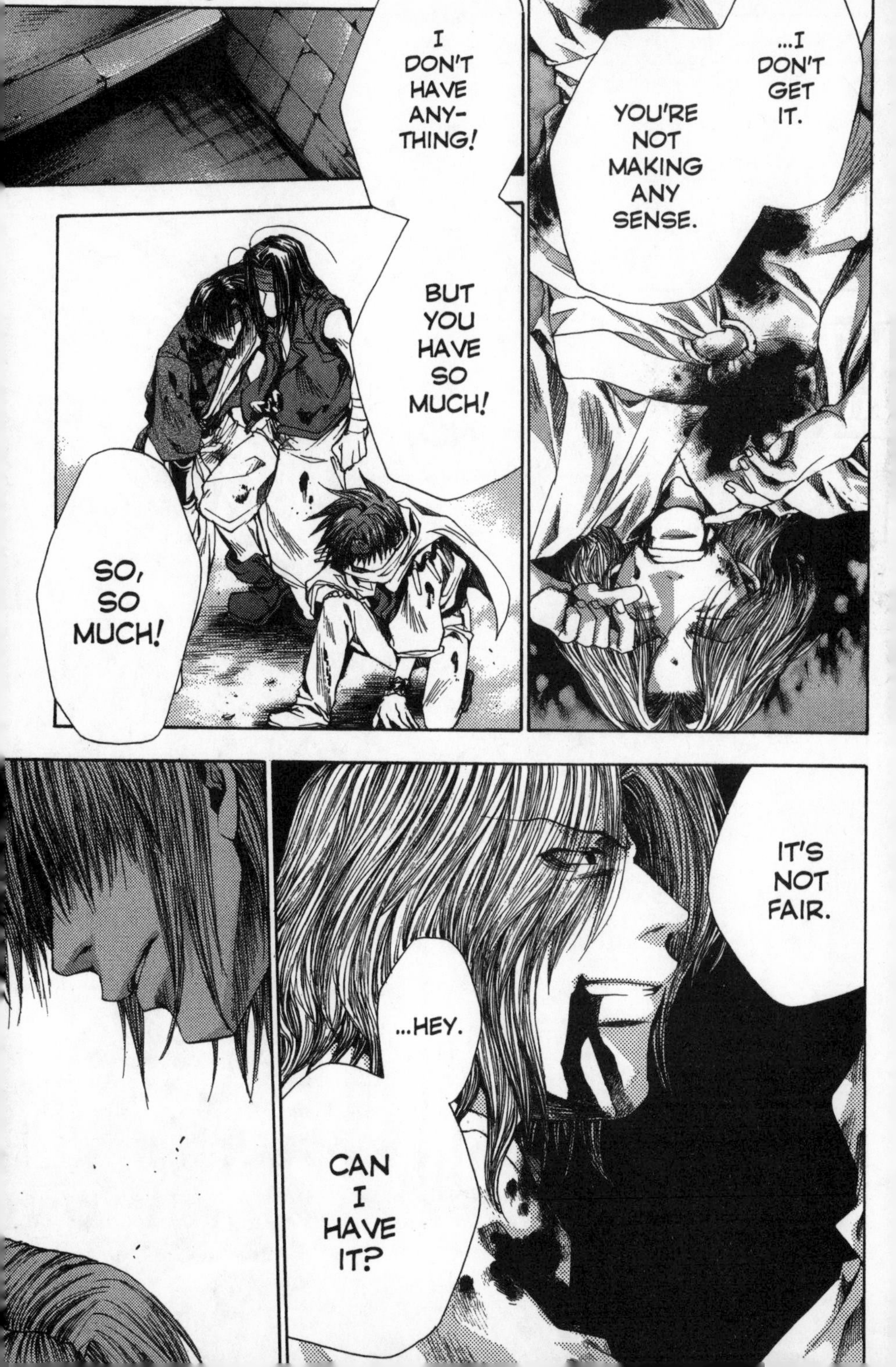
...I DON'T GET IT.
YOU'RE NOT MAKING ANY SENSE.
I DON'T HAVE ANY-THING!
BUT YOU HAVE SO MUCH!
SO, SO MUCH!
IT'S NOT FAIR.
...HEY.
CAN I HAVE IT?

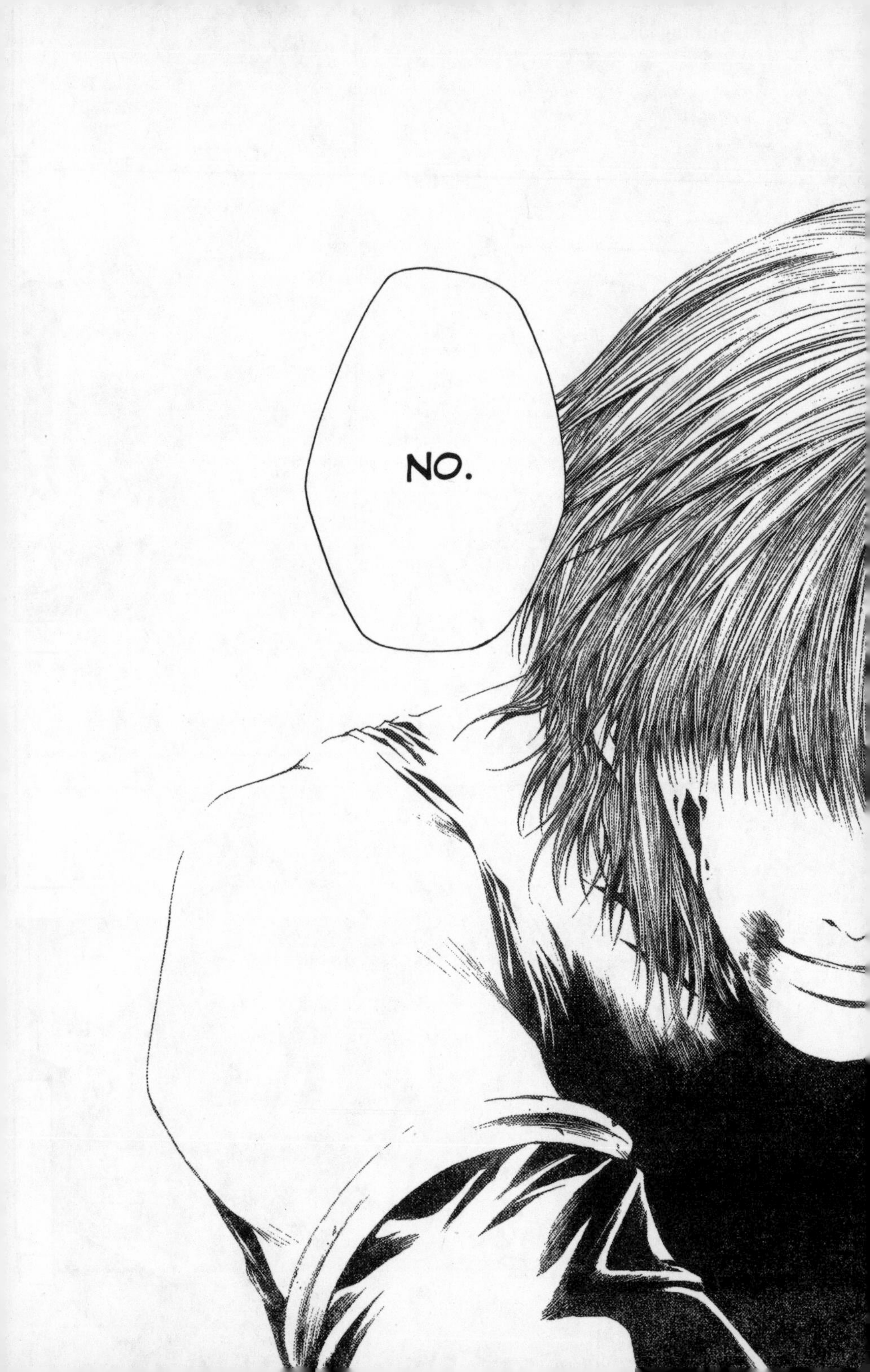
NO.

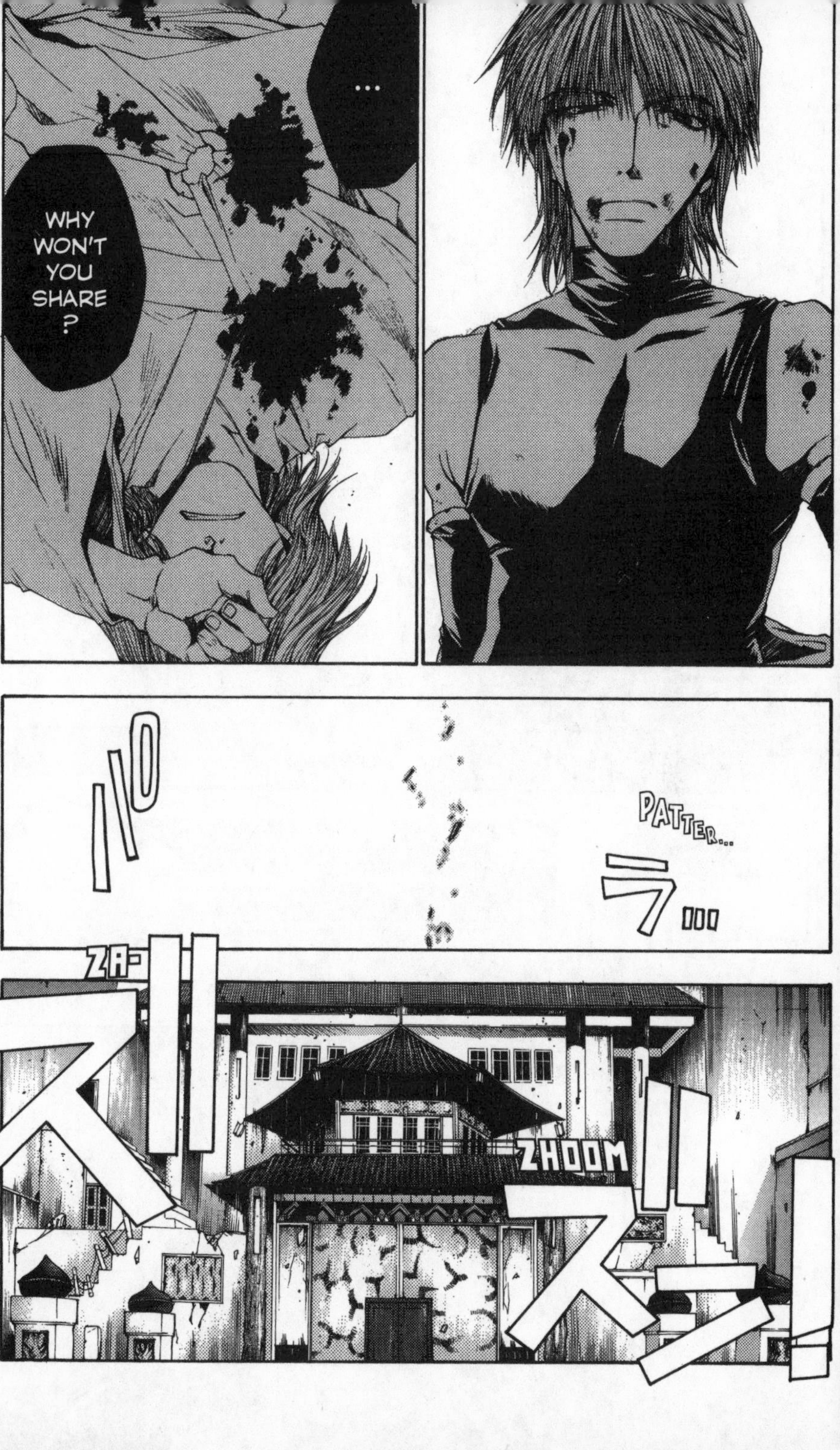
...
WHY WON'T YOU SHARE ?
PATTER...
ZHOOM
ZA-

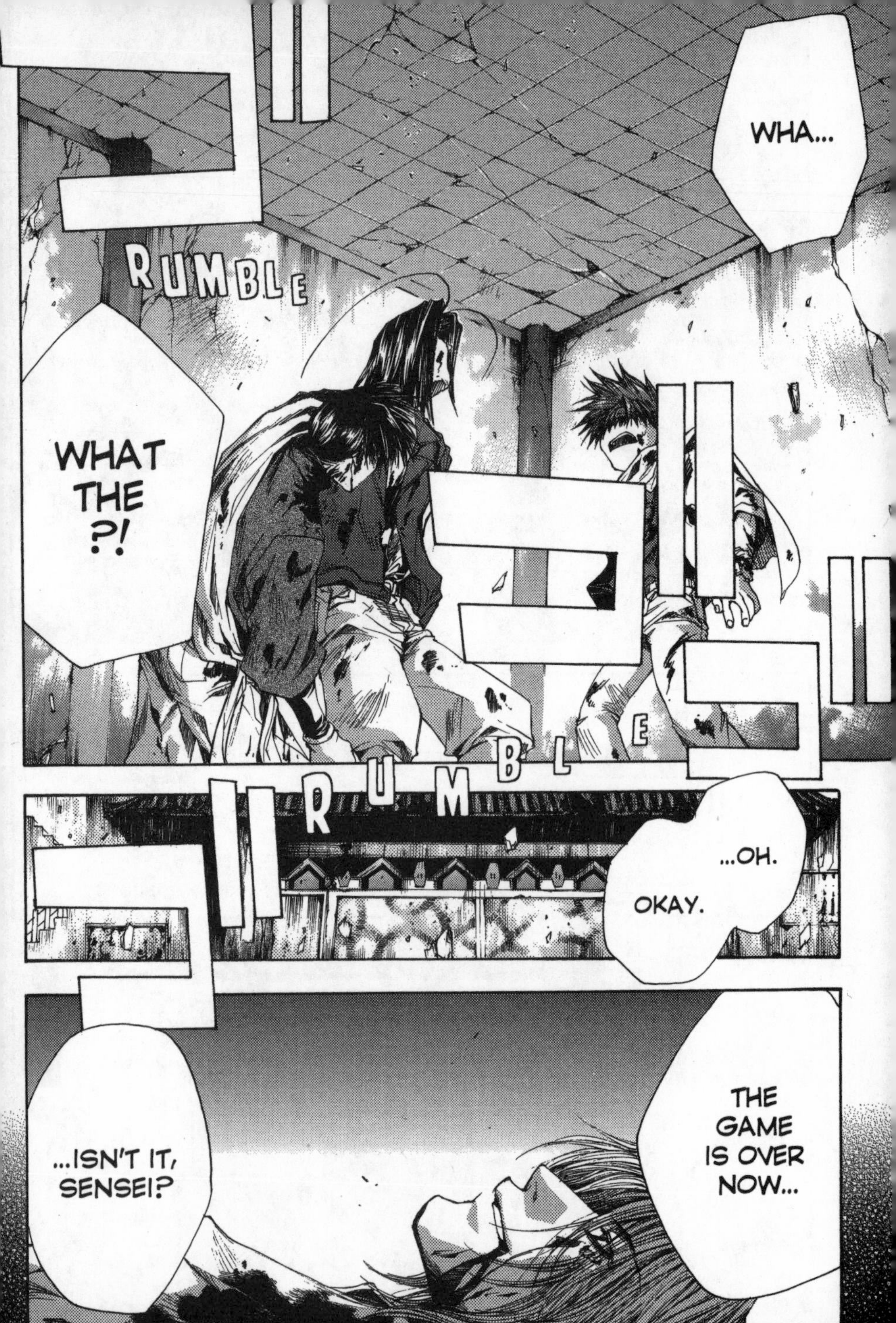
WHA...
RUMBLE
WHAT THE ?!
RUMBLE
...OH. OKAY.
THE GAME IS OVER NOW...
...ISN'T IT, SENSEI?

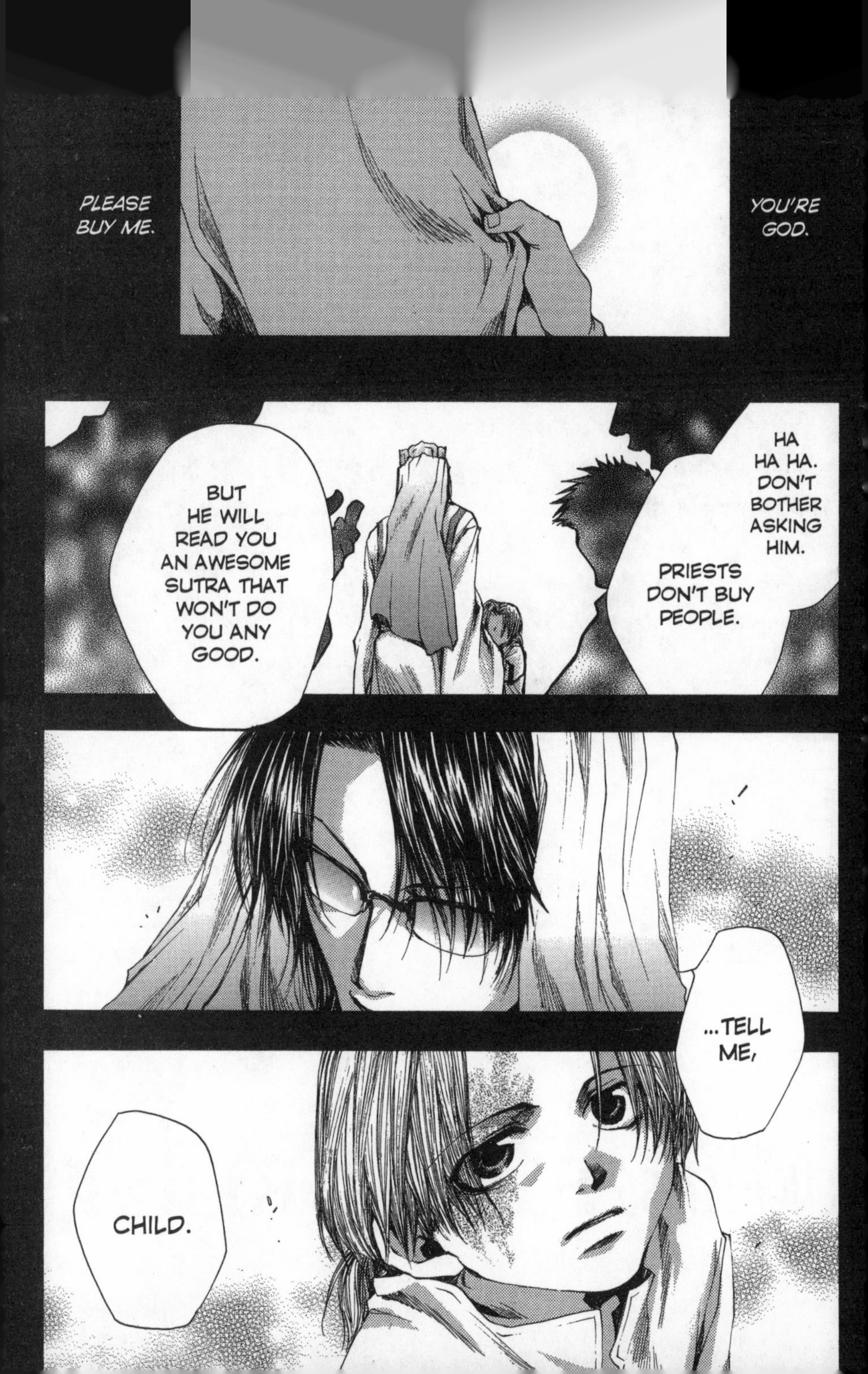
YOU'RE GOD.
PLEASE BUY ME.
HA HA HA. DON'T BOTHER ASKING HIM.
PRIESTS DON'T BUY PEOPLE.
BUT HE WILL READ YOU AN AWESOME SUTRA THAT WON'T DO YOU ANY GOOD.
...TELL ME,
CHILD.

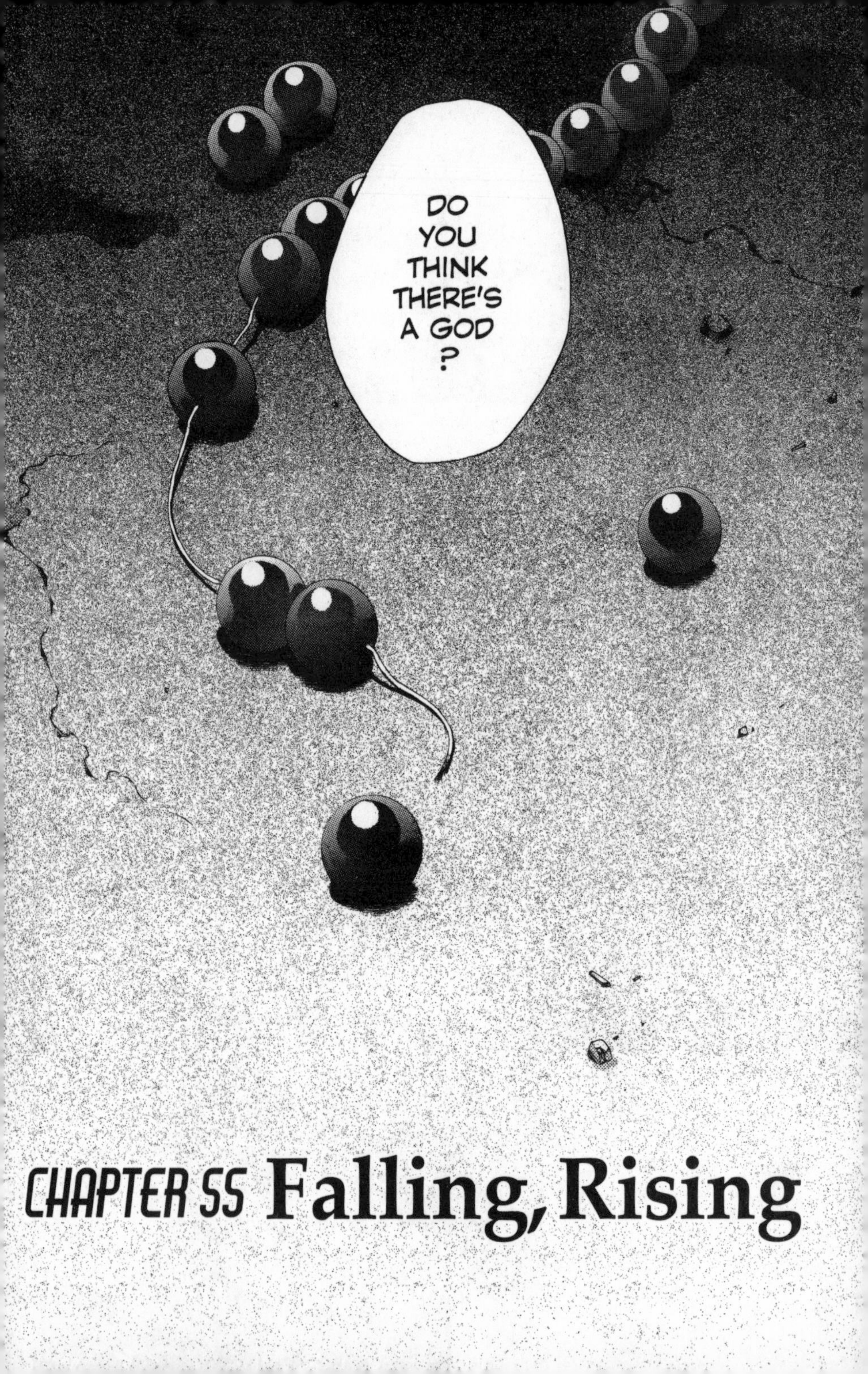
DO YOU THINK THERE'S A GOD ?

CHAPTER 55 Falling, Rising

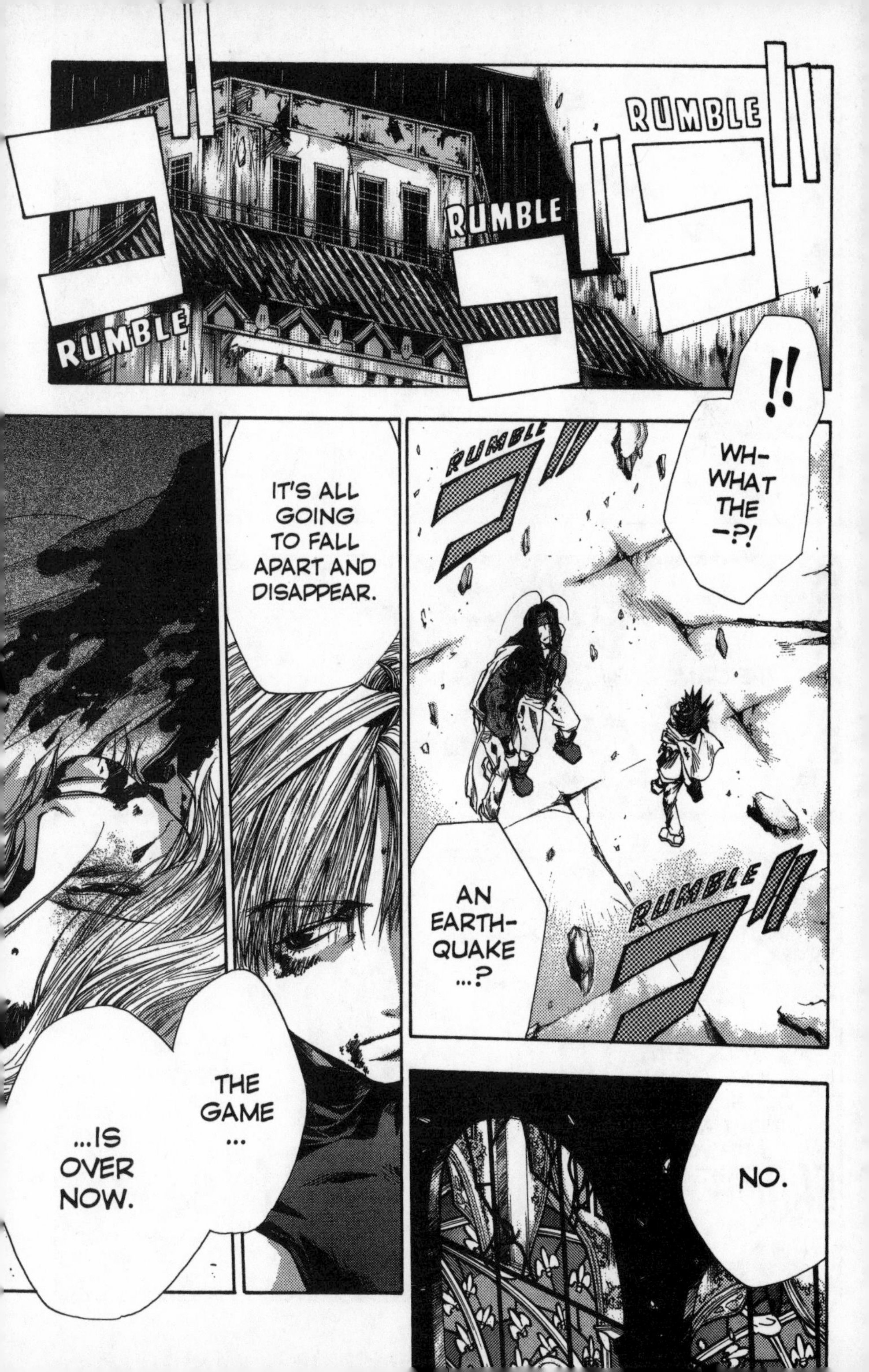
RUMBLE
RUMBLE
RUMBLE
!!
WH- WHAT THE —?!
RUMBLE
AN EARTH-QUAKE ...?
RUMBLE
IT'S ALL GOING TO FALL APART AND DISAPPEAR.
THE GAME ...
...IS OVER NOW.
NO.

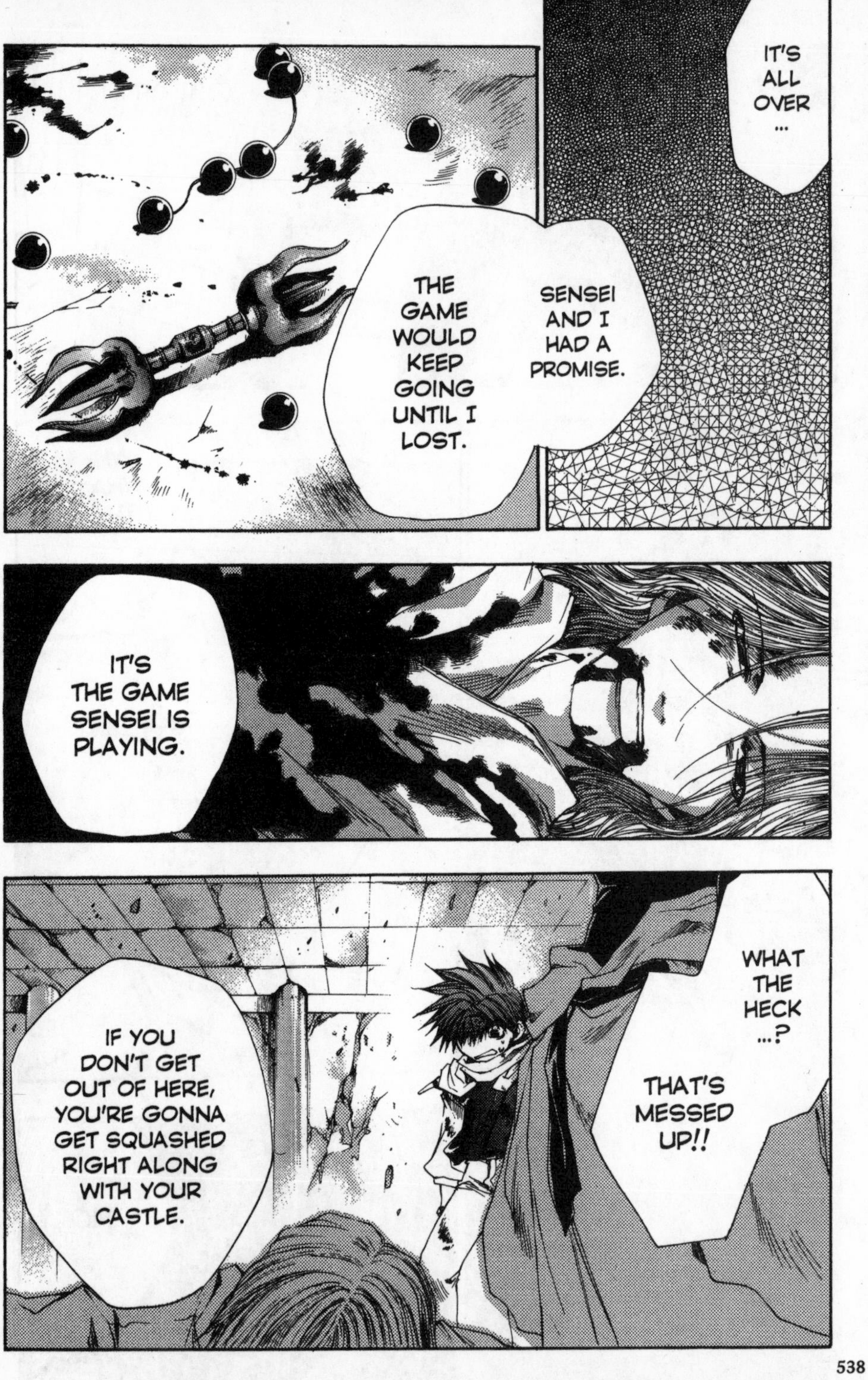
IT'S ALL OVER ...
SENSEI AND I HAD A PROMISE.
THE GAME WOULD KEEP GOING UNTIL I LOST.
IT'S THE GAME SENSEI IS PLAYING.
WHAT THE HECK ...?
THAT'S MESSED UP!!
IF YOU DON'T GET OUT OF HERE, YOU'RE GONNA GET SQUASHED RIGHT ALONG WITH YOUR CASTLE.

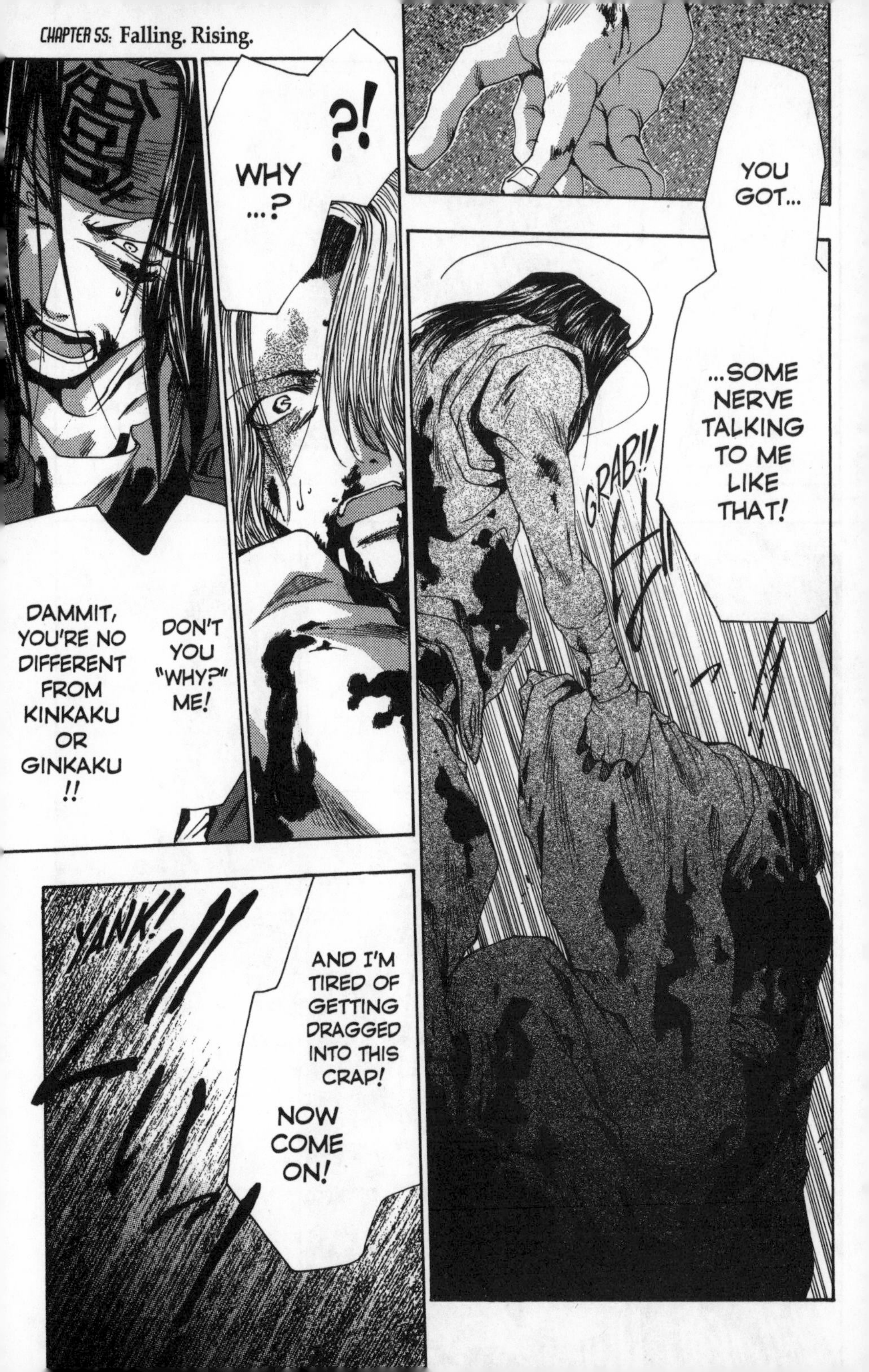
YOU GOT...
...SOME NERVE TALKING TO ME LIKE THAT!
GRAB!!
?!
WHY ...?
DON'T YOU "WHY?" ME!
DAMMIT, YOU'RE NO DIFFERENT FROM KINKAKU OR GINKAKU !!
YANK!
AND I'M TIRED OF GETTING DRAGGED INTO THIS CRAP!
NOW COME ON!

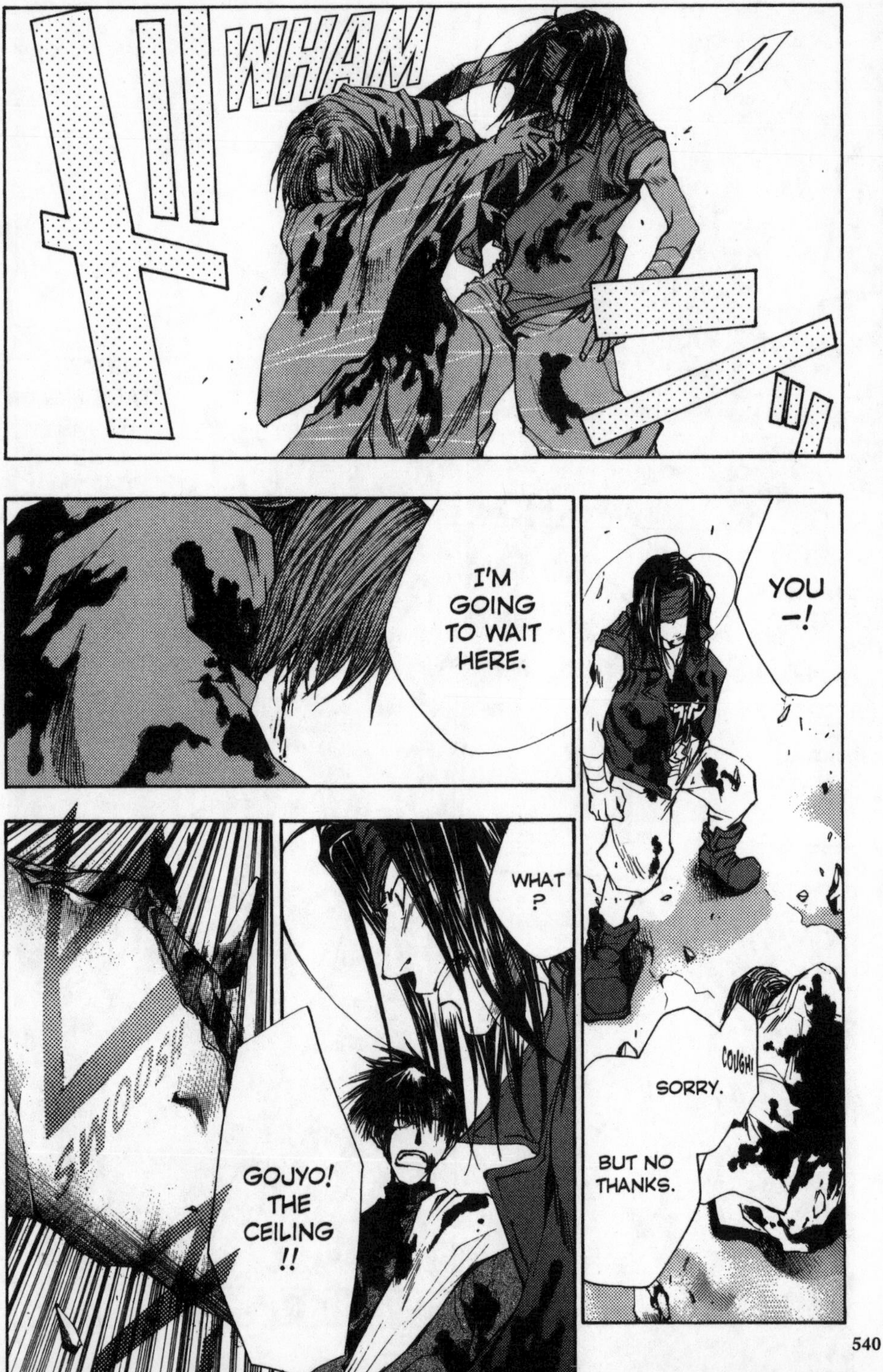
WHAM
YOU —!
COUGH!
SORRY.
BUT NO THANKS.
I'M GOING TO WAIT HERE.
WHAT?
GOJYO! THE CEILING!!
SWOOSH

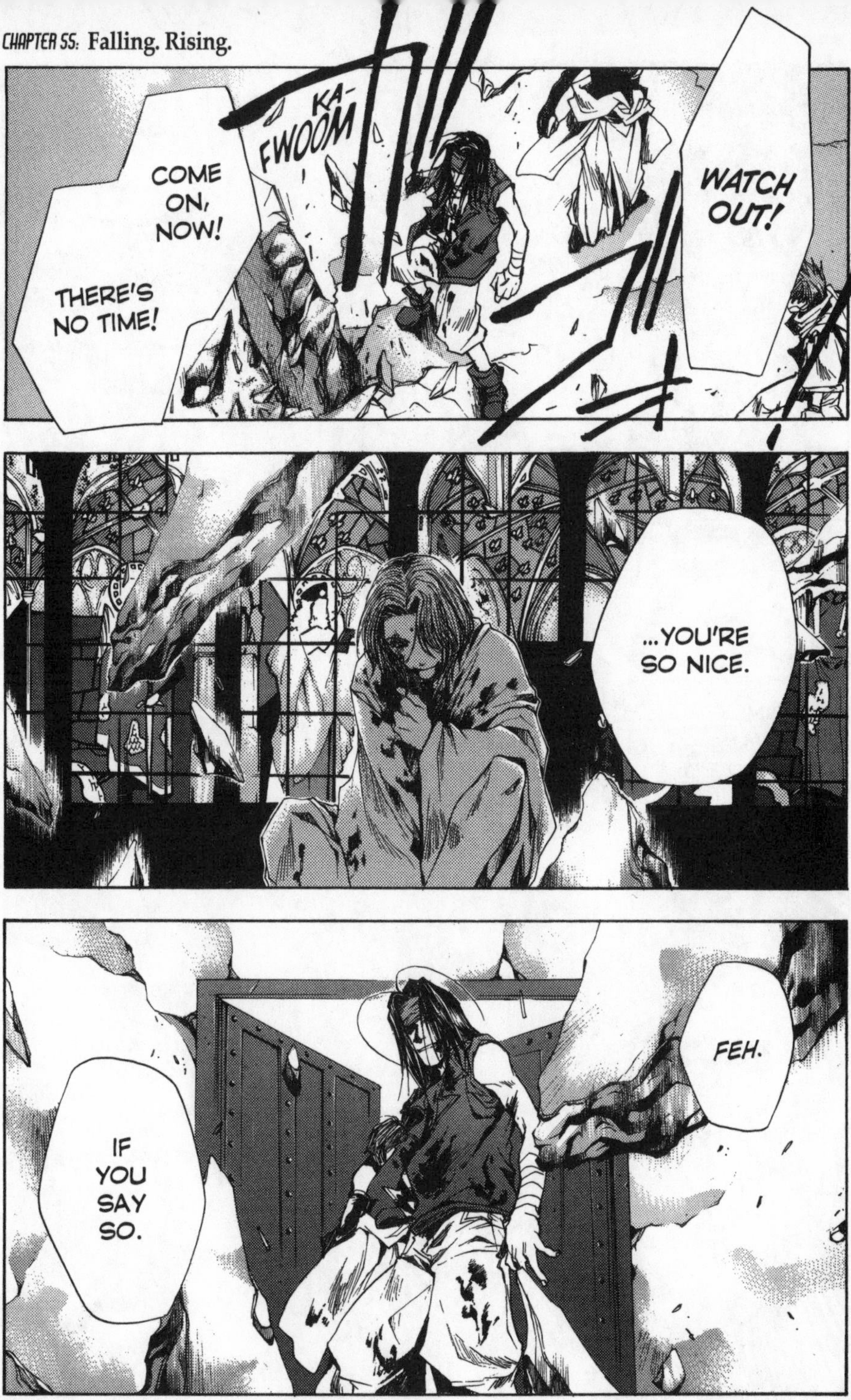
WATCH OUT!
KA-FWOOM
COME ON, NOW!
THERE'S NO TIME!
...YOU'RE SO NICE.
FEH.
IF YOU SAY SO.

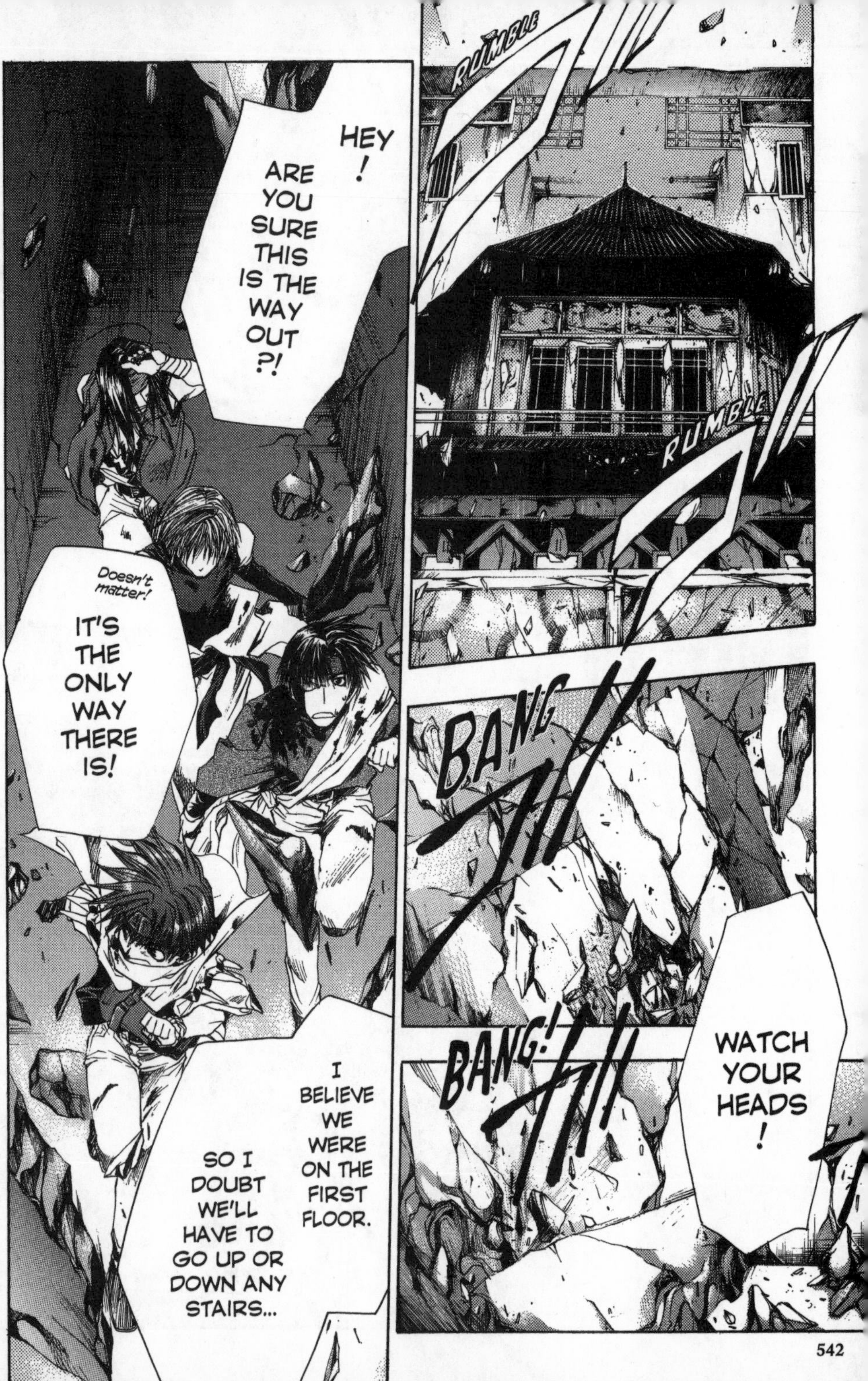
RUMBLE
RUMBLE
BANG
BANG!
WATCH YOUR HEADS!
HEY! ARE YOU SURE THIS IS THE WAY OUT?!
Doesn't matter!
IT'S THE ONLY WAY THERE IS!
I BELIEVE WE WERE ON THE FIRST FLOOR.
SO I DOUBT WE'LL HAVE TO GO UP OR DOWN ANY STAIRS...

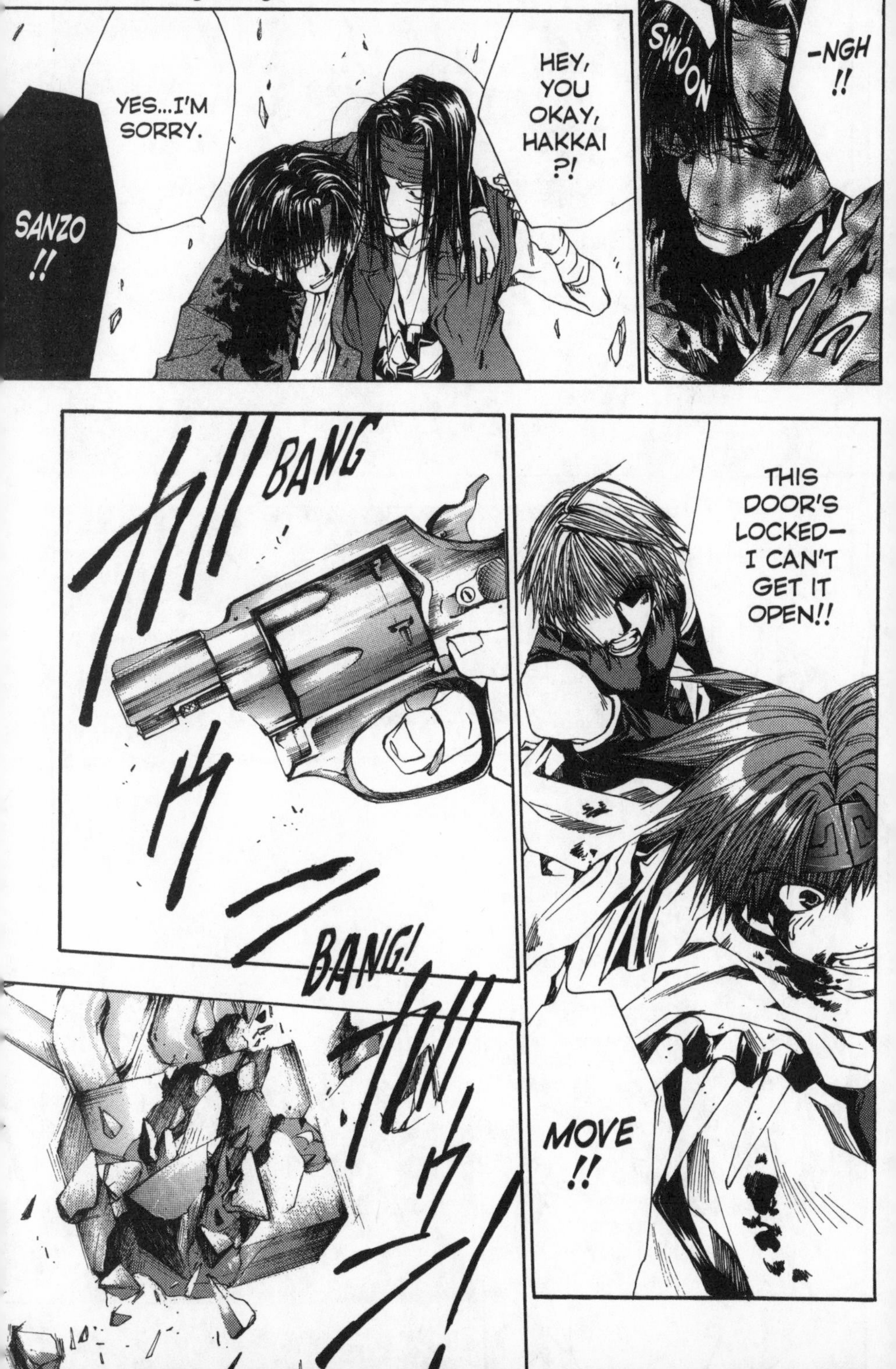
SWOON
-NGH!!
HEY, YOU OKAY, HAKKAI?!
YES...I'M SORRY.
SANZO!!
THIS DOOR'S LOCKED— I CAN'T GET IT OPEN!!
MOVE!!
BANG
BANG!

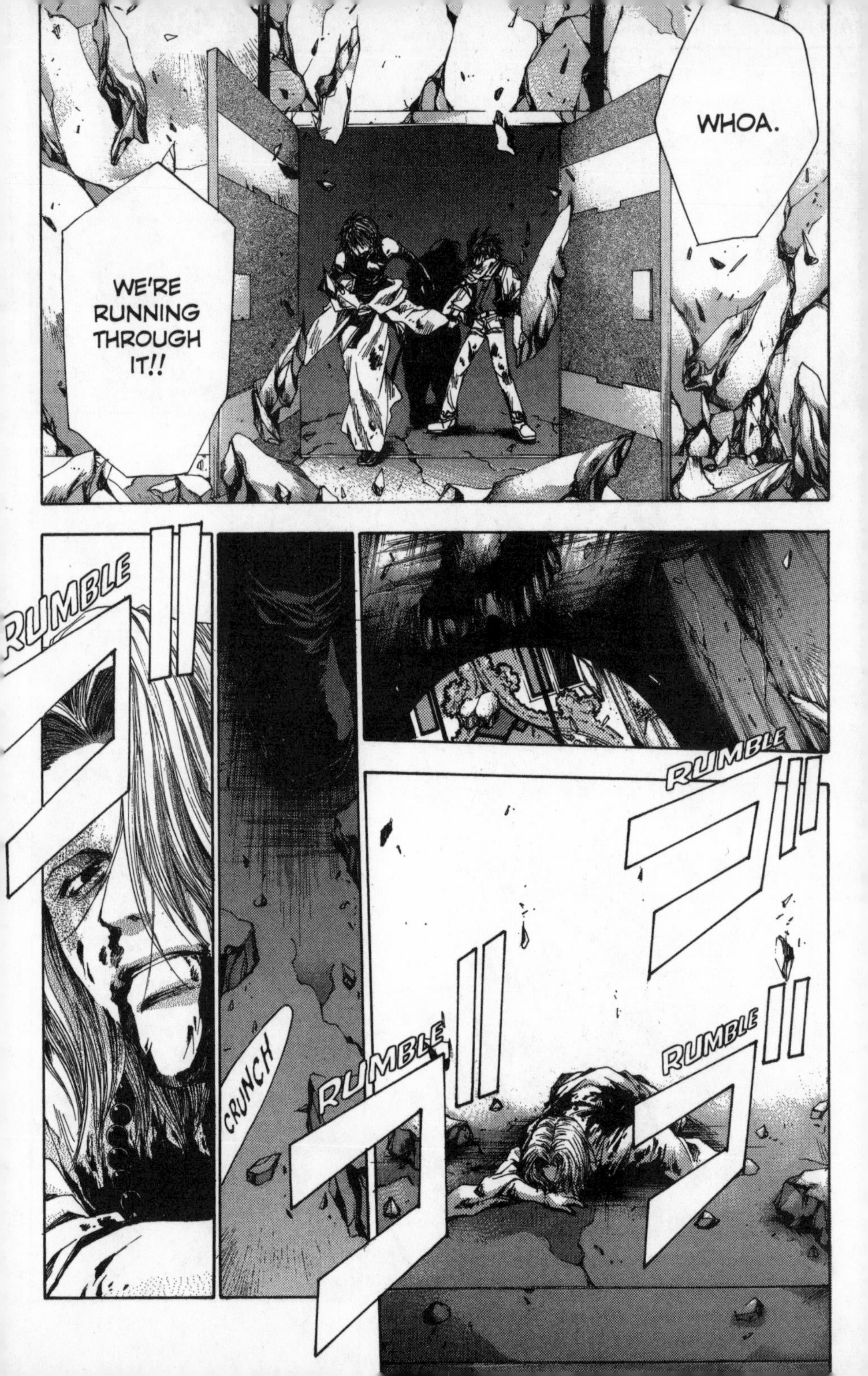
WHOA.
WE'RE RUNNING THROUGH IT!!
RUMBLE
RUMBLE
RUMBLE
CRUNCH
RUMBLE

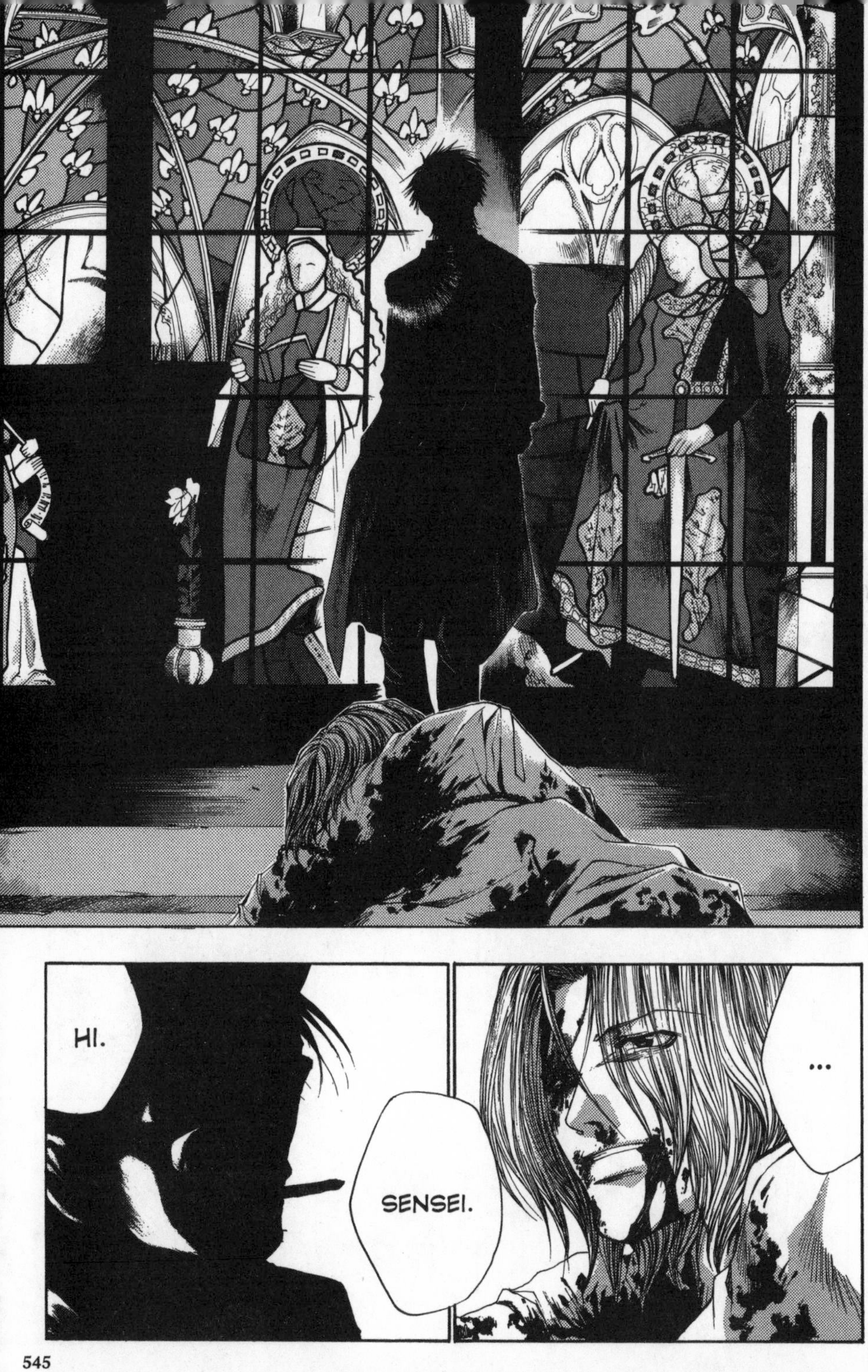
...
SENSEI.
HI.

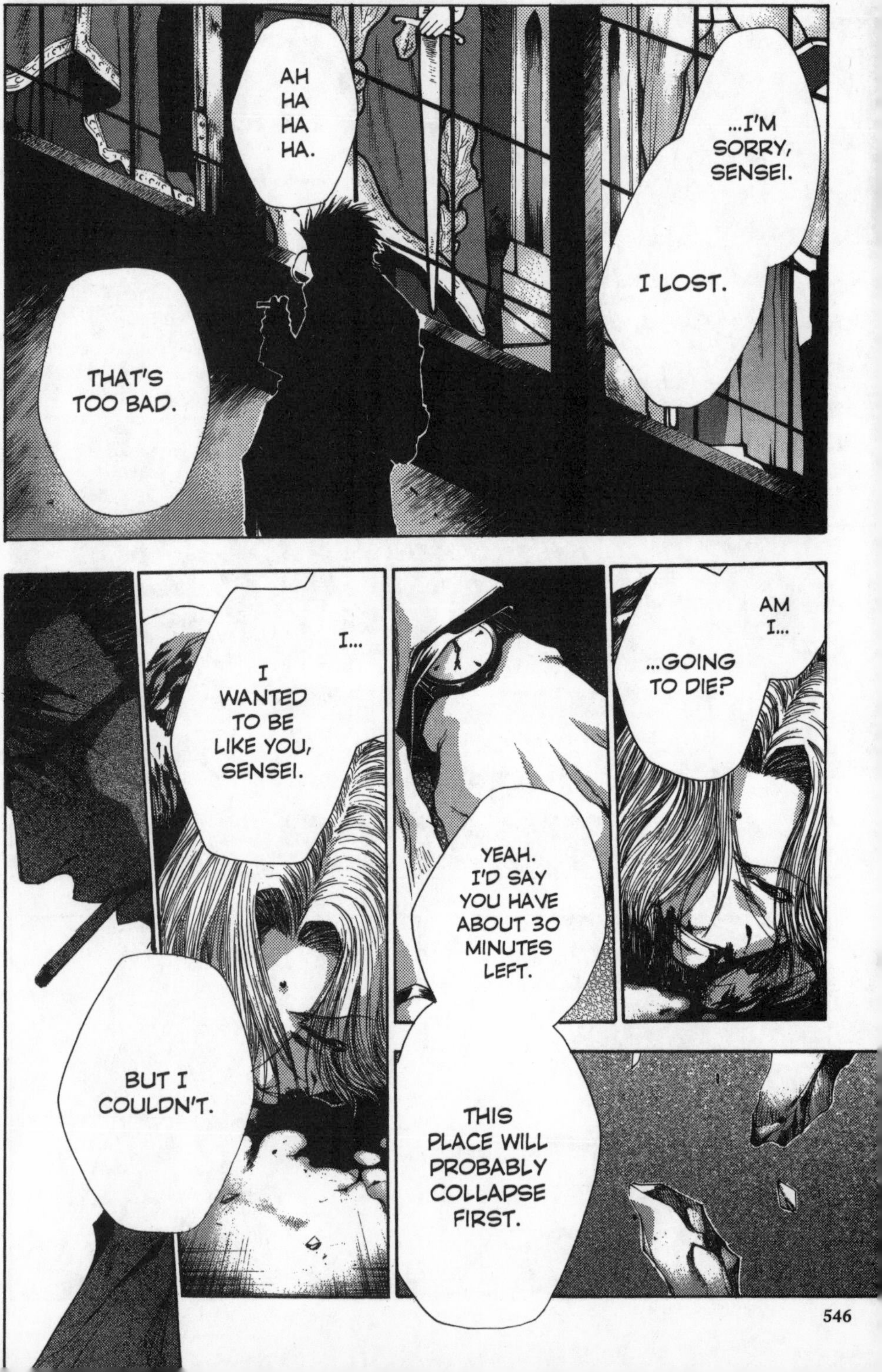
...I'M SORRY, SENSEI.
I LOST.
AH HA HA HA.
THAT'S TOO BAD.
AM I...
...GOING TO DIE?
YEAH. I'D SAY YOU HAVE ABOUT 30 MINUTES LEFT.
THIS PLACE WILL PROBABLY COLLAPSE FIRST.
I...
I WANTED TO BE LIKE YOU, SENSEI.
BUT I COULDN'T.

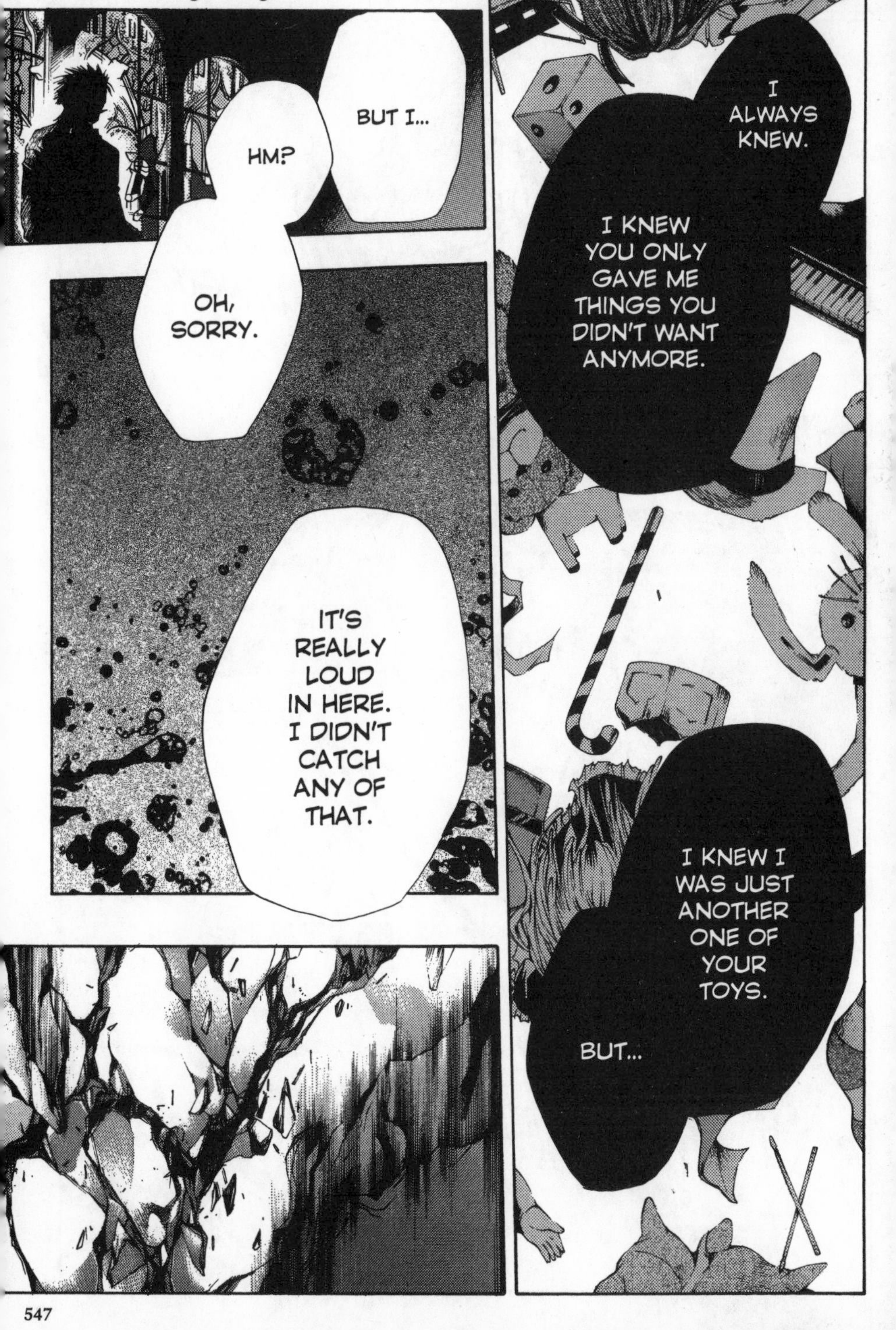
I ALWAYS KNEW.
I KNEW YOU ONLY GAVE ME THINGS YOU DIDN'T WANT ANYMORE.
I KNEW I WAS JUST ANOTHER ONE OF YOUR TOYS.
BUT...
BUT I...
HM?
OH, SORRY.
IT'S REALLY LOUD IN HERE. I DIDN'T CATCH ANY OF THAT.

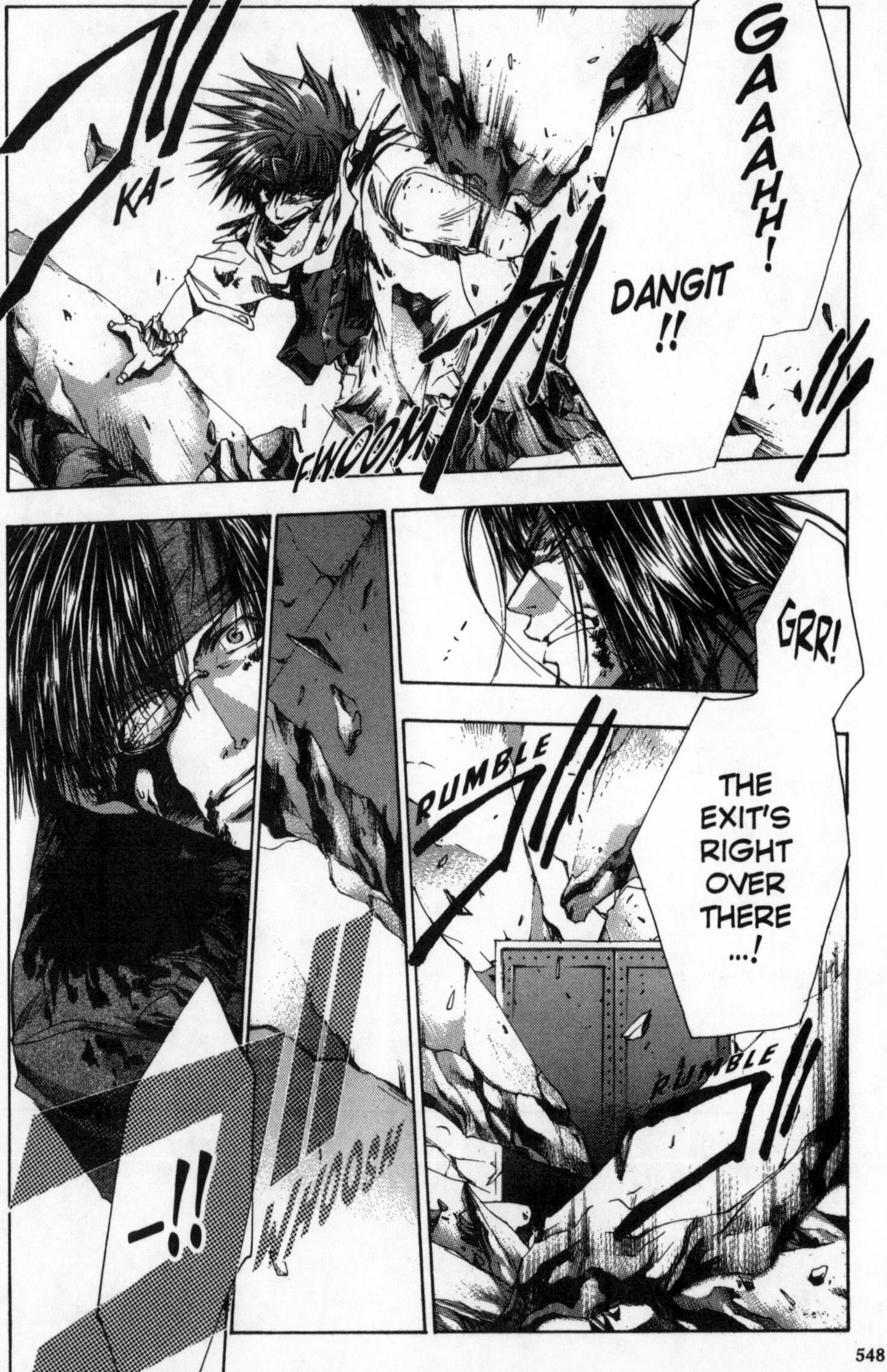
GAAAAHH!
DANGIT !!
KA-
FWOOM
GRR!
THE EXIT'S RIGHT OVER THERE ...!
RUMBLE
RUMBLE
WHOOSH
—!!

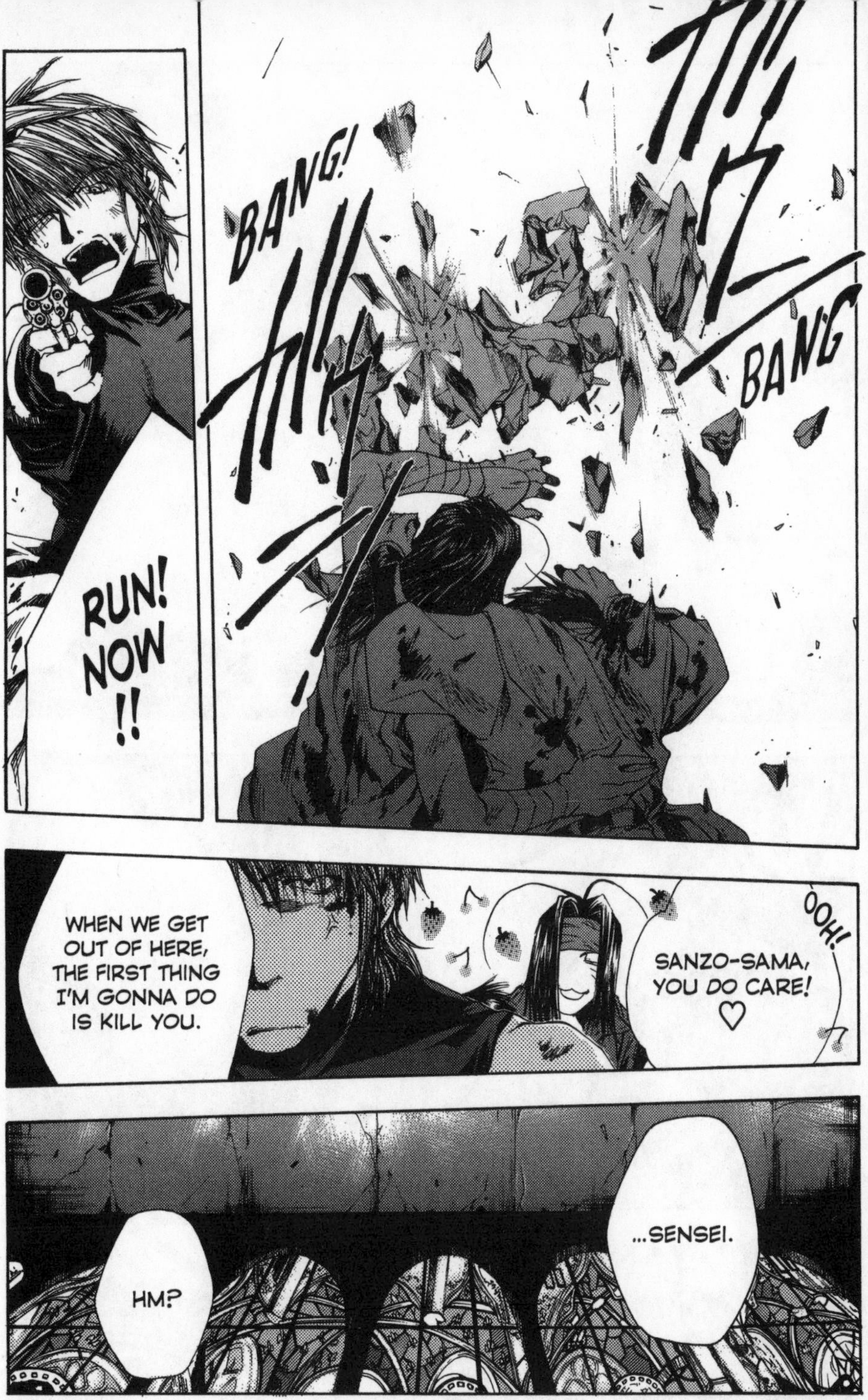
BANG!
BANG
RUN! NOW !!
OOH!
SANZO-SAMA, YOU DO CARE! ♡
WHEN WE GET OUT OF HERE, THE FIRST THING I'M GONNA DO IS KILL YOU.
...SENSEI.
HM?

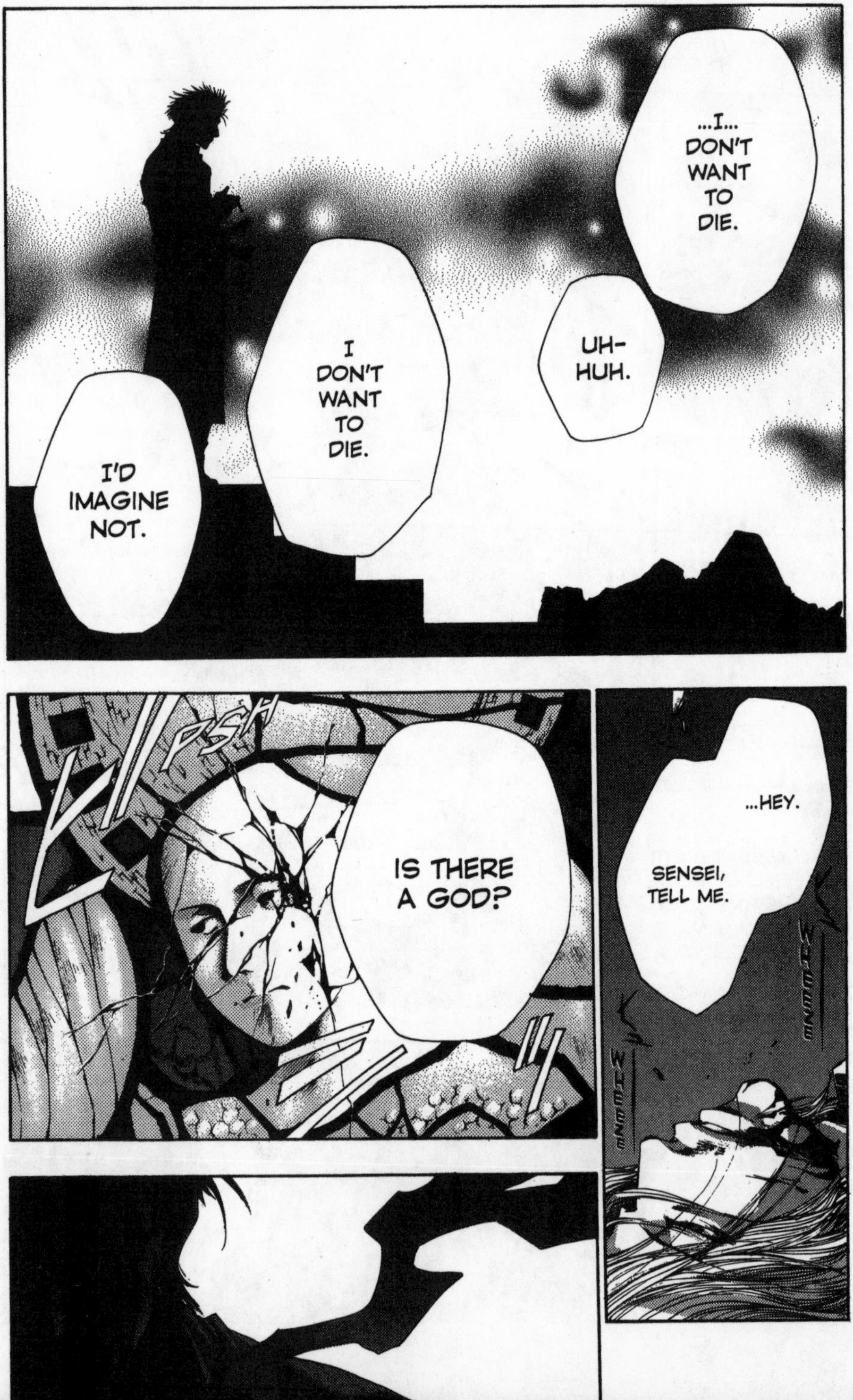
...I... DON'T WANT TO DIE.
UH-HUH.
I DON'T WANT TO DIE.
I'D IMAGINE NOT.
...HEY.
SENSEI, TELL ME.
WHEEZE
WHEEZE
PSH
IS THERE A GOD?

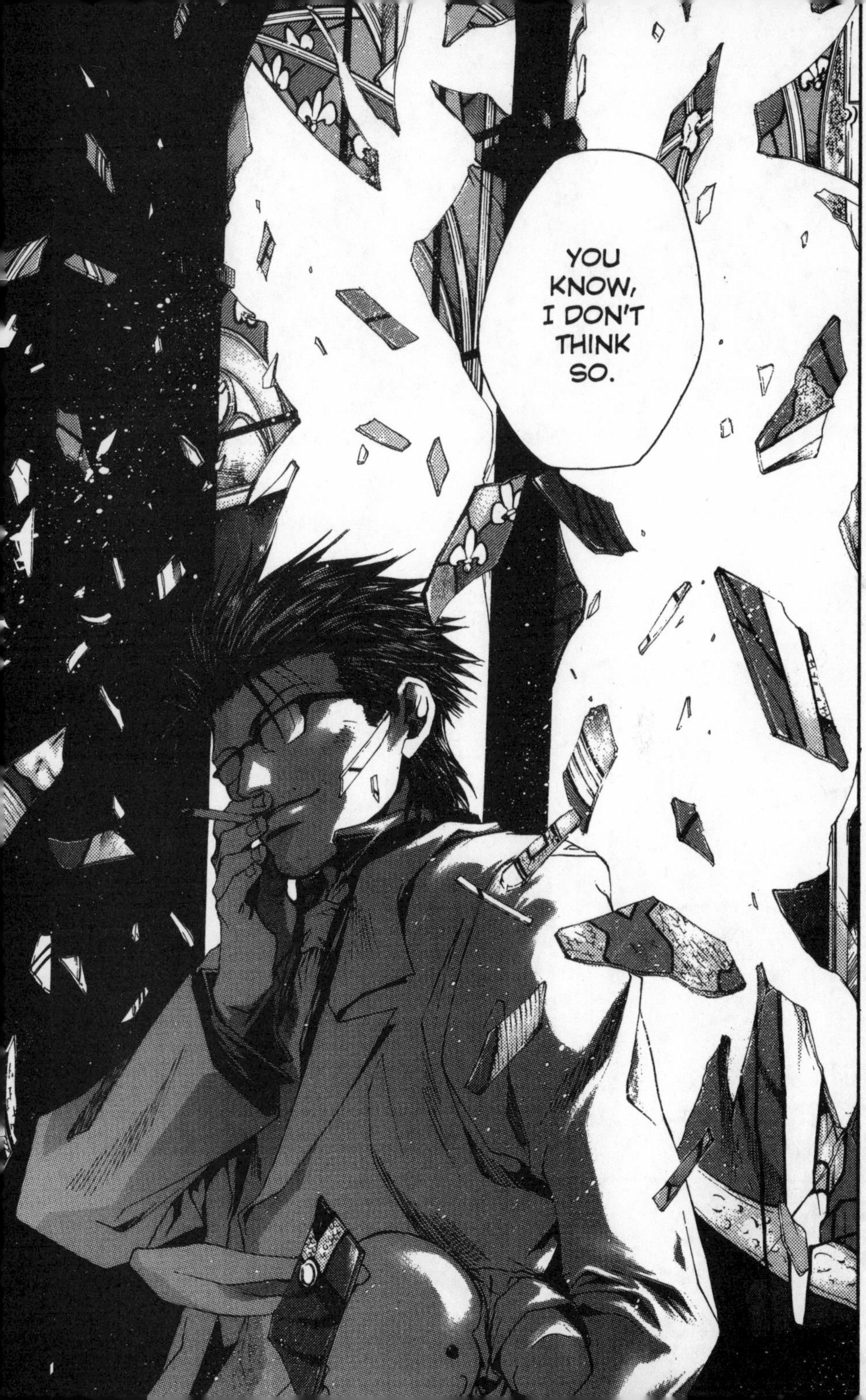
YOU KNOW, I DON'T THINK SO.

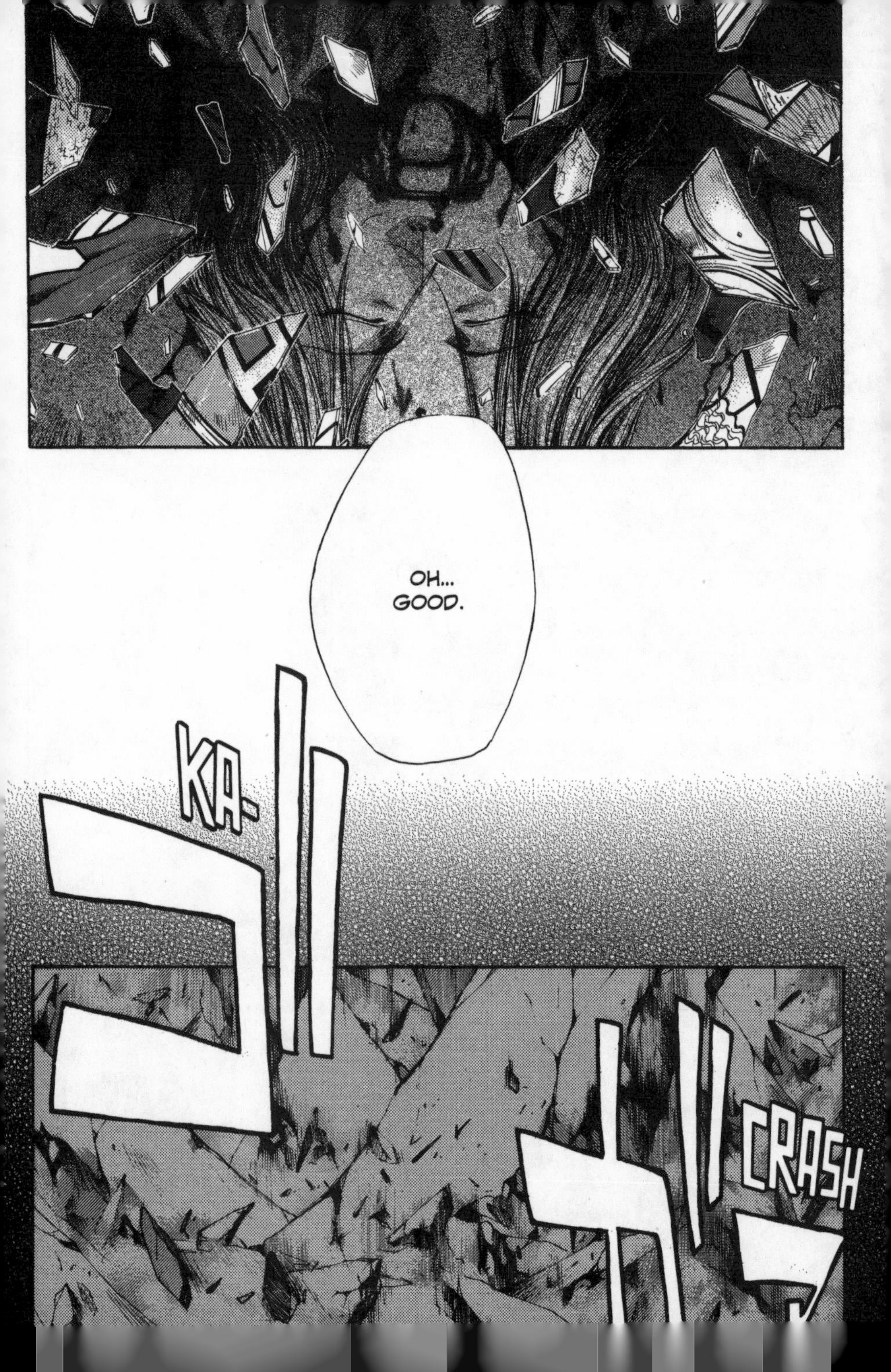
OH... GOOD.
KA-
CRASH

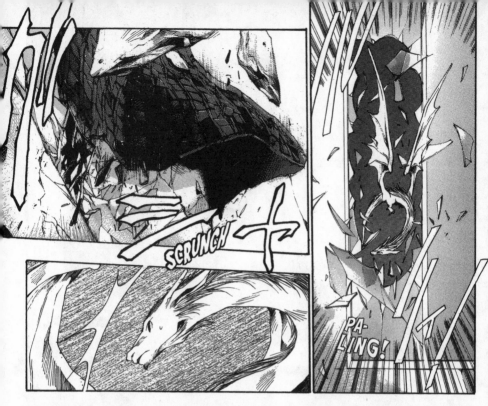

SCRUNCH

PA-LING!

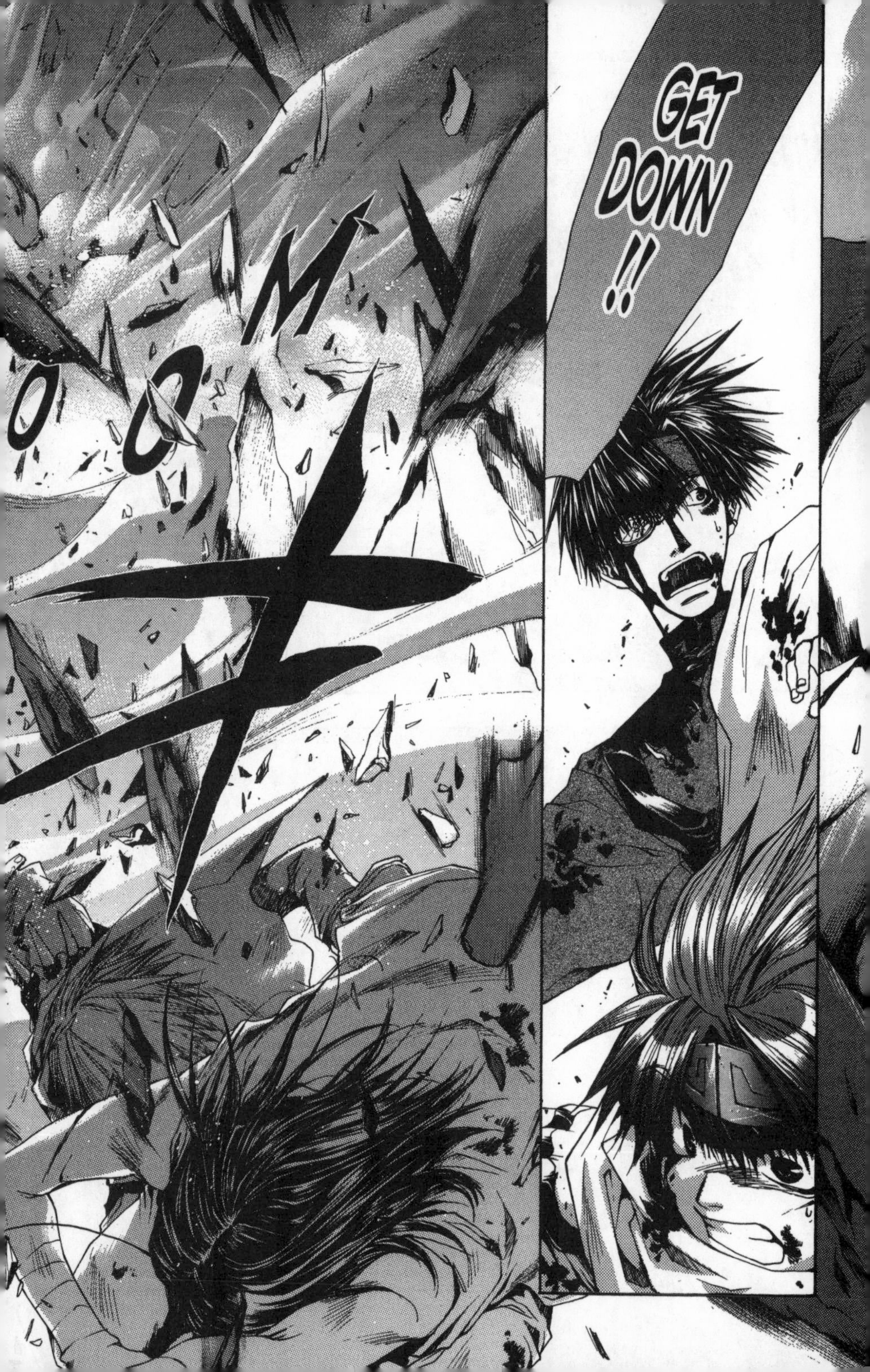
GET DOWN!!

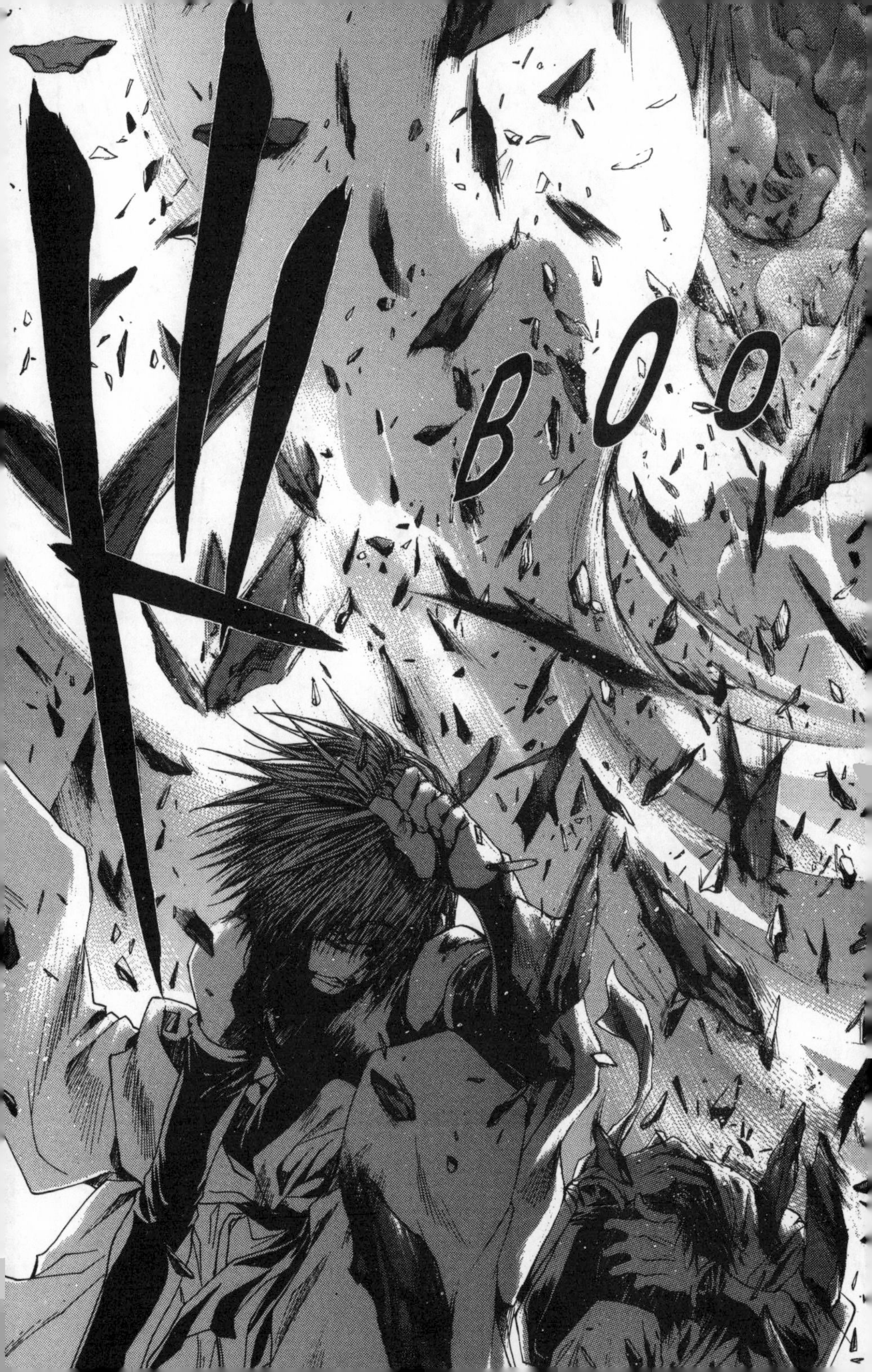
BOOO

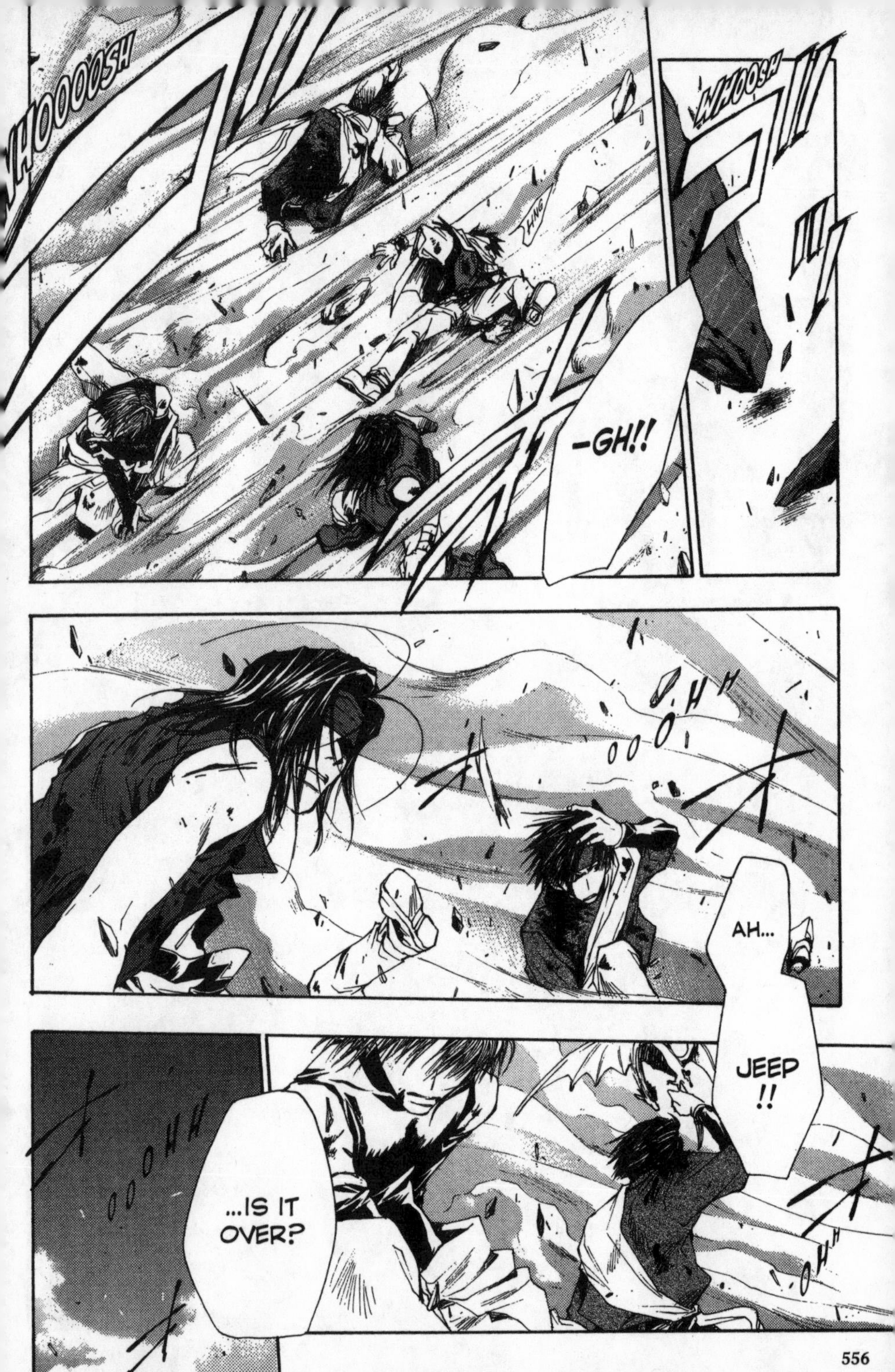
WHOOSH
-GH!!
HNG
WHOOOOSH
OOOHH
AH...
JEEP !!
OHH
...IS IT OVER?
OOOHH

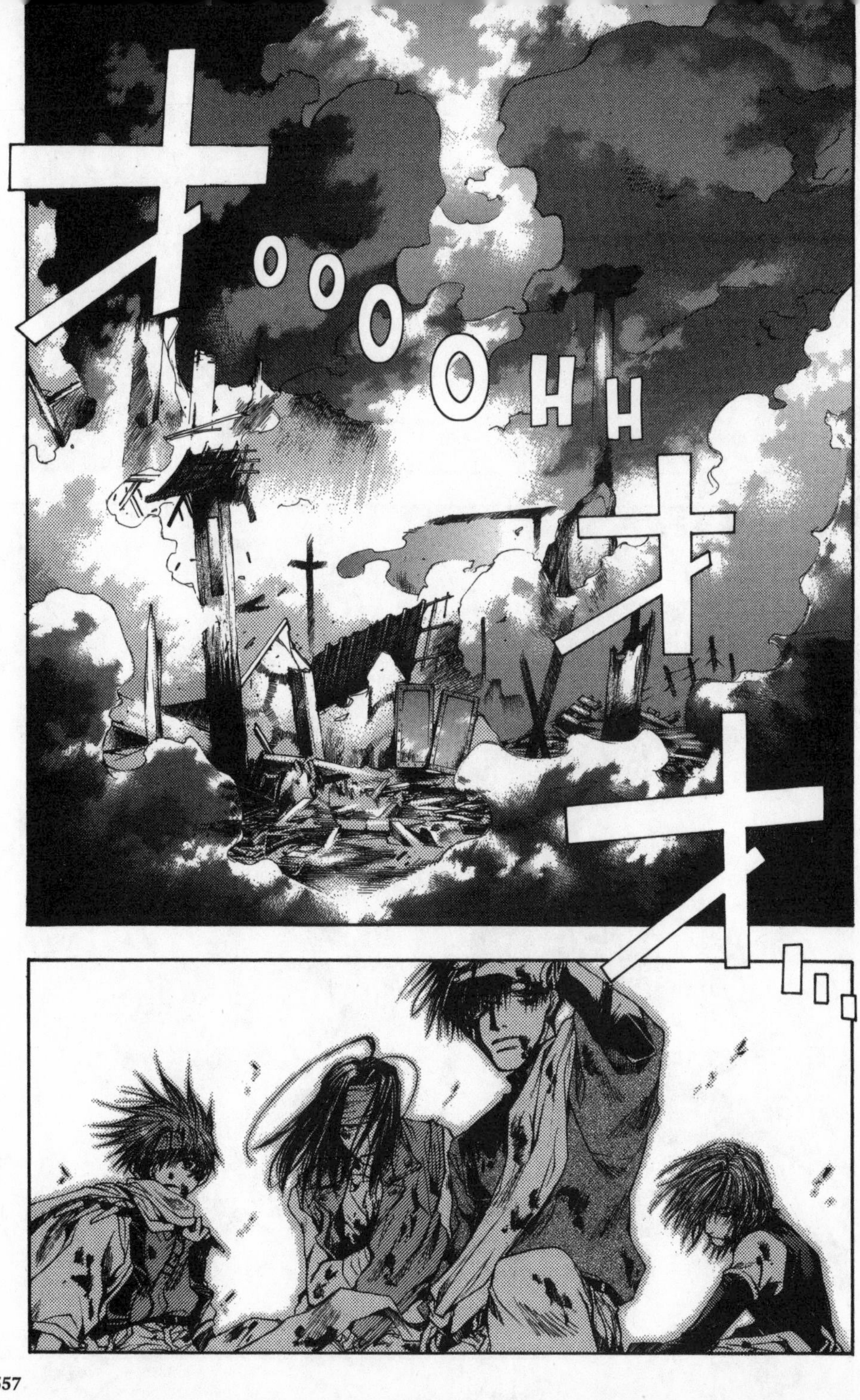
オOOOOHH
オオオ...

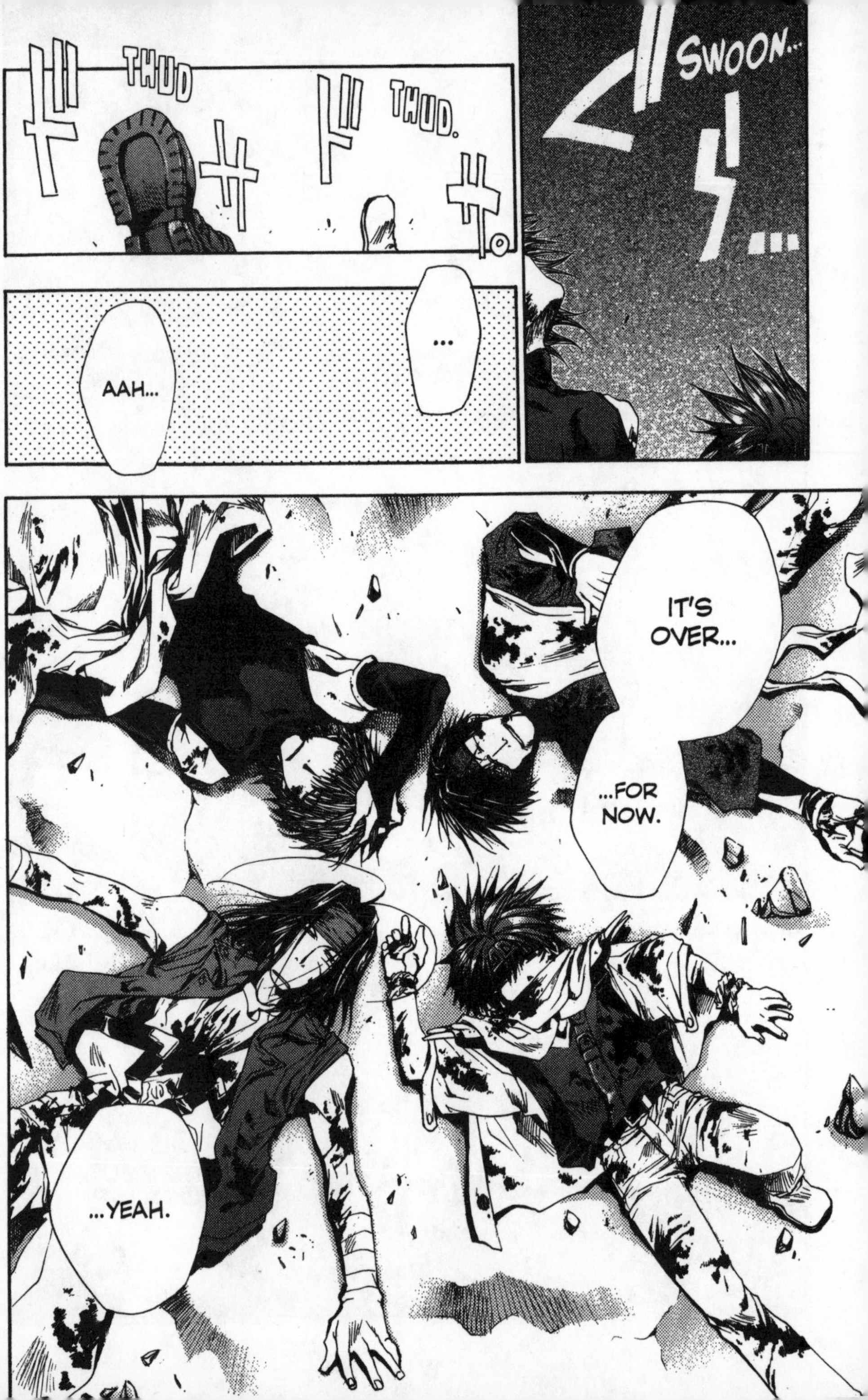
SWOON...
THUD
THUD.
...
AAH...
IT'S OVER...
...FOR NOW.
...YEAH.

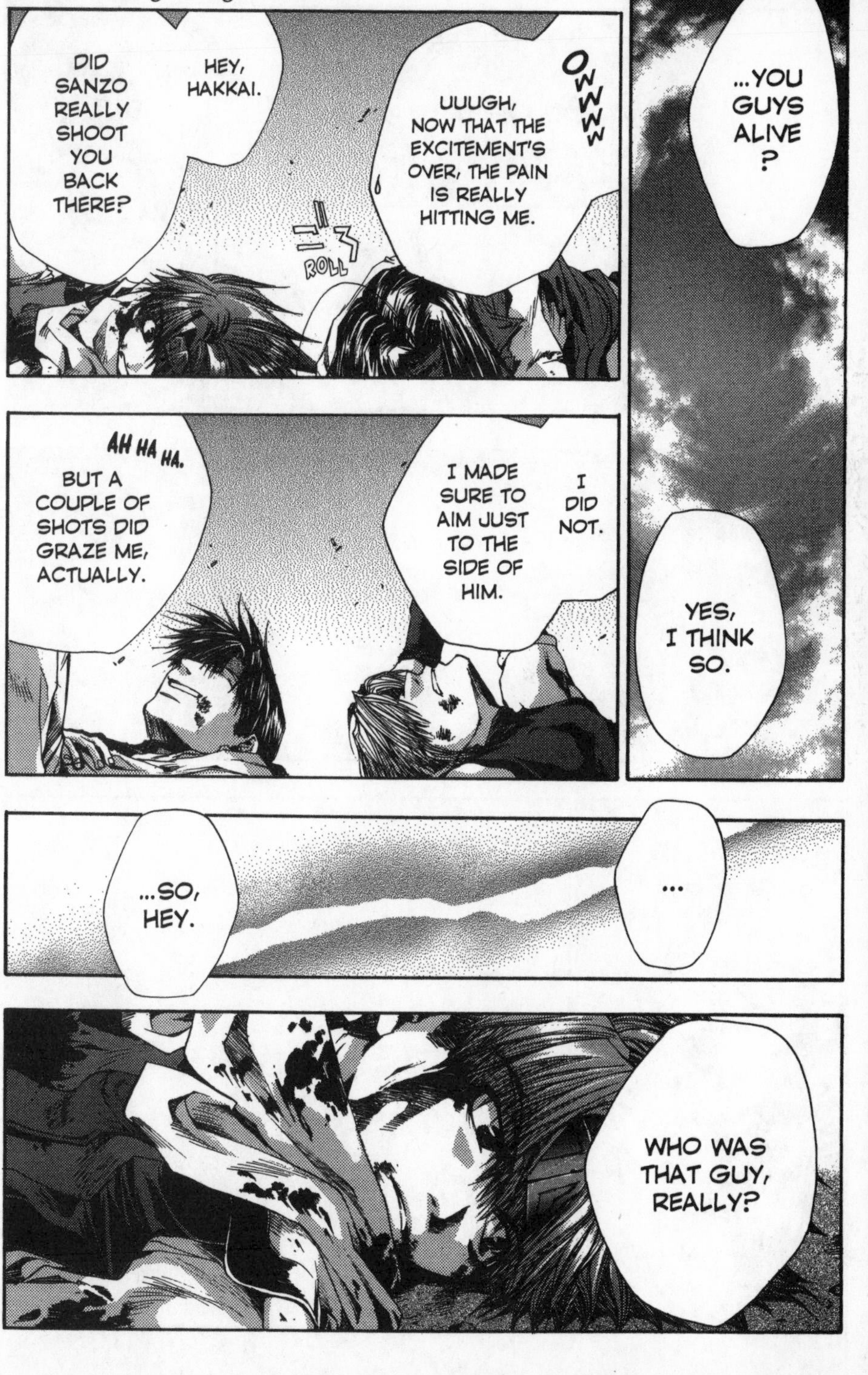
...YOU GUYS ALIVE?
YES, I THINK SO.
OWWWW
UUUGH, NOW THAT THE EXCITEMENT'S OVER, THE PAIN IS REALLY HITTING ME.
ROLL
HEY, HAKKAI.
DID SANZO REALLY SHOOT YOU BACK THERE?
I DID NOT.
I MADE SURE TO AIM JUST TO THE SIDE OF HIM.
AH HA HA.
BUT A COUPLE OF SHOTS DID GRAZE ME, ACTUALLY.
...
...SO, HEY.
WHO WAS THAT GUY, REALLY?

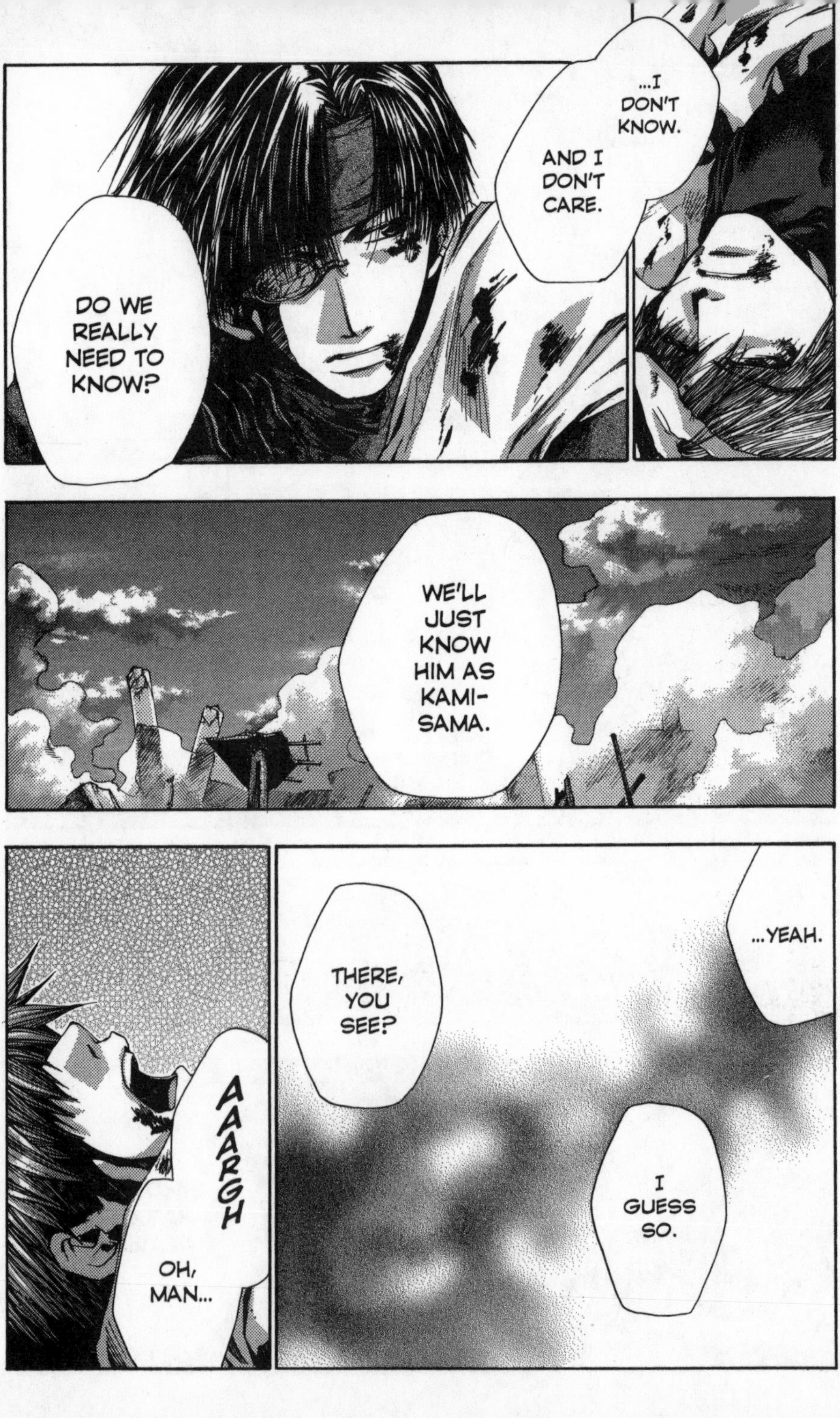
...I DON'T KNOW.
AND I DON'T CARE.
DO WE REALLY NEED TO KNOW?
WE'LL JUST KNOW HIM AS KAMI-SAMA.
...YEAH.
THERE, YOU SEE?
I GUESS SO.
AAARGH
OH, MAN...

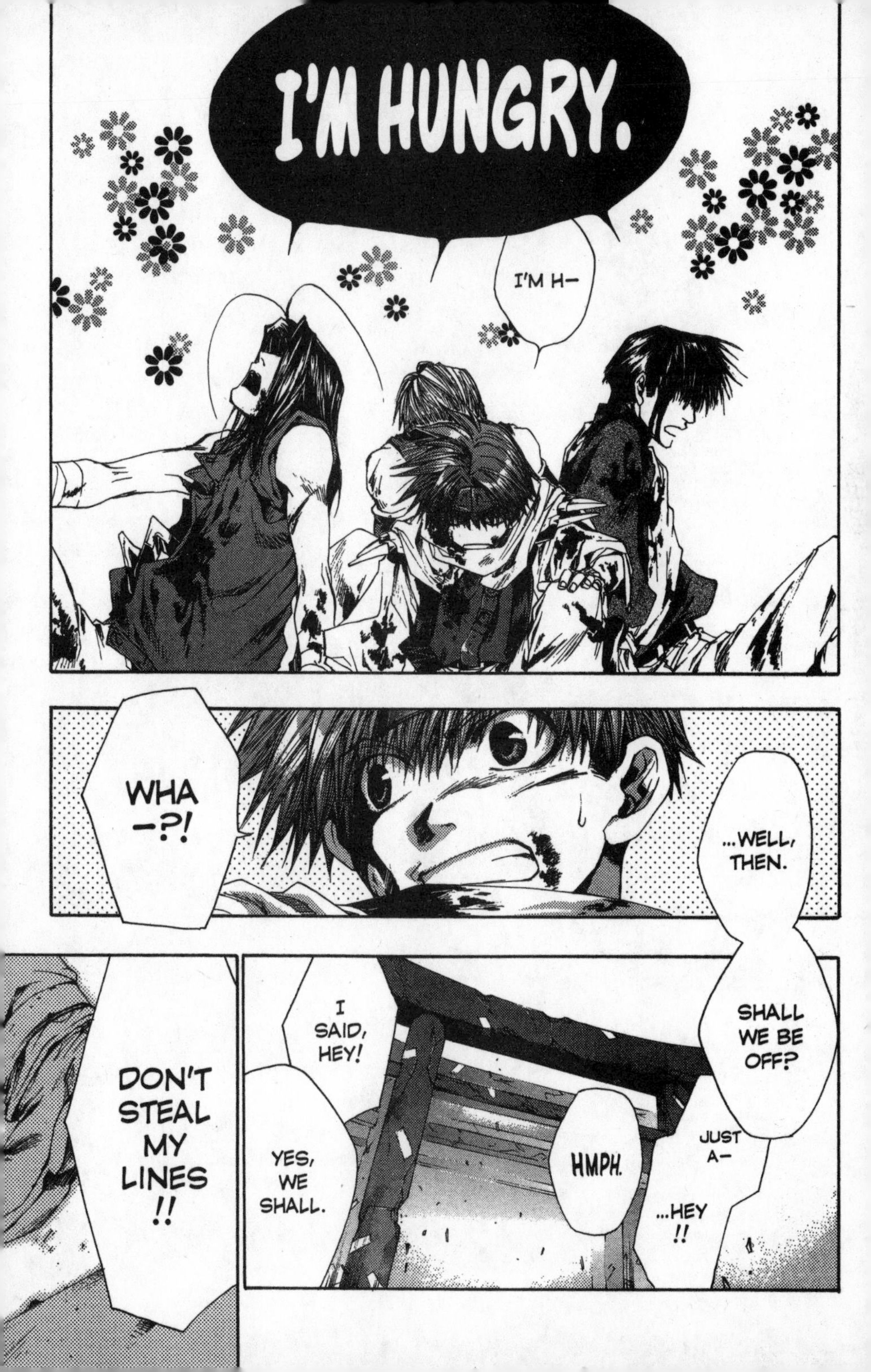
I'M HUNGRY.
I'M H—
WHA —?!
...WELL, THEN.
SHALL WE BE OFF?
YES, WE SHALL.
HMPH.
JUST A—
...HEY !!
I SAID, HEY!
DON'T STEAL MY LINES !!

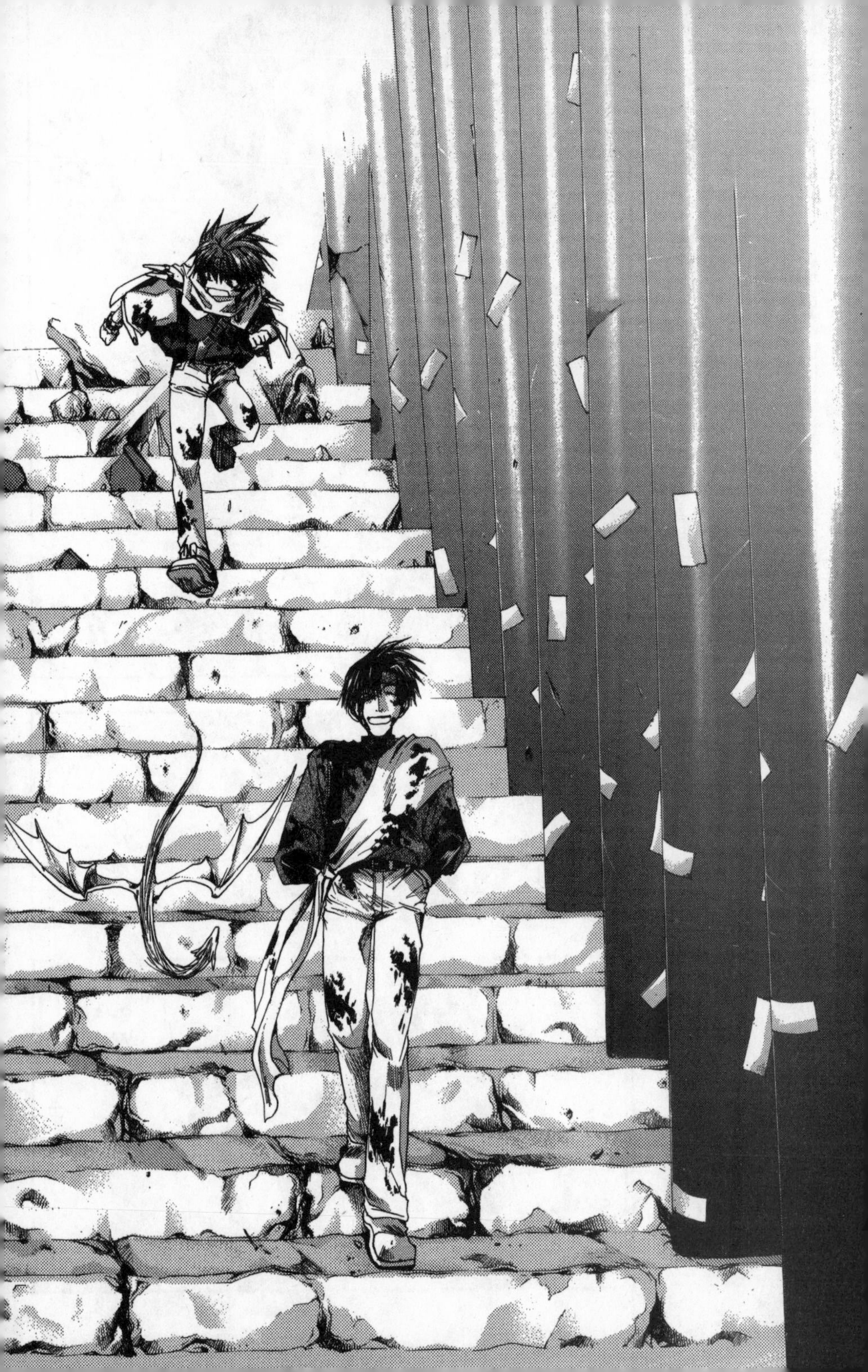

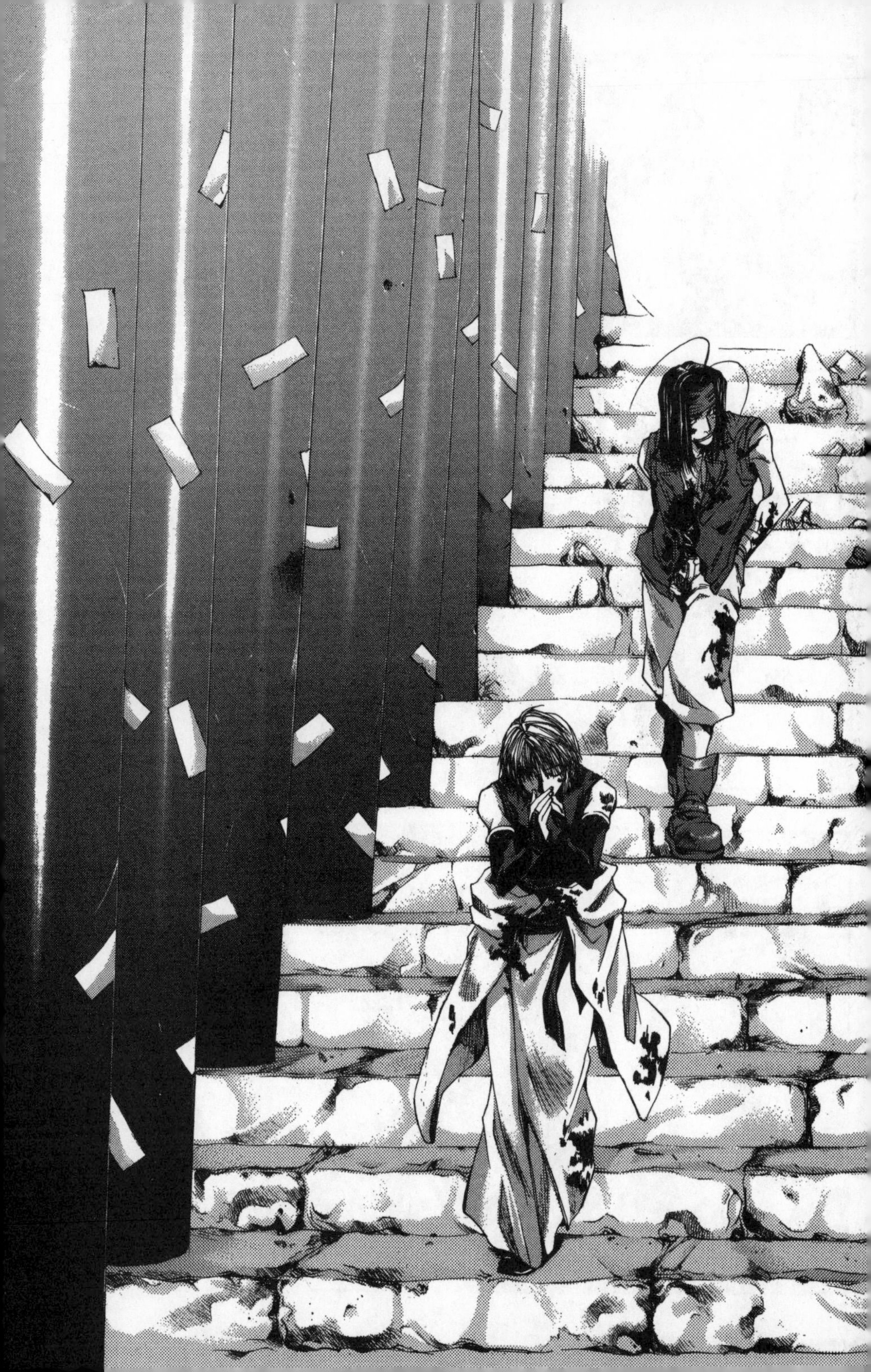

...MY, MY, MY.

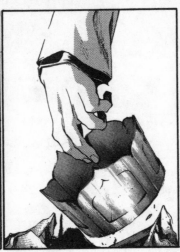

NOW, THEN...

YOU HAVE LEFT ME SOMETHING VERY INTERESTING,

HAVEN'T YOU, KOUMYOU?

CHAPTER 55: Falling. Rising.

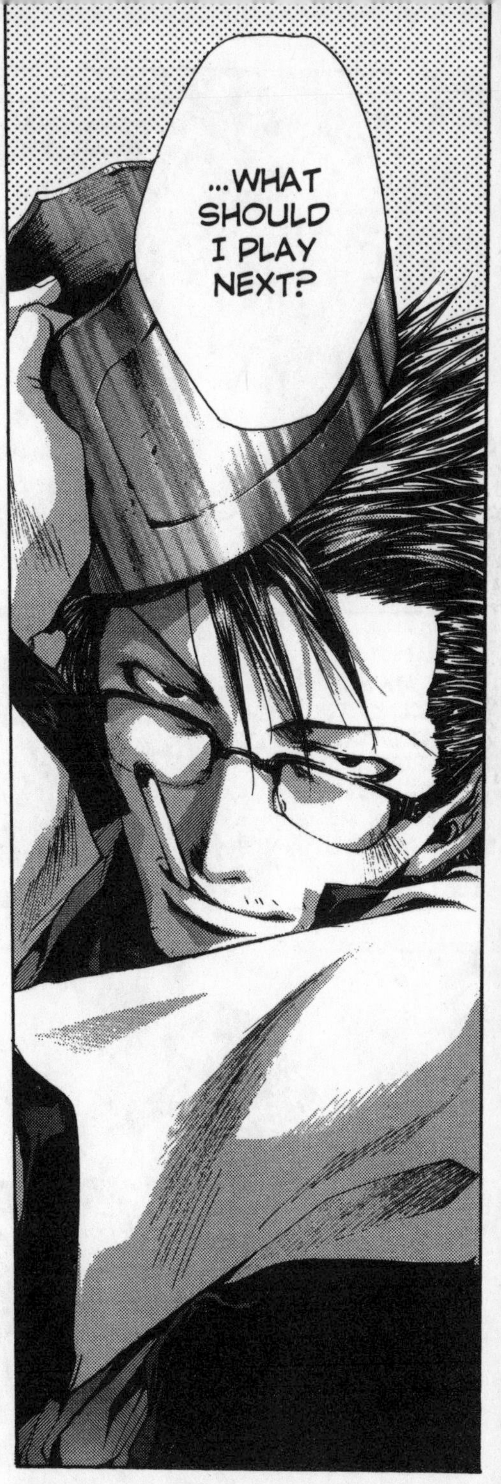
...WHAT SHOULD I PLAY NEXT?

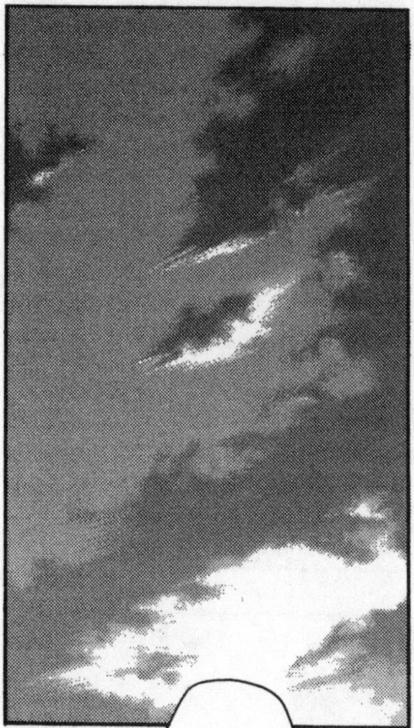

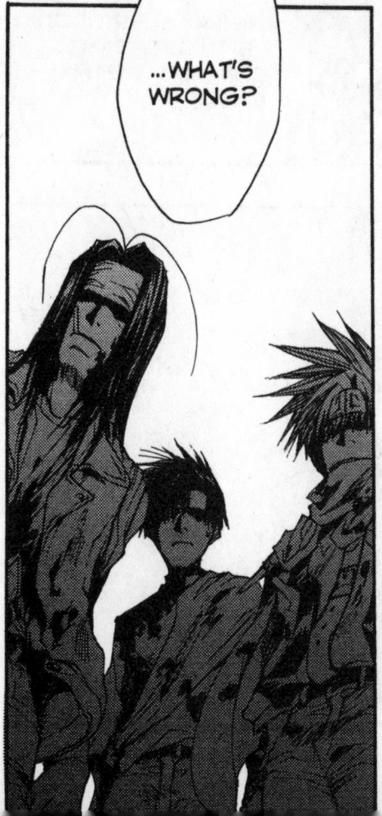
...WHAT'S WRONG?

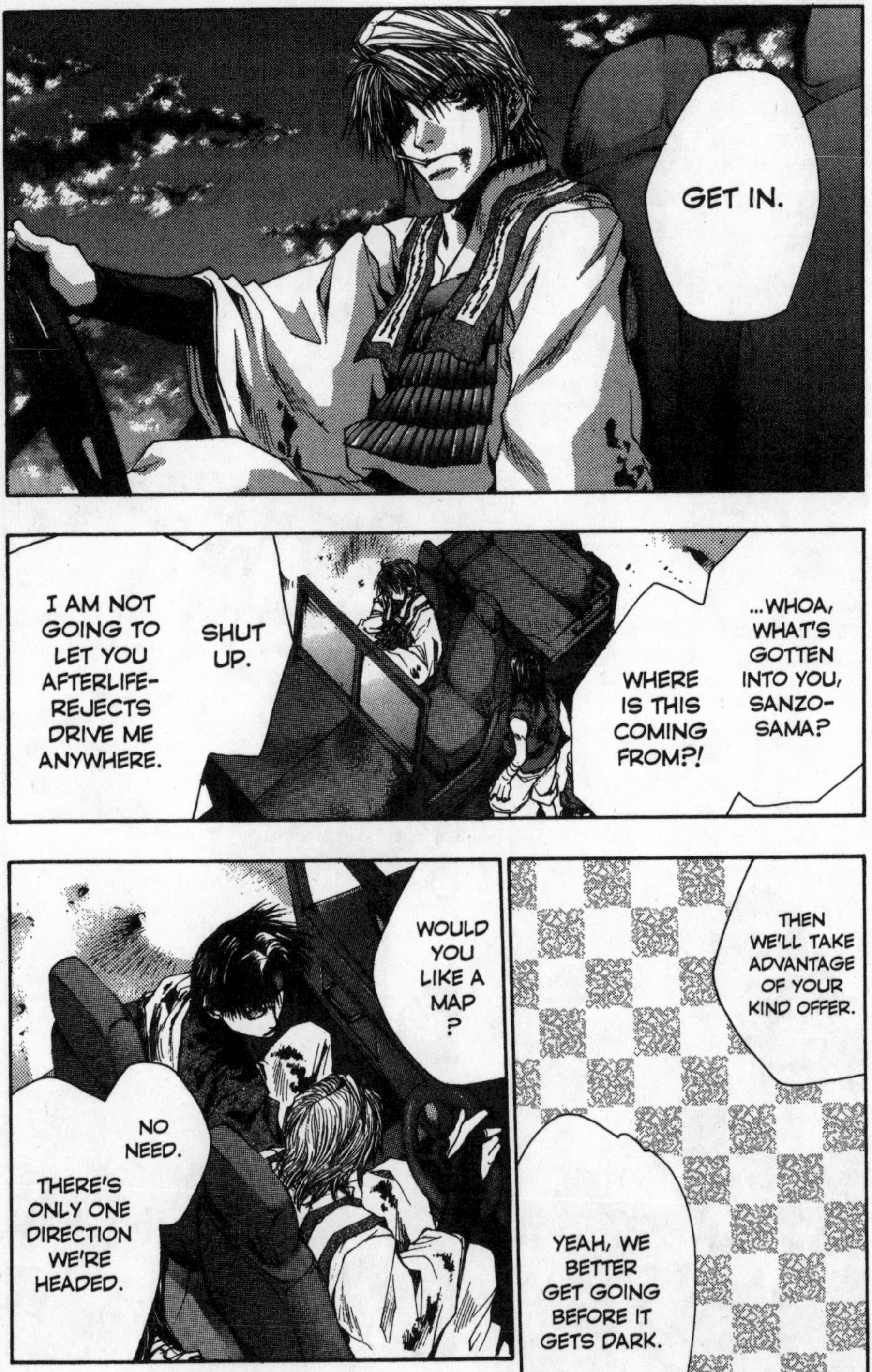
GET IN.
...WHOA, WHAT'S GOTTEN INTO YOU, SANZO-SAMA?
WHERE IS THIS COMING FROM?!
SHUT UP.
I AM NOT GOING TO LET YOU AFTERLIFE-REJECTS DRIVE ME ANYWHERE.
THEN WE'LL TAKE ADVANTAGE OF YOUR KIND OFFER.
YEAH, WE BETTER GET GOING BEFORE IT GETS DARK.
WOULD YOU LIKE A MAP?
NO NEED.
THERE'S ONLY ONE DIRECTION WE'RE HEADED.

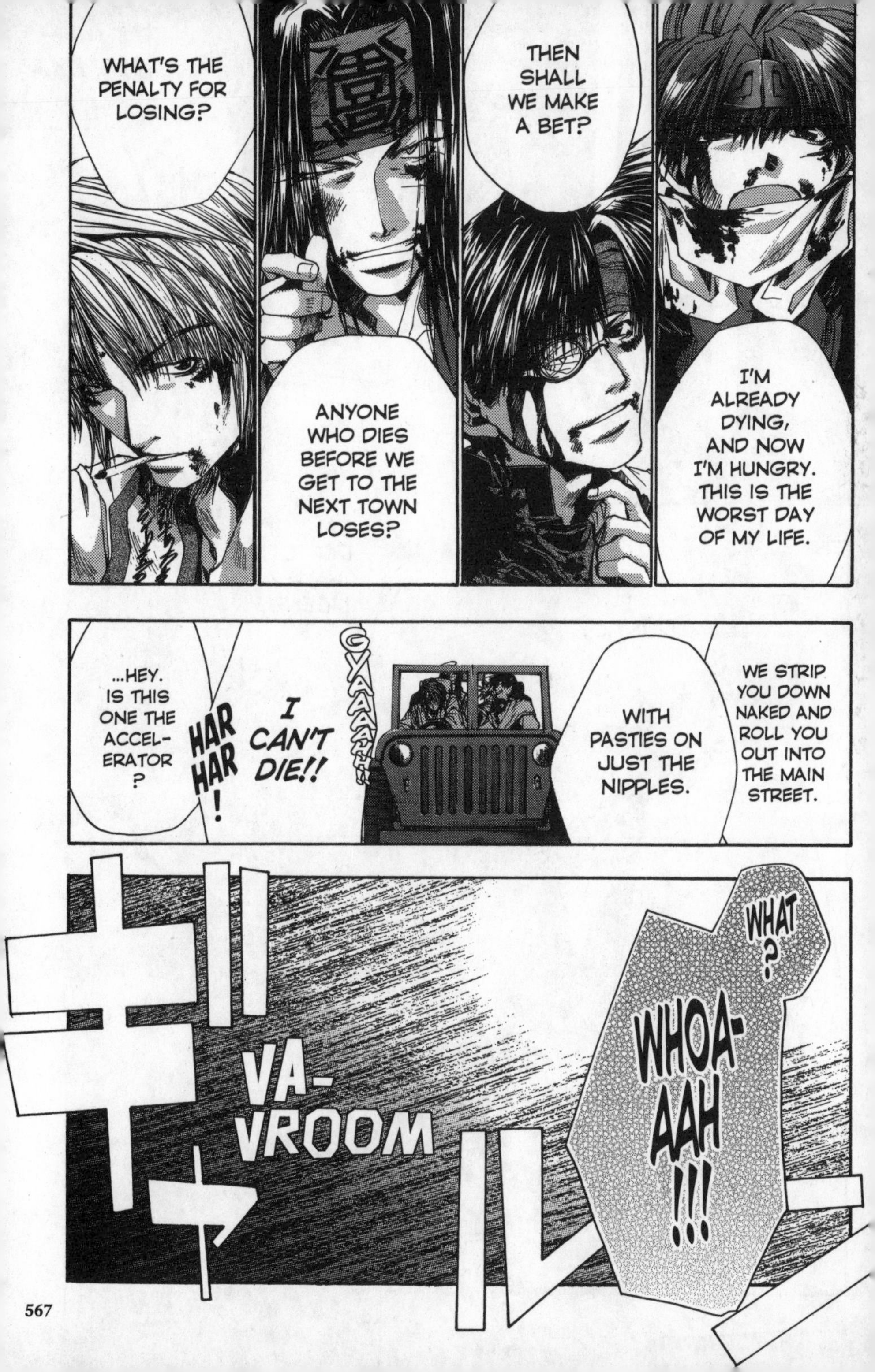
I'M ALREADY DYING, AND NOW I'M HUNGRY. THIS IS THE WORST DAY OF MY LIFE.
THEN SHALL WE MAKE A BET?
ANYONE WHO DIES BEFORE WE GET TO THE NEXT TOWN LOSES?
WHAT'S THE PENALTY FOR LOSING?
WE STRIP YOU DOWN NAKED AND ROLL YOU OUT INTO THE MAIN STREET.
WITH PASTIES ON JUST THE NIPPLES.
GYAAAAH!
I CAN'T DIE!!
HAR HAR!
...HEY. IS THIS ONE THE ACCELERATOR?
WHAT?
WHOA-AAH!!!
VA-VROOM

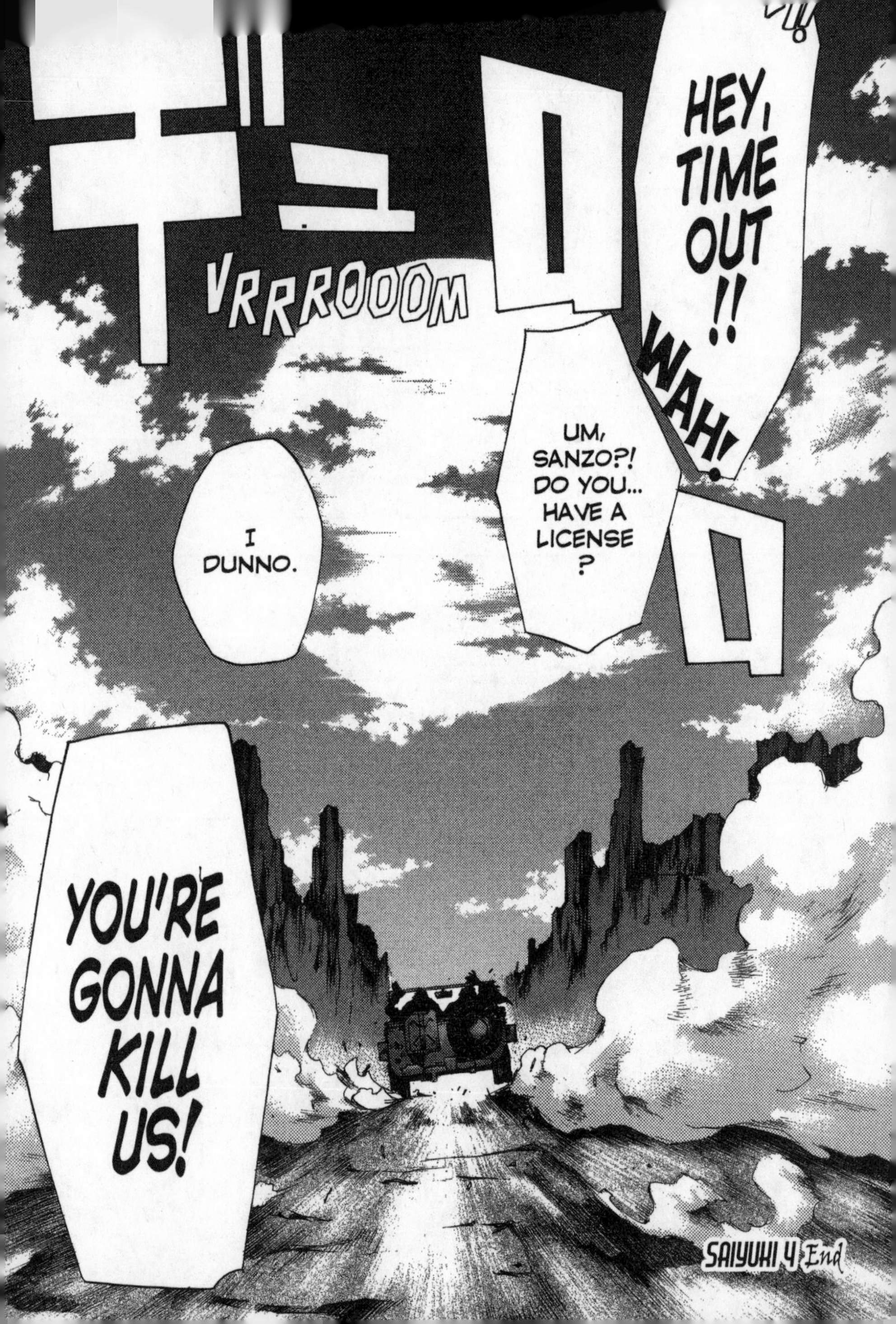
HEY, TIME OUT!!
VRRROOOM
WAH!
UM, SANZO?! DO YOU... HAVE A LICENSE?
I DUNNO.
YOU'RE GONNA KILL US!
SAIYUKI 4 End

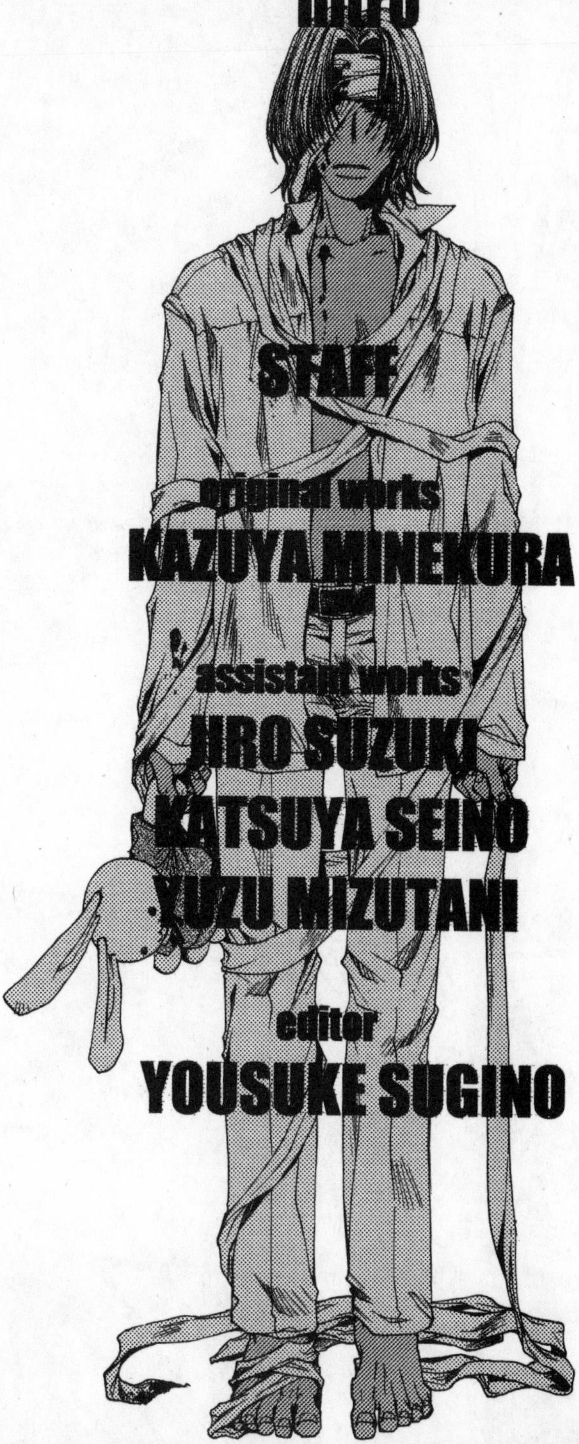
"nitro"
STAFF
original works
KAZUYA MINEKURA
assistant works
JIRO SUZUKI
KATSUYA SEINO
YUZU MIZUTANI
editor
YOUSUKE SUGINO

From the storyboard

THE KAMI-SAMA ARC,
ALSO KNOWN AS THE DETOUR ARC.

MINEKURA: THIS ARC HAS BEEN KIND OF AN EXPERIMENT, WHERE I TRIED ALL KINDS OF THINGS. FOR SANZO AND HIS GANG, NOT ONLY WAS IT LONG, ARDUOUS, AND FREAKING ANNOYING, BUT IT DIDN'T TAKE THEM A SINGLE STEP FORWARD IN THEIR JOURNEY (HA HA). ...JUST LIKE THE BOYS THEMSELVES, IT SEEMS LIKE SOMETHING HAS CHANGED, BUT ACTUALLY NOTHING HAS CHANGED. AND I'M LIKE, EH, THAT'S OKAY. I'M SURE THAT'S HOW THEY FELT AS THEY STARTED UP THEIR JOURNEY AGAIN.

RIGHT SIDE (clockwise from top left)
pages 525, 522, & 526

LEFT SIDE (clockwise from top left)
pages 523, 527, 518, 524, 528

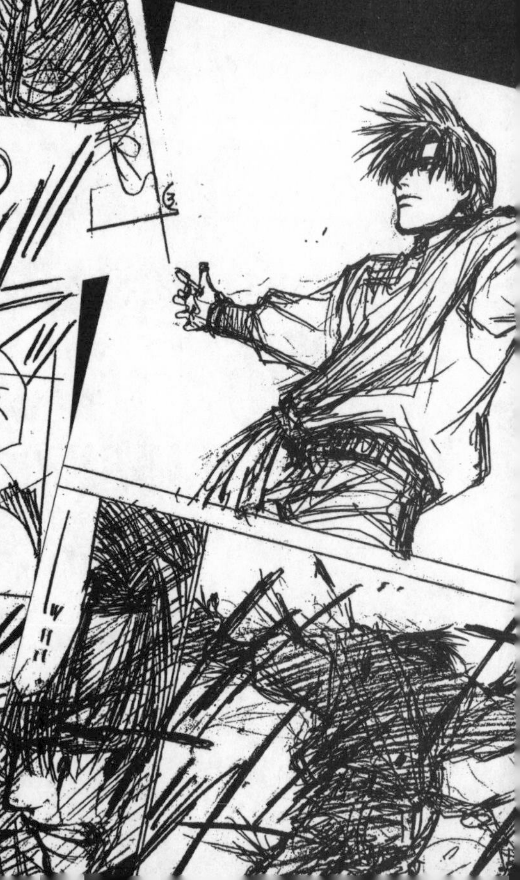

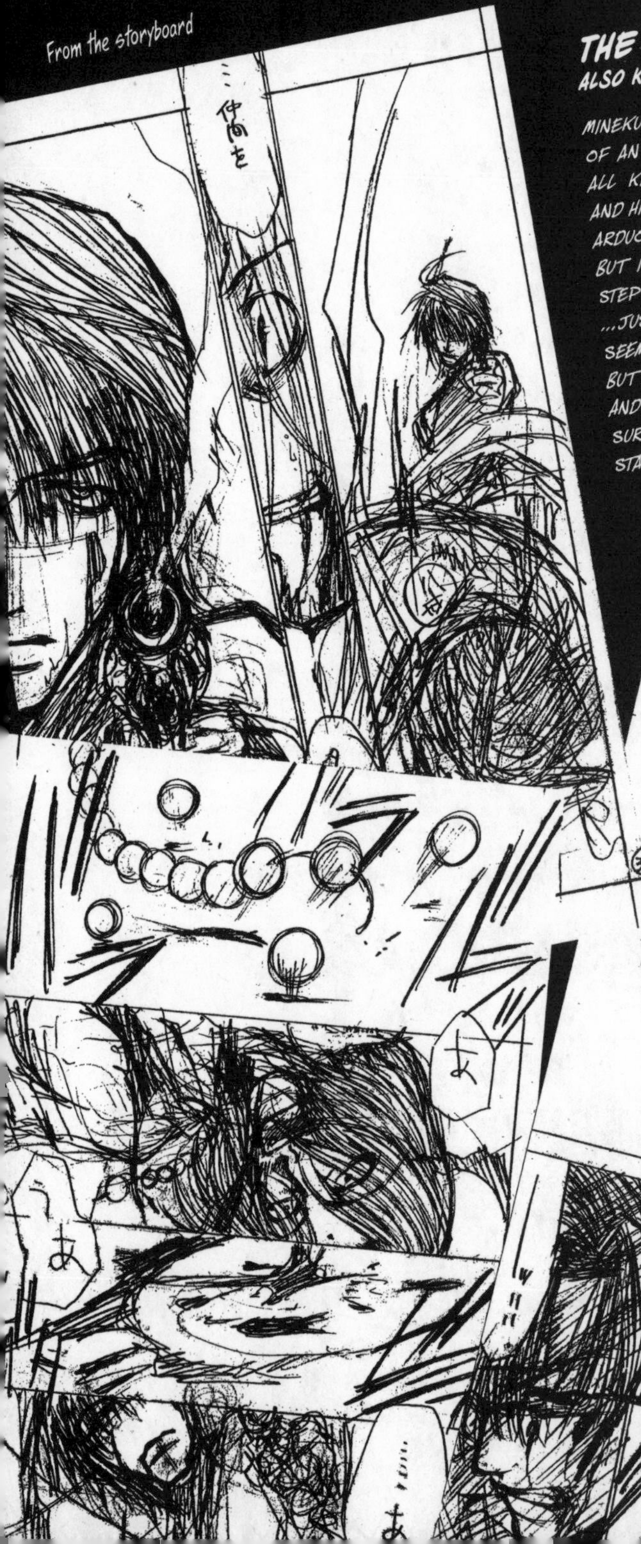

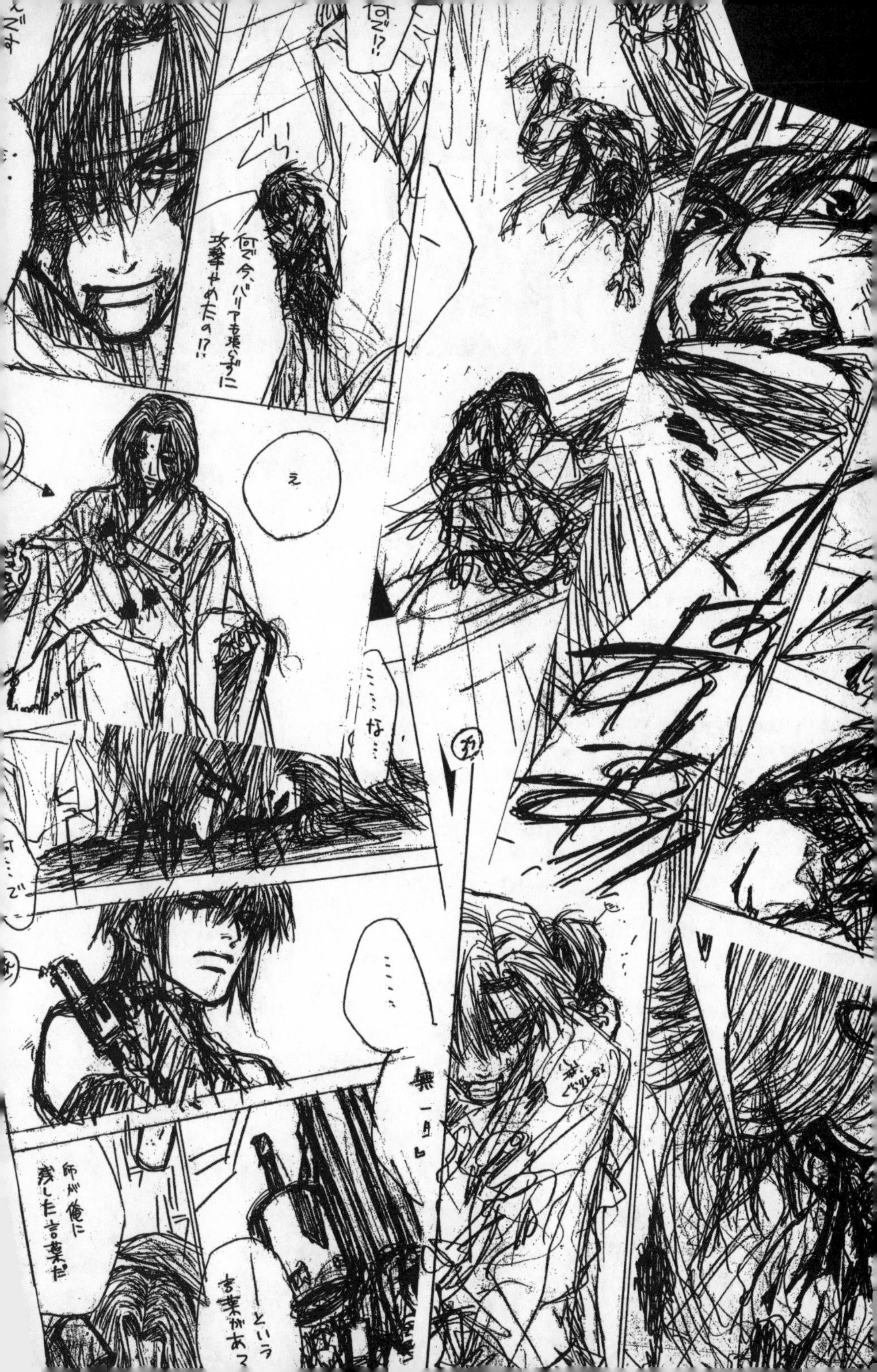

・・・
何で!?
ぐら
何で今、バリアも張らずに攻撃やめたの!?
んです
……
え
……な……
何……で……
……
——という言葉があって
師が俺に残した言葉だ

Interview with Saiyuki Creator

KAZUYA MINEKURA

EXCERPTED FROM THE SAIYUKI CHARACTER BOOK: SANZO AND GOKU

"Every character has someone to console them when they get down and someone to support them."

are four characters to work with. Recently, Sanzo and Goku have a full-on grandfather-grandson relationship going on (lol). In the past, Sanzo was still like a father, though…

Sanzo's the only one who ended up aging (lol).

MINEKURA: For the most part, the grandson is also growing, but the father got pretty far ahead and became a grandpa (lol). But even though it would be strange to say that's the reason why, you can see the most unexpected side of Sanzo when he's with Goku. Sanzo's expressions are softest when he's just speaking alone with Goku. When he's talking with the other two, if the topic of could have these two characters tag into the scene when I want the story to progress, or I could have these other two characters together when I want to take my time and explain things in a settled manner. Sanzo and Hakkai are a good example. When just those two appear together, I set things up so that Sanzo brings something up by asking, "What do you think?" and Hakkai goes into "explanation time" in reply. Each character has someone to console them when they get down and someone to support them. Moreover, the way things are presented changes depending on the characters involved, so it's convenient—or rather, I'm glad that there

THE MOST COMFORTABLE COMBINATION...

♦ ♦ ♦

In addition to the amusing interactions between the four main characters in *Saiyuki,* some of the more appealing aspects of the series are the different moods and relationships between each pairing. Were you aware of certain "pairs" as you were working on this manga?

MINEKURA: I enjoyed being able to draw the characters in various forms depending on the specific combination. It was helpful, too. Like, I

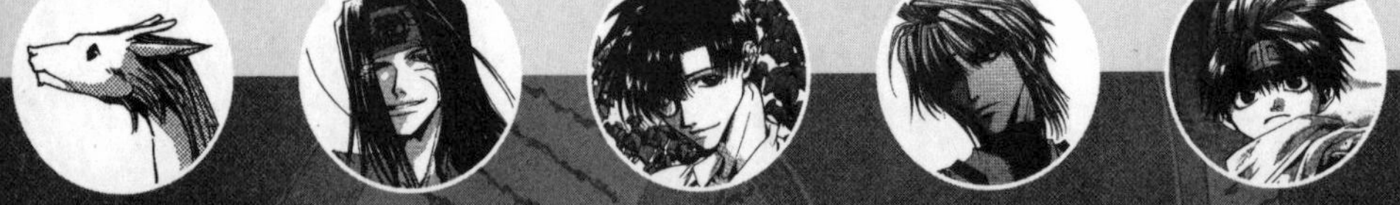

who he is, interprets that as, "Sanzo is entrusting me with this, so I'll move things forward," and then he just moves ahead with things on his own. And no one around Hakkai has any complaints. If Sanzo says something, Goku and Gojyo might be against it, but in Hakkai's case, they would be like, "Well, if Hakkai says so…" (lol).

It seems like Gojyo just says whatever he wants even when he's with someone like Hakkai.

MINEKURA: Being with Hakkai is most natural for Gojyo—or rather, he feels the most relaxed around Hakkai. They're friends of equal standing, or there's a feeling of them being on the same level. Hakkai is particularly nagging when it comes to Gojyo, but all of his lecturing goes in one ear and out the other for Gojyo. He can be like a bad husband who disregards his wife's constant pleas to put his socks in the washing machine.

And yet it seems like Hakkai doesn't get fed up with him.

Sanzo also treats Hakkai as if he were the adult of the group.

MINEKURA: The original relationship between Hakkai and Sanzo was that of a criminal and his probation officer. And because of that, at first, Sanzo was very distant to Hakkai. But somewhere along the way, Sanzo started to say things like, "You decide," and came to pass off all the decision-making to Hakkai. To Sanzo, Hakkai's in a secretary-like position. In the beginning, there were times where he wondered if it would be all right to let him handle this or that, and he would worry about entrusting things to Hakkai. But now he just has him take care of things. He figures that if it's Hakkai, it'll be all right.

So, you're saying that the trust between them deepened?

MINEKURA: Yeah, you could say that. The truth is that part of the reason Sanzo is passing stuff off to Hakkai is that those things are a pain in the ass (lol). Still, Hakkai, being

the conversation isn't very serious, then he basically spaces out. But in one scene, where a near-death Goku is alone with Sanzo, Sanzo sees Goku's condition and says, "What's wrong?" The expression on his face in this scene caused a commotion among the fans, and they were wondering if Sanzo was actually smiling in this panel (lol). The truth is that I wanted to draw Sanzo with a subtle expression then. He's not really smiling, but I intended to draw him with a softness that you don't usually see from him. I think he only has that sort of expression when he's with Goku.

Meanwhile, Goku is basically the same person no matter who he's paired with. I guess there are times where he's scared of Hakkai, though. Like, the way he eats in a slightly more well-mannered way when Hakkai's around (lol). It's the same as a child who acts that way in front of their mother with the expectation that they'll be scolded otherwise. And in Goku's case, that's instinctual, but whether he's actually conscious of that or not is a different story.

the same green room. They ask not to be put together because it will be awkward. Probably the only connection they have with each other is that they're both smokers. They're companions who understand each other from being persecuted for being smoky and scattering ash (lol). People who smoke cigarettes will do things together just to smoke cigarettes. Next thing you know, they're next to each other silently puffing on their cigarettes—that's the kind of relationship they have. Oh, but I guess Sanzo is at his most talkative when he's fighting with Gojyo. He'll talk up a storm just to verbally abuse Gojyo. I think Gojyo's just about the only person that can get Sanzo worked up enough to talk like that. He seriously gets annoyed.

It seems like you could say the same for Gojyo, though (lol).

MINEKURA: Of course. The veins on Gojyo's temples stick out when he gets annoyed, so it's easy to tell when he's mad. He usually makes fun of people and cracks jokes with a laid-back attitude, but when much the only time that those two have done things together for an extended period was when Goku and Hakkai got sucked up into Kami-sama's magical gourd. They constantly fought during that time, but under a similarly high-pressure situation, the same thing would happen even if I drew those two together now. The relationship between Gojyo and Sanzo hasn't really changed. Even after traveling together for so long, Sanzo sees Gojyo as someone that's pretty much useless. And Gojyo being Gojyo, his impression of Sanzo hasn't really changed. The relationship between those two is one that has always remained the same. But that's precisely why it's amusing to imagine what would happen when they're alone together at an inn or the like (lol).

It seems like it would be one of two extremes if they shared a room: they would either not speak to each other at all, or they would be fighting.

MINEKURA: It's the same as entertainer duos that say they don't want to be together in

MINEKURA: Yeah. Gojyo's bad because he thinks that even though Hakkai complains about it, he'll still put the socks in the washing machine, anyway. Maybe if Gojyo actually put his socks in the washing machine, Hakkai would be pleasantly surprised to see him do that, but he would quickly come to his senses and realize that he shouldn't be so happy for something that should be a matter of fact. Those two have had that relationship from the beginning, and it hasn't changed since.

Which pairing has resulted in a particularly large response from readers?

MINEKURA: Well, each and every combination had its own requests and responses, but I guess there was a lot of that for Sanzo-Goku and Gojyo-Hakkai. As far as their respective positions go, those combinations might be the most comfortable, I think. Also, I guess there's always been a large number of people who are very vocal about asking me to draw a story about Gojyo and Sanzo, too. Pretty

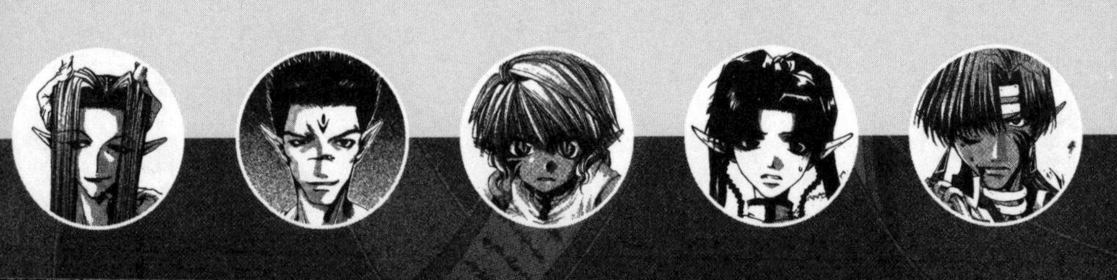

MINEKURA: But my assistants tell me that Goku has had some moments where he looks crafty lately. Like when he's posing in some illustrations, he's posing in a way that says, "I totally know you think I'm cute." The person seeing that knows that Goku has grown up, so I think they feel that he's doing that on purpose, but when that was pointed out to me, I was like, "You got me!" (lol). Hakkai has had some moments where he looked crafty, and sometimes the readers could tell that it was completely intentional, but since he was originally a calculating character, well, I guess it's calculated (lol).

Contrary to that, what have people said about Goku, whose actual character has grown considerably in the series?

MINEKURA: The opinions are pretty split, with some people saying that they feel sad to see Goku grow up, and others who say they like the current Goku better. I guess the former is a case of people who place Goku in a "cute position," and the latter keep him in a "cool position." Also, people who like the innocent Goku like *Saiyuki Gaiden.* They liked the juvenile version of Goku when he had long hair—that's the Goku from *Gaiden* and the time when he was in the temple before going on the journey. Personally, I'm drawing the current Goku with a sense of parental love and hope that he'll become a good man. But if Goku grows up too much, that would put the other three in too awkward a position, so... (lol).

Because he has naturally high potential.

he seriously gets angry, his veins pop out, and he'll be like, "What'd you say?!"

Still, Gojyo has gotten more fans lately! I think it might be because the readers have become a little older, but young people hate Gojyo... People say they don't like that he's a womanizer, or that they don't know what's good about him, or that Gojyo is the only one that they hate out of the four main characters, and many of the people that say those things are young people.

Wow, people really hate him, huh?

MINEKURA: Somehow or other, I've continued to draw this manga for 15 years, so some people first read this when they were in elementary school, or junior high, or even high school, and those people are now older than the four characters in the manga. So, I've heard from quite a lot of people who tell me they've reached an age where they understand what's good about Gojyo (lol).

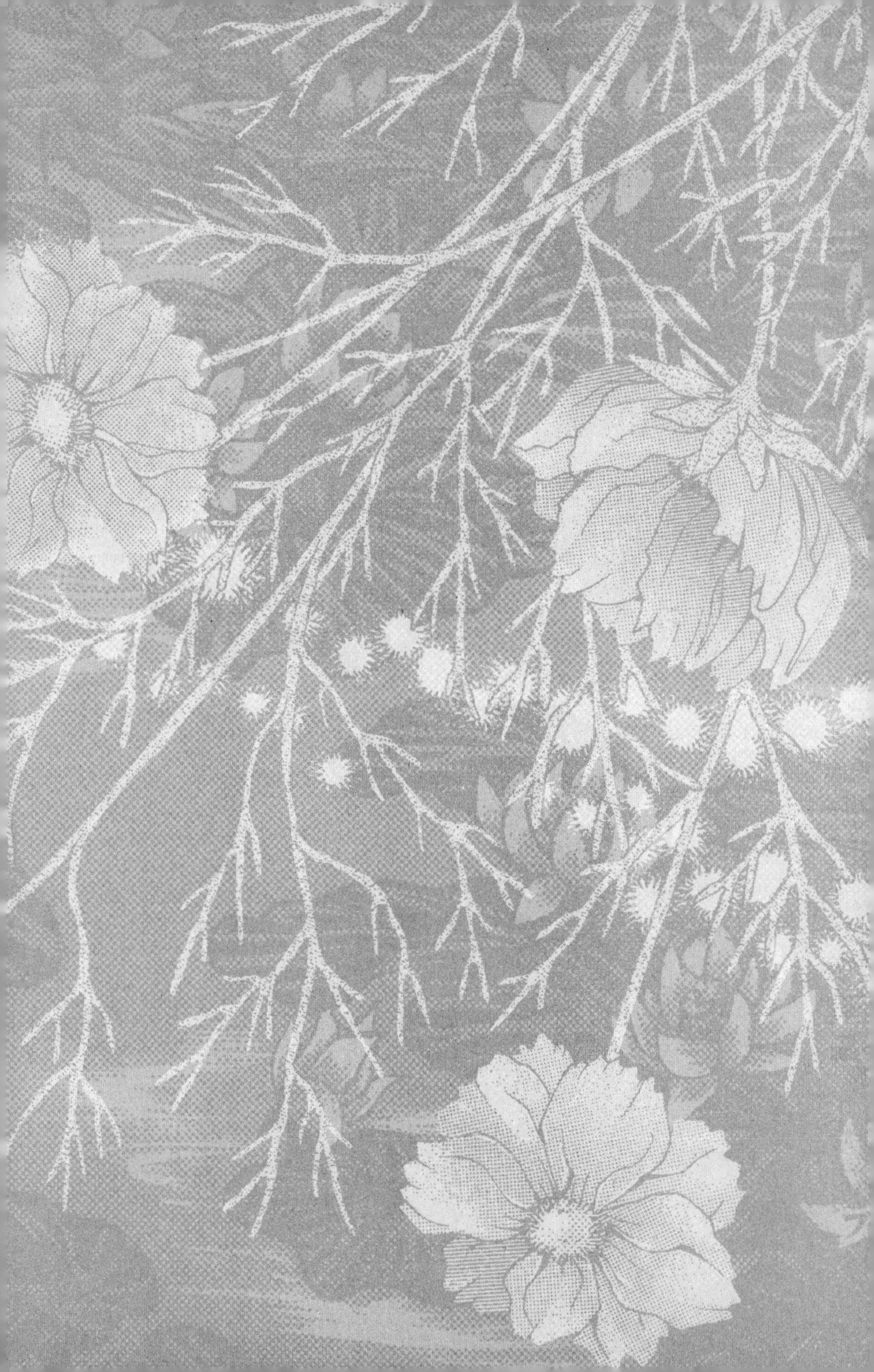

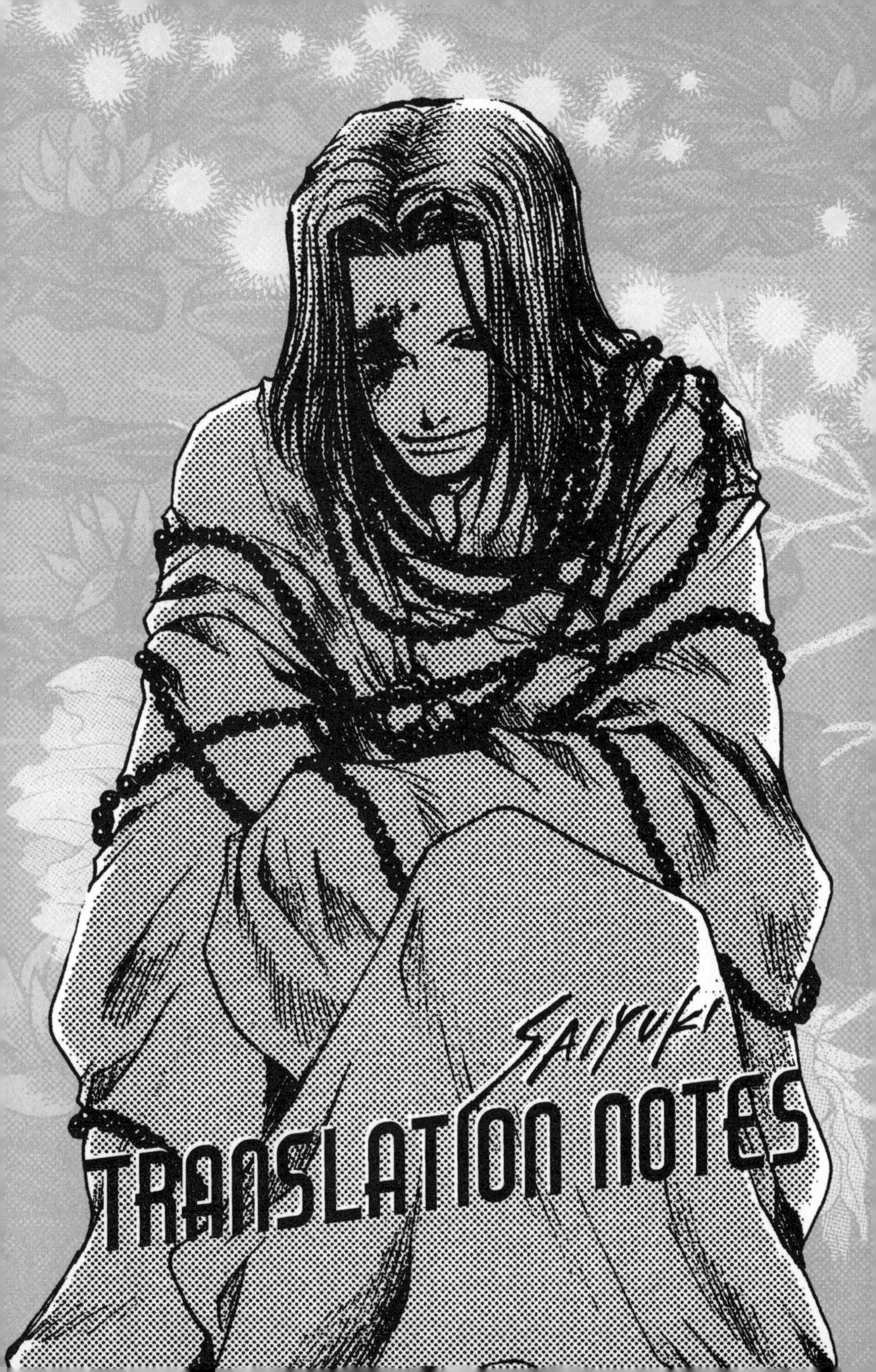
SAIYUKI
TRANSLATION NOTES

PAGE 41

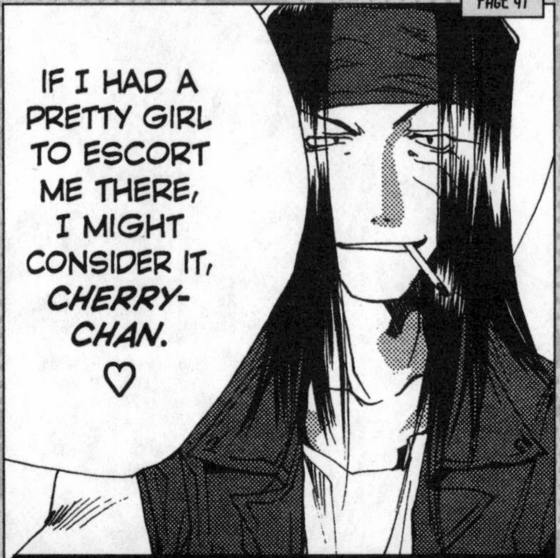
IF I HAD A PRETTY GIRL TO ESCORT ME THERE, I MIGHT CONSIDER IT, CHERRY-CHAN. ♡

Cherry-chan

From the Japanese slang "cherry boy," this nickname for Sanzo refers to the assumption that the priest has not had sexual relations.

PAGE 101

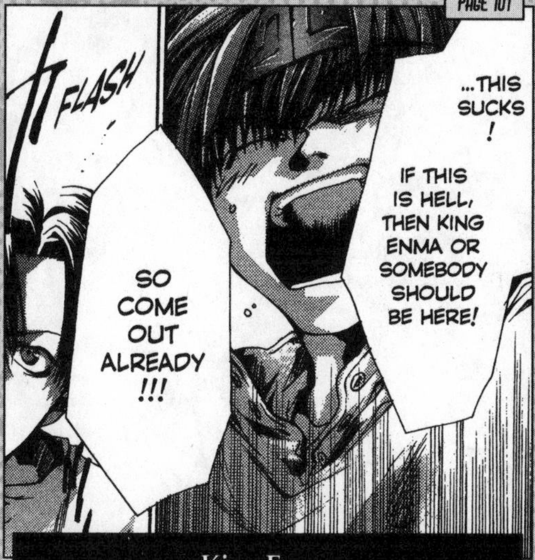
...THIS SUCKS!
IF THIS IS HELL, THEN KING ENMA OR SOMEBODY SHOULD BE HERE!
SO COME OUT ALREADY!!!
FLASH

King Enma

As implied by Goku's exclamation, King Enma is the king of Hell, whose job it is to make sure sinners are appropriately punished for the wrongs they committed in life.

PAGE 114

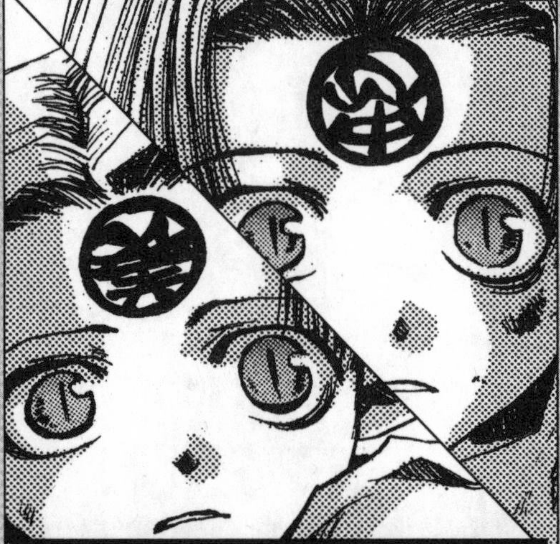

Kinkaku and Ginkaku

These twins are based on two of the more famous characters from *Journey to the West,* the Golden Horned King and the Silver Horned King, who used a gourd in their attempt to capture Sun Wukong (Goku). Like the other characters who show up in the original story, their tale is much different in this version.

Their yokai markings are inverted Chinese characters. On Kinkaku's forehead (left) is the upside down character meaning "loyalty" or "faithfulness." On Ginkaku's forehead (right) is the upside-down character for "righteousness." Together, the two characters mean "loyalty" or "devotion."

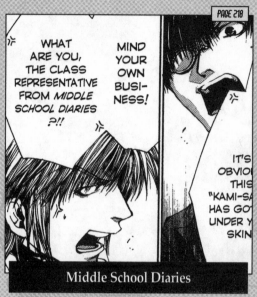

PAGE 218

IT'S OBVIO
THIS
"KAMI-SA
HAS GOT
UNDER Y
SKIN
MIND YOUR OWN BUSI-NESS!
WHAT ARE YOU, THE CLASS REPRESENTATIVE FROM *MIDDLE SCHOOL DIARIES* ?!!

Middle School Diaries

Known in Japanese as *Chūgakusei Nikki, Middle School Diaries* is a long-running TV drama that started in 1972 and continued into 2012 about the problems middle school students face in life. Sanzo may be referring to a specific episode from 1977, in which a boy reluctantly becomes his class's representative. He is frustrated by his class's failure to show responsibility, but eventually realizes he was being selfish himself.

PAGE 245

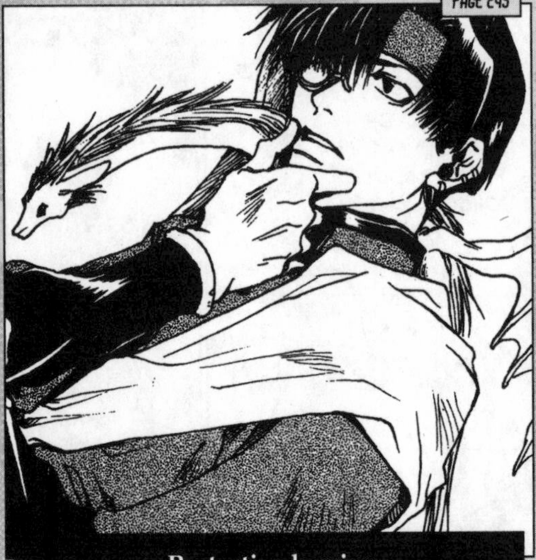

Protective barrier

The word Hakkai uses here for "protective barrier" is *kekkai,* literally "bound world." Often translated to "barrier," a *kekkai* is a boundary marking off the border between the sacred and the profane. The area inside the barrier is supposed to be protected from unwanted outsiders.

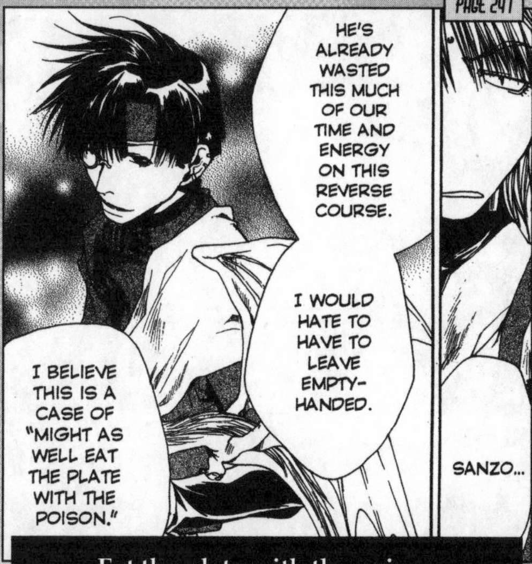
PAGE 247
SANZO...
HE'S ALREADY WASTED THIS MUCH OF OUR TIME AND ENERGY ON THIS REVERSE COURSE.
I WOULD HATE TO HAVE TO LEAVE EMPTY-HANDED.
I BELIEVE THIS IS A CASE OF "MIGHT AS WELL EAT THE PLATE WITH THE POISON."

Eat the plate with the poison

This is a roughly literal translation of the Japanese version of "in for a penny, in for a pound," or "might as well be hanged for a sheep as a lamb." The reasoning behind the Japanese version is that if you've already ingested the poison in a meal, you may as well finish the meal and even lick the plate, because you're going to die, anyway.

PAGE 263

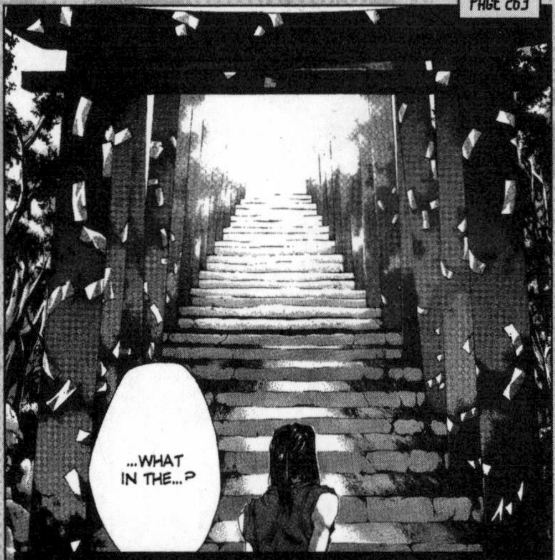
...WHAT IN THE...?

Torii

This stairway is lined by special gates called *torii.* The *torii* are the symbol of a Shinto shrine, and represents the transition from the profane to the sacred—once someone walks through the *torii* onto the shrine grounds, they have entered sacred, or godly, territory.

PAGE 298

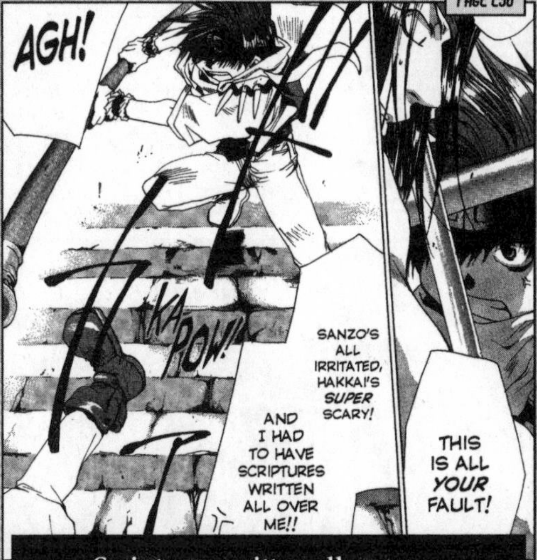
THIS IS ALL *YOUR* FAULT!
AGH!
KA-POW!
SANZO'S ALL IRRITATED, HAKKAI'S *SUPER* SCARY!
AND I HAD TO HAVE SCRIPTURES WRITTEN ALL OVER ME!!

Scriptures written all over me

Writing scriptures on one's body is considered a protective or empowering practice within Japanese religious traditions.

PAGE 308

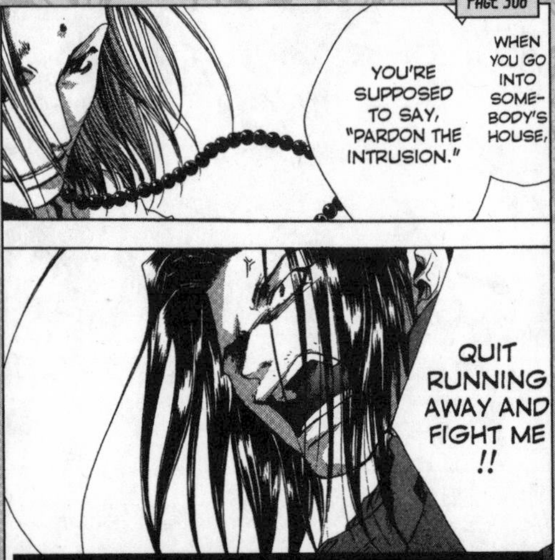
WHEN YOU GO INTO SOME-BODY'S HOUSE,
YOU'RE SUPPOSED TO SAY, "PARDON THE INTRUSION."
QUIT RUNNING AWAY AND FIGHT ME !!

Pardon the intrusion

When entering Japanese homes, the polite thing to say is "*ojama shimasu,*" which literally means "I humbly intrude." This can be translated in a number of ways, including, "Pardon the intrusion," and "Thank you for having me."

PAGE 336

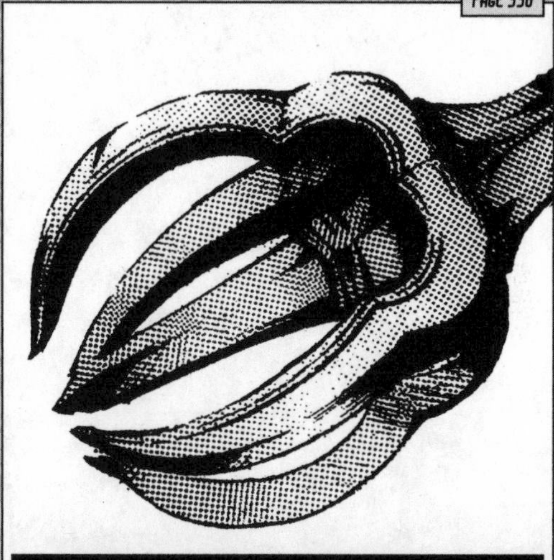

Vajra

Kami-sama uses a *gokosho,* or five-pronged vajra, to enhance his mystical powers. As mentioned in previous notes (see Volume 3), the vajra represents the indestructibility of diamond and the force of the thunderbolt.

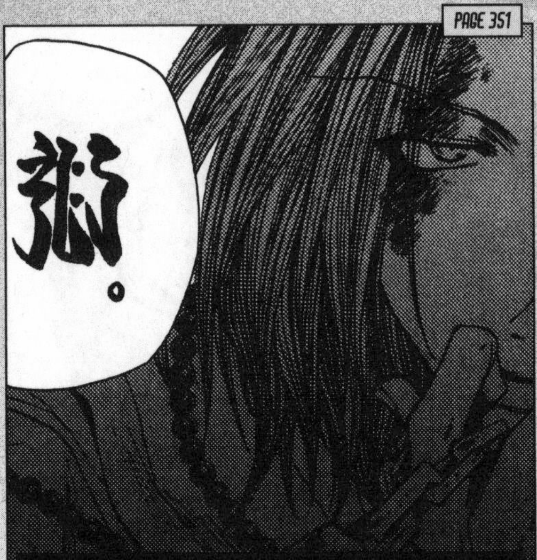
PAGE 351
術。

Kami-sama's spell

The character displayed here is a calligraphic version of the one representing *jutsu*, or “spell.” It refers to a skill or art performed through training and/or magic.

MAHJONG

PAGE 407

CHII. GIMME THAT TILE.

Chii

Chii is called when the player to your left discards a tile that will complete a sequence in your hand. It would appear Sanzo just discarded the seven of Characters, meaning that Gojyo must have either the five and six of Characters or the eight and nine of Characters. After he takes the discarded tile, he must lay all three of the tiles in that sequence flat for the other players to see.

PAGE 404

PINFU, A THOUSAND POINTS!!
DAH!

Pinfu

Pinfu, also known as "all sequences," is a winning hand in Mahjong that contains all sequences. Similar to "straights" in poker, a sequence is a set of three tiles in the same suit that have consecutive numbers. For example, the reader can see that Goku's hand includes a sequence with one, two, and three Circles.

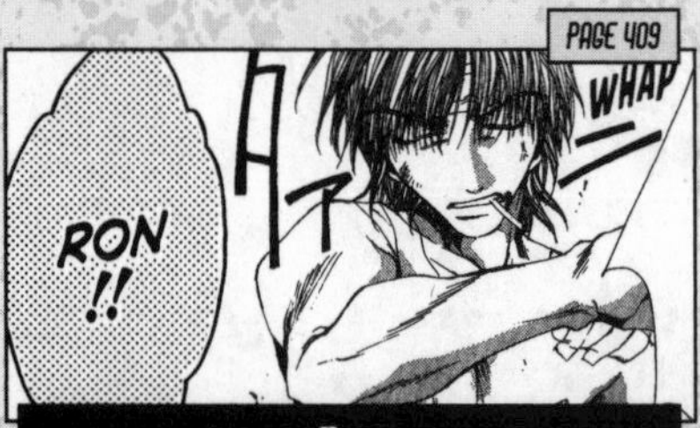
PAGE 409
WHAP
RON!!

Ron

When someone discards the last tile a player needs to win, that player will call ron, take the tile, and win the round.

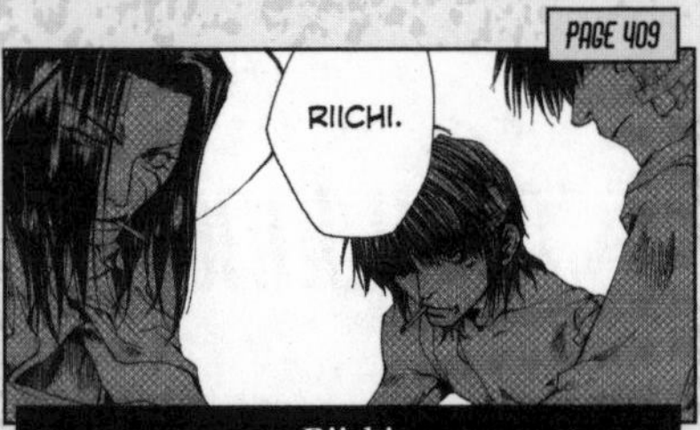
PAGE 409
RIICHI.

Riichi

Goku has a closed hand, meaning all of his tiles are still hidden from the other players. As such, they don't know that he only needs one more tile to win—or they didn't, until he called *riichi*, which is something like calling "Uno." Calling *riichi* is not required, but it does allow certain advantages, such as a higher score for his hand if he wins.

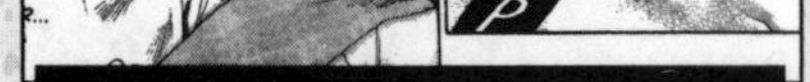
PAGE 419
KAN.
TAP
THIS SEEMS LIKE A JOKE, BUT IN ALL SERIOUSNESS...
SEEING GOKU PLAY FOR SO LONG...

Kan

Kan means a player has four of the same tile.

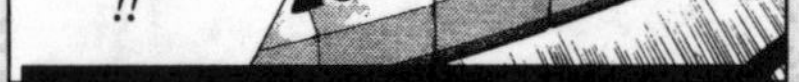
PAGE 410
TA-
MENTANPIN, IPPATSU, TRIPLE SEQUENCE, DOUBLE SEQUENCE, ONE DORA !!

Goku's score

Goku first scores points for *mentanpin,* which means he called *riichi* (men); his hand was *tanyao* (tan), meaning his hand contained only tiles numbered 2-8, no 1s or 9s; and it was *pinfu* (pin).

His hand was also *ippatsu* (one hit), meaning he completed his winning hand after calling *riichi* and by using a discarded tile before drawing again.

Triple sequence means he has three sequences in his hands, and double sequence means he has two identical sequences.

One *dora* means that one of Goku's tiles is a *dora* tile—a tile specially designated at the beginning of the round as one that would give bonus points if found in a winning hand. Additionally bonus tiles, called *uradora,* can be revealed if the hand is completed after calling *riichi.*

PAGE 420

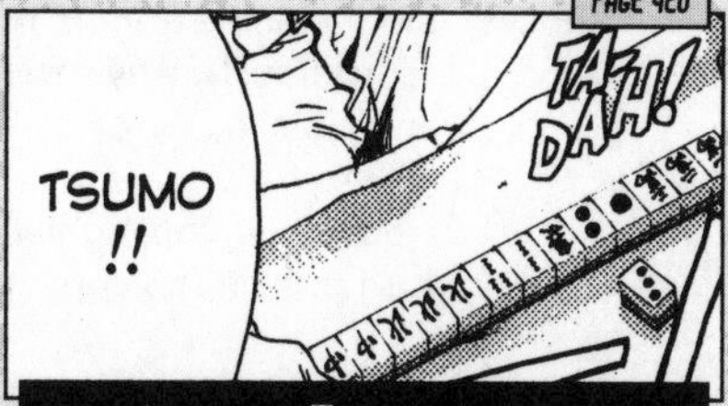
TA DAH!
TSUMO !!

Tsumo

Tsumo is what you call when you win without using any discarded tiles.

PAGE 420

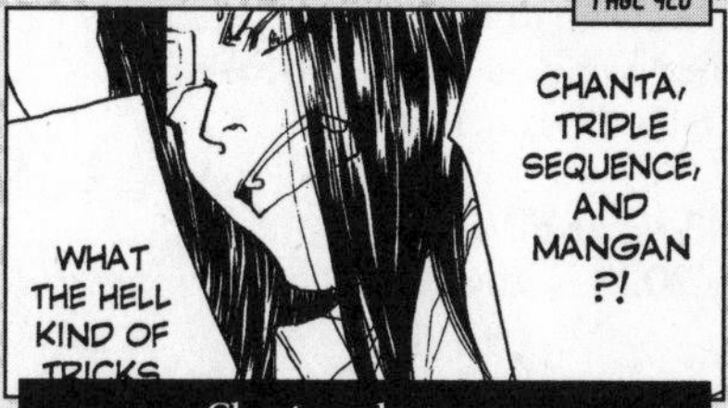
CHANTA, TRIPLE SEQUENCE, AND MANGAN ?!
WHAT THE HELL KIND OF TRICKS

Chanta and mangan

Chanta is a type of hand in which every meld (set of three or four tiles) contains a one, a nine, a wind, or a dragon. Mangan is when the score reaches the score cap and ceases to be calculated any higher.

PAGE 424

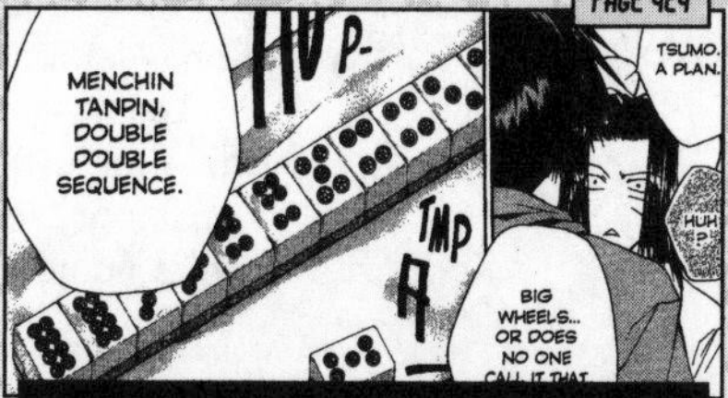
TSUMO. A PLAN.
HUH ?
BIG WHEELS... OR DOES NO ONE
HUP-
MENCHIN TANPIN, DOUBLE DOUBLE SEQUENCE.
TMP

Hakkai's hand

Big Wheels is an apparently old-fashioned term for a hand consisting of only tiles in the Circles suit. *Menchin* is the name of a *chin iisou* hand (meaning it's all the same suit) that is obtained when the player still has a closed hand. *Tanpin* means he has no 1s or 9s, and his hand consists of all sequences (no triplets). Double double sequence means he has two sets of identical sequences.

PAGE 434

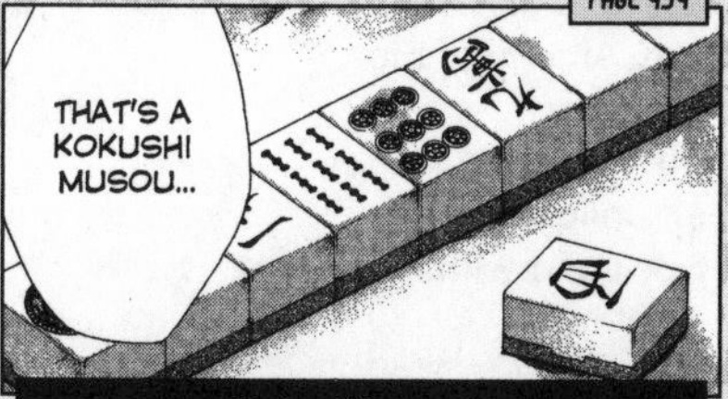
THAT'S A KOKUSHI MUSOU...

Kokushi musou

Kokushi musou, also known in English as "thirteen orphans," is a *yakuman* hand, which makes it one of the highest scoring hands in the game. In this hand—the "thirteen wait" version, which sometimes earns double the points—Sanzo has the 1 and the 9 in each of the three suits, one of each of the three dragon tiles, and one of each of the four wind tiles. One more of any of these tiles would turn his hand into a winning one. Naturally, Sanzo's winning tile is the west wind.

Published in the United States by Kodansha Comics, an imprint of
Kodansha USA Publishing, LLC, New York.

Publication rights for this English edition arranged through
Kodansha Ltd., Tokyo.

First published in Japan in 2003 by Ichijinsha Inc., Tokyo
as *Saiyuki*, volumes 7, 8, and 9.

ISBN 978-1-64651-002-3

Printed in the United States of America.

www.kodansha.us

2nd Printing
Translation: Alethea Nibley & Athena Nibley
Lettering: Evan Hayden
Additional layout: Paige Pumphrey
Editing: Nathaniel Gallant
Kodansha Comics edition cover design by Phil Balsman

8389141

Publisher: Kiichiro Sugawara

Director of publishing services: Ben Applegate
Associate director of operations: Stephen Pakula
Publishing services managing editor: Noelle Webster
Assistant production manager: Emi Lotto, Angela Zurlo

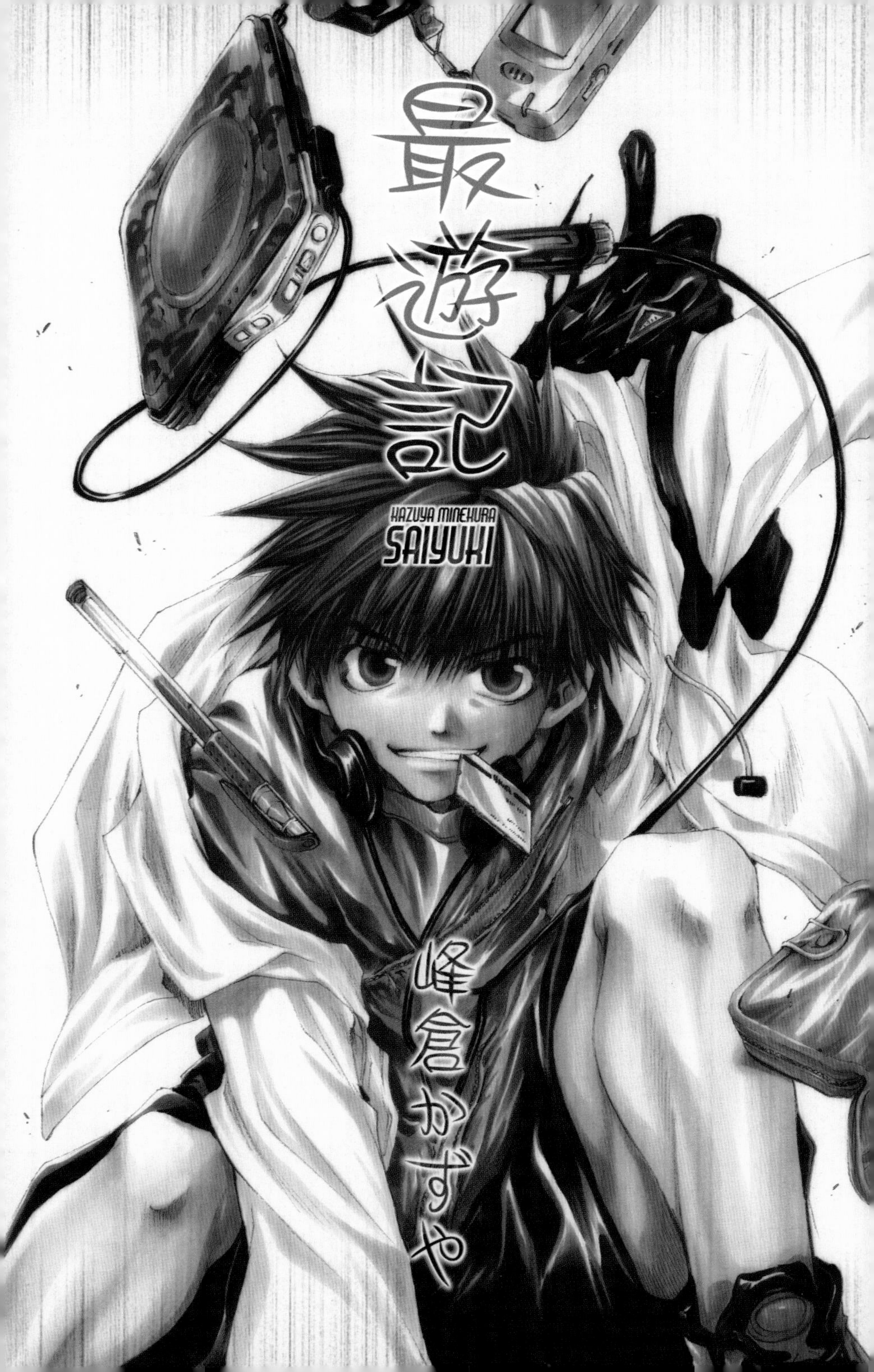
最遊記
KAZUYA MINEKURA
SAIYUKI
峰倉かずや

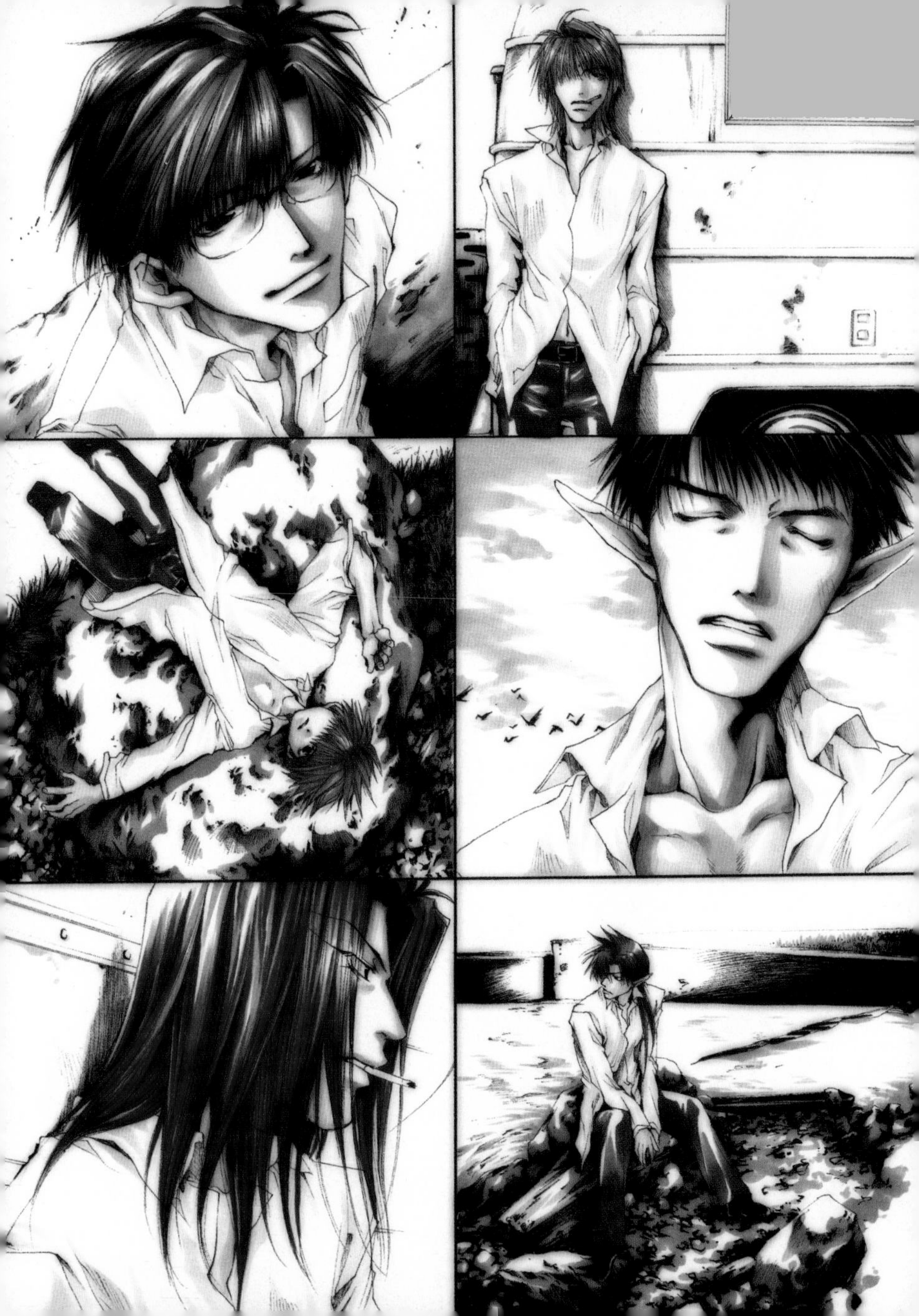

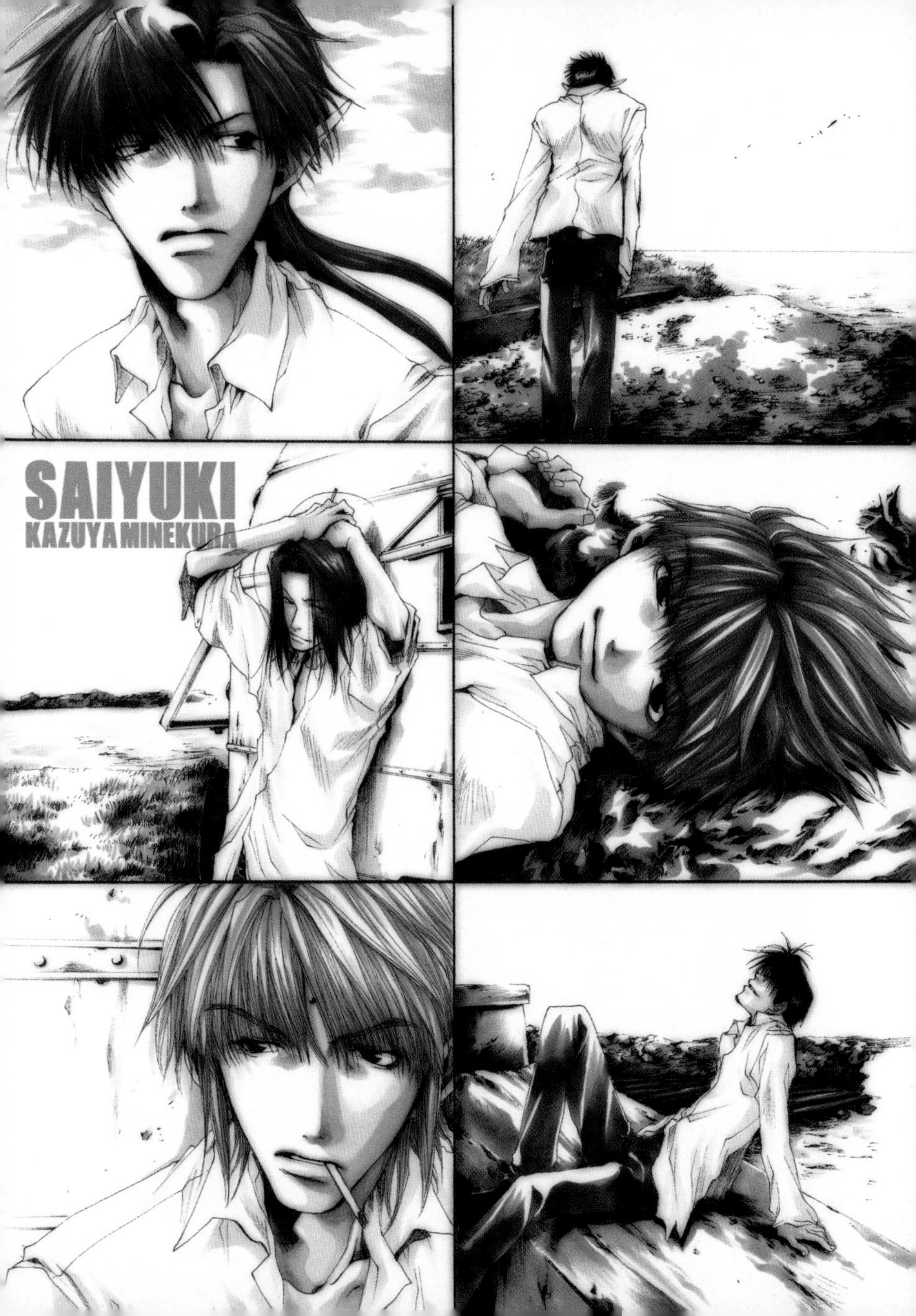
SAIYUKI
KAZUYA MINEKURA

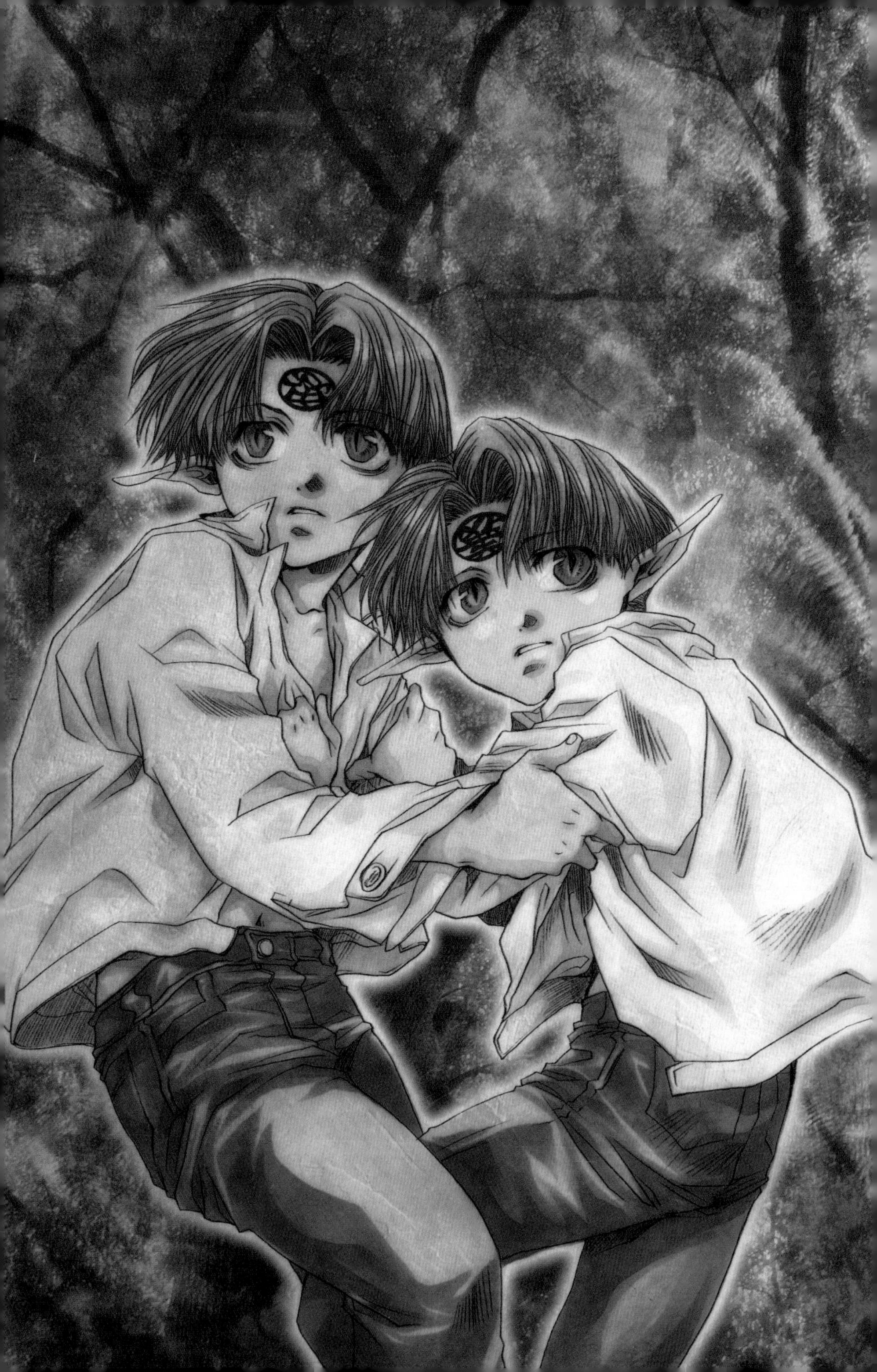

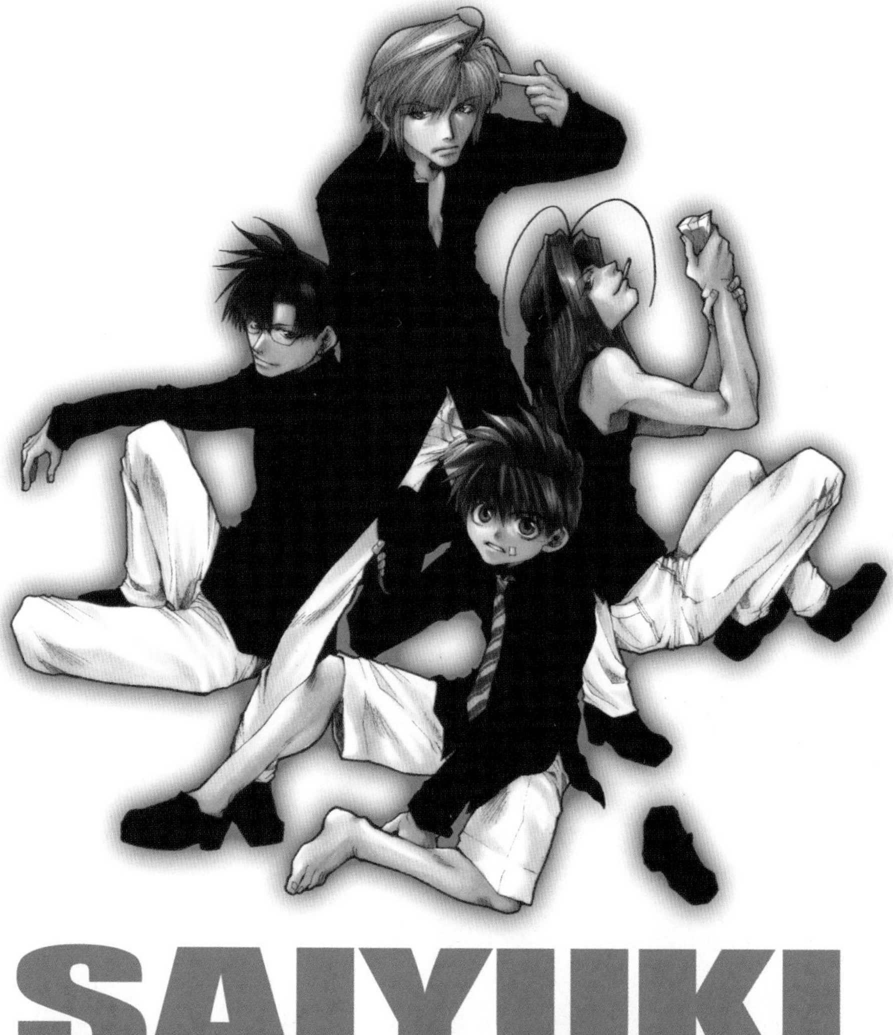

SAIYUKI

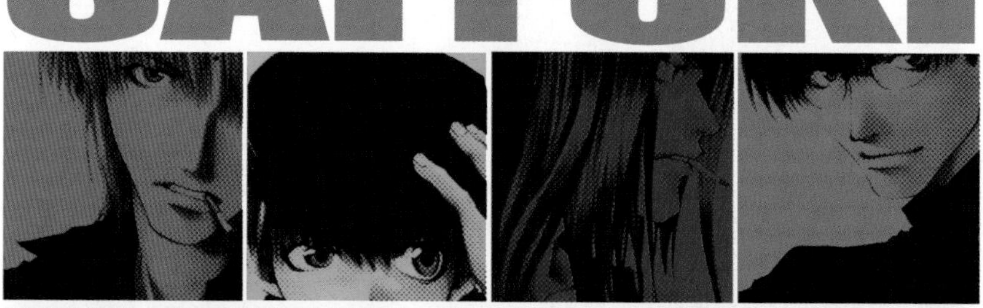

KAZUYA MINEKURA

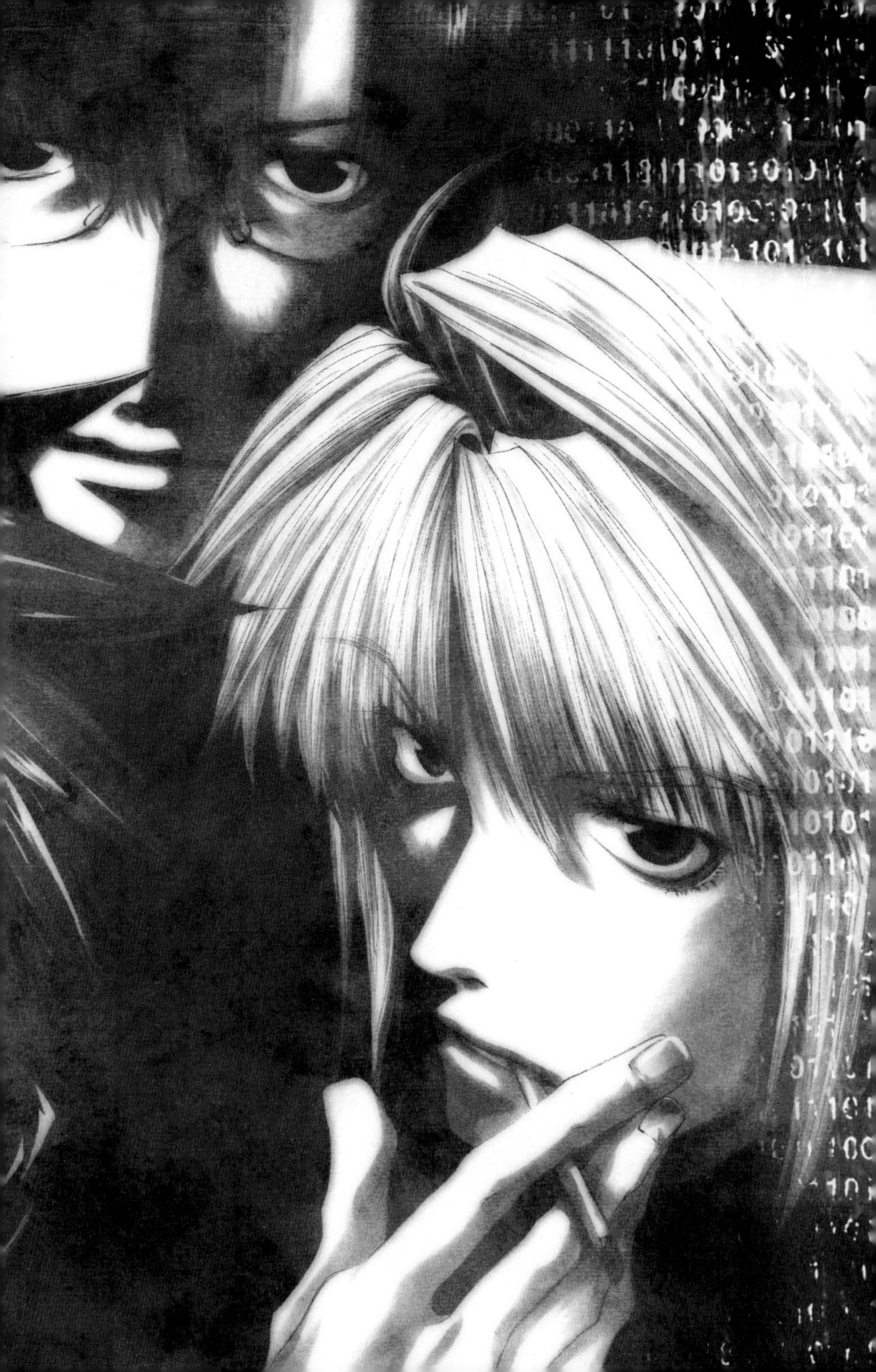

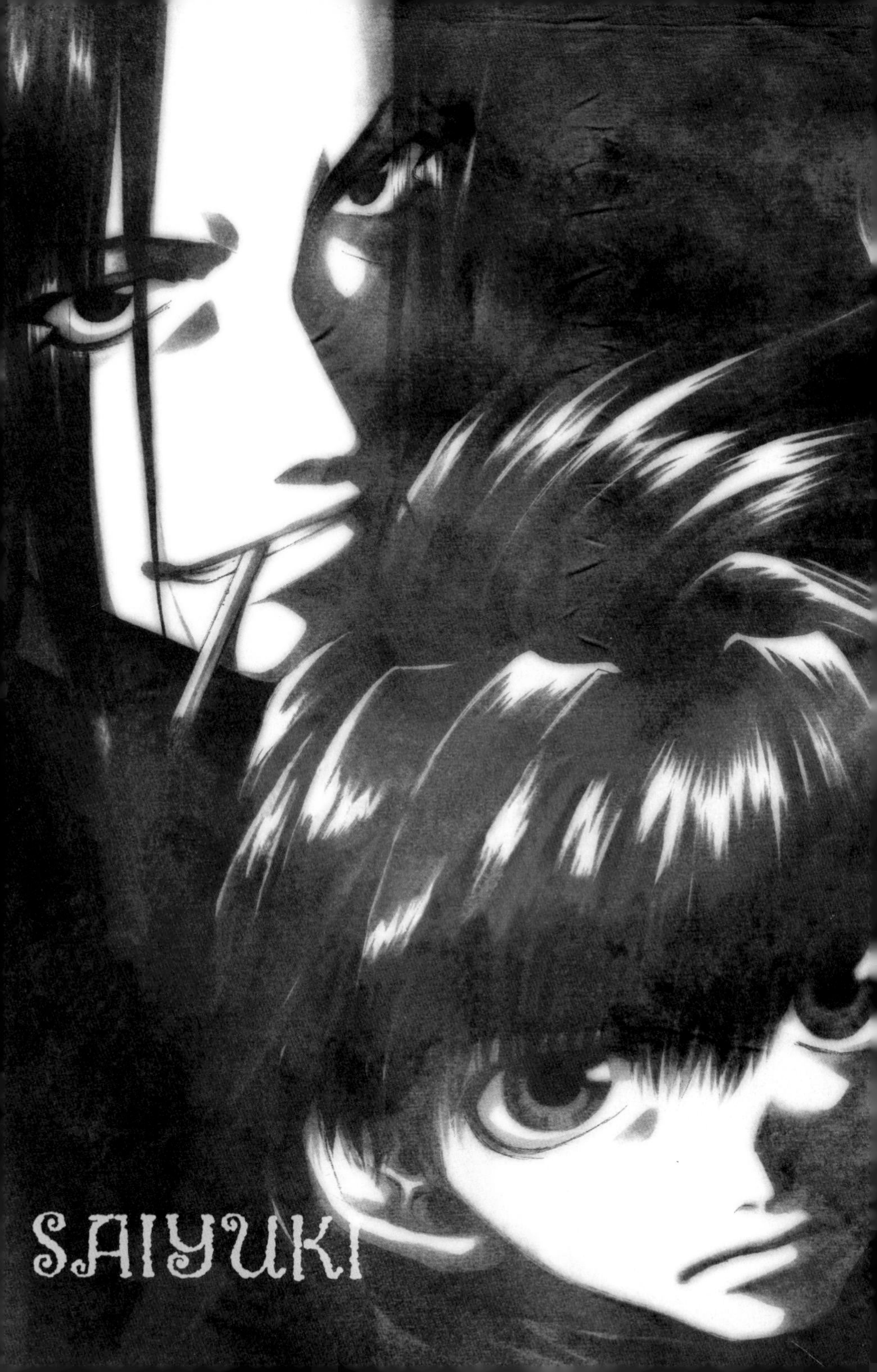
SAIYUKI

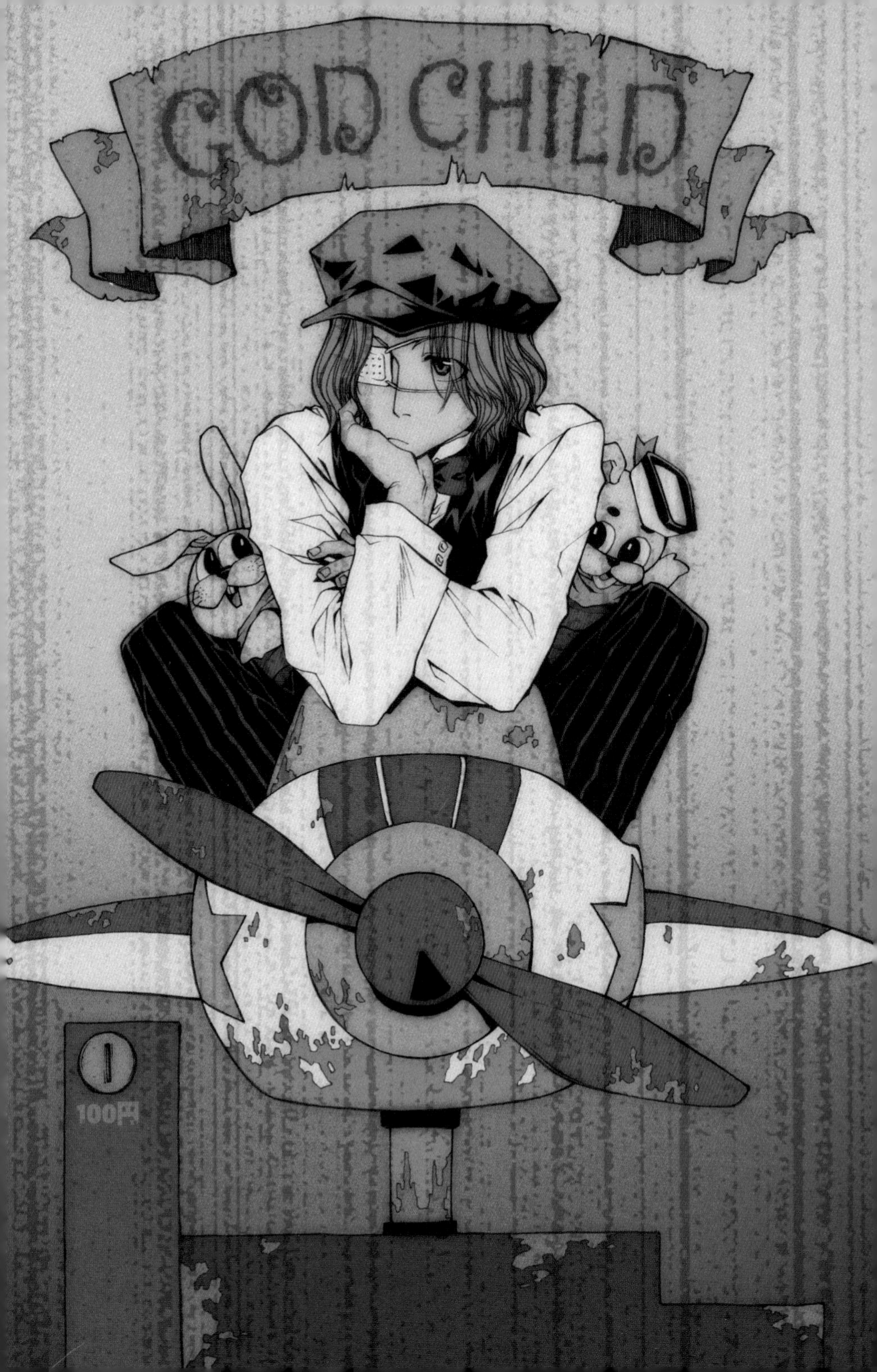
GOD CHILD
1
100円

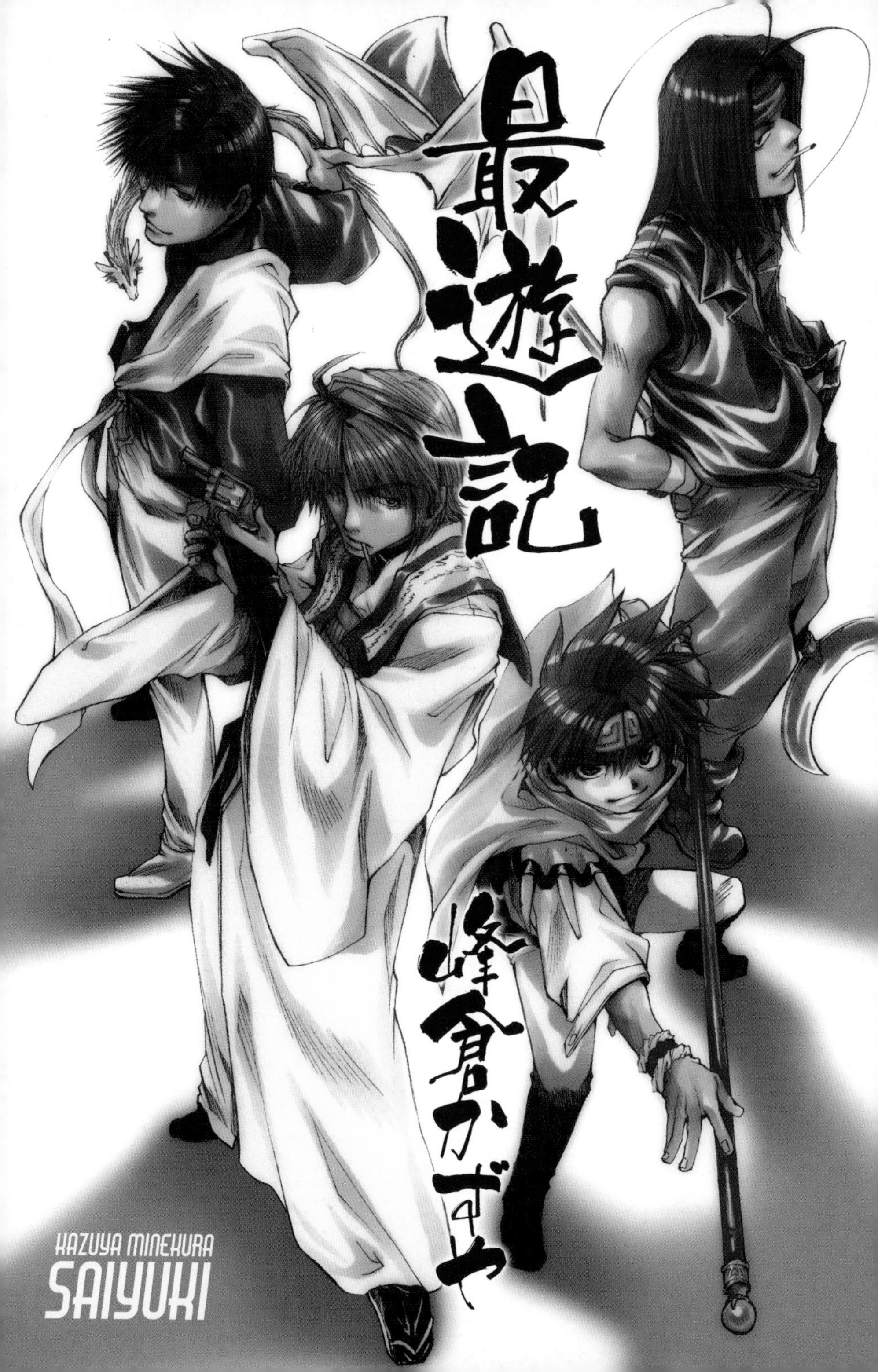
最遊記
峰倉かずや
KAZUYA MINEKURA
SAIYUKI

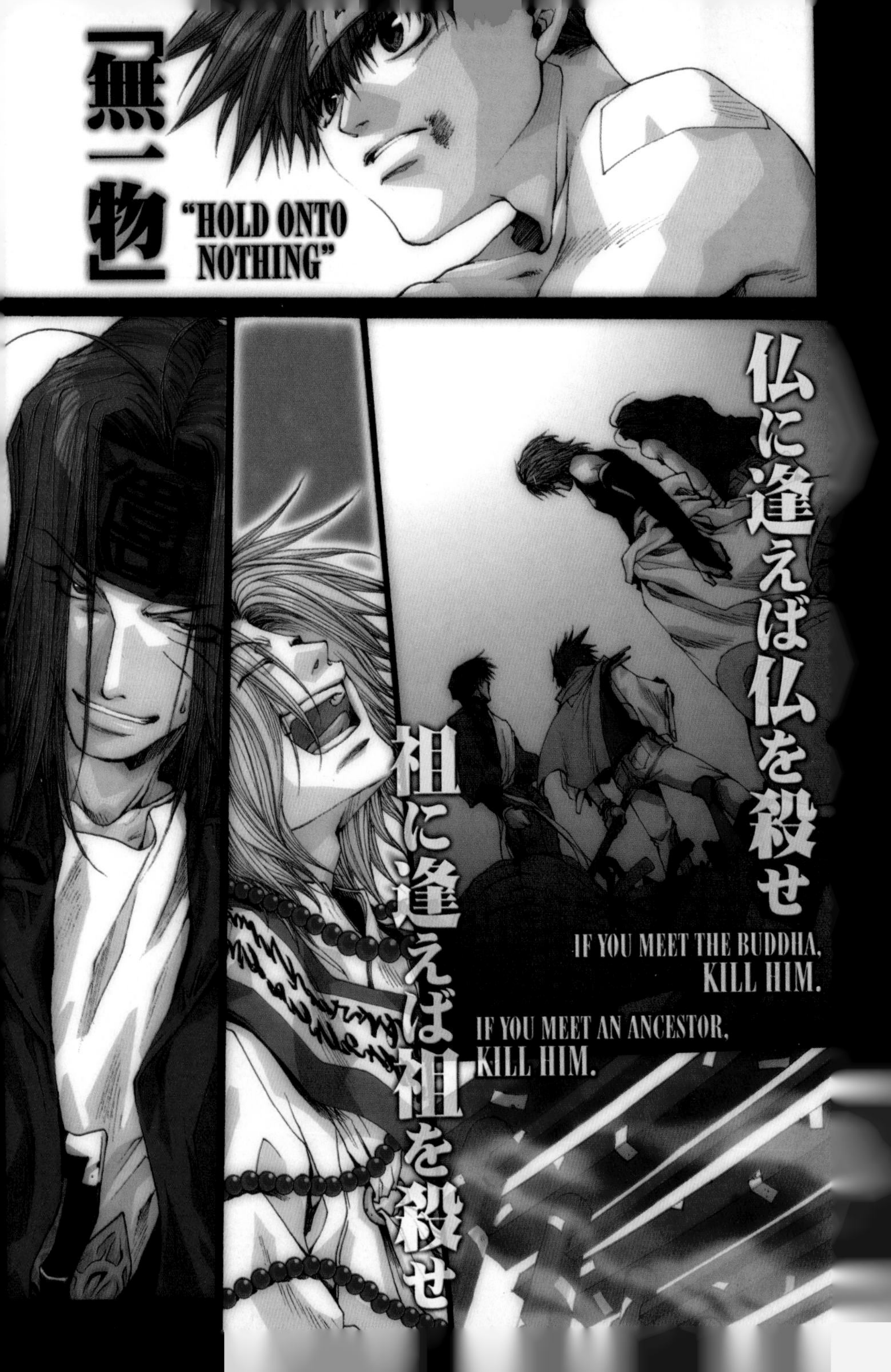
「無一物」
"HOLD ONTO NOTHING"
仏に逢えば仏を殺せ
IF YOU MEET THE BUDDHA, KILL HIM.
祖に逢えば祖を殺せ
IF YOU MEET AN ANCESTOR, KILL HIM.

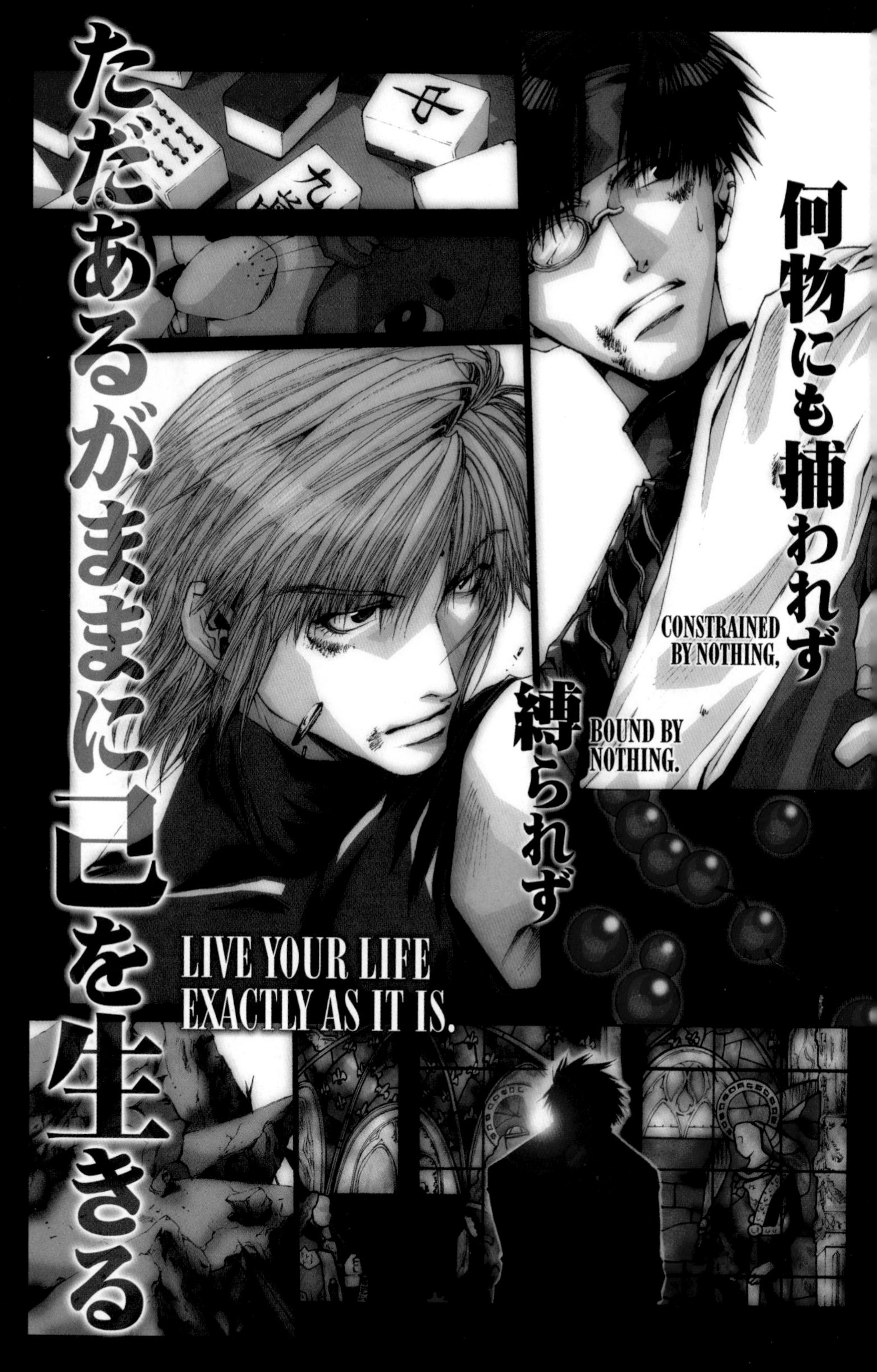
何物にも捕われず
CONSTRAINED BY NOTHING,
縛られず
BOUND BY NOTHING.
ただあるがままに己を生きる
LIVE YOUR LIFE EXACTLY AS IT IS.

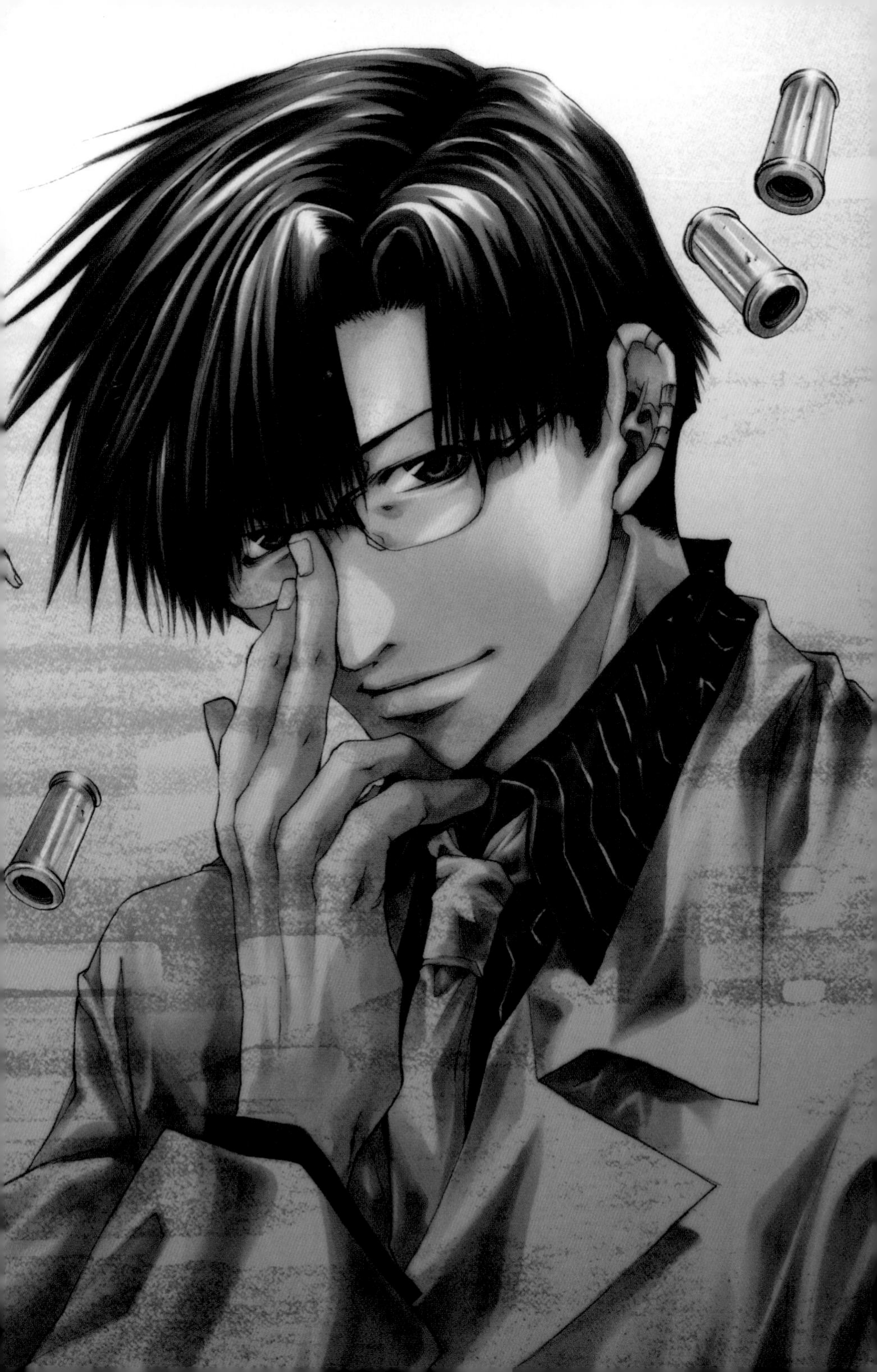

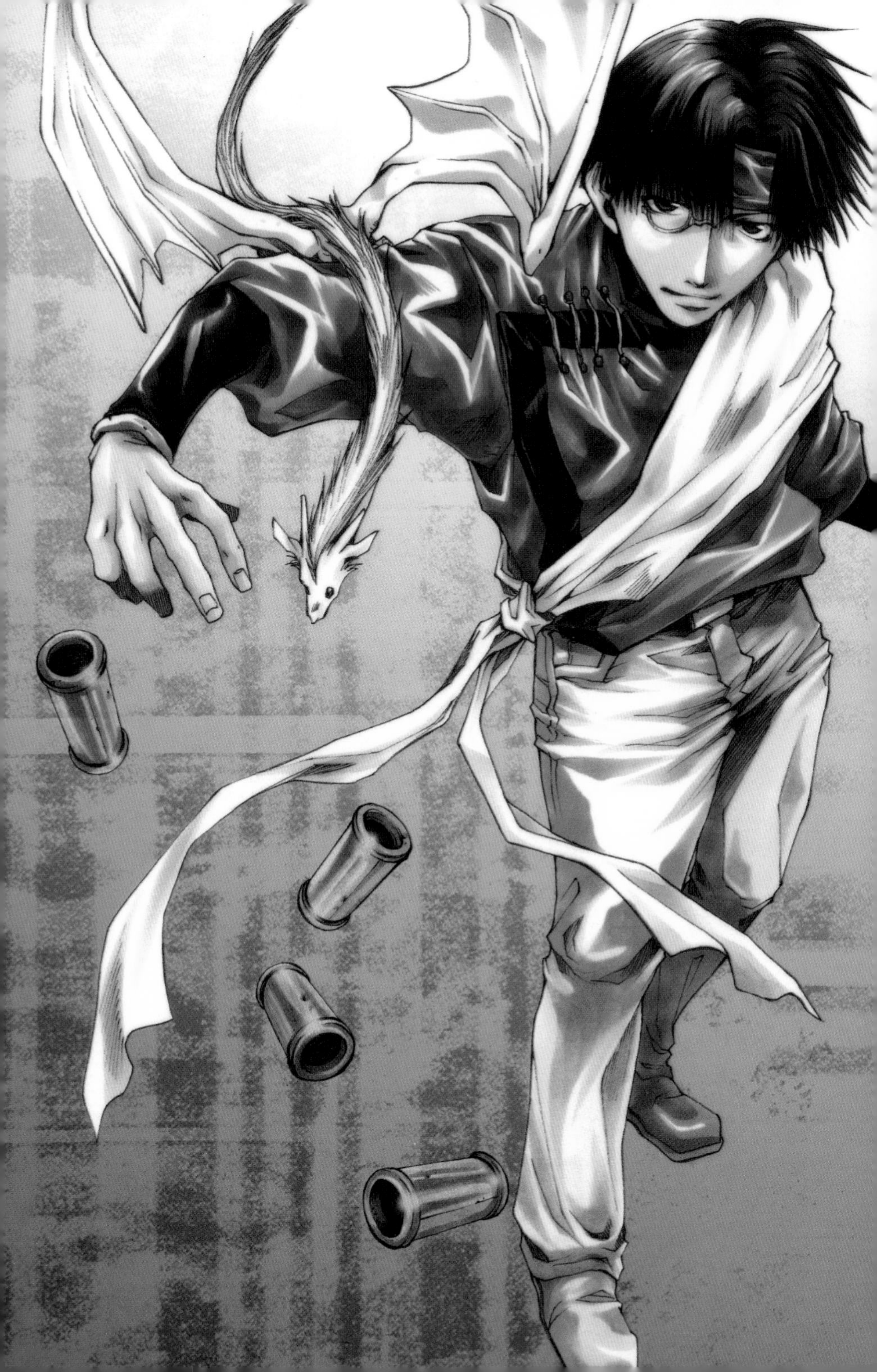

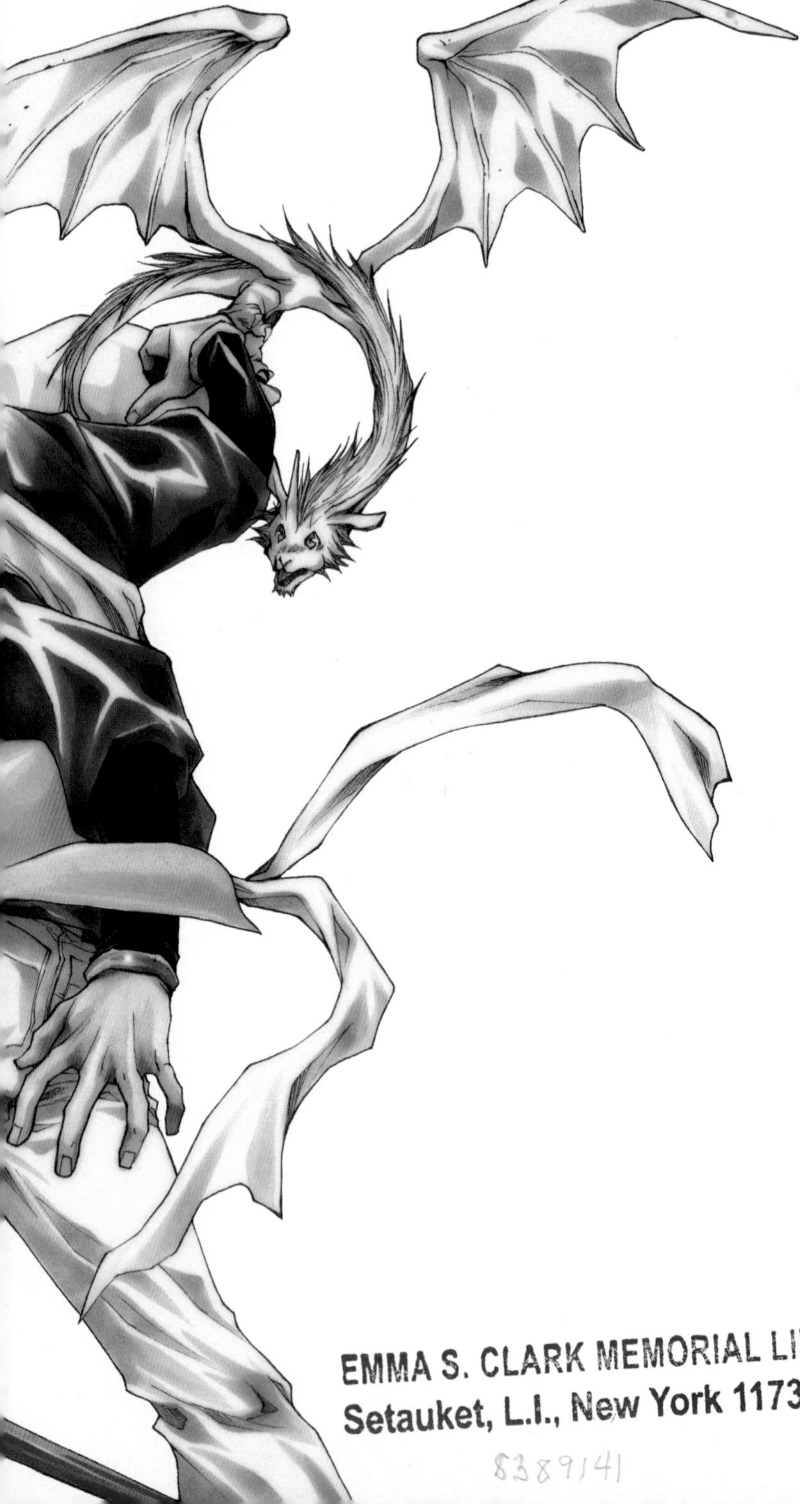

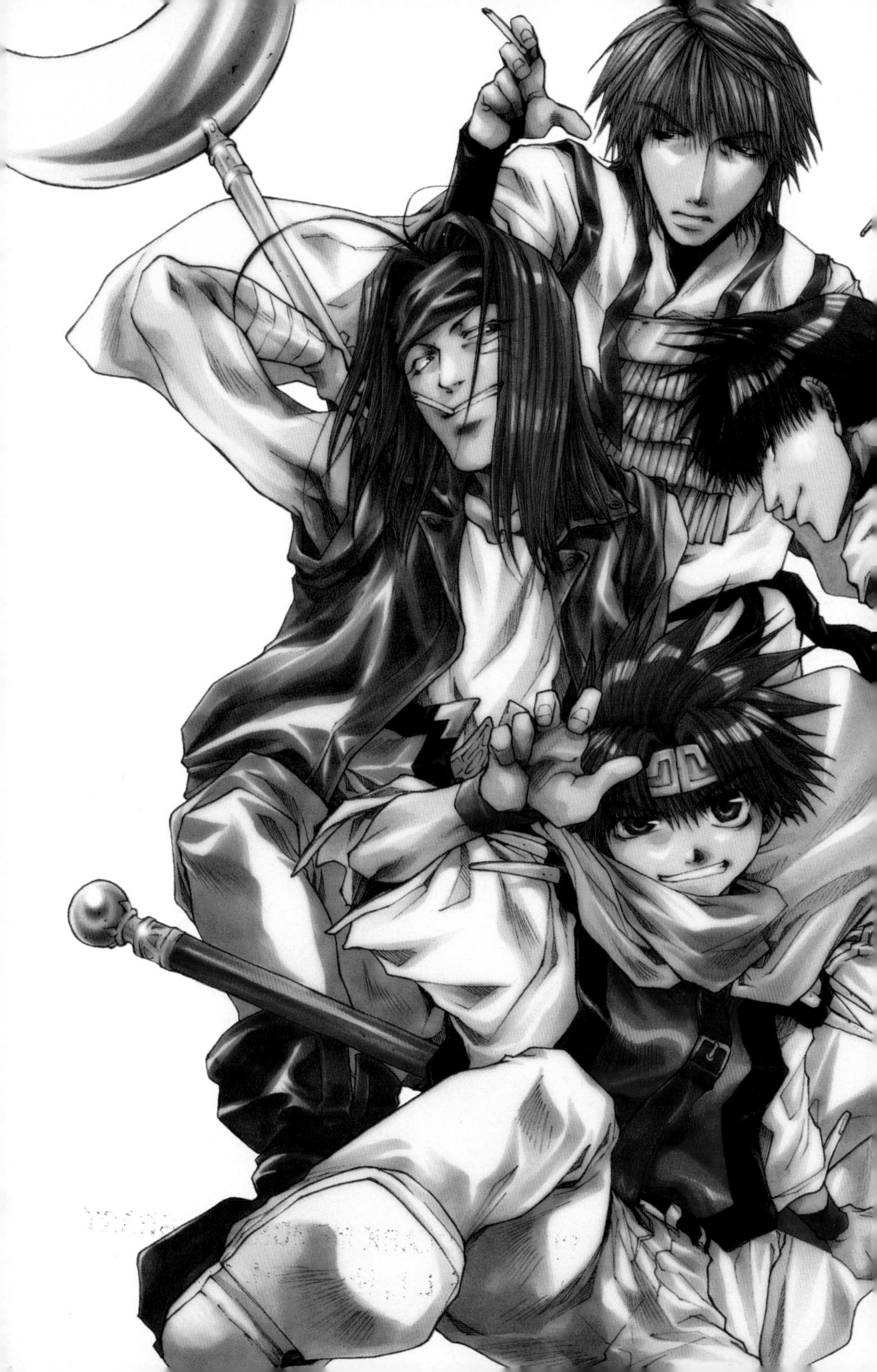

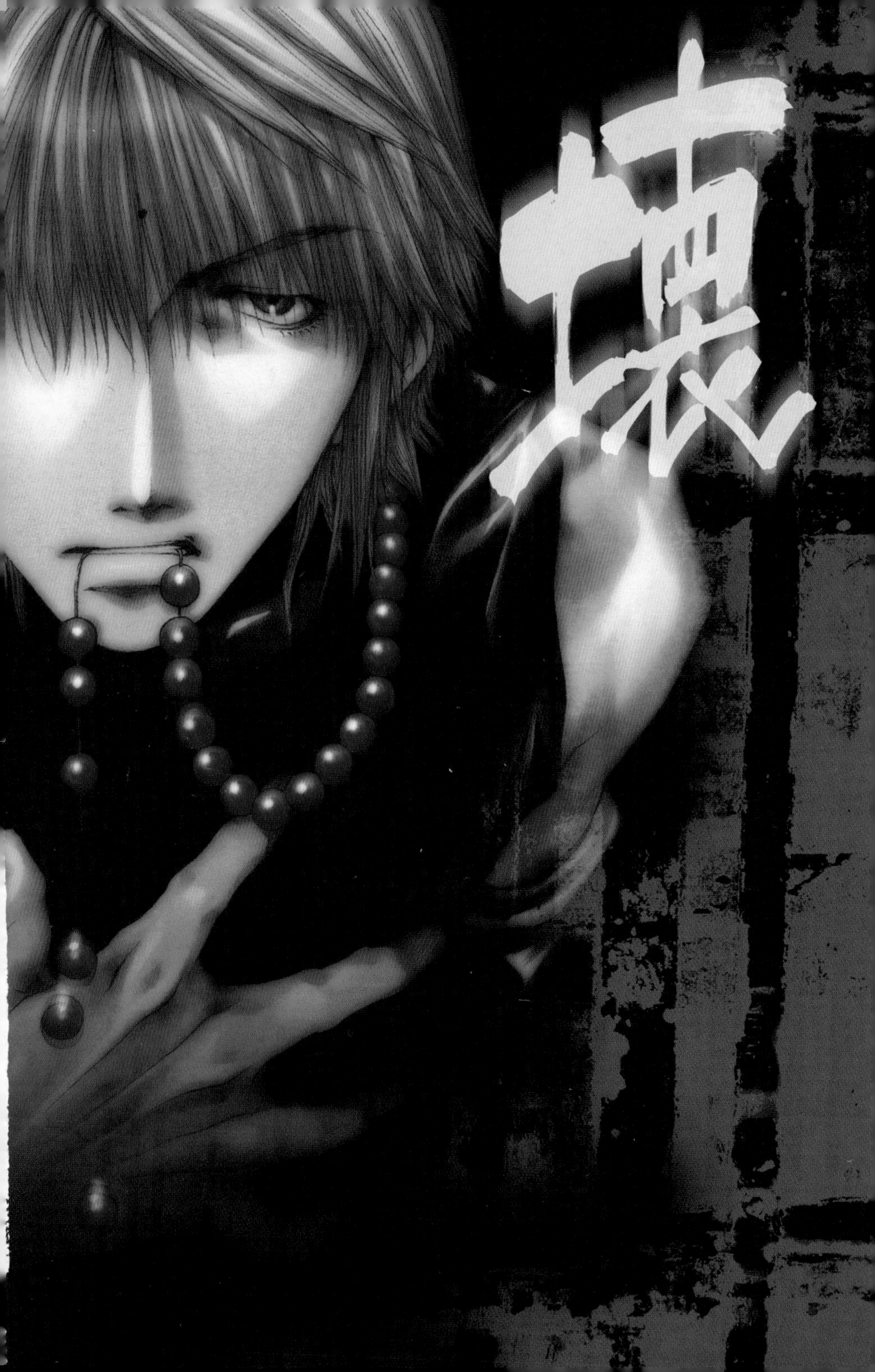
壊